GOOD HOUSEKEEPING

# COOKERY BOOK

# GOOD HOUSEKEEPING

# COOKERY BOOK

EBURY PRESS LONDON

First published in Great Britain 1948
by Ebury Press
National Magazine House, 72 Broadwick Street,
London W1V 2BP

Completely revised and reset
1962, 1966, 1976, 1985

© The National Magazine Company Limited 1962,
1966, 1976, 1985

ISBN 0 85223 420 1

Edited by Laurine Croasdale, Felicity Jackson,
Beverly LeBlanc
Designed by Grub Street Design, London
Illustrations by Terry Pottle, Julie Carpenter,
Gabriel Izen
Commissioned photographs by James Jackson,
Anne Morris, Julie Fisher
Jacket photograph by Peter Myers
Cookery by Susanna Tee, Heather Owen, Shirley Gill

Filmset by Advanced Filmsetters (Glasgow) Ltd
Printed and bound in Italy by
New Interlitho, S.p.a., Milan

# FOREWORD TO THE NEW EDITION

This completely rewritten edition represents a landmark in the long and successful history of The Good Housekeeping Cookery Book: it remains unrivalled as the one essential source of inspiration and reference for every cook and in every kitchen.

Hundreds of new recipes have been developed, and the classics revised, in line with current cookery methods and trends towards healthier eating. The result is the most comprehensive and varied collection of recipes available today. Many of them are beautifully illustrated in over 175 mouthwatering photographs, specially commissioned for this edition.

All recipes have been double tested by the staff of the Good Housekeeping Institute in their purpose-designed test kitchens. While the majority of dishes reflect British cooking at its best, there are also recipes from all over the world which incorporate the wide range of fruit and vegetables now available here.

The Good Housekeeping Cookery Book is not only a book of superlative recipes: it is a complete guide to success in the kitchen and at the table, from the organisation of your kitchen and utilising the latest equipment to new culinary skills and successful entertaining. There is invaluable reference information on important subjects such as freezing, preserving, microwave cookery, cooking for large numbers and wine. An important section on eating wisely and well shows how to plan a balanced diet while still enjoying a wide variety of foods. Glossaries of herbs, spices, fruit, vegetables, cheeses and game explain when they are in season (whether home grown or imported), what to look for when buying, what they taste like and how to cook them.

With over one million copies sold since the first 1948 edition, the Good Housekeeping Cookery Book has proved its worth in countless kitchens. This new edition continues the tradition of providing up to date knowledge and ideas from the Good Housekeeping Institute which has remained one of the leading authorities on food and cookery since its foundation over 60 years ago.

# CONTENTS

# COOKERY NOTES AND CHARTS

**1.** Follow either metric or imperial measures for the recipes in this book as they are not interchangeable.

**2.** All spoon measures are level unless otherwise stated.

**3.** Sets of measuring spoons are available in both metric and imperial size to give accurate measurement of small quantities.

**4.** When measuring milk the exact conversion of 568 ml (1 pint) has been used.

**5.** Size 4 and 3 eggs should be used except where otherwise stated.

**6.** Where margarine is stated use either block or soft tub margarine. Otherwise use as specified in the recipe.

**7.** Plain or self raising flour can be used unless otherwise stated. Use white, brown or wholemeal flour but see individual chapters for use in pastry, bread and cake making.

**8.** Use white or brown granulated sugar unless otherwise stated.

**9.** Brown or white breadcrumbs can be used unless otherwise stated.

## METRIC CONVERSION SCALE

| LIQUID | | | SOLID | | |
|---|---|---|---|---|---|
| *Imperial* | *Exact conversion* | *Recommended ml* | *Imperial* | *Exact conversion* | *Recommended g* |
| $\frac{1}{4}$ pint | 142 ml | 150 ml | 1 oz | 28.35 g | 25 g |
| $\frac{1}{2}$ pint | 284 ml | 300 ml | 2 oz | 56.7 g | 50 g |
| 1 pint | 568 ml | 600 ml | 4 oz | 113.4 g | 100 g |
| $1\frac{1}{2}$ pints | 851 ml | 900 ml | 8 oz | 226.8 g | 225 g |
| $1\frac{3}{4}$ pints | 992 ml | 1 litre | 12 oz | 340.2 g | 350 g |
| | | | 14 oz | 397.0 g | 400 g |
| For quantities of $1\frac{3}{4}$ pints and over, litres and fractions of a litre have been used. | | | 16 oz (1 lb) | 453.6 g | 450 g |
| | | | 1 kilogram (kg) equals 2.2 lb. | | |

## OVEN TEMPERATURE SCALES

| °Celsius Scale | Electric Scale °F | Gas Oven Marks |
|---|---|---|
| 110°C | 225°F | $\frac{1}{4}$ |
| 130 | 250 | $\frac{1}{2}$ |
| 140 | 275 | 1 |
| 150 | 300 | 2 |
| 170 | 325 | 3 |
| 180 | 350 | 4 |
| 190 | 375 | 5 |
| 200 | 400 | 6 |
| 220 | 425 | 7 |
| 230 | 450 | 8 |
| 240 | 475 | 9 |

# EATING WISELY AND WELL

*F*ood is vital to everyone, not simply because it is pleasurable to eat, but because it is essential to health. It contains nutrients (proteins, fats, carbohydrates, vitamins and minerals) which are needed for growth, repair and normal body functioning.

◆

In general, most people in the developed world eat reasonably adequate diets, often taking in more nutrients than their bodies actually need. The wide variety of foods available mean that on a balanced diet it's virtually impossible to be seriously deficient in any vital nutrients. Nevertheless, doctors and nutritionists are concerned about people's eating patterns and how these affect their health.

Over the past hundred years or so, the average western diet has changed dramatically. People now eat more meat, dairy foods, sugary and salty foods, refined carbohydrates and drink more alcohol. Fewer cereals (particularly the unrefined ones) and less fresh fruit and vegetables are consumed. In nutritional terms, this has meant a diet high in saturated fat, sugar and salt and low in the dietary fibre which is an essential part of healthy eating.

These changes seem to be associated with a high incidence of certain diseases which were previously rare and remain rare in those countries which still eat a diet equivalent to ours of a century ago. These include coronary heart disease, certain cancers, maturity onset diabetes and dental caries (tooth decay). Coronary heart disease is currently the biggest single killer in the west. In Britain over 150,000 people die from it each year and it is estimated that two out of every five men will suffer some form of heart disease before they reach retirement age. Tooth decay doesn't kill, but its treatment is time-consuming and costly.

Some people eat a healthy diet with little or no room for improvement. Most could improve their diet by consuming less fat—particularly saturated fat—less sugar, salt and alcohol and more dietary fibre. This does not mean cutting out certain foods altogether; just eating less of some and more of others. It does not mean constant vigilance over what you eat; a few basic changes will automatically produce a healthy diet.

### FAT AND CHOLESTEROL

Fat from food is the most concentrated source of energy. The average westerner eats around 100 g (4 oz) of fat each day, which supplies almost 40 per cent of energy intake. This means that for every 100 calories consumed 40 come from fat.

Fats can be divided into three categories; saturated, monosaturated and polyunsaturated. Saturated fats are mainly found in meats and dairy products, but some fats can be made more saturated by manufacturing processes. Saturated fats are usually solid at room temperature, but there are some exceptions; palm oil and coconut oil are highly saturated vegetable oils.

Saturated fats tend to increase the amount of cholesterol in the blood. The body manufactures its own supply of cholesterol in the liver, and a certain amount of cholesterol is essential to make bile acids and various hormones (cortisol, oestrogen, testosterone). However, excess cholesterol in the blood can lead to heart disease.

As well as its own manufactured supply, the body uses both cholesterol and saturated fats from foods to make blood cholesterol. Of the two, saturated fats have the most impact on blood cholesterol.

Monosaturated fats have no effect on blood cholesterol—they neither raise or lower it. They include the fats in avocados, cashew nuts, olives and olive oil, peanuts and peanut butter.

Polyunsaturated fats may lower the level of cholesterol in the blood and could protect against heart disease. These fats are usually liquid at room temperature, such as corn oil, safflower oil, sesame oil and sunflower oil. Some margarines are high in polyunsaturated fat and are recommended by most nutritionists as a healthy alternative to those high in saturated fats.

From the point of view of weight control, it is best to cut down on *all* fats and eat more bread, cereals, fresh fruit and vegetables.

### CARBOHYDRATES AND FIBRE

These are important suppliers of energy to the body and, although in the past people were often advised to cut down on carbohydrates as a means of controlling weight, research has shown that everyone should be eating more foods which are high in the *unrefined* carbohydrates, such as wholemeal bread, wholemeal flour and brown rice. When these are refined into white bread, flour and rice most of the dietary fibre is removed, reducing their food value.

## TYPICAL EXAMPLE OF 30 g OF FIBRE

| | |
|---|---|
| 25 g (1 oz) high fibre breakfast cereal | 7.5 g |
| 2 slices wholemeal bread | 4.5 g |
| 1 large apple | 2.5 g |
| 1 large orange | 3.0 g |
| 1 jacket potato, weighing about 200 g (7 oz) | 5.0 g |
| 2 medium raw carrots | 3.0 g |
| 1 banana | 3.5 g |
| *Total fibre* | 30.0 g |

**Other fibre**

| | |
|---|---|
| 50 g (2 oz) uncooked wholewheat spaghetti or macaroni | 5.5 g |
| 50 g (2 oz) uncooked brown rice | 2.5 g |

Dietary fibre, known as roughage, is found only in plant foods, where it gives structure to plant cell walls. It is indigestible and remains in the intestine after the nutrients have been absorbed. Although it is of no nutritional value, it plays a vital role in keeping the body healthy. It prevents constipation and may also prevent certain diseases of the intestine, such as diverticulosis, cancer of the large bowel and possibly other disorders like varicose veins and heart disease, although this has yet to be proved.

Dietary fibre works by holding a lot of water. The more fibre that is eaten, the more moisture is absorbed and it becomes easy for the intestine to push the soft, bulky waste matter along without pressure or straining. It also means that any potentially harmful substances are diluted and eliminated quickly from the body, spending little time in contact with the wall of the intestine.

The fibre found in cereals is particularly effective at absorbing moisture, but the fibre in vegetable foods may have other roles in preventing disease, so it is sensible to eat fibre from a variety of sources.

There is no recommended daily intake for dietary fibre, but experts agree that at least 25 g (1 oz) a day, rather than the average 20 g ($\frac{3}{4}$ oz) would be beneficial. In parts of Africa, where diseases of civilisation such as cancer of the colon are rare, the average intake of fibre is around 150 g (5 oz) a day, proving to a large extent the damage lack of fibre can do.

Increasing fibre intake doesn't mean adding bran to everything. It is much better to eat more foods that are naturally high in fibre, like whole grain cereals (including wholemeal and brown bread which include brans or fibres), wholegrain breakfast cereals, muesli, wholewheat pasta and rice, fruit, vegetables and pulses. There's little danger of eating too much fibre. An excess of uncooked bran can reduce the absorption of zinc and certain other minerals but an adult would have to eat quite a bit for this to happen. Children under the age of two, however, should not be given uncooked bran.

### SUGAR

This is the one carbohydrate that everyone should eat less of. It is a very concentrated form of energy— 10 ml (2 tsp) contains around 40 calories. It has few nutrients and little bulk, which means it is easy to eat large amounts.

*It is essential to eat a wide variety of foods to maintain the well-balanced diet the body needs.*

There is no significant nutritional difference between refined white sugar and brown sugar; both are detrimental to teeth. It's particularly damaging in sticky forms like cakes, sweets and biscuits and the more often it's eaten the more damage it does, so frequent sugary snacks are worse than the same amount of sugar in one meal.

Experts recommend that the average sugar intake of 38 kg (86 lb) per person each year should be reduced. The best way to do this is by cutting down on the sugar added to food and drinks in the home, consuming fewer soft drinks, cakes, sweets, biscuits and sugar-laden snacks. Replace them with fresh fruit, salad or vegetables. Change to low calorie or sugar-free drinks (check labels for dextrose, maltose, glucose and fructose, which are all common examples of hidden sugar). Use artificial sweeteners like saccharine, aspartame or acesulfame K, which are low in calories and do not cause tooth decay.

### SALT

Salt is a compound of sodium and chloride, both of which are minerals essential for regulating the amount of water in body cells and transmitting nervous impulses. Chloride also produces hydrochloric acid in the stomach, which aids digestion, and sodium is important for muscle contraction and the regulation of blood pressure.

Sodium occurs naturally in many foods and is also added in the form of salt or other sodium-containing compounds. It has important implications for health. The theory is that a high sodium intake is an important factor in the development of high blood pressure (hypertension) in certain susceptible individuals. In communities where salt intake is very low, so too is the incidence of high blood pressure. In Japan, where salt intake is very high, roughly 40 per cent of middle-aged adults have high blood pressure.

High blood pressure is a major risk factor in the development of heart and blood vessel disease and greatly increases the risk of heart attacks and strokes. Nutritionists and many within the medical profession feel the evidence is strong enough to recommend that we cut down on the amount of salt we eat. However, other experts claim there is not enough evidence available to justify recommending major changes to our diet.

Approximately 70 per cent of the salt we eat is present in food, much of it added during manufacture. The other 30 per cent is added at the table or in cooking. It would seem advisable to at least reduce the amount of salt we eat, by using smaller amounts in cooking and eating less of the products with a high salt content, such as preserved meats and meat products, smoked food and savoury snacks like salted peanuts.

### PROTEIN

Protein forms 75 per cent of the body's solid mass and is needed in every body cell. All enzymes and many hormones are made from protein and it is essential for body growth and repair.

Protein is made up of small units called amino acids. When protein is eaten, it breaks down into over 20 different amino acids and reassembles in many different combinations to form the 10,000 or so proteins which the body needs. Unused protein becomes a source of calories, which are either used up as energy or stored as body fat.

The body can make some amino acids itself, but others—known as the essential amino acids—must come from food. The quality of a protein depends on its essential amino acid composition. If a protein contains all the essential amino acids, but the amount of one of them is relatively low, this is said to be the 'limiting amino acid' because it limits the value of the protein.

## AVERAGE DAILY PROTEIN REQUIREMENTS

| Group | Protein required | Food |
|---|---|---|
| Children 1–3 | 20–39 g (1–1½ oz app.) | **20 g**—568 ml (1 pint) milk. **39 g**—100 g (4 oz) fish + 1 egg + 75 g (3 oz) baked beans + 1 glass of pasteurised milk. |
| Boys 15–18 | 67–90 g (2½–3½ oz app.) | **67 g**—4 slices bread + 568 ml (1 pint) milk + 50 g (2 oz) cheese + 2 medium potatoes + 100 g (4 oz) lean meat. **90 g**—as above + 400 g (14 oz) baked beans + 25 g (1 oz) peanuts. |
| Women 18–54 Moderately active | 54 g (2 oz app.) | 100 g (4 oz) fish + 2 slices bread + 50 g (2 oz) cheese + 2 medium potatoes + 150 g (5 oz) spaghetti + 1 small glass of milk. |
| Men 18–54 Moderately active | 70 g (3 oz app.) | As women (above) + 50 g (2 oz) lean meat. |

By mixing proteins containing differing amino acids, you can produce a meal of high quality protein. For example, the protein in animal foods such as meat contains roughly the necessary amount of amino acids, so it is high quality protein. Protein from a vegetable source is of a lower value because it lacks or is low in one or more of the essential amino acids. However, one source of vegetable protein can make up for the deficiency in another, so a combination of vegetables, pulses and grains will together provide all the necessary amino acids.

Individual protein requirements vary considerably, depending on many factors such as age, sex, weight and level of activity. Early childhood, adolescence, pregnancy and lactation are periods when protein requirements are relatively high because of the growth and development taking place. The chart opposite gives average daily allowances for certain groups of people with an example of the foods which provide this amount of protein.

### PROTEIN IN VEGETARIAN DIETS

The term 'vegetarian' covers a wide range of eating habits and, in order to analyse the nutritional content, it is important to differentiate between the types. Vegetarians exclude meat, fish and poultry from their diet although most eat eggs and dairy produce and are sometimes known as lacto-vegetarians.

*Vegans* or *strict vegetarians* do not eat any animal products and they must take special care when planning their diet to ensure that they eat a wide variety of wholewheat cereals, pulses, nuts and legumes (podded plants such as peas and beans). Soya bean protein is comparable with meat protein, so is valuable to vegans.

### VITAMINS

Vitamins, which are vital for proper body functioning, can be divided into two different types— the fat soluble and the water soluble ones. Vitamins A, D, E and K dissolve in fats and are mostly found in foods which contain fat. They are stored in the liver in amounts large enough to last for several months. The water soluble vitamins, C and the B complex, dissolve in water and cannot be stored in the body in large quantities. Small amounts are found in body cells and added together they form what nutritionists call the vitamin pool. Once the pool is full or saturated, any excess is simply excreted from the body. As the vitamins are used up, the pool needs to be topped up.

The amounts of vitamins needed by the body are tiny. Most people in Britain obtain all the vitamins they need from food, provided their diet is varied enough. Those who believe they have special needs should ask their doctor for advice. If extra vitamins are recommended, a multi-vitamin tablet should fulfil the need, but do not exceed the recommended dose. The body is a finely-tuned machine and taking large doses of fat soluble vitamins can upset its chemical balance and cause illness and even death—large amounts of vitamins A and D stored in the body can have fatal consequences.

However, it is highly unlikely that toxic amounts of vitamins come from food, unless unnatural quantities of, for example, carrot juice or liver are consumed to excess. Most problems occur when high dosage vitamin tablets are regularly taken. For instance, although excess amounts of water soluble vitamins are generally eliminated from the body in the urine, taking large amounts of vitamin C over a period of time has been linked with kidney stones and 'rebound scurvey'. In the case of the latter, the body gets used to high doses of the vitamin and reacts by developing the deficiency disease when vitamin C intake levels return to normal.

Vitamins and minerals (see page 14) often work together, one complementing the work of the other. Iron absorption can be increased significantly if vitamin C is present in the body, so a fresh orange eaten after liver ensures that the iron in the liver is well absorbed.

Some vitamins are easily lost or destroyed by bad storage, preparation or cooking. If fruit and vegetables are cooked for too long, most of their vitamin C is destroyed. If milk is left on the doorstep, sunlight will reduce its riboflavin (vitamin B2) content (see page 14).

Buy fresh fruit and vegetables in prime condition and store in a cool place. Prepare them just before they are needed, do not leave them soaking in water. To keep vitamin loss to a minimum, cook in a small amount of water for as short a time as possible, or steam them. Wherever possible, eat raw fruit and vegetables which then retain all their vitamins.

**Folic acid (folacin)** is needed to produce healthy red blood cells. Deficiency is being increasingly recognised in pregnant women, old people and Asian immigrants, who may need supplements. Good food sources include liver, green leafy vegetables, pulses, bread, oranges and bananas. Other fruit, meat and dairy products contain little.

**Pantothenic acid** is needed for all tissue growth as it plays a large part in releasing energy from fats and carbohydrates. It is found in a wide variety of foods, particularly animal produce, cereals and legumes.

**Vitamin A (retinol)** is needed for growth, good vision in dim light, healthy skin and surface tissues, especially those that secrete mucus. Vitamin A is the vitamin in its active form and is known as retinol. Provitamin A, vitamin A precursors or caratenoids are substances which the body can turn into vitamin A. These are found in animal foods, dairy products and vegetables. Good sources include offal, green leafy vegetables, yellow and orange-coloured fruit and vegetables, e.g. carrots, tomatoes, apricots, peaches and Cantaloupe melons, butter and margarine.

**Vitamin B** was originally thought to be one vitamin, but has turned out to be a complex of substances. There are at present thought to be about eight vitamins in the B group and they often appear in the same foods. The three best known are thiamin (vitamin B1), riboflavin (vitamin B2) and niacin or nicotinic acid (which used to be referred to as vitamin B3). These three are always known by their chemical names, while most of the others are known by their numbers.

**Thiamine (B1)** helps the body release energy from carbohydrates. Good sources include milk, offal, eggs, vegetables, fruit, wholegrain and fortified cereals—including bread and breakfast cereals—pulses and nuts.

**Riboflavin (B2)** is also vital for the release of energy from food. About one third of our daily intake comes from milk. Other good sources include offal, eggs, cheese and yeast extract.

**Niacin** helps in the conversion of food to energy. The main sources are meat, fish, fortified breakfast cereals, vegetables and yeast extract.

**Vitamin B6 (pyridoxine)** helps the body utilise protein and contributes to the formation of haemoglobin for red blood cells. It is found in a wide range of foods including meat, fish, eggs, wholegrain cereals, some vegetables, pulses and yeast extract.

**Vitamin B12 (cyanocobalamin)** is essential for the production of healthy red blood cells. Deficiency leads to a type of anaemia. The only people at risk of not getting enough of this vitamin are vegans, as it is found only in animal foods. Useful sources include liver, meat, eggs, fish, milk and cheese.

**Vitamin B13 (orotic acid)** is little known; its function and its deficiency effects are not known.

**Biotin** also belongs to the B complex. It is made by bacteria in the intestine and is also found in offal, egg yolk, vegetables, cereals, fruit and nuts.

**Vitamin C (ascorbic acid)** is needed to keep the connective tissue between cells healthy. Vitamin C is found almost exclusively in fresh fruit and vegetables, including potatoes. A glass of orange juice will supply a day's requirements. Despite the popular belief that vitamin C will prevent or cure colds, the evidence is not conclusive.

**Vitamin D (cholecalciferol)** is needed for the growth and formation of bones and teeth as it helps in the absorption of calcium and controls the amount that is retained. Children, pregnant women and lactating women have particularly high requirements, while elderly people and Asian women and children may be at risk of deficiency.

Vitamin D is obtained by the action of sunlight on a substance in the skin. It is also found in a few sources such as some dairy products, some fish and margarine. Most of the body's supply comes from sunlight.

**Vitamin E** can be found in different forms under the names tocopherols and tototrienols—tocopherols is the most common name. It is thought to be essential for muscular health and blood circulation. Rich sources include wheatgerm, vegetable oils, some vegetables and nuts.

**Vitamin K** is needed for the normal clotting of the blood. It is found in green and some other vegetables, cereals and pulses. It is also made by bacteria in the intestines.

## MINERALS

These cannot be manufactured by the body and must be obtained from food. At present, 15 minerals have been identified as being essential to health and others are still under investigation. The majority of people obtain enough minerals provided a good variety of food is eaten.

**Calcium** is essential for the growth and development of bones, teeth and tissues. It is also needed for muscle contraction, nerve functioning, the action of several enzymes and for the normal clotting of blood. Calcium is found in milk, yogurt, cheese (including reduced and low fat varieties), white or brown bread and flour (which are fortified with calcium), eggs and green vegetables. It is also present in the soft bones of canned fish and in small quantities in many other foods.

**Iron** is used to make the haemoglobin in red blood cells and is stored in the muscles and liver. Haemoglobin carries oxygen to supply all the body's cells and a shortage leads to anaemia. Iron deficiency is fairly common in Britain, particularly in women of child bearing age since iron requirements are increased by menstrual loss and pregnancy.

The body can adapt to increased needs by increasing its absorption from the intestine, but some women still need to be prescribed iron tablets or supplements. Iron is found in meat (particularly liver), some fish, cereals, pulses and vegetables. The iron in vegetable foods is less well absorbed than the iron in animal foods, but vitamin C increases the absorption of iron from all foods.

**Magnesium** is concentrated in the bones and provides strength for them. Minute amounts are also found in body cells. It is necessary for the functioning of some enzymes and also plays a part in breaking down foods to release energy. It is found in cocoa, some nuts and green vegetables.

**Phosphorous** is mainly laid down in the skeleton with calcium. The rest interacts with some B complex vitamins to release energy from foods and is present in small quantities in many body cells. It is found in a wide variety of foods.

**Potassium**, together with sodium (see Salt on page 12) plays a vital part in the functioning of nerves and in determining blood pressure. It is found in many foods, particularly fruit, vegetables, cereals, eggs, cheese, fish and some meats, such as offal beef and pork.

**Sodium and Chlorine** (see Salt on page 12).

**Sulphur** is found in minute quantities in every cell in the body. All protein foods contain sulphur, so there is no danger of deficiency.

**Trace elements** are mineral substances present in the body in very small amounts. With the varied diet eaten in Britain, there is unlikely to be a deficiency of any of the important ones known so far. Considerable work is being done on trace elements and new ones may well yet emerge. Those recognised as being essential for health include cobalt, copper, chromium, fluoride, iodine, manganese and zinc.

## GUIDELINES FOR HEALTHY EATING

Obviously no-one needs to eat a perfectly balanced diet every day. The odd junk meal or day of snacks will even itself out over a week of varied eating. Fresh foods which have not undergone any processing are obviously better than packaged versions, but make sure that they really are fresh. Canned, dried and frozen foods can be just as good as fresh.

Read the list of ingredients on manufactured food packaging, so you can avoid those foods containing excessive amounts of sugar, salt or undesirable additives such as colouring or preservatives.

### FOOD LABELLING

To comply with food labelling regulations, most prepacked foods have to include certain information, such as the name and a description of the food, how to use it if that is not clear, and the name and address of the manufacturer.

The label must list the ingredients in the food in descending order of weight, including water if it is more than 5 per cent of the weight of the finished product. With certain exceptions, such as canned food, the label should show a date. Food which has a life of 6 weeks or less will have a 'Sell by' date; food which has a life of 6 weeks to 3 months will have a 'Best before' date, showing the day and the month; food that will last from 3–18 months will have either a 'Best before' date, followed by a date which includes the day, month and year or it will say 'End of' followed by the month and year. Use these dates to check the freshness of foods in your store cupboard.

**For most people a healthy diet means**
- Eating less fat. Aim to cut total fat intake by at least a quarter and saturated fat by half.
- Eating less sugar. Aim to cut sugar intake by at least half.
- Eating less salt.
- Eating more dietary fibre (roughage).

**Aim towards**
- Being the correct weight for your height and bone structure.
- Drinking in moderation.
- Not smoking.

**Foods to eat less of**
- Fatty meats such as pork, lamb, beef and bacon. Meat products such as pies, sausages, pâtés, burgers. Cooked and cured meats such as salami, corned beef, luncheon meat.
- Dairy foods such as butter, full fat milk and cheese, cream, ice cream.
- Hard margarines, dripping, lard and other animal shortenings.
- Cakes, biscuits and pastries. Refined and sweetened breakfast cereals, ready-made desserts, confectionery, soft drinks, snacks such as crisps and salted nuts.
- Cut down the amount of sugar added to food and drinks and reduce the number of snacks between meals.
- Cut down the amount of salt added to foods.
- Limit the number of egg yolks consumed to only three to five a week.

## Foods to eat more of

- Poultry such as chicken and turkey, game, rabbit (all low in saturated fat) and offal. Lean cuts of other meats with visible fat trimmed off.
- Fish, both white and oily types. The latter contains a type of fatty acid which may actually protect against heart disease. Eat at least one oily fish meal each week (mackerel, herring, sardine).
- Low fat dairy foods such as skimmed or semi-skimmed milk (the latter is virtually indistinguishable from full fat milk), low or medium fat cheese and low fat yogurt.
- Fresh fruit and vegetables, including potatoes. Leave skins on and eat raw wherever possible to retain maximum nutrients.
- Unrefined cereal products, such as wholemeal flour and bread and wholegrain breakfast cereals.
- Pulses, beans, rice, pasta and noodles, especially the unrefined varieties.
- Soft margarine labelled 'high in polyunsaturates' which is relatively low in saturated fats. Pure vegetable oils, such as sunflower, soya, safflower corn and olive. Use these as alternatives to other fats like butter and hard margarines, but still try and cut down on them.

## Meal planning

Aim to eat daily:

- Bread and cereals including rice and pasta: 4 servings or more.
- Vegetables and fruit: 4 servings or more, including at least one raw.
- Meat, offal, poultry, fish, eggs, cheese or pulses: 1–2 servings, vary the choice throughout the week and, eat lean meats and low fat cheeses.
- Milk: children and adolescents, 568 ml (1 pint); adults, 300 ml ($\frac{1}{2}$ pint). Apart from infants, switch to semi or skimmed milk.
- Up to 15–25 g ($\frac{1}{2}$–1 oz) of butter, margarine or cooking oils: remember part of this intake will come from the preparation of other foods. Also, do not forget to take account of the hidden fats in baked goods, such as cakes, pies and biscuits.

### WATCHING WEIGHT

The energy value of a food indicates its value to the body as a fuel. Traditionally, this has been measured in calories: one calorie is the amount of heat required to raise the temperature of 1 g of water by one degree Celcius. More recently, the word joule has been appearing on some food labels and diet charts. The joule is the unit of energy which is largely used in scientific work and throughout the EEC. It is a smaller unit than a calorie, and enables tests to be carried out to a greater degree of accuracy. One calorie is equal to 4.17 joules.

Both units are too small for everyday use, so for convenience the next unit up is used. What we count when watching our diet are not calories but units of 1,000 calories, known as kilocalories or Calories with a capital C. Just as there are Calories, there are kilojoules, units of 1,000 joules, or megajoules which are 1,000 kilojoules. In practical terms, a 1,000 Calorie diet is 4,200 kilojoules or 4.2 megajoules.

The amount of energy produced by our calorie intake should be the same as the amount needed for our bodies to function. Eating too many calories too often gradually increases the amount of fat stored in the body and leads to overweight.

People who are overweight are more likely than those of normal weight to suffer from heart disease, strokes, high blood pressure, maturity onset diabetes, gallstones and varicose veins. Even relatively small amounts of excess weight increase the chances of disease.

To lose weight and maintain the loss, you need to make permanent changes to your dietary habits. Crash diets and cures may promise rapid weight loss, but they are rarely successful in the long term. They usually amount to expensive ways of calorie counting and some can actually be dangerous if followed for too long.

For permanent weight loss, cut down on fatty and sugary foods and eat more fresh fruit, vegetables (including potatoes which are an excellent source of dietary fibre) and salads. Carbohydrate foods like wholemeal bread, wholegrain breakfast cereals and wholewheat pasta contain a good range of nutrients and because they are bulky they satisfy hunger. Also, carbohydrate has to be converted into fat in the body and one quarter is lost as energy in the process, unlike fat which can be absorbed directly into the body's fat store.

Low calorie soft drinks and artificial sweeteners allow slimmers to cut down on calories without feeling deprived.

Slimming clubs are helpful if you are weak willed and they also work on changing eating habits, as well as offering encouragement and support. Once you have lost weight, weigh yourself regularly each week to make sure it does not creep back on.

Exercise can also help by increasing the amount which makes you look and feel trimmer; you lose weight and inches.

# SOUPS

The term soup covers an astonishingly wide range of liquid dishes, ranging from thin light consommé to thick hearty stews containing chunks of meat and vegetables which serve as a meal in themselves. Soups are great for using up small quantities of leftovers —just put them in a blender or food processor with some stock or other flavoursome liquid—but may also require time and skill to create perfect flavour and texture.

♦

There is nothing to beat the flavour of really good homemade soup: you know exactly what has gone into it; there are no additives in the form of preservatives or colourants and you can adjust flavour and texture to suit your taste. With the use of electrical equipment, soups can easily be processed to exactly the right texture.

When serving soup as a starter, allow about 150–200 ml (5–7 fl oz) per person, depending on how substantial it is; for soup that's a meal in itself, allow about 250–300 ml (8–10 fl oz), depending on appetites and the ratio of solids to liquid.

Hot soup should be served piping hot, unless it's a type with cream added that would curdle. Warm the soup bowls well and, if possible, don't pour it out until people are seated and ready to eat.

Chilled soup should not be so cold that its flavour is masked.

### STOCK OR STOCK CUBES?

Cubes (and stock powders) tend to be strong and salty. If you find them too salty, use less of the cube than recommended and do not add extra salt to the soup. If you make your own stock, you can reduce it to quite small quantities which can be diluted with water when required. It also freezes well. Making stock takes about 3 hours in an ordinary pan on the cooker; 1–1¼ hours in a pressure cooker. When it's done, allow the stock to cool and remove the layer of fat from the top before storing. Stock can be kept in the refrigerator for up to a week but boil up every 1–2 days.

### ACCOMPANIMENTS FOR SOUP

Some soups have a traditional accompaniment like the croûtons and grated cheese that are served with French onion soup; others such as Vichyssoise can look pale and bland unless garnished with chopped chives or parsley. Most soups, especially those served in wide soup plates, look better garnished, while others can be bulked out or given a contrasting texture by adding an accompaniment.

**Croûtons** are fried or toasted cubes of bread. For fried croûtons, cut the bread into small dice and fry in vegetable oil until golden brown. Drain on absorbent kitchen paper and serve in a separate bowl so they remain crisp. For toasted croûtons, toast the bread and then cut it into dice. Croûtons can be made in advance and stored in an airtight container. Add to the soup just before serving.

**Cream or yogurt** swirled on top of a soup just before serving looks attractive.

**Rice and pasta** make a soup more substantial. Either add cooked leftovers and heat through just before the soup is served or cook the rice

*Cut bacon into fine dice to garnish a bowl of soup.*

or pasta in the soup itself (see page 293). Use small pasta shapes in soups or break up large varieties so that it is easy to eat with a soup spoon.

**Fried vegetables** such as onion rings, chopped leeks and sliced mushrooms add colour, texture and flavour to bland soups such as Potato or Bean soup. Cook then drain well before using.

**Bacon rashers** rinded and cut into small strips or dice, can be fried or grilled until crisp and then crumbled. Sprinkle over a soup to add flavour and texture but take care that the soup itself is not salty to start with.

**Fresh vegetables** like thin slices of cucumber, snipped celery tops, julienne strips of carrot will decorate the soup and add a crunchy texture. They are best used on chilled soups.

Lemon, thinly sliced, or curls of lemon rind are good with clear soups. Orange slices and rind go well with tomato.

**Grated hard cheese** such as Cheddar and Parmesan melts deliciously into hot soups. Serve separately in a bowl and sprinkle on the soup just before it is served.

**Fresh herbs**, whether of one or several types, will liven up almost any hot or cold soup. Dried herbs will always look dried if sprinkled on top and are best cooked in the soup itself.

## MELBA TOAST

*4 slices of ready-sliced white or brown bread*

1. Preheat the grill to high and toast the bread lightly on both sides. Cut off the crusts, then holding the toast flat, slide the knife between the toasted edges to split the bread.
2. Cut each piece into 4 triangles, then toast under the grill, untoasted side uppermost, until golden and the edges curl. Serve warm. Alternatively, make earlier in the day and warm for a short time

in the oven at 170°C (325°F) mark 3 before serving.
*Serves 4*

*Hold the toast flat and, using a sharp knife, cut the slices in half.*

## DUMPLINGS

*100 g (4 oz) self raising flour*

*50 g (2 oz) shredded suet*

*salt and pepper*

1. In a bowl, mix the flour, suet and seasoning with sufficient cold water to make an elastic dough.
2. Divide into about 16 portions and with lightly floured hands, roll into small balls.
3. Add to the soup and simmer for about 15–20 minutes.
*Serves 4*

**Variations**
Plain or flavoured dumplings may be added to almost any meat or vegetable soup to make it more substantial. Flavour the above recipe with any of the following ingredients:
25 g (1 oz) Cheddar cheese, finely grated
½ small onion, skinned and finely chopped
15 ml (1 level tbsp) grated Parmesan cheese
2.5 ml (½ level tsp) mild curry powder
15 ml (1 level tbsp) chopped fresh watercress
7.5 ml (1½ tsp) chopped fresh parsley
7.5 ml (1½ tsp) snipped fresh chives
5 ml (1 tsp) chopped fresh tarragon
2.5 ml (½ level tsp) mixed dried herbs
2.5 ml (½ level tsp) paprika
15 ml (1 level tbsp) canned sweetcorn, drained
5 ml (1 level tsp) caraway seeds

# BASIC BONE STOCK

*900 g (2 lb) meat bones, fresh or from cooked meat*

*2 medium onions, skinned and chopped*

*2 celery sticks, chopped*

*2 medium carrots, scrubbed and chopped*

*5 ml (1 level tsp) salt*

*3 black peppercorns*

*bouquet garni or sprig of parsley and thyme, a bay
  leaf, blade of mace, etc*

**1.** Chop the bones. Place in a saucepan with
2 litres (3½ pints) water, the vegetables, salt,
peppercorns and herbs. Bring to the boil and
skim off any scum. Cover and simmer for about
3 hours. Strain the stock and, when cold, remove
all traces of fat.

**2.** If using a pressure cooker, add the bones and
1.4 litres (2½ pints) water, bring to the boil and
skim. Add the vegetables, salt, peppercorns and
herbs. Bring to High (15 lb) pressure and cook
for 1–1¼ hours. If you are using marrow bones,
increase the water to 1.7 litres (3 pints) and
cook for 2 hours. Reduce pressure at room
temperature.

*Makes about 900 ml–1.1 litres (1½–2 pints)*

# BEEF STOCK

*450 g (1 lb) shin of beef, cut into pieces*

*450 g (1 lb) marrow bone or knuckle of veal, chopped*

*bouquet garni*

*1 medium onion, skinned and sliced*

*1 medium carrot, scrubbed and sliced*

*1 celery stick, washed and sliced*

*2.5 ml (½ level tsp) salt*

**1.** To give a good flavour and colour, brown the
bones and meat in the oven before using them. Put
in a saucepan with 1.7 litres (3 pints) water, herbs,
vegetables and salt. Bring to the boil, skim, cover
and simmer for about 3 hours.

**2.** Or pressure cook on High (15 lb) pressure for
1–1¼ hours as for Basic Bone Stock (see above),
using 1.4 litres (2½ pints) water. If using marrow
bones, increase the water to 1.7 litres (3 pints) and
cook for 2 hours. Strain the stock and, when cold,
remove all traces of fat.

*Makes about 900 ml–1.1 litres (1½–2 pints)*

# CHICKEN STOCK

*1 chicken carcass*

*1 medium onion, skinned and sliced*

*1 medium carrot, scrubbed and sliced*

*1 celery stick, washed and sliced*

*1 bay leaf*

**1.** Break up the carcass and put in a large saucepan
with any skin and chicken meat. Add 1.4–1.7 litres
(2½–3 pints) water, the flavouring vegetables and
bay leaf. Bring to the boil, skim, cover and simmer
for about 3 hours.

**2.** Or pressure cook on High (15 lb) for about
1 hour as for Basic Bone Stock (see above).

**3.** Strain the stock and, when cold, remove all
traces of fat.

*Makes about 900 ml (1½ pints)*

# FISH STOCK

*1 fish head or fish bones and trimmings*

*salt*

*bouquet garni*

*1 medium onion, skinned and sliced*

**1.** Put the head and fish trimmings into a
saucepan, cover with 450 ml (¾ pint) water and
season with salt. Bring to the boil, then skim.

**2.** Reduce the heat and add the bouquet garni and
onion. Cover and simmer for 20 minutes. Strain.

**3.** Use on the same day, or store in the
refrigerator for not more than 2 days.

*Makes about 300 ml (½ pint)*

# CONSOMMÉ AND VARIATIONS

## CLASSIC CONSOMMÉ

A completely clear, well flavoured broth, made from good brown stock. Both the stock and the utensils must be quite free from any trace of grease, to prevent droplets of fat forming on the surface of the soup.

| |
|---|
| *1.4 litres (2½ pints) Beef Stock (see page 19)* |
| *100 g (4 oz) lean beef steak, eg rump* |
| *150 ml (¼ pint) cold water* |
| *1 medium carrot, peeled and quartered* |
| *1 small onion, skinned and quartered* |
| *bouquet garni* |
| *1 egg white* |
| *salt* |
| *10 ml (2 tsp) dry sherry (optional)* |

**1.** Remove any fat from the stock. Shred the meat finely and soak it in the water for 15 minutes. Put the meat and water, vegetables, stock and bouquet garni into a deep saucepan and add the egg white. Heat gently, whisking continuously until a thick froth starts to form. Stop whisking and bring to the boil. Reduce the heat immediately, cover and simmer for 2 hours. If the liquid boils too rapidly, the froth will break and cloud the consommé.

*Pour through a jelly bag.*

**2.** Scald a clean cloth or jelly bag, by pouring boiling water through it, wring it out, tie it to the four legs of an upturned stool and place a bowl underneath. Pour the soup through the cloth, keeping the froth back at first with a spoon, then let it slide out on to the cloth. Again pour the soup through the cloth and through the filter of egg white. The consommé should now be clear and sparkling.

**3.** Reheat the consommé, season with salt if necessary, and if you like, a little sherry to improve the flavour.
*Serves 4*

**To serve** Consommé may be served hot or cold, plain or with one of the following variations— in which case the consommé takes its name from the garnish. To prevent the consommé becoming cloudy, rinse the garnish in water and add it to the hot liquid just before it is served.

## Variations

### CONSOMMÉ JULIENNE

Cut small quantities of vegetables such as carrot, turnip and celery into thin strips and boil separately; rinse well before adding to the soup.

### CONSOMMÉ À LA ROYALE

The garnish consists of steamed savoury egg custard cut into tiny fancy shapes. Make the custard by mixing 1 egg yolk, 15 ml (1 tbsp) Beef Stock, milk or cream and salt and pepper to taste; strain it into a ramekin dish, cover with foil or greaseproof paper and stand the basin in a saucepan containing enough hot water to come half-way up its sides. Steam the custard slowly until it is firm; turn it out and cut into fancy shapes. Add to the soup before serving.

*Cut the savoury custard into decorative shapes.*

### JELLIED CONSOMMÉ

Cold consommé should be lightly jellied. Jellied consommé is a good soup for summer days. Use the recipe for Classic Consommé (see above). Leave the soup to cool, then chill until set. Chop roughly and serve in individual dishes.

**Variations for Jellied Consommé**

**1.** Add 30–45 ml (2–3 tbsp) chopped fresh herbs (chives, parsley and tarragon) to the consommé. Garnish with whipped cream flavoured with curry powder or sprinkled with toasted flaked almonds.

**2.** Add 30–45 ml (2–3 tbsp) chopped fresh mint leaves to the consommé. Garnish with whipped cream mixed with chopped mint.

### CONSOMMÉ À LA JARDINIÈRE

Prepare a mixture of vegetables such as finely diced carrots and turnips, tiny florets of cauliflower and green peas. Cook in boiling salted water until just tender, rinse and add to the soup before serving.

# CREAM OF ARTICHOKE SOUP

900 g (2 lb) Jerusalem artichokes, peeled

salt

2 lemon slices

25 g (1 oz) butter or margarine

1 medium onion, skinned and chopped

30 ml (2 level tbsp) cornflour

450 ml ($\frac{3}{4}$ pint) milk

15–30 ml (1–2 tbsp) lemon juice

15–30 ml (1–2 tbsp) chopped fresh parsley

60 ml (4 tbsp) single cream (optional)

pepper

croûtons, to garnish

1. Place the artichokes in a large saucepan with 900 ml (1½ pints) cold salted water and the lemon slices. Bring to the boil, cover and simmer gently for 25 minutes, until tender.

2. Drain, reserving 600 ml (1 pint) of the cooking liquid. Discard the lemon slices and mash the artichokes.
3. Melt the butter in a saucepan, add the onion and cook for about 5 minutes, until soft but not coloured. Remove the pan from the heat, stir in the cornflour and gradually add the artichoke cooking liquid and the milk.
4. Add the artichokes and bring to the boil, stirring. Cook for 2–3 minutes.
5. Cool the soup slightly, then purée in a blender or food processor or rub through a sieve. Return the purée to the rinsed out pan and stir in the lemon juice, parsley and cream if using, and season with salt and pepper.
6. Reheat gently but do not boil. Garnish with croûtons and serve immediately.
*Serves 6*

# LETTUCE SOUP

50 g (2 oz) butter or margarine

350 g (12 oz) lettuce leaves, roughly chopped

125 g (4 oz) spring onions, trimmed and sliced

15 ml (1 level tbsp) flour

600 ml (1 pint) Chicken Stock (see page 19)

150 ml ($\frac{1}{4}$ pint) milk

salt and pepper

1. Melt the butter in a saucepan, add the lettuce and spring onions and cook until very soft.
2. Stir in the flour, then add the stock. Bring to the boil, cover and simmer for about 20 minutes.
3. Allow the soup to cool slightly, then sieve or purée in a blender or food processor until smooth. Return to the pan and add the milk and seasoning. Reheat gently.
*Serves 4*

# FRESH TOMATO SOUP WITH BASIL

50 g (2 oz) butter or margarine

2 medium onions, skinned and thinly sliced

900 g (2 lb) tomatoes

45 ml (3 level tbsp) flour

900 ml (1½ pints) Chicken Stock (see page 19)

30 ml (2 level tbsp) tomato purée

7.5 ml (1½ tsp) chopped fresh basil or 2.5 ml ($\frac{1}{2}$ level tsp) dried

salt and pepper

150 ml (5 fl oz) single cream (optional)

1. Melt the butter in a saucepan, add the onions and fry gently until golden brown.
2. Meanwhile, wipe and halve the tomatoes, scoop out the seeds into a sieve placed over a bowl. Press the seeds to remove all the tomato pulp and juice; discard the seeds and reserve the juice.
3. Remove the pan from the heat. Stir in the flour and cook gently for 1 minute, stirring. Remove the pan from the heat and gradually stir in the stock. Bring to the boil slowly and continue to cook, stirring, until thickened.
4. Stir in the tomato purée, herbs and the tomatoes with reserved juice and season. Cover the pan and simmer gently for about 30 minutes.
5. Leave the soup to cool slightly, then sieve or purée in a blender or food processor. Strain through a sieve into a clean pan and reheat gently. Taste and adjust seasoning if necessary.
6. Ladle the soup into individual soup bowls and, if wished swirl a little cream through each bowl just before serving.
*Serves 6*

## CARROT AND ORANGE SOUP

| |
|---|
| 25 g (1 oz) butter or margarine |
| 700 g (1½ lb) carrots, peeled and sliced |
| 2 medium onions, skinned and sliced |
| 1.1 litres (2 pints) Chicken Stock (see page 19) |
| salt and pepper |
| 1 medium orange |

1. Melt the butter in a saucepan, add the carrots and onions and cook gently until the vegetables begin to soften.
2. Add the stock, season with salt and pepper and bring to the boil. Reduce the heat, cover and simmer for about 40 minutes, until the vegetables are tender.
3. Allow the soup to cool slightly, then sieve or purée in a blender or food processor.
4. Finely grate half the rind from the orange and add to the soup. Thinly pare the remainder of the rind, using a potato peeler, and cut into fine shreds. Cook the shreds in simmering water for 2–3 minutes until tender, then drain.
5. Squeeze the juice from the orange and add to the pan. Reheat gently and adjust seasoning, if necessary. Garnish with shreds of orange rind just before serving.
*Serves 6*

## WATERCRESS SOUP

| |
|---|
| 2 bunches of watercress |
| 50 g (2 oz) butter or margarine |
| 1 medium onion, skinned and chopped |
| 25 g (1 oz) flour |
| 568 ml (1 pint) milk |
| 450 ml (¼ pint) Chicken Stock (see page 19) |
| salt and pepper |
| 90 ml (6 tbsp) single cream (optional) |

1. Wash the watercress and reserve a few sprigs to garnish. Cut away any coarse stalks. Chop the leaves and remaining stalks.
2. Melt the butter in a large saucepan, add the watercress and onion and cook gently for about 15 minutes, until soft but not browned.
3. Stir in the flour and cook gently for 1 minute, stirring. Remove pan from the heat and gradually stir in milk, stock and seasoning. Bring to the boil slowly and continue to cook, stirring, until thickened. Simmer gently for about 30 minutes, stirring occasionally.
4. Allow to cool slightly, then purée in a blender or food processor.
5. To serve hot, return to the pan, reheat gently, adjust seasoning and stir in the cream, if using. Garnish with watercress sprigs. To serve chilled, place in the refrigerator for at least 4 hours or overnight. Serve garnished with swirls of cream, if using, and watercress sprigs.
*Serves 6*

*Watercress Soup*

## CAULIFLOWER AND ALMOND CREAM SOUP

*few saffron strands*

*60 ml (4 tbsp) boiling water*

*100 g (4 oz) flaked almonds*

*50 g (2 oz) butter or margarine*

*1 medium onion, skinned and chopped*

*1 small cauliflower, broken into florets*

*1.3 litres (2¼ pints) Chicken Stock (see page 19)*

*freshly grated nutmeg*

*salt and pepper*

*150 ml (5 fl oz) single cream*

*Cauliflower and Almond Cream Soup*

**1.** Soak the saffron in the boiling water for 2 hours. Toast half the almonds on a sheet of foil under the grill, turning them frequently. Leave to cool.

**2.** Melt the butter in a large saucepan, add the onion and fry gently until soft. Add the cauliflower and the untoasted almonds and stir, cover and cook gently for 10 minutes.

**3.** Add the stock and stir well, then strain in the yellow saffron liquid. Add a pinch of nutmeg and season to taste. Bring to the boil, lower the heat, cover and simmer for 30 minutes, or until the cauliflower is very tender.

**4.** Purée the soup in a blender or food processor until very smooth (you may have to do this twice to break down the almonds). Return to the rinsed-out pan, add half the cream and reheat gently. Taste and adjust seasoning, then pour into a warmed tureen.

**5.** Swirl in the remaining cream and sprinkle with the toasted almonds and a little nutmeg, if liked. Serve immediately.

*Serves 6*

## FRENCH ONION SOUP

*50 g (2 oz) butter or margarine*

*2 medium onions, skinned and sliced*

*30 ml (2 level tbsp) flour*

*900 ml (1½ pints) Beef Stock (see page 19)*

*salt and pepper*

*1 bay leaf*

*4 slices of French bread*

*75 g (3 oz) Gruyère cheese, grated*

**1.** Melt the butter in a saucepan, add the onions and fry for 5–10 minutes, until browned.

**2.** Stir in the flour and cook gently for 1 minute, stirring. Remove pan from the heat and gradually stir in the stock, seasoning and bay leaf. Bring to the boil slowly and continue to cook, stirring, until thickened. Cover and simmer for about 30 minutes. Remove the bay leaf. Adjust the seasoning.

**3.** Put a slice of bread into each individual soup bowl, pour on the soup and top with cheese. Alternatively, put all the soup into a flameproof casserole, float the slices of bread on it, cover with grated cheese and put under the grill, or in a hot oven, until the cheese is melted and bubbling.

*Note* Gruyère is the cheese traditionally used in this soup. Cheddar is a good alternative.

*Serves 4*

*Cover the surface of the soup with French bread slices, sprinkle over the grated cheese and brown under the grill.*

# CURRIED PARSNIP SOUP

40 g (1½ oz) butter or margarine

1 medium onion, skinned and sliced

700 g (1½ lb) parsnips, peeled and finely diced

5 ml (1 level tsp) curry powder

2.5 ml (½ level tsp) ground cumin

1.1 litres (2 pints) Chicken Stock (see page 19)

salt and pepper

150 ml (5 fl oz) single cream or milk

paprika, to garnish

1. Melt the butter in a large saucepan, add the onion and parsnips and fry gently for about 3 minutes.
2. Stir in the curry powder and cumin and cook for a further 2 minutes.
3. Add the stock, season and bring to the boil, then reduce the heat, cover and simmer for about 45 minutes, until the vegetables are tender.
4. Allow to cool slightly, then sieve or purée in a blender or food processor until smooth.
5. Return the purée to the pan and adjust the seasoning. Add the cream and reheat but do not boil. Serve sprinkled with paprika.
*Serves 6*

# CREAM OF SPINACH SOUP

50 g (2 oz) butter or margarine

450 g (1 lb) fresh spinach, washed and roughly chopped
    or 175 g (6 oz) packet frozen spinach, thawed

1 medium onion, skinned and finely chopped

25 g (1 oz) flour

450 ml (¾ pint) Chicken Stock (see page 19)

568 ml (1 pint) milk

salt and pepper

pinch of freshly grated nutmeg

30 ml (2 tbsp) single cream (optional)

1. Melt the butter in a large saucepan, add the spinach and onion and fry gently for 5–6 minutes. Stir in the flour and cook gently for 1 minute, stirring, then remove from the heat and gradually stir in the stock. Bring to the boil slowly and continue to cook, stirring, until the mixture thickens.
2. Carefully blend in the milk and bring back to the boil, stirring. Cover and simmer for 15–20 minutes, then add the seasoning and nutmeg.
3. Allow to cool slightly, then sieve or purée in a blender or food processor until smooth. Thin with a little milk if necessary. Reheat gently and adjust the seasoning.
4. Pour into a warmed soup tureen or individual dishes and stir in the cream, if using, just before serving.
*Serves 6*

# CELERY AND STILTON SOUP

40 g (1½ oz) butter or margarine

4 celery sticks, trimmed and chopped

45 ml (3 level tbsp) flour

300 ml (½ pint) milk

600 ml (1 pint) Chicken Stock (see page 19)

225 g (8 oz) Stilton cheese, grated

salt and pepper

1. Melt the butter in a saucepan, add the celery and cook gently for about 5 minutes, until softened but not coloured.
2. Stir in the flour and cook gently for 1 minute, stirring. Remove from the heat and gradually stir in the milk and stock. Bring to the boil, cover and simmer for about 15 minutes, until the celery is tender.
3. Gradually add the Stilton and stir in until melted. Season to taste and reheat gently.
*Serves 4 as a main course*

# SHROPSHIRE PEA SOUP

50 g (2 oz) butter or margarine

1 small onion, skinned and finely chopped

900 g (2 lb) fresh peas, shelled

1.1 litres (2 pints) Chicken Stock (see page 19)

2.5 ml (½ level tsp) sugar

2 large sprigs of fresh mint

salt and pepper

2 egg yolks

150 ml (5 fl oz) single cream or milk

mint sprig, to garnish

1. Melt the butter in a large saucepan, add the onion and cook for 5 minutes, until soft. Add the peas, stock, sugar and sprigs of mint. Bring to the boil, cover and cook for about 30 minutes.
2. Allow to cool slightly, then sieve or purée in a blender or food processor until smooth. Return to the pan and season to taste.
3. In a bowl, beat together the egg yolks and cream and add to the soup. Heat gently, stirring, but do not boil otherwise it will curdle. Adjust the seasoning.
4. Transfer to a soup tureen and garnish with a sprig of fresh mint.
Serves 6

# MUSHROOM SOUP

25 g (1 oz) butter or margarine

25 g (1 oz) flour

600 ml (1 pint) Chicken Stock (see page 19)

300 ml (½ pint) milk

15 ml (1 tbsp) chopped fresh parsley

175 g (6 oz) mushrooms, wiped and finely chopped

salt and pepper

15 ml (1 tbsp) lemon juice

30 ml (2 tbsp) cream (optional)

1. Place all the ingredients except the lemon juice and cream in a large saucepan. Bring to the boil over a moderate heat, whisking continuously. Cover and simmer for about 10 minutes.
2. Remove from the heat and add the lemon juice and cream, if using, stirring well. Adjust seasoning and reheat gently without boiling.
3. Pour the soup into a warmed tureen or individual soup bowls and serve immediately.
Serves 4

# MULLIGATAWNY SOUP

50 g (2 oz) butter or margarine

1 medium onion, skinned and finely chopped

1 medium carrot, peeled and finely chopped

125 g (4 oz) swede, peeled and finely chopped

1 small eating apple, peeled, cored and finely chopped

50 g (2 oz) streaky bacon, rinded and finely chopped

25 g (1 oz) flour

15 ml (1 level tbsp) mild curry paste

15 ml (1 level tbsp) tomato purée

30 ml (2 level tbsp) mango chutney

1.4 litres (2½ pints) Beef Stock (see page 19)

5 ml (1 level tsp) dried mixed herbs

pinch of ground mace

pinch of ground cloves

salt and pepper

50 g (2 oz) long grain white rice

1. Melt the butter in a saucepan, add the onion, carrot, swede, apple and bacon and fry until lightly browned.
2. Stir in the flour, curry paste, tomato purée and chutney and cook gently for 1 minute stirring. Remove from the heat and gradually stir in the stock, herbs, spices and seasoning. Bring to the boil slowly and continue to cook, stirring, until thickened.
3. Cover and simmer for 30–40 minutes.
4. Cool slightly, then sieve or purée in a blender or food processor until smooth. Return the soup to the pan, bring to the boil, add the rice and boil gently for about 12 minutes, stirring occasionally.
5. Adjust seasoning, then pour the soup into a tureen or individual soup bowls and serve immediately.
Serves 6

Left: Bean Soup. Right: Traditional Italian Pasta Soup.

## BEAN SOUP (Minestra di fagioli)

225 g (8 oz) dried white haricot beans, soaked in cold
water overnight

1.7 litres (3 pints) Chicken Stock (see page 19)

salt and pepper

30 ml (2 tbsp) olive oil

2 garlic cloves, skinned and chopped

45 ml (3 tbsp) chopped fresh parsley

extra olive oil, to garnish (optional)

**1.** Drain the soaked beans, rinse under cold
running water, then place in a large saucepan.
Cover with the stock or water and bring to the
boil. Simmer half covered for 2–2½ hours, or until
the beans are very tender.
**2.** Remove half the beans with a slotted spoon and
purée in a blender or food processor with a little
of the cooking liquid. Purée the remaining beans.
Return to the pan and season to taste.
**3.** Heat the 30 ml (2 tbsp) olive oil in a small pan,
add the garlic and fry gently until soft but not
brown. Stir in the parsley.
**4.** Add the garlic and parsley mixture to the soup,
stir well, then taste and adjust seasoning.
**5.** Pour the hot soup into a warmed soup tureen,
drizzle over a little olive oil and serve immediately.
Serves 4 as a main course

## TRADITIONAL ITALIAN PASTA SOUP (Pasta in brodo)

1.4 litres (2½ pints) Chicken or Beef Stock (see page 19)
or three 450 ml (15 fl oz) cans consommé

400 g (14 oz) medium pasta shapes, eg shells and bows

salt and pepper

freshly grated Parmesan cheese, to serve

**1.** In a large saucepan, bring the stock or
consommé to the boil. Add the pasta and cook
until just tender.
**2.** Taste and adjust seasoning, then pour into six
soup bowls and serve immediately with freshly
grated Parmesan cheese handed separately.
Serves 4 as a main course

## CLEAR VEGETABLE SOUP WITH BARLEY

1 medium carrot, peeled

3 celery sticks, trimmed

225 g (8 oz) swede, peeled

2 medium onions, skinned

25 g (1 oz) butter or margarine

1.7 litres (3 pints) Chicken Stock (see page 19)

30 ml (2 level tbsp) tomato purée

1 bay leaf

50 g (2 oz) pearl barley

1 garlic clove, skinned and crushed

salt and pepper

croûtons, to serve

**1.** Cut the vegetables into fine strips about 5 cm × 2.5 mm (2 × $\frac{1}{8}$ inch), making them as evenly sized as possible.
**2.** Heat the butter in a saucepan, add the vegetables and fry gently until just browned.
**3.** Pour in the stock with the tomato purée, bay leaf, barley and garlic.
**4.** Bring to the boil slowly and season, then cover and simmer for about 50 minutes. The vegetables should be tender and the barley soft.
**5.** Adjust seasoning and serve with croûtons.
*Serves 4 as a main course*

## JEWISH CHICKEN SOUP WITH DUMPLINGS

1.1–1.4 kg (2½–3 lb) oven-ready chicken, skinned

1 medium onion, skinned and chopped

1 litre (1¾ pints) Chicken Stock (see page 19)

350 g (12 oz) carrots, peeled and sliced

salt and pepper

100 g (4 oz) celery sticks with leaves, chopped

**For the dumplings**

75 g (3 oz) matzo meal

120 ml (8 tbsp) boiling water

1 egg, beaten

salt

**1.** Put the chicken, onion, stock, carrots and seasoning into a large saucepan and bring to the boil. Reduce the heat, cover and simmer for about 1 hour, until the chicken is tender. Remove the chicken and leave to stand for a few minutes. Strain the stock into a saucepan and heat to just simmering while you make the dumplings.
**2.** Mix together the matzo meal, boiling water, egg and salt. Shape the mixture into small marble-sized dumplings with your hands.
**3.** Add the dumplings and celery to the simmering soup and cook gently for about 20 minutes.
**4.** Carve the chicken off the bones. Cut the meat into small chunks, stir into the soup and heat through. Taste and adjust seasoning and serve immediately.
*Serves 4 as a main course*

*Jewish Chicken Soup with Dumplings*

## Vichyssoise (Chilled Leek and Potato Soup)

| |
|---|
| 25 g (1 oz) butter or margarine |
| 2 medium leeks, trimmed and sliced |
| 1 small onion, skinned and finely chopped |
| 350 g (12 oz) potatoes, peeled and finely sliced |
| 600 ml (1 pint) Chicken Stock (see page 19) |
| salt and pepper |
| 1 blade of mace |
| 150 ml (5 fl oz) single cream |
| 30 ml (2 tbsp) snipped fresh chives or finely chopped watercress, to garnish |

1. Melt the butter in a saucepan, add the leeks and onion and cook gently without browning for 7–10 minutes. Add the potatoes with the stock, seasoning and mace.
2. Bring to the boil, cover and simmer very gently for 20 –30 minutes, until the vegetables are tender.
3. Allow to cool slightly, then sieve or purée in a blender or food processor until smooth. Chill thoroughly.
4. To serve, stir in the cream, adjust the seasoning and sprinkle with snipped chives or chopped watercress.
*Serves 4*

## Chilled Asparagus Soup

| |
|---|
| 700 g (1½ lb) asparagus |
| salt |
| 100 g (4 oz) butter or margarine |
| 2 medium onions, skinned and thinly sliced |
| 1.4 litres (2½ pints) Chicken Stock (see page 19) |
| pepper |
| 150 ml (5 fl oz) single cream or natural yogurt |
| small brown uncut loaf |
| lemon slices, to garnish |

1. Wash the asparagus thoroughly under running cold water. Cut off the heads and simmer them very gently in salted water for 3–5 minutes, until just tender. Drain carefully and leave to cool.
2. Scrape the asparagus stalks with a potato peeler or knife to remove any scales and cut off the woody ends. Thinly slice the stalks.
3. Melt 50 g (2 oz) butter in a large saucepan. Add the asparagus stalks and the onions, cover and cook for 5–10 minutes, until beginning to soften.
4. Add the stock and seasoning and bring to the boil. Cover and simmer for about 30–40 minutes, until the asparagus and onion are tender.
5. Allow to cool slightly, then purée in a blender or food processor until smooth. Sieve, to remove any stringy particles, then stir in the cream and adjust the seasoning. Cover and chill in the refrigerator for 2–3 hours.
6. To make asparagus rolls: cut thin slices of brown bread and cut off the crusts and halve lengthways, then butter. Place one asparagus head on each piece of bread and roll up with the asparagus inside. Cover with cling film and chill until required.
7. Serve the soup chilled, garnished with lemon slices and accompanied by the asparagus rolls.
*Serves 6*

## Chilled Avocado Soup

| |
|---|
| 2 ripe avocados |
| 1 small onion, skinned and chopped |
| grated rind and juice of 1 lemon |
| 142 g (5 oz) natural yogurt |
| 142 ml (5 fl oz) soured cream |
| 600 ml (1 pint) Chicken Stock (see page 19) |
| salt and pepper |
| snipped fresh chives, to garnish |

1. Halve the avocados, remove the stones and scoop out the flesh.
2. Put in a blender or food processor with the onion, lemon rind and juice, yogurt and soured cream and purée until smooth.
3. Turn out into a large bowl and gradually whisk in the stock. Season to taste.
4. Cover tightly and chill well in the refrigerator. Serve the soup garnished with snipped chives.
*Serves 6*

## BORSHCH

6 small raw beetroot, about 1 kg (2¼ lb), peeled

2 medium onions, skinned and chopped

1.1 litres (2 pints) Beef Stock (see page 19)

salt and pepper

30 ml (2 tbsp) lemon juice

90 ml (6 tbsp) dry sherry

142 ml (5 fl oz) soured cream or natural yogurt and
    snipped fresh chives or dill, to garnish

1. Grate the beetroot coarsely and put in a saucepan with the onions, stock and seasoning. Bring to the boil, cover and simmer for about 45 minutes.
2. Strain, discarding the vegetables, then add the lemon juice and sherry to the liquid and adjust the seasoning. Leave to cool, then chill in the refrigerator. Serve well chilled, garnished with a whirl of soured cream and snipped chives.
*Serves 4*

## GAZPACHO

30 ml (2 level tbsp) fresh breadcrumbs

15 ml (1 tbsp) olive oil

25 ml (5 tsp) red wine vinegar

450 g (1 lb) tomatoes, skinned

225 g (8 oz) cucumber, skinned and finely chopped

1 medium green pepper, seeded and chopped

1 medium onion, skinned and chopped

450 ml (¾ pint) water

salt and pepper

3 slices fresh white bread

vegetable oil for frying

1 garlic clove, skinned and crushed

1. Place the breadcrumbs, olive oil and vinegar together in a large mixing bowl. Leave to soak for 20 minutes.

2. Halve the tomatoes, remove the seeds and finely chop the flesh.
3. Reserve about 30 ml (2 tbsp) of each chopped vegetable. Cover and refrigerate.
4. Purée the remaining vegetables with half the water until very smooth.
5. Gradually stir into the oil and breadcrumb mixture until thoroughly combined. Stir in the remaining water. Season well.
6. Cover and chill in the refrigerator for at least 2 hours before serving.
7. Evenly dice the bread. Heat the oil with the garlic, add the bread and fry until golden brown. Drain well on absorbent kitchen paper.
8. Serve the soup well chilled with the chopped vegetables and croûtons served in separate dishes. Place one or two ice cubes in each soup bowl before serving, if wished.
*Serves 4*

## LENTIL AND BACON SOUP

175 g (6 oz) red lentils

1.7 litres (3 pints) Chicken Stock (see page 19)

1 garlic clove, skinned and crushed

1 clove

200 g (7 oz) lean bacon rashers, rinded and diced

226 g (8 oz) can tomatoes

1 medium onion, skinned and chopped

salt and pepper

450 g (1 lb) potatoes, peeled and diced

30 ml (2 tbsp) lemon juice

crisply fried bacon rolls, chopped fresh parsley, grated
    cheese or croûtons, to garnish

1. Wash the lentils and put them in a saucepan with the stock. Add the garlic, clove, bacon, tomatoes, onion and seasoning.
2. Bring to the boil, cover and simmer for about 1 hour, until the lentils are soft.
3. Add the potatoes and cook for a further 20 minutes, until tender.
4. Remove the clove. Allow the soup to cool slightly, then sieve or purée in a blender or food processor until smooth.
5. Return the soup to the pan, add the lemon juice and reheat gently. Adjust the seasoning and garnish with bacon rolls, chopped parsley, grated cheese or croûtons just before serving.
*Serves 6 as a main course*

## CHESTNUT AND ORANGE SOUP

*450 g (1 lb) fresh whole chestnuts or a 238 g (10 oz)*
*can whole chestnuts (drained weight)*

*40 g (1½ oz) butter or margarine*

*1 medium carrot, peeled and finely chopped*

*2 medium onions, skinned and finely chopped*

*125 g (4 oz) mushrooms, wiped and finely chopped*

*5 ml (1 level tsp) flour*

*1.4 litres (2½ pints) Beef Stock (see page 19)*

*salt and pepper*

*15 ml (1 level tbsp) finely grated orange rind*

*chopped fresh parsley, to garnish*

*Chestnut and Orange Soup*

1. If using fresh chestnuts, nick the brown outer skins of the chestnuts with a pair of scissors, or the tip of a sharp knife. Cook the chestnuts in boiling water for 3–5 minutes, then lift out using a slotted spoon, a few at a time. Peel off both the brown and inner skins and discard.
2. Melt the butter in a large saucepan, add the vegetables and fry together until lightly browned. Mix in the flour and cook, stirring for a further 3–4 minutes, or until the flour begins to colour.
3. Off the heat, stir in the stock, prepared chestnuts and seasoning. Bring slowly to the boil, stirring. Simmer, covered, for 40–45 minutes, or until the chestnuts are quite tender.
4. Cool a little, then sieve or purée in a blender or food processor until smooth a small quantity at a time. Add half the orange rind and reheat for serving.

5. Adjust seasoning, add the remaining orange rind and garnish with the parsley.
*Serves 6*

## MUSSEL BISQUE

*40 g (1½ oz) butter or margarine*

*45 ml (3 level tbsp) flour*

*900 ml (1½ pints) milk*

*150 ml (¼ pint) white wine*

*3.4 litres (6 pints) mussels, cooked (see page 82)*

*2 egg yolks*

*45 ml (3 tbsp) double cream*

*salt and pepper*

*15 ml (1 tbsp) chopped fresh parsley, to garnish*

1. Melt the butter in a saucepan, stir in the flour and cook gently for 1 minute, stirring. Remove pan from the heat and gradually stir in the milk.

Bring to the boil slowly and continue to cook, stirring, until thickened slightly.
2. Add the wine and mussels and, stirring all the time, cook over low heat for 10 minutes to reheat the fish thoroughly.
3. Mix the egg yolks with the cream in a small bowl. Add a little of the fish soup to the cream, then pour into the soup. Reheat without boiling, stirring all the time.
4. Adjust the seasoning. Sprinkle over the parsley for serving.
*Note* If you wish, use four 113 g (4 oz) cans mussels, drained and add with the wine.
*Serves 4 as a main course*

## BOUILLABAISSE

*900 g (2 lb) mixed fish and shellfish, e.g. monkfish, red mullet, John Dory, bass, prawns*

*few saffron strands*

*150 ml (¼ pint) olive oil*

*2–3 medium onions, skinned and sliced*

*1 celery stick, trimmed and chopped*

*225 g (8 oz) tomatoes, skinned and sliced*

*2 garlic cloves, skinned and crushed*

*1 bay leaf*

*2.5 ml (½ level tsp) dried thyme or fennel*

*few fresh parsley sprigs*

*finely shredded rind of ½ an orange*

*salt and pepper*

*French bread, to serve*

**1.** Clean and wash the fish and pat dry with absorbent kitchen paper. Skin and fillet if necessary, then cut into fairly large, thick pieces. If using shellfish, remove them from their shells.

**2.** Put the saffron in a small bowl. Pour in 150 ml (¼ pint) boiling water and leave to soak for 30 minutes.

**3.** Heat the oil in large saucepan, add the onions and celery and fry gently for 5 minutes, until beginning to soften.

**4.** Stir in the tomatoes with the garlic, herbs, orange rind and seasoning.

**5.** Arrange the fish in a layer over the vegetables, pour over the saffron liquid and just enough water to cover the fish. Bring to the boil and simmer uncovered for about 8 minutes.

**6.** Add the shellfish and cook for a further 5–8 minutes, until the fish pieces are cooked but still hold their shape. Serve with French bread.

*Serves 6 as a main course*

## SMOKED FISH CHOWDER

*450 g (1 lb) smoked haddock or cod fillet*

*50 g (2 oz) butter or margarine*

*2 medium onions, skinned and sliced*

*30 ml (2 level tbsp) flour*

*225 g (8 oz) potatoes, peeled and cut into 1 cm (½ inch) dice*

*1 large carrot, peeled and coarsely grated*

*150 ml (5 fl oz) single cream or milk*

*pepper*

*chopped fresh parsley, to garnish*

**1.** Simmer the fish in 1.1 litres (2 pints) water for about 10 minutes, until tender. Strain and reserve the cooking liquid, then flake the fish coarsely, discarding the skin and any bones.

**2.** Melt the butter in a saucepan, add the onions and fry gently until soft. Stir in the flour and cook gently for 1 minute, stirring. Remove pan from the heat and gradually stir in the strained fish stock. Bring to the boil, stirring, until thickened. Add the potatoes and carrot. Simmer for about 10 minutes, until the vegetables are tender.

**3.** Stir in the cream and flaked fish. Season well with pepper and heat gently without boiling. Garnish with chopped parsley.

*Serves 4 as a main course*

**Variation**

CORN CHOWDER

Omit the fish. Roughly chop 100 g (4 oz) rinded streaky bacon and fry with the onion. Add 1.1 litres (2 pints) chicken stock in place of the fish stock. Finish the soup as above, adding 350 g (12 oz) sweetcorn kernels with the cream.

Smoked Fish Chowder

## Leek and Split Pea Soup

75 g (3 oz) green split peas, washed

75 g (3 oz) streaky bacon, rinded and chopped

1.1 litres (2 pints) Chicken Stock (see page 19)

salt and pepper

700 g (1½ lb) leeks, trimmed and sliced

**1.** Cover the split peas with boiling water and leave to soak for 2 hours. Drain thoroughly.

**2.** Put the bacon in a large saucepan and heat gently until the fat runs out of the bacon.
**3.** Add the split peas, stock and seasoning. Bring to the boil, cover and simmer gently for about 45 minutes.
**4.** Add the leeks to the pan and continue cooking for a further 30 minutes, until the leeks are tender. Adjust the seasoning.
*Serves 4 as a main course*

## Scotch Broth

700 g (1½ lb) shin of beef, trimmed of excess fat and cut into small pieces

salt and pepper

1 medium carrot, peeled and chopped

1 medium turnip, peeled and chopped

1 medium onion, skinned and chopped

2 medium leeks, trimmed and thinly sliced

45 ml (3 level tbsp) pearl barley

15 ml (1 tbsp) chopped fresh parsley, to garnish

**1.** Put the meat in a saucepan, cover with 2.3 litres (4 pints) water and season. Bring to the boil, cover and simmer for 1½ hours.
**2.** Add the vegetables and the barley. Cover and simmer for about 1 hour, until the vegetables and barley are soft.
**3.** Skim off any fat from the surface and adjust seasoning. Serve the soup garnished with parsley.
**4.** Traditionally, the meat is served with a little of the broth and the remaining broth is served separately.
*Serves 4 as a main course*

## Minestrone

25 g (1 oz) butter or margarine

2 rashers streaky bacon, rinded and diced

1 small leek, trimmed and sliced

1 small onion, skinned and chopped

1 garlic clove, skinned and crushed

1 small carrot, peeled and cut into thin strips

1 medium turnip, peeled and cut into thin strips

1 celery stick, trimmed and sliced

1.4 litres (2½ pints) Chicken Stock (see page 19)

175 g (6 oz) cabbage, washed and shredded

100 g (4 oz) runner beans, thinly sliced

45 ml (3 tbsp) fresh or frozen peas

25 g (1 oz) short cut macaroni

5 ml (1 level tsp) tomato purée or 4 tomatoes, skinned, seeded and chopped

salt and pepper

grated Parmesan cheese, to serve

**1.** Melt the butter in a large saucepan, add the bacon and fry gently until brown. Remove the bacon from the pan with a slotted spoon and set aside.
**2.** Add the leek, onion and garlic to the fat in the saucepan and cook gently for about 8 minutes, until beginning to soften.
**3.** Add the carrot and turnip strips to the pan with the celery and the stock. Bring to the boil, cover and simmer for about 20 minutes.
**4.** Stir in the cabbage, beans and peas and the macaroni. Cover and simmer for a further 20 minutes until the ingredients are tender.
**5.** Add the tomato purée or tomatoes and the bacon. Bring back to the boil and season to taste. Serve with grated Parmesan cheese.
*Serves 4 as a main course*

# STARTERS

$S$tarters are a very important part of a meal; they stimulate the appetite and set the scene for the rest of the meal that is to follow. Starter portions should be small, so they do not take the edge off the appetite, and attractively presented. Also included in this chapter are canapés (little cocktail savouries) and other savoury finger food that can be eaten with drinks before a meal, hors d'oeuvre and savouries to eat at the end of a meal.

◆

Starters may be soups, salads, mousses, pâtés, fruit or cold meats—the variations are endless, but they should be planned with the other courses in mind. In that way you can achieve a balance of flavour, colour and texture, and if you know you are serving a substantial main course, you can make sure the starter is light. Check also that it does not include the same ingredients as other courses.

Cold starters are probably the easiest as they can be prepared in advance; a hot starter such as soup may require attention just before the meal, but is a good idea in winter or if the other courses are cold. If serving large numbers choose one which can be put on the table before guests sit down.

### FINGER FOOD WITH DRINKS

Savoury finger food can be served in small quantities with pre-meal drinks or a selection can be served as the starter before sitting down at the table. Some of the simplest foods to serve with drinks can be bought ready to eat. They include small savoury biscuits and crackers, olives (black, green or stuffed with pimientos or anchovies) and nuts of different varieties. Small cocktail onions and sausages can be served on cocktail sticks, radishes can be served whole and pickled cucumber and gherkins can be chopped into bite-sized pieces.

Dips make excellent accompaniments to pre-meal drinks and if you serve a number of different flavours in reasonable quantities they can act as the starter to the meal.

It is very easy to make your own dips, especially if you have a blender or food processor. Hot dips are usually based on white sauce, while cold ones are often based on soft cheese, mayonnaise or yogurt. They should be light and full of flavour and soft enough for people to be able to dip food into easily. Tasty foods for dipping include sticks of fresh vegetables (crudités) such as celery, cucumber, carrot, cauliflower florets, peppers and whole radishes, crackers, grissini (crisp Italian bread sticks) and small chunks of French bread. For more filling dippers, serve tiny chipolatas, fried scampi or small meat balls on cocktail sticks. Thin strips of pitta bread and tortilla are also good for serving as dippers.

### HORS D'OEUVRE

These are small dishes, served cold, as a starter. A mixed hors d'oeuvre of five or six different dishes contrast in colours, shapes and flavours (see Hors d'Oeuvre Variés, page 34).

### AFTER-DINNER SAVOURIES

It is not essential to serve an after-dinner savoury, but they may be served at formal dinner parties after the dessert and instead of the cheese course. After-dinner savouries include dishes such as Devils on Horseback and Scotch Woodcock (see page 52).

## CANAPÉS

Canapés are probably the most widely served cocktail savoury, consisting of a base made from either fried or toasted bread, small shapes of shortcrust, cheese, puff or flaky pastry or ready-prepared bases such as water biscuits.

The base is spread with Savoury Butter (see page 209) or a soft cheese mixture (see Cheese Boats, page 48) and topped with one or more of the following:

- Thin slices of cold meat, rolled or chopped
- Flaked fish or very small whole fish
- Slices of cheese or grated cheese
- Slices or segments of tomato
- Thin slices of cucumber, flat or in cones
- Segments of fruit
- Whole or chopped nuts
- Olives, plain or stuffed

Canapés can be decorated with piped savoury butter or any simple savoury garnish. For a more formal occasion, garnish canapés with a thin coating of aspic jelly—they should be served fairly quickly, so that the base does not become soggy.

## HORS D'OEUVRE VARIÉS

It is usual to include at least one meat and one fish dish, which can be bought ready-made—sliced cooked ham, salami and fresh, canned or pickled fish—and then add one or two salads or vegetable dishes. Suggestions for Hors d'Oeuvre Variés:

- Potato salad
- Artichoke hearts
- Tomato Salad with Basil (see page 250)
- Palm hearts
- Mixed Bean Salad (see page 254)
- Mushrooms à la Grecque (see page 37)
- Stuffed eggs
- Pasta, Prawn and Apple Salad (see page 258)
- Selection of fish and shellfish hors d'oeuvre (see below)

Serve hors d'oeuvre variés in a series of small dishes, or choose a large tray, line it with lettuce leaves and arrange the dishes on the lettuce.

## FISH AND SHELLFISH HORS D'OEUVRE

**Anchovies**
Choose from fresh (see page 58) or canned (in brine or oil). If canned, drain and serve on a bed of lettuce, garnished with the chopped white and sieved yolk of a hard-boiled egg.

**Caviar**
Caviar is the salted hard roe of the sturgeon fish. Most is caught in the Caspian Sea, by the Russians in the North and the Iranians in the South. In colour it varies from yellow brown to soft grey to grey black, and the quality is judged by the time of year, age of the fish and method of preservation. Also, the less salt the better the caviar. Red caviar is much cheaper than the black. However, even less expensive lump fish roe is often substituted for caviar.

Caviar should be served ice-cold from the jar it comes in, embedded in cracked ice or turned out into a glass dish and surrounded by ice, with freshly made toast or crisp biscuits and chilled butter. It deteriorates when exposed to the air so should not be opened until serving time. Lemon juice may be sprinkled over it if you wish, or serve wedges of lemon. Alternatively, spread the caviar directly on croûtes of fried bread or toast and sprinkle with a few grains of cayenne pepper.

**Cockles**
Choose fresh (see page 85) or purchase cooked. Season and add a little vinegar. Serve with brown bread and butter.

**Fresh Salmon**
Cold poached salmon can be divided into small portions, dressed with mayonnaise and served on a bed of lettuce. Garnish with cucumber slices or cones (see page 249).

**Herrings**
Choose pickled wrapped around gherkins or soused (see page 64). Slice if wished for serving.

**Mussels**
Choose from fresh (see page 82) or canned. Serve fresh in the half shell with tomato mayonnaise or a light horseradish sauce.

**Oysters**
Serve raw oysters on the half shell (see page 82) and, if possible, on a bed of chopped ice. Thin brown bread and butter, slices of lemon and cayenne or freshly ground black pepper are the usual accompaniments. Tabasco sauce may also be served with them.

**Sardines**
Choose from fresh (see page 60) or canned (in brine, oil or tomato sauce). Drain and serve on a

bed of lettuce, garnished with strips of pimiento and chopped parsley.

**Smoked eel**
Choose from smoked or canned. Remove the skin from smoked eel. Arrange on a bed of lettuce and serve with thin brown bread slices, butter, lemon wedges and black pepper or horseradish relish.

**Smoked haddock**
Poach and skin the haddock and serve cold coated with Mayonnaise (see page 261), on a bed of lettuce. Garnish with sliced cucumber or cucumber cones (see page 249).

**Smoked (canned) oysters** Remove from the can and drain. Serve with thin brown bread slices, butter, lemon wedges and pepper.

**Smoked salmon**
Serve thinly sliced, with thin brown bread slices, butter, lemon wedges and paprika.

**Smoked trout or mackerel**
Remove the skin from the body of the fish, but leave the head and tail intact. Serve with lemon wedges and Horseradish Cream Sauce (see page 207). Or, skin the fish, remove the fillets from the bone and serve on lettuce leaves with lemon and brown bread. Smoked mackerel is served in a similar way.

**Smoked tunny fish**
Serve as smoked salmon.

**Whelks**
Choose fresh (see page 84) or purchase cooked. Season and add a little vinegar. Serve with brown bread and butter.

*Seafood Hors d'Oeuvre*

**Whitebait**
See page 61 for method of cooking. Serve with wedges of lemon and garnish each portion with a sprig of parsley.

**Winkles**
Choose fresh (see page 84) or purchase cooked, with or without shell.

# FRUIT AND VEGETABLE STARTERS

## GRAPEFRUIT

2 grapefruit

caster sugar, for sprinkling

4 maraschino or glacé cherries (optional)

1. Cut each grapefruit in half and cut around each half, loosening the flesh from the outer skin. Cut between the segments to loosen the flesh from the membranes, sprinkle with sugar and chill before serving.
2. If liked, decorate the centre with a maraschino or glacé cherry.
*Serves 4*

## SPICED HOT GRAPEFRUIT

2 grapefruit

30 ml (2 level tbsp) brown sugar

2.5–5 ml (½–1 level tsp) ground cinnamon

a little butter or margarine

1. Prepare the grapefruit as above.
2. Mix the brown sugar and cinnamon together and sprinkle over the grapefruit, dot with butter.
3. Grill lightly under a medium grill until the sugar has melted and the grapefruit is heated through; serve hot.
*Serves 4*

## FLORIDA COCKTAILS

2 small grapefruit

2 large oranges

curaçao or any orange-flavoured liqueur

sugar

1. Working over a plate, prepare the grapefruit: remove all the skin. Holding the fruit in one hand, remove the flesh of each segment by cutting down at the side of the membrane and then scraping the segment off the membrane on the opposite side on to the plate.
2. Repeat the process for the oranges. Mix the segments, together with any of the juice collected on the plate. Add the curaçao and sugar to taste.
3. Divide the fruit between four glasses and pour a little juice into each. Serve chilled.
Serves 4

## MINTED PEAR VINAIGRETTE

100 g (4 oz) streaky bacon, rinded

120 ml (8 tbsp) French Dressing (see page 260)

30 ml (2 tbsp) chopped fresh mint

3 large ripe dessert pears

1 small lettuce, washed

1. Grill the bacon until crisp, cool and snip into tiny pieces.
2. Place the French Dressing in a bowl or screw-topped jar with the mint and whisk or shake well together.
3. One at a time, peel and halve the pears and scoop out the cores with a teaspoon. Brush both sides of each pear half immediately with a little of the dressing to prevent discoloration. Cover the pears tightly with cling film until required.
4. To serve, arrange lettuce leaves on six individual serving plates. Place a pear half, cut-side up, on each plate and spoon over the dressing. Sprinkle with the bacon.
Serves 6

## STUFFED TOMATOES

4 large tomatoes

salt and pepper

15 ml (1 tbsp) vegetable oil

1 small red pepper, halved, seeded and finely chopped

100 g (4 oz) mushrooms, wiped and finely chopped

4 spring onions, trimmed and finely chopped

90 ml (6 tbsp) Mayonnaise (see page 261)

a few lettuce leaves

parsley sprigs, to garnish

1. Cut the tops off the tomatoes, scoop out the seeds using a teaspoon and discard. Roughly chop the tops and put them in a bowl.
2. Sprinkle the insides of the tomatoes with salt, turn upside-down and leave to drain.
3. Heat the oil in a frying pan, add the pepper and mushrooms and fry gently for about 5 minutes, until soft.
4. Remove from the pan, drain on absorbent kitchen paper and add to the bowl with the spring onions and plenty of seasoning. Add the Mayonnaise and mix well.
5. Spoon the mixture into the tomato cases. Place on lettuce leaves on individual serving plates and garnish with parsley sprigs.
Serves 4

## MOZZARELLA SALAD

2 ripe avocados

150 ml (¼ pint) French Dressing (see page 260)

175 g (6 oz) mozzarella cheese, thinly sliced

6 medium tomatoes, thinly sliced

chopped fresh parsley and mint, to garnish

1. Halve the avocados lengthways and remove the stones. Peel and cut the avocados into slices. Pour the French Dressing over the avocado. Stir to coat thoroughly and prevent discoloration.
2. Arrange slices of mozzarella, tomato and avocado on four individual serving plates.
3. Spoon over the dressing and sprinkle with chopped herbs.
Serves 4

## DRESSED AVOCADOS

ripe avocados (allow half per person)

lemon juice

a few lettuce leaves (optional)

black pepper, paprika or parsley sprigs, to garnish


IDEAS FOR FILLINGS

Diced tomatoes with mayonnaise.

Caper Dressing (see page 261).

Mayonnaise (see page 261).

Shrimps or prawns.

Lobster or crabmeat, with mayonnaise.

**1.** Halve the avocados lengthways using a stainless steel knife and remove the stones. Brush the cut surfaces of the avocados with lemon juice to prevent discoloration.

**2.** Place the avocado halves in avocado dishes, or on serving plates lined with lettuce leaves. If serving on flat plates, cut a thin slice from the rounded side of each avocado so that they will sit firmly on the plates.

**3.** Fill the cavities with a little of the chosen filling and garnish.

## STUFFED MUSHROOMS WITH DILL

100 g (4 oz) long grain brown rice

salt and pepper

8 large flat or cup mushrooms, total weight about
     450 g (1 lb), wiped

25 g (1 oz) butter or margarine

1 medium onion, skinned and finely chopped

198 g (7 oz) can sweetcorn niblets, drained

15 ml (1 tbsp) chopped fresh dill or 5 ml (1 level tsp)
     dried dill weed

175 g (6 oz) blue cheese, e.g. Gorgonzola, cut into
     small pieces

30 ml (2 tbsp) lemon juice

fresh dill, to garnish

**1.** Cook the rice in plenty of boiling salted water for about 35 minutes until tender. Drain well.

**2.** Ease out the mushroom stalks and finely chop them.

**3.** Melt the butter in a frying pan. Add the chopped mushroom stalks and onion. Fry for 2–3 minutes, stirring occasionally, until the onion is beginning to brown and all excess moisture has been driven off.

**4.** Remove from the heat and stir in the sweetcorn, cooked rice, dill and cheese. Season with plenty of pepper.

**5.** Place the mushrooms stalk side up in a large shallow ovenproof dish. Spoon the sweetcorn mixture on top of each one. Sprinkle over the lemon juice.

**6.** Bake in the oven at 200°C (400°F) mark 6 for about 20 minutes. Serve hot, garnished with fresh dill.

Serves 8

## MUSHROOMS À LA GRECQUE (Greek-style Mushrooms)

30 ml (2 tbsp) olive or vegetable oil

1 medium onion, skinned and chopped

1 garlic clove, skinned and crushed

30 ml (2 level tbsp) tomato purée

300 ml (½ pint) red wine

bouquet garni

15 ml (1 tbsp) coriander seeds, lightly crushed

5 ml (1 level tsp) sugar

salt and pepper

450 ml (1 lb) button mushrooms, wiped

225 g (8 oz) tomatoes, skinned, quartered and seeded

chopped fresh coriander, to garnish

**1.** Heat the oil in a large frying pan, add the onion and garlic and cook for 5 minutes.

**2.** Stir in the tomato purée, wine, bouquet garni, coriander seeds, sugar and seasoning.

**3.** Add the mushrooms and tomatoes and cook gently, uncovered, for about 10 minutes, until just tender.

**4.** Remove the bouquet garni and spoon the mushrooms and cooking liquid into a serving dish. Chill well and serve sprinkled with coriander.

Serves 4

*Smoked Chicken and Orange Appetiser*

## SMOKED CHICKEN AND ORANGE APPETISER

*900 g (2 lb) smoked chicken*

*4 oranges*

*135 ml (9 tbsp) sunflower or vegetable oil*

*juice of 1 orange*

*1.25 ml (¼ level tsp) ground allspice or mixed spice*

*pinch of sugar*

*salt and pepper*

*sprigs of curly endive, to garnish*

**1.** Remove all the meat from the chicken carcass, cutting the slices as thinly and evenly as possible.
**2.** Remove the skin and pith from the oranges with a sharp, serrated knife, working in a spiral and using a sawing action.
**3.** Cut the oranges crossways into thin, even rounds.
**4.** Arrange the chicken and orange slices in a fan shape on four individual serving plates. Set aside.
**5.** Make the dressing, put the oil, orange juice, spice and sugar in a screw-top jar with salt and pepper to taste. Shake vigorously to combine, then taste and adjust spice and seasoning.
**6.** Pour the dressing over the salad, then chill in the refrigerator for at least 30 minutes so that the flavours are absorbed. Garnish each plate with a sprig or two of endive just before serving.
*Serves 6*

## MELON BALLS

*1 medium melon, such as Cantaloupe, Charentais or Ogen*

*caster sugar, to dredge*

*30 ml (2 tbsp) Madeira or sherry*

**1.** Cut the top off the melon, remove the seeds from the centre and scoop out the flesh with a melon baller or a teaspoon.
**2.** Dredge the melon balls with sugar, sprinkle with Madeira or sherry and chill.
**3.** Serve in small bowls or stemmed glasses, set if possible in crushed ice.
*Serves 4*

## MELON SLICES

*1 medium melon, such as Cantaloupe, Charentais or Ogen*

*ground ginger and caster sugar or lemon wedges, to serve*

**1.** Chill the melon thoroughly and cut into wedge-shaped slices. Remove the seeds and loosen the flesh from the skin. Cut the flesh at right angles to the skin into wedge-shaped pieces. Leave on the skin.
**2.** Serve with ground ginger and caster sugar or with wedges of lemon.
*Serves 4*

**Variation**
These melon slices are also delicious flavoured with finely crushed almonds or walnut halves or freshly grated nutmeg.

## MELON AND PARMA HAM

900 g (2 lb) Cantaloupe melon, chilled

8 thin slices Parma ham

Juice of 1 lemon

pepper

1. Cut the melon in half lengthways and scoop out the seeds. Cut each half into four wedges.
2. With a sharp knife and a sawing action, separate the flesh from the skin, keeping it in position on the skin.
3. Cut the flesh across into bite-sized slices, then push each in opposite directions to make an attractive pattern.
4. Roll up each slice of ham into a cigar shape. Place on serving dishes with the melon wedges and sprinkle with lemon juice and pepper.
Serves 4

Melon and Parma Ham

# SEAFOOD STARTERS

## SMOKED SALMON PÂTÉ

175 g (6 oz) smoked salmon scraps

75 g (3 oz) unsalted butter or margarine

20 ml (4 tsp) lemon juice

60 ml (4 tbsp) single cream

pepper

cucumber slices, to garnish

½ a packet aspic jelly

1. A day ahead, roughly cut up the salmon pieces, reserving a few for garnishing, and place in a blender or food processor.
2. Melt the butter and add the lemon juice and cream. Pour into the blender or food processor.
3. Blend mixture until smooth. Season to taste with pepper. Salt is not usually needed.
4. Spoon into a 300 ml (½ pint) dish to within 1 cm (½ inch) of the rim. Refrigerate to set. Make up the aspic jelly to 150 ml (¼ pint) with water, according to the manufacturer's instructions.
5. Garnish the pâté with twists of smoked salmon and cucumber slices and spoon over the aspic jelly when almost setting. Refrigerate again to set the aspic. Leave at room temperature for 30 minutes before serving.
Serves 6

## SHELLFISH COCKTAILS

60 ml (4 level tbsp) Mayonnaise (see page 261)

60 ml (4 tbsp) single cream

10 ml (2 level tsp) tomato purée

10 ml (2 tsp) lemon juice

dash of Worcestershire sauce

dash of dry sherry

salt and pepper

225 g (8 oz) peeled prawns or shrimps or flaked crab

few lettuce leaves, shredded

lemon slices, to garnish

1. In a small bowl, mix together the Mayonnaise, cream, tomato purée, lemon juice, Worcestershire sauce and sherry. Season to taste. Add the fish and stir well to coat.
2. Place the shredded lettuce into four glasses and top with the fish mixture.
3. Garnish each glass with a lemon slice. Serve brown bread.
Serves 4

## BAKED CRAB RAMEKINS

25 g (1 oz) butter or margarine

1 small onion, skinned and finely chopped

225 g (8 oz) white crab meat or white and brown mixed

50 g (2 oz) fresh brown breadcrumbs

10 ml (2 level tsp) French mustard

142 g (5 oz) natural yogurt

45 ml (3 tbsp) single cream or milk

cayenne pepper

salt

40 g (1½ oz) Cheddar cheese, grated

**1.** Melt the butter in a saucepan, add the onion and fry until golden brown.
**2.** Flake the crab meat, taking care to remove any membranes or shell particles. Mix the onion, crab meat and breadcrumbs well together.
**3.** Stir in the mustard with the yogurt and cream. Sprinkle generously with cayenne pepper, then add salt to taste.
**4.** Spoon the mixture into six ramekin dishes and sprinkle a little cheese over the surface of each.
**5.** Stand the dishes on a baking sheet. Bake in the oven at 170°C (325°F) mark 3 for 25–30 minutes, until really hot. Serve with crispbreads.
*Serves 6*

## SEAFOOD PANCAKES

100 g (4 oz) plus 30 ml (2 level tbsp) plain flour

pinch of salt

1 egg

568 ml (1 pint) milk

vegetable oil for frying

350 g (12 oz) smoked haddock fillets

1 bay leaf

onion slices for flavouring

40 g (1½ oz) butter or margarine

150 ml (5 fl oz) single cream

2 eggs, hard-boiled, shelled and chopped

45 ml (3 tbsp) chopped fresh parsley

snipped fresh chives, to garnish

**1.** Sift 100 g (4 oz) flour and the salt into a mixing bowl. Make a well in the centre and break in the egg. Gradually add 150 ml (¼ pint) milk, vigorously beating in the flour with a wooden spoon until a thick smooth batter is formed. Pour in 150 ml (¼ pint) milk, and beat again until quite smooth.
**2.** Heat a little oil in a small frying pan or omelette pan and when it is very hot pour in a small amount of batter. Tip the pan quickly so that the batter runs over the bottom of the pan. Cook over a high heat until the underside is golden brown, then turn the pancake over either by tossing it, or

*Cook pancake until golden on bottom, then turn over.*

using a fish slice. Cook the other side until golden brown. Cook eight pancakes and keep warm.
**3.** Place the fish in a saucepan, pour over the remaining milk and add the bay leaf and onion slices. Cover the pan and simmer until the fish begins to flake. Strain off and reserve the milk. Flake the fish and discard the skin and bones.
**4.** Melt the butter in a pan, stir in the remaining flour and cook gently for 1 minute, stirring. Remove pan from the heat and gradually stir in the reserved milk. Bring to the boil slowly and continue to cook, stirring, until the sauce thickens.
**5.** Off the heat, stir in the cream, fish, three-quarters of the chopped egg and the parsley and season with pepper. Cool slightly.
**6.** Divide the fish mixture between the pancakes, fold over and place in individual dishes or one large ovenproof dish. Cover with buttered foil and cook in the oven at 200°C (400°F) mark 6 for about 20 minutes.
**7.** Scatter over the remaining egg and the chives for serving.
*Makes 8*

**Variations**
Substitute the smoked haddock fillets with any of the following:
- 350 g (12 oz) peeled prawns, cooked
- 200 g (7 oz) can tuna, drained and flaked, and mixed with a can sweetcorn, drained
- 600 ml (1 pint) cockles, cooked and drained
- 350 g (12 oz) cooked cod, flaked

## Tuna Pasta Hors d'Oeuvre

75 g (3 oz) pasta shells

225 g (8 oz) small courgettes, wiped and trimmed

200 g (7 oz) can tuna fish

142 g (5 oz) natural yogurt

30 ml (2 tbsp) milk

5 ml (1 tsp) anchovy essence

15 ml (1 tbsp) lemon juice

salt and pepper

12 small black olives, halved and stoned

paprika, to garnish

1. Cook the pasta shells in boiling salted water according to manufacturer's instructions, until just tender. Meanwhile, cut the courgettes diagonally into 0.5 cm (¼ inch) slices. Add to the boiling pasta for the last 2 minutes of the cooking time. Drain well and rinse in cold water.

2. Drain the tuna fish, reserving the oil, and flake the fish. Place the tuna oil, yogurt, milk, anchovy essence, lemon juice and salt and pepper in a large bowl and mix.

3. Add the pasta, courgettes, tuna and olives to the dressing and stir gently to mix. Cover and chill. *Serves 4*

# PÂTÉS AND MOUSSES

## Vegetable Terrine

900 g (2 lb) chicken joints

1 small slice white bread, crusts removed

450 ml (15 fl oz) double cream, chilled

salt and pepper

1 small bunch watercress

125 g (4 oz) small young carrots, washed, stems
   removed and chopped

125 g (4 oz) French beans

275 g (10 oz) peas in the pod, shelled

75 g (3 oz) small even-sized button mushrooms, wiped

200 g (7 oz) can artichoke hearts, drained

**For the sauce**

225 g (8 oz) ripe tomatoes, skinned and quartered

100 ml (4 fl oz) vegetable oil

50 ml (2 fl oz) white wine vinegar

75 ml (5 level tbsp) tomato purée

1. Cut all the chicken flesh away from the chicken bones; discard the skin and any fatty areas. Finely mince the chicken and the bread. Chill for 30 minutes. Stir the cream, a little at a time, into the chicken mixture with salt and pepper to taste.

2. Stir one third of the mixture into the watercress. Cover both bowls and chill for 2 hours.

3. Peel the carrots, then cut them into neat matchstick-shaped pieces, 2.5 cm (1 inch) by 2.5 mm (⅛ inch). Top, tail and string the beans and cut into similar length pieces; wash and drain. Blanch the carrots, beans and peas for 2 minutes in separate pans of boiling water. Drain.

4. Trim the mushroom stalks level with the caps. Cut the mushrooms across into slices 5 mm (¼ inch) thick. Dice the artichoke bases into 5 mm (¼ inch) pieces. The careful preparation of vegetables is essential to the final presentation.

5. Grease a 1.1 litre (2 pint) terrine dish and base-line with an oblong piece of paper, grease the top of the paper. Take half the watercress farce and spread evenly over the base of the terrine. Arrange the carrots in neat crossways lines over this, then spread one quarter of the chicken farce carefully over the carrots.

6. Lightly seasoning the vegetables as they are layered, sprinkle the peas over the farce and put another thin layer of chicken farce on top. Next, place the mushrooms in crossways lines and top with the remaining watercress farce. Arrange the artichokes on top, cover with half the remaining farce, arrange the beans in crossways lines, and cover with the remaining farce.

7. Place a double sheet of greased greaseproof paper on top and cover tightly with the lid. Put the terrine in a roasting tin with water to come halfway up the side. Bake in the oven at 170°C (325°F) mark 3 for about 1 hour, until firm.

8. Cool a little, drain off any juices, then invert the terrine on to a serving plate. Cool, then refrigerate for 1 hour before serving.

9. Meanwhile, make the sauce. Purée the tomatoes in a blender or food processor with the oil, vinegar, tomato purée and seasoning. Rub through a sieve. Chill lightly before serving. *Serves 8–10*

## DUCK AND ORANGE TERRINE

*1.8 kg (4 lb) oven-ready duckling*

*350 g (12 oz) belly of pork, skin and bones removed*

*125 g (4 oz) lamb's liver*

*1 medium onion, skinned and quartered*

*2 oranges*

*1 garlic clove, skinned and crushed*

*salt and pepper*

*2.5 ml (½ level tsp) ground mace*

*15 ml (1 tbsp) chopped fresh parsley*

*30 ml (2 tbsp) sherry*

*half a 25 g (1 oz) packet aspic jelly*

*celery leaves, to garnish (optional)*

*Duck and Orange Terrine*

**1.** Prepare two days ahead. Discard the skin and fat layer from the duckling. Cut away breast portion. Remove rest of flesh—about 350 g (12 oz).
**2.** Finely mince the duckling flesh (except breast), pork, liver and the onion. Grate in the rind of one orange.
**3.** Segment this orange, removing the membrane, over a bowl to collect any juice. Cut the segments into small pieces.
**4.** Combine meats, orange juice and segments and remaining ingredients, except the aspic, breast meat and garnish.
**5.** Press half the mixture into a 1.1 litre (2 pint) terrine. Lay the breast portions on top and spread over the remaining mixture.

**6.** Cover with foil or a lid. Put the dish in a roasting tin half filled with boiling water. Cook in the oven at 170°C (325°F) mark 3 for 3 hours.
**7.** Place a weight on top of the pâté and refrigerate until cold. Scrape off any solidified fat and drain away the juices.
**8.** Make up the aspic jelly to 300 ml (½ pint) with water, according to the manufacturer's instructions. Garnish with remaining orange, sliced, and celery leaves. Spoon over the aspic when nearly set. Leave at room temperature for 30 minutes before serving.
*Serves 8–10*

## AVOCADO MOUSSE

*15 ml (1 tbsp) gelatine*

*150 ml (¼ pint) Chicken Stock (see page 19)*

*3 small or 2 large ripe avocados*

*salt and pepper*

*10 ml (2 tsp) Worcestershire sauce*

*150 ml (5 fl oz) double cream*

*150 ml (¼ pint) Mayonnaise (see page 261)*

*thinly sliced cucumber, to garnish*

**1.** Sprinkle the gelatine in 150 ml (¼ pint) water in a small bowl and leave to soak. Place the bowl over a saucepan of simmering water and stir until dissolved.
**2.** Stir in the stock and set aside to cool for a few minutes.

**3.** Lightly whip the cream.
**4.** Halve the avocados and remove the stones, scoop out the flesh with a fork and mash until smooth, or purée in a blender or food processor. Season with salt and pepper and Worcestershire sauce.
**5.** Slowly pour the gelatine mixture into the avocado mixture and stir until just beginning to thicken. Then gently fold in the Mayonnaise and the cream.
**6.** Pour into a dampened 1 litre (1½ pint) mould and chill until firm. Just before serving, remove from the mould and place on a serving platter. Garnish with cucumber slices.
*Serves 6*

# SALMON MOUSSE

350 g (12 oz) salmon steaks

1 small onion, skinned and sliced

1 medium carrot, peeled and sliced

2 bay leaves

4 black peppercorns

salt and pepper

75 ml (5 tbsp) white wine

15 ml (1 level tbsp) gelatine

300 ml ($\frac{1}{2}$ pint) milk

25 g (1 oz) butter or margarine

30 ml (2 level tbsp) flour

75 ml (5 level tbsp) Lemon Mayonnaise (see page 261)

150 ml (5 fl oz) whipping cream

red food colouring (optional)

1 egg white

**Aspic jelly for garnish**

7.5 ml (1$\frac{1}{2}$ level tsp) gelatine

60 ml (4 tbsp) white wine

15 ml (1 tbsp) medium sherry

5 ml (1 tsp) rosemary vinegar

5 cm (2 inch) piece cucumber

1. Place the salmon steaks in a small shallow pan. Add half the onion and carrot slices, 1 bay leaf, 2 peppercorns and a good pinch of salt. Spoon over the wine with 75 ml (5 tbsp) water and bring slowly to the boil. Cover the pan and simmer gently for 10–15 minutes, until the fish flakes easily when tested with a knife. Flake the fish, discarding bones and skin. Place the fish in a small bowl and set aside. Boil the cooking liquid until reduced by half, strain off and reserve.
2. Sprinkle the gelatine in 45 ml (3 tbsp) water in a small basin and leave to soak.
3. Place the milk in a saucepan with the remaining sliced onion, carrot, bay leaf and peppercorns. Bring to the boil slowly, remove from the heat, cover and leave to infuse for 30 minutes.
4. Melt the butter in a pan, stir in the flour and cook gently for 1 minute, stirring. Remove the pan from the heat and gradually strain in the infused milk, stirring until smooth. Bring to the boil slowly and continue to cook, stirring, until the sauce thickens. Pour into a bowl and while still warm add the soaked gelatine and stir until dissolved.
5. Stir the fish into the cool sauce with the

reserved cooking juices. Spoon half at a time into a blender or food processor and switch on for a few seconds only; the fish should retain a little of its texture. Pour into a large mixing bowl and repeat with the remaining sauce and fish mixture.
6. Stir the mayonnaise gently into the salmon mixture. Whip the cream until soft peaks form and fold into the mousse, adjust seasoning and add a little red food colouring if wished. Whisk the egg white until stiff and fold lightly into the mousse until no traces of egg white are visible.
7. Pour the mousse into an oiled 18 cm (7 inch) soufflé dish, smooth the surface, cover and refrigerate for about 2 hours, until set.
8. Meanwhile, make the aspic jelly: soak the gelatine in 30 ml (2 tbsp) water in a small bowl and leave to soak. Place the bowl over a pan of simmering water and stir until dissolved. Stir in the white wine, sherry, vinegar, 90 ml (6 tbsp) water and seasoning. Refrigerate until set.
9. Turn out on to a flat platter and gently dab the surface with absorbent kitchen paper to absorb any oil. Turn the aspic out on to a sheet of damp greaseproof or non-stick paper and chop roughly with a wet knife. Run a fork down the cucumber to form grooves in the skin, slice thinly. Garnish the mousse with cucumber and aspic.
*Serves 6*

*Salmon Mousse*

## SMOKED TROUT MOUSSE

300 ml (½ pint) milk

1 piece of carrot

1 piece of onion

1 bay leaf

3 black peppercorns

225 g (8 oz) smoked trout

7.5 ml (1½ level tsp) gelatine

25 g (1 oz) butter or margarine

30 ml (2 level tbsp) flour

15 ml (1 tbsp) creamed horseradish

30 ml (2 tbsp) lemon sauce

75 ml (5 tbsp) double cream

salt and pepper

2 egg whites

watercress sprigs or cucumber slices, to garnish

1. Put the milk in a saucepan with the carrot, onion, bay leaf and peppercorns. Bring to the boil slowly, remove from the heat, cover and leave to infuse for 30 minutes.

2. Meanwhile, skin the smoked trout and flake the flesh finely, discarding any bones. Keep the flesh covered with cling film until required.

3. Sprinkle the gelatine in 30 ml (2 tbsp) water in a small bowl and leave to soak for at least 10 minutes.

4. Melt the butter in a small pan, stir in the flour and cook gently for 1 minute, stirring. Remove the pan from the heat and gradually strain in the infused milk, stirring until smooth. Bring to the boil slowly and continue to cook, stirring, until the sauce thickens.

5. Remove from the heat and stir in the soaked gelatine until dissolved. Pour into a bowl, cover with a sheet of dampened greaseproof paper and set aside to cool.

6. Mix the fish into the sauce with the horseradish and lemon juice. Whip the cream to soft peaks and fold into the fish mixture. Adjust the seasoning.

7. Whisk the egg whites until stiff, then fold them gently into the fish mixture. Spoon into six 150 ml (¼ pint) individual soufflé dishes, cover and chill until lightly set. Garnish with watercress or slices of cucumber.

*Serves 6*

## PRAWN AND ASPARAGUS MOUSSE

300 ml (½ pint) milk

1 piece of carrot

1 piece of onion

1 bay leaf

3 black peppercorns

1 mace blade

25 g (1 oz) butter or margarine

30 ml (2 level tbsp) flour

15 ml (1 level tbsp) gelatine

425 g (15 oz) can green asparagus

salt and pepper

75 ml (5 tbsp) double cream

225 g (8 oz) peeled prawns

2 egg whites

tomato slices, to garnish

1. Put the milk into a saucepan with the carrot, onion, bay leaf, peppercorns and mace. Bring to the boil slowly, remove from the heat, cover and leave to infuse for 30 minutes. Strain, reserving the milk.

2. Melt the butter in a saucepan, stir in the flour and cook gently for 1 minute, stirring. Remove the pan from the heat and gradually stir in the milk. Bring to the boil slowly and continue to cook, stirring, until the sauce thickens.

3. Meanwhile, sprinkle the gelatine in 45 ml (3 tbsp) water in a small bowl and leave to soak. Place the bowl over a pan of simmering water and stir until dissolved.

4. Beat the gelatine mixture into the hot sauce. Turn into a bowl, cover closely with a sheet of dampened greaseproof paper and allow to cool but not set.

5. Reserve a few pieces of asparagus for the garnish, then purée the rest in a blender or food processor with the sauce. Season.

6. Softly whip the cream and stiffly whisk the egg whites, then fold first the cream then the egg into the pureed mixture with the prawns.

7. Pour into individual dishes. Chill until set. Garnish with the remaining asparagus and tomato.

*Serves 6*

## SMOKED MACKEREL PÂTÉ

*275 g (10 oz) smoked mackerel*

*50 g (2 oz) butter or margarine, softened*

*45 ml (3 level tbsp) creamed horseradish sauce*

*30 ml (2 tbsp) single cream*

*pepper*

*parsley sprig, to garnish*

**1.** The day before, skin the mackerel and discard the bones. Mash the flesh in a bowl.
**2.** Mix the butter with the fish and add the horseradish sauce and cream. Season with pepper. Salt is not usually needed.
**3.** Spoon the mixture into a serving dish, cover tightly and refrigerate until required.

**4.** Leave the pâté at room temperature for 30 minutes before serving. Decorate the surface of the pâté with indentations made using a blunt edged knife and garnish with a parsley sprig.
*Serves 6*

**Variation**
*HERBY MACKEREL PÂTÉ*
**1.** Cream together 100 g (4 oz) butter or margarine, 30 ml (2 tbsp) chopped fresh parsley and 5 ml (1 tsp) lemon juice and beat well.
**2.** In a 600 ml (1 pint) dish, layer the fish mixture and parsley butter, beginning and ending with a thick layer of fish.

## CHICKEN LIVER PÂTÉ

*450 g (1 lb) chicken livers*

*50 g (2 oz) butter or margarine*

*1 medium onion, skinned and chopped*

*1 garlic clove, skinned and crushed*

*75 ml (5 tbsp) double or single cream*

*15 ml (1 level tbsp) tomato purée*

*15 ml (1 tbsp) brandy*

*salt and pepper*

*parsley sprigs, to garnish*

*Melba Toast or French bread, for serving*

**1.** Clean the chicken livers and dry with

absorbent kitchen paper.
**2.** Melt the butter in a saucepan, add the onion and garlic and cook for about 5 minutes, until the onion is soft. Add the chicken livers and cook for a further 5 minutes.
**3.** Cool, then add the cream, tomato purée and brandy and season well.
**4.** Purée the mixture in a blender or food processor, then transfer to a serving dish and chill in the refrigerator. Garnish with parsley sprigs and serve with Melba Toast or crusty French bread.
*Note* Melted butter can be poured over the pâté to prevent it drying out.
*Serves 8*

## PORK AND LIVER PÂTÉ WITH BLACK OLIVES

*275 g (10 oz) streaky bacon, rinded*

*450 g (1 lb) belly of pork*

*275 g (10 oz) diced pie veal*

*175 g (6 oz) lamb's liver*

*2 medium onions, skinned and quartered*

*1 garlic clove, skinned and crushed*

*75 g (3 oz) black olives, halved, stoned and roughly chopped*

*salt and pepper*

*5 ml (1 tsp) chopped fresh sage*

*30 ml (2 tbsp) olive oil*

*15 ml (1 tbsp) lemon juice*

*30 ml (2 tbsp) brandy*

**1.** Make the pâté one day before needed. Stretch the bacon rashers with the back of a knife. Finely mince the belly of pork, veal, liver and onion. Add remaining ingredients, except the bacon, and mix well.
**2.** Layer the bacon and minced ingredients in a 1.1 litre (2 pint) terrine, topping with rashers.
**3.** Cover with foil or a lid and place in a roasting tin, half filled with boiling water. Cook at 170°C (325°F) mark 3 for about 2 hours.
**4.** Pour off the juices and reserve. Place a weight on top of the pâté and refrigerate overnight.
**5.** Skim the fat off the jellied juices, warm the juices to liquefy, then spoon over the pâté. Refrigerate to set. Leave at room temperature for 30 minutes before serving.
*Serves 10–12*

## COARSE GARLIC PÂTÉ

450 g (1 lb) ox liver

60 ml (4 tbsp) milk

450 g (1 lb) belly of pork, skinned and boned

225 g (8 oz) pork fat

225 g (8 oz) stewing steak

1 medium onion, skinned and quartered

100 g (4 oz) mushrooms, wiped and roughly chopped

4 garlic cloves, skinned and crushed

45 ml (3 tbsp) red wine

1.25 ml ($\frac{1}{4}$ level tsp) freshly grated nutmeg

salt and pepper

**1.** Make the pâté two days before needed. Soak the liver in the milk for about 1 hour, then drain.

**2.** Mince the liver, belly pork, pork fat, steak and onion. Stir the mushrooms into the minced mixture.
**3.** Add the garlic to the pâté ingredients with the wine, nutmeg and seasoning.
**4.** Pack mixture tightly into a 1.4 litre ($2\frac{1}{2}$ pint) terrine. Cover tightly with the lid or foil and stand in a roasting tin with sufficient water to come halfway up the sides. Bake in the oven at 170°C (325°F) mark 3 for about 2 hours.
**5.** When cooked, remove from the roasting tin and place a heavy weight on the pâté.
**6.** Refrigerate until required. Leave at room temperature for 30 minutes before serving.
*Serves 10–12*

## POTTED PRAWN PÂTÉ

225 g (8 oz) peeled prawns

75 g (3 oz) butter, softened

10 ml (2 tsp) lemon juice

20 ml (4 tsp) chopped fresh parsley

salt and pepper

peeled prawns and lemon slices, to garnish

French bread, to serve

**1.** Finely chop the prawns. Beat into 50 g (2 oz) butter with the lemon juice, parsley and seasoning.
**2.** Spoon into a serving dish and level the surface. Melt the remaining butter and pour over the prawn mixture. Chill in the refrigerator for 1 hour. Garnish with prawns and lemon slices. Serve with French bread.
*Serves 4*

*Potted Prawn Pâté*

## TARAMASALATA

225 g (8 oz) smoked cod's roe, skinned and broken up

1 garlic clove, skinned and crushed

50 g (2 oz) fresh bread crumbs

1 small onion, skinned and finely chopped

grated rind and juice of 1 lemon

150 ml ($\frac{1}{4}$ pint) olive oil

pepper

lemon slices, to garnish

pitta bread or toast, to serve

**1.** Place the cod's roe in a blender or food processor and blend to form a purée.
**2.** Add the garlic to the cod's roe with the bread crumbs, onion and lemon rind and juice and blend for a few more seconds.
**3.** Gradually add the oil and blend well after each addition until smooth. Blend in 90 ml (6 tbsp) hot water with the pepper.
**4.** Spoon into a serving dish and chill for at least 1 hour. Garnish with lemon slices and serve with pitta bread or toast.
*Serves 6*

# DIPS

## GUACAMOLE

| | |
|---|---|
| 2 avocados | |
| 2 medium tomatoes, skinned | |
| 1 small onion, skinned and chopped | |
| 15 ml (1 tbsp) chopped fresh parsley | |
| 1 green chilli, seeded and chopped | |
| salt and pepper | |
| wholemeal toast or corn chips, to serve | |

1. Peel, stone and mash the avocado flesh.
2. Halve the tomatoes and discard the seeds. Chop the flesh and add with the onion, parsley and green chilli to the avocado pulp.
3. Adjust the seasoning and serve in small bowls with fingers of wholemeal toast or corn chips.
*Serves 4*

## MUSTARD DIP

45 ml (3 level tbsp) Mayonnaise (see page 261)

60–90 ml (4–6 tbsp) soured cream

45 ml (3 level tbsp) whole grain mustard

30 ml (2 level tbsp) finely chopped gherkins

1. Whisk together the Mayonnaise and cream until blended.
2. Stir in the mustard and gherkins. Leave for several hours for the flavours to develop.
3. Serve with chipolatas or small meat balls.
*Serves 4*

## BLUE CHEESE DIP

142 ml (5 fl oz) soured cream

1 garlic clove, skinned and crushed

175 g (6 oz) Blue Stilton cheese, crumbled

juice of 1 lemon

salt and pepper

snipped fresh chives, to garnish

1. Blend all the ingredients, except the chives, to a smooth paste. Sprinkle over the chives and serve with chunks of French bread or crudités.
*Serves 6–8*

## ASPARAGUS DIP

48 g (2 oz) packet asparagus soup

142 ml (5 fl oz) soured cream

5 ml (1 tsp) herb vinegar

salt and pepper

paprika, to garnish

1. Make up the soup following the packet instructions, but using 200 ml (7 fl oz) boiling water.
2. Stir in the soured cream, vinegar and seasoning, and mix well until smooth and the ingredients are well combined.
3. Before serving, transfer to a bowl and sprinkle with paprika. Serve with crudités or cheese crackers.
*Serves 6–8*

## SPICY CHEESE AND TOMATO DIP

125 g (4 oz) Cheddar or Cheshire cheese, grated

50 g (2 oz) butter or margarine, softened

1 small onion, skinned and finely grated

5 ml (1 level tsp) mustard powder

15 ml (1 tbsp) tomato ketchup

30 ml (2 tbsp) single cream

few drops of Worcestershire sauce

pinch of cayenne pepper

1. In a bowl, beat together the cheese and butter with a wooden spoon.
2. Mix in the onion, add the mustard powder, tomato ketchup, cream, Worcestershire sauce and season with cayenne pepper. Mix well.
3. Transfer to a serving dish and chill.
*Serves 4*

## HUMMUS

225 g (8 oz) dried chick-peas, soaked overnight and
  drained or two 400 g (14 oz) cans chick-peas,
  drained

juice of 2 large lemons

150 ml (¼ pint) tahini

60 ml (4 tbsp) olive oil

1 or 2 garlic cloves, skinned and crushed

salt and pepper

black olives and chopped fresh parsley, to garnish

warm pitta bread, to serve

1.  Place the dried chick-peas in a saucepan and cover with cold water. Bring to the boil and simmer gently for 2 hours or until tender. Drain, reserving a little of the cooking liquid.

2.  Put the drained, cooked chick-peas in a blender or food processor, reserving a few for garnish, and gradually add the lemon juice, blending well after each addition in order to form a smooth purée.

3.  Add the tahini paste, oil, reserving 10 ml (2 tbsp), garlic and seasoning. Blend until smooth.

4.  Spoon into a serving dish and sprinkle with the reserved oil and chick-peas, and garnish with the olives and parsley. Serve with warm pitta bread.
*Serves 8*

# SAVOURY FINGER FOOD

## CHEESE AND OLIVE PICK-UPS

100 g (4 oz) blue cheese

100 g (4 oz) cottage cheese

15 ml (1 tbsp) snipped fresh chives

50 g (2 oz) black olives, stoned and finely chopped

15 ml (1 tbsp) brandy

50 g (2 oz) chopped almonds, browned

buttered cracker biscuits, to serve

1.  Blend the cheeses together. Work in the chives, olives and brandy and shape into a roll about 2.5 cm (1 inch) across. Roll in the nuts, coating evenly, then chill on a plate.

2.  Just before serving, slice with a sharp knife and serve with crackers.
*Makes 30–36*

## CHEESE BOATS

100 g (4 oz) flour

pinch of salt

pinch of mustard powder or cayenne pepper (optional)

25 g (1 oz) butter or block margarine

25 g (1 oz) lard

50 g (2 oz) Cheddar or other hard cheese, finely grated

little beaten egg or water

225 g (8 oz) flavoured full fat or low fat soft cheese

paprika or chopped fresh parsley, to garnish

1.  Mix together the flour, salt and mustard, if using, in a bowl. Cut the butter and lard into small pieces and rub into the flour until the mixture resembles fine breadcrumbs. Mix in the cheese.

2.  Add a little egg or 15–30 ml (1–2 tbsp) water, stirring with a round-bladed knife until the ingredients begin to stick together in large lumps. With one hand, collect the mixture together and knead for a few seconds to give a smooth dough.

3.  On a floured surface, roll out the pastry and use to line about 30 boat-shaped moulds. Prick the bottom of the pastry well and bake blind (see page 371) in the oven at 200°C (400°F) mark 6 for 10–15 minutes, until golden brown. Leave to cool on a wire rack.

4.  Pile the cheese mixture into the pastry cases and smooth with a knife. Garnish with paprika or sprinkle with parsley.

Flavour the softened cheese by blending with one of the following:

- *Pimiento Cheese:* 45 ml (3 tbsp) sieved canned pimiento.
- *Guava Cheese:* 4 mashed canned guavas and 2.5 ml (½ level tsp) salt.
- *Ham Cheese:* 75 g (3 oz) finely minced ham.
- *Tuna Cheese:* 90–135 ml (6–9 level tbsp) finely mashed tuna fish mixed with 15 ml (1 tbsp) vinegar or 45 ml (3 level tbsp) Mayonnaise (see page 261).

*Makes about 30*

# STILTON BITES

*50 g (2 oz) butter or margarine*

*50 g (2 oz) flour*

*300 ml (½ pint) milk*

*175 g (6 oz) Stilton cheese, crumbled*

*salt and pepper*

*paprika*

*4 gherkins, each cut into 16 pieces*

*1 egg, beaten*

*50 g (2 oz) dry white breadcrumbs*

*vegetable oil for frying*

**1.** Melt the butter in a saucepan, stir in the flour and cook gently for 1 minute, stirring. Remove the pan from the heat and gradually stir in the milk. Bring to the boil slowly and continue to cook, stirring, until the sauce thickens, then add the cheese and seasonings and stir well.

**2.** Turn into a non-stick 17.5 cm (7 inch) square tin. Chill for several hours.

**3.** Remove from the tin and cut into 64 dice. Using floured hands, press a piece of gherkin into each dice, then carefully coat in egg and breadcrumbs.

**4.** Heat the oil in a deep-fat fryer to 190°C (375°F) and cook the Stilton Bites in batches for several minutes until golden. Drain on absorbent kitchen paper and keep warm in a low oven whilst frying the others.

*Cut the cheese bites into dice, then press a piece of gherkin into each one.*

*Note* For a more economical version of these delicious snacks, substitute Danish blue cheese for the Stilton.

*Makes 64*

# CHEESE STRAWS

*75 g (3 oz) flour*

*salt and pepper*

*40 g (1½ oz) butter or margarine*

*40 g (1½ oz) Cheddar cheese, finely grated*

*1 egg, beaten*

*5 ml (1 level tsp) French mustard*

**1.** Mix the flour and seasoning together and rub in the butter until the mixture resembles fine breadcrumbs. Add the cheese and stir until mixed evenly.

**2.** Combine half the egg with the mustard and stir into the flour mixture to form a soft dough. Turn out on to a floured work surface and knead lightly until just smooth.

**3.** Roll out the dough to a 15 cm (6 inch) square and place on a baking sheet. Brush with the remaining beaten egg. Divide the dough into 7.5 × 1 cm (3 × ½ inch) oblongs and separate them.

**4.** Bake in the oven at 180°C (350°F) mark 4 for 12–15 minutes, until golden. Cool on a wire rack. Store in an airtight container.

*Makes about 24*

# INDIVIDUAL QUICHES

*100 g (4 oz) plain flour*

*pinch of salt*

*25 g (1 oz) butter or block margarine, diced*

*25 g (1 oz) lard, diced*

*75 g (3 oz) matured Cheddar cheese, grated*

*150 ml (¼ pint) milk*

*1 egg*

*5 ml (1 tsp) chopped fresh parsley or 1.25 ml (¼ level tsp) mixed dried herbs*

*salt and pepper*

**1.** Place the flour and salt in a bowl. Add the butter and lard to the flour. Using both hands, rub in until the mixture resembles fine breadcrumbs. Add enough cold water to bind the mixture together. Knead lightly for a few seconds to give a firm, smooth dough.

**2.** Roll out the pastry on a floured surface and use it to line twelve to fourteen 5 cm (2 inch) patty tins. Divide the cheese between the pastry cases.

**3.** Lightly whisk together the milk, egg and parsley. Season to taste.

**4.** Spoon the mixture evenly over the cheese. Bake in the oven at 180°C (350°F) mark 4 for 20–25 minutes. Serve warm.

*Makes 12–14*

## SMOKED SALMON PINWHEELS

*1 large brown sliced loaf, crusts removed*

*100 g (4 oz) butter or margarine, softened*

*350 g (12 oz) smoked salmon, thinly sliced*

*lemon juice*

*pepper*

**1.** Butter each slice and cover with salmon, sprinkle with lemon juice and season with pepper.
**2.** Roll up, then wrap in foil and chill for up to 1 hour before slicing.
*Makes about 96*

## ASPARAGUS ROLLS

*25 slices of fresh brown bread, crusts removed*

*50 g (2 oz) butter or margarine, softened*

*salt and pepper*

*350 g (12.3 oz) can asparagus tips, drained*

**1.** Spread each slice with butter, sprinkle with salt and pepper and roll up with an asparagus tip inside. Store wrapped in foil until required, but preferably serve the day made. Halve to serve.
*Note* The bread slices can be lightly rolled with a rolling pin before buttering; this gives a thinner roll and prevents the bread cracking.
*Makes about 50*

# PASTRY STARTERS

## TARRAGON EGG TARTLETS

*75 g (3 oz) Shortcrust Pastry (see page 372)*

*1 pimiento cap, finely chopped*

*salt and pepper*

*pinch of sugar*

*4 eggs*

*60 ml (4 tbsp) single cream*

*sprig of fresh tarragon or 1.25 ml ($\frac{1}{4}$ level tsp) dried*

*2.5 ml ($\frac{1}{2}$ tsp) lemon juice*

*tarragon sprigs, to garnish (optional)*

**1.** On a lightly floured surface, roll out the pastry thinly. Cut or stamp out four 10 cm (4 inch) rounds and use to line four 7.5 cm (3 inch) tartlet tins. Chill for 30 minutes.
**2.** Bake the tartlets blind (see page 371) in the oven at 190°C (375°F) mark 5 for 15–20 minutes, until pale golden. Turn out and leave to cool on a wire rack.
**3.** Season the pimiento with salt and pepper and sugar.
**4.** Not more than 30 minutes before serving, softly poach the eggs (see page 265). Drain and place on greaseproof paper. Trim neatly and cover with damp greaseproof paper.
**5.** To serve, spread the pimiento over the base of each tartlet. Place an egg in each. Stand the tartlets on a baking sheet and cover with damp greaseproof paper. Warm gently in the oven at 180°C (350°F) mark 4 for about 3 minutes. Transfer to a serving dish.
**6.** Meanwhile, gently warm the cream with the tarragon, salt, pepper and lemon juice. Spoon around the warmed tartlets and garnish.
*Serves 4*

**Variation**
*MUSTARD EGG TARTLETS*
Substitute the tarragon sprig or dried tarragon with 7.5 ml (1$\frac{1}{2}$ level tsp) Dijon mustard. Mix it in well with the cream. Garnish with fresh dill.

*Tarragon Egg Tartlet*

## SAVOURY CHOUX

*50 g (2 oz) Choux Pastry (see page 379)*

*fillings (see below)*

**1.** Put the pastry into a piping bag fitted with a 1 cm (½ inch) plain nozzle and pipe about 24 walnut-sized balls on to a dampened baking sheet.
**2.** Bake in the oven at 200°C (400°F) mark 6 for 15–20 minutes, until golden brown and crisp. Remove from the oven and make a short slit in the side of each to let out the steam. If necessary, return the cases to the oven to dry out completely. Either spoon or pipe the filling into the cases.
*Makes about 24*

*FILLINGS*
**1.** Cream together 100 g (4 oz) full fat or low fat soft cheese and 50 g (2 oz) softened butter or margarine. Add 5 ml (1 tsp) lemon juice and salt and pepper to taste.
**2.** Cream together 175 g (6 oz) liver pâté, 5 ml (1 level tsp) French mustard and 30 ml (2 tbsp) soured cream.
**3.** Cream together 100 g (4 oz) full fat or low fat soft cheese, 30 ml (2 tbsp) soured cream, 100 g (4 oz) finely chopped smoked salmon trimmings, 15 ml (1 tbsp) lemon juice and pepper.

## CHEESE PALMIERS

*212 g (7½ oz) packet frozen puff pastry, thawed*

*beaten egg, to glaze*

*75 g (3 oz) Gruyère cheese, finely grated*

*salt and pepper*

*paprika*

**1.** Roll out the pastry to an oblong 30.5 × 25.5 cm (12 × 10 inches). Brush with beaten egg.
**2.** Scatter over the grated cheese and sprinkle

with salt and pepper and paprika.
**3.** Roll up tightly lengthways, rolling from each side until the rolls meet in the centre. Cut across into ten pieces.
**4.** Place on a greased baking sheet and flatten with a round-bladed knife.
**5.** Bake in the oven at 200°C (400°F) mark 6 for 15–18 minutes, until brown and crisp. Ease off the baking sheet and cool on a wire rack.
*Makes 10*

## BOUCHÉES

*225 g (8 oz) Puff Pastry (see page 376) or 368 g (13 oz) packet frozen puff pastry, thawed*

*beaten egg, to glaze*

*fillings (see below)*

**1.** Roll out the pastry 0.5 cm (¼ inch) thick and cut out twenty-five 5 cm (2 inch) rounds, using a plain cutter. Place the rounds on dampened baking sheets.
**2.** Using a 4 cm (1¼ inch) plain cutter, cut partway through the centre of each round. Glaze the tops with beaten egg. Bake at 230°C (450°F) mark 8 for 10 minutes, until well risen and golden brown.
**3.** Remove the lid and soft pastry centres, and either use the cases hot with a hot filling or cool them on a wire rack and use cold with a cold filling.
*Note* When making Bouchées for a party, it is better to fill cold cases with a cold filling and reheat in the oven at 180°C (350°F) mark 4 for about 15 minutes.
*Makes 25*

*FILLINGS*
*(Each enough to fill 25 Bouchée cases)*
**Mushroom** Melt a knob of butter in a small saucepan and fry 75 g (3 oz) chopped button mushrooms. Put on one side, wipe the pan and melt a further 25 g (1 oz) butter. Stir in 45 ml (3 level tbsp) flour and cook for 2 minutes. Remove from the heat and add 150 ml (¼ pint) milk. Bring to the boil and cook for about 2 minutes, stirring continuously. Fold in the mushrooms and about 45 ml (3 tbsp) single cream. Season to taste with salt, pepper and a dash of Worcestershire sauce.
**Prawn** Fry 100 g (4 oz) peeled prawns to replace the mushrooms (see previous recipe) and add 5 ml (1 tsp) chopped fresh parsley and a little lemon juice instead of the Worcestershire sauce.
**Chicken** Fry 1 small skinned and finely chopped onion to replace the mushrooms (see previous recipe); replace the Worcestershire sauce with Tabasco, and add 100 g (4 oz) diced cooked chicken meat before reheating.

# AFTER-DINNER SAVOURIES

An after-dinner savoury may be served instead of a cheese course after the dessert. They are usually hot and should have a distinctive flavour that contrasts with the main course. The portions should be small. The recipes in this section are some of the most popular after-dinner savouries.

## SCOTCH WOODCOCK

two 50 g (1¾ oz) can anchovies, drained

2 bread slices

butter or margarine for spreading

60–90 ml (4–6 tbsp) milk

2 eggs

salt and pepper

pieces of canned pimiento or paprika, to garnish

1.  Reserve 2 anchovy fillets for a garnish and sieve the rest.
2.  Toast the bread, remove the crusts, and spread with butter, then cut into triangles and spread with the anchovy purée. Keep warm.
3.  Melt the butter in a saucepan. Whisk together the milk, egg and seasoning, pour into the pan and stir slowly over a gentle heat until the mixture begins to thicken. Remove from the heat and stir until creamy.
4.  Spread the mixture on top of the anchovy toast; garnish with thin strips of anchovy fillet and add pieces of pimiento or a sprinkling of paprika.
*Makes 8*
*Note* Gentleman's Relish may be used to replace the sieved anchovies.

## DEVILS ON HORSEBACK

8 blanched almonds

olive oil

salt and cayenne pepper

8 large prunes, stoned

4 thin rashers of streaky bacon, rinded

8 rounds of bread, about 5 cm (2 inches) in diameter

50 g (2 oz) butter or margarine

watercress, to garnish

1.  Fry the almonds for 2–3 minutes in a little oil, until they are golden brown and toss in a little salt and cayenne pepper. Remove the stones from the prunes and put the almonds in their place.
2.  Stretch the bacon rashers with the back of a knife, cut in half and roll around the prunes.

Secure with a wooden cocktail stick or small skewer and cook under a medium grill, turning, until all the bacon is golden brown.
3.  Meanwhile, fry the bread for 2–3 minutes in the butter, until golden. Put a prune on each piece, garnish with watercress and serve at once.
*Makes 8*

**Variation**
*ANGELS ON HORSEBACK*
Omit the almonds and prunes and replace with 8 oysters sprinkled with cayenne papper and lemon juice. Place one roll on top of each croûte of bread and bake in the oven at 200°C (400°F) mark 6 for about 15 minutes, or until the bacon is lightly cooked. Serve at once, garnished with a little watercress.

## CHICKEN LIVERS ON TOAST

100 g (4 oz) chicken livers

15–30 ml (1–2 level tbsp) seasoned flour

4 rounds of bread about 5 cm (2 inches) in diameter

50 g (2 oz) butter or margarine

30 ml (2 tbsp) sherry or Madeira

50 g (2 oz) mushrooms, wiped and sliced (optional)

1.  Wash and dry the livers, cut them in small pieces and coat with the seasoned flour.
2.  Toast the bread and lightly butter.
3.  Melt the remaining butter in a frying pan, add the livers and cook until browned, stirring. Add the sherry or Madeira and the mushrooms if using, mix well and cook slowly for 10–15 minutes.
4.  Serve the livers on the toast.
*Makes 4*

# FISH

*F*ish are an excellent source of protein and are low in fat and carbohydrates. Most of the fat they do contain is polyunsaturated, unlike animal fat which is saturated (see page 9). White fish have a more delicate flavour than oily fish. They have less than 2 per cent fat and contain only 50–80 calories per 100 g (4 oz). Oily fish, such as mackerel, generally have darker, richer flesh. They have 8–20 per cent fat and contain 80–160 calories per 100 g (4 oz).

This chapter includes some varieties previously unavailable in this country; try experimenting by using them in recipes instead of the more familiar ones. Some fish are available all year around, others have a close season (period when they cannot be fished) which is usually the spawning time. General availability for each fish is given in the individual entries, but it can vary by several weeks in different parts of the country.

♦

### BUYING FRESH FISH

Look for fish that are as fresh as possible and preferably cook on the day they are bought. Whole fish should have clear, bright eyes, bright red or pink gills, shiny bodies and close-fitting scales. Fillets, steaks and cutlets should not show signs of dryness or discoloration, nor should they be wet and shiny. All fresh fish should have a mild, clean smell; do not buy any strong smelling fish.

Shellfish should be very fresh as they are more perishable than other fish. They should have a clean sea smell and clear fresh colour; avoid any that are dull looking. Prawns and shrimps should have tails curled well under them. Look for tightly closed shells where applicable (see individual entries).

### BUYING FROZEN FISH

Frozen fish are sold in a variety of ways—whole, filleted, as cutlets or as fingers or cakes. Shellfish are also available frozen. Use frozen fish like fresh, but be sure to carefully follow the manufacturer's instructions concerning the storage, thawing and cooking times.

### CLEANING FISH

The fishmonger will nearly always prepare fish for you, but you can do it yourself if you follow these instructions:

**1.** Using the back of a knife, remove any scales, scraping from tail to head (the opposite way to the direction the scales lie). Rinse frequently under cold running water.

**2.** To remove the entrails from round fish, such as herrings or trout, make a slit along the abdomen from the gills to the tail vent. Draw out the insides

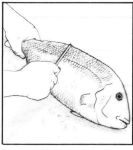
*Scrape off the scales.*

*Slit along abdomen to gut.*

and clean away any blood. Rub with a little salt to remove the black skin and blood. Rinse under cold running water and pat dry with absorbent kitchen paper.

**3.** To remove the entrails from flat fish, such as sole and plaice, open the cavity which lies in the upper part of the body under the gills and clean out the entrails in the same way. Rinse under cold running water.

**4.** Cut off the fins and gills, if wished, if the fish is to be served whole. The head and tail may also be cut off, if wished. Rinse the fish under cold running water and pat dry with absorbent kitchen paper.

**5.** Fillets and cutlets should be rinsed under cold running water, then patted dry with absorbent kitchen paper.

## SKINNING FISH

### Whole flat fish

**1.** Rinse the fish and cut off the fins, if not already removed. Make an incision across the tail, slip the thumb between the skin and the flesh and loosen the dark skin around the sides of the fish. Salt your fingers, then hold the fish down firmly with one hand and hold the skin with the other hand. Then pull the skin upwards towards the head. The white skin can be removed in the same way, but unless the fish is particularly large, this layer of skin is usually left on.

*To skin flat fish, make an incision across the tail. Use salted fingers and pull the skin away.*

### Fillets of flat fish

**1.** Lay the fillet on a board, skin side down. Salt your fingers and hold the tail end of the skin firmly.

*Firmly hold tail while skinning the fish.*

Insert a sharp knife between the flesh and the skin and work from head to tail, sawing with the knife from side to side and pressing the flat side of the blade against the skin. Keep the edges of the blade close to the skin while cutting, but do not press it down at too sharp an angle or you will slice through the fish's skin.

### Round fish

These are usually cooked with the skin on, but may be skinned if wished.

**1.** Using a sharp knife, cut along the spine and across the skin just below the head. Loosen the skin under the head with the point of the knife. Salt the fingers, then gently pull the skin down towards the tail, working carefully to avoid breaking the flesh. Skin the other side in the same way.

*With salted fingers, carefully pull the skin towards the tail.*

## FILLETING FISH

### Flat fish

**1.** Four fillets are taken from flat fish, two from each side. Using a small, sharp, pointed knife, make an incision straight down the back of the fish, following the line of the bone and keeping the fish flat on the board.

**2.** Insert the knife between the flesh and the bone and carefully remove the flesh with

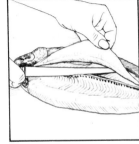

*Place a knife between the flesh and bones and slice away the fillet.*

long, clean strokes, cutting the first fillet from the left-hand side of the fish, carefully working from the head to the tail.

**3.** Turn the fish and cut off the second fillet from tail to head. Fillet the other side using the same method. There should not be any flesh left on the fish's bone.

**Key.**
1. Cod; 2. Grey mullet; 3. Monkfish; 4. Turbot; 5. Dover sole; 6. Sea bass; 7. Whiting; 8. Red mullet; 9. Skate; 10. Halibut; 11. Plaice; 12. Mackerel; 13. Herring; 14. Sardine; 15. Whitebait; 16. Conger eel; 17. Salmon; 18. Salmon cutlets; 19. Trout.

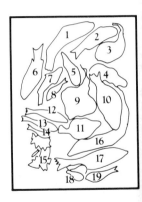

**Round fish**
1. Two fillets are taken from round fish. Keeping the fish flat on the board, cut along the centre of the back to the bone, using a sharp knife. Then cut along the abdomen of the fish.
2. Remove the flesh cleanly from the bones, working from the head down, pressing the knife against the bones and working with short, sharp strokes. Remove the fillet from the other side in the same way. If the fish is large, cut the fillets into serving-size pieces.

**Herring and mackerel**
These are small fish and are often cooked whole rather than first being divided into fillets. This is

how to remove the bones:
1. Cut off the head, tail and fins. Split the fish along the underside and remove the entrails. Salt the fingers and rub off the black inner skin and blood.
2. Put the fish on a board, cut side down, and press lightly with the fingers down the middle of the back to loosen the bone.
3. Turn the fish over and ease the backbone up with the fingers, removing with it as many of the small bones as possible. If the fish contains roes, remove these before easing out the backbone (they can be cooked and served with the fish or served separately).

## POACHED FISH

Fish can be poached very gently, so that it does not break up and the texture is not spoilt by overcooking. It can be poached on the top of the stove in a fish kettle or saucepan, or in the oven. The poaching liquid may be wine, milk or salted water, flavoured with parsley sprigs, a small piece of onion and/or carrot, a few mushroom stalks, a squeeze of lemon juice, a bay leaf and some peppercorns. Alternatively, poach in Court Bouillon (see below).

Fillets, steaks or whole fish, e.g. halibut, turbot, brill, haddock, flounder, salmon, sea

trout, smoked haddock and kippers can be poached.
1. Heat the liquid in a fish kettle or saucepan until simmering, then add the fish. Cover and simmer very gently until tender, allowing 10–15 minutes per 450 g (1 lb), according to the thickness of the cut, or about 20 minutes in all for a small piece.
2. Drain the fish, transfer to a warmed serving dish and serve with a sauce made from the cooking liquid. Alternatively, serve the fish cold, in aspic or with Mayonnaise (see page 261).

## COURT BOUILLON

*1 litre (1¾ pint) water or dry white wine and water mixed*

*1 small carrot, scrubbed and sliced*

*1 small onion, skinned and sliced*

*1 small celery stick, washed and chopped (optional)*

*15 ml (1 tbsp) wine vinegar or lemon juice*

*few fresh parsley sprigs*

*1 bay leaf*

*3–4 black peppercorns*

*10 ml (2 level tsp) salt*

1. Place all the ingredients in a saucepan and simmer for about 30 minutes. Allow to cool and strain the liquid before using, if wished.
*Makes about 900 ml (1½ pints)*

## STEAMED FISH

Fillets, e.g. sole, trout and monkfish, can be steamed.

1. Season the prepared fish with salt and pepper. Heat the water in the base of a steamer to simmering point (line the top of the steamer with buttered foil to keep in the flavour, if wished).

2. Put the fish into the steamer and cover with a tight fitting lid. Steam for 10–15 minutes or until the fish is firm to touch and just flaking from the bones.
*Note* If you do not have a steamer, the fish can be placed between two greased plates over a saucepan of simmering water.

# GRILLED FISH

Small fish, thin fillets and thicker cuts, e.g. sole, plaice, halibut, turbot, hake, brill, cod, haddock, flounder, salmon, sea trout, trout, herring, mackerel, kippers, red mullet and monkfish, can be grilled.

1. Put the prepared fish in the grill pan, season and make two or three diagonal cuts in the body on each side, to allow the heat to penetrate through the flesh.
2. Brush with melted butter, oil or margarine and cook under a moderate heat, allowing 4–5 minutes for thin fillets, 10–15 minutes for thicker fillets, steaks and small whole fish, adjusting times according to size and thickness.

**Variation**
*BARBECUED FISH*
Many types of fish can be barbecued—trout, bass, red mullet, mackerel, sardines and shellfish such as lobster, oysters, prawns, clams and scallops are all suitable. Use a special grilling basket or wrap in foil to prevent it breaking up. Alternatively, thread the fish on to long skewers. Leave the shells on shellfish to protect the delicate flesh during cooking.

# SHALLOW-FRIED FISH

Fillets, steaks and whole fish, e.g. sole, plaice, dabs, bass, monkfish, bream, cod, haddock, mackerel, herring, trout, perch and pike, can be shallow-fried.

1. Coat the prepared fish with either a coating of seasoned flour, or egg and breadcrumbs.
2. Heat either clarified butter (see page 571), vegetable oil, or oil and butter until fairly hot.
3. Add the fish and fry for 3–4 minutes for small fillets, steaks or whole fish and 8–10 minutes for larger cuts, turning once.
4. Drain well on crumpled absorbent kitchen paper and serve with lemon and parsley or Maître d'Hôtel Butter (see page 209).

# DEEP-FRIED FISH

Fillets from large fish coated with batter or egg and breadcrumbs, small whole fish, e.g. cod, haddock, hake, whiting, coley, monkfish and skate, can be deep-fried.

1. Heat vegetable oil in a deep-fat fryer to 190°C (375°F). Coat the fish with flour, egg and breadcrumbs or coating batter (see page 328).
2. Lower the fish gently into the oil, using a basket for egg-and-crumbed pieces, and deep-fry for 4–5 minutes or until golden brown and crisp. (Take care when cooking small fish like whitebait, as they will cook in little more than a minute.)
3. Drain well on absorbent kitchen paper before serving.

# BAKED FISH

Fillets, steaks, whole fish and cuts from large fish, e.g. cod, haddock, hake, whiting, sole, plaice, trout, halibut, salmon, herring and monkfish, can be baked.

1. Place the prepared fish in an ovenproof dish, season, add a knob of butter or margarine and pour over a little water, milk, lemon juice stock or wine.
2. Cover with foil and bake in the oven at 180°C (350°F) mark 4 for whole fish, allowing 25–30 minutes, and at 200°C (400°F) mark 6 for smaller fish or fillets, allowing 15–20 minutes or until tender. (Never allow the liquid to boil as this results in the flesh flaking and a dry texture.)
3. Alternatively, wrap the prepared fish in greased foil and add a squeeze of lemon juice and a sprinkling of salt and pepper.
4. Place the fish on a baking sheet and bake in the oven at 180°C (350°F) mark 4 allowing 20 minutes for steaks and 8 minutes per 450 g (1 lb) plus 10 minutes extra for whole fish, according to size, unless otherwise directed in a particular recipe.

# Sea Fish

## Anchovy

The anchovy is a small round fish, which is usually filleted and cured, by salting or brining, and then canned or bottled. Because they are very salty, cured anchovies are only used in small amounts in appetisers and cocktail nibbles, as pizza topping and in Salade Niçoise (see page 256). They can also be used to make Anchovy Butter (see page 209) for use in savouries.

Anchovies are rarely available fresh, but they are easily recognised by their extraordinarily large mouth, which stretches back almost as far as their gills. They have a strong flavour, but are not salty like the cured ones.

## Bass

Bass is a round fish, similar to salmon in shape, which can weigh up to 4.5 kg (10 lb). It has steel grey or blue scales covering the back and sides and a white or yellowish belly. It has white flesh and is sold whole or as steaks or fillets. Large bass, which have a good flavour, are usually poached or baked; small fish can be grilled or fried. Available May to September.

## Bream (Sea)

Bream is a round, red-backed fish with a silvery belly and red fins. It has firm white flesh which has a mild flavour. It is usually sold whole and can be stuffed and baked, poached, fried or grilled. Available July to March.

## Brill

This is a flat fish with a good flavour and texture resembling turbot. The flesh is firm and slightly yellowish; avoid any with a bluish tinge. It is sold whole or as fillets and may be poached, served cold with Mayonnaise (see page 261), or cooked like turbot (see page 61). Available April to July.

## Catfish

Catfish gets its name from its head, which has cat-like whiskers. The flesh is firm and white with a pinkish tinge and has a strong flavour. It is ideal for casseroles or stews. It can also be grilled or cooked as for Cod (see below). It is sold as fillets, portions or cutlets. Available February to July.

## Cod

Cod is a large round fish with close, white flesh. Small cod are known as *codling*. Cod may be sold whole when young and small, or as fillets or steaks when large. It can be grilled, baked, fried in batter or used in various cooked dishes. Available all year, best from October to May.

**Cod's roe** is also available either fresh, canned or smoked.

**Salt cod fillets** are sold in some ethnic shops. Look for fillets that are thick and have white flesh; when not fresh, salt cod takes on a yellow appearance. To use: soak for 24 hours in cold water, changing the water several times. Drain and remove any skin and bones before cooking. Salt cod tends to be uninteresting cooked alone, but is good made up with other well-flavoured ingredients.

## Coley (Saithe)

Coley is a member of the cod family with bluish-black skin. It is usually sold as fillets or cutlets, but may be sold whole. The well-flavoured meaty flesh is pinkish-grey and turns white when cooked. Use in the same way as Cod (see left), but as it is inclined to be dry, add moisture during cooking. Best September to February.

## Conger Eel

The conger eel is a sea fish which is a greyish-brown colour on top and silver underneath. The full-flavoured flesh is white and firm; larger eels have a coarser texture than small ones. The conger eel is larger than the common (freshwater) eel, but it can be prepared and cooked in the same way. Eels can be jellied, fried, grilled, poached or baked. Available March to October.

## Cuttlefish

The cuttlefish is a member of a group of aquatic creatures known as *cephalopods*—a name which comes from the Greek words for head and feet—so called because they have tentacles protruding from their heads. Octopus and squid are also cephalopods. Cuttlefish and squid have ten tentacles, octopus eight. In prehistoric times, they had external shells and, although they no longer have them, they are still regarded as part of the mollusc family (see Shellfish, page 81).

Cuttlefish are mostly sold frozen. If buying fresh, clean and prepare as for Squid (see page 61).

## Dab

Dab is a small flat fish belonging to the plaice family. It has white flesh and is excellent fried or baked. It may be sold whole or as fillets. Best August to December.

## FLOUNDER

Flounder is a flat fish which resembles plaice, but does not have such a good texture and flavour. It is sold whole or as fillets and can be cooked like Plaice (see page 60). Available all year.

## GURNET, GURNARD

This is a small round fish with a large, distinctive, boney head and three rays of the pectoral fins extending downwards. There are three types of gurnet, the grey, yellow and red. It has firm white flesh and can be baked, grilled or poached and is especially good for fish soups.

## HADDOCK

This round fish is a cousin of the cod and is distinguished from it by a dark streak, which runs down the back, and the two black 'thumb marks' above the gills. Haddock has firm, white flesh and may be cooked by any method suitable for white fish; it is particularly useful for cooked dishes such as fish pie. It is sold as fillets or cutlets. Available all year, best May to February. Haddock does not take salt as well as cod does, and it is traditionally cured by smoking (see page 79).

## HAKE

Hake belongs to the same family as cod and is similar in shape, but has a closer white flesh and a better flavour. It can be cooked like Cod (see left). Small hake are sold whole; large ones are sold as fillets, steaks or cutlets. Hake is available June to January.

## HALIBUT

Halibut is a very large flat fish and like turbot is regarded as one of the best flavoured fish. It is sold as fillets or steaks. It is usually baked or grilled, but may also be cooked by any recipe suitable for Turbot (see page 61) or Cod (see page 58). Available all the year, best June to March.

## HERRING

Herring is a fairly small, round, oily fish with creamy-coloured flesh which has a distinctive flavour. It is usually grilled, fried, sautéed or stuffed and baked. Though generally sold whole, the fishmonger will fillet them for you on request. Available all year. Herrings are also sold prepared in various ways:

**Salt herrings** are gutted and preserved in wooden casks between layers of salt. Salt herrings are usually sold at delicatessen counters.

**Matjes herrings** are herrings cured in salt, sugar and a little saltpetre. They are sold whole or as fillets and have a better flavour than salt herrings.

**Rollmops and bismarcks** are boned herrings marinated in spiced vinegar. Rollmops are rolled with chopped onions, gherkins and peppercorns. Bismarcks are flat fillets covered with sliced onion.

**Canned herrings** are most popular in tomato sauce. Canned kippers and bloaters are available too, as are herring roes.

## HUSS

Huss is a long, pointed fish with light brown skin and a cream-coloured belly. It is also known as dogfish and used to be known as rock salmon. The firm flesh is white with a tinge of pink and is excellent fried. It is usually sold as fillets or cutlets. Available all year, best September to January.

## JOHN DORY

This ugly, flat fish has very large jaws and a body that is nearly oval in shape and olive-brown skin with a black 'thumb mark' on each side just behind the head. It has firm, white flesh with a delicate flavour. The head and fins can be removed and the fish poached or baked whole, but it is more usually filleted and cooked like Sole (see page 60). Available June to September.

## MACKEREL

Mackerel is a fairly small, round, oily fish with blue-black markings on the back, cream-coloured flesh and a very distinctive flavour. It is sold whole. It can be cooked whole or filleted and cooked by any method suitable for Herring (see left). Mackerel must be eaten very fresh. Available all year, best August to May.

**Horse mackerel** (scad) are sometimes available. They are a darker colour than ordinary mackerel and their flavour is not as good.

## MONKFISH (ANGLER FISH)

A round fish with a very large, ugly head. Only the tail is eaten and it is sold as fillets. The firm white flesh is not unlike lobster. Available all year, best October to January.

## MULLET (GREY)

Grey mullet is a round fish which looks and tastes similar to sea bass. It is sold whole or as fillets. The white flesh is firm with a mild, nutty flavour and is suitable for baking, grilling, steaming or poaching.

## MULLET (RED)

No relation to the grey mullet, red mullet is smaller, crimson in colour with a unique and delicate flavour. The liver is a delicacy and should not be discarded. Red mullet is sold whole and may be grilled, fried or baked. Available all year, best during summer months.

## OCTOPUS

The octopus is a member of the cephalopod group (see Cuttlefish, page 58) and has eight tentacles. Octopus vary in size and can grow up to 3 metres (12 feet). Small octopus may be sold whole; larger ones, ready-prepared in pieces. Octopus can be poached in water or red wine, then skinned and served cold or reheated in a sauce. It can also be used in soups and casseroles.

**To prepare octopus**

**1.** Rinse the octopus, then hold the body in one hand and with the other firmly pull off the head and tentacles. The soft contents of the body will come out and can be discarded. Cut the tentacles just in front of the eyes.

**2.** Rinse the body and the tentacles, then beat well with a wooden mallet. Cut the flesh into rings or pieces or keep whole for stuffing. The ink sac has a musky flavour and is not usually used.

## PILCHARD

This is a small, round, oily fish, called sardine when young and pilchard when mature. Most pilchards are caught off the coasts of Devon and Cornwall and are sold canned. Fresh pilchards can be grilled or fried whole. Available February to July.

## PLAICE

Plaice is a flat fish with warm brown skin with orange or red spots on the top side. The underside is white. The flesh is soft and white with a very delicate flavour. It is sold whole or as fillets and can be cooked by most methods, including steaming, frying, grilling and baking. Available all year, best April to December.

## RED FISH (NORWAY HADDOCK)

This is a fish with a flattened body and bright orange-red skin with dark blotches. It is sold whole or as fillets. The white flesh is lean and firm and has a good flavour. It is excellent for soup, but can also be cooked like Bream (see page 58).

## RED SNAPPER

This round fish has a distinctive red skin and delicious white flesh. It is usually sold whole, but steaks and fillets are also available. Whole fish may be baked with scales left on, or stuffed and baked. Alternatively, grill, braise or steam with scales removed. Available all year.

## SARDINE

Sardines are strictly speaking young pilchards, but the name is also applied to the young of other fish (sprats and herrings). The majority are canned in olive oil or tomato sauce but fresh sardines are becoming more readily available. Sardines can be grilled or baked or fried like Smelts, Sprats and Whitebait (see right). They are available February to July.

## SKATE

Skate is a flat-bodied, kite-shaped fish. Its upper side is bluish-grey and its belly is greyish-white. Only the wings (side parts) and nuggets of flesh known as 'nobs' are eaten and they are usually sold already cut from the body. They can be fried, grilled or poached.

The wings of small skate are often sold whole, but those of larger fish are usually sold cut into slices. Pieces of small skate can be cooked without any preparation, but large skate tend to be rather tough and flavourless and are better if first simmered in salted water or Court Bouillon (see page 56) until just tender. They can then be skinned, cut into 5–7.5 cm (2–3 inch) pieces and cooked in any way you wish.

Skate nobs are nuggets of flesh cut from under the boney part of the fish and sold separately. Best September to February.

## SMELT

This is a small round, silvery fish, which can be very oily. Its flavour is similar to trout. Smelts are usually served as a starter. They are prepared by making a small cut with scissors just below the gills and gently pressing out the entrails. They can be threaded on to skewers through the eye sockets and deep fried or larger ones may be baked. Available in November to February.

## SOLE

The name sole is given to several species of flat fish which resemble the sole of a sandal. *Dover sole* is the only true sole. Sole is sold whole or as fillets and is delicious grilled, fried, baked or steamed.

**Dover sole** is considered one of the finest flat fish. It has dark brown-grey skin and pale, firm flesh with a delicious flavour. Available all year, however they are best November to April.

**Lemon sole** is lighter in colour, slightly longer and its head is more pointed than Dover sole. The flesh is more stringy and has less flavour. Best December to March.

**Witch or Torbay sole** is shaped like Dover sole and has slightly greyish-pinkish skin. Its flesh is similar to that of lemon sole. Sole is best August to April.

### SPRAT

A fairly small, round fish of the same family as the Herring (see page 59). To prepare sprats, wash and draw them through the gills, as for Smelt (see left). Coat in seasoned flour and fry as for Whitebait (see below right), but allow 4–5 minutes frying. They may also be grilled. Available September to March.

### SQUID

Squid is the most commonly available member of the cephalopod group (see Cuttlefish, page 58) in Britain. There are several species, varying in size. Only the tentacles and body pouch are eaten, the other parts are discarded. The tentacles are usually chopped and the body is either sliced into rings, cut into sections or kept whole and the body cavity stuffed.

A popular practice in Mediterranean cookery is to cook the squid in their ink, the ink sac must, therefore, be removed intact. Small squid can be sautéed, poached, grilled or deep-fried; larger ones are often stewed.

**To clean squid**

**1.** Rinse the squid, then hold the body in one hand and with the other, firmly pull on the head and tentacles. As you do this, the soft contents of the body will come out and can be discarded. Cut

Firmly holding the squid, pull on the head and tentacles to remove the body cavity's contents, then discard.

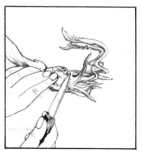

Using a small sharp knife, cut the tentacles away from the head just by the eyes, then discard.

the tentacles just in front of the eyes. Remove the ink sac from the head, if wished.

**2.** Remove the plastic-like quill and rinse the body under cold running water to remove any white substance.

**3.** Rub the fine dark skin off the outer body and rinse again under cold running water. Cut the flesh into rings, pieces or keep whole for filling with stuffing.

### STURGEON

Sturgeon is not usually available in Britain. It is a large fish—it can grow up to 4 metres (13 feet)—and has a head covered with hard boney plates and a snout with four barbels (thin feelers) hanging from it. Its flesh is white to pink with a flavour similar to veal. Caviar (see page 34) is the roe of the female sturgeon.

### TUNA (TUNNY)

Fresh tuna is not widely available in Britain—it is usually sold canned. Tuna is a very large round fish with a dark blue back and silvery grey sides and belly. The deep reddish-pink flesh is oily and much heavier than the flesh of other fish, it is almost like meat. It may be sold in slices or pieces, the belly is the best part. Fresh tuna can be braised, poached in foil, grilled or fried. Canned tuna can be used in both hot and cold dishes.

### TURBOT

Turbot is a flat diamond-shaped fish with very small scales. The upper sides can be various shades of dappled brown. It has creamy white flesh with a delicious flavour and is considered to be the finest of the flat fish. It is usually cut into steaks and grilled, baked or poached—often with wine. In season all year, but it is most tasteful March to August.

### WHITEBAIT

These are the tiny, silvery fry (young) of sprats or herring which are eaten whole and require no gutting. Rinse thoroughly and drain well. Whitebait are usually coated in flour, either seasoned with salt and pepper and/or cayenne pepper, and deep fried. Best February to June.

### WHITING

Whiting is a smallish fish with a pale brown to olive-green back and a cream-coloured belly. The flesh is soft, white and flaky with a delicate flavour. It is sold whole or as fillets. It can be poached, steamed or shallow fried. Available all year.

## Barbecued Bass

100 g (4 oz) unsalted butter

20 ml (4 level tsp) dried dill weed

finely grated rind and juice of 1 lemon

salt and pepper

1.5 kg (3 lb) bass, cleaned

75 ml (3 fl oz) dry white wine

lemon slices and fresh dill sprigs, to garnish

**1.** In a bowl, work the butter with the dill weed, lemon rind and seasoning to taste. Form into a roll, wrap in foil and chill in the refrigerator for 2–3 hours, until firm.

**2.** Cut a sheet of foil large enough to enclose the fish. Place the fish in the centre of the foil.

**3.** Using a sharp knife, cut the flavoured butter into slices. Peel off and discard the foil after cutting.

**4.** Place the butter slices inside the belly of the fish. Sprinkle the outside of the fish with salt and pepper, then slowly pour over the wine and lemon juice.

**5.** Fold the foil over the fish to form a loose package so that the wine and juices do not leak out. Place the foil package on the barbecue and grill for 45 minutes. Serve hot, straight from the foil, garnished with a few lemon slices and fresh dill sprigs.

Serves 4

Barbecued Bass

# Cod in White Wine

*50 g (2 oz) butter or margarine*

*450 g (1 lb) courgettes, thinly sliced*

*2 large onions, skinned and sliced*

*30 ml (2 level tbsp) flour*

*15 ml (1 level tbsp) paprika*

*300 ml (½ pint) dry white wine*

*397 g (14 oz) can tomatoes*

*15 ml (1 tbsp) chopped fresh basil or 5 ml (1 level tsp) dried*

*1 garlic clove, crushed*

*salt and pepper*

*1.1 kg (2½ lb) cod fillets, skinned and cut into 5 cm (2 inch) pieces*

*190 g (6¾ oz) can pimiento, drained and sliced*

*fried French bread croûtes*

Cod in White Wine

1. Melt the butter in a large frying pan, add the courgettes, onions, flour and paprika and fry gently for 3–4 minutes, stirring.
2. Stir in the wine, tomatoes, basil, garlic and seasoning. Bring to the boil.
3. In a large ovenproof dish, layer up the fish, pimiento and sauce mixture, seasoning well.
4. Cover the dish and cook at 170°C (325°F) mark 3 for 50–60 minutes. Garnish with the croûtes.
*Serves 8*

**Variation**
Use haddock or other firm white fish.

# Hot Fish Terrine with Gruyère Sauce

*65 g (2½ oz) butter or margarine*

*1 garlic clove, skinned and crushed*

*60 ml (4 level tbsp) flour*

*700 ml (1¼ pints) milk*

*550 g (1¼ lb) hake fillets, skinned and cut into pieces*

*150 ml (5 fl oz) double cream*

*10 ml (2 tsp) anchovy essence*

*3 eggs*

*1 egg yolk*

*salt and pepper*

*30 ml (2 tbsp) chopped fresh parsley*

*125 g (4 oz) peeled prawns, finely chopped*

*125 g (4 oz) Gruyère cheese, grated*

1. Grease and base-line a 1.6 litre (2¾ pint) loaf tin or terrine.
2. Melt 40 g (1½ oz) butter in a saucepan, add the garlic and 45 ml (3 level tbsp) flour and cook for 1 minute, stirring. Remove from the heat and gradually stir in 450 ml (¾ pint) milk. Bring to the boil, stirring, until the sauce thickens.
3. In a blender or food processor, purée the sauce, raw fish, cream, anchovy essence, eggs and egg yolk. Season lightly.
4. Spoon half the mixture into the tin. Sprinkle with parsley and half the prawns. Spoon in the rest of the fish mixture.
5. Cover tightly with greased greaseproof paper. Place in a roasting tin with water to come halfway up the sides of the terrine and cook in the oven at 150°C (300°F) mark 2 for about 1¾ hours.
6. Just before the end of the cooking time, make the cheese sauce. Melt the remaining butter in a saucepan. Stir in 15 ml (1 level tbsp) flour and cook gently for 1 minute, stirring. Remove the pan from the heat and gradually stir in the remaining milk.
7. Bring to the boil stirring and continue to cook, stirring, until the sauce thickens. Simmer for 3 minutes. Remove from the heat and stir in the grated cheese and the remaining prawns. Check the seasoning. Invert the terrine on to a warmed serving dish and tilt slightly to drain off the juice.
8. To serve, spoon a little sauce over terrine and hand the rest of the sauce separately.
*Serves 6*

## HAKE GOUJONS

450 g (1 lb) hake fillets, skinned, boned and cut into
   20 even-sized pieces

1 egg, beaten

50 g (2 oz) fresh breadcrumbs

vegetable oil for deep frying

Tartare Sauce (see page 261), to serve

**1.** Coat the fish pieces in egg, then in the
breadcrumbs.
**2.** Heat the oil in a deep-fat fryer to 180°C

(350°F), add the fish and fry until golden. Drain on
absorbent kitchen paper.
**3.** Serve the goujons on cocktail sticks with the
sauce handed separately.
*Serves 4*

**Variation**
Other firm fish such as haddock, coley, cod,
monkfish and huss can be cooked in the same
way.

## FISH CAKES

350 g (12 oz) fish, e.g. cod, haddock or coley, cooked
   and flaked

350 g (12 oz) potatoes, cooked and mashed

25 g (1 oz) butter or margarine

15 ml (1 tbsp) chopped fresh parsley

salt and pepper

few drops of anchovy essence (optional)

milk or beaten egg, to bind

100 g (4 oz) fresh breadcrumbs

vegetable oil for frying

**1.** Mix the fish with the potatoes, butter, parsley,
seasoning and anchovy essence, if using, binding if
necessary with a little milk or egg.
**2.** On a lightly floured board, form the mixture
into a roll, cut into eight slices and shape into flat
cakes. Coat them with egg and breadcrumbs.
**3.** Heat the oil in a frying pan, add the fish cakes
and fry, turning once, until crisp and golden.
Drain well on absorbent kitchen paper.
*Serves 4*

**Variations**
Replace the cod, haddock or coley with smoked
haddock, herrings, canned tuna or salmon.

## HERRINGS IN OATMEAL

4 herrings, weighing 175–225 g (6–8 oz) each, cleaned
   boned and heads and tails removed

salt and pepper

100 g (4 oz) fine oatmeal

$\frac{1}{2}$ a lemon, cut into wedges

chopped fresh parsley, to garnish

**1.** Sprinkle the herrings with salt and pepper and
coat with oatmeal, pressing it well into the fish.
**2.** Arrange the herrings in a grill pan. Cook under
a fairly hot grill for 6–8 minutes, turning once,
until tender and slightly flaky.
**3.** Serve garnished with lemon wedges and
chopped parsley.
*Serves 4*

## SOUSED HERRINGS

salt and pepper

4 large or 6–8 small herrings, cleaned, boned and
   heads and tails removed

1 small onion, skinned and sliced into rings

6 black peppercorns

1–2 bay leaves

fresh parsley sprigs

150 ml ($\frac{1}{4}$ pint) malt vinegar

**1.** Season fish, roll up and secure. Arrange in a
shallow ovenproof dish with onion, peppercorns
and herbs.
**2.** Pour in the vinegar and enough water to almost
cover the fish. Cover with greaseproof paper or
foil and bake in the oven at 180°C (350°F) mark 4
for about 45 minutes or until tender.
**3.** Leave the herrings to cool in the cooking liquid
before serving as an appetiser or with salad.
*Serves 4*

# MONKFISH WITH LIME AND PRAWNS

| |
|---|
| 550 g (1¼ lb) monkfish fillets, skinned, boned and cut into 5 cm (2 inch) pieces |
| 30 ml (2 level tbsp) seasoned flour |
| 30 ml (2 tbsp) vegetable oil |
| 1 small onion, skinned and chopped |
| 1 garlic clove, skinned and chopped |
| 225 g (8 oz) tomatoes, skinned and chopped |
| 150 ml (¼ pint) dry white wine |
| grated rind and juice of 1 lime |
| pinch of sugar |
| salt and pepper |
| 100 g (4 oz) peeled prawns |
| lime slices, to garnish |

*Monkfish with Lime and Prawns*

1. Coat the fish in seasoned flour. Heat the oil in a flameproof casserole, add the onion and garlic and fry gently for 5 minutes, until softened. Add the fish and fry for 5 minutes, until golden.
2. Stir in the tomatoes, wine, lime rind and juice, sugar and seasoning. Bring to the boil.
3. Cover and cook in the oven at 180°C (350°F) mark 4 for 15 minutes. Add the prawns and continue to cook for a further 15 minutes, until the monkfish is tender. Garnish with lime slices.
*Serves 4*

# MONKFISH AND MUSSEL BROCHETTES

| |
|---|
| 36 mussels, cooked (see page 82) |
| 18 streaky bacon rashers, rinded and halved |
| 900 g (2 lb) monkfish fillets, skinned, boned and cut into 42 cubes |
| 50 g (2 oz) butter or margarine, melted |
| 60 ml (4 tbsp) chopped fresh parsley |
| grated rind and juice of 1 lime or lemon |
| 4 garlic cloves, skinned and crushed |
| salt and pepper |
| shredded lettuce, bay leaves and lime or lemon wedges, to garnish |
| saffron rice, to serve (optional) |

1. Using a sharp knife, shell the mussels, discarding the shells.
2. Roll the bacon rashers up neatly. Thread the cubed fish, mussels and bacon alternately on to six oiled kebab skewers.
3. Mix together the melted butter, parsley, lime rind and juice, garlic and salt and pepper to taste. (Take care when adding salt as both the mussels and the bacon are naturally salty.)
4. Place the brochettes on an oiled grill or barbecue rack. Brush with the butter mixture, then grill under a moderate grill for 15 minutes, turning frequently and brushing with the butter mixture.
5. Arrange the hot brochettes on a serving platter lined with shredded lettuce. Garnish with bay leaves and lime wedges and serve at once with saffron rice, if wished.
*Serves 6*

*Monkfish and Mussel Brochettes*

## RED MULLET IN TOMATO SAUCE

| |
|---|
| 25 g (1 oz) butter or margarine |
| 1 small onion, skinned and finely chopped |
| 1 garlic clove, skinned and crushed (optional) |
| 450 g (1 lb) tomatoes, skinned and quartered |
| salt and pepper |
| 10 ml (2 level tsp) sugar |
| 1 bay leaf |
| 4 red mullet, about 550 g (1¼ lb) each, cleaned |
| 30 ml (2 level tbsp) seasoned flour |
| 45 ml (3 tbsp) vegetable oil for frying |
| 30 ml (2 level tbsp) fresh breadcrumbs |
| 15 ml (1 tbsp) chopped fresh parsley |

1. Melt the butter in a saucepan, add the onion and the garlic, if using, and fry for about 5 minutes, until soft but not coloured. Add the tomatoes, seasoning, sugar and bay leaf. Cover and simmer gently for about 30 minutes, until soft and pulped. Remove the bay leaf.
2. Meanwhile, coat the fish in seasoned flour. Heat the oil in a large frying pan, add the fish and fry for 6–8 minutes, turning them once.
3. Place half the tomato sauce in a shallow ovenproof dish, lay the fish on top, then cover with the rest of the sauce. Sprinkle the breadcrumbs over the top and brown under a hot grill. Sprinkle with parsley and serve at once.
*Serves 4*

## FRESH SARDINES WITH HERBS

| |
|---|
| 900 g (2 lb) fresh sardines (at least 12), cleaned if wished |
| 60 ml (4 tbsp) chopped fresh mixed herbs, e.g. mint, parsley, sage |
| grated rind of 2 lemons |
| 120 ml (8 tbsp) lemon juice |
| 300 ml (½ pint) olive or sunflower oil |
| 2 medium onions, skinned and finely sliced |
| salt and pepper |
| lemon wedges, to garnish |

1. Wash the sardines well. Mix together 45 ml (3 tbsp) herbs with the lemon rind and juice, oil, onions and seasoning.
2. Grill the sardines for 5–7 minutes each side, basting with the herb dressing. Serve immediately or leave in the dressing to cool completely.
3. Sprinkle with the reserved herbs before serving. Garnish with lemon wedges.
*Serves 4*

## SKATE WITH BLACK BUTTER

| |
|---|
| 700–900 g (1½–2 lb) skate wings |
| salt |
| 50 g (2 oz) butter |
| 15 ml (1 tbsp) white wine vinegar |
| 10 ml (2 level tsp) capers |
| 10 ml (2 tsp) chopped fresh parsley |

1. Put the fish in a saucepan and cover with salted water. Bring to the boil, then simmer for 10–15 minutes, until tender. Drain and place on a warm serving dish. Cover and keep warm.
2. Melt the butter in a saucepan, cook until it turns golden brown, add the vinegar and capers and cook for a further 2–3 minutes. Pour over the fish, sprinkle with parsley and serve immediately.
*Serves 4*

**Variation**
*SKATE IN PEPPER BUTTER*
1. Prepare the skate as described in the recipe above.
2. Melt 75 g (3 oz) butter in a saucepan, add 30 ml (2 level tbsp) black peppercorns, crushed, 1 small garlic clove, crushed and 5 ml (1 level tsp) dried sage. Stir over a medium heat for about 1 minute, until the butter is golden brown. Pour over the skate and serve immediately.

## STUFFED RED SNAPPER

*1 red snapper, about 550 g (1¼ lb) in weight, cleaned*

*25 g (1 oz) butter or margarine*

*1 large bunch of watercress, about 75 g (3 oz), washed and finely chopped*

*50 g (2 oz) spring onions, trimmed and finely chopped*

*175 g (6 oz) firm Brie, rinded and roughly chopped*

*salt and pepper*

**1.** Place the fish in a shallow ovenproof dish. Melt the butter in a frying pan, add the watercress and all but 15 ml (1 tbsp) onions and fry gently for 1–2 minutes, until softened.

**2.** Remove from the heat and stir in the chopped Brie. Season. Spoon two thirds of the mixture into the cavity of the fish. Spread the remainder over the fish to cover completely, excluding the head and tail.

**3.** Bake in the oven at 200°C (400°F) mark 6 for about 30 minutes. Place under a hot grill for 3–4 minutes, until well browned. Remove head and tail before serving. Sprinkle with the reserved chopped onion.

*Serves 2*

## OLD FASHIONED FISH PIE

*450 g (1 lb) haddock, cod or coley fillets*

*300 ml (½ pint) milk*

*1 bay leaf*

*6 black peppercorns*

*onion slices for flavouring*

*salt and pepper*

*65 g (2½ oz) butter or margarine*

*45 ml (3 level tbsp) flour*

*150 ml (5 fl oz) single cream*

*2 eggs, hard-boiled, shelled and chopped*

*30 ml (2 tbsp) chopped fresh parsley*

*90 ml (6 tbsp) milk*

*900 g (2 lb) potatoes, cooked and mashed*

*1 egg, beaten, to glaze*

**1.** Put the fish in a frying pan, pour over the milk and add the bay leaf, peppercorns, onion slices and a good pinch of salt. Bring slowly to the boil, cover and simmer for 8–10 minutes, until the fish flakes when tested with a fork.

**2.** Lift the fish out of the pan using a fish slice and place on a plate. Flake the fish, discarding the skin and bone. Strain and reserve the milk.

**3.** Melt 40 g (1½ oz) butter in a saucepan, stir in the flour and cook gently for 1 minute, stirring. Remove the pan from the heat and gradually stir in the reserved milk. Bring to the boil slowly and continue to cook, stirring until the sauce thickens. Season.

**4.** Stir in the cream and fish together with any juices. Add the chopped egg and parsley and adjust the seasoning. Spoon the mixture into a 1.1 litre (2 pint) pie dish or similar ovenproof dish.

**5.** Heat the milk and remaining butter in a saucepan, then beat into the potato. Season and leave to cool slightly.

**6.** Spoon the cooled potato into a large piping bag fitted with a large star nozzle. Pipe shell-shaped lines of potato across the fish mixture. Alternatively, spoon potato on top and roughen the surface with a fork.

**7.** Place the dish on a baking sheet and cook in the oven at 200°C (400°F) mark 6 for 10–15 minutes or until the potato is set.

**8.** Beat the egg with a good pinch of salt then brush over the pie. Return to the oven for about 15 minutes, until golden brown.

*Serves 4*

### Variations

● Stir 100 g (4 oz) grated Cheddar cheese into the sauce.

● Beat 100 g (4 oz) grated Cheddar or Red Leicester cheese into the mashed potatoes.

● Stir 175 g (6 oz) canned sweetcorn, drained, and 1.25 ml (¼ tsp) cayenne pepper into the fish mixture.

● Fry 100 g (4 oz) sliced button mushrooms in 25 g (1 oz) butter for 3 minutes. Stir into the fish mixture.

● Sprinkle the potato topping with 50 g (2 oz) mixed grated Parmesan cheese and fresh breadcrumbs after the first 10–15 minutes.

● Cover the pie with puff pastry instead of the mashed potatoes.

## Ceviche

This is a traditional Mexican recipe. The acidic lime juice pickles and tenderises the fish so that it does not need cooking.

| |
|---|
| 450 g (1 lb) haddock fillets, skinned and cut diagonally into thin strips |
| 5 ml (1 level tsp) coriander seeds |
| 5 ml (1 level tsp) black peppercorns |
| juice of 6 limes |
| 5 ml (1 level tsp) salt |
| 30 ml (2 tbsp) olive oil |
| bunch of spring onions, washed, trimmed and sliced |
| 4 tomatoes, skinned and chopped |
| dash of Tabasco sauce, or to taste |
| 30 ml (2 tbsp) chopped fresh coriander |
| 1 avocado, lime slices and fresh coriander, to garnish |

1. Place the fish strips in a bowl. Using a pestle and mortar, crush the coriander seeds and peppercorns to a fine powder, mix with the lime juice and salt, then pour over the fish. Cover and chill in the refrigerator for 24 hours, turning the fish occasionally.
2. The next day, heat the oil in a frying pan, add the spring onions and fry gently for 5 minutes.

Ceviche

Add the tomatoes and Tabasco sauce to taste and toss together over brisk heat for 1–2 minutes. Remove from the heat and cool for 20–30 minutes.
3. To serve, drain the fish from the marinade, discarding the marinade, and mix with the spring onion and tomatoes and the chopped coriander.
4. Halve the avocado, peel and remove the stone. Slice the flesh crossways. Arrange the slices around the inside of a serving bowl and pile the fish mixture in the centre. Garnish. Serve chilled.
Serves 4

## Indonesian Fish Curry

| |
|---|
| 1 small onion, skinned and roughly chopped |
| 1 garlic clove, skinned and chopped |
| 2.5 cm (1 inch) piece root ginger, skinned and chopped |
| 5 ml (1 level tsp) ground turmeric |
| 2.5 ml (½ level tsp) laos powder (see page 194) |
| 1 dried red chilli or 1.25 ml (¼ level tsp) chilli powder |
| 30 ml (2 tbsp) vegetable oil |
| salt |
| 450 g (1 lb) haddock fillets, skinned and cut into bite-sized pieces |
| 450 ml (¾ pint) coconut milk |
| juice of 1 lime |
| shredded coconut, to garnish |

1. Put the first seven ingredients in a blender or food processor with 2.5 ml (½ level tsp) salt. Work to a thick paste.
2. Transfer the paste to a flameproof casserole and fry gently, stirring, for 5 minutes. Add the haddock pieces and fry for a few minutes more, shaking the pan constantly.

3. Pour in the coconut milk, shake the pan and turn the fish gently in the liquid. (Take care not to break up the pieces of fish.) Bring to the boil slowly, then lower the heat, cover and simmer for 10–15 minutes, until the fish is tender.
4. Add the lime juice, taste and adjust seasoning, then transfer to a warmed serving dish and sprinkle with coconut. Serve immediately.
Serves 4

Indonesian Fish Curry with rice and lime pickle

*Fish Croquettes*

# FISH CROQUETTES

*350 g (12 oz) haddock or cod fillets*

*300 ml (½ pint) milk*

*1 small onion, sliced*

*1 small carrot, peeled*

*1 bay leaf*

*salt and pepper*

*50 g (2 oz) butter or margarine*

*50 g (2 oz) flour*

*30 ml (2 tbsp) chopped fresh parsley*

*30 ml (2 level tbsp) capers, roughly chopped*

*5 ml (1 tsp) lemon juice*

*cayenne pepper*

*1 egg, beaten*

*50 g (2 oz) fresh breadcrumbs*

*vegetable oil for frying*

*Tartare Sauce (see page 126), to serve*

**1.** Place the fish in a frying pan, pour over the milk and add the onion, carrot and bay leaf with a pinch of salt. Bring to the boil slowly, then cover and simmer gently for about 8–10 minutes, until the fish flakes when tested with a fork.

**2.** Using a fish slice, lift the fish out of the milk and place on a plate. Flake the fish, discarding the skin and bones. Strain and reserve the milk.

**3.** Melt the butter in a saucepan, stir in the flour and cook gently for 1 minute, stirring. Remove the pan from the heat and gradually stir in the reserved milk. Bring to the boil slowly and continue to cook, stirring, until the sauce thickens. (It will be very thick.)

**4.** Remove from the heat and stir in the fish, beating until smooth. Stir in the parsley, capers and lemon juice, mixing well. Season to taste and add a sprinkling of cayenne pepper.

**5.** Turn the fish mixture into a shallow square dish—not metallic. Form the mixture into a 15 cm (6 inch) square and leave until cold. Cover tightly with cling film and refrigerate for several hours.

**6.** Divide the mixture into twelve portions, then with lightly floured hands, roll each portion into a sausage shape, about 7.5 cm (3 inches) long.

**7.** Brush a few croquettes at a time with beaten egg and coat with crumbs. Chill for 30 minutes.

**8.** Heat the oil in a deep-fat fryer to 180°C (350°F). Place a few croquettes at a time into a frying basket and lower gently into the oil. Fry for 2–3 minutes or until golden brown, then drain on absorbent kitchen paper and keep warm while frying the remaining croquettes. Serve with Tartare Sauce.

*Makes 12*

## LEMON AND MUSTARD MACKEREL

*40 g (1½ oz) butter or margarine*

*1 small onion, skinned and finely chopped*

*75 g (3 oz) fresh breadcrumbs*

*30 ml (2 level tbsp) mustard seeds*

*grated rind and juice of 1 lemon*

*15 ml (1 level tbsp) French mustard*

*1 egg yolk*

*salt and pepper*

*2 mackerel, each weighing 350 g (12 oz), cleaned, boned and heads removed*

*15 ml (1 level tbsp) flour*

*lemon rind shreds and fresh coriander, to garnish*

**1.** Heat 15 g (½ oz) butter in a frying pan, add the onion and fry until softened. Remove from the heat and stir in the breadcrumbs, mustard seeds, grated rind of 1 lemon rind, the mustard and egg yolk. Season with salt and pepper.

**2.** Press the breadcrumb mixture well into the cavity of the fish. Place in a greased shallow ovenproof dish just large enough to hold the mackerel and make deep slashes along each fish.

**3.** Dust the mackerel lightly with the flour. Pour over the lemon juice and dot with the remaining butter. Cook, uncovered, in the oven at 190°C (375°F) mark 5 for about 30 minutes. Baste frequently during cooking.

**4.** Garnish with lemon rind shreds and coriander before serving.

*Serves 2*

## SOLE VÉRONIQUE

*700 g (1½ lb) Dover or lemon sole fillets, skinned*

*2 shallots, skinned and chopped*

*fresh parsley sprigs*

*1 bay leaf*

*salt and pepper*

*150 ml (¼ pint) dry white wine*

*25 g (1 oz) butter or margarine*

*30 ml (2 level tbsp) flour*

*about 150 ml (¼ pint) milk*

*100 g (4 oz) seedless white grapes, skinned*

*squeeze of lemon juice*

*30 ml (2 tbsp) single cream (optional)*

**1.** Arrange the fish in a shallow ovenproof dish with the shallots, herbs, salt and pepper, wine and 150 ml (¼ pint) water. Cover with foil and bake in the oven at 200°C (400°F) mark 6 for about 15 minutes, until tender.

**2.** Strain the liquid from the fish and reduce it slightly by boiling rapidly, transfer the fish to a serving dish and keep warm.

**3.** Melt the butter in a saucepan, stir in the flour and cook for 1 minute, stirring. Remove the pan from the heat and gradually stir in the reduced fish liquid, made up to 300 ml (½ pint) with the milk. Bring to the boil slowly and continue to cook, stirring, until the sauce thickens.

**4.** Remove from the heat and stir in most of the grapes, the lemon juice and the cream.

**5.** Pour over the fish and serve decorated with the remaining grapes.

*Note* Fillets of plaice and John Dory or large dabs may also be cooked in the same way.

*Serves 4*

**Variation**

*SOLE BONNE FEMME*

Omit the white grapes and lemon juice. Add the finely chopped stalks of 100 g (4 oz) button mushrooms to the shallots, herbs, salt and pepper, wine and water. Fry the mushroom caps lightly in 20 g (¾ oz) butter and serve as a garnish.

## SOLE MEUNIÈRE

*4 small Dover or lemon soles, skinned and fins removed*

*30 ml (2 level tbsp) seasoned flour*

*75 g (3 oz) Clarified Butter (see page 571)*

*15 ml (1 tbsp) chopped fresh parsley*

*juice of 1 lemon*

*lemon slices or wedges, to garnish*

**1.** Coat the fish with seasoned flour. Fry in 50 g (2 oz) butter for 5 minutes each side. Drain and keep warm.

**2.** Wipe the pan clean with absorbent kitchen paper. Melt the remaining butter in the pan and heat until lightly browned. Add the parsley and lemon juice and pour over fish. Garnish.

*Serves 4*

# SOLE COLBERT

*4 small Dover or lemon soles, skinned*

*30 ml (2 level tbsp) seasoned flour*

*2 eggs, beaten*

*50–75 g (2–3 oz) fresh breadcrumbs*

*vegetable oil for deep-frying*

*Maître d'Hôtel Butter (see page 209)*

**1.** Remove the black skin by holding firmly at the tail and pull it off up to the head. Rinse and wipe the soles. With a sharp knife make a cut down the centre of the backbone on one side of the fish. Raise the fillets on this side only away from the bone to form a pocket.

**2.** With the points of scissors, cut the backbone through just below the head and above the tail, so that it may be more easily removed after the fish is cooked.

**3.** Dip the soles in seasoned flour and coat with beaten egg and breadcrumbs, pressing the crumbs on well.

**4.** Heat the oil in a deep-fat fryer to 180°C (350°F), add the fish and fry for about 6–7 minutes, until golden brown. Drain on absorbent kitchen paper.

**5.** Using scissors or a knife, cut the backbone and ease it from the cooked fish. Fill the centre cavity of each fish with Maître d'Hôtel Butter and serve. *Serves 4*

*1. Carefully cut down the backbone, then raise the fillets. 2. Use scissors to cut away the backbone so it can be removed after cooking. 3. After frying, fill the cavity of each fish with Maître d'Hôtel Butter.*

# CHUNKY FISH CASSEROLE (CASSOLA)

*125 g (4 oz) small dried pasta shells*

*50 g (2 oz) butter or margarine*

*1 medium green pepper, seeded and cut into squares*

*1 medium yellow pepper, seeded and cut into squares*

*2 medium onions, skinned and sliced*

*225 g (8 oz) button mushrooms, wiped and sliced*

*450 g (1 lb) sole fillets, skinned and cut into finger-sized strips*

*6 scallops, prepared (see page 83) and cut into chunks*

*60 ml (4 level tbsp) seasoned flour*

*1 garlic clove, skinned and crushed*

*300 ml (½ pint) dry vermouth*

*150 ml (¼ pint) Fish or Chicken Stock (see page 19)*

*15 ml (1 tbsp) chopped fresh sage, or 5 ml (1 level tsp) dried*

*salt and pepper*

*200 g (7 oz) can whole artichoke hearts, drained and quartered*

*225 g (8 oz) peeled prawns*

*chopped fresh parsley, to garnish*

**1.** Cook the pasta shells in boiling salted water for three quarters of the time recommended on the packet. Drain in a colander and run cold water over the pasta.

**2.** Melt 25 g (1 oz) butter in a large frying pan, add the peppers, onions and mushrooms and fry over a high heat for a few minutes. Remove from the pan with a slotted spoon and place in a deep 2.8 litre (5 pint) ovenproof dish.

**3.** Toss the prepared fish in the seasoned flour. Melt the remaining butter in the pan, add the sole and scallops with the garlic and fry gently for a few minutes, turning gently to avoid breaking up the fish.

**4.** Stir in the vermouth, stock, sage and seasoning and bring to the boil. Pour over the vegetables. Add the artichoke hearts, prawns and pasta shells and stir gently to mix the ingredients.

**5.** Cover the dish and bake in the oven at 180°C (350°F) mark 4 for about 40 minutes. Serve garnished with chopped parsley. *Serves 6*

*Stuffed Sole Paupiettes*

## STUFFED SOLE PAUPIETTES

| |
|---|
| 75 g (3 oz) butter or margarine |
| 1 small onion, skinned and chopped |
| 225 g (8 oz) button mushrooms, wiped and trimmed |
| 75 g (3 oz) fresh breadcrumbs |
| finely grated rind of 1 lemon |
| 15 ml (1 tbsp) chopped fresh tarragon leaves |
| salt and pepper |
| 18 lemon sole quarter-cut fillets (two from each side of fish), skinned |
| 300 ml (½ pint) dry white wine |
| 30 ml (2 level tbsp) flour |
| about 90 ml (6 tbsp) double cream, at room temperature |
| fresh tarragon sprigs, to garnish |

1. Make the stuffing. Melt 25 g (1 oz) of the butter in a saucepan, add the onion and fry gently until lightly coloured.
2. Meanwhile, slice half the mushrooms and chop the remainder very finely. Put the chopped mushrooms in a bowl with the breadcrumbs, lemon rind and tarragon.
3. Add the softened onion, season to taste and stir well.
4. Place a sole fillet, skinned side uppermost, on a board. Put a teaspoonful of stuffing on one end of the fillet. Roll the fish up around it. Secure with a

wooden cocktail stick.
5. Stand in an upright position in a well-buttered baking dish. Repeat with remaining sole fillets, placing them side by side in the dish.
6. Mix together the wine and 150 ml (¼ pint) water and pour over the fish. Cover loosely with foil and bake in the oven at 190°C (375°F) mark 5 for 15 minutes.
7. Remove the fish from the cooking liquid with a slotted spoon and discard the cocktail sticks. Place the fish in a single layer in a warmed serving dish, cover and keep warm. Strain the liquid and reserve.
8. Melt 25 g (1 oz) butter in a saucepan, sprinkle in the flour and cook for 1–2 minutes, stirring. Remove from the heat, then gradually stir in the reserved cooking liquid. Bring to the boil, reduce the heat and simmer gently for 5 minutes, stirring until thick.
9. Meanwhile, melt the remaining butter in a frying pan, add the finely sliced mushrooms and fry gently.
10. Whisk the cream into the sauce. Pour a little sauce over each paupiette; then garnish with sliced mushrooms and tarragon sprigs. Pour any remaining sauce into a warmed sauceboat and hand separately.
*Serves 6*

# FRITTO MISTO DI MARE

| |
|---|
| 450 g (1 lb) squid, cleaned |
| 225 g (8 oz) whitebait |
| 4 small red mullet, cleaned and heads and tails removed, sliced |
| 225 g (8 oz) firm, white fish fillets, e.g. cod, haddock or sole, skinned, and cut into long thin strips |
| 8–12 large prawns, peeled |
| 60 ml (4 tbsp) seasoned flour |
| vegetable oil for deep-frying |
| fresh parsley sprigs and lemon wedges, to garnish |

1. Slice the body of the squid into rings 0.5 cm ($\frac{1}{4}$ inch) thick and the tentacles into 1 cm ($\frac{1}{2}$ inch) pieces. Toss all the fish in seasoned flour to coat.
2. Heat the oil in a deep-fat fryer to 190°C (375°F). Add the fish pieces a few at a time and fry until crisp and golden brown. Drain on absorbent kitchen paper and keep each batch warm while frying the rest.
3. Divide the fish between six warmed plates and garnish with lemon wedges and sprigs of parsley.
*Serves 6*

**Variation**
Dip the fish in Fritter Batter (see page 328) before frying.

# FISH KOULIBIAC

| |
|---|
| 350 g (12 oz) whiting fillets |
| 150 ml ($\frac{1}{4}$ pint) dry white wine |
| salt and pepper |
| 75 g (3 oz) butter or margarine |
| 125 g (4 oz) spring onions, trimmed and chopped |
| 75 g (3 oz) long grain white rice |
| 1.25 ml ($\frac{1}{4}$ level tsp) dried dill weed |
| 125 g (4 oz) small button mushrooms, wiped and quartered |
| 213 g ($7\frac{1}{2}$ oz) can red salmon, drained |
| 3 eggs, hard-boiled and chopped |
| 30 ml (2 tbsp) lemon juice |
| 225 g (8 oz) Puff Pastry (see page 367) or 368 g (13 oz) packet frozen puff pastry, thawed |
| 1 egg, lightly beaten |
| lime wedges and parsley sprigs, to garnish |

1. Place the whiting in a shallow saucepan. Pour over the wine with 150 ml ($\frac{1}{4}$ pint) water, season and bring to the boil. Cover and poach gently for 5–8 minutes or until tender, then strain and reserve the juices. Flake the fish and place in a large bowl, discarding skin and any bones.
2. Melt the butter in a saucepan, add the onions and fry until lightly browned. Stir in the rice with the reserved fish juices, dill weed and seasoning.

Bring to the boil, then cover and simmer for 10 minutes. Stir in the mushrooms and cook until the rice is tender and the liquid absorbed.
3. Flake the salmon, discarding any skin and bone. Combine the salmon, eggs, whiting and rice mixture. Stir in the lemon juice and adjust the seasoning; allow to cool.
4. Roll one third of the pastry to an oblong about 35.5 cm × 15 cm (14 inch × 6 inch) and place on a large baking sheet. Spoon the filling down the centre of the pastry, leaving a 2.5 cm (1 inch) strip round the edge. Dome the filling up well—the finished koulibiac should look high and narrow.
5. Brush the rim of pastry with beaten egg. Roll out the remaining dough to a rectangle 43 cm × 23 cm (17 inch × 9 inch) and wind loosely round a floured rolling pin. Unroll over filling and press edges well together. Neaten them with a sharp knife, leaving a 2.5 cm (1 inch) pastry rim all round.
6. Roll cut edges inwards, and press firmly. Mark new edge at regular intervals with the back of a knife. Chill for at least 30 minutes.
7. Add a pinch of salt to the beaten egg and use to glaze the pastry. Bake in the oven at 220°C (425°F) mark 7 for 35 minutes or until well browned. Serve hot, garnished with parsley sprigs and lime wedges.
*Serves 6–8*

# QUENELLES

*450 g (1 lb) whiting, pike or brill fillets, skinned and*
   *bones removed*

*1 egg white*

*1 quantity of Choux Pastry (see page 379), chilled*

*salt and pepper*

*150 ml (5 fl oz) double cream*

*18 fresh cooked prawns (in the shell)*

*100 g (4 oz) butter*

*150 ml (¼ pint) dry white wine*

*30 ml (2 level tbsp) flour*

**1.** Mince the fish twice, using the finest blade
of the mincer, or purée in a blender or food
processor. Cover and chill in the refrigerator for
1 hour.
**2.** Place the fish mixture in a large bowl placed in
a saucepan of iced water. Break up the egg white
with a fork. Beat into the fish, a little at a time,
using a wooden spoon or electric hand mixer and
keep the mixture stiff. Steady the bowl with one
hand to prevent any iced water splashing into it.
**3.** Gradually add the choux paste, beating well
between each addition. Add 2.5 ml (½ level tsp)
salt and plenty of pepper, then beat into the fish
with 60 ml (4 tbsp) cream, a little at a time. The
mixture should be the consistency of creamed
cake mixture. Cover and refrigerate for at least
1 hour.
**4.** Meanwhile, twist the heads off the prawns and
discard them. Carefully ease the body shell and
any roe away from the prawn flesh. Reserve the
prawns for garnish. Pound the shells and roes with
50 g (2 oz) butter until well mixed, using a pestle
and mortar or the end of a rolling pin in a strong

bowl. Sieve the prawn butter to remove the shells.
Cover and refrigerate with the prawns.
**5.** Pour 900 ml (1½ pint) water into a large frying
pan and add the wine
with 1.25 ml (¼ level tsp)
salt. Bring to the
boil. Using two wet
dessertspoons, shape
the quenelle mixture
into ovals and push
them gently out of
the spoons into the
simmering liquid. Add
sufficient quenelle
shapes to half fill the
pan; they will swell on
cooking.

*Spoon the quenelle mixture into simmering water.*

**6.** Cover the pan and simmer very gently for
10–12 minutes. Do not boil or the quenelles will
break up. When the quenelles are well puffed up
and firm to the touch, lift them out of the pan
using slotted spoons. Drain on absorbent kitchen
paper, then transfer to a warm serving dish, cover
and keep warm while poaching the remaining
quenelles.
**7.** Boil the cooking liquid until reduced to 250 ml
(8 fl oz). Melt the remaining butter in a saucepan,
stir in the flour and cook gently for 1 minute,
stirring. Remove the pan from the heat and
gradually stir in the reduced stock.
**8.** Bring to the boil slowly and continue to
cook, stirring, until the sauce thickens. Cook for
1–2 minutes. Remove from the heat, stir in the
remaining cream, then whisk in the prawn butter.
Reheat gently without boiling. Adjust seasoning.
Spoon over the quenelles. Garnish with prawns.
*Serves 6 as a starter, 4 for a mean meal*

# FRIED WHITEBAIT

*450 g (1 lb) whitebait*

*90 ml (6 level tbsp) seasoned flour*

*vegetable oil for deep-frying*

*fresh parsley sprigs, to garnish*

*lemon wedges and brown bread and butter, to serve*

**1.** Toss the whitebait in the seasoned flour until
well coated.

**2.** Heat the oil in a deep-fat fryer to 180°C (350°F).
Add the whitebait, about one quarter at a time,
and fry for 2–3 minutes, until crisp. Drain on
absorbent kitchen paper. Keep warm, uncovered,
in the oven set at 200°C (400°F) mark 6 until all
the fish are cooked.
**3.** Garnish with lemon and parsley and serve with
brown bread and butter.
*Serves 4*

# FRESHWATER FISH Salmon and trout are the main freshwater fish sold at fishmongers—though you may also find pike and eel occasionally.

### CARP

There are several varieties of carp found in ponds, lakes and rivers in most parts of the world. Carp feeds on vegetation in the mud and its flesh tends to have a slightly muddy flavour: soak in salted water for 3–4 hours and rinse well before cooking. Some carp are very scaley and need careful scaling (see page 53). Carp can be stuffed and baked, poached or braised over vegetables.

### CHAR

Char belongs to the salmon family. It has firm white to pink flesh, similar in flavour to salmon and trout. It can be cooked like Trout (see right).

### FRESHWATER EEL (COMMON EEL)

A long, snake-like fish with shiny, dark green to black skin and dense, fatty flesh which is enhanced by strong flavoured sauces. As eels must be fresh, they are sold alive and should be cooked soon after killing. Eels can be jellied, fried, stewed or made into pies. Young eels, called *elvers*, are best eaten stewed in garlic, sautéed or deep-fried. Eels are also sold jellied, whole or as fillets.

### GRAYLING

A silvery fish belonging to the salmon family. It has a thyme-like scent and firm white flesh, similar to trout. It can be cooked like Trout (see right).

### PERCH

A large round fish with firm, sweet white flesh, perch should be cleaned and scaled as soon as possible after being caught (see page 53). Treat the dorsal fins with respect as they can wound. Fry or poach. If poaching, cook first, then scale.

### PIKE

Pike is a sharp-nosed, duck-billed fish with large jaws and sharp teeth. It is found in lakes and streams, where it feeds on other fish—hence its other names of *waterwolf* and *fresh water shark*. The flesh is quite dry, but has an excellent flavour. Smaller fish up to 900 g (2 lb) are best. Used for quenelles and stuffings and it can also be poached or stuffed and baked.

If the fish has a muddy film on it, it can be soaked in cold water for a few hours before cooking.

### SALMON

Salmon is a round fish with bright, silvery scales and flesh which is deep pink when raw and pale pink when cooked. The flesh is firm and rich. It is sold whole or as steaks or cutlets. It is also available smoked (see page 79). When buying a whole fish, look for a small head and broad shoulders, as the head can represent up to one fifth of the weight.

Home-caught salmon has such a delicious flavour and excellent texture that the simplest cooking is the best. While fish can be baked or poached and steaks and cutlets can be baked, poached or grilled. Canadian, Norwegian, Alaskan and Japanese salmon tend to be less tender and delicate, but can be made more interesting with sauces.

Salmon is in season in England and Scotland from February to August and in Ireland from January to September, but it is imported and sold frozen all year round. Farmed Scottish salmon, reared in large numbers in the remote lochs of the Western Highlands and Islands, is always available.

### TROUT

There are several different varieties of trout.

**Sea trout (Salmon trout)**

Sea trout is a trout which has spent a season or more in the sea, living on a diet of crustaceans so that its flesh takes on a pink colour and flavour similar to that of salmon. However, because its flesh is coarser and less succulent than salmon, it is slightly cheaper. Sea trout can be prepared and cooked like Salmon (see page 76).

**Rainbow trout**

This trout spends all its life in fresh water. It is readily available all year around, as it is reared on trout farms. The delicate-flavoured flesh may be white or pink. Farmed fish which are fed on shrimps have pinkish-red flesh and may be called *red trout*. Rainbow trout is sold, and usually cooked, whole. This can be either grilled, poached or baked in foil.

**River or brown trout**

River trout is a golden brown fish with whitish flesh. It spends all its life in rivers or streams and is considered to have a better flavour than rainbow trout. It is rarely available in the shops. It can be cooked like rainbow trout. Best March to September.

## FOIL-BAKED SALMON

*1 salmon*

*melted butter*

*salt and pepper*

**1.** To prepare the salmon, slit the fish along the underside between the head and rear gill opening. Cut out the entrails and discard. Rinse the fish to remove all the blood.
**2.** Snip off the fins and trim the tail into a neat 'V' shape. Leave on the head if wished. Pat dry with absorbent kitchen paper and weigh the fish before cooking.
**3.** Brush a large piece of foil with butter. Place the fish in the centre and season lightly. Wrap loosely in the foil and place on a baking sheet.
**4.** Bake in the oven at 140–150°C (275–300°F) mark 1–2 for the following time:
● Whole fish—over 2.3 kg (5 lb): 8 minutes per 450 g (1 lb)

● Whole fish or middle cuts—between 900 g– 2.3 kg (2–5 lb): 10 minutes per 450 g (1 lb)
● Whole fish—under 900 g (2 lb): 10–15 minutes per 450 g (1 lb).
**5.** Leave the salmon for 10 minutes in the foil if serving hot. Remove the skin while still warm and, if wished, lift the flesh from the bones (see below). If the salmon is to be eaten cold, remove the skin, then allow it to cool.

*SKINNING AND BONING A COOKED SALMON*
Whilst still hot, lay the fish on a firm surface and snip the skin below the head and above the tail. Gently peel off the skin. Turn the fish over and remove the skin from the other side. Ease out all the fine bones and leave the head and tail intact.

With a sharp pointed knife, slit the fish along the backbone, without disturbing the flesh, and ease out the backbone through the slit.

## POACHED SALMON

**1.** Prepare the salmon as above. Fill a fish kettle or large saucepan with water, water and wine mixed or Court Bouillon (see page 56). Bring to the boil, then lower the fish into the kettle or pan. A piece of muslin wrapped around the salmon will enable it to be lifted out.
**2.** Bring the liquid back to the boil, then simmer for 7–8 minutes per 450 g (1 lb) if eating hot.
**3.** If eating cold, bring the liquid back to the boil, then cook for 5 minutes for fish under 3.2 kg (7 lb), 10–15 minutes for fish over 3.2 kg (7 lb), allow to cool completely in the liquid, then skin and bone (see above).

**Variation**
Salmon can also be poached in the oven.
**1.** Place the fish in a deep roasting tin—it must fit snugly. Pour over enough water, water and wine or Court Bouillon (see page 56) to three-quarters cover it. Cover tightly with buttered foil.
**2.** Cook in the oven at 150°C (300°F) mark 2, allowing 10 minutes per 450 g (1 lb). If serving the fish hot, allow an extra 10 minutes at the end of the cooking time.

## POACHED SALMON STEAKS

**1.** Place the fish in a deep frying pan (preferably not a saucepan, as a shallow utensil makes removal of the fish much easier), with Court Bouillon (see page 56) to cover. Cover the pan and simmer gently for 5–10 minutes.

**2.** To test the fish is cooked, insert a skewer into the thickest part of the flesh. If cooked, the flesh will offer no resistance to the skewer, Serve the steaks hot or cold.

## GRILLED SALMON STEAKS

**1.** Season the prepared fish and brush well with melted butter. Grill in a greased pan under a medium heat.
**2.** When the top side is cooked and tinged light brown, turn over, brush with more butter

and continue to cook for about 10–20 minutes altogether.
**3.** Serve hot with poached diced cucumber, new potatoes and asparagus or peas.

*Salmon in fish kettle before preparation*

## SALMON STEAKS AND CUTLETS

Steaks should be cut about 2 cm (¾ inch) thick and are cut from below the belly. Cutlets are taken from the head end. If they are very large, serve one between two people, rather than cut the steaks thinly. Wipe the fish, and remove any blood from the backbone area. Close the flaps and, to keep the pieces a good shape, secure with a cocktail stick.

When individual portions of cold salmon are required for coating with mayonnaise, and especially for small numbers, it is sometimes easier to cook cutlets, which are smaller. After cooking, carefully ease away the bones, remove the skins and portion the fish as required.

## BAKED SALMON STEAKS

**1.** Line a baking sheet with a large piece of foil, and butter the surface. Place the prepared salmon on the foil. Dot each steak with butter and season with salt, pepper and lemon juice.

**2.** Wrap loosely and bake in the oven at 170°C (325°F) mark 3 for 20–40 minutes, according to the thickness of the fish.

**3.** Serve with Maître d'Hôtel Butter (see page 209) or Hollandaise Sauce (see page 205) or garnish with poached diced cucumber, sliced lemon and parsley sprigs. If serving cold, leave the salmon to cool wrapped in the foil. Remove the skin if wished.

## Salmon in Aspic

*1 small salmon or sea trout about 1.8 kg (4 lb), cleaned
    with head and tail left on*

*450 ml (¾ pint) aspic jelly*

*radishes, cucumber, tomato skins, olives, parsley sprigs
    and prawns, to garnish*

**1.** Poach or bake the salmon (see page 76).
Remove the skin, leaving on the head and tail.
**2.** Place the fish on a wire rack with a large plate
or tray underneath, then leave to cool. Make up
the aspic according to the packet instructions and
when it is just beginning to thicken, coat the fish
thinly.
**3.** Meanwhile, prepare the garnish. Cut the
radishes into thin rings, cut strips of cucumber
skin or thin cucumber slices, diamonds or strips
of tomato skin and rings of olive.
**4.** Decorate the fish with the prepared garnishes
and the parsley sprigs and prawns. Cover with
further layers of aspic until the decoration is held
in place. When the aspic has set, transfer the fish
to a large serving dish.
**5.** Leave any remaining aspic to set, chop it on
damp greaseproof paper and use as a garnish.

*Chop the remaining aspic
and use it as a garnish.*

Note For a really
professional finish and
easy carving, remove
the salmon bones
before the fish is
glazed. Loosen the flesh
along the ridge of
the backbone and use
scissors to cut the bone
through just below the
head and above the tail.
Gently pull and ease
out the bone.
*Serves 4*

## Baked Trout with Lemon

*6 rainbow trout, about 200 g (7 oz) each, cleaned*

*75 g (3 oz) butter*

*90 ml (6 tbsp) lemon juice*

*90 ml (6 tbsp) chopped fresh parsley*

*salt and pepper*

*watercress sprigs, to garnish*

**1.** Make three or four diagonal slashes about
0.5 cm (¼ inch) deep on either side of each fish.
Place the fish, side by side, in a shallow, ovenproof
dish.
**2.** Melt the butter in a small saucepan. Leave to
cool, then mix in the lemon juice, parsley and
seasoning and pour over the fish.
**3.** Cover with cling film and leave in a cool
place—not the refrigerator—for 2 hours, turning
and basting once.
**4.** Remove the cling film. Cover the dish with foil
and bake in the oven at 180°C (350°F) mark 4 for
about 40 minutes.
**5.** Remove the foil for serving and garnish with
watercress sprigs.
*Serves 6*

## Trout and Almonds

*4 rainbow or river trout, about 200 g (7 oz) each,
    cleaned with heads left on*

*30 ml (2 tbsp) seasoned flour*

*65 g (2½ oz) butter*

*50 g (2 oz) flaked almonds*

*juice of ½ a lemon*

**1.** Coat the fish with seasoned flour. Melt 50 g
(2 oz) butter in a large frying pan, add the fish two
at a time, and fry for 12–15 minutes, turning them
once, until they are tender and golden on both
sides.
**2.** Drain on absorbent kitchen paper, transfer to a
serving dish and keep warm. Clean out the pan
with absorbent kitchen paper.
**3.** Melt the remaining butter in the pan, add the
almonds and fry until lightly browned, add a
squeeze of lemon juice and pour over the fish.
Serve at once, with the remaining lemon juice.
*Serves 4*

# SMOKED FISH

There are two methods of smoking—hot and cold. Cold smoking is done at relatively low temperatures and most cold-smoked fish need to be cooked before eating. The exception is salmon, which is smoked for a long period and can be eaten raw. Hot smoking is done at higher temperatures and the fish is ready to eat. Smoking is done more for flavour than as a means of preserving these days and smoked fish should only be kept in the refrigerator for 3–5 days.

## SMOKED COD

**Smoked fillets**

These are taken from large fish, skinned and cold-smoked. They are dyed, often to a bright orange yellow. To cook, poach the fillets in milk, water or Court Bouillon (see page 56) for 10–15 minutes.

**Smoked cod's roe**

This is firm roe taken from a large cod and smoked for a long period with slight heat. It does not need cooking. Used to make Taramasalata (see page 46).

## SMOKED EEL

Smoked eel is not widely available, but may be found either whole or as chunks of fillet in some delicatessens and fishmongers. It is ready to eat. Serve as a starter with cayenne pepper, lemon wedges and brown bread and butter.

## SMOKED HADDOCK

**Smoked fillets**

These are taken from large fish and cold-smoked with the skin on. They are dyed, often to bright orange yellow. Cook as for Smoked Cod.

**Finnan haddock**

These are named after the village of Findon near Aberdeen in Scotland. Before smoking, the fish are split and lightly brined, but not usually dyed. They are a light straw colour and darken during cooking. Cook as for Smoked Cod.

**Golden cutlets**

These are small haddock with the heads removed, which are split and boned before smoking. Cook as for Smoked Cod.

**Smokies**

These are also whole haddock, or whiting, with the heads removed. They are hot-smoked and only need reheating in the oven or under the grill. Originally, smokies came from Arbroath in Scotland and were very dark in colour. Nowadays, they are smoked mechanically and are much lighter.

## SMOKED HALIBUT

This is not widely available, but may be found as slices of fillet. It does not need cooking.

## SMOKED HERRING

**Bloater**

This is a lightly smoked, dry salted herring with bones, head and tail removed. Bloaters should be eaten within 24 hours of buying. Lightly grill or fry.

**Buckling**

This is a whole smoked herring ready to eat.

**Kipper**

The fish are split, lightly brined, then cold-smoked. To cook, grill or poach for about 5 minutes, or place in a jug of boiling water and leave in a warm place for 5–10 minutes, or wrap in foil and bake in the oven at 190°C (375°F) mark 5 for 10–15 minutes.

**Red herring**

These are heavily smoked and highly salted. They are rarely available. Lightly grill or fry.

## SMOKED MACKEREL

Mackerel may be whole or filleted and some are coated with peppercorns, and hot or cold-smoked. Cold-smoked mackerel may also be known as *kippered mackerel*. They can be poached or grilled.

## SMOKED SALMON

Smoked salmon is cold smoked for a long period and is ready to eat. Scottish smoked salmon, which is quite pale in colour, is the best quality. Canadian and Pacific smoked salmon are a deeper colour.

## SMOKED SPRATS

These are smoked whole and are grilled or fried.

## SMOKED STURGEON

This is not widely available, but is sometimes sold sliced very thinly. It does not need cooking.

## SMOKED TROUT

Smoked trout is usually rainbow trout, cleaned with the head left on. They are hot smoked and do not need cooking.

## SMOKED TUNA

This is not widely available, but may be found in slices of fillet. It does not need cooking.

## Smoked Haddock Kedgeree

175 g (6 oz) long-grain rice

salt

450 g (1 lb) smoked haddock fillets

2 hard-boiled eggs, shelled

75 g (3 oz) butter or margarine

cayenne pepper

chopped fresh parsley, to garnish

1. Cook the rice in a saucepan of fast-boiling salted water until tender. Drain well and rinse under cold water.

2. Meanwhile, put the haddock in a large frying pan with just enough water to cover. Bring to simmering point, then simmer for 10–15 minutes, until tender. Drain, skin and flake the fish, discarding the bones.

3. Chop one egg and slice the other into rings. Melt the butter in a saucepan, add the cooked rice, fish, chopped egg, salt and cayenne pepper and stir over a moderate heat for about 5 minutes, until hot. Pile on to a warmed serving dish and garnish with parsley and the sliced egg.
*Serves 4*

## Smoked Haddock Gougère

**For the choux pastry**

75 g (3 oz) butter or margarine

200 ml (7 fl oz) water

100 g (4 oz) plain or strong plain flour

3 eggs, lightly beaten

**For the filling**

450 g (1 lb) smoked haddock fillets

25 g (1 oz) butter or margarine

1 medium onion, skinned and chopped

25 g (1 oz) flour

300 ml (½ pint) milk

10 ml (2 level tsp) capers

2 eggs, hard-boiled, shelled and chopped

2 tomatoes, skinned, seeded and cut into thin strips

salt and pepper

about 30 ml (2 tbsp) lemon juice

15 ml (1 level tbsp) fresh breadcrumbs

15 ml (1 level tbsp) grated hard cheese

chopped fresh parsley, to garnish

1. Make the choux pastry. Sift the flour on to a plate or piece of paper. Put the fat and water together in a saucepan, heat gently until the fat has melted, then bring to the boil. Remove from the heat. Tip all the flour at once into the hot liquid. Beat thoroughly with a wooden spoon, then return the pan to the heat.

2. Continue beating the mixture until it is smooth and forms a ball in the centre of the pan (take care not to over-beat or the mixture will become fatty). Remove from the heat and leave the mixture to cool for a minute or two.

3. Beat in the egg, a little at a time, adding just enough to give a piping consistency.

4. Using a 1 cm (½ inch) plain nozzle, pipe the mixture in two circles (one on top of the other) round the bottom of each of four 12.5 cm (5 inch) diameter ovenproof dishes. Bake in the oven at 220°C (425°F) mark 7 for about 25 minutes.

5. Meanwhile, put the haddock in a large frying pan with just enough water to cover. Bring to simmering point, then simmer for 10–15 minutes, until tender. Drain, skin and flake the fish, discarding the bones.

6. Melt the butter in a saucepan, add the onion and fry gently until golden brown. Stir in the flour and cook for 1 minute, stirring. Remove the pan from the heat and gradually stir in the milk. Bring to the boil slowly and continue to cook, stirring, until the sauce thickens.

7. Stir in the capers, eggs, fish and tomatoes. Season well; add the lemon juice to taste.

8. Spoon the mixture into the centre of each gougère, dividing it equally between them. Combine the crumbs and cheese, sprinkle over and cook in the oven for a further 10 minutes. Garnish with chopped parsley.
*Note* Golden cutlets could be used instead of smoked fillets.
*Serves 4*

# SHELLFISH
Shellfish can be divided into two different types—molluscs and crustaceans. Molluscs, such as cockles and winkles, have soft bodies and live inside a solid, hard shell. Some molluscs, such as clams and mussels, have a pair of shells and are known as bivalves. The exceptions are the cephalopods, such as Cuttlefish, Octopus and Squid (see pages 58, 60 and 61), which belong to the mollusc family, but have no shells. Crustaceans have hard external skeletons, which are segmented to allow for movement. All shellfish, except crayfish, are sea fish.

## CLAM

There are many different species of this bivalve, varying considerably in size. The *carpet shell* is whitish, yellow or light brown in colour, sometimes with darker brown markings. It grows up to about 7.5 cm (3 inches). The *common otter shell* is white, fawn-coloured or light yellow. It has a longer-shaped shell than other clams. It grows up to 12.5 cm (5 inches). The *quahog* (little-neck, hard-shell) *clam* is dirty white, greyish or brown. It grows up to about 12.5 cm (5 inches). The *rayed-trough shell* is cream-coloured with purplish markings. It grows up to about 12.5 cm (5 inches). The *soft-shelled clam* (long-neck, steamer) is a dirty white or fawn colour. It grows up to 15 cm (6 inches). The *venus shell* is shiny red or pink and looks as if it has been varnished. It grows up to about 7.5 cm (3 inches). *Warty venus* is dirty white or brownish-coloured. Its shell is quite plump with ridges that develop into wart-like spines. It grows up to about 7.5 cm (3 inches). The *wedge shell* (bean clam) is a small clam, generally under 4 cm (1½ inches). Its colour varies from white or yellow to brown or purple.

Clams are sold live in their shells and smaller ones can be eaten raw. Large ones can be cooked as for Mussels (see page 82). In season all year, best in the autumn. They are also available frozen, canned and smoked throughout the year from supermarkets.

*To prepare raw clams*
**1.** Scrub the clams with a stiff scrubbing brush. Hold each clam in a cloth or glove in the palm of one hand and prise open the shells at the hinge (it is helpful if you get a special clam knife for doing this).
**2.** Loosen the clams, leaving them in one half-shell.

*Use a cloth to protect your hands and prise open the clam shell.*

## CRAB

There are many different species of this crustacean. All are encased in a hard shell which is shed periodically to allow the crab to grow. The *blue crab* (Atlantic blue crab) gets its name from its blue claws. It has the finest flavour of all the crabs. It is extremely popular in America, where it is eaten in the soft-shell state when it has shed its shell and before it grows a new one. It is also found in the Mediterranean. It grows to a maximum width of about 20.5 cm (8 inches).

The *common crab* has a brownish-red shell. It grows to a width of about 20.5 cm (8 inches). The *rock crab* has a yellowish shell marked with purple or brown spots. It grows to a width of about 10 cm (4 inches). The *shore* (green crab) has a green shell, sometimes with yellow spots. It grows up to a width of about 7.5 cm (3 inches). In Venice, the *shore crab* is very popular in its soft-shell state. The *southern stone crab* has a greyish shell and enormous claws in proportion to its size; one claw is bigger than the other. It grows to a width of about 12.5 cm (5 inches). The *spider crab* (spiny crab) has a shell which varies in colour from brown to reddish-orange and is covered with prickly spines. It has a round body and long legs—hence its name. This variety of crab grows up to a width of about 20.5 cm (8 inches).

Crabs are sometimes sold alive, but more often they are ready-cooked. Some fishmongers will also dress a crab (see page 85). The crab's edible part consists of white meat in the claws and legs and brown meat in the shell. Best May to November. They are also available canned and frozen throughout the year.

## CRAWFISH

Often called the *spiny lobster*, the crawfish resembles a lobster without the big claws. Prepare and cook like Lobster (see page 82). It is also delicious cooked in casseroles and stews. Often used in creole-style cooking. Available May to October. Crawfish is also available canned and frozen.

### CRAYFISH

The crayfish is a freshwater crustacean which looks like a miniature lobster. It varies in colour from dark purple to red. Small crayfish can be used for soups and garnishes, larger ones can be served hot in a cream sauce or cold with salad and brown bread and butter.

*To prepare crayfish*

**1.** Rinse well, then remove the intestinal tube under the tail, using a pointed knife. Put the fish in a saucepan of cold salted water, bring to the boil and cook for about 10 minutes.

### LOBSTER

There are several types of this crustacean; the most common are the *European lobster*, which has the finest flavour, the *spiny lobster* (*crawfish*) and the *flat lobster*. Lobster is dark blue when alive and bright pink when cooked. It is often sold ready-boiled. Female lobsters may contain eggs in the form of an orange coral. In season all year, but best in the summer months; may be difficult to obtain from December to April. Lobster meat is often available frozen.

*To prepare lobster*

If a lobster has been bought alive, ask the fishmonger to weigh it, then kill and cook by one of the following methods.

**1.** Boil a large saucepan of water vigorously, then let it become completely cold. Immerse the lobster in the water and leave for 30 minutes. The lack of oxygen renders the lobster unconscious before it is put over the heat. Bring to the boil slowly, then simmer gently for 8 minutes per 450 g (1 lb). Lift the lobster out of the pan, set it aside and leave to cool completely.

**2.** Or bring a large saucepan of water to the boil, grasp the lobster by the back and drop it into the water, covering the pan with a lid and weight it down for the first 2 minutes. Then simmer gently for 12 minutes for the first 450 g (1 lb), 10 minutes for the next 450 g (1 lb) and 5 minutes more for each additional 450 g (1 lb). Lift out of the pan, set aside and leave to cool completely.

**3.** Or you can kill a lobster before cooking it or before grilling it, so it is not overcooked. Keeping your hands clear of the claws, put the lobster, shell side up on a work surface. Place a cleaver in the centre of the cross-shaped mark behind the head and hammer it down with one sharp blow. The lobster may still twitch a little, but that is only reflex action. Cook the lobster in the same way as for method 2 above or prepare and grill it (see page 87).

### MUSSELS

Mussels are bivalves with very dark blue shells. They are usually sold by the quart (1.1 litres) which is approximately the same as 900 g (2 lb). Never buy mussels with cracked or open shells. Available September to March.

*To prepare mussels*

**1.** Put the mussels in a large bowl and, under running cold water, scrape off any mud, barnacles, seaweed and 'beards' with a small sharp knife. Discard any that are open and do not close when sharply tapped with the back of a knife. Rinse again until there is no trace of sand in the bowl.

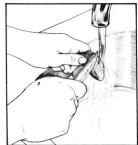

*Scrape the mussels clean under cold running water.*

**2.** Put the mussels in a frying pan and cover. Cook on a high heat for about 5 minutes, until the shells open. Discard any whose shells do not open.

**3.** Alternatively, put the mussels in a saucepan of water or wine, flavoured with onion and herbs. Cover and cook for 3–5 minutes, until the mussels open, shaking the pan frequently. Discard any whose shells do not open and do not attempt to prise open.

### OYSTERS

Oysters are bivalves which are farmed intensively in oyster beds and sea lochs. There are many species: in Britain, the smaller ones from the Essex and Kent beds are the best for eating raw, while *Portuguese oysters* or the *American Blue Points* (now cultivated in Britain) are best cooked.

The shells should be firmly closed. To keep fresh oysters, pack in a bowl, deep shell downwards and cover with a damp cloth. Place in the refrigerator and eat within 2 days. Under no circumstances should the oysters be covered with water and do not make any attempt to feed them while they are in the refrigerator.

Oysters can be served raw 'on the half-shell'; open as for Clams (see page 81). Alternatively, they can be cooked in various ways—as patties, as oysters au gratin, or added to steak and kidney puddings. Available August to April. Shelled (shucked) oysters are available frozen or canned, or dried from oriental shops. Oysters stuffed with various fillings are also available frozen, as are canned smoked oysters.

## PRAWNS

Prawns are crustaceans which are available in a variety of sizes, called by many different names. The *common prawns* from the cold waters of the North Atlantic have a better flavour than those from the warm waters of the Indian and Pacific Oceans, such as *Malaysian prawns* and *Pacific (jumbo) prawns*. The Mediterranean has several different species, known as *Mediterranean prawns*.

Fresh prawns are usually sold ready-boiled in the shell and may be sold by volume or weight. Frozen prawns come from different areas around the world and are usually peeled. Available all year. Also available canned, or dried from oriental stores.

*To peel prawns*

**1.** Hold the head of the prawn between the thumb and forefinger of the right hand. Using the fingers of the left hand, hold the tail and gently pinch and pull off the tail shell. Holding the body, gently pull off the head, the body shell and the claws.

**2.** Using a skewer or the point of a knife, carefully remove and discard the black vein running down the prawn's back.

## SCAMPI (DUBLIN BAY PRAWN)

This crustacean, which is related to the lobster, has a variety of names. It is known as *Norway lobster*, *languostine* in France, *cigale* in Spain and *scampi* in Italy. In Britain it is usually called *Dublin Bay prawn* when whole and the peeled, uncooked tail meat is known as *scampi*.

It can be cooked whole as for Lobster (see page 82) and served cold with Mayonnaise (see page 261), or the tail meat can be fried or used in hot dishes. Available all year.

## SCALLOPS

Scallops are bivalves with ribbed shells that are almost circular. There are several types which vary in size; the *great scallop* and the *queen scallop* are the varieties most commonly available in Britain. The colour of their shells varies from whitish, brown, yellow or orange to pinkish or purple.

Look for shells that are tightly closed. If slightly open, tap the shell sharply and, if fresh, they will close up instantly. Do not buy any that do not close. Scallops are in season October to March. Frozen scallops are available all year from supermarkets.

*To prepare scallops*

**1.** Scrub the scallop shells under cold running water to remove as much sand as possible. Discard any that are open and do not close when sharply tapped. Place on a baking sheet with their rounded side uppermost. Cook in the oven at 150°C (300°F) mark 2 for about 10 minutes, or until the shells open, then set aside and leave until they are cold.

**2.** Using your fingers, gently push the shells slightly apart until there is a gap into which a knife blade can be slipped. Slide the blade through the opening against the rounded upper shell, then gradually ease the scallop flesh away from the top shell.

**3.** Detach the scallop from the top shell and prise apart the top and bottom shells by pushing the shell backwards until the small black hinge at its back snaps. Rinse the scallops, still attached to the lower shells, under cold running water to remove as much sand as possible.

*Slide knife into shells.*

**4.** Using a small knife, cut and ease away all the grey-coloured beard-like fringe surrounding the scallop. Make sure that you don't detach the orange roe and try not to tear the flesh.

**5.** Slide the point of a small knife under the black thread on the side of the scallop. Ease this up and gently pull it off, with the attached black intestinal bag. Ease the scallop away from the bottom shell, wash in a bowl of cold water until all traces of sand have gone. Scrub the rounded shells thoroughly to remove all traces of sand and grit; drain carefully under cold running water and gently pat dry with absorbent kitchen paper.

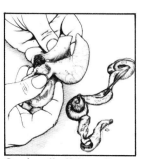
*Gently pull off the scallop's intestinal bag.*

## SHRIMPS

In Britain, only very small crustaceans are called shrimps. They are greyish-brown and translucent when alive and pink when cooked. In America, larger crustaceans—which are known as prawns in Britain—are called shrimps. Shrimps are available fresh nearly all the year. They are also available throughout the year frozen, canned and potted in butter from supermarkets.

## WHELKS

These are molluscs with greyish or brownish shells. They are usually sold ready-cooked and shelled and can be eaten plain with vinegar. Available all year, best September to February.

*To prepare raw whelks*

Wash the whelks in several changes of water, then leave to soak for 2–3 hours. Cook in a saucepan of boiling salted water for 15–20 minutes, until tender.

**Key**
1. Crab; 2. Great scallops; 3. Queen scallops; 4. Prawns; 5. Lobster; 6. Crayfish; 7. Jumbo prawns; 8. Brown shrimps; 9. Oysters; 10. Clams; 11. Mussels; 12. Raw jumbo prawns; 13. Dublin bay prawns.

## WINKLES

These small molluscs are usually sold ready-cooked, with or without shells. A long pin is needed to remove the flesh from the shells. Prepare and cook raw winkles as Whelks (see left). Eaten with vinegar and bread. Available September to April.

# COCKLES

These molluscs are usually sold cooked and shelled. They can be eaten plain with vinegar or used in dishes in place of mussels or oysters. Available most of the year, best September to April.

*To prepare cockles*

1. Rinse well under cold running water, then leave to soak for 2–3 hours before cooking.
2. Place the cockles in a saucepan with a little water and heat gently, shaking the pan, for about 5 minutes, until the shells open.
3. Take cockles out of their shells and cook for a further 4 minutes.

# DRESSING A CRAB

*1 medium uncooked crab, weighing about 900 g (2 lb)*

*salt*

*1 bay leaf*

*15 ml (1 tbsp) lemon juice*

1. Place the crab in a large saucepan in enough cold, salted water to cover. Add the bay leaf and lemon juice. Bring slowly to boiling point, cover and boil fairly rapidly for 10–20 minutes. Allow the crab to cool in the water.
2. Place the crab on its back on a large chopping board. Take a claw firmly in one hand, holding it as close to the body of the crab as possible. Twist it off, steadying the body with the other hand.
3. Remove the other claw and the legs in the same way. Snap the claws in half by bending them backwards at the joint.
4. Hold the claws at the top end and, with a hammer or heavy weight, tap the shell smartly on the rounded edge to crack the claws open. Try not to shatter the shell. Repeat with second claw.
5. Using a blunt knife, ease the white meat out of the claws. Keep the blade as close to the edges of the shell as possible.
6. Using a teaspoon handle or skewer, reach well into the crevices to make sure all the white meat is removed. Discard any membrane.
7. Crack the larger legs open and scrape out the white meat. Keep the small legs for decoration. Reserve all the scooped-out white meat in one bowl.
8. Place the crab on its back with the tail flap towards you, head away from you. Hold the shell firmly and press the body section upwards from beneath the tail flap and ease out with your thumbs until the body is detached.
9. Pull off the inedible, grey feather-like gills (known as dead men's fingers) from the body section and discard them.
10. Use a spoon to remove stomach bag and mouth which are attached to the back shell. If the bag breaks, make sure you remove all the greenish or grey-white matter.

Hold the crab securely and twist off claws.

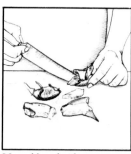

Use a blunt knife to ease meat out of claws.

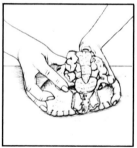

Press the shell down firmly to ease out the body.

Remove grey feather-like gills from the crab's body.

11. Ease the brown meat out of the shell, running a knife around the edge to bring it out smoothly. Put in a separate bowl.
12. Discard any membrane and scrape out corners of the shell with the handle of a teaspoon.
13. Protect your hand with a cloth. Hold the shell firmly and tap with a hammer just inside natural line of shell until inner shell breaks smoothly away.
14. Scrub the shell well under cold running water. Then dry the empty shell on absorbent kitchen paper and rub the outside lightly with oil.
15. Place the body on its back on the board. Cut through the body to divide it in two.
16. Spoon any creamy brown meat out into the bowl with the rest. Discard the body pieces. Complete dressing the crab as on page 86.

## Dressed Crab

*shell and meat from 1 medium cooked crab weighing*
*about 900 g (2 lb) (to remove the crab meat and*
*prepare the shell, see Dressing a Crab, page 85)*

*salt and pepper*

*15 ml (1 tbsp) lemon juice*

*30 ml (2 level tbsp) fresh breadcrumbs*

*1 egg, hard-boiled and shelled*

*chopped fresh parsley*

*lettuce or endive, to serve*

1. Using two forks, flake all the white crab meat, removing any shell or membrane. Season and add about 5 ml (1 tsp) lemon juice.
2. Pound the brown meat and work in the breadcrumbs with the remaining lemon juice and seasoning to taste.
3. Using a small spoon, place the white meat in both ends of the crab's empty shell, making sure that it is well piled up into the shell. Keep the inside edges neat.
4. Spoon the brown meat in a neat line down the centre, between the two sections of white crab meat.
5. Hold a blunt knife between the white and brown crab meat and carefully spoon lines of parsley, sieved egg yolk and chopped egg white across the crab, moving the knife as you go to keep a neat edge.
6. To serve, place the shell on a bed of lettuce or endive, surrounded by the small crab legs.
*Serves 2–3*

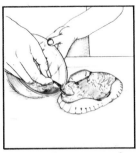

*Arrange white meat in sides of the empty shells.*

*Neatly spoon brown meat down the shell's centre.*

## Lobster Salad

*1 medium lobster, weighing 450 g (1 lb), cooked*

*1 lettuce, washed*

*fresh parsley sprigs, to garnish*

*French Dressing (see page 260) or Mayonnaise (see*
*page 261), to serve*

1. Place the cooked lobster on a firm surface and twist off the claws and pincers.
2. Crack open the large claws and remove the flesh, discarding the membrane from the claw centre. Reserve the smaller claws, which are used only for garnishing.
3. Using a sharp pointed knife split the lobster in two from head to tail.
4. Remove and discard the intestine (which looks like a small vein running through the centre of the tail), the stomach (which lies near the head), and

*Remove the lobster meat from the cracked claws.*

the spongy-looking gills, which are not edible.
5. Take out the tail flesh, reserving the coral if there is any. Scrape the meat from the rear legs with a skewer.
6. Wash and dry the two halves of the shell. Pile the meat back into the shell halves.
7. Line a serving dish with the lettuce leaves, arrange the lobster on top, garnish with the claws, parsley and chopped coral if there is any. Serve with French Dressing or Mayonnaise.
*Serves 2*

### Variation
LOBSTER MAYONNAISE
1. Remove the meat from the lobster (see above) retaining the claws and coral for garnish.
2. Flake the flesh and mix with 150 ml (¼ pint) Mayonnaise (see page 261).
3. Arrange the shredded leaves of the lettuce in a salad bowl and pile the lobster in the centre.
4. Garnish with the claws and the coral, sieved if liked.

# GRILLED LOBSTER

*For grilled lobster, kill the lobster by method 3 on page 82, but do not precook*

**1.** Split the lobster lengthways and remove the intestine, stomach and gills.
**2.** Brush the shell and flesh with melted butter and grill the flesh side for 8–10 minutes, then turn the lobster and grill the shell side for 5 minutes.
**3.** Dot the flesh with small pieces of butter, sprinkle with a little salt and cayenne pepper and serve with melted butter.
*Serves 2*

# LOBSTER NEWBURG

*2 small lobsters, weighing 225 g (8 oz) each, cooked*

*25 g (1 oz) butter or margarine*

*salt and cayenne pepper*

*60 ml (4 tbsp) Madeira or sherry*

*2 egg yolks*

*150 ml (5 fl oz) single cream*

*buttered toast or boiled rice, to serve*

*chopped fresh parsley, to garnish*

**1.** Cut the lobsters in half lengthways and remove the lobster meat from the shells (see left).
**2.** Melt the butter, add the lobster, season and heat gently for 5 minutes.

**3.** Pour over the Madeira or sherry, increase the heat and cook until liquid is reduced by half.
**4.** Beat the egg yolks with a little seasoning and add the cream. Remove the lobster from the heat, pour over the cream mixture and mix gently over a low heat until the sauce is the consistency of cream.
**5.** Adjust the seasoning, pour at once on to hot buttered toast or boiled rice and sprinkle with parsley.
*Serves 2*

**Variation**
As an alternative, make Prawns Newburg, using 225 g (8 oz) peeled prawns or shrimps.

# LOBSTER THERMIDOR

*2 small lobsters, weighing 225 g (8 oz) each, cooked*

*50 g (2 oz) butter or margarine*

*15 ml (1 tbsp) chopped shallot*

*10 ml (2 tsp) chopped fresh parsley*

*5–10 ml (1–2 tsp) chopped fresh tarragon*

*60 ml (4 tbsp) dry white wine*

*300 ml (½ pint) Béchamel Sauce (see page 202)*

*45 ml (3 level tbsp) grated Parmesan cheese*

*mustard powder, salt and paprika*

**1.** Cut the lobsters in half lengthways and remove the lobster meat from the shells. Chop the claw and head meat roughly and cut the tail meat into thick slices.
**2.** Melt half the butter, add the shallot, parsley and tarragon and fry gently for a few minutes. Add the wine and simmer for 5 minutes.
**3.** Add the Béchamel Sauce and simmer until it is reduced to a creamy consistency. Add the lobster meat to the sauce, with 30 ml (2 tbsp) of the cheese, the remaining butter, in small pieces, and mustard, salt and paprika to taste.
**4.** Arrange the mixture in the shells, sprinkle with the remaining cheese and put under the grill to brown the top quickly. Serve at once.
*Serves 2*

# OYSTERS AU NATUREL

*12 oysters*

*salt and pepper*

*brown bread and butter, lemon wedges and Tabasco sauce, to serve*

**1.** Scrub the oysters with a stiff scrubbing brush, then prise open.
**2.** Remove the beard from each and loosen the oysters, leaving them in the deeper half-shell. Season lightly and serve with brown bread, lemon wedges and Tabasco sauce.
*Serves 4*

## Malaysian-style Prawns

| |
|---|
| 30 ml (2 tbsp) vegetable oil |
| 1 medium onion, skinned and very finely chopped |
| 2 garlic cloves, skinned and crushed |
| 2.5 cm (1 inch) piece root ginger, skinned and crushed |
| 2 dried red chillis, finely chopped |
| 15 ml (1 level tbsp) ground coriander |
| 10 ml (2 level tsp) ground turmeric |
| salt |
| 700 g (1½ lb) peeled prawns |
| half a 200 g (7 oz) block creamed coconut, crumbled |
| about 300 ml (½ pint) boiling water |
| juice of 1 lime or lemon |
| 15–25 g (½–1 oz) coconut shreds or shredded coconut (optional) |
| lime or lemon slices, whole prawns (optional) and fresh coriander sprigs, to garnish |

**1.** Heat the oil in a wok or large frying pan, add the onion, garlic and ginger and fry gently for 5 minutes. Sprinkle in the chillis, spices and salt and stir-fry for 2–3 minutes more.
**2.** Add the prawns to the pan and stir-fry for 5 minutes until heated through and evenly coated in the spice mixture.
**3.** Crumble in the coconut, then gradually add the water and bring to the boil, stirring all the time (add just enough water to make a thick gravy that coats the prawns). Simmer for 5 minutes, stirring frequently. Taste and add more salt, if necessary.
**4.** Transfer to a warmed serving dish and sprinkle the juice from the lime evenly over the top. Scatter over the coconut shreds, if using, then garnish with lime or lemon slices, whole prawns, if using, and coriander. Serve immediately.
Serves 6

*Malaysian-style Prawns*

## Moules Marinières

| |
|---|
| 2.3 litres (2 quarts) fresh mussels |
| 40 g (1½ oz) butter or margarine |
| 1 medium onion, skinned and finely chopped |
| 1 small garlic clove, skinned and crushed |
| 300 ml (½ pint) medium dry white wine |
| 1 bay leaf |
| salt and pepper |
| 10 ml (2 level tsp) plain flour |
| 15–30 ml (1–2 tbsp) chopped fresh parsley |

**1.** Clean the mussels (see page 82) under cold water. Melt 25 g (1 oz) butter in a large heavy-based saucepan, add the onion and fry gently until lightly brown. Add the mussels, garlic, wine, bay leaf, salt and plenty of pepper.
**2.** Cover, bring to the boil, and cook for 3–5 minutes, until the mussels open, shaking the pan frequently.
**3.** Pour off the cooking juices into a small saucepan, discarding the bay leaf, and boil until reduced by about one third.

**4.** Lift the mussels out of the pan and discard any that have not opened. Pull away and discard each empty shell, leaving the mussel attached to the half-shell. Do this over the pan to catch any juices. Transfer the mussels to a warmed soup tureen or individual soup bowls, cover and keep warm.
**5.** Work the remaining butter and the flour together, using a blunt-edged knife on a flat plate, until a smooth paste is formed. Off the heat, whisk the kneaded butter into the reduced cooking juices.

**6.** Return to the heat and bring to the boil, stirring constantly. Adjust the seasoning and add the parsley. Pour over the mussels and serve immediately.
*Note* Marinièr is a French term meaning 'in the style of the fisherman'. Moules Marinières is a classic French dish suitable to be served as a starter or main course accompanied by hot garlic bread.
*Serves 4 as a starter or 2 as a main course*

# DEEP-FRIED SCAMPI

225 g (8 oz) scampi, fresh or frozen, thawed if frozen

15–30 ml (1–2 tbsp) seasoned flour

100 g (4 oz) plain flour

pinch of salt

15 ml (1 tbsp) vegetable oil

1 egg, separated

30–45 ml (2–3 tbsp) water or milk and water

vegetable oil for deep-frying

Tartare Sauce (see page 261), to serve

lemon wedges, to garnish

**1.** If fresh scampi or prawns are used, discard their heads, remove the flesh from the shells and remove the dark veins.

**2.** Dip the scampi in the seasoned flour. Mix the plain flour, salt, oil and egg yolk with enough liquid to give a stiff batter which will coat the back of a spoon. Beat until smooth.
**3.** Just before cooking, whisk the egg white until stiff and fold into the batter.
**4.** Heat the oil in a deep-fat fryer to 180°C (350°F). Dip the scampi in the batter, then fry, a few at a time, until golden brown. Drain on absorbent kitchen paper and keep warm while frying the rest. Serve with Tartare sauce and lemon wedges.
*Serves 2*

**Variation**
Coat the scampi with beaten egg and 25–50 g (1–2 oz) fresh breadcrumbs and fry until golden.

# SCAMPI PROVENÇAL

25 g (1 oz) butter or 45 ml (3 tbsp) vegetable oil

1 medium onion, skinned and finely chopped

1 garlic clove, skinned and finely chopped

450 g (1 lb) tomatoes, skinned and chopped, or 397 g
    (14 oz) can tomatoes, drained

90 ml (6 tbsp) dry white wine

salt and pepper

15 ml (1 tbsp) chopped fresh parsley

450 g (1 lb) frozen scampi, thawed and drained

**1.** Heat the butter or oil in a saucepan, add the onion and garlic and fry gently for about 5 minutes, until soft but not coloured.
**2.** Add the tomatoes, wine, seasoning and parsley, stir well and simmer gently for about 10 minutes.
**3.** Add the scampi and continue simmering for about 5 minutes, or until they are just heated through. Serve with crusty French bread or boiled rice.
*Serves 4*

# COQUILLES ST. JACQUES

8 medium scallops, prepared

60 ml (4 tbsp) medium white wine

1 bay leaf

salt and pepper

40 g (1½ oz) butter or margarine

45 ml (3 level tbsp) flour

60 ml (4 tbsp) single cream

50 g (2 oz) Gruyère cheese, grated

450 g (1 lb) potatoes, boiled and creamed

**1.** Reserve four of the round scallop shells. Place the scallops in a small saucepan; add 150 ml (¼ pint) water, the wine, bay leaf and a good pinch of salt.
**2.** Bring slowly to the boil, cover, and simmer gently for about 5 minutes or until the scallops are just tender when tested with a sharp knife. Lift out with a slotted spoon. Strain and reserve the juices.

**3.** Melt the butter in a saucepan. Stir in the flour and cook gently for 1 minute, stirring. Remove the pan from the heat and gradually stir in the reserved juices.
**4.** Bring to the boil slowly and continue to cook, stirring, until the sauce thickens. Season and simmer gently for 4–5 minutes. Lower the heat and stir in the cream and half the grated cheese. Cut each scallop into two or three pieces and stir in.
**5.** Pipe a border of mashed potato around the edges of the rounded scallop shells. Spoon the sauce mixture into the centre and sprinkle the remaining grated cheese over the top.
**6.** Bake in the oven at 220°C (425°F) mark 7 for about 15 minutes or until sauce and piped potato are golden.
*Serves 4*

# MEAT

Meat is not just the basis of a good satisfying meal, it is a major supplier of nutrients including protein, some of the B vitamins and iron. It need not be the most expensive ingredient in a dish since price varies according to the type of cut. You pay most for those parts of the animal which are least exercised and thus tender enough to roast, fry or grill. Tougher cuts, which have more muscle, are cheaper and need long, gentle, moist cooking to soften them. Nutritionally there is nothing to choose between tender and tough meat, and the flavour of both is good if correctly cooked.

◆

Modern methods of transport and developments in cold storage have done away with seasons for meat and you can buy good-quality beef, lamb and pork at any time of the year. Most butchers sell both fresh and frozen meat and it is worth searching out a good local butcher who is prepared to offer a wide choice of cuts. Bear in mind that he is an expert on meat and take advantage of this. A friendly butcher can take away a lot of preparation problems by being prepared to bone, chop or mince to a particular degree of fineness for you.

### CHOOSING MEAT

A butcher will sometimes sell meat that has been frozen and that he has thawed, so do not refreeze unless cooked first. If it still contains ice crystals allow it to thaw thoroughly at room temperature before cooking. Pouring hot water over it or putting it straight into a hot oven will lead to flavour loss.

Do not worry about the colour of meat. Bright red does not necessarily indicate good eating quality. The colour of cut lean beef displayed in butchers' shops will, for example, vary from bright red to dark brown. Exposure to atmosphere makes meat develop a brownish-red shade so some butchers use red-tinted lighting to disguise it.

It is important to cut down the amount of fat we eat, but when cooking meat a little fat is essential to prevent the meat drying out. It also enhances the flavour. Fat on meat should be firm and free from dark marks or discoloration. Meat for roasting, frying and grilling should be finely grained, firm and slightly elastic, with a fine marbling of fat throughout. Meat that is to be stewed or braised will have coarser-grained, lean areas and more fat. Trim off all but a little of the fat before cooking.

### CALCULATING QUANTITIES FOR ALL MEATS

Although servings vary according to the age, taste

and appetite of the people being served, as a guide, allow 100–175 g (4–6 oz) raw meat without bone and 175–350 g (6–12 oz) with bone for each person.

### STORING MEAT

Meat should always be removed from the paper in which it is wrapped when bought. Either put it on a plate or wrap it in cling film, leaving the ends open for ventilation. Before using it wipe with absorbent kitchen paper to remove any blood.

Meat should be stored in a cool place; the most suitable is just below the frozen food storage compartment in the refrigerator. Although the low, controlled temperature means that uncooked meat can be stored thus for 3–5 days, a refrigerator should not be regarded as a place for the long-term storage of meat. The low temperature merely slows down the process of deterioration; it does not completely prevent it. When no refrigerator is available, store meat in a cool, well ventilated place, loose-wrapped. It must be used within 2 days.

Minced raw meat, sausages and offal are especially perishable and should be used within a day of being purchased.

Cooked meats should be wrapped to prevent drying out before they are put into a refrigerator. Leftover stews and casseroles should first be allowed to cool and then put into the refrigerator or a cool place in a covered dish. They should be used within the next couple of days and reheated thoroughly before they are eaten. Bring the dish to boiling point and boil gently for at least 10 minutes.

### ROASTING MEAT

The process known as oven roasting is in fact baking. The oven should be preheated to 180°C (350°F) mark 4. This low temperature will produce succulent meat with less shrinkage. The traditional, high temperature cooking is only suitable for top-quality meat.

Weigh the joint as it is to be cooked (i.e. on the bone or boned and rolled or stuffed as appropriate). Put in a shallow roasting tin, preferably on a grid. Cook for the time shown below:

### ROASTING AT 180°C (350°F) MARK 4

| | |
|---|---|
| Beef | 20 minutes per 450 g (1 lb) + 20 minutes |
| Lamb | 25 minutes per 450 g (1 lb) + 25 minutes |
| Pork | 30 minutes per 450 g (1 lb) + 30 minutes |
| Veal | 40 minutes per 450 g (1 lb) + 40 minutes |

Use a meat thermometer to accurately determine whether the meat is cooked. Insert it into the thickest part of the joint before cooking, making sure the tip of the thermometer is well clear of the bone. Cook to 60°C (140°F), 70°C (160°F), 80°C (180°F) for rare, medium and well done. To allow for thermometer inaccuracy, the cook should discover which final internal temperature produces the desired result.

*Note* Covering the cooking container, covering in foil or cooking in a roasting bag is strictly pot roasting and the recommended roasting times will not be relevant.

### Roasting on a Spit—Rotisserie Cooking

The meat is placed on a revolving spit, or skewers, and cooked under a direct source of heat, either in the oven or on a grill attachment. Allow 15 minutes per 450 g (1 lb) plus 15 minutes extra.

### BOILING MEAT

The term boiling is a misnomer since meat cooked by this method should not be boiled but gently simmered. Boiling produces tough and tasteless meat. For this type of cooking the meat should be covered with liquid in a pan with a well-fitting lid so that evaporation is kept to a minimum. Vegetables and herbs added to the cooking liquid will produce excellent stock for soup.

Meat for boiling is usually salted and should first be soaked in cold water for several hours or overnight to remove excess salt. Change the water before bringing it slowly to the boil, then reduce to a gentle simmer. Large salted joints should be cooked for 25 minutes per 450 g (1 lb) plus an extra 30 minutes. Small joints should be cooked for a minimum of 1½ hours. Calculate the cooking time from the moment the water reaches the boil. With vacuum packs, follow the instructions given.

Pressure cooking will cut the time needed to 'boil' meat by about two thirds, and less liquid is needed. Follow the pressure cooker manufacturer's instructions for exact times and quantities.

### GRILLING MEAT

Grilling is a quick method of cooking by radiant heat which is only suitable for best-quality meat, such as tender chops, steaks, liver, kidneys, gammon, back and streaky bacon. Grilling toughens inferior cuts of meat as the fibres cannot be broken down.

An electric grill should be preheated but this is not necessary with gas. As the heat is fierce the meat must be basted with oil or melted butter before cooking. Meat for grilling is often greatly improved by first being marinated for at least 2 hours.

### FRYING MEAT

It is the heat of the fat that cooks the meat when frying, and as it cooks, the meat absorbs some of the fat. Frying is not a suitable cooking method for anyone who is trying to cut down on fat.

Frying may be done in shallow fat that comes about halfway up the sides of the meat or deep fat in which it is completely immersed.

### BRAISING MEAT

Braising is a combination of stewing, steaming and roasting. The meat is cooked in a saucepan or casserole, over a bed of vegetables, with just sufficient liquid for the steam to keep it moist. This gives a good flavour and texture to meat that otherwise would be tough and flavourless.

### STEWING AND CASSEROLING MEAT

Strictly speaking, both stewing and casseroling describe a long, slow method of cooking in a simmering liquid at 96°C (205°F). The only difference between the two is that casseroling refers to the actual dish in which the food is cooked. This method of cooking is particularly suitable for tougher cuts of meat and since all the liquid is served, none of the flavour or food value is lost. A good, strong saucepan or casserole is needed to avoid burning; it should have a tightly fitting lid to prevent evaporation. Keep the temperature below boiling—as boiling can often cause meat to become tough to chew.

### CARVING MEAT

Carving is not the mystery some people like to pretend it is provided you understand a few basic facts. The only things needed are a large, sharp carving knife, a knife sharpener and a two-pronged carving fork with a finger guard.

Boned and rolled joints are just sliced through. The backbone of rib or loin cuts of lamb or pork helps to keep the joint in shape during cooking. Get the butcher to 'chine' it (partially chop through the bone lengthways) when you buy it so you can then remove the bone just before serving, for easier carving.

Place the cooked joint on a meat dish, wooden board or spiked metal carving dish with recesses to catch the meat juices and leave to stand for 15 minutes before carving. Always carve on a non-slip surface. Before starting to carve, loosen the cooked meat from any exposed bones. Take off all or at least some of the crackling before carving pork.

Aim to cut across the grain of the lean in order to shorten the muscle fibres. This makes the meat easier to chew and thus more tender. This procedure will usually mean cutting at right angles to the bone.

### Carving Beef

**Fore rib** Ask the butcher to chine the backbone. After cooking, remove the backbone and run a sharp knife between meat and bone. Carve the meat downwards, on to and between the rib bones.
**Sirloin** Sirloin of beef comprises the fillet and sirloin muscles with a T-shaped bone between and a portion of flank. Sometimes the fillet is removed and sold separately. When carving, gradually loosen the meat from the bones with a sharp knife as you carve along the joint. Carve slices of meat down to the bone, first on one side, then the other. If the entire joint is to be carved at one time, it may be easier to remove the three pieces of meat first.

### Carving Lamb

**Leg** With the meatier side of the leg uppermost, carve a narrow, wedge-shaped piece of meat from the middle of the leg right down to the bone. Then carve slices from either side of the cut, slanting the knife to obtain larger slices. The underside of the joint can be carved, after removing any excess fat, by slicing along the length of the leg.
**Shoulder** Secure the joint at the shank end, with the crisp skin uppermost. Cut a wedge-shaped slice through the middle of the joint in the angle between the shoulder blade and the leg bone. Carve slices

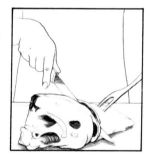

*To carve a leg of lamb, begin by cutting a narrow, wedge-shaped piece of meat from the middle of the leg through the meat down to the bone. Continue carving from either side, cutting at an angle.*

from each side of the first cut until the shoulder blade and shank bones are reached. Turn the joint over and carve horizontal slices from the underside.
**Best end of neck** Get the butcher to chine the joint. After cooking, remove the chined bone and cut the meat into cutlets between the rib bones.

### Carving Pork

**Loin** Ask the butcher to chine the bone. After cooking, remove it and cut through the fat just

*When carving a shank end leg of pork, the first step is to carefully remove the crackling from the uppermost surface.*

beneath the crackling and remove a section or all of it before carving thinly, downwards to the bones.

**Leg (shank end)** Remove some of the crackling. Cut thin slices down to and around the bone as far as possible. When the shank bone is reached, carve slanting slices over the top of the bone. Turn the whole joint over and cut slanting slices down towards the thin end of the bone.

**Leg (fillet end)** Carve slices through to the bone, on either side of it.

### TEXTURISED VEGETABLE PROTEIN

Otherwise known as novel protein, TVP is derived mainly from soya beans but also from cotton seed, peanuts, sesame seeds, oats and sunflower seeds.

It has a nutritional value almost identical to meat though short in one or two essential amino acids.

In the proportion of 25% TVP to 75% meat, people are unlikely to detect anything different, especially in granule form which integrates easily into dishes designed to use minced meat.

When using TVP in recipes it is important to remember that it has greater absorption powers than fresh meat and so it is well to check on the liquid and adjust accordingly. Reconstitute TVP according to manufacturers' directions. Because TVP is pre-cooked, it needs less cooking time than fresh meat (extra cooking doesn't help to tenderise) and so sauces and other basic mixtures are best cooked for a while before the TVP is added.

As a meat-extender, ground TVP is suitable for using with fresh mince in hamburgers, Cottage Pie, meat balls and Bolognese Sauce. Generally speaking for replacement value 25 g (1 oz) TVP is equal to 100 g (4 oz) fresh mince.

TVP can be used instead of meat to make appetising stews, as a stuffing for cannelloni, in lasagne and other similar dishes. TVP has little taste so needs to be well seasoned. It's best mixed with vegetables in casseroles and is particularly good in curries where the sauce provides the flavour.

# BEEF

The quality of beef is very dependent on all sorts of factors, such as the age, breed and sex of the animal and the hanging, storing and the cutting up of the joints. It is worth seeking out a butcher who supplies the sort of beef you like.

Beef should look fresh and moist but not watery with small flecks of fat through the lean—this fat (called marbling) helps to keep the meat moist and tender when cooking. Choose meat with little gristle between the fat and the lean.

## CUTS AND METHODS OF COOKING

**Shin (foreleg) and leg (hindleg)** are lean meat with a high proportion of connective tissue. Suitable for stews, casseroles, stock, soup and brawn.

**Neck and clod** are usually cut into pieces and sold as stewing 'steak' or mince.

**Silverside** traditionally is salted and sold for boiling. Today, more often sold for roasting but, because it is lean, needs constant basting.

*Note* Uncooked salted beef is grey, but turns pink during cooking.

**Fore rib** is the traditional cut of roast beef and is sold on the bone or boned and rolled.

**Wing rib** is a popular roasting joint, but often boned, sliced and sold as frying or grilling steaks.

**Sirloin** is a tender and delicious cut of beef, sold on the bone or boned and rolled with or without the fillet, for roasting. The fillet is the smaller 'eye' on the inside of the rib bone, which is usually removed. It is sold in slices as fillet steak, or whole for Beef Wellington. Sirloin steaks are slices of the larger 'eye' of the lean.

**Chuck and blade steak** is a large, fairly lean cut of high-quality meat, removed from the bone and sold as 'chuck steak'. Suitable for braising, stewing and pie fillings.

**Thick flank (top rump)** is a lean cut suitable for roasting, pot roasting and braising or, when sliced, for braising and frying.

**Thin flank** is ideal for braising and stewing. Often salted or pickled. Frequently sold minced.

**Brisket**, sold either on the bone or boned and rolled, is suitable for braising or boiling, and is often sold salted. Good served cold.

**Thin ribs and thick ribs**, usually sold boned and rolled, are ideal for braising and pot roasting.

**Rump** is an excellent large lean and tender cut, sold in slices for grilling and frying.

**Topside**, a lean cut of beef, with little or no fat, is often sold with a layer of fat tied around it. It can be roasted or pot roasted.

**Steaks** are slices of the most tender cuts of meat, such as sirloin, fillet, rump, tournedos, chateaubriand, T-bone, porterhouse, entrecôte and filet mignon.

**'Flash fry'** is a term used for slices from lean cuts which have been passed between knife covered rollers. This makes the meat more tender and reduces the cooking, i.e. can be flash (quickly) fried.

**Calculating quantities for all meats**, see page 91.

**General roasting**, see page 92.

---

# STEAKS are lean slices taken from the tenderest cuts of beef. They take very little time to cook and need careful watching to ensure they do not overcook.

Steaks need very little preparation; trim them to a good shape if necessary and wipe well. Trim off excess fat but do not remove it all, then slash the remaining fat at regular intervals before cooking to prevent the meat curling while it is cooking.

## CUTS OF STEAK

**Rump** is the joint next to the sirloin and one of the commonest cuts used for grilling or frying. The 'point' is considered the best part for tenderness and flavour.

**Fillet**, the undercut of the sirloin, is probably one of the best-known and the most expensive of the cuts used for grilling or frying. Very tender, although it usually has less flavour than rump. The 'centre' or 'eye' of the fillet is considered the best part. The fillet is often cut and shaped into small rounds, known as tournedos, weighing 100 g (4 oz) each.

A *filet mignon tournedos* is a small round steak, weighing 75 g (3 oz), cut from the end of the fillet.

**Chateaubriand**, a thick slice taken from the middle of the fillet, is generally regarded as the most superb cut of all. It can weigh about 350 g (12 oz). Grill and serve with Maître d'Hôtel Butter (see page 209.

**Sirloin** (or *Contre-filet*) is cut into two parts. Porterhouse steak is cut from the thick end of the sirloin, giving a large juicy piece that can weigh 800 g (1¼ lb); when it is cooked on the bone it is called T-bone steak. *Minute steak* is a very thin steak from the upper part of the sirloin, weighing 125–150 g (4–5 oz), without any trimmings of fat.

**Entrecôte**, by definition, is the part of the meat between the ribs of beef, but a slice cut from the sirloin or rump is often served under this name.

**Steak Tartare** is not a cut of steak, but a dish of finely chopped or minced steak served raw. It is garnished with egg yolks and served with capers, onions, anchovies and seasoning.

## COOKING STEAKS

**To grill** Brush with melted butter or oil and put under a preheated grill. Cook under a medium heat, turning them regularly with a blunt tool so as not to pierce the meat and allow the sealed in juices to escape.

**To fry** If the steak is large, brown it quickly on both sides in hot shallow oil and/or butter, then reduce the heat and cook gently for the remaining time. With small steaks, fry over medium heat for half the cooking time on one side, then turn them and cook for remaining time. Use a heavy-based frying pan, heating it well before adding the fat.

**To serve** To make quick sauces for fried steaks remove them from the pan and keep warm. Add whisky or brandy to the pan juices and ignite. Pour the sauce over the steaks. Another variation is to add mustard and single or double cream to the pan juices and heat without boiling, then pour over the steaks.

A piece of Maître d'Hôtel Butter (see page 209) placed on each steak before it is served, is one traditional accompaniment. Other accompaniments are matchstick or chipped potatoes, grilled tomatoes and fried mushrooms, or a green or mixed salad, or green vegetables.

### COOKING TIMES FOR STEAKS
#### (total in minutes)

| Thickness | Rare | Medium Rare | Well-done |
|---|---|---|---|
| 2 cm (¾ inch) | 5 | 9–10 | 12–15 |
| 2.5 cm (1 inch) | 6–7 | 10 | 15 |
| 4 cm (1½ inches) | 10 | 12–14 | 18–20 |

## ROAST BEEF WITH YORKSHIRE PUDDING

Traditionally, beef was roasted at a high temperature to allow the Yorkshire pudding to be cooked with the joint. If you are roasting at the lower temperature of 180°C (350°F) mark 4, you will need to keep the joint warm and covered, while cooking the Yorkshire pudding. If cooking roast potatoes, leave them in the oven while cooking the Yorkshire pudding to give them a crisp finish.

Yorkshire pudding is made from a batter mixture and should be cooked in a baking or small roasting tin (not a pie dish or ovenproof dish as this tends to make it soggy), and cut into pieces after it is cooked. The original way to eat it was at the start of a meal with some of the meat gravy to take the edge off the appetite and in this way less of the expensive meat was eaten. Today, it is a traditional accompaniment. Roast the meat according to the chart on page 92. Make the gravy as directed on page 204.

*sirloin, rib, rump or topside*

*50 g (2 oz) beef dripping (optional)*

*pepper*

*5 ml (1 tsp) mustard powder (optional)*

**For the Yorkshire pudding**

*125 g (4 oz) plain flour*

*pinch of salt*

*1 egg*

*200 ml (7 fl oz) milk*

*25 g (1 oz) lard or dripping or 30 ml (2 tbsp) vegetable oil*

**1.** Weigh the meat and calculate the cooking time (see page 92). Put the meat into a shallow roasting tin, preferably on a grid, with the thickest layer of fat uppermost and the cut sides exposed to the heat. Add dripping if the meat is lean. Season with pepper and mustard, if wished.

**2.** Roast the joint at 180°C (350°F) mark 4 and cook for the calculated time, basting occasionally with the juices from the tin.

**3.** To make the Yorkshire pudding, mix the flour and salt in a bowl, make a well in the centre and break in the egg.

**4.** Add half the milk and using a wooden spoon gradually work in the flour. Beat the mixture until it is smooth then add the remaining milk and 100 ml (3 fl oz) water. Beat until well mixed and the surface is covered with tiny bubbles.

**5.** Put the fat in a small roasting or other baking tin and place it in the oven at 220°C (425°F) mark 7 for about 10 minutes until the fat shows a haze.

**6.** Pour in the batter and return to the oven to cook for 40–45 minutes, until risen and golden brown. Do not open the oven door for 30 minutes.

*Serves 4–6*

**Variation**

For individual Yorkshire Puddings or Popovers, use 50 g (2 oz) plain flour, a pinch of salt, 1 egg, 150 ml (¼ pint) milk and water mixed. Cook for 15–20 minutes. This quantity will fill 12 patty tins.

*Roast Beef with Yorkshire Pudding*

# FILLET OF BEEF WELLINGTON

*(Boeuf en Croûte)*

*1.4 kg (3 lb) fillet of beef*

*pepper*

*30 ml (2 tbsp) vegetable oil*

*225 g (8 oz) button mushrooms, wiped and sliced*

*50 g (2 oz) butter or margarine*

*175 g (6 oz) smooth liver pâté*

*368 g (13 oz) packet frozen puff pastry, thawed*

*beaten egg, to glaze*

**1.** Trim and tie up the fillet at intervals to retain its shape. Season with pepper. Heat the oil in a large frying pan, add the meat and fry briskly on all sides to brown. Press down with a wooden spoon while frying to seal the surface well.
**2.** Roast in the oven at 220°C (425°F) mark 7 for 20 minutes, then cool the beef and remove the string. Fry the mushrooms in the butter until soft; leave them to go cold, then blend with the pâté.
**3.** On a lightly floured surface roll out the pastry to a large rectangle about 33 × 28 cm (13 × 11 inches) and 0.5 cm (¼ inch) thick.
**4.** Spread the pâté mixture down the centre of the pastry. Place the meat in the centre. Brush the edges of the pastry with egg.
**5.** Fold the pastry edges over lengthways and turn the parcel over so that the join is underneath. Fold the ends under the meat on a baking sheet.

*Fillet of Beef Wellington*

**6.** Decorate with leaves cut from the pastry trimmings. Bake in the oven at 220°C (425°F) mark 7 for 50 minutes, covering with foil after 25 minutes.
*Serves 8*

# BRAISED BRISKET WITH RED WINE

*1.1 kg (2½ lb) piece of lean boned and rolled brisket*

*15 ml (1 level tbsp) seasoned flour*

*15 ml (1 tbsp) vegetable oil*

*2 medium carrots, peeled and cut into chunks*

*2 medium parsnips, peeled and cut into chunks*

*2 medium onions, skinned and diced*

*150 ml (¼ pint) Beef Stock (see page 19)*

*15 ml (1 level tbsp) tomato purée*

*60 ml (4 tbsp) red wine*

*2.5 ml (½ level tsp) dried thyme*

*1 bay leaf*

*salt and pepper*

*10 ml (2 level tsp) cornflour*

**1.** Roll the brisket joint in the seasoned flour until well coated.
**2.** Heat the oil in a 2.3 litre (4 pint) flameproof casserole and brown the joint well. Remove.
**3.** Stir the vegetables into the fat remaining in the pan and fry gently for 2 minutes, then add the stock, tomato purée, wine, thyme, bay leaf and seasoning. Bring to the boil. Replace the meat, placing it in the centre of the vegetables.
**4.** Cover tightly and cook in the oven at 170°C (325°F) mark 3 for about 2¼ hours, until the meat is tender when pierced with a fine skewer.
**5.** Remove the meat and carve into slices. Arrange on a warmed serving dish with the vegetables, cover and keep warm.
**6.** Mix the cornflour to a smooth paste with 30 ml (2 tbsp) water. Stir into the meat juices, then bring slowly to the boil. Boil for 1 minute, adjust seasoning and serve separately.
*Serves 6*

## BRAISED BEEF

| |
|---|
| 1.4 kg (3 lb) piece of boned unsalted silverside |
| 2 medium carrots, peeled |
| 2 medium parsnips, peeled |
| 2 medium onions, skinned and thickly sliced |
| 3 celery sticks, washed and thickly sliced |
| 2 small turnips, peeled and thickly sliced |
| 25 g (1 oz) lard or dripping or 30 ml (2 tbsp) vegetable oil |
| 75 g (3 oz) streaky bacon rashers, rinded and chopped |
| 1 bay leaf |
| salt and pepper |
| 150 ml (¼ pint) Beef Stock (see page 19) |
| 150 ml (¼ pint) cider |
| 15 ml (1 level tbsp) arrowroot |
| chopped fresh parsley, to garnish |

1. Tie up the meat to form a neat joint. Cut the carrots and parsnips into slices about 1 cm (½ inch) thick, halving them if large.
2. Heat the fat in a 3.4 litre (6 pint) deep flameproof casserole. Add the bacon and fry until it begins to brown. Remove the bacon with a slotted spoon and reserve.
3. Reheat the fat in the casserole for a few seconds. Brown the meat all over, turning it with long handled spoons. When browned evenly, remove from casserole and keep warm.
4. Add the vegetables to the pan and fry over a high heat. Add the bacon pieces and bay leaf to the vegetables and season well. Place the joint in the centre of the bed of vegetables.
5. Pour the stock and cider into the casserole. Bring to the boil. Fit a piece of kitchen foil over the meat and vegetables to form a 'tent'. Cover the dish with a close-fitting lid.

*When browning, turn meat with a long handled spoon.*

6. Cook in the oven at 160–170°C (300–325°F) mark 2–3 for 2–2½ hours. Halfway through the cooking time, turn the joint over and re-cover firmly. After 2 hours test the meat—if done a fine skewer will glide easily and smoothly into the joint.
7. Lift the joint on to a board and cut into slices no more than 5 mm (¼ inch) thick. Remove the vegetables from the casserole and place on a shallow, warmed serving dish. Arrange the meat across the top, cover with foil and keep warm in a low oven.
8. Mix the arrowroot to a smooth paste with 45 ml (3 tbsp) water. Skim off excess fat from the juices. Off the heat, stir the paste into the juices, return to the heat then bring slowly to boil, stirring. Boil for 1 minute, then adjust the seasoning. Spoon a little gravy over the meat and sprinkle with parsley. Serve the rest of the gravy separately.
*Serves 6*

## SPICED SILVERSIDE

| |
|---|
| 1.8 kg (4 lb) piece of boned salted silverside |
| 1 medium onion, skinned and sliced |
| 4 medium carrots, peeled and sliced |
| 1 small turnip, peeled and sliced |
| 1–2 celery sticks, trimmed and chopped |
| 8 cloves |
| 100 g (4 oz) soft brown sugar |
| 2.5 ml (½ level tsp) mustard powder |
| 5 ml (1 level tsp) ground cinnamon |
| juice of 1 orange |

1. Soak the meat in cold water for several hours or overnight, then rinse and put in a large saucepan with the vegetables. Cover with water and bring slowly to the boil. Remove any scum, cover with a lid and simmer for 3–4 hours until tender. Allow to cool in the liquid.
2. Drain well, then put the meat into a roasting tin and stick the cloves into the fat. Mix together the remaining ingredients and spread over the meat.
3. Bake in the oven at 180°C (350°F) mark 4 for ¾–1 hour, basting from time to time. Serve hot or cold.

If you wish, you can press the meat after cooking it until tender. Fit it snugly into a casserole or foil-lined tin, spoon a few spoonfuls of the liquid over and cover with a board or plate then place a heavy weight on top. Leave in a cold place for several hours.
*Serves 6*

# STEAK DIANE

4 pieces of fillet steak, 0.5 cm (¼ inch) thick, trimmed
    of excess fat

25 g (1 oz) butter or margarine

30 ml (2 tbsp) vegetable oil

30 ml (2 tbsp) Worcestershire sauce

15 ml (1 tbsp) lemon juice

1 small onion, skinned and grated

10 ml (2 tsp) chopped fresh parsley

**1.** Fry the steaks in the butter and oil for 1–2 minutes on each side. Remove with a slotted spoon and keep warm. Stir the Worcestershire sauce and lemon juice into the pan juices.
**2.** Warm through, then add the onion and parsley and cook gently for 1 minute. Serve the sauce spooned over the steaks.
*Serves 4*

# STEAK AU POIVRE

30 ml (2 level tbsp) black or green peppercorns

4 sirloin, rump or fillet steaks, trimmed of excess fat

salt

25 g (1 oz) butter or margarine

15 ml (1 tbsp) vegetable oil

30 ml (2 tbsp) brandy

150 ml (¼ pint) double cream

**1.** Crush the peppercorns coarsely using a pestle and mortar, or in a polythene bag, or a board with a rolling pin.
**2.** Place the steaks on the peppercorn mixture and press hard to encrust the surface of the meat; repeat with the other side.
**3.** Heat the butter and oil in a frying pan and fry the steaks for 2 minutes on either side. Reduce the heat and continue cooking until cooked to taste (see page 95 for cooking chart). Season with salt.
**4.** Remove the steaks from the pan and keep warm. Add the brandy to the pan, remove from the heat and set it alight. Take off the heat until the flames have died down, then stir in the cream. Season and reheat gently. Pour over the steaks.
*Serves 4*

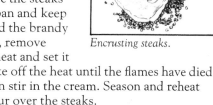

*Encrusting steaks.*

# BEEF OLIVES

75 g (3 oz) streaky bacon, rinded and chopped

10 ml (2 tsp) chopped fresh parsley

125 g (4 oz) fresh breadcrumbs

50 g (2 oz) shredded suet

1.25 ml (¼ level tsp) dried mixed herbs

rind and juice of 1 lemon

salt and pepper

1 egg, beaten

8 thin slices beef topside, 700 g (1½ lb) total weight

45 ml (3 level tbsp) seasoned flour

60 ml (4 tbsp) vegetable oil

450 ml (¾ pint) Beef Stock (see page 19)

2 medium onions, skinned and sliced into rings

**1.** Combine the first six ingredients for the stuffing, season and bind with the egg. Spread each slice of meat with stuffing, roll up, secure with string and toss in seasoned flour.
**2.** Heat the oil in a frying pan and brown the beef olives lightly, remove and place in a casserole.
**3.** Add remaining seasoned flour to the frying pan, brown well, then gradually add the stock and bring to the boil. Season and pour over the olives.
**4.** Add the onion slices, cover and cook in the oven at 180°C (350°F) mark 4 for 1½ hours. Remove the strings before serving the beef olives.
*Serves 4*

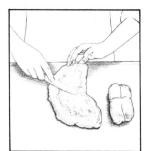

*Spread each slice of meat with stuffing, leaving a small space around the edge. Roll up and secure neatly with fine kitchen string.*

## FONDUE BOURGUIGNONNE

*This dish is cooked at the table with each guest cooking their own share of the meat.*

*700 g (1½ lb) fillet or rump steak, trimmed of excess fat and cut into 2.5 cm (1 inch) cubes*

*vegetable oil for deep frying*

*Spicy Cheese and Tomato, Mustard and Blue Cheese dips (see page 47)*

*1 onion or shallot, finely chopped*

*finely chopped fresh parsley*

*chutney (optional)*

*gherkins (optional)*

*French bread, cubed*

**1.** Arrange the steak on individual plates.

**2.** Fill a fondue dish one-third full of oil and heat on a fondue burner on the table to 190°C (375°F).

**3.** Put the remaining ingredients in individual dishes or bowls.

**4.** Give each guest a two-pronged fondue fork for spearing the meat cubes, which they cook in the hot oil for a few minutes. The cooked meat is then dipped into one of the dips and served with the remaining ingredients.

*Serves 4*

## CLASSIC BEEF STEW

*50 g (2 oz) lard or 45 ml (3 tbsp) vegetable oil*

*700–900 g (1½–2 lb) stewing steak, trimmed and cut into 4 cm (1½ inch) cubes*

*4 medium onions, skinned and halved lengthways*

*350 g (12 oz) carrots, peeled and cut into chunks*

*30 ml (2 level tbsp) flour*

*600 ml (1 pint) Beef Stock (see page 19)*

*15 ml (1 level tbsp) tomato purée*

*salt and pepper*

*2 bay leaves*

**1.** Melt the lard in a medium flameproof casserole. Increase the heat and when the fat is just beginning to smoke, add the meat about one quarter at a time. Fry each batch until well browned. Remove with a slotted spoon.

*Classic Beef Stew*

**2.** Reduce the heat, add the onions and carrots and fry until the vegetables are lightly browned. Remove from the casserole.

**3.** Sprinkle the flour into the fat remaining in the pan and stir well until evenly blended. Return the pan to the heat and cook slowly, stirring constantly, until the roux begins to turn a light brown colour.

**4.** Add the stock, tomato purée and seasoning and stir until the mixture is quite smooth. Bring slowly to the boil, stirring, then add the meat and vegetables with their juices and the bay leaves.

**5.** Cover the casserole tightly and cook in the oven at 170°C (325°F) mark 3 for about 2½ hours. Uncover and stir once during cooking; recover and return to the oven. Alternatively, cover and simmer gently on top of the stove for about 2 hours, stirring occasionally to prevent the stew from sticking. Remove the bay leaves before serving.

*Serves 4*

**Variation**

*CARBONADE OF BEEF*

Proceed as in recipe for Classic Beef Stew omitting the carrots and slicing the onions after halving them. Add 300 ml (½ pint) brown ale and 5 ml (1 tsp) cider or wine vinegar to the stock; cover and cook for 2 hours only. Cut 8 medium-sized slices of French bread and spread one side with French mustard. Uncover the casserole and push the bread down into the meat juices, with the mustard side up. Return to the oven and cook, uncovered, for about 30 minutes, or until the bread forms a good crust.

*Beef Stewed in Red Wine*

## BEEF STEWED IN RED WINE

*(Manzo stufato di vino rosso)*

| |
|---|
| 1.4 kg (3 lb) piece top rump or chuck steak, trimmed |
| 150 ml (¼ pint) red wine |
| 1 medium onion, skinned and finely sliced |
| 3 garlic cloves, skinned and sliced |
| 3 parsley stalks, lightly crushed |
| 8 black peppercorns |
| sprig of fresh thyme or 2.5 ml (½ level tsp) dried thyme |
| 30 ml (2 tbsp) olive oil |
| about 150 ml (¼ pint) Beef Stock (see page 19) |
| 100 g (4 oz) lean gammon, cut into cubes |
| salt and pepper |

**1.** Place the piece of beef in a polythene bag or bowl, pour in the wine and add the onion, garlic, parsley stalks, peppercorns and thyme. Mix well.

**2.** Seal the bag or cover the dish, and leave in a cool place to marinate for 4–5 hours. (Alternatively, the beef can be cut into large pieces first.)

**3.** Remove the beef from the marinade. Set aside. Strain the marinade and set aside. Reserve the onion slices.

**4.** Heat the oil in a heavy flameproof casserole, add the reserved onion slices and fry gently for 5 minutes until soft but not coloured. Add the beef and fry for about 10 minutes, until brown on all sides.

**5.** Pour over the marinade and the stock, then add the gammon. Season. Bring to the boil and boil rapidly for 2–3 minutes.

**6.** Cover tightly and cook in the oven at 180°C (350°F) mark 4 for 2¼–3 hours, until the beef is tender. Check every 30 minutes, turning the beef and making sure that the liquid has not evaporated. If necessary, top up with a little stock or water.

**7.** To serve, remove the cooked beef from the casserole and slice neatly. Arrange the slices overlapping on a warmed serving plate. Taste and adjust the seasoning of the sauce, then serve immediately with the sliced beef.
*Serves 6*

## BOEUF BOURGUIGNONNE

| |
|---|
| 50 g (2 oz) butter or margarine |
| 30 ml (2 tbsp) vegetable oil |
| 100 g (4 oz) streaky bacon rashers, rinded and diced |
| 900 g (2 lb) lean braising steak, cut into 2.5 cm (1 inch) cubes |
| 1 garlic clove, skinned and crushed |
| 45 ml (3 level tbsp) flour |
| salt and pepper |
| bouquet garni |
| 150 ml (¼ pint) Beef Stock (see page 19) |
| 300 ml (½ pint) burgundy |
| 12 small onions, skinned |
| 175 g (6 oz) button mushrooms, wiped |
| chopped fresh parsley, to garnish |

**1.** Melt half the butter and oil in a large flameproof casserole. Quickly brown the bacon, then drain on absorbent kitchen paper.

**2.** Reheat the fat and brown the meat in batches. Return the bacon to the casserole with the garlic. Sprinkle in the flour and stir well.

**3.** Add salt and pepper, the bouquet garni, stock and wine. Bring to the boil, stirring, then cover and cook in the oven at 170°C (325°F) mark 3 for about 2½ hours.

**4.** Meanwhile, heat the remaining butter and oil together. Add the whole onions and fry gently until they are glazed and golden brown. Remove from the pan and fry the mushrooms.

**5.** Add the mushrooms and onions to the casserole and cook for a further 30 minutes. Remove the bouquet garni, adjust the seasoning. Serve garnished with chopped parsley.
*Note* This classic French dish is usually made with topside or rump steak but lean braising steak is a cheaper alternative.

Other red wine can be used instead of burgundy but the flavour will not be quite as good.
*Serves 6*

## BOEUF STROGANOFF

*700 g (1½ lb) rump or fillet steak, trimmed of excess fat and thinly sliced into 0.5 cm (¼ inch) × 5 cm (2 inch) strips*

*45 ml (3 level tbsp) seasoned flour*

*50 g (2 oz) butter or margarine or vegetable oil*

*1 medium onion, skinned and thinly sliced*

*225 g (8 oz) mushrooms, wiped and sliced*

*salt and pepper*

*284 ml (10 fl oz) soured cream*

**1.** Coat the steak strips with the seasoned flour, then fry in 25 g (1 oz) butter or half the oil for about 5–7 minutes, until golden brown.
**2.** Cook the onion and mushrooms in the remaining butter or oil for 3–4 minutes, season to taste and add to the beef.
**3.** Stir the soured cream into the meat mixture and warm through gently. Serve with boiled or buttered noodles.
*Serves 4*

## STEAK AND KIDNEY PUDDING

*550 g (1¼ lb) piece stewing steak, trimmed and cut into 1 cm (½ inch) cubes*

*225 g (8 oz) ox kidney, cut into small even-sized cubes*

*1 medium onion, skinned and finely chopped*

*30 ml (2 tbsp) chopped fresh parsley*

*45 ml (3 level tbsp) flour*

*grated rind of 1 lemon*

*salt and pepper*

*275 g (10 oz) self raising flour*

*150 g (5 oz) shredded suet*

*butter or margarine for greasing*

*parsley sprig, to garnish*

**1.** Place the beef and kidney in a bowl with the onion and the parsley. Sprinkle in the plain flour and lemon rind and season well. Stir well.
**2.** Mix together the self raising flour, suet and a good pinch of salt. Stir in about 200 ml (7 fl oz) water, until a soft dough is formed. Knead lightly, then on a lightly floured surface, roll out to a 35 cm (14 inch) round. Cut out one-quarter of the dough in a fan shape to within 2.5 cm (1 inch) of the centre.
**3.** Lightly grease a 1.7 litre (3 pint) pudding basin. Dust the top surface of the pastry with flour and fold the dough in half, then in half again. Lift the dough into the basin, unfold, press into the base and up the sides, taking care to seal the join well. The pastry should overlap the basin top by about 2.5 cm (1 inch).
**4.** Spoon the meat mixture into the lined pudding basin. Spread the meat out evenly. Add about 120 ml (8 tbsp) water. This should come about two thirds of the way up the meat mixture.

**5.** Roll out the remaining piece of dough to a round 2.5 cm (1 inch) larger than the top of the basin. Dampen the exposed edge of the dough lining the basin. Lift the round of dough on top of the filling and push the pastry edges together to seal. Trim around the top of the basin to neaten. Roll the sealed edges inwards around the top of the basin.
**6.** Cut a piece of greaseproof paper and a piece of foil large enough to cover the basin. Place them together and pleat across the middle. Lightly butter the greaseproof side and put them over the pudding, greaseproof side down. Tie securely on to the basin, running the string just under the lip. Make a string handle across the basin top.
**7.** Bring a large pan of water to the boil. Fit a steamer over the pan and put the pudding inside. Cover with lid. Steam for about 5 hours. Top up with boiling water as necessary and do not allow the water to go off the boil. To serve, uncover and place on a serving plate. Garnish with parsley.
*Serves 6*

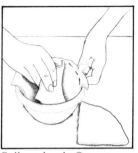

*Roll out dough. Cut out one quarter of the dough. Fold remaining dough in half, then in half again. Lift into basin, unfold and seal.*

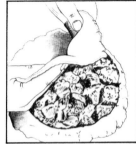

*Spoon the filling into pastry-lined basin. Roll out reserved quarter of dough and place on top of the filling.*

# STEAK AND MUSHROOM PIE

*Illustrated on page 375*

*700 g (1½ lb) stewing steak, cut into small even pieces*

*30 ml (2 level tbsp) seasoned flour*

*1 medium onion, skinned and sliced*

*450 ml (¾ pint) Beef Stock (see page 19)*

*salt and pepper*

*100 g (4 oz) button mushrooms, wiped*

*212 g (7½ oz) packet frozen puff pastry, thawed*

*1 beaten egg, to glaze*

**1.** Coat the meat with seasoned flour, then put in a large saucepan with the sliced onion and stock.
**2.** Bring to the boil, reduce the heat and simmer for 1½–2 hours, until the meat is tender. Season to taste. Alternatively, cook for 2 hours in a covered casserole in the oven at 170°C (325°F) mark 3.

**3.** Chill the meat and the mushrooms, then put into a 1.1 litre (2 pint) pie dish with enough of the gravy to half fill it.
**4.** Roll out the pastry 2.5 cm (1 inch) larger than the top of the dish. Cut off a 1 cm (½ inch) strip from round the edge of the pastry and put this strip round the dampened rim of the dish. Dampen the edges of the pastry with water and put on the top of the pie, without stretching the pastry; trim if necessary and knock up the edges (see page 370). Use the trimmings to make decorations if wished. Brush the top of the pie with beaten egg.
**5.** Bake in the oven at 220°C (425°F) mark 7 for 20 minutes. Reduce the heat to 180°C (350°F) mark 4 and cook for about a further 20 minutes.
*Serves 4*

# CORNISH PASTIES

*450 g 1 lb) stewing steak, trimmed and cut into small pieces*

*175 g (6 oz) potatoes, peeled and diced*

*175 g (6 oz) swede, peeled and diced*

*1 medium onion, skinned and chopped*

*2.5 ml (½ level tsp) dried mixed herbs*

*salt and pepper*

*400 g (14 oz) Shortcrust Pastry made with 400 g (14 oz) plain flour (see page 372)*

*25 g (1 oz) butter or margarine*

*1 egg, beaten, to glaze*

**1.** Place the meat, potato, swede and onion in a bowl and mix in the herbs and seasoning.
**2.** Divide the pastry into six and roll out each piece to a 20 cm (8 inch) circle. Spoon the filling on to half of each circle and top with a little butter.

**3.** Brush the edges of the pastry with water, then fold over and press the edges firmly together to seal.
**4.** Place the pasties on a baking sheet. Brush with the beaten egg and bake at 220°C (425°F) mark 7 for 15 minutes. Reduce the heat to 170°C (325°F) mark 3 for a further 1 hour. Serve warm or cold.
*Serves 6*

*Divide pastry into six and roll out each piece to a 20 cm (8 inch) circle. Spoon filling on to half of each circle, top with butter and moisten edges with water. Fold over and seal.*

# RISSOLES

*225–350 g (8–12 oz) cooked beef, minced*

*1 small onion, skinned*

*450 g (1 lb) potatoes, boiled and mashed*

*dash of Worcestershire sauce*

*salt and pepper*

*1 egg, beaten*

*25 g (1 oz) fresh breadcrumbs*

*45 ml (3 tbsp) vegetable oil*

**1.** Mince together the meat and onion. Add the potatoes, the Worcestershire sauce and season well. Stir until well blended.
**2.** Using floured hands, form into eight round patties, coat with the beaten egg and then with breadcrumbs.
**3.** Heat the oil in a frying pan, add the rissoles and fry on both sides until golden brown. Drain well on absorbent kitchen paper before serving.
*Serves 4*

## COTTAGE PIE *(Shepherd's pie)*

| |
|---|
| 900 g (2 lb) potatoes, peeled |
| 45 ml (3 tbsp) milk |
| knob of butter or margarine |
| salt and pepper |
| 15 ml (1 tbsp) vegetable oil |
| 1 large onion, skinned and chopped |
| 450 g (1 lb) cold cooked beef or lamb, minced |
| 150 ml (¼ pint) Beef Stock (see page 19) |
| 30 ml (2 tbsp) chopped fresh parsley or 10 ml (2 level tsp) dried mixed herbs |

**1.** Cook the potatoes in boiling salted water for 15–20 minutes, then drain and mash with the milk, butter and seasoning.
**2.** Heat the oil in a frying pan, add the onion and fry for about 5 minutes, then stir in the minced meat with the stock, seasoning and parsley.
**3.** Spoon the meat mixture into an ovenproof dish and cover the top with the mashed potato. Mark the top with a fork and bake in the oven at 190°C (375°F) mark 5 for 25–30 minutes, until the surface is crisp and browned.
*Serves 4*

**Variation**
Use 450 g (1 lb) fresh minced beef in place of the cooked meat, add it to the softened onion and cook until well browned. Add 30 ml (2 level tbsp) flour and cook for 2 minutes, then add 300 ml (½ pint) beef stock. Bring to the boil and simmer for 30 minutes. Put the meat in an ovenproof dish and proceed as above.

## MEAT LOAF

| |
|---|
| 25 g (1 oz) butter or margarine |
| 1 medium onion, skinned and finely chopped |
| 5 ml (1 level tsp) paprika |
| 450 g (1 lb) minced beef |
| 50 g (2 oz) fresh breadcrumbs |
| 45 ml (3 level tbsp) natural wheatgerm |
| 1 garlic clove, skinned and crushed |
| 15 ml (1 tbsp) chopped fresh herbs or 5 ml (1 level tsp) dried mixed herbs |
| 60 ml (4 level tbsp) tomato purée |
| 1 egg, beaten |
| salt and pepper |
| Fresh Tomato Sauce, to serve (see page 209) |

**1.** Grease and base line a 450 g (1 lb), capacity 900 ml (1½ pints), loaf tin.
**2.** Melt the butter in a frying pan, add the onion and cook until softened. Add the paprika and cook for 1 minute, stirring, then turn the mixture into a large bowl.
**3.** Add all the remaining ingredients, except the sauce, and stir thoroughly until evenly mixed.
**4.** Spoon the mixture into the loaf tin, level the surface and cover tightly with foil.
**5.** Stand the loaf tin in a roasting tin and pour in water to a depth of 2.5 cm (1 inch).
**6.** Bake in the oven at 180°C (350°F) mark 4 for 1½ hours. Turn out and serve with the sauce.
*Serves 4*

## CHILLI CON CARNE

| |
|---|
| 225 g (8 oz) dried red kidney beans, soaked in cold water overnight |
| 15 ml (1 tbsp) vegetable oil |
| 2 medium onions, skinned and chopped |
| 700 g (1½ lb) minced beef |
| 1 garlic clove, skinned and crushed |
| salt and pepper |
| 2.5 ml (½ level tsp) hot chilli powder or 30–45 ml (2–3 level tbsp) chilli seasoning |
| 15 ml (1 level tbsp) flour |
| 30 ml (2 level tbsp) tomato purée |
| 793 g (28 oz) can tomatoes |

**1.** Drain the beans, rinse, then put into a large saucepan with enough water to cover. Bring to the boil, boil rapidly for 10 minutes, then reduce the heat and simmer gently for about 35 minutes, until tender.
**2.** Heat the oil in a large saucepan, add the onions and fry until softened, then add the mince and cook until browned.
**3.** Add the garlic, salt, pepper and chilli powder.
**4.** Sprinkle in the flour and stir well, then add the tomato purée and tomatoes with their juice. Bring to the boil and add drained beans.
**5.** Simmer for 30 minutes, stirring occasionally.
*Serves 6*

# MEAT BALLS IN TOMATO SAUCE

*150 g (5 oz) crustless stale white bread*

*150 ml (¼ pint) milk*

*15 g (½ oz) butter or margarine*

*20 ml (4 level tsp) flour*

*200 ml (7 fl oz) Beef Stock (see page 19)*

*397 g (14 oz) can tomatoes, sieved*

*5 ml (1 level tsp) sugar (optional)*

*2.5 ml (½ level tsp) dried thyme*

*salt and pepper*

*1 large onion, skinned and finely chopped*

*450 g (1 lb) minced beef*

*5 ml (1 level tsp) paprika*

*45 ml (3 tbsp) vegetable oil*

**1.** Crumble the white bread into a bowl, pour over the milk and leave to soak for about 30 minutes.

**2.** Melt the butter in a large saucepan, stir in the flour and cook gently for 1 minute, stirring. Remove from the heat and gradually stir in the stock. Return to the heat, bring to the boil and continue to cook, stirring, until the sauce thickens. Add the tomatoes, sugar, if using, and thyme. Season well and simmer, covered, for 30 minutes.

**3.** Meanwhile, put the onion and the mince in a bowl and add the soaked bread together with any remaining milk, the paprika and seasoning. Using floured hands shape the mixture into 18 balls.

**4.** Heat the oil in a frying pan, add the meat balls a few at a time and fry until browned all over.

**5.** Place the meat balls in a single layer in a shallow ovenproof dish and pour over the sauce. Cover and bake at 180°C (350°F) mark 4 for about 30 minutes.

*Serves 6*

# BEEFBURGERS *(Hamburgers)*

*450 g (1 lb) lean beef, e.g. chuck, shoulder or rump*
  *steak, minced*

*½ a small onion, skinned and grated (optional)*

*salt and pepper*

*melted butter or oil for coating or a little fat for*
  *shallow frying*

**1.** Mix the minced beef well with the onion, if using, and a generous amount of salt and pepper. Shape lightly into 4–8 round flat patties.

**2.** To cook, brush sparingly with melted butter or oil and grill for 4–6 minutes for small burgers and 8–10 minutes for larger, turning once, or fry in a little fat in a frying pan, turning them once and allowing the same amount of time.

*Note* Hamburgers can be served rare or well done, according to personal preference, hence the variation in cooking time.

*Serves 4*

## Variations

Traditionally, beefburgers contain no other ingredients, but they can be varied by adding any of the following when combining the mixture:

- 50–100 g (2–4 oz) grated cheese
- 15 ml (1 tbsp) sweet pickle
- 5–10 ml (1–2 level tsp) prepared mustard
- 5 ml (1 level tsp) dried mixed herbs

*Beefburgers*

# VEAL comes from a young animal so the flesh should be comparatively light in colour—fine-textured, pale pink, soft and moist. Avoid really flabby, wet meat. The fat—of which there is very little—should be firm and pinkish or creamy white. Veal bones make excellent jellied stock or gravy when simmered—they give the special flavour to veal stews and fricassees.

## CUTS AND METHODS OF COOKING

**Leg** is a prime cut, used mainly for escalopes (also known as *schnitzels*) for frying. Occasionally sold as small joints for roasting.

**Fillet**, which is usually the most expensive cut, is sold in a piece for roasting. It can also be cut in thin slices, which are beaten and fried. It is also sold as medallions.

**Knuckle**, usually sold as osso bucco, already sawn into 5 cm (2 inch) pieces, for stewing.

**Loin** is usually sold as cutlets (with rib in) and chops. It can be boned and sold as entrecôte steak. Otherwise rolled for roasting.

**Shoulder** is usually boned and rolled into oyster and shoulder roasting joints. The oyster cut is slightly leaner than the shoulder.

**Breast** is usually the least expensive. It is divided into breast and flank joints, boned and rolled and sometimes ready stuffed for roasting.

**Pie or diced veal** consists of trimmings and small pieces of shoulder, breast, neck or knuckle, bought ready cut up. This needs long slow cooking.

**Best neck** is a good-value cut. It can be chined and roasted on the bone, or boned, stuffed and rolled for roasting, or used for braising and stewing. Cutlets can be cut if the 'eye' muscle is sufficiently large.

**Calculating quantities for all meats**, see page 91.
**General roasting**, see page 92.

## VEAL CHOPS WITH SPINACH PURÉE

6 veal chops, weighing about 175 g (6 oz) each, trimmed

finely grated rind of 2 lemons

90 ml (6 tbsp) lemon juice

150 ml (¼ pint) dry vermouth

1 large garlic clove, skinned and crushed

salt and pepper

225 g (8 oz) fresh spinach, trimmed

50 g (2 oz) butter or margarine

2.5 ml (½ level tsp) grated nutmeg

45 ml (3 tbsp) vegetable oil

1 egg, hard-boiled and finely chopped

bunch of spring onions, trimmed and shredded

1. Place the chops in a large shallow dish. Whisk together the lemon rind and juice, vermouth, garlic and seasoning and pour over the chops. Cover and marinate in a cool place overnight.
2. Wash the spinach well in several changes of cold water. Put in a saucepan with just the water that clings to the leaves, cover and cook for 3–4 minutes. Drain well in a colander, pressing the spinach with the back of a wooden spoon to extract as much liquid as possible. Finely chop.
3. Sauté the spinach with 25 g (1 oz) butter and the nutmeg for 1–2 minutes to dry off any excess moisture. Transfer to a bowl. Cool and cover.
4. Remove chops from marinade, drain and pat dry with absorbent kitchen paper. Heat oil with the remaining butter in a large pan until foaming. Brown the chops well on both sides, one or two at a time. Place in a single layer in one or two shallow ovenproof dishes.
5. Pour the marinade into the pan. Bring to the boil, stirring any sediment from the base. Strain over the chops. Cover tightly and cook in the oven at 180°C (350°F) mark 4 for about 50 minutes, or until chops are tender.
6. Transfer the chops to a warmed serving dish and keep warm. Purée the spinach mixture with the reserved pan juices in a blender or food processor until smooth. Pour into a small saucepan and simmer gently for 5–10 minutes, until hot.
7. Garnish the chops with the chopped egg and spring onion. Serve the purée separately.
*Serves 6*

## ESCALOPES FINES HERBES

4 veal escalopes, weighing about 450 g (1 lb)

60 ml (4 level tbsp) seasoned flour

50 g (2 oz) butter or margarine

10 ml (2 level tsp) tomato purée

60 ml (4 tbsp) sherry

100 ml (4 fl oz) red wine

50 g (2 oz) mushrooms, sliced

2.5 ml (½ level tsp) dried mixed herbs

60 ml (4 tbsp) single cream

salt and pepper

225 g (8 oz) tomatoes, skinned and chopped

50 g (2 oz) mature Cheddar cheese, grated

1. Flatten each escalope between two sheets of damp greaseproof paper, then coat in seasoned flour.
2. Melt 25 g (1 oz) of the butter in a frying pan and fry the escalopes gently for 3–5 minutes on each side, then remove and keep warm.
3. Add the remaining flour to the frying pan, stir in the tomato purée, sherry and wine and bring the mixture slowly to the boil. Add the mushrooms, herbs and the cream. Season and cook very gently for about 5 minutes, without boiling.
4. Heat the remaining butter in a pan, add the tomatoes and heat through. Pour the tomato mixture into a shallow ovenproof dish, arrange the meat on top, pour over the sauce, sprinkle with the cheese and brown under the grill.
Serves 4

## VEAL KIEV

4 veal escalopes, weighing about 450 g (1 lb)

100 g (4 oz) butter or margarine

finely grated rind of ½ a lemon

15 ml (1 tbsp) lemon juice

30 ml (2 tbsp) chopped fresh parsley

salt and pepper

30 ml (2 level tbsp) seasoned flour

1 egg, beaten

50 g (2 oz) fresh breadcrumbs

vegetable oil for deep-fat frying

lemon wedges and chopped fresh parsley, to garnish

1. Halve each veal escalope, trim and flatten between two sheets of damp greaseproof paper.
2. Cream the butter, then mix in the lemon rind and juice, the parsley and seasoning.
3. Divide the butter between the eight escalopes, roll up each one with the butter inside to completely enclose and tie with fine string. Chill.
4. Coat the escalopes in flour, egg and breadcrumbs, and chill again while heating the oil.
5. Heat the oil in a deep-fat fryer to 185°C (365°F), add the escalopes and fry for 6–8 minutes, until golden brown. Drain on absorbent kitchen paper, remove string and garnish.
Serves 4

## VEAL ESCALOPES WITH HAM AND MARSALA (Saltimbocca Alla Romana)

8 veal escalopes, weighing about 900 g (2 lb)

15–30 ml (1–2 tbsp) lemon juice

pepper

8 fresh sage or basil leaves or sprigs of marjoram

8 thin slices of prosciutto

50 g (2 oz) butter or margarine

15 ml (1 tbsp) vegetable oil

30 ml (2 tbsp) Marsala

fried croûtons, to garnish

1. Flatten escalopes between greaseproof.
2. Season each escalope with lemon juice and pepper. Place a sage or basil leaf or marjoram in the centre and cover with a slice of prosciutto

Roll up and secure with a cocktail stick.
3. Heat the butter and oil in a frying pan, add the veal rolls and fry gently until golden brown. Stir in the Marsala, bring to simmering point, then cover the pan and simmer gently for about 10 minutes. Serve with the juices poured over and surround with croûtons. Note Prosciutto is a special Italian smoked ham.
Serves 8

Roll the escalopes.

*Wiener Schnitzel*

## WIENER SCHNITZEL *(Fried Veal Escalopes)*

*4 veal escalopes, weighing about 450 g (1 lb)*

*salt and pepper*

*1 egg, beaten*

*150 g (5 oz) fresh breadcrumbs*

*75 g (3 oz) butter or margarine*

*30 ml (2 tbsp) vegetable oil*

*8 anchovy fillets, drained and halved (optional)*

*1 egg, hard-boiled and the yolk and white chopped separately (optional)*

*lemon slices and capers, to garnish*

**1.** Flatten each escalope thinly between two sheets of damp greaseproof paper.
**2.** Season the meat, then coat in beaten egg and breadcrumbs, pressing the crumbs on well.
**3.** Heat the butter and oil in a large frying pan and fry the escalopes, two at a time, for 3–5 minutes each side, until golden. Drain on absorbent kitchen paper and keep warm whilst cooking the remaining escalopes.
**4.** Serve garnished with the anchovy fillets, egg, if using, the lemon slices and capers.
*Serves 4*

**Variations**
*ESCALOPES WITH PARMESAN CHEESE*
Prepare the escalopes as above, cooking only 2 minutes on each side. Lay a slice of cooked ham over each escalope and sprinkle 15 ml (1 level tbsp) Parmesan cheese on top of each. Cover the pan and cook a further 2–3 minutes until the cheese just melts.

*ESCALOPES WITH MARSALA AND CHEESE*
Coat the escalopes in 60 ml (4 level tbsp) seasoned flour and cook only 2 minutes each side. Stir 45–60 ml (3–4 tbsp) Marsala into the pan and sprinkle 15 ml (1 level tbsp) Parmesan on each escalope. Cover and cook for a further 2–3 minutes.

## VEAL GOULASH

*75 g (3 oz) butter or margarine*

*1.4 kg (3 lb) stewing veal or braising steak, cut into 4 cm (1½ inch) pieces*

*700 g (1½ lb) onions, skinned and thinly sliced*

*450 g (1 lb) carrots, peeled and thinly sliced*

*45–60 ml (3–4 tbsp) paprika*

*30 ml (2 tbsp) flour*

*900 ml (1½ pints) Chicken Stock (see page 19)*

*60 ml (4 tbsp) dry white wine*

*salt and pepper*

*142 ml (5 fl oz) soured cream*

**1.** Melt the butter in a frying pan and fry the veal, a little at a time, until browned. Remove from the pan with a slotted spoon and place in an ovenproof dish.
**2.** Fry the onions and carrots in the butter remaining in the pan for about 5 minutes until lightly browned. Add the paprika and flour and fry for 2 minutes. Gradually stir in the stock, wine and seasoning. Bring to the boil and pour over the veal.
**3.** Cover tightly and cook in the oven at 150°C (300°F) mark 2 for 2¾ hours. When cooked, pour the soured cream over the goulash and serve.
*Serves 8*

*Veal Goulash*

*Blanquette de Veau*

# BLANQUETTE DE VEAU

*700 g (1½ lb) pie veal, trimmed and cubed*

*2 medium onions, skinned and chopped*

*2 medium carrots, peeled and chopped*

*squeeze of lemon juice*

*bouquet garni*

*salt and pepper*

*25 g (1 oz) butter or margarine*

*45 ml (3 level tbsp) flour*

*1 egg yolk*

*30–45 ml (2–3 tbsp) single cream*

*4–6 bacon rolls*

*chopped fresh parsley, to garnish*

**1.** Put the meat, onions, carrots, lemon juice, bouquet garni and seasoning into a large saucepan with enough water to cover. Cover and simmer gently for about 1 hour, until the meat is tender.

**2.** Strain off the cooking liquid, reserving 600 ml (1 pint) and keep the meat and vegetables warm.

**3.** Melt the butter in a pan, stir in the flour and cook gently for 1 minute, stirring. Remove from the heat and gradually stir in the reserved liquid. Return to the heat, bring to the boil slowly and continue to cook, stirring, until the sauce thickens.

**4.** Adjust the seasoning, remove from the heat and when slightly cooled stir in the egg yolk and cream. Add the meat, vegetables and bacon rolls and reheat without boiling for 5 minutes. Serve garnished with parsley.

*Serves 4–6*

# RAGOÛT OF VEAL

| | |
|---|---|
| 900 g (2 lb) pie veal, trimmed and cubed | 1. Toss the veal in the flour and quickly fry in the oil. Transfer to a large casserole. |
| 45 ml (3 level tbsp) seasoned flour | 2. Add the bacon and onions to the pan and fry for 3 minutes. Transfer to the casserole. |
| 75 ml (5 tbsp) vegetable oil | |
| 175 g (6 oz) lean bacon rashers, rinded and roughly chopped | 3. Add the tomatoes to the casserole with the wine, paprika and seasoning. |
| 16 button onions, skinned | 4. Cover and cook in the oven at 150°C (300°F) mark 2 for about 2½ hours. About 20 minutes |
| 397 g (14 oz) can tomatoes, drained | before cooking is finished, stir in the peas and |
| 150 ml (¼ pint) dry white wine | return to the oven. |
| 2.5 ml (½ level tsp) paprika | 5. Swirl the soured cream into the sauce and |
| salt and pepper | sprinkle with parsley just before serving. |
| 112 g (4 oz) packet frozen peas | *Serves 6–8* |
| 45 ml (3 tbsp) soured cream | |
| chopped fresh parsley, to garnish | |

# OSSO BUCO *(Braised Veal in White Wine)*

| | |
|---|---|
| 50 g (2 oz) butter or margarine | 1. Melt the butter with the oil in a flameproof casserole, add the onion and fry gently for |
| 15 ml (1 tbsp) olive oil | 5 minutes, until soft but not coloured. |
| 1 medium onion, skinned and finely chopped | 2. Coat the veal in the flour, add to the casserole and fry for about 10 minutes, until browned. |
| 4 large or 8 small ossi buchi (veal shin, hind cut), weighing about 1.75 kg (3½ lb) sawn into 5 cm (2 inch) lengths | 3. Pour over the wine and boil rapidly for 5 minutes, then add the stock. |
| 45 ml (3 tbsp) seasoned flour | 4. Cover the pan tightly and simmer for 1½–2 hours, basting and turning the meat occasionally. |
| 300 ml (½ pint) dry white wine | 5. Transfer the meat to a warmed serving dish, |
| 300 ml (½ pint) Veal or Chicken Stock (see page 19) | cover and keep warm. If necessary, boil the sauce rapidly to thicken, then pour over the meat. |
| finely grated rind of 1 lemon | 6. Mix together the lemon rind, garlic and parsley |
| 1 garlic clove, skinned and finely chopped | and sprinkle over the dish. Serve with the risotto. |
| 45 ml (3 tbsp) chopped fresh parsley | *Serves 4* |
| Risotto alla Milanese, to serve (see page 306) | |

# VITELLO TONNATO *(Veal in Tuna Fish Sauce)*

| | |
|---|---|
| 700 g (1½ lb) leg of veal, boned, with bone reserved | 1. Tie the meat into a neat roll and put into a saucepan with the bone, carrot, onion, celery, |
| 1 small carrot, peeled and sliced | peppercorns, 5 ml (1 level tsp) salt and 300 ml |
| 1 medium onion, skinned and quartered | (½ pint) water. |
| 1 celery stick, trimmed and chopped | 2. Bring to the boil, cover and simmer for about 1 hour, or until tender. Remove the meat and cool. |
| 4 black peppercorns | 3. Meanwhile, mash together the tuna and |
| salt and pepper | anchovies with a fork or in a blender or food |
| 99 g (3½ oz) can tuna in oil, drained | processor. Stir in the egg yolks, pepper and lemon juice. Add the oil, a little at a time, until the sauce |
| 4 anchovy fillets, drained | resembles thin cream. Season. |
| 2 egg yolks | 4. Cut the meat into thin slices, arrange in a |
| 15 ml (1 tbsp) lemon juice | shallow dish and coat completely with the sauce. |
| 150 ml (¼ pint) olive oil | Cover and leave overnight. |
| capers, black olives and lemon slices, to garnish | 5. Garnish and serve. |
| | *Serves 4–6* |

$LAMB$ is a particularly tender meat and all the joints can be roasted. This is because lambs are slaughtered before their connective tissues become tough, so the tissues dissolve easily in the meat's natural moisture during cooking. Cuts such as chops and cutlets from the neck, are also suitable for grilling or frying. Other neck cuts are ideal for casseroles, stews and pies.

The fat in lamb should be crisp and white with the lean, fine-grained, firm and pinky-brown. There is usually very little gristle. Freshly cut surfaces should look slightly moist and the bones be pinkish-white.

## CUTS AND METHODS OF COOKING

**Scrag and middle neck** are usually sold as neck cuts on the bone and used for stewing or braising. Traditional cuts for Irish stew or Lancashire hot pot. The main 'eye' of lean meat from the middle neck is now sold as 'fillet of lamb' and is ideal for grilling.

**Shoulder** is a succulent, tender roasting joint, whether on the bone, or boned, stuffed and rolled. Sold whole or halved into blade and knuckle, both of which are good for roasting or braising. The shoulder or forequarter can be cut into chop-size portions which are ideal for grilling or braising.

**Best end of neck** can be purchased as a roasting joint with a row of 6 or 7 rib bones. The butcher will chine (remove) the backbone, to make carving easier. This is sometimes called 'rack of lamb'. It can be roasted on the bone, or boned, stuffed and rolled. Also sold as chops with one rib bone to each, for grilling or frying. Two best end necks joined together and curved, bones outwards, make a 'Crown roast'. Facing each other, fat side outwards, they make a 'Guard of honour'. Both these special occasion dishes can be stuffed before roasting. This cut is recognisable by the dot of lean beneath the main 'eye' of lean.

**Loin,** the whole loin consists of both chump and loin chops. It can be roasted in the piece, or boned, stuffed and rolled. Loin is usually divided into loin

end and chump end, and cut into chops for grilling or frying. Chump chops are recognisable by the small round bone in the centre. Loin chops are recognisable by the small T bone.

**Saddle of lamb** is a large roasting joint for special occasions, which is the whole loin from both sides of the animal, left in one piece. Double loin chops (Barnsley chops) are cut from a saddle of lamb. It is advisable to give the butcher notice for these cuts.

**Leg** is an excellent roasting joint on the bone, or boned, stuffed and rolled. The leg is often divided into fillet end and shank end. The round leg bone steaks are better for baking or braising than grilling or frying.

**Breast** is a long, thin cut, streaked with fat and lean. When boned, rolled and stuffed, it is the most economical cut for roasting or braising. Riblets of lamb breast make a suitable alternative to pork spare ribs for barbecuing, pan roasting, etc.

**Minced or diced lamb** is a quick and convenient way to purchase lamb for dishes such as Shepherd's Pie, Moussaka, Kebabs, etc.

**Calculating quantities for all meats**, see page 91.
**General roasting**, see page 92.

**Accompaniments**, with roast lamb or grilled chops serve mint sauce or jelly or redcurrant jelly. With boiled leg of lamb (mutton) serve onion or caper sauce.

## GRILLING AND FRYING LAMB

*4 lamb chump or loin chops*

*15 ml (1 tbsp) vegetable oil*

**Frying**
1. Heat the oil in a frying pan and add the chops. Cook for about 15 minutes, turning frequently.

**Grilling**
1. Brush the chops with the oil. Place on the grill pan and grill under a moderate heat for about 6–8 minutes each side. Serve with mint sauce and redcurrant jelly.
*Serves 4*

# CROWN ROAST OF LAMB

2 best end necks of lamb, chined, each with 6 cutlets

25 g (1 oz) butter or margarine

1 medium onion, skinned and chopped

3 celery sticks, trimmed and chopped

1 eating apple, peeled, cored and chopped

40 g (1½ oz) dried apricots, soaked overnight

125 g (4 oz) fresh breadcrumbs

30 ml (2 tbsp) chopped fresh parsley

finely grated rind of ½ a lemon

15 ml (1 tbsp) lemon juice

1 egg

salt and pepper

50 g (2 oz) lard or 30 ml (2 tbsp) vegetable oil

30 ml (2 level tbsp) flour

450 ml (¾ pint) Beef Stock (see page 19)

1. Trim each cutlet bone to a depth of 2.5 cm (1 inch). Bend the joints around, fat side inwards, and sew together using strong cotton or fine string to form a crown. Cover the exposed bones with foil.
2. Melt the butter in a saucepan and cook the onion, celery and apple until brown. Drain, dry and chop the apricots and stir into the pan with the breadcrumbs, parsley, lemon rind and juice, egg and seasoning. Allow to cool, then fill the centre of the joint with the stuffing and weigh.
3. Place the joint in a small roasting tin with the lard or oil. Roast at 180°C (350°F) mark 4 for 25 minutes per 450 g (1 lb) plus 25 minutes. Baste occasionally and cover with foil if necessary.
4. Transfer the crown roast to a warmed serving dish and keep warm. Drain off all but 30 ml (2 tbsp) of the fat in the roasting tin, add the flour and blend well. Cook for 2–3 minutes, stirring continuously. Add the stock and boil for 2–3 minutes. Season and serve hot with the joint. Serves 6

**Variation**

GUARD OF HONOUR

This is also prepared from two best ends of neck. Trim as above but interlace the bones, fat side outwards, to form an arch. Fill the cavity with the stuffing (as above) and fasten together with strong thread or fine string.

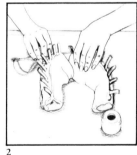

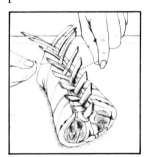

1. Bend joints around, fat side inwards. 2. Sew joints together using strong cotton or fine kitchen string to form a crown. 3. For Guard of Honour, interlace the bones, fat side outwards, to form an arch.

Guard of Honour

# ROLLED STUFFED BREASTS OF LAMB

25 g (1 oz) butter or margarine

1 medium onion, skinned and chopped

411 g (14½ oz) can apricot halves

175 g (6 oz) fresh breadcrumbs

45 ml (3 tbsp) chopped fresh parsley

25 g (1 oz) chopped mixed nuts

finely grated rind of ½ a lemon

30 ml (2 tbsp) lemon juice

salt and pepper

1 egg, beaten

2 large breasts of lamb, boned and trimmed

45 ml (3 tbsp) vegetable oil

1. Melt the butter in a saucepan and lightly brown the onion. Drain and roughly chop three-quarters of the apricots, reserving the rest for garnishing.

2. Mix together the onion, chopped apricots, breadcrumbs, parsley and nuts and stir in the lemon rind and juice, seasoning and egg.
3. Lay the breasts of lamb fat side down on a work surface, overlapping slightly, and spread the stuffing evenly over them. Roll up the lamb breasts loosely and tie in several places with string to hold their shape. Weigh the joints.
4. Heat the oil in a small roasting tin and roast the joint at 180°C (350°F) mark 4 for 25 minutes per 450 g (1 lb) plus 25 minutes, basting occasionally. Serve garnished with the reserved apricots.
Serves 4

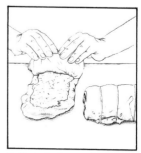

Roll up the breasts loosely.

# LAMB CUTLETS EN CROÛTE

25 g (1 oz) butter or margarine

1 medium onion, skinned and chopped

25 g (1 oz) fresh breadcrumbs

1 egg, beaten

30 ml (2 tbsp) chopped fresh mint

salt and pepper

squeeze of lemon juice

12 lamb cutlets, trimmed

two 368 g (13 oz) packets frozen puff pastry, thawed

beaten egg, to glaze

fresh mint sprig, to garnish

1. To make the stuffing, melt the butter in a pan and fry the onion for about 5 minutes, until soft but not brown. Remove from the heat. Stir in the breadcrumbs and bind with the egg. Mix in the mint, seasoning and lemon juice.
2. Grill or fry the cutlets for 3 minutes on both sides. They should be browned, but pink inside. Leave to cool.
3. Thinly roll out each piece of pastry on a lightly floured surface and cut into six squares.
4. Place each of the lamb cutlets on a square of pastry so that the bone extends over the edge of the pastry.
5. Press even amounts of stuffing on the eye of each cutlet. Dampen the pastry edges, wrap the pastry over the cutlets and seal.

6. Place on a dampened baking sheet, folded sides underneath. Use any pastry trimmings to decorate the cutlets. Brush with a little beaten egg.
7. Bake in the oven at 220°C (425°F) mark 7 for 15–20 minutes, then reduce the temperature to 190°C (375°F) mark 5 and bake for a further 15 minutes, until the pastry is golden. Serve hot, garnished with a sprig of fresh mint.
Serves 6

Lamb Cutlets en Croûte

## LAMB EN CROÛTE

2.2 kg (4½ lb) leg of lamb, boned

150 ml (¼ pint) red wine

350 g (12 oz) pork sausagemeat

100 g (¼ lb) streaky bacon, rinded and chopped

15 ml (1 tbsp) almonds or pistachio nuts, blanched and
    chopped

salt and pepper

30 ml (2 tbsp) vegetable oil

2 medium onions, skinned and sliced

few thyme sprigs or a pinch of dried thyme

1 bay leaf

3 parsley stalks

1 garlic clove, skinned and crushed

411 g (15 oz) can chicken consommé or 450 ml (¾ pint)
    Chicken Stock (see page 19)

368 g (13 oz) packet frozen puff pastry, thawed

1 egg, beaten

30 ml (2 level tbsp) cornflour

1. Trim the lamb of excess fat, then marinate in the wine for 2–3 hours, turning it occasionally.
2. Mix the sausagemeat, bacon and nuts and season. Remove the meat from the wine and dry. Reserve marinade. Stuff the cavity with the sausagemeat and sew both ends with string.
3. Heat the oil in a large flameproof casserole and quickly fry the lamb to brown. Add the onions and cook for 2–3 minutes until browned. Add the thyme, bay leaf, parsley, garlic, consommé and reserved marinade. Cover, and cook in the oven at 170°C (325°F) mark 3 for 2 hours. Remove the meat and cool. Reserve the juices.
4. On a lightly floured surface, roll out the pastry to an oblong 50 cm × 25 cm (20 inch × 10 inch). Remove the string from the meat. Place the lamb in the centre and brush the edges of the pastry with egg. Make a parcel by folding the pastry edges over lengthways and turn the parcel over so that the join is underneath. Fold the ends under the meat on a baking sheet. Decorate with the pastry trimmings. Chill for about 30 minutes until the pastry is firm. Brush with beaten egg, then bake in the oven at 230°C (450°F) mark 8 for about 45 minutes, covering with foil if overbrowning.
5. For the gravy, strain the juices into a pan. Blend the cornflour with 30 ml (2 tbsp) water. Stir into the pan, bring to the boil. Serve separately.
*Serves 8–10*

## KASHMIRI-STYLE LAMB

1.4 kg (3 lb) leg of lamb

15 ml (1 level tbsp) poppy seeds

45 ml (3 level tbsp) grated fresh or desiccated coconut

2 medium onions, skinned and coarsely chopped

5 cm (2 inch) piece root ginger, peeled and coarsely
    chopped

25 g (1 oz) blanched almonds, chopped

cinnamon stick, 5 cm (2 inch) long

6 green cardamoms

3 black cardamoms, ground

4 cloves

small piece of mace

2.5 ml (½ level tsp) grated nutmeg

7.5 ml (1½ level tsp) mild chilli powder

5 ml (1 level tsp) salt

142 g (5 fl oz) natural yogurt

150 g (5 oz) ghee or butter, melted

4 bay leaves, crushed

30 ml (2 level tbsp) ground aniseed

1. Remove all traces of fat and the white membrane from the meat. Prick the meat thoroughly with a sharp knife so that the fibres are completely broken up. It should virtually be falling off the bone. Place in a deep baking dish or a roasting tin.
2. Soak the poppy seeds and the coconut in a little warm water for 10 minutes. Drain and put in a blender or food processor with the next 11 ingredients and blend to a smooth paste.
3. Pour the paste over the meat and spread all over coating well. Again, prick the meat with a knife all over to help the mixture to penetrate.
4. Mix together the yogurt and remaining ingredients and spread it over the lamb. Cook in the oven at 170°C (325°F) mark 3 for 2¼–2½ hours, basting frequently. Turn the leg over once, halfway during cooking time. Remove from the oven and transfer to a warmed serving dish. Carve and serve hot.
*Serves 6*

# SPINACH STUFFED SHOULDER OF LAMB

2 medium onions, skinned and finely chopped

15 ml (1 tbsp) vegetable oil

227 g (8 oz) packet frozen chopped spinach, thawed
    and drained

1 garlic clove, skinned and crushed

2.5 ml (½ level tsp) grated nutmeg

salt and pepper

1.4 kg (3 lb) shoulder of lamb, boned

1–2 garlic cloves, cut into slivers

10 ml (2 level tsp) flour

300 ml (½ pint) Beef Stock (see page 19)

15 ml (1 level tbsp) redcurrant jelly

dash of gravy browning

1. Soften the onion in the oil in a saucepan, then add the spinach, garlic, nutmeg and seasoning, adding plenty of pepper. Cool.
2. Fill the bone cavity of the lamb with the spinach mixture and sew up using cotton or fine string. Make small cuts in the fat and insert the garlic slivers into them.
3. Place the lamb on a rack in a roasting tin. Roast in the oven at 180°C (350°F) mark 4 for about 2¼ hours, basting several times during cooking.
4. Transfer the joint to a shallow serving plate and keep warm. Drain off all but 15 ml (1 tbsp) fat from the roasting tin, stir in the flour and cook for 1–2 minutes, stirring. Add the stock, jelly, seasoning and a dash of gravy browning and boil for 2–3 minutes, stirring. Serve the gravy separately.
*Serves 6*

# BREASTS OF LAMB WITH TARTARE SAUCE

2 large breasts of lamb, trimmed

1 medium onion, skinned and quartered

1 medium carrot, peeled and sliced

2 bay leaves

salt and pepper

30 ml (2 level tbsp) seasoned flour

2 eggs, beaten

125 g (4 oz) fresh breadcrumbs

60 ml (4 tbsp) vegetable oil

watercress sprigs, to garnish

Tartare Sauce, to serve (see page 161)

1. Place the lamb in a large saucepan with the onion, carrots, bay leaves and seasoning. Cover with water and simmer gently for 1½ hours, skimming occasionally.
2. Remove the meat from the pan, allow to cool slightly, then ease out all the bones. Lay the meat flat on a baking sheet, cover with a board with weights on top and leave for several hours.
3. Cut the lamb into 7.5 cm (3 inch) cubes, coat in flour, egg and breadcrumbs and chill for 1 hour.
4. Heat the oil in a frying pan and gently fry the coated lamb pieces until golden brown and crisp. Drain on absorbent kitchen paper.
5. Garnish with watercress sprigs and serve with Tartare Sauce.
*Serves 4*

# LAMB PAPRIKA

40 g (1½ oz) butter or margarine

8 best end of neck chops, trimmed

2 medium onions, skinned and chopped

450 g (1 lb) tomatoes, skinned, quartered and seeded

15 ml (1 tbsp) chopped fresh parsley

5–10 ml (1–2 level tsp) paprika

salt

142 ml (5 fl oz) soured cream or natural yogurt

1. Melt the butter in a large frying pan and brown the chops on both sides, then remove from the pan. Fry the onions in the fat for about 5 minutes, or until golden brown.
2. Add the tomatoes, parsley, paprika and salt to taste, replace the chops, cover and simmer gently for about 30 minutes, until tender.
3. Stir in the cream, adjust the seasoning and reheat without boiling.
*Serves 4*

## GREEK LAMB

| |
|---|
| 45 ml (3 tbsp) olive oil |
| 900 g (2 lb) small new potatoes, scraped, or old potatoes, peeled and cut into cubes |
| 1.25 kg (2½ lb) boned shoulder of lamb, cut into cubes |
| 2 large onions, skinned and sliced |
| 15 ml (1 tbsp) flour |
| 300 ml (½ pint) dry white wine |
| 350 g (12 oz) tomatoes, skinned and chopped |
| 30 ml (2 tbsp) wine vinegar |
| 2 cinnamon sticks |
| 2 bay leaves |
| 15 ml (1 tbsp) chopped fresh thyme or 5 ml (1 tsp) dried |
| salt and pepper |
| thyme sprigs, to garnish |

Greek Lamb

**1.** Heat 30 ml (2 tbsp) of the oil in a large flameproof casserole. Pierce each potato (or potato cube) with a sharp knife, add to the casserole and fry over moderate heat until golden on all sides. Remove from the oil with a slotted spoon and drain on absorbent kitchen paper.
**2.** Heat the remaining oil in the casserole, add the lamb and onions and fry over moderate heat until browned on all sides. Sprinkle in the flour and fry 1 further minute, stirring until absorbed.
**3.** Pour the wine into the casserole and add the tomatoes and wine vinegar. Bring slowly to the boil, then lower the heat and add the cinnamon, bay leaves, chopped thyme and seasoning to taste. Cover and simmer gently for 1 hour, stirring occasionally.

**4.** Add the fried potatoes to the casserole and continue simmering for a further 1 hour, or until the lamb and potatoes are tender. Remove the cinnamon sticks and bay leaves, then taste and adjust seasoning. Garnish with thyme sprigs and serve immediately.
Note If you find the thought of boning a shoulder of lamb yourself too daunting, ask your butcher to do it. Be sure to give enough advance notice.
Serves 4–6

## LAMB AND KIDNEY BEAN CASSEROLE

| |
|---|
| 125 g (4 oz) dried red kidney beans, soaked overnight |
| 15 ml (1 tbsp) vegetable oil |
| 1 large breast of lamb, trimmed and cut into 5 cm (2 inch) pieces |
| 450 g (1 lb) leeks, washed, trimmed and cut into 1 cm (½ inch) pieces |
| 1 bay leaf |
| 450 ml (¾ pint) Chicken Stock (see page 19) |
| 1 garlic clove, skinned and crushed |
| salt and pepper |
| 125 g (4 oz) garlic sausage, cut into bite-size pieces |

**1.** Drain the beans and place in a large saucepan. Cover with fresh water, bring to the boil and boil for 10 minutes, then reduce the heat and simmer for 30 minutes. Drain.
**2.** Meanwhile, heat the oil in a flameproof casserole and fry the lamb until browned. Remove from the casserole with a slotted spoon, then brown the leeks in the remaining fat.
**3.** Replace the meat with the drained beans, bay leaf, stock, garlic and seasoning and bring to the boil.
**4.** Add the garlic sausage to the casserole. Cover tightly and simmer gently for about 1¼ hours.
Serves 4

## NAVARIN OF LAMB

1 kg (2¼ lb) best end of neck or shoulder of lamb,
    trimmed and cut into 2.5 cm (1 inch) cubes

30 ml (2 tbsp) vegetable oil

5 ml (1 level tsp) sugar

15 ml (1 level tbsp) flour

900 ml (1½ pints) Beef Stock (see page 19)

30 ml (2 level tbsp) tomato purée

salt and pepper

bouquet garni

225 g (8 oz) button onions, skinned

4 medium carrots, peeled and sliced

1–2 small turnips, peeled and quartered

8 small, even-sized potatoes, peeled

113 g (4 oz) packet frozen peas (optional)

chopped fresh parsley, to garnish

1. Lightly fry the lamb on all sides in the oil. Stir in the sugar and heat until it browns slightly, then add the flour, stirring until it browns.

2. Remove from the heat and gradually stir in the stock. Bring to the boil, add the tomato purée, seasoning and bouquet garni, then cover and simmer for about 1 hour.

3. Remove the bouquet garni, add the onions, carrots and turnips and continue cooking for a further 30 minutes. Add the potatoes and continue cooking for about 20 minutes, until tender. Add the peas for the last 10 minutes, if using.

4. Transfer the meat to a warmed serving dish and garnish with the parsley.

Serves 4

Navarin of Lamb

## SPICED LAMB WITH WHOLEWHEAT

350 g (12 oz) wholewheat grain, washed and soaked in
   cold water overnight

75 ml (5 tbsp) vegetable oil or ghee

2 medium onions, skinned and finely chopped

2 garlic cloves, skinned and finely chopped

5 cm (2 inch) piece root ginger, peeled and finely
   chopped

5 ml (1 level tsp) black cumin seeds

4 green cardamoms

4 cloves

5–7.5 ml (1–1½ level tsp) mild chilli powder

2.5 ml (½ level tsp) ground turmeric

30 ml (2 tbsp) chopped fresh coriander leaves

15 ml (1 tbsp) chopped fresh mint leaves

700 g (1½ lb) fillet of lamb, cut into 2.5 cm (1 inch)
   pieces

7.5 ml (1½ level tsp) salt

284 g (10 oz) natural yogurt

75 ml (5 tbsp) lemon juice

fresh coriander, to garnish

1.  Drain the wheat and place in a saucepan.
Add 1.4 litres (2½ pints) water and boil for about
40 minutes, until tender. Drain.
2.  Heat the oil in a large heavy-based saucepan.
Add the onions and fry for about 10 minutes,
stirring, until a deep golden colour. Remove with
a slotted spoon and place in a blender or food
processor. Add the garlic and the ginger and blend
to a smooth paste.
3.  Reheat the oil in the pan, add the ground
onion mixture and continue frying for another
few minutes. Then add the cumin seeds,
cardamoms, cloves, chilli powder, turmeric and
the chopped coriander and mint. Fry for a further
8–10 minutes, stirring frequently, until a rich
golden colour.
4.  Add the meat and salt and fry for about 40
minutes, stirring frequently, until the meat is well
browned and nearly tender. Stir in the yogurt and
fry for another 10 minutes, stirring, until the meat
is tender and the yogurt well blended. Add 300 ml
(½ pint) water, stir well and simmer for another 10
minutes.
5.  Add the reserved wheat and the lemon juice
and stir well. Reheat but do not allow to boil.
Garnish with fresh coriander and serve with
chapatis and poppadums.
*Serves 4*

**Chapatis** are large unleavened griddle cakes which
can be bought from shops specialising in Eastern
foods, or made at home (see page 452).
**Poppadums** are wafer-thin savoury biscuits that
can be bought dried. To cook, fry one at a time in
a little hot fat until crisp, holding them down with
a spoon as they swell in cooking; alternatively heat
for 1–2 minutes under a hot grill.

## LANCASHIRE HOT POT

8 middle neck chops, about 900 g (2 lb) in weight,
   trimmed

175 g (6 oz) lamb's kidneys

40 g (1½ oz) lard or dripping or 45 ml (3 tbsp) vegetable
   oil

450 g (1 lb) leeks, trimmed, cut into 1 cm (½ inch) slices
   and washed

2 medium carrots, peeled and thickly sliced

900 g (2 lb) potatoes, peeled and thinly sliced

5 ml (1 level tsp) dried thyme

salt and pepper

600 ml (1 pint) Beef Stock (see page 19)

1.  Skin, halve and core the kidneys and divide
each half into three or four pieces.
2.  Heat the lard in a frying pan and brown the
lamb, a few chops at a time. Lightly brown the
kidneys.
3.  In a 3.4 litre (6 pint) ovenproof casserole, layer
the meats, leeks, carrots and three quarters of
the potatoes, sprinkling the thyme and seasoning
between the layers. Pour in the stock and top with
a neat layer of overlapping potato slices. Brush
with the lard remaining in the frying pan.
4.  Cover the casserole and cook in the oven
at 170°C (325°F) mark 3 for 2 hours. Uncover,
increase the temperature to 220°C (425°F) mark 7
and continue cooking for about 30 minutes, until
the potatoes are golden brown and crisp.
*Serves 4*

# IRISH STEW

8 middle neck chops, about 900 g (2 lb) in weight,
    trimmed

900 g (2 lb) potatoes, peeled and sliced

2 large onions, skinned and sliced

15 ml (1 level tbsp) pearl barley

salt and pepper

**1.** Place alternate layers of meat and vegetables in a saucepan, sprinkling each layer with a little pearl barley; season and finish with a layer of potatoes.
**2.** Add sufficient water to half cover. Cover and simmer very slowly for 3 hours. Alternatively, cook the stew in a casserole in the oven at 180°C (350°F) mark 4 for about 2½ hours. Serve sprinkled with chopped parsley, if liked.
*Serves 4*

# MOUSSAKA

450 g (1 lb) aubergines, sliced

salt and pepper

2 large onions, skinned and sliced

1 garlic clove, skinned and finely chopped

90 ml (6 tbsp) vegetable oil

700 g (1½ lb) minced lamb

15 ml (1 level tbsp) flour

397 g (14 oz) can tomatoes

284 g (10 oz) natural yogurt

2 eggs, beaten

1.25 ml (¼ level tsp) grated nutmeg

25 g (1 oz) grated Parmesan cheese

**1.** Place the aubergine slices in a colander, sprinkling each layer with salt. Cover and leave for 30 minutes to extract the bitter juices.

**2.** Meanwhile, fry the onions and garlic in 30 ml (2 tbsp) oil for 5 minutes, until golden. Add the meat and fry for a further 10 minutes, until browned, then add the flour and cook for 1 minute. Add the tomatoes with their juice, season and simmer for 20 minutes.
**3.** Drain the aubergine slices, rinse and pat dry. Heat the remaining oil in a frying pan and fry the aubergine slices for 4–5 minutes, turning once. Add more oil, if necessary.
**4.** Arrange a layer of aubergine in the bottom of a large ovenproof dish and spoon over a layer of meat. Continue the layers until all the meat and aubergines are used.
**5.** Beat the yogurt, eggs, seasoning and nutmeg together and stir in half the Parmesan. Pour over the dish and sprinkle with the remaining cheese. Bake in the oven at 180°C (350°F) mark 4 for about 45 minutes, until golden.
*Serves 4–6*

# STUFFED VINE LEAVES (Dolmas)

227 g (8 oz) packet vine leaves in brine

15 ml (1 tbsp) olive oil

1 medium onion, skinned and finely chopped

450 g (1 lb) minced lamb

50 g (2 oz) long grain white rice, cooked

30 ml (2 tbsp) chopped fresh mint or 5 ml (1 level tsp)
    dried mint

salt and pepper

450 ml (¾ pint) Chicken Stock (see page 19)

natural yogurt, to serve

**1.** Drain the brine from the vine leaves, put them in a large bowl and pour over boiling water. Rinse well to remove excess salt.
**2.** Heat the oil in a frying pan, add the onions and

cook for 5 minutes, until browned. Remove from the heat and add the lamb, rice, mint and seasoning. Mix well.
**3.** Spread out three quarters of the vine leaves on a flat surface and spoon a little of the lamb mixture over each. Fold the leaves over to make small, neat parcels. Arrange some of the remaining vine leaves in a large saucepan.
**4.** Arrange half the dolmas close together in a layer, then cover with more vine leaves. Add another layer of dolmas. Pour over the stock and cover with a small plate. Bring to the boil and simmer for 45 minutes.
**5.** Lift the dolmas from the cooking liquid and arrange on a warmed serving dish. Serve with natural yogurt.
*Serves 4–6*

## LAMB KEBABS

thick slice of lamb taken from the leg, about 700 g
    (1½ lb) in weight, trimmed and cut into 2.5 cm
    (1 inch) cubes

45 ml (3 tbsp) olive oil

15 ml (1 tbsp) lemon juice

15 ml (1 tbsp) chopped fresh rosemary

salt and pepper

1 garlic clove, skinned and crushed

8 small tomatoes, halved

16 button mushrooms

bay leaves

4 small onions, quartered

1 sweetcorn cob, boiled and sliced

**1.** Marinate the lamb for 2 hours (or preferably overnight) in the olive oil, lemon juice, rosemary, seasoning and garlic.
**2.** Remove with a slotted spoon, reserving the marinade.
**3.** Thread eight skewers alternately with meat cubes, tomatoes, mushrooms, bay leaves, onions and slices of sweetcorn.
**4.** Brush with the marinade and cook under a low grill for 10–15 minutes, turning the kebabs about three times, until the meat is tender. Serve on boiled rice with lemon wedges.
*Serves 4*

Lamb Kebabs

# MIDDLE EASTERN MEATBALLS

2 medium aubergines, sliced

salt and freshly ground pepper

150 ml (¼ pint) vegetable oil

450 g (1 lb) boneless lamb

2 thick slices of white bread, crusts removed

1 small onion, skinned

10 ml (2 level tsp) ground cumin

plain flour, for coating

450 g (1 lb) tomatoes, skinned and chopped

15 ml (1 tbsp) tomato purée

150 ml (¼ pint) Chicken Stock (see page 19)

2.5 ml (½ level tsp) ground allspice

vegetable oil for deep frying

*Middle Eastern Meatballs*

1. Layer the aubergine slices in a colander, sprinkling each layer with salt. Cover with a plate, weight down and leave for 30 minutes.
2. Drain the aubergine slices, rinse and dry well. In a large frying pan, fry for 4–5 minutes in the oil, turning once. Drain on absorbent kitchen paper.
3. Put the lamb through the blades of a mincer or food processor twice with the fried aubergines, bread and onion.
4. In a bowl, mix the minced meat with the cumin and seasoning to taste. Chill for 30 minutes until firm.
5. Meanwhile put the tomatoes, tomato purée, allspice and stock in a large flanged casserole. Season. Bring to the boil and simmer for 10 minutes until thick.

6. With well-floured hands, form the mixture into 30 balls. Chill in the refrigerator for 30 minutes.
7. Heat the oil for deep fat frying and fry the meatballs in batches until golden, about 3 minutes. Drain and add to the casserole.
8. Bring slowly to boiling point, then cover and simmer gently for 30 minutes. Shake the casserole frequently during this time so that the meatballs become saturated in the sauce.
9. Taste and, if necessary, adjust the seasoning of the tomato sauce before serving.
*Serves 6*

# BLANQUETTE OF LAMB

700 g (1½ lb) lean shoulder of lamb, diced

100 g (4 oz) carrots, peeled and sliced

1 medium onion, skinned and sliced

2 celery sticks, trimmed and sliced

1 bay leaf

5 ml (1 level tsp) dried thyme

salt and pepper

300 ml (½ pint) Beef Stock (see page 19)

30 ml (2 tbsp) butter or margarine, softened

45 ml (3 level tbsp) flour

1 egg yolk

30 ml (2 tbsp) single cream

chopped fresh parsley, to garnish

1. Put the meat, carrots, onion, celery, herbs and seasoning in a large saucepan. Pour in the stock, cover and simmer for 1½ hours.
2. Blend together the butter and flour, then add to the stew in small knobs and stir until thickened. Simmer for 10 minutes.
3. Blend together the egg yolk and cream, add to the stew and reheat without boiling. Adjust the seasoning. Garnish with parsley before serving.
*Serves 4*

PORK can be bought all the year round due to modern refrigeration. It is particularly good value during the summer. All joints can be roasted and the individual cuts from them grilled or fried. In addition, the forequarter cuts can be used for casseroles, stews and pies.

The lean part of pork should be pale pink, moist and slightly marbled with fat. There should be a good outer layer of firm, white fat with a thin, elastic skin. Small pinkish bones denote a young animal. If the joint is to be roasted either get the butcher to score the rind or use a sharp knife.

## CUTS AND METHODS OF COOKING

**Neck End (spare rib and blade bone)** is a large, economical roasting joint, particularly good when boned, stuffed and rolled. Often divided into *blade* and *spare rib*. These two smaller cuts can also be roasted, braised or stewed. Spare rib pork makes the best filling for pies. Spare rib chops are suitable for braising, grilling or frying.

**Hand and spring** is a large roasting joint, often divided into the smaller cuts, *hand* and *shank*. As well as being suitable for roasting, hand and shank can be used for casseroles and stews.

**Belly** is a long, thin cut with streaks of fat and lean meat. Stuffed thick end of belly makes an economical roast. Because belly is sometimes rather fatty, it is better used sliced for grilling and frying, rather than for braising and stewing.

**Spare ribs (American)** are from the belly and are removed in one piece, leaving the meat between the rib bones. Chinese spare ribs are bones with a very small amount of meat on them. They are usually barbecued or used in Chinese dishes.

**Leg** can be cut into four or more succulent and popular roasting joints, often divided into *fillet end* and *knuckle end*. The fillet end (the top of the leg) is the prime roasting joint, which can be boned and stuffed. It is sometimes sliced into steaks for grilling

and frying. The feet (trotters) are usually salted and boiled or used to make brawn.

**Loin** is a popular roast on the bone or boned, stuffed and rolled. Often divided into *loin chops* (with or without kidney) and large, meaty *chump chops*, both of which are excellent for grilling, frying or roasting. Produces good crackling.

**Tenderloin** is a tender, lean cut, found underneath the backbone of the loin, in the same position as beef fillet. It is sometimes called pork fillet, not to be confused with the fillet end of the leg. Most often served sliced or cubed for frying, or coated with a sauce. Can be stuffed and rolled for roasting.

**Crackling** For good crackling, score the rind deeply and evenly. Brush the cut surface with oil and rub salt into the scoring. Place the joint, with the rind uppermost, in a roasting tin. Do not baste the pork during cooking. Alternatively, the rind can be removed before cooking, treated in the same way, and roasted separately until crisp and golden.

**Calculating quantities for all meats**, see page 91.

**General roasting**, see page 92.

**Accompaniments** apple, gooseberry or cranberry sauce with sage and onion stuffing when appropriate. Try baked or fried apples or redcurrant jelly as an alternative.

## GRILLING AND FRYING PORK

*4 pork chops*

*30 ml (2 tbsp) vegetable oil*

Trim any excess fat from the chops. Large loin chops often have a thick strip of fat around the edge. To prevent this fat curling during cooking, snip it with scissors at 2.5 cm (1 inch) intervals.

**Frying**

1. Heat the oil in a large frying pan and add the chops. Cook for about 20 minutes, turning them frequently.

**Grilling**

1. Brush the chops with the oil. Place on the grill pan. Grill the chops for about 8–10 minutes each side. Serve with Apple Sauce (see page 207).

*Serves 4*

# ROAST PORK TENDERLOIN

3 pork tenderloins, about 900 g (2 lb) total weight

125 g (4 oz) streaky bacon, rinded

150 ml (¼ pint) dry white wine

300 ml (½ pint) Chicken Stock (see page 19)

10 ml (2 level tsp) arrowroot

parsley sprigs, to garnish

**For the stuffing**

175 g (6 oz) mushrooms, wiped and roughly chopped

1 medium onion, skinned and finely chopped

50 g (2 oz) butter or margarine

125 g (4 oz) fresh breadcrumbs

15 ml (1 tbsp) chopped fresh sage or 5 ml (1 level tsp) dried rubbed sage

salt and pepper

1 egg, beaten

**1.** To make the stuffing, fry the mushrooms and onion in 25 g (1 oz) butter until golden, then remove from the heat. Mix in the breadcrumbs and sage with seasoning and bind with egg, cool.

**2.** Carefully trim any skin and excess fat from the pork tenderloins and slit lengthways, three quarters of the way through each tenderloin. Open the meat out so that it is as flat as possible.

**3.** Spread one piece of meat with half of the mushroom mixture. Top with another of the tenderloins. Spread over the remaining stuffing and top with remaining tenderloin.

**4.** Stretch out each bacon rasher thinly, using a knife. Wrap up the meat in the bacon rashers and tie with string to form a joint.

**5.** Put the pork parcel in a small roasting tin and spread the remaining butter over the top and season well. Pour the wine around and roast in the oven at 180°C (350°F) mark 4 for about 1¼ hours, basting frequently. Lift on to a warmed serving platter, and remove string. Keep warm.

**6.** Add the stock to the pan and bring to the boil. Blend the arrowroot with 20 ml (4 tsp) water to a smooth paste and add to pan, stirring. Boil for 1 minute, then adjust the seasoning. Garnish.
*Serves 6*

# CROWN ROAST OF PORK

two 2–2.3 kg (4½–5 lb) fore loins of pork, chined, each with 7–8 cutlets

salt

½ quantity Sage and Onion Stuffing (see page 184)

watercress, to garnish

**1.** With fat side of pork skin uppermost, slice skin across the width into 0.5 mm (¼ inch) strips. Then slice into 6.5 cm (2½ inch) lengths. Retain a third, placing the rest on a mesh wire trivet in a roasting tin. Sprinkle with salt. Roast below the joint until the crackling is crisp (1½–2 hours).

**2.** Cut along length of joint through to the bones and trim each bone to a depth of 1 cm (½ inch)— not further as flesh shrinks during cooking. Finely chop the lean meat and add to the stuffing.

**3.** Lay the joint on the board with fat side down, eye towards you. Make a narrow incision between cutlet bones.

*Cut around the bones.*

Slice down through the eye of the meat to a depth of 2.5 cm (1 inch). Cut through the fat at base of the joint. (As pork is thicker than lamb it's necessary to open out joint.)

**4.** Prepare the second loin in the same way as the first. Sew the joints together to form one long piece using a trussing needle and fine string. Make sure that the string goes around the end bone on each joint to prevent it tearing the flesh away.

**5.** Stand the joints up with the eye of the meat as the base, bend around with the fat inside and sew together to form a crown shape.

**6.** Place the crown in a large roasting tin and tie two rows of string around the base. Spoon the stuffing into the centre, pushing down well to plump out the crown shape. Shape the stuffing into a dome at the level of the bone tips. Cover the exposed bones with foil and place the reserved strips of pork on top of the stuffing. Sprinkle with salt and weigh the joint.

**7.** Roast in the oven at 180°C (350°F) mark 4 for 30 minutes per 450 g (1 lb) plus 30 minutes, basting frequently. (When done the juices should run clear, not pink.) To serve, lift on to a serving plate. Remove foil and string and garnish with watercress.
*Serves 7–8*

*Pork Loin in Cider*

## PORK LOIN IN CIDER

600 ml (1 pint) dry cider

1.8 kg (4 lb) loin of pork, boned with rind on

salt and pepper

1 medium onion, skinned

30 ml (2 tbsp) vegetable oil

175 g (6 oz) carrots, peeled and cut into matchsticks

2 bay leaves

15 ml (1 level tbsp) cornflour

**For the stuffing**

50 g (2 oz) butter or margarine

125 g (4 oz) streaky bacon, rinded and diced

1 medium onion, skinned and chopped

225 g (8 oz) button or cup mushrooms, chopped

15 ml (1 tbsp) chopped fresh sage or 5 ml (1 level tsp)
    dried rubbed sage

125 g (4 oz) fresh breadcrumbs

1 egg, beaten

**1.** Pour the cider into a small saucepan and boil to reduce by half. Remove the rind and most of the fat from the pork and cut into thin fingers. Place these in a small roasting tin. Sprinkle with salt and set aside.

**2.** Slit the loin of pork along the eye of the meat three quarters of the way through, from the centre outwards. Open out so that it forms a long roll.

**3.** To make the stuffing, melt half the butter in a frying pan, add the bacon and onion and cook slowly until the bacon fat runs and the ingredients begin to brown. Increase the heat, add the mushrooms and cook until all excess moisture has evaporated.

**4.** Turn out into a large bowl and stir in the sage, breadcrumbs and enough egg to bind. Season, mix well and cool.

**5.** Spread the cold stuffing over the pork, roll up and tie at regular intervals. Slice the remaining onion. Heat the oil and remaining butter in a flameproof casserole and brown the joint. Remove from the pan.

*Spread the cold stuffing over the pork, then roll up before securely tying.*

**6.** Add the sliced onion and carrots to the remaining fat in the casserole and lightly brown. Replace the meat and pour the reduced cider around. Add the bay leaves and seasoning and bring to the boil.

**7.** Cover tightly and bake in the oven at 170°C (325°F) mark 3. Place the roasting tin of pork rind and fat above and cook both for about 2 hours.

**8.** Lift the pork out of the casserole with any stuffing that has oozed out and slice, discarding the string. Remove the vegetables from the casserole and arrange on a warmed serving plate with the sliced pork, cover and keep warm.

**9.** Mix the cornflour to a smooth paste with 30 ml (2 tbsp) water and stir into the pan juices. Bring to the boil, stirring. Boil for 2 minutes. To serve, garnish with the crackling strips. Serve the gravy separately.

*Serves 6*

# ROAST HAND OF PORK

2.5 kg (5½ lb) hand of pork

10 ml (2 level tsp) dried sage

vegetable oil

salt and pepper

20 ml (4 level tsp) flour

450 ml (¾ pint) Beef Stock (see page 19)

gravy browning

**1.** Score the pork rind all over with a sharp knife.
**2.** Rub the sage into the score lines, then rub in oil and sprinkle liberally with salt.

**3.** Place the joint on a trivet (or strong wire cooling rack) in or over a roasting tin. Roast in the oven at 180°C (350°F) mark 4 for 30 minutes per 450 g (1 lb) plus 30 minutes, until the pork is tender.
**4.** Slip the crackling off the pork and divide into pieces using a sharp knife; keep warm uncovered. Carve the meat and keep warm, loosely covered.
**5.** Drain off all but 30 ml (2 tbsp) of the fat in the roasting tin, then stir in the flour and cook until brown. Stir in the stock, cook until thickened, then add a dash of gravy browning and season. Serve the gravy separately.
*Serves 8*

# BEAN AND PORK PATTIES

125 g (4 oz) dried aduki beans, soaked in cold water
    overnight

225 g (8 oz) minced pork

2 garlic cloves, skinned

25 g (1 oz) fresh breadcrumbs

7.5 ml (1½ level tsp) crushed dried rosemary

1 large onion, skinned and finely chopped

1 egg, beaten

salt and pepper

30 ml (2 level tbsp) flour

45 ml (3 tbsp) vegetable oil

450 g (1 lb) tomatoes, skinned, seeded and roughly
    chopped

5 ml (1 level tsp) sugar

10 ml (2 tsp) Worcestershire sauce

10 ml (2 tsp) soy sauce

20 ml (4 level tsp) mango chutney

5 ml (1 tsp) cider vinegar

450 ml (¾ pint) Chicken Stock (see page 19)

15 ml (1 level tbsp) cornflour

**1.** Drain the beans, rinse under cold running water, then place in a large saucepan. Cover with water and bring to the boil. Simmer for 30 minutes, until the beans are tender. Drain well.
**2.** Mash the beans and mix with the pork, 1 crushed garlic clove, the breadcrumbs, rosemary, half the onion and bind with the egg. Season. Shape into sixteen balls, roll in the flour and flatten into patties.

*Bean and Pork Patties*

**3.** Fry the patties in the oil for about 15 minutes, until well browned. Drain on absorbent kitchen paper and place in an ovenproof dish.
**4.** Crush the remaining garlic clove and fry with the remaining onion and tomatoes in the oil left in the pan. Add the rest of the ingredients, except the cornflour, season well and simmer for about 10 minutes. Mix the cornflour to a smooth paste with 30 ml (2 tbsp) water and stir into the sauce. Bring to the boil, stirring. Boil for 2 minutes, then pour over the patties.
**5.** Cover and cook in the oven at 180°C (350°F) mark 4 for about 30 minutes.
*Serves 4*

## PORK CHOPS WITH ORANGE SAUCE

| 4 large pork chump chops, rinded |
| 30 ml (2 level tbsp) seasoned flour |
| 30 ml (2 tbsp) vegetable oil |
| 2 large thin-skinned oranges |
| 60 ml (4 level tbsp) light soft brown sugar |
| 15 ml (1 level tbsp) cornflour |
| 150 ml (¼ pint) dry white wine |
| 300 ml (½ pint) orange juice |
| salt and pepper |
| 1 medium onion, skinned and sliced |
| watercress, to garnish |

1. Coat the chops in seasoned flour.
2. Heat the oil in a large frying pan and fry the chops quickly on either side until well browned.

Drain and place in a shallow casserole.
3. Peel the oranges, removing all traces of white pith. Slice, discarding the pips, and cut each slice in half, reserving any juice. Sprinkle with 30 ml (2 tbsp) sugar and set aside.
4. Blend the cornflour with a little of the wine. Pour the rest of the wine into a small pan, with the reserved orange juice and the 300 ml (½ pint) orange juice and remaining sugar. Add the blended cornflour mixture and bring to the boil, stirring. Season, then pour over the chops.
5. Arrange the onion over the chops, cover tightly and cook in the oven at 180°C (350°F) mark 4 for 1¼–1½ hours. Remove the lid, arrange the orange slices over the onion and cook for a further 15–20 minutes, basting occasionally. Garnish.
*Serves 4*

## BAKED STUFFED PORK CHOPS

| 50 g (2 oz) long grain brown rice |
| salt and pepper |
| 30 ml (2 tbsp) vegetable oil |
| 4 spare rib pork chops, trimmed and boned |
| 1 small onion, skinned and finely chopped |
| 50 g (2 oz) raisins |
| 226 g (8 oz) can pineapple cubes, drained with juice reserved |
| 45 ml (3 tbsp) chopped fresh parsley |

1. Cook the rice in plenty of boiling salted water for about 35 minutes, until tender. Drain well.

2. Heat the oil in a large frying pan and brown the chops. Allow to cool, then slit three quarters of the way through each chop to form a large pocket.
3. Meanwhile, brown the onion in the oil remaining in the pan. Stir in the raisins with the pineapple, cooked rice, parsley and seasoning.
4. Place the chops in a shallow ovenproof dish and spoon the rice mixture into the prepared pockets. Spoon over 60 ml (4 tbsp) pineapple juice. Season.
5. Cover the dish tightly and cook in the oven at 180°C (350°F) mark 4 for 1–1¼ hours. Baste once with the juice during cooking.
*Serves 4*

## NORMANDY PORK

| 300 ml (½ pint) dry white wine |
| 225 g (8 oz) button mushrooms, wiped and sliced |
| 900 g (2 lb) pork fillet, cut into thick strips |
| 30 ml (2 level tbsp) seasoned flour |
| 25 g (1 oz) butter or margarine |
| 15 ml (1 tbsp) vegetable oil |
| 30 ml (2 tbsp) Calvados |
| 2 large cooking apples, peeled, cored and thinly sliced |
| 30 ml (2 tbsp) chopped fresh parsley |
| 150 ml (5 fl oz) double cream |
| salt and pepper |

1. Bring the wine to the boil in a small saucepan, add the mushrooms and simmer, covered, for 10–15 minutes.
2. Toss the pork strips in the seasoned flour.
3. Heat the butter and oil in a frying pan and brown the pork. Warm the Calvados in a small pan, set it alight and when the flames die down, pour it over the meat.
4. Add the wine, mushrooms and apples to the pork and simmer, covered, for 30 minutes, until tender.
5. Add the parsley and cream to the juices in the pan and simmer without boiling until the sauce thickens slightly. Adjust the seasoning.
*Serves 6*

## PORK ESCALOPES WITH SAGE

450 g (1 lb) pork fillet, trimmed and cut into 0.5 cm
   (¼ inch) slices

1 egg, beaten

125 g (4 oz) fresh breadcrumbs

10 ml (2 level tsp) dried sage

grated rind of 1 lemon

50 g (2 oz) butter or margarine

15 ml (1 tbsp) vegetable oil

lemon wedges, to garnish

**1.** Flatten the pork between two sheets of damp greaseproof paper into thin escalopes.
**2.** Dip the escalopes in the egg.
**3.** Mix together the breadcrumbs, sage and lemon rind and coat the pork escalopes.
**4.** Heat the butter and oil in a large frying pan, add half the escalopes and cook for 2–3 minutes each side, until golden brown. Keep warm whilst cooking the remaining escalopes. Garnish with lemon wedges to serve.
*Serves 4*

## BARBECUED SPARE RIBS

30 ml (2 tbsp) vegetable oil

2 medium onions, skinned and chopped

1 garlic clove, skinned and crushed

30 ml (2 level tbsp) tomato purée

60 ml (4 tbsp) malt vinegar

1.25 ml (¼ level tsp) dried thyme

1.25 ml (¼ level tsp) chilli seasoning

45 ml (3 level tbsp) honey

150 ml (¼ pint) Beef Stock (see page 19)

1 kg (2¼ lb) spare ribs (American cut)

**1.** Heat the oil in a saucepan, add the onions and cook for 5 minutes, until softened. Add all the remaining ingredients, except the spare ribs, and simmer gently for 10 minutes.
**2.** Place the spare ribs in a roasting tin in a single layer and brush with a little of the sauce.
**3.** Roast in the oven at 190°C (375°F) mark 5 for 30 minutes, then pour off the fat and spoon the remaining sauce over the meat. Cook for a further 1–1¼ hours, basting occasionally.
*Serves 4*

## SWEET-SOUR PORK BALLS

450 g (1 lb) pork, minced

1 garlic clove, skinned and crushed

45 ml (3 level tbsp) flour

50 g (2 oz) fresh breadcrumbs

salt and pepper

1 egg yolk, beaten

30 ml (2 tbsp) vegetable oil

**For the sauce**

75 g (3 oz) soft brown sugar

60 ml (4 tbsp) cider vinegar

45 ml (3 tbsp) soy sauce

45 ml (3 level tbsp) tomato ketchup

227 g (8 oz) can pineapple pieces in natural juice,
   drained with juice reserved

30 ml (2 level tbsp) cornflour

300 ml (½ pint) water

1 medium green pepper, blanched and cut in thin strips

**1.** Mix together the pork, garlic, 15 ml (1 level tbsp) flour, breadcrumbs and seasoning. Stir in the egg yolk and mix well.
**2.** Form into twenty-four balls and toss in the remaining flour.
**3.** Heat the oil in a frying pan, add the balls and fry gently for 20 minutes, turning frequently, until golden. Drain on absorbent kitchen paper.
**4.** Meanwhile, put the sugar, vinegar, soy sauce and tomato ketchup in a saucepan. Make up the pineapple juice to 300 ml (½ pint) with water, blend in the cornflour and add to the pan. Bring to the boil, stirring, then simmer gently for 5 minutes. Add the pineapple and green pepper and simmer for a further 5–10 minutes.
**5.** Transfer the pork balls to a warmed dish and pour over the sauce.
*Serves 4*

*Cassoulet*

# CASSOULET

225 g (8 oz) salt pork or bacon, in one piece

450 g (1 lb) loin or shoulder or pork, boned, rinded and
     cubed

30 ml (2 tbsp) vegetable oil or fat from preserved goose

2 medium onions, skinned and thinly sliced

3 garlic cloves, skinned and finely chopped

1.4 kg (3 lb) shoulder of lamb (or ½ a large shoulder),
     boned and cubed

1 piece of preserved goose

450 g (1 lb) piece coarse pork and garlic sausage, cut
     into large cubes

60 ml (4 tbsp) tomato purée

750 g (1½ lb) dried haricot beans, soaked overnight

salt and pepper

1 bouquet garni

100 g (4 oz) fresh breadcrumbs

1.  Remove the rind from the salt pork or bacon.
2.  Heat the oil or goose fat in a large frying
pan and fry the onions and garlic for 5 minutes,
until softened. Add the pieces of pork rind and
fry gently for 5 minutes. Using a slotted spoon,
remove the onion and rind and set aside.

3.  Raise the heat and add, in turn, the pork and
salt pork, the shoulder of lamb, the piece of goose
and the sausage, and fry until browned on all
sides. Remove each from the pan. Set aside.

4.  Add the tomato purée to the pan with 300 ml
(½ pint) cold water, stir well to amalgamate any
sediment and bring quickly to the boil.

5.  Drain the beans, rinse them under cold running
water and put them in a flameproof casserole
with 1.4 litres (2½ pints) cold water. Bring to the
boil, then add the contents of the frying pan with
salt and pepper to taste and stir well. Bury the
salt pork or bacon, the pork, shoulder of lamb,
preserved goose and sausage among the beans, add
the bouquet garni, and bring to simmering point.

6.  Sprinkle over a thick layer of breadcrumbs
(approximately one-third of the crumbs). Cook in
the oven at 150°C (300°F) mark 2 for 2–3 hours,
until the meat and beans are tender.

7.  From time to time press down the crust which
will have formed on top and sprinkle on two
further layers of breadcrumbs. Cut up larger
pieces of meat before serving.
*Serves 12*

# FRIKADELLER

450 g (1 lb) lean pork, cubed

1 small onion, skinned and quartered

salt and pepper

30 ml (2 level tbsp) flour

1 egg, beaten

a little milk

vegetable oil for deep frying

1.  Mince the meat and onion together twice.
Season and stir in the flour, egg and enough milk
to give a soft mixture that holds its shape; roll it
into small balls.

2.  Heat the oil in a deep fat fryer to 190°C (375°F)
and cook the meat balls for about 6 minutes, until
brown. Drain on absorbent kitchen paper and
serve with Fresh Tomato Sauce (see page 209).
*Serves 4*

# PORK KEBABS

450 g (1 lb) minced pork or lamb

1 large onion, skinned and grated

2 garlic cloves, skinned and crushed

1 green chilli, seeded and finely chopped

5 ml (1 level tsp) ground cumin

salt and pepper

grated rind and juice of 1 lemon

vegetable oil

lemon wedges and pitta bread to serve

1.  Thoroughly blend all ingredients except the oil
in a bowl. Cover and chill for at least an hour.

2.  Divide the meat mixture into 16 pieces and
shape into a thin strip about 10 cm (4 inch) long
and then roll up; or form into tight balls.

3.  Place four meat rolls on each lightly greased
skewer and brush lightly with the oil.

4.  Place the skewers under a hot grill rack and
grill for about 10 minutes, turning frequently for
even browning. Serve with lemon wedges and pitta
bread.
*Serves 4*

## RAISED PORK PIE

| |
|---|
| 3 or 4 small veal bones |
| 1 small onion, skinned |
| 1 bay leaf |
| 4 black peppercorns |
| 900 g (2 lb) boneless leg or shoulder of pork, cubed |
| 1.25 ml ($\frac{1}{4}$ level tsp) cayenne pepper |
| 1.25 ml ($\frac{1}{4}$ level tsp) ground ginger |
| 1.25 ml ($\frac{1}{4}$ level tsp) ground mace |
| 1.25 ml ($\frac{1}{4}$ level tsp) dried sage |
| 1.25 ml ($\frac{1}{4}$ level tsp) dried marjoram |
| 15 ml (1 level tbsp) salt |
| 2.5 ml ($\frac{1}{2}$ level tsp) pepper |
| 300 ml ($\frac{1}{2}$ pint) milk and water mixed |
| 150 g (5 oz) lard |
| 450 g (1 lb) plain flour |
| beaten egg, to glaze |

**1.** Put the bones, onion, bay leaf and peppercorns in a saucepan and cover with water. Simmer for 20 minutes, then boil to reduce the liquid to 150 ml ($\frac{1}{4}$ pint). Strain and cool.

**2.** Mix the pork with the spices and herbs, 5 ml (1 level tsp) salt and the pepper.

**3.** Bring the milk, water and lard to the boil in a saucepan, then gradually beat it into the flour and remaining salt in a bowl. Knead for 3–4 minutes.

**4.** Roll out two thirds of the pastry on a lightly floured surface and mould into a 20.5 cm (8 inch) base-lined, spring release cake tin. Cover and chill for 30 minutes. Keep the remaining pastry covered.

**5.** Spoon the meat mixture and 60 ml (4 tbsp) cold stock into the pastry case. Roll out the remaining pastry to make a lid and place on top of the meat mixture, sealing the pastry edges well. Decorate with pastry trimmings and make a hole in the centre. Glaze with the egg.

**6.** Bake at 220°C (425°F) mark 7 for 30 minutes. Cover loosely with foil, reduce heat to 180°C (350°F) mark 4 and bake for a further 2$\frac{1}{2}$ hours. Cool.

**7.** Warm the remaining jellied stock until liquid, then pour into the centre hole of the pie. Chill.
*Note* If you have no bones available for stock, use 10 ml (2 level tsp) gelatine to 300 ml ($\frac{1}{2}$ pint) stock.
*Serves 8*

### Variation
*RAISED VEAL AND HAM PIE*
Mix together 700 g (1$\frac{1}{2}$ lb) diced pie veal and 225 g (8 oz) diced cooked ham, 15 ml (1 tbsp) chopped fresh parsley, grated rind and juice of 1 lemon and seasoning and use to half fill the pie. Put one hard-boiled egg in the centre and cover with remaining veal mixture. Proceed as above.

*Raised Pork Pie*

BACON is made by curing fresh pork. There are several methods of curing which result in different flavours of bacon. The most common is the 'Wiltshire' cure which involves injecting whole sides, under pressure, with a special 'brine' or 'pickle'. This ensures even distribution of the curing salts throughout the muscles of the carcass. The brine contains permitted preservatives, which colour and flavour the meat.

A side of bacon (half a carcass, without the head and feet) may be cured whole, as in the Wiltshire cure, or cuts such as the middle may be cured separately, with or without their bones.

Bacon may be smoked after curing—hung over smouldering wood sawdust. Oak chippings or sawdust give the most distinctive flavouring. Unsmoked bacon is known as 'green', 'pale' or 'plain' bacon.

Quick cures Smaller cuts of meat may be cured by modern 'quick' cures. Parts of the side, such as middle and shoulder are cured separately. The curing solution is injected by machine into the lean and, unlike the Wiltshire method, the bacon is not then immersed in brine. The pieces are simply hung for 2–3 days. Bacon sold in vacuum packs as 'sweet', 'mild' or 'tender cure' has had sugar added to the curing brine.

Traditional cures As well as new quick methods of curing, developed by modern British curers, there are other traditional methods. In Scotland, the 'Ayrshire' method is as old as the Wiltshire cure. Instead of curing the whole side, the carcass is skinned, jointed, boned and formed into rolls, usually called Ayrshire gigot (hind leg), Ayrshire middle or Ayrshire shoulder. The rolls are injected with brine and then immersed in a brine cure.

## CUTS AND METHODS OF COOKING

Bacon is sold sliced and unpacked ('loose') or in airtight vacuum packs. Vacuum-packed bacon will remain moist until opened. After being opened it will gradually dry and deteriorate in a similar way to 'loose' bacon. Fresh 'loose' bacon has moist, lean, firm white fat and smooth rind. Green bacon has a pale rind and smoked bacon a deep brown rind. Local methods of cutting bacon sides make it difficult to describe all the available cuts. Gammon is the name given to whole hind legs cut from a side of bacon after curing. Joints of gammon and bacon vary in saltiness.

**Prime back** is lean and usually sold as rashers or boneless chops (thick rashers), which are grilled or fried. Alternatively, a thick piece can be used for boiling or braising.

**Prime streaky rashers** combine lean and fat and are best grilled or fried. Streaky bacon is used to line pâté dishes and can be chopped for casseroles, soups and rice dishes, stretched and rolled to make bacon rolls, or crispy fried snippets can be used as a garnish. A joint of streaky bacon is excellent boiled and pressed, to eat cold.

**Middle or throughcut rashers** are the back and streaky cut together, giving a long rasher with a balanced mix of lean and fat—an economical buy.

Use them for grilling or have a piece of middle cut rolled and use for boiling or baking—delicious used as a stuffed joint. With the rind removed, this is sometimes called Ayrshire Roll, as it is traditionally prepared in Scotland.

**Long back lean rashers** are best cut fairly thin for frying or grilling. Thick slices cut up well for casseroles, flans or pies.

**Middle gammon** is a prime, lean, meaty cut for boiling, braising or baking. Gammon rashers or steaks, about 1 cm ($\frac{1}{2}$ inch) thick, are usually cut from this joint. They are excellent grilled or fried.

**Corner gammon** is a small, economical, triangular cut off the gammon which can be boiled and served hot, with a parsley sauce, then sliced when cold for sandwiches.

**Gammon hock** gives succulent meat as a small boiling joint or cut up meat for casseroles, soups and pies.

**Prime collar** makes a good family joint boiled or braised. The collar joint can also be sliced into rashers. As a joint it may need to be soaked.

**Prime forehock**, another joint that is sometimes better soaked. A good meaty cut for casseroles or boiled as a joint, it is also a suitable cut for mincing.

**Bacon pieces** These offcuts when available are worth having for the occasions when small amounts of bacon are required minced or to lard lean joints of meat or poultry. Don't buy if they look on the dry side.

### BACON IN THE BAG

Joints are sometimes sold ready packed in film bags with special instructions for cooking. They can be cooked without the bags being removed; this has the advantage of keeping the joint a good shape and retaining the natural juices of the meat. Unlike vacuum packs of bacon, the film bag does not extend the keeping qualities of the contents.

### VACUUM-PACKED BACON

Bacon is widely sold in vacuum packets, which are hygienic and convenient both for the customer and the shopkeeper. Mostly rashers come packed in this way, but also small joints and gammon steaks. Vacuum packing extends the keeping qualities of bacon and packets are usually marked with a 'sell by' or 'best before' date. Once opened, use and treat as loose bacon.

As a guide, vacuum-packed rashers, chops, steaks and joints keep about 5 days without refrigeration, 15 days with refrigeration.

### STORAGE OF BACON

Store loose bacon in the refrigerator. Wrap closely in kitchen foil or cling film. Do not use greaseproof paper, which is porous and allows the bacon to dry out. Refrigerate for up to about a week.

### PREPARING RASHERS

Rind rashers thinly with kitchen scissors or a sharp knife, unless, of course, the bacon is bought already rinded. Remove any bone. Thick rashers, steaks or chops should be snipped at intervals along the fat edge to help them remain flat during cooking. If you suspect that chops, collar or gammon steaks are salty, soak them for a short time or poach in water for a few minutes, then throw away the water. Pat dry, using absorbent kitchen paper, and cook as desired.

For bacon rolls, use thin cut streaky rashers and remove the rind. Stretch the rashers by stroking along the length with the back of a knife. Do this on the work surface or a board. Either roll up the whole rasher or cut each in half crossways before rolling.

### COOKING RASHERS

For frying, overlap back bacon rashers in a cold pan with the lean parts over the fat. For grilling, heat the pan gently first, then arrange the bacon rashers on the rack with the fat parts overlapping the lean. Turn rashers halfway through cooking time, 3–5 minutes. Lean rashers are better brushed with fat or oil for grilling. Grill under a high heat, reducing the heat and turning the bacon over halfway through the cooking time, 3–5 minutes for rashers, 12–15 minutes for chops, 10–15 minutes for steaks, depending on thickness.

---

# HAM, strictly speaking, is the hind leg of a pig cut from the whole carcass, then cured and matured separately. Nowadays, cooked gammon is often described as ham. When selecting a whole ham, choose a short, thick leg without too much fat and a thin rind. More often than not hams are cooked prior to purchase but if not cook as for bacon.

## SOME OF THE BEST-KNOWN CURES

**York ham** is cured with dry salt and lightly smoked before being boiled. York ham is cut from the side near the oyster bone, which makes it a long shape. It is then rounded off. The meat is pale with a mild, delicate flavour. Average weight is 7–11 kg (16–24 lb).

**Bradenham ham**, rarely found today, is expensive. It is cured in a similar way to York ham and then pickled in molasses for a month. The cure turns the skin black and the meat rather red with a slightly sweet flavour. To cook, soak for 48–72 hours, drain and put in fresh cold water. Boil as for bacon.

**Suffolk ham** is sweet cured and has a rich red-brown meat with a 'blue' bloom. This ham, cured in beer and sugar or black molasses, has a deep golden, toasted look to the skin. It is not widely available today.

**Cumberland ham** is dry salted, with the addition of brown sugar.

**Belfast ham** is now almost entirely found in the West of Scotland. These hams are dry salted and traditionally smoked over peat.

**Honey-baked ham** is baked with a coating of honey, or honey and brown sugar.
**Virginia ham** is an American ham. A true Virginia ham comes from pigs fed on peanuts and peaches.
**Kentucky ham** is an American ham from pigs fattened on acorns, beans and cloves.

**Raw hams** All English hams need to be cooked but there are several hams from other countries produced specially for eating raw. The most famous is the proscuitto (raw ham) from Parma in Italy. Bayonne in France and Westphalia in Germany also produce notable raw hams.

## BOILED BACON JOINT

*1.4 kg (3 lb) piece of gammon, collar or forehock bacon*

*2 medium onions, skinned*

*2 medium carrots, peeled and thickly sliced*

*1 bay leaf*

*4 black peppercorns*

*Parsley or Onion Sauce (see page 201), to serve*

**1.** Weigh the joint. To remove the salt, place the joint in a large saucepan with enough cold water to cover, bring to the boil, then discard the water.
**2.** Calculate the cooking time allowing 20 minutes per 450 g (1 lb) plus 20 minutes. If the joint is over 4.5 kg (10 lb), allow 15–20 minutes per 450 g (1 lb) plus 15 minutes.
**3.** Place the joint in a large saucepan or preserving pan, add the flavouring vegetables, bay leaf and peppercorns, cover with cold water and bring slowly to the boil. Remove any scum with a slotted spoon. Cover and calculate the cooking time from this point.
**4.** When the bacon is cooked, ease off the rind and any excess fat and serve hot, sliced, with Parsley or Onion Sauce.
*Serves 6–8*

**Variations**
**1.** Add 300 ml ($\frac{1}{2}$ pint) cider after the flavouring vegetables and peppercorns and cover the joint with cold water.
**2.** To serve the joint cold, remove the rind and excess fat and roll it in toasted breadcrumbs. Leave to cool.

## BRAISED BACON

*1.4 kg (3 lb) piece of gammon, collar or forehock bacon*

*1 medium onion, skinned and sliced*

*4 medium carrots, peeled and sliced*

*1 small turnip, peeled and sliced*

*2 celery sticks, trimmed and sliced*

*45 ml (3 tbsp) vegetable oil*

*Chicken Stock (see page 19)*

*bouquet garni*

*salt and pepper*

*Parsley or Onion Sauce (see page 201), to serve*

**1.** Soak the gammon or bacon in plenty of cold water for 2–3 hours or place the joint in a large saucepan with enough cold water to cover, bring to the boil, then discard the water. Weigh the joint and calculate the cooking time, allowing 20 minutes per 450 g (1 lb) plus 20 minutes.
**2.** Place the joint in a large saucepan, cover with cold water and bring slowly to the boil. Remove any scum, cover and calculate the cooking time from this point.

**3.** Lightly fry the vegetables in the oil for 3–4 minutes. Put them in a casserole, put the bacon on top and add enough stock to cover the vegetables. Add the bouquet garni and the seasoning, cover and cook in the oven at 180°C (350°F) mark 4 for the remainder of the cooking time.
**4.** About 30 minutes before the end of the cooking time, remove the rind and continue cooking, uncovered, for the final 30 minutes. Remove the bouquet garni and serve with Parsley or Onion Sauce.
*Note* Some gammon or bacon joints are more salty than others and the soaking time will therefore vary accordingly. If possible, ask your butcher which cure was used and he will be able to advise more specifically on the length of the soaking time.
*Serves 6–8*

## BAKED AND GLAZED BACON JOINTS

Bacon joints may be boiled for half their cooking time (as calculated in Boiled Bacon Joint recipe) and then baked for the remainder of the cooking time.

Weigh the joint to calculate the cooking time and boil as above. Drain and wrap in foil. Place in a roasting tin and bake in the oven at 180°C (350°F) mark 4 until 30 minutes before the cooking time is complete. Increase the oven temperature to 220°C (425°F) mark 7. Remove the foil and rind from the bacon, score the fat in diamonds and stud with cloves. Sprinkle the surface with demerara sugar and pat in.

*Score the bacon fat and stud with cloves.*

Return the joint to the oven for 30 minutes, until crisp and golden. Alternatively glaze with one of the glazes below, and serve with Cumberland Sauce (see page 207).

**Spiced marmalade and honey glaze** In a small bowl, blend together 60 ml (4 level tbsp) fine shred marmalade, 75 ml (5 tbsp) clear honey and 4–5 drops Tabasco sauce. Brush about one third of the glaze over the bacon fat 30 minutes before the end of cooking time. Return to the oven for 10 minutes before applying the second glaze. Don't use the glaze that has run into the pan as this will dull the shine. Repeat with the final third.

**Sharp honey glaze** In a small saucepan, warm 15 ml (1 tbsp) clear honey and 30 ml (2 tbsp) vinegar. Strip off bacon rind. Pour the glaze over the bacon fat. Mix together equal quantities of brown sugar and golden breadcrumbs and sprinkle over the top. Return to the oven, basting frequently.

*Baked Bacon Joint served with Cumberland Sauce*

## BACON AND EGG PIE

*225 g (8 oz) Shortcrust Pastry (see page 372), made with 225 g (8 oz) flour*

*4 bacon rashers, rinded and chopped*

*4 eggs*

*60 ml (4 tbsp) milk*

*salt and pepper*

*2 tomatoes or 4 mushrooms, sliced (optional)*

1. Divide the pastry into two pieces—one slightly larger than the other. On a lightly floured surface, roll out the larger piece to a circle 2.5 cm (1 inch) wider than the top of an 18 cm (7 inch) deep pie dish and line the dish. Roll out the remaining pastry to form a lid.

2. Fry the bacon lightly in its own fat until transparent, then spread over the pastry base.
3. Whisk the eggs in a bowl and add the milk and seasoning. Pour over the bacon and add the tomatoes or mushrooms (if using).
4. Damp the edges of the pastry and cover with the lid, pressing the edges well together; flake and scallop the edge. Brush the top of the pie with the little egg remaining in the bowl.
5. Bake the pie on a baking sheet in the oven at 220°C (425°F) mark 7 for 15 minutes, then reduce the temperature to 180°C (350°F) mark 4 and cook for a further 30 minutes. Serve hot or cold. *Serves 4*

# HAM AND LEEKS AU GRATIN

| |
|---|
| medium leeks, washed and trimmed |
| salt and pepper |
| 50 g (2 oz) butter or margarine |
| 75 ml (5 level tbsp) flour |
| 568 ml (1 pint) milk |
| 100 g (4 oz) Cheddar cheese, grated |
| thin slices of cooked ham |
| 25 g (1 oz) fresh breadcrumbs |

1. Cook the leeks, in boiling, salted water for 10–15 minutes, until soft. Drain and keep warm.
2. Meanwhile, melt 40 g (1½ oz) butter, stir in the flour and cook gently for 1 minute. Remove the pan from the heat and gradually stir in the milk. Bring to the boil slowly and continue to cook, stirring until the sauce thickens. Stir in 75 g (3 oz) of the cheese and season.
3. Wrap each leek in a slice of ham, place in a flameproof dish and coat with sauce.
4. Mix together the breadcrumbs and remaining cheese and sprinkle over the top. Dot with the remaining butter and brown under the grill until golden.
Serves 4

**Variation**
Use 4 heads of chicory instead of the leeks, cooking for 15 minutes, until tender. Use only 4 slices of ham for wrapping the chicory heads.

# BACON CHOPS EN CROÛTE

| |
|---|
| 15 ml (1 level tbsp) flour |
| 5 ml (1 level tsp) soft brown sugar |
| 5 ml (1 level tsp) mustard powder |
| pepper |
| bacon chops, rinded |
| few drops of Tabasco sauce |
| fresh or canned pineapple rings |
| 125 g (4 oz) Bel Paese cheese, cut into 4 slices |
| 368 g (13 oz) packet frozen puff pastry, thawed |
| egg, beaten |

1. Mix together the flour, sugar, mustard and pepper. Toss the bacon chops in this mixture, one at a time. Place the chops on a board, sprinkle each with a little Tabasco sauce, place a pineapple ring in the centre and top with a slice of cheese.
2. Roll out the pastry thinly on a lightly floured surface. Cut into 4 squares, large enough to encase the chops. Place a chop in the centre of each piece of pastry. Moisten the edges of the pastry with a little water and fold over to cover the chops completely. Seal well. Place on a baking sheet. Chill for 30 minutes.
3. Glaze with a little beaten egg and cook in the oven at 220°C (425°F) mark 7 for 15–20 minutes. Reduce heat to 180°C (350°F) mark 4 for a further 25 minutes. Cover with foil if over browning.
Serves 4

# BREADED PORK TROTTERS

| |
|---|
| fresh or lightly pickled pig's trotters |
| salt and pepper |
| clove |
| bay leaf |
| celery stick, trimmed and roughly chopped |
| 100 g (4 oz) fresh breadcrumbs |
| medium onion, skinned and minced |
| vegetable oil for deep frying |
| chopped fresh parsley, to garnish |
| mustard, to serve |

1. Wash the trotters, place in tepid water with the salt, pepper, clove, bay leaf and celery and simmer gently for 2½ hours. Remove any scum that comes to the surface with a slotted spoon. Cut each trotter in half and remove the bones.
2. Mix together the breadcrumbs and onion and season with salt and pepper. Heat the oil in a deep fat fryer to 180°C (350°F). Dip the trotters in breadcrumb mixture, then fry until golden brown. Sprinkle with parsley and serve with mustard.
Serves 4

OFFAL is one of the most economical meats to buy; the strong flavour and lack of bones in most offal means that only small amounts are needed. The most popular offal meats are probably liver and kidney, but all offal can be used to make interesting and nutritious meals.

Offal must be very fresh and should be cooked as soon as possible as it goes off more quickly than other meat. It must not be overcooked or it will be tough.

## TYPES OF OFFAL

**Liver** The best liver is calf's, followed by lamb's, pig's and ox, which is coarse and strong flavoured. Calf's, lamb's and pig's liver can be grilled, fried or used in braised dishes. Pig's and ox livers are mainly used in stews and casseroles or minced for pâtés and stuffings. The strong flavour of ox and pig's livers can be mellowed by soaking for an hour in milk.

**Kidney** Calf's kidney is light in colour, delicately flavoured and considered the best. Lamb's kidney is darker than calf's, smaller and with a good flavour. Pig and ox kidneys have a much stronger flavour; ox kidney needs slow moist cooking. They are traditionally used in casseroles and pies. Kidneys should be cooked quickly to be tender and are most frequently grilled or fried. Remove the outer membrane, split in half lengthways and, using scissors, remove the white core and as many of the tubes as possible.

**Heart** Whole lamb's and pig's hearts are the most commonly available and one per portion is usually sufficient. Best results are achieved by pot roasting, braising or casseroling. An ox heart will weigh up to 1.8 kg (4 lb) and is best cut into cubes for stews and casseroles. Whole hearts are frequently stuffed. Wash thoroughly in cold water, trim away fat and tubes and snip the cavity walls. Leave to soak for an hour in clean, salt water. Rinse and drain. Cut across an ox heart and thus across the grain to increase tenderness.

**Tripe** Tripe is the stomach linings from the ox. The smooth first stomach is known as 'blanket', the second 'honeycomb' and the third 'thick seam'. All should be thick, firm and white and there is no difference in taste. Tripe is sold bleached (dressed) and partly boiled.

**Tongue** Ox and lamb's tongues are the most common, calf's and pig's usually being sold with the head. Lamb's and ox tongues can be bought fresh or salted. Lamb's tongues weigh about 225 g (8 oz) but an ox tongue can weigh from 1.8–3 kg (4–6½ lb). Lamb's tongue: soak 1–2 hours if fresh or 3–4 hours if salted. Ox tongue: soak 2–3 hours if fresh or overnight if salted. Drain, place in cold water (salt only if fresh) and bring slowly to the boil. Skim, then add peppercorns, bay leaves and root vegetables. Simmer gently for 2–3 hours, until tender. Remove skin carefully and use as required.

**Tail** Oxtail is usually the main type sold, ready skinned and jointed (pigs' tails are sometimes available). There should be a good proportion of lean with a layer of firm, white fat. One oxtail weighs about 1.4 kg (3 lb).

**Sweetbreads** These consist of two portions of calf's or lamb's thymus gland, are sold in pairs and are considered a delicacy. Calf's sweetbreads are considered the finest, while lamb's are smaller and have a less pronounced flavour. Ox sweetbreads are large, reddish, tough and coarse in flavour. They may have a strong smell, which will disappear during preparation. Buy 450 g (1 lb) sweetbreads to serve 3–4 people. Soak in cold water or milk for 2 hours. Rinse. Cover with cold water, flavoured with the juice of half a lemon and 5 ml (1 level tsp) of salt and bring to simmering point. Simmer for 15 minutes and plunge into cold water to firm the meat. Remove the tubes and outer membrane. Use as required.

**Brains** Calf's brains have the most delicate flavour but are not widely available. Ox or lamb's brains are more plentiful and are usually sold in sets. One set of lamb's brains is sufficient for 1 portion, while a set of calf's or ox brains will serve 2. When fresh they should look shiny, pinkish-grey, plump and moist. Soak for 1–2 hours in cold water to remove all traces of blood. Remove arteries and membranes with a sharp, pointed knife. Cover with water and parboil for 5–15 minutes, depending on size. Vinegar or lemon juice can be added to the cooking water to help retain the pale colour. Add other ingredients for flavour, such as a whole onion or a bay leaf, if required. After parboiling plunge into cold water or allow to cool in the cooking liquid to firm the meat. Discard the water and any loose particles of meat which will have solidified.

**Head** These are usually sold whole or split in half; pig's and sheep's heads are the most commonly seen. The best brawn is made from boiled pig's head, although some is made from calf's head. Pig's cheek is sold as Bath Chaps. Head meat can also be used for pie fillings. On gala occasions a pig's head is sometimes roasted whole, glazed and decorated as a Boar's head. Ask the butcher to prepare the head as for roasting. Cook and remove the meat for brawns or pies.

**Feet** When cooked, trotters (feet) produce a protein-rich gelatin. Pig's trotters are the most frequently available, either fresh or salted. Calf's foot and cow heel, once widely used for jellied stock and meat moulds, are now rarely seen and must be ordered in advance. Pig's trotters may be boned, stuffed and roasted, or the meat from them used in brawn.

Singe off any hairs over an open flame. Scrub well and pat dry. Parboil in salted water for 5 minutes before using in a recipe.

**Lungs** Also known as 'lights', lungs are not commonly eaten in this country but can be used as an ingredient in forcemeats or stuffing.

**Melts** (spleen) These are not commonly eaten in this country but can be used in stuffings.

## LIVER AND ONIONS

25 g (1 oz) butter or margarine

450 g (1 lb) onions, skinned and chopped

salt and pepper

2.5 ml (½ level tsp) dried sage or mixed herbs (optional)

450 g (1 lb) calf's or lamb's liver, cut into thin strips

1. Melt the butter in a frying pan, add the onions and fry gently until they begin to colour, then add the seasoning and the herbs, if using. Cover the frying pan and simmer very gently for about 10 minutes, until the onions are soft.
2. Add the liver strips to the onions, increase the heat slightly and continue cooking for about 5–10 minutes, stirring all the time, until the liver is just cooked. Transfer to a warmed serving dish.
*Serves 4*

## LIVER MARSALA

450 g (1 lb) lamb's liver, cut into wafer-thin strips

30 ml (2 tbsp) Marsala or sweet sherry

salt and pepper

225 g (8 oz) tomatoes, skinned

30 ml (2 tbsp) vegetable oil

1 large onion, skinned and finely sliced

150 ml (¼ pint) Beef Stock (see page 19)

1. Place the liver in a shallow bowl with the Marsala and season well with pepper. Cover the liver and leave to marinate for several hours in a cool place.

2. Quarter the tomatoes, remove the seeds and reserve the juices. Slice into fine strips and set aside.
3. Heat the oil in a frying pan and add the liver strips, a few at a time. Shake the pan briskly for about 1 minute so that the strips cook quickly. Remove from the pan when cooked and keep warm.
4. Add the onion to the oil remaining in the pan and cook, covered, for about 5 minutes. Add the stock and seasoning, return the liver to the pan and add the tomatoes and their juice. Bring to the boil, adjust seasoning if necessary and serve immediately.
*Serves 4*

## LIVER GOUJONS WITH ORANGE SAUCE

350 g (12 oz) lamb's liver, thinly sliced

1 egg, beaten

125 g (4 oz) medium oatmeal

1 medium onion, skinned and sliced

300 ml (½ pint) Beef Stock (see page 19)

grated rind and juice of a medium orange

salt and pepper

60 ml (4 tbsp) vegetable oil

1. Coat the liver pieces in egg and oatmeal.
2. In a saucepan, fry the onion in half the oil until golden, add the flour and cook for 2 minutes.
3. Add the stock, orange rind and juice. Bring to the boil and simmer for 15 minutes. Season.
4. Fry the goujons gently in the remaining oil for about 3–4 minutes until tender.
*Serves 4*

## EASTERN SPICED LIVER

| |
|---|
| 25 g (1 oz) desiccated coconut |
| 445 ml (3 tbsp) vegetable oil |
| 25 g (1 oz) butter or margarine |
| 450 g (1 lb) lamb's liver, cut into strips |
| 2 medium onions, skinned and sliced |
| 15 ml (1 level tbsp) chilli seasoning |
| 15 ml (1 level tbsp) ground coriander |
| 5 ml (1 level tsp) paprika |
| 2.5 ml (½ level tsp) ground turmeric |
| 30 ml (2 level tbsp) flour |
| 450 ml (¾ pint) Beef Stock (see page 19) |
| 30 ml (2 tbsp) mango chutney |
| salt and pepper |
| lemon twists and coriander sprig, to garnish |
| poppadums, to serve |

*Eastern Spiced Liver*

1. Soak the coconut in 150 ml (¼ pint) boiling water for 15 minutes. Strain, reserving the 'milk'.
2. Heat the oil and butter in a frying pan, add the liver and fry until browned, about 2 minutes. Remove from the pan with a slotted spoon.
3. Add the onions to the pan and fry until golden. Stir in the chilli, coriander, paprika, turmeric and flour and cook for 1 minute, stirring.
4. Add the stock with the coconut 'milk', chutney and seasoning and bring to the boil.
5. Return the liver to the pan, cover and simmer for 15–20 minutes. Garnish with lemon twists and coriander and serve with poppadums.
*Serves 4*

## CHINESE-STYLE FRIED LIVER

| |
|---|
| 4 fresh mushrooms, wiped and chopped or 25 g (1 oz) dried mushrooms |
| 450 g (1 lb) lamb's liver, cut into thin strips |
| 10 ml (2 level tsp) cornflour |
| 30 ml (2 tbsp) sherry |
| 2.5 cm (1 inch) piece root ginger, peeled and sliced |
| 1 small onion, skinned and finely chopped |
| 30 ml (2 tbsp) vegetable oil |
| 175 g (6 oz) can bamboo shoots, drained |
| 10 ml (2 tsp) soy sauce |

1. If using dried mushrooms, soak in hot water for 10 minutes, until soft, then cut into small pieces.
2. Mix the liver with the cornflour, sherry, ginger and onion.
3. Heat the oil in a frying pan and fry the liver briskly for about 1 minute, then add the vegetables. Stir until every piece is golden, about 3–4 minutes, then pour in the soy sauce and serve hot.
*Serves 4*

## GRILLED KIDNEYS

| |
|---|
| 550–700 g (1¼–1½ lb) lamb's kidneys, washed, skinned and cored |
| 45 ml (3 tbsp) vegetable oil |
| salt and pepper |
| grilled bacon, to serve |

1. Thread the kidneys on to 4 skewers, cut side uppermost.
2. Brush with oil and sprinkle with salt and pepper.
3. Cook under a hot grill for 3 minutes, uncut side uppermost, then turn over to allow the juices to gather in the cut side and grill a further 3 minutes. Serve immediately with grilled bacon.
*Serves 4*

# ROGNONS SAUTÉS TURBIGO

26 pickling onions

50 g (2 oz) butter or margarine

350 g (12 oz) cocktail pork sausages

30 ml (2 tbsp) vegetable oil

350 g (12 oz) button mushrooms, wiped and halved

15 lamb's kidneys, washed, skinned and cored

45 ml (3 level tbsp) plain flour

15 ml (1 level tbsp) tomato purée

45 ml (3 tbsp) sherry

600 ml (1 pint) Beef Stock (see page 19)

2 bay leaves

salt and pepper

6 slices white bread

vegetable oil

chopped fresh parsley, to garnish

1. Pour boiling water over the onions, leave for 2–3 minutes, then drain and peel.
2. Melt 25 g (1 oz) butter in a large frying pan and cook the sausages until brown on all sides, then remove from the pan. Heat the remaining butter and the oil and cook the onions and mushrooms over brisk heat for 3–4 minutes, shaking the pan. Remove from the pan.
3. Add the kidneys and cook briskly for about 5 minutes until evenly coloured. Remove from pan.
4. Stir the flour, tomato purée, sherry and stock into the juices. Bring to the boil, stirring, then add the bay leaves and seasoning. Return the sausages, mushrooms, onions and kidneys to the pan, cover and simmer for 20–25 minutes. Transfer to a warmed serving dish.
5. Meanwhile, trim the bread into small triangles or cut into heart shapes with a pastry cutter. Fry in oil until golden brown. Drain well and arrange around the kidneys. Garnish with parsley.
*Serves 6*

*Rognons Sautés Turbigo*

## KIDNEY STUFFED ONIONS

| |
|---|
| six 175 g (6 oz) onions, skinned |
| 6 lamb's kidneys, washed, skinned and cored |
| 150 ml (¼ pint) red wine |
| 60 ml (4 tbsp) Beef Stock (see page 19) |
| 15 ml (1 tbsp) wine vinegar |
| 5 ml (1 level tsp) sugar |
| 75 g (3 oz) seedless raisins |
| salt and pepper |
| chopped fresh parsley, to garnish |

1. Blanch the onions in boiling water for 10 minutes. Run under cold water to cool.
2. Remove the centre from the onions to give a cavity large enough to fit the kidneys. (Use the onion centres for another recipe.) Ease the kidneys into the onions, then arrange them upright in a casserole.
3. Pour over the wine, stock and vinegar, add the sugar and raisins and season well. Cover the casserole tightly and cook in the oven at 180°C (350°F), mark 4 for about 45 minutes.
4. Serve garnished with chopped parsley.
*Serves 6*

## LAMB'S HEART CASSEROLE

| |
|---|
| 50 g (2 oz) butter or margarine |
| 1 medium onion, skinned and chopped |
| 125 g (4 oz) mushrooms, wiped and chopped |
| 125 g (4 oz) streaky bacon, rinded and chopped |
| 2.5 ml (½ level tsp) dried sage or thyme |
| 225 g (8 oz) fresh breadcrumbs |
| finely grated rind of 1 lemon |
| salt and pepper |
| 1 egg, beaten |
| 8 lamb's hearts, washed and trimmed |
| 60 ml (4 level tbsp) flour |
| 30 ml (2 tbsp) vegetable oil |
| 300 ml (½ pint) Chicken Stock (see page 19) |
| 45 ml (3 tbsp) sherry |

1. Melt half the butter in a saucepan and cook the onion, mushroom and bacon until browned. Remove from the heat and stir in the herb, breadcrumbs, lemon rind and seasoning. Bind with the egg.
2. Fill the hearts with the stuffing and sew up neatly with strong cotton.
3. Toss the hearts in the flour and brown well in the remaining butter and oil in a flameproof casserole. Pour over the stock and sherry, season well and bring to the boil.
4. Cover the casserole and cook in the oven at 150°C (300°F) mark 2 for about 2 hours or until tender.
5. To serve, slice the hearts and pour over the juices.
*Serves 8*

## RICH CASSEROLED HEART

| |
|---|
| 1 ox heart, weighing 1–1.4 kg (2¼–3 lb), washed and cut into 1 cm (½ inch) slices |
| 45 ml (3 tbsp) vegetable oil |
| 2 medium onions, skinned and sliced |
| 45 ml (3 level tbsp) flour |
| 300 ml (½ pint) Beef Stock (see page 19) |
| salt and pepper |
| 2 medium carrots, peeled and grated |
| ½ a small swede, peeled and grated |
| 1 orange |
| 25 g (1 oz) walnut pieces, chopped |

1. In a frying pan fry the heart slices in the oil until slightly browned and put them into a casserole. Fry the onions until lightly browned and add them to the casserole.
2. Add the flour to the fat remaining in the pan and brown slightly. Pour in the stock, bring to the boil and simmer for 2–3 minutes, season, then add to the casserole. Cover and cook for 3½–4 hours in the oven at 150°C (300°F) mark 2, adding the carrots and swede after 2½–3 hours.
3. Pare the rind from the orange, shred it finely, cook in boiling water for 10–15 minutes, then drain.
4. Add the walnuts and orange rind to the casserole 15 minutes before cooking is complete.
*Serves 4*

# BRAISED OXTAIL

2 oxtails, total weight about 1.6 kg (3½ lb), trimmed
  and cut into pieces

30 ml (2 level tbsp) seasoned flour

60 ml (4 tbsp) vegetable oil

2 large onions, skinned and sliced

900 ml (1½ pints) Beef Stock (see page 19)

150 ml (¼ pint) red wine

15 ml (1 level tbsp) tomato purée

finely grated rind of ½ a lemon

2 bay leaves

salt and pepper

2 medium carrots, peeled and chopped

450 g (1 lb) parsnips, peeled and chopped

chopped fresh parsley, to garnish

**1.** Coat the oxtail pieces in the seasoned flour. Brown a few pieces at a time in the oil in a large flameproof casserole. Remove from the casserole with a slotted spoon.
**2.** Add the onions to the casserole and lightly brown. Stir in any remaining flour, the stock, red wine, tomato purée, lemon rind and bay leaves and season well. Bring to the boil and replace the meat. Cover and simmer for 2 hours, then skim well.
**3.** Stir the carrots and parsnips into the casserole.
**4.** Re-cover the casserole and simmer for a further 2 hours, until the meat is quite tender.
**5.** Skim all fat off the surface of the casserole, adjust seasoning and garnish with parsley.
*Serves 6*

# FRICASSÉE OF LAMB'S TONGUES

900 g (2 lb) lamb's tongues

salt and pepper

1 medium onion, skinned and sliced

1 medium carrot, peeled and sliced

1 bay leaf

6 black peppercorns

50 g (2 oz) butter or margarine

60 ml (4 level tbsp) flour

60 ml (4 tbsp) double cream

45 ml (3 tbsp) chopped fresh parsley

20 ml (4 tsp) lemon juice

bacon snippets and bread croûtons, to garnish

**1.** Rinse the tongues under cold water. Turn into a large bowl and cover with cold water, add 2.5 ml (½ level tsp) salt and leave to soak for 1–2 hours.
**2.** Rinse and drain well. Place in a large saucepan with the onion and carrot, bay leaf and peppercorns and water to cover. Add a large pinch of salt, bring slowly to the boil and skim off any scum rising to the surface. Cover and simmer gently for about 2 hours, or until tender.
**3.** Remove the tongues with a slotted spoon and place in a large bowl of cold water. Leave to go quite cold. Boil down the cooking liquid to strengthen the flavour, strain off and reserve 450 ml (¾ pint).

**4.** When the tongues are cold, ease a finger or thumb between the skin and flesh and gradually peel the skin off. Using a small pointed knife, gradually ease out the small bones and pieces of gristle lying at the base of the tongue.
**5.** Place the tongues on a chopping board and, using a very sharp knife, slice diagonally into 1 cm (½ inch) slices, starting from the tip end.
**6.** Melt the butter in a pan, stir in the flour and cook gently for 1 minute, stirring. Remove the pan from the heat and gradually stir in the reserved stock. Bring to the boil slowly and cook, stirring until the sauce thickens. Blend in the cream and season. Lower the heat and stir in the parsley.
**7.** Stir the tongue into the sauce, cover the pan and leave over a low heat for 10–15 minutes to warm through, stirring occasionally to prevent sticking. Just before serving, stir in the lemon juice and adjust seasoning. Garnish the dish with bacon snippets and small croûtons.
*Note* To make bacon snippets, remove the rinds from six prime streaky bacon rashers and chop into small pieces. It is easier to use kitchen scissors for this operation. Fry in a heavy-based frying pan with no extra fat until crisp and golden. Drain on absorbent kitchen paper and keep hot until required.
*Serves 6*

## OXTAIL PAPRIKA

2 oxtails, total weight about 1.6 kg (3½ lb), trimmed and
cut into pieces

75 ml (5 tbsp) vegetable oil

2 medium onions, skinned and sliced

30 ml (2 level tbsp) paprika

60 ml (4 level tbsp) flour

700 g (1½ lb) fresh tomatoes, skinned and chopped or
397 g (14 oz) can tomatoes

2 caps canned pimiento, sliced

600 ml (1 pint) Beef Stock (see page 19)

salt and pepper

142 ml (5 fl oz) soured cream

chopped fresh parsley, to garnish

1. The day before heat the oil in a large
flameproof casserole and brown the oxtail pieces,
a few at a time. Remove from the pan with a
slotted spoon.

2. Brown the onions in the oil remaining in the
pan. Stir in the paprika and flour and cook gently
for 1 minute.

3. Stir in the tomatoes, pimientos, stock and
plenty of seasoning. Bring to the boil. Replace the
meat.

4. Cover the casserole tightly and cook in
the oven at 170°C (325°F) mark 3 for about
3 hours, until the meat is really tender. Cool and
refrigerate.

5. Next day, shortly before serving, skim all fat
from the surface of the casserole. Bring slowly to
the boil, cover and simmer gently for 10 minutes.
Stir in the soured cream and heat gently. Garnish
with chopped parsley.
Serves 6

Oxtail Paprika

# PRESSED OX TONGUE

*1.6–1.8 kg (3½–4 lb) pickled ox tongue*

*1 medium onion, skinned*

*1 medium carrot, peeled*

*4 celery sticks*

*30 ml (2 tbsp) wine vinegar*

*2 bay leaves*

*12 black peppercorns*

*5 ml (1 level tsp) gelatine*

*Pressed Ox Tongue*

**1.** The day before, scrub and rinse the tongue under cold water. Place in a large bowl, cover with cold water and leave to soak overnight. Drain the tongue, then roll into a neat shape and secure with a skewer. Wrap in a single thickness of muslin, tying the ends together.

**2.** Next day, place the tongue in a large saucepan. Cover the cold water and bring to the boil. Boil for 1 minute only. Drain the tongue, rinse with cold water, then cover with fresh water. Thickly slice the vegetables and add to the pan with the vinegar, bay leaves and peppercorns. Bring to the boil, cover and simmer for about 4 hours.

**3.** Lift the tongue on to a large plate, reserving the cooking liquid. Unwrap, ease out the skewer and use to pierce the thickest piece of flesh; if it slips in easily, the tongue is cooked.

**4.** Place the tongue in a colander and rinse with cold water until cool enough to handle. This will help to loosen the skin. Using a sharp knife, make a shallow slit along the underside. Peel the skin off in strips, starting from the tip end. Ease out the bones and gristle lying at the base.

**5.** Tightly curl the warm tongue and fit into a

15 cm (6 inch) deep-sided soufflé dish or non-stick cake tin. It is important for the finished look of the tongue that it fits tightly into the container.

**6.** Strain the stock, reserving 600 ml (1 pint). Pour into a saucepan and boil rapidly to reduce to 150 ml (¼ pint). Meanwhile, pour 30 ml (2 tbsp) water into a small bowl and sprinkle over the gelatine. Soak for 10 minutes, then spoon the gelatine into the stock; stir gently and cool.

**7.** Gently pour the stock over the tongue. Put a small plate that will just fit inside the soufflé dish on top of the tongue. Put weights on the plate and chill overnight.

**8.** Lift the weights off the tongue and then ease off the plate. To release the tongue, run a blunt-edged knife around the inside of the dish, then immerse the base and sides in hot water for a few seconds only. Invert on to a serving plate, shaking well to release the tongue. Slice the tongue for serving.

*Serves 10–12*

# CREAMED SWEETBREADS

*450 g (1 lb) sweetbreads, rinsed and soaked in cold*
*    water for two hours*

*1 small onion, skinned and chopped*

*1 medium carrot, peeled and chopped*

*few parsley stalks*

*1 bay leaf*

*salt and pepper*

*40 g (1½ oz) butter or margarine*

*60 ml (4 level tbsp) flour*

*300 ml (½ pint) milk*

*squeeze of lemon juice*

*chopped fresh parsley, to garnish*

**1.** Put the sweetbreads, vegetables, herbs and seasoning in a saucepan with water to cover and simmer gently for about 15 minutes, until the sweetbreads are tender. Drain, reserving 300 ml (½ pint) of the cooking liquid, and keep hot.

**2.** Melt the butter in a saucepan, stir in the flour and cook gently for 1 minute, stirring. Remove from the heat and gradually stir in the milk and cooking liquid. Bring to the boil and continue to cook, stirring, until the sauce thickens. Season and add a squeeze of lemon juice.

**3.** Add the sweetbreads to the sauce and simmer gently for 5–10 minutes. Garnish with parsley.

*Serves 4*

## LANCASHIRE TRIPE AND ONIONS

450 g (1 lb) dressed tripe, washed

225 g (8 oz) shallots, skinned

568 ml (1 pint) milk

salt and pepper

pinch of grated nutmeg

1 bay leaf (optional)

25 g (1 oz) butter or margarine

45 ml (3 level tbsp) flour

chopped fresh parsley, to garnish

1. Put the tripe in a saucepan and cover with cold water. Bring to the boil, then drain and rinse under running cold water. Cut into 2.5 cm (1 inch) pieces.
2. Put the tripe, shallots, milk, seasonings and bay leaf (if using) into the rinsed out pan. Bring to the boil, cover and simmer for about 2 hours, until tender. Strain off the liquid and reserve 600 ml (1 pint).
3. Melt the butter in a pan, stir in the flour and cook gently for 1 minute, stirring. Remove pan from the heat and gradually stir in the cooking liquid. Bring to the boil and continue to cook, stirring, until the sauce thickens.
4. Add the tripe and shallots and reheat. Adjust the seasoning and sprinkle with parsley.
*Serves 4*

## TRIPE PROVENÇALE

450 g (1 lb) dressed tripe, washed

300 ml (½ pint) Chicken Stock (see page 19)

salt and pepper

15 g (½ oz) butter or margarine

1 medium onion, skinned and chopped

1 garlic clove, skinned and crushed

450 g (1 lb) tomatoes, skinned and chopped

pinch of dried thyme

30 ml (2 tbsp) dry white wine

30 ml (2 tbsp) chopped fresh parsley

1. Put the tripe in a saucepan and cover with cold water. Bring to the boil, then drain and rinse under cold running water. Cut into 2.5 cm (1 inch) pieces. Bring the stock to the boil and add the tripe and a pinch of salt.
2. Bring back to the boil, cover and simmer for about 2 hours.
3. Melt the butter in a frying pan, add the onion and fry until transparent. Add the garlic to the frying pan with the tomatoes, thyme, wine, parsley and seasoning. Bring to the boil and boil the sauce for 15 minutes. When the tripe is cooked, drain and stir into the tomato mixture. Cook over a low heat for a further 10 minutes.
*Serves 4*

## BRAINS IN BLACK BUTTER SAUCE

4 sets of lamb's brains

30 ml (2 tbsp) wine vinegar

salt and pepper

100 g (4 oz) butter or margarine

chopped fresh parsley, to garnish

1. Soak the brains for 1–2 hours in cold water. Remove as much of the skin and membrane as possible and put the brains into a saucepan with half the vinegar, 2.5 ml (½ level tsp) salt and enough water to cover well. Bring to simmering point and cook gently for 15 minutes.
2. Drain and place in cold water, then dry on absorbent kitchen paper.
3. Melt half of the butter in a frying pan, add the brains, brown on all sides and put on to a very hot dish. Add the rest of the butter to the pan and heat until dark brown, without allowing it to burn. Add the remaining vinegar, then pour it over the brains and sprinkle with salt, pepper and parsley.
*Serves 4*

# BRAWN

*2 large pig's trotters*

*900 g (2 lb) belly of pork*

*30 ml (2 tbsp) white wine vinegar*

*10 ml (2 level tsp) salt*

*12 black peppercorns*

*8 whole allspice berries*

*2 cloves*

*5 ml (1 level tsp) dried mixed herbs*

*1 medium onion, skinned and roughly chopped*

*2 eggs, hard-boiled*

**1.** Ask your butcher to split the trotters. Put them and the belly of pork into a large saucepan. Pour over 1.7 litres (3 pints) water and add the vinegar, salt, peppercorns, allspice, cloves, mixed herbs and onion.

**2.** Bring slowly to the boil, cover and simmer for 2½ hours. Every 20–30 minutes skim off any scum that rises to the surface.

**3.** Remove the meat and strain the liquid into a clean saucepan. Boil to reduce to about 300 ml (½ pint). Leave until cool but not set, then skim.

**4.** When the meat is cool enough to handle, skin and dice the belly of pork, discarding bones, and remove all the meat from the trotters.

**5.** Slice the hard-boiled eggs and arrange on the bottom and sides of a 900 ml (1½ pint) bowl or soufflé dish. Arrange the meat in layers on top.

**6.** Gently pour in enough of the reduced liquid to cover the meat. Place a small saucer and light weight on top. Chill until set into a firm but not solid jelly. Remove any fat from the surface before turning out for serving.

*Serves 6*

# SAUSAGES

**Fried sausages**

Melt a little fat in the frying pan, add the sausages and fry for 15–20 minutes, keeping the heat low to prevent them burning and turning them several times to brown evenly.

**Grilled sausages**

Heat the grill to hot, put the sausages on the grill rack in the pan and cook until one side is lightly browned, then turn them; continue cooking and turning frequently for about 15–20 minutes, until the sausages are well browned.

**Baked sausages**

Heat the oven to 200°C (400°F) mark 6. Put the sausages in a greased baking tin and cook in the oven for about 30 minutes. Alternatively, make kilted sausages by wrapping rinded streaky bacon rashers around pairs of chipolatas and baking in the same way at 190°C (375°F) mark 5.

# SAUSAGE ROLLS

*175 g (6 oz) Shortcrust Pastry, made with 175 g (6 oz) plain flour (see page 372)*

*225 g (8 oz) pork sausagemeat*

*flour, for dusting*

*a little milk*

*beaten egg, to glaze*

**1.** On a lightly floured surface, roll out the pastry thinly to an oblong, then cut it lengthways into 2 strips. Divide the sausagemeat into 2 pieces, dust with flour, and form into 2 rolls the length of the pastry.

**2.** Lay a roll of sausagemeat down the centre of each strip, brush the edges of the pastry with a little milk, fold one side of the pastry over the sausagemeat and press the two edges firmly together. Seal the long edges together.

**3.** Brush the length of the two rolls with milk, then cut each into slices 4–5 cm (1½–2 inch). Place on a baking sheet and bake in the oven at 200°C (400°F) mark 6 for 15 minutes. Reduce the temperature to 180°C (350°F) mark 4 and cook for a further 15 minutes.

*Makes 16*

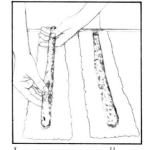

*Lay a sausagemeat roll down the centre of each strip of pastry.*

**Variation**

Sausage rolls can also be made with bought frozen puff pastry. Use a 212 g (7½ oz) packet and allow it to reach room temperature before rolling out. Cook at 220°C (425°F) mark 7 for 10–15 minutes.

## SAUSAGE AND LIVER RAGOÛT

| |
|---|
| 30 ml (2 tbsp) vegetable oil |
| 225 g (8 oz) pork chipolata sausages |
| 225 g (8 oz) lamb's liver, sliced |
| 4 small onions, skinned and quartered |
| 30 ml (2 level tbsp) flour |
| 450 ml (¾ pint) Chicken Stock (see page 19) |
| 15 ml (1 level tbsp) French mustard |
| salt and pepper |
| 30 ml (2 tbsp) sherry (optional) |

1. Heat the oil in a large frying pan and brown the sausages, add the liver and quickly brown. Remove from the pan.
2. Add the onions and brown lightly in the oil remaining in the pan. Stir in the flour and cook gently for 1 minute, stirring. Remove pan from the heat and gradually stir in the stock, mustard and seasoning. Bring to the boil slowly and continue to cook, stirring, until thickened.
3. Replace the liver and sausages. Cover the pan tightly and simmer gently for about 15 minutes, until the meat and vegetables are just tender.
4. Adjust seasoning and stir in the sherry, if using.
Serves 4

## TOAD IN THE HOLE

| |
|---|
| 30 ml (2 tbsp) vegetable oil |
| 450 g (1 lb) sausages |
| 125 g (4 oz) plain flour |
| pinch of salt |
| 1 egg |
| 300 ml (½ pint) milk and water mixed |

1. Put the vegetable oil in a small roasting tin and add the sausages. Place the tin in the oven at 220°C (425°F) mark 7 for about 10 minutes, until

browned and the fat is hot.
2. Meanwhile, sift the flour and salt into a bowl and make a well in the centre. Add the egg and half the liquid.
3. Gradually mix the flour into the centre of the bowl and add the remaining liquid. Beat until smooth.
4. Pour into the roasting tin and bake in the oven for 40–45 minutes, until the batter is well risen and golden.
Serves 4

## LAYERED SAUSAGE PIE

| |
|---|
| 225 g (8 oz) self raising flour |
| salt |
| 100 g (4 oz) lard |
| 1 small onion, skinned and grated |
| 225 g (8 oz) pork sausagemeat |
| 15 ml (1 tbsp) snipped fresh chives |
| 225 g (8 oz) potatoes, peeled and sliced |
| 50 g (2 oz) streaky bacon, rinded and chopped |
| 225 g (8 oz) cooking apples, peeled, cored and sliced |
| beaten egg, to glaze |

1. Place the flour and 1.25 ml (¼ level tsp) salt in a bowl. Cut the lard into small pieces and add to the flour. Using both hands, rub the fat into the flour until the mixture looks like fine breadcrumbs.

Add the onion and enough water to bind the mixture together. Knead lightly for a few seconds, to give a firm, smooth dough.
2. On a lightly floured surface roll out three quarters of the pastry and use to line a 20.5 cm (8 inch) sandwich tin.
3. Mix together the sausagemeat and chives. Layer up the potatoes, sausage mixture, bacon and apples in the pastry shell, seasoning lightly between the layers.
4. Roll out the remaining pastry to make a lid and place on top of the filling, sealing the edges well.
5. Place on a baking sheet. Glaze with the egg. Bake in the oven at 200°C (400°F) mark 6 for about 1 hour, covering lightly if overbrowning. Turn out of the tin and serve hot or cold.
Serves 4

# POULTRY

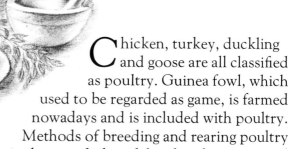

Chicken, turkey, duckling and goose are all classified as poultry. Guinea fowl, which used to be regarded as game, is farmed nowadays and is included with poultry. Methods of breeding and rearing poultry have changed dramatically, so that now it is cheap and plentiful and no longer served only on special occasions.

♦

## BUYING CHICKEN

It is usually cheaper to buy a whole chicken and cut it up yourself. This way you also get the whole carcass which can be made into good stock (see page 19) for use in soups, sauces and casseroles. Chicken pieces are ideal to use if you are short of time. All weights given are for oven-ready birds.

**Poussins** are very small chickens, 450–575 g (1–1¼ lb) 4–8 weeks old; one serves 1–2 people.

**Spring chickens** are small birds, 1.1 kg (2½ lb) 12 weeks old; one serves 2–3 people.

**Roasters** are generally young cockerels or hens, but may be capons. They are 1.8–2.3 kg (4–5 lb) and one serves 5–6 people.

**Boiling fowls** are older, tougher birds; 1.8–3.2 kg (4–7 lb). They should be 18 months old, but may in some cases be older. Usually served in casseroles. A 2.3–3.2 kg (5–7 lb) one will serve 6–8 people.

**Capons** are young cockerels that have been castrated and specially fattened. They weigh 2.3–3.6 kg (5–8 lb) and one serves 6–10 people.

**Corn-fed chickens** are yellow in colour because of their diet of sweetcorn (maize) and cost more than chickens fed on standard feed.

**Halves and quarters** are available and can be used instead of jointing a whole chicken.

**Breasts** are usually bought with the skin and some bones attached. Also sold as fillets and escalopes. They vary quite considerably in size.

**Suprêmes** are a French cut of breast sold with the wing bone attached.

**Thighs and drumsticks** are dark meat portions which can be baked, fried, grilled or casseroled.

**Wings** are available in packs in some supermarkets. They are best casseroled.

## BUYING TURKEY

**Oven-ready turkeys** are available in sizes ranging from 2.3 kg (5 lb) up to 13.5 kg (30 lb). See page 164 for a guide to calculating serving portions.

**Frozen turkeys** are also available in a range of sizes from 2.3 kg (5 lb) upwards. Some are self-basting oven-ready frozen birds with fat incorporated. Follow the cooking instructions on the wrapping.

**Chilled oven-ready**, these are prepared as for frozen but sold chilled and loosely wrapped.

**Turkey roast** is rolled dark or light meat of a convenient size for about four people. Roast as other joints allowing about 20 minutes per 450 g (1 lb) at 170°C (325°F), mark 3.

**Turkey steaks** look similar to gammon steaks. They can be fried or grilled.

**Turkey escalopes** are thin slices carved from the breast of the bird for frying or grilling.

**Turkey drumsticks, wings and thighs** can be either roasted or casseroled.

**Turkey chops** are cut from the top of the drumstick or the thigh and can be grilled fried or casseroled. They are sold fresh or frozen.
**Turkey casserole meat** is sold in packs of dark or light meat. It needs less cooking time than stewing beef, veal or lamb and there is no fat to trim.
**Turkey sausages** are made from turkey meat with a little pork fat and flavoured with herbs and spices. They can be bought fresh or frozen.
**Turkey burgers** are also flavoured with herbs and spices and come plain or coated with crumbs. When cooked they shrink less than beef burgers because of their lower fat content.

## JOINTING AND BONING POULTRY

### JOINTING POULTRY

**1.** With the bird breast side up, cut through the skin between leg and breast. Bend the leg back until the joint cracks. Remove leg from body by cutting through joint. Repeat with other leg.
**2.** Separate the thighs from the drumsticks by bending each leg to crack the joint. Cut through the joint with a sharp knife to separate. Remove wings by bending them back and cutting the joint at the breast.
**3.** Place carcass on its side; with poultry shears, cut from leg joint to backbone and along backbone to neck. Turn and cut along the other side to detach the breast. (The backbone will remain intact.)
**4.** Hold the breast skin-side down and bend it back to crack breastbone. With poultry shears, cut along each side of breastbone and remove.

### HALVING A BIRD

**1.** With the bird breast side up, using poultry shears or a sharp knife, cut straight along one side of breastbone from body cavity to neck cavity. Spread open, cut along side of the backbone to halve.

### BONING POULTRY

Use a small very sharp knife, strong scissors, a darning or trussing needle with a large eye.

Bone turkey or chicken like this.
**1.** If using a frozen bird, first remove the giblets. Snip off the wing pinions at the second joint and remove the parson's nose. Wipe and pat dry.
**2.** Place bird on its breast, cut straight down the back to the bone. Ease flesh and skin away from backbone and rib-cage. Work down towards the joints, turning the bird as you go.
**3.** Clasping one leg in each hand, press firmly outwards to release the ball and socket joints. Ease the knife point into joints and separate legs from the body. Repeat for wings.
**4.** Return to the main body and fillet flesh from breastbone. There is little flesh below the skin. Work down both sides and continue along the tip until the whole carcass is free.
**5.** Taking hold of the thigh end of the leg joint in one hand, scrape the flesh down from the bone towards the hinge joint.
**6.** Use the point of the knife—a cartilage has to be removed too. Continue filleting the flesh off the lower leg joint until the knobbly end is reached.
**7.** Clasp the exposed bones in one hand and the skin and flesh in the other. Pull the leg completely inside out to remove the bone, snipping any sinews.
**8.** Remove the wings similarly, easing out any pieces of breast bone, and remove the wishbone.

## STORING POULTRY

Remove any wrappings from the bird as soon as possible, and the giblets if there are any. The bird can be stored on a plate, covered with greaseproof paper, in the refrigerator for 2–3 days. The giblets are best cooked the same day (see below).

Frozen birds should be transferred to the freezer while still solidly frozen. If possible, freeze the giblets separately as they only have a freezer life of 1 month.

## ROASTING BIRDS

### TRUSSING

Trussing is done to keep the bird in a compact shape. You need a trussing needle or fine skewer and thin thread.
**1.** Fold the neck skin under the body and fold the wing tips back towards the backbone so they hold the neck skin in position. Put the bird on its back and press the legs well into the side. Slit the skin above the vent, push the parson's nose through.
**2.** Thread the needle with a length of string and insert it close to the second joint of the right wing; push it right through the body, to catch the cor-

responding joint on the left side.

**3.** Insert the needle again in the first joint of the left wing, pass it through the flesh at the back of the body, catching the tips of the wings and the neck skin, and pass it out through the first joint of the wing on the right side. Tie the ends in a bow.

**4.** To truss the legs, re-thread the needle and insert it through the gristle at the right side of the parson's nose. Pass the string over the right leg, over the left leg, through the gristle at the left side of the parson's nose, carry it behind the parson's nose and tie the ends of the string firmly.

**5.** If using a skewer, insert it right through the body of the bird just below the thigh bone and turn the bird over on to its breast. First, catching in the wing tips, pass the string under the ends of skewer and cross it over the back. Turn the bird over and tie the ends of the string together around the tail, at the same time securing each of the drumsticks.

### TESTING

To test when the bird is cooked, push a fine skewer into the thickest part of the thigh. If the juices run clear, the bird is cooked but if they are still pink, it needs longer cooking.

### CARVING

**1.** Remove the trussing thread and place the bird so that one wing is towards your left hand, with the breast diagonally towards you. Prise the leg outwards with the fork. Sever the leg.

**2.** Divide the thigh from the drumstick by cutting through the joint; in a big bird the thigh is further divided. Hold wing with fork and cut through outer layer of breast and wing joint. Ease wing away from body. Repeat with other wing.

**3.** Slice the breast, cutting parallel with the bone. Slice stuffed birds from front of the breast.

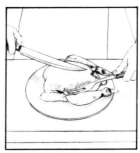

*Use fork to prise leg outward, then sever through the joint.*

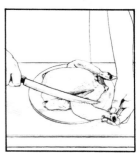

*Divide the thigh from the drumstick by cutting the joint.*

# ROASTING CHICKEN Originally the term roasting meant cooking by a fierce dry heat over an open fire. Nowadays, it refers to oven-roasting, or baking. The heat is still fierce but confined to the oven space, so the meat retains its juices. A well-roasted chicken has crispy brown skin with juicy flesh.

## ROAST CHICKEN

*1.4–1.8 kg (3–4 lb) oven-ready chicken*

*stuffing (see pages 184–188)*

*1 onion, skinned*

*1 lemon wedge*

*butter, melted, or vegetable oil*

*salt and pepper*

*streaky bacon rashers (optional)*

**1.** Wash the bird, dry thoroughly and stuff with chosen stuffing at the neck end before folding the neck skin over. Put the onion and lemon wedge in the body cavity.

**2.** Truss the bird (see page 148) and weigh it. Place it in a deep roasting tin, brush with melted butter or oil and sprinkle with salt and pepper. A few strips of streaky bacon may be laid over the breast to prevent it from becoming dry. Roast in the oven at 200°C (400°F) mark 6, basting from time to time, allowing 20 minutes per 450 g (1 lb) plus 20 minutes.

**3.** Put a piece of foil over the breast if it shows signs of becoming too brown.

*Serves 4–6*

### ACCOMPANIMENTS FOR CHICKEN

**Stuffing Balls** See page 184.

**Bread Sauce** See page 208.

**Thin gravy**

Pour off all the fat except 15 ml (1 tbsp) from the roasting tin. Sprinkle in 10 ml (2 level tsp) flour and stir in 300 ml (½ pint) Giblet Stock. Bring to the boil, stirring, season with salt and pepper.

**Giblet Stock**

Wash giblets. Put in a saucepan, cover with water and cook for 45–60 minutes.

*Italian Stuffed Capon*

# ITALIAN STUFFED CAPON

| |
|---|
| *75 g (3 oz) butter or margarine* |
| *1 medium onion, skinned and finely chopped* |
| *45 ml (3 tbsp) Marsala* |
| *450 g (1 lb) minced pork* |
| *100 g (4 oz) fresh breadcrumbs* |
| *50 g (2 oz) green olives, stoned and roughly chopped* |
| *50 g (2 oz) pine nuts, roughly chopped* |
| *15 ml (1 tbsp) chopped fresh marjoram or 5 ml (1 level tsp) dried* |
| *pinch of freshly grated nutmeg* |
| *salt and pepper* |
| *1 egg, beaten* |
| *3 kg (6½ lb) capon, boned (see page 148)* |
| *450 g (1 lb) piece Italian salami, skinned* |
| *watercress, to garnish* |

**1.** Melt 25 g (1 oz) of butter in a frying pan and cook the onion for 5 minutes, until soft but not brown. Add the Marsala and boil rapidly for 2 minutes. Cool for 5 minutes.

**2.** Mix together the onion, pork, breadcrumbs, olives, pine nuts, marjoram, nutmeg and salt and pepper to taste. Bind with the egg.

**3.** Place the capon, skin side down, on a work surface. Push the legs and wings inside and flatten with a rolling pin to evenly distribute the flesh. Spread one half of the stuffing mixture over the centre of the capon, then place the salami on top. Cover with the remaining stuffing mixture.

**4.** Tuck the neck end in towards the filling, draw the long sides of the bird over the stuffing and sew it neatly together with fine string or cotton, reshaping the bird. Use overlapping stitches and do not roll too tightly or the bird will burst during cooking. Secure the string loosely for easy removal. Weigh the bird.

**5.** Place the capon in a roasting tin. Sprinkle with salt and pepper, then dot with the remaining butter. Roast in the oven at 190°C (375°F) mark 5, basting occasionally, allowing 25 minutes per 450 g (1 lb).

**6.** Cool completely for 3–4 hours, then refrigerate overnight. Remove the string before slicing. Garnish with watercress to serve.
*Serves 12–16*

# FRENCH-STYLE ROAST CHICKEN

1.4 kg (3 lb) oven-ready chicken

50 g (2 oz) butter or margarine

salt and pepper

5–6 fresh tarragon or parsley sprigs

melted butter

2 rashers bacon, rinded

300 ml (½ pint) Chicken Stock (see page 19) or 150 ml (¼ pint) Chicken Stock and 150 ml (¼ pint) white wine

1. Prepare the bird as for ordinary roasting.

2. Cream the butter with a good sprinkling of salt and pepper and put the butter and sprigs of herb inside the bird.

3. Brush the breast with melted butter and cover with the rashers of bacon.

4. Place the bird in a roasting tin and add the stock. Roast in the oven at 190°C (375°F) mark 5 for about 1 hour 20 minutes, basting with the stock every 15 minutes.

5. Remove the bacon during the last 15 minutes of the cooking to brown the breast. Reserve the stock to make gravy.

*Serves 4*

# PEACH GLAZED CHICKEN LEGS

50 g (2 oz) long grain brown rice

15 ml (1 level tbsp) ground turmeric

salt

50 g (2 oz) butter or margarine

125 g (4 oz) spring onions, trimmed and finely chopped

25 g (1 oz) Brazil nuts, finely chopped

2.5 ml (½ level tsp) ground ginger

411 g (14½ oz) can peach halves, drained and juice reserved

pepper

4 chicken legs, about 1 kg (2.2 lb) total weight

15 ml (1 level tbsp) golden syrup

5 ml (1 level tsp) cornflour

15 ml (1 tbsp) malt vinegar

1. Cook the brown rice with the turmeric in fast boiling salted water for about 35 minutes. Drain well.

2. Melt 25 g (1 oz) butter in a saucepan, add the spring onions, nuts and ginger and fry gently for 2–3 minutes. Remove from the heat and stir in the rice and one chopped peach half. Season and leave to cool.

3. Cut and ease the bones out of the chicken legs, keeping the skin and flesh as intact as possible.

4. Spoon a little stuffing into each chicken leg. Carefully fold over to enclose stuffing. Sew up neatly.

5. Purée the remaining peaches with half the juice, the golden syrup, cornflour and vinegar in a blender or food processor. Pour into a saucepan and boil until reduced to half its original quantity, stirring all the time.

*Peach Glazed Chicken Legs*

6. Melt the remaining butter in a 1.1 litre (2 pint) flameproof casserole. Add the chicken parcels and fry until browned. Pour over the peach sauce and bake in the oven at 200°C (400°F) mark 6 for about 40 minutes. Skim off any fat before serving.

*Serves 4*

# CHICKEN GALANTINE

50 g (2 oz) butter or margarine

125 g (4 oz) button mushrooms, wiped and coarsely
    chopped

1 medium onion, skinned and coarsely chopped

3 celery sticks, trimmed and coarsely chopped

225 g (8 oz) fresh breadcrumbs

5 ml (1 level tsp) dried marjoram

1 egg, beaten

salt and pepper

1.4 kg (3 lb) oven-ready chicken, boned (see page 148)

125 g (4 oz) piece of garlic sausage

**1.** Melt half the butter in a large frying pan, add
the vegetables and fry for about 4 minutes, then
leave to cool.
**2.** Place the breadcrumbs in a mixing bowl, add
the marjoram and cooked vegetables. Mix well
with a wooden spoon, adding enough egg to bind.
Season well.

**3.** Spread the bird out, skin side down and spoon
some of the stuffing into the leg and wing cavities.
Spread the remaining stuffing over the bird. Place
the garlic sausage lengthways down the centre.
**4.** Tuck the neck end in towards the filling, draw
the long sides of the bird over the stuffing and
sew it neatly together with fine string or strong
thread. Use overlapping stitches and do not roll
too tightly or the bird will burst during cooking.
Secure the string loosely for easy removal.
**5.** Weigh the chicken and calculate the cooking
time to allow 25 minutes to the 450 g (1 lb). Place
the chicken in a roasting tin and dot with the
remaining butter. Season well. Roast in the oven
at 180°C (350°F) mark 4, basting frequently. When
cooked, remove from the tin and leave to cool.
Remove skewers, then chill in the refrigerator. To
serve, remove the thread and thinly slice the
chicken.
*Serves 6–8*

# DEVILLED POUSSINS

15 ml (1 level tbsp) mustard powder

15 ml (1 level tbsp) paprika

20 ml (4 level tsp) ground turmeric

20 ml (4 level tsp) ground cumin

60 ml (4 level tbsp) tomato ketchup

15 ml (1 tbsp) lemon juice

75 g (3 oz) butter or margarine, melted

3 poussins, about 700 g (1½ lb) each

15 ml (1 level tbsp) poppy seeds

**1.** Put the mustard powder, paprika, turmeric and
ground cumin into a small bowl. Add the tomato
ketchup and lemon juice and beat well to form a
thick, smooth paste. Slowly pour in the melted
butter, stirring all the time.
**2.** Place the poussins on a chopping board, breast

side down. With a small sharp knife cut right
along the backbone of each bird through the skin
and flesh. With scissors cut through the backbone
to open them up. Turn the birds over, breast side
up. Continue cutting along the breastbone which
will split the birds into two equal halves. Lie them
skin side uppermost in a roasting tin.
**3.** Spread the paste evenly over the surface of the
birds. Sprinkle with the poppy seeds. Loosely
cover with cling film and leave in a cool place for
at least 1–2 hours. Cook the poussins, uncovered,
in the oven at 220°C (425°F) mark 7 for 15
minutes.
**4.** Remove from the oven and place under a hot
grill until the skin is well browned and crisp.
Return to the oven, reduce temperature to 180°C
(350°F) mark 4 for a further 20 minutes.
*Serves 6*

## Variations

*HERBY ORANGE POUSSINS*
Replace the spicy marinade with a mixture of
150 ml (¼ pint) dry white wine, 45 ml (3 tbsp)
olive oil, juice of 2 oranges, 5 ml (1 tsp) each
chopped fresh rosemary, thyme and marjoram
and 1 skinned and crushed garlic clove.

*ORIENTAL-STYLE POUSSINS*
Replace the spicy marinade with 100 ml (4 fl oz)
soy sauce, 30 ml (2 tbsp) dry sherry, 2 thinly sliced
spring onions, 30 ml (2 tbsp) soft light brown
sugar, 2.5 ml (½ tsp) salt and 2.5 ml (½ tsp) ground
ginger.

## TANDOORI CHICKEN

4 chicken quarters, skinned

30 ml (2 tbsp) lemon juice

1 garlic clove, skinned

2.5 cm (1 inch) piece root ginger, peeled and roughly
 chopped

1 green chilli, seeded

60 ml (4 tbsp) natural yogurt

5 ml (1 level tsp) ground cumin

5 ml (1 level tsp) Garam Masala (see page 198)

15 ml (1 level tbsp) paprika

5 ml (1 level tsp) salt

30 ml (2 tbsp) melted ghee or vegetable oil

lemon wedges and onion rings, to garnish

1. Using a sharp knife or skewer, pierce the
chicken pieces all over. Put the chicken in an
ovenproof dish, add the lemon juice and rub it
into the flesh. Cover and leave for 30 minutes.
2. Meanwhile, make the marinade. Put the garlic,
ginger and green chilli in a blender or food processor with 15 ml (1 tbsp) water and grind to a
smooth paste.
3. Add the paste to the yogurt with the ground
cumin, garam masala, paprika, salt and the melted
ghee. Mix all the ingredients together, then pour
them over the chicken pieces.
4. Coat the pieces liberally with the yogurt
marinade. Cover and leave to marinate at room
temperature for 5 hours. Turn once or twice.
5. Roast the chicken in the oven at 170°C (325°F)
mark 3 for 1¾–2 hours, basting frequently and
turning once, until tender and most of the
marinade has evaporated. Alternatively, grill or
barbecue the chicken. Garnish with lemon wedges
and onion rings.
*Serves 4*

## BAKED CHICKEN JOINTS

4 chicken joints or pieces

salt and pepper

45 ml (3 level tbsp) flour

50–75 g (2–3 oz) butter or margarine

1. Wipe the chicken joints and pat dry with
absorbent kitchen paper. Season.
2. Toss in the flour until completely coated and
place in a roasting tin. Melt the butter and pour it
over the chicken. Bake in the oven at 200°C
(400°F) mark 6 for 45 minutes, turning once, until
tender.
*Serves 4*

**Variation**
For a crisp coating, dip the chicken pieces in 1
lightly beaten egg and then in 50 g (2 oz) dry breadcrumbs. Bake as above.

# FRIED AND GRILLED CHICKEN

## FRIED CHICKEN

4 chicken joints or pieces

salt and pepper

45 ml (3 level tbsp) flour

50 g (2 oz) butter or margarine or 45 ml (3 tbsp)
 vegetable oil

1. Wipe the chicken joints or pieces and pat dry
with absorbent kitchen paper. Season to taste with
salt and pepper.
2. Toss the chicken in the flour until completely
coated.
3. Heat the butter in a frying pan or flameproof
casserole and add the chicken pieces. Cook until
golden brown on both sides, then lower the heat
and cook for about 30–40 minutes, until tender.
Drain on absorbent kitchen paper.
*Serves 4*
*Note* To ensure that the chicken pieces remain
moist the surface should be browned at a high
temperature to seal in the juices and give a good
colour, then the heat reduced for the remaining
cooking time.

## CHICKEN WITH CUMIN AND CIDER

| |
|---|
| 15 ml (1 tbsp) vegetable oil |
| 50 g (2 oz) butter or margarine |
| 4 chicken leg portions |
| 2 small cooking apples, peeled and sliced |
| 1 small onion, skinned and sliced |
| 5 ml (1 level tsp) ground cumin |
| 15 ml (1 level tbsp) flour |
| 300 ml (½ pint) Chicken Stock (see page 19) |
| 150 ml (¼ pint) dry cider |
| salt and pepper |
| 1 large red skinned eating apple |

**1.** Heat the oil and 25 g (1 oz) butter in a flame-proof casserole, add the chicken joints and fry until golden. Remove from the pan with a slotted spoon.

**2.** Add the cooking apples and onion to the pan, cook for 3 minutes, then stir in the cumin and flour and cook for 1 minute, stirring. Remove from the heat and gradually stir in the stock and cider.

**3.** Bring to the boil slowly and continue to cook, stirring, until thickened. Return the chicken to the pan and adjust the seasoning.

**4.** Cover the pan and simmer gently for 15 minutes. Turn the chicken pieces over. Re-cover the pan and cook for a further 15 minutes, until the chicken is quite tender.

**5.** Meanwhile, quarter and core the eating apple, halve each quarter lengthways. Melt the remaining butter and fry until golden but still crisp.

**6.** Garnish the dish with the fried apple slices and serve immediately.
*Serves 4*

## CHICKEN WITH TARRAGON SAUCE

| |
|---|
| 6 chicken breasts |
| 75 g (3 oz) butter or margarine |
| 25 g (1 oz) flour |
| 450 ml (¾ pint) Chicken Stock (see page 19) |
| 30 ml (2 tbsp) tarragon vinegar |
| 10 ml (2 level tsp) French mustard |
| 15 ml (1 tbsp) fresh tarragon, chopped, or 5 ml (1 level tsp) dried |
| 50 g (2 oz) Cheddar cheese, grated |
| 150 ml (5 fl oz) single cream |
| salt and pepper |

**1.** Wipe the chicken breasts and pat dry with absorbent kitchen paper.

**2.** Melt 50 g (2 oz) butter in a frying pan or flame-proof casserole and add the chicken breasts. Cook until golden on both sides, then lower the heat and cook for about 20 minutes until tender, turning once.

**3.** Meanwhile, melt the remaining butter in a saucepan, stir in the flour and cook gently for 1 minute, stirring. Remove pan from the heat and gradually stir in the stock and vinegar. Bring to the boil slowly and continue to cook, stirring, until the sauce thickens.

**4.** Stir in the mustard, tarragon, cheese and cream. Season. Heat gently without boiling.

**5.** Drain the chicken breasts on absorbent kitchen paper and transfer to a warmed serving dish.

*Chicken with Tarragon Sauce*

Spoon over the sauce and serve immediately.
*Serves 6*

# SPICED CHICKEN WITH CASHEW NUTS

8 chicken breast fillets, about 75–100 g (3–4 oz) each

2.5 cm (1 inch) piece root ginger, peeled and roughly
    chopped

5 ml (1 level tsp) coriander seeds

4 cloves

10 ml (2 level tsp) black peppercorns

284 g (10 oz) natural yogurt

1 medium onion, skinned and roughly chopped

50 g (2 oz) cashew nuts

2.5 ml (½ level tsp) hot chilli powder

10 ml (2 level tsp) ground turmeric

40 g (1½ oz) ghee or clarified butter (see page 571)

salt

chopped toasted cashew nuts and chopped fresh
    coriander, to garnish

1. Make shallow slashes across each chicken breast. Put the ginger, coriander seeds, cloves, peppercorns and yogurt in a blender or food processor and purée until almost smooth. Pour the yogurt mixture over the chicken, cover and marinate in the refrigerator for about 24 hours, turning once.
2. Put the onion, cashew nuts, chilli powder, turmeric and 150 ml (¼ pint) water in a blender or food processor and purée until almost smooth.
3. Lift the chicken out of the marinade. Melt the ghee in a large frying pan, add the chicken and fry until browned.
4. Stir in the marinade with the nut mixture and bring slowly to the boil. Season.
5. Cover the pan and simmer for about 20 minutes, until the chicken is tender, stirring occasionally. Adjust seasoning. Garnish with cashew nuts and coriander.
*Serves 8*

# CHICKEN KIEV

175 g (6 oz) butter, softened

grated rind of ½ a lemon

15 ml (1 tbsp) lemon juice

salt and pepper

15 ml (1 tbsp) chopped fresh parsley

1 garlic clove, skinned and crushed

6 large chicken breasts, boned and skinned

25 g (1 oz) seasoned flour

1 egg, beaten

100 g (4 oz) fresh breadcrumbs

vegetable oil for deep frying

lemon wedges and parsley sprigs, to garnish
    (optional)

1. Combine the butter with lemon rind, juice, salt and pepper, parsley and garlic. Beat well together, form into a roll and chill well.
2. Place the chicken breasts on a flat surface and pound them to an even thickness with a meat mallet or rolling pin.
3. Cut the butter into six pieces and place one piece on the centre of each chicken breast.
4. Roll up, folding the ends in to enclose the butter completely.
5. Secure the rolls with wooden cocktail sticks, then coat each one with seasoned flour.
6. Dip the rolls in the beaten egg, then coat them with breadcrumbs, patting the crumbs firmly on to the chicken.
7. Place the rolls on a baking sheet, cover lightly with non-stick or greaseproof paper and refrigerate for 2 hours or until required, to allow the coating to dry.
8. In a deep-fat fryer, heat the oil to 160°C (325°F). Put two chicken rolls in a frying basket and lower into the oil. Fry for 15 minutes. The chicken is cooked when it is browned and firm when pressed with a fork. Do not pierce.
9. Remove from the fryer, drain on absorbent kitchen paper and keep warm while cooking the remaining chicken. Remove the cocktail sticks before serving.
*Serves 6*

**Variation**
SPICY CHICKEN KIEV
To make the butter filling, sauté 1 finely chopped shallot with 20 ml (2 level tsp) cayenne pepper in 15 ml (1 level tbsp) butter or margarine until soft but not brown. Stir in 15 ml (1 tbsp) fresh chopped parsley. Combine with 175 g (6 oz) softened butter and season. Proceed from step 2 as above.

## CHICKEN MARYLAND

1.4 kg (3 lb) oven-ready chicken, jointed (see page 148)

45 ml (3 level tbsp) seasoned flour

1 egg, beaten

100 g (4 oz) fresh breadcrumbs

25 g (1 oz) butter or margarine

45–60 ml (3–4 tbsp) vegetable oil

4 Fried Bananas, Corn Fritters and 4 Bacon Rolls (see
     right), to serve

1. Divide the chicken into fairly small pieces, coat
with seasoned flour, dip in beaten egg and coat
with breadcrumbs.
2. Heat the butter and oil in a large frying pan,
add the chicken and fry until lightly browned.
Continue frying gently, turning the pieces once,
for about 20 minutes, until tender.
   Alternatively, fry them in deep fat for 5–10

minutes at a frying temperature of 190°C (375°F).
3. Serve the chicken with Fried Bananas, Corn
Fritters and Bacon Rolls.
**Fried Bananas**
Peel and slice the bananas lengthways and fry
gently for about 3 minutes in a little hot butter or
margarine until lightly browned.
**Corn Fritters**
Make up a batter from 100 g (4 oz) flour, a pinch of
salt, 1 egg and 150 ml (¼ pint) milk. Fold in a
312 g (11 oz) tin sweetcorn kernels, drained. Fry
spoonfuls in a little hot fat until crisp and golden,
turning them once. Drain well on absorbent
kitchen paper.
**Bacon Rolls**
Roll up rashers of rinded streaky bacon, thread on
a skewer and grill for 3–5 minutes, until crisp.
*Serves 4*

## SESAME LEMON CHICKEN

8 small chicken drumsticks, about 75 g (3 oz) each

30 ml (2 level tbsp) cornflour

1 egg, beaten

1 lemon

15 ml (1 tbsp) soy sauce

15 ml (1 tbsp) cider vinegar

15 ml (1 level tbsp) demerara sugar

60 ml (4 tbsp) dry sherry

15 ml (1 tbsp) sesame oil

30 ml (2 tbsp) peanut oil

2 medium leeks, washed, trimmed and cut into 1 cm
     (½ inch) slices

45 ml (3 level tbsp) sesame seeds

salt and pepper

1. Put the drumsticks in a large saucepan and
cover with cold water. Bring to the boil, cover and
simmer for about 30 minutes. Drain and dry with

absorbent kitchen paper.
2. Mix together the cornflour and egg; use to
thoroughly coat the chicken drumsticks.
3. Grate the lemon rind and whisk together with
the soy sauce, cider vinegar, sugar and sherry. Peel
and thinly slice the lemon and reserve for the
garnish.
4. Heat the sesame and peanut oils in a wok or
large frying pan until just beginning to smoke.
Brown the drumsticks a few at a time. Remove
with a slotted spoon and keep warm.
5. Fry the leeks and sesame seeds for 1–2 minutes,
adding more oil if necessary. Return the
drumsticks with the sauce mixture to the pan.
Bring to the boil, then simmer for 3–4 minutes,
stirring occasionally. Season.
6. Transfer to a warmed serving dish. Lightly fry
the lemon slices in the wok or frying pan. Garnish
the drumsticks with the lemon.
*Serves 4*

## GRILLED CHICKEN OR POUSSIN

4 chicken joints or whole poussins

salt and pepper

50–75 g (2–3 oz) butter or margarine, melted, or
     45–60 ml (3–4 tbsp) vegetable oil

1. If using chicken joints, season and brush with
melted butter, margarine or oil and grill under a
medium heat for 20 minutes.

2. To prepare poussins for grilling, place them
breast side down on a board. Cut through the
backbone, open the bird out and flatten.
3. Brush all over with the melted butter or oil and
season lightly. Place in the grill pan.
4. Grill under a medium heat, turning once or
twice for about 30 minutes, until tender.
*Serves 4*

# POACHED CHICKEN

## POACHED CHICKEN

*1.4 kg (3 lb) oven-ready chicken*

*juice of ½ a lemon*

*salt*

*1 medium onion, skinned and stuck with 3–4 cloves*

*1 medium carrot, peeled*

*6 black peppercorns*

*bouquet garni*

**1.** Rub the bird with lemon juice. Put in a large pan and just cover with water. Add the salt, onion, carrot, peppercorns and bouquet garni.
**2.** Bring to the boil, cover and simmer for about 50 minutes, until tender. Remove from stock and cool.
**3.** Dice and use for fricassées, curries or salads. Use the cooking liquid to make sauce or soup.
*Serves 4*

## CHICKEN AU GRATIN

*4 chicken joints, skinned*

*6 black peppercorns*

*1 bay leaf*

*1 medium carrot, peeled and sliced*

*1 medium onion, skinned and sliced*

*2 cloves*

*thinly pared rind of 1 lemon*

*salt and pepper*

*25 g (1 oz) butter or margarine*

*25 g (1 oz) flour*

*pinch of grated nutmeg*

*pinch of ground bay leaves*

*125 g (4 oz) Cheddar cheese, grated*

*30 ml (2 tbsp) lemon juice*

*30 ml (2 level tbsp) fresh breadcrumbs*

**1.** Put the chicken joints in a large saucepan with the peppercorns, bay leaf, carrot, onion, cloves, pared lemon rind and a pinch of salt. Cover with cold water and bring to the boil. Cover and simmer gently, for 45 minutes, until tender. Remove joints and keep warm. Boil the stock until reduced to 300 ml (½ pint), strain and reserve.
**2.** Melt the butter in a heavy-based pan, stir in the flour, nutmeg and ground bay leaves and cook for 1 minute, stirring. Remove pan from the heat and gradually stir in the reserved chicken stock. Bring to the boil slowly and cook, stirring, until thick. Remove from the heat and add three quarters of the cheese and all the lemon juice. Season well.
**3.** Arrange chicken in a shallow ovenproof serving dish. Coat with the sauce. Combine remaining cheese and breadcrumbs. Scatter over the sauce. Grill until golden and bubbling.
*Serves 4*

## FRICASSEE OF CHICKEN

*1.6 kg (3½ lb) oven-ready chicken*

*1 medium onion, skinned and chopped*

*2 celery sticks, sliced*

*salt and pepper*

*bouquet garni*

*30 ml (2 tbsp) lemon juice*

*65 g (2½ oz) butter or margarine*

*175 g (6 oz) button mushrooms, wiped and sliced*

*50 g (2 oz) flour*

*45 ml (3 tbsp) double cream*

*parsley sprigs and bacon rolls, to garnish*

**1.** Put the chicken in a large saucepan with the onion, celery, seasoning, bouquet garni and 15 ml (1 tbsp) lemon juice. Add just enough water to cover. Bring to the boil, cover and simmer for about 1 hour, until tender.
**2.** Drain, reserving the vegetables and 600 ml (1 pint) of the stock. Dice the flesh.
**3.** Melt 15 g (½ oz) butter in a saucepan, add the mushrooms and fry for 2–3 minutes.
**4.** In a separate pan melt the remaining butter, stir in the flour and cook gently for 1 minute, stirring. Remove pan from the heat and gradually stir in the reserved stock. Bring to the boil slowly and continue to cook, stirring, until the sauce thickens. Add 15 ml (1 tbsp) lemon juice, the chicken, vegetables and mushrooms. Stir in the cream and adjust the seasoning. Garnish.
*Serves 4*

## Chicken Puff Pie

| |
|---|
| 900 g (2 lb) oven-ready chicken |
| 1 bay leaf |
| 2 fresh rosemary or marjoram sprigs, or 10 ml (2 level tsp) dried |
| salt and pepper |
| 4 medium leeks, trimmed, cut into 2 cm (¾ inch) lengths and washed |
| 2 large carrots, peeled and thickly sliced |
| 100 g (4 oz) boiled ham, cut into bite-sized pieces |
| 25 g (1 oz) butter or margarine |
| 1 medium onion, skinned and chopped |
| 45 ml (3 level tbsp) flour |
| 150 ml (¼ pint) milk |
| 60 ml (4 tbsp) single cream |
| 225 g (8 oz) frozen puff pastry, thawed |
| 1 egg, beaten, to glaze |

1. Put the chicken in a large saucepan with the herbs and salt and pepper to taste. Cover with water and bring to the boil, then reduce the heat, cover and simmer for 45–60 minutes, until the chicken is tender.
2. Remove the chicken from the liquid and leave to cool slightly. Meanwhile, add the leeks and carrots to the liquid, bring to the boil and simmer for about 7 minutes, until tender but still crunchy. Remove from the pan with a slotted spoon. Strain the cooking liquid and reserve 600 ml (1 pint).
3. Remove the chicken meat from the bones, discarding the skin. Cut into bite-sized chunks.
4. Mix the chicken with the ham and vegetables in a 1.1 litre (2 pint) pie dish.
5. Melt the butter in a clean saucepan, add the onion and fry gently until soft. Stir in the flour and cook gently for 1 minute, stirring, then gradually add the reserved cooking liquid.
6. Bring to the boil and simmer, stirring, until thick, then stir in the milk and cream, with salt and pepper to taste. Pour the sauce into the pie dish and leave for about 50 minutes, until cold.
7. Roll out the pastry on a floured surface until about 2.5 cm (1 inch) larger all round than the pie dish. Cut off a strip from all round the edge of the pastry. Place the strip on the rim of the pie dish, moisten, then place pastry lid on top.
8. Press the edge firmly to seal, then knock up and flute. Make a hole in the centre of the pie and use the pastry trimmings to make decorations, sticking them in place with water.
9. Brush the pastry with the egg, then bake in the oven at 190°C (375°F) mark 5 for 30 minutes, until puffed up and golden brown. Serve hot.
*Serves 4–6*

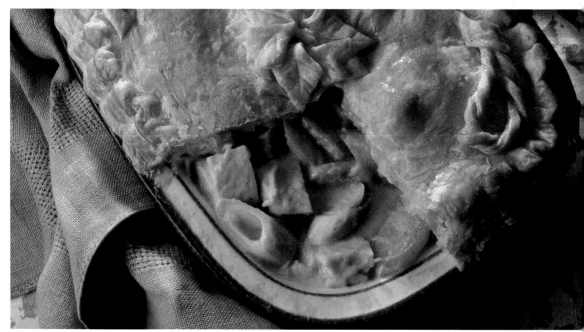

*Chicken Puff Pie*

# CHICKEN AND CUCUMBER MOUSSE

*1.4 kg (3 lb) oven-ready chicken*

*slices of carrot and onion for flavouring*

*15 ml (1 level tbsp) chopped fresh tarragon or 5 ml (1 level tsp) dried*

*salt and pepper*

*1 cucumber, about 275 g (10 oz) weight*

*10 ml (2 level tsp) gelatine*

*25 g (1 oz) butter or margarine*

*30 ml (2 level tbsp) flour*

*30 ml (2 tbsp) lemon juice*

*142 ml (5 fl oz) whipping cream*

*1 egg white*

*fresh tarragon sprigs, to garnish*

*Chicken and Cucumber Mousse*

**1.** Put the chicken, flavouring vegetables, herbs and seasoning into a large saucepan. Add just enough water to cover. Bring to the boil, cover and simmer for about 50 minutes, until tender.

**2.** Cool the chicken and remove skin. Cut the flesh into small pieces and mince. Boil the cooking liquid until reduced to 450 ml (¾ pint), then strain and reserve.

**3.** Peel and finely dice three quarters of the cucumber.

**4.** Sprinkle the gelatine in 30 ml (2 tbsp) water in a small bowl and leave to soak. Place the bowl over a pan of simmering water and stir until dissolved.

**5.** Melt the butter in a pan, stir in the flour and cook gently for 1 minute, stirring. Remove from

the heat and gradually stir in the strained stock.

**6.** Bring to the boil and continue to cook, stirring, until the sauce thickens. Remove from the heat and stir in the gelatine. Stir in the chicken and leave to cool.

**7.** When cold, add the diced cucumber, lemon juice, salt and plenty of pepper.

**8.** Lightly whip the cream and stiffly whisk the egg white. Fold in the cream, then the egg white into the sauce.

**9.** Spoon into a 1.7 litre (3 pint) serving dish, cover and refrigerate to set. Serve cold, decorated with cucumber slices and tarragon sprigs.
*Serves 6*

# CHICKEN WITH WALNUTS

*1.6 kg (3½ lb) oven-ready chicken*

*1 large carrot, peeled and sliced*

*1 medium onion, skinned and sliced*

*1 bay leaf*

*salt and pepper*

**For the walnut sauce**

*50 g (2 oz) butter or margarine*

*175 g (6 oz) walnut halves*

*2 medium onions, skinned and sliced*

*284 ml (10 oz) natural yogurt*

*1.25 ml (¼ level tsp) paprika*

*150 ml (¼ pint) Chicken Stock (see page 19)*

**1.** Put the chicken in a large saucepan with the carrot, onion, bay leaf and seasoning and cover

with cold water.

**2.** Bring to the boil, cover, and simmer for about 1 hour until tender.

**3.** Remove the chicken from the pan, discard the skin and cut the meat into large pieces.

**4.** To make the sauce, heat the butter in a frying pan, add 50 g (2 oz) of the walnut halves and fry gently until light golden brown, then remove from the pan with a slotted spoon.

**5.** Add the onions and fry until soft, then add the yogurt, paprika and Chicken Stock.

**6.** Place the remaining walnuts in a blender or food processor until finely ground, then add to the sauce.

**7.** Stir in the walnut halves and the chicken, heat through and adjust the seasoning.
*Serves 4*

# CASSEROLED CHICKEN

## POULET EN COCOTTE *(Chicken Casserole)*

| |
|---|
| *1.4 kg (3 lb) oven-ready chicken* |
| *50 g (2 oz) butter or margarine* |
| *225 g (8 oz) lean back bacon in one slice* |
| *450 g (1 lb) potatoes, peeled and cut into 2.5 cm (1 inch) dice* |
| *3 celery sticks, trimmed and sliced* |
| *450 g (1 lb) small new carrots, peeled* |
| *50 g (2 oz) button mushrooms, wiped* |
| *25 g (1 oz) shelled walnuts* |
| *chopped fresh parsley, to garnish* |
| **For the stuffing** |
| *100 g (4 oz) sausagemeat* |
| *30 ml (2 level tbsp) fresh breadcrumbs* |
| *1 chicken liver, chopped* |
| *30 ml (2 tbsp) chopped fresh parsley* |
| *salt and pepper* |

1. To make the stuffing, mix all the ingredients together in a bowl until well blended. Season well.
2. Stuff the chicken at the neck end, then truss the bird as for roasting. Season well.
3. Melt the butter in a large frying pan, add the chicken and fry, turning it until well browned all over.
4. Place the chicken and butter in a large ovenproof casserole.
5. Rind the bacon and cut into 2 cm (¾ inch) cubes. Add to the casserole, cover, and cook in the oven at 180°C (350°F) mark 4 for 15 minutes.
6. Remove the casserole from the oven and baste the chicken. Surround it with the vegetables and walnuts, turning them in the fat.
7. Return the casserole to the oven and cook for a further 1½ hours. Transfer the chicken to a warmed serving plate and garnish with chopped parsley. Serve the vegetables and juices straight from the casserole.
*Serves 4*

## CHICKEN WITH VERMOUTH AND OLIVES

| |
|---|
| *8 chicken thighs, skinned, total weight about 900 g (2 lb)* |
| *40 g (1½ oz) seasoned flour* |
| *50 g (2 oz) butter or margarine* |
| *300 ml (½ pint) Chicken Stock (see page 19)* |
| *150 ml (¼ pint) dry French vermouth or dry white wine* |
| *1 small garlic clove, skinned and crushed* |
| *142 ml (5 fl oz) soured cream* |
| *50 g (2 oz) black olives, stoned and sliced* |
| *salt and pepper* |
| *Pastry Crescents (see right) and parsley sprigs, to garnish* |

1. Toss the chicken thighs in seasoned flour and reserve any remaining flour. Melt the butter in a flameproof casserole and brown the chicken well all over. Carefully remove the chicken from the fat with a large slotted spoon and set aside and keep warm.
2. Stir in the reserved seasoned flour, cook gently for 1 minute stirring. Remove pan from the heat and gradually stir in the stock, vermouth and crushed garlic. Bring to the boil slowly and continue to cook, stirring constantly, until the sauce is thickened.
3. Return the chicken to the pan, cover and simmer gently for about 1 hour.
4. Transfer the chicken pieces to a serving dish and keep warm. Stir the soured cream into the pan juices. Heat gently for 3–4 minutes, without boiling.
5. Just before serving, add the olives, adjust the seasoning and spoon the sauce over the chicken. Garnish with pastry crescents and parsley.

**Pastry Crescents (fleurons)**
Cut about 50 g (2 oz) Shortcrust Pastry made with 50 g (2 oz) flour (see page 372) into crescents, place on dampened baking sheet and bake in the oven at 220°C (425°F) mark 7 for about 12 minutes, until golden brown and well risen.
*Serves 4*

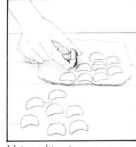

*Using a biscuit cutter, cut crescent shapes from thinly rolled pastry.*

## CHICKEN MARENGO

4 chicken joints

½ a lemon, cut into wedges

50 g (2 oz) flour

60 ml (4 tbsp) vegetable oil

50 g (2 oz) butter or margarine

30 ml (2 tbsp) brandy

salt and pepper

397 g (14 oz) can tomatoes, with their juice

1 garlic clove, skinned and crushed

150 ml (¼ pint) Chicken Stock (see page 19)

125 g (4 oz) button mushrooms, wiped

30 ml (2 tbsp) chopped fresh parsley

1. Rub the chicken joints all over with the lemon and coat in the flour.
2. Heat the oil in a large frying pan, add the chicken joints and fry on both sides, until golden brown, about 5–10 minutes.
3. Remove from the frying pan and place, skin-side up, in a large saucepan or flameproof casserole together with 25 g (1 oz) of the butter. Sprinkle with the brandy and seasoning, then turn the joints over. Roughly chop the tomatoes and add them to the chicken with the garlic and stock.
4. Cover and simmer gently for about 1 hour, until the meat is tender.
5. Ten minutes before serving, melt the remaining butter in a pan and cook the mushrooms for about 5 minutes, until soft. Drain and add to the chicken.

*Chicken Cacciatora*

6. When the chicken is cooked add the parsley and stir. Adjust the seasoning.
7. Transfer the chicken joints to a warmed serving dish. If the sauce is too thin, boil briskly to reduce. Spoon the sauce over the chicken and serve garnished with the fried bread.

### Variation

CHICKEN CACCIATORA

To make Chicken Cacciatora, increase the mushrooms to 225 g (8 oz) and fry with 1 skinned and finely chopped onion. Replace the stock with dry white wine.
*Serves 4*

## CHICKEN AND WATERCRESS CASSEROLE

1 large bunch watercress

1.4 kg (3 lb) oven-ready chicken

15 g (½ oz) butter

15 ml (1 tbsp) vegetable oil

2 medium onions, skinned and sliced

100 g (4 oz) peas

200 ml (7 fl oz) Chicken Stock (see page 19)

salt and pepper

60 ml (4 tbsp) soured cream

croûtons of fried bread, to garnish

1. Trim, wash and chop the watercress, keeping a few sprigs for garnishing.
2. Joint the chicken into eight pieces (see page 149), leaving the skin on. Heat the butter and oil in a shallow flameproof casserole, add

the chicken pieces and fry until well browned. Remove from the casserole with a slotted spoon.
3. Add the onions to the residual fat and cook until soft. Stir in the watercress and cook, stirring, for 2 minutes. Return the chicken to the pan with the peas.
4. Pour over the stock and add the seasoning. Cover tightly and bake in the oven at 180°C (350°F) mark 4 for about 50 minutes, until the chicken is tender.
5. Remove the chicken and keep warm. Purée the cooking liquid and vegetables in a blender or food processor, return to the casserole and bring to the boil. Remove from the heat and stir in the soured cream.
6. Spoon the sauce over the chicken and serve, garnished with croûtons and watercress sprigs.
*Serves 4*

## ITALIAN STYLE POUSSIN

| |
|---|
| 15 ml (1 tbsp) vegetable oil |
| 25 g (1 oz) butter or margarine |
| 4 small poussins |
| 450 g (1 lb) potatoes, peeled and cut into small fingers |
| 175 g (6 oz) button onions, skinned |
| 125 g (4 oz) button mushrooms, wiped |
| 450 ml (¾ pint) Chicken Stock (see page 19) |
| 30 ml (2 level tbsp) tomato purée |
| 5 ml (1 level tsp) dried oregano |
| 45 ml (3 tbsp) dry sherry |
| salt and pepper |
| 50 g (2 oz) cooked ham, shredded |
| 30 ml (2 level tbsp) cornflour |

1. Heat the oil and butter in large flameproof casserole, add the poussins and fry until browned.

Remove with a slotted spoon and drain on absorbent kitchen paper.
2. Add the potatoes to the casserole with the onions and mushrooms and cook until golden brown. Return the poussins to the casserole, arranging them side by side.
3. Mix together the stock, tomato purée, oregano and sherry and season well. Pour over the poussins, cover and cook in the oven at 180°C (350°F) mark 4 for about 1 hour, until all the ingredients are tender.
4. Transfer the birds and vegetables to a warmed serving plate, leaving the juices in the pan. Add the ham to the juices, adjust the seasoning and stir in the cornflour blended with a little water. Bring to the boil, stirring, until thickened. Spoon over the poussins and serve.
*Serves 4*

## COQ AU VIN

| |
|---|
| 1 large chicken, jointed, or 6–8 chicken joints |
| 30 ml (2 level tbsp) flour |
| salt and pepper |
| 90 g (3½ oz) butter or margarine |
| 100 g (4 oz) lean bacon, diced |
| 1 medium onion, skinned and quartered |
| 1 medium carrot, peeled and quartered |
| 60 ml (4 tbsp) brandy |
| 600 ml (1 pint) red wine |
| 1 garlic clove, skinned and crushed |
| bouquet garni |
| 1 sugar lump |
| 30 ml (2 tbsp) vegetable oil |
| 450 g (1 lb) button onions, skinned |
| pinch of sugar |
| 5 ml (1 tsp) wine vinegar |
| 225 g (8 oz) button mushrooms, wiped |
| 6 slices of white bread, crusts removed |

1. Coat the chicken pieces with 15 ml (1 tbsp) of the flour, liberally seasoned with salt and pepper.
2. Melt 25 g (1 oz) of the butter in a flameproof casserole, add the chicken pieces and fry gently until they are golden brown on all sides. Add the bacon, onion and carrot and fry until softened.
3. Heat the brandy in a small saucepan, pour over the chicken and ignite, shaking the pan so that

all the chicken pieces are covered in flames. Pour on the wine and stir to remove any sediment from the bottom of the casserole. Add the garlic, bouquet garni and sugar lump. Bring to the boil, cover and simmer for 1–1½ hours, until tender.
4. Meanwhile, melt another 25 g (1 oz) of the butter with 10 ml (2 tsp) of the oil in a frying pan. Add the onions and fry until they begin to brown. Add the sugar and the vinegar, together with 15 ml (1 tbsp) water. Cover and simmer for 10–15 minutes, until just tender. Keep warm.
5. Melt 25 g (1 oz) of the butter with 10 ml (2 tsp) oil in a pan and add the mushrooms. Cook for a few minutes. Keep warm. Remove chicken from the casserole and place in serving dish. Surround with onions and mushrooms. Keep hot.
6. Discard the bouquet garni. Skim the excess fat off the cooking liquid and boil the liquid in the casserole briskly for 3–5 minutes to reduce it.
7. Add the remaining oil to the fat in the frying pan and fry the pieces of bread until golden brown on both sides. Cut each slice into triangles.
8. Work the remaining flour and butter to make a *beurre manié* (see page 570). Take the casserole off the heat and add the beurre manié in small pieces to the cooking liquid. Stir until smooth, then bring just to the boil. The sauce should now be thick and shiny. Adjust the seasoning and pour over the chicken. Garnish with fried bread.
*Serves 6–8*

## CHICKEN AND STILTON ROULADES

125 g (4 oz) Stilton cheese, crumbled

100 g (4 oz) butter or margarine, softened

4 chicken breast fillets, about 75–100 g (3–4 oz) each

8 rashers smoked back bacon, rinded

15 ml (1 tbsp) vegetable oil

150 ml (¼ pint) red wine

150 ml (¼ pint) Chicken Stock (see page 19)

salt and pepper

5 ml (1 level tsp) arrowroot

watercress sprigs, to garnish

1. Cream the Stilton and 75 g (3 oz) butter to a smooth paste in a small bowl.
2. Flatten chicken breasts between two sheets of damp greaseproof paper. Spread the Stilton butter evenly on one side of each breast.
3. Roll up the chicken breasts and wrap each one in two bacon rashers. Secure each roll with a wooden cocktail stick.
4. In a flameproof casserole, heat the oil and remaining butter and brown the chicken rolls well.
5. Pour in the red wine and stock and season. Bring to the boil, cover and simmer very gently for 35–40 minutes, turning occasionally. Transfer the rolls to a warmed serving dish, remove the cocktail sticks and keep warm.
6. Blend the arrowroot with 10 ml (2 tsp) water in a small bowl. Add to the pan juices and boil until thickened. Season to taste. Spoon the sauce over the chicken. Garnish with watercress sprigs.
Serves 4

*Using a rolling pin, flatten the chicken breasts between two sheets of dampened greaseproof paper or on a wooden board.*

# COOKED CHICKEN DISHES

## CHICKEN CHAUDFROID

half a 28.35 g (1 oz) packet aspic powder

6 boneless chicken portions, cooked

300 ml (½ pint) Béchamel Sauce (see page 202)

cucumber, pickled walnuts, radishes and strips of
    lemon rind, to garnish

1. Make up the aspic to 300 ml (½ pint) as directed on the packet and leave it until it has almost reached setting point.
2. Place the cold chicken portions on a wire rack over a tray or large plate.
3. Add half the aspic to the Béchamel Sauce, stir in lightly and allow it to thicken but not set. (Keep the remaining aspic in a basin standing in a bowl of warm water.) Coat the chicken portions by pouring the sauce steadily over them to give a smooth, even surface, allowing the excess to run off and collect in the tray.
4. The chicken portions can be decorated with strips of cucumber skin or pieces of pickled walnut, slices of radish and strips of lemon rind, then carefully spoon over the remaining aspic (which should be at setting point), so that the coated chicken portions are completely covered with aspic, but the decorations are not disturbed.
Serves 6

*Place the chicken portions on a wire rack and pour over the sauce to give a smooth, even coating. Allow the excess sauce to collect in a tray under the rack.*

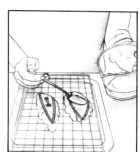

*Use finely cut strips of cucumbers, radishes and lemon rind and walnuts to decorate the chicken pieces. Then spoon over aspic.*

## PANCAKE ROLLS

225 g (8 oz) cooked chicken, boned and skinned

15 ml (1 tbsp) sesame or vegetable oil

1 small bunch spring onions, trimmed and chopped

3 garlic cloves, skinned and crushed

2.5 cm (1 inch) piece of fresh root ginger, peeled and
   crushed

100 g (4 oz) beansprouts

1 medium carrot, peeled and grated

15 ml (1 tbsp) soy sauce

2.5 ml ($\frac{1}{2}$ level tsp) soft brown sugar

salt and pepper

8 squares of frozen spring roll pastry, thawed

vegetable oil for deep-frying

Pancake Rolls

1. Cut the chicken into thin strips. Set aside.
2. Heat the 15 ml (1 tbsp) oil in a wok or frying
pan, add the spring onions, garlic and ginger
and fry gently for 5 minutes until soft. Add the
beansprouts and carrot and fry for a further
2 minutes, stirring constantly.
3. Turn the vegetables into a bowl and mix with
the chicken, soy sauce, sugar and salt and pepper.
4. Divide the filling mixture equally into eight,
then form each portion into a roll shape.
5. Place one roll on one sheet of pastry, towards

the nearest corner. Fold the corner over the roll.
6. Fold in the corner at right angles to the first
corner, then fold in the opposite corner.
7. Roll up the filling in the pastry until the last
corner is reached, so that the filling is completely
enclosed. Seal the end with a little water.
8. Heat the oil in a deep-fat fryer to 180°C (350°F)
and fry in batches for about 10 minutes until
golden. Drain before serving.
Makes 8

# ROASTING TURKEY When roasting a turkey, remember you are
cooking two different types of meat, the delicate light breast meat, which must not be
allowed to dry out, and the darker leg meat which takes longer to cook. The turkey
must be roasted long enough for the legs to cook so frequent basting is necessary.

## ROAST TURKEY

1 oven-ready turkey (see Note)

a little melted butter or vegetable oil

salt and pepper

streaky bacon rashers, rinded (optional)

1. Wash the inside of the bird and stuff at the
neck end before folding the neck skin over.
2. Make the turkey plump and as even in shape as
possible, then truss it with the wings folded under
the body and the legs tied together.
3. Weigh the turkey and calculate the cooking
time, allowing 20 minutes per 450 g (1 lb) plus
20 minutes.
4. Place the turkey in a roasting tin, brush with
melted butter and sprinkle with salt and pepper.

5. Place streaky bacon rashers over the breast to
prevent it from becoming dry, if wished. Roast in
the oven at 180°C (350°F) mark 4, basting from
time to time. Put a piece of foil over the bird if it
shows signs of becoming too brown.
   Serve with gravy and Bread Sauce (see page
208). Small sausages, Bacon Rolls (see page 156)
and watercress may be used to garnish the turkey.
Cranberry Sauce (see page 208) or some other
sharp sauce can also be served.
Note To calculate the required size, use the
following guidelines: 3.6–5 kg (8–11 lb) serves
10–15; 5–6.8 kg (11–15 lb) serves 15–20; 6.8–9 kg
(15–20 lb) serves 20–30.

# Festive Turkey Galantine

3.9 kg (8½ lb) oven-ready turkey

100 g (4 oz) butter or margarine

1 medium onion, skinned and chopped

3 celery sticks, washed and finely chopped

450 g (1 lb) cooking apples, peeled, cored and roughly
    chopped

700 g (1½ lb) pork sausagemeat

50 g (2 oz) fresh breadcrumbs

grated rind and juice of 1 orange

50 g (2 oz) chopped walnuts

2.5 ml (½ level tsp) dried thyme

salt and pepper

2 eggs, size 6, beaten

1.4 kg (2½ lb) boneless bacon joint, boiled and skinned

1. Bone the turkey (see page 149) or ask the butcher to do this for you. Melt half the butter in a saucepan and gently fry the onion, celery and apples together for 5 minutes. Leave to cool.

2. Stir the cooled mixture into the sausagemeat and breadcrumbs, adding the grated orange rind, walnuts, thyme and seasoning. Bind with the eggs.

3. Place the turkey, skin side down, on a work surface and spread the stuffing over the bird, more generously in the thigh positions. Place the cooked bacon joint lengthways down the centre of the bird.

4. Tuck the neck end in towards the filling, draw the long sides of the bird over the stuffing and sew it neatly together with fine string to completely encase the stuffing. Use overlapping stitches and do not roll too tightly or the bird will burst during cooking. Secure the string loosely for easy removal. Weigh the bird.

5. Place it, breast side up, on a large piece of foil in a roasting tin. Spread with the remaining butter and add the orange juice. Wrap over the edges of the foil to make a parcel.

6. Roast in the oven at 180°C (350°F) mark 4 for 15 minutes per 450 g (1 lb) plus 15 minutes. Unwrap for the last 30 minutes, to brown.

7. Cool completely for 4–5 hours, then refrigerate overnight. Remove the string before slicing.
*Serves about 20*

*Festive Turkey Galantine*

## STUFFED TURKEY DRUMSTICKS

*2 turkey drumsticks, at least 900 g (2 lb) total weight*

*225 g (8 oz) pork sausagemeat*

*15 ml (1 tbsp) chopped fresh tarragon or 5 ml (1 level tsp) dried*

*10 ml (2 tsp) chopped fresh parsley*

*salt and pepper*

*50 g (2 oz) mushrooms, wiped and thinly sliced*

*flour for dusting*

*1 egg white, beaten*

*175 g (6 oz) fresh breadcrumbs*

*100 g (4 oz) butter or margarine, softened*

*15 ml (1 level tbsp) French mustard*

*Onion Sauce (see page 201), to serve*

1. Skin the turkey drumsticks, slit the flesh and ease out the bone and large sinews.
2. Mix the sausagemeat, herbs and seasoning and spread one quarter in each boned leg. Cover with a layer of sliced mushrooms and top with more sausagemeat stuffing. Reshape the legs and sew up neatly.
3. Dip joints in flour, brush with the egg white and place seam-side down in a greased roasting tin.
4. Beat together the breadcrumbs, butter and mustard, then spread it over the top and sides of the drumsticks.
5. Bake in the oven at 190°C (375°F) mark 5 for about 1 hour 40 minutes, until the meat is tender and has a crisp, golden crust. Remove the string and serve sliced with Onion Sauce.
*Serves 6*

# FRIED AND GRILLED TURKEY

## DEVILLED TURKEY DRUMSTICKS

*2 cooked turkey drumsticks*

*50 g (2 oz) butter or margarine, melted*

*5 ml (1 level tsp) French mustard*

*5 ml (1 level tsp) prepared English mustard*

*10 ml (2 level tsp) chutney, finely chopped*

*pinch of ground ginger*

*pinch of cayenne pepper*

*salt and pepper*

*watercress sprigs, to garnish*

1. Score the drumsticks with a sharp knife, then brush with melted butter.
2. Mix together the French and English mustards, chutney, ground ginger, cayenne and salt and pepper.
3. Spread the mixture over and into the cuts and leave the turkey legs to marinate for at least 1 hour.
4. Grill the drumsticks on a greased grid under a medium heat until crisp and brown, turning regularly to ensure even cooking. Serve halved, garnished with watercress.
*Serves 4*

## TURKEY STROGANOFF

*15 ml (1 tbsp) vegetable oil*

*50 g (2 oz) butter or margarine*

*450 g (1 lb) turkey fillets, cut into pencil-thin strips*

*30 ml (2 tbsp) brandy*

*1 garlic clove, skinned and crushed*

*salt and pepper*

*225 g (8 oz) button mushrooms, wiped and sliced*

*1 medium green pepper, seeded and thinly sliced*

*60 ml (4 tbsp) soured cream*

1. Heat the oil and butter in a large frying pan and brown the turkey strips. Pour over the brandy and set alight, then add the garlic and seasoning.
2. Cover the pan and simmer for 4–5 minutes, or until the turkey is just tender.
3. Increase the heat, add the mushrooms and pepper and cook for 3–4 minutes, turning occasionally.
4. Reduce the heat, stir in the soured cream (if on the thick side, stir before adding to the pan) and adjust seasoning.
*Serves 4*

## TURKEY KEBABS WITH CHILLI PEANUT SAUCE

450 g (1 lb) turkey fillets or escalopes, cut into 2.5 cm
    (1 inch) pieces

225 g (8 oz) button mushrooms, wiped or 185 g (7½ oz)
    can button mushrooms, drained

150 ml (¼ pint) vegetable oil

30 ml (2 tbsp) lemon juice

5 ml (1 level tsp) ground cumin

5 ml (1 level tsp) sugar

5 ml (1 level tsp) salt

300 ml (½ pint) milk

45 ml (3 level tbsp) desiccated coconut

60 ml (4 level tbsp) crunchy peanut butter

pinch of mild chilli powder or 20 ml (4 level tsp) chilli
    seasoning

pepper

beansprouts and spring onions, to garnish

1. Thread eight skewers alternately with turkey
meat and whole mushrooms.
2. Mix together the oil, lemon juice, cumin,

sugar and salt. Pour over the kebabs. Cover and
marinate for at least 2 hours, turning occasionally.
3. Bring the milk to the boil and add the coconut.
Remove from the heat, cover and leave to infuse
for 10 minutes, then strain.
4. In a heavy-based saucepan, heat the peanut
butter with the chilli powder. Cook gently for
1 minute. Gradually stir in coconut milk, bring to
the boil, then simmer for 2–3 minutes. Add pepper.

Thread the turkey cubes and
mushrooms on to eight long
skewers.

5. Cook kebabs under
a low grill for 10–15
minutes, turning two or
three times and basting
with the marinade.
6. Spoon a little sauce
over kebabs and serve
the rest separately.
Garnish the kebabs
with beansprouts and
spring onions.
Serves 4

## CURRIED TURKEY WITH AVOCADO

1 ripe but firm avocado

15 ml (1 tbsp) lemon juice

30 ml (2 level tbsp) flour

15 ml (1 level tbsp) ground cumin

15 ml (1 level tbsp) ground ginger

450 g (1 lb) turkey fillets, cut into thin 5 cm (2 inch)
    long strips

1 egg, beaten

about 45 ml (3 tbsp) peanut oil

1 garlic clove, skinned and crushed

225 g (8 oz) can bamboo shoots, drained and thinly
    sliced

1 bunch spring onions, roughly chopped

salt and pepper

Boiled Rice (see page 302), to serve

1. Peel, halve and stone the avocado. Thickly slice
and coat the flesh with the lemon juice to prevent
discoloration.
2. Mix together the flour, cumin and ginger and
toss the turkey in it. Stir in the beaten egg until the
strips are well coated.
3. Heat the oil with the garlic in a wok or large
frying pan until beginning to smoke. Gradually
add the turkey strips, fry over a high heat, stirring
all the time, until the turkey strips are a golden
brown colour, adding a little more oil if necessary.
4. Reduce the heat, stir in the bamboo shoots
and spring onions. Continue cooking, stirring
constantly, for 1–2 minutes.
5. Off the heat, gently fold in the avocado and
lemon juice. Season with salt and pepper and serve
immediately with Boiled Rice.
Serves 4

**Variation**
CURRIED CHICKEN WITH AVOCADO
Substitute the turkey fillets with 450 g (1 lb)
chicken breasts, skinned and cut into 5 cm (2 inch)

strips. Proceed as above. Serve with the Boiled
Rice or Fried Rice (see page 304).

## TURKEY SAUTÉ WITH LEMON AND WALNUTS

| |
|---|
| 450 g (1 lb) turkey fillets or escalopes, cut into thin 5 cm (2 inch) long strips |
| 30 ml (2 level tbsp) cornflour |
| 30 ml (2 tbsp) vegetable oil |
| 40 g (1½ oz) walnut halves or pieces |
| 1 medium green pepper, seeded and cut into strips |
| 25 g (1 oz) butter or margarine |
| 60 ml (4 tbsp) Chicken Stock (see page 19) |
| 30 ml (2 tbsp) lemon juice |
| 45 ml (3 level tbsp) lemon marmalade |
| 5 ml (1 tsp) malt vinegar |
| 1.25 ml (¼ tsp) soy sauce |
| salt and pepper |

*Turkey Sauté with Lemon and Walnuts*

**1.** Toss the turkey in the cornflour until coated.
**2.** Heat the oil in a large sauté or deep frying pan, add the walnuts and pepper and fry for 2–3 minutes. Remove from the pan with a slotted spoon.
**3.** Melt the butter in the residual fat, add the turkey strips a few at a time and fry until golden.

**4.** Return all the turkey to the pan and stir in the stock and lemon juice, stirring well to remove any sediment at the bottom of the pan. Add the lemon marmalade, vinegar, soy sauce and seasoning. Stir in the walnuts and pepper.
**5.** Cook gently for a further 5 minutes. Adjust seasoning if necessary, and serve at once.
*Serves 4*

## TURKEY AND HAM PARCELS

| |
|---|
| 700 g (1½ lb) turkey escalopes |
| 8 thin slices of cooked ham |
| 100 g (4 oz) Cotswold cheese |
| 30 ml (2 level tbsp) creamed horseradish |
| salt and pepper |
| 20 ml (4 level tsp) flour |
| 1 egg, beaten |
| 90 ml (6 level tbsp) dried breadcrumbs |
| vegetable oil |
| lime slices, to garnish |

*Turkey and Ham Parcels*

**1.** Cut the escalopes into sixteen even-sized pieces. Using a rolling pin or meat mallet, flatten thinly between two sheets of dampened grease-proof paper.
**2.** Halve each of the eight slices of ham and cut the cheese into sixteen pieces. Then wrap a piece of cheese, a little creamed horseradish and seasoning in each of the slices of ham.
**3.** Enclose each ham roll in a slice of the turkey meat, securing firmly with wooden cocktail sticks pierced through the centre of each roll.

**4.** Coat the turkey parcels in the flour, egg and breadcrumbs, then chill in the refrigerator for at least 2 hours.
**5.** Brush the turkey and ham parcels with plenty of oil and grill them for about 8 minutes on each side. Serve hot, garnished with lime slices.
*Serves 8*

## TURKEY IN SPICED YOGURT

7.5 ml (1½ level tsp) ground cumin

7.5 ml (1½ level tsp) ground coriander

2.5 ml (½ level tsp) ground turmeric

2.5 ml (½ level tsp) ground ginger

salt and pepper

284 g (10 oz) natural yogurt

30 ml (2 tbsp) lemon juice

900 g (2 lb) turkey meat, cut into 2.5 cm (1 inch) cubes

45 ml (3 tbsp) vegetable oil

2 medium onions, skinned and sliced

45 ml (3 level tbsp) desiccated coconut

30 ml (2 level tbsp) flour

150 ml (¼ pint) Chicken Stock (see page 19)

chopped fresh parsley, to garnish

**1.** In a large bowl, mix the spices with the seasoning, yogurt and lemon juice. Stir well until evenly blended.
**2.** Fold in the turkey meat until coated with the yogurt mixture. Cover tightly with cling film and refrigerate for several hours.
**3.** Heat the oil in a medium flameproof casserole, add the onions and fry until lightly browned. Add the coconut and flour and fry gently, stirring, for about 1 minute.
**4.** Remove from the heat and stir in the turkey with its marinade and the stock. Return to the heat and bring slowly to the boil, stirring all the time. Cover tightly and cook in the oven at 170°C (325°F) mark 3 for 1–1¼ hours until the turkey is tender.

*Turkey in Spiced Yogurt*

**5.** Adjust the seasoning and serve garnished with chopped fresh parsley.
*Serves 6–8*

# COOKED TURKEY

## TURKEY À LA KING

50 g (2 oz) butter or margarine

125 g (4 oz) mushrooms, wiped and sliced

1 medium green pepper, chopped, or 1 small canned
    pimiento, chopped

50 g (2 oz) flour

568 ml (1 pint) milk or milk and chicken stock, mixed

450 g (1 lb) skinned, cooked turkey meat, diced

salt and pepper

paprika and grated nutmeg

15–30 ml (1–2 tbsp) sherry (optional)

Boiled Rice (see page 302) or buttered noodles, to serve

**1.** Melt the butter in a saucepan, add the mushrooms and pepper and fry until soft.
**2.** Stir in the flour and cook gently for 1 minute, stirring. Remove the pan from the heat and gradually stir in the milk. Bring to the boil slowly and continue to cook, stirring constantly, until the sauce thickens.
**3.** Add the turkey, season to taste with salt, pepper and paprika and add the sherry, if using. Heat through, stirring occasionally. Serve with Boiled Rice or buttered noodles.
*Serves 4*

# GOOSE

GOOSE The main season for fresh geese is September to December, although a limited number are usually available throughout the year, especially at Easter. They are also sold frozen ready for the oven. Fresh goose may be dressed or 'rough plucked' (with head and feet on and not drawn). Deep yellow fat indicates an old goose.

## BUYING GEESE

It is advisable to order a goose in advance, as butchers, poulterers and supermarkets tend not to keep extensive stocks.

Geese range in weight from about 3 kg (7 lb) to as much as 6.75 kg (15 lb), with the most popular sizes being 3.6–5.5 kg (8–12 lb). A 4.5 kg (10 lb)

goose will serve 6–8 people.

It is important to remember that the breast meat will cook faster than the leg and underside and care must be taken that it does not dry out so cover it with foil. The legs are cooked if the juices run clear when a skewer is inserted.

## ROAST GOOSE

*4–5 kg (9–11 lb) oven-ready goose*

*salt*

*Sage and Onion Stuffing (see page 184)*

*Apple Sauce (see page 207)  to serve*

**1.** Prick the skin of the goose with a fork in several places. Pull the inside fat out of the bird. Rub salt over the skin.
**2.** Spoon the stuffing into the neck end of the goose, skewer the neck skin to the back of the

bird, then truss (see page 148) or tie up the goose with string. Weigh the bird.
**3.** Put on a rack placed over a roasting tin. Cover the breast with foil. Roast in the oven at 200°C (400°F) mark 6 for 15 minutes per 450 g (1 lb) plus 15 minutes, basting frequently. Remove foil for last 20 minutes to brown.
**4.** Serve the goose with the Apple Sauce and thin gravy (see page 149).
*Serves 8*

# DUCKLING

DUCKLING is sold both fresh and frozen ready for the oven and is usually killed before the second feather stage, at about 7–8 weeks. A smaller number are also sold New York dressed or 'rough plucked' (with heads and feet on and not drawn). When choosing a rough plucked bird check that the beak and feet are pliable and the breast plump.

Oven-ready weights range from 1.4–2.7 kg (3–6 lb) and you should allow a minimum of 450 g (1 lb) dressed weight per person. Portions of fresh or frozen duckling can be used when a recipe calls for jointing.

## ROAST DUCKLING

*1 oven-ready duckling*

*salt and pepper*

*Sage and Onion Stuffing (see page 184)*

*Apple Sauce (see page 207)*

**1.** If frozen, thaw the duckling completely. Leave it in its bag and thaw at room temperature. Remove the giblets as soon as possible. Wash and pat the carcass dry both inside and out.
**2.** Rub the skin with salt and prick it all over with a sharp skewer or fork to allow the fat to run during cooking. Weigh the bird.

**3.** Place the duckling on a wire rack over a roasting tin and roast in the oven at 180°C (350°F) mark 4, allowing 30–35 minutes per 450 g (1 lb).

Traditionally, roast duckling is served with Sage and Onion Stuffing and accompanied by Apple Sauce and thin brown gravy (see page 204). *Note* Only young ducklings should be used for roasting and older birds reserved for slower cooking methods, such as braising, or for using in pâtés.

PORTIONING A DUCKLING
1. Cut off any excess neck skin and discard. Pull out the clusters of fat from inside the body cavity and discard.
2. With the bird breast side up, starting at the vent end, cut along one side of the breastbone to the neck cavity.

3. Cut along both sides of the backbone to halve the duckling and remove the bone.
4. Cut each half of the duckling into two to give equal portions of meat. If poultry shears are not sharp enough, first cut through the flesh, then the bone.

## ROAST STUFFED DUCKLINGS

*125 g (4 oz) tenderised prunes*
*225 g (8 oz) fresh breadcrumbs*
*1 large orange*
*5 ml (1 level tsp) dried thyme*
*salt and pepper*
*1 egg*
*two 1.8 kg (4 lb) oven-ready ducklings, trimmed of
    excess fat*
*30 ml (2 level tbsp) flour*
*450 ml (¾ pint) Chicken Stock (see page 19)*
*30 ml (2 tbsp) medium dry sherry*
*gravy browning*
*watercress sprigs, to garnish*

1. Cut the prunes into small pieces, then place in a large bowl with the breadcrumbs.
2. Finely grate in the orange rind and strain in the orange juice—there should be about 90 ml (6 tbsp) of juice.
3. Add the thyme, seasoning and egg and stir well until evenly blended.

4. Divide the stuffing between the birds, then truss (see page 148). Weigh the birds.
5. Place the ducklings on a wire rack over a large roasting tin. Prick the ducklings well all over, then sprinkle with salt. Roast in the oven at 180°C (350°F) mark 4, allowing 30–35 minutes per 450 g (1 lb).
6. To test the ducklings, pierce the thickest part of the leg with a fine skewer. The juices will run clear if the bird is cooked.
7. Remove the string and place the ducklings on a warmed serving dish and keep warm, uncovered, in a low oven.
8. Pour off all but 30 ml (2 tbsp) of fat from the roasting tin, then stir in the flour and cook gently until golden brown.
9. Stir in the stock and seasoning, bring to the boil and boil for 2–3 minutes, add the sherry with a dash of gravy browning and keep warm on the side of the cooker.
10. Garnish the duckling with watercress and serve with the gravy.
*Serves 6*

## DUCKLING WITH ORANGE SAUCE (CANETON À LA BIGARADE)

*1.8–2.6 kg (4–6 lb) oven-ready duckling*
*salt and pepper*
*150 ml (¼ pint) white wine*
*4 oranges (use bitter oranges when available)*
*1 lemon*
*15 ml (1 level tbsp) sugar*
*15 ml (1 tbsp) white wine vinegar*
*30 ml (2 tbsp) brandy or orange-flavoured liqueur*
*15 ml (1 level tbsp) cornflour*
*1 bunch watercress, to garnish*

1. Rub the duckling skin with salt and prick the skin all over.
2. Put the duckling in the roasting tin with the wine and roast in the oven at 180°C (350°F) mark 4 for 30–35 minutes per 450 g, basting occasionally.

3. Meanwhile, grate the rind from 1 orange and squeeze the juice from 3 of the oranges and the lemon. Separate the remaining orange into segments and reserve for the garnish.
4. Melt the sugar in a pan with the vinegar and heat until it is a dark brown caramel.
5. Add the brandy and the orange and lemon juice and simmer gently for 5 minutes.
6. When the duckling is cooked, remove it from the roasting tin, joint it (see above) and place the pieces on a serving dish and keep warm.
7. Drain excess fat from the tin and add the grated rind and the orange sauce to the sediment.
8. Blend the cornflour with 30 ml (2 tbsp) water, stir it into the pan juices, bring to the boil and cook for 2–3 minutes, stirring. Season and pour the sauce over the joints. Garnish and serve.
*Serves 4*

*Sweet and Sour Duckling Joints*

## SWEET AND SOUR DUCKLING JOINTS

| |
|---|
| *4 duckling joints* |
| *salt and pepper* |
| *60 ml (4 tbsp) soy sauce* |
| *45 ml (3 level tbsp) soft brown sugar* |
| *45 ml (3 tbsp) honey* |
| *45 ml (3 tbsp) wine or cider vinegar* |
| *30 ml (2 tbsp) dry sherry* |
| *juice of 1 orange* |
| *150 ml (¼ pint) water* |
| *2.5 ml (½ level tsp) ground ginger* |
| *few orange slices and watercress, to garnish* |

**1.** Prick the duckling joints all over with a fork, then sprinkle the skin with salt and pepper.
**2.** Place on a rack in a roasting tin and roast in the oven at 190°C (375°F) mark 5 for 45–60 minutes, until the skin is crisp and the juices run clear when the thickest part is pierced with a skewer.
**3.** Meanwhile, make the sauce. Mix together all the remaining ingredients in a saucepan and bring to the boil. Simmer, stirring constantly, for about 5 minutes to allow the flavours to blend and the sauce to thicken slightly. Add salt and pepper to taste.
**4.** Trim the duck joints neatly by cutting off any knuckles or wing joints. Arrange on a warmed serving platter and coat with the sauce. Garnish each portion with orange slices and watercress. Serve immediately.
*Serves 4*

---

# GUINEA FOWL
These are available all the year round, but are at their best from February to June. A guinea fowl has grey plumage with white spots and is about the same size as a pheasant, though it can be as large as a small chicken. It has a more gamey flavour than chicken. When choosing one, look out for the same points as in a fresh chicken, especially a plump breast and smooth-skinned feet. An average-sized bird will serve 4 people. Guinea fowl are not usually available jointed.

All methods for cooking chicken or pheasant (see pages 149 and 173) are applicable, especially braising or casseroling, but take care to use plenty of fat when roasting it, otherwise the flesh will be dry.

## ROAST GUINEA FOWL

Singe, draw and wipe the bird, then truss it for roasting (see page 148). Roast in the oven at 200°C (400°F) mark 6 for 45–60 minutes, or longer according to size, basting frequently with butter or dripping. Garnish with watercress and serve with thin gravy and orange or mixed green salad or with Bread Sauce (see page 208).

# GAME

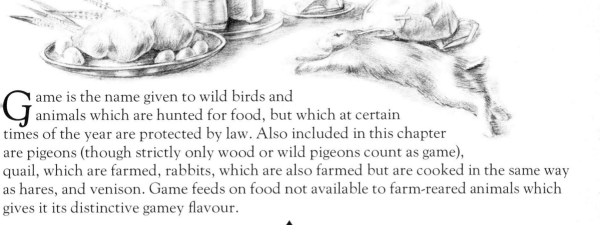

Game is the name given to wild birds and animals which are hunted for food, but which at certain times of the year are protected by law. Also included in this chapter are pigeons (though strictly only wood or wild pigeons count as game), quail, which are farmed, rabbits, which are also farmed but are cooked in the same way as hares, and venison. Game feeds on food not available to farm-reared animals which gives it its distinctive gamey flavour.

◆

## GAME BIRDS

GAME BIRDS are best eaten young. The plumage is a guide as all young birds have soft even feathers. With pheasants and partridge, the long wing feathers are V-shaped in a young bird, as distinct from the rounded ones of an older bird. Smooth, pliable legs, short spurs and a firm, plump breast are other points to look for. Most game birds need to be hung so ask the butcher or poulterer if the bird has been hung and for how long. If it is not hung, the flesh will be tough and tasteless.

Alternatively, order game from your butcher or poulterer and he will hang the bird for the specified time and supply it ready plucked and drawn on the required day. If you are given game, you can hang it yourself in a cold, dry, airy place for the time specified in the chart overleaf. The birds should be hung by the neck without being plucked or drawn.

If you are given a bird that has been damaged by shot or is wet, it will not keep as long as a bird in good condition. Check it frequently and cook it as soon as the tail feathers will pluck out easily.

### STORING GAME BIRDS

A bird that has been hung and is ready for cooking can be stored for 1–2 days in the refrigerator or it can be frozen. If necessary, a bird can be frozen for a short time with its feathers on and plucked after thawing, but it is best to pluck and draw first.

### COOKING AND SERVING

The more simply game is cooked, the better. For a young bird, there is no better way than roasting, but for older birds, which are likely to be tough if plainly roasted, braising or casseroling is a better method.

Game birds lack fat, so it is usual to cover the breast before roasting with pieces of fat bacon (this is called 'barding') and to baste frequently with butter or margarine during the cooking. When the bird is nearly cooked, the bacon can be removed in order to brown the meat.

### ACCOMPANIMENTS

**Thin gravy**, can be served with any roast game bird. Add 150 ml ($\frac{1}{4}$ pint) water or meat stock to the roasting tin and, with a spoon, rub down any cooking juices left in the tin. Bring to the boil and boil for 2–3 minutes. Remove all grease from the surface with a metal spoon, season to taste and strain before serving.

**Fried Crumbs**, fry 50–100 g (2–4 oz) fresh breadcrumbs in 25 g (1 oz) butter or margarine until golden brown. Stir from time to time to ensure even browning.

**Game Chips**, see page 222.

**Bread Sauce**, see page 208.

**Toast**, small birds such as grouse are roasted on a slice of toast or bread. The bird is served on the toast or bread on which it is roasted.

CARVING GAME

Large game birds are carved in the same way as chicken (see page 148). Small birds like partridges and pigeons are usually cut in half. If very small, the whole bird may be served as one portion; woodcock, snipe and quail are among the birds which are served whole, on the toast or fried bread on which they were cooked. Special poultry shears are for cutting birds in half, or use a game carver or a short, pointed knife. Insert the point of the knife in the neck end of the breast and cut firmly through in the direction of the breast bone and tail.

## OPEN SEASONS FOR GAME BIRDS

| Bird | Shooting Season | Hanging (Days) | Cooking | No. of Servings |
|---|---|---|---|---|
| Blackgame (black grouse) | 20 Aug–10 Dec | 3–10 | Roast at 190°C (375°F) mark 5 for about 45 minutes | 2 servings |
| Capercaillie | 1 Oct–31 Jan | 7–14 | Roast at 200°C (400°F) mark 6 for about 40 minutes | 2–3 servings |
| Grouse | 12 Aug–10 Dec | 2–4 | Roast at 200°C (400°F) mark 6 for about 40 minutes | 1 per person |
| Partridge (Grey and Red-legged) | 1 Sept–1 Feb | 3–5 | Roast at 200°C (400°F) mark 6 for 40 minutes | 1 per person |
| Pheasant | 1 Oct–1 Feb (10 Dec in Scotland) | 3–10 | Roast at 230°C (450°F) mark 8 for 10 minutes, then reduce to 200°C (400°F) mark 6 for 30–50 minutes | Female birds give 2 servings, male birds give 3 servings |
| Ptarmigan | 12 Aug–10 Dec | 2–4 | Braise or casserole at 190°C (375°F) mark 5 for 40 minutes | 1 per person |
| Quail | not applicable | not applicable | Roast at 190°C (375°F) mark 5 for 15–20 minutes | 2 per person |
| Snipe | 12 Aug–31 Jan | 3–4 | Roast at 190°C (375°F) mark 5 for 15–20 minutes | 1–2 per person |
| Wild Duck–Mallard–Teal and Wigeon | 1 Sept–31 Jan | 2–3 (may be drawn before hanging) | Roast at 220°C (425°F) mark 7 for about 30 minutes | 2 servings |
| Wild Geese–Pink Footed and Greylag | 1 Sept–31 Jan | 2–9 | Roast at 220°C (425°F) mark 7 for 20 minutes. Reduce heat to 180°C (350°F) mark 4 allowing 13–15 minutes per 480 g (1 lb). | A 4.5 kg (10 lb) bird will serve 6–8 people |
| Woodcock | 1 Oct–31 Jan (1 Sept–31 Jan in Scotland) | 3–5 | Roast at 190°C (375°F) mark 5 for 15–20 minutes | 1 per person |
| Woodpigeon | No close season (best May–Oct) | Requires no hanging | Roast at 230°C (450°F) mark 8 for about 15–20 minutes | 1 per person |

## CASSEROLED PIGEONS WITH CIDER AND APPLE

4 pigeons, oven-ready

1 large onion, skinned and sliced into rings

2–3 celery sticks, washed and chopped

450 g (1 lb) apples, peeled, cored and thinly sliced

pinch of cayenne pepper

pinch of freshly grated nutmeg

1 bay leaf

salt

600 ml (1 pint) medium or dry cider

Worcestershire sauce (optional)

watercress sprigs and apple slices, to garnish

1. Put the pigeons into a large casserole, either whole or cut in half.

2. Arrange the vegetables and apples round them, add the cayenne, nutmeg and bay leaf and season well with salt. Pour over the cider.

3. Cover the casserole and cook in the oven at 150°C (300°F) mark 2 for 2 hours, until the birds are quite tender and the vegetables soft.

4. Remove the birds and the bay leaf with a slotted spoon and keep warm. Purée the cooking liquid and the vegetables in a blender or food processor.

5. Taste the sauce and if it is too sweet (which will depend on the apples and cider used) add a dash of Worcestershire sauce.

6. Pour the sauce over the birds and garnish with watercress and apple slices.
*Serves 4*

## SALMIS OF PHEASANT

a brace of older pheasants

butter or margarine

salt and pepper

300 ml (½ pint) Chicken Stock (see page 19)

slices of carrot and onion for flavouring

1 bay leaf

225 g (8 oz) carrots, peeled

1 medium onion, skinned

3 celery sticks, washed and trimmed

45 ml (3 level tbsp) flour

60 ml (4 tbsp) port

fried croûtons (see page 17), to garnish

1. Place the birds in a small roasting tin. Rub a small knob of butter over the breast of each bird. Season well and pour the Chicken Stock into the tin. Roast at 200°C (400°F) mark 6 for 40 minutes, basting occasionally.

2. Lift the birds out on to a large chopping board. Pour off the pan juices and reserve. Slice through the flesh, cutting through the breast of the bird to the bone. Using strong scissors or game shears, snip right through the breast bone to open out the bird.

3. Cut through the skin around the legs then push the joints away from the carcass until completely detached. Snip firmly down either side of the backbone to remove it; reserve the bone. Divide each breast portion into two, snipping through the bone. Place the joints on a plate, cover loosely and store in a cool place.

4. Place the backbones in a small saucepan. Pour over the reserved roasting juices. Add the flavouring vegetables with the bay leaf and seasoning and sufficient water to just cover the bones. Bring slowly to the boil, simmer uncovered for about 30 minutes, until about 450 ml (¾ pint) stock remains. Strain off and reserve.

5. Cut the carrots, onions and celery into 5 mm (¼ inch) slices.

6. Melt 50 g (2 oz) butter in a flameproof casserole. Add the prepared vegetables, cover and cook over a moderate heat until the vegetables soften, about 10 minutes. Stir in the flour and cook gently for 1 minute, stirring. Remove the casserole from the heat and gradually stir in the 450 ml (¾ pint) stock and the port. Season, then bring to the boil and continue to cook, stirring, until thickened.

7. Remove from the heat and add the pheasant joints. Bring slowly to the boil, cover and cook in the oven at 170°C (325°F) mark 3 for about 1¼ hours. Garnish with the croûtons.
*Serves 4–6*

*Using strong scissors or game shears, snip through the breast bone to open out the bird.*

*Pheasant with Port*

## PHEASANT WITH PORT

| |
|---|
| *30 ml (2 tbsp) vegetable oil* |
| *3 young pheasants, well wiped* |
| *300 ml (½ pint) Chicken Stock (see page 19)* |
| *120 ml (8 tbsp) port* |
| *finely grated rind and juice of 2 oranges* |
| *50 g (2 oz) sultanas* |
| *salt and pepper* |
| *20 ml (4 level tsp) cornflour* |
| *25 g (1 oz) flaked almonds, toasted, to garnish* |

**1.** Heat the oil in a large flameproof casserole. When hot, add the pheasants and brown all over.
**2.** Pour the stock and port over the birds. Add the orange rind and juice with the sultanas and season well. Bring to the boil. Cover tightly and cook in the oven at 170°C (325°F) mark 3 for 1–1½ hours.
**3.** Remove the birds from the casserole, then joint each pheasant into two or three pieces, depending on size, and arrange on a serving dish; keep warm.
**4.** Mix the cornflour to a smooth paste with 60 ml (4 tbsp) water. Stir into the juices in the casserole and bring to the boil. Adjust the seasoning and spoon over the pheasant. Garnish with toasted flaked almonds.
*Serves 6*

## PHEASANT WITH CHESTNUTS

30 ml (2 tbsp) vegetable oil

50 g (2 oz) butter or margarine

brace of pheasants, oven-ready

225 g (8 oz) fresh chestnuts, peeled

2 medium onions, skinned and sliced

45 ml (3 level tbsp) flour

450 ml ($\frac{3}{4}$ pint) Beef Stock (see page 19)

100 ml (4 fl oz) red wine

salt and pepper

grated rind and juice of $\frac{1}{2}$ an orange

10 ml (2 level tsp) redcurrant jelly

bouquet garni

chopped fresh parsley, to garnish

1. Heat the oil and butter in a large frying pan, add the pheasants and fry for about 5–6 minutes until golden brown. Remove from the pan with a slotted spoon and put into a casserole.
2. Fry the chestnuts and onions in the oil and butter for about 5 minutes, until golden brown, and add to the pheasant.
3. Stir the flour into the remaining fat and cook gently for 1 minute, stirring. Remove the pan from the heat and gradually stir in the stock and wine. Bring to the boil slowly and continue to cook stirring until it thickens. Season and pour over the pheasant.
4. Add the orange rind and juice, redcurrant jelly and bouquet garni, cover and cook in the oven at 180°C (350°F) mark 4 for 1 hour, until the pheasant is tender.
5. Remove the bouquet garni before serving and adjust the seasoning to taste, if necessary. Sprinkle with chopped parsley.
Serves 4

# QUAIL

## ROAST QUAIL

8 quail

8 rounds of bread, toasted or fried

thin rashers of fat bacon

Game Chips, to serve

watercress, to garnish

1. Pluck and singe the birds but do not draw. Cut off the head and neck and take out the crop.
2. Place each bird on a round of toast or fried bread and cover the breast with thin rashers of fat bacon. Roast in the oven at 220°C (425°F) mark 7 for about 25 minutes, basting with butter.
3. Serve on the toast or fried bread with the bacon, thin gravy and Game Chips. Garnish with watercress.
Serves 4

Roast Quail

## CREAMED QUAIL CASSEROLE

| |
|---|
| 4 quail |
| 30 ml (2 tbsp) seasoned flour |
| 50 g (2 oz) butter or margarine |
| 100 g (4 oz) button mushrooms, wiped |
| 60 ml (4 tbsp) dry sherry |
| salt and pepper |
| 142 ml (5 fl oz) soured cream |
| chopped fresh parsley, to garnish |

1. Coat the quail in the seasoned flour.
2. Melt the butter in a flameproof casserole, add the quail and fry until evenly browned.
3. Add the mushrooms and fry them, then add the sherry and seasoning.
4. Cover and cook in the oven at 190°C (375°F) mark 5 for 40 minutes.
5. Stir in the soured cream, adjust the seasoning and serve sprinkled with chopped parsley.
*Serves 2*

## RAISED GAME PIE

| |
|---|
| 1 pheasant |
| 4 rabbit joints, total weight about 450 g (1 lb) |
| 450 g (1 lb) shoulder venison |
| 1 medium onion, skinned |
| 450 g (1 lb) pork sausagemeat |
| 1 garlic clove, skinned and crushed |
| 5 ml (1 level tsp) dried marjoram |
| pinch ground mace |
| 6 juniper berries, crushed |
| salt and pepper |
| slices of onion, carrot, 6 black peppercorns and 1 bay leaf for flavouring |
| **For the pastry** |
| 400 g (14 oz) plain flour |
| 7.5 ml (1½ level tsp) salt |
| 90 g (3½ oz) lard |
| 225 ml (8 fl oz) water |
| beaten egg, to glaze |
| 5 ml (1 level tsp) gelatine |

1. Remove the flesh from the pheasant and rabbit joints and cut into small pieces, discarding skin. Reserve the pheasant carcass and rabbit bones. Cut the venison into similar sized pieces. Place the meats in a bowl, add the onion, sausagemeat, garlic, spices, juniper and seasoning. Cover and leave in a cool place overnight.
2. Place the pheasant carcass and rabbit bones into a large saucepan, add the flavouring ingredients and 1.4 litres (2½ pints) water. Bring the contents to the boil, skim, then cover and simmer for about 2½ hours. Strain, then if necessary, boil to reduce the stock to 300 ml (½ pint). Cool, then refrigerate until needed.
3. Next day, make the pastry: sift the flour and salt into a bowl. Make a well in the centre. Heat the lard and water together, bring to the boil, then pour into the well. Using a wooden spoon, beat the ingredients together, then knead lightly against the side of the bowl until smooth. Cover with cling film, then leave for up to 30 minutes. Use the pastry whilst still warm.
4. Keep one quarter of the pastry covered. On a lightly floured surface, roll out the remaining pastry to a 35.5 cm (14 inch) circle. Fold loosely over the rolling pin, then lift over a 20.5 cm (8 inch) spring release tin. Ease the pastry into the corners and press evenly up the sides of the tin. Fold excess pastry outwards.
5. Spoon the meat mixture into the lined tin, pressing down with the back of the spoon. Roll out the remaining pastry to 23 cm (9 inch) round and use to top the pie. Seal well, then trim the edges and reserve the trimmings.
6. Flute the edges and make a small hole in the centre of the pie, and two near the edge—to pour the stock through later. Use trimmings to make 'leaves', arrange around the edge of the pie top.
7. Place the pie on a baking sheet and brush with the beaten egg. Bake in the oven at 220°C (425°F) mark 7 for 20 minutes, then reduce the temperature to 180°C (350°F) mark 4 and cook for a further 2¾ hours, covering with foil if necessary. To test it is cooked, insert a skewer through the centre hole—the meat should feel tender. Cool.
8. Sprinkle the gelatine in 20 ml (4 tsp) water in a small bowl and leave to soak. Place the bowl over a pan of simmering water and stir until dissolved. Heat the reserved stock in a saucepan and add the gelatine. Remove from the heat and leave to cool until beginning to set. Place on a plate, and ease off the tin. Pour the stock into the pie. Cover loosely, then refrigerate overnight. Serve cold.
*Serves 10–12*

# HARES AND RABBITS look similar but are two different species.
Hares are available from late summer to early spring. Rabbits are available all the year around and may be tame (farmed) or wild. Hares have a darker more gamey flavoured flesh than rabbits.

Hares are hung by the hind feet without being paunched (entrails removed) for 5–7 days to improve the flavour. During this time, the blood collects in the chest cavity. When paunching (see below) collect the blood if using for Jugged Hare (see page 180) and add 5 ml (1 tsp) malt vinegar to it to stop it coagulating. It can be stored, covered, in the refrigerator for 2–3 days.

If you want the butcher to collect the blood, you will probably have to order the hare and specify that you want the blood. Add vinegar to it as above. The butcher will skin and paunch the hare after hanging.

Very young hares (*leverets*) may be roasted whole but for larger hares, the body alone is used. This is known as saddle or baron of hare.

Rabbits are available both fresh and frozen. Unlike hares, they are paunched within a few hours of killing and are not hung. Tame rabbits, which have a delicate flavour, are always tender. Wild rabbits have darker stronger flavoured flesh and they should be eaten young. Fresh rabbit can be cooked in the same way as hare. Frozen rabbit is best used for pies and casseroles.

## PREPARING A HARE OR RABBIT

### SKINNING
1. Cut off the feet at the first joint. Loosen the skin round the back legs. Hold the end of one leg and bend at the joint, then pull the skin over the hind leg. Do the same with the other legs.
2. If keeping the head on for roasting, cut the skin around the eyes and mouth and remove the eyes (if not, cut the head off), then pull the skin towards the head, stripping it off inside out.

### PAUNCHING
1. Using kitchen scissors, snip the skin at the fork and cut it up the breastbone, then open the paunch by cutting the inside skin in the same direction. Draw out the entrails. Cut away the gall-bladder and the flesh it rested on and discard. Reserve the kidneys and liver. Cut the diaphragm and draw out the heart and lungs. Discard the lungs but keep the heart. If paunching hare, reserve the blood.

### TRUSSING
1. Cut the sinews in the hind legs at the thigh, bring the legs forward and press closely against the body. Bend forelegs back in the same way. Secure with two skewers or a trussing needle and thread.

### JOINTING
1. Cut off the hind legs at the thighs and the forelegs round the shoulder bone. Cut off the head. Cut the back into pieces, giving the back of the knife a sharp tap with a hammer to cut through the bone, then cut the ribs in two lengthways.

## ROAST HARE

*1.6 kg (3½ lb) hare or saddle of larger hare*

*Veal Stuffing (see page 186)*

*streaky bacon rashers*

*dripping or margarine*

*gravy and redcurrant or guava jelly, to serve*

1. Stuff the hare, fold the skin over and sew in position (see Trussing, above). Lay slices of bacon over the back and cover with greased greaseproof paper.
2. Put in a roasting tin, dot with dripping and roast in the oven at 180°C (350°F) mark 4 for 1½–2 hours. Baste frequently as the flesh is apt to be dry.
3. Remove the paper and bacon 15 minutes before the end of the cooking time to allow the joint to brown.
4. Remove the skewers and trussing thread and serve the hare with gravy and redcurrant or guava jelly.
*Note* The heart, liver and kidneys may be added to the stuffing, if wished. Wash well, put into a saucepan, cover with cold water, bring to the boil, then strain and chop finely.
*Serves 4*

## JUGGED HARE

*1.6 kg (3½ lb) hare, paunched and jointed, with its*
  *blood (see page 179)*

*75 ml (5 level tbsp) seasoned flour*

*125 g (4 oz) streaky bacon, rinded and diced*

*50 g (2 oz) butter or margarine*

*900 ml (1½ pints) Beef Stock (see page 19)*

*150 ml (¼ pint) port*

*5 ml (1 level tsp) dried marjoram*

*45 ml (3 level tbsp) redcurrant jelly*

*2 medium onions, skinned and stuck with 12 cloves*

*salt and pepper*

*chopped fresh parsley, to garnish*

1. Wipe the hare and toss in the seasoned flour.
2. Brown the bacon in its own fat in a large flameproof casserole, then remove and drain.
3. Add the butter to the casserole and lightly brown the hare portions. Add the stock, port, marjoram and redcurrant jelly with the onions. Replace the bacon and season.
4. Bring to the boil, cover and cook in the oven at 170°C (325°F) mark 3 for 3 hours, until tender.
5. Transfer the hare to a deep serving dish, cover and keep warm. Discard onions.
6. Mix the blood with cooking juices until smooth. Pour into the casserole and heat gently, adjust seasoning and pour over hare. Garnish.
*Serves 6*

## POACHER'S PIE

*4 rabbit portions, total weight about 550 g (1¼ lb),*
  *boned and cut into cubes*

*100 g (4 oz) bacon rashers, rinded and chopped*

*2 medium potatoes, peeled and sliced*

*1 medium leek, trimmed, sliced and washed*

*salt and pepper*

*15 ml (1 tbsp) chopped fresh parsley*

*1.25 ml (¼ level tsp) mixed dried herbs*

*Chicken Stock (see page 19) or water*

*225 g (8 oz) Shortcrust Pastry made with 225 g (8 oz)*
  *plain flour (see page 372)*

*beaten egg, to glaze*

1. Fill a 1.7 litre (3 pint) pie dish with alternate layers of rabbit, bacon and vegetables, sprinkling with seasoning and herbs. Half-fill with stock.
2. Roll out the pastry to 5 cm (2 inches) wider than the top of the dish. Cut a 2.5 cm (1 inch) strip from the outer edge and line the dampened rim of the dish. Dampen the pastry rim and cover with the pastry lid. Trim and seal the edges. Make a hole in the centre to let the steam escape.
3. Decorate with pastry leaves and brush with egg. Bake in the oven at 190°C (375°F) mark 5 for 30 minutes. Cover loosely with foil, then reduce to 180°C (350°F) mark 4 for a further hour.
*Serves 4*

## SWEET-SOUR RABBIT WITH PRUNES

*1 kg (2¼ lb) rabbit, jointed*

*2 medium onions, skinned and sliced*

*300 ml (½ pint) dry white wine*

*300 ml (½ pint) Chicken Stock (see page 19)*

*1 bay leaf*

*30 ml (2 tbsp) redcurrant jelly*

*a few black peppercorns*

*8 whole prunes, stoned*

*15 ml (1 tbsp) malt vinegar*

*10 ml (2 level tsp) cornflour*

*salt and pepper*

*chopped fresh parsley and toasted almonds, to garnish*

1. Put the rabbit in a dish with the onions, pour over the wine and marinate overnight.

2. Discard the onions, then place the rabbit and wine in a flameproof casserole and add the stock, bay leaf, redcurrant jelly and a few peppercorns. Bring to the boil.
3. Add the prunes and submerge them in the liquid. Cover the casserole tightly and cook in the oven at 170°C (325°F) mark 3 for about 1½ hours, until the rabbit is really tender and the prunes plump.
4. Remove the meat from the joints and discard the bones. Blend the vinegar with the cornflour and add to the liquid in the pan. Adjust the seasoning, then boil for 1–2 minutes.
5. Arrange the rabbit and prunes in a hot casserole and pour over the thickened juices. Garnish with parsley and toasted almonds.
*Serves 4*

# RABBIT AND FORCEMEAT PIE

4 rabbit portions, total weight 550 g (1¼ lb)

30 ml (2 level tbsp) flour

25 g (1 oz) lard

225 g (8 oz) button onions, skinned and quartered

225 g (8 oz) button mushrooms, wiped and trimmed

1 garlic clove, skinned and crushed

100 ml (4 fl oz) port

300 ml (½ pint) Chicken Stock (see page 19)

12 juniper berries, crushed

350 g (12 oz) sausagemeat

45 ml (3 tbsp) chopped fresh parsley

30 ml (2 level tbsp) prepared English mustard

salt and pepper

225 g (8 oz) Shortcrust Pastry made with 225 g (8 oz)
    plain flour (see page 372)

Rabbit and Forcemeat Pie

1. Toss the rabbit portions in the flour.
2. Heat the lard in a large frying pan, add
the onions, mushrooms and garlic and fry until
beginning to brown. Using a slotted spoon,
transfer them to a 1.7 litre (3 pint) pie dish.
3. Add the rabbit portions and fry until browned,
then transfer to the pie dish. Stir the port, stock
and juniper berries into the pan. Bring to the boil,
scraping sediment from the base. Add to dish.
4. Mix together the sausagemeat, parsley, mustard
and seasoning. Shape into eight balls. Add to pie
dish.
5. Roll out the pastry on a lightly floured surface
to 5 cm (2 inches) wider than the top of the dish.
Cut a 2.5 cm (1 inch) strip from the outer edge and
use to line the dampened rim of the dish. Dampen
the pastry rim with water and cover with the pastry
lid. Trim off any excess and seal the edges firmly.
Make a hole in the centre to let the steam escape.
6. Bake in the oven at 190°C (375°F) mark 5 for
30 minutes. Cover with foil. Reduce temperature
to 180°C (350°F) mark 4 for a further 1 hour.
*Serves 4*

# FRICASSÉE OF RABBIT

1 kg (2¼ lb) rabbit, jointed

3 medium onions, skinned

3 cloves

bouquet garni

450 ml (¾ pint) Chicken Stock (see page 19)

25 g (1 oz) butter or margarine

100 g (4 oz) bacon rashers, rinded and chopped

45 ml (3 level tbsp) flour

150 ml (¼ pint) white wine

2 egg yolks

salt and pepper

pinch of freshly grated nutmeg

sliced lemon, to garnish

1. Place the rabbit joints in a saucepan with one
onion, the cloves and bouquet garni. Add the
stock and simmer for about 45 minutes.
2. Slice remaining onions. Melt the butter in a
large saucepan, add the bacon and sliced onions
and cook for 5 minutes, until browned. Stir in
the flour and cook for 1 minute. Remove from
the heat.
3. Strain the stock from the rabbit and stir
gradually into the flour. Bring to the boil and
continue to cook, stirring, until it thickens.
4. Add the rabbit and simmer for about
30 minutes.
5. Remove the rabbit joints to a serving plate,
cover and keep warm. Blend the wine and egg
yolks together to a smooth cream, add a little of
the sauce and return the blended mixture to the
pan. Add salt, pepper and nutmeg and allow to
heat through, but do not boil.
6. Pour the sauce over the rabbit joints.
7. Garnish with lemon slices and serve with
boiled rice if liked.
*Serves 4*

# VENISON is the meat of the red, fallow or roe deer. The meat is inclined to be tough so it is hung for 1–2 weeks before cooking. Unless your butcher specialises in game, you will probably have to order the venison, though venison roasting joints such as legs, saddles and shoulders are becoming more widely available at butchers and supermarkets and some stewing venison is now sold cut up ready for cooking. The meat should be dark and firm with clear white fat. As there is only a little fat on venison, the meat tends to be dry, so additional fat or liquid is added for cooking. This is done either by marinating the meat overnight or adding melted fat or oil and basting frequently during cooking.

## ROAST VENISON

*saddle, leg or shoulder of venison*

*melted butter or margarine or vegetable oil*

*Thick Gravy (see page 204) and redcurrant jelly*

**1.** Pat the joint dry with absorbent kitchen paper and place on a large piece of foil. Brush generously with butter. Fold the foil to make a parcel. Weigh.
**2.** Place the parcel in a roasting tin and roast in the oven at 170°C (325°F) mark 3 allowing 25 minutes per 450 g (1 lb). Fold back the foil

20 minutes before the end of the cooking time to allow to brown. Serve with gravy and jelly.

*MARINADE*
Place 2 chopped carrots and small onions, 1 chopped celery stick, 6 black peppercorns, parsley stalks, 1 bay leaf and 3 blades mace in a large dish. Add venison and sufficient wine to half-cover. Soak for 12 hours, turning the meat 2–3 times. Remove meat and cook as liked. Boil marinade to reduce by half; use for gravy.

## RICH VENISON CASSEROLE

*1 kg (2 lb) stewing venison, trimmed of excess fat or gristle and cut into cubes*

*150 ml (¼ pint) red wine*

*100 ml (4 fl oz) vegetable oil*

*12 juniper berries, lightly crushed*

*4 cloves*

*8 black peppercorns*

*1 garlic clove, skinned and crushed*

*25 g (4 oz) streaky bacon rashers, rinded*

*2 medium onions, skinned and sliced*

*30 ml (2 level tbsp) flour*

*150 ml (¼ pint) beef stock*

*30 ml (2 tbsp) redcurrant jelly*

*salt and pepper*

*chopped fresh parsley, to garnish*

**1.** Place the venison in a bowl and add the wine, half the oil, the juniper berries, cloves, peppercorns and garlic. Stir well and leave to marinate for at least 24 hours, stirring occasionally.
**2.** Stretch each bacon rasher using a knife, cut in half and roll up. Heat the remaining oil in a

flameproof casserole, add the bacon rolls and fry for about 3 minutes, until coloured. Remove from the casserole with a slotted spoon.
**3.** Strain the venison from the marinade and quickly fry the meat pieces, in several batches, until coloured. Add the onions and cook for 3 minutes.

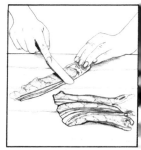

*Using the back of a knife, stretch each bacon rasher.*

Then add the flour and cook for 2 minutes, stirring.
**4.** Remove the casserole from the heat and gradually stir in the stock, redcurrant jelly and the marinade. Bring to the boil slowly and continue to cook, stirring, until thickened. Return the venison to the casserole. Season and place the bacon rolls on the top of the casserole.
**5.** Cover and cook in the oven at 170°C (325°F) mark 3 for 3 hours, until the venison is tender. Garnish with chopped parsley. Serve with extra redcurrant jelly, braised cabbage and creamed potatoes.
*Serves 4*

# STUFFINGS

S tuffings, also known as forcemeats,
fillings and, sometimes, farces, may
be used in various ways. They can help keep
a dry food moist during cooking or absorb some of the fat and
juices from meat, or they can be used to extend small amounts of ingredients
into meal-sized portions. They can also be used to provide contrasting colour, flavour
or texture to a dish. Stuffings are most commonly used with meat and poultry, but
they are equally good with fish or vegetables such as peppers and tomatoes.

◆

### STUFFING INGREDIENTS

Most stuffings are based on one of the following:

**Breadcrumbs**, homemade ones are best, as bought ones are dry and powdery and often artificially coloured. Use brown or white bread that is 2–3 days old and make the breadcrumbs in a blender or food processor. A grater can also be used to make them.

**Rice**, this should be cooked first (see page 302), then mixed with a little fat, egg or liquid to bind it with the other ingredients.

**Suet**, this adds flavour and moisture to a stuffing. Suet is available in packets, shredded, ready for use.

**Sausagemeat**, this can be bought fresh from the butcher or frozen.

Small amounts of other foods such as meat, sausagemeat, fish, nuts, vegetables and cheese can be added to the basic ingredient. Depending on the mixture, it may need moistening with a little water, stock or fruit juice or binding with egg.

### MAKING STUFFINGS

When making a stuffing, assemble all the ingredients but do not mix with any egg or liquid until ready to use. Do not put the stuffing into poultry, meat or fish until ready to cook it; bacteria could penetrate the stuffing which might not reach a sufficiently high temperature during cooking to kill them. When cooking food that is stuffed, calculate the cooking time on the total weight of the food to make sure it is cooked thoroughly.

### WATCHPOINTS

- Do not make the stuffing too wet or too dry; if too wet it will be stodgy and if it is too dry it will be crumbly and difficult to handle.
- Season stuffings well as the flavours may well need to penetrate a fairly solid mass.
- If stuffing poultry, put the stuffing in to neck end only as it might not cook sufficiently in the body cavity.

● Do not pack the stuffing too tightly into meat and poultry as the meat juices will make the stuffing swell during cooking and it may burst the skin and spill out. If you have too much stuffing, cook the surplus in a separate casserole or form into small balls and cook with the meat. *Note* It is not advisable to stuff meat or poultry prior to freezing.

## SAGE AND ONION STUFFING

*Sufficient for a 4–5 kg (9–11 lb) oven-ready goose.*

| |
|---|
| 50 g (2 oz) butter or margarine |
| 450 g (1 lb) onions, skinned and chopped |
| 10 ml (2 level tsp) dried sage |
| 225 g (8 oz) fresh breadcrumbs |
| 125 g (4 oz) medium oatmeal |
| salt and pepper |

1. Melt the butter in a saucepan, add the onions and sage and fry for 4–5 minutes. Stir in the breadcrumbs.
2. Toast the oatmeal under the grill for a few minutes, then stir into the breadcrumb mixture and season well. Cool before use.

## EASTERN FRUIT STUFFING

*Sufficient for a 1.4 kg (3 lb) oven-ready chicken.*

| |
|---|
| 50 g (2 oz) butter or margarine |
| 1 small onion, skinned and finely chopped |
| 1 garlic clove, skinned and crushed |
| 50 g (2 oz) blanched almonds, roughly chopped |
| 50 g (2 oz) long grain white rice |
| salt and pepper |
| 50 g (2 oz) seedless raisins |
| 50 g (2 oz) dried apricots, chopped |
| 2.5 ml (½ level tsp) ground cinnamon |

1. Melt 25 g (1 oz) butter in a saucepan, add the onion and garlic and fry gently for 5 minutes, until softened. Add the almonds and fry until turning colour, then add the rice and stir-fry until the grains begin to swell.
2. Pour 150 ml (¼ pint) water into the pan (it will boil furiously), then season. Cover and simmer for 15 minutes, until the water has been absorbed.
3. Remove from the heat, add the remaining butter, raisins, apricots and cinnamon and mix well.

*Eastern Fruit Stuffing*

# MINT AND ROSEMARY STUFFING

*Sufficient for a 4.5–5.4 kg (10–12 lb) oven-ready turkey.*

| |
|---|
| 75 g (3 oz) butter or margarine |
| 2 medium onions, skinned and finely chopped |
| 2 celery sticks, trimmed and finely chopped |
| 225 g (8 oz) fresh breadcrumbs |
| 30 ml (2 level tbsp) mint sauce |
| 10 ml (2 level tsp) dried rosemary |
| grated rind of 1 lemon |
| salt and pepper |
| 1 egg, beaten |

**1.** Melt the butter in a saucepan, add the onions and celery and fry gently for about 10 minutes.
**2.** Put the breadcrumbs, mint sauce, rosemary and lemon rind in a bowl. Stir in the celery and onion and season. Mix well together, then bind with the beaten egg.

*Mint and Rosemary Stuffing*

# LIVER AND BACON STUFFING

*Sufficient for a 4.5–5.4 kg (10–12 lb) oven-ready turkey.*

| |
|---|
| 125 g (4 oz) turkey liver (from the turkey giblets) |
| 50 g (2 oz) butter or margarine |
| 225 g (8 oz) streaky bacon, rinded and finely chopped |
| 1 medium onion, skinned and finely chopped |
| 30 ml (2 level tbsp) chopped fresh parsley |
| 225 g (8 oz) fresh breadcrumbs |
| salt and pepper |
| 1 egg, beaten |

**1.** Wash the liver, remove any fat and roughly chop.
**2.** Melt the butter, add the liver, bacon and onion and fry for 5 minutes.
**3.** Mix the parsley with the breadcrumbs in a bowl, then stir in the liver and bacon mixture and season well.
**4.** Stir in the egg to bind the mixture, then knead together.

# RICE STUFFING

*Sufficient for a 1.4 kg (3 lb) oven-ready chicken. Also use for meat, fish or vegetables.*

| |
|---|
| 50 g (2 oz) long grain rice, cooked |
| 1 medium onion, skinned and chopped |
| 50 g (2 oz) raisins |
| 50 g (2 oz) almonds, blanched and chopped |
| 30 ml (2 tbsp) chopped fresh parsley |
| 25 g (1 oz) butter or margarine, melted |
| salt and pepper |
| 1 egg, beaten |

**1.** Combine all the ingredients in a bowl, except the egg, then season. Add sufficient egg to bind.

**Variations**
1 celery stick, washed and finely chopped, to replace the onion
30 ml (2 tbsp) chopped fresh coriander, to replace the parsley
Use brown rice instead of white.

## OATMEAL AND PRUNE STUFFING

*Sufficient for a 4.5–5.4 kg (10–12 lb) oven-ready turkey.*

100 g (4 oz) prunes

60 ml (4 tbsp) port

175 g (6 oz) fresh brown breadcrumbs

100 g (4 oz) shelled Brazil nuts, chopped

100 g (4 oz) coarse oatmeal

1 large cooking apple, peeled and cored

50 g (2 oz) butter or margarine, melted

50 g (2 oz) shredded suet

salt and pepper

2 eggs, beaten

**1.** Soak the prunes in the port and 300 ml ($\frac{1}{2}$ pint) water overnight. Drain, reserving the liquid. Chop the prunes into small pieces.
**2.** In a bowl, mix together the prunes, breadcrumbs and nuts. Toast the oatmeal for a few minutes under the grill, then stir into the breadcrumb mixture. Coarsely grate the cooking apple into the mixture.
**3.** Stir in the butter, suet and seasoning and bind together with the eggs.
*Note* Use the reserved liquid for the gravy.

## VEAL STUFFING

*Use for veal or lamb; double the quantities for a 6 kg (13 lb) oven-ready turkey.*

100 g (4 oz) lean veal

75 g (3 oz) lean bacon, rinded

25 g (1 oz) butter or margarine

1 small onion, skinned and finely chopped

75 g (3 oz) fresh breadcrumbs

25 g (1 oz) mushrooms, wiped and finely chopped

5 ml (1 tsp) chopped fresh parsley

salt and pepper

a pinch of cayenne pepper

a pinch of ground mace

1 egg, beaten

**1.** Put the veal and bacon through a mincer or food processor twice, then beat them well in a bowl.
**2.** Melt the butter in a saucepan, add the onion and fry for 2–3 minutes, until soft but not coloured, then add to the meat.
**3.** Add the breadcrumbs, mushrooms, parsley and seasonings. Mix together well, then bind with the egg.

## NUT STUFFING

*Sufficient for a 4–4.5 kg (9–10 lb) oven-ready turkey.*

50 g (2 oz) butter or margarine

2 small onions, skinned and finely chopped

100 g (4 oz) mushrooms, wiped and finely chopped

50 g (2 oz) shelled walnuts, finely chopped

45 ml (3 tbsp) shelled cashew nuts, finely chopped

6 shelled Brazil nuts, finely chopped

pinch of dried mixed herbs

15 ml (1 tbsp) chopped fresh parsley

175 g (6 oz) fresh breadcrumbs

1 egg, size 2, beaten

salt and pepper

**1.** Melt the butter, add the onions and fry for 5 minutes. Add the mushrooms and fry for a further 5 minutes. In a bowl, mix together the nuts, mixed herbs, parsley and breadcrumbs.
**2.** Stir in the mushroom mixture with the egg. Season to taste.

**Variations**
Replace cashew nuts with peanuts. If preferred, use one type of nut only. Almonds could be used in this stuffing.

## APPLE AND CELERY STUFFING

*Sufficient for a 4–5 kg (9–11 lb) oven-ready goose.*

50 g (2 oz) butter or margarine

100 g (4 oz) bacon, rinded and chopped

4 medium onions, skinned and chopped

4 celery sticks, trimmed and chopped

700 g (1½ lb) cooking apples, peeled, cored and sliced

175 g (6 oz) fresh breadcrumbs

60 ml (4 tbsp) chopped fresh parsley

sugar, to taste

salt and pepper

**1.** Melt the butter in a frying pan, add the bacon and fry for 2–3 minutes, until golden brown. Remove from the pan with a slotted spoon and put in a bowl.

**2.** Fry the onions and celery for 5 minutes, then remove from the pan with the slotted spoon and add to the bacon.

**3.** Fry the apples for 2–3 minutes, until soft, then add to the bowl.

**4.** Stir in all the remaining ingredients and mix well together. Season well.

## BACON OR HAM STUFFING

*Use as a stuffing for vegetables, tomatoes, small marrows, peppers, etc. Sufficient for a 1.4 kg (3 lb) oven-ready chicken.*

15 ml (1 tbsp) vegetable oil

1 small onion, skinned and chopped

25 g (1 oz) mushrooms, wiped and chopped

50–75 g (2–3 oz) cooked bacon or ham, chopped

25 g (1 oz) fresh breadcrumbs

salt and pepper

pinch of mustard powder

few drops of Worcestershire sauce

1 egg, beaten

**1.** Heat the oil in a frying pan, add the onion and fry gently for 1–2 minutes. Add the mushrooms and bacon and fry until the onion is soft but not coloured.

**2.** Remove from the heat and add the breadcrumbs, seasoning, mustard powder and Worcestershire sauce. Mix together well, then bind with the egg.

## CHESTNUT STUFFING

*Sufficient for a 4.5–5.4 kg (10–12 lb) oven-ready turkey.*

450 g (1 lb) fresh chestnuts or 225 g (8 oz) can whole chestnuts (unsweetened), drained and roughly chopped

25 g (1 oz) butter or margarine

2 medium onions, skinned and chopped

350 g (12 oz) fresh breadcrumbs

75 g (3 oz) shredded suet

45 ml (3 level tbsp) creamed horseradish

5 ml (1 tsp) lemon juice

salt and pepper

**1.** If using fresh chestnuts, make a small cut along the flat side of each. Bake in the oven at 200°C (400°F) mark 6 for 10 minutes, until the skins crack. Peel when cooled. Simmer the chestnuts in salted water for 20 minutes or until tender. Drain and chop roughly.

**2.** Melt the butter in a frying pan, add the onions

and fry until soft but not coloured.

**3.** Remove from the heat and stir in the chestnuts, breadcrumbs, suet, horseradish, lemon juice and seasoning.

**4.** Continue to fry slowly on top of the cooker, stirring occasionally, for 15–20 minutes, or spoon into an ovenproof dish, cover and bake in the oven at 200°C (400°F) mark 6 for 30–35 minutes. Uncover and bake for a further 15 minutes. Cool before use.

### Variation

*SAUSAGEMEAT AND CHESTNUT STUFFING*
Put 225 g (8 oz) fresh breadcrumbs, 450 g (1 lb) pork sausagemeat, finely grated rind of 1 orange, 5 ml (1 level tsp) dried sage, salt and pepper in a large bowl. Stir well to mix. Drain and roughly chop a 440 g (15½ oz) can whole chestnuts in water. Add to the bowl with juice of 1 orange and gently bind. Sufficient for a 4.5–5.4 kg (10–12 lb) oven-ready turkey.

## PEACH AND NUT STUFFING

*Sufficient for a 1.4 kg (3 lb) oven-ready chicken.*

50 g (2 oz) long grain brown rice

15 ml (1 level tbsp) ground turmeric

25 g (1 oz) butter or margarine

100 g (4 oz) spring onions, trimmed and finely chopped

25 g (1 oz) Brazil nuts, finely chopped

2.5 ml ($\frac{1}{2}$ level tsp) ground ginger

1 fresh peach, skinned and chopped

salt and pepper

**1.** Cook the brown rice with the turmeric in boiling salted water for about 45 minutes. Drain well.
**2.** Melt the butter, add the spring onions, nuts and ginger and fry gently for 5 minutes.
**3.** Remove from the heat and stir in the rice and peach. Season and cool.

## MUSHROOM STUFFING

*Sufficient stuffing for a 1.4–1.8 kg (3–4 lb) oven-ready chicken; double these amounts for a 4.5 kg (10 lb) goose or turkey. The mixture may also be used to stuff tomatoes or green peppers, but reduce the amount of breadcrumbs to 50 g (2 oz).*

25 g (1 oz) butter or margarine

100 g (4 oz) mushrooms, wiped and chopped

1 small onion, skinned and chopped

15 ml (1 tbsp) chopped fresh parsley

salt and pepper

100 g (4 oz) fresh breadcrumbs

1 egg, beaten

**1.** Melt the butter in a saucepan, add the mushrooms and onion and fry gently for 2–3 minutes, until soft but not coloured.
**2.** Add the parsley, seasoning and breadcrumbs and mix together well, then bind with a little beaten egg.

## APRICOT STUFFING

*Sufficient stuffing for a 1.8 kg (4 lb) oven-ready duckling.*

175 g (6 oz) fresh breadcrumbs

100 g (4 oz) dried apricots, finely chopped

50 g (2 oz) salted peanuts, finely chopped

15 ml (1 tbsp) chopped fresh parsley

50 g (2 oz) butter or margarine

1 large onion, skinned and finely chopped

grated rind and juice of 1 small orange

5 ml (1 level tsp) curry powder

salt and pepper

1 egg, beaten

**1.** Place the breadcrumbs in a bowl and add the apricots, peanuts and parsley.
**2.** Melt the butter in a small saucepan, add the onion and orange rind, cover and cook gently until soft. Remove from the pan and add to the breadcrumb mixture.
**3.** Sprinkle in the curry powder and cook gently for 1 minute, then pour over the orange juice and boil gently for 30 seconds.
**4.** Stir the curried orange juice into the breadcrumbs. Season well, then bind with the egg.

**Variation**
*APRICOT, APPLE AND PRUNE STUFFING*
Cut 100 g (4 oz) soaked and stoned prunes into quarters. Mix the prunes, 50 g (2 oz) chopped dried apricots, 175 g (6 oz) peeled, cored and roughly chopped cooking apples, 100 g (4 oz) cooked rice, 50 g (2 oz) shredded suet and 50 g (2 oz) blanched and chopped almonds in a bowl. Season to taste. Add the grated rind and juice of $\frac{1}{2}$ lemon, and bind with 1 beaten egg. Sufficient stuffing for a 1.4 kg (3 lb) rolled pork joint.

# HERBS, SPICES, FLAVOURINGS AND ESSENCES

Herbs and spices have been used with food since time immemorial. Originally, one of their main purposes was to disguise the flavour and colour of perishable foods which were past their best, or even starting to rot. Today, they are appreciated for the distinctive tastes they add to heighten or improve the flavour of meat, fish, vegetables, rice, pulses and fruit. The cuisines of different countries use them in different ways and the spread of ethnic food shops means that people have a greater selection.

◆

HERBS are sold fresh or dried; fresh have a better appearance than dried and are essential for adding to salads, but many dried herbs have a good flavour and it is virtually impossible to detect the difference in cooked dishes such as casseroles. Dried herbs have a stronger flavour than fresh and should be used more sparingly; as a rule, you need about one third the amount specified for fresh herbs if substituting dried.

The majority of herbs, even if they do not originate in this country, can be grown successfully either outdoors or under glass. Some are annuals and need to be sown each year, others are perennial.

Ideally, fresh herbs should be picked just before using, but if necessary they can be stored in the refrigerator in a plastic box or glass jar with a top for 1–2 days. Herbs can be dried very easily or they can be frozen and used in soups or casseroles.

## DRYING AND STORING HERBS

Dry home-grown herbs in a slow oven, microwave oven, in the sun or by hanging them in a cool airy place, covered with muslin to keep the dust off them.

When dry, strip the leaves carefully from the stems and leave them whole. This will preserve more flavour than crumbling them.

Dried herbs keep best in airtight jars away from the light. Choose wood, earthenware or dark-coloured glass.

In a cool place, dried herbs will keep their flavour for 6–8 months. After that, any left can be scattered around the herb garden or sprinkled round pot plants to keep away insects.

## HERBS AND THEIR USES

**Angelica** Tall plant with all parts used for flavouring, though only the candied stem is available commercially. Use the leaves as a vegetable, add to salads or cook with fish. The stems can be eaten raw like celery or candied and crystallised and used in ice creams, cakes and as a cake decoration. The root imparts sweetness when cooked, so it is good for stewing with acid fruits such as rhubarb or gooseberries.

**Balm (lemon balm)** This has green, heart-shaped leaves and a tendency, like mint, to take over a whole garden unless controlled by planting it in a bottomless container sunk in the earth to contain the roots. It has a lemony smell and taste and is good with fish, poultry and ham dishes and in marinades. It also adds flavour to punches and fruit drinks and makes an excellent herbal tea.

**Basil (sweet basil)** Has a distinctive, pungent taste and aromatic scent and is generally used with tomatoes and in Italian cookery. It is also good in salads, with lamb, in Basil Butter, to be served on grilled meat, with green vegetables, in tomato soup and in Pesto Sauce. Basil grows for a short period in summer and needs plenty of sun.

**Bay** Has a strong, spicy flavour and can be used fresh or dried—when the flavour is even more pronounced. One or two leaves are all that is needed to flavour a dish. Bay is one of the ingredients in a bouquet garni. Although mainly used in meat and fish casseroles and marinades for fish and poultry, it is also used in soups and stocks and to flavour infusions of milk for use in sauces such as Béchamel or milk puddings. Bay trees are very ornamental and can be pruned like hedges to a desired shape.

**Borage** Both the slightly hairy leaves and the bright blue flowers have a flavour of salt and cucumber. It is mainly used in Claret Cup, Pimms and other cool drinks, but can be used in salads. The flowers can be candied and used as decorations for cakes and sweets. Borage is easy to grow and is not sold dried.

**Burnet (salad burnet)** Has a nutty flavour with a hint of cucumber and is good in salads, especially in winter when it continues to flourish. It can also be used in soups and stews.

**Chervil** Has a delicate, sweet flavour and is used in a similar way to parsley, especially in French dishes. It is good in salads, as a garnish, with a variety of vegetables, especially new potatoes, and as a flavouring for sauces such as Hollandaise. It also blends well with egg, cheese and chicken dishes.

**Chives** Members of the onion family with narrow, green leaves which are the part you eat. They are best used raw to flavour salads and dressings and as a garnish for soups and savoury dishes. They should be snipped into short lengths before use.

**Coriander** Mainly grown for its seeds (see page 193) but the leaves have an unusual flavour and are good in Middle Eastern and Indian dishes, salads and chilled soups.

**Curry plant** The green, spiky leaves of this shrubby perennial have a strong curry flavour. Although not used in Indian curries, add the fresh or dried leaves sparingly to soups and stews.

**Dill** The feathery leaves (known as dill weed) are used as a herb and the dried dill seeds as a spice. Dill weed has a mild, sweet, caraway flavour and needs to be used in fairly large quantities. The dried dill seeds are more pungent. Dill is used in salads, as a garnish, in scrambled eggs, white meat dishes and, classically, with salmon.

**Fennel** Both the feathery leaves and seeds are used. It has a slightly aniseed flavour and the seed is a good aid to digestion. It is a classical flavouring for fish—especially oily fish where it counteracts the richness—and in marinades, soups and sauces.

**Fines herbes** A mixture of finely chopped leaves of chives, chervil, parsley and tarragon which are used in omelettes, with fish, poultry and salads.

**Garlic** Not a herb but often used in conjunction with fresh herbs. Garlic is the most pungent of the onion family and is available in three varieties, white, red and pink. Choose cloves that are hard and firm. The strong taste of garlic is held in its oil and is passed through the lungs on the breath and, if enough is eaten, through the pores of the skin. It is used widely in savoury dishes, usually only a clove at a time. See page 209 for Garlic Butter.

**Horseradish** A root of the mustard family, which has a hot, biting, pungent taste and should be used sparingly. It is used raw, grated into dressings of cream and is classically served with roast beef. Horseradish is also good with some fish and as a flavouring for sandwich fillings.

**Lemon Grass** Lemon grass is grown mostly in tropical and sub-tropical countries but is imported to the West, in fresh and dried forms and as a powder (*sereh*). It has thick, grass like leaves which smell and taste strongly of lemon. It is most often used in the cooking of Sri Lanka and South Asia to flavour curries and meat dishes. It can also be used with fish and to flavour sweet puddings.

**Lovage** Has a sharp peppery flavour, which is good in all strong tasting savoury dishes and soups. Lovage leaves add an unusual tang to salads and are good in cold roast beef sandwiches.

**Marjoram** Has a spicy, slightly bitter, nutmeg-type flavour and can be used to replace basil if not available. It is good in stuffings, rubbed over roasts such as pork, in meat soups, on pizza and in homemade sausages. It is also used in egg dishes, on buttered vegetables and in cream soups.

**Mint** There are many culinary varieties of mint with different flavours and scents, e.g. peppermint, spearmint, applemint. It is usually sold dried but is very easy to grow. Use fresh for Mint Sauce (see page 207) or jelly with lamb, as a flavouring for potatoes, peas and other vegetables and to garnish wine and fruit cups.

**Mixed herbs** A mixture of dried herbs, usually parsley, sage, thyme, marjoram and tarragon, used for seasoning savoury dishes which do not require individual herbs, e.g. soups and casseroles.

Oregano A member of the marjoram family and sometimes referred to as Wild Marjoram, which can be interchanged, although oregano is much more aromatic and strongly flavoured. Use with meat, sausages, soups, pizza and other Italian dishes, tomatoes, in salads, with cooked vegetables and in egg and cheese dishes.

Parsley A mild, pleasantly flavoured herb with flat or curly leaves which make an attractive garnish sprinkled on food. Most of the flavour is in the stalks which are used as a classic ingredient for bouquet garni and fines herbes. Use in sauces for ham and fish, with vegetables, in stuffings and butters, salads and as a garnish.

Rosemary Strong pungent herb with spikey leaves. The flavour overpowers other herbs so use it on its own and sparingly in meat, fish, poultry and some sweet dishes. It marries well with all lamb dishes and is excellent used with barbecued meats.

Sage A large-leaved herb with a strong, slightly bitter taste. Use on its own, sparingly, in stuffings, casseroles, salads, meat dishes such as pork and sausages, egg and cheese dishes.

Savory Comes in summer and winter varieties and is best when fresh. It has a distinctive peppery flavour which has a particular affinity with beans and brings out their taste. Use also with egg dishes, tomatoes and other vegetables, soups and cheese.

Tarragon Has a distinctive, unusual flavour. There are two main species, the French variety being better than the Russian. It is one of the herbs used in the fines herbes mixture and is also used in Hollandaise, Bearnaise and Tartare Sauces. Use also to flavour wine vinegar, in marinades, with fish and chicken, in aspic glaze, tarragon butter and sauce for ham.

Thyme Comes in many varieties of which garden and lemon are the most common. Has a strong aromatic flavour and is a constituent of bouquet garni. Rub over beef, lamb and veal before roasting and use in soups, stuffings, Bread Sauce, with carrots, onions and mushrooms and in dishes cooked with wine. Lemon thyme is especially good in stuffings for veal and in egg and fish dishes.

SPICES are the dried parts of aromatic plants and may be the fruit, bark, seed, root or flower bud. Most come from hot countries. Once rare and expensive commodities, spices are now some of the most useful ingredients available to every cook.

Most spices are sold dried, either whole or ground. Whole spices which you grind yourself will give a more pungent flavour than those which are ready ground. For the strongest flavour, grind the spice immediately before use. Use either a pestle and mortar or an electric coffee bean grinder. If the latter, first clean it by grinding a slice of stale bread which will absorb the flavour of coffee. If you grind spices regularly it is worth keeping a separate grinder for this purpose. Spices should be bought in small quantities since their flavour deteriorates quite quickly. Keep them in small, airtight jars stored away from the light as this affects their flavour. Discard them if not used up within a year.

### SPICES AND THEIR USES

Allspice Also called Jamaica Pepper, it is sold as small dried berries or ready ground. The whole spice is an ingredient of pickling spice. Its flavour is a mixture of cloves, cinnamon and nutmeg and it can be used whole in marinades, meat dishes, pickles, chutneys and with poached fish or ground in pickles, relishes, soups, sauces, vegetable dishes, beef stews, baked ham, lamb dishes, boiled fish, oyster stew, cakes, milk puddings and fruit pies.

Aniseed (anise) These small seeds have a strong, distinctive flavour which aids digestion. They are used mainly to flavour cakes and biscuits, but also in salad dressings, with sugar and butter on carrots and red cabbage, in cheese, fish and shellfish dishes and with Baked Apples. Aniseed is the main flavouring ingredient in drinks such as Pernod, Ricard, Anisette, Ouzo and Raki.

Anise pepper Also called Szechuan pepper, it is a hot aromatic spice made from the dried red berries of a Chinese tree. It is one of the ingredients of Five-Spice Powder (see page 197).

Asafoetida This is not a true spice but is derived from the resin of a plant native to Afghanistan and Iran. It can be bought in solid form but as it is very hard is best bought ground, in powder form. The flavour is pungent, a little like spicy garlic, so it is used in very small quantities, mainly in Indian cooking for pickles, fish and vegetables. It is often used as a substitute for salt in India.

Caraway Small brown seeds with tapering ends with a pleasant, sharp, liquorice-like taste. Widely used in central European and Jewish cookery.

Used mainly for flavouring cakes, biscuits and bread but also in soups, salads, sauerkraut, with vegetables, in cheese dishes, omelettes and pork dishes. It is also an ingredient of the liqueur Kummel. Like aniseed, caraway aids digestion.

**Cardamom** A member of the ginger family sold both whole either green or black, and ground. It has a strong, bitter-sweet, slightly lemony flavour and should be used sparingly. Widely used in Indian, Eastern and continental European cooking. Cardamom is an expensive spice as the seed pods have to be snipped individually from the plant by hand. It is an ingredient of most curry powders and can also be used in pickles, soups, beef and pork dishes, with sweet potato, pumpkin and apples and in bread, buns, biscuits and cakes, with iced melon and in Custard and Rice Pudding. It is also added to Turkish coffee.

**Cayenne** Comes from the red pepper (capsicum) family and is prepared from the smallest, hottest chillies. It is always sold ground and is sweet, pungent and very hot. Use it sparingly to flavour meats and sauces, especially barbecue and devilled recipes, eggs, fish, vegetables, cheese sauces and pastry, chicken croquettes, cheese and vegetable soups. Unlike paprika, it cannot be used for colouring as it is far too strong.

**Celery seeds** These are seeds from a different plant than salad celery and have a strong taste which resembles the vegetable. They are sold whole or ground and can be used sparingly in pickles and chutney, meat and fish dishes, salads, bread, marinades, dressings and dips.

**Chilli powder** A very hot spice which should be used extremely sparingly in Mexican dishes, pickles, chutneys, ketchups, soup, tomato dishes, casseroles, spaghetti and meat sauces. Some pre-mixed commercial chilli powders often called mild chilli powder or seasoned chilli powder contain a mixture of chilli and other spices such as cumin,

oregano, salt and garlic and are less hot. Test before using.

**Cinnamon** Available ground or in sticks of bark. It has a sweet, pungent flavour and is widely used in all sweet, spicy baking, as a flavouring for chocolate dishes, on cheese cakes, in pork dishes, pickles and chutneys and to flavour hot drinks, Mulled Wine and punches.

**Cloves** These look like small nails when whole, and are also sold ground. They have a distinctive, pungent flavour and are used mainly to flavour apple dishes, Christmas Pudding, mincemeat, Bread Sauce and to stud ham and pork. They are good with pumpkin and in Mulled Wine. Whole cloves are best removed before a dish is eaten.

**Coriander** Coriander seeds have a mild, sweet, orangey flavour and are sold whole or ground. Coriander is an ingredient of most curry powders and pickling spice and is also used in chutney, meat dishes, especially pork, in casseroles, Greek-style dishes, apple pies, pea soup and baked goods.

**Cumin** Seeds with a strong, spicy, slightly bitter taste which are sold whole or ground. An ingredient of curry powders and some chilli powder mixtures, they are also used in pickles, chutney, cheese dishes, soups, with cabbage and rice dishes, in Mexican and Eastern dishes, meat loaves, marinades and fruit pies.

**Fenugreek** Seeds with a slightly harsh, hot flavour which are an ingredient of commercial curry powders. Also used in chutneys, pickles and sauces, but rarely as the sole spice.

**Ginger** A root with a hot sweetish taste sold in various forms. Root ginger is available fresh or dried, or it may be dried and ground. Stem (green) ginger is available preserved in syrup or crystallised. Root ginger needs to be cooked to release the true flavour; peel and slice and use in marinades, curries, sauces, chutneys and Chinese cooking. Ground ginger is used in curries, sauces, preserves, cakes and sprinkled on to melon. Preserved ginger is used in sweet dishes.

**Juniper** Small purple-black berries with an aromatic scent and pine tang. They should be crushed before being added to a dish to release maximum flavour. Use with game, venison, pork and mutton, in marinades and casseroles with these ingredients, also in pâtés and sauerkraut. Juniper is a flavouring agent in gin.

**Laos powder** It is related to ginger and is similar in that the root is the part used. It has a peppery ginger taste and is used in the hot dishes of South-east Asia. In Europe it is used to flavour liqueurs and bitters. It is also known as *galangal* or *galingale*.

**Key**
1. Sage; 2. Parsley; 3. Chives;
4. Garlic; 5. Bay leaves; 6. Rosemary;
7. Tarragon; 8. Basil; 9. Dill;
10. Marjoram; 11. Mint; 12. Chives;
13. Fennel; 14. Curly leafed parsley;
15. Italian parsley; 16. Coriander;
17. Thyme.

**Mace** The outer covering of the nutmeg which is bright red when harvested and dries to a deep orange. Is sold as blades (useful for infusing) or ground. It has a stronger flavour than nutmeg. Use it in Mulled Wine and punches, potted meat, fish dishes, Béchamel Sauce, Meat Loaf, stews, pies and some puddings and cooked fruit dishes.

**Mustard** Made from the black, brown and white seeds of the mustard plant. The dark seeds give aroma and white ones pungency and most made-up mustards are a combination of the two in varying proportions. The seeds are either left whole for whole-grain mustard or are ground to make mustard flour and then liquid such as wine, vinegar and cider are added to moisten it and add the characteristic flavours. Some English mustard is sold as a dry yellow powder made from black mustard seeds which you mix up with water; other mustards are sold ready mixed. Mustard is used as a condiment like salt and pepper with a wide variety of savoury dishes and also to flavour dressings and sauces, with cheese dishes, especially Welsh Rarebit and in beef, ham and bacon dishes.

**Nutmeg** The seed of the nutmeg fruit. Nutmeg is sold whole or ground. As the flavour evaporates quickly, it is best bought whole and a little grated when required. Use it in chicken and cream soups, sprinkled on buttered corn, spinach, carrots, beans, and Brussels sprouts, in cheese dishes, fish cakes, with chicken and veal, in custards, milk puddings, Christmas Pudding and cakes.

**Paprika** A sweet mild spice which is always sold ground to a red powder. It is good for adding colour to pale egg and cheese dishes. Some varieties (particularly Hungarian) are hotter than others. It keeps poorly so buy little and often. Use it in salads, fish, meat and chicken dishes, with vegetables, on canapés and, classically, in Goulash where it adds the characteristic rich red colour.

**Pepper** The berry of the pepper tree is sold in several forms; green, black or white. Green or unripe berries are picked and either dried, canned or bottled. They have a milder flavour than black or white pepper and are used whole as a separate spice in pâtés, with rich meat like duck and in sauces and casseroles. They are sometimes lightly crushed. Black pepper consists of berries which are picked while green and dried in the sun which shrivels and darkens them. It has a strong, pungent, hot flavour and is best used freshly ground to season virtually all savoury dishes.

White pepper is made from the fully-ripened berries and is more aromatic and less hot in flavour than black pepper. It can be interchanged with it, but its main use is in light-coloured dishes and sauces whose appearance could be marred by dark flecks.

**Poppy seeds** Small black seeds from the opium poppy, which have no narcotic effect, but are nutty-flavoured, very hard and usually sold whole. They are used to add flavour and give an attractive appearance to baked goods, also in curry powder, dips, spreads, Onion Soup, salads and dressings and pasta dishes. They are widely used in Jewish and central European cookery. Also available cream coloured from Indian shops.

**Saffron** The most expensive of the spices, saffron is the dried stigmas of the saffron crocus flower. It has an aromatic, slightly bitter taste and only a pinch is needed to flavour and colour dishes such as Bouillabaisse, Chicken Soup, rice and Paella, fish sauces, buns and cakes—traditionally cornish saffron cake. Where just a touch of colour is needed, a pinch of turmeric can be used, but the flavour will not be the same.

**Sesame seeds** Small seeds with a rich, sweet, slightly burnt flavour which is enhanced by toasting or frying in butter. Use in salads and dressings, with mashed potato, sprinkled on to fish and chicken dishes, in fruit salads, pastry for meat pies and baked goods.

**Star anise** The star-shaped fruit of an evergreen tree native to China. When dried it is a red-brown colour and the flavour is one of pungent aniseed. It can be used to flavour stewed and simmered duck, beef, chicken and lamb. It can also be placed under whole fish for steaming. It is used whole and one star is quite sufficient to flavour a large dish. Star anise is one of the ingredients of Five-Spice Powder (see page 197).

**Tamarind** Tamarind is the large pod that grows on the Indian tamarind tree. It is seeded, peeled and pressed into a dark-brown pulp which is sold dried. It is made into a juice and used to add a sour

flavour to chutneys, sauces and curries. To make Tamarind Juice, see recipe on page 198.

**Turmeric** The dried root of a plant of the ginger family. Whole pieces of turmeric are available—they look like fresh ginger but are bright orange inside the peel—but it is most commonly sold ground. It has an aromatic, slightly bitter flavour and should be used sparingly in curry powder,

pickles and relishes and to colour cakes and rice dishes.

**Vanilla** The dried pods of a climbing orchid which are sold whole or as a synthetic bottled flavouring. Infuse a pod in the milk or cream when making custard or sweet sauces. A pod left in a jar of caster sugar will impart its flavour to it. Use in ice cream, chocolate and coffee dishes and custards.

# FLAVOURINGS AND ESSENCES There are some

concentrated flavourings that do not fall into the category of herbs or spices. These include flavouring agents such as salt and monosodium glutamate as well as the most common bottled flavourings and essences. True essences are made by naturally extracting the flavour from the food itself, flavourings are synthetic and tend to be cheaper. Both flavourings and essences have very strong flavours and usually only a few drops are needed in a recipe.

**Almond** The essence is made from bitter almonds. It is not widely available but is sold at herbalists. Almond flavouring is sold in most supermarkets. Either can be used in baking.

**Anchovy essence** A strong essence made from cured anchovies. It is very salty and should be used sparingly.

**Angostura bitters** A liquid made from a secret formula which includes cloves, cinnamon, nutmeg, citrus peel, prunes, quinine and rum. Originally medicinal; now used in drinks mixtures and sometimes as a flavouring in casseroles.

**Coffee essence** Bottled coffee concentrate which is used to impart flavour to both sweet and savoury dishes, and also for making quick iced coffee.

**Monosodium glutamate (msg)** A powder with little taste of its own but it enhances the flavour of meat and vegetables. It is widely used in processed foods for home use. It is also called taste powder and gourmet powder, particularly when used in Chinese cooking.

**Orange flower water** Orange-flavoured water used in small quantities in baking and sweet dishes.

**Peppermint oil** is similar to essence as it is made from the natural plant. The oil is mostly used for making sweets.

**Rose water** Highly fragrant rose-flavoured water, used in Turkish Delight, baking and sweet dishes and in other Middle Eastern dishes.

**Salt** A mineral used for seasoning savoury dishes. Sea salt and bay salt are fairly coarse and are evaporated naturally or over a fire. Rock salt is mined or pumped up with water, then evaporated.

Table salt is mixed with magnesium carbonate and ground small so that it flows freely.

Salt substitutes are available for people who want to reduce their salt intake. These may be low sodium or sodium reduced and are bulked out with potassium chloride.

**Sweeteners** Low calorie artificial sweeteners can be used to replace sugar in many recipes. Follow the instructions for cooking given on the sweetener pack or bottle.

**Soy sauce** Light or dark brown sauce with a salty sweetish taste made from soya beans which have been boiled and then fermented. Light soy sauce has a more delicate flavour and is not as salty as the dark soy sauce. It is widely used in oriental cookery and for flavouring a variety of savoury dishes.

**Tabasco** is made from a secret recipe. It is a hot sauce made from chillies mixed with spirit vinegar and salt. It is very strong and used in drink mixers such as Bloody Mary (see page 543), with shellfish and in savoury dishes.

**Vanilla** True vanilla essence is extracted from vanilla pods. It is not widely available but is sold at some high-class food shops and herbalists. It may be sold as an essence or natural vanilla. Vanilla flavouring, which is made from an ingredient in clove oil, is sold in supermarkets. Both can be used to flavour sweet dishes, particularly to bring out the flavour of coffee and chocolate.

**Worcestershire sauce** Pungent anchovy-flavoured sauce made from a secret recipe. Can be used to flavour sauces, meat casseroles and cheese dishes.

# HERB AND SPICE MIXTURES

## BOUQUET GARNI

This is a small bunch of herbs, tied together with string so it can be suspended in soups, casseroles and sauté dishes and removed before serving. The classic ingredients are bay leaves, parsley stems and thyme, but other herbs can be added to suit a particular dish.

When dried herbs are used for a bouquet garni they are tied in a small muslin bag. Tie together 5 ml (1 level tsp) dried parsley, 2.5 ml ($\frac{1}{2}$ level tsp) dried thyme and half a bay leaf, crumbled.

- If liked, 1 sprig of fresh marjoram can be added with the thyme; or 2.5 ml ($\frac{1}{2}$ level tsp) dried.
- To go with lamb, add 1 rosemary sprig to the basic bunch of fresh herbs; 1.25 ml ($\frac{1}{4}$ level tsp) dried crumbled rosemary to the muslin bag.
- To go with pork, add 1 sprig each of sage and savory; or 1.25 ml ($\frac{1}{4}$ level tsp) each of dried.
- To go with beef, add 1 thinly pared strip of orange rind and 1 sprig of celery leaves.
- To go with chicken, use lemon thyme instead of thyme and tie in 1 strip lemon rind; or add 2.5 ml ($\frac{1}{2}$ level tsp) dried lemon thyme.
- To go with fish, replace the thyme with lemon thyme and add a sprig of fresh fennel; or add 2.5 ml ($\frac{1}{2}$ level tsp) dried lemon thyme and 1.25 ml ($\frac{1}{4}$ level tsp) dried fennel.

You can buy bouquet garni made from dried herbs and these should be stored in dark airtight jars and used up quickly.

## FINES HERBES

*90 ml (6 level tbsp) finely chopped fresh parsley*

*45 ml (3 level tbsp) finely chopped fresh chervil*

*45 ml (3 level tbsp) finely chopped fresh chives*

*30 ml (2 level tbsp) finely chopped fresh tarragon*

**1.** Mix the herbs together and use to flavour omelettes and other egg dishes, fish, poultry and salads.

## CURRY POWDER

The flavourings for authentic Indian curries are made up of different mixtures of ground spices which include cumin, coriander, chilli powder and other aromatics.

Besides using it in ethnic dishes, curry powder can add spice to many other types of dishes. Add it to salad dressings, sprinkle it into sauces and casseroles, and rub it into chicken skin before poaching.

Bought curry powders are available but for the best flavour make your own.

*30 ml (2 level tbsp) cumin seeds*

*30 ml (2 level tbsp) whole fenugreek*

*7.5 ml (1$\frac{1}{2}$ level tsp) mustard seeds*

*15 ml (1 level tbsp) black peppercorns*

*120 ml (8 level tbsp) coriander seeds*

*15 ml (1 level tbsp) poppy seeds*

*15 ml (1 level tbsp) ground ginger*

*5 ml (1 level tsp) hot chilli powder*

*60 ml (4 level tbsp) ground turmeric*

**1.** Combine all the ingredients in a blender or coffee grinder and blend to a fine powder. Store in an airtight container for up to 3 months.

## FIVE-SPICE POWDER

A ground mixture of star anise, anise pepper, fennel seeds, cloves and cinnamon or cassia. Five-Spice Powder is used in authentic Chinese cookery. It is cocoa coloured and very pungent and should be used sparingly. Five-Spice Powder is used to season Chinese red-cooked meats (meats simmered in soy sauce) and roast meats and poultry. It can also be added to marinades and sprinkled over whole steamed fish and vegetable dishes.

*25 ml (5 tsp) anise pepper*

*25 ml (5 tsp) star anise*

*12.5 cm (5 inch) cassia bark or cinnamon stick*

*30 ml (6 tsp) whole cloves*

*35 ml (7 tsp) fennel seeds*

**1.** Grind together all the spices. Store in an airtight jar for up to one month.

## GARAM MASALA

This is a mixture of spices used in Indian cookery. Grind together 4 black cardamoms or 10 green cardamoms, 15 ml (1 level tbsp) black peppercorns and 10 ml (2 level tsp) cumin seeds. The amounts can be increased or decreased according to taste and spices such as dried red chillies or whole coriander seeds may be added.

## HARISSA

Harissa is a hot mixture of chilli and other spices that is used in Middle Eastern cooking. It can be bought in powder and paste form and may contain up to twenty spices. It is often served with Couscous and other North African dishes: it is put into a separate bowl, stock from the main dish is poured in to dilute it and it is spooned back over the dish to taste.

| |
|---|
| *25 g (1 oz) dried red chillies* |
| *1 garlic clove, skinned and chopped* |
| *5 ml (1 level tsp) caraway seeds* |
| *5 ml (1 level tsp) cumin seeds* |
| *5 ml (1 level tsp) coriander seeds* |
| *pinch of salt* |
| *olive oil* |

1. Soak chillies in hot water for 1 hour. Drain well, then grind into a paste using a pestle and mortar or coffee bean grinder together with the garlic clove and spices. Add a pinch of salt.
2. Put into a jar, cover with olive oil and seal. It will keep in the refrigerator for up to 2 months. The oil can be used in salad dressings.

## TAMARIND JUICE

| |
|---|
| *15 ml (1 level tbsp) dried tamarind pulp* |
| *60 ml (4 tbsp) warm water* |

1. Soak the dried pulp in warm water for 15 minutes. Strain the liquid through a sieve, pressing down hard with a wooden spoon to extract as much of the pulp as possible.
2. Discard the pulp left in the sieve and use the juice according to the recipe.

## MIXED SPICE

This is a mixture of sweet-flavoured ground spices. Mixed Spice is most often used in sweet dishes, cakes, biscuits and confectionery, but it can be added sparingly to curries and spiced Middle Eastern dishes.

| |
|---|
| *30 ml (6 level tsp) whole cloves* |
| *25 ml (5 level tsp) whole allspice berries* |
| *12.5 cm (5 inch) cinnamon stick* |
| *60 ml (4 level tbsp) freshly grated nutmeg* |
| *30 ml (6 level tsp) ground ginger* |

1. Grind the whole spices together and mix with the nutmeg and ginger. Store in an airtight, screw-topped jar. Keeps well for up to 1 month. Use for baking and in puddings.

## PICKLING SPICE

Pickling spice is a pungent mixture of varying spices added to the vinegar when making pickles. Varying proportions of black peppercorns, mace, red chillies, allspice, cloves, ginger, mustard seeds or coriander may be included.

| |
|---|
| *30 ml (2 level tbsp) mace blades* |
| *15 ml (1 level tbsp) allspice berries* |
| *15 ml (1 level tbsp) whole cloves* |
| *18 cm (7 inch) cinnamon stick* |
| *6 black peppercorns* |
| *1 bay leaf, crumbled* |

1. Mix all the ingredients together well. Store in an airtight, screw-topped jar. Keeps well for up to 1 month. Tie in a muslin bag to use.

## DRY-FRYING SPICES

Heating in a frying pan will mellow the flavour of spices. They can be dry-fried individually or in mixtures before using. Put the hardest ones, such as fenugreek, in first and add softer ones, like coriander and cumin, after a few minutes. Stir constantly until evenly browned. Cool and grind.

# SAUCES

Sauces provide the finishing touch to many dishes and it is important that their flavour complements the dish they are served with. For this reason it is well worth making your own; commercial packet sauces are often highly seasoned and coloured, as well as more expensive. Once you have mastered the basic techniques of sauce making, the variations are endless and you can easily create original and distinctive sauces.

♦

A great deal of mystique is attached to successful sauce making, but in fact all that is required is a little time and your undivided attention. Roux-based sauces are probably the most common type, but there are also egg-based types and the classic British favourites like bread, mint and apple sauce. Savoury butters and sweet sauces are also included.

### ROUX-BASED SAUCES
These are made by melting butter (or another fat), adding flour and cooking, then adding liquid. For a white sauce the butter and flour, i.e. the *roux*, are cooked but not coloured; for a blond sauce they are allowed to cook to a light biscuit colour; while for a brown sauce the roux is cooked until brown.

### LIQUID CHOICE
For white and blond sauces, as Velouté, the liquid used is usually milk or milk and white stock. Brown sauces need meat stock and/or vegetable water. Fish should be served with a sauce made from a liquid produced by boiling up the fish bones in water and adding milk if necessary.

There is no doubt that real stock (see page 19) does add an excellent flavour to sauces. If you are short of time, or do not have any stock, you can use a cube flavoured with beef, chicken, ham, fish or vegetables, but bear in mind that many contain monosodium glutamate and other sodium compounds and give a salty flavour. Check the seasoning.

### CORNFLOUR SAUCES
Cornflour is used in a different way to wheat flour. Blend the required amount with a little cold liquid, bring the rest of the liquid to the boil and gradually stir in the cornflour mixture and cook for a few minutes.

Cornflour tends to give a more glutinous texture to a sauce than the roux-based sauce.

### ARROWROOT SAUCES
Arrowroot can be used in the same way as cornflour to thicken a clear liquid. It gives the sauce a gloss, unlike cornflour which makes a cloudy sauce. Once added to the sauce, bring to the boil, then remove from the heat.

### VEGETABLE PURÉE SAUCES
Leaf vegetables can be briefly cooked and puréed

to make sauces. Root vegetables and pulses need to be cooked until they are really soft.

Purées such as onion, need to be thickened with equal quantities of white sauce to give the desired consistency, while others, like pulses, need thinning with stock or their cooking liquid.

### USEFUL TIPS

- You can make a sauce before it is needed and leave it to stand with a piece of damp greaseproof paper pushed down on the surface to prevent a skin forming. Reheat when required.
- A lumpy sauce can sometimes be rescued by vigorous beating with a wire whisk, although you should not do this in a non-stick pan a it will damage the lining. Otherwise, strain through a sieve or put it in a blender or foo processor to remove the lumps.
- Make a sauce slowly, stirring all the time, an don't turn your back on it until you hav finished cooking.
- Give a sauce a glossy finish by adding a spoonfu or two of cream, a knob of butter or margarir or an egg yolk at the last minute. Do not bo after this or the sauce may curdle.
- If a cream-based sauce starts to separate, ad a little warm water, stir well and the origin consistency will re-appear.

## WHITE SAUCE Roux method

| |
|---|
| 15 g (½ oz) butter or margarine |
| 15 g (½ oz) flour |
| 300 ml (½ pint) milk |
| salt and pepper |

### 1. POURING SAUCE

1. Melt the butter in a saucepan, stir in the flour and cook gently for 1 minute, stirring.
2. Remove the pan from the heat and gradually stir in the milk. Bring to the boil slowly and continue cooking, stirring all the time, until the sauce comes to the boil and thickens.
3. Simmer very gently for a further 2–3 minutes. Season with salt and pepper.
*Makes 300 ml (½ pint)*

### 2. COATING SAUCE

Follow recipe for Pouring Sauce (see above), increasing butter and flour to 25 g (1 oz) each.

### 3. BINDING SAUCE

Follow recipe for Pouring Sauce (see left), increasing butter and flour to 50 g (2 oz) each.

### 4. ONE-STAGE METHOD

1. Use ingredients in same quantities as for Pouring or Coating Sauce (see above).
2. Place the butter, flour, milk and seasonings in a saucepan. Heat, whisking continuously, until th sauce thickens and is cooked.

### 5. BLENDER OR FOOD PROCESSOR METHOD

1. Use ingredients in same quantities as for Pouring or Coating Sauce (see left).
2. Place the butter, flour, milk and seasonings in the machine and blend until smooth.
3. Pour into a saucepan and bring to the boil, stirring, until the sauce thickens.

## WHITE SAUCE Blending method

| |
|---|
| 25 ml (5 level tsp) cornflour |
| 300 ml (½ pint) milk |
| knob of butter or margarine |
| salt and pepper |

### 1. POURING SAUCE

1. Put the cornflour in a bowl and blend with 75 ml (5 tbsp) milk to a smooth paste. Heat the remaining milk with the butter until boiling, then pour on to the blended mixture, stirring all the time to prevent lumps forming.
2. Return the mixture to the saucepan. Bring to the boil slowly and continue to cook, stirring all the time, until the sauce comes to the boil and thickens.
3. Simmer gently for a further 2–3 minutes, to make a white, glossy sauce. Add salt and pepper to taste.
*Note* For a savoury sauce, half stock and half milk can be used.
*Makes 300 ml (½ pint)*

### 2. COATING SAUCE

Increase the quantity of cornflour to 30 ml (2 level tbsp) and blend with 90 ml (6 tbsp) milk.

# WHITE SAUCE
**Variations**

## PARSLEY SAUCE
A traditional sauce for bacon, ham and fish.
1. Follow the recipe for the Pouring Sauce or Coating Sauce (see opposite).
2. After seasoning with salt and pepper, stir in 15–30 ml (1–2 tbsp) finely chopped fresh parsley.

## ONION SAUCE
For grilled and roast lamb, tripe and freshly hard-boiled eggs.
1. Follow the recipe for the Pouring Sauce or Coating Sauce (see opposite).
2. Soften 1 large onion, skinned and finely chopped, in the butter before adding the flour.

## ANCHOVY SAUCE
Serve with fish.
1. Follow the recipe for the Pouring Sauce or Coating Sauce (see opposite), using half milk and half fish stock.
2. Before seasoning with salt and pepper, stir in 5–10 ml (1–2 tsp) anchovy essence to taste, a squeeze of lemon juice and a few drops of red colouring to tint a pale pink (if liked).

## MUSHROOM SAUCE
Serve with fish, meat or eggs.
1. Follow the recipe for the Pouring Sauce or Coating Sauce (see opposite).
2. Fry 50–75 g (2–3 oz) sliced button mushrooms in the butter before adding the flour.

## CAPER SAUCE
For lamb dishes.
1. Follow the recipe for the Pouring Sauce or Coating Sauce (see opposite), using all milk or—to give a better flavour—half milk and half stock.
2. Before seasoning with salt and pepper, stir in 15 ml (1 level tbsp) capers and 5–10 ml (1–2 tsp) vinegar from the capers, or lemon juice. Reheat gently before serving.

## EGG SAUCE
Serve with poached or steamed fish or kedgeree.
1. Follow the recipe for the Pouring Sauce or Coating Sauce (see opposite), using all milk or (if possible) half milk and half fish stock.
2. Before seasoning with salt and pepper, add 1 hard-boiled egg, shelled and chopped, and 5–10 ml (1–2 tsp) snipped chives. Reheat gently before serving.

## CHEESE SAUCE
Delicious with fish, poultry, ham, bacon, egg and vegetable dishes.
1. Follow the recipe for the Pouring Sauce or Coating Sauce (see opposite).
2. Before seasoning with salt and pepper, stir in 50 g (2 oz) finely grated Cheddar cheese or 50 g (2 oz) crumbled Lancashire cheese, 2.5–5 ml ($\frac{1}{2}$–1 level tsp) prepared mustard and a pinch of cayenne pepper.

---

# MILD CURRY SAUCE

Use for vegetables such as marrow and cabbage wedges, hard-boiled eggs or combining with pieces of cooked fish, chicken or meat.

50 g (2 oz) butter or margarine

1 medium onion, skinned and finely chopped

15–20 ml (3–4 level tsp) mild curry powder

45 ml (3 level tbsp) flour

450 ml ($\frac{3}{4}$ pint) milk or half stock and half milk

30 ml (2 level tbsp) mango or apple chutney, roughly chopped

salt and pepper

1. Melt the butter in a saucepan, add the onion and fry until golden.
2. Stir in the curry powder and cook for 3–4 minutes. Add the flour and cook gently for 2–3 minutes.
3. Remove the pan from the heat and gradually stir in the milk. Bring to the boil slowly and continue to cook, stirring, until the sauce thickens.
4. Add the chutney and seasoning. Reheat gently before serving.
*Note* Curry sauce is useful when you want to make a curry in a hurry, and makes good use of leftovers of meat, poultry and fish. Because some people like a hottish curry flavour and others prefer a very mild taste, it is best to start with the smaller amount of curry powder in the recipe.
*Makes 450 ml ($\frac{3}{4}$ pint)*

## MUSTARD CREAM SAUCE

Use for carrots, celery hearts, herring, mackerel, cheese, ham and bacon dishes.

| |
|---|
| 40 g (1½ oz) butter or margarine |
| 45 ml (3 level tbsp) flour |
| 450 ml (¾ pint) milk |
| 30 ml (2 level tbsp) mustard powder |
| 20 ml (4 tsp) malt vinegar |
| salt and pepper |
| 30 ml (2 tbsp) single cream |

1. Melt the butter in a saucepan, stir in the flour and cook for 1 minute, stirring.
2. Remove the pan from the heat and gradually stir in the milk. Bring to the boil slowly and continue to cook, stirring, until the sauce thickens. Simmer for about 5 minutes.
3. Blend the mustard powder with the vinegar and whisk into the sauce, then season. Stir in the cream. Reheat but do not boil.
*Note* To vary the flavour, use different mustards, such as whole grain, Dijon or herb flavoured mustards, such as tarragon or chive.
*Makes 450 ml (¾ pint)*

## BÉCHAMEL SAUCE

This classic sauce is the basis of many other sauces (see below). Use for fish, poultry, egg and vegetable dishes.

| |
|---|
| 300 ml (½ pint) milk |
| 1 shallot, skinned and sliced, or a small piece of onion, skinned |
| 1 small carrot, peeled and sliced |
| ½ celery stick, washed and chopped |
| 1 bay leaf |
| 3 black peppercorns |
| 25 g (1 oz) butter or margarine |
| 25 g (1 oz) flour |
| salt and white pepper |
| 30 ml (2 tbsp) single cream (optional) |

1. Put the milk, vegetables and flavourings in a saucepan and slowly bring to the boil. Remove from the heat, cover and set aside to infuse for 30 minutes, then strain, reserving the milk liquid.

2. Melt the butter in a saucepan. Stir in the flour and cook gently for 1 minute, stirring. Remove the pan from the heat and gradually stir in the flavoured milk.
3. Bring to the boil and continue to cook, stirring, until the sauce thickens. Simmer very gently for 3 minutes. Remove from the heat and season with salt and pepper. Stir in the cream, if using.
*Makes 300 ml (½ pint)*

**Variations**
MORNAY SAUCE
Serve with eggs, chicken or fish.
Before seasoning, stir in 50 g (2 oz) finely grated, mature Cheddar cheese or 25 g (1 oz) grated Parmesan or 50 g (2 oz) grated Gruyère. Do not reheat or the cheese will become overcooked and stringy.

## CHAUDFROID SAUCE

| |
|---|
| 28.35 g (1 oz) packet aspic jelly powder |
| 300 ml (½ pint) warm Béchamel Sauce (see above) |
| 150 ml (¼ pint) single cream |
| salt and pepper |

1. Sprinkle the aspic powder in 150 ml (¼ pint) water. Place the bowl over a pan of simmering water and stir until dissolved, taking care not to overheat the mixture.
2. Add to the Béchamel Sauce, beating well, then stir in the cream and extra seasoning, if necessary.

3. Strain the sauce and leave to cool, stirring frequently, so it remains smooth and glossy. When at the consistency of thick cream, use as a coating sauce.
*Note* This is a classic sauce which is used for coating chicken, fish or eggs. A final decoration of anchovy, pimiento, hard-boiled egg slices or cucumber slices is often added.
*Makes about 450 ml (¾ pint)*

## SOUBISE SAUCE

Use for fish, egg and meat dishes.

25 g (1 oz) butter or margarine

2 medium onions, skinned and chopped

300 ml (½ pint) Béchamel Sauce (see opposite)

15–30 ml (1–2 tbsp) Chicken Stock (see page 19) or water

salt and pepper

1. Melt the butter in a saucepan, add the onions and cook gently for 10–15 minutes, until soft.
2. Sieve or purée with the Béchamel Sauce and the stock in a blender or food processor until smooth.
3. Season and reheat gently for 1–2 minutes before serving.

*Makes about 300 ml (½ pint)*

## VELOUTÉ SAUCE

Serve with poultry, fish or veal.

knob of butter

30 ml (2 level tbsp) flour

450 ml (¾ pint) Chicken or other white stock (see page 19)

30–45 ml (2–3 tbsp) single cream

few drops of lemon juice

salt and pepper

1. Melt the butter in a saucepan, stir in the flour and cook gently for 1 minute, stirring well, until the mixture is a light golden colour.
2. Remove the pan from the heat and gradually stir in the stock. Bring to the boil and continue to cook, stirring, until the sauce thickens. Simmer until slightly reduced and velvety.
3. Remove from the heat and add the cream, a few drops of lemon juice and seasoning.

*Makes 450 ml (¾ pint)*

### Variations
#### SUPRÊME SAUCE

Serve with poultry or fish. Suprême Sauce is sometimes used in meat and vegetable dishes.

300 ml (½ pint) warm Velouté Sauce (see above)

1 egg yolk

30–45 ml (2–3 tbsp) single or double cream

knob of butter

1. Remove the Velouté Sauce from the heat and stir in the egg yolks and the cream, then add the butter a little at a time. Reheat if necessary, but do not allow to boil, or the sauce will curdle.

*Makes 300 ml (½ pint)*

#### AURORE SAUCE

Serve with eggs, chicken or fish.

15–30 ml (1–2 level tbsp) tomato purée

25 g (1 oz) butter or margarine

300 ml (½ pint) warm Velouté Sauce (see above)

salt and pepper

1. Blend the tomato purée with the butter and stir into the Velouté Sauce, a little at a time. Season with salt and pepper.

*Makes 300 ml (½ pint)*

#### NORMANDY SAUCE

Serve with poached, grilled or steamed white fish dishes, or hot crab and lobster dishes.

300 ml (½ pint) warm Velouté Sauce (see above), made with Fish Stock (see page 19)

1 egg yolk

25 g (1 oz) unsalted butter

1. Remove the Velouté Sauce from the heat and beat in the egg yolk.
2. Gradually add the butter, a small piece at a time, rotating the pan in a circular fashion gently until the butter melts. Do not stir or reheat after adding the butter.

*Makes 300 ml (½ pint)*

# BROWN SAUCES are made by cooking a roux until it is brown, thus giving the sauce its colour. Brown sauces range from simple gravies made with meat juices to the classic Espanole Sauce and sauces based on it. For the best flavour, use homemade Beef Stock (see page 19) when making brown sauces.

## GRAVY

A rich brown gravy is served with all roast joints—thin with roast beef and thick with other meats. If the gravy is made in the baking tin, there should be no need to use colouring. Remove the joint from the tin and keep it hot while making the gravy.

### THIN GRAVY
Pour the fat very slowly from the tin, draining it off carefully from one corner and leaving the sediment behind. Season well with salt and pepper and add 300 ml (½ pint) hot vegetable water or stock. Stir thoroughly, until all the sediment is scraped from the tin and the gravy is a rich brown; return the tin to the heat and boil for 2–3 minutes to reduce. Serve very hot.

You may prefer to make a slightly thickened version, using half the amount of flour used for thick gravy (see below).
*Makes about 300 ml (½ pint)*

### THICK GRAVY
Pour off most of the fat from the roasting tin leaving about 30 ml (2 tbsp) of the sediment. Stir in about 15 ml (1 level tbsp) flour, blend well and cook over the heat until it turns brown, stirring. Slowly stir in 300 ml (½ pint) Beef Stock (see page 19) or hot vegetable water and boil for 2–3 minutes. Season well, strain and serve very hot. A little gravy browning may be added.
*Makes about 300 ml (½ pint)*

## ESPAGNOLE SAUCE

Serve with red meats and game.

| |
|---|
| 25 g (1 oz) butter or margarine |
| 1 rasher streaky bacon, rinded and chopped |
| 1 shallot, skinned and chopped, or a small piece of onion, skinned and chopped |
| 60 ml (4 tbsp) mushroom stalks, wiped and chopped |
| 1 small carrot, peeled and chopped |
| 30–45 ml (2–3 level tbsp) flour |
| 450 ml (¾ pint) Beef Stock (see page 19), or beef stock from a cube |
| bouquet garni |
| 30 ml (2 level tbsp) tomato purée |
| salt and pepper |
| 15 ml (1 tbsp) sherry (optional) |

1. Melt the butter in a saucepan, add the bacon and fry for 2–3 minutes. Add the vegetables and fry for a further 3–5 minutes, until lightly browned. Stir in the flour, mix well and continue cooking until it turns brown.
2. Remove from the heat and gradually add the stock, stirring after each addition.
3. Bring to the boil slowly and continue to cook, stirring, until the sauce thickens. Add the bouquet garni, tomato purée, salt and pepper.
4. Reduce the heat and allow to simmer very gently for 1 hour, stirring from time to time to prevent it sticking; alternatively, cook in the oven at 170°C (325°F) mark 3 for 1½–2 hours.
5. Strain the sauce, reheat and skim off any fat, using a metal spoon. Adjust seasoning and add the sherry, if using, just before serving.
*Makes about 300 ml (½ pint)*

## Variations

### DEMI-GLACE SAUCE
Serve with red meats and game.

| |
|---|
| 150 ml (¼ pint) jellied stock from under beef dripping |
| 300 ml (½ pint) Espagnole Sauce (see above) |

1. Add the stock to the sauce and boil, uncovered, until the sauce has a glossy appearance and will coat the back of a spoon with a shiny glaze.

This is a simplified version of the classic demi-glace, but gives quite a satisfactory result for ordinary use.
*Makes 450 ml (¾ pint)*

## ROBERT SAUCE

Serve with pork.

25 g (1 oz) butter or margarine

1 small onion, skinned and finely chopped

150 ml (¼ pint) dry white wine

15 ml (1 tbsp) wine vinegar

300 ml (½ pint) Espagnole Sauce (see opposite)

5–10 ml (1–2 level tsp) mild prepared mustard

pinch of sugar

salt and pepper

1. Melt the butter in a saucepan, add the onion and fry gently for about 10 minutes, without browning.
2. Add the wine and vinegar and boil rapidly until reduced by half. Stir in the sauce and simmer for 10 minutes.
3. Add the mustard, sugar and extra seasoning, if necessary.

Makes about 450 ml (¾ pint)

## REFORME SAUCE

45–60 ml (3–4 tbsp) vinegar

few parsley stalks

1 bay leaf

sprig of fresh thyme

6 black peppercorns

300 ml (½ pint) Espagnole Sauce (see opposite)

1 gherkin, finely sliced

15 g (½ oz) tongue, finely sliced

1 hard-boiled egg white, finely chopped

1. Put the vinegar, parsley stalks, bay leaf, thyme and peppercorns into a saucepan and boil, uncovered, until reduced by half.
2. Stir in the Espagnole Sauce and simmer for 10–15 minutes, then strain.
3. Add the gherkin, tongue and egg white and serve, without further cooking, with lamb or beef.

Makes about 300 ml (½ pint)

---

# EGG YOLKS rather than flour are the thickening agent with these sauces. They must be cooked very slowly and gently. The water in the double saucepan should be barely simmering; a fierce heat will produce a granular texture and, if overcooked, the eggs will scramble. If not serving immediately, remove the sauce from the heat and keep warm over warm (not hot) water.

## HOLLANDAISE SAUCE

A classic sauce for fish, egg, chicken and vegetable dishes.

30 ml (2 tbsp) wine or tarragon vinegar

15 ml (1 tbsp) water

3 egg yolks

225 g (8 oz) unsalted butter, softened

salt and white pepper

1. Put the vinegar and water into a saucepan. Boil gently until the liquid has reduced by half. Set aside until cool.
2. Put the egg yolks and reduced vinegar liquid into a double saucepan or bowl standing over a pan of very gently simmering water and whisk until the mixture is thick and fluffy.
3. Gradually add the butter, a tiny piece at a time. Whisk briskly until each piece has been absorbed

by the sauce and the sauce itself is the consistency of the mayonnaise. Season with salt and pepper. If the sauce is too sharp add a little more butter — it should be slightly piquant, and warm rather than hot when served.

Makes about 300 ml (½ pint)

### Variation
MOUSSELINE SAUCE
This is a richer sauce suitable for asparagus and broccoli and poached fish, egg and chicken dishes.
    Stir 45 ml (3 tbsp) whipped double cream into the sauce just before serving.

## BÉARNAISE SAUCE

A classic sauce for meat grills and roasts.

| |
|---|
| *60 ml (4 tbsp) wine or tarragon vinegar* |
| *1 shallot or ¼ onion, skinned and finely chopped* |
| *few fresh tarragon sprigs, chopped* |
| *2 egg yolks* |
| *75 g (3 oz) butter, softened* |
| *salt and white pepper* |

*Béarnaise Sauce*

**1.** Put the vinegar, onion and tarragon into a saucepan and boil gently until the liquid has reduced by about one-third. Leave to cool.

**2.** Put the egg yolks and reduced vinegar liquid into a double saucepan or bowl standing over a pan of very gently simmering water and whisk until thick and fluffy.

**3.** Gradually add the butter, a tiny piece at a time. Whisk briskly until each piece has been absorbed by the sauce and the sauce itself has thickened. Season with salt and white pepper.

*Note* 15 ml (1 tbsp) vinegar can be replaced by 15 ml (1 tbsp) water—this gives a slightly less piquant sauce, which some people prefer.

*Makes about 200 ml (⅓ pint)*

### Variation

CHORON SAUCE

This sauce is tinted and flavoured with tomato purée. Serve with grilled steaks, salmon or egg dishes.

Make up the Béarnaise Sauce. Just before serving, stir in 30 ml (2 tbsp) tomato purée.

RESCUE REMEDIES

● Have ready a bowl containing a little iced water. If the sauce shows signs of curdling, put the pan or bowl of sauce in the cold water and stir briskly. Alternatively, add a small ice cube to the sauce itself, then stir quickly.

● If the sauce curdles, beat 5 ml (1 tsp) lemon juice and 15 ml (1 tbsp) curdled sauce in a warm mixing bowl until it thickens. Then beat in the remaining curdled sauce 15 ml (1 tbsp) at a time.

● If the above remedies do not work, beat two egg yolks with some seasoning in a bowl and beat in 30 ml (2 tbsp) of the curdled sauce. Cook as originally, stirring constantly, adding the rest of the mixture slowly. It will taste more eggy than usual.

# TRADITIONAL SAUCES like bread, apple, horseradish and mint, as well as various hot and cold savoury sauces for serving with fish, cutlets, beefburgers, pasta and croquettes and for barbecues are included in this section.

## BARBECUE SAUCE

Serve with chicken, sausages, hamburgers or chops.

| |
|---|
| *50 g (2 oz) butter or margarine* |
| *1 large onion, skinned and chopped* |
| *5 ml (1 level tsp) tomato purée* |
| *30 ml (2 tbsp) vinegar* |
| *30 ml (2 level tbsp) demerara sugar* |
| *10 ml (2 level tsp) mustard powder* |
| *30 ml (2 tbsp) Worcestershire sauce* |

**1.** Melt the butter in a saucepan, add the onion and fry for 5 minutes, until soft. Stir in the tomato purée and continue cooking for a further 3 minutes.

**2.** Blend together the remaining ingredients with 150 ml (¼ pint) water until smooth, then stir into the onion mixture. Bring to the boil and boil, uncovered, for a further 10 minutes.

*Serves 4*

# HORSERADISH CREAM

Serve with beef, trout or mackerel.

30 ml (2 level tbsp) grated fresh horseradish

10 ml (2 tsp) lemon juice

10 ml (2 level tsp) sugar

pinch of mustard powder (optional)

150 ml (¼ pint) double cream

**1.** Mix together the horseradish, lemon juice, sugar and mustard, if using.

**2.** Whip the cream to soft peaks, then fold in the horseradish mixture.

*Serves 4*

# APPLE SAUCE

This slightly acidic sauce is traditionally served with roast pork and goose to counteract their fattiness.

450 g (1 lb) cooking apples, peeled, cored and sliced

25 g (1 oz) butter or margarine

little sugar

**1.** Put the apples in a saucepan with 30–45 ml (2–3 tbsp) water and cook gently, uncovered, until soft and thick, about 10 minutes.

**2.** Beat to a pulp with a wooden spoon or potato masher, then, if you wish, sieve or purée in an electric blender or food processor.

**3.** Stir in the butter and add a little sugar if the apples are very tart.

*Serves 4*

# MINT SAUCE

Serve with lamb.

small mint bunch, washed and stalks removed

10 ml (2 level tsp) caster sugar

15 ml (1 tbsp) boiling water

15–30 ml (1–2 tbsp) wine vinegar

**1.** Chop the mint leaves finely and place in a sauceboat with the sugar.

**2.** Stir in the boiling water and leave for about 5 minutes to dissolve the sugar.

**3.** Add the vinegar and leave for about 1 hour before serving.

*Serves 4*

# CUMBERLAND SAUCE

Usually served cold with ham, venison or lamb.

1 orange

1 lemon

60 ml (4 level tbsp) redcurrant jelly

5 ml (1 tsp) Dijon mustard

60 ml (4 tbsp) port

salt and pepper

pinch of ground ginger (optional)

**1.** Pare the rind thinly from the orange and lemon, free of all the white pith. Cut it in fine strips, cover with water and simmer for 5 minutes. Drain.

**2.** Squeeze the juice from both fruits. Put the redcurrant jelly, orange juice and lemon juice and mustard in a saucepan and heat gently, stirring, until the jelly dissolves. Simmer for 5 minutes,

*Cumberland Sauce served with cold, sliced gammon*

then add the port. Season with salt and pepper and ginger, if wished.

*Serves 4*

# GOOSEBERRY SAUCE

A lovely eighteenth century sauce for mackerel and other oily fish.

| |
|---|
| 350 g (12 oz) gooseberries |
| 25 g (1 oz) butter or margarine |
| 25 g (1 oz) sugar |
| 1.25 ml ($\frac{1}{4}$ level tsp) freshly grated nutmeg |
| salt and pepper |

**1.** Put the gooseberries in a saucepan with 150 ml ($\frac{1}{4}$ pint) water and cook for 4–5 minutes, until tender and pulped. Drain and rub through a sieve or purée in a blender or food processor.
**2.** Add the butter, sugar, nutmeg and salt and pepper. Reheat and serve.
*Serves 4*

# BREAD SAUCE

A tasty accompaniment to roast chicken, turkey or pheasant.

| |
|---|
| 2 cloves |
| 1 medium onion, skinned |
| 1 small bay leaf |
| 450 ml ($\frac{3}{4}$ pint) milk |
| 75 g (3 oz) fresh breadcrumbs |
| salt and white pepper |
| 15 g ($\frac{1}{2}$ oz) butter or margarine |
| 30 ml (2 tbsp) single cream |

**1.** Stick the cloves into the onion and place in a heavy saucepan with the bay leaf and milk.

**2.** Bring slowly to the boil, remove from the heat, cover and leave to infuse for 10 minutes, then remove the onion and bay leaf.
**3.** Add the bread-crumbs and seasoning, return to the heat, cover and simmer gently, for 10–15 minutes, stirring occasionally. Stir in the butter and cream.
*Serves 4*

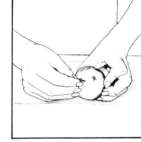

*Stick the cloves into the onion.*

# CRANBERRY SAUCE

Serve with turkey.

| |
|---|
| 225 g (8 oz) cranberries, washed |
| 225 g (8 oz) sugar |
| 15 ml (1 tbsp) port (optional) |

**1.** Put the cranberries in a saucepan, cover with 300 ml ($\frac{1}{2}$ pint) cold water and bring slowly to the boil over a moderate heat.

**2.** Simmer, uncovered, for a further 10 minutes or until the berries have burst.
**3.** Add the sugar and port, if using, and cook very gently until the sugar has dissolved. Cool before serving.
*Serves 4–6*

# CHESTNUT SAUCE

Rich and satisfying with turkey and other poultry.

| |
|---|
| 225 g (8 oz) chestnuts, peeled |
| 300 ml ($\frac{1}{2}$ pint) Chicken Stock (see page 19) |
| 1 small piece of onion, skinned |
| 1 small piece of carrot, peeled |
| 40 g (1$\frac{1}{2}$ oz) butter or margarine |
| 45 ml (3 level tbsp) flour |
| salt and pepper |
| 30–45 ml (2–3 tbsp) single cream or milk |

**1.** Put the chestnuts into a saucepan with the

stock and vegetables, cover, and simmer for about 20 minutes, until soft, then mash, sieve or purée in a blender or food processor.
**2.** Melt the butter in a pan, stir in the flour and cook gently for 1 minute, stirring. Remove pan from the heat and gradually stir in the chestnut purée. Bring to the boil, stirring—the sauce should be thick, but it may be necessary at this point to add a little milk or extra stock.
**3.** Season well with salt and pepper, remove from the heat and stir in the cream. Reheat without boiling and serve at once.
*Serves 4*

# FRESH TOMATO SAUCE

Serve with croquettes, pasta, cutlets, beefburgers and other meats.

25 g (1 oz) butter or margarine

1 small onion, skinned and chopped

1 small carrot, peeled and chopped

25 ml (5 level tsp) flour

450 g (1 lb) tomatoes, quartered

300 ml (½ pint) Chicken Stock (see page 19)

1 bay leaf

1 clove

5 ml (1 level tsp) sugar

15 ml (1 tbsp) chopped fresh parsley or basil

salt and pepper

1. Melt the butter in a pan, add the onion and carrot and lightly fry for 5 minutes until soft.
2. Stir in the flour and cook gently for 1 minute, stirring. Remove pan from the heat and gradually stir in the tomatoes, stock, bay leaf, clove, sugar, parsley and seasoning. Bring to the boil slowly and continue to cook, stirring, until the sauce thickens. Cover and simmer for 30–45 minutes, until the vegetables are cooked.
3. Sieve or purée in a blender or food processor. Reheat and serve.
Note If you wish, add 10 ml (2 level tsp) tomato purée to give a full flavour and better colour. 15–60 ml (1–4 tbsp) dry white wine or dry sherry may also be added just before serving.
Serves 4

# TOMATO SAUCE (made from canned tomatoes)

Serve as for Fresh Tomato Sauce.

knob of butter or margarine

1 small onion, skinned and chopped

2 bacon rashers, rinded and chopped

25 ml (5 level tsp) flour

397 g (14 oz) can tomatoes

1 clove, 1 bay leaf and a few fresh sprigs rosemary, basil or parsley, or 5 ml (1 level tsp) dried mixed herbs or oregano

pinch of sugar

salt and pepper

1. Melt the butter in a saucepan, add the onion and bacon and fry for 5 minutes.
2. Stir in the flour and cook for 1 minute, stirring. Remove pan from the heat and gradually stir in the tomatoes with their juice, the herbs, sugar and seasoning. Simmer gently for 15 minutes, then sieve or purée in a blender or food processor.
3. Reheat and adjust seasoning if necessary.
Serves 4

# SAVOURY BUTTERS may be added to sauces, or used as a garnish for meat, fish and vegetable dishes and as toppings for canapés. On average allow 25 g (1 oz) of butter per person. Make them at least a few hours beforehand and leave in a cool place to become firm before you use them.

Add one of the following flavouring ingredients to 100 g (4 oz) softened butter:
**Anchovy butter** 6 anchovies, mashed with a fork.
**Blue cheese butter** 50 g (2 oz) soft blue cheese.
**Curry butter** 10 ml (2 level tsp) curry powder.
**Garlic butter** 2 cloves garlic, skinned and crushed and 5–10 ml (1–2 tsp) chopped fresh parsley.
**Golden butter** Sieved yolks of 2 hard-boiled eggs.
**Green butter** 50 g (2 oz) chopped watercress.
**Ham butter** 100 g (4 oz) minced cooked ham.
**Horseradish butter** 30 ml (2 level tbsp) creamed horseradish.

**Lobster butter** 50 g (2 oz) lobster coral.
**Maître d'hôtel (parsley) butter** 30 ml (2 tbsp) finely chopped fresh parsley and a squeeze of lemon juice, with salt and cayenne pepper.
**Onion butter** 30 ml (2 level tbsp) finely grated onion.
**Sardine butter** 4 sardines, mashed with a fork.
**Tomato butter** 30 ml (2 level tbsp) tomato ketchup or 10 ml (2 level tsp) tomato purée and 5 ml (1 level tsp) sugar.
**Tarragon butter** 30 ml (2 tbsp) chopped fresh tarragon.

# SWEET SAUCES in this section can be served either hot or cold and you do not necessarily have to serve a hot sauce with a hot dessert; a piping hot pudding tastes delicious with a chilled spicy cream sauce.

## SWEET WHITE SAUCE Roux method

20 g (¾ oz) butter or margarine

about 30 ml (2 level tbsp) flour

300 ml (½ pint) milk

about 25 ml (5 level tsp) sugar

1. Melt the butter in a saucepan, stir in the flour and cook gently for 1 minute, stirring.
2. Remove the pan from the heat and gradually stir in the milk.
3. Bring to the boil and continue to cook, stirring, until the sauce thickens. Add the sugar to taste.
*Makes 300 ml (½ pint)*

## SWEET WHITE SAUCE Blended method

25 ml (5 level tsp) cornflour

300 ml (½ pint) milk

about 25 ml (5 level tsp) sugar

1. Place the cornflour in a bowl and blend with 15–30 ml (1–2 tbsp) milk to a smooth paste.
2. Heat the remaining milk until boiling, then pour on to the blended mixture, stirring.
3. Return the mixture to the pan and bring to the boil, stirring continuously. Cook for 1–2 minutes after the mixture has thickened to make a white, glossy sauce. Add sugar to taste.
*Note* For a thicker sauce, increase the quantity

of cornflour to 30 ml (2 level tbsp). This will be necessary if you add cream, rum or any other form of liquid when the sauce has been made.
*Makes 300 ml (½ pint)*

**Variations**
Flavour with any of the following when the sauce has thickened:
5 ml (1 level tsp) mixed spice or grated nutmeg
30 ml (2 level tbsp) jam
grated rind of ½ an orange or lemon
15–30 ml (1–2 tbsp) rum
1 egg yolk (must be reheated but not re-boiled)
 Use 15 ml (1 level tbsp) cocoa powder for cornflour.

## EGG CUSTARD SAUCE

2 eggs

15 ml (1 level tbsp) sugar

300 ml (½ pint) milk

few strips of thinly pared lemon rind or ½ a vanilla pod, split

1. In a bowl, beat the eggs, sugar and 45 ml (3 tbsp) milk. Put the rest of the milk in a pan with the

lemon rind and bring slowly to the boil. Remove from heat, cover and infuse for 10 minutes.
2. Pour the milk on to the eggs and strain the mixture into the top of a double boiler or into a heavy-based saucepan.
3. Cook, stirring, until custard will thinly coat the back of a spoon. Do not boil.
*Makes 300 ml (½ pint)*

## BUTTERSCOTCH SAUCE

Serve poured over ice cream.

50 g (2 oz) butter or margarine

60 ml (4 level tbsp) soft brown sugar

30 ml (2 tbsp) golden syrup

90 ml (6 level tbsp) chopped nuts

squeeze of lemon juice (optional)

1. Put the butter, sugar and syrup in a saucepan and heat gently, stirring until well blended.
2. Bring to the boil and boil for 1 minute, then stir in the nuts and lemon juice, if using. Serve at once.
*Serves 4*

# RICH CHOCOLATE SAUCE

*175 g (6 oz) plain chocolate*

*50 g (2 oz) light soft brown sugar*

**1.** Break up the chocolate and place in a heavy-based saucepan with the sugar and 150 ml (¼ pint) water.
**2.** Heat gently until the chocolate and sugar have dissolved. Add a further 150 ml (¼ pint) water, bring to the boil and simmer uncovered for 20–30 minutes, or until of a thick pouring consistency. Stir occasionally.
*Serves 6*

*Rich Chocolate Sauce*

# COFFEE SAUCE

Serve warm with baked puddings.

*25 ml (5 level tsp) instant coffee powder*

*7.5 ml (1½ level tsp) arrowroot*

*170 g (6 oz) can evaporated milk*

*30 ml (2 level tbsp) soft light brown sugar*

**1.** Mix the coffee powder and arrowroot to a smooth paste with a little water, then make up to 150 ml (¼ pint) with more water.
**2.** Pour into a saucepan, add the evaporated milk and brown sugar and slowly bring to the boil, stirring. Simmer for 1 minute.
*Serves 4*

# LEMON OR ORANGE SAUCE

Serve hot with baked or steamed puddings or cold with ice cream.

*grated rind and juice of 1 large lemon or orange*

*15 ml (1 level tbsp) cornflour*

*30 ml (2 level tbsp) sugar*

*knob of butter or margarine*

*1 egg yolk (optional)*

**1.** Make up the fruit rind and juice with water to 300 ml (½ pint). Blend the cornflour and sugar with a little of the liquid to a smooth cream.
**2.** Heat the remaining liquid until boiling, then pour on to the blended mixture, stirring all the time. Return it to the pan and bring to the boil, stirring until the sauce thickens and clears. Add the butter.
**3.** Cool, beat in the egg yolk, if using, and reheat, stirring, without boiling.
*Serves 4*

# GINGER SAUCE

Serve over steamed or baked puddings or fruit desserts.

*30 ml (2 level tbsp) sugar*

*squeeze of lemon juice*

*4–6 pieces of stem ginger, sliced*

*30 ml (2 tbsp) ginger syrup from the jar*

**1.** Put the sugar in a saucepan with 60 ml (4 tbsp) water and heat gently until the sugar has dissolved. Bring to the boil and boil until thickened.
**2.** Add the lemon juice, ginger and syrup and serve at once.
*Serves 4*

## Melba Sauce

Serve poured over ice cream.

| |
|---|
| 60 ml (4 level tbsp) redcurrant jelly |
| 50 g (2 oz) sugar |
| 150 ml (¼ pint) raspberry purée, from 225 g (8 oz) raspberries, sieved |
| 10 ml (2 level tsp) arrowroot or cornflour |
| 15 ml (1 tbsp) cold water |

1. Put the jelly, sugar and raspberry purée in a saucepan and slowly bring it to the boil.
2. Blend the arrowroot with the cold water to a smooth cream, stir in a little of the raspberry mixture, then stir into the mixture in the pan off the heat. Bring to the boil, stirring with a wooden spoon, until the sauce thickens and clears. Cool before serving.
*Serves 4*

## Sweet Mousseline Sauce

Serve over light steamed or baked puddings, fruit desserts or Christmas pudding.

| |
|---|
| 1 egg |
| 1 egg yolk |
| 45 ml (3 level tbsp) sugar |
| 15 ml (1 tbsp) sherry |
| 60 ml (4 tbsp) single cream |

1. Place all the ingredients in a bowl over a pan of boiling water and whisk until pale and frothy and of a thick creamy consistency. Serve at once.
*Serves 4*

## Sabayon Sauce (Cold)

Serve with cold fruit desserts.

| |
|---|
| 50 g (2 oz) caster sugar |
| 2 egg yolks, beaten |
| grated rind of ½ a lemon |
| juice of 1 lemon |
| 30 ml (2 tbsp) rum or sherry |
| 30 ml (2 tbsp) single cream |

1. Put the sugar in a saucepan with 60 ml (4 tbsp) water and heat gently until the sugar has dissolved. Bring to the boil and boil for 2–3 minutes, until syrupy. Pour slowly on to the yolks, whisking constantly until pale and thick.
2. Add the lemon rind, lemon juice and rum and whisk for a further few minutes. Fold in the cream and chill well.
*Serves 4*

## Brandy Butter (Hard Sauce)

Traditionally served with Christmas pudding and mince pies.

| |
|---|
| 75 g (3 oz) butter |
| 75 g (3 oz) caster sugar |
| 30–45 ml (2–3 tbsp) brandy |

1. Cream the butter until pale and soft.
2. Beat in the sugar gradually, then add the brandy a few drops at a time, taking care not to allow the mixture to curdle. The finished sauce should be pale and frothy.

3. Pile into a small dish and chill well before serving.
*Note* If you prefer a less granular texture, use sifted icing sugar or half icing and half caster sugar.
*Serves 6–8*

**Variation**
*RUM BUTTER*
Make this as for Brandy Butter, but use soft brown sugar, replace the brandy with 60 ml (4 tbsp) rum and add the grated rind of ½ a lemon and a squeeze of lemon juice.

# VEGETABLES

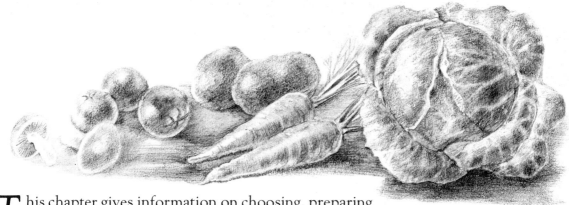

$T$ his chapter gives information on choosing, preparing
and cooking most of the vegetables which are currently available. Vegetables
should be prepared as simply as possible as vitamins are usually found just under the
skin, so peel thinly and only cut the vegetables if necessary or the nutrients will be lost.
For information on storing vegetables see page 567 and for freezing see page 511.

♦

## ARTICHOKE (GLOBE)

A type of thistle native
to North Africa but
now grown in Europe
and America as a
vegetable.

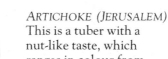

*To buy:* Look for heads
with a clear green
colour and leaves which
have no dry edges.
Choose artichokes
which are tightly curled rather than wide open.
*To prepare:* Cut off the stalks and remove a few of
the rough outer leaves with scissors so that any
brown or dried edges are removed.
*To cook:* Cook in boiling salted water for 35
minutes or until you can pull out a leaf easily.
*To eat:* Serve hot with melted butter or
Hollandaise Sauce (see page 205) or cold with
Mayonnaise (see page 261) or French Dressing (see
page 260). Pull off the leaves one by one, dip in the
dressing, then suck off the fleshy part. Once all the
leaves are off, slice off or spoon out the hairy
choke (easily visible) and use a knife and fork to
eat the base (fond).

Allow 1 artichoke per person as a starter or
light lunch dish. If only the hearts are being
served, allow 2–3 per person.

## ARTICHOKE (JERUSALEM)

This is a tuber with a
nut-like taste, which
ranges in colour from
beige to brownish-red.

*To buy:* Choose the
smoothest ones
available as they are easier to peel.
*To prepare:* Scrub well and peel thinly. If they
are very knobbly and difficult to peel, cook them
first and then peel. Like other tubers, Jerusalem
artichokes can be cubed, diced, sliced or cut into
julienne slices.
*To cook:* Cook in boiling salted water with 15 ml
(1 tbsp) lemon juice or vinegar added to prevent
discoloration for 15–20 minutes.
*To eat:* Serve as a vegetable accompaniment, purée
or make into soup.

Allow 175–225 g (6–8 oz) per person.

## ASPARAGUS

There are two basic types, blanched (white)
asparagus which is cut below the soil when the tips
are 5 cm (2 inches) above it, and green asparagus
which is cut at soil level.
*To buy:* Choose stems which look fresh and tender.
Avoid wilted stems, ones with brown patches or
coarse looking woody ones.

*To cook:* Use a special asparagus pan or wedge the bundles upright in a deep saucepan. Cover the tips with a cap made of foil and simmer gently for about 15 minutes, until tender. This way the stalks are poached while the delicate tips are gently steamed. Untie the bundles and serve hot with melted butter or Hollandaise Sauce (see page 205) or cold with Mayonnaise (see page 261) or French Dressing (see page 260). Asparagus is eaten with the fingers. Hold one stem at a time and dip the tip into the sauce. Eat only as far as the stem is tender and tasty, then discard the rest.

Allow 6–10 stems per person depending on size.

### Aubergine (Egg Plant)
Aubergines range in colour from white and whitish green through dark green to yellowish purple to red purple or black.
*To buy:* Choose firm, shiny aubergines free from blemishes. They may be round or oval.
*To prepare:* Cut off the stem, trim the ends and halve or slice. Sprinkle the flesh with salt and leave for half an hour to extract the bitter juices. Rinse and dry with absorbent kitchen paper.
*To cook:* Grill or fry the slices and serve as accompaniments, or stuff and bake and serve as a starter or main dish. Aubergine is included in many dishes, such as Ratatouille and Moussaka.

Allow 175–225 g (6–8 oz) per person.

### Bamboo Shoots
These are the conical-shaped shoots of a bamboo plant native to Asia. The shoots are cut when they are 15 cm (6 inches) long. Fresh bamboo shoots are available in Chinese stores.
*To prepare and cook:*
They should be peeled and cooked in boiling water for about 40 minutes or until tender. Canned bamboo shoots are more readily available and these are already cooked. Either sort are excellent in stir-fried dishes or salads.

Allow 50–75 g (2–3 oz) per person.

### Beans, Broad
*To buy:* Choose young, small, tender pods.
*To cook:* Where the pods are less than 5–7.5 cm (2–3 inches) long, both pods and beans can be cooked and eaten. Larger than that, the beans should be removed from the pods. Cook beans in boiling salted water for 15–20 minutes, then serve with melted butter or in a White Sauce (see page 200). Old large beans should be cooked, then made into soup or puréed.

Allow about 225–275 g (8–10 oz) weight of whole beans per person.

### Beans, French (Green Beans)
*To buy:* Choose slim French beans which break with a crisp snap.
*To cook:* Cut off the ends and steam or cook in boiling salted water for about 10 minutes.
*To eat:* Serve hot or cold in a French Dressing (see page 260).

Allow 100–175 g (4–6 oz) per person.

Other varieties of French beans include bobby beans, which are shorter and fatter, and haricot verts which are slim and delicate. Cook both as for French beans, for about 8 minutes.

### Beans, Runner
Choose beans that break with a crisp snap.
*To prepare:* Cut off the ends and remove the strings from the sides. Cut into chunks or lengths (a bean slicer makes this task quicker).
*To cook:* Steam or cook in boiling salted water for about 10 minutes. Serve hot.

Allow 100–175 g (4–6 oz) per person.

### Bean Sprouts
*To buy:* Choose crisp, small, fresh shoots or grow them yourself at home. Bean sprouts take only 5–6 days to sprout from mung beans (see page 244).
*To cook:* Cook as soon as possible after buying or harvesting. Rinse in cold water, then either blanch for 30 seconds in boiling salted water or stir-fry for 1–2 minutes. Serve hot as an accompaniment, cold in salads or stir-fried with other ingredients.

Allow about 100 g (4 oz) per person.

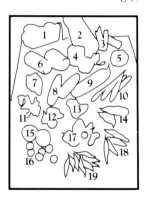

Key
1. Mooli—white radish; 2. Chinese Leaves; 3. Fennel; 4. Kohlrabi; 5. Celeriac; 6. Yam; 7. Dasheen; 8. Sweet Potato; 9. Cassava; 10. Scorzonera; 11. Radish; 12. Globe Artichoke; 13. Eddoe; 14. Karella; 15. Beef Tomatoes; 16. Cherry Tomatoes; 17. Peppers (left) and Chilli Peppers (right); 18. Okra; 19. Mange Tout Peas.

## BEETROOT

*To buy:* Choose firm, smallish beetroots with crisp tops. There are two types of beetroot available, long and globe-shape. Small, globe-shaped beetroots, available in early summer, are usually sold in bunches. Maincrop beetroot, which grow larger, are sold by weight and it is common practice for them to be sold cooked.

*To prepare:* Cut off the stalk about 2.5 cm (1 inch) above the root and wash the beetroot. Take care not to pierce the skin or juices will bleed into the cooking water.

*To cook:* Cook in boiling salted water until soft; this may take up to 1½ hours for large beetroot. Alternatively, bake in the oven at 180°C (350°F) mark 4 for 2–3 hours. Peel, slice or dice and serve hot or cold with a sauce or dressing.

Allow 100–175 g (4–6 oz) per person.

## BROCCOLI

There are several types of broccoli, the sprouting ones which produce many purple, white or green shoots and the heading type with one large close head like a cauliflower. Originally from Italy *Calabrese* is another variety with green heads.

*To buy:* Choose firm, tightly packed heads with strong stalks. The purple and green varieties have a more delicate flavour than the white.

*To prepare:* Trim the stalks and leaves. Halve the shoots if large.

*To cook:* Simmer upright in boiling salted water for 10–15 minutes, or steam for 10–15 minutes. Broccoli florets can be stir-fried or added to casseroles. Serve hot.

Allow 100–175 g (4–6 oz) per person.

## BRUSSELS SPROUTS

*To buy:* Choose small round sprouts with tightly packed heads and no wilted leaves.

*To prepare:* Remove any damaged or wilted leaves and cut off the stem. Cut a cross on the stump to allow the thick part to cook as quickly as the leaves. Wash and drain.

*To cook:* Cook in boiling salted water for 8–10 minutes, or steam for about 15 minutes. Serve hot. Very young Brussels sprouts can be served raw in salads.

Allow 100–175 g (4–6 oz) per person.

## CABBAGE, SEASONAL

*To buy:* Available all year round. In spring the thinnings from the main crop are sold as *spring greens* before the heart has formed. *Spring cabbages* are on sale a little later and these have a small heart. The *summer cabbages* are firm and green. The *winter cabbages* are coarser, not as sweet as the summer ones, and are more strongly flavoured.

*To buy:* Choose fresh looking cabbage with no wilted leaves.

*To prepare:* Prepare and cook as for Dutch cabbage (below).

Allow 175–225 g (6–8 oz) per person.

## CABBAGE, RED AND WHITE

*To buy:* Choose those with either a deep, bright red or pale yellowish white colour, round, heavy for their size and firmly packed.

*To prepare:* Cabbage can be shredded for using raw in salads or, for cooking briefly, cut into thick wedges, or the centre can be removed and the cabbage stuffed.

*To cook:* Cook in boiling salted water for 2–3 minutes (shredded), 10 minutes (wedges). Serve hot, immediately.

Allow 175–225 g (6–8 oz) per person.

## CABBAGE, DUTCH (SAVOY)

*To buy:* Choose one that is heavy for its size.

*To prepare:* Remove the coarse outer leaves and cut the rest in half. Take out the centre stalk, wash, shred finely or cut into wedges.

*To cook:* Cook in boiling salted water for 2–3 minutes (shredded), 10 minutes (wedges), or steam for the same length of time. Serve hot.

Allow 175–225 g (6–8 oz) per person.

## CARDOON

An edible thistle related to the artichoke, which grows in the Mediterranean. Its stalks are like celery and it can be eaten in the same way.

*To prepare:* To eat raw, separate the stalks and remove the strings and inner white skin. Cut the stalks into lengths and thinly slice the heart. Leave in cold water acidulated with lemon juice to prevent browning until ready to serve.

*To cook:* To cook, separate the heart and stalks and slice. Cook in boiling salted water with added lemon juice for 30–40 minutes, until tender, then peel away the strings and skin. Serve hot.

Allow 225–275 g (8–10 oz) per person.

## CARROTS

*To buy:* Choose carrots which are brightly coloured, firm, well shaped and with smooth skins.

*To prepare:* Small new carrots should have their stalks cut off and be scrubbed well. Pare the skins from older carrots and cut lengthways or slice.

*To cook:* Cook in boiling salted water for 10–15 minutes, until tender.

Serve hot as an accompaniment or make into purée or soup. Carrots can also be eaten raw, either grated or cut into sticks.

Allow 100–175 g (4–6 oz) per person.

## CASSAVA (MANIOC, YUCLA)

A long, brown-skinned tuber with white starchy flesh. In the Caribbean there are two varieties: a sweet one and a bitter one, which is poisonous unless it is specially prepared. Only the sweet variety is available in Britain.

*To prepare:* Peel and cut into slices.

*To cook:* Cook in boiling salted water for 20 minutes or until tender.

Allow 100–175 g (4–6 oz) per person.

## CAULIFLOWER

*To buy:* Choose cauliflowers with firm white heads surrounded by fresh green leaves. Cauliflowers can be eaten raw in salads or cooked and served hot. Cook as soon as possible after buying.

*To prepare:* Cut away the outer leaves and chop off the stem. Cut a cross on the stump to help the thick part cook more quickly. Wash and drain.

*To cook:* Cook in boiling salted water for 10–15 minutes, keeping the stem immersed, but the florets out of the water. Cover the pan so that the florets cook in the steam.

A medium cauliflower serves 4 people.

## CELERIAC

Sometimes known as turnip rooted celery, celeriac is a swollen root with a pronounced celery flavour.

*To buy:* Choose bulbs which are firm, heavy and free from blemishes.

*To prepare:* Scrub well, cut off the roots and peel thickly. Leave whole, grate or slice into julienne strips. Leave in cold water with a little lemon juice until you are ready to cook.

*To cook:* Cook in boiling salted water for about 20 minutes (slices and strips), 35–45 minutes (whole). Drain well. Serve hot with melted butter or a sauce or blanch strips and use in salads.

Allow 100–225 g (4–8 oz) per person.

## CELERY

*To buy:* Pale green celery is available all year round, while white winter celery is usually available from October through the new year. Winter celery is usually sold with black soil still attached. Choose celery with thick unblemished sticks and fresh leafy tops. The green tops will tell you if the plant is fresh.

*To prepare:* Separate the stalks and scrub well to remove any dirt. Leave whole or cut into slices. Serve raw in salads or with cheese. To serve hot, boil or steam for about 20 minutes. The leaves can be used to garnish soup.

Allow 3–4 sticks per person.

## CHAYOTE

Pear-shaped gourd with a smooth or ridged skin and white to green flesh with a high water content. They have a delicate flavour which  becomes more insipid as they become larger. They are available in West Indian shops and some supermarkets.

*To buy:* Choose firm ones with no blemishes or soft spots.

*To cook:* Small ones can be cooked like courgettes, larger ones can be peeled and cooked in boiling salted water for 15–20 minutes until tender, stuffed and baked, made into chutney.

Allow 2–3 small ones per person, 175–225 g (6–8 oz) for larger ones.

## CHICORY

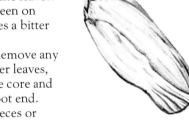

*To buy:* Choose heads
with crisp white leaves.
Too much green on
them indicates a bitter
flavour.

*To prepare:* Remove any
damaged outer leaves,
scoop out the core and
cut off the root end.
Chop into pieces or
leave whole.

*To cook:* Plunge the heads into boiling salted water
and cook for 5 minutes, drain and cook in about
60 ml (4 tbsp) water and a little lemon juice for
about 25 minutes. Serve hot or serve raw in salads.

Allow half a head per person in salads and
1 head per person when cooked.

## CHINESE LEAVES

*To buy:* Choose heads
that are heavy and look
fresh. Chinese leaves
can be served raw in
salads or cooked and
served hot.

*To prepare:* Cut off the
stem and cut the leaves
widthways into about
8 thin slices.

*To cook:* Cook as for cabbage or stir-fry.

Allow 100–175 g (4–6 oz) per person.

## COURGETTES

There are green and yellow varieties of this
miniature marrow.

*To buy:* Choose small, tender courgettes with skins
that are free from blemishes. Large ones tend to be
tough and are best stuffed and baked.

*To prepare:* Slice off both ends, wash or wipe the
skin and slice or dice.

*To cook:* Cook in boiling salted water for about
5 minutes, steam for 5 minutes, coat in batter and
deep fry for 2–3 minutes or slice and sauté in
butter for about 5 minutes. Serve hot.

Allow 2–3 courgettes, 100–175 g (4–6 oz) per
person.

## CUCUMBER

*To buy:* Choose smallish cucumbers with skins
that are free from blemishes.

*To prepare:* They may be sliced or diced.

*To cook:* Cucumber is usually served raw but may
also be boiled, steamed or sautéed and eaten hot.

Allow 100–175 g (4–6 oz) per person if serving
as a hot vegetable, 50–100 g (2–4 oz) per person
in salads. Cucumber goes well with chervil, dill,
chives, fennel or parsley.

## DUDI

The dudi is a member
of the marrow family. It
grows up to 60 cm
(2 feet) long and is
thinner at the stalk end,
becoming wide at the
other end. It has a
yellowy-green skin and
a creamy taste.

*To buy:* Choose
smooth-skinned ones with no bruising.

*To prepare:* Top and tail and cut into thick slices
(there is no need to peel), leaving the seeds in.

*To cook:* Cook in boiling salted water for
10–20 minutes, until tender, or shallow fry. It
can be eaten with melted butter or used to make
ratatouille.

1 dudi will serve 4 people.

## EDDOE

A root vegetable with a
small central bulb
surrounded by
tuberous growths. It
has white mealy flesh
and a potato-like
flavour.

*To prepare and cook:* Both parts can be peeled,
cooked and used like potatoes. It can be boiled,
baked or chopped and fried.

Allow 175–225 g (6–8 oz) cooked weight per
person.

## FENNEL

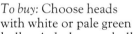

Known as Florence
fennel to distinguish it
from the herb. The
bulb resembles celery
but is more bulbous at
the base with long green
feathery leaves. Fennel
has a strong aniseed
flavour.

*To buy:* Choose heads
with white or pale green
bulbs. A dark green bulb indicates a sharp
bitterness.

*To prepare:* Trim both root and stalk ends. Chop

or grate if it is to be eaten raw.
*To cook:* Quarter, cook in boiling salted water for
about 30 minutes, then drain and slice. If liked,
the slices can then be sautéed in butter. Serve hot
or raw in salads. Always use the feathery leaves,
they are good for garnishing or in salads.
Allow 100–175 g (4–6 oz) per person.

## KALE

There are many varieties, both flat and curly, of
this leafy winter vegetable. It has a tough texture
but is a good source of vitamins in the winter.
*To buy:* Choose kale that is firm and green with no
wilted yellow leaves.
*To prepare and cook:* Trim off the tough stalks
and cook the leaves in boiling salted water for
8–10 minutes, until tender but still crisp. Drain
and shred. Serve hot. Allow 175–225 g (6–8 oz)
per person.

## KARELLA

Long pod-like vegetable
which comes from
Kenya. It looks like a
large okra with knobbly
skin and edible red
seeds.
*To buy:* Choose firm
green pods, avoid
brown or withered
ones.
*To prepare and cook:* Top and tail and scrape off the
knobs. Slice the pods, place in a colander, sprinkle
with salt and leave for 1 hour. Wash, drain and pat
dry, then fry gently until tender. Sprinkle with a
little sugar and serve as a side dish with curry.
Allow 100 g (4 oz) per person.

## KOHLRABI

An unusual looking
vegetable, similar in size
to a turnip. It is a
swollen stalk, not a
root, with leaves
growing out from the
surface. It can be white
or purple skinned.
*To buy:* Choose small
ones, no more than
5 cm (2 inches) in diameter as larger ones can be
very tough. Do not buy any with decaying leaves.
*To prepare:* Trim the base, cut off the leaves and
stalks and peel the globe thinly.
*To cook:* Cook in boiling salted water for 30–40

minutes, steam or fry and serve hot. Kohlrabi can
also be sliced very thinly and eaten raw.
Allow 100–175 g (4–6 oz) per person.

## LEEKS

*To buy:* Choose small young firm leeks which
have white stalks and fresh green leaves. Trim the
root and top and slit down the length or slice
crossways. Wash well under cold running water to
remove all dirt and grit. It may require several
washings to remove all the grit between the layers.
*To cook:* Cook in boiling salted water for
10–15 minutes, steam for 5–7 minutes or braise
whole, in enough stock to cover, for about 1 hour.
Serve hot with herbs or a sauce. Alternatively,
allow to cool and serve with French Dressing (see
page 260) or serve raw in salads.
Allow 1–2 leeks per person.

## LETTUCE

*To buy:* Choose lettuce with crisp green leaves and
no brown or slimy patches.
**Webb's Wonder, Iceberg and Great Lakes** are
large compact solid lettuces which stay very crisp.
**Cos (Kos)** lettuces have long crisp green leaves,
pale green hearts and a sweeter taste.
**Baby cos lettuce (Little Gem, Sugar Cos)** is
excellent in salads.
**Round (cabbage)** lettuces are available all year
round but have less flavour than these other
summer varieties and their soft leaves have a
tendency to bruise.
*To prepare:* Trim the base of the stalk and remove
any damaged outer leaves. Separate the remaining
leaves and wash in a bowl of cold water, *not* under
running cold water which could wilt them. Dry
thoroughly and tear the leaves into pieces. Try not
to cut with a knife as this damages them, causing
loss of vitamins and may cause discoloration.
Other vegetables which are similar to lettuce
and prepared in the same way are *lamb's lettuce*
(corn salad) and *dandelion leaves*.
Lettuce is usually served raw in salads but can
be braised for 25–30 minutes or cut into small
pieces and stir-fried. It also makes good soup.
Allow 1 lettuce per person when cooked; $\frac{1}{4}$–$\frac{1}{2}$
of a medium lettuce served raw.

## MARROW

*To buy:* Look for firm marrows with no blemished
or soft parts. Choose ones which are about 30 cm
(12 inches) long and weigh about 900 g (2 lb). Over
this size they tend to be full of seeds and rather
fibrous.

*To prepare:* Wash the skin and if thick, peel it off. Cut into small pieces or into halves, lengthways if it is to be stuffed. Discard the seeds and centre fibres. Place in a colander and sprinkle with salt. Leave for 30 minutes to extract the bitter juices. Rinse and pat dry with absorbent kitchen paper.
*To cook:* Cook in boiling salted water for 10–20 minutes, steam for 20–25 minutes or sauté for 5–10 minutes. Stuffed marrow should be baked in the oven covered with foil at 190°C (375°F) mark 5 for about 45 minutes, until tender.
   Allow 175–225 g (6–8 oz) per person.

### SPAGHETTI MARROW

This marrow is available in the winter. It is shaped like a short marrow and is cooked in its skin. The white flesh inside, which resembles spaghetti, is eaten seasoned with butter or a tomato sauce.

### MUSHROOMS

There are many edible species of mushrooms. The ones below are the most commonly available in Britain.
*To buy:* Choose mushrooms which are firm-textured, with fresh looking stalks that are not brown or withered. Use fresh mushrooms as soon as possible since they deteriorate quickly.
*To prepare:* Wipe with a damp cloth. If very dirty, wash them quickly but do not let them soak. Soak dried mushrooms for 15–20 minutes in warm water before using in cooked dishes.
*To cook:* Sauté in butter or oil, steam or cook in a little salted water for 3–5 minutes and serve hot. Young mushrooms can be eaten raw in salads.
   Allow 100 g (4 oz) fresh mushrooms per person, 75 g (3 oz) dried mushrooms when reconstituted will be equal to about 450 g (1 lb).
**Cultivated mushrooms** are the most commonly available. They may be gathered young as **button mushrooms**, as **cup mushrooms** when the cap has partially opened or as **flat mushrooms** when the cap has opened out and become flat. **Oyster mushrooms**, which have a stronger flavour, are available in some places.
**Chanterelles** grow throughout Europe but cannot be cultivated and are usually available dried or canned in Britain. They have a delicious delicately perfumed flavour.
**Cèpes and morels** also have a very delicate flavour and are used in many European dishes. They are usually only available dried.
**Truffles**, which are renowned for their flavour and scent, are actually tubers which grow near the roots of oak and beech trees, particularly in France and Italy. The two main, highly prized, varieties are the black **Perigord** which is used as a garnish (for *pâté de foie gras* in particular) and the white **Piedmontese** which is usually used grated raw on pasta or egg dishes.

### OKRA

These are dark green and look like ribbed chillies. They are about 7.5 cm (3 inches) in length and both pods and seeds are eaten.
*To buy:* Choose those which have no brown marks as they indicate staleness.
*To prepare:* Top and tail and if the ridges are tough or damaged, scrape them. Slice or leave whole.
*To cook:* Cook in boiling salted water for 5 minutes or sauté for about 10 minutes, until tender. Serve hot.
   Allow 100 g (4 oz) per person.

### ONIONS

There are different varieties of onions, some more strongly flavoured than others (see below).
*To buy:* Choose clean, firm onions with dry, papery skins.
*To prepare onions:* Cut a slice from the top and peel off the skin. Cut the onion in half lengthways and cut each half separately. Laying it flat on the chopping board, slice it through in one direction, turn and slice it in the other direction for chopped onion.
*To cook:* Boil whole onions for 30–40 minutes, bake for 1–1½ hours, steam for 40 minutes, braise for 30–40 minutes or slice and gently fry in butter until soft.
   Allow 1 onion per person if serving whole onions as a vegetable, 100 g (4 oz) if serving shallots as a vegetable, 2–3 spring onions per person in salads.
**Globe onions** are the most commonly used variety for cooking.
**Spanish onions** are larger and more delicately flavoured. They are more suitable for frying or serving raw.
**Italian red onions** are oblong-shaped and smaller than globe onions. They have a mild, sometimes sweet flavour, and are attractive cut into thin rings raw. If cooked they become white.
**Pickling (button) onions** are about 2.5 cm (1 inch) in diameter.

Shallots are also small and have a stronger flavour than globe onions.

Silverskin onions have white flesh and a silver skin. They are very small and are popular for pickling.

Spring onions are nearly always used raw. They are slim and mild in flavour when young, with a more pronounced taste as they increase in size. Cut off the roots and trim the green part to about 2.5 cm (1 inch) above the white. Use whole or sliced in salads or chop and add to stir-fried dishes.

## PALM HEARTS

These are the edible inner part of palm tree shoots. The firm, creamy coloured flesh has a delicate flavour rather like artichoke or asparagus. They are rarely available fresh in Britain but canned ones are sold in specialist food shops. They can be added to salads or sauces, eaten hot as a vegetable or sliced and fried.

## PARSNIPS

A root vegetable with a nutty, sweet flavour which improves after several frosts.

To buy: Choose those which are small and young with firm clean skins and no side shoots or brown marks.

To prepare: Scrub well, trim the top and root ends and peel thinly. Either leave young parsnips whole or slice large old ones into quarters and remove the central core.

To cook: Boil or steam for 15–20 minutes, or blanch and sauté in butter or oil, or roast around a joint of meat after first boiling in water for 2 minutes. Serve hot.

Allow 175–225 g (6–8 oz) per person.

## PEAS

To buy: Choose crisp, well filled pods with some air space between the peas. Very full pods may have tough peas inside. The fresh pea season is short but they are available all year round frozen, dried and canned.

To prepare: Shell the peas and discard any that are discoloured or blemished. Wash and cook immediately.

To cook: Cook in a little boiling salted water for 8–10 minutes. Serve hot with butter, sprinkled with chopped fresh mint.

Allow 100–175 g (4–6 oz) prepared weight per person. You will need to buy about 225–350 g (8–12 oz) per person in the pods.

Petit pois are tiny peas which are prepared in the same way.

## MANGE-TOUT PEAS

In French, mange tout means eat all. The whole pods are eaten very young when the peas are underdeveloped.

To buy: Choose pods in which the peas are very small and underdeveloped.

To prepare: Trim the ends and wash.

To cook: Cook in boiling salted water for 2–4 minutes. They can also be included in stir-fried dishes.

Allow about 100 g (4 oz) per person.

## PEPPERS

Peppers belong to the capsicum family. There is a great variety of colours ranging from white, yellow, red and green to black. They all taste similar.

To buy: Choose those with firm shiny skins and no sign of shrivelling. They can be eaten cooked or raw.

To prepare: Rinse the skins, then slice off the stem and remove the seeds and membrane. Leave whole, slice into rings or dice. When peppers are to be eaten raw they are more digestible with the skins removed. Grill or turn the whole pepper over a gas flame until the skin is charred, then plunge into cold water. The skin will rub off between your fingers.

To cook: Blanch or stuff and bake in the oven at 190°C (375°F) mark 5 for about 45 minutes.

Allow 1 pepper per person when stuffed.

## CHILLI PEPPERS

The volatile oils in the flesh and seeds of the chilli can make your skin tingle, so treat with care. They are sometimes eaten on their own in Indian and Far Eastern cookery but otherwise they are added in small quantities to soups and casseroles for flavour. Prepare as for large peppers and discard the seeds if you do not want a very hot flavour.

## POTATOES

New or early British potatoes are available from May to August. Maincrop British potatoes are lifted during September and October and stored for sale over the next eight months.

*To buy:* Choose potatoes with smooth, firm skins. New potatoes should have skins that can be rubbed off. Buy new potatoes in small quantities and use up quickly. See below for the most common varieties and the best methods of cooking them.

*To prepare:* Prepare potatoes just before you cook them; leaving them in water after peeling causes loss of their vitamin C. Scrub or scrape new potatoes. They contain more vitamin C than maincrop potatoes which is why they are only scrubbed or scraped and eaten with their skin on.

Allow 175–225 g (6–8 oz) per person.

**Boiled** Peel and, if necessary, cut into smallish, even-sized pieces. Place in cold salted water and bring to the boil. Cook for about 10–15 minutes (new potatoes), 15–20 minutes (maincrop) or until tender.

**Chipped** Peel and cut into slices, then into sticks. Put into a bowl of cold water for 30 minutes to remove excess starch. Drain and dry in a clean tea towel or on absorbent kitchen paper. In a deep frying pan or electric deep fat fryer, heat the oil to 190°C (375°F). If you do not have a thermostat on the pan, nor a cooking thermometer, check the temperature by dropping in one chip which should rise to the surface immediately, surrounded by bubbles. Put enough chips into the frying basket to quarter-fill it, lower into the oil and cook for 6–7 minutes, until starting to colour. Raise the basket and drain the chips on absorbent kitchen paper. When all the chips have had their first frying, repeat the process and fry this time for 3 minutes, until they are golden and crisp. Drain and serve at once.

For **Game Chips**, cut very thin slices. Then deep fry until golden.

**Jacket Potatoes** Wash, dry and prick with a fork or impale on a potato baking spike. For crisp skins, brush with oil or melted butter. Bake near the top of the oven at 200°C (400°F) mark 6 for 1–1½ hours, until tender right through. Cut a cross in the top or cut in half and serve with a knob of butter.

**Mashed and creamed** Boil, then mash until smooth with a fork or potato macher. Season, then put on a low heat and dry for 2–3 minutes, stirring continuously. For creamed potatoes, add a little butter or margarine, a little warm milk and beat until fluffy.

**Roasted** Place peeled potatoes in cold salted water and bring to the boil. Cook for 2–3 minutes, then drain thoroughly. Either add to the fat around a joint at 180°C (350°F) mark 4 for about 1¼–1½ hours or heat vegetable oil or dripping in a roasting tin in the oven at 220°C (425°F) mark 7 and put the potatoes into it. Cook for about 45 minutes–1 hour, basting regularly and turning once or twice, until golden brown all over.

**Steamed** Scrub the potatoes and remove a 1 cm (½ inch) strip of peel from around the centre of each. Steam for about 45 minutes, until tender.

**Sautéed** Boil the potatoes for 15 minutes, until just cooked. Drain, peel and cut into large chunks. Sauté gently in hot butter and oil until golden and crisp on both sides. Drain thoroughly on absorbent kitchen paper and sprinkle with salt.

### NEW POTATOES

**Arran Comet** has creamy white flesh which does not break up when cooked. Good for boiling, sautéeing, potato salad and chips.

**Home Guard** has creamy white flesh which does not break up or discolour when cooked. Good for boiling and potato salad.

**Maris Peer** has pale yellow firm flesh. Good for boiling, sautéeing, potato salad, chips or roasting.

**Pentland Javelin** has very white firm flesh. Good for boiling and potato salad.

**Red Craigs Royal** has creamy close textured flesh. Good all rounder.

**Ulster Sceptre** is a very early variety with white flesh which does not discolour. Good all rounder.

**Wilja** has pale yellow flesh and a soft texture when cooked. Good for boiling and potato salad.

### MAINCROP POTATOES

**Desiree** has pinkish-red skin and pale yellow flesh which is consistently good quality and not as dry as many maincrop varieties. Good all-rounder.

**King Edward** has a patchy red skin and pale yellow floury flesh. Good all rounder.

**Maris Piper** has a pale skin and creamy white floury flesh which does not discolour after cooking. Good for chips, cooking in its jacket, boiling, sautéeing, mashing and roasting.

**Majestic** has a white skin and creamy white floury flesh. It does tend to discolour after cooking. Good for chips, sautéeing and roasting.

**Pentland Crown** has pale skin and creamy white

flesh but is of only moderate cooking quality as it tends to be wet. It is best used for jacket potatoes.
**Pentland Dell** has a pale skin and tends to disintegrate. It is best for jacket potatoes.
**Pentland Hawk** has pale skin and creamy flesh but only moderate cooking quality. It is best for boiling, mashing and cooking in its jacket.

## PUMPKIN

One of the largest of the squashes (the same family as the marrow), pumpkin can be used as a vegetable or a fruit.
*To buy*: Choose firm pumpkins weighing about 4.5–6.8 kg (10–15 lb).
*To prepare*: Cut in half and scoop out the seeds. Cut into sections and peel and chop the flesh into even-sized pieces. Alternatively, you can buy slices of pumpkin, sold by weight.
*To cook*: Cook pumpkin in boiling salted water for about 15 minutes, until tender, steam or roast—like potatoes—around a joint or in hot fat. It can also be stuffed and baked or used in stews—it makes a good thickener for gravies.
Allow 225 g (8 oz) per person.

## RADISHES

There are several varieties and sizes of this root vegetable.
*To buy*: Choose those with fresh green tops or, if these have been cut off, look for ones with firm bright flesh.
Allow 3–4 red radishes per person; 175–225 g (6–8 oz) raw weight, 100–175 g (4–6 oz) cooked weight white or black radish per person.
**Red radish**, the cultivated varieties of this small radish are sold all year round. They have a peppery flavour which is milder in the spring. They are usually eaten raw in salads or with bread and butter as an hors d'oeuvre or they can be made into attractive garnishes (see Radish Roses, page 249). The leaves add pungent flavour to salads.
**Daikon radish (Japanese radish)** is the traditional white Japanese variety, often sold in Oriental food shops. It is milder than other types and is grated and used as a garnish or pickled.
**Mooli** is a long, white tube-like vegetable which can be grated and eaten raw or cooked.
**Spanish black radish** is a round radish the size of a small turnip which can be eaten raw or cooked.

## SALSIFY AND SCORZONERA

These two root vegetables are closely related. They both have long, tapering roots. Salsify has a white skin and a flavour similar to oysters—it is also known as *oyster plant* or *vegetable oyster*. Scorzonera has a brownish black skin and is also known as *black salsify*. It has a stronger flavour than salsify and is at its best in the late autumn.
*To buy*: Choose roots that are as smooth as possible and firm. Avoid flabby ones.
*To prepare*: Top and tail the roots and scrub well with a scrubbing brush under cold running water.
*To cook*: Cook in boiling salted water with a little added lemon juice for 25–30 minutes, until tender but still crisp. Drain well. Serve hot with lemon juice, melted butter and chopped fresh herbs, purée for soups, use in casseroles or as a salad ingredient.
Allow 100–175 g (4–6 oz) per person.

## SEAKALE

This looks like a cross between blanched forced rhubarb and celery. It has crisp white stalks topped with tiny green leaves. The variety most commonly available in greengrocers' is forced in a greenhouse.

Seakale grown outdoors like celery is available in specialist shops in the spring.
*To buy*: Choose stalks which are not discoloured or wilting. Trim the stalks and wash well.
*To cook*: Tie in bunches of five or six stalks as for asparagus. Steam for 20–25 minutes, or alternatively, boil in a lightly salted water with a little lemon juice for 15–20 minutes. Drain well.
*To eat*: Serve hot with melted butter, Hollandaise or cheese sauce.
Allow 100–175 g (4–6 oz) per person.

## SORREL

There are several varieties but the main ones are *wild sorrel* and *French sorrel*.
*To buy*: Choose leaves which are small, fresh looking and bright green. Sorrel is not widely available commercially, but is

easily grown in a garden. It should be picked when young before it flowers.

*To prepare:* Wash well and tear up any large leaves into smaller pieces. Use raw in salads or soften the leaves in butter or margarine and use in soups, sauces or as a filling for omelettes. Sorrel has a distinctive acidic flavour and cannot be used alone in salad.

Allow 50 g (2 oz) per person.

## SPINACH

*To buy:* Choose bright green leaves and avoid spinach that is yellow or wilted. *Summer spinach* is light green and fine textured, while *winter spinach* is darker and coarser.

*To prepare:* Wash spinach well as it collects dirt. Use several changes of water and handle the leaves gently as they bruise easily.

*To cook:* Summer spinach is best steamed for 5–10 minutes in just the water that clings to it after rinsing. Winter spinach needs to have the stalks and central ribs removed before boiling in salted water for 5–10 minutes, until tender. Drain well and press the water out of the leaves with the back of a wooden spoon.

Allow at least 225 g (8 oz) per person.

As spinach can be quite a difficult vegetable to grow, hardier varieties have been developed. The 'spinach substitutes' available are listed here— plants that produce leaves similar in colour, texture and flavour:

**Spinach beet (perpetual spinach)** This looks very much like winter spinach but the leaves have a coarser centre rib and stalk and a stronger flavour.

**Seakale beet** This is two vegetables in one. Although unrelated, its leaves are used as spinach and the centre ribs cooked as for seakale.

**Good King Henry** This vegetable, with its charming name, is a native of Britain. It has been grown for centuries in cottage gardens and has recently become popular again. The plant produces leaves on a centre stalk rather than many leaves grown from the root.

## SWEDE

A heavy, coarse-skinned root vegetable with orange flesh.

*To buy:* Choose small swedes as large ones can be tough. Avoid those with damaged skins.

*To prepare:* Peel thickly to remove all the skin and roots. then cut into chunks.

*To cook:* Place in cold salted water and boil for 20 minutes or steam for the same amount of time, then mash or purée with a knob of butter and seasoning. Alternatively, roast chunks of swede in hot fat or around a joint of meat for 1–1½ hours at 200°C (400°F) mark 6.

Allow 175–225 g (6–8 oz) per person.

## SWEETCORN

Sweetcorn originated in America but it is now grown all over the world. The cob's sweet nutty flavour is at its best just after picking. Once the cob is cut from the plant the natural sugar in the kernels changes to starch and the cob loses the sweetness and flavour quite quickly.

*To buy:* Choose cobs with a pale green, tightly fitting husk with kernels inside that are not dry. Once they turn gold some of the sweetness goes and the corn becomes tougher. *Baby sweetcorn,* which looks like miniature corn on the cob, is sometimes sold fresh and also in cans. When cooked, the whole cob is eaten.

*To prepare:* Remove the stem, leaves and silky fibres. Trim the pointed end if the corn is not fully formed there.

*To cook:* Cook in boiling unsalted water (salt makes corn tough) for 5–15 minutes, until a piece of corn comes away from the cob easily.

*To eat:* Serve with melted butter or margarine. The easiest way to eat corn on the cob is from special cob-shaped dishes, holding it between two forks or special tiny skewers. If the corn is to be served off the cob, remove it by holding the cob upright on a work surface and cutting off the corn with a sharp knife, working downwards. Cook the loose corn in a little unsalted boiling water for 5–10 minutes, then drain. Serve hot with melted butter, or cool and add to salads.

Allow 1 whole cob per person and 75–100 g (3–4 oz) loose corn.

## SWEET POTATOES

Despite their name, these are not related to potatoes. They are a tuber vegetable, usually an elongated shape though there are some round varieties. The flesh is usually white and is sweet and slightly perfumed. The outer skin may be white or pulplish red.

*To buy:* Choose those which are small and firm; large ones tend to be fibrous.

*To prepare:* Scrub them well and if boiling, peel after they are cooked as the flesh is soft and floury.

*To cook:* Boil, bake, fry or roast as for ordinary potatoes.

Allow 225 g (8 oz) per person.

## SWISS CHARD

This is related to Seakale beet and is grown mainly for its leaves which look very similar to spinach. The leaves have coarse, crisp central ribs.

*To buy:* Choose fresh looking bulbs with unblemished ribs and crisp leaves.

*To prepare and cook:* The leaves are prepared and cooked in the same way as winter spinach. The central ribs, once removed from the leaves, are prepared and cooked in the same way as seakale.

Allow 225 g (8 oz) leaves per person and 100–175 g (4–6 oz) ribs per person.

## TOMATOES

Although strictly speaking a fruit, the tomato is nearly always used as a vegetable and has come to be classed under that heading. The varieties range in colour from red to orange, yellow to green.

*To buy:* Look for firm tomatoes with not too dark a colour. The following are the most common varieties:

*To prepare:* Prepare tomatoes according to their final use. For cooked dishes they are usually skinned: cover with boiling water for about 30 seconds, then plunge into cold water and the skins will slide off. Slice or quarter tomatoes if using raw, or remove the top and the seeds and flesh and cut a small sliver from the base if they are to be stuffed. Over-ripe tomatoes can be used to make juice or sauces for pasta, meat, fish and vegetables.

Serve in salads or with herbs and a dressing as a starter. When stuffed, they may be served hot or cold.

Allow 1–2 tomatoes per person when served raw, 1 large one when stuffed.

**Spanish tomatoes** are large and misshapen with skin varying from deep pink to green. They are good raw or stuffed.

**Italian plum tomatoes** are bright red with a strong flavour. They are excellent for soups, sauces and casseroles.

**Cherry tomatoes** are tiny tomatoes about the size of large marbles, which are very sweet and delicious eaten raw.

**Beef and marmande varieties** are very large, weighing up to 450 g (1 lb) each. They can be stuffed or used raw.

## TURNIPS

Sweet, tender early turnips are slightly mustard flavoured. They have green and white skins and are sold from April to July. Maincrop turnips, which are available for the rest of the year, have thicker skins and coarser flesh.

*To buy:* Choose turnips that are smooth and unblemished.

*To prepare:* Peel young turnips thinly, older ones thickly, then slice, dice or cut into chunks.

*To cook:* Place in cold salted water and boil for 20–30 minutes until tender. Young turnips can be cooked whole, but older ones should be cut up and served either in chunks or mashed. Their strong flavour benefits from being mashed with an equal part of mashed potato or carrots. Use older turnips sparingly, diced or thinly sliced, in soups and casseroles.

Young turnips can be served raw, sliced thinly or grated into salads.

Allow 175–225 g (6–8 oz) per person.

## VINE LEAVES

These are the young leaves of the grape vine which originated in the Mediterranean region and are now found all over the world.

*To buy:* Vine leaves are sold fresh, canned or packed in brine. Choose fresh leaves that are undamaged.

*To prepare:* If using fresh vine leaves, plunge a few at a time into boiling water for a few minutes until softened. When using vine leaves packed in brine, drain them, then pour over boiling water and leave to soak for about 20 minutes. Drain, then soak in fresh cold water for a further 20 minutes, drain again, then soak once more to remove any remaining excess salt.

*To eat:* Serve in salads or stuffed. They can also be wrapped around game or used as an attractive base for fresh fruit dishes and salads or stuffed.

Allow 4–5 leaves per person if stuffing.

## WATERCRESS

*To buy:* Choose watercress that looks fresh with dark green leaves and no sign of yellowing.

*To prepare:* Wash well and trim off the tough stalks before use.

*To eat:* Watercress is usually eaten raw in salads or used as a garnish on hot or cold dishes.

Allow 1 bunch for four people when raw.

## YAMS

A member of the tuber family, yams originated in Africa but have become widely available in British markets and supermarkets. Yams have a brownish-pink skin and white flesh. Choose undamaged yams when buying.

*To prepare:* Wash and peel, then dice.

*To cook:* Cook in boiling salted water with a little added lemon juice to avoid discoloration for 20 minutes, until tender, or steam. Yams can also be roasted, baked or fried like ordinary potatoes and served with meat.

Allow 175–225 g (6–8 oz) per person.

## UNUSUAL VEGETABLES

Although this glossary covers the range of vegetables likely to be found reasonably widely, there are a considerable number of others which are indigenous to particular cuisines such as West Indian and Eastern European. In general, if a recipe calls for something you have never used before, it is best to buy it from an ethnic shop and get extra advice you need on cooking it from the shop's owner. As a rough rule of thumb it is usually correct if you cook the vegetable in the same way that you would a familiar one which it resembles. For example, *Dasheen* is a West Indian root similar to potato with a dark bark-like skin and *Padr shka* a root from Eastern Europe which is like celeriac. Some supermarkets now stock a range of less familiar vegetables and provide advice on how to cook them in the form of leaflets.

*Stuffed Globe Artichoke*

## STUFFED GLOBE ARTICHOKES

| 6 medium globe artichokes |
| 45 ml (3 tbsp) lemon juice |
| salt and pepper |
| 2 medium onions, skinned and finely chopped |
| 350 g (12 oz) streaky bacon, rinded and finely sliced |
| 75 g (3 oz) butter or margarine |
| 700 g (1½ lb) ripe tomatoes, skinned, quartered, seeded and chopped |
| 175 g (6 oz) fresh breadcrumbs |
| finely grated rind and juice of 2 medium oranges |
| 90 ml (6 tbsp) chopped fresh parsley |
| 2 eggs, beaten |
| melted butter, to serve |

**1.** Strip away discoloured leaves. Slice off stem of artichoke as close as possible to the base of leaves. Level up so artichokes stand upright.
**2.** Using scissors, snip off the leaf tips. Soak the artichokes in cold water acidulated with 15 ml (1 tbsp) lemon juice for about 30 minutes while preparing the rest.
**3.** Drain the artichokes and place them in a large saucepan of boiling salted water with the remaining lemon juice.
**4.** Cover and boil gently for 30–45 minutes, depending on size. The artichokes will float, so turn them during cooking and keep covered, to steam the leaves above the water.
**5.** Meanwhile, make the stuffing. Fry the onions

and bacon in the butter until onions are soft and bacon golden.

**6.** Add the tomatoes to the pan, cook for a few minutes, then stir in the breadcrumbs, grated orange rind, parsley, eggs and seasoning, beating well to mix.

**7.** Test whether the artichokes are cooked. To do this, gently pull an outer leaf; if cooked, it will come out easily.

**8.** Drain the cooked artichokes upside down in a colander and hold briefly under cold tap. This helps to bring out and set the green colour and cools down the leaves for handling.

**9.** Gradually peel back leaves, working from the outside inwards (be careful not to snap any off). Continue peeling back the leaves until the hairy

choke of the artichoke is exposed.

**10.** With a teaspoon, scrape away and discard hairs. Hollow out heart slightly.

**11.** Spoon stuffing generously over hearts; divide it evenly between the six artichokes.

**12.** Gently fold the leaves back around the stuffing. Tie string around each one to hold it together.

**13.** Pack artichokes into a well-buttered deep ovenproof dish or shallow casserole. Pour over the strained orange juice and cover tightly with buttered greaseproof paper or foil and the lid. Bake in the oven at 190°C (375°F) mark 5 for 25 minutes. To serve, remove string and hand the melted butter separately.
*Serves 6*

## JERUSALEM ARTICHOKES IN NUTMEG CREAM

700 g (1½ lb) Jerusalem artichokes, washed and peeled

1 lemon

salt and pepper

50 g (2 oz) butter or margarine

150 ml (5 fl oz) single cream

little freshly grated nutmeg

**1.** Place the artichokes in a saucepan with a slice of lemon. Cover with cold salted water, bring to the boil and simmer gently for 10 minutes. Drain.

**2.** Melt the butter in a clean pan, add the artichokes with the juice of ½ a lemon. Cover and cook for 10 minutes, shaking occasionally.

**3.** Remove from the heat, add the cream, seasoning and nutmeg. Heat gently for 5 minutes.
*Serves 4*

## ASPARAGUS MALTAISE

450 g (1 lb) asparagus, washed and trimmed

salt and pepper

3 egg yolks

grated rind and juice of 1 orange

100 g (4 oz) unsalted butter, softened

15 ml (1 tbsp) lemon juice

30–45 ml (2–3 level tbsp) double cream

orange twists, to garnish

**1.** Tie the asparagus in bundles of six to eight stalks. Cover the tips with foil and stand them upright in a pan of boiling salted water and cook for 10–15 minutes, until tender.

**2.** Meanwhile, make the sauce. Beat together the egg yolks, orange rind and seasoning in a bowl with a knob of the softened butter.

**3.** Place the bowl over a pan of hot water and whisk in the orange and lemon juice. Cook over a gentle heat and gradually beat in remaining butter, a little at a time.

**4.** Once the sauce begins to thicken, remove from

the heat and continue heating for 1 minute. Adjust seasoning to taste. Stir in the cream.

**5.** Remove the asparagus from the pan and drain well. To serve, remove the string, arrange on a serving plate and garnish with the orange twists. Serve immediately with the orange butter sauce handed separately.
*Serves 6*

*Asparagus Maltaise*

# AUBERGINES WITH HAM

2 even-sized aubergines, 450 g (1 lb) total weight

salt and pepper

vegetable oil

1 medium onion, skinned and finely chopped

50 g (2 oz) butter or margarine

1 garlic clove, skinned and crushed

30 ml (2 level tbsp) flour

10 ml (2 level tsp) chopped fresh basil or 2.5 ml
($\frac{1}{2}$ level tsp) dried

50 g (2 oz) fresh breadcrumbs

125 g (4 oz) cooked lean ham, finely chopped

5 ml (1 level tsp) French mustard

5 ml (1 tsp) lemon juice

60 ml (4 tbsp) single cream or top of the milk

1. Cut the aubergines in half lengthways, sprinkle with salt and leave for 30 minutes to extract the bitter juices. Rinse and pat dry.

2. Score the cut side, brush with oil and place in an ovenproof dish with 60 ml (4 tbsp) water. Cover with foil or a lid and bake in the oven at 190°C (375°F) mark 5 for about 50 minutes. Do not overcook.
3. Scoop out as much flesh as possible, leaving the shell intact. Chop the flesh.
4. Brown the onion in half the butter, add the crushed garlic and aubergine flesh and fry for a few minutes.
5. Sprinkle over the flour and basil and cook for a few minutes, stirring. Reserve 30 ml (2 tbsp) of the breadcrumbs and add the rest to the pan with the ham, mustard, lemon juice, cream and seasoning.
6. Fill the aubergine shells with stuffing. Sprinkle over the reserved breadcrumbs and dot with the remaining butter.
7. Bake, uncovered, in the oven at 190°C (375°F) mark 5 for about 30 minutes.
*Serves 2*

# BROAD BEANS IN LEMON PARSLEY SAUCE

900 g–1.1 kg (2–2$\frac{1}{2}$ lb) broad beans, shelled

salt

**For the sauce**

25 g (1 oz) butter or margarine

45 ml (3 level tbsp) flour

150 ml ($\frac{1}{4}$ pint) Chicken Stock (see page 19)

60 ml (4 tbsp) milk

salt and pepper

1 egg yolk

30 ml (2 tbsp) single cream

grated rind and juice of $\frac{1}{2}$ a lemon

15 ml (1 tbsp) chopped fresh parsley

1. Cook the broad beans in boiling salted water for 15–20 minutes, until just tender. Drain well.
2. Meanwhile, make the sauce, melt the butter in a saucepan, stir in the flour and cook gently for 1 minute, stirring. Remove the pan from the heat and gradually stir in the stock. Bring to the boil slowly and continue to cook for 1–2 minutes, until the sauce thickens.
3. Stir in the milk and the seasoning.
4. Beat the egg yolk and cream together in a bowl. Add 45 ml (3 tbsp) of the sauce to the cream, then stir the mixture into the pan. Cook over a very low heat, stirring, until the sauce thickens. Stir in the lemon rind and juice, parsley and the drained beans.
*Serves 4*

# FRENCH BEANS WITH THYME

25 g (1 oz) butter or margarine

1 medium onion, skinned and finely sliced

4 rashers streaky bacon, rinded and chopped

700 g (1$\frac{1}{2}$ lb) French beans, topped and tailed

5 ml (1 tsp) chopped fresh thyme

salt and pepper

1. Melt the butter in a large saucepan, add the onion and bacon and cook for 10 minutes, until the onion begins to colour.
2. Add the beans to the pan with the thyme, seasoning and 90 ml (6 tbsp) cold water. Cover and simmer gently for about 10 minutes, until the beans are tender but still crisp.
*Serves 4*

# FRENCH BEANS WITH TOMATOES

*700 g (1½ lb) French beans, topped and tailed*

*salt*

*30 ml (2 tbsp) vegetable oil*

*4 tomatoes, skinned and chopped*

*1 garlic clove, skinned*

*chopped fresh parsley, to garnish*

1. Cook the beans whole in boiling salted water for about 5 minutes. Drain well.
2. Heat the oil in a saucepan, add the tomatoes, garlic and beans. Cover and cook for 10 15 minutes, until the tomatoes and beans are tender.
3. Remove the garlic and turn the beans into a warmed serving dish. Sprinkle with parsley before serving.
*Serves 4*

# SPICED RUNNER BEANS

*700 g (1½ lb) runner beans, topped and tailed*

*25 g (1 oz) butter or margarine*

*15 ml (1 tbsp) vegetable oil*

*1.25 ml (¼ level tsp) mustard powder*

*1.25 ml (¼ level tsp) ground cumin*

*5 ml (1 level tsp) ground turmeric*

*1.25 ml (¼ level tsp) cayenne pepper*

*salt and pepper*

1. Cut the beans into 5 cm (2 inch) lengths and then into thin strips. Heat the butter and oil in a saucepan, add the spices and cook for 1 minute, stirring.
2. Add the beans and seasonings, cover and cook over a very gentle heat for about 10 minutes, until the beans are tender. Shake the pan from time to time to prevent sticking.
*Serves 4*

# BEAN SPROUTS WITH CHINESE EGG STRIPS

*45 ml (3 tbsp) vegetable oil*

*3 eggs, beaten*

*1 medium onion, skinned and finely chopped*

*1 garlic clove, skinned and crushed*

*1 medium red or green pepper, seeded and sliced*

*4 celery sticks, washed and chopped*

*175 g (6 oz) button mushrooms, wiped and sliced*

*225 g (8 oz) bean sprouts, washed*

*15 ml (1 tbsp) soy sauce*

*salt and pepper*

1. Heat 15 ml (1 tbsp) oil in a frying pan, add the beaten eggs and cook over a gentle heat for about 10 minutes, until set like a thin omelette. Remove from the pan, cut into thin strips, then cut each strip into three or four pieces.
2. Heat the remaining oil in the pan, add the onion, garlic, pepper and celery and cook for about 10 minutes, until soft. Increase the heat, add the mushrooms and cook until golden brown.
3. Stir in the bean sprouts, soy sauce, seasoning and the egg strips and cook for 3–4 minutes, stirring, until heated through. Serve immediately.
*Serves 4*

# OVEN-COOKED BEETROOTS

*4 large beetroots*

*vegetable oil for brushing*

*25–50 g (1–2 oz) butter or margarine*

*grated rind of 1 orange*

*salt and pepper*

1. Scrub the beetroots well and place on a baking sheet. Brush the skins with a little oil and cook in the oven at 180°C (350°F) mark 4 for 2–3 hours, according to size. The flesh is cooked when it can be pierced with a knife.
2. While still warm, peel, then slice or chop coarsely. Melt the butter in a saucepan, add the orange rind and the beetroots and heat through.
3. Season to taste and turn into a warmed serving dish.
*Serves 4*

## BROCCOLI AMANDINE

| |
|---|
| 700 g (1½ lb) broccoli, trimmed |
| salt |
| 50 g (2 oz) butter or margarine |
| 50 g (2 oz) flaked almonds |
| 30 ml (2 tbsp) lemon juice |
| pepper |

1. Cook the broccoli in boiling salted water for 10–15 minutes. Drain well and turn into a warmed serving dish.
2. Melt the butter in a frying pan, add the almonds and cook over a gentle heat for about 5 minutes, until golden brown.
3. Stir in the lemon juice and seasoning and spoon over the broccoli.
*Serves 4*

## BROCCOLI AND CURRIED EGGS

| |
|---|
| 700 g (1½ lb) broccoli |
| 6 eggs, hard-boiled |
| 30 ml (2 level tbsp) mango chutney, chopped |
| salt and pepper |
| 50 g (2 oz) butter or margarine |
| 225 g (8 oz) onion, skinned and finely chopped |
| 20 ml (4 level tsp) mild curry paste |
| 5 ml (1 level tsp) ground turmeric (optional) |
| 30 ml (2 level tbsp) flour |
| 300 ml (½ pint) milk |
| 284 ml (10 fl oz) soured cream |
| toasted flaked almonds, to garnish |

1. Trim about 175 g (6 oz) off the broccoli stalks. Wash the stalks and head, drain well. Cook the stalks in boiling salted water until tender; drain and chop finely.
2. Halve the eggs, sieve the yolks and mix with the chopped broccoli, chopped chutney and seasoning. Spoon the mixture back into the egg halves.
3. Melt the butter in a saucepan, add the onion, curry paste and turmeric and cook gently until the onion is soft.
4. Stir in the flour and cook gently for 1 minute, stirring. Remove pan from the heat and gradually stir in the milk. Bring to the boil slowly and continue to cook, stirring, until the sauce thickens. Stir in the soured cream and seasoning.
5. Meanwhile, cook the broccoli in boiling salted water for about 8 minutes until just tender, drain well.
6. Arrange the eggs and broccoli in a serving dish and spoon the sauce over the eggs. Garnish with flaked almonds.
*Serves 4*

*Broccoli and Curried Eggs*

## BRUSSELS SPROUTS AND CHESTNUTS

350 g (12 oz) fresh chestnuts

300 ml (½ pint) Chicken Stock (see page 19)

1 celery stick, trimmed

5 ml (1 level tsp) sugar

700 g (1½ lb) Brussels sprouts, trimmed

salt

25 g (1 oz) butter or margarine

1. Place the chestnuts in a saucepan of cold water and bring to the boil. Drain and remove skins.

2. Return the chestnuts to the pan, with the stock, celery and sugar. Bring to the boil and allow to simmer gently for about 35–40 minutes, until the nuts are soft. Remove and discard the celery, then drain the nuts.

3. Meanwhile, cook the Brussels sprouts separately in boiling salted water for 8–10 minutes. Drain.

4. Melt the butter and toss the cooked nuts and sprouts together.

*Serves 4*

## WHOLE STUFFED CABBAGE

winter cabbage, about 900 g (2 lb) in weight

50 g (2 oz) butter or margarine

125 g (4 oz) onion, skinned and finely chopped

50 g (2 oz) celery, trimmed and finely chopped

10 ml (2 level tsp) ground coriander

240 g (8½ oz) smoked pork sausage, finely chopped

50 g (2 oz) fresh breadcrumbs

30 ml (2 tbsp) chopped fresh parsley

10 ml (2 tsp) lemon juice

1 egg, beaten

salt and pepper

300 ml (½ pint) Chicken Stock (see page 19)

soy sauce

1. Trim the coarse outer leaves from the cabbage. Using a potato peeler, gouge out some of the stem. Cut a 2 cm (¾ inch) slice off the top. Tie with string around the middle. Blanch in boiling salted water for 8–10 minutes, then rinse under cold running water to cool and drain well. Scoop out and reserve the centre of cabbage leaving a 1 cm (½ inch) shell.

2. Melt the butter in a saucepan, add the onion, celery and coriander and cook gently until the onion and celery are softened. Stir the pork sausage into the onion and celery with the breadcrumbs, parsley, lemon juice and the egg. Season.

3. Pack the stuffing well into the cabbage shell. Place in a shallow ovenproof dish, pour in the stock and a dash of soy sauce. Cover loosely with buttered foil. Bake in the oven at 190°C (375°F) mark 5 for about 1¼ hours. Cut into wedges and serve with the cooking juices, accompanied by the reserved cabbage heated in butter and seasoned.

*Serves 4*

*Whole Stuffed Cabbage*

## SAVOURY WHITE CABBAGE

50 g (2 oz) butter or margarine

700 g (1½ lb) white cabbage, finely shredded

1 medium onion, skinned and grated

2 rashers streaky bacon, rinded and chopped

pinch of freshly grated nutmeg

1. Melt the butter in a large saucepan. Add all the remaining ingredients, cover and cook very gently for 20–30 minutes, until the cabbage is just tender, shaking the pan frequently.
*Serves 4*

## BRAISED RED CABBAGE WITH APPLE

1.1 kg (2½ lb) red cabbage

2 medium onions, skinned and sliced

2 medium cooking apples, peeled, cored and chopped

10 ml (2 level tsp) sugar

salt and pepper

bouquet garni

30 ml (2 tbsp) red wine vinegar

25 g (1 oz) margarine or butter

1. Shred the cabbage finely, discarding any

discoloured outside leaves and coarse stems.
2. Layer the cabbage in a 3.4 litre (6 pint) casserole with the onions, apples, sugar and seasoning. Put the bouquet garni in the centre and pour over 30 ml (2 tbsp) water and the vinegar.
3. Cover tightly and cook in the oven at 200°C (400°F) mark 6 for 1 hour. Remove the lid and continue cooking for about 30 minutes, until the liquid has evaporated.
4. Add butter or margarine and mix with the cabbage at the end of the cooking time.
*Serves 6*

## CAROTTES À LA VICHY

700 g (1½ lb) new carrots, trimmed and scrubbed

50 g (2 oz) butter or margarine

salt and pepper

450 ml (¾ pint) Chicken Stock (see page 19) or water

5 ml (1 level tsp) sugar

chopped fresh parsley, to garnish

1. Put the carrots in a saucepan with half the butter, salt, stock and sugar. Bring to the boil, then cook, uncovered, for 45 minutes, until the liquid has evaporated.
2. Add the remaining butter and pepper and toss the carrots until evenly glazed. Turn into a serving dish and sprinkle with parsley.
*Serves 4*

## CAULIFLOWER POLONAISE

1 medium cauliflower, trimmed and divided into
    florets

salt

1 egg, hard-boiled

50 g (2 oz) butter or margarine

50 g (2 oz) fresh breadcrumbs

chopped fresh parsley, to garnish

1. Cook the cauliflower in boiling salted water for 5–10 minutes, until tender but still crisp.

Drain well, then place in a shallow serving dish and keep hot.
2. Sieve the egg yolk, chop the egg white and reserve.
3. Melt the butter in a frying pan, stir in the breadcrumbs and cook until the breadcrumbs are golden brown.
4. Spoon the golden crumbs over the cauliflower, then sprinkle the egg yolk, egg white and parsley in neat rows over the cauliflower.
*Serves 4*

# CELERIAC AND ONION BAKE

900 g (2 lb) celeriac, peeled and cut into 0.5 cm
  (¼ inch) slices

1 large onion, skinned and thinly sliced

salt and pepper

50 g (2 oz) butter or margarine

150 ml (¼ pint) milk

1. Layer the celeriac and onion slices in a greased ovenproof dish. Sprinkle each layer with seasoning and dot with butter.
2. Pour over the milk and cook, uncovered, in the oven at 190°C (375°F) mark 5 for about 1¼ hours, until the celeriac is soft and golden brown on top.
Serves 4

# BRAISED CELERY WITH WALNUTS

1 large head of celery, trimmed and washed

50 g (2 oz) butter or margarine

1 medium onion, skinned and chopped

150 ml (¼ pint) Chicken Stock (see page 19)

50 g (2 oz) walnuts, roughly chopped

chopped fresh parsley, to garnish

1. Cut the celery sticks into 2.5 cm (1 inch) lengths.
2. Melt the butter in a saucepan, add the onion and celery and cook for 5–10 minutes, until soft but not coloured. Add the stock, cover and simmer gently for 20 minutes, until the celery is tender and the stock absorbed.
3. Stir in the walnuts and heat through. Turn into a warmed serving dish and sprinkle with parsley.
Serves 4

# BRAISED CHICORY

4 chicory heads, trimmed and washed

25 g (1 oz) butter or margarine

1.25 ml (¼ level tsp) freshly grated nutmeg

juice of ½ a lemon

150 ml (¼ pint) Chicken Stock (see page 19)

10 ml (2 level tsp) cornflour

salt and pepper

30 ml (2 tbsp) single cream

chopped fresh parsley, to garnish

1. Blanch the chicory in boiling water for 1 minute. Drain, refresh in cold water and drain

again. Place the chicory heads in a single layer in a greased ovenproof dish and dot with the butter.
2. Stir the nutmeg and lemon juice into the stock and pour over the chicory. Cover and cook in the oven at 170°C (325°F) mark 3 for 1½ hours, until the chicory is tender.
3. Blend the cornflour with 30 ml (2 tbsp) water to a smooth paste. Drain the juice from the dish into a small pan, add the cornflour mixture and the seasoning. Bring to the boil, stirring, and cook for 1 minute. Add the cream.
4. Arrange the chicory in a warmed serving dish, pour over the sauce and sprinkle with parsley.
Serves 4

# STIR-FRIED CHINESE LEAVES

1 head Chinese leaves, coarsely shredded

450 g (1 lb) firm tomatoes, skinned

30 ml (2 tbsp) sunflower oil

salt and pepper

1. Wash the Chinese leaves in cold water and drain well, patting dry with absorbent kitchen paper.
2. Quarter the tomatoes, or if large, cut into eighths. Using a teaspoon, scoop out the seeds and discard.

3. Heat the oil in a wok or large deep frying pan, stir in the Chinese leaves and continue stirring for 4 minutes, until the leaves are transparent but still crisp.
4. Stir in the tomatoes and season well with salt and pepper. Stir again.
5. Using a large spoon, arrange in a warmed serving dish.
Serves 6

*Creamy Courgettes and Almonds*

## CREAMY COURGETTES AND ALMONDS

| |
|---|
| 450–700 g (1–1½ lb) courgettes, trimmed and cut into 1 cm (½ inch) slices |
| 45 ml (3 level tbsp) seasoned flour |
| 25 g (1 oz) butter or margarine |
| 30 ml (2 tbsp) vegetable oil |
| 50 g (2 oz) blanched almonds |
| 142 ml (5 fl oz) soured cream |
| salt and pepper |
| paprika, to garnish |

1. Coat the courgettes in the seasoned flour.
2. Heat the butter and oil in a frying pan, add the courgette slices, a few at a time, and fry until golden brown on both sides. Drain on absorbent kitchen paper and keep warm.
3. Add the almonds to the pan and fry gently until golden brown. Stir in the cream and seasoning and heat gently, stirring.
4. Spoon the courgettes into a warmed serving dish, pour over the cream and almonds and sprinkle with paprika.
*Serves 4*

## SAUTÉED CUCUMBER WITH HERBS

| |
|---|
| 1 cucumber |
| salt |
| 50 g (2 oz) butter or margarine |
| 2 shallots or 1 small onion, skinned and finely chopped |
| 15 ml (1 tbsp) fresh chopped rosemary or 5 ml (1 level tsp) dried |
| 2.5 ml (½ tsp) sugar |
| pepper |
| 60 ml (4 tbsp) soured cream |
| fresh rosemary sprigs, to garnish |

1. Using a sharp fork, run the prongs down the length of the cucumber to score the skin.
2. Using a sharp knife, cut the cucumber into 5 cm (2 inch) lengths, then cut each piece lengthways into quarters.
3. Remove the seeds from the cucumber, then put the cucumber in a colander and sprinkle with the salt. Cover with a plate and leave to drain for 30 minutes, pressing the plate down occasionally to press out the liquid from the cucumber. Rinse and pat dry with absorbent kitchen paper.
4. Melt the butter in a large, heavy-based frying pan. Add the shallots and fry gently for 5 minutes, until they are soft and lightly coloured.
5. Add the cucumber pieces to the pan, together with the rosemary, sugar and pepper to taste. Cook for 5 minutes only, stirring frequently to ensure even cooking.
6. Remove the pan from the heat and stir in the soured cream. Taste and garnish. Serve.
*Serves 6*

*Sautéed Cucumber with Herbs*

## BRAISED FENNEL

25 g (1 oz) butter or margarine

1 medium onion, skinned and chopped

2 large carrots, peeled and chopped

2 celery sticks, trimmed and chopped

4 small fennel heads, trimmed

450 ml ($\frac{3}{4}$ pint) Chicken Stock (see page 19)

salt and pepper

bouquet garni

1. Melt the butter in a saucepan, add the onion, carrots and celery and sauté gently for 5 minutes.

Remove the vegetables with a slotted spoon and place in a shallow ovenproof dish. Cut each fennel in half and place, cut side down, on the vegetables.
2. Pour over the stock and add seasoning and the bouquet garni. Cover and cook in the oven at 180°C (350°F) mark 4 for about 1 hour, until the fennel is tender.
3. Transfer the fennel to a warmed serving dish. Remove the bouquet garni and sieve the remaining vegetables or purée in a blender or food processor until smooth. Pour the sauce over the fennel before serving.
*Serves 4*

## SCALLOPED KOHLRABI

700 g (1$\frac{1}{2}$ lb) kohlrabi, washed, peeled and cut into
    0.5 cm ($\frac{1}{4}$ inch) slices

1 large onion, skinned and chopped

salt and pepper

50 g (2 oz) butter or margarine

150 ml ($\frac{1}{4}$ pint) milk

1. Arrange the kohlrabi in layers with the onion in a greased ovenproof dish. Sprinkle each layer with seasoning and dot with butter.
2. Pour over the milk, cover, and cook in the oven at 190°C (375°F) mark 5 for 1 hour. Remove the lid and continue cooking for 15 minutes, until the top is golden brown.
*Serves 4*

## LEEKS AU GRATIN

4 medium leeks, trimmed

salt and pepper

25 g (1 oz) butter or margarine

45 ml (3 level tbsp) flour

300 ml ($\frac{1}{2}$ pint) milk

2.5 ml ($\frac{1}{2}$ level tsp) mustard powder

100 g (4 oz) Cheddar cheese, grated

50 g (2 oz) fresh breadcrumbs

1. Remove the outer leaves of the leeks. Cut each leek in half lengthways and wash thoroughly under running cold water. Cook in boiling salted water for 10–15 minutes and drain thoroughly.
2. Melt the butter in a saucepan, stir in the flour and cook gently for 1 minute, stirring. Remove the pan from the heat and gradually stir in the milk. Bring to the boil slowly and continue to cook, stirring, until the sauce thickens. Stir in the seasoning, mustard and half the cheese.
3. Arrange the leeks in a greased shallow flameproof serving dish and pour over the cheese sauce.
4. Mix together the remaining cheese and

*Leeks au Gratin*

breadcrumbs and spoon over the dish. Brown under a hot grill or in the oven.
*Serves 2 for supper or 4 as an accompanying vegetable*

## STIR-FRIED MANGE-TOUT

| |
|---|
| 30 ml (2 tbsp) vegetable oil |
| 1 small onion, skinned and chopped |
| 50 g (2 oz) button mushrooms, wiped and chopped |
| 450 g (1 lb) mange-tout, trimmed |
| 100 g (4 oz) bean sprouts, washed |
| 15 ml (1 tbsp) soy sauce |
| salt and pepper |

1. Heat the oil in a wok, add the onion and cook over a high heat, stirring for 2–3 minutes.
2. Add mushrooms and cook until lightly browned, then add mange-tout and cook for 2–3 minutes.
3. Stir in the bean sprouts and cook for 1 minute, then add 30 ml (2 tbsp) water, the soy sauce and seasoning. Continue cooking for 2 minutes. Serve.
*Serves 4*

## SPICED MARROW

| |
|---|
| 1 marrow, about 900 g (2 lb) |
| 15 ml (1 tbsp) vegetable oil |
| 25 g (1 oz) butter or margarine |
| 1 large onion, skinned and chopped |
| 1 garlic clove, skinned and crushed |
| 15 ml (1 level tbsp) paprika |
| 15 ml (1 level tbsp) flour |
| 150 ml (¼ pint) Beef Stock (see page 19) |
| 15 ml (1 level tbsp) tomato purée |
| salt and pepper |
| 4 large tomatoes, skinned and chopped |

1. Peel the marrow thinly. Cut into 7.5 cm (3 inch) pieces and scoop out the seeds, then cube.
2. Heat the oil and butter in a large saucepan, add the onion and garlic and cook for 5 minutes. Stir in the paprika and flour and cook for 1 minute, stirring. Remove pan from the heat and gradually stir in the stock. Bring to the boil slowly and continue to cook, stirring, until thickened.
3. Stir in the tomato purée, seasoning and tomatoes and simmer, uncovered, for 15 minutes, until thick. Stir in the marrow and cook for a further 10–15 minutes.
*Serves 4*

## CREAMED MUSHROOMS

| |
|---|
| 25 g (1 oz) butter or margarine |
| 450 g (1 lb) button mushrooms, wiped and sliced |
| 20 ml (4 level tsp) cornflour |
| 150 ml (¼ pint) milk |
| 60 ml (4 tbsp) single cream |
| salt and pepper |
| 4 large slices of bread |
| butter or margarine for spreading |

1. Melt the butter in a saucepan, add the mushrooms and sauté gently for 5 minutes.
2. Blend the cornflour to a smooth paste with a little of the milk. Stir into the remaining milk, then add to the pan. Bring to the boil, stirring, and cook for 1–2 minutes, until the sauce thickens.
3. Mix in the cream and seasoning, and reheat without boiling. Toast the bread and spread with butter. Pile the creamed mixture on top.
*Serves 4*

## CURRIED OKRA

| |
|---|
| 15 ml (1 tbsp) vegetable oil |
| 25 g (1 oz) butter or margarine |
| salt and pepper |
| 5 ml (1 level tsp) ground cumin |
| 5 ml (1 level tsp) ground turmeric |
| 5 ml (1 level tsp) ground coriander |
| 450 g (1 lb) okra, trimmed and sliced |
| 142 g (5 oz) natural yogurt |
| 5 ml (1 level tsp) tomato purée |

1. Heat the oil and butter in a large saucepan, stir in the salt and all the spices and cook for 1–2 minutes, stirring. Add the okra, cover and cook for about 10 minutes, until just tender.
2. Stir in the yogurt, tomato purée and pepper and reheat for 2–3 minutes, stirring occasionally.
*Serves 4*

## Jacket Baked Onions

4 large even-sized onions

25 g (1 oz) butter or margarine

50 g (2 oz) Cheddar cheese, grated

15 ml (1 tbsp) chopped fresh parsley

salt and pepper

**1.** Wash the onions well and trim off the base. Place in a baking tin and cook in the oven at 180°C (350°F) mark 4 for 1–1½ hours, until tender.
**2.** Remove from the oven, cut a cross in the top of each onion, scoop out the centre and chop finely. Mix the chopped onions with the butter, cheese, parsley and seasoning, then spoon the mixture back into the onions. Return to the oven for 10–15 minutes to reheat.
*Serves 4*

## Glazed Onions

700 g (1½ lb) shallots, skinned

75 g (3 oz) butter or margarine

15 ml (1 level tbsp) sugar

salt and pepper

chopped fresh parsley, to garnish

**1.** Put the shallots in a saucepan and cover with cold water. Bring to the boil and cook for 10 minutes. Drain the shallots well.
**2.** Melt the butter in a frying pan, add the sugar, seasoning and shallots. Cover and cook for about 15 minutes, until the shallots are tender and well glazed, stirring occasionally to prevent the sugar from burning.
**3.** Turn into a warmed serving dish and sprinkle with parsley.
*Serves 4*

## Parsnip Bake

700 g (1½ lb) parsnips, washed and thickly sliced

salt and pepper

75 g (3 oz) butter or margarine

2 medium onions, skinned and sliced

3 eggs

45 ml (3 tbsp) single cream

8 large thin cut slices brown bread

butter or margarine for spreading

vegetable extract for spreading

**1.** Cook the parsnips in boiling salted water for 15–20 minutes, until tender. Drain and peel.
**2.** Melt 50 g (2 oz) butter in a saucepan, add the onion slices and fry until lightly browned. Reserve a few slices for garnishing.
**3.** Purée the parsnips, onions, eggs, cream and remaining butter. Season well.
**4.** Cut the crusts off the bread and roll out thinly, using a rolling pin. Butter and spread sparsely with vegetable extract. Cut each into two triangles.
**5.** Butter four 300 ml (½ pint) ovenproof dishes. Line each dish with four triangles of bread. Spoon in the parsnip mixture, garnish with reserved onion slices. Bake in the oven at 200°C (400°F) mark 6 for 30–35 minutes, until set and golden.
*Serves 4*

## Petits Pois à la Française

1 firm-hearted lettuce

50 g (2 oz) butter or margarine

900 g (2 lb) young peas, shelled

12 spring onions, trimmed and sliced

5 ml (1 level tsp) sugar

salt and pepper

150 ml (¼ pint) Chicken Stock (see page 19)

**1.** Remove the outer leaves of the lettuce and cut the heart into quarters.
**2.** Melt the butter in a large saucepan, add the peas, spring onions, lettuce, sugar, seasoning and stock. Bring to the boil, cover and simmer gently for 15–20 minutes.
*Serves 4*

## Ratatouille (Pepper Casserole)

| |
|---|
| 450 g (1 lb) aubergines, cut into thin slices |
| salt and pepper |
| 120 ml (8 tbsp) olive oil |
| 1 garlic clove, skinned and crushed |
| 450 g (1 lb) onions, skinned and chopped |
| 450 g (1 lb) tomatoes, skinned, seeded and chopped, or one 397 g (14 oz) can tomatoes, drained |
| 30 ml (2 level tbsp) tomato purée |
| 450 g (1 lb) courgettes, cut into thin slices |
| 3 medium red or green peppers, seeded and cut into rings |
| bouquet garni |

Ratatouille (Pepper Casserole)

1. Sprinkle the aubergines with salt and leave for 30 minutes to extract the bitter juices. Rinse under cold running water and pat dry with absorbent kitchen paper.
2. Heat the oil and garlic in a large saucepan. Add the onions and cook gently for about 10 minutes, until soft and golden.
3. Add the tomatoes and purée and cook for a few more minutes, then add the aubergines, courgettes, peppers, bouquet garni and salt and pepper. Cover and simmer gently for 1 hour. The vegetables should be soft and well mixed, but retain their shape and most of the cooking liquid should have evaporated.
4. To reduce the liquid, remove the lid and cook gently for another 20 minutes. Check the seasoning and serve hot or cold.
*Serves 6*

## Scalloped Potatoes

| |
|---|
| 700 g (1½ lb) potatoes, peeled and finely sliced |
| salt and pepper |
| 45 ml (3 level tbsp) flour |
| 25 g (1 oz) butter or margarine |
| 150 ml (¼ pint) milk |

1. Arrange the potatoes in layers in a greased ovenproof dish. Season each layer, dredge with flour and dot with butter.
2. Repeat the layers until all the slices are used, then pour over the milk. Cook in the oven at 190°C (375°F) mark 5 for about 1¼ hours, until the potatoes are cooked and the top golden brown.
*Serves 4*

## Gratin Dauphinois

| |
|---|
| 900 g (2 lb) potatoes, peeled and cut into small pieces |
| salt and pepper |
| 1 garlic clove, skinned and crushed |
| pinch of freshly grated nutmeg |
| 150 ml (5 fl oz) single cream |
| 75 g (3 oz) Gruyère cheese, grated |

1. Cook the potatoes in boiling salted water for 5 minutes, then drain well. Turn into a greased 1.1 litre (2 pint) ovenproof dish.
2. Stir the seasoning, garlic and nutmeg into the cream and pour over the potatoes.
3. Sprinkle with cheese, cover and cook in the oven at 180°C (350°F) mark 4 for about 45 minutes, until the potatoes are tender.
4. Uncover the dish and brown under a hot grill.
*Serves 4–6*

## POTATO PUFFS WITH FRIED PARSLEY

| |
|---|
| 700 g (1½ lb) potatoes, peeled and cut into chunks |
| salt |
| 75 g (3 oz) butter or margarine |
| 65 g (2½ oz) flour |
| 2 eggs, beaten |
| vegetable oil for deep frying |
| parsley sprigs |

1. Cook the potatoes in boiling salted water for 15–20 minutes, until tender. Drain well, then sieve or mash to a purée with 25 g (1 oz) butter.
2. Melt the remaining butter in 150 ml (¼ pint) water in a saucepan. Bring to the boil, remove from the heat and quickly beat in the flour. Leave to cool slightly, then beat in the eggs and salt. Stir the mashed potatoes into the mixture.
3. Heat the oil in a deep fat fryer to 190°C (375°F) and cook spoonfuls of the mixture for about 5 minutes, until they are puffed up and golden brown. Drain on absorbent kitchen paper.
4. Fry the parsley in the oil for a few seconds until bright green, then drain. Place the potato puffs in a warmed serving dish with the fried parsley. Serve immediately.
*Serves 4*

*Potato Puffs with Fried Parsley*

## NEW POTATOES WITH TARRAGON CREAM

| |
|---|
| 15 g (½ oz) butter or margarine |
| 4 spring onions, washed, trimmed and chopped |
| 142 ml (5 fl oz) soured cream |
| salt and pepper |
| 3 sprigs of fresh tarragon |
| 700 g (1½ lb) cooked new potatoes, drained and kept hot |

1. Melt the butter in a saucepan, add the onions and cook for 5 minutes, until soft. Stir in the cream, seasoning, and two tarragon sprigs and heat without boiling.
2. Add the cooked potatoes to the creamy onion and tarragon mixture in the pan. Reheat gently, do not boil.
3. Turn the potatoes and the sauce into a warm serving dish and serve garnished with the remaining tarragon sprig.
*Serves 4*

*New Potatoes with Tarragon Cream*

## CHÂTEAU POTATOES

50 g (2 oz) butter or margarine

700 g (1½ lb) new potatoes, scraped

salt and pepper

chopped fresh parsley, to garnish

1. Melt the butter in a frying pan and add the potatoes. Cover and cook gently, shaking the pan occasionally, for 15–20 minutes, until golden brown.
2. If the new potatoes are fairly large, pour the butter and potatoes into an ovenproof dish, cover and cook in the oven at 190°C (375°F) mark 5 for about 15 minutes, until cooked.
3. Season well and garnish with parsley.
*Serves 4*

## HASSELBACK POTATOES

8 potatoes, weighing about 75 g (3 oz) each

vegetable oil for brushing

salt and pepper

1. Cut the potatoes across their width at 0.5 cm (¼ inch) intervals three-quarters of the way through.
2. Place in a layer in an oiled baking tin. Brush with oil and season. Roast, uncovered, in the oven at 220°C (425°F) mark 7 for 45 minutes.
*Serves 4*

## SWISS ROSTI

350 g (12 oz) potatoes

salt and pepper

75 g (3 oz) butter or margarine

1 small onion, skinned and grated

1. Scrub the potatoes and cook in boiling salted water for 7 minutes. Drain well, remove the skins and grate the potato into a bowl.
2. Melt 25 g (1 oz) butter in a pan, add the onion and cook for 5 minutes, until soft. Stir into the grated potato and add the seasoning.
3. Melt the remaining butter in a 20.5 cm (8 inch) frying pan, add the potato mixture and form into a cake the size of the pan. Fry for 5–7 minutes, until golden brown.
4. Using a wide spatula, turn and brown the second side. Serve cut into wedges.
*Serves 2*

## DUCHESSE POTATOES

Pipe into pyramids to serve as a vegetable or use to garnish serving dishes for a dinner party.

700 g (1½ lb) potatoes, peeled and cut into pieces

salt and pepper

50 g (2 oz) butter or margarine

1 egg, beaten

grated nutmeg

1. Cook the potatoes in boiling salted water for 15–20 minutes, until tender, then drain well.
3. Sieve or mash the potatoes, then beat in the butter, egg, seasoning and nutmeg. Cool.
3. Spoon into a piping bag fitted with a large rosette nozzle and pipe on to a greased baking sheet. Cook in the oven at 200°C (400°F) mark 6 for about 25 minutes, until set and golden brown.
*Serves 4*

## CREAMED SPINACH

900 g (2 lb) spinach, washed, trimmed and chopped

3–4 spring onions, trimmed and finely chopped

25 g (1 oz) butter or margarine

150 ml (5 fl oz) double cream

salt and pepper

grated nutmeg

1. Place the spinach in a pan with the spring onions and butter and cook for about 10 minutes, stirring occasionally, until tender. Drain well.
2. Sieve or chop the spinach and return to the pan with the cream, seasoning and nutmeg. Reheat gently without boiling.
*Serves 4*

# SWEDE AND BACON BAKE

25 g (1 oz) butter or margarine

1 large onion, skinned and chopped

1 garlic clove, skinned and crushed

6 smoked streaky bacon rashers, rinded and chopped

100 g (4 oz) mushrooms, wiped and sliced

45 ml (3 level tbsp) flour

300 ml (½ pint) Beef Stock (see page 19)

salt and pepper

450 g (1 lb) swede, peeled and cut into 0.5 cm (¼ inch)
    slices

**1.** Melt the butter in a saucepan, add the onion,
garlic and bacon and fry gently for 5 minutes.

Add the mushrooms and continue cooking for
3–4 minutes.
**2.** Stir in the flour and cook for 1 minute.
Remove the pan from the heat and gradually
stir in the stock and seasoning. Bring to the
boil slowly and continue to cook, stirring, until
thickened.
**3.** Arrange the swede slices in layers with the
bacon and mushroom sauce in a 1.1 litre (2 pint)
ovenproof dish.
**4.** Cover and cook in the oven at 190°C (375°F)
mark 5 for about 1 hour, until the swede slices are
tender.
*Serves 4*

# SWEET POTATOES WITH ORANGE

900 g (2 lb) medium sweet potatoes, scrubbed

salt

2 large oranges

15 ml (1 tbsp) black peppercorns

30 ml (2 tbsp) vegetable oil

25 g (1 oz) butter or margarine

2.5 ml (½ level tsp) ground cinnamon

30 ml (2 level tbsp) chopped fresh parsley

**1.** Cook the potatoes in boiling, salted water for
about 20 minutes, until almost tender.
**2.** Meanwhile, peel and segment one orange and

squeeze the juice from the other. Crush the
peppercorns using a pestle and mortar or the end
of a rolling pin in a strong bowl.
**3.** Drain the potatoes and peel off their skins
while still hot. Cut the potatoes into large chunks.
**4.** Heat the oil and butter in a large frying pan and
when it is frothing, tip in all the potatoes. Fry,
turning occasionally, until the potatoes are golden
brown and beginning to flake.
**5.** Remove the pan from the heat and stir in the
cinnamon, peppercorns, parsley, orange juice and
segments and salt. Mix well, then transfer to a
warmed serving dish and serve immediately.
*Serves 4*

# TURNIPS IN MUSTARD SAUCE

1 kg (2¼ lb) turnips, peeled and cut into pieces

450 ml (¾ pint) chicken stock

**For the mustard sauce**

25 g (1 oz) butter or margarine

45 ml (3 level tbsp) flour

300 ml (½ pint) milk

15 ml (1 level tbsp) mustard powder

10 ml (2 level tsp) sugar

15 ml (1 tbsp) vinegar

salt and pepper

**1.** Put the turnip pieces in a saucepan and add the
stock. Cover, bring to the boil and cook for about
30 minutes, until tender.
**2.** Meanwhile, make the sauce: melt the butter
in a pan, stir in the flour and cook gently for
1 minute, stirring. Remove pan from the heat and
gradually stir in the milk. Bring to the boil slowly
and continue to cook, stirring, until the sauce
thickens.
**3.** Blend the mustard and sugar with the vinegar,
add to the sauce and reheat. Drain the turnips, add
to the mustard sauce, season and reheat gently.
*Serves 4–6*

# GRAINS are the edible seeds of different grasses. They are high in vitamins and minerals and, though widely used in the form of flour, they can also be used whole, cracked or flaked to add interest and nutrients to a wide range of dishes. Also included in this section are buckwheat, tapioca and sago, which are not grains but are used in the same way.

### BARLEY
One of the earliest grains to be cultivated, it is now seldom used to make bread—it makes a moist, heavy bread. It is used mostly in Scotch whiskies, malt drinks and malt extract. Pearl barley, which is the husked, polished grain, is used to thicken soups and stews and to make barley water.

### BUCKWHEAT
Although cooked and eaten as a cereal grain, buckwheat is actually the fruit of a plant related to rhubarb. It is a triangular-shape, rather like a beech nut. It is widely used in Russia to make porridge known as *kasha*, and in Japan to make noodles called *soba*. It is often sold lightly roasted, which enhances the mild flavour, and can then be used without further preparation. It is also made into flour (see page 440).

### BULGHUR, BURGUL OR BULGAR WHEAT
Bulghur is cooked wheat which is spread out to dry, then broken into pieces. It can be used in salads or it can be used as a stuffing mixture (see Spiced Wheat Peppers, right).

### CORN (MAIZE)
Corn grain has a tough outer layer which makes it difficult to cook whole. It is often ground to a meal or flour. Cornmeal may be yellow or white; Italian yellow cornmeal is called *polenta* and *masa harina* is a specially processed cornflour which is used for making Tortillas (see page 453). Hominy is whole dried corn without the yellow husk. Grits are coarsely ground dried corn and may be yellow or white depending on whether the outer husk has been removed. Cornflour is used as a thickening agent. It is lighter than wheat flour. Corn is also used to make corn syrup and corn oil, which provides a subtle flavour for salad dressing.

### COUSCOUS
Couscous is processed semolina processed into tiny pellets. It is used to make the North African dish of the same name (see Vegetable Couscous, page 246). Pre-cooked couscous is also available in packets, follow the manufacturer's instructions.

### CRACKED AND KIBBLED WHEAT
Cracked wheat is crushed under light pressure, kibbled wheat is pricked by a machine and split into small pieces.

### MILLET
Although thought of as a bird food, millet is in fact the third most important grain in the world after rice and wheat. There are many different varieties. The grains are small round and pale golden to yellow. Millet flakes are also available and can be used in porridge or muesli.

### OATS
Oats are available as whole grains, rough cut (sometimes called *groats*), medium or fine meal or as rolled or flaked oats. Grains are used for porridge or rolled oats for quick porridge, rough cut for thickening stews and making oatcakes, medium oatmeal for cakes (see Oatmeal Parkin, page 395) and for mixing with flours for scones, and fine oatmeal for pancakes and coating grilled herrings (see page 64).

### RYE
The grains are seldom cooked on their own, but can be used with other grains in casseroles. Rye flour is used in bread making (see page 440). Rye flakes can be used in mixed grain porridge or muesli.

### SEMOLINA
Tiny particles of hard durum wheat. Used for making pasta, gnocchi (see page 308) and for milk puddings.

### SAGO
Dried starch granules from the sago, a palm tree native to Asia. Used mainly in milk puddings. Sago is also made into flour.

### TAPIOCA
Small white balls or flakes made from starch extracted from the cassava plant (see page 217). It is used to make milk puddings.

## WHEAT

Whole wheat grains are grains with just the outer husk removed. They look like brown grains of rice with a split down the middle. Can be added to casseroles or breakfast cereals. Its most important use is as flour (see page 439).

## WHEAT GERM

Wheat germ is the heart of the grain which is removed when milling white flour. It is high in vitamins and is sold plain or toasted. It can be added to cooked dishes or sprinkled over the top of breakfast cereals.

# HOT WHEAT WITH CORIANDER

*225 g (8 oz) bulgar wheat*

*25 g (1 oz) butter or margarine*

*30 ml (2 tbsp) chopped fresh coriander*

*45 ml (3 tbsp) chopped fresh parsley*

*335 g (11.8 oz) can sweetcorn kernels, drained*

*salt and pepper*

*120 ml (8 tbsp) Chicken Stock (see page 19)*

1. Place the wheat in a large bowl, cover with cold water to a level 1 cm ($\frac{1}{2}$ inch) above the wheat. Soak for 20 minutes or until the water has been absorbed.

2. Using half the butter, lightly grease a shallow ovenproof dish. Transfer the soaked wheat to the prepared dish.
3. Stir the coriander, parsley, sweetcorn and seasoning into the wheat. Pour over the stock.
4. With the remaining butter, grease a large piece of greaseproof paper. Cover the dish tightly with the paper and then foil.
5. Bake in the oven at 180°C (350°F) mark 4 for about 45 minutes. Fork through lightly before serving.
*Serves 8*

# SPICED WHEAT PEPPERS

*175 g (6 oz) bulgar wheat*

*2 medium green peppers*

*2 medium yellow peppers*

*25 g (1 oz) butter or margarine*

*2 medium onions, skinned and chopped*

*15 ml (1 level tbsp) chilli seasoning*

*175 g (6 oz) tomatoes, skinned and chopped*

*salt and pepper*

*284 g (10 oz) natural yogurt*

*75 g (3 oz) cucumber*

1. Cover the bulgar wheat with cold water and soak for 20 minutes, then drain well.
2. Cut a thin slice from the stalk end of each pepper. Reserve. Remove the seeds. Cut each pepper in half horizontally and place alternate colours side by side in a shallow buttered ovenproof dish.
3. Melt the butter in a saucepan and gently fry the onion with the chilli seasoning for 3–4 minutes. Add the tomatoes and well-drained bulgar wheat. Cook, stirring, for 1–2 minutes, season. Fill the peppers with the chilli mixture. Replace the tops.
4. Cover tightly with buttered foil. Bake in the oven at 190°C (375°F) mark 5 for about 40 minutes.
5. Gently heat together the natural yogurt and

*Spiced Wheat Peppers*

finely chopped cucumber, whisking. Season. Serve the peppers with the sauce handed separately.
*Serves 4*

$P_{ULSE}$ is the generic name given to dried beans, peas and lentils and there are many varieties in different shapes, sizes and colours. Pulses are very versatile ingredients and can be used in savoury dishes of all kinds. Nutritionally they are an excellent food; they contain plenty of dietary fibre, protein, B group vitamins, iron and potassium. They have virtually no fat and are best eaten with a cereal such as bread, rice or pasta.

Pulses are sold in packets or loose and should be bought in fairly small quantities from a shop with a good turnover. Use them up within 6–9 months, or they will start to shrivel and become tough. Before cooking, wash them thoroughly and pick out any pieces of dirt or damaged beans.

All pulses, except lentils, need to be soaked, preferably overnight, before cooking. If you do not have enough time for this, put the pulses in water and bring to the boil, simmer for 2 minutes, then leave them to soak in the water for 2–3 hours. Cook according to the chart on page 245.

When cooking, allow double the volume of water to beans and do not add salt until the end of the cooking time or it will make the pulses tough.

### ADUKI (ADZUKI) BEANS
Small, reddish-brown round beans with a delicious sweet flavour when cooked.

### BLACK BEANS
Oval beans with a shiny black casing and white flesh. They are used mainly in soups and the Chinese black bean sauce, but can be interchanged with red kidney beans.

### BLACK-EYED BEANS
Cream-coloured with a black spot with an earthy taste that goes well with pork and in casseroles.

### BUTTER BEANS (LIMA BEANS)
Large, oval, flat and white. Cook them gently so that they don't break up.

### CANNELLINI BEANS
These are white and are very popular in Italian cooking.

### CHICK PEAS (GARBANZOS)
Round, beige-coloured pulses which are virtually impossible to overcook.

### DALS
The collective name for pulses cooked in India. There are many different types available. A large selection can be found in Indian shops and larger supermarkets and health stores stock a good range.

### DRIED PEAS
These may be whole or split, green or yellow. They cook quickly and are good in soups and puréed.

### FLAGEOLET BEANS
These may be white or pale green. They are small and oval and served hot or cold.

### HARICOT BEANS
Small, white oval beans which come in a number of varieties, the best known being the navy bean.

### LENTILS
Small pulses which may be red, brown or green. The red lentils cook quickly to a purée and are good in soups and sauces. Brown lentils also cook quickly and keep their shape for use in casseroles or salads. Lentils do not need soaking.

### MUNG BEANS
These are small, round and green and are used in Indian cookery or as seeds for sprouting bean sprouts (see page 214). When cooked, they tend to be sticky but are good in stuffings and salads.

### RED KIDNEY BEANS
Dark red beans with white flesh and a full, strong flavour. It is essential to boil for at least 10 minutes at the start of the cooking time to kill the toxic haemoglutinens. Do not include red kidney beans in a slow cooking casserole unless pre-boiled.

### SOYA BEANS
Round brown beans which are the most useful of all pulses nutritionally. They contain first class protein and so do not need to be eaten with a cereal to release it. They are widely used in vegetarian cookery, are used to make bean curd (tofu) and also for meat substitutes (soya protein or texturised vegetable protein). Soya beans with a yellow tinge have a mild flavour; the blacker ones taste sweet.

## PULSES COOKING TIME

| Type | Approx. Cooked Weight 100–125 g (4 oz) Dried | Approx. Boiling Time | Pressure Cooking High (15 lb) pressure |
|---|---|---|---|
| Aduki beans | 250 g (9 oz) | 30 minutes | 15 minutes |
| Black beans | 250 g (9 oz) | 1 hour | 20 minutes |
| Black-eye beans | 275 g (10 oz) | 45 minutes | 12 minutes |
| Butter beans | 275 g (10 oz) | 50 minutes | 17 minutes |
| Cannellini beans | 250 g (9 oz) | 1½ hours | 25 minutes |
| Chick peas and peas | 225 g (8 oz) | 1½ hours | 20 minutes |
| Dal and lentils | 200 g (7 oz) | 1 hour | 15 minutes |
| Flageolet beans | 250 g (9 oz) | 1¼ hours | 14 minutes |
| Haricot beans | 275 g (10 oz) | 1½ hours | 18 minutes |
| Mung beans | 300 g (11 oz) | 30 minutes | 10 minutes |
| Red kidney beans | 250 g (9 oz) | 50 minutes | 17 minutes |
| Soya beans | 250 g (9 oz) | 1½ hours | 25 minutes |
| Split peas | 225 g (8 oz) | 45 minutes | 15 minutes |

## BUTTER BEAN HOT POT

125 g (4 oz) dried butter beans
25 g (1 oz) butter or margarine
1 medium onion, skinned and chopped
3 celery sticks, trimmed and sliced
1 medium carrot, peeled and sliced
15 ml (1 level tbsp) flour
300 ml (½ pint) Chicken Stock (see page 19)
salt and pepper
125 g (4 oz) French beans, trimmed
2 medium courgettes, wiped and sliced
25 g (1 oz) fresh wholemeal breadcrumbs
75 g (3 oz) Cheddar cheese, grated

1. Soak the beans overnight. Drain, then cook for about 50 minutes, until tender.
2. Melt the butter in a large saucepan, add the onion and fry gently until soft. Add the celery and carrots and cook gently, covered, for 5 minutes.
3. Stir in the flour and cook gently for 1 minute, stirring. Remove the pan from the heat and gradually stir in the stock. Bring to the boil, slowly and continue to cook, stirring, until thickened. Season and simmer for 5 minutes.
4. Add the French beans and simmer for a further 5 minutes, then add the courgettes and cook until the vegetables are tender, but still crisp.
5. Drain the butter beans and add to the vegetables. Heat through, adjust the seasoning and turn into a deep ovenproof dish.
6. Combine the breadcrumbs and cheese, sprinkle over the top and brown under the grill until crisp and crusty.
Serves 4

## BOSTON BEANS

275 g (10 oz) dried haricot or cannellini beans
15 ml (1 tbsp) vegetable oil
2 medium onions, skinned and chopped
5 ml (1 level tsp) mustard powder
15 ml (1 tbsp) black treacle
150 ml (¼ pint) tomato juice
30 ml (2 level tbsp) tomato purée
10 ml (2 level tsp) dark soft brown sugar
300 ml (½ pint) Beef Stock (see page 19)

1. Soak the beans overnight, then cook in boiling water for 25 minutes. Drain.
2. Heat the oil in a flameproof casserole, add the onions and fry until soft.
3. Remove from the heat and stir in the remaining ingredients.
4. Bring contents to the boil, cover and cook in the oven at 140°C (275°F) mark 1 for about 2½–3 hours, until the beans are tender and the sauce is syrup-like. Stir occasionally.
Serves 4

## PEASE PUDDING

*225 g (8 oz) split peas, washed and soaked overnight*

*1 medium onion, skinned and quartered (optional)*

*sprigs of fresh herbs (optional)*

*1 ham bone or some bacon scraps*

*25 g (1 oz) butter or margarine*

*1 egg, beaten*

*pinch of sugar*

*salt and pepper*

1. Tie the peas loosely in a cloth, place in a saucepan with the onion and herbs, if using, the bone or bacon scraps and enough boiling water to cover. Bring to the boil and cook for 2–2½ hours, until soft.
2. Lift out the bag of peas, sieve, then add the butter, egg, sugar and seasoning. Mix.
3. Tie up tightly in a floured cloth and boil for another 30 minutes. Serve.
*Serves 4*

## VEGETABLE COUSCOUS

*100 g (4 oz) chick peas, soaked overnight*

*350 g (12 oz) couscous (not precooked)*

*2 medium leeks, trimmed, cut into 1 cm (½ inch) diagonal slices and washed*

*100 g (4 oz) butter or margarine*

*1 medium carrot, peeled and cut into 0.5 cm (¼ inch) slices*

*1 medium parsnip, peeled and cut into wedge-shaped pieces*

*225 g (8 oz) swede, peeled and cut into wedge-shaped pieces*

*5 ml (1 level tsp) ground cumin*

*5 ml (1 level tsp) ground coriander*

*2.5 ml (½ level tsp) ground turmeric*

*1.1 litres (2 pints) chicken stock*

*30 ml (2 level tbsp) tomato purée*

*salt and pepper*

*1 medium red pepper, seeded and diced*

*1 medium green pepper, seeded and diced*

*450 g (1 lb) tomatoes, skinned and quartered*

*225 g (½ lb) courgettes, sliced*

*1 small cauliflower, divided into florets*

*chopped fresh parsley for garnish*

1. Cook the chick peas for 1 hour.
2. Place the couscous in a bowl and pour over 200 ml (7 fl oz) warm water. Work the water into the couscous with the fingertips using a 'rubbing-in' motion to ensure all grains are separate. Leave to stand for 15 minutes, then repeat twice more. Use a total of 600 ml (1 pint) water.
3. Melt 50 g (2 oz) butter in a large pan of at least 4 litres (7 pints) capacity over which a perforated steamer will fit snugly. Add the prepared vegetables and sprinkle over the spices. Fry gently until lightly browned, then add the drained chick peas with the stock, tomato purée and seasoning and bring to the boil.
4. Line a steamer with a double thickness of muslin and spoon in the couscous, seasoning well. Place over the vegetables and cover the steamer tightly. Bring up to a fast boil, then lower the heat and simmer gently for about 30 minutes.
5. Take pan and steamer off the heat and spoon the couscous out into a large bowl. Cut the remaining butter into small pieces and add to the couscous with seasoning. Stir well until the butter has melted and every grain is separate. Season.
6. Add the remaining prepared vegetables to the pan and stir well. Return to the heat and bring slowly to the boil. Spoon the couscous back into the lined steamer and place over the pan. Cover the steamer tightly, lower the heat and simmer for another 15 minutes.
7. Turn couscous into a dish and fork through. Serve the vegetable mixture separately. Garnish.
*Serves 6*

*Vegetable Couscous*

# Salads

S alads are quick and easy to make and there are any number of interesting combinations of flavour and texture. All ingredients mentioned can be eaten either raw or cooked. Follow the instructions for preparing and dressing salads and enjoy refreshing salads all year round.

◆

## PREPARING SALAD VEGETABLES

For crisp flavoursome salads use only fresh vegetables in good condition. Most salad ingredients can be prepared in advance, but it is best not to assemble the salad until you are ready to serve it.

### AVOCADOS

Although strictly a fruit, they are used like a vegetable. Prepare just before serving. Cut in half, remove stone, peel and slice. Brush with lemon juice to prevent the flesh browning.

### BEETROOT

Thinly peel cooked beetroot, dice or grate large ones and thinly slice small ones. Beetroot tends to 'bleed' into salads, so either add at the last minute or serve in a separate dish.

### CARROTS

Carrots give colour and a crunchy texture to salads; tender new ones are especially good. Trim and either scrub or scrape. Cut into thin sticks or serve tiny new ones whole.

### CABBAGE

Choose young green leaved varieties as well as white and red cabbage. Wash in salted water to kill any insects. Dry well, then shred.

### CELERIAC

Peel, wash and slice the celeriac. Cut into dice or julienne strips using a grater or food processor. Immediately toss in French Dressing or Mayonnaise flavoured with mustard (known as Celeriac Rémoulade).

### CELERY

Separate the sticks and wash in cold water. Use a small brush to scrub along the grooves and remove any dirt. Slice into the lengths required or make into curls (see page 249).

### CHICORY

Trim off the root end and remove any damaged leaves. Either separate the leaves or slice across the whole vegetable. If the central core is very hard, remove it.

### CHINESE CABBAGE (CHINESE LEAVES)

Trim off the root end and remove any damaged leaves. Wash thoroughly, then shred finely.

### CUCUMBER

Wipe the skin and peel if wished. Alternatively, make attractive striped patterns on it using a cannelle knife or by running a fork down the skin. For crisp cucumber, slice it thinly just before serving.

## ENDIVE

Trim off the root end and remove coarse outer leaves. Separate the remaining leaves, wash and dry well, then tear into bite-sized pieces.

## FENNEL

Trim off top stems and slice off base. Wash in cold water and slice thinly or grate. Blanch if wished.

## LETTUCE

Trim the base and remove coarse outer leaves. Wash the remainder in cold water and dry thoroughly. Tear the lettuce into manageable pieces when ready to make the salad.

## LAMB'S LETTUCE (ALSO CALLED CORN SALAD OR MÂCHE)

Separate the leaves, wash in cold water and dry thoroughly. Keep in the refrigerator until needed.

## MUSHROOMS

Trim the base of the stalks, wipe and thoroughly dry, if necessary. Halve or thinly slice.

## MUSTARD AND CRESS

Snip the tops and stems off as low down as possible. Place in a sieve and wash in cold water. Dry and remove any seeds which have stuck to the tops.

## NASTURTIUM

The round, hot flavoured leaves are occasionally eaten in salads. Choose young leaves and use either whole or shredded. The flowers may be used to garnish salads.

## PEPPERS

Red, green, yellow and black peppers add colour to plain salads. Cut off the top and stalk and remove the seeds and membrane. Wash, dry and slice thinly or cut into dice.

## RADICCHIO

Cut off the root end and separate the leaves, discarding any that are damaged. Wash and dry, then tear into manageable pieces.

## RADISHES

Trim off the root end and leaves and wash in cold water. Serve whole, sliced thinly or cut into fancy shapes (see opposite).

## SPRING ONIONS

Trim off the root end, slide the onion out of its papery skin and remove the green leaves. Wash and serve whole, chopped into smaller pieces or made into curls (see opposite).

## TOMATOES

Remove the stem wash the tomatoes and cut into wedges, slices or lilies (see opposite). To skin tomatoes, dip into boiling water for 30 seconds, then into cold. The skin will then slide off easily.

## WATERCRESS

Snip off the coarse ends of the stalks and remove any yellow leaves. Wash in cold water and drain well before using.

## HERBS AND FLAVOURINGS

Fresh herbs are excellent in salads, they look attractive as well as giving a delicious flavour. Add basil or chives to a tomato salad and try dill with cucumber or savory with a bean salad. Dried herbs are not as good as fresh in salads; if using they are best mixed into the dressing. Other flavourings like salt, pepper, garlic and mustard are also best added to the dressing.

## DRESSING INGREDIENTS

Most salad dressings are made from combinations of oil and vinegar or lemon juice, though other ingredients like yogurt, soured cream and various fruit juices can be used.

Different oils and vinegars have their own distinct flavours. *Olive oil* is traditional for salads and very popular with its distinctive flavour. Virgin oil is best with a dark green colour and a strong rich flavour and aroma. *Corn or maize oil* has a bland flavour which is useful with strongly flavoured salad ingredients. *Groundnut (peanut, arachide) oil* is also bland and light, while *soya bean oil* has a strong flavour which some people dislike. *Sunflower and safflower seed oil* are also fairly bland and have a high polyunsaturated content. *Sesame seed oil* is expensive but has a delicate nutty flavour that goes well in dressings, while *walnut oil*—the most expensive of all—has a strong nutty flavour and is thought by many people to be the best of all for salad dressings. *Hazelnut oil* also has a delicate nutty flavour.

*Blended vegetable oil* and *salad oil* are usually a mixture of different oils and are acceptable in dressings, provided the flavour is not too pronounced.

Wine and cider vinegars are in general more suitable than malt vinegars which tend to mask other flavours in salad dressings. Vinegars flavoured with garlic, herbs such as tarragon, or fruit such as raspberries add unusual flavours to dressings. You can buy them or make your own more cheaply.

For herb vinegars, place the herbs or mixture of herbs in clean bottles. Fill up with good quality red or white wine or cider vinegar, cork or cap the bottles and leave for 6 weeks in a dark place. Strain through muslin and re-bottle. If you are giving some as a present, it looks attractive if you place a fresh spray of herb in the bottle.

Fruit vinegars are usually made with soft fruits like raspberries, strawberries, blackberries or blackcurrants. Wash the fruit and mash it gently with a wooden spoon. Place in wide-mouthed jars and add 600 ml (1 pint) white wine vinegar for each 450 g (1 lb) fruit. Cover and leave for 3–4 days, shaking the jars occasionally. Strain again through muslin, bottle and seal (see Pickles, page 478).

### DRESSING A SALAD

It is important not to drown a salad in dressing. There should be just enough to coat the ingredients without leaving a pool in the bottom of the bowl.

Some salads need to be dressed in advance so that the flavours have time to blend. This applies particularly to cooked ingredients, which are best dressed when warm so they absorb the flavours while cooling. Others, like a plain green salad, should be tossed in dressing just before serving. If you are serving the salad in individual dishes, you will find it easier to dress the salad in a large bowl and then divide it. Thicker dressings like Mayonnaise or Aïoli may be served separately at the table.

### GARNISHING A SALAD

A salad can be simply garnished with a sprinkling of chopped fresh herbs or sesame seeds, but for a really special effect try making some vegetable garnishes.

**Celery curls,** Cut sticks of celery into strips about 1 cm (½ inch) wide and 5 cm (2 inches) long. Make small horizontal cuts along the length as close to each other as possible. Leave in iced water for 1–2 hours, until the strips curl. Drain before use.

**Cucumber cones,** Cut thin slices and make a single cut on each slice from the centre to edge. Fold edges over each other.

**Gherkin fans,** Use long thin gherkins and cut them lengthways into thin slices but leave these joined at one end. Fan out the strips until they just overlap each other.

*Cut the gherkins in long strips to form fan shapes.*

**Radish roses,** Cut a narrow slice from the root end of each radish, then cut thin 'petals' from stem to root. Put into iced water until the cuts open to form petals.

**Radish waterlilies,** Make 4–8 small deep cuts, crossing the centre of the radish at the root end, and leave in iced water to open out.

**Spring onion curls,** Trim the root end and all but 5 cm (2 inches) of the leaves. Remove the skin and cut along each green leaf two or three times. Put into iced water until the leaves curl up.

**Tomato lilies,** Choose firm even-sized tomatoes. With a small, sharp pointed knife make a series of V-shaped cuts right round the middle, cutting through to the centre. Carefully pull the halves apart.

## GREEN SALAD

| |
|---|
| 1 lettuce, washed, and 2 or more of the following: |
| 1 punnet mustard and cress, snipped |
| 1 bunch watercress, washed and trimmed |
| 1 endive, washed |
| 2 chicory heads, trimmed, washed and chopped |
| 1 medium green pepper, seeded and chopped |
| ½ a cucumber, chopped |
| ½ a green cabbage, finely shredded |
| 60 ml (4 tbsp) French Dressing (see page 260) |
| 5–10 ml (1–2 tsp) chopped fresh parsley, chives, mint, tarragon or other herbs, as available |

1. Tear the lettuce into bite-sized pieces and place in a salad bowl with two or more of the other green ingredients.
2. Pour over the French Dressing and toss well into the salad. Sprinkle with herbs and serve immediately.

*Serves 4 as a side salad*

# TZAZIKI

½ a medium cucumber, diced

142 g (5 oz) natural yogurt (preferably firm set)

10 ml (2 tsp) olive oil

15 ml (1 tbsp) chopped fresh mint

1 garlic clove, skinned and crushed

salt and pepper

1. Place the cucumber in a serving bowl. Pour over the yogurt, olive oil, add the mint, garlic, season and mix well. Cover and chill before serving.
*Serves 4 as a side salad*

# TOMATO SALAD WITH BASIL

750 g (1½ lb) ripe tomatoes, skinned

135 ml (9 tbsp) olive oil

45 ml (3 tbsp) wine vinegar

1 small garlic clove, skinned and crushed

30 ml (2 tbsp) chopped fresh basil

salt and pepper

1. Slice the tomatoes thinly and arrange on six individual serving plates.
2. Place the oil, vinegar, garlic, basil and seasoning in a bowl or screw-topped jar and whisk or shake

well together. Spoon over the tomatoes.
3. Cover the plates tightly with cling film and chill in the refrigerator for about 2 hours.
*Serves 6 as a side salad*

**Variation**
TOMATO AND ONION SALAD
Arrange the tomato slices and 3 medium onions, skinned and very thinly sliced, alternately on the serving plates. Spoon over 90 ml (6 tbsp) French Dressing (see page 260) mixed with 10 ml (2 tsp) snipped fresh chives.

# POTATO SALAD

1 kg (2 lb) potatoes

4 spring onions, trimmed and finely chopped

salt and pepper

150 ml (¼ pint) Mayonnaise (see page 261)

15–30 ml (1–2 tbsp) boiling water or milk (optional)

snipped fresh chives, to garnish

1. Place the potatoes in cold, salted water, bring to the boil and cook for 15–20 minutes, until just tender. Drain, remove the skins and leave until quite cold.

2. Cut the potatoes into a small dice and place in a bowl. Add the spring onions and season to taste with salt and pepper.
3. Thin the Mayonnaise, if wished, with a little boiling water or milk, stir it into the potatoes and toss gently.
4. Leave the salad to stand for at least 1 hour. Sprinkle with snipped chives before serving.
*Serves 6 as a side salad*

**Variation**
Replace the Mayonnaise with 150 ml (¼ pint) French Dressing (see page 260).

# CRISPY CAULIFLOWER SALAD

1 medium cauliflower, trimmed

1 red eating apple, cored and chopped

2 eggs, hard-boiled, shelled and chopped

50 g (2 oz) walnut pieces, chopped

150 ml (¼ pint) Mayonnaise (see page 261)

15 ml (1 tbsp) lemon juice

salt and pepper

1. Break the cauliflower into small florets and wash and drain well.
2. Put all the ingredients in a salad bowl, season with salt and pepper and toss well together.
*Serves 4 as a side salad*

# COLESLAW

½ a white cabbage, about 900 g (2 lb) weight, trimmed
    and finely shredded

1 large carrot, peeled and grated

1 large onion, skinned and finely chopped

45 ml (3 tbsp) chopped fresh parsley

4 celery sticks, trimmed and sliced

salt and pepper

200 ml (7 fl oz) Mayonnaise (see page 261)

watercress, to garnish (optional)

1. In a large bowl, combine the cabbage, carrot,
onion, parsley and celery, tossing well together.
2. Season the Mayonnaise well, pour over the
vegetables and toss until well coated.
3. Cover and chill for several hours before
serving. Garnish with watercress, if wished.
If preferred, the ingredients can be prepared
beforehand and left covered. Add the dressing
2–3 hours before serving.
Serves 8 as a side salad

*From the top: Coleslaw, Greek Salad*

# RED CABBAGE AND APPLE SALAD

½ a red cabbage, about 900 g (2 lb) weight, trimmed
    and very finely shredded

3 eating apples

1 small garlic clove, skinned and crushed

300 ml (½ pint) salad oil

150 ml (¼ pint) cider vinegar

60 ml (4 level tbsp) natural yogurt

salt and pepper

1. Blanch the cabbage for 2–3 minutes in boiling
salted water, taking care not to over-blanch it,
otherwise it will lose its crisp texture. Drain and
leave to cool.
2. Peel, core and slice the apples and place in
a bowl with the cabbage. Place the remaining
ingredients in a bowl and whisk together. Pour at
once over the cabbage and apple and toss together.
3. Cover the salad and refrigerate overnight. Toss
again to mix well just before serving.
Serves 8 as a side salad

# GREEK SALAD

2 Mediterranean or beefsteak tomatoes, cut into eighths

1 medium green pepper, seeded and thinly sliced

½ a medium cucumber, thickly sliced

50 g (2 oz) black or stuffed olives, stoned

100–175 g (4–6 oz) Feta cheese, diced

120 ml (8 tbsp) olive oil

30–45 ml (2–3 tbsp) lemon juice

salt and pepper

pitta bread, to serve

1. Arrange the tomatoes, pepper, cucumber and
olives in a salad bowl. Add the cheese to the bowl,
reserving a few dice for garnish.
2. Pour over the olive oil, followed by the lemon
juice and season well. Toss the salad together.
Crumble over the remaining cheese cubes and
serve with pitta bread.
Serves 4 as a side salad or 2 as a main course

## WALDORF SALAD

| |
|---|
| 450 g (1 lb) eating apples |
| juice of ½ a lemon |
| 5 ml (1 level tsp) sugar |
| 150 ml (¼ pint) Mayonnaise (see page 261) |
| 1 lettuce |
| ½ a head of celery, trimmed and sliced |
| 50 g (2 oz) walnut pieces, chopped |
| a few walnut halves, to garnish (optional) |

1. Peel and core the apples, slice one and dice the rest. Dip the slices in lemon juice to prevent discoloration. Toss the diced apples in the lemon juice, the sugar and 15 ml (1 tbsp) Mayonnaise and leave to stand for about 30 minutes.
2. Just before serving, wash and dry the lettuce leaves and use to line a salad bowl. Add the celery, walnuts and remaining Mayonnaise to the diced apples and toss together. Spoon into the salad bowl and garnish with the apple slices and a few whole walnuts, if wished.
*Serves 4 as a side salad*

## RICE SALAD RING

| |
|---|
| 225 g (8 oz) long grain white rice |
| 1 green pepper, seeded and diced |
| 3 caps canned pimiento, diced |
| 198 g (7 oz) can corn niblets, drained |
| 75 ml (5 tbsp) chopped fresh parsley |
| 50 g (2 oz) salted peanuts |
| 45 ml (3 tbsp) lemon juice |
| celery salt |
| pepper |
| vegetable oil for greasing |
| watercress, to garnish |

1. Cook the rice in plenty of boiling salted water for 10–15 minutes, until tender, then drain. Rinse through with cold water and drain thoroughly. Leave to cool completely.
2. Blanch the pepper in boiling water for 1 minute, drain, rinse in cold water and drain again.
3. In a large bowl, mix the cold rice, pepper and pimiento, corn niblets, parsley, peanuts and lemon juice, and season well with celery salt and pepper. Press the salad into a lightly oiled 1.4 litre (2½ pint) ring mould and chill well.
4. To serve, turn out on to a flat serving plate and fill the centre of the salad ring with watercress.
*Serves 8 as a side salad*

**Variation**
This ring can be made using brown rice. Follow the cooking instructions on page 303.

## CRANBERRY AND ORANGE RING

| |
|---|
| grated rind and juice of 1 orange |
| 25 g (1 oz) gelatine |
| 200 ml (7 fl oz) red wine vinegar |
| 1.25 ml (¼ level tsp) salt |
| 3 large oranges |
| two 382 g (12½ oz) jars cranberry sauce |
| celery sticks, trimmed and cut into strips |

1. Place the orange juice in a small bowl. Sprinkle in the gelatine and leave to soak for 1–2 minutes. Stand the bowl over a saucepan of hot water and heat gently until the gelatine has dissolved. Remove from the heat.
2. In a saucepan, gently heat the vinegar, salt and orange rind to infuse the flavours. Add the gelatine liquid, remove from the heat and leave to cool.
3. Peel the oranges, removing all the pith, and slice thinly. Cut each slice into four and mix with the cranberry sauce in a bowl. Gently fold in the vinegar and gelatine liquid, then pour into a 1.4 litre (2½ pint) plain ring mould. Chill until firm.
4. When set, gently ease the cranberry and orange ring away from the edges of the mould with your fingers, and dip the mould in hot water. Place a serving plate upside-down over the mould and invert the ring on to the plate.
5. Remove the mould and fill the centre of the ring with the celery sticks.
*Note* This salad is ideal to serve with cold sliced meats.
*Serves 8 as a side salad*

# MARINATED MUSHROOMS

450 g (1 lb) small button mushrooms, wiped

150 ml (¼ pint) French Dressing (see page 260)

chopped fresh parsley, to garnish

1. Place the mushrooms in a bowl and pour over the dressing. Coat the mushrooms well, then cover and leave to marinate in the refrigerator for 6–8 hours, stirring occasionally.

2. Serve in individual shallow dishes and sprinkle the mushrooms with chopped parsley.

*Serves 4–6 as a side salad*

**Variation**

Use other fresh herbs as available.

# BEAN SPROUT AND BROWN RICE SALAD

225 g (8 oz) long grain brown rice

salt

225 g (8 oz) fresh bean sprouts

1 large green pepper

90 ml (6 tbsp) French Dressing (see page 260)

1. Cook the rice in a large pan of boiling salted water for about 35 minutes, until just tender. Drain and rinse through with hot water.

2. Wash the bean sprouts and drain well. Halve the pepper, discard the seeds, dice and mix in a bowl with the bean sprouts and rice.

3. Spoon the dressing over the salad and stir well. Cover and chill for 2 hours before serving.

*Serves 6 as a side salad*

# RADICCHIO AND ALFALFA SALAD

2 heads radicchio (see Note)

50–75 g (2–3 oz) alfalfa sprouts

90 ml (6 tbsp) vegetable oil

30 ml (2 tbsp) white wine vinegar

1 small garlic clove, skinned and crushed

1.25 ml (¼ level tsp) sugar

15 ml (1 tbsp) single cream

salt and pepper

1. Tear the radicchio into bite-sized pieces. Wash, drain and pat dry on absorbent kitchen paper. Wash and dry the alfalfa sprouts.

2. Mix the alfalfa and radicchio together and refrigerate in a large polythene bag.

3. Place the remaining ingredients in a bowl and whisk together until well blended. Toss the dressing with the radicchio and alfalfa when ready to serve.

*Note* If radicchio is unobtainable use 350 g (12 oz) thinly shredded red cabbage.

*Serves 6 as a side salad*

# CAESAR SALAD

1 large garlic clove, skinned and crushed

150 ml (¼ pint) olive oil

75 g (3 oz) stale white bread

1 Cos lettuce

salt and pepper

1 egg

30 ml (2 tbsp) lemon juice

25 g (1 oz) Parmesan cheese, freshly grated

4 anchovies, finely chopped

1. Add the garlic to the oil and leave to stand for 30 minutes. Cut the bread into 0.5 cm (¼ inch) dice. Heat a little of the garlic oil in a frying pan and fry the bread until golden brown on all sides. Remove and drain on absorbent kitchen paper.

2. Wash and dry the lettuce leaves and tear into bite-sized pieces. Place in a salad bowl. Pour over the remaining garlic oil and toss until the leaves are completely coated. Season well.

3. Boil the egg for 1 minute only, break it into the salad and toss well. Add the lemon juice, cheese, anchovies and croûtons and give a final toss. Serve immediately.

*Serves 4 as a side salad*

## FENNEL AND TOMATO SALAD

*90 ml (6 tbsp) vegetable oil or half vegetable, half*
   *walnut oil*

*45 ml (3 tbsp) lemon juice*

*salt and pepper*

*12 black olives, halved and stoned*

*450 g (1 lb) Florence fennel*

*450 g (1 lb) ripe tomatoes*

*Fennel and Tomato Salad*

**1.** In a medium mixing bowl, whisk the oils, lemon juice and seasoning together. Add the olives to the dressing.
**2.** Snip off the feathery ends of the fennel and refrigerate them in a polythene bag until required.
**3.** Halve each bulb of fennel lengthways, then slice thinly crossways, discarding the roots. Blanch in boiling salted water for 2–3 minutes, then drain. While it is still warm, stir into the dressing.
**4.** Leave to cool, cover tightly with cling film and refrigerate until required. Meanwhile, skin and slice the tomatoes, cover and refrigerate.

**5.** Just before serving, arrange the tomatoes and fennel mixture on individual serving plates and snip the fennel tops over them.
*Note* This salad can also be made with chicory and garnished with parsley.
*Serves 6 as a side salad*

## BEETROOT IN CARAWAY DRESSING

*450 g (1 lb) small beetroots*

*5 ml (1 level tsp) caraway seeds*

*30 ml (2 tbsp) boiling water*

*30 ml (2 tbsp) wine vinegar*

*5 ml (1 level tsp) salt*

*10 ml (2 level tsp) caster sugar*

*pepper*

**1.** Cook the beetroots in boiling salted water for 1–1½ hours according to size. While still warm, remove the skins and cut into 0.5 cm (¼ inch) slices.
**2.** For the dressing, place the caraway seeds in a bowl, pour over the boiling water and leave for 30 minutes. Stir in the remaining dressing ingredients.
**3.** Pour over the beetroot slices and leave to marinate for 1–2 hours or overnight.
*Serves 4 as a side salad*

## MIXED BEAN SALAD

*175 g (6 oz) mixed dried beans, e.g. aduki, red kidney,*
   *black or haricot, soaked separately overnight*

*2.5 ml (½ level tsp) ground coriander*

*100 ml (4 fl oz) French Dressing (see page 260)*

*1 small onion, skinned and very finely sliced*

*salt and pepper*

add them halfway through the cooking time.) Alternatively, cook the beans in a pressure cooker at High (15 lb) pressure for 15–20 minutes. (Do not use aduki beans in a pressure cooker with other beans as they only need 5–10 minutes cooking.) Drain and place in a large bowl.
**2.** Add the coriander to the French Dressing and pour over the beans while they are still warm. Toss thoroughly and leave to cool.
**3.** Add the onion to the beans, stir well and season. Chill, then transfer to a salad bowl or individual serving plates.
*Serves 6 as a side salad*

**1.** Drain the beans, place in a saucepan and cover with fresh water. Bring to the boil and boil for 10 minutes, then cover and simmer for about 1 hour, until tender. (If aduki beans are included,

*Fresh Spinach Salad with Hot Bacon Dressing*

## FRESH SPINACH SALAD WITH HOT BACON DRESSING

*225 g (8 oz) fresh young spinach, washed and trimmed*

*4 large slices of white bread*

*45 ml (3 tbsp) vegetable oil*

*1 garlic clove, skinned and crushed*

*6 rashers streaky bacon, rinded and chopped*

*15 ml (1 tbsp) white wine vinegar*

*salt and pepper*

**1.** Shred any large spinach leaves into small strips and place in a salad bowl. Set aside until required.
**2.** Make the croûtons. Remove the crusts from the bread and cut the bread into 1 cm (½ inch) cubes. Heat the oil in a frying pan and fry the bread cubes until golden brown.

**3.** Stir the crushed garlic into the bread croûtons, then drain them on absorbent kitchen paper.
**4.** Add the bacon to the pan and fry for about 5 minutes until crisp and golden brown. Pour the fried bacon and any fat over the spinach leaves.
**5.** Add the vinegar to the pan, stir well, then pour over the salad. Add seasoning, toss quickly, scatter the croûtons on top and serve at once.
*Serves 4 as a side salad*

**Variations**
If fresh spinach isn't available, substitute 1 head of Lamb's lettuce (see page 248), washed and gently torn into bite-sized pieces. To make a more filling salad, add 50 g (2 oz) very thinly sliced mushrooms.

## FLORIDA CHICORY SALAD

| |
|---|
| 1 small grapefruit |
| 2 medium oranges |
| 225 g (8 oz) tomatoes, skinned |
| 30 ml (2 tbsp) vegetable oil |
| 15 ml (1 tbsp) lemon juice |
| 10 ml (2 level tsp) light soft brown sugar |
| salt and pepper |
| 45 ml (3 tbsp) chopped fresh parsley |

1. Prepare the grapefruit and oranges over a bowl to catch any juice. Using a serrated knife, cut away all the peel and pith from the grapefruit and oranges and divide the flesh into segments, discarding the pips and as much of the membrane as possible. Add the segments to the juice in the bowl.

2. Quarter the tomatoes, scooping the seeds and juice into a nylon sieve placed over the bowl. Discard the seeds. If large, slice the tomato quarters into eighths and add to the bowl.
3. Trim off the root and wash the chicory, removing any outer damaged leaves. Slice diagonally into 1 cm ($\frac{1}{2}$ inch) pieces. Open out the slices and add to the tomato, grapefruit and orange mixture.
4. Place the oil, lemon juice, sugar, seasoning and parsley in a bowl or screw-topped jar and whisk or shake well together. Pour over the fruit and vegetable mixture and stir well. Adjust the seasoning and, if the fruit is very acidic, add a little more sugar.
5. Cover the bowl and chill well in the refrigerator.
*Serves 6 as a side salad*

## LEMON-DRESSED AVOCADO SALAD

| |
|---|
| $\frac{1}{2}$ a small cucumber, diced |
| salt |
| 2 ripe avocados, peeled and thickly sliced |
| 150 ml ($\frac{1}{4}$ pint) vegetable oil |
| 60 ml (4 tbsp) lemon juice |
| 10 ml (2 tsp) thin honey |
| pepper |
| 4 celery sticks, trimmed and thinly sliced |
| 50 g (2 oz) salted peanuts |
| paprika, to garnish |

1. Place the oil, lemon juice, honey and seasoning in a bowl or screw-topped jar and whisk or shake well together.
2. Place the celery and peanuts in a bowl with the cucumber and avocado, pour over the dressing and toss well. Pile into a serving dish, dust with paprika and serve immediately.
*Serves 6 as a side salad*

## SALADE NIÇOISE

| |
|---|
| 198 g (7 oz) can tuna fish, drained |
| 225 g (8 oz) tomatoes, skinned and quartered |
| 50 g (2 oz) black olives, stoned |
| $\frac{1}{2}$ a small cucumber, thinly sliced |
| 225 g (8 oz) French beans, cooked |
| 2 eggs, hard-boiled, shelled and quartered |
| 15 ml (1 tbsp) chopped fresh parsley |
| 15 ml (1 tbsp) chopped fresh basil |
| 150 ml ($\frac{1}{4}$ pint) garlic-flavoured French Dressing (see page 260) |
| 8 anchovies, halved lengthways |

1. Flake the tuna into fairly large chunks. Arrange in a salad bowl with the tomatoes, olives, cucumber, beans and egg quarters.
2. Add the parsley and basil to the French Dressing, mix well and pour over the salad.
3. Arrange the anchovy fillets in a lattice pattern over the salad and allow to stand for 30 minutes before serving.
*Serves 4 as a side salad or 2 as a main course*

# Wholewheat and Apricot Salad

225 g (8 oz) wholewheat grain

125 g (4 oz) dried apricots, washed

3 celery sticks, trimmed and sliced

90 ml (6 tbsp) French Dressing (see page 260)

1. Soak the wholewheat overnight in plenty of cold water. Drain and place in a large saucepan of boiling water. Simmer gently for 25 minutes, or until the grains are tender but retain a little bite. Drain well, rinse under cold running water and place in a bowl.

2. Snip the apricots into small pieces and add to the wholewheat with the celery. Pour the dressing over the salad and toss well.

3. Cover and chill for several hours. Stir again just before serving.

*Serves 4 as a side salad or 2 as a main course*

# Spiced Duckling and Orange Salad

1.8 kg (4 lb) oven-ready duckling

2 medium oranges

salt and pepper

45 ml (3 tbsp) vegetable oil

15 ml (1 tbsp) white wine vinegar

30 ml (2 level tbsp) Mayonnaise (see page 261)

10 ml (2 level tsp) curry powder

30 ml (2 level tbsp) orange marmalade

125 g (4 oz) peas, cooked

snipped fresh chives or chopped fresh parsley, to
    garnish

1. Wipe the duckling and prick well all over with a fork. Using a potato peeler or sharp knife, pare the rind from one orange and place it inside the duckling. Place the duckling on a rack or trivet in a roasting tin. Sprinkle with salt and pepper inside and out then roast in the oven at 180°C (350°F) mark 4 for about 2 hours, or until the juices run clear and the flesh is tender. While still warm, strip the breast skin off the duck and reserve. Carve off all the meat and shred finely.

2. In a large bowl, mix the oil, vinegar, Mayonnaise, curry powder and marmalade and season with salt and pepper. Stir in the duckling.

3. Using a serrated knife, remove all the peel and pith from the oranges and divide into segments, discarding the pips and as much of the membrane as possible. Add to the duck with the peas. Cover and refrigerate.

4. Cut the reserved duck skin into strips and grill until crisp. Just before serving, sprinkle over the salad, with the snipped chives or chopped parsley.

*Serves 4 as a main course*

# Coronation Chicken

2.3 kg (5 lb) chicken, cooked, flesh removed and diced

15 ml (1 tbsp) vegetable oil

1 small onion, skinned and finely chopped

15 ml (1 level tbsp) curry paste

15 ml (1 level tbsp) tomato purée

100 ml (4 fl oz) red wine

1 bay leaf

juice of $\frac{1}{2}$ a lemon

4 canned apricot halves, drained and finely chopped

300 ml ($\frac{1}{2}$ pint) Mayonnaise (see page 261)

100 ml (4 fl oz) whipping cream

salt and pepper

watercress, to garnish

1. In a small saucepan, heat the oil, add the onion and cook for about 3 minutes, until softened. Add the curry paste, tomato purée, wine, bay leaf and lemon juice.

2. Simmer, uncovered, for about 10 minutes until well reduced. Strain and leave to cool.

3. Purée the chopped apricot halves in a blender or food processor or through a sieve. Beat the cooled sauce into the Mayonnaise with the apricot purée.

4. Whip the cream to stiff peaks and fold into the mixture. Season, adding a little extra lemon juice if necessary.

5. Fold the chicken pieces into the sauce and garnish with watercress.

*Serves 8 as a main course*

*Pasta, Prawn and Apple Salad*

## PASTA, PRAWN AND APPLE SALAD

| |
|---|
| *175 g (6 oz) pasta shells* |
| *150 ml (¼ pint) unsweetened apple juice* |
| *5 ml (1 tsp) chopped fresh mint* |
| *5 ml (1 tsp) white wine vinegar* |
| *salt and pepper* |
| *225 g (8 oz) peeled prawns* |
| *2 crisp dessert apples, peeled, cored and roughly chopped* |
| *lettuce leaves* |
| *paprika, to garnish* |

**1.** Cook the pasta in boiling salted water for 6–12 minutes until tender. Drain well, rinse in cold running water and drain again.
**2.** Meanwhile, make the dressing. Whisk together the apple juice, mint, vinegar and seasoning.
**3.** Dry the prawns with absorbent kitchen paper. Quarter, core and roughly chop the apples. Stir the prawns, apple and cooked pasta into the dressing until well mixed. Cover tightly with cling film and refrigerate for 2–3 hours.
**4.** Wash the lettuce leaves, dry and shred finely. Arrange the lettuce in a bowl and spoon the prawn salad on top. Sprinkle with paprika.
*Serves 2 as a main course*

# SEAFOOD SALAD

1.1 litres (2 pints) fresh mussels, cleaned and cooked,
    with cooking liquid reserved (see page 82)

1 medium onion, skinned and roughly chopped

1 bay leaf

salt

350 g (12 oz) squid, cleaned (see page 61)

350 g (12 oz) shelled scallops (see page 82)

350 g (12 oz) peeled prawns, thawed and thoroughly
    dried if frozen

1 small green pepper, cored, seeded and finely sliced
    into strips

1 small red pepper, cored, seeded and finely sliced into
    strips

1 medium carrot, peeled

150 ml (¼ pint) olive oil

60 ml (4 tbsp) lemon juice

30 ml (2 tbsp) capers

45 ml (3 tbsp) chopped fresh parsley

1 garlic clove, skinned and crushed

pepper

black olives, to garnish

1. In a large saucepan, mix together the cooking
liquid from the mussels and 1.75 litres (3 pints) of
water. Add the onion, bay leaf and a pinch of salt
and bring to the boil. Add the squid and simmer
gently for 20 minutes, or until tender.
2. Remove the squid from the liquid and set
aside.
3. Bring the liquid back to the boil, add the
scallops and poach gently for 3 minutes. Remove
the scallops with a slotted spoon and set aside.
(Reserve the cooking liquid for making a fish
soup.)

Seafood Salad

4. Cut the squid into 1 cm (½ inch) wide rings.
5. Cut the scallops into four, removing the tough
muscle (found near the coral or roe).
6. Reserve a few mussels in their shells for the
garnish. Remove the shells from the remaining
mussels, put the mussels in a large serving bowl
with the squid, prawns and scallops. Add the
sliced peppers.
7. With a potato peeler, shred the carrot into
ribbons and add this to the seafood.
8. Make the dressing. Mix together the oil, lemon
juice, capers, parsley, garlic and pepper and pour
over the seafood. Mix lightly but thoroughly.
Taste and add salt if necessary.
9. Chill for at least 2 hours and then serve
garnished with black olives and the reserved
mussels in their shells.
Serves 6 as a main course

# SMOKED MACKEREL SALAD

450 g (1 lb) small new potatoes

350 g (12 oz) smoked mackerel fillets

142 ml (5 fl oz) soured cream

60 ml (4 level tbsp) Mayonnaise (see page 261)

45 ml (3 level tbsp) Horseradish Cream (see page 207)

salt and pepper

½ a head of celery, trimmed and sliced

paprika, to garnish

lemon wedges, to serve

1. Cook the potatoes in their skins in boiling
salted water for 10–15 minutes, until tender.
Drain, halve and leave to cool. Skin the mackerel
fillets and divide the flesh into bite-sized pieces.
2. In a large bowl, mix the soured cream with the
Mayonnaise, Horseradish Cream and seasoning.
Stir in the fish, celery and potatoes, cover and
chill well in the refrigerator.
3. Serve the salad sprinkled with paprika and
accompanied by lemon wedges.
Serves 4 as a main course

## RUSSIAN SALAD

| |
|---|
| 1 small cauliflower, trimmed |
| 1 medium turnip, peeled and diced |
| 1 medium carrot, peeled and diced |
| 225 g (8 oz) potatoes, peeled and diced |
| 1 small cooked beetroot, skinned |
| 2 medium tomatoes, skinned |
| salt and pepper |
| 150 ml (¼ pint) Mayonnaise |
| lemon juice |
| 125 g (4 oz) peas, cooked |
| 125 g (4 oz) tongue, diced |
| 125 g (4 oz) prawns, peeled |
| 4 gherkins, chopped |
| 30 ml (2 level tbsp) capers |
| 6 black olives, halved |
| 6 anchovies, sliced |

1. Break the cauliflower into small florets and cook in boiling salted water for about 8 minutes, until tender. Drain, rinse in cold water and drain again.
2. Cook the turnip, carrot and potato, rinse and drain as above. Dice the beetroot and tomatoes, discarding the tomato seeds.
3. Place a layer of cauliflower in a deep salad bowl and season well. Thin the Mayonnaise with a little lemon juice and spread a little over the cauliflower. Layer the turnips, carrots, potatoes, peas, beetroot, tomatoes, tongue and prawns in the same way, ending with a layer of Mayonnaise.
4. Sprinkle over the gherkins and capers and garnish with the olives and anchovies.
*Serves 4 as a main course.*

## FRENCH DRESSING *(Vinaigrette Sauce)*

| |
|---|
| 90 ml (6 tbsp) oil (see page 248) |
| 30 ml (2 tbsp) vinegar (see below) or lemon juice |
| 2.5 ml (½ level tsp) sugar |
| 2.5 ml (½ level tsp) mustard, e.g. whole grain, Dijon, French, or mustard powder |
| salt and pepper |

1. Place all the ingredients in a bowl or screw-topped jar and whisk or shake until well blended. The oil separates out on standing, so whisk or shake the dressing again, if necessary, immediately before use.

2. The dressing can be stored in a bottle or screw-topped jar for a few months in the refrigerator, but shake it vigorously just before serving.
*Makes 120 ml (8 tbsp)*
*Note* The proportion of oil to vinegar can be varied according to taste. Here it is in the ratio of three to one. Use less oil if a sharper dressing is preferred.

Wine, herb, cider or flavoured vinegars (see page 249), or lemon juice, may be used, or use a mixture of half vinegar and half lemon juice.

If a recipe calls for 150 ml (¼ pint) dressing, add an extra 30 ml (2 tbsp) oil.

## MUSTARD DRESSING

| |
|---|
| 15 ml (1 level tbsp) flour |
| a pinch of cayenne pepper |
| 25 ml (5 level tsp) sugar |
| 5 ml (1 level tsp) mustard powder |
| 2.5 ml (½ level tsp) salt |
| 150 ml (¼ pint) milk |
| 2 egg yolks, beaten |
| 60 ml (4 tbsp) cider vinegar |

1. Mix the dry ingredients to a smooth cream with a little of the milk.
2. Heat the remainder of the milk and, when boiling, stir in the blended ingredients. Return the mixture to the boil, stirring all the time.
3. Cool slightly, stir in the egg yolks and again return the pan to the heat. Cook gently until the mixture thickens, but do not allow it to boil.
4. Remove from the heat, allow to cool, then stir in the vinegar.
*Makes 300 ml (½ pint)*

# MAYONNAISE

1 egg yolk (see Note)

2.5 ml (½ level tsp) mustard powder or 5 ml
(1 level tsp) Dijon mustard

2.5 ml (½ level tsp) salt

1.25 ml (¼ level tsp) pepper

2.5 ml (½ level tsp) sugar

15 ml (1 tbsp) white wine vinegar or lemon juice

about 150 ml (¼ pint) oil (see page 248)

**1.** Put the egg yolk into a bowl with the mustard, seasoning, sugar and 5 ml (1 tsp) of the vinegar or lemon juice. Mix thoroughly, then add the oil drop by drop, whisking constantly, until the sauce is thick and smooth. If it becomes too thick, add a little more of the vinegar or lemon juice. When all the oil has been added, add the remaining vinegar or lemon juice gradually and mix thoroughly.
*Note* The ingredients for Mayonnaise should be at room temperature. Never use eggs straight from the refrigerator or cold larder as this may result in curdling. (See right for rescue remedies.)

If a recipe requires thin mayonnaise, thin it down with a little warm water, single cream, vinegar or lemon juice. Add the extra liquid slowly—too much will spoil the consistency.
*Makes about 150 ml (¼ pint)*

**Making Mayonnaise in an electric blender or food processor** Most blenders and food processors need at least a two-egg quantity in order to ensure that the blades are covered. Put the yolks, seasoning and half the vinegar or lemon juice into the blender goblet or food processor bowl and blend well. If your machine has a variable speed control, run it at a slow speed. Add the oil gradually while the machine is running. Add the remaining vinegar and season.
**Rescue remedies** If the Mayonnaise separates save it by beating the curdled mixture into a fresh base. This base can be any one of the following: 5 ml (1 tsp) hot water; 5 ml (1 tsp) vinegar or lemon juice; 5 ml (1 level tsp) Dijon mustard or 2.5 ml (½ level tsp) mustard powder; or an egg yolk. Add the curdled mixture to the base, beating hard. When the mixture is smooth, continue adding the oil as above. (If you use an extra egg yolk you may find that you need to add a little extra oil.)
**Storing Mayonnaise** Homemade Mayonnaise does not keep as long as bought varieties because it lacks their added emulsifiers, stabilisers and preservatives. However, Mayonnaise should keep for 3–4 days at room temperature and for at least a month in a screw-topped glass jar in the refrigerator. Allow to come to room temperature before stirring or the Mayonnaise may curdle.

## Variations

These variations are made by adding the extra ingredients to 150 ml (¼ pint) Mayonnaise.

### CAPER MAYONNAISE

Add 10 ml (2 tsp) chopped capers, 5 ml (1 tsp) chopped pimiento and 2.5 ml (½ tsp) tarragon vinegar (see page 249). Caper Mayonnaise makes an ideal accompaniment for fish.

### CUCUMBER MAYONNAISE

Add 30 ml (2 tbsp) finely chopped cucumber and 2.5 ml (½ level tsp) salt. This mayonnaise goes well with fish salads, especially crab, lobster or salmon.

### BLUE CHEESE DRESSING

Add 142 ml (5 fl oz) soured cream, 75 g (3 oz) crumbled blue cheese, 5 ml (1 tsp) vinegar and 1 garlic clove, skinned and crushed, and pepper to taste.

### RÉMOULADE SAUCE

Add 5 ml (1 tsp) chopped gherkins, 5 ml (1 tsp) chopped capers, 5 ml (1 tsp) chopped fresh parsley and 1 anchovy, finely chopped.

### TARTARE SAUCE

Add 5 ml (1 tsp) chopped fresh tarragon or snipped chives, 10 ml (2 tsp) chopped capers, 10 ml (2 tsp) chopped gherkins, 10 ml (2 tsp) chopped fresh parsley and 15 ml (1 tbsp) lemon juice or tarragon vinegar. Allow to stand for at least 1 hour before serving, to allow the flavours to blend.

### THOUSAND ISLAND MAYONNAISE

Add 15 ml (1 tbsp) chopped stuffed olives, 5 ml (1 tsp) finely chopped onion, 1 egg, hard-boiled, shelled and chopped, 15 ml (1 tbsp) finely chopped green pepper, 5 ml (1 tsp) chopped fresh parsley and 5 ml (1 level tsp) tomato purée.

## AÏOLI (Garlic Mayonnaise)

| |
|---|
| 4 garlic cloves, skinned |
| 1.25 ml (¼ level tsp) salt |
| 2 egg yolks |
| 300 ml (½ pint) olive oil |
| 30 ml (2 tbsp) lemon juice |

**1.** In a bowl, crush the garlic cloves with a little of the salt until a smooth paste is formed. Add the egg yolks and remaining salt and beat well.
**2.** Gradually beat in the oil, a little at a time, as for Mayonnaise, until the mixture is thick and smooth.
**3.** When all the oil has been added, beat in the remaining lemon juice. Store for up to 4 days in a screw-topped jar in the refrigerator.
*Makes 300 ml (½ pint)*

Aïoli with selection of fresh vegetables

## PESTO

| |
|---|
| 50 g (2 oz) fresh basil leaves |
| 2 garlic cloves, skinned |
| 30 ml (2 tbsp) pine nuts |
| salt and pepper |
| 50 g (2 oz) freshly grated Parmesan cheese |
| 100 ml (4 fl oz) olive oil |

**1.** Put the basil, garlic, pine nuts and seasoning in a mortar and grind with a pestle until a paste forms. Add the cheese and blend well.
**2.** Transfer to a bowl and beat in the oil, a little at a time, stirring vigorously with a wooden spoon.
*Note* This sauce can also be made in an electric blender or food processor. Place the basil, garlic, pine nuts, seasoning and olive oil in a blender or food processor and blend at high speed until very creamy. Transfer the mixture to a bowl, fold in the cheese and cream and mix thoroughly. Store for up to 2 weeks in a screw-topped jar in the refrigerator.
*Makes 300 ml (½ pint)*

## YOGURT DRESSING

| |
|---|
| 142 g (5 oz) natural yogurt or sour cream |
| 15 ml (1 tbsp) oil (see page 248) |
| 5–10 ml (1–2 tsp) vinegar |
| 5 ml (1 tsp) wholegrain mustard |

**1.** Place all the ingredients in a bowl and whisk together until well blended, then chill before serving. Store for up to 1 week in a screw-topped jar in the refrigerator.
*Note* Yogurt can be used as a substitute for soured cream in many recipes. It will give a slightly sharper dressing. Yogurts vary a little in acidity—season to taste.
*Makes 150 ml (¼ pint)*

**Variation**
TOMATO AND YOGURT DRESSING
Place 60 ml (4 tbsp) olive or corn oil, 5 ml (1 level tsp) salt, 5 ml (1 level tsp) caster sugar, 30 ml (2 tbsp) vinegar and 300 ml (½ pint) tomato juice in a bowl and whisk well together. Gradually whisk in 142 g (5 oz) natural yogurt, 10 ml (2 level tsp) grated onion and 30 ml (2 tbsp) Horseradish Cream. Season well with pepper. Store for up to 1 week in a screw-topped jar in the refrigerator.
*Makes 600 ml (1 pint)*

# EGGS

*E*ggs are versatile good value food and have a tremendous number of uses in all kinds of cooking. They are the essential ingredients of most cakes and of many other dishes such as sauces and hot and cold puddings. Nutritionally, they are rich in protein (one egg contains about the same amount as 50 g (2 oz) meat) and fat and also contain vitamin A, vitamins of the B complex and useful amounts of iron and calcium.

◆

### EGG SIZES

Eggs are graded for size as follows:

| Size 1 | over 70 g |
|--------|-----------|
| Size 2 | 65–70 g |
| Size 3 | 60–65 g |
| Size 4 | 55–60 g |
| Size 5 | 50–55 g |
| Size 6 | 45–50 g |
| Size 7 | below 45 g |

Unless a particular egg size is specified in a recipe, use Size 3 or 4 eggs. It does not matter if they are white or brown, there is no difference in taste or nutritional value; the simple explanation is that varying breeds of hen produce different coloured eggs.

When buying pre-packed eggs in shops you can get some idea of how old they are by checking the week number given on the box. Week 1 falls at the end of December or beginning of January. If the eggs are fresh, they can be stored for 2–3 weeks in the refrigerator.

The small air space inside every egg increases with age and it is possible to carry out a simple test at home to see if an egg is fresh. Place an uncooked egg in a bowl of water; if it lies on the bottom it is fresh; if it tilts it is older (and should be used for frying or scrambling rather than boiling) and if it floats it is likely to be bad. However, this test should only be done just before using the egg as immersing it in water makes the shell porous and open to bacteria.

### STORING EGGS

Eggs are best kept in a rack in a cool place. If you have to store them in a refrigerator keep them well away from the ice compartment (there is often a special egg storage rack) and away from foods like cheese, fish or onions whose smells may transfer to the eggs.

Store eggs pointed end down and use them at room temperature; eggs that are too cold will crack when boiled and are also difficult to whisk.

Since eggs are usually in plentiful supply all year around, there is little point in preserving them unless you keep your own hens and have a sudden glut.

If eggs have been separated and only one part used the remaining part can be stored in the refrigerator; yolks will keep for 2–3 days covered with water, whites for up to 7 days in a covered container or whites may be frozen. If freezing, label the container with the number of whites it holds. If you forget, an egg white measures about 25 ml (1 fl oz).

# COOKING WITH EGGS

Eggs have three main functions in cooking:

- Emulsifying. The yolk only is used as an emulsifying agent in mixtures like Mayonnaise (see page 270).
- Thickening and binding. Beaten eggs will thicken sauces (page 205) and custard mixtures (page 210). They will also bind flaky ingredients like fish for fish cakes and coat foods which are likely to disintegrate during cooking, such as fish for frying, fritters and croquettes.
- Raising. Eggs are used as a raising agent for batters and for many cakes.

Where an extra light mixture is needed, whisk the egg whites separately before incorporating them. Whisked egg whites are also used for making meringues (see page 365), soufflé omelettes (see page 272), soufflés (see opposite) and light foamy sweets and icings.

Eggs should be cooked gently except when hard-boiled. Cooking them at too high a temperature or for too long makes them tough. Custards and mousses containing eggs should be cooked very slowly, preferably in a double saucepan or water bath.

### HOW TO SEPARATE AN EGG

Tap the egg sharply on the side of a bowl or cup and break the shell in half. Tapping it gently two or three times is liable to crush the shell instead of breaking it cleanly and may cause the yolk to break and mingle with the white. Egg whites will not whisk well if any yolk is present.

Collect all the egg in one half of the shell, then pass the yolk back and forth between the two halves, allowing the white to drop into a bowl below. Put the completely separated yolk into another container.

When separating more than one egg, use a third container and crack each egg over this, so that if you do break a yolk you will only spoil one white. As each egg is successfully separated you can add the white and yolk to separate bowls.

### OTHER BIRDS' EGGS

**Ducks' eggs** are larger and richer than hens'. They must be thoroughly cooked to ensure that all bacteria are killed; allow at least 10 minutes for boiling. They can be included in cakes and puddings, but should not be used in meringues or any sweet which is cooked for only a short time or at a low temperature. They should only be stored for up to 4 days.

**Turkey and goose eggs** taste similar to hens' eggs but are much larger. They can be cooked by any of the methods given for hens' eggs and can be used in all cakes and puddings. Allow about 7 minutes for a soft boil. They can be stored for up to 4 days.

**Quails' eggs** are much smaller than hens' eggs; boil for 1 minute.

### DIFFERENT WAYS OF COOKING EGGS

#### Boiled Eggs

Although called boiled eggs, they should in fact be simmered rather than boiled. Using a spoon, lower them into boiling water, reduce the heat and simmer for $3\frac{1}{2}$ minutes for a light set and up to 5 minutes for a firmer set. Alternatively, put them in cold water and bring slowly to the boil, then cook for 3–4 minutes—they will then be lightly set. The water in each case should be just sufficient to cover the eggs.

If the egg cracks in the pan, quickly add a little salt or vinegar to the water to prevent a stream of egg escaping.

#### Hard-boiled Eggs

Put the eggs into boiling water, bring back to the boil and simmer gently for 10–12 minutes.

Once they are cooked, hard-boiled eggs should be placed under cold running water, then tap the shells and leave them until cold (this prevents a discoloured rim forming round the outside of the yolk and enables the shell to be removed easily. Crack the shell all over, then peel it off.

#### Soft-boiled Eggs (Oeufs Mollets)

Soft-boiled eggs can be served hot or cold. Cold, they are ideal for eggs in aspic; hot they can be served in a savoury sauce. They can also be used as an alternative to poached eggs.

Put the eggs into a pan of boiling water, reduce the heat and simmer gently, allowing 6 minutes from the time the water comes back to the boil. Small eggs take 3–4 minutes. Plunge at once in cold water, leave about 8 minutes, then carefully peel away the shell from the centre, remembering that the egg is only lightly set.

#### Coddled Eggs

Place the eggs in boiling water, cover, remove from the heat and keep in a warm place for 8–10 minutes; they will then be lightly set. Alternatively, the eggs can be cooked in a china egg coddler.

## Poached Eggs

The eggs may be cooked in a poaching pan or in water in a frying pan.

To use an egg poacher, half-fill the lower container with water, place a small knob of butter in each cup and heat. When the water boils, break the eggs into the cups, season and cover the pan. Simmer gently until the eggs are set, then loosen them with a knife before turning out.

To use a frying pan, half-fill it with water and add a pinch of salt or a little vinegar to help the eggs keep their shape and give added flavour. Swirl the water with a spoon and slip the eggs into the water. Cook gently until lightly set, then lift out with a slotted spoon or fish slice.

## Fried Eggs

Melt a little butter or oil in a frying pan. Break each egg separately into a cup and slide into the hot fat. Cook gently, basting with the fat, so the eggs cook evenly on top and underneath. When just set, remove from the pan with a fish slice or broad palette knife.

## Baked Eggs

Place the required number of ovenproof dishes on a baking sheet, with a knob of butter in each dish. Put them in the oven until the butter has melted. Break an egg into each dish, season, and cook at 180°C (350°F) mark 4 for about 8–10 minutes, until the eggs are just set. Serve at once.

## Scrambled Eggs

Mealt a knob of butter in a small saucepan. Whisk 2 eggs with 30 ml (2 tbsp) milk or water and season. Pour into the saucepan and stir slowly over a gentle heat until the mixture begins to thicken. Remove from the heat and stir until creamy. Pile on to hot buttered toast and serve immediately.
*Serves 1*

---

# SOUFFLÉS
It is traditional to use a special soufflé dish, which is fairly deep, smooth inside and fluted outside. The basic soufflé mixture, or *panada*, consists of flour, butter or margarine and milk. The egg yolks are always separated from the whites and are beaten into the panada, the stiffly beaten whites are folded in as the last step. The preparation of the panada is important, for unless it is smoothly blended and thoroughly amalgamated with the egg yolks, the soufflé may be leathery. When making the panada, choose a rather large saucepan—big enough not only to beat the egg yolks in, but also to fold in the whites.

This section also includes roulades—a roulade is a soufflé mixture baked in a paper case, which is then turned out and rolled up with a filling or sauce inside.

## Hot Spinach Soufflé

| |
|---|
| 30 ml (2 level tbsp) grated Parmesan cheese |
| 450 g (1 lb) fresh spinach, cooked or 250 g (8.82 oz) packet chopped spinach, thawed |
| 50 g (2 oz) butter or margarine |
| 45 ml (3 level tbsp) flour |
| 200 ml (7 fl oz) milk |
| salt and pepper |
| 3 eggs, separated, and 1 extra egg white |
| 100 g (4 oz) Gruyère or Emmenthal cheese, grated |

**1.** Grease a 1.3 litre (2¼ pint) soufflé dish and dust with Parmesan cheese.

**2.** Place the spinach in a sieve and press to remove all moisture.

**3.** Melt the butter in a medium saucepan, add the spinach and cook for a few minutes to drive off any liquid.

**4.** Stir in the flour and cook gently for 1 minute, stirring. Remove pan from the heat and gradually stir in the milk and seasoning. Bring to the boil slowly, and continue to cook, stirring until thickened. Cool slightly. Beat in the yolks one at a time and 75 g (3 oz) grated cheese.

**5.** Stiffly whisk the egg whites and fold into the mixture. Spoon into the soufflé dish. Sprinkle with the remaining cheese.

**6.** Stand the dish on a baking sheet and bake in the oven at 190°C (375°F) mark 5 for about 30 minutes or until well risen and just set.
*Serves 3–4*

*Cheese Soufflé*

## CHEESE SOUFFLÉ

| |
|---|
| 15 ml (1 level tbsp) grated Parmesan cheese |
| 200 ml (7 fl oz) milk |
| slices of onion and carrot, 1 bay leaf, 6 black peppercorns, for flavouring |
| 25 g (1 oz) butter or margarine |
| 30 ml (2 level tbsp) flour |
| 10 ml (2 level tsp) Dijon mustard |
| salt and pepper |
| cayenne pepper |
| 4 whole eggs, separated and 1 extra egg white |
| 75 g (3 oz) mature Cheddar cheese, finely grated |

**1.** Grease a 1.3 litre (2¼ pint) soufflé dish. Sprinkle the grated Parmesan into the dish. Tilt the dish, knocking the sides gently until they are evenly coated with cheese.

**2.** Place the milk in a medium saucepan together with the flavouring ingredients. Bring slowly to the boil, remove from the heat, cover, and leave to infuse for 30 minutes. Strain off and reserve the milk.

**3.** Melt the butter in a medium saucepan, stir in the flour, mustard and seasoning and cook gently for 1 minute, stirring. Remove from the heat and gradually stir in the milk. Bring to the boil slowly and continue to cook, stirring until the sauce thickens. Cool a little.

**4.** Beat the yolks into the cooled sauce one at a time. Sprinkle the cheese over the sauce, reserving 15 ml (1 level tbsp). (At this stage the mixture can be left to stand for several hours if necessary.)

**5.** Stir in the cheese until evenly blended. Using a hand or electric mixer, whisk the egg whites until the egg whites stand in stiff peaks.

**6.** Mix one large spoonful of egg white into the sauce to lighten its texture. Gently pour the sauce over the remaining egg whites and cut and fold the ingredients together. Do not overmix; fold lightly, using a metal spoon or plastic spatula, until the egg whites are just incorporated.

**7.** Pour the soufflé mixture gently into the prepared dish. The mixture should come about three quarters of the way up the side of the dish. Smooth the surface of the soufflé with a palette knife and sprinkle over the reserved cheese.

**8.** Place the soufflé on a baking sheet and cook in the oven at 180°C (350°F) mark 4 for about 30 minutes. It should be golden brown on the top, well risen and just firm to the touch with a hint of softness in the centre.
*Serves 4*

### Variations
Don't use too great a weight of filling or the soufflé will be heavy. Omit the cheese and add one of the following:
**Cheese** Other cheese can be used. Use a hard cheese such as Gruyère or Stilton.
**Ham** 75 g (3 oz) cooked ham, or finely chopped pork.
**Fish** 75 g (3 oz) cooked smoked haddock, finely flaked.
**Mushroom** 75–100 g (3–4 oz) mushrooms, chopped and cooked in butter until tender.
**Sweet soufflés** See page 353.

# HADDOCK ROULADE

225 g (8 oz) smoked haddock

300 ml (½ pint) milk

6 black peppercorns

3 eggs, separated

50 g (2 oz) butter or margarine

50 g (2 oz) flour

10 ml (2 tsp) lemon juice

salt and pepper

chopped fresh parsley, to garnish

**For the mushroom sauce**

milk

125 g (4 oz) button mushrooms, wiped and thinly sliced

25 g (1 oz) butter or margarine

30 ml (2 level tbsp) flour

30 ml (2 tbsp) chopped fresh parsley

5 ml (1 tsp) lemon juice

Haddock Roulade

**1.** Cut out a 35.5 × 25.5 cm (14 × 10 inch) rectangle of strong greaseproof or non-stick paper. Mark a 3.5 cm (1½ inch) border all round, then fold up the edges to form a case. Make a cut along one of the creases at each corner and secure with paper clips. Place on a baking sheet and brush the inside with melted lard or oil.

**2.** Put the fish into a small saucepan, add the milk and the peppercorns. Simmer, covered, for about 10 minutes, until the fish is beginning to flake. Strain and reserve the flavoured milk. Flake the fish, discarding any skin and bones. Place the flesh in a small bowl, add the egg yolks and mix until smooth.

**3.** Melt the butter in a large saucepan, stir in the flour and cook gently for 1 minute, stirring. Remove the pan from the heat and gradually stir in 150 ml (¼ pint) of the reserved milk (keep the rest). Bring to the boil slowly and cook, stirring, until the sauce thickens. Remove from the heat and beat in the fish and lemon juice. Season.

**4.** Stiffly whisk the egg whites. Beat 15 ml (1 tbsp) of egg white into the roulade mixture—this will lighten the mixture and so make it easier to incorporate the remaining egg whites. Gently fold in remainder. Pour the mixture into the prepared case and level with a spatula.

**5.** Cook in the oven at 200°C (400°F) mark 6 for about 12 minutes.

**6.** Meanwhile, make the mushroom sauce. Make the reserved fish cooking juices up to 300 ml

(½ pint) with milk. Melt the butter in a saucepan, add the mushrooms and fry for 2–3 minutes. Stir in the flour, taking care not to break up the mushrooms, and cook for 1 minute. Remove from the heat and gradually stir in the milk. Bring to the boil and continue to cook, stirring, until the sauce thickens. Stir in the parsley, lemon juice and seasoning.

**7.** When cooked, turn out the roulade. Place a damp sheet of greaseproof paper on a flat working surface. Take the roulade from the oven and immediately remove the paper clips. Ease the paper case away from the edges of the roulade. Quickly flip the roulade on to the damp paper, then using a sharp knife ease away the paper case.

**8.** Make a shallow cut right across 2.5 cm (1 inch) from the bottom edge of the roulade. Spread half the sauce over the bottom two-thirds; keep the rest of the sauce warm. Using the paper beneath as a support, carefully roll up from the cut end. Lift on to a flat serving dish using fish slices. Garnish with parsley. Serve the remaining sauce separately.
Serves 4

Spread the sauce on to the roulade.

Using the paper, carefully roll it up.

# MISCELLANEOUS EGG DISHES

## EGGS FLORENTINE

| |
|---|
| 900 g (2 lb) spinach |
| salt and pepper |
| 40 g (1½ oz) butter or margarine |
| 45 ml (3 level tbsp) flour |
| 300 ml (½ pint) milk |
| 75 g (3 oz) Gruyère or Cheddar cheese, grated |
| 4 eggs |

1. Wash the spinach well in several changes of water. Put into a saucepan with a little salt and just the water that clings to the leaves, cover and cook for 10–15 minutes, until tender. Drain well, chop roughly and reheat with 15 g (½ oz) butter.
2. Melt the remaining 25 g (1 oz) butter, stir in the flour and cook gently for 1 minute, stirring.
3. Remove the pan from the heat and gradually stir in the milk; bring to the boil and continue to stir until the sauce thickens. Add 50 g (2 oz) cheese and season. Do not allow to boil.
4. Poach the eggs (see page 265). Place the spinach in an ovenproof dish, arrange the eggs on top and pour the cheese sauce over.
5. Sprinkle with the remaining cheese and brown under the grill.
*Serves 4*

*Arrange the eggs decoratively over the spinach then cover with sauce.*

## BAKED EGGS WITH MUSHROOMS

| |
|---|
| 25 g (1 oz) butter or margarine |
| 100 g (4 oz) button mushrooms, wiped and finely chopped |
| 30 ml (2 tbsp) chopped fresh tarragon or parsley |
| salt and pepper |
| 2 eggs |

1. Melt the butter (keeping some in reserve) in a frying pan, add the mushrooms and fry until all excess moisture has evaporated. Add the tarragon or parsley and season.
2. Divide the mushroom mixture between two ramekin or cocotte dishes and make a well in the centre of each.
3. Carefully break an egg into each dish, dot with reserved butter and stand the ramekins in a roasting tin. Pour boiling water into the tin to come halfway up the sides of the ramekins.
4. Cover the roasting tin tightly with foil and place in the oven. Bake at 180°C (350°F) mark 4 for 10–12 minutes, until the eggs are just set. Serve at once.
*Serves 2*

## PIPÉRADE  *(Ragout of eggs, peppers and tomatoes)*

| |
|---|
| 30 ml (2 tbsp) olive oil |
| 2 large onions, skinned and thinly sliced |
| 1 garlic clove, skinned and finely chopped (optional) |
| 1 medium red or yellow pepper, seeded and sliced |
| 1 medium green pepper, seeded and sliced |
| 450 g (1 lb) tomatoes, skinned and roughly chopped |
| 6 eggs |
| 5 ml (1 tsp) finely chopped fresh parsley or basil |
| salt and pepper |
| fried bread triangles, to garnish |

1. Heat the oil in a deep frying pan or shallow flameproof casserole, add the onions and garlic and fry gently until golden.
2. Add the peppers and cook for 10–15 minutes, until they are soft.
3. Stir in the tomatoes, raise the heat a little and cook until most of the moisture has evaporated and the tomatoes have reduced to a thick pulp.
4. Beat the eggs together with the herbs, adding salt and pepper to taste and pour it into the pan. Stir gently until they begin to set.
5. Remove the pan from the heat while the mixture is still creamy.
6. Serve garnished with the fried bread triangles.
*Serves 4–6*

# EGG FRICASSÉE

200 ml (7 fl oz) milk

slice of onion, carrot, 1 bay leaf, 6 black peppercorns
    for flavouring

25 g (1 oz) butter or margarine

30 ml (2 level tbsp) flour

142 ml (5 fl oz) soured cream

10 ml (2 tsp) fresh snipped tarragon or 2.5 ml
    ($\frac{1}{2}$ level tsp) dried

salt and pepper

6 eggs, hard-boiled

fresh tarragon sprig, snipped, to garnish

212 g (7$\frac{1}{2}$ oz) packet frozen puff pastry, thawed, for
    pastry triangles (see below)

1. Pour the milk into a saucepan and add the flavourings. Bring slowly to the boil, remove from the heat, cover and leave to infuse for 30 minutes. Strain.

2. Melt the butter in a pan, stir in the flour and cook gently for 1 minute, stirring. Remove from the heat and gradually stir in the milk, soured cream, tarragon and seasoning. Bring slowly to the boil and continue to cook, stirring, until the sauce thickens. Simmer for about 5 minutes.

3. Slice the eggs, reserving the yolk from one. Add the egg slices to the sauce and simmer to warm the eggs; adjust seasoning.

4. Sieve the reserved egg yolk and use with the snipped tarragon to garnish the dish. Serve accompanied by pastry triangles.

PASTRY TRIANGLES
Roll out the pastry to an oblong 25.5 × 10 cm (10 × 4 inches). Divide into two, lengthwise, and cut each strip into ten triangles. Bake in the oven at 220°C (425°F) mark 7 for 12–15 minutes, until golden brown and well risen.
Serves 4

# STUFFED EGGS WITH PÂTÉ

6 eggs, hard-boiled

100 g (4 oz) soft liver pâté

salt and pepper

stuffed green olives, sliced, to garnish

1. Cut the eggs in half lengthways, carefully remove the yolks and rub through a nylon sieve into a bowl.

2. Add the pâté and beat well. Season with salt and pepper.

3. Put the pâté mixture into a piping bag fitted with a 1 cm ($\frac{1}{2}$ inch) plain nozzle and pipe into the egg whites.

4. Garnish with slices of olive.
Serves 2–4

# STUFFED EGG MAYONNAISE

4 eggs, hard-boiled

75 g (3 oz) soft blue cheese (Cambazola)

75 g (3 oz) full fat soft cheese

45–60 ml (3–4 tbsp) single cream

salt and pepper

225 g (8 oz) tomatoes, skinned

150 ml ($\frac{1}{4}$ pint) Mayonnaise (see page 261)

parsley sprigs, to garnish

1. Halve the eggs lengthways, carefully remove the yolks and rub through a nylon sieve into a bowl. Rinse and carefully dry the egg whites.

2. Cut the rind off the Blue Brie and beat the cheese until smooth. Work in the full fat soft cheese with the sieved egg yolks, cream and seasoning, beating until it is a smooth and pipeable consistency.

3. Put the cheese mixture into a piping bag fitted with a 1 cm ($\frac{1}{2}$ inch) star nozzle and pipe into the egg whites.

4. Slice half the tomatoes and arrange in four individual serving dishes; place the stuffed eggs on top. Refrigerate for 30 minutes.

5. Halve, seed and roughly chop the remaining tomatoes and stir into the Mayonnaise.

6. Spoon a little Mayonnaise over each egg and garnish with parsley sprigs.
Serves 4

*Chilled Egg and Cucumber Mousse*

## CHILLED EGG AND CUCUMBER MOUSSE

*1 medium cucumber*

*4 eggs, hard-boiled*

*300 ml (½ pint) Mayonnaise, made with tarragon vinegar (see page 261)*

*15 ml (3 level tsp) gelatine*

*2 egg whites*

*salt and pepper*

*mustard powder*

*fresh chervil, to garnish*

1. Cut a 5 cm (2 inch) piece off the cucumber and reserve. Peel and coarsely grate the remainder.
2. Finely chop three of the eggs and stir into the Mayonnaise with the well drained cucumber.
3. Sprinkle the gelatine in 45 ml (3 tbsp) water in a small bowl and leave to soak. Place the bowl over a pan of simmering water and stir until dissolved. Stir into the Mayonnaise mixture.
4. Stiffly whisk the egg whites and fold into the mixture. Spoon into a 1.4 litre (2½ pint) soufflé dish. Refrigerate to set.
5. Serve well chilled, garnished with the reserved egg and cucumber, finely sliced, and the chervil.
*Serves 6*

## EGG MAYONNAISE

*4 eggs, hard-boiled*

*few lettuce leaves*

*150 ml (¼ pint) Mayonnaise (see page 261)*

*chopped fresh parsley or paprika, to garnish*

1. Halve the eggs lengthways. Wash and drain the lettuce and arrange in a shallow dish.
2. Place the eggs on the lettuce, cut side down and coat with the Mayonnaise. Garnish with parsley or paprika to serve.
*Serves 2–4*

## EGGS BÉNÉDICT

*4 slices bread, cut from a barrel loaf*

*4 eggs*

*150 ml (¼ pint) Hollandaise Sauce (see page 205)*

*4 thin slices lean ham*

*parsley sprigs, to garnish*

1. Toast the bread on both sides.
2. Poach the eggs (see page 265) and gently warm the Hollandaise Sauce.
3. Top each slice of toast with a folded slice of ham, then the hot poached egg and finally coat with Hollandaise Sauce.
4. Garnish each with a sprig of parsley.
*Serves 4*

*Eggs Bénédict*

*From the left: Bacon and Egg Croquettes and Scotch Eggs (see page 272) with nasturtium salad*

## BACON AND EGG CROQUETTES

200 ml (7 fl oz) milk

slice of carrot, onion, 1 bay leaf, 6 black peppercorns, for flavouring

25 g (1 oz) butter or margarine

125 g (4 oz) streaky bacon rashers, rinded and roughly chopped

105 ml (7 level tbsp) flour

30 ml (2 tbsp) single cream, on top of milk

1 egg yolk

4 eggs, hard-boiled and chopped

salt and pepper

1 egg, beaten

50 g (2 oz) fresh breadcrumbs

oil for deep frying

parsley sprigs, to garnish

**1.** Bring the milk to the boil in a saucepan with the flavourings, cover and leave to infuse for at least 15 minutes, then strain.

**2.** Meanwhile, melt the butter in a heavy-based frying pan, add the bacon and fry until golden brown.

**3.** Stir in 75 ml (5 level tbsp) flour and cook gently for 1 minute, stirring. Remove pan from heat and gradually stir in the milk. Bring to the boil, stirring, then blend in the cream, egg yolk, hard-boiled eggs and seasoning to taste. Transfer the mixture to a bowl, cool and then chill in the refrigerator.

**4.** Roll the egg mixture into sausage shapes on a floured board, brush with beaten egg and coat in dry white crumbs—leave 15 minutes for a crisper coat. At this stage croquettes can be refrigerated for an hour.

**5.** Heat the oil in a deep fat fryer to a temperature of 180°C (350°F) and fry the croquettes, a few at a time, until golden. Drain on absorbent kitchen paper; serve at once garnished with parsley.
*Makes 12*

## SCOTCH EGGS

| |
|---|
| 4 eggs, hard-boiled |
| 10 ml (2 level tsp) seasoned flour |
| Worcestershire sauce |
| 225 g (8 oz) sausagemeat |
| 1 egg, beaten |
| fresh breadcrumbs |
| vegetable oil for deep frying |

1. Dust the eggs with the seasoned flour.
2. Add a few drops of Worcestershire sauce to the sausagemeat and divide it into 4 equal portions. Form each quarter into a flat cake and shape it round an egg, making it as even as possible, to keep the egg a good shape, and making sure there are no cracks in the sausagemeat.
3. Brush with egg and roll in the breadcrumbs.
4. Heat the oil in a deep fat fryer to a temperature of 160°C (325°F), gently lower the Scotch Eggs into the oil and fry for 7–8 minutes. (As the sausagemeat is raw, it is essential that the fat must not be too hot so the meat has time to cook.)
5. When they are golden brown on the outside, remove them from the fat and drain on absorbent kitchen paper.
6. Cut the eggs in half lengthways and serve either hot with Tomato Sauce (see page 209) or cold with a green salad.
*Serves 4*

# OMELETTES With care, anyone can master the art of omelette making.

Delicate handling and a little practice is needed—don't be discouraged if your first two or three omelettes are not successful. Two good points about omelettes are the short preparation time and the way they can be combined with cooked meat, fish or vegetables—either in the omelette itself, as a filling, or as an accompaniment.

Have everything ready before beginning to make an omelette, including a hot plate on which to serve it—an omelette must never wait, but rather be waited for.

### THE PAN

Special omelette pans are obtainable and should be kept for omelettes only. If you do not own such a pan, however, a heavy-based frying pan can also be used. Non-stick pans are ideal for omelettes and do not require seasoning before use. Whether of cast iron, copper, enamelled iron or aluminium, the pan should be thick, so that it will hold sufficient heat to cook the egg mixture as soon as it is put in. This means the omelette can be cooked in about 2 minutes; both slow cooking and overcooking make an omelette tough. A 15–18 cm (6–7 inch) pan takes a 2–3 egg omelette.

To season an omelette pan (to treat it before using for the first time), put 15 ml (1 level tbsp) salt in the pan, heat it slowly, then rub in well with a piece of absorbent kitchen paper. Tip out the salt and wipe the pan. To clean an omelette pan after use, don't wsh it, but rub it over with absorbent kitchen paper, then rub the surface again with a clean cloth.

Gently heat the pan before use to ensure that it is heated evenly right to the edges—a fierce heat would cause the pan to heat unevenly. When the pan is ready for the mixture it will feel comfortably hot if you hold the back of your hand about 2.5 cm (1 inch) away from the surface.

*Note* Manufacturers of non-stick pans advise that heating the empty pan will damage the surface, so carefully read the instructions and add the fat before heating the pan.

### FAT FOR GREASING OMELETTE PANS

Undoubtedly butter gives the best flavour, but margarine or oil can be used as a substitute. Bacon fat can also be used.

### TYPES OF OMELETTE

Basically there are only two different kinds, the plain, and the soufflé omelette in which the egg whites are whisked separately, then folded into the yolk mixture to give it a fluffy texture. Plain omelettes are usually savoury and soufflé omelettes are most commonly served as a sweet but there is no fixed rule and the fillings can be interchanged. There are also many different omelette variations, where the different ingredients are added to the eggs or used in the filling.

# PLAIN OMELETTE

*Allow 2 eggs per person*

Whisk the eggs just enough to break them down; don't make them frothy as overbeating spoils the texture of the finished omelette. Season with salt and pepper and add 15 ml (1 tbsp) water or milk. Place the pan over a gentle heat and when it is hot, add a knob of butter or margarine to grease it lightly. Add the beaten eggs. Stir gently with a fork or wooden spatula, drawing the mixture from the sides to the centre as it sets and letting the liquid egg from the centre run to the sides. When the eggs have set, stop stirring and cook for another minute until the omelette is golden underneath and still creamy on top. Tilt the pan away from you slightly and use a palette knife to fold over a third of the omelette to the centre, then fold over the opposite third. Turn the omelette out on to the warmed plate, with the folded sides underneath, and serve at once. Don't overcook or the omelette will be tough.

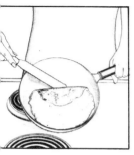

*Use a palette knife to fold the omelette over.*

## OMELETTE FILLINGS

**Fines herbes** Add 15 ml (1 tbsp) finely chopped fresh herbs or 5 ml (1 level tsp) mixed dried herbs to the beaten egg mixture before cooking. Parsley, chives, chervil and tarragon are all suitable.

**Cheese** Grate 40 g (1½ oz) cheese and mix 45 ml (3 tbsp) of it with the eggs before cooking; sprinkle the rest over the omelette after it is folded.

**Tomato** Skin and chop 1–2 tomatoes and fry in a little butter or margarine in a saucepan for 5 minutes, until soft and pulpy. Put in the centre of the omelette before folding.

**Mushroom** Wipe and slice 50 g (2 oz) mushrooms and cook in butter in a saucepan until soft. Put in the centre of the omelette before folding.

**Bacon** Rind and snip 2 rashers of bacon and fry in butter in a saucepan until crisp. Put in the centre of the omelette before folding.

**Ham or tongue** Add 50 g (2 oz) chopped meat and 5 ml (1 tbsp) chopped fresh parsley to the beaten egg before cooking.

**Fish** Flake some cooked fish and heat gently in a little cheese sauce. Put in the centre of the omelette before folding.

**Shrimp or prawn** Thaw 50 g (2 oz) frozen shrimps or prawns (or use the equivalent from a can) and fry gently in melted butter or margarine in a saucepan, with a squeeze of lemon juice. Put into the centre of the omelette before folding.

# SOUFFLÉ OMELETTE

*2 eggs, separated*

*salt and pepper*

*30 ml (2 tbsp) water*

*knob of butter or margarine*

**1.** Whisk the egg yolks until creamy. Add the seasoning and the water and beat again.

**2.** Stiffly whisk the egg whites.

**3.** Melt the butter in an omelette pan over a low heat without browning.

**4.** Turn the egg whites into the yolk mixture and fold in carefully, using a metal spoon, but don't overmix.

**5.** Grease the sides of the pan with the butter by tilting it in all directions, then pour in the egg mixture. Cook over a moderate heat until the omelette is golden brown on the underside. Put under a preheated grill until the omelette is brown on top.

**6.** Remove at once, as overcooking tends to make it tough. Run a spatula gently around the edge and underneath the omelette to loosen it. Make a mark across the middle at right angles to the pan handle and add any required filling—see suggestions below—then double the omelette over. Turn it gently on to a warmed serving plate and serve at once.

*Serves 1*

**Variations**

Any of the fillings given for plain omelettes can be used for soufflé omelettes. For sweet fillings, add 50 g (2 oz) chopped fresh or canned fruit, drained, flavoured with a liqueur, if wished. Drain again before adding to the omelette. Serve at once. (For Rum Soufflé Omelette, see page 356.)

*Spanish Omelette*

## SPANISH OMELETTE

45 ml (3 tbsp) olive oil

2 large potatoes, peeled and cut into 1 cm (½ inch) cubes

2 large onions, skinned and coarsely chopped

salt and pepper

6 eggs, lightly beaten

1. In a medium frying pan, gently heat the olive oil. Add the potatoes and onions and season with salt and pepper. Fry, stirring occasionally, for 10–15 minutes, until golden brown.

2. Drain off excess oil and quickly stir in the eggs. Cook for 5 minutes, shaking the pan occasionally to prevent sticking. If you wish, place under a hot grill to brown the top. Serve.

*Serves 4*

*Note* This is a basic Spanish Omelette, but other vegetables may be added, such as chopped red pepper, tomatoes, peas, mushrooms, spinach. Either add them raw at the beginning or stir cooked vegetables into the eggs (peas and spinach should be added already cooked).

## OMELETTE ARNOLD BENNETT

100 g (4 oz) smoked haddock

50 g (2 oz) butter or margarine

150 ml (5 fl oz) double or single cream

3 eggs, separated

salt and pepper

50 g (2 oz) Cheddar cheese, grated

1. Place the fish in a saucepan and cover with water. Bring to the boil and simmer gently for 10 minutes. Drain and flake the fish, discarding the skin and bones.

2. Place the fish in a pan with half the butter and 30 ml (2 tbsp) of the cream. Toss over a high heat until the butter melts. Leave to cool.

3. Beat the egg yolks in a bowl with 15 ml (1 tbsp) cream and seasoning. Stir in the fish mixture. Stiffly whisk the egg whites and fold in.

4. Heat the remaining butter in an omelette pan. Fry the egg mixture, but make sure it remains fairly fluid. Do not fold over. Slide it on to a flameproof serving dish.

5. Top with the cheese and remaining fresh cream blended together, then brown under the grill.

*Serves 2*

# CHEESE

Cheese is a solid derivative of milk.
It is produced by coagulating the protein (casein) so
that it forms curds—usually by adding rennet—and draining off the liquid (whey).
Cheese then undergoes a ripening process, during which it changes in taste, texture and
appearance and each variety takes on its own particular characteristics.

◆

Most cheese is made from cow's milk with a small amount made from ewe's or goat's milk. The type of milk and the different techniques used to separate the curds and whey and ripen the cheese result in the many different types of cheese. Climate, vegetation and seasonal changes can also influence the finished cheese and means that some varieties can only be produced in a certain area and cannot be produced in large quantities or under factory conditions. Cheddar, however, lends itself well to factory techniques.

Although casein makes up 78 per cent of the milk protein, there are other proteins present in smaller quantities, but they are soluble and are drained out with the whey (they are known as whey proteins). The whey may then be processed to curdle the remaining protein and used to make low fat cheese such as Ricotta—a moist, unsalted Italian cheese.

Much of the cheese bought in this country is factory produced but increasingly cheese is being made by the traditional methods on farms using unpasteurised milk. Traditional Cheddar, Single and Double Gloucester, Cheshire, Lancashire, Leicester, Wensleydale and Caerphilly are all being produced.

## BUYING AND STORING CHEESE

At specialist cheese shops, cheese is kept in exactly the right conditions for each type and you can often taste a sliver of a particular cheese before you buy. If buying pre-packed cheese, check that it does not look sweaty or excessively runny and that it is within the life of its date stamp: if the date is many weeks ahead it may mean that the cheese is immature.

Store cheese in a covered, ventilated china dish or bowl with a plate on top or wrap in foil or cling film and store in the refrigerator. Keep it in the door, dairy compartment or bottom of the refrigerator, so it does not get too cold. Leave cheese at room temperature, still in its paper or other wrappings to prevent drying out for about 30 minutes before serving.

If you want cheese to become hard and dry for grating, leave it exposed to the air in a cool, dry place for a couple of days, turning it from time to time. Grated cheese can be stored in a polythene bag in the refrigerator for several weeks.

Cheese can be frozen (see page 515). Some varieties freeze better than others and once thawed all cheese should be eaten as soon as possible as it deteriorates quickly.

## SERVING CHEESE

Cheese may be served at the end of a meal or it may form the main course for a light lunch. When planning a cheese board serve some of the following with it:

- Biscuits which may be savoury or salty, plain or semi-sweet. Rolls or bread (French, granary, wholemeal or rye) cut into chunks and put into a separate bowl or basket. Fruit Bread is also delicious with cheese.
- Butter, margarine which is low in saturated fats or a low-fat spread.
- Vegetables such as lettuce, celery, chicory, tomato wedges, small whole radishes, watercress, carrot sticks and spring onions.
- Fresh fruit such as grapes.

Cheese and wine have a natural affinity; they can be served together for informal parties, lunches or dinner parties. For a dinner party, the cheese can either be served French-style between the main course and the dessert (in which case it is eaten with the wine served with the main course) or at the end of the meal. As a general rule for serving wine with cheese, serve richer cheeses with full-bodied wines and lighter, creamier cheeses with lighter red or white wine.

## COOKING WITH CHEESE

Cheese goes well with many other ingredients such as eggs and pasta and is a flavouring for many sauces and toppings. When cooking cheese remember that too fierce a heat can make it stringy. It should melt rather than bubble fiercely and when added to a sauce, it should not be allowed to boil. Hard cheese can be grated for cooking, but softer cheeses are best sliced, shredded or crumbled before adding to a dish.

It is important to think carefully about what cheese you use in which dish. If a recipe specifies a particular type of cheese it is usually because of its individual flavour and texture, and substituting another variety may alter the taste of the dish. However, some cheeses can be used as substitutes for each other and the recipes in this chapter indicate which these are.

Well matured cheese gives the best flavour; if using a mild Cheddar add a little mustard for extra flavour if wished—adding an extra quantity of a mild cheese will not give a greater depth of flavour. Cheddar is good in baking; use Lancashire, Cheshire or Leicester for toasting; Mozzarella for pizzas, while crumbly cheeses such as Feta or Roquefort are best for mixing into salads and dressings.

## BRITISH CHEESES

**Applewood** A type of Cheddar which is smoked over apple branches and coated with paprika. It is very similar to a type called Charnwood.

**Arran** An individual rindless Dunlop cheese in a 1 kg (2¼ lb) pack made on the island of Arran. It is a hard cheese, moist and close-textured.

**Caboc** Originated from the Western Highlands in the fifteenth century. The recipe is believed to have been handed down from mother to daughter through the centuries. This is a very rich, soft double cream cheese rolled in oatmeal.

**Caerphilly** Originally a Welsh cheese, this is now made also in Somerset, Wiltshire, Devon and Dorset. It is made from whole milk, pressed only lightly and eaten in its 'green' state, when about ten days old. Caerphilly is soft and white, with a creamy mild flavour, and is best served uncooked.

**Cheddar** Cheddar is perhaps the best known and most widely used of the English cheeses.

The name 'Cheddar' is given to any cheese which undergoes the 'cheddaring' process, regardless of where it is made. Cheddar is now produced in various other parts of England and also in Scotland, Ireland, Canada, Australia and New Zealand.

English Farmhouse Cheddar is made with whole milk from a single herd of cows. The process is the same as ordinary Cheddar but Farmhouse is allowed to mature longer to produce a richer and more mellow flavour. Flavours vary from mild to quite strong and are equally good cooked or uncooked.

The mellow, slightly salty Cheddar made in Canada is similar to Farmhouse Cheddar. Its strong, mature flavour makes it excellent for cooking. Australian and New Zealand cheddars are also widely available and are of a mild quality.

Cheddar cheese is also available smoked.

**Cheshire** Said to be the oldest English cheese, Cheshire is another very well known type. Like Cheddar, it is a hard cheese, but rather more crumbly in texture, with a mild yet mellow flavour. There are two main varieties—the red, which is coloured by the addition of vegetable dye, and the white. There is no significant difference in the flavour. Blue Cheshire is also made but is less widely available. Farmhouse Cheshire, which is made from a single herd of cows, is also available. Cheshire is good cooked or uncooked.

**Cheviot** Cheddar with chives.

**Cotswold** A variant of Double Gloucester which is flavoured with chives and chopped onion.

**Derby** A hard, close-textured cheese, mild in flavour when young, it develops a fuller flavour as it matures and is at its best when it is six months old.

Sage Derby was originally made by layering with sage leaves to give a pleasant, sharp tangy flavour. It must be eaten fresh or the flavour becomes very sharp. Nowadays, sage oil is used in place of the leaves to retain the flavour.

**Dunlop** A Scottish cheese made originally in Dunlop, Ayrshire, but now fairly general throughout Scotland. It is not unlike Cheddar, but moister and of a closer texture.

**Gloucester** Gloucester is an orange-yellow, hard cheese with a close, crumbly texture and a good rich flavour, rather similar to that of a mature Cheddar. Originally there were 'double' and 'single' Gloucesters, one being twice the size of the other, but now only the 'double' is made.

**Highland Crowdie** Similar to cottage cheese but more finely ground. It is high in protein and low in fat with a light, fresh flavour.

**Hramsa** This is a soft cheese made from fresh double cream which is delicately flavoured with wild garlic. It is excellent served on savoury biscuits or made into a dip.

**Huntsman** An attractive looking cheese made from layering Double Gloucester and Stilton.

**Ilchester** Double Gloucester and mustard pickle.

**Islay** A miniature Dunlop which is excellent for melting and is best eaten when fairly mature.

**Lancashire** A fairly hard cheese, crumbly in texture when cut. When new it has a mild, tangy flavour, which develops considerably as it matures. It can be enjoyed cooked or uncooked.

**Leicester** A hard cheese with a mild, slightly sweet flavour and orange-red colour.

**Lymeswold** The first mild soft blue British cheese. As it matures, Lymeswold develops from a firmer, more curd-textured and fresh-flavoured cheese to a softer, more mellow richness. The rind can be eaten.

**Melbury** A mild, white mould ripened soft cheese. It has a mellow taste and is made in a distinctive loaf shape.

**Nutwood** Cheddar with cider, nuts and raisins.

**Orkney** This cheese which is made in Orkney was originally made in various farms, but is now made in a modern creamery. Each cheese weighs 454 g (1 lb), is similar to Dunlop cheese and is available as white cheese, red cheese and the more subtle smoked cheese.

**Rutland** Cheddar with beer, garlic and parsley.

**Sherwood** Double Gloucester with chives and onions.

**Shropshire Blue** Created in the 1970s, this cheese is a cross between Stilton and Blue Cheshire.

**Stilton** Stilton, one of the best known of English cheeses, is made in Leicestershire, Nottinghamshire and Derbyshire. It is a white full-cream milk cheese now produced all the year round although it used to be a seasonal cheese. Stilton is semi-hard and has a blue veining, caused by a mould which in most cases is a natural growth throughout the curd, accelerated by the use of stainless steel skewers piercing the cheese to allow the mould to enter. The veins of blue mould should be evenly distributed throughout. The rind, of a dull, drab colour, should be well crinkled and regular and free from cracks. Stilton is at its best when fully ripe, that is 4–5 months after it has been made. If bought in small quantities eat it as soon as possible. A whole or half Stilton will keep well if the cut surface is covered and the cheese is kept in a dry airy larder. It needs no port or anything else added to it. It should be cut in slices from the top and not scooped out.

White Stilton bears little resemblance to Blue Stilton in flavour but it is the same cheese before the blue mould has grown into it. It has a slightly crumbly texture and is white in colour without the characteristic blue-veining. This cheese has a pleasant, mild flavour.

**Vegetarian cheese** This is made with a non-animal rennet and is similar to Cheddar in texture and flavour. Use it in the same way.

**Walton** Cheddar and Stilton with walnuts.

**Windsor Red** A mature Cheddar cheese flavoured and coloured with English fruit wine. This produces a cheese with a red-veining and gives a very mature flavour.

**Wensleydale** Made in the vale of Wensleydale in Yorkshire. Originally it was a double cream cheese, cylindrical in shape, which matured until it became blue—in this form it was considered one of the best English blue cheeses, next only to Stilton. Since 1954 much of the Wensleydale production has been sold when white and in this form it is a mild, creamy-coloured cheese with a rather flaky texture. Blue Wensleydale is also obtainable.

### LOW FAT CHEESES

Low fat hard cheeses such as Cheddar and Cheshire have been produced in response to the needs of people who want to have less fat in their diet. They are made in a similar way to traditional hard cheeses but with half their fat content and a consequent reduction in calories. Low fat cheeses tend

o be mild flavoured. For use in cooking where stronger flavour is required, either add a pinch of mustard or keep the cheese in the refrigerator for 2–3 weeks to allow the flavour to mature and develop.

## SOFT CHEESES

A true soft cheese is made by coagulating milk with rennet. The addition of a 'starter' just before rennet is added ensures a clean acid flavour. The majority of soft cheeses, such as Camembert, are foreign in origin. English soft cheeses include York and Colwick. The British cheeses are usually marketed in a fresh or unripened state, whilst the better known of those made abroad are consumed when fully mature. This requires the growth of specific bacteria and moulds to produce the desired ripening action. The British varieties of unripened soft cheese are usually made from cow's milk, but goat's milk can equally well be used.

Today many soft cheeses are made from skimmed milk, which means they are lower in calories and fat content. Varieties of soft cheese are defined and labelled according to the amount of milk fat and water they contain.

Skimmed milk soft cheese must by law contain less than 2 per cent milk fat and not more than 80 per cent water. They are generally low in calories, soft and smooth with a bland or slightly acid taste. Examples include Fromage frais.

Those labelled as low fat soft cheese have 2–10 per cent milk fat and up to 80 per cent water. Textures may vary from smooth and yogurt-like to lumpy-textured cottage cheese (see right).

Medium fat soft cheese must contain 10–20 per cent milk fat and not more than 70 per cent water. It is white with a smooth but slightly granular texture and lightly acid flavour.

Full fat soft cheeses are often called 'creamy' and frequently confused with the higher fat cream cheeses. Full fat means they must contain at least 20 per cent milk fat and not more than 60 per cent water.

The higher fat cream cheeses are often referred to as double cream cheese (see below). One example is Caboc.

**Cream cheese** can be classified as a soft cheese. Its manufacture is very similar to that described above, but it is made from cream rather than milk. A typical cream cheese is a soft bodied, unripened cheese with a rich, full and mildly acid flavour. It has a rather granular texture, buttery consistency and a high content of milk fat which gives it a creamy appearance. It is usually moulded into small cylindrical, square, rectangular or round shapes of varying sizes. There are two recognised varieties of cream cheese—single or double cream cheese.

Single cream cheese is made from single cream with an optimum fat content of 20–25 per cent. 1.2 litres (2 pints) of this cream will yield about six cheeses weighing 100–125 g (about 4 oz) each. Carefully prepared, it will keep for a week in a refrigerator, after which it deteriorates quickly both in flavour and appearance.

Double cream cheese is produced from cream containing about 50–55 per cent butterfat. Usually 1.2 litres (2 pints) of this cream will yield eight double cream cheeses weighing 100–125 g (about 4 oz) each. This cheese does not keep quite as long as single cream cheese.

## ACID CURD CHEESE

Acid curd cheese is frequently classed as a soft cheese, but is fundamentally different. The curds are formed solely by the action of lactic acid upon the casein. Acid curdling is a completely different action from rennet coagulation and yields a curd of high acidity, quick drainage properties and somewhat granular texture. The cheese has a clean, acid flavour, and a slightly granular, soft, spreadable texture. It has a short shelf life and must be eaten in a fresh state.

**Cottage cheese** is an acid curd cheese, but is made from pasteurised, skimmed milk. The curd is cut into small cubes and slowly heated to develop the right body and texture. The whey is drained off, and the curd washed several times and cooled. The washing of the curd produces the familiar lumpy appearance of cottage cheese. Salt and single cream are then added and the cheese is packaged in cartons. The addition of the cream gives a final fat content of 4 per cent in the cottage cheese. This, combined with the high moisture content gives the cheese its soft velvety texture. Cottage cheese has a short keeping quality and should be eaten while fresh.

**Key**
1. Double Gloucester; 2. Farmhouse Cheddar; 3. Blue Stilton; 4. Shropshire Blue; 5. Edam; 6. Caerphilly; 7. Sage Derby; 8. Emmenthal; 9. Huntsman; 10. Fourme d'Ambert; 11. Smoked German; 12. Rutland; 13. Torta San Gaudenzio; 14. Tomme au Raisin; 15. Roule (Garlic and Herbs); 16. Bel Paese; 17. Walnut Crédioux; 18. Roule (Peppers and Chives); 19. Bûche de Chèvre; 20. Mozzarella; 21. Cambazola; 22. Brie; 23. Camembert.

## CONTINENTAL CHEESES

**Bel Paese** A rich, creamy cheese of mild flavour, made in various parts of Italy, usually from October to June. The cheeses weigh about 2.3 kg (5 lb) each.

**Bleu de Bresse** A soft and creamy blue cheese from France with a rich, subtle flavour. It has a grey-coloured rind and should not be allowed to over-ripen as it develops a strong, and unpleasant flavour.

**Boursin** This is the brand name of a fresh cream cheese made in France and usually flavoured with garlic, herbs or rolled in crushed peppercorns.

**Brie** A soft-textured farm cheese, produced in the north of France. It is made from whole milk and is mould-inoculated. Brie is flat and round, usually 35 cm (14 inches) in diameter and about 2.7 kg (6 lb) in weight; it has a white floury crust instead of the more usual hard rind. It should be eaten fresh when soft all through. It doesn't keep well. Some Brie cheeses have added flavourings of herbs or peppercorns.

**Bûche de Chèvre** A soft French goat's milk cheese.

**Cambazola** A full fat soft German cheese with a white Camembert mould on the rind and a blue Gorgonzola mould internally. Creamy in texture with a light bite coming from the blue.

**Camembert** A French soft cheese, made of cow's milk, the curd being inoculated with a white mould. The cheese was made originally in Normandy, but is made now also in other parts of France. Camembert is at its best when it begins to get soft; if allowed to over-ripen, it develops a smell which many people find unpleasant.

**Crédioux** A processed cheese shaped either as a small cake or round log. It is creamy with a highly refined flavour and is coated with walnuts.

**Danish Blue** A white softish cheese made in Denmark; it has a blue mould veining and a sharp, salty taste.

**Demi-sel** A fresh cream cheese, usually sold in small squares wrapped in foil. It is made in France, mainly in Normandy.

**Dolcelatte** A mild, blue cheese version of Gorgonzola but slightly softer and creamier.

**Edam** A Dutch ball-shaped cheese, bright red outside and deep yellow inside, and about 2.3 kg (5 lb) in weight. It is firm and smooth in texture and has a mild flavour.

**Emmenthal** A Swiss cheese similar to Gruyère but larger and slightly softer in texture, with larger 'eyes'.

**Esrom** Made in Denmark, this is a semi-hard yellow cheese and has a pleasant, mild flavour.

**Feta** (also called Fetta) Made from ewe's milk originally in Greece but now made in many other countries. It is stored in barrels in brine which accounts for its salty flavour. It is a fairly hard cheese that crumbles easily for use in salads and other raw dishes. It can also be sprinkled on to stews, used in pastries and in vegetable stuffings.

**Fontainebleau** A French cream type cheese; soft and fresh; it is made in the country round Fontainebleau, mostly in the summer.

**Fourme d'Ambert** A firm but soft French blue cheese produced in the Auvergne with cow's milk.

**Fromage blanc** A very low fat cheese with a light fresh, clean taste, useful for calorie-watchers.

**Gorgonzola** A semi-hard, blue-veined sharp flavoured cheese, made in Italy near Milan.

**Gouda** A wheel-shaped Dutch cheese, not unlike Edam in taste and texture, but flatter in shape with a yellow skin and very much larger, approximately 5 kg (9 lb) in weight, and an excellent cheese for cooking. There are also small Goudas, about 450 g (1 lb) in weight, known as Midget Goudas. Mature Gouda has a black skin.

**Gruyère** A hard, large cheese, weighing anything up to 45 kg (100 lb). Originally it came exclusively from Switzerland but is now made also in France, Italy and other parts of Europe. It is pale yellow in colour and is honeycombed with 'eyes' or holes caused by the rapid fermentation of the curd; it has a distinctive and fairly sweet taste. It is served uncooked, but is also used in such classic cooked dishes as fondue.

**Jarlsberg** originates in Norway. The whole cheese (usually sold in wedges) is wheel-shaped with a yellow wax rind. The cheese itself has a sweet nutty flavour like Emmenthal and has similar holes.

**Limburger** A semi-hard, whole milk cheese made in Belgium (and also in Germany and Alsace) from December to May. It is full flavoured and strong smelling.

**Mascarpone** A rich cream cheese made in Italy.

**Mozzarella** An Italian cheese, pale-coloured and egg-shaped. When fresh, it is very soft, dripping with buttermilk. Traditionally made from buffalo milk, it is now more often made from cows' milk. Mozzarella should be eaten fresh, as the cheese ripens quickly and is past its best in a few days. Available only from specialist Continental shops, it can be used in salads and is also splendid for pizzas, lasagnes, and other Italian dishes. Bel Paese may be used as a substitute.

**Mycella** This cheese gets its name from the mould mycelium which produces the blue veins. It is a full fat cheese similar to Danish Blue but has a milder flavour.

**Mysöst (Gietöst)** A whey cheese, principally made from goat's milk, which is produced in Norway. It is hard and dark brown, with a sweetish flavour.

**Parmesan** This Italian cheese is the hardest of all. After being specially processed, the curd is broken up, heated, packed into a large mould the shape of a millstone and matured for at least two and usually three years. When it is ripe the crust is almost black, but the cheese itself should be of a pale straw colour and full of tiny holes, like pinpricks. Parmesan has a strong and distinctive flavour and is used finely grated for cooking or as a traditional accompaniment for soups such as Minestrone and for rice and pasta dishes.

**Petit Suisse (Petit Gervais)** An unsalted cream cheese, cylindrical in shape, made in France. It is very mild in flavour. Often sold in small foil-wrapped packs.

**Pipo Crem'** Blue-veined cheese sold in a log shape. It is semi-soft with a flavour similar to Bleu de Bresse.

**Pommel** A double cream cheese, unsalted and not unlike Petit Suisse, which is made in France all the year round.

**Pont l'Evêque** A soft paste cheese with a thickish orange rind, about 10 cm (4 inches) square and 4 cm (1½ inches) thick. It is made practically all the year round in the Pont l'Evêque district of Normandy. The smell is stronger than the taste.

**Quark** A soft cheese that is often eaten on its own with a spoon. It is sometimes flavoured with fruit or herbs. It may be made from skimmed or whole milk or buttermilk and may also include added cream. The name, which is German, means simply curds and the cheese is also sold as Buttermilchquark, Labquark and Speisequark.

**Raclette** To most people this means a Swiss method of toasting cheese over an open fire or in a special appliance. But raclette is generically a semi-hard cheese (the name means scraper) which is golden with a few small holes and a rough, grey-brown rind. It tastes full and fruity and somewhat like Gruyère. There are many local Swiss varieties.

**Ricotta** A fragrant Italian cheese made from the whey left over when producing other cheeses. It has a delicate, smooth flavour and is very suitable for cooking in such things as ravioli or cannelloni. It can also be eaten with sugar or used layered in fruit tarts and puddings.

**Roquefort** This is the only ewe's milk cheese which has obtained a world-wide reputation. It is made during the lambing season in the village of Roquefort in the Cevennes mountains of France. It can be made only in this district, partly because the sheep-grazing land here is particularly suitable, but also because of the limestone caverns of Roquefort itself, which play a very important part in the maturing of the Roquefort cheese. The same mould as that used in the making of Stilton is introduced into the curd as a maturing agent. This delicious blue cheese has a sharp, pungent flavour and a soft creamy, crumbly texture. Very good for salads, mixed with the dressing.

**Roule** This resembles a Swiss roll in shape and comes in two versions. Both are full fat soft cheese but one is rolled in fines herbes and garlic and the other (Roule Acapulco) in spices which include cumin, pepper and chilli.

**Saint Paulin** A French semi-hard cheese, round in shape, it was made originally by the monks of Port du Salut and is sometimes sold as Port Salut, but is now made in various other parts of France. It is creamy yellow in colour and has a very mild and delicate flavour; it should be eaten while still slightly soft.

**Samsoe** Named after the Danish island of Samsoe. This is a firm cheese, made from unskimmed cow's milk. It has a few irregular-sized small holes and a delicate, nutty flavour. The flavour acquires greater pungency as it matures. Samsoe is best used uncooked, and is a popular addition to open sandwiches.

**Smoked Cheese (Austrian and German)** Sold in small rounds or 'sausages' wrapped in brown plastic, the cheese is a pale creamy colour. Mild and smoky in flavour, with a very smooth, soft texture, excellent with wine.

**Taleggio** An Italian unpressed, uncooked cheese with a pinkish-grey rind and white soft flesh. The flavour becomes stronger and more aromatic as the cheese ripens. Taleggio made with unpasteurised milk is considered a special Italian delicacy.

**Tomme** Is the name given to the various small cheeses produced during the summer months in Savoie. They are mostly from skimmed cow's milk.

Tomme au Raisin is ripened in a mixture of grape skins, pips and stalks to give the cheese its distinctive flavour.

Tomme de Savoie is cylindrical in shape and has a pleasant, light flavour resembling Saint Paulin.

**Torta San Gaudenzio** A mixture of the semi-hard blue veined Gorgonzola and the rich creamy Mascarpone cheeses which are layered together to form a gateau effect. A variety sometimes flavoured with anchovy and caraway seeds. This cheese is also known as Torta Gorgonzola.

## CHEESE ON TOAST

| |
|---|
| 225 g (8 oz) hard cheese, grated |
| 5 ml (1 level tsp) mustard powder |
| salt and pepper |
| 2.5–5 ml (½–1 tsp) Worcestershire sauce |
| milk to mix |
| 4 slices of bread, crusts removed |

**1.** Mix the cheese and seasonings and bind to a paste with milk.
**2.** Lightly toast the bread on one side.

**3.** Pile the cheese thickly on the uncooked sides and cook under a hot grill until golden.
*Serves 4*

**Variation**
CHEESE AND ONION CRISP
Skin 1 medium onion, slice into thin rings and parboil in salted water for 5–10 minutes. Drain well and lay on slices of buttered toast. Sprinkle with salt and pepper, crumble over some Lancashire cheese and cook under a hot grill until golden and bubbling.

## WELSH RAREBIT

| |
|---|
| 225 g (8 oz) Cheddar cheese, grated |
| 25 g (1 oz) butter or margarine |
| 5 ml (1 level tsp) mustard powder |
| salt and pepper |
| 60 ml (4 tbsp) brown ale |
| 4 slices of bread, crusts removed |

**1.** Place all the ingredients except the bread in a heavy-based saucepan and heat very gently until a

creamy mixture is obtained.
**2.** Lightly toast the bread on one side.
**3.** Pour the sauce over the uncooked sides and put under a hot grill until golden and bubbling.
*Serves 4*

**Variation**
BUCK RAREBIT
This is Welsh Rarebit topped with a poached egg.

## CROQUE MONSIEUR

| |
|---|
| 16 thin slices bread, crusts removed |
| 5–10 ml (1–2 level tsp) prepared mustard |
| 225 g (8 oz) Gruyère cheese, sliced |
| 225 g (8 oz) cooked ham, thinly sliced |
| 75 g (3 oz) butter or margarine, melted |

**1.** Spread half the slices of bread on one side with the mustard; trim the cheese slices to fit and put them on top.
**2.** Trim the ham slices to fit and arrange them on top of the cheese. Top with the remaining bread.
**3.** Brush the sandwiches lightly with melted butter and fry for 3–5 minutes, until they are lightly browned.
**4.** Turn the sandwiches over and fry for a further 3–5 minutes.
**5.** Cut the sandwiches in half and serve hot.
*Note* 90 ml (6 tbsp) vegetable oil may be used instead of the butter. Heat in the frying pan and cook the sandwiches as above.
*Serves 4–8*

*Croque Monsieur*

**Variation**
For a more economical version of Croque Monsieur, use Cheddar cheese instead of Gruyère. Serve with salad for a light lunch.

## FETA CHEESE PUFFS

225 g (8 oz) Feta cheese, grated

142 g (5 oz) natural yogurt

15 ml (1 tbsp) chopped fresh basil or 5 ml (1 level tsp)
   dried

pepper

368 g (13 oz) packet puff pastry, thawed

1 egg, beaten

fresh basil leaves, to garnish

1. Mix the cheese with the yogurt, basil and
pepper. (Do not add salt as the cheese is salty.)
2. Roll out the pastry thinly on a lightly floured
surface and cut out sixteen 7.5 cm (3 inch) rounds.
3. Place half the rounds on two baking sheets.
Spoon the cheese mixture into the centre of each
one.
4. Brush the pastry edges with beaten egg. Cover
with remaining rounds, knocking up the pastry
edges to seal. Make a small slit in the top of each
puff and glaze the tops with beaten egg.
5. Bake in the oven at 220°C (425°F) mark 7 for
about 15 minutes, until well browned and crisp.
Serve warm, garnished with basil leaves.
*Makes 8*

*From the top: Cheese Aigrettes and Feta Cheese Puffs*

## CHEESE AIGRETTES

50 g (2 oz) butter or margarine

150 ml (¼ pint) water

65 g (2½ oz) plain flour, sifted

2 eggs, beaten

50 g (2 oz) mature Cheddar cheese, grated

salt, pepper and cayenne pepper

vegetable oil for deep frying

1. Heat the butter and water in a saucepan until
the fat dissolves, then bring to the boil. Remove
from the heat, add the flour all at once and beat
well until the paste is smooth and leaves the sides
of the pan.
2. Allow to cool slightly, then beat in the eggs
gradually. Add the cheese and season well.
3. Heat the oil in a deep-fat fryer to 190°C (375°F),
then drop in teaspoonfuls of the mixture and fry
until golden. Drain well on absorbent kitchen
paper and serve hot.
*Serves 4*

Drop a teaspoonful of
mixture into the preheated
fat and fry in small batches.

**Variations**
Gruyère could be used instead of Cheddar cheese.
   Sprinkle the hot aigrettes with grated Parmesan
cheese.
   Serve with a tossed green salad for a light meal.

## Cheese and Potato Cakes

| |
|---|
| 450 g (1 lb) potatoes, boiled and mashed |
| 25 g (1 oz) butter or margarine |
| 100 g (4 oz) hard cheese, grated |
| 15 ml (1 tbsp) snipped fresh chives |
| salt and pepper |
| 15 ml (1 level tbsp) flour |
| 2 eggs, beaten |
| 40 g (1½ oz) fresh breadcrumbs |
| 30–45 ml (2–3 tbsp) oil for frying (optional) |

1. Mix the potatoes with the butter, cheese, chives, seasoning, flour and 1 egg and beat until smooth. Leave until cold.
2. Turn on to a lightly floured surface and form into a roll. Cut into 2.5 cm (1 inch) slices and, using lightly floured hands, shape into round cakes.
3. Brush with the remaining egg and coat with breadcrumbs. Place on a greased baking sheet and chill in the refrigerator for 30 minutes. Bake in the oven at 190°C (375°F) mark 5 for about 20 minutes. Alternatively, fry the cakes in the oil until golden brown. Serve hot.
*Serves 4*

## Scotch Cheesies

| |
|---|
| 125 g (4 oz) Cheddar cheese |
| 450 g (1 lb) sausagemeat |
| 15 ml (1 level tbsp) French mustard |
| salt and pepper |
| flour |
| 1 egg, beaten |
| 25 g (1 oz) fresh breadcrumbs |
| vegetable oil for deep frying |

*Encase each piece of cheese in sausagemeat by moulding it firmly with your hands.*

1. Divide the cheese into twelve even-sized pieces.
2. Pound the sausagemeat with the mustard and seasoning until well blended.
3. Roll each piece of cheese in sausagemeat, making sure the cheese is completely encased.
4. Coat the balls lightly in flour, beaten egg and breadcrumbs in that order, pressing the crumbs on well. Chill for 30 minutes to set the crumbs.
5. Heat the oil in a deep fat fryer to 190°C (375°F), add the cheesies and fry until golden brown. Drain well on absorbent kitchen paper. Leave until cold.
*Makes 12*

## Camembert Frappé

| |
|---|
| 125 g (4 oz) Camembert, rinded |
| 225 g (8 oz) full fat soft cheese |
| 150 g (5 oz) butter or margarine |
| 50 g (2 oz) flour |
| 300 ml (½ pint) milk |
| 15 ml (1 tbsp) chopped fresh parsley |
| salt and pepper |
| 50 g (2 oz) ground hazelnuts |

1. Cream together the Camembert, full fat soft cheese and 75 g (3 oz) butter.
2. Melt the remaining 50 g (2 oz) of butter in a saucepan, stir in the flour and cook gently for 1 minute, stirring. Remove pan from the heat and gradually stir in the milk. Bring to the boil slowly and continue to cook, stirring, until the sauce thickens. Leave to cool slightly.
3. Beat together the cheese mixture, cooked sauce and parsley. Season lightly.
4. Base line an 18 cm (7 inch) wide, fairly deep sandwich tin with greaseproof paper. Spoon in the cheese mixture and smooth the top. Chill well for 10–12 hours.
5. Turn out on to a serving dish and sprinkle with ground hazelnuts, patting the nuts on lightly.
*Serves 6*

# CAULIFLOWER CHEESE

1 medium cauliflower, trimmed

40 g (1½ oz) butter or margarine

45 ml (3 level tbsp) flour

300 ml (½ pint) milk

100 g (4 oz) Cheddar cheese, grated

salt and pepper

1. Cook the cauliflower in fast-boiling salted water until just tender, then drain and place in an ovenproof serving dish.
2. Meanwhile, melt the butter in a saucepan, stir in the flour and cook gently for 1 minute. Remove pan from the heat and gradually stir in the milk. Bring to the boil and continue to cook, stirring, until the sauce thickens, then add 75 g (3 oz) cheese and seasoning to taste.
3. Pour the sauce over the hot cauliflower, sprinkle with the remaining cheese and brown under a hot grill.
Serves 4

# POTTED CHEESE WITH MINT

75 g (3 oz) butter

225 g (8 oz) Leicester cheese, grated

15 ml (1 tbsp) chopped fresh mint

60 ml (4 level tbsp) soured cream

pepper

fresh mint leaves, to garnish

brown bread or crispbread, to serve

1. Beat the butter until really soft, then gradually beat in the cheese.
2. Stir in the chopped mint and soured cream and add pepper to taste. Salt should not be required as the cheese should add sufficient.
3. Spoon into a serving dish; cover and refrigerate for at least 2 hours.
4. To serve, leave at room temperature for about 20 minutes, to soften a little, then garnish with fresh mint leaves. Spread on slices of brown bread or crispbread.
Serves 4–6

# QUICK PIZZA

225 g (8 oz) self raising flour

salt and pepper

50 g (2 oz) butter or margarine

150 ml (½ pint) milk

5 large tomatoes, skinned and finely chopped

2 medium onions, skinned and finely chopped

30 ml (2 level tbsp) tomato purée

2.5 ml (½ level tsp) dried mixed herbs

4 anchovy filets

6 black olives, stoned and chopped

175 g (6 oz) Cheddar, Bel Paese or Mozzarella cheese, thinly sliced

1. Sift the flour and 2.5 ml (½ level tsp) salt into a bowl, then rub in the butter until the mixture resembles fine breadcrumbs. Add the milk and mix to a soft dough.
2. Roll out the pizza dough on a lightly floured surface to form a 23 cm (9 inch) round. Place the dough on a lightly greased baking sheet.
3. Mix together the tomatoes, onions, and tomato purée and season with salt and pepper.
4. Spread the tomato mixture on top of the dough and sprinkle with mixed herbs. Arrange the anchovy fillets and olives over the mixture and top with the cheese slices.
5. Bake in the oven at 220°C (425°F) mark 7 for 20–25 minutes, until cooked and golden. Serve hot.
Serves 4

**Variations**
Omit the anchovies and make a lattice with 2 rashers of streaky bacon, cut into narrow strips.

Use drained canned sardines or sausages, sliced lengthways, instead of the bacon lattice.

## NEAPOLITAN PIZZA

| |
|---|
| 15 g (½ oz) fresh yeast or 7.5 ml (1½ level tsp) dried and 5 ml (1 level tsp) caster sugar |
| about 120 ml (4 fl oz) tepid water |
| 225 g (8 oz) plain flour |
| 7.5 ml (1½ level tsp) salt |
| 50 g (1¾ oz) can anchovy fillets, drained and sliced lengthways |
| 60 ml (4 tbsp) milk |
| 60 ml (4 tbsp) olive oil |
| 350 g (12 oz) tomatoes, skinned and thinly sliced |
| 7.5 ml (1½ tsp) chopped fresh oregano or 2.5 ml (½ level tsp) dried |
| salt and pepper |
| 100 g (4 oz) Mozzarella cheese, grated |
| 16 black olives, halved and stoned |
| fresh oregano, to garnish |

*Left: Neapolitan Pizza. Right: Quiche Lorraine*

1. Crumble the fresh yeast into a small basin; pour in the tepid—not hot— water and stir gently until smooth. For dried yeast, dissolve the sugar in the tepid water, then sprinkle the yeast over the surface; leave this to stand in a warm place for 15 minutes until frothy.

2. Sift the flour and salt into a mixing bowl and stir in the sugar; if dried yeast is being used the sugar will already be in. Make a well in the centre of the dry ingredients and pour in the yeast liquid. Using a wooden spoon or fork, gradually beat and 'lap' the flour into the well of liquid to form a soft dough, adding a little more liquid if necessary.

3. Turn the dough on to a lightly floured surface and knead for at least 5 minutes to form a smooth elastic dough.

4. Put the dough in a bowl, cover with a clean tea towel and leave in a warm place until doubled in size.

5. Turn the dough out on to a floured surface and knead with floured hands to remove any large air bubbles. Divide the dough into two equal pieces. Lightly knead each piece into a smooth ball. Leave on the floured surface, covering each with an upturned mixing bowl for about 15 minutes.

6. Meanwhile, put the anchovies to soak in the milk for 10 minutes, then drain off the milk.

7. Take each piece of dough and roll out on a lightly floured surface to a 23 cm (9 inch) round. Place the dough bases on to oiled baking sheets and crimp the edges.

8. Brush 15 ml (1 tbsp) oil over each pizza base and cover with sliced tomatoes. Sprinkle with oregano, plenty of seasoning and the remaining oil. Scatter over the grated cheese. Garnish with anchovies and olives. Bake the pizzas in the oven at 230°C (450°F) mark 8 for 15–18 minutes, until well browned and crisp. Serve warm, garnished with oregano.

*Serves 2 as a main course*

### Variation

This pizza base can also be made with a mixture of plain and wholemeal flour—use 100 g (4 oz) of each.

## QUICHE LORRAINE

175 g (6 oz) Shortcrust Pastry (see page 372)
75–100 g (3–4 oz) lean bacon, rinded and chopped
75–100 g (3–4 oz) Gruyère cheese, thinly sliced
2 eggs, beaten
150 ml (5 fl oz) single cream or milk
salt and pepper

1. Roll out the pastry on a lightly floured surface and use to line a 20.5 cm (8 inch) plain flan ring placed on a baking sheet. Bake blind in the oven at 200°C (400°F) mark 6 for 10–15 minutes, until set.

2. Scatter the bacon over the pastry base and top with the cheese.

3. Beat together the eggs, cream and seasoning and pour into the pastry case. Bake in the oven at 200°C (400°F) mark 6 for about 30 minutes, until well risen and golden. Serve hot or cold.

### Variations

Lightly fried rings of onion or leeks can be used instead of, or as well as, the bacon.
*Serves 4*

## CRAB AND RICOTTA QUICHE

| |
|---|
| 175 g (6 oz) Shortcrust Pastry (see page 372) |
| salt and pepper |
| 2 eggs |
| 150 ml (5 fl oz) single cream |
| 150 ml (¼ pint) milk |
| 225 g (8 oz) crab meat |
| 175 g (6 oz) Ricotta cheese |
| 30 ml (2 level tbsp) grated Parmesan |

1. Roll out the pastry on a lightly floured surface and use to line a 20.5 cm (8 inch) flan dish or ring placed on a baking sheet.
2. Bake blind in the oven at 200°C (400°F) mark 6 for 10–15 minutes.
3. Whisk the eggs, milk and cream together in a bowl. Flake the crab meat, crumble the Ricotta and add to the egg mixture with the Parmesan and plenty of seasoning. Pour into the flan case and bake in the oven at 190°C (375°F) mark 5 for 35 minutes until golden. Serve hot.
*Serves 6*

## ROQUEFORT QUICHE

| |
|---|
| 175 g (6 oz) Shortcrust Pastry (see page 372) |
| 75 g (3 oz) Roquefort or other blue cheese, shredded |
| 175 g (6 oz) full fat or low fat soft cheese |
| 2 eggs, beaten |
| 150 ml (5 fl oz) single cream |
| 5–10 ml (1–2 tsp) grated onion or 15 ml (1 tbsp) snipped fresh chives |
| salt and pepper |

1. Roll out the pastry and use to line a 20.5 cm (8 inch) flan ring placed on a baking sheet.
2. Bake blind in the oven at 200°C (400°F) mark 6 for 10–15 minutes, until set.
3. Cream together the two cheeses and stir in the eggs, cream, onion and salt and pepper.
4. Pour into the pastry case. Bake in the oven at 190°C (375°F) mark 5 for about 30 minutes, until well risen and golden. Serve at once.
*Serves 6*

## BLUE CHEESE SPREAD

| |
|---|
| 100 g (4 oz) butter or margarine |
| 225 g (8 oz) Stilton cheese, crumbled |
| 30 ml (2 tbsp) port |

1. Beat all the ingredients together well. Chill in the refrigerator. Serve with savoury biscuits.
*Serves 4*

## CHEESE AND ASPARAGUS TART

| |
|---|
| 175 g (6 oz) Shortcrust Pastry (see page 372) |
| 25 g (1 oz) butter or margarine |
| 45 ml (3 level tbsp) flour |
| 300 ml (½ pint) milk |
| 100 g (4 oz) hard cheese, grated |
| salt and pepper |
| 340 g (12 oz) can green asparagus spears, drained |

1. Roll out the pastry and use to line a 20.5 cm (8 inch) flan ring placed on a baking sheet. Bake blind in the oven at 200°C (400°F) mark 6 for 10–15 minutes, until set. Remove the baking beans and return to the oven and bake for a further 15 minutes, until firm and golden brown.
2. Melt the butter in a saucepan, stir in the flour and cook gently for 1 minute, stirring. Remove pan from the heat and gradually stir in the milk. Bring to the boil slowly and continue to cook, stirring, until the sauce thickens.
3. Remove from the heat and stir in 75 g (3 oz) of the cheese and salt and pepper to taste.
4. Place the drained asparagus in the pastry case, reserving a few for garnish, pour over the sauce and garnish with the remaining asparagus.
5. Sprinkle with the remaining cheese and brown under a hot grill or in a hot oven.
*Serves 4*

**Variation**
For a healthy alternative, use wholemeal flour for the pastry case.

# TOMATO AND CHEESE TART

200 g (7 oz) full fat soft cheese

75 g (3 oz) butter or margarine, softened

2 whole eggs plus 1 egg yolk

10 ml (2 level tsp) whole grain mustard

225 g (8 oz) plain wholemeal flour

450 g (1 lb) firm ripe tomatoes

75 ml (5 tbsp) milk

15 ml (1 tbsp) finely chopped fresh rosemary or 5 ml
(1 level tsp) dried

salt and pepper

1. Beat 75 g (3 oz) cheese with the butter, egg yolk and mustard. When evenly blended, cut and mix in the flour, then knead well until smooth.
2. Roll out the pastry and use to line a 25.5 cm (10 inch) loose-based flan tin. The pastry will be short and so difficult to handle; patch up the flan case if necessary.
3. Bake blind in the oven at 200°C (400°F) mark 6 for 10–15 minutes, until set.
4. Meanwhile, skin the tomatoes and cut into neat wedges. Whisk together the eggs, milk, remaining cheese, rosemary and seasoning.
5. Arrange the tomatoes in the flan case. Pour in the cheese mixture.
6. Bake in the oven at 180°C (350°F) mark 4 for about 30 minutes or until just set. Serve warm.
*Serves 6*

# SAVOURY CHEESECAKE

75 g (3 oz) plain potato crisps (preferably unsalted)

50 g (2 oz) water biscuits

50 g (2 oz) butter or margarine

175 g (6 oz) full low or fat soft cheese

175 g (6 oz) Roquefort cheese

3 eggs

200 ml (7 fl oz) single cream

10 ml (2 level tsp) grated onion

7.5 ml (1½ tsp) chopped fresh rosemary or 2.5 ml
(½ level tsp) dried

pepper

gherkin fans (see page 249), to garnish

1. Crush the crisps and biscuits to crumbs. Melt the butter in a saucepan and stir in the crumbs. Press the crumb mixture into the base of a 23 cm (9 inch) flan dish; cover with cling film and refrigerate.
2. Beat the cheeses together until smooth, then beat in the eggs, cream, onion, rosemary and pepper.
3. Pour the cheese mixture into the flan case and cook in the oven at 180°C (350°F) mark 4 for about 40 minutes, until well risen, just set and golden brown. Serve warm, garnished with gherkin fans.
*Serves 4–6*

**Variations**
Instead of Roquefort cheese, other blue cheeses such as Stilton or Danish Blue, could be substituted.

Garnish with overlapping cucumber slices in place of the gherkin fans.

*Savoury Cheesecake*

## TUNA AND CHEESE SOUFFLÉ FLAN

| 175 g (6 oz) Cheese Pastry (see page 372) |
| 200 g (7 oz) can tuna fish, drained |
| 50 g (2 oz) butter or margarine |
| 50 g (2 oz) flour |
| 200 ml (7 fl oz) milk |
| 5 ml (1 tsp) lemon juice |
| 100 g (4 oz) smoked cheese, grated |
| 2 eggs, separated |
| salt and pepper |

1. Roll out the pastry on a lightly floured surface and use to line a 20.5 cm (8 inch) plain flan ring placed on a baking sheet. Bake blind in the oven at 200°C (400°F) mark 6 for about 20 minutes, until set but not browned.

2. Lightly break up the tuna fish with a fork. Melt the butter in a saucepan, stir in the flour and cook gently for 1 minute, stirring. Remove from the heat and gradually stir in the milk and lemon juice. Bring to the boil slowly and continue to cook, stirring, until the sauce thickens. At this stage the sauce will be very thick.
3. Gently stir in the tuna. Add 75 g (3 oz) of the cheese and stir in with the egg yolks. Season lightly
4. Whisk the egg whites until stiff and gently fold them into the tuna mixture. Spoon into the pastry case.
5. Sprinkle over the remaining cheese. Bake in the oven at 200°C (400°F) mark 6 for 30–35 minutes, until risen and golden. Serve immediately.
*Serves 4*

## CHEESE FONDUE

| 1 garlic clove, skinned |
| 300 ml (½ pint) dry white wine |
| 450 g (1 lb) cheese (half Gruyère and half Emmenthal), coarsely grated |
| 20 ml (4 level tsp) cornflour |
| pepper |
| pinch of grated nutmeg |
| 45 ml (3 tbsp) kirsch (optional) |
| French bread, to serve |

1. Rub the inside of a fondue pot or flameproof dish with the garlic. Pour in the wine, place the pot over a fondue burner on the table and warm the liquid.
2. Add the cheese gradually and continue to heat gently, stirring, until all the cheese has melted.

3. Add the cornflour and seasonings, blended to a smooth paste with the kirsch, if using, and continue cooking for a further 2–3 minutes. When the fondue reaches a very smooth consistency, it is ready to serve.
4. Fondue is traditionally served in the centre of the table, kept warm over a fondue burner. Crusty cubes of bread are speared on long handled forks and dipped into it.
*Note* If liked, small glasses of kirsch can be served with the fondue—guests should dip the cubes of bread first in the kirsch, before dipping in the fondue.
*Serves 4*

**Variation**
Replace the Gruyère and Emmenthal with mature Cheddar cheese, grated, and use dry cider, instead of the white wine.

## RACLETTE

| 450 g (1 lb) Raclette cheese |
| pepper or paprika |

1. Using a sharp knife, cut the rind from the cheese and slice the cheese thinly.
2. Place the slices, overlapping slightly, in a shallow ovenproof dish and bake in the oven at 190°C (375°F) mark 5 for 4–6 minutes, until the cheese has just melted and the surface is smooth.

3. Sprinkle with pepper or paprika and serve in the cooking dish to keep hot. It can be eaten by itself or may be served with hot boiled potatoes, pickled cucumbers and cocktail onions.
*Serves 4*
*Note* This dish is traditionally made in Switzerland by holding a large piece of Raclette cheese over an open fire and scraping off the melting cheese.

# PASTA, RICE AND GNOCCHI

P asta and rice are cheap, nutritious and extremely versatile; they can be used as accompaniments to dishes or as the main ingredient. There are numerous types of rice and pasta. Gnocchi, a semolina or flour based dumpling, is baked or poached and served with a sauce like pasta.

---

♦

---

*PASTA* The word pasta simply means dough in Italian but it is also used to describe spaghetti, macaroni, lasagne and many other pasta shapes made from the basic dough mixture. Also included in this chapter are egg and rice noodles which are widely used in Japanese and Chinese cooking.

There are said to be over 500 different varieties of pasta throughout Italy today, although only about 50 of these are widely known. It falls into two main types—commercially dried pasta sold in packets *(pasta secca)* and fresh pasta *(pasta all'uovo* or *pasta fatta in casa)*. The best commercially dried pasta is made from 100 per cent hard durum wheat *(semola di grano duro)*, so check the packet before buying.

As for nutritional value, pasta is mainly a carbohydrate food, although good-quality brands can contain as much as 13 per cent protein, and all contain some vitamins and minerals.

Ingredients vary from one brand to another, but in general the tubular types are not made with eggs, whereas the flat ones are usually made with the addition of eggs. Although made with good-quality ingredients, commercially produced pasta cannot compare with the flavour and freshness of home-made pasta (see page 294).

### DIFFERENT TYPES OF PASTA

There is an increasingly wide choice of both fresh and dried pasta now available. Coloured pasta adds interest to meals—green pasta *(pasta verde)* is flavoured with spinach, pink or red pasta *(pasta rosso)* with tomatoes. Fresh pasta is also available flavoured with basil or garlic. Wholewheat pasta is also available. This contains more fibre than pasta made with ordinary flour and is consequently more chewy and tasty.

The variety of pasta shapes is endless and new shapes are constantly being introduced. Below is a guide to the most common shapes, although you may see slightly different shapes or the same shape under different names—especially if visiting Italy. This is simply because the different regions of Italy have their own individual pasta shapes and names—and so do the manufacturers.

**Spaghetti** comes in long straight strands of varying thickness. When cooking long dried spaghetti, coil it gently into the pan as it softens on contact with the boiling water.

**Macaroni** is a thicker hollow tube, sometimes cut into short lengths; *bucatini, tubetti lunghi, zite* and *penne* are all short macaroni.

**Lasagne** is the widest of the ribbon pastas. It comes in flat strips, rectangles or squares with either a smooth or ridged edge. Some varieties do

not need pre-cooking before incorporating into a dish which is to be baked.

**Noodles** are narrow flat pasta strips which are either straight ribbons or are folded into a nest-shaped mass, which is easier to drop into boiling water. *Tagliatelle* and *fettucine* are the commonest.

**Vermicelli** is the finest ribbon pasta, which comes in a nest-shaped mass and is mostly used in soups.

**Cannelloni** are large hollow tubes which can be stuffed with meat or vegetable mixtures and served with sauce.

**Rigatoni** are slightly narrower than cannelloni and can be served with a sauce.

**Lumache (snails), conchiglie (shells), fusilli (spirals), ruotini (wheels) and fiochetti (bows)** are all small shapes.

**Rings, hoops and rollers** are small hollow circles of pasta, sometimes with spokes like a wheel.

**Ditalini** are tiny pasta shapes served in soup.

**Ravioli, cappelleti, tortellini and tortelli** are stuffed pasta shapes.

## QUANTITIES OF PASTA

When calculating quantities of pasta per person, allow the same amount whether it is fresh or dried. Allow 50–75 g (2–3 oz) uncooked pasta per person if serving pasta as a starter before a substantial main course dish. If serving pasta as a main course dish for an informal meal, then increase the quantity to 100–175 g (4–6 oz) per person.

## STORING PASTA

Fresh pasta should be used within 24 hours of purchase; after this time it begins to dry out. Fresh pasta freezes very successfully and can be cooked from frozen. Freeze it in usable quantities in well-sealed polythene bags or containers and use within 2–3 months. It can be frozen in the manufacturer's packaging as long as it is overwrapped. Unopened packets of dried pasta will keep for months in a cool, dry cupboard, but once opened, the packet should be used up quickly as exposure to the air makes the pasta become brittle and tasteless—this is especially true of pasta made with eggs.

Leftover cooked pasta without a sauce should be cooled and stored in a covered container in the refrigerator for 1–2 days or up to 1 month in the freezer. To reheat, simply drop into boiling water and simmer gently until heated through.

## MAKING YOUR OWN PASTA

Making pasta at home is very easy—the actual dough is a simple mixture of flour, salt, eggs and olive oil. The best flour to use is semolina flour: a hard, very fine wheat flour. As this is difficult to obtain, a strong flour of the type used for making bread is a satisfactory alternative. General household plain flour can be used, but it produces a dough which cannot be rolled out as thinly by hand—it is best to use this only if you have a pasta machine. These can cut larger quantities more evenly and quickly than you can by hand. They can also cut various shapes such as spaghetti, macaroni and long strips for lasagne.

## COOKING PASTA

Pasta should be cooked in fast-boiling salted water in a large saucepan. Allow about 2–3 litres (3½–5¼ pints) per 450 g (1 lb) of pasta. Adding 15 ml (1 tbsp) oil to the water will prevent it boiling over and stop the pasta sticking together. Cooking time depends on the size; long pasta takes about 8–10 minutes, short cut pasta 6–12 minutes and tiny pasta shapes 2–6 minutes. Lasagne takes about 12 minutes. Fresh pasta takes about 3 minutes.

Check just before the end of the cooking time by biting a piece of pasta. It should be what the Italians call *al dente*, firm but not too hard or soft. Once it has reached this stage it should be drained thoroughly. If it is for a cold dish, rinse it under cold running water. If for a hot dish, it is best eaten or mixed with the other ingredients immediately, although it can be kept hot in a colander over a pan of boiling water for a short time before serving.

## NOODLES

Noodles, which feature strongly in Chinese, Japanese and Asian cooking, are very similar to pasta and may be used in the same way as thin ribbon pastas. The following are the most widely available from supermarkets and specialist shops. Fresh noodles are obtainable in Chinese supermarkets.

**Egg noodles** are the best known noodles and are used a great deal in Chinese cooking. They are made

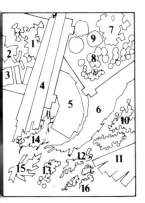

**Key**
1 Fiochetti—bows; 2 Tubetti lunghi—Short cut macaroni; 3 Cannelloni; 4 Spaghetti; 5 Lasagne; 6 Tagliatelle; 7 Ravioli; 8 Tortelli and tortellini; 9 Tagliatelle; 10 Conchiglie rigate—shells; 11 Lasagne; 12 Fusilli—spirals; 13 Ruotini—wheels; 14 Fettucine; 15 Penne—short cut macaroni; 16 Zite—short cut macaroni.

from flour, egg and water, and are usually sold in compressed bundles of varying sizes.

**Rice noodles** come in various thickness. They are made in long strands which are folded over for packaging. Very thin rice noodles are sold in compressed bundles, and these are known as vermicelli.

**Transparent or cellophane noodles** are made from mung bean, pea starch or wheat. They are made in long strands which are folded over for packaging.

Noodles may also be made from soya beans, buckwheat, corn or chick-peas.

## HOMEMADE PASTA DOUGH

| about 200 g (7 oz) semolina flour or strong plain flour |
| 2 eggs |
| pinch of salt |
| 15 ml (1 tbsp) olive oil |

**1.** Sift the flour into a mound on a clean working surface. With your fist, make a well in the centre and add the eggs, salt and oil.
**2.** Using your fingertips, gradually stir in the flour from the sides of the well. Continue until the dough comes together.
**3.** Then, using both hands, knead the dough for about 10 minutes until smooth and not sticky.
**4.** Wrap in cling film and leave to rest for 30 minutes before shaping as required.
*Makes about 350 g (12 oz) dough*

**Variation**
*PASTA VERDE (SPINACH PASTA)*
Wash, drain and discard coarse stalks from 225 g (8 oz) fresh spinach. Cook in a saucepan, with no additional water until tender, about 5 minutes. Cool, then squeeze out all excess moisture with your hands. Finely chop. Increase the flour to 225 g (8 oz) and add the spinach with the eggs.

*SHAPING THE DOUGH*
Roll out the pasta on a floured work surface to a large rectangle which is nearly paper thin.

If you are making cut pasta such as tagliatelle, fettucine or lasagne, the dough must be allowed to dry. Place the dough on a clean tea towel, allowing one third to hang over the edge of a table or work surface and turn every 10 minutes. The pasta is ready to cut when it is dry to the touch and begins to look leathery, about 30 minutes.

**1. Tagliatelle**
Fold the dough over into a roll about 8 cm (3 inches) in depth. With a sharp knife, cut into 1 cm (½ inch) wide strips. Try to cut them all the same width. When it has been cut, unfold and leave to dry for a minimum of 10 minutes.

**2. Fettucine**
Proceed as for tagliatelle but cut into 0.5 cm (¼ inch) wide strips.

**3. Lasagne**
Cut into 10 × 15 cm (4 × 6 inch) rectangles.

1

2

3

*1. Roll out dough on floured surface until paper thin.*
*2. To dry, leave dough on a towel with one third hanging over the edge.*
*3. Roll up and cut into noodles. Unfold and dry on a floured tray.*

# SPAGHETTI AL BURRO (*Spaghetti with butter and Parmesan cheese*)

225–350 g (8–12 oz) spaghetti

50 g (2 oz) butter or margarine

50 g (2 oz) Parmesan cheese, grated

**1.** Cook the spaghetti in a large saucepan of fast-boiling salted water for about 10 minutes for dried pasta or 3 minutes for fresh pasta or until tender.

**2.** Drain well and return to the pan. Add the butter and 15 g ($\frac{1}{2}$ oz) of Parmesan cheese. Stir and leave for a few minutes for the butter and cheese to melt. Serve with the remaining cheese in a separate dish.

*Note* Any form of tubular or ribbon pasta can be cooked and served in this way.

*Serves 4 as a starter*

# SPAGHETTI BOLOGNESE

25 g (1 oz) butter or margarine

45 ml (3 tbsp) olive oil

2 slices of unsmoked streaky bacon, rinded and finely chopped

225 g (8 oz) minced beef

1 small onion, skinned and finely chopped

1 small carrot, peeled and finely chopped

1 small celery stick, finely chopped

1 small garlic clove, skinned and finely chopped

1 bay leaf

15 ml (1 level tbsp) tomato purée

150 ml ($\frac{1}{4}$ pint) dry white wine

150 ml ($\frac{1}{4}$ pint) Beef Stock (see page 19)

salt and pepper

450–700 g (1–1$\frac{1}{2}$ lb) spaghetti

**1.** Heat the butter and oil in a saucepan, add the bacon and cook for 2–3 minutes until soft.

**2.** Add the minced beef and cook for a further 5 minutes, until lightly browned.

**3.** Add the onion, carrot, celery, garlic and bay leaf. Stir and cook for 2 minutes. Add the tomato purée, wine, stock and seasoning.

**4.** Bring to the boil, then simmer uncovered for 1–1$\frac{1}{2}$ hours, stirring occasionally.

**5.** Cook the spaghetti in a large saucepan of fast-boiling salted water for about 10 minutes for dried pasta or 3 minutes for fresh pasta or until just tender. Drain well and mix with the sauce on a warmed dish.

*Serves 4 as a main course*

# SPAGHETTI MILANESE (*Spaghetti with mushrooms, ham and tongue in tomato sauce*)

25 g (1 oz) butter or margarine

1 medium onion, skinned and chopped

50 g (2 oz) mushrooms, wiped and chopped

450 g (1 lb) tomatoes, skinned and chopped, or 397 g (14 oz) can tomatoes, drained

1 bay leaf

pinch of dried thyme

pinch of freshly grated nutmeg

5 ml (1 level tsp) sugar

salt and pepper

50 g (2 oz) ham, chopped

50 g (2 oz) tongue, chopped

450–700 g (1–1$\frac{1}{2}$ lb) spaghetti

Parmesan cheese, grated, to serve

**1.** Melt the butter in a saucepan, add the onion and mushrooms and fry for 3–5 minutes, until soft.

**2.** Stir in the tomatoes, herbs, nutmeg, sugar and seasoning, cover and simmer gently for about 20 minutes, until the sauce has thickened.

**3.** Add the ham and tongue and simmer uncovered for a further 5–10 minutes.

**4.** Cook the spaghetti in a large saucepan of fast-boiling salted water for about 10 minutes for dried pasta or 3 minutes for fresh pasta or until just tender. Drain well, return to the pan and mix with the sauce.

**5.** Pour into a warmed serving dish. Serve the cheese in a separate dish.

*Serves 4 as a main course*

*Spaghetti alla Carbonara*

## SPAGHETTI ALLA CARBONARA *(Spaghetti with eggs and bacon)*

| |
|---|
| *15 ml (1 tbsp) olive or vegetable oil* |
| *1 garlic clove, skinned* |
| *175 g (6 oz) lean unsmoked bacon, cut into thin strips* |
| *450–700 g (1–1½ lb) spaghetti* |
| *4 eggs, lightly beaten* |
| *90 ml (6 level tbsp) grated Parmesan cheese* |
| *60 ml (4 tbsp) single cream* |
| *salt and pepper* |
| *50 g (2 oz) butter or margarine* |

**1.** Heat the oil and the whole garlic clove in a large frying pan, add the bacon and fry for about 10 minutes, until the bacon is golden brown.

Discard the garlic.

**2.** Meanwhile, cook the spaghetti in a large saucepan of fast-boiling salted water for about 10 minutes for dried pasta or 3 minutes for fresh pasta or until just tender. Combine the eggs with the cheese and cream and season with salt and pepper.

**3.** Drain the pasta well, return to the saucepan and toss with the butter, then add the bacon. Cook for 1 minute, stirring all the time. Remove from the heat and pour over the egg and cheese mixture. Mix well, then transfer to a warmed serving dish and serve at once.

*Serves 4 as a main course*

# SPAGHETTI NAPOLETANA *(Spaghetti with tomato sauce)*

| |
|---|
| 1.1 kg (2½ lb) tomatoes |
| 30 ml (2 tbsp) olive oil |
| 1 small garlic clove, skinned and crushed |
| 7.5 ml (1½ tsp) chopped fresh basil or 2.5 ml (½ level tsp) dried |
| 5 ml (1 level tsp) ground bay leaves |
| 10 ml (2 level tsp) sugar |
| salt and pepper |
| 450–700 g (1–1½ lb) spaghetti |
| small knob of butter or margarine |
| Parmesan cheese, grated, to serve |

1. Skin the tomatoes and cut flesh into quarters. Put the seeds in a nylon sieve placed over a bowl and press lightly to extract any juices.
2. Heat the oil in a heavy based saucepan, add the tomatoes and juices, garlic, herbs, sugar and seasoning and simmer gently, uncovered, until tomatoes cook down to a thick pulp. Adjust the seasoning.
3. Meanwhile, cook the spaghetti in a large saucepan of fast-boiling salted water for about 10 minutes for dried pasta or 3 minutes for fresh pasta until just tender, drain, return to the pan and toss in a little butter. Transfer to a warmed serving dish.
4. Pour over the tomato sauce and top with plenty of grated Parmesan cheese.
*Serves 4 as a main course*

# LEEK AND MACARONI AU GRATIN

| |
|---|
| 175 g (6 oz) short cut macaroni |
| 75 g (3 oz) butter or margarine |
| 350 g (12 oz) leeks, trimmed, washed and chopped |
| 40 g (1½ oz) flour |
| 900 ml (1½ pints) milk |
| 225 g (8 oz) Double Gloucester or Cotswold cheese, grated |
| salt and pepper |
| 40 g (1½ oz) fresh breadcrumbs |
| 30 ml (2 tbsp) snipped fresh chives |

1. Cook the macaroni in a large saucepan of fast-boiling water for about 10 minutes for dried pasta or 3 minutes for fresh pasta, or until just tender. Drain well.
2. Melt the butter in a frying pan, add the leeks and fry for 2 minutes. Stir in the flour and cook gently for 1 minute, stirring. Remove pan from the heat and gradually stir in the milk. Bring to the boil slowly and continue cooking, stirring, until the sauce thickens. Remove from the heat and add all but 30 ml (2 level tbsp) of the grated cheese and the cooked macaroni. Season.
3. Spoon into a greased shallow, ovenproof dish. Mix together the breadcrumbs, chives and remaining cheese. Sprinkle in lines evenly across the dish.
4. Bake in the oven at 190°C (375°F) mark 5 for 30–35 minutes, until golden. Serve immediately.
*Note* It is important to clean leeks well—they contain a surprising amount of dirt between their

*Leek and Macaroni au Gratin*

layers. Remove the coarse outer leaves and cut off the tops and roots. Slit the leeks in half lengthwise and place in a bowl of cold water. Shake gently to remove all the grit, then remove from the water and chop roughly.
*Serves 4*

**Variation**
It is possible to use other cheeses. Substitute Cheddar or Lancashire cheeses for the above.

## MACARONI CHEESE

| |
|---|
| 225 g (8 oz) short cut macaroni |
| 65 g (2½ oz) butter or margarine |
| 90 ml (6 level tbsp) flour |
| 900 ml (1½ pints) milk |
| salt and pepper |
| pinch of freshly grated nutmeg or 2.5 ml (½ level tsp) prepared mustard |
| 225 g (8 oz) mature Cheddar cheese, grated |
| 45 ml (3 level tbsp) fresh breadcrumbs |

1. Cook the macaroni in a large saucepan of fast-boiling salted water for about 10 minutes for dried pasta or 3 minutes for fresh pasta until just tender and drain well. Keep warm.
2. Meanwhile, melt the butter in a saucepan, stir in the flour and cook gently for 1 minute. Remove pan from the heat and gradually stir in the milk. Bring to the boil and continue to cook, stirring, until the sauce thickens, then remove from the heat and add seasonings, 175 g (6 oz) cheese and the macaroni.
3. Pour into an ovenproof dish and sprinkle with the remaining cheese and breadcrumbs.
4. Place on a baking sheet and bake in the oven at 200°C (400°F) mark 6 for about 20 minutes, until golden and bubbling, or brown under a very hot grill.
*Serves 4*

## FISH-STUFFED CANNELLONI WITH CHEESE SAUCE

| |
|---|
| 50 g (2 oz) butter or margarine |
| 100 g (4 oz) mushrooms, wiped and chopped |
| 115 g (4 oz) can pimientos, drained and diced |
| 1 garlic clove, skinned and crushed |
| 210 g (7½ oz) can salmon or tuna steak, drained and flaked |
| 50 g (2 oz) fresh breadcrumbs |
| 12 oven-ready cannelloni |
| **For the sauce** |
| 50 g (2 oz) butter or margarine |
| 60 ml (4 level tbsp) flour |
| 568 ml (1 pint) milk |
| 175 g (6 oz) Cheddar cheese, grated |
| salt and pepper |

1. Melt the butter in a saucepan, add the mushrooms and fry gently for 2–3 minutes, until soft. Add the pimiento, garlic, fish and breadcrumbs. Cook over a low heat for 5 minutes, stirring.
2. Make the sauce: melt the butter in a saucepan. Stir in the flour and cook for 1 minute, stirring. Remove the pan from the heat and gradually stir in the milk. Bring to the boil slowly and continue to cook, stirring, until the sauce has thickened. Remove from the heat and stir in 150 g (5 oz) of the cheese until melted. Season well.
3. Spoon the fish filling into the pasta tubes so that it protrudes slightly at each end.
4. Pour enough sauce into an ovenproof dish to just cover the bottom. Arrange the cannelloni side by side in the dish and pour over the remaining sauce. Sprinkle over the rest of the cheese.
5. Bake in the oven at 200°C (400°F) mark 6 for 30 minutes, until golden brown.
*Serves 4*

## TAGLIATELLE WITH PARMA HAM IN CREAM SAUCE

| |
|---|
| 225–350 g (8–12 oz) tagliatelle |
| 50 g (2 oz) butter or margarine |
| 1 large onion, skinned and finely sliced |
| 100 g (4 oz) Parma ham, cut into thin strips |
| 100 g (4 oz) peas, cooked |
| 60 ml (4 tbsp) single cream |
| 50 g (2 oz) Parmesan cheese, grated |
| salt and pepper |

1. Cook the pasta in a large saucepan of fast-boiling salted water until just tender. Drain.
2. Meanwhile, melt the butter in a saucepan, add the onion and cook for about 3 minutes, until the onion is soft. Add the ham and peas and cook for a further 5 minutes.
3. Add the drained pasta, stir well, then add the cream and half the cheese. Toss gently, add seasoning and serve at once in a warmed serving dish with the remaining cheese in a separate dish.
*Serves 4*

## LASAGNE VERDI AL FORNO *(Baked green lasagne)*

| |
|---|
| 30 ml (2 tbsp) vegetable oil |
| 1 small onion, skinned and chopped |
| 1 carrot, peeled and chopped |
| 125 g (4 oz) button mushrooms, wiped and sliced |
| 50 g (2 oz) streaky bacon, rinded and chopped |
| 1 garlic clove, skinned and chopped |
| 450 g (1 lb) minced beef |
| 350 g (12 oz) fresh tomatoes, skinned and chopped, or a 227 g (8 oz) can tomatoes |
| 15 ml (1 level tbsp) tomato purée |
| 150 ml (¼ pint) dry white wine |
| 150 ml (¼ pint) Beef Stock (see page 19) |
| 2 bay leaves |
| salt and pepper |
| 900 ml (1½ pints) milk |
| few slices of onion, carrot and celery |
| 6 black peppercorns |
| 225 g (8 oz) lasagne verdi |
| 125 g (4 oz) butter or margarine |
| 75 g (3 oz) flour |
| 75 g (3 oz) grated Parmesan cheese |

1. Heat the oil in a large saucepan and add the onion, carrot, mushrooms, bacon and garlic. Fry, stirring, for 1–2 minutes, then add the beef and cook over a high heat for a further 2 minutes. Stir in the tomatoes, tomato purée, wine, stock and a bay leaf. Season. Bring to the boil, reduce heat to a simmer, cover and cook for about 35 minutes.

2. Meanwhile, pour the milk into a saucepan, add the onion, carrot, celery, peppercorns and remaining bay leaf. Bring slowly to the boil, remove from the heat, cover and leave to infuse for about 15 minutes.

3. Cook the lasagne, several at a time, in a large pan of fast-boiling salted water, for about 12 minutes for dried pasta or 3 minutes for fresh pasta or until just tender. Stir gently from time to time with a fork, to prevent the pasta sticking together.

4. Drain the lasagne and rinse in cold water to prevent further cooking. Drain and lay on a clean cloth.

5. Strain the milk. Melt the butter in a pan, stir in the flour and cook gently for 1 minute, stirring. Remove pan from the heat and gradually stir in the milk. Bring to the boil slowly and continue to cook, stirring, until the sauce thickens. Season.

6. Grease a 2.8 litre (5 pint) shallow ovenproof dish. Spoon half the meat sauce over the base of the dish. Cover this with half the pasta and spread over half of the sauce. Repeat these layers topping with the sauce to cover the pasta completely. Sprinkle with the Parmesan.

7. Cook in the oven at 180°C (350°F) mark 4 for about 45 minutes, or until the top is golden brown.

*Serves 4–6*

## CURRIED CHICKEN LASAGNE

| |
|---|
| 2 kg (4½ lb) oven-ready chicken |
| 350 g (12 oz) dried lasagne |
| 50 g (2 oz) butter or margarine |
| 30 ml (2 level tbsp) flour |
| 45 ml (3 level tbsp) medium curry powder |
| 1.1 litres (2 pints) milk |
| salt and pepper |
| 40 g (1½ oz) desiccated coconut |
| 15 ml (1 level tbsp) fresh breadcrumbs |

1. Skin chicken and remove flesh. Trim off the fat and cut meat into 1 cm (½ inch) chunks.

2. Cook the lasagne, several at a time in a large saucepan of fast-boiling salted water until just tender. Drain, rinse in cold water, then drain on a clean cloth.

3. Melt the butter in a saucepan, stir in the flour and curry powder and cook for 1 minute, stirring. Remove from the heat and gradually stir in the milk. Bring to the boil slowly and continue to cook, stirring, until the sauce thickens. Simmer for 5 minutes, then season and add 25 g (1 oz) of the coconut.

4. Spoon some sauce over the base of a 2.3 litre (4 pint) shallow dish. Arrange the lasagne and chicken in single layers, adding a little sauce to each layer. Finish with lasagne, pour the rest of the sauce over the top. Sprinkle with the remaining coconut and breadcrumbs.

5. Bake in the oven at 180°C (350°F) mark 4 for about 1 hour, until the top is brown.

*Serves 6*

*Ravioli Stuffed with Spinach served with a French bean and pine nut salad*

## TORTELLINI AL FORNO

*450 g (1 lb) aubergines, washed and trimmed*

*salt*

*25 g (1 oz) butter or margarine*

*450 g (1 lb) tomatoes, skinned and chopped*

*1 garlic clove, skinned and crushed*

*pepper*

*225 g (8 oz) tortellini*

*150 ml (¼ pint) milk*

*225 g (8 oz) full fat soft cheese*

*15 ml (1 level tbsp) grated Parmesan cheese*

*30 ml (2 level tbsp) dried breadcrumbs*

**1.** Chop the aubergines, sprinkle with salt and leave for 15–20 minutes. Rinse well and pat dry.

**2.** Melt the butter in a frying pan, add the aubergines, tomatoes and garlic and cook gently for 5–10 minutes, until very soft. Season well.

**3.** Cook the tortellini in fast-boiling salted water for about 15 minutes for dried pasta, 8 minutes for fresh pasta or until just tender. Drain well.

**4.** Spoon the vegetable mixture into a shallow, ovenproof dish. Layer the tortellini on top.

**5.** In a bowl, gradually beat the milk into the cheese whisking until smooth. Stir in 5 ml (1 level tsp) Parmesan. Spoon evenly over the tortellini. Sprinkle the top with breadcrumbs and the remaining Parmesan.

**6.** Bake in the oven at 200°C (400°F) mark 6 for 25–30 minutes, until the top is golden brown.
*Serves 4*

# RAVIOLI STUFFED WITH SPINACH

1½ quantities of Homemade Pasta Dough (see
  page 294)

75 g (3 oz) butter or margarine

450 g (1 lb) fresh spinach, cooked, or 226 g (8 oz)
  packet frozen spinach, thawed and chopped

50 g (2 oz) Parmesan cheese, grated

pinch of freshly grated nutmeg

salt and pepper

melted butter, grated Parmesan cheese and chopped
  fresh parsley, to serve

1. Make the dough as described on page 294, then
wrap in cling film and leave for 30 minutes.
2. Meanwhile, make the filling. Melt the butter
and add it to the drained spinach with the cheese
and nutmeg. Season well.
3. Halve the dough. Roll it out, then stretch by
drawing the fingertips underneath until each half
is 32.5 × 40 cm (13 × 16 inches).
4. Place 8 small mounds of spinach along the
length and 6 across the width, equally spaced.
Brush around the mounds with water.
5. Cover with the remaining dough and seal
around each spinach mound. Cut with a serrated
pastry wheel between the mounds.
6. Place the ravioli in gently boiling salted water,
adding about 12 pieces at a time, and cook for
about 10 minutes until tender. Remove with a
slotted spoon and keep warm until all are cooked.
Drain well and toss in melted butter with the
grated cheese and chopped parsley.
*Serves 4*

**Variation**
The cooked ravioli can be layered with Tomato
Sauce (see page 209) in a greased ovenproof dish,
sprinkled with grated Parmesan cheese and baked
in the oven at 200°C (400°F) mark 6 for about
15 minutes, until golden brown.

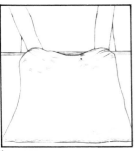

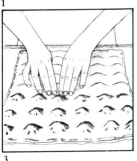

1. *Roll out dough as thinly*
*as possible, then stretch by*
*'drawing out' with your*
*fingertips.*
2. *Spoon small mounds of*
*spinach on to the dough.*
3. *Press firmly around the*
*mounds to seal.*

# PASTA AND FRANKFURTER SCRAMBLE

4 eggs

45 ml (3 tbsp) milk

salt and pepper

175 g (6 oz) pasta shapes, eg shells

112 g (4 oz) packet frozen peas

25 g (1 oz) butter or margarine

213 g (7½ oz) packet frankfurters, thinly sliced

bunch of spring onions, trimmed and chopped

5 ml (1 level tsp) ground cumin

1. In a bowl, whisk together the eggs, milk and
seasoning.
2. Cook the pasta in fast-boiling salted water until
tender, adding the peas for the last 5 minutes of
cooking time. Drain well.
3. Melt the butter in a large frying pan, add the
frankfurters, spring onions and cumin and fry
gently for about 5 minutes.
4. Add the drained pasta and peas with plenty of
seasoning and reheat, stirring, for 2–3 minutes.
5. Lower the heat and pour in the egg mixture,
stirring all the time, until the eggs lightly scramble
through the pasta. Transfer to a warmed serving
dish.
*Serves 4*

$RICE$ may have long, medium or short grains. It may be sold as brown, natural, unpolished or wholegrain rice, still retaining its outer bran layers, or as white or polished rice, having been milled to remove the bran. All rice contains protein, carbohydrate, vitamins and minerals, but no fat. The brown types also contain dietary fibre, which makes them a better choice nutritionally, but they do need longer cooking than white rice.

Some rice is sold as easy-cook, pre-cooked or pre-fluffed. This has usually been steam treated before the husk is removed. This helps retain some of the vitamins and minerals which would normally be removed with the husk and also helps to keep the grains separate during cooking.

### TYPES OF RICE

**Long grain rice** consists of slender grains about four times as long as they are wide. When cooked they become fluffy and dry and remain separate. Long grain rice is particularly suitable for savoury dishes. The two main types are *patna* and *basmati*. Basmati is the best rice to eat with Indian food, with its slimmer, dense grains giving a delicate nutty flavour when cooked. It should be rinsed before cooking to remove excess starch.

**Medium grain rice** is about three times as long as it is wide. It absorbs more liquid than long grain and is moister and stickier when cooked. It can be used in both sweet and savoury dishes.

**Short grain rice** has small, chalky round or oval grains which absorb a large quantity of liquid and produce a moist sticky mass when cooked. It is used mainly for milk puddings and other sweet dishes.

Italians use a special short grain rice, called *arborio* for making risottos (see recipe for Risotto alla Milanese, page 306). *Arborio* rice swells during cooking and the grains cling together—unlike most other savoury rice dishes in which long grain rice needs to be fluffy and the individual grains separate. It is available in specialist delicatessens and Italian shops. Two other varieties which can also be used for risottos are *superfino* and *avorio*, which are pre-fluffed and a golden yellow colour.

**Glutinous rice** (also sold as sticky or sweet rice) has oval cream-coloured grains which cook into a sticky mass. It is popular in Chinese and other eastern cuisines.

**Wild rice** is not rice at all but the seed of an aquatic grass. It has long dark brown grains which are cooked in the same way as long grain rice and served with savoury dishes. It is considerably more expensive than other types of rice, but has a very distinctive flavour.

### COOKING RICE

During cooking, the starch in rice swells, the grain softens and the rice increases to two or three times its original weight and bulk. Allow about 50 g (2 oz) uncooked rice per person as an accompaniment and about 40–50 g ($1\frac{1}{2}$–2 oz) when it is to be mixed with other ingredients.

Rice can be cooked either on the top of the stove or in the oven. Check when it is done by biting a grain between your teeth, like pasta it should be *al dente*. For easy-cook, pre-cooked or pre-fluffed rice, follow the manufacturer's instructions on the can or packet.

Cooked rice can be stored, covered, in the refrigerator for up to 1 week or frozen for up to 6 months. To reheat, either put it in a pan with a little water, steam in a colander over boiling water or place in a tightly covered greased dish in the oven.

## BOILED RICE

*3.4 litres (6 pints) water*

*salt*

*225 g (8 oz) long grain white rice*

**Method One**

**1.** Bring a large saucepan of water to a fast boil, then add salt and the rice.

**2.** Stir once to loosen the grains at the base of the pan, then leave uncovered to cook for 12 minutes, until tender.

**3.** Drain well, rinse with hot water and drain again. Pour into a warmed serving dish and separate the grains with a fork.

## Method Two

An alternative method is to use an exact amount of water which is completely absorbed by the rice. For this method allow 600 ml (1 pint) water, 5 ml (1 level tsp) salt to 225 g (8 oz) long grain white rice. Place the rice, salt and water in a large pan and bring quickly to the boil, stir well and cover with a tightly fitting lid. Reduce the heat and simmer gently for about 15 minutes or until tender and the water has been absorbed. Remove from the heat and separate the grains with a fork before serving. *Note* Cook brown rice in plenty of fast-boiling salted water for about 35 minutes until just tender. *Serves 4*

## Variations

Although rice is most usually cooked in water, it can also be cooked in other liquids to give extra flavour and variety. The water may be replaced by any of the following:
Chicken or beef stock (fresh or made from a cube), canned tomato juice, undiluted or used half-and half with water.

*HERBY RICE*
Add a pinch of dried herbs with the cooking liquid (eg sage, marjoram, thyme, mixed herbs).

*SAFFRON RICE*
Add a pinch of ground saffron to the cooking water to give the rice a delicate yellow colour.

Soak a good pinch of saffron strands in a little boiling water for 15 minutes, then add to the rice before cooking.

*TURMERIC RICE*
Also used to give rice a yellow colour, but add only a pinch of turmeric to the cooking water as it has a more pronounced colour.

## OVEN-COOKED RICE

*225 g (8 oz) long grain white rice*
*600 ml (1 pint) water*
*5 ml (1 level tsp) salt*

1. Place the rice in an ovenproof dish. Bring the water and salt to a fast boil, pour over the rice and stir well with a fork.
2. Cover tightly with a lid or foil and bake in the oven at 180°C (350°F) mark 4 for 35–40 minutes, or until the grains are just soft and all the cooking liquid has been absorbed by the rice. *Serves 4*

## SAVOURY RICE

*25 g (1 oz) butter or margarine*
*1 medium onion, skinned and chopped*
*1 medium pepper, seeded and chopped*
*1 celery stick, trimmed and chopped*
*2 rashers bacon, rinded and chopped*
*225 g (8 oz) long grain white rice*
*salt and pepper*
*600 ml (1 pint) water or Chicken Stock (see page 19)*

1. Melt the butter in a large saucepan, add the vegetables and bacon and fry gently for about 5 minutes, until soft.
2. Add the rice and seasoning and stir well. Cover with water or chicken stock. Bring to boil, cover and cook for about 15 minutes, until tender and liquid is absorbed. *Serves 4*

**Variations**
Add any of the following ingredients to the above:
50 g (2 oz) salami, finely diced
198 g (7 oz) can tuna, drained and flaked
200 g (7 oz) canned salmon, drained and flaked
100 g (4 oz) peeled prawns
1 medium canned pimiento, chopped
25 g (1 oz) toasted almonds, chopped
50 g (2 oz) button mushrooms, thinly sliced
2 spring onions, finely chopped
50 g (2 oz) frozen peas
15 ml (1 tbsp) soy sauce
1 garlic clove, skinned and crushed
pinch of turmeric

## CURRIED RICE

25 g (1 oz) butter or margarine

1 medium onion, skinned and finely chopped

225 g (8 oz) long grain white rice

25–50 g (1–2 oz) currants or seedless raisins

15 ml (1 tbsp) curry powder

600 ml (1 pint) Chicken Stock (see page 19)

salt and pepper

25 g (1 oz) blanched almonds, slivered and toasted
    (optional)

1. Melt the butter in a saucepan, add the onion and fry for about 5 minutes, until soft.
2. Add the rice and fry for a further 2–3 minutes, stirring all the time. Add the currants, curry powder, stock and seasoning and bring to the boil.
3. Stir and cover with a lid, reduce the heat and simmer gently for 15 minutes, until tender but still firm.
4. Stir in the almonds and spoon into a warmed serving dish.
Serves 4

## FRIED RICE

100 g (4 oz) long grain brown or white rice

2 eggs, beaten

60 ml (4 tbsp) vegetable oil

1 small onion, skinned and finely chopped

50 g (2 oz) mushrooms, thinly sliced

30 ml (2 tbsp) frozen peas

50 g (2 oz) cooked ham, diced

salt and pepper

10 ml (2 tsp) soy sauce

1. Cook the rice (see page 302).
2. Make an omelette from the eggs (see page 273), cut it into thin strips and set aside.
3. Heat 30 ml (2 tbsp) oil in a frying pan or wok, add the rice and fry for about 5 minutes, stirring gently all the time. Remove from the pan and set aside.
4. Fry the onion in the remaining oil for about 3 minutes until lightly browned, then add the remaining vegetables, rice, ham and seasoning and fry lightly for a further 3 minutes, stirring gently.
5. Stir in the soy sauce and shredded omelette. Serve the mixture as soon as it is hot.
Serves 2

**Variation**
FRIED RICE WITH SEAFOOD

175–225 g (6–8 oz) long grain brown rice

salt and pepper

75 g (3 oz) butter or margarine

1 medium onion, skinned and sliced

15 ml (1 level tbsp) mild curry powder

50 g (2 oz) salted peanuts

226 g (8 oz) packet frozen prawns, thawed

two 125 g (4¼ oz) cans mackerel fillets in oil, drained

50 g (2 oz) seedless raisins

1. Cook the rice until just tender. Drain well.
2. Melt the butter in a large frying pan, add the onion and fry gently for 5 minutes.
3. Stir in the curry powder with the nuts, prawns, mackerel, raisins, cooked rice and seasoning.
4. Fry over a moderate heat turning frequently, until heated through.
Serves 4

Fried Rice

*Paella*

# PAELLA

60 ml (4 tbsp) olive oil

6 chicken drumsticks

1 medium onion, skinned and chopped

1 garlic clove, skinned and crushed

225 g (8 oz) tomatoes, skinned and chopped

1 medium red or green pepper, seeded and finely sliced

112 g (4 oz) packet frozen peas

5 ml (1 level tsp) paprika

450 g (1 lb) Italian risotto rice or long grain white rice

few saffron strands

900 ml (1½ pints) Chicken Stock (see page 19)

600 ml (1 pint) mussels in their shells

100 g (4 oz) peeled prawns

salt and pepper

lemon wedges, to garnish

**1.** Heat the oil in a paella pan or large saucepan, add the drumsticks and fry for 15–20 minutes.
**2.** Remove from the pan with a slotted spoon and keep warm. Add the onion and garlic to the fat remaining in the pan and fry for 3–5 minutes.
**3.** Add the tomatoes, pepper, peas and paprika and cook, stirring, for 5 minutes.

**4.** Return the chicken to the pan, and stir in the rice, saffron and stock. Bring to the boil, stirring all the time. Reduce the heat and simmer uncovered for 20–25 minutes, or until most of the stock has been absorbed and the rice is tender.
**5.** Meanwhile, to prepare the mussels, put them in a large bowl and under running water, scrape off the mud, barnacles, seaweed and 'beards' with a small sharp knife. Discard any that are open. Rinse again until there is no trace of sand in the bowl.
**6.** Cook the prepared mussels in 1 cm (½ inch) of boiling salted water for 5 minutes. Drain.
**7.** Stir the mussels and prawns into the rice mixture and reheat for a further 5 minutes.
**8.** Season with salt and pepper. Arrange the lemon wedges around the rim of the pan and serve immediately.
*Serves 6*

**Variation**
A more elaborate paella may be made using the flesh of 1 small cooked lobster, about 700–900 g (1½–2 lb) in weight, and 12 clams, scrubbed and added to the pan and cooked for 5 minutes before cooking is complete (the clams should open in the steam, discard any that do not).

## Spiced Rice with Chicken

| |
|---|
| *1.4 kg (3 lb) oven-ready chicken* |
| *75 ml (5 tbsp) vegetable oil* |
| *2 medium onions, skinned and sliced* |
| *175 g (6 oz) long grain white rice* |
| *15 ml (3 level tsp) ground cumin* |
| *10 ml (2 level tsp) ground coriander* |
| *1.25 ml (¼ level tsp) chilli powder* |
| *2.5 ml (½ level tsp) ground turmeric* |
| *284 g (10 oz) natural yogurt* |
| *350 ml (12 fl oz) Chicken Stock (see page 19)* |
| *salt and pepper* |
| *parsley sprigs, to garnish* |

**1.** Remove flesh from chicken and cut into 2.5 cm (1 inch) pieces. Heat the oil in a flameproof casserole, add the chicken, half at a time, and fry until browned. Remove from the pan and set aside.
**2.** Add the onions to the casserole and lightly brown, then stir in the rice, spices, yogurt and stock. Season well and bring to the boil.
**3.** Return the chicken to the casserole, cover and bake in the oven at 170°C (325°F) mark 3 for about 35 minutes, or until the rice and chicken are tender and the liquid absorbed.
**4.** Stir the rice with a fork and garnish with parsley sprigs.
*Serves 4*

## Risotto alla Milanese

| |
|---|
| *1.1 litres (2 pints) Chicken or Beef Stock (see page 19)* |
| *75 g (3 oz) butter or margarine* |
| *1 small onion, skinned and finely chopped* |
| *350 g (12 oz) arborio rice (see page 302)* |
| *few saffron strands* |
| *salt and pepper* |
| *50 g (2 oz) Parmesan cheese, freshly grated* |

**1.** Bring the stock to the boil in a large saucepan and keep at barely simmering point.
**2.** Meanwhile, in a large, heavy-based saucepan, melt 25 g (1 oz) butter, add the onion and fry gently for 5 minutes, until soft but not coloured.
**3.** Add the arborio rice to the pan and stir with a fork for 2–3 minutes, until the rice is well coated with the butter.
**4.** Add a ladleful of stock to the pan, cook gently, stirring frequently, until the stock is absorbed. Add more stock as soon as each ladleful is absorbed, stirring frequently.
**5.** When the rice becomes creamy, sprinkle in the saffron with salt and pepper to taste. Continue adding stock and stirring until the risotto is thick, creamy and tender but not sticky. This process should take about 20–25 minutes to complete. It must not be hurried.
**6.** Just before serving, stir in the remaining butter and the Parmesan, then taste and adjust seasoning. Serve hot.
*Serves 4*

## Chicken and Prawn Risotto

| |
|---|
| *175 g (6 oz) chicken fillet, cut into 2.5 cm (1 inch) pieces* |
| *1 small onion, skinned and sliced* |
| *1 garlic clove, skinned and crushed* |
| *1 litre (1¾ pints) Chicken Stock (see page 19)* |
| *225 g (8 oz) brown rice* |
| *50 g (2 oz) small button mushrooms, wiped* |
| *pinch of ground saffron* |
| *salt and pepper* |
| *125 g (4 oz) peeled prawns* |
| *50 g (2 oz) petits pois* |
| *12 whole prawns, to garnish* |

**1.** Place all the ingredients except the prawns and petits pois in a large saucepan. Bring to the boil and simmer, uncovered, for 35 minutes, until the chicken is tender.
**2.** Stir in the prawns and petits pois. Cook over a high heat for about 5 minutes, stirring occasionally until most of the liquid has been absorbed.
**3.** Adjust seasoning. Place in a warmed serving dish and garnish with the whole prawns.
*Serves 4*

# BROWN RICE RISOTTO

45 ml (3 tbsp) vegetable oil

2 medium onions, skinned and sliced

225 g (8 oz) brown rice

5 ml (1 level tsp) ground turmeric

600 ml (1 pint) Chicken Stock (see page 19)

salt and pepper

chopped fresh parsley, to garnish

1. Heat the oil in a medium flameproof casserole, add the onions, rice and turmeric and fry gently for 1–2 minutes. Stir in the stock and seasoning and bring to the boil.

2. Cover the dish tightly and cook in the oven at 170°C (325°F) mark 3 for about 1 hour, until the rice is tender and the stock absorbed. Adjust the seasoning and garnish with plenty of chopped parsley.

*Serves 4*

# BASIC PILAU

50 g (2 oz) butter

225 g (8 oz) long grain white rice

750 ml (1¼ pints) boiling Chicken Stock (see page 19)

salt and pepper

knob of butter

1. Melt the butter in a saucepan, add the rice and gently fry for about 5 minutes, stirring all the time, until it looks transparent.

2. Add the stock, pouring it in slowly, as it will tend to bubble at first. Add the seasoning, stir well, cover with a tightly fitting lid and leave over a very low heat for about 15 minutes, until the water has been absorbed and the rice grains are just soft. (The idea is that the rice should cook in its own steam, so don't stir it while it is cooking.)

3. Remove the lid, cover the rice with a cloth, replace the lid and leave in a warm place for at least 15 minutes to dry out before serving. (This is a traditional part of making a pilau, although not included in many European versions of this dish.)

4. To serve, stir lightly with a fork to separate the grains, add a knob of butter and serve at once.

*Serves 4*

# SPICED FISH PILAU

25 g (1 oz) butter or margarine

2 medium onions, skinned and sliced

1 garlic clove, skinned and crushed

225 g (8 oz) long grain white rice

5 ml (1 level tsp) ground turmeric

2.5 ml (½ level tsp) ground coriander

2.5 ml (½ level tsp) ground cumin

salt and pepper

350 g (12 oz) tomatoes, skinned and roughly chopped

450 g (1 lb) coley fillet, skinned and cut into 2.5 cm
(1 inch) strips

7.5 ml (1½ tsp) chopped fresh mint or 2.5 ml (½ level
tsp) dried

300 ml (½ pint) Chicken Stock (see page 19) or water

fresh mint or parsley sprigs, to garnish

1. Melt the butter in a saucepan, add the onion and fry for 5 minutes.

2. Stir in the garlic and rice and fry until transparent. Add the spices, seasoning and tomatoes and cook for 1 minute.

3. Mix the coley with the mint. Spread some of the rice in the base of a 600 ml (1 pint) casserole which has tight-fitting lid. Alternate with layers of fish and rice, ending with a layer of rice.

4. Pour over the stock, cover tightly and cook in the oven at 180°C (350°F) mark 4 for about 45 minutes.

5. Stir through and garnish with mint or parsley sprigs.

*Serves 4*

# GNOCCHI This name is given to several different dishes. Gnocchi are small dumplings which are cooked in boiling water and served like pasta with a sauce. But the gnocchi mixture may also be spread in a dish, cooled and cut into rounds or squares. These are arranged in a dish, sprinkled with cheese and browned under the grill, then served with a sauce.

Gnocchi are sometimes made with flour, water and egg, or some or all of the flour can be replaced with semolina, cornmeal, cooked potato and grated raw potato.

## GNOCCHI ALLA ROMANA

568 ml (1 pint) milk

100 g (4 oz) fine semolina

salt and pepper

pinch of freshly grated nutmeg

1 egg, beaten

25 g (1 oz) butter or margarine

75 g (3 oz) Parmesan cheese, grated

little butter and extra grated cheese, for topping

grated cheese and Tomato Sauce (see page 209)

1. In a large saucepan, bring the milk to the boil, sprinkle in the semolina and seasonings and stir over a gentle heat until the mixture is really thick. Beat until smooth.
2. Remove from the heat and stir in the egg, butter and cheese. Return the pan to a low heat and stir for 1 minute.
3. Spread this mixture, about $\frac{1}{2}$–1 cm ($\frac{1}{4}$–$\frac{1}{2}$ inch) thick, in a shallow buttered dish and allow to cool. Cut into 2.5 cm (1 inch) rounds or squares and arrange in a shallow greased ovenproof dish.
4. Put a few knobs of butter over the top, sprinkle with a little extra cheese and brown under the grill or towards the top of the oven at 200°C (400°F) mark 6. Serve with cheese and Tomato Sauce.
*Serves 4*

## CHEESE GNOCCHI

225 g (8 oz) Ricotta, curd or full fat soft cheese, sieved

50 g (2 oz) butter or margarine

60 ml (4 level tbsp) grated Parmesan cheese

2 eggs, beaten

50–75 g (2–3 oz) flour

salt and pepper

pinch of freshly grated nutmeg

melted butter or margarine and grated Parmesan
    cheese, to serve

1. Mix all the ingredients together except the butter and cheese, and beat until smooth.
2. Dust your hands with flour and shape the dough into small balls. Roll them in flour, then chill in the refrigerator for 30 minutes.
3. To cook the gnocchi, poach about ten at a time in boiling salted water for about 5 minutes, until they rise to the top of the pan. Transfer to a warmed serving dish. Serve tossed in melted butter and sprinkled with grated Parmesan cheese.
*Serves 4*

## SPINACH GNOCCHI

450 g (1 lb) frozen spinach, thawed, drained and finely
    chopped

225 g (8 oz) Ricotta or curd cheese

2 eggs, beaten

225 g (8 oz) flour, plus extra for dusting

1.25 ml ($\frac{1}{4}$ level tsp) freshly grated nutmeg

100 g (4 oz) Parmesan cheese, freshly grated

salt and pepper

melted butter or margarine, to serve

1. Mix together the spinach, Ricotta, eggs, flour, nutmeg, half the Parmesan and seasoning.
2. Dust your hands with flour and shape the dough into small balls. Roll them in flour, then chill in the refrigerator for at least 30 minutes.
3. To cook the gnocchi, poach about ten at a time in boiling salted water for 5–10 minutes, until they rise to the top of the pan.
4. Serve tossed in melted butter and sprinkled with the remaining Parmesan.
*Serves 4*

# FRUIT AND NUTS

*I*mproved methods of storage and transport mean that a wide variety of fresh fruit is now available all year round.

Fruit is important both as a source of dietary fibre and of Vitamin C, and nutritionists stress that everyone should eat more fresh fruit and less sugar-laden confectionery. This chapter shows you how to choose and use familiar and unfamiliar fruits.

♦

## APPLES

The many varieties of apples can be divided into two groups: dessert and cooking. Dessert apples often have more flavour than cooking apples. *Cox's Orange Pippin, Newton Wonder, Laxton Superb, Worcester Pearmain* and *Granny Smith* are all popular dessert apples with distinctive flavours.

Cooking apples are too tart to eat on their own, but are delicious cooked with sugar. Look for *Bramley's Seedling, Lord Derby* and *Grenadier*.

Choose firm apples with unblemished skins. Keep apples cool and dry. Apples kept at room temperature should be eaten within 2 weeks.

Wipe and wash dessert apples before using. They make good additions to raw fruit salads, or they can be used in pies, tarts and puddings or served with cheese. Apple slices should be brushed with lemon juice to prevent browning.

## APRICOTS

These are stone fruits, round and about the size of a plum with velvety, yellowish-orange skin and fairly soft, juicy flesh of much the same colour. Unripe apricots are hard and sour; over-ripe ones mealy and tasteless. Choose firm, unwrinkled fruit with a deep colour or leave unripened fruit to ripen at room temperature. Once ripe they should be eaten within 2–3 days.

Prepare apricots by washing, cutting them in half and removing the stone. To peel apricots, blanch in boiling water for 30 seconds to loosen the skins, then peel. Sliced apricots should be brushed with lemon juice to prevent browning.

Serve apricots raw as a dessert or halve, stone and poach in syrup or use in puddings and pies. They also make very good jam.

## AVOCADOS

These are the fruit of a tree grown in sub-tropical climates. They are the same shape as pears and have a shiny green or bumpy purple-brown skin according to variety. They have a soft, oily, pale green flesh of the consistency of butter and have a large central stone.

A ripe avocado always 'gives' slightly when pressed at the pointed end. A hard, under-ripe avocado will ripen in 1–2 days if kept at room temperature or in about a week in the refrigerator.

To open an avocado, cut in half lengthways and turn the halves in opposite directions until they come apart. Brush the slices with lemon juice to prevent browning.

Avocados are normally eaten as a savoury, either as a starter or in salads, or they can be made into dips and mousses.

## BANANAS

Tropical fruit with bright yellow skins and pale, sweet flesh. Bananas are picked in large bunches called 'hands' when they are still hard and green, but they have usually turned yellow by the time they reach the shops.

Choose bananas with evenly coloured skins. They are ready to eat when yellow and slightly flecked brown. Black patches on the surface indicate the fruit is over-ripe. They will ripen if kept in the dark (such as in a bag) at room temperature.

Once peeled, bananas should be brushed with lemon juice to prevent browning. They can be eaten raw, used in sweet and savoury salads, cakes, ice creams, and in various Indian and Chinese dishes. They can also be baked or fried in butter or made into fritters. For cooking, choose slightly under-ripe fruit as they slice better. Green bananas are also cooked as vegetables either by frying, boiling or baking whole in their skins.

Plantains, which are related to bananas, are unsuitable for eating raw but are used widely in West Indian cooking in soups and stews. They have a higher starch and lower sugar content than ordinary bananas.

## BILBERRIES (BLUEBERRIES, WHORTLEBERRIES OR HUCKLEBERRIES)

Bilberries are small dark blue or mauve berries which grow on open moorland and are also cultivated. They may also be sold as whortleberries or huckleberries. Blueberries which come mostly from America are plumper, sweeter and juicier.

To prepare, remove the stalk and any leaves, rinse under cold running water and dry thoroughly. Ripe berries can be kept in a covered container in the refrigerator for a week or so.

Bilberries can be eaten raw, though they have a distinctive acid taste or they can be stewed with sugar, cooked in pies or made into jam.

## BLACKBERRIES

These small soft fruit, dark red to black in colour, are available wild and cultivated. The cultivated varieties tend to be larger and juicier.

Once picked, blackberries lose their flavour rapidly and should be eaten on the day of purchase.

To prepare, wash them and remove the stalks. They can be eaten raw, stewed (they are especially good cooked with apple), included in fruit puddings and pies or made into jams and jellies.

## CAPE GOOSEBERRIES (CHINESE LANTERN)

These are the fruit of the Chinese lantern and get their name from the lantern-shaped papery calyx which surrounds each fruit. They are round and golden with juicy flesh which has a delicate, scented flavour and many edible seeds.

To prepare, remove the skin and eat raw or cook in pies or compotes.

Canned cape gooseberries are usually labelled goldenberries.

## CHERRIES

Cherries vary in colour from white, through red to a very dark red. They are mainly eaten raw but some varieties have sour flesh and are used for pies and jams. Popular varieties of sweet cherries are *Napoleon Bigarreau*, *Frogmore Early*, *Merton Heart* and *White Heart*. The best variety for cooking is *Morello*.

Avoid split, diseased or immature fruit. Look for large soft berries for eating raw. Remove the stalks and rinse the fruit in a colander. The stones can be removed with a cherry stoner or the fruit can be slit with the point of a knife and the stones prised out.

## COCONUTS

These are the nuts of the coconut palm with hard, hairy brown shells containing sweet white flesh and a liquid called coconut milk which makes a delicious drink. When choosing, test a coconut for freshness by shaking it to make sure it contains liquid.

To prepare a coconut, puncture the shell with a hammer and screwdriver at the top of the nut where there are three indentations (eyes). Drain off the milk. Store, covered, in the refrigerator for up to 2 days. Crack the shell by hitting the widest part of the coconut all around. Separate the halves and prise the flesh from the shell with a small sharp knife. The flesh can be eaten raw, puréed in a blender with the milk to make coconut cream or it can be shredded and used as an ingredient in baking or oriental cooking. Freshly grated coconut can be toasted in the oven at 180°C (350°F) mark 4 until golden brown. It can be stored for up to 4 days.

### CRAB APPLES

The common European crab is the original wild apple. The small fruit have a shiny red or yellow skin and firm flesh, which is usually very sour. They are chiefly used to make jelly and other preserves.

### CRANBERRIES

These small American fruit are similar to bilberries but with skins coloured pink to dark red. The flesh is sharp-tasting and cranberries are mostly used for sauces and jellies to serve with poultry and game or in tarts and puddings. Americans traditionally serve turkey with Cranberry Sauce (see page 208).

To prepare cranberries, remove all the stalks and any leaves and rinse well under cold running water.

### CURRANTS

Currants are small fruit which may be black, red or white. Blackcurrants are more common than red or white. They are normally on a strip or stalk and are more expensive when not. Avoid withered or dusty currants; choose only ones with a distinct gloss.

To remove currants from the stalks, use a fork to rake them off.

Blackcurrants have a rich flavour but tend to be slightly sour; they are best known for their use in making the liqueur cassis and other drinks, but can also be used in puddings and pies. Redcurrants are sweeter and can be eaten raw, but are mainly used in preserves, syrups and puddings. Whitecurrants are less common than other varieties, but are similar in flavour to redcurrants, although slightly less acid and can be used in the same ways.

### CUSTARD APPLES

These are a group of tropical fruit also known as Anona fruit. They include *cherimoyas*, *sweet sops*, *sour sops* and *bullocks' hearts*. They look similar to apples with green, purple-green or yellow-brown skin and flesh that varies from sweet to acid. The best known variety is cherimoya, which has a patterned skin and pineapple flavoured flesh the colour and texture of custard.

To prepare, cut off the top and remove the flesh, discarding the seeds. Use in fruit salads, ice cream and creamy sweets.

### DATES

Dates are the fruit of the date palm tree with firm sweet flesh and a long inedible stone.

Dates are mainly cultivated in the deserts of Tunisia and Southern Algeria.

Fresh dates should be plump and shiny, with smooth golden brown skins. Squeeze the stem end to remove the tough skin, then slit open and remove the stone. Dates can be eaten raw, used in salads or sweets or may be stuffed with cream cheese.

### DURIANS

These very large fruit can weigh up to 9 kg (20 lb). They have a thick dull yellow skin covered with rough spines and a cream coloured flesh which has an unpleasant smell but delicious taste.

To prepare, slit the fruit at segment joints with a sharp knife and prise open, taking care of the sharp spines. The flesh can be eaten raw or added to Indonesian rice and meat dishes. The large seeds can be lightly roasted and eaten like nuts.

### ELDERBERRIES

These are the fruit of the elder tree which grows wild in hedgerows and similar places. The berries are small, round and shiny, almost black in colour, and ripen in late summer. Elderberries are used to make elderberry wine or preserves.

### FEIJOAS (PINEAPPLE GUAVA)

These are large berries native to Brazil but are now also grown in New Zealand. They have a tough reddish-green skin, scented flesh and a soft centre containing edible seeds. They taste like a combination of pineapple, strawberry and guava.

They are ripe when slightly soft and sweet smelling. Peel off the thin outer skin. The rest of the fruit can be eaten, either raw, sliced into fruit salads or made into jams or jellies.

### FIGS

There are green, white, purple or black varieties of figs. They have juicy flesh full of tiny edible seeds. Most figs have thin skins which are edible.

Figs are available fresh or dried. Fresh fruit

should be soft to the touch and have skins with a distinct bloom. To prepare, rinse, remove the stalk and eat as a dessert.

### GOOSEBERRIES

There are many varieties, round or long, hairy or smooth, cooking or dessert. Cooking gooseberries are usually green with very sour, firm flesh and a fairly large number of edible seeds. Dessert gooseberries can be green, yellow-white or russet colour, often with hairy skin and usually with soft pulpy flesh and large seeds.

Choose evenly coloured fruit, keep it refrigerated and eat within 3 days. Wash the berries and snip off the stem and flower ends (top and tail). Dessert varieties can be eaten raw; cooking varieties can be used in pies, puddings and for jam.

### GRAPEFRUIT

These large citrus fruits with thick yellow skins may have either yellow or pink flesh. The pink fleshed varieties are sweeter than the yellow.

They will keep for 4 days at room temperature or 2 weeks in the refrigerator. Prepare grapefruit by cutting in half and separating the flesh from the skin with a serrated knife, then divide the segments.

Grapefruit can be eaten raw on their own or with other fruits or used to make mixed fruit marmalades. They are often used in slimming diets as they are believed to contain an enzyme which stimulates the metabolism.

### GRAPES

Grapes can range from pale amber to a deep blue colour. Popular dessert varieties include *Muscat* with white or golden coloured berries, *Almeria*, with golden-yellow or pale green berries and *Alicante* with purple-black berries.

Choose plump, unbruised grapes with a distinct bloom to them; where possible buy in bunches and avoid any with shrivelled or squashed berries or any with signs of mould near the stem. Keep grapes refrigerated and use within 3 days. They should be left unwashed until ready to serve.

Grapes can be used in fruit salads and other raw fruit dishes; they are rarely cooked. Pips can be removed by halving the fruit with a knife and flicking out the pips with the point of a knife. To leave the fruit whole, push the tip of a skewer into the grape and push out the pips.

### GUAVAS

Tropical fruit of South American and Indian origin, which may be round or pear-shaped. They have whitish-yellow to red skins and musky smelling flesh containing edible seeds.

Choose firm, unblemished fruit. To prepare, cut in half and peel. Guavas can be eaten raw—they have one of the highest vitamin C contents of all fruit—or they can be baked.

### JACKFRUIT

Widely cultivated in the tropical lowlands of Asia, Africa and America, jackfruit can grow up to 31.75 kg (70 lb) in weight. They have a rough, spiky green skin and yellow fibrous flesh which contains juicy pulp surrounding walnut-sized seeds.

The pulp tastes like a cross between banana and pineapple with the texture of lychee.

To prepare, remove the skin and eat the pulp, discarding the seeds.

### JAPONICAS

The fruit of the japonica tree is the ornamental version of the quince. They do not always ripen on the tree but can be picked whilst green and stored for about a month until they begin to turn slightly yellow. They have a distinctive flavour and are often mixed with apples in a pie or when stewed or can be made into jelly.

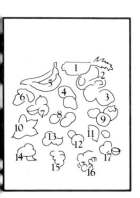

**Key**
1. Pineapple; 2. Papayas; 3. Custard Apples; 4. Mangoes—yellow and green; 5. Green Bananas and Plantain; 6. Guavas; 7. Pomegranates; 8. Kiwi Fruit; 9. Persimmons; 10. Prickly Pears; 11. Tamarillos; 12. Medlars; 13. Figs; 14. Dates; 15. Kumquats; 16. Cape Gooseberries (Chinese Lanterns); 17. Passion Fruit.

### KIWI FRUIT (CHINESE GOOSEBERRY)

Kiwi fruit are egg-shaped fruit with brown hairy skins and bright green flesh pitted with edible black seeds. They are grown mainly in New Zealand.

Choose firm fruit. Cut in half and eat with a teaspoon or peel and slice to use in fruit or savoury salads or as an attractive decoration. Kiwi fruit is usually eaten raw but can be poached. It has a very high vitamin C content.

### LEMONS

Lemons have many culinary uses, although they are too acid to eat raw on their own. Look for lemons which are a strong 'lemon yellow' colour, have a moist looking skin and feel heavy for their size. A shrivelled skin indicates that some of the juice has evaporated.

When grating lemon rind, make sure that none of the bitter tasting white pith is grated. To thinly pare lemons, peel the rind with a vegetable peeler, avoiding any white pith.

The rind and juice can be used in puddings, cakes, pies, fruit drinks and in preserves such as lemon curd and marmalade, as well as in many savoury dishes and sauces. Lemon juice is an excellent source of pectin and is used in jams.

### LIMES

Limes are like small lemons but with greener skin and a stronger, sharper flavour. Prepare in the same way as lemons. The juice and rind are used in some ice creams and sorbets, curries and preserves.

### LOGANBERRIES AND TAYBERRIES

Loganberries are a hybrid of a blackberry and a raspberry. They are dark red with a flavour similar to raspberries but stronger. Tayberries are a hybrid of loganberries and blackberries. Both these fruits can be used in the same way as raspberries.

### LOQUATS (JAPANESE MEDLAR)

Originally an oriental fruit, loquats are now grown in Mediterranean countries and the US. They look similar to a small plum with sweet, scented, slightly tart flesh. The seeds are

within the large stone. Look for firm fruit with smooth golden yellow skins. To eat raw, cut crossways and remove the stone. The outer skin can be eaten. To cook, remove the stone, quarter the fruit and poach in a light syrup. Skin them, if wished, and serve chilled. Loquats can also be made into preserves.

### LYCHEES

Originally a Chinese fruit, lychees are now grown in many other countries. They are stone fruit the size of plums, which grow in bunches. They have hard skins, ranging from pink to brown, and sweet, juicy white flesh.

Avoid fruit with shrivelled dry skins. Peel and eat raw, discarding the skin and stone, or serve in fruit salads, with Chinese dishes or poach in syrup and serve chilled.

### MANGOES

Mangoes are large stone fruit which grow all over the tropical and sub-tropical regions of the world. Some are round, others long and narrow or pear-shaped. Their juicy fibrous flesh has a distinctive, delicate flavour.

Ripe mangoes are very juicy with a yellow or orange skin and 'give' if gently squeezed. Avoid soft or shrivelled mangoes. Ripe mangoes are best used within 3 days.

To prepare, cut a large slice from one side of the fruit cutting close to the stone. Cut another slice from the opposite side. Cut the flesh in the segments lengthways and crossways without breaking the skin, then push the skin inside out to expose the cubes of flesh. Peel the remaining centre section and cut the flesh away from the stone in chunks or slices.

Mangoes can be served with ice cream, added to fruit salads, or puréed for mousses or ice cream. Green, unripe mangoes, can be made into chutney.

## MANGOSTEENS

Tropical fruit with a deep purple, fibrous outer shell and juicy segments of creamy white flesh.

To prepare, cut the shell through the centre and remove the top part to reveal the fruit which can be eaten raw.

## MEDLARS

These are small brown fruit about the size of an apple with sharp-flavoured flesh.

The fruit is ripe when soft and almost disintegrating. To prepare, wash and halve and spoon out the flesh which can be eaten raw or used to make preserves.

## MELONS

Depending on the variety, melons can be smooth skinned or have a light or heavy netting. All melons have perfumed, sweet juicy flesh; usually the more fragrant the melon, the sweeter and juicier its flesh.

Melons should feel heavy for their size and slightly soft at the stalk end when ripe. Soft patches on the rind indicate bruising rather than ripeness. Some varieties smell fragrant when ripe. Melons should be stored tightly wrapped in the refrigerator as they can easily pick up the flavours of other foods. Buy slices or wedges only if they have been kept with the cut surface covered with cling film.

The flesh is usually eaten raw; cut in wedges and discard the seeds. Melon can be served as a starter, sometimes with smoked ham or other cold meat, or as a dessert, or it can be puréed for ice creams and sorbets. The following are the best-known types:

**Charentais** Small round melons with green skin and fragrant orange flesh.

**Cantaloupe** Has a green to yellow rough, segmented skin. The flesh is orange-yellow and extremely fragrant.

**Galia** Round with green flesh and a lightly netted skin which ranges from green to yellow.

**Honeydew** Oval in shape, usually with bright yellow skin. The flesh is pale green, sweet and delicate tasting.

**Ogen** Round with yellow to orange skin marked with faint green stripes and very sweet juicy flesh.

**Watermelons** Large round or oblong melons with dark green or striped green and yellow skin and pink to deep red watery flesh with black inedible seeds.

## MULBERRIES

Similar in shape to a blackberry but larger; the two most common varieties are the black and white. Black mulberries are a wine-red colour with a sharp flavour; white mulberries are sweeter.

They require careful washing. Place in a colander and dip into a bowl of water once or twice, then leave to dry in the colander. They are generally eaten raw or used to make jams and wines.

## NECTARINES

Nectarines are a variety of peach, but with a smooth skin that is a brighter red-orange colour.

Look for plump rich-coloured fruit softening along the indent. Avoid hard, extremely soft or shrivelled fruit. Nectarines will ripen at room temperature but once ripe should be refrigerated and used within 5 days.

To prepare, simply wash then brush the exposed flesh with lemon juice to prevent browning. Eat on their own, in fruit salads or made into jams.

## ORANGES

These are the best-known of the citrus fruits and are high in vitamin C. There are two main types; bitter and sweet. The two main bitter varieties, which are never eaten raw, are *Seville*, which are used for making marmalade and occasionally in meat and fish dishes, and *Bergamot*, which are used for perfumes and for extracting their oil. Sweet oranges include *Jaffas*, *Navels*, *Bloods* and *Valencia Lates*. They are very juicy and can be squeezed for their juice or sliced for fruit salads.

Choose firm fruit that feel heavy and have a glossy skin. Avoid ones with hard or dry-looking skins. Oranges will keep for 4 days at room temperature and if wrapped and stored in the refrigerator they will keep for at least 2 weeks.

When serving sliced oranges, remove the white pith and peel. To use orange peel in cooking, peel the rind with a vegetable peeler avoiding any white pith, then blanch the peel for 3 minutes, rinse under cold water and then shred before using.

In addition to the bitter and sweet types there are several small varieties of oranges:

**Mandarins and tangerines**, generally thought of as being the same thing, are smaller than oranges and have loose skin which is easy to remove.

**Satsumas** are similar to tangerines but contain no pips.

**Clementines** are similar to satsumas and tangerines but are smaller with stiffer skin with a few pips.

**Ortaniques** have a thin orange-yellow skin and sweet flesh.

**Tangelos** (*ugli fruit*) are a cross between a tangerine and a grapefruit.

**Mineolas** are smaller than tangelos and taste sweeter and more orangey.

**Kumquats** are tiny oranges about half the size of plums which are eaten whole, peel and pips included.

### PAPAYAS (PAW PAW)

Large tropical fruit with smooth skins which ripen from green to yellow or orange. They have juicy orange-pink flesh the texture of avocado with lots of black inedible seeds in the centre.

They are ripe when the skin is yellow and feels soft. Prepare and use like a melon, removing the seeds. Serve in wedges or add to fruit salads.

### PASSION FRUIT

These are tropical vine fruit that look like large wrinkled plums. The inedible skin is deeply wrinkled when ripe. The yellow flesh is sweet and juicy and pitted with small edible black seeds.

To eat raw, cut in half and scoop out the flesh with a spoon. The juice can be used to make drinks or flavour ice cream.

### PEACHES

Peaches can be roughly divided into two main types, the 'freestone' type with a stone that separates easily from the flesh, which are good for eating, and the 'clingstone' type, which are good for cooking. The 'freestone' type can either be eaten on their own as a dessert or added to fruit salads; 'clingstones' can be poached or made into jams or chutneys.

Ripe peaches are slightly soft and have a yellow to orange skin. Avoid green, bruised or 'sale' fruit. Eat within 2 days if kept at room temperature or if wrapped and kept in the refrigerator within 5 days. Peaches can be peeled by immersing them in boiling water for about 15 seconds, then cooling in cold water. Very ripe peaches are best skinned and stoned under running water, as scalding them will soften and slightly discolour the flesh. Brush cut fruit with lemon juice to prevent browning.

### PERSIMMONS (SHARON FRUIT)

Large tomato-like fruit with leathery skins which turn from yellow to bright orangey red. The most common variety of persimmon found in the UK is the *sharon fruit*. Unlike other persimmons, it is seedless and both skin and the flesh can be eaten.

To prepare, wash the fruit and slice. The flesh can be spooned out and added to fruit salads or puréed and used in ice creams and mousses.

### PEARS

There are many varieties of pears, each with a different shape, size and colour. Most ripe pears are suitable for eating raw; *Williams*, *Conference*, *Comice* and *Lacton's* are good dessert pears.

Choose well formed firm pears with no oozing or softness. Ripe pears 'give' a little at the stem end. They become overripe very quickly so are best refrigerated and eaten within 3 days.

Pears can be eaten with cheese or added to fruit salads. Smaller firm pears can be stewed or puréed. Prepare pears by washing and peeling. Brush peeled pears with lemon juice to prevent browning.

### PINEAPPLES

Large oval fruit with hard knobbly skins that grow in most tropical and sub-tropical countries. The skin varies from deep yellow to orange-brown.

Ripe pineapples give off a sweet aroma and a leaf pulls easily from the crown. Avoid pineapples that are bruised, discoloured or have wilting leaves. Pineapples continue to ripen after picking and are often sold slightly unripe. However an unripe fruit with no aroma will not ripen properly.

To prepare, cut off the leaf crown and cut the fruit into thick slices crossways. Trim off the outer skin and remove the brown spots from the flesh. Remove the central core.

The flesh can be eaten raw on its own or mixed with other fruit. Pineapple can also be served with ham or bacon. Alternatively, cut off the leaf crown and carefully cut out the flesh in chunks, leaving skin intact to use as a bowl for fruit salad.

## PLUMS

There are many different varieties of this stone fruit, varying in size and colour of skin and flesh. Sweet plums can be eaten raw on their own or added to fruit salads, and all varieties can be cooked. They can be stewed, used in pies and puddings or made into preserves. To prepare, wash and halve the plums.

**Greengages** are sweet, amber-coloured plums with a good flavour.

**Damsons** are small dark blue to purple coloured plums with yellow flesh. They need to be cooked as they are sour. They are usually stewed, made into pies or preserves, particularly Damson Cheese.

**Cherry plums** are usually stewed or bottled.

## POMEGRANATES

Pomegranates are the size of oranges with thin, tough pink or red rind and juicy red flesh packed with seeds.

Buy fruit with hard undamaged skins. Keep refrigerated and use within 7 days. To prepare, cut a slice off the stem end, then slice the skin sections lengthways and draw the sections apart. The seeds can be eaten or juiced—the juice is purple and pleasantly sharp. Pomegranates are used in Middle Eastern dishes, soups and stews. The seeds can be used to decorate some dishes.

## PRICKLY PEARS (INDIAN FIG)

This pear-shaped fruit with a greenish-orange skin is covered with fine, needle-sharp prickles. The sweet juicy pink flesh has edible seeds.

These have to be prepared carefully because of the prickles. Wash and scrub off the prickles, cut off each end, slice downwards and peel back the skin. Slice the flesh and serve with a squeeze of lemon juice.

## QUINCES

Small, pear-shaped fruit with yellow skin and scented flesh. Avoid scabby, split or very small fruit. They make good jams and jellies or they can be stewed with apples and pears. Simply peel and slice.

## RAMBUTANS

These are the dark red-brown fruit of an Indonesian tree. The shell, which is covered with soft spines, is peeled off to reveal white translucent flesh similar in taste to a lychee. It can be eaten on its own, or chopped and added to fruit salads.

## RASPBERRIES

Soft juicy fruit with a central hull, raspberries have a delicious sweet yet slightly acidic flavour. Most raspberries are red, but white and black varieties are also available.

Raspberries are sold hulled which makes them liable to crushing. When buying, avoid stained containers and wet fruit. After damp weather they are likely to go mouldy quickly. They can be eaten fresh with cream, used in desserts with other fruit, lightly stewed or made into jams.

## RHUBARB

Rhubarb is officially a vegetable as it is the stem of a plant, but it is always eaten in sweet dishes. Forced rhubarb is pink and tender looking and sweet tasting; maincrop rhubarb has a stronger colour, a thicker stem and is more acid tasting. Look for young pink rhubarb; once the stems are thick and green they are coarse and acid tasting.

To prepare, cut off the leaves and root, then wash and chop the stems. Rhubarb is always cooked and can be used for pies, puddings and jams. The leaves must not be eaten as they are poisonous.

## SLOES

Sloes are the small, round, bluish-black fruit of the blackthorn tree which grows wild. They are used to make Sloe Gin and country wines.

## STAR FRUIT (CARAMBOLOS)

Fluted yellow, waxy-looking fruit with a sweet and sour taste which forms star shapes when sliced.

To prepare, peel off the skin and slice, eat on its own or add to fruit salads.

### STRAWBERRIES

Widely grown in the UK, strawberries are one of the most popular summer fruits. The juicy red fruit grows round a central hull and has tiny seeds embedded in the outer surface.

When buying, check the base of the punnet for staining as this indicates squashed fruit. Buy plump glossy berries with the green hulls still attached. Only wash the strawberries just before hulling.

Strawberries can be eaten raw or stewed and used in flans, pies and/or made into a variety of preserves.

### TAMARILLOS

The large yellow or red hard fruit are related to the tomato and the kiwi fruit.

Peel and eat raw, including the edible seeds, or add to fruit salads.

# DRIED FRUIT
Drying fruit is one of the oldest ways of preserving it and, although the methods have changed—much of the dried fruit is now dried by artificial heat rather than the sun—the principle is the same. The water content is drawn out, preventing the growth of mould and bacteria and leaving the natural sugar in the fruit to act as a preservative. Most dried fruit needs washing and soaking for at least 3 hours, and preferably overnight, before using.

### APPLES

Apples are one of the few fruits which do not lose any vitamin C content in the drying process. They are usually sold as rings and can be eaten as a snack, added to muesli and other breakfast cereals, or they can be soaked and used to make purées or added to other fruits in crumbles and pies.

### APRICOTS

The flavour of dried apricots is often better than the fresh fruit. Some types are specially tenderised so that there is no need to soak them before use. They can be used for fruit salads, purées, pies, sauces and stuffings.

### BANANAS

Bananas are peeled and dried whole or sliced lengthways. Soak and use in compotes, fruit salads or in baking, especially teabreads.

### DATES

Dried dates are available whole with stones or as pressed blocks of stoned fruit. Whole dates can be stoned and used without soaking for teabreads. The pressed blocks need to be soaked overnight and are best used for puddings, breads and cakes. Chopped dates rolled in sugar are also available and these can be used in baking without soaking.

### FIGS

Dried figs may be sold loose or in pressed blocks. They should not be too sticky. Soak and use to make compotes, fruit salads or hot puddings or use without soaking in biscuits, cakes or scones.

### PEACHES

Unlike apricots, dried peaches lack the flavour of the fresh fruit. They are usually sold in packets of mixed dried fruits. Soak and use in fruit salads, pies, teabreads, crumble toppings and stuffings for poultry.

### PEARS

These are also usually sold in packets of dried mixed fruit and can be used in the same way as peaches.

### PRUNES

These are whole dried plums, with or without the stones. Some varieties are tenderised and do not need soaking before using; otherwise, soak in cold tea or red wine rather than water for a better flavour.

They can be eaten on their own or they can be used in biscuits, puddings, cakes and stuffings.

### VINE FRUITS

Currants, raisins and sultanas are all types of dried grapes. They do not need soaking and are often sold pre-washed. Currants are dried small black seedless grapes. Seedless raisins are dried seedless grapes and are the most popular type for cooking. The largest and sweetest raisins come from the Spanish Muscatel grapes. Sultanas are dried small white seedless grapes.

The main use of all the vine fruits is in baking, such as cakes and steamed puddings, and desserts.

# NUTS

The term nut is used to describe any seed or fruit with an edible kernel inside a hard shell. Nuts are a highly concentrated food, rich in protein, vitamins, minerals, fats and fibre. As well as being popular snacks, they are widely used in baking, sauces and sweet making. Mixed with vegetables, they make a good substitute for meat, fish and eggs.

Shelled, flaked, chopped and ground nuts are best bought loose in small quantities or vacuum packed. Store them in airtight containers, preferably in the refrigerator. Nuts bought in their shells should feel heavy; if they feel light they are likely to be stale. Store them in a cool, dark place for up to 3 months.

## ALMONDS

Almonds are the seeds of a tree belonging to the peach family which grows in hot dry climates such as Sicily, Spain and California. There are two varieties of almonds—bitter and sweet. Bitter almonds contain prussic acid and are seldom eaten raw (if they are eaten, they must only be eaten in small quantities). They are used mainly for making essences and oils.

Sweet almonds are available in their shells at Christmas and shelled the rest of the year.

Whole and split almonds are used in baking—whole almonds are a traditional decoration for Dundee Cake. Flaked almonds are often toasted and used as a garnish or decoration. Ground almonds are used to make Almond Paste (see page 495) and Macaroons.

To blanch almonds, cover with boiling water and leave for 10 seconds, then rinse in cold water and rub off the skin.

## BRAZIL NUTS

These are large, oval, creamy-coloured nuts with a high percentage of fat. They grow, grouped together in their individual shells, inside the round fruit of a South American tree.

They are eaten raw, used in sweet making or added to vegetarian dishes, such as nut roasts and rissoles.

## CASHEW NUTS

These whitish-coloured nuts come from the tropical cashew tree. The tree bears reddish pear-shaped fruit and one kidney-shaped nut grows from the base of each fruit. As there is toxic oil in the shells of cashews, they are always sold shelled.

They are sold whole (often salted), in pieces, or roasted. They have a slightly crumbly texture and delicate sweet flavour. They are often served with drinks or used in stir-fried dishes.

## CHESTNUTS

These are the fruit of the sweet chestnut tree, which grows mainly in European countries. They are sold in their skins, dried, cooked and canned or as a purée (sweetened or unsweetened) in cans or tubes. Chestnuts in their skins must be peeled and cooked before eating.

To peel, make a tiny slit in the skin near the pointed end, then cover with boiling water and leave for 5 minutes. Remove from the water, one at a time, and peel off the thick outer skin and thin inner skin while warm. To cook, simmer the peeled nuts for 30–40 minutes. Alternatively, bake the nuts in their skins in the oven at 200°C (400°F) mark 6 for 20 minutes, then peel.

Chestnuts have a rich flavour and are used to make soups and stuffings, served with vegetables such as Brussels sprouts and cabbage or preserved in sugar to make Marrons Glacés (see page 503). Chestnut purée is used in gateaux and desserts. Dried chestnuts should be soaked in hot water for 30 minutes, then cooked and used as for raw chestnuts.

## HAZELNUTS

Hazelnuts, filberts and cobs are all fruits of different varieties of hazel tree. Cobs are not as common as the other two. They are available in their shells, as shelled whole nuts (plain or roasted), flaked or ground. Remove the skin as for Almonds.

Hazelnuts have a distinct flavour which goes well with chocolate; they are often used in sweet making.

## PEANUTS (GROUND NUTS, MONKEY NUTS)

Peanuts are a type of underground bean which grows in India, Africa and parts of America and the Far East. They consist of two kernels which grow in a crinkly shell. They are available as whole nuts roasted in their shells or as shelled nuts,

which may be plain, dry roasted or roasted and salted. Ground peanuts are used to make peanut butter. Peanuts are also used to make oil (usually called groundnut oil).

They are the most popular nuts for eating as snacks. They can be added to salads or used in vegetable dishes. Peanut butter, as well as being a spread, can be used in biscuits and sauces.

### PECAN NUTS

Pecan nuts belong to the walnut family and grow in North America where they are also known as hickory nuts. They are available in their shells or shelled.

They are used to make Pecan Pie, but can be used instead of walnuts in any recipe.

### PINE NUTS (PINE KERNELS, INDIAN NUTS, PIGNOLIAS, PIGNOLI)

These are the small, pale cream-coloured seeds of the Mediterranean pine tree. They are always sold shelled and may be roasted and salted. They have a strong resinous flavour and soft oily texture.

They are popular in Middle Eastern rice dishes and stuffings and are also used to make the Italian Pesto Sauce (see page 262). They can also be eaten raw, sprinkled over cooked vegetables or added to fruit salads.

### PISTACHIO NUTS

These are the fruit of a small tree native to the Middle East and Central Asia, but now grown in other parts of the world. The bright green kernels have purple skins and beige-coloured shells. The shell splits when the kernels are ripe.

They are available in their shells or shelled (plain or salted). Skin as for Almonds. They can be eaten as a snack or used as a colourful garnish or ingredient in sweets, ice creams, pâtés, terrines and rice dishes.

**Key**
1. Figs; 2. Peaches; 3. Pears; 4. Apricots and Hunza Apricots; 5. Apple Rings; 6. Bananas; 7. Banana Chips; 8. Dates; 9. Raisins; 10. Sultanas; 11. Currants; 12. Prunes; 13. Pistachio Nuts; 14. Hazelnuts; 15. Chestnuts; 16. Cashews; 17. Peanuts; 18. Almonds; 19. Pine Kernels; 20. Brazils; 21. Tiger Nuts; 22. Pumpkin Seeds; 23. Pecans; 24. Walnuts.

### WALNUTS

These are one of the most popular nuts and are grown in many parts of the world. They have a round, crinkly shell with a wrinkled looking kernel.

They are available in their shells, shelled, chopped or ground. Fresh unripe green walnuts are sometimes available pickled in jars.

Walnuts have a moist, oily flavour and are used in cakes, stuffings and salads.

# PUDDINGS

**B**ritain is famous throughout the world for its baked and steamed puddings and delicious fruit and cream desserts. This chapter includes all the family favourites, from traditional pies, crumbles and charlottes to fresh fruit salads and fools, as well as exotic dinner party desserts and meringue gateaux.

◆

**B**AKED PUDDINGS range from light sponge puddings, flavoured with fruit or jam, to crumbles, charlottes and baked apples filled with brown sugar, mincemeat or dates. Baked puddings take less time to cook than steamed ones as they are cooked in the oven with more direct heat.

## BAKED JAM SPONGE

45 ml (3 level tbsp) jam

75 g (3 oz) butter or block margarine

75 g (3 oz) caster sugar

1 egg, beaten

150 g (5 oz) self raising flour

2.5 ml (½ tsp) vanilla flavouring

milk, to mix

Egg Custard Sauce (see page 210), to serve

1. Grease a 600–900 ml (1–1½ pint) pie dish. Spread the jam in an even layer in the bottom of the dish.

2. Cream the fat and sugar until pale and fluffy. Add the egg, a little at a time, beating after each addition. Fold in the flour with the flavouring and little milk to give a dropping consistency.

3. Spoon into the prepared dish and bake in the oven at 180°C (350°F) mark 4 for 30–40 minutes, until well risen and golden. Serve with Egg Custard Sauce.

Serves 3–4

### Variations

BAKED CASTLE PUDDINGS

Grease eight small individual foil dishes or dariole moulds and put 5–10 ml (1–2 level tsp) jam in the bottom of each. Divide the mixture between the dishes or moulds, bake for 20 minutes.

ORANGE AND LEMON SPONGE

Add the grated rind of an orange or lemon to the creamed mixture and replace the milk with fruit juice.

CHOCOLATE SPONGE

Add 45 ml (3 level tbsp) cocoa, sifted with the flour, or stir 25 g (1 oz) chocolate dots or chips into the mixture. Serve with Rich Chocolate Sauce (see page 211).

GINGER SPONGE

Sift 2.5 ml (½ level tsp) ground ginger with the flour, or add 2 pieces of preserved ginger, finely chopped, and 10 ml (2 tsp) of the ginger syrup.

*Eve's Pudding*

## EVE'S PUDDING

| |
| --- |
| 450 g (1 lb) cooking apples, peeled and cored |
| 75 g (3 oz) demerara sugar |
| grated rind of 1 lemon |
| 75 g (3 oz) butter or block margarine |
| 75 g (3 oz) caster sugar |
| 1 egg, beaten |
| 150 g (5 oz) self raising flour |
| a little milk, to mix |

1. Grease a 900 ml (1½ pint) ovenproof dish. Slice the apples and place in the dish. Sprinkle over the sugar and lemon rind.
2. Cream the fat and caster sugar until pale and fluffy. Add the egg, a little at a time, beating well after each addition.
3. Fold in the flour with enough milk to give a dropping consistency and spread the mixture over the apples.
4. Bake in the oven at 180°C (350°F) mark 4 for 40–45 minutes, until the apples are tender and the sponge mixture golden brown.
*Serves 4*

**Variation**
Add 25 g (1 oz) ground almonds with the flour and sprinkle 25 g (1 oz) flaked almonds over the top of the pudding.

## LEMON LAYER PUDDING

| |
| --- |
| grated rind and juice of 2 lemons |
| 50 g (2 oz) butter or block margarine |
| 100 g (4 oz) caster sugar |
| 2 eggs, separated |
| 50 g (2 oz) self raising flour |
| 300 ml (½ pint) milk |

1. Grease a 1.1 litre (2 pint) ovenproof dish.
2. Cream together the lemon rind, butter and sugar until pale and fluffy. Add the egg yolks and flour and beat well to combine.
3. Stir in the milk and lemon juice. Whisk the egg whites until stiff and fold into the mixture, then pour into the dish.
4. Stand the dish in a shallow tin of cold water and bake in the oven at 180°C (350°F) mark 4 for about 45 minutes, or until the top is set and spongy to the touch.
*Note* This pudding separates out in the cooking into a custard layer with a sponge topping.
*Serves 4*

# PINEAPPLE UPSIDE-DOWN PUDDING

150 g (6 oz) butter or block margarine

50 g (2 oz) soft dark brown sugar

226 g (7 oz) can pineapple rings, drained

2 glacé cherries, halved

100 g (4 oz) caster sugar

2 eggs, beaten

175 g (6 oz) self raising flour

30–45 ml (2–3 tbsp) pineapple juice or milk

1. Grease and base-line an 18 cm (7 inch) round cake tin. Cream together 50 g (2 oz) butter and brown sugar and spread it over the bottom of the tin. Arrange the pineapple rings and cherries on this layer in the bottom of the tin.
2. Cream together the remaining butter and

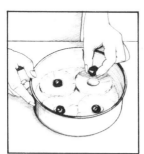

*Arrange pineapple rings and cherries in a layer in the bottom of the tin.*

sugar until pale and fluffy. Add the beaten egg, a little at a time, beating well after each addition. Fold in the flour, adding some pineapple juice or milk to give a dropping consistency, then spread on top of the pineapple rings.
3. Bake in the oven at 180°C (350°F) mark 4 for about 45 minutes. Turn out on to a warmed serving dish and serve.
*Serves 4*

**Variations**
CHOCOLATE PEAR UPSIDE-DOWN PUDDING
Use canned pear halves instead of pineapple. Substitute 25 g (1 oz) cocoa powder for 25 g (1 oz) flour and sift with the flour into the sponge mixture.

SPICED APRICOT UPSIDE-DOWN PUDDING
Replace the pineapple rings with canned apricot halves, well drained with a little syrup reserved for giving a dropping consistency. Add 2.5 ml (½ level tsp) ground cinnamon to the pudding mixture.

# COLLEGE PUDDING

100 g (4 oz) shredded suet

100 g (4 oz) fresh breadcrumbs

50 g (2 oz) sultanas

50 g (2 oz) seedless raisins

pinch of ground cinnamon

pinch of ground cloves

pinch of freshly grated nutmeg

50 g (2 oz) sugar

2.5 ml (½ level tsp) baking powder

pinch of salt

2 eggs, beaten

1. Grease four dariole moulds.
2. Mix the suet with the breadcrumbs and add the fruit, spices, sugar, baking powder and salt. Mix very well together, then add the eggs.
3. Pour into the prepared dariole moulds and bake in the oven at 180°C (350°F) mark 4 for about 30 minutes.
*Makes 4*

*College Pudding*

## FRUIT CRUMBLE

50 g (2 oz) butter or block margarine

100 g (4 oz) plain flour

100 g (4 oz) sugar

450 g (1 lb) prepared fruit (sliced apples, peaches,
rhubarb, plums or gooseberries)

custard, to serve

**1.** Rub the butter into the flour until the mixture resembles fine breadcrumbs, then stir in 50 g (2 oz) caster sugar.
**2.** Arrange half the prepared fruit in a 1.1 litre (2 pint) pie dish and sprinkle over the remaining sugar, then top with the remaining fruit.
**3.** Spoon the crumble mixture over the fruit and lightly press it down.
**4.** Bake in the oven at 200°C (400°F) mark 6 for about 45 minutes, until the fruit is soft. Serve hot with custard or cold.
*Serves 4*

**Variations**
**1.** Add 5 ml (1 level tsp) ground cinnamon, mixed spice or ginger to the flour before rubbing in the fat.
**2.** Add the grated rind of an orange or lemon to the crumb mixture before sprinkling it on the fruit.

## APPLE AND BLACKBERRY CHARLOTTE

450 g (1 lb) cooking apples, peeled and cored

450 g (1 lb) blackberries

rind and juice of ½ a lemon

1.25 ml (¼ level tsp) ground cinnamon

175–225 g (6–8 oz) sugar

30 ml (2 level tbsp) bread or cake crumbs

6 large bread slices

50 g (2 oz) butter or margarine, melted

custard, to serve

**1.** Grease a 1.4 litre (2½ pint) charlotte mould or a 17 cm (6 inch) round cake tin.
**2.** Thickly slice the apples and put in a saucepan with the blackberries, lemon rind and juice and cinnamon and cook gently for 10 minutes, until the apples have softened slightly. Add the sugar and crumbs.
**3.** Cut the crusts off the bread. Trim one piece to a round the same size as the base of the tin, dip it into the melted butter and fit into the bottom of the tin. Dip the remaining slices of bread in the butter and arrange closely around the side of the tin, reserving one piece for the top.

*Arrange bread around side. of the mould or tin.*

**4.** Spoon in the stewed fruit and cover with the remaining slice of bread, trimmed to fit the top of the mould.
**5.** Bake in the oven at 190°C (375°F) mark 5 for about 1 hour. Turn out and serve with custard
*Note* This is the traditional charlotte recipe. It can be made with apples alone.
*Serves 4*

## BAKED APPLES

4 medium cooking apples

demerara sugar

knob of butter or margarine

**1.** Wipe and core the apples, then make a shallow cut through the skin around the middle of each.
**2.** Stand the apples in an ovenproof dish. Pour 60 ml (4 tbsp) water around them, fill each apple with sugar and top with a small knob of butter.
**3.** Bake in the oven at 200°C (400°F) mark 6 for about 45–60 minutes, until the apples are soft.
*Serves 4*

**Variations**
**1.** Stuff the centre of the apples with mincemeat instead of demerara sugar.
**2.** Stuff the apples with currants, sultanas, stoned raisins, chopped dried apricots, mixed peel or glacé fruits, or with a mixture of chopped dates and walnuts or other nuts.
**3.** Pack the centres with chopped dates, grated orange rind and soft brown sugar.

# STEAMED AND BOILED PUDDINGS are made by a very

gentle method of cooking in a bowl in a steamer or saucepan of boiling water or wrapped and boiled in a preserving pan. Follow the rules below and the result will always be soft and moist. These puddings are turned out and often served with a sauce.

## GENERAL RULES FOR STEAMING

Half-fill the steamer with water and heat so that it is boiling by the time the pudding is made. If you have no steamer, fill a large saucepan or preserving pan with water to come halfway up the pudding basin. Cover and bring to the boil. Use a baking sheet or foil to make a lid for the preserving pan.

Grease the pudding basin well.

Cut double greaseproof paper or a piece of foil to cover the pudding basin and grease well. If you wish, put a pleat in the paper or foil to allow the pudding to rise.

- Fill the basin not more than two-thirds full with mixture.
- Cover the basin tightly with the paper or foil to prevent steam or water entering. Secure with string and make a string handle to lift the basin in and out of the pan.
- Keep the water in the steamer boiling rapidly all the time and have a kettle of boiling water ready to top it up regularly, or the steamer will boil dry. If you are using a saucepan, put an old saucer or metal pastry cutter in the base to keep the basin off the bottom.

## AM SPONGE PUDDING

| |
|---|
| 0 ml (2 level tbsp) jam |
| 00 g (4 oz) butter or block margarine |
| 00 g (4 oz) caster sugar |
| eggs, beaten |
| ew drops of vanilla flavouring |
| 75 g (6 oz) self raising flour, sifted |
| little milk, to mix |
| ustard, to serve |

. Half-fill a steamer or large saucepan with water nd put it on to boil. Grease a 900 ml (1½ pint)

pudding basin and spoon the jam into the bottom.
2. Cream together the fat and sugar until pale and fluffy. Add the beaten eggs and the flavouring, a little at a time, beating well after each addition.
3. Using a metal spoon, fold in half the sifted flour, then fold in the rest, with enough milk to give a dropping consistency.
4. Pour the mixture into the prepared basin, cover with greased greaseproof paper or foil and secure with string. Steam for 1½ hours. Serve with custard.
*Serves 4*

**Variations**

SYRUP SPONGE PUDDING
Put 30 ml (2 tbsp) golden syrup into the bottom of the basin instead of the jam.

FRUIT SPONGE PUDDING
Put a shallow layer of drained canned fruit or a layer of stewed fruit in the basin before adding the sponge mixture.

MINCEMEAT SURPRISE PUDDING
Line the bottom and sides of the basin with a thin layer of mincemeat and fill with the pudding mixture. When the pudding is cooked, turn it out carefully so that the outside remains completely covered with the mincemeat.

CHOCOLATE SPONGE PUDDING
Omit the jam. Blend 60 ml (4 level tbsp) cocoa powder to a smooth cream with 15 ml (1 tbsp) hot water; add gradually to the creamed fat and sugar.

LEMON OR ORANGE SPONGE
Add the grated rind of 1 orange or lemon when creaming the fat and sugar.

STEAMED CASTLE PUDDINGS
Divide the jam and the sponge mixture between greased dariole moulds, filling them two-thirds full. Cover each mould with greased foil and secure with string. Steam for 30–45 minutes (depending on size) over rapidly boiling water.

## JAM ROLY-POLY

Illustrated on page 378.

175 g (6 oz) Suetcrust Pastry (see page 378)

60–90 ml (4–6 level tbsp) jam

a little milk

custard, to serve

1. Half-fill a steamer with water and put on to boil. Grease a piece of foil 23 × 33 cm (9 × 13 inches).
2. Roll out the suetcrust pastry on a lightly floured surface to an oblong about 23 × 25 cm (9 × 11 inches). Spread the jam on the pastry, leaving 0.5 cm (¼ inch) clear along each edge. Brush the edges with milk and roll up the pastry evenly, starting from one short side.
3. Place the roll on the greased foil and wrap the foil around it loosely, to allow room for expansion, but seal the edges well.
4. Steam for 1½–2 hours. Remove from the foil and serve with custard.
Serves 4

## SPOTTED DICK

100 g (4 oz) fresh breadcrumbs

75 g (3 oz) self raising flour

75 g (3 oz) shredded suet

50 g (2 oz) caster sugar

175 g (6 oz) currants

finely grated rind of 1 lemon

75 ml (5 tbsp) milk

custard, to serve

1. Half-fill a preserving pan or large saucepan with water and put on to boil.
2. Place the crumbs, flour, suet, sugar, currants and lemon rind in a bowl and stir well until thoroughly mixed.
3. Pour in the milk and stir until well blended. Using one hand, bring the ingredients together to form a soft, slightly sticky dough.
4. Turn the dough on to a floured surface and knead gently until just smooth. Shape into a neat roll about 15 cm (6 inches) in length.
5. Make a 5 cm (2 inch) pleat across a clean tea towel or pudding cloth. Or pleat together sheets of greased greaseproof paper and strong foil. Encase the roll in the cloth or foil, pleating the open edges tightly together.
6. Tie the ends securely with string to form a cracker shape. Make a string handle

*Encase the Spotted Dick in foil or paper and pleat to close.*

across the top. Lower the suet roll into the pan of boiling water and boil for 2 hours.
7. Lift the spotted dick out of the water using the string handle. Place on a wire rack standing over a plate and allow excess moisture to drain off.
8. Snip the string and gently roll the pudding out of the cloth or foil on to a warmed serving plate. Serve sliced with custard.
Serves 4

## JAM SUET PUDDING

30 ml (2 level tbsp) jam

175 g (6 oz) self raising flour

pinch of salt

75 g (3 oz) shredded suet

50 g (2 oz) caster sugar

about 150 ml (¼ pint) milk

custard, to serve

1. Half-fill a steamer or large saucepan with water and put on to boil. Grease a 900 ml (1½ pint) pudding basin and spoon the jam into the bottom.
2. Mix together the flour, salt, suet and sugar. Make a well in the centre and add enough milk to give a soft dropping consistency.
3. Pour into the prepared basin, cover with greased greaseproof paper or foil and secure with string.
4. Steam for 1½–2 hours. Serve with custard.
Serves 4

**Variation**
Add 225 g (8 oz) cooking apples, peeled and finely chopped or grated, to the dry ingredients.

# RICH CHRISTMAS PUDDING

| |
|---|
| 00 g (4 oz) prunes |
| 75 g (6 oz) currants |
| 75 g (6 oz) seedless raisins |
| 75 g (6 oz) sultanas |
| 00 g (4 oz) plain flour |
| .25 ml (¼ level tsp) grated nutmeg |
| .25 ml (¼ level tsp) ground cinnamon |
| .5 ml (½ level tsp) salt |
| 5 g (3 oz) fresh breadcrumbs |
| 00 g (4 oz) shredded suet |
| 00 g (4 oz) dark soft brown sugar |
| 5 g (1 oz) blanched almonds, chopped |
| nely grated rind of ½ lemon |
| 50 ml (¼ pint) brown ale |
| eggs, beaten |

1. Snip the prunes into small pieces, discarding the stones.
2. Half-fill a steamer or large saucepan with water and put it on to boil. Grease a 1.3 litre (2½ pint) pudding basin.
3. Place the prunes in a large mixing bowl and stir in the remaining ingredients. Stir well until evenly mixed.
4. Put the mixture into the prepared basin, pushing down well. Cover with greased, pleated greaseproof paper and foil. To cook, steam for about 8 hours.
5. Leave the greaseproof paper in position, allow to cool, then cover with a clean dry cloth or foil and store in a cool place for at least 2 weeks before serving.
6. To reheat, steam for 2½ hours. Turn out on to a warmed serving plate and serve with brandy or Rum Butter (see page 212).
*Serves 8*

# BATTER PUDDINGS There are two main types of batter used for puddings: pouring batter, which is used for pancakes and baked batter puddings, and coating batter, which is used for fritters. Coating batter is thicker than pouring batter, so it will cling to fruit dipped into it, which can then be deep-fried.

# PANCAKES

| |
|---|
| 00 g (4 oz) plain flour |
| inch of salt |
| egg |
| 00 ml (½ pint) milk |
| egetable oil for frying |
| ugar and lemon juice, to serve |

Repeat with the remaining batter to make eight pancakes. Pile the cooked pancakes on top of each other with greaseproof paper in between each one
5. Serve as soon as they are all cooked, sprinkled with sugar and lemon juice.
*Note* Pancake batter may also be made in an electric blender or food processor. Put the liquid in first, egg next and the flour last.
*Makes 8*

1. Sift the flour and salt into a bowl and make a well in the centre. Break in the egg and beat well with a wooden spoon, then gradually beat in the milk, drawing in the flour from the sides to make smooth batter.
2. Heat a little oil in an 18 cm (7 inch) heavy-based frying pan, running it around the base and sides of the pan, until hot. Pour off any surplus.
3. Pour in just enough batter to thinly coat the base of the pan. Cook for 1–2 minutes, until golden brown, turn or toss and cook the second side until golden.
4. Transfer the pancake to a plate and keep hot.

**Variations**
1. Add 5–10 ml (1–2 level tsp) icing sugar to the flour before mixing.
2. Add the grated rind of ½ a lemon or orange to the flour before mixing.

## APRICOT PANCAKES
Stew 225 g (8 oz) dried apricots (see page 318), then purée in a blender or food processor. Divide between the pancakes then roll up. Place in a greased ovenproof dish, cover and bake at 220°C (425°F) mark 7 for about 20 minutes.

## CRÊPES SUZETTE

| |
|---|
| *50 g (2 oz) butter or margarine* |
| *25 g (1 oz) caster sugar* |
| *finely grated rind and juice of 1 large orange* |
| *30 ml (2 tbsp) orange-flavoured liqueur* |
| *45 ml (3 tbsp) brandy or rum* |
| *8 freshly cooked pancakes (see page 327)* |
| *cream, to serve* |

**1.** Melt the butter in a large frying pan. Remove from the heat and add the sugar, orange rind and juice and the liqueur. Heat gently to dissolve the sugar.
**2.** Fold each pancake in half and then in half again to form a fan shape. Place the pancakes in the frying pan in overlapping lines.
**3.** Warm the brandy, pour it over the pancakes and set alight. Shake gently, then serve at once with cream.
*Makes 8*

## FRITTER BATTER

| |
|---|
| *125 g (4 oz) plain flour* |
| *pinch of salt* |
| *1 egg* |
| *150 ml (¼ pint) milk or milk and water mixed* |

**1.** Sift the flour and salt into a bowl and make a well in the centre. Break in the egg and beat well with a wooden spoon, then gradually beat in the liquid, drawing in the flour from the sides to make a smooth batter.
*Makes 200 ml (7 fl oz)*

**Variation**
To make a lighter batter, use 15 ml (1 tbsp) vegetable oil instead of the egg. Just before cooking, whisk two egg whites stiffly and fold them into the batter. Use the batter immediately.

*APPLE FRITTERS*
**1.** Peel and core 3 medium cooking apples and cut into rings 0.5 cm (¼ inch) thick.
**2.** Dip in Fritter Batter and deep-fry in oil at 180°C (350°F) for 2–3 minutes, until golden.
**3.** Drain on absorbent kitchen paper, toss in caster sugar and ground cinnamon and serve.
*Serves 4*

*PINEAPPLE FRITTERS*
Use a well drained 226 g (8 oz) can pineapple rings.
*Serves 4*

*BANANA FRITTERS*
Use 4 small bananas, peeled and cut in half lengthways.
*Serves 4*

## WAFFLES

These crisp, light wafers, made from batter, are cooked in a special waffle iron. The cooking time varies with different kinds of waffle irons, but as a rule 2–3 minutes is sufficient. Follow manufacturer's instructions carefully.

| |
|---|
| *125 g (4 oz) self raising flour* |
| *pinch of salt* |
| *15 ml (1 level tbsp) caster sugar* |
| *1 egg, separated* |
| *30 ml (2 tbsp) butter or margarine, melted* |
| *150 ml (¼ pint) milk* |
| *2.5 ml (½ tsp) vanilla flavouring (optional)* |
| *butter and golden or maple syrup, to serve* |

**1.** Heat the waffle iron according to the manufacturer's instructions.

**2.** Mix the dry ingredients together in a bowl. Add the egg yolk, melted butter, milk and flavouring and beat to give a smooth coating batter.
**3.** Whisk the egg white until stiff and fold into the batter. Pour just enough batter into the iron to run over the surface.
**4.** Close the iron and cook for 2–3 minutes, turning the iron if using a non-electric type. When the waffle is cooked, it should be golden brown and crisp and easily removed from the iron—if it sticks, cook for a minute longer.
**5.** Serve immediately with butter and golden or maple syrup. Alternatively, layer the waffles with whipped cream or vanilla ice cream and fresh fruit.
*Serves 4*

# PASTRIES AND FLANS

Sweet fillings in a crispy, light-textured pastry are delicious and very popular desserts for both everyday and special occasions. Flans can be made with a pastry base or with sponge cake, and there are also recipes for uncooked cases made from biscuits. These desserts have the added advantage that most—if not all—the cooking can be done beforehand.

## EGG CUSTARD TART

150 g (5 oz) Shortcrust Pastry, made with 150 g (5 oz)
    flour (see page 372)

2 eggs

30 ml (2 level tbsp) sugar

300 ml (½ pint) milk

freshly grated nutmeg

1. Roll out the pastry on a floured surface and use it to line an 18 cm (7 inch) flan ring or fluted flan dish. Chill in the refrigerator for 30 minutes.

2. Meanwhile, whisk the eggs with the sugar; warm the milk and pour on to the egg mixture. Strain the custard into the pastry case and sprinkle the top with nutmeg.

3. Bake in the oven at 220°C (425°F) mark 7 for about 10 minutes, then reduce the temperature to 180°C (350°F) mark 4 and continue cooking for about 20 minutes, or until the custard is just set. Serve cold.
*Serves 4*

## PECAN PIE

200 g (7 oz) Shortcrust Pastry, made with 200 g (7 oz)
    flour (see page 372)

3 eggs

15 ml (1 tbsp) milk

175 g (6 oz) demerara sugar

150 ml (¼ pint) maple or corn syrup

50 g (2 oz) butter or margarine, softened

2.5 ml (½ tsp) vanilla flavouring

175 g (6 oz) pecan nuts, halved

cream, to serve

1. Roll out the pastry on a floured surface and use to line a 23 cm (9 inch) flan ring or fluted flan dish.

Chill in the refrigerator for 30 minutes.

2. Meanwhile, make the filling. Beat the eggs and milk together. Boil the sugar and syrup together in a saucepan for 3 minutes. Slowly pour on to the beaten eggs and stir in the butter and vanilla flavouring.

3. Use half the nuts to cover the base of the pastry case, spoon the syrup mixture over and cover with the remaining nuts. Bake in the oven at 220°C (425°F) mark 7 for 10 minutes.

4. Reduce the temperature to 170°C (325°F) mark 3 and cook for a further 45 minutes, until the filling is set. Serve warm or cold with cream.
*Serves 6–8*

## BAKEWELL PUDDING

212 g (7½ oz) packet frozen puff pastry, thawed

2 eggs

2 egg yolks

100 g (4 oz) butter or margarine, melted

100 g (4 oz) caster sugar

50 g (2 oz) ground almonds

30 ml (2 level tbsp) raspberry jam

1. Roll out the pastry on a floured surface and use to line an 18 cm (7 inch) pie plate or flan ring.

2. Beat the eggs and extra yolks together, add the butter, sugar and almonds and mix well.

3. Spread the bottom of the pastry case with the jam and pour on the egg mixture.

4. Bake in the oven at 200°C (400°F) mark 6 for 30 minutes, until the filling is firm to the touch.
*Serves 4*

## ALMOND AND CHERRY FLAN

200 g (8 oz) Flan Pastry (see page 373)

350 g (12 oz) fresh black cherries, stoned

50 g (2 oz) butter or block margarine

50 g (2 oz) caster sugar

125 g (4 oz) ground almonds

5 ml (1 tsp) almond flavouring

15 ml (1 tbsp) almond-flavoured liqueur (optional)

1 egg yolk

50 g (2 oz) self raising flour

2.5 ml (½ level tsp) baking powder

30 ml (2 tbsp) milk

2 egg whites

25 g (1 oz) flaked almonds

cream, to serve

*Almond and Cherry Flan*

1. Roll out the pastry on a floured surface and use to line a 24 cm (9½ inch) flan ring or fluted flan dish. Chill in the refrigerator for 30 minutes.
2. Bake blind (see page 371) in the oven at 200°C (400°F) mark 6 for 10–15 minutes, then remove the paper and beans and bake for a further 5 minutes until set. Cool slightly.
3. Scatter the cherries over the pastry. Then cream the remaining butter and sugar well together and beat in the ground almonds, almond flavouring, liqueur, if using, and the egg yolk. Sift together the flour and baking powder and fold into the mixture, then lightly stir in the milk.
4. Whisk the two egg whites until they are stiff, and fold them into the creamed mixture.
5. Spread over the cherries in the flan case and scatter the flaked almonds on top. Bake in the oven at 180°C (350°F) mark 4 for about 30 minutes. Serve warm with cream.
*Serves 6*

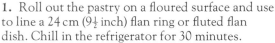

*Old-Fashioned Treacle Tart*

## OLD-FASHIONED TREACLE TART

175 g (6 oz) Shortcrust Pastry (see page 372)

225 g (8 oz) golden syrup

finely grated rind and juice of 1 lemon

75 g (3 oz) fresh breadcrumbs

beaten egg, to glaze

1. Roll out the pastry on a floured surface and use to line a 20.5 cm (8 inch) fluted flan dish. Reserve trimmings. Chill for 30 minutes.
2. Meanwhile, to make the filling, warm the golden syrup in a saucepan with the lemon rind and juice. Sprinkle the breadcrumbs evenly over the base of the pastry case, then slowly pour in the syrup.
3. Make strips from the reserved pastry trimmings and place these over the tart in a lattice pattern, brushing the ends with water to stick them to the pastry case. Glaze with a little egg.
4. Bake in the oven at 190°C (375°F) mark 5 for about 25 minutes until the filling is just set.
*Serves 4–6*

# APPLE PIE

*900 g (2 lb) cooking apples, peeled, cored and sliced*

*50 g (2 oz) sugar*

*225 g (8 oz) Shortcrust Pastry, made with 225 g (8 oz)*
*    flour (see page 372)*

*caster sugar for sprinkling*

**1.** Layer the apples and sugar in a 1.1 litre (2 pint) pie dish. Sprinkle over 15 ml (1 tbsp) water.
**2.** Roll out the pastry on a floured surface to a circle 2.5 cm (1 inch) larger than the dish. Cut off a strip, dampen the rim of the dish and press on the strip. Dampen the strip and cover with the pastry, pressing the edges well together. Scallop the edges (see page 370) and make a slit in the centre.
**3.** Bake in the oven at 200°C (400°F) mark 6 for 30–35 minutes, until the pastry is lightly browned. Sprinkle with caster sugar for serving.
*Serves 4–6*

# FRENCH APPLE FLAN

*200 g (8 oz) Flan Pastry (see page 373)*

*900 g (2 lb) cooking apples*

*50 g (2 oz) butter or margarine*

*120 ml (9 level tbsp) apricot jam*

*50 g (2 oz) sugar*

*finely grated rind of ½ lemon*

*30 ml (2 tbsp) apple brandy or brandy*

*225 g (8 oz) eating apples*

*about 30 ml (2 tbsp) lemon juice*

*5 ml (1 level tsp) caster sugar*

**1.** Roll out the pastry on a floured surface and use to line a 20.5 cm (8 inch) fluted flan ring or dish placed on a baking sheet. Chill in the refrigerator for 30 minutes.
**2.** Bake blind (see page 371) in the oven at 200°C (400°F) mark 6 for 10–15 minutes, then remove paper and beans and bake for a further 5 minutes until the base is set.
**3.** Cut the cooking apples into quarters, core and roughly chop the skin and flesh. Melt the butter in a saucepan and add the apples with 30 ml (2 tbsp) water. Cover the pan tightly and cook gently for about 15 minutes until soft and mushy.
**4.** Rub the apples through a sieve into a large clean pan. Add half the apricot jam with the sugar, lemon rind and brandy. Cook over a high heat for about 15 minutes, stirring, until all excess liquid has evaporated and the mixture is thickened.
**5.** Spoon the thick apple purée into the flan case and smooth the surface. Peel, quarter, core and slice the dessert apples very thinly. Arrange in an overlapping circle around the edge of the flan. Brush lightly with lemon juice; sprinkle with the caster sugar.
**6.** Return the flan to the oven and bake for a further 25–30 minutes, or until the pastry

*French Apple Flan*

*Decoratively arrange the peeled and thinly sliced apples around the top.*

and apples are lightly coloured. Slide on to a serving plate and remove the flan ring. Cool for 10 minutes.
**7.** Gently warm the remaining jam with 15 ml (1 tbsp) lemon juice, then sieve into a small bowl. Brush over the top and sides of the flan. Serve.
*Serves 6*

## LEMON MERINGUE PIE

*175 g (6 oz) Shortcrust Pastry made with 175 g (6 oz)*
*    flour (see page 372)*

*finely grated rind and juice of 2 lemons*

*100 g (4 oz) granulated sugar*

*75 ml (5 level tbsp) cornflour*

*2 eggs, separated*

*75 g (3 oz) caster sugar*

*cream, to serve*

1. Roll out the pastry on a floured surface and use to line a 20.5 cm (8 inch) flan ring or fluted flan dish. Chill in the refrigerator for 30 minutes.
2. Bake blind (see page 371) in the oven at 200°C (400°F) mark 6 for 10–15 minutes, then remove the paper and beans and bake for a further 5 minutes until the base is set.
3. Put the lemon rind and juice, granulated sugar and 300 ml (½ pint) water in a saucepan. Heat gently until the sugar dissolves.
4. Mix the cornflour to a smooth paste with 90 ml (6 tbsp) water and stir into the saucepan until well blended. Bring to the boil, stirring and cook for 1 minute, until thickened.
5. Cool slightly, then beat in the egg yolks, one at a time.

6. Pour the warm filling into the pastry case, levelling the surface. Whisk the egg whites until stiff. Whisk in half the caster sugar until completely incorporated, then carefully fold in the remaining sugar.
7. Spoon the meringue on to the filling and spread with a palette knife. The filling must be completely covered, but the meringue must not overlap the flan ring or removing the ring will ruin the final appearance of the pie. Flick it up with the tip of the knife and bake in the oven at 150°C (300°F) mark 2 for about 35 minutes. Ease off the flan ring and serve the pie with cream.

### Variations

*LIME MERINGUE PIE*
Prepare as for Lemon Meringue Pie, substituting the finely grated rind and juice of 3 limes for the lemons. To decorate, shred a few strips of lime rind and blanch in boiling water for 1 minute, then drain well. Sprinkle over the top of the pie.

*LEMON SNOW PIE*
Prepare the pie as above, however gently fold the meringue into the hot filling using a large metal spoon.

## FRESH APRICOT FLAN

*150 g (5 oz) flour*

*pinch of salt*

*50 g (2 oz) ground almonds*

*75 g (3 oz) butter or block margarine*

*1 egg yolk mixed with 15 ml (1 tbsp) water*

*2 eggs*

*150 ml (5 fl oz) single cream or milk*

*15 ml (1 level tbsp) caster sugar*

*few drops of almond flavouring*

*120 ml (8 level tbsp) apricot jam, sieved*

*450 g (1 lb) fresh apricots, skinned, halved and stoned*
*    or 411 g (14 oz) can apricot halves, drained*

*15 ml (1 tbsp) lemon juice*

*15 ml (1 tbsp) almond-flavoured liqueur*

1. Mix the flour and salt in a bowl with half the ground almonds. Rub in the butter until the mixture resembles fine breadcrumbs. Bind to a firm dough with the egg yolk mixture; knead lightly until smooth.

2. Roll out the dough on a floured surface and use to line a 20.5 cm (8 inch) fluted flan dish or ring. Chill in the refrigerator for 30 minutes.
3. Bake blind (see page 371) in the oven at 190°C (375°F) mark 5 for 10–15 minutes, then remove paper and beans and bake for a further 5 minutes until set.
4. Meanwhile, mix together the eggs, cream, sugar, remaining ground almonds and almond flavouring.
5. Warm the jam gently in a small saucepan. Spread 45 ml (3 tbsp) jam over the pastry case, then pour the cream mixture into the flan case.
6. Reduce the temperature to 170°C (325°F) mark 3 and bake for 20 minutes, or until the filling is just set. Leave for about 1 hour to cool.
7. Arrange the apricot halves neatly over the custard filling in the flan. Add the lemon juice to the remaining jam together with the liqueur and reduce the mixture to a glaze. Brush the glaze over the apricots to cover them completely. Chill in the refrigerator for 2 hours before serving.
*Serves 6*

# Double-Crust Blackcurrant Pie

450 g (1 lb) blackcurrants, stringed and washed

75 g (3 oz) sugar

30 ml (2 level tbsp) cornflour

350 g (12 oz) Shortcrust Pastry made with 350 g (12 oz)
    flour (see page 372)

milk, to glaze

caster sugar for sprinkling

1. Mix together the blackcurrants, sugar and cornflour.
2. Roll out two-thirds of the pastry on a floured surface and use it to line a 20.5 cm (8 inch) deep pie plate or sandwich tin.
3. Fill the plate with the fruit mixture and roll out the remaining pastry to form a lid, pressing the edges well together. Scallop the edges (see page 370) and make a slit in the centre. Brush the top with milk. Put the plate on a baking sheet and bake in the oven at 200°C (400°F) mark 6 for about 1 hour. Cover it loosely with foil after 30 minutes to prevent over-browning. Sprinkle with caster sugar for serving.
Serves 4–6

# Mince Pies

225 g (8 oz) Shortcrust Pastry (see page 372)

350–450 g (12 oz–1 lb) mincemeat

icing or caster sugar for dusting

1. Roll out the pastry on a floured surface to about 0.3 cm ($\frac{1}{8}$ inch) thick.
2. Cut out about 20 rounds with a 7.5 cm (3 inch) fluted cutter and 20 smaller rounds with a 5.5 cm ($2\frac{1}{4}$ inch) fluted cutter.
3. Line 6.5 cm ($2\frac{1}{2}$ inch) patty tins with the larger rounds and fill with mincemeat. Dampen the edges of the small rounds with water and place firmly on top. Make a small slit in each top.
4. Bake in the oven at 220°C (425°F) mark 7 for 15–20 minutes, until light golden brown. Leave to cool on a wire rack. Serve dusted with sugar.
Makes about 20

**Variation**
Mince pies can be made using a 368 g (13 oz) packet puff pastry. Roll out the pastry to 0.3 cm ($\frac{1}{8}$ inch) thick. Cut into 16 rounds with a 6.5 cm ($2\frac{1}{2}$ inch) cutter. Re-roll the scraps, cut another 16 rounds to use for the bases.
    Place the bases on a dampened baking sheet. Put a heaped 5 ml (1 tsp) mincemeat on each and dampen edges. Cover and press the edges lightly together; glaze with beaten egg.
    Bake in the oven at 230°C (450°F) mark 8 for about 20 minutes.
Makes 16

# Chocolate Ginger Flan

175 g (6 oz) ginger biscuits, crushed

50 g (2 oz) flour

75 g (3 oz) butter or block margarine

200 g (7 oz) natural quark (low fat soft cheese)

3 eggs, separated

30 ml (2 level tbsp) cocoa powder

2 pieces stem ginger, finely chopped

15 ml (1 tbsp) stem ginger syrup or 15 ml (1 level tbsp)
    ginger marmalade

50 g (2 oz) plain chocolate

150 ml (5 fl oz) whipping cream

Chocolate Caraque (see page 418), to decorate

1. In a bowl, mix together the biscuits and flour. Rub in the butter until the mixture is soft and just begins to bind.
2. Press evenly over the base and up the sides of a 20.5 cm (8 inch) fluted flan dish or ring. Bake in the oven at 200°C (400°F) mark 6 for 15–20 minutes, or until quite firm to the touch.
3. Whisk together the quark, egg yolks, cocoa, chopped ginger and the syrup. Whisk the egg whites until just holding their shape. Fold into the ginger mixture, then pour into the flan tin.
4. Bake in the oven at 180°C (350°F) mark 4 for about 20 minutes or until just set and firm to the touch. Leave to cool.
5. Place the chocolate with 30 ml (2 tbsp) water in a small bowl. Melt over a pan of simmering water and stir until smooth. Spread evenly over the cooked flan. Leave to cool.
6. Lightly whip the cream. Spoon over the chocolate and decorate with Chocolate Caraque.
Serves 8–10

*Rhubarb and Orange Chiffon Pie*

# RHUBARB AND ORANGE CHIFFON PIE

*150 g (6 oz) digestive biscuits, crushed*

*50 g (2 oz) demerara sugar*

*75 g (3 oz) unsalted butter, melted*

*560 g (1 lb 4 oz) can rhubarb, drained*

*finely grated rind and juice of 1 large orange*

*2 eggs, separated*

*50 g (2 oz) caster sugar*

*30 ml (2 level tbsp) cornflour*

*2.5 ml (½ level tsp) ground ginger*

*orange slices, to decorate*

**1.** In a bowl, mix together the biscuits and demerara sugar, then stir in the butter.

**2.** Press evenly over the base and up the sides of a 20.5 cm (8 inch) fluted flan dish. Chill in the refrigerator while preparing the filling.
**3.** Purée the rhubarb in a blender or food processor, then pour into a bowl. Put the orange rind and juice into a heavy-based saucepan. Add the egg yolks, caster sugar, cornflour and ginger. Heat gently, stirring, until thick. Stir into the rhubarb purée.
**4.** Whisk the egg whites until stiff. Fold into the rhubarb custard, then spoon the mixture into the biscuit crust. Chill in the refrigerator for at least 4 hours, or overnight. Decorate with orange slices just before serving.
*Serves 4*

# GLAZED FRUIT SPONGE FLAN

*50 g (2 oz) caster sugar plus 10 ml (2 level tsp)*

*50 g (2 oz) flour plus 5 ml (1 level tsp)*

*2 eggs, size 2*

*225 g (8 oz) strawberries, hulled and sliced*

*45 ml (3 level tbsp) redcurrant jelly*

**1.** Grease a 20.5 cm (8 inch) raised-based flan tin. Sprinkle over 10 ml (2 tsp) caster sugar and tilt the tin to coat evenly. Add 5 ml (1 level tsp) flour and coat similarly, knocking out any excess.
**2.** Place the eggs and remaining sugar in a deep bowl and whisk until the mixture is very thick. Sift the flour over the surface of the mixture. Fold gently through with a metal spoon, then turn into

the prepared tin and tilt to level the surface.
**3.** Place on a baking sheet and bake in the oven at 180°C (350°F) mark 4 for 20–25 minutes, until a light golden brown and the sponge springs back when pressed lightly. Turn out on to a wire rack. Leave to cool.
**4.** Arrange the sliced fruit in the flan case. Put the redcurrant jelly and 15 ml (1 tbsp) water in a small saucepan and heat gently together until liquid. Cool a little, then brush over the fruit.
*Serves 6*

**Variations**
Use fresh raspberries, apricots, gooseberries or black and green grapes instead of strawberries.

# GOOSEBERRY BISCUIT FLAN

| |
|---|
| 75 g (3 oz) ginger biscuits, crushed |
| 75 g (3 oz) digestive biscuits, crushed |
| 75 g (3 oz) butter or block margarine, melted |
| 1 large orange |
| 10 ml (2 level tsp) gelatine |
| 350 g (12 oz) fresh gooseberries |
| 75–100 g (3–4 oz) sugar |
| 170 g (6 oz) can creamed rice |
| 150 ml (5 fl oz) double cream |

1. Mix together the biscuits and butter in a bowl.
2. Press evenly over the base and up the sides of an 18 cm (7 inch) fluted flan dish or ring. Chill in the refrigerator for 30 minutes.
3. Pare off a few strips of orange rind with a potato peeler and cut into very fine shreds. Blanch, drain and reserve.
4. Sprinkle the gelatine in 30 ml (2 tbsp) water in a small bowl and leave to soak. Place the bowl over a pan of simmering water and stir until dissolved.
5. Cook the gooseberries in a saucepan with the remaining orange rind, finely grated, and 45 ml (3 tbsp) orange juice, for about 10 minutes, until thick and pulpy.
6. Push the gooseberries through a nylon sieve, or purée in a blender or food processor, then sieve to remove the pips. While still warm, stir in the sugar to taste and the gelatine. Mix until both have dissolved, then chill in the refrigerator to setting point.
7. Spoon the creamed rice into the crumb crust and level. Spread the gooseberry mixture over the top. Refrigerate to set.
8. Lightly whip the cream. Spoon into a piping bag fitted with a large star nozzle and pipe cream on the flan. Decorate with the reserved orange shreds.

*Serves 6*

# APPLE STRUDEL

| |
|---|
| 225 g (8 oz) Strudel Pastry (see page 380) |
| 700 g (1½ lb) cooking apples, peeled, cored and sliced |
| 50 g (2 oz) currants |
| 50 g (2 oz) sultanas |
| 45 ml (3 level tbsp) caster sugar |
| 5 ml (1 level tsp) ground mixed spice |
| 40 g (1½ oz) butter or margarine, melted |
| 100 g (4 oz) fresh breadcrumbs |
| 25 g (1 oz) flaked almonds |
| icing sugar, to decorate |
| lemon-flavoured cream, to serve |

1. Roll out the Strudel Pastry as instructed on page 380 and leave to rest on the cloth for 15 minutes.
2. Put the apples, currants, sultanas, sugar and spice in a bowl and mix thoroughly. Brush the dough with half the melted butter and sprinkle with breadcrumbs.
3. Spread the apple mixture over the dough, leaving a 5 cm (2 inch) border uncovered all around the edge. Fold these edges over the apple mixture.
4. With a long side towards you, lift the corners of the cloth and roll up the strudel. Stop after each turn to pat into shape and to keep the roll even.
5. Form the roll carefully into a horseshoe shape and slide it on to an oiled baking sheet. Brush with the remaining melted butter and sprinkle over the top of the almonds.
6. Bake in the oven at 190°C (375°F) mark 5 for about 40 minutes, until pale golden brown. Dredge with icing sugar to serve. Serve warm or cold with cream.

*Serves 8–10*

*Apple Strudel*

## GÂTEAU ST. HONORÉ

*100 g (4 oz) Pâte Sucrée (see page 373)*

*beaten egg, to glaze*

*65 g (2½ oz) Choux Pastry (see page 379)*

*300 ml (10 fl oz) double cream*

*45 ml (3 level tbsp) sugar*

*angelica and glacé cherries, to decorate*

**For the Crème Pâtissière**

*2 eggs*

*50 g (2 oz) caster sugar*

*30 ml (2 level tbsp) flour*

*30 ml (2 level tbsp) cornflour*

*300 ml (½ pint) milk*

*few drops vanilla flavouring*

**1.** Roll out the Pâte Sucrée on a floured surface to an 18 cm (7 inch) round. Place on a baking sheet and prick all over with a fork. Chill in the refrigerator for 30 minutes, then brush a 1 cm (½ inch) band around the edge with beaten egg.
**2.** Put the pastry into a piping bag fitted with a medium plain nozzle and pipe a circle around the edge of the pastry round. Brush with beaten egg. Dampen a baking sheet and pipe about twenty walnut-sized choux balls on to it. Brush with beaten egg.
**3.** Bake both the flan and the choux balls in the oven at 190°C (375°F) mark 5 for about 15 minutes or until the choux pastry is well risen and golden brown. Make a slit in the side of each bun and the ring to release the steam, then transfer with the flan case on to a wire rack and leave for

15–20 minutes to cool.
**4.** Meanwhile, to make the Crème Pâtissière, cream the eggs and sugar together until pale and thick. Sift the flour and cornflour into the bowl and beat in with a little cold milk until smooth. Heat the rest of the milk until almost boiling and pour on to the egg mixture, stirring well.
**5.** Return the custard to the saucepan and stir over a low heat until the mixture boils. Add the vanilla flavouring to taste and cook for a further 2–3 minutes. Cover and allow to cool.
**6.** Whip the cream until stiff. Reserving a little cream for the top of the gâteau, put the rest into a piping bag fitted with a medium plain nozzle and pipe some into each of the cold choux buns.
**7.** Put the sugar and 45 ml (3 tbsp) water into a heavy-based saucepan and boil until the edge just begins to turn straw-coloured. Dip the bun tops in this syrup, holding with a skewer or tongs.
**8.** Use the remainder of the syrup to stick the buns on to the choux pastry border to form a wall. Fill the centre of the gâteau with the crème pâtissière mixture.
**9.** Pipe the reserved cream around the edge in between the choux balls. Decorate with angelica and cherries. *Serves 6*

*Use the choux buns to form a border around flan.*

## BAKLAVA

*225 g (8 oz) shelled walnuts, ground*

*50 g (2 oz) light soft brown sugar*

*2.5 ml (½ level tsp) ground cinnamon*

*450 g (1 lb) packet phyllo or strudel pastry*

*150 g (5 oz) butter, melted*

*175 g (6 oz) clear honey*

**1.** Grease a 24 × 18 cm (9½ × 7 inch) roasting tin. Mix the walnuts, sugar and cinnamon together in a bowl. Halve each sheet of pastry to measure a 25 cm (10 inch) square.
**2.** Fit one sheet of pastry into the bottom of the tin, allowing it to come up the sides, and brush

with melted butter. Repeat with five more pastry sheets. Sprinkle with one-fifth of the nut mixture.
**3.** Repeat stage 2 four more times to produce five layers of walnut mixture. Top with remaining pastry and trim the sheets to fit the tin. Mark the surface of the pastry into 20 squares with the tip of a sharp knife.
**4.** Bake in the oven at 220°C (425°F) mark 7 for 15 minutes, then at 180°C (350°F) mark 4 for 10–15 minutes, until golden brown.
**5.** Meanwhile, warm the honey in a saucepan over a low heat, spoon over the cooked baklava, and leave to cool in the tin for 1–2 hours. Cut out the marked squares.
*Makes 20*

## MILLE-FEUILLES

*212 g (7½ oz) packet frozen puff pastry, thawed, or*
  *¼ quantity Puff Pastry (see page 376)*

*100 g (4 oz) raspberry jam*

*1 quantity Crème Pâtissière (see page 336)*

*175 g (6 oz) Glacé Icing (see page 422), to decorate*

*few drops red food colouring*

**1.** Roll out the pastry on a lightly floured surface into a rectangle measuring 25 × 23 cm (10 × 9 inches) and place on a dampened baking sheet. Prick all over with a fork.
**2.** Bake in the oven at 220°C (425°F) mark 7 for 10 minutes, until well risen and golden brown. Transfer to a wire rack and leave for 30 minutes to cool.
**3.** When cold, trim the pastry edges, cut in half lengthways and cut each half across into six slices. Spread half with raspberry jam, then cover with the crème pâtissière or cream.
**4.** Spread jam on the bases of the remaining pastry pieces and place jam side down on top of the first layers.
**5.** Mix 15 ml (1 tbsp) of the Glacé Icing with the red colouring. Set aside. Spread remaining glacé icing over the pastries.
**6.** Pour the pink icing into a greaseproof paper piping bag (see page 418). Cut off the tip and carefully pipe fine pink lines 1 cm (½ inch) apart on top of the white glacé icing, across each pastry.
**7.** Draw a skewer down the length of the Mille-Feuilles at 1 cm (½ inch) intervals to make a 'feathering' design. Leave for 1 hour to set.
*Makes 6*

## PROFITEROLES

*65 g (2½ oz) Choux Pastry (see page 379)*

*150 ml (5 fl oz) whipping or double cream*

*icing sugar, to decorate*

*Rich Chocolate Sauce (see page 211)*

**1.** Dampen the surface of two or three baking sheets with water. Fill a piping bag fitted with a medium plain nozzle with the choux pastry and pipe small balls, about the size of walnuts, on to the baking sheets.
**2.** Bake in the oven at 200°C (400°F) mark 6 for 15–20 minutes until crisp. Make a slit in the side of each profiterole to release the steam and leave to cool on a wire rack.
**3.** Whisk the cream until stiff and spoon into a piping bag fitted with medium plain nozzle and pipe some into each of the profiteroles. Dredge with icing sugar and pile them into a pyramid.
**4.** Pour a little of the sauce over and serve immediately with the sauce handed separately.
*Serves 6*

# CHEESE PUDDING AND CHEESECAKES Coeurs à la
Crème is a classic example of a cheese pudding. Cheesecakes are a flavoured mixture of cheese, cream and, usually, eggs. There are two basic kinds, the cooked cheesecake, which usually has a pastry or sponge base, and the uncooked cheesecake, which may be set with gelatine and often has a base of crushed biscuits.

## COEURS À LA CRÈME

*225 g (8 oz) cottage cheese*

*25 g (1 oz) caster sugar*

*300 ml (10 fl oz) double cream*

*5 ml (1 tsp) lemon juice*

*2 egg whites*

*150 ml (5 fl oz) single cream and fresh raspberries or*
  *strawberries, to serve*

**1.** Press the cottage cheese through a nylon sieve into a bowl. Add the sugar and mix well.
**2.** Whip the cream until stiff, then add the lemon juice. Stir into the cheese mixture.
**3.** Line four or six small heart-shaped moulds with muslin (this is unnecessary if serving in the moulds). Whisk the egg whites until stiff and fold into the cheese mixture. Spoon into moulds and drain overnight in the refrigerator. Serve with cream and fruit.
*Serves 4–6*

## TRADITIONAL BAKED CHEESECAKE

| |
|---|
| 50 g (2 oz) self raising flour |
| 2.5 ml (½ level tsp) baking powder |
| 50 g (2 oz) butter or margarine, softened |
| 275 g (10 oz) caster sugar |
| 5 eggs, size 2 |
| 450 g (1 lb) full fat soft or curd cheese |
| 40 g (1½ oz) plain flour |
| grated rind and juice of 1 lemon |
| 150 ml (5 fl oz) soured cream |
| 75 g (3 oz) sultanas |

*Traditional Baked Cheesecake*

**1.** Grease and base-line a 20.5 cm (8 inch) round spring-release cake tin.
**2.** Sift the self raising flour and baking powder into a bowl. Add the butter, 50 g (2 oz) sugar and 1 egg. Mix well and beat for 2–3 minutes. Spread the mixture evenly over the bottom of the prepared tin.
**3.** Separate the remaining eggs. Whisk the egg yolks with the remaining sugar until the mixture is thick and creamy.
**4.** Beat the cheese lightly. Add the whisked egg mixture and mix until smooth. Sift in the plain flour and stir it in, add the lemon rind and juice, the soured cream and the sultanas and stir in.
**5.** Whisk the egg whites until stiff, then fold into the mixture. Pour into the tin.
**6.** Bake in the oven at 170°C (325°F) mark 3 for 1 hour or until firm but still spongy to the touch. Turn off the heat and leave in the oven for 1 hour with the door ajar.

**7.** Remove from the oven and cool completely for 2–3 hours. Carefully remove the cheesecake from the tin to serve.
*Serves 8–10*

## LEMON CHEESECAKE

| |
|---|
| 75 g (3 oz) butter or margarine |
| 175 g (6 oz) digestive biscuits, finely crushed |
| 15 ml (1 level tbsp) gelatine |
| finely grated rind and juice of 1 lemon |
| 225 g (8 oz) cottage cheese, sieved |
| 142 ml (5 fl oz) soured cream |
| 75 g (3 oz) caster sugar |
| 2 eggs, separated |
| fresh fruit such as strawberries, sliced, black and green grapes, halved and seeded, or kiwi fruit, skinned and sliced, to decorate |

**1.** Melt the butter in a saucepan and mix in the biscuit crumbs. Press into the base of a 20.5 cm (8 inch) loose-bottomed or spring-release cake tin. Chill in the refrigerator for 30 minutes.
**2.** Sprinkle the gelatine in 60 ml (4 tbsp) water in a small bowl. Place over a pan of simmering water and stir until dissolved. Cool slightly.
**3.** Put the lemon rind, juice and cottage cheese into a bowl and add the soured cream and sugar and mix well together. Add the egg yolks and gelatine.
**4.** Whisk the egg whites until stiff and then fold lightly into the mixture. Carefully pour into the tin and chill for several hours, preferably overnight.
**5.** Remove the cheesecake from the tin and place on a flat serving plate. Decorate with fresh fruit.
*Serves 6*

# Hot Chocolate Cheesecake

*100 g (4 oz) unsalted butter, melted*

*225 g (8 oz) chocolate digestive biscuits, crushed*

*2 eggs, separated*

*75 g (3 oz) caster sugar*

*225 g (8 oz) curd cheese*

*40 g (1½ oz) ground or very finely chopped hazelnuts*

*150 ml (5 fl oz) double cream*

*25 g (1 oz) cocoa powder*

*10 ml (2 tsp) dark rum*

*icing sugar, to decorate*

Hot Chocolate Cheesecake

**1.** Melt the butter in a saucepan and mix in the biscuit crumbs. Press into the base and 4 cm (1½ inches) up the sides of a 20 cm (8 inch) loose-bottomed or spring-release cake tin. Chill in the refrigerator for 30 minutes.

**2.** Whisk the egg yolks and sugar together until thick enough to leave a trail on the surface when the whisk is lifted.

**3.** Whisk in the cheese, nuts, cream, cocoa powder and rum until evenly blended.

**4.** Whisk the egg whites until stiff, then fold into the cheese mixture. Pour into the biscuit base, then bake in the oven at 170°C (325°F) mark 3 for 1½–1¾ hours, until risen.

**5.** Remove carefully from the tin, sift the icing sugar over the top to coat lightly and serve immediately while still hot.

*Serves 8–10*

# Tropical Cheesecake

*75 g (3 oz) butter or margarine*

*175 g (6 oz) chocolate digestive biscuits, finely crushed*

*50 g (2 oz) desiccated coconut*

*2 medium mangoes*

*150 ml (¼ pint) pure orange juice*

*30 ml (2 level tbsp) gelatine*

*350 g (12 oz) full fat soft cheese*

*100 g (4 oz) caster sugar*

*2 eggs, separated*

*30 ml (2 tbsp) lemon juice*

*300 ml (10 fl oz) double cream*

*3 kiwi fruit, to decorate*

**1.** Lightly oil a 22 cm (8½ inch) spring-release cake tin. Base-line with greaseproof paper and grease the paper.

**2.** Melt the butter in a saucepan and stir in the biscuit crumbs and coconut. Press into the base of the prepared tin. Chill in the refrigerator for 30 minutes.

**3.** Peel the mangoes and cut the flesh from the flat oval stone. Discard the stone.

**4.** Roughly chop or mash the flesh. Put the orange juice into a bowl and sprinkle in the gelatine and leave to soak.

**5.** Place over a pan of simmering water and stir

until dissolved. Leave to cool for 5 minutes.

**6.** Beat the cheese and sugar until smooth, then beat in the egg yolks and lemon juice. Stir in the mango flesh and gelatine mixture. Lightly whip the cream and fold into the mixture.

**7.** Whisk the egg whites until stiff and carefully fold into the cheese mixture. Pour into the prepared tin and place in the refrigerator for 3–4 hours, until firm.

**8.** To serve, carefully remove the cheesecake from the tin. Decorate with kiwi fruit, peeled and sliced.

*Serves 8*

Tropical Cheesecake

# FRUIT PUDDINGS
Fruit can be served raw with cream or yogurt as a quick and simple dessert, made into fresh fruit salads or used for a whole range of delectable hot and cold puddings. Although this section is Fruit Puddings, many of the other recipes in this chapter, such as the baked puddings also include fruit.

## POACHED OR STEWED FRUITS IN SUGAR SYRUP

Use firm fruits, as soft fruits will not hold their shape well. Poach in a heavy-based pan large enough to take the fruit in one layer so that it cooks evenly.

*50–100 g (2–4 oz) sugar*

*450 g (1 lb) fresh fruit, prepared (see pages 309–318)*

**1.** Slowly dissolve the sugar in 300 ml (½ pint) water over a gentle heat. Bring to the boil and boil for 1 minute.
**2.** Add the fruit and simmer very gently in the sugar syrup until almost cooked, turning occasionally with a slotted spoon.
**3.** To prevent the fruit becoming mushy, remove the pan from the heat, cover and leave for several more minutes while the fruit finishes cooking.

*FLAVOURINGS FOR 450 g (1 lb) POACHED FRUIT*
**Apples** Add a squeeze of lemon juice, a strip of lemon rind, 1 or 2 cloves or a small piece of cinnamon stick.
**Gooseberry** Add a piece of bruised root ginger or a pinch of ground ginger.
**Peaches** Add 45–60 ml (3–4 tbsp) brandy after the fruit has cooked.
**Pears** Add 1 or 2 cloves or a piece of cinnamon stick.
**Plums** Add the plum kernels or a few almonds while the fruit is cooking.
**Rhubarb** Add a piece of bruised root ginger, a piece of cinnamon stick or a strip of lemon or orange rind.

## STEWED DRIED FRUIT

*450 g (1 lb) dried fruit, e.g. prunes, apricots, peaches, figs, apples, pears or a mixture*

*strip of lemon rind*

*granulated or demerara sugar, to taste*

**1.** Wash the fruit thoroughly, put in a bowl with 600 ml (1 pint) water and soak for 12 hours.

**2.** Put the fruit into a saucepan with the water in which it soaked. Add the lemon rind, bring to the boil and simmer gently until tender. Add the sugar.
**3.** Remove the fruit with a slotted spoon, boil the juice for a few minutes until syrupy, then strain it over the fruit.
*Serves 4*

## GOOSEBERRY FOOL

*450 g (1 lb) gooseberries, washed and topped and tailed*

*100 g (4 oz) sugar*

*15 ml (1 level tbsp) custard powder*

*150 ml (¼ pint) milk*

*few drops green food colouring*

*150 ml (5 fl oz) whipping cream*

*chopped nuts, to decorate*

**1.** Put the gooseberries and sugar in a saucepan with 30 ml (2 tbsp) water, cover and cook for about 20 minutes.
**2.** Sieve or purée the fruit in a blender or food processor.
**3.** Blend the custard powder with a little milk and heat the remaining milk. Pour hot milk on to

blended custard powder, stirring, then return to the pan and stir over a gentle heat until thickened.
**4.** Beat the custard into the fruit pulp and allow to cool. Add the food colouring, remembering that the cream will lighten the colour.
**5.** Whip the cream until stiff, then fold into the purée.
**6.** Pour into a glass dish or individual glasses and chill in the refrigerator.
**7.** Decorate with nuts for serving.
*Serves 4*

**Variations**
Use 450 g (1 lb) raspberries, strawberries, blackberries or damsons instead of gooseberries. Do not cook but purée and add sugar to taste. Sieve if necessary to remove seeds.

# FRUIT SALAD

*50–100 g (2–4 oz) sugar*

*juice of ½ lemon*

*selection of at least three fruit, e.g. 2 red-skinned apples, 2 oranges, 2 bananas, 100 g (4 oz) black or green grapes, 1 small pineapple*

1. Dissolve the sugar in 300 ml (½ pint) water over a gentle heat, bring to the boil and boil for 5 minutes. Cool and add the lemon juice.
2. Prepare the fruits: Quarter, core and slice the apples; peel and segment the oranges; slice the bananas, and halve and seed the grapes. Cut the pineapple into 1 cm (½ inch) slices, remove the skin and cut flesh into cubes. Put each fruit into the syrup as it is ready.
3. Mix them all together and if possible leave to stand for 2–3 hours before serving, to blend the flavours.
*Serves 4–6*

**Variations**

1. Add 15–30 ml (1–2 tbsp) fruit liqueur, brandy or rum to the syrup.
2. Substitute orange, pineapple or grape juice for the sugar syrup.

Any other combinations of fresh fruits can be used, such as dessert pears, strawberries, raspberries, cherries and melon.

Fruit salad can be served in a hollowed-out melon or pineapple; in either case the flesh which has been removed should be cut into chunks and used in the salad.

Canned fruit such as apricot halves, peach slices and pineapple chunks can also be used in fruit salads, or the more exotic canned guavas and lychees. If you use canned fruit, use some of the syrup from the can, with a little added lemon juice, to replace the sugar syrup.

# ORANGES IN CARAMEL

*8 medium juicy oranges*

*225 g (8 oz) caster sugar*

*30 ml (2 tbsp) orange-flavoured liqueur*

1. Thinly pare the rind from half the oranges and cut into very thin julienne strips. Place in a small saucepan and cover with water. Cover the pan and cook for 5 minutes until tender. Drain and rinse under cold water.
2. Cut away the pith from the oranges and both rind and pith from the four remaining oranges.
3. Slice the orange flesh into rounds, reserving any juice and discarding pips, and arrange in a serving dish. (If liked, the orange rounds can be reassembled in the shape of oranges and secured with wooden cocktail sticks.)
4. Place the sugar and 300 ml (½ pint) water in a saucepan and heat gently until the sugar has dissolved. Bring to the boil and boil until caramel-coloured.
5. Remove the pan from the heat, add 45 ml (3 tbsp) water and return it to a low heat to dissolve the caramel. Add the reserved orange juice and the liqueur.
6. Leave the caramel syrup to cool for 10 minutes, then pour over the oranges. Top with the julienne strips. Chill in the refrigerator for 2–3 hours, turning the oranges occasionally.
*Serves 8*

# PEARS IN PORT

*150 ml (¼ pint) port*

*75 g (3 oz) sugar*

*thinly pared rind of 1 lemon*

*4 large ripe pears*

*30 ml (2 level tbsp) redcurrant jelly*

*crisp sweet biscuits, to serve*

1. Put the port, sugar and lemon rind in a saucepan with 150 ml (¼ pint) water and heat gently until the sugar dissolves, stirring occasionally.
Bring to the boil.
2. Meanwhile, peel the pears and remove the cores. Add to the syrup, bring to the boil, cover and simmer gently until tender, about 15 minutes.
3. Using a slotted spoon, transfer the pears to a serving dish. Add the redcurrant jelly to the syrup and boil rapidly for about 5 minutes until well reduced.
4. Remove the lemon rind and pour the syrup over the pears. Cool. Serve with the biscuits.
*Serves 4*

## FLAMBÉ BANANAS

25 g (1 oz) butter or margarine

grated rind and juice of 1 large orange

2.5 ml (½ level tsp) ground cinnamon

4 large bananas, peeled

50 g (2 oz) demerara sugar

60 ml (4 tbsp) dark rum

orange shreds and slices, to decorate

cream or vanilla ice cream, to serve

**1.** Melt the butter in a frying pan and add the orange rind and juice. Stir in the cinnamon, then add the bananas and cook for a few minutes, until softened.
**2.** Add the sugar and stir until dissolved. Add the rum, set alight and stir gently to mix.
**3.** Decorate with orange shreds and slices and serve immediately with cream or ice cream.
*Serves 4*

*Flambé Bananas*

### Variation
This recipe can be cooked on a barbecue. Put each peeled banana in and prick with a skewer.

Mix together the rum, sugar, orange juice and cinnamon and pour over the bananas. Dot with the butter. Fold over the foil tightly and cook on the barbecue for 15 minutes.

## APRICOT SAVARIN

75 g (3 oz) dried apricots, soaked overnight

25 g (1 oz) fresh yeast or 15 ml (1 level tbsp) dried yeast
      and 5 ml (1 level tsp) sugar

90 ml (6 tbsp) tepid milk

225 g (8 oz) strong white flour

2.5 ml (½ level tsp) salt

30 ml (2 level tbsp) caster sugar

4 eggs, beaten

100 g (4 oz) butter or block margarine, softened

90 ml (6 tbsp) clear honey

45 ml (3 tbsp) brandy

450 g (1 lb) fresh or canned apricot halves

150 ml (5 fl oz) whipping cream

15 g (½ oz) flaked almonds, toasted

**1.** Grease a 1.4 litre (2½ pint) ring mould. Drain the apricots and chop roughly.
**2.** Blend the yeast, milk and 50 g (2 oz) of the flour together in a bowl. If using dried yeast, add the 5 ml (1 level tsp) sugar and leave in a warm place for 15 minutes until frothy.
**3.** Add the remaining flour with the salt, sugar, eggs, butter and dried apricots. Beat thoroughly for 3–4 minutes.
**4.** Pour into the ring mould and cover with a clean tea towel. Leave to rise in a warm place for 15 minutes.
**5.** Bake in the oven at 200°C (400°F) mark 6 for about 30 minutes. Turn out on to a plate.
**6.** Simmer the honey and 90 ml (6 tbsp) water together for 3–5 minutes. Add the brandy and, while still hot, spoon over the savarin. Cool.
**7.** Transfer carefully to a serving plate and spoon the apricots into the middle of the savarin. Whip the cream until stiff and pipe a border of cream at the top and bottom of the savarin and sprinkle with toasted flaked almonds.
*Serves 4*

# FRESH PEAR SHORTCAKE

150 g (5 oz) self raising flour

25 g (1 oz) ground rice

grated rind of 1 lemon

50 g (2 oz) dark soft brown sugar

150 g (5 oz) butter or block margarine

3 ripe large, even-sized pears, about 450 g (1 lb) in
    weight

125 g (4 oz) full fat soft cheese

1 egg

few drops almond flavouring

1. Lightly grease a 20.5 cm (8 inch) loose-based fluted flan tin and set aside. In a mixing bowl, stir together the flour, ground rice and lemon rind.
2. Sieve the sugar into the bowl. Rub in the butter and continue lightly kneading the mixture until it forms a dough.
3. Press the dough into the prepared tin with floured fingertips. Mark into six portions and prick well with a fork.

4. Bake in the oven at 190°C (375°F) mark 5 for 30–35 minutes until light brown and cooked through. Leave in the tin to cool slightly.
5. Using a sharp knife, peel and halve the pears. Then scoop out the cores using a teaspoon or corer.
6. Slice each pear half crossways into pieces 0.3 cm ($\frac{1}{8}$ inch) thick, keeping the slices together. Then place a sliced pear half on each portion of shortcake, fanning out the slices a little.
7. Beat together the soft cheese, egg and almond flavouring until smooth, then spoon over the pears, completely covering both fruit and shortcake.
8. Bake in the oven at 180°C (350°F) mark 4 for 40 minutes until golden. Ease out of the tin and serve warm or cold.
Note Flaked almonds can be scattered over the top before baking, if desired.
Serves 6

Fresh Pear Shortcake

## SUMMER PUDDING

*450 g (1 lb) mixed redcurrants, cherries and raspberries*

*150 g (5 oz) sugar*

*100–175 g (4–6 oz) white bread, thinly sliced and crusts removed*

*cream, to serve*

**1.** Strip the redcurrants off their stalks. Stone the cherries. Hull the raspberries. Place the fruits in a colander and wash under cold running water.
**2.** Put the sugar in a saucepan with 100 ml (4 fl oz) water, stir, then bring slowly to the boil. Add the fruits and cook gently for 5–10 minutes, until they are soft but retain their shape.
**3.** Meanwhile, line the base and sides of a 900 ml (1½ pint) pudding basin with the bread so that there are no spaces between the slices.
**4.** Add the fruit and cover with more slices of bread. Place a saucer with a weight on it on top of the pudding, leave to cool, then refrigerate overnight.
**5.** To serve, turn the pudding out on to a flat plate and serve with cream.
*Serves 4*

**Variation**
Use a mixture of fruits such as blackcurrants, blackberries and loganberries, using at least two fruits.

# MILK, CUSTARD AND CREAM PUDDINGS Milk
is the basis of many puddings; on its own as in easy-to-digest yogurt and junket or mixed with eggs or cream for a whole range of nutritious and tasty desserts.

### TYPES OF MILK
All milk sold in Britain is heat-treated in some way unless it has a solid or striped green foil top.
**Pasteurised milk** has a silver top. It is a white milk with thin cream on top.
**Channel Islands and South Devon milk** has a gold top and comes only from Jersey, Guernsey and South Devon cows. It has a richer colour and thicker cream than silver-top.
**Homogenised milk** has a red top. The milk is forced through a tiny valve under pressure so that the fat (cream) globules are reduced in size and do not separate from the milk.
**Semi-skimmed milk** has a red and silver striped top. It has some of the fat removed.
**Skimmed milk** has all the fat removed.
**Sterilised milk** is usually sold in tall bottles capped like beer. The milk is heated, homogenised, bottled and sealed, then heated for 30–40 minutes. The milk has a slight cooked flavour. It can be kept unopened for 2–3 months without refrigeration.
**UHT or Long-Life milk** is heated to 132°C (270°F) for 1 second, then packed under sterile conditions into aluminium foil-lined containers. It lasts un-opened for months but is like ordinary milk once opened.
**Buttermilk** is the liquid left after churning cream to make butter. However, most buttermilk is made from skimmed milk with a culture added to it which makes it thicker and slightly acidic.
**Goat's milk** is more easily available nowadays, as many people cannot digest cow's milk.

### TYPES OF CREAM
Creams vary in their fat content, which is why some are richer than others. In order to whip successfully, cream must have a fat content of at least 35 per cent.
**Half cream and single cream** have a minimum fat content of 12 per cent and 18 per cent. They are ideal pouring creams.
**Soured cream** has the same fat content as single cream. Its flavour results from incubating cream with a harmless bacteria and culture to turn it slightly acid.
**Crème fraîche** is double cream which has been fermented under controlled conditions long enough to have a lactic taste which is neither sweet nor sour.
**Spooning cream** is homogenised cream, suitable for pouring or adding to coffee. It has the same fat content as whipping cream.
**Whipping cream** has a fat content of at least 35 per cent and will whip to at least double its volume. It is good for folding into mousses.
**Double cream** has a fat content of 48 per cent.

It will whip to slightly less volume than whipping cream, but adding 15 ml (1 tbsp) milk for every 150 ml (5 fl oz) cream will help it achieve greater volume. It is good for piping and cake fillings.

**Extra thick double cream** also has a fat content of 48 per cent but has been homogenised.

**Clotted cream** has a fat content of 55 per cent. It has a slightly nutty flavour and a thick consistency but cannot be whipped.

**UHT cream** is available as half, single, whipping and double. It will keep unopened for 2–4 months depending on its fat content.

**Aerosol cream** This is heat-treated cream which may contain up to 13 per cent added sugar, stabilisers and a propellant to make it flow from its container. It is very light textured but loses its volume quickly.

**Frozen cream** This is fresh cream which has been frozen at very low temperatures. It is available as single, double, whipped and clotted.

**Sterilised cream** This type of cream is in cans and has been heat-treated and homogenised. The sterilisation process gives it a distinctive caramel flavour. It will not whip.

**Extended life cream** This is packed in vacuum-sealed bottles and keeps in the refrigerator, unopened for 2–3 weeks. It is spoonable double cream and can be whipped.

## Yogurt

Homemade yogurt is very easy to make using unpasteurised yogurt containing live bacteria, which remain dormant as long as the yogurt is kept cool. Pasteurised yogurt (it will say on the label) is not suitable. Use pasteurised, sterilised or UHT milk. Yogurt can be made in a vacuum flask or in an electric yogurt maker.

*568 ml (1 pint) milk*

*15 ml (1 tbsp) natural yogurt (not pasteurised)*

*15 ml (1 level tbsp) skimmed milk powder (optional)*

**1.** Sterilise a vacuum flask and a small saucepan with boiling water or recommended sterilising solution. Warm the vacuum flask.

**2.** Reserve 30 ml (2 tbsp) of the milk and heat the rest to blood temperature (about 37°C/98.4°F).

**3.** Blend the reserved milk with the yogurt and skimmed milk powder (if using) to a smooth paste. Gradually stir into the warm milk.

**4.** Pour into the warmed vacuum flask. Replace the lid and leave for 6–8 hours, undisturbed. Transfer to a bowl and chill in the refrigerator.

*Makes about 600 ml (1 pint)*

## Junket

It is important to use pasteurised milk for junket. Do not use homogenised milk or it will not set properly. Do not overheat the milk, or cool the junket too rapidly as this may kill the rennet enzyme. Junket should not be disturbed until it is served as once it is cut it separates into curds and whey.

*568 ml (1 pint) pasteurised milk*

*15 ml (1 level tbsp) caster sugar*

*5 ml (1 tsp) liquid rennet*

*freshly grated nutmeg, to serve*

**1.** Gently heat the milk in a saucepan until just warm to the finger. Remove from the heat and stir in the sugar until dissolved. Add the rennet, stirring gently.

**2.** Pour into a shallow dish and leave 1–1½ hours in a warm place, undisturbed, until set.

**3.** Chill in the refrigerator and sprinkle the top with nutmeg to serve.

*Note* Rennet is sold as a liquid or in tablet form, with or without added colouring and flavouring. Use according to the directions on the packet.

*Serves 4*

## Rice Pudding

*50 g (2 oz) short grain white rice*

*30 ml (2 level tbsp) sugar*

*568 ml (1 pint) milk*

*knob of butter or margarine*

*freshly grated nutmeg*

**1.** Grease a 900 ml (1½ pint) ovenproof dish.

**2.** Add the rice, sugar and milk and stir; dot with shavings of butter and sprinkle nutmeg on top.

**3.** Bake in the oven at 150°C (300°F) mark 2 for about 2 hours; stir it after about 30 minutes.

*Serves 4*

# BLANCMANGE

60 ml (4 level tbsp) cornflour

568 ml (1 pint) milk

strip of lemon rind

45 ml (3 level tbsp) sugar

1. Blend the cornflour to a smooth paste with 30 ml (2 tbsp) of the milk.
2. Put the remaining milk in a saucepan with the lemon rind, bring to the boil, then strain it on to the blended mixture, stirring well.
3. Return the mixture to the pan and bring to the boil, stirring all the time, until the mixture thickens and cook for a further 3 minutes. Add sugar to taste.
4. Pour into a 600 ml (1 pint) dampened jelly mould and leave for several hours until set. Turn out to serve.
*Serves 4*

**Variations**
CHOCOLATE
Omit the lemon rind and add 50 g (2 oz) melted chocolate to the cooked mixture.

COFFEE
Omit the lemon rind and add 15–30 ml (1–2 tbsp) coffee essence.

ORANGE
Substitute the lemon rind with 5 ml (1 level tsp) grated orange rind.

# CREAMED RICE

50 g (2 oz) short grain white rice

568 ml (1 pint) milk

30 ml (2 level tbsp) sugar

150 ml (5 fl oz) whipping cream

1. Put the rice, milk and sugar into a heavy-based or double saucepan. Cover and cook gently for about 30 minutes or up to 2 hours in a double pan, until creamy. Remove the lid after half the time and cook uncovered, stirring occasionally.
2. Allow to cool for 3–4 hours. Whip the cream, then fold in just before serving.
*Serves 4*

# SEMOLINA PUDDING

568 ml (1 pint) milk

knob of butter or margarine

60 ml (4 level tbsp) semolina

50 g (2 oz) sugar

1. Heat the milk and butter and sprinkle on the semolina. Bring to the boil, then cook for a further 2–3 minutes, stirring all the time.
2. Remove from the heat and stir in the sugar. Pour the pudding into a greased ovenproof dish.
3. Bake in the oven at 200°C (400°F) mark 6 for about 30 minutes, until lightly browned.
*Note* Alternatively, do not bake but cook for a further 10–15 minutes in the pan.
*Serves 4*

**Variations**
1. Add the grated rind of an orange or lemon to the milk.

*FINE SAGO AND FLAKED GRAINS*
Prepare as for semolina, but cook in the oven for 40–50 minutes or for 15–20 minutes in the pan.

# BAKED CUSTARD

568 ml (1 pint) milk

3 eggs

30 ml (2 level tbsp) caster sugar

freshly grated nutmeg

1. Warm the milk in a saucepan but do not boil. Whisk the eggs and sugar lightly in a bowl, then pour on the hot milk, stirring.
2. Strain the mixture into a greased ovenproof dish. Sprinkle the nutmeg on top and bake in the oven at 170°C (325°F) mark 3 for about 45 minutes, until set and firm to the touch. Serve hot or cold.
*Serves 4*

# CRÈME CARAMEL

*125 g (4 oz) sugar plus 15 ml (1 level tbsp)*

*4 eggs*

*568 ml (1 pint) milk*

*1.25 ml (¼ tsp) vanilla flavouring*

*pouring cream, to serve*

**1.** Place the 125 g (4 oz) sugar in a small saucepan and carefully pour in 150 ml (¼ pint) water. Heat gently until all the sugar has dissolved, stirring occasionally.

**2.** Bring the syrup to a fast boil and cook rapidly until the caramel is a golden brown. Remove from the heat and leave for a few seconds to darken. Pour into a 15 cm (6 inch) soufflé dish and cool.

**3.** Whisk the eggs and remaining sugar in a bowl. Warm the milk and pour on to the egg mixture. Whisk in the vanilla flavouring, then strain the custard on to the cool caramel.

**4.** Stand the dish in a roasting tin containing enough hot water to come halfway up the sides of the dish. Bake in the oven at 170°C (325°F) mark 3 for about 1 hour. The custard should be *just* set and firm to the touch, but not solid.

**5.** When cold, cover tightly with cling film and refrigerate for several hours, preferably overnight. Take out of the refrigerator 30 minutes before serving.

**6.** Using the fingertips, gently loosen and ease the edges of custard away from the dish. Take a rimmed serving dish and place over the Crème Caramel. Hold the two dishes firmly together and turn over quickly until the cooking dish is uppermost.

**7.** Still holding the dishes together, give a few sharp sideways shakes until the suction is heard to release. Leave the cooking dish upturned for a few minutes until all the caramel has drained

*Crème Caramel*

out. Then stand the dish in a pan of hot water to soften remaining caramel and pour over the Crème Caramel.

*Serves 4*

**Variation**

Divide the mixture between 6 ramekin dishes. Cook for 40 minutes only.

# BREAD AND BUTTER PUDDING

*6 thin slices of bread, crusts removed*

*50 g (2 oz) butter or margarine*

*50 g (2 oz) currants or sultanas, or mixture of both*

*40 g (1½ oz) caster sugar*

*2 eggs*

*568 ml (1 pint) milk*

**1.** Thickly spread bread slices with butter. Cut into fingers or small squares. Put half into a greased 1.1 litre (2 pint) ovenproof dish. Sprinkle

with all the fruit and half the sugar.

**2.** Top with the remaining bread, buttered side uppermost. Sprinkle with the rest of the sugar.

**3.** Beat the eggs and milk well together. Strain into the dish over the bread.

**4.** Leave to stand for 30 minutes, so that the bread absorbs some of the liquid. Bake in the oven at 170°C (325°F) mark 3 for 45 minutes–1 hour, until set and the top is crisp and golden.

*Serves 4*

## QUEEN OF PUDDINGS

4 eggs

568 ml (1 pint) milk

100 g (4 oz) fresh breadcrumbs

45–60 ml (3–4 level tbsp) raspberry jam

75 g (3 oz) caster sugar

1. Separate three eggs and beat together the three egg yolks and one whole egg. Add to the milk and mix well. Stir in the breadcrumbs.

2. Spread the jam on the bottom of a pie dish. Pour over the milk mixture and leave for 30 minutes.

3. Bake in the oven at 150°C (300°F) mark 2 for 1 hour, until set.

4. Whisk the egg whites until stiff, then fold in the sugar. Pile on top of the custard and return to the oven for a further 15–20 minutes until the meringue is set.

*Serves 4*

## COFFEE BAVAROIS

125 g (4 oz) well roasted coffee beans

900 ml (1½ pints) milk

6 egg yolks

75 g (3 oz) caster sugar

20 ml (4 level tsp) gelatine

300 ml (10 fl oz) double cream

30 ml (2 tbsp) coffee flavoured liqueur, such as
    Tia Maria (optional)

coffee dragées and grated chocolate, to decorate

1. Put the coffee beans in a saucepan and place over a low heat, warm very gently for 2–3 minutes, shaking the pan frequently. Remove from the heat, pour the milk into the pan, return to the heat and bring up to the boil.

2. Remove from the heat, cover and leave to infuse for 30 minutes.

3. Place the egg yolks and caster sugar in a deep mixing bowl and beat until the mixture is thick and light in colour. Strain the coffee infusion on to the egg yolks, then stir well.

4. Return the custard mixture to the rinsed out saucepan and cook very gently, stirring, until the custard thickens very slightly. Do not boil. Strain into a large bowl and cool.

5. In a small bowl, sprinkle the gelatine over 60 ml (4 tbsp) water. Place over a pan of hot water and

stir until dissolved.

6. Stir the gelatine into the cool custard. Stand the custard in a roasting tin of water and surround with ice cubes. Stir the custard frequently while it cools to setting point.

7. Meanwhile, lightly whip half the cream and grease a 1.4 litre (2 pint) soufflé dish or mould.

8. When the custard is well chilled and beginning to thicken, fold in the whipped cream. Pour the setting custard into the dish and refrigerate until completely set.

9. With a dampened finger, gently ease the edges of the cream away from the dish. Moisten a flat plate and place over the dish. Invert the plate and shake gently. Ease off the dish and slide the cream into the centre of the plate.

10. Whisk the remaining cream until it holds its shape, then gradually whisk in the Tia Maria. Spoon into a piping bag fitted with a 1 cm (½ inch) star vegetable nozzle. Pipe the coffee cream around the top edge in a shell pattern. Decorate with coffee dragées and grated chocolate.

*Serves 6*

### Variation
CHOCOLATE BAVAROIS
Omit the coffee beans, liqueur and coffee dragées. Dissolve 75 g (3 oz) plain chocolate in a little milk, whisk in the remaining milk. Complete as above.

## SYLLABUB

150 ml (¼ pint) dry white wine

finely grated rind and juice of 1 lemon

75 g (3 oz) caster sugar

300 ml (10 fl oz) double cream

1. Put the wine, lemon rind and juice and sugar in

a bowl. Leave to infuse for at least 3 hours.

2. Add the cream and whisk until the mixture just holds its shape. Do not overwhip or the mixture may curdle.

3. Spoon into six glass dishes and chill in the refrigerator for several hours before serving.

*Serves 6*

## OLD ENGLISH TRIFLE

| |
|---|
| 568 ml (1 pint) milk |
| ½ vanilla pod |
| 2 eggs, plus 2 egg yolks |
| 30 ml (2 level tbsp) caster sugar plus extra for sprinkling |
| 1 Victoria Sandwich Cake (see page 395) or 8 trifle sponges |
| 175 g (6 oz) raspberry or strawberry jam |
| 100 g (4 oz) macaroons, lightly crushed |
| 100 ml (4 fl oz) medium sherry |
| 300 ml (10 fl oz) double cream |
| 40 g (1½ oz) flaked almonds, toasted and 50 g (2 oz) glacé cherries, to decorate |

1. Bring the milk to the boil with the vanilla pod. Remove from the heat, cover and leave to infuse for 20 minutes.
2. Beat together the eggs, egg yolks and sugar and strain on to the milk. Cook gently, without boiling, stirring, until the custard thickens slightly. Pour into a bowl; lightly sprinkle the surface with sugar and cool.
3. Spread the sponge cake with jam, cut up and place in a 2 litre (3½ pint) shallow serving dish with the macaroons. Spoon over the sherry and leave for 2 hours. Pour over the cold custard.
4. Lightly whip the cream. Top the custard with half the cream. Pipe the remaining cream on top and decorate.
*Serves 6*

## CHARLOTTE RUSSE

| |
|---|
| 135 g (4¾ oz) packet lemon jelly |
| 45 ml (3 tbsp) lemon juice |
| 2 glacé cherries, quartered |
| piece of angelica, cut into triangles |
| 300 ml (½ pint) milk |
| vanilla pod |
| 15 ml (1 level tbsp) gelatine |
| 3 egg yolks |
| 45 ml (3 level tbsp) caster sugar |
| 18 sponge (boudoir) fingers |
| 300 ml (10 fl oz) whipping cream |

1. Dissolve the jelly in a measuring jug making up to 500 ml (1 pint) with the lemon juice and water. Spoon a thin covering of cool jelly into the base of a 1.1 litre (2 pint) charlotte mould; refrigerate.
2. When set, arrange the cherries and angelica on top. Carefully spoon over the liquid jelly to a depth of about 2.5 cm (1 inch). Refrigerate to set, along with remaining jelly.
3. Pour the milk into a medium saucepan and add the vanilla pod. Bring slowly to the boil, remove from the heat, cover and leave to infuse for at least 10 minutes.
4. In a small bowl, sprinkle the gelatine in 45 ml (3 tbsp) water and leave to soak for about 10 minutes.
5. Beat together the egg yolks and sugar, then stir in the strained milk. Return to the pan and cook gently, stirring, until the custard thickens sufficiently to just coat the back of a spoon. Do

not boil. Pour into a large bowl and stir in the gelatine. Cool.
6. Trim a small amount off each sponge finger so that they just fit the charlotte mould, without rising above the rim; reserve trimmings. Stand the fingers closely together, rounded side down, sugar side out around the edge of the mould.

*Line inside of mould with sponge fingers trimmed to the correct length.*

7. Whip the cream until it just holds its shape and stir into the custard. Place the bowl in a roasting tin with iced water to come halfway up its sides. Stir occasionally until on the point of setting and has a thick consistency. Pour into the mould.
8. Trim the sponge fingers level with the custard. Lay all the trimmings on top of the custard. Cover tightly and refrigerate to set for at least 3 hours.
9. Using fingertips, ease the sponge fingers away from the edge, then tilt it slightly to allow an airlock to form between the two. Dip the base of the mould in hot water for about 5 seconds only, then invert on to a damp plate to unmould.
10. Take the remaining set jelly out of the refrigerator and loosen by dipping the jug in hot water. Turn out on to a board lined with damp greaseproof paper and chop into small pieces. Spoon around the Charlotte Russe.
*Serves 6*

## BOODLE'S ORANGE FOOL

*4–6 trifle sponge cakes, cut into 1 cm (½ inch) thick*
*slices*

*grated rind and juice of 2 oranges*

*grated rind and juice of 1 lemon*

*25–50 g (1–2 oz) sugar*

*300 ml (10 fl oz) double cream*

*orange slices or segments, to decorate*

**1.** Use the sponge cake slices to line the bottom and halfway up the sides of a deep dish or bowl.

**2.** Mix the orange and lemon rinds and juice with the sugar and stir until the sugar has completely dissolved.

**3.** In another bowl, whip the cream until it just starts to thicken, then slowly add the sweetened fruit juice, continuing to whip until the cream is light and thickened and the juice all absorbed.

**4.** Pour the mixture over the sponge cakes and refrigerate for at least 2 hours. Decorate with orange slices.

*Serves 6*

## CRÈME BRÛLÉE

*600 ml (20 fl oz) double cream*

*1 vanilla pod*

*4 egg yolks*

*100 g (4 oz) caster sugar*

**1.** Pour the cream into the top of a double saucepan or into a mixing bowl placed over a pan of simmering water. Add the vanilla pod and warm gently until almost boiling, then remove from the heat. Remove the vanilla pod.

**2.** Beat together the egg yolks and 50 g (2 oz) of the caster sugar until light in colour. Gradually pour on the cream, stirring until evenly mixed.

**3.** Stand 6 individual ramekin dishes in a roasting tin, then pour in enough hot water to come

halfway up the sides of the dishes. Pour the custard mixture slowly into the ramekins, dividing it equally between them.

**4.** Bake in the oven at 150°C (300°F) mark 2 for about 1 hour until set. Do not allow the skin to colour. Remove from the tin and leave to cool, then refrigerate overnight.

**5.** Sprinkle the remaining sugar evenly over the top of each Crème Brûlée and put under a preheated hot grill for 2–3 minutes until the sugar turns to a caramel. Leave to cool, then chill before serving.

*Note* This is delicious served with a selection of fruit, such as freshly sliced strawberries and peaches and stoned cherries.

*Serves 6*

*Crème Brûlée*

## CUSTARD CREAM

*300 ml (½ pint) Egg Custard Sauce (see page 210)*

*5–10 ml (1–2 tsp) vanilla flavouring*

*10 ml (2 level tsp) gelatine*

*300 ml (10 fl oz) double cream*

*sugar to taste*

**1.** Make up the custard, add the vanilla flavouring and stir occasionally as it cools. To prevent a skin forming, press a piece of wetted greaseproof paper down on to the surface of the custard.

**2.** In a small bowl, sprinkle the gelatine over 30 ml (2 tbsp) water and leave to soak. Place the bowl over a pan of simmering water and stir until dissolved. Cool slightly. Pour into the custard in a steady, thin stream, stirring.

**3.** Whip the cream until stiff, then fold into the custard, check the sweetness and when the mixture is just on the point of setting, pour into a dampened 900 ml (1½ pint) jelly mould and leave to set. Unmould just before serving.

*Serves 4*

**Variation**

GINGER CREAM

Add 50 g (2 oz) preserved ginger, chopped.

## FLOATING ISLANDS

*5 egg yolks, beaten*

*450 ml (¾ pint) milk*

*50 g (2 oz) caster sugar plus 75 ml (5 tbsp)*

*2.5 ml (½ tsp) vanilla flavouring*

*1 egg white*

**1.** Make custard, put the egg yolks, milk and 50 g (2 oz) sugar in the top of a double boiler, or in a heavy-based saucepan. Cook gently for about 15 minutes, stirring, until the mixture thickens and coats the back of the spoon. Stir in the vanilla flavouring.

**2.** Divide the custard between four dessert dishes. Cover and refrigerate for 1 hour.

**3.** Meanwhile, whisk the egg white until stiff. Add 30 ml (2 tbsp) sugar and whisk again until the sugar is dissolved.

**4.** Put some cold water into a shallow tin. Bring to a gentle simmer and spoon on the meringue in four even mounds. Poach for about 5 minutes until set, turning once.

**5.** Remove the meringues with a slotted spoon, drain for a minute on absorbent kitchen paper and spoon on to the custard in the glasses.

**6.** Put the remaining sugar into a heavy-based saucepan and cook, stirring, for about 3 minutes, until it forms a golden syrup.

**7.** Remove from the heat and leave for 2 minutes to cool slightly, then drizzle a little of the warm syrup over the top of each meringue.

*Serves 4*

## BANANA CHARTREUSE

*135 g (4¾ oz) packet lemon jelly, broken into squares*

*3 bananas*

*juice of ½ a lemon*

*about 6 shelled pistachio nuts, cut in half lengthways*

*15 ml (3 tsp) gelatine*

*60 ml (4 tbsp) dark rum*

*150 ml (5 fl oz) double cream*

*50 g (2 oz) icing sugar, sifted*

**1.** Make up the jelly according to the packet instructions, but making up to only 300 ml (½ pint). Cool for 30 minutes.

**2.** Pour about one-third of the jelly into a chilled 18 cm (6 inch) charlotte mould. Chill for 30 minutes until set.

**3.** Peel 1 banana, slice and add lemon juice.

**4.** Arrange the banana slices on top of the set jelly and place the pistachios between the bananas.

**5.** Slowly spoon over the remaining cool jelly, taking care not to dislodge the bananas and pistachios. Chill for 30 minutes, until set.

**6.** In a small bowl, sprinkle the gelatine over the rum and remaining lemon juice. Place over a pan of hot water and stir until dissolved. Cool slightly.

**7.** Whip the cream with the icing sugar. Peel and mash the remaining bananas, then combine with the cream and cooled gelatine liquid. Spoon on top of the set jelly and chill in the refrigerator for about 2 hours, until set.

**8.** Dip base of mould in hot water for a few seconds, then invert on to a serving plate. Chill.

*Serves 4–6*

# Soufflés and Mousses

Hot soufflés are a rich creamy mixture with whisked egg white in them. As the soufflé cooks, the air expands making the soufflé rise. They are usually based either on a sweet white sauce called a panada (or panade), to which egg yolks and flavourings are added, or on a crème pâtissière, a sauce in which the egg yolks are already incorporated.

Cold soufflés are not true soufflés but mousses which are set in a dish with a collar to give a 'soufflé-like' appearance. When the collar is removed, the soufflé looks as if it has risen like a baked soufflé. Mousses are an egg mixture, flavoured with fruit, liqueur or chocolate. They are usually lightened with egg white and may be set with gelatine. They are usually served cold.

### Watch Points

- Ideally, beat egg whites in a metal bowl, copper is best but stainless steel is also good. If beating by hand, use a balloon or rotary whisk or electric beater.
- Make sure the bowl and whisk are spotlessly clean, if there is any grease the egg whites will not whisk to maximum volume.
- Start whisking with a slow circular movement and gradually work faster, lifting the eggs high out of the bowl to help incorporate as much air as possible.
- Do not overbeat or the foam will become dry and brittle.

### To Prepare a Cold Soufflé Dish

- Cut a strip of double greaseproof paper long enough to go right around the soufflé dish with the ends overlapping slightly, and deep enough to reach from the bottom of the dish to about 7 cm (2¾ inches) above the top.
- Tie the paper around the outside of the dish with string, or stick it with adhesive tape, so that it fits closely to the rim of the dish and prevents any mixture escaping.
- Place the prepared soufflé dish on a baking tray. This makes it easier to move the filled dish from the work surface to the refrigerator for chilling.
- To take off the paper when the soufflé has set, remove the string and ease the paper away from the mixture with a knife dipped in hot water.

## Lemon Soufflé

| |
|---|
| grated rind of 3 lemons |
| 90 ml (6 tbsp) lemon juice |
| 100 g (4 oz) caster sugar |
| 4 eggs, separated |
| 15 ml (1 level tbsp) gelatine |
| 300 ml (10 fl oz) double cream |
| angelica leaves and mimosa balls, to decorate |

1. Prepare a 900 ml (1½ pint) soufflé dish with a paper collar.
2. In a deep bowl, whisk the lemon rind, juice, sugar and egg yolks together over a pan of hot water until thick.
3. Sprinkle the gelatine in 45 ml (3 tbsp) water in a small bowl and leave to soak. Place over a pan of simmering water and stir until dissolved. Stir into the soufflé mixture and chill.
4. Lightly whip the cream. Whisk the egg whites until stiff. Fold half the cream into the soufflé, then the egg whites, until evenly blended.
5. Pour into the soufflé dish and level the surface. Chill in the refrigerator for at least 4 hours, until set.
6. Remove the paper from the edge of the soufflé. Decorate the soufflé with the remaining cream, angelica leaves and mimosa balls.
*Serves 4*

**Variation**
*Chilled Strawberry Soufflé*
Substitute the lemon rind and juice with 450 g (12 oz) strawberries, puréed. Fold into the thickened sugar and egg yolks mixture before folding in the gelatine. Decorate the top of the soufflé with fresh strawberry slices and rosettes of piped cream.

## RASPBERRY SOUFFLÉ

450 g (1 lb) raspberries, hulled

4 eggs, separated

100 g (4 oz) caster sugar

15 ml (1 level tbsp) gelatine

15 ml (1 tbsp) orange flavoured liqueur (optional)

450 ml (15 fl oz) whipping cream

1. Prepare a 1.1 litre (2 pint) soufflé dish with a paper collar.

2. Reserve six raspberries for decoration. Purée the remainder in a blender or food processor, then sieve the purée to remove the seeds.

3. In a deep bowl, whisk the egg yolks and sugar together over a pan of hot water until thick. Stir in the raspberry purée.

4. Sprinkle the gelatine in 30 ml (2 tbsp) water and the curaçao, if using, in a small bowl and leave to soak. Place the bowl over a pan of simmering water and stir until dissolved. Add the gelatine to the raspberry mixture and leave to chill.

5. Lightly whip the cream. Whisk the egg whites until stiff. Fold two-thirds of the cream into the soufflé, then gently fold in the egg whites, until evenly blended.

6. Pour into the soufflé dish and level the surface. Chill in the refrigerator for at least 4 hours, until set.

7. Remove the paper from the edge of the soufflé. Decorate with the reserved raspberries and whipped cream.
*Serves 6*

## CHOCOLATE SOUFFLÉ

150 ml (¼ pint) milk

175 g (6 oz) plain chocolate

4 eggs, separated, plus 1 egg white

75 g (3 oz) caster sugar

15 ml (1 level tbsp) gelatine

300 ml (10 fl oz) whipping cream

1. Prepare a 900 ml (1½ pint) soufflé dish with a paper collar.

2. Heat the milk and 150 g (5 oz) chocolate together. Bring to the boil and boil for 2 minutes, whisking, then remove from the heat.

3. Beat the egg yolks with the sugar until light. Pour on the flavoured milk, return to the pan and cook over a gentle heat, without boiling, until the custard coats the back of a spoon. Pour into a bowl and cool.

4. Sprinkle the gelatine in 45 ml (3 tbsp) water in a small bowl and leave to soak. Place over a pan of simmering water and stir until dissolved. Stir into the custard and cool.

5. Lightly whip the cream. Stir half into the custard on the point of setting. Whisk the four egg whites until stiff, then fold into the mixture.

6. Pour into the soufflé dish and chill in the refrigerator for at least 4 hours, until set. Remove the paper and decorate with remaining cream and grated chocolate.
*Serves 4*

## HOT VANILLA SOUFFLÉ

50 g (2 oz) caster sugar

4 eggs, size 2

60 ml (4 level tbsp) plain flour

300 ml (½ pint) milk

2.5 ml (½ tsp) vanilla flavouring

icing sugar for dusting (optional)

1. Grease a 1.7 litre (3 pint) soufflé dish.

2. In a saucepan, cream the sugar with one whole egg and one yolk until pale cream in colour. Stir in the flour, then pour on the milk and mix until smooth. Bring to the boil, stirring, and simmer for 2 minutes.

3. Cool slightly, then beat in the remaining yolks and vanilla flavouring. Whisk the egg whites until stiff and gently fold into the sauce.

4. Pour into the soufflé dish and bake in the oven at 180°C (350°F) mark 4 for about 45 minutes, until well risen, firm to the touch and pale golden. If you wish, after 30 minutes cooking, quickly dust the soufflé with icing sugar and continue to bake.
*Serves 4*

## HOT CHOCOLATE SOUFFLÉ

*75 g (3 oz) plain chocolate or chocolate dots*

*150 ml (¼ pint) milk*

*50 g (2 oz) caster sugar*

*60 ml (4 level tbsp) flour*

*knob of butter or margarine*

*3 egg yolks*

*4 egg whites*

*icing sugar for dusting*

**1.** Grease a 1.1 litre (2 pint) soufflé dish.

**2.** Put the chocolate in a bowl with 30 ml (2 tbsp) water and melt over a pan of simmering water.

**3.** Heat the milk, reserving a little, with the sugar, then pour on to the melted chocolate.

**4.** Blend the flour to a smooth paste with the remaining milk, and stir in the chocolate mixture. Return to the pan, bring to the boil, stirring, then cook for 2 minutes, stirring occasionally. Add the butter, in small pieces, then leave until lukewarm.

**5.** Stir in the egg yolks. Whisk the egg whites until stiff and fold into the mixture.

**6.** Pour into the soufflé dish and bake in the oven at 200°C (400°F) mark 6 for about 35 minutes, until well risen and firm to the touch. Dust with icing sugar before serving.

*Serves 4*

*Hot Apricot Soufflé*

## HOT APRICOT SOUFFLÉ

*450 g (1 lb) fresh apricots, halved and stoned*

*40 g (1½ oz) butter or margarine*

*60 ml (4 level tbsp) plain flour*

*150 ml (¼ pint) milk*

*50 g (2 oz) caster sugar*

*4 eggs, size 2, separated*

*15 ml (1 tbsp) apricot brandy*

*icing sugar for dusting*

*single cream, to serve*

**1.** Put the apricots in a saucepan with 30 ml (2 tbsp) water and cook until soft. Meanwhile, grease a 2 litre (3½ pint) soufflé dish.

**2.** Rub the fruit through a sieve or purée in a blender or food processor. Discard the skins.

**3.** Melt the butter in a saucepan, stir in the flour and cook gently for 1 minute, stirring. Remove from the heat and gradually stir in the milk and apricot purée. Bring to the boil, and continue to cook, stirring, until the sauce thickens.

**4.** Remove from heat and stir in sugar, egg yolks and brandy. Whisk egg whites until stiff and fold into mixture.

**5.** Pour into the soufflé dish and bake in the oven at 180°C (350°F) mark 4 for 45 minutes, until well risen. Dust with icing sugar and serve with cream.

*Serves 4*

# BLACKCURRANT MOUSSE

*225 g (8 oz) fresh blackcurrants, stringed and washed*

*caster sugar to taste*

*3 egg yolks*

*150 ml (5 fl oz) double cream*

*3 egg whites*

Cook the blackcurrants with 30 ml (2 tbsp)
water, until soft enough to sieve or purée in a
blender or food processor. (This should give
150 ml (¼ pint) purée.)

Put the purée, sugar and egg yolks into a large
bowl over a saucepan of hot water and whisk until
thick and creamy—the mixture should be stiff
enough to retain the impression of the whisk for a
few seconds.

**3.** Remove from the heat and whisk until cool.
Lightly whip the cream, then fold into mixture.

**4.** Whisk the egg whites until stiff and gently fold
into the blackcurrant mixture.

**5.** Pour the mixture into a shallow dish or
individual soufflé dishes, chill in the refrigerator
for about 2 hours, until set. Serve the same day.
*Serves 4–6*

# MANGO MOUSSE

*2 ripe mangoes, about 350 g (12 oz) each*

*finely grated rind and juice of 1 orange*

*2 whole eggs, plus 1 egg yolk*

*40 g (1½ oz) caster sugar*

*15 ml (1 level tbsp) gelatine*

*300 ml (10 fl oz) double cream*

Stand the mangoes on a board on their long
rounded edges. Cut a thick slice down either side
of the mango keeping the knife as close to the
stone as possible.

Scrape the mango flesh out of the skin. Purée
in a blender or food processor. Rub through a
nylon sieve. Add the orange rind.

Place the whole eggs and egg yolk in a large
bowl, add the caster sugar and whisk until the
mixture is very pale, thick and creamy.

Whisk the mango purée, a little at a time, into
the mixture, whisking well after each addition.

Sprinkle the gelatine over the orange juice in a
small bowl and leave to soak. Place the bowl over
a pan of simmering water and stir until dissolved.

Meanwhile, pour half the cream into a bowl.
Lightly whip the cream, then, using a metal spoon,
lightly fold the cream into the mango mixture.
Pour the gelatine in a thin stream into the mango
mixture, stirring gently.

**7.** Gently put the mixture into a 2 litre (3½ pint)
shallow serving dish. Chill in the refrigerator for
about 1 hour until beginning to set, then cover
with cling film and chill for several hours, or
overnight, until set.

**8.** Lightly whisk the remaining cream until it just
holds its shape. Spoon the cream into a piping bag
fitted with a star nozzle and pipe small rosettes
around the edge of the mousse.
*Serves 6*

**Variation**

*RHUBARB MOUSSE*

In place of mangoes, use 450 g (1 lb) pink rhubarb;
wipe, then cut into 2.5 cm (1 inch) pieces. Place the
rhubarb in a saucepan with 45 ml (3 tbsp) of water.
Cover the pan tightly and cook gently until the
rhubarb is soft and pulpy.

Purée in a blender or food processor until
smooth. (Do not sieve.) Cool, and complete the
mousse as from step 2, using 65 g (2½ oz) caster
sugar in place of the 40 g (1½ oz) caster sugar.

# ZABAGLIONE

*6 egg yolks*

*65 g (2½ oz) caster sugar*

*100 ml (4 fl oz) Marsala*

*sponge fingers, to serve*

Put the egg yolks and sugar in a large heatproof
bowl. Beat together, then add the Marsala and beat
until mixed.

**2.** Place the bowl over a saucepan of simmering
water and heat gently, whisking the mixture until it
is very thick and creamy and forms soft peaks.

**3.** To serve, pour the Zabaglione into six glasses,
and serve immediately, with sponge fingers.

*Note* A classic rich Italian dessert, Zabaglione is
best served after a light main course such as grilled
chicken and steaks or boiled fish.
*Serves 6*

*Rum Soufflé Omelette*

## RUM SOUFFLÉ OMELETTE

| |
|---|
| *2 eggs, separated* |
| *5 ml (1 level tsp) caster sugar* |
| *15 ml (1 tbsp) dark rum* |
| *15 g (½ oz) butter or margarine* |
| *15 ml (1 level tbsp) apricot jam, warmed* |
| *30 ml (2 level tbsp) icing sugar* |

**1.** Put the egg yolks in a bowl with the caster sugar and rum. Mix well together. Whisk the egg whites until stiff.

**2.** Melt the butter in a heavy-based omelette pan until foaming. Fold the egg whites quickly into the egg yolk mixture, then pour into the foaming butter.

**3.** Cook over moderate heat for 2–3 minutes until the underside of the omelette is golden brown, then place the pan under a hot grill and cook for a few minutes more until the top is a golden brown colour.

**4.** Slide the omelette on to a warmed serving plate. Spread with the warmed jam, then fold over half of the omelette.

**5.** Sift the icing sugar thickly over the top of the omelette, then mark in a criss-cross pattern with a metal skewer, if liked. Serve immediately.
*Makes 1*

**Variations**
Omit the rum and serve plain with the apricot filling. Replace the apricot jam with raspberry or strawberry jam.

# CHOCOLATE MOUSSE

350 g (12 oz) plain chocolate

eggs, separated

0 ml (2 tbsp) rum or brandy

50 ml (5 fl oz) double cream

Chocolate Caraque (see page 418), to decorate

. Break the chocolate into a bowl. Place the bowl over a pan of simmering water and heat until melted, stirring occasionally.

**2.** Remove from heat and beat in the egg yolks and rum. Whisk the egg whites until stiff and fold into the chocolate mixture.

**3.** Spoon into six ramekin dishes and chill in the refrigerator for 2–3 hours, until set. Whip the cream until stiff. Decorate the mousses with piped cream and Chocolate Caraque.

*Serves 6*

# STRAWBERRY AND ORANGE MOUSSE

00 g (1½ lb) fresh strawberries, hulled

finely grated rind and juice of 1 large orange

5 ml (3 level tbsp) icing sugar

egg yolks and 2 egg whites

00 g (4 oz) caster sugar

5 ml (1 level tbsp) gelatine

00 ml (10 fl oz) double cream

50 ml (5 fl oz) single cream

. Thinly slice enough strawberries to line the sides of a 2.3 litre (4 pint) shallow glass dish.

. Purée half the remainder in a blender or food processor with the orange rind, 75 ml (5 tbsp) juice and the icing sugar. Pass through a nylon sieve to give a very smooth texture. Reserve the remaining strawberries to use for decoration.

**3.** Whisk the egg yolks and caster sugar until thick and light. Then gradually whisk in the strawberry purée.

**4.** Sprinkle in the gelatine in 45 ml (3 tbsp) water in a small bowl and leave to soak. Place the bowl over a saucepan of simmering water and stir until dissolved. Leave to cool, then stir it into the mousse mixture.

**5.** Lightly whip the creams together. Fold one-third through the mousse and keep the rest covered in refrigerator. Whisk the two egg whites until stiff and fold through the mixture. Pour into the strawberry-lined dish, and chill in the refrigerator for 2–3 hours, until set.

**6.** Pipe cream on top and decorate.

*Serves 6*

*Strawberry and Orange Mousse*

# JELLIES AND JELLY SWEETS

Homemade jellies containing fresh fruit and fruit juice are very simple to prepare. The flavour is much better than jellies made with commercial jelly tablets and crystals which contain mostly sugar, flavouring and colouring.

Most jellies are made with gelatine, a colourless, tasteless animal substance which sets liquid.

**Powdered gelatine** is the most commonly used setting agent in jellies. It is sold loose in cartons or in envelopes each containing exactly 11 g (0.4 oz), which will set 600 ml (1 pint) liquid.

To use powdered gelatine, always add the gelatine to the liquid. Place the required amount of water or liquid in a heatproof cup or bowl. Sprinkle over the gelatine. Leave for 10 minutes and then heat gently until the gelatine has dissolved. The gelatine must not be allowed to boil.

**Leaf gelatine** is a more expensive alternative Four sheets of leaf gelatine is equivalent to 15 m (1 level tbsp) powdered gelatine and will set 600 m (1 pint) liquid. Snip into small pieces and soak ir about 45 ml (3 tbsp) liquid per four sheets fo about 10 minutes before dissolving in the same way as powdered gelatine.

**Agar-agar** can also be used as a setting agent. It is a tasteless white powder derived from seaweed. It i available from health food shops and is particu larly popular with vegetarians. Follow the manu facturer's instructions if using.

## MAKING A JELLY

When making fruit jellies, warm the liquid, sweeten and flavour it, then quickly stir in the dissolved gelatine. The more closely the two are to the same temperature, the more easily the gelatine can be evenly blended with the liquid. To hasten the set, heat one-half of the liquid, add the gelatine, then combine with the remaining cold liquid.

For the best flavour, allow jellied desserts to come to room temperature for 1 hour before serving.

### TO SET FRUIT IN JELLY

Use fresh fruits such as black grapes, bananas, raspberries or orange segments. Do not use fresh pineapple and kiwi fruit as they contain an enzyme which breaks down gelatine and destroys its setting powers. Boil fresh pineapple juice for 2–3 minutes before using.

Pour about 2.5 cm (1 inch) clear jelly into a mould, and arrange a little of the fruit in this. Allow the jelly to set. Add more jelly and fruit and allow to set; continue until the mould is filled.

### TO LINE OR MASK A MOULD WITH JELLY

First prepare any decorations (e.g. sliced glacé cherries and pistachio nuts, cut angelica). Fill a large basin with chips of ice and rest the wetted mould in it. Pour 30–45 ml (2–3 tbsp) cold bu liquid jelly into the mould and rotate this slowly until the inside is evenly coated. Continue pouring in and setting cold liquid jelly until the whole surface is lined with a layer about 0.3 cm ($\frac{1}{8}$ inch thick. Using 2 fine skewers, dip the decoration pieces into liquid jelly and place in position in the mould, allowing each piece to set firmly. Pour a thin coating over the decorations and allow to se before adding the cream mixture or other filling.

### TO UNMOULD A JELLY OR MOUSSE

Draw the tip of a knife or your finger around the rim of the mould to loosen the edge of the jelly Immerse the mould in hot water for 2–3 second and place a wetted serving plate on top of the mould. Hold in position with both hands, ther quickly invert together giving sharp shakes.

## CLARET JELLY

| |
|---|
| *300 ml ($\frac{1}{2}$ pint) water or raspberry juice* |
| *300 ml ($\frac{1}{2}$ pint) claret* |
| *50 g (2 oz) sugar* |
| *finely grated rind and juice of $\frac{1}{2}$ lemon* |
| *20 ml (4 level tsp) gelatine* |
| *red food colouring (optional)* |

**1.** Slowly bring all the ingredients except the food colouring to simmering point. Do not boil. Strain through muslin, add a few drops of colouring, if necessary, and pour into a wetted mould.
**2.** Chill in the refrigerator for several hours until set. Turn out and serve.
*Serves 4*

## LEMON CHEESE JELLY

35 g (4¾ oz) packet lemon jelly

200 g (7 oz) natural quark (low fat soft cheese)

finely grated rind of 1 lemon

5 ml (1 tsp) lemon juice

**1.** Make up the jelly according to packet instructions; cool until beginning to set.
**2.** Purée the jelly with the cheese, grated rind and lemon juice in a blender or food processor. Pour into a shallow dish and chill until set.
*Serves 4*

## MILK JELLY

50 g (2 oz) caster sugar

3 thin strips of lemon rind

568 ml (1 pint) milk

20 ml (4 level tsp) gelatine

stewed fruit, to serve

**1.** Add the sugar and lemon rind to the milk and allow to infuse over a gentle heat for 10 minutes.

Cool in the refrigerator.
**2.** Sprinkle the gelatine in 45 ml (3 tbsp) water in a small bowl and leave to soak. Place over a pan of simmering water and stir until dissolved. Leave until lukewarm, then add the cooled milk.
**3.** Pour into a 600 ml (1 pint) dampened mould and chill in the refrigerator until set. Unmould on to a plate and serve with stewed fruit.
*Serves 4*

# ICES AND ICED PUDDINGS Nowadays, there is a vast range of ready-made ice creams available, and by combining them with sweet sauces (see page 210) and other ingredients such as fresh fruit, nuts, chocolate and cream it is easy to make simple yet delicious desserts. However, for a richer, creamier ice with more flavour, you cannot beat homemade ice cream; or experiment with flavoursome iced puddings, water ices and sorbets.

## ICE CREAMS

These are seldom made entirely of cream, but are usually a mixture of equal parts of cream and custard (the best being egg custard made with yolks only), cream and fruit purée or cream and egg whites. If wished, the cream may be replaced by evaporated milk or a commercial cream substitute. Flavourings and colourings are then added.

### EQUIPMENT FOR MAKING ICE CREAM

Ice cream can be made with everyday kitchen equipment or with a specially designed machine.
**Large bowl, flat whisk or fork** are needed for beating if not using an ice cream maker.
**Bombe mould or freezerproof bowl** for bombes.
**Rigid freezer containers** for freezing the mixture if not using a machine. The mixture will set more quickly in a shallow one, but transfer to a deep container if you want to serve in scoops.
**Manually operated ice cream maker** has an inner and outer container. The space between is filled with salt or ice while beating the mixture.
**Electric ice cream makers** are available in two

types; a small one that fits into the freezer or one that has its own freezer unit. They produce smoother, creamier ice with a greater volume.

### WATER ICES AND SORBETS

Water ices are made from a sugar and water syrup, usually flavoured with fruit juice or purée, and egg white. Wine or liqueur is often added. Sorbets are similar, but have a higher proportion of egg white. Because of their softness they are not moulded but usually served in tall glasses.

### FREEZING MIXTURES

Use maximum freezing power, the quicker the mixture freezes, the better the texture. Everything should be cold, ingredients and equipment. If using a refrigerator, set the dial of the frozen food compartment at maximum about 1 hour before you freeze the mixture. Don't forget to return the dial to normal afterwards or other foods in the refrigerator could suffer. If using a freezer, set the dial or switch to fast freeze 1 hour ahead.

## PRALINE ICE CREAM

| |
|---|
| 50 g (2 oz) whole unblanched almonds |
| 50 g (2 oz) sugar |
| 300 ml (½ pint) milk |
| 1 vanilla pod |
| 1 egg |
| 2 egg yolks |
| 75 g (3 oz) caster sugar |
| 200 ml (7 fl oz) double cream |

**1.** Place the almonds and sugar in a heavy-based saucepan, heat slowly until the sugar caramelises, turning occasionally. Pour on to an oiled baking sheet to cool and harden for about 15 minutes. Then use a mouli grater, blender or food processor or rolling pin to grind to a powder.

**2.** Bring the milk and vanilla pod to the boil, remove from the heat and infuse for 30 minutes.

**3.** Beat the egg, egg yolks and sugar until pale in colour, then strain in the milk. Cook slowly for about 10 minutes, until the custard coats the back of the spoon. Do not boil. Pour into a chilled freezer container, cool then freeze for 2 hours until mushy.

**4.** Lightly whip the cream and fold into the custard. Pour into a freezer container and freeze for 2 hours, until mushy.

**5.** Turn into a large, chilled bowl, beat with a flat whisk or fork, then fold in the praline. Return to the freezer container and freeze until firm.

**6.** Transfer to the refrigerator to soften for 30 minutes before serving.

*Serves 6*

*Praline Ice Cream*

*Snowcap Iced Pudding*

# SNOWCAP ICED PUDDING

150 ml ($\frac{1}{4}$ pint) kirsch

60 ml (4 tbsp) water

about 15 sponge fingers

450 ml ($\frac{3}{4}$ pint) chocolate chip ice cream

225 g (8 oz) ripe cherries, pitted and roughly chopped

450 ml ($\frac{3}{4}$ pint) vanilla ice cream

150 ml (5 fl oz) double cream

**1.** Cut out a circle of greaseproof paper and use it to line the base of a 1.1 litre (2$\frac{1}{2}$ pint) pudding basin.

**2.** Mix the kirsch with the water and dip the sponge fingers one at a time into the mixture. Use to line the sides of the pudding basin, trimming them to fit so that there are no gaps in between. Fill the base with leftover pieces of sponge. Refrigerate for 15 minutes.

**3.** Stir any remaining kirsch liquid into the chocolate ice cream and mash the ice cream well with a fork to soften it slightly and make it smooth without any ice crystals.

**4.** Spoon the chocolate ice cream into the basin and work it up the sides of the sponge fingers to the top of the basin so that it forms an even layer. Freeze for about 2 hours until firm.

**5.** Mix the cherries into the vanilla ice cream and mash well with a fork as in step 3.

**6.** Spoon the vanilla ice cream into the centre of the basin and smooth it over the top so that it covers the chocolate ice cream and sponge fingers. Cover with foil and freeze overnight.

**7.** To serve, whip the cream until it will just hold its shape. Run a knife around the inside of the basin, then turn the ice cream out on to a well chilled serving plate.

**8.** Spoon the cream over the top and let it just start to run down the sides, then freeze immediately for about 15 minutes or until the cream has frozen solid. Serve straight from the freezer.

*Serves 6–8*

# VANILLA ICE CREAM

568 ml (1 pint) milk

1 vanilla pod

6 egg yolks

175 g (6 oz) sugar

600 ml (20 fl oz) whipping cream

1. Bring the milk and vanilla pod almost to the boil. Remove from the heat and leave to infuse for 30 minutes.
2. Beat the egg yolks and sugar together, stir in the milk and strain back into the pan. Cook the custard gently over a low heat, stirring until it coats the back of a wooden spoon. Do not boil.
3. Pour into a chilled freezer container, cool, then freeze for 2 hours until mushy.
4. Turn into a chilled bowl and beat well with a flat whisk or fork. Lightly whip the cream and fold into the mixture. Return to the freezer container and freeze for 2 hours.
5. Turn into a chilled bowl and beat well again. Return to the freezer and freeze until firm.
6. Transfer to the refrigerator to soften for 30 minutes before serving.
Serves 8–10

**Variations**
1. Break up 175 g (6 oz) plain chocolate and heat with the milk, whisking until smooth.
2. Stir 60 ml (4 tbsp) coffee essence into the made custard.
3. Purée 350 g (12 oz) strawberries with 25 g (1 oz) icing sugar and 10 ml (2 tsp) lemon juice and stir into the custard.

# BROWN BREAD ICE CREAM

125 g (4 oz) fresh fine brown breadcrumbs

50 g (2 oz) soft brown sugar

300 ml (10 fl oz) double cream

150 ml (5 fl oz) single cream

15 ml (1 tbsp) dark rum

50 g (2 oz) icing sugar, sifted

1. Spread the breadcrumbs on a baking sheet and sprinkle over the brown sugar. Bake in the oven at 200°C (400°F) mark 6 for about 10 minutes, stirring occasionally, until the sugar caramelises. and the crumbs are golden. Cool, then break up.
2. Whisk together the creams until stiff. Gently fold in the rum and icing sugar.
3. Pour into a freezer container and freeze for 2 hours, until mushy.
4. Turn into a chilled bowl and beat with a fork or whisk. Stir in the breadcrumbs. Return to the freezer container and freeze until firm.
5. Transfer to the refrigerator to soften for 30 minutes before serving.
Serves 4

# ICED CHRISTMAS PUDDING

225 g (8 oz) mixed dried fruit

50 g (2 oz) glacé cherries, halved

75 ml (5 tbsp) brandy

3 eggs

140 g (4½ oz) caster sugar

450 ml (¾ pint) milk

300 ml (10 fl oz) double cream

150 ml (5 fl oz) single cream

1. Place the mixed dried fruit and glacé cherries in a bowl, spoon over the brandy, cover and leave to soak for 2–3 hours.
2. Beat the eggs and the sugar until well mixed. Bring the milk nearly to the boil, then stir the milk into the egg mixture.
3. Strain back into the pan and cook gently, without boiling, until the custard coats the back of the spoon. Cool for 30 minutes.
4. Lightly whip the creams together and mix into the custard with the fruit and brandy mixture.
5. Turn into a large bowl and freeze for 2 hours until mushy. Mix well and pack into a 1.7 litre (3 pint) pudding basin base-lined with non-stick paper. Freeze for 2–3 hours until firm.
6. Remove from the freezer 20 minutes before serving. Turn out and decorate with holly. Serve immediately.
Serves 8

# ICED RASPBERRY MERINGUE

700 g (1½ lb) fresh raspberries, hulled

60 ml (4 level tbsp) icing sugar

60 ml (4 tbsp) orange-flavoured liqueur

300 ml (10 fl oz) double cream

150 ml (5 fl oz) single cream

18 meringue nests made from 3 egg whites (see
    page 365)

1. Put half the raspberries into a bowl. Sift over the icing sugar, add the liqueur and mix gently. Cover and leave in a cool place for 3–4 hours or overnight.

2. Purée the raspberry mixture in a blender or food processor, then press through a nylon sieve to remove the pips.

3. Whip the creams together until they just hold their shape. Break up the meringues into 3–4 pieces each and stir through the cream with the raspberry purée until just mixed but still marbled in appearance.

4. Oil a 1.7 litre (3 pint) ring mould. Spoon the mixture into the prepared mould, overwrap and freeze for at least 6 hours.

5. Serve straight from the freezer; ease out of the mould and pile the remaining raspberries in the centre.

*Serves 6*

# KNICKERBOCKER GLORY

one quarter of a 135 g (4¾ oz) packet raspberry or
    strawberry jelly

one quarter of a 135 g (4¾ oz) packet lemon jelly

210 g (7½ oz) can peach slices, drained and chopped

210 g (7½ oz) can pineapple chunks, drained

483 ml (17 fl oz) block of vanilla ice cream

150 ml (5 fl oz) double cream

6 glacé cherries

1. Make up the jellies as directed on the packet, allow to set and then chop them.

2. Put small portions of the fruit into the bottom of 6 tall sundae glasses. Cover with a layer of red jelly. Put a scoop of ice cream on top and add a layer of yellow jelly.

3. Repeat the layering finishing with a layer of cream and a cherry.

*Serves 6*

# BAKED ALASKA

225 g (8 oz) plus 10 ml (2 level tsp) caster sugar

50 g (2 oz) plus 5 ml (1 level tsp) plain flour

2 eggs, size 2

finely grated rind of 1 orange

225 g (8 oz) fresh or frozen raspberries

30 ml (2 tbsp) orange-flavoured liqueur

4 egg whites, at room temperature

483 ml (17 fl oz) block vanilla ice cream

1. Grease a 20.5 cm (8 inch) non-stick flan tin. Sprinkle over 10 ml (2 level tsp) caster sugar and tilt the tin to give an even coating of sugar. Add 5 ml (1 level tsp) plain flour and coat similarly.

2. Place the eggs and 50 g (2 oz) of the caster sugar in a bowl and whisk until the mixture is very thick. Fold in the orange rind and sifted flour.

3. Pour the mixture into the tin and level the surface by tilting the tin. Bake in the oven at 180°C (350°F) mark 4 for 20–25 minutes, until golden. Turn out on to a wire rack to cool.

4. Place the raspberries in a shallow dish and sprinkle over the liqueur. Cover and leave in a cool place for 2 hours, turning occasionally.

5. Place the cold sponge flan on a large ovenproof serving dish and spoon the raspberries together with all their juices into the centre of the flan.

6. Stiffly whisk the egg whites. Whisk in half the remaining sugar, then carefully fold in the rest.

7. Fit a piping bag with a large star nozzle and fill with the meringue mixture. Place the ice cream on top of the raspberries. Pipe the meringue on top. Start from base and pipe the meringue around and over the ice cream until completely covered.

8. Immediately, bake in the oven at 230°C (450°F) mark 8 for 3–4 minutes, until the meringue is tinged with brown. Watch the meringue carefully as it burns easily. Serve.

*Cover in meringue.*

*Serves 6–8*

## ORANGE WATER ICE

*100 g (4 oz) caster sugar*

*15 ml (1 tbsp) lemon juice*

*grated rind of 1 orange*

*grated rind of 1 lemon*

*juice of 3 oranges and 1 lemon, mixed, about 300 ml (½ pint)*

*1 egg white*

**1.** Dissolve the sugar in 300 ml (½ pint) water over a low heat, bring to the boil and boil gently for 10 minutes. Add the lemon juice.

**2.** Put the grated fruit rinds in a basin, pour the boiling syrup over and leave until cold. Add the mixed fruit juices and strain into a freezer container and freeze about 2 hours, until mushy.
**3.** Whisk the egg white until stiff. Turn the mixture into a bowl, fold in the egg white, mixing thoroughly, then replace in the container and freeze until firm.
**4.** Transfer to the refrigerator for about 45 minutes before serving.
*Serves 8*

## LEMON SORBET

*225 g (8 oz) sugar*

*grated rind and juice of 4 lemons*

*2 egg whites*

**1.** Dissolve the sugar in 600 ml (1 pint) water over a low heat, then bring to the boil and boil for 2 minutes. Remove from the heat, add the lemon rinds, cover and leave to infuse for 10 minutes.

**2.** When cool, add the lemon juice, then strain into a shallow freezer container. Freeze for about 2 hours, until mushy.
**3.** Whisk the egg whites until stiff. Turn the mixture into a bowl, fold in the egg whites, then replace in the container and freeze until firm. Transfer to the refrigerator for 45 minutes before serving.
*Serves 8*

## STRAWBERRY SORBET

*700 g (1½ lb) strawberries, hulled*

*175 g (6 oz) sugar*

*15 ml (1 tbsp) lemon juice*

*2 egg whites*

**1.** Purée the strawberries in a blender or food processor, then sieve to remove the seeds.
**2.** Dissolve the sugar in 300 ml (½ pint) water over a low heat, bring to the boil and boil for

3–4 minutes until syrupy. Stir into the strawberry purée with the lemon juice. Cool.
**3.** Pour the mixture into a shallow freezer container and freeze 3–4 hours, until mushy.
**4.** Whisk the egg whites until stiff. Turn the mixture into a bowl, fold in the egg whites, then replace in the container and freeze until firm.
**5.** Transfer to the refrigerator for about 45 minutes before serving.
*Serves 6*

## MELON AND GINGER SORBET

*75 g (3 oz) sugar*

*1 medium honeydew melon*

*45 ml (3 tbsp) lemon juice*

*1 piece preserved stem ginger, finely chopped*

*few drops green food colouring (optional)*

*2 egg whites*

*fan wafers, to serve (optional)*

**1.** Dissolve the sugar in 300 ml (½ pint) water over a low heat, bring to the boil for 2 minutes. Cool.
**2.** Halve the melon, remove the seeds and scoop

out the flesh. Purée the flesh in a blender or food processor until smooth. Stir into the cool syrup with the lemon juice. Add the chopped ginger and food colouring, if wished.
**3.** Pour the mixture into a freezer container and freeze for 2–3 hours, until mushy.
**4.** Whisk the egg whites until stiff. Turn the mixture into a bowl, fold in the egg whites, then replace in the container and freeze until firm.
**5.** Transfer to the refrigerator for about 45 minutes before serving. Serve with fan wafers.
*Serves 6*

# MERINGUES are a mixture of whisked egg white and sugar, which is very slowly baked in the oven so it dries out and becomes crisp and firm. The light texture is the perfect foil to creamy fillings and soft fruit. Making meringues is the ideal way of using up leftover egg whites and the meringues will keep for up to six weeks in an airtight tin.

There are three basic types of meringue, although for home cooking Meringue Suisse is the most commonly used. Meringue Suisse is made by incorporating sugar into stiffly whisked egg whites. Half the sugar is very gradually added, about 15 ml (1 tbsp) at a time, whisking after each addition, until the sugar is fully mixed in and partially dissolved. Sugar added in large amounts at this state may result in a sticky meringue.

The remaining sugar is added by sprinkling it over the whisked whites and folding it in with a metal spoon. The egg whites should be firm and have a glossy appearance.

Meringue Cuite is made by cooking the egg whites over boiling water while whisking them. This means that the meringue can be stored if necessary before shaping. These meringues are harder, whiter and more powdery than Meringue Suisse and are used mostly by professional bakers as they require great care and long whisking.

Italian Meringue is made by adding a hot sugar syrup to egg whites. It requires a sugar thermometer and is rarely used at home as other methods are simpler.

## MERINGUE SUISSE

*3 egg whites, size 2*

*75 g (3 oz) granulated sugar and 75 g (3 oz) caster sugar or 175 g (6 oz) caster sugar*

1. Grease a baking sheet or line it with foil or non-stick paper.
2. Whisk egg whites until stiff. Gradually whisk in half the sugar, whisking after each addition until thoroughly incorporated, then fold in the remaining sugar very lightly with a metal spoon.
3. Spoon the meringue into a piping bag fitted with a large star nozzle and pipe small rounds on to the prepared baking sheet. Alternatively, spoon the mixture in small mounds.
4. Bake in the oven at 110°C (225°F) mark $\frac{1}{4}$ for about $2\frac{1}{2}$–3 hours, until firm and crisp, but still white. If they begin to brown, prop open the oven door a little. Transfer to a wire rack and leave until cold.

*Makes about 20 individual meringue shapes*

### Variations

SANDWICHED MERINGUES
Sandwich the meringue shapes together with 300 ml ($\frac{1}{2}$ pint) whipped cream.

MERINGUE FLAN CASE
Draw a 20.5 cm (8 inch) circle on a sheet of non-stick paper and place the paper mark side down on a baking sheet. Spread some of the meringue over the circle to form the base of the flan.

Using a large star nozzle, pipe the remainder to form the edge of the flan, or make a rim with the aid of a spoon. Bake in the bottom of the oven for $1\frac{1}{2}$–2 hours.

MERINGUE BASKET
Grease a 23 cm (9 inch) pie dish and spoon in the meringue. Pile the meringue high around the sides of the dish to make a basket.

To pipe a meringue basket, line three baking sheets with non-stick paper. Draw an 18 cm (7 inch) circle on each. Spoon one third of the meringue mixture into a piping bag and pipe rings of meringue about 1 cm ($\frac{1}{2}$ inch) thick inside two of the circles. Fill the bag again and starting from the centre pipe a continuous coil of meringue on to the third circle. Cook in the oven at 100°C (200°F) gas low for $2\frac{1}{2}$–3 hours to dry out. Use an extra egg white and 50 g (2 oz) sugar to make more meringue as above. Remove the cooked meringue rings from the oven and pipe more meringue between the base and ring layers. Return to the oven for a further $1\frac{1}{2}$–2 hours.

MERINGUE NESTS
Spoon the meringue into six mounds, spaced well apart on the prepared baking sheet; hollow out centres with the back of a spoon.

# RASPBERRY PAVLOVA

3 egg whites

175 g (6 oz) caster sugar

2.5 ml (½ tsp) vanilla flavouring

2.5 ml (½ tsp) white wine vinegar

5 ml (1 level tsp) cornflour

300 ml (10 fl oz) double cream

350 g (12 oz) fresh raspberries, washed and hulled

1. Draw an 18 cm (7 inch) circle on a sheet of non-stick paper and place the paper mark side down on a baking sheet.
2. Whisk the egg whites until stiff. Whisk in half the sugar, then carefully fold in the remaining sugar, the vanilla flavouring, vinegar and cornflour with a metal spoon.
3. Spread the meringue over the circle and bake in the oven at 150°C (300°F) mark 2 for about 1 hour, until crisp and dry. Transfer to a wire rack to cool, then carefully peel off the non-stick paper.
4. Whisk the cream until stiff. Slide the meringue on to a flat plate, pile the cream on it and arrange the raspberries on top.
*Serves 6*

**Variations**
Replace the raspberries with strawberries, grapes, passion fruit or pineapple.

# MERINGUE CUITE

2 egg whites

125 g (4½ oz) icing sugar

1. Line a baking sheet with non-stick paper or use greaseproof paper very lightly greased with oil.
2. Place the egg whites and icing sugar in a bowl over a pan of boiling water and whisk until the mixture forms a meringue stiff enough to hold a shape.
3. Use as for a Meringue Suisse (see page 365). Bake in the oven at 150°C (300°F) mark 1 for about 1 hour, until crisp and dry.

# CHOCOLATE MERINGUE GÂTEAU

3 egg whites and 2 egg yolks

225 g (8 oz) caster sugar

50 g (2 oz) plain chocolate

50 g (2 oz) unsalted butter, softened

150 ml (5 fl oz) double cream

Chocolate Caraque (see page 418), to decorate

1. Draw two 20.5 cm (8 inch) circles on non-stick paper and place them mark side down on baking sheets.
2. Whisk the egg whites until stiff. Whisk in 75 g (3 oz) sugar, then carefully fold in another 75 g (3 oz) of the sugar with a metal spoon.
3. Spoon the mixture into a piping bag fitted with a large star nozzle and pipe the mixture on to the circles on the baking sheets. Or, using a palette knife, spread the mixture evenly.
4. Bake in the oven at 110°C (225°F) mark ¼ for about 1¾ hours or until dry. Transfer to a wire rack to cool.
5. Meanwhile, prepare the filling. Beat the egg yolks in a bowl. Put the remaining sugar and 45 ml (3 tbsp) water into a small saucepan and heat until the sugar has dissolved.
6. Bring to the boil and boil to 113°C (235°F) on a sugar thermometer, or until the mixture reaches the soft ball stage (see page 492).
7. Pour the syrup on to the egg yolks in a steady stream, whisking all the time. Continue to whisk until thick.
8. Break the chocolate into a heatproof bowl and place over simmering water. Stir until melted, then remove from heat and leave to cool slightly. Gradually beat the butter and chocolate into the syrup mixture.
9. Peel the paper from the meringues, then sandwich the rounds together with the chocolate filling. Whip the cream until stiff, then spoon into a piping bag with a large star nozzle and pipe on to the gâteau. Decorate with chocolate curls.
*Serves 6–8*

# PASTRY

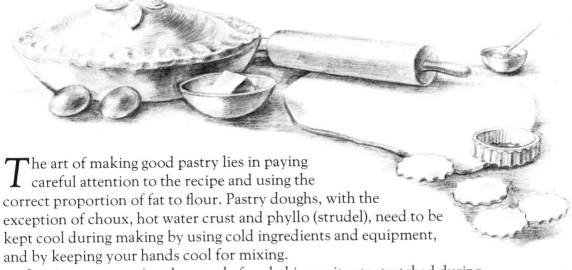

The art of making good pastry lies in paying careful attention to the recipe and using the correct proportion of fat to flour. Pastry doughs, with the exception of choux, hot water crust and phyllo (strudel), need to be kept cool during making by using cold ingredients and equipment, and by keeping your hands cool for mixing.

It is important to 'rest' pastry before baking as it gets stretched during shaping. If not allowed to 'rest' and firm up, it may shrink away from the sides of the tin during baking. Flaked pastries need 'resting' before and after shaping as they are handled a great deal.

Each kind of pastry produces a different texture and variation in flavour and is suited to a certain range of recipes. Some pastries are more difficult than others, but with practice, care and patience you will obtain successful results with your pastry making every time.

◆

## PASTRY INGREDIENTS

**Flour** For most pastries plain flour is the best. Wholemeal flour can be used for shortcrust or suetcrust pastry. Wholemeal flour in shortcrust produces a dough which is more difficult to roll out but has a distinctive flavour and texture when cooked. Shortcrust can also be made with self raising flour but this gives a softer more crumbly texture.

Suetcrust, unlike other pastries, needs a flour and a raising agent to lighten the dough. Puff pastry and phyllo (strudel) pastry need to be made with strong plain flour, as this contains extra gluten which strengthens the dough for the rolling and folding of puff pastry and allows phyllo pastry to be stretched out very thinly. Strong plain flour can also be used for choux pastry, making it rise more, but it may also slightly toughen the resulting pastry.

**Raising agent** Suetcrust pastry needs a raising agent; either plain flour sifted with 12.5 ml (2½ level tsp) baking powder to each 225 g (8 oz) or self raising flour can be used. Do not add baking powder to self raising flour as this produces an unpleasant flavour. Steam acts as the raising agent in flaked pastries in combination with the air enclosed in the layers of dough. In choux pastry the raising agents are eggs and steam.

**Salt** The quantity of salt varies according to the type of pastry. Only a pinch of salt is added to shortcrust pastry for flavour, while a measured quantity is added to hot water crust to strengthen the gluten in the flour and allow for the amount of handling during shaping. Salt is also needed to strengthen the gluten in the flour with flaked pastries.

**Fat** Butter, margarine and lard are the fats most commonly used, but proprietary vegetable shortenings (both blended and whipped) and pure vegetable oils can give excellent results. When using oil, remember to follow the directions in the recipe on page 374, as a smaller quantity of oil is recommended in proportion to the flour than is usual with other kinds of fat. Generally, the firmer block margarine should be used rather than soft tub margarine. A recipe is given using soft tub margarine, called One Stage Short Pastry (see page 374).

For shortcrust pastry, butter, margarine, lard or vegetable fat can be used alone, though margarine tends to give a firmer pastry which is rather yellow in colour. Good results are achieved with an equal mixture of fats—butter or margarine for flavour with lard for shortness. For the richer pastries, it is better to keep to the amount of fat specified in the recipes.

For suetcrust pastry, suet is used. Suet is the fat around the kidneys, heart and liver of beef and mutton. It is available ready shredded in packets from grocers.

**Liquid** Use chilled water to make pastry dough and add just enough to make the dough bind. It is important to add the liquid carefully, as too much will make the cooked pastry tough and too little will produce a crumbly baked pastry. Egg yolks are often used as the binding liquid to enrich the pastry. Lemon juice is added to flaked pastries to soften the gluten in the flour and make the dough more elastic.

**Sugar** Caster sugar may be added to rich shortcrust or flan pastries if the pastry is to be used for a sweet dish.

## SHAPING PASTRY

*LINING A FLAN CASE*
See quantity chart on page 372. Choose a plain or fluted flan ring placed on a baking sheet; a loose-bottomed flan tin, china fluted flan dish or sandwich tin.
1. Roll out the pastry thinly to a circle about 5 cm (2 inch) wider than the ring. With a rolling pin, lift the pastry and lower it into the ring or fold the pastry in half and position it in the ring.
2. Lift the edges carefully and ease the pastry into the flan shape, lightly pressing the pastry against the edges—with a fluted edge press your finger edge into each flute to ensure a good finish. No air should be left between the container and pastry.
3. Turn any surplus pastry outwards over the rim and roll across the top with the rolling pin or use a knife to trim the edges.

*LINING INDIVIDUAL TARTLET TINS OR MOULDS*
1. Arrange the tins close together on a baking sheet. Roll out the pastry to a size large enough to cover the whole area of the tins. Lift the pastry on to the rolling pin and lay loosely over the tins.
2. With a small knob of dough, press the pastry into each tin. With a rolling pin, roll across the complete set of tins and lift the surplus pastry away.
3. Prick the bases and sides lightly with a fork. With a sheet of patty tins, cut rounds of thinly rolled pastry slightly larger than the top of the tin and ease one round into each shape.

*COVERING A PIE DISH*
1. Roll out the pastry to the required thickness and 5 cm (2 inch) wider than the pie dish, using the inverted dish as a guide. Cut a 2.5 cm (1 inch) wide strip from the outer edge and place it on the dampened rim of the dish. Seal the join and brush the whole strip with water.
2. Fill the pie dish generously, so that the surface is slightly rounded; use a pie funnel if insufficient filling is available.
3. Lift the remaining pastry on the rolling pin and lay it over the pie dish. Press the lid lightly on to the pastry-lined rim to seal. Trim

*Using a rolling pin place the bottom layer of pastry in the flan ring.*

*Use a rolling pin to trim excess pastry from the top of the flan ring.*

*Place a thin strip of pastry on to the dampened rim.*

ff any excess pastry with the cutting edge of a
nife held at a slight angle away from the dish.

. Seal the edges firmly so that they do not open
p during cooking (see Knock Up, page 370). If
ou wish, scallop the edges (see page 370) and use
rimmings rolled thinly as decorative leaf shapes
tc. Cut a slit in the centre of the pie crust for the
team to escape.

### DOUBLE CRUST PIE

. Divide the pastry into two parts, one slightly
igger than the other. Shape the larger piece into a
all and roll it out. Rotate the pastry as you roll it,
 keep it circular. Pinch together any cracks that
ppear at the edge. Roll it out to about 2.5 cm
 inch) wider than the inverted pie plate.

. To move the pastry, roll the dough loosely
round the rolling pin, lift and unroll it over the
ie dish. Press into the dish, taking care not to
tretch it.

. Add the cold filling, keeping the surface
ightly rounded. Roll out remaining pastry for
d, making it about 1 cm (½ inch) wider than rim.

. Brush the pastry rim
ith water, then lift the
d into position as for
overing a pie. Seal the
dge either by folding
he surplus edge of the
d over the rim of
he base pastry or by
ressing the two layers
gether and trimming
 for covering a pie.
nock up the edges (see
age 370) and make a
ort slit in the centre
r the steam to escape.

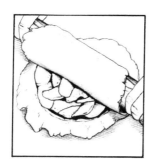
*Using a rolling pin, place
the top crust over the pie
filling.*

### SHAPING FREE-STANDING RAISED PIES

his method can be used for small or large pies
epending on the size of jar you are using to shape
e pastry. Make up 450 g (1 lb) Hot Water Crust
astry (see page 377) and keep it warm. This is
fficient to make six small pies based on covering
x 350 g (12 oz) or 450 g (1 lb) jam jars. You can
so use a traditional wooden raised pie mould—
vailable in 450 g (1 lb) or 900 g (2 lb) sizes.

Cut off one third of the pastry dough and set
ide, covered with a cloth or upturned bowl.
ivide the remaining two thirds into six equal
ortions. Roll each piece into a 15 cm (6 inch)

*Mould the pastry round over
an up-turned jar.*   *Gently twist to ease the
pastry away from the jar.*

round and trim the edges. Turn a jar upside down
and place a round over it. Mould it into shape
with your fingertips and smooth down the folds.
Repeat the process with the remaining five jars.
2. Cut out a double thickness of greaseproof
paper large enough to fit around the pie. Wrap
paper around the pastry and secure with string.
Repeat for all six jars. Cover the jars with a tea
towel and leave in a cool place for 2 hours to firm.
3. Turn the jar upright and carefully ease the
pastry away from the jar and greaseproof paper,
gently twisting to loosen and produce a cup shape.
Place the shaped pastry cases on a lightly greased
baking sheet.
4. Fill with a meat mixture using spoon to push
firmly down at the base and sides to hold the pie's
shape. Brush the edge of the pastry with water.
5. Divide the remaining pastry into six roughly
equal portions and roll each into a round slightly
bigger than the filled case diameter. Place each on
top of a pie and press the edges together to seal.
6. Trim away any surplus pastry and paper with a
pair of scissors and then cut a cross with a sharp
knife in the centre of each pie. Fold back the
pastry and glaze and decorate it to taste. Finish
with a tassel (see page 370). Bake as directed.

### SHAPING A LARGE RAISED PIE IN A MOULD

Use this method for making Raised Game Pie (see
page 178).

1. Make up 450 g (1 lb) Hot Water Crust Pastry
(see page 377) and keep it warm. Grease a 1.75 litre
(3 pint) hinged pie mould or use a loose-based
round cake tin or loaf tin with the same capacity.
Place the mould on a baking sheet.
2. Roll out two thirds of the pastry 0.5 cm (¼ inch)
thick and use to line the tin.
3. Fill and put on the lid as above. Bake as
directed in the recipe.

## DECORATIVE TOUCHES

### KNOCK UP

After the pastry edges have been trimmed all pies should then be 'knocked up' to seal the edges firmly before decorating. Press your index finger along the rim and holding a knife horizontally, tap the edge of the pastry sharply with the blunt side of the blade to give a 'flaky' appearance.

*Knock up the pastry edge with the blunt edge of a knife.*

### SCALLOP/FLUTE

Press a thumb on the rim of the pastry and at the same time draw back the floured blade of a round-bladed or table knife about 1 cm ($\frac{1}{2}$ inch) towards the centre. Repeat around the edge of the pie. Traditionally sweet dishes should have about 0.5 cm ($\frac{1}{4}$ inch) scallops and savoury dishes 2.5 cm (1 inch) scallops.

*Use your thumb and a sharp knife to scallop the pastry edge.*

### CRIMP

Push the thumb or finger of one hand into the rim of the pastry. Use the thumb and first finger of the other hand to gently pinch the pastry pushed up by this action. Continue around the edge of the pie. Crimp is traditionally used to seal Cornish Pasties as well as to decorate pie edges.

*Press the pastry against your fingertips to crimp the pastry's rim.*

### LEAVES

Cut thinly rolled out pastry trimmings into 2.5 cm (1 inch) wide strips. Cut these diagonally to form diamond shapes and mark the veins of a leaf on each one with the back of a knife blade. Pinch one of the long ends to form a stem.

*Score diamond shaped pieces of pastry trimmings to make leaves.*

### TASSEL

Cut a strip from the rolled out pastry trimmings 2.5 cm (1 inch) wide and 10–15 cm (4–6 inches) long. Use a knife to make 2 cm ($\frac{3}{4}$ inch) slits at short intervals to resemble a fringe. Roll up and stand on the uncut end while you spread out the cut strips.

*Use pastry trimmings to make decorative tassels.*

### LATTICE WORK

Lattice is probably the best known decoration for open pie tarts. They may be either simple or interwoven.

**1.** Use either a knife or pastry wheel to cut the rolled out pastry into 1 cm ($\frac{1}{2}$ inch) wide strips of the same length as the tart.

**2.** Lay half the strips at intervals across the surface an equal distance apart. Place the other half diagonally across the first. Flatten the ends and moisten and press firmly to seal.

**3.** An interwoven lattice may be achieved by folding back alternate strips of the first layer and adding strips at right angles. Replace the folded back strips, lift back the alternate ones and continue.

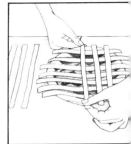

*Arrange the top layer of pastry strips diagonally across the first layer.*

## BAKING BLIND

This is the term used to describe the cooking of pastry cases without any filling. The pastry may be partially prebaked to be cooked for a further period when filled, or completely cooked if the filling requires no further cooking. All shortcrust pastries and puff pastries may be baked blind.

The pastry shell is lined with foil or greaseproof paper and then, for larger cases, filled with baking beans before cooking. Baking beans may be any dried pulse or ceramic 'beans'.

· Make the pastry and line the flan case (see page 368). Chill in the refrigerator for 30 minutes, possible, to 'rest' the pastry.

· Cut out a piece of foil or greaseproof paper rather larger than the tin. Remove the case from the refrigerator and prick the base thoroughly.

· Press the paper or foil against the pastry, then form a 1 cm (½ inch) layer of beans.

· For partially prebaked cases, bake in the oven at 200°C (400°F) mark 6 for 10–15 minutes until set. Lift out the paper or foil and beans, and bake for a further 5 minutes, until the base is just firm and lightly coloured.

Pastry cases which need complete baking should be returned to the oven for a further 15 minutes or until firm and golden brown.

For small pastry cases, it is usually sufficient to prick the pastry well with a fork before baking.

Pastry cases which have been baked blind keep several days in an airtight tin and freeze well, in freezer foil and stored in a rigid container.

### RECIPE QUANTITIES

When a recipe specifies, for example, 100 g (4 oz) pastry, this means pastry made using 100 g (4 oz) flour, with the other ingredients in proportion, not the combined ingredients' weight.

# SHORT PASTRIES are some of the easiest to make and the most versatile. They can be plain or flavoured, savoury or sweet, and form the basis of a wide range of flans, pies and tartlets. They are made by rubbing fat into flour until it is broken down into flour-coated crumbs which then bake to a light crisp texture.

Cool ingredients and conditions are essential and the dough should be handled as little as possible. It is not necessary to grease the baking equipment when cooking this type of pastry.

*Shortcrust Pastry, used here in a pie with cherries*

# SHORTCRUST PASTRY

This plain short pastry is probably the most widely used of all pastries.

*225 g (8 oz) plain flour*

*pinch of salt*

*50 g (2 oz) butter or block margarine, chilled and diced*

*50 g (2 oz) lard, chilled and diced*

*chilled water*

**1.** Place the flour and salt in a bowl and add the fat to the flour.

**2.** Using both hands, rub the fat lightly into the flour until the mixture resembles fine breadcrumbs.

**3.** Add 45–60 ml (3–4 tbsp) water, sprinkling it evenly over the surface. (Uneven addition may cause blistering when the pastry is cooked.)

**4.** Stir in with a round-bladed knife until the mixture begins to stick together in large lumps.

**5.** With one hand, collect the dough mixture together to form a ball.

**6.** Knead lightly for a few seconds to give a firm, smooth dough. Do not overhandle the dough.

**7.** To roll out, sprinkle a very little flour on a working surface and the rolling pin (not on the pastry) and roll out the dough evenly in one direction only, turning it occasionally. The usual thickness is 0.3 cm (⅛ inch). Do not pull or stretch the pastry.

### Shortcrust Pastry Quantity Guide for Flans

| Dish Size<br>Plain or Fluted Flan Ring | Pastry<br>(Flour weight,<br>see page 371) |
| --- | --- |
| 15 cm (6 inch) | 100 g (4 oz) |
| 18 cm (7 inch) | 150 g (5 oz) |
| 20.5 cm (8 inch) | 175 g (6 oz) |
| 23 cm (9 inch) | 200 g (7 oz) |

Loose-bottomed metal flan tins are shallower than flan rings, china dishes or sandwich tins and require less pastry and filling than indicated in the recipe.

**8.** The pastry can be baked straight away, but it is better if allowed to 'rest' for about 30 minutes in the tin or dish, covered in foil or cling film, in the refrigerator.

**9.** Bake at 200–220°C (400–425°F) mark 6–7, except where otherwise specified, until lightly browned (see individual recipes).

*Note* For shortcrust pastry, the proportion of flour to fat is 2 : 1, or twice the quantity. Therefore, for a recipe using quantities of shortcrust pastry other than 225 g (8 oz) simply use half the quantity of fat to the flour weight specified.

## Variations

### WHOLEMEAL PASTRY

Follow the recipe and method for Shortcrust Pastry but use plain wholemeal flour instead of white. You may need a little extra water due to the absorbency of wholemeal flour.

### NUT PASTRY

Follow the recipe and method for Shortcrust Pastry but stir in 25 g (1 oz) very finely chopped, shelled walnuts, peanuts, cashew nuts, hazelnuts or almonds before adding the water. When using salted nuts, do not add salt to the flour.

### CHEESE PASTRY

Follow the recipe and method for Shortcrust Pastry, but stir in 100 g (4 oz) finely grated Cheddar or other hard cheese and a pinch of mustard powder before adding the water.

### SHORTCRUST PASTRY MADE IN A MIXER

A mixer makes excellent shortcrust pastry in a very short time. It is important to remember, however, that the machine works quickly, so never let it overmix as the resulting pastry will be disappointing. As the hands do not touch the pastry, it remains cool, thus improving the end result. Ingredients: as basic shortcrust recipe.

**1.** Place the flour and salt in the mixer bowl. Add the diced fat. Switch on to minimum speed until the ingredients are incorporated.

**2.** Gradually increase the mixer speed as the fat breaks up, until the mixture resembles fine breadcrumbs.

**3.** Switch off the mixer and quickly sprinkle over 45 ml (3 tbsp) chilled water. Incorporate this on medium speed and switch off the machine as soon as the mixture forms a compact dough. Roll out as for shortcrust pastry.

## SHORTCRUST PASTRY MADE IN A FOOD PROCESSOR

A food processor makes shortcrust pastry very quickly and gives good results. It is most important not to overmix the dough as a food processor works in seconds not minutes. For even 'rubbing in', turn the machine on in short bursts rather than letting it run continuously. Make sure you know the capacity of your food processor and never overload the processor bowl. If making a large quantity of pastry, make it in two batches. Ingredients: as basic shortcrust recipe.

1. Mix the flour and salt together in the bowl of the food processor.
2. Cut the fat into pieces and add it to the flour. Mix for a few seconds until the mixture resembles fine breadcrumbs.
3. Add 45–60 ml (3–4 tbsp) chilled water and switch on until the mixture forms a smooth dough. Roll out as for shortcrust pastry.

## RICH SHORTCRUST OR FLAN PASTRY

Rich shortcrust or flan pastry is made by the same rubbing in method as shortcrust, but the liquid used is beaten egg instead of water. It is usually sweetened with caster sugar which improves the flavour and is ideal for flan cases, small tarts and other sweet pastries. If the sugar is omitted, it can be used for savoury flans and tarts. Quick and easy to prepare, flan pastry benefits from being chilled in the refrigerator for at least 30 minutes before being used.

100 g (4 oz) flour

pinch of salt

75 g (3 oz) butter or block margarine and lard, diced

5 ml (1 level tsp) caster sugar

1 egg, beaten

1. Place the flour and salt in a bowl. Rub the fat into the flour as for shortcrust pastry, until the mixture resembles fine breadcrumbs. Stir in the sugar.

2. Add the egg, stirring with a round-bladed knife until the ingredients begin to stick together in large lumps.
3. With one hand, collect the mixture together and knead lightly for a few seconds to give a firm, smooth dough. Roll out as for shortcrust pastry.
4. Bake at 200°C (400°F) mark 6, unless otherwise stated, until lightly browned.

## PÂTE SUCRÉE (SWEET PASTRY)

This French, rich, sweet, short pastry is the best choice for Continental pâtisserie. Pâte Sucrée is thin, crisp yet melting in texture; it keeps its shape, shrinks very little and does not spread during baking. It is fairly quick and easy to make. Although it can be made in a mixing bowl, the classic way to make it is on a flat, cold surface such as marble.

100 g (4 oz) flour

pinch of salt

50 g (2 oz) caster sugar

50 g (2 oz) butter (at room temperature)

2 egg yolks

1. Sift the flour and salt on to a working surface. Make a well in the centre and add the sugar, butter and egg yolks.

2. Using the fingertips of one hand, pinch and work the sugar, butter and egg yolks together until well blended.
3. Gradually work in all the flour to bind the mixture together.
4. Knead lightly until smooth. Wrap the pastry in foil or cling film and leave to 'rest' in the refrigerator or a cool place for about 1 hour, or overnight if possible.
5. Bake at 190°C (375°F) mark 5, unless otherwise stated, until lightly browned.

## CHEESE PASTRY

There are two types and methods of making cheese pastry. The plainer version is made by the shortcrust pastry technique with grated cheese added (see page 372) and is easy to handle and less liable to crack when shaped. That type is better to use for pies, tarts and flans.

This cheese pastry is a little more difficult to make and handle; the fat and cheese are creamed together, then the flour is worked in. This type is best used for small savouries, such as pastry and cocktail appetisers and savouries. Use a hard, dry, well flavoured cheese with a 'bite', such as Cheddar, Cheshire or Leicester, and grate it finely. A pinch of dry mustard added to the flour with the salt helps to bring out the cheese taste. Another flavour which blends well with cheese pastry is a pinch of cayenne pepper.

| |
|---|
| 40 g (1½ oz) butter or block margarine |
| 40 g (1½ oz) lard |
| 75 g (3 oz) Cheddar or other hard cheese, finely grated |
| 100 g (4 oz) flour |
| pinch of salt |

1. Cream the butter, lard and cheese together until soft. Gradually work in the flour and salt with a wooden spoon or a palette knife until the mixture sticks together.
2. With one hand, collect the mixture together and knead very lightly for a few seconds to give a smooth dough. Cover with greaseproof paper or cling film and leave in a cool place until required.
3. Bake at 200°C (400°F) mark 6, unless stated otherwise, until lightly browned.

## ONE STAGE SHORT PASTRY

This quick method for making pastry is completely different from the rubbed-in method for shortcrust. Soft tub margarine, water and a little of the flour are creamed together, then the remaining flour is mixed in until a dough is formed. One Stage Short Pastry can be used in any recipe using shortcrust pastry.

| |
|---|
| 100 g (4 oz) soft tub margarine |
| 175 g (6 oz) flour, sifted |
| 15 ml (1 tbsp) chilled water |
| pinch of salt |

1. Place the margarine, 30 ml (2 level tbsp) flour and the water in a bowl.
2. Cream with a fork for about 30 seconds until well mixed. Mix in the remaining flour with the salt to form a fairly soft dough and knead lightly until smooth. Roll out as for shortcrust pastry.
3. Bake at 190°C (375°F) mark 5 until lightly browned, or for the length of time stated in the individual shortcrust pastry recipes.

## OIL OR FORK-MIX PASTRY

Oil Pastry is very quick to make and can be used instead of shortcrust pastry. As it is naturally slightly more greasy, it is best used for savoury rather than sweet dishes. Short and flaky in texture, oil pastry should be mixed quickly and used straight away, as it dries out and is too difficult to roll if left for even a short while or chilled.

| |
|---|
| 40 ml (8 tsp) vegetable oil |
| 15 ml (1 tbsp) chilled water |
| 100 g (4 oz) flour |
| pinch of salt |

1. Put the oil and water into a bowl. Beat well with a fork to form an emulsion.
2. Mix the flour and salt together and gradually add to the mixture to make a dough.
3. Roll out on a floured surface or between pieces of greaseproof paper.
4. Bake at 200°C (400°F) mark 6 for the same length of time as shortcrust pastry.

# FLAKED PASTRIES

The light layered texture of flaked pastries is achieved by rolling and folding the dough to trap pockets of air between the layers of dough.

The proportion of fat to flour is much higher in all flaked pastries than shortcrust, and the methods of mixing it into the dough vary with the different types of flaked pastries.

Remember to rest all flaked pastries in the refrigerator for about 30 minutes after making and again after shaping and before baking. During baking, the air expands and the fat melts and is absorbed by the flour which leaves more air spacing. This gives the pastry its characteristic flaky texture.

## FLAKY PASTRY

This pastry can be used instead of puff pastry in many savoury and sweet dishes where a great rise is not needed. The fat should be of about the same consistency as the dough with which it is to be combined, which is why it is 'worked' on a plate beforehand.

*225 g (8 oz) plain flour*

*pinch of salt*

*175 g (6 oz) butter or a mixture of butter and lard*

*120 ml (8 tbsp) chilled water and a squeeze of lemon juice*

*beaten egg, to glaze*

**1.** Mix the flour and salt together in a bowl. Soften the fat by 'working' it with a knife on a plate, then divide it into four equal portions.
**2.** Add one quarter of the fat to the flour and rub it into the flour between finger and thumb tips until the mixture resembles fine breadcrumbs.
**3.** Add enough water and lemon juice, stirring with a round-bladed knife, to make a soft, elastic dough. Turn the dough on to a lightly floured surface, knead until smooth, then roll out into an oblong three times as long as it is wide.
**4.** Using a round-bladed knife, dot a second quarter of the fat over the top two thirds of the pastry in flakes, so that it looks like buttons on a card.

*Flaky Pastry on a Steak and Mushroom Pie (see page 103)*

**5.** Fold the bottom third of the pastry up and the top third down, then turn it so that the folded edges are at the sides.
**6.** Seal the edges of the pastry by pressing with a rolling pin. Wrap the pastry in greaseproof paper and leave in the refrigerator to rest for 15 minutes. Re-roll as before and repeat twice more until the remaining fat has been used up.

*Dot the butter and lard over the top two thirds of the rolled pastry.*

**7.** Wrap the pastry loosely in greaseproof paper and leave it to 'rest' in the refrigerator for at least 30 minutes before using.
**8.** Roll out the pastry on a lightly floured working surface to 0.3 cm (⅛ inch) thick and use as required. Leave to rest in the refrigerator for 30 minutes before baking. Brush with beaten egg before baking to give the characteristic glaze.
**9.** Bake at 200°C (400°F) mark 6, unless otherwise stated.

## Rough Puff Pastry

Similar in texture to flaky pastry, rough puff can be used instead of flaky, except when even rising and appearance are particularly important. Rough puff is quicker and easier to make than puff or flaky pastry.

| |
|---|
| *225 g (8 oz) plain flour* |
| *pinch of salt* |
| *75 g (3 oz) butter or block margarine, well chilled* |
| *75 g (3 oz) lard* |
| *about 150 ml (¼ pint) chilled water and a squeeze of lemon juice* |
| *beaten egg, to glaze* |

**1.** Mix the flour and salt together in a bowl. Cut the butter into 2 cm (¾ inch) cubes. Stir into the flour without breaking up the pieces.
**2.** Add enough water and lemon juice to mix to a fairly stiff dough using a round-bladed knife. On a lightly floured surface, roll out into an oblong three times as long as it is wide.
**3.** Fold the bottom third up and the top third down, then turn the pastry so that the folded edges are at the sides. Seal the ends of the pastry with a rolling pin. Wrap the pastry in greaseproof paper and chill for 15 minutes.

**4.** Repeat this rolling and folding process three more times, turning the dough so that the folded edge is on the left hand side each time. Wrap the pastry in paper and chill for 30 minutes.
**5.** Roll out the pastry to 0.3 cm (⅛ inch) thick and use as required. Leave to 'rest' in the refrigerator for 30 minutes before baking. Brush with beaten egg before baking to give the characteristic glaze.
**6.** Bake at 220°C (425°F) mark 7.

*Add butter to the flour.*     *Fold up bottom third.*

## Puff Pastry

The richest of all the pastries, puff requires patience, practice and very light handling. Whenever possible it should be made the day before use. It is not practical to make in a quantity with less than 450 g (1 lb) flour weight. This is equivalent to two 368 g (13 oz) frozen packets.

| |
|---|
| *450 g (1 lb) strong plain flour* |
| *pinch of salt* |
| *450 g (1 lb) butter or block margarine* |
| *300 ml (½ pint) chilled water* |
| *15 ml (1 tbsp) lemon juice* |
| *beaten egg, to glaze* |

**1.** Mix the flour and salt together in a bowl. Cut off 50 g (2 oz) of butter and flatten the remaining butter with a rolling pin to a slab 2 cm (¾ inch) thick.
**2.** Cut the 50 g (2 oz) butter into small pieces, add to the flour and rub in. Using a round-bladed knife, stir in enough water and lemon juice to make a soft, elastic dough.
**3.** Quickly knead the dough until smooth and shape into a round. Cut through half the depth in the shape of a cross. Open out to form a star.

**4.** Roll out, keeping the centre four times as thick as the flaps. Place the slab of butter in the centre of the dough and fold the flaps envelope-style.
**5.** Press gently with a rolling pin and roll out into a rectangle measuring about 40 × 20 cm (16 × 8 inches).
**6.** Fold the bottom third up and the top third down, keeping the edges straight. Seal the edges.
**7.** Wrap the pastry in greaseproof paper and leave in the refrigerator to 'rest' for 30 minutes. Put the pastry on a lightly floured working surface with the folded edges to the sides and repeat the rolling, folding and resting sequence five times.
**8.** Shape the pastry as required, then leave to 'rest' in the refrigerator for 30 minutes before baking. Brush with beaten egg before baking.
**9.** Bake at 220°C (425°F) mark 7, for about 15 minutes on its own or longer if filled, except where otherwise specified.

*MAKING BOUCHÉES*

**1.** Roll out ½ quantity Puff Pastry (see page 376), 0.5 cm (¼ inch) thick, or use a 368 g (13 oz) packet of puff pastry, rolled thinner. Using a 5 cm (2 inch) plain cutter, cut out 20–25 rounds and put them on a dampened baking sheet.
**2.** Cut part-way through the centre of each round with a 4 cm (1¼ inch) plain cutter.
**3.** Glaze the tops with beaten egg and bake in the oven at 230°C (450°F) mark 8 for 10 minutes, until golden brown.
**4.** Remove the lid and soft pastry from the centre and cool the cases on a rack. Before serving, reheat in the oven at 180°C (350°F) mark 4 for about 15 minutes, then fill with a hot savoury sauce, or fill cold bouchées with cold sauce and reheat as above. Individual Vol-au-Vents are made in a similar way but are cut with a 7.5 cm (3 inch) plain cutter and a 5 cm (2 inch) plain cutter for marking the lid.

*MAKING A LARGE VOL-AU-VENT*

**1.** Roll out ½ quantity Puff Pastry, 2.5 cm (1 inch) thick, or use a 368 g (13 oz) packet of puff pastry, rolled thinner. Put on to a dampened baking sheet and cut into an oval or large round to take in nearly all the pastry. Try not to cut nearer than 1 cm (½ inch) to the edge of the slab of pastry.
**2.** With a small knife mark an oval or round 1–2 cm (½–¾ inch) inside the larger one, to form a lid, cutting about halfway through the pastry.
**3.** Brush the top with beaten egg. Bake in the oven at 230°C (450°F) mark 8 for 30–35 minutes, covering the pastry with greaseproof paper when it is sufficiently brown. Remove the lid, scoop out any soft pastry inside and dry out the case in the oven for a further 5–10 minutes.
**4.** Serve hot or cold, filled with a savoury sauce as suggested for Bouchées (see left), or make a cold sweet by filling with soft fruit, peaches or apricots and whipped cream.

# MISCELLANEOUS PASTRIES This section includes the pastries like suetcrust, hot water crust, choux and phyllo that are not made by either the traditional rubbing in or flaked pastry methods.

## HOT WATER CRUST PASTRY

This pastry is used to make savoury raised pies such as Veal and Ham Pie and Game Pie. It is mixed with boiling water, which makes it pliable enough to mould into a raised pie that will hold its shape as it cools and during the baking. It is a 'strong' pastry, fit to withstand the extra handling that it must receive during the shaping and also the weight of the savoury filling it must hold. Care must be taken when moulding hot water crust pastry to ensure that there are no cracks through which the meat juices can escape during baking. Keep the part of the pastry that is not actually being used covered with a cloth or an upturned bowl, to prevent it hardening before use. If you do not wish to 'raise' the pie by hand (see page 369), you can use a cake tin. For a more elaborate raised pie, you can buy a special metal mould, made in two parts, joined by a hinge, so that they can easily be removed when the pie is cooked.

*450 g (1 lb) plain flour*
*10 ml (2 level tsp) salt*
*100 g (4 oz) lard*
*250 ml (9 fl oz) water*

**1.** Mix the flour and salt together in a bowl. Make a well in the centre. In a small saucepan, melt the lard in the water, then bring to the boil and pour into the well.
**2.** Working quickly, beat the mixture with a wooden spoon to form a fairly soft dough.
**3.** Use one hand to pinch the dough lightly together and knead until smooth and silky.
**4.** Cover with cling film or a damp tea towel. Leave in a warm place to rest for 20–30 minutes so the dough becomes elastic and easy to work. Use as required but do not allow it to cool. See page 369 for the method of shaping a raised pie by hand and in a cake tin.
**5.** Bake at 220°C (425°F) mark 7, reducing to 180°C (350°F) mark 4 (see individual recipes).

*Jam Roly-Poly (see page 326) made with Suetcrust Pastry*

## SUETCRUST PASTRY

This pastry may be used for both sweet and savoury basin puddings, roly-poly puddings and dumplings. It can be steamed, boiled or baked; the first two methods are the most satisfactory, as baked suetcrust pastry is inclined to be hard. Suetcrust pastry is quick and easy to make, and should be light and spongy in texture—the correct mixing, quick light handling and long, slow cooking will achieve this. For a lighter texture or if using wholemeal flour, replace 50 g (2 oz) of the flour with 50 g (2 oz) fresh breadcrumbs.

| |
|---|
| *225 g (8 oz) self raising flour* |
| *2.5 ml (½ level tsp) salt* |
| *100 g (4 oz) shredded suet* |
| *about 150 ml (¼ pint) chilled water* |

1. Mix the flour, salt and suet together in a bowl.
2. Using a round-bladed knife, stir in enough water to give a light, elastic dough. Knead very lightly until smooth.
3. Roll out to 0.5 cm (¼ inch) thick and use as required.
4. Steaming or boiling basin and roly-poly puddings takes about 2–4 hours, depending on filling and size. Roly-poly puddings can also be wrapped in foil and baked at 200°C (400°F) mark 6 for about 45 minutes, unless otherwise stated. Dumplings cooked in simmering liquid take about 25 minutes.

## LINING A PUDDING BASIN WITH SUETCRUST

Sweet and savoury filled and layered suet puddings in basins are a constant family favourite. The basin may be made of any heatproof material from glass or earthenware to certain kinds of plastic. It is important to use the size of basin given in a recipe. The correct size basin should allow a space of about 1 cm (½ inch) at the top when the uncooked pudding is complete. Always grease the basin to prevent the pastry from sticking and if you do not have a steamer cook the pudding on a trivet in a saucepan at least 5 cm (2 inch) wider than the diameter of the basin, in boiling water that comes halfway up the basin.

1. For a 1.7 litre (3 pint) pudding basin, roll out the pastry to a round about 35.5 cm (14 inches) in diameter. Using a sharp knife cut out one quarter of the dough and reserve. Lightly grease the pudding basin.
2. Dust the top surface of the large piece of pastry with flour and fold in half, then in half again. Lift the pastry into the basin, unfold, press into the base and up the sides, taking care to seal the join well. The pastry should overlap the basin top by about 2.5 cm (1 inch).
3. Spoon the filling into the lined pudding basin, taking care not to puncture the pastry lining. Gently spread out the filling so it is evenly distributed.
4. Roll out the remaining one quarter of pastry to a round 2.5 cm (1 inch) wider than the top of the basin. Dampen the exposed edge of pastry lining the basin.
5. Lift the round of pastry on top of the filling. Push the pastry edges together to seal.
6. Cut a piece of greaseproof paper and a piece of foil large enough to cover the basin. Place them together and pleat across the middle to allow for expansion. Lightly grease the greaseproof side and put them over the pudding with the greaseproof side down.
7. Tie securely on to the basin, running the string just under the rim. Make a string handle across the basin top. Bring a large pan of water to the boil. Fit a steamer over the pan and put the pudding inside and cover. Steam for the specified time.

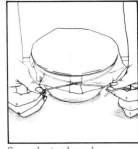

*Securely tie pleated greaseproof paper and foil over the pudding basin.*

# CHOUX PASTRY

This light, crisp-textured pastry is used for making sweet and savoury éclairs, cream puffs, aigrettes and gougère. As long as the recipe instructions are strictly adhered to, choux pastry will always give good results. Always collect the ingredients together before starting to make choux pastry as all the flour needs to be added quickly as soon as the mixture has come to the boil.

Raw choux paste is too soft and sticky to be rolled out and is, therefore, piped or spooned on to a dampened baking sheet for baking. During baking, the moisture in the dough turns to steam and puffs up the mixture leaving the centre hollow. Thorough cooking is important; if insufficiently cooked, the choux may collapse when taken from the oven and there will be uncooked pastry in the centre to scoop out.

When the cooked choux has cooled and dried out, it can be filled with whipped cream or a savoury filling. Choux pastry can also be deep fried—pipe or spoon it directly into hot oil.

65 g (2½ oz) plain or strong plain flour

50 g (2 oz) butter or block margarine

150 ml (¼ pint) water

2 eggs, lightly beaten (use size 2 when using an electric mixer)

**1.** Sift the flour on to a plate or piece of paper. Put the fat and water together in a saucepan, heat gently until the fat has melted, then bring to the boil. Remove the pan from the heat. Tip the flour at once into the hot liquid. Beat thoroughly with a wooden spoon.
**2.** Continue beating the mixture until it is smooth and forms a ball in the centre of the pan (take care not to overbeat or the mixture will become fatty). Remove from the heat and leave the mixture to cool for a minute or two.
**3.** Beat in the eggs a little at a time, adding only just enough to give a piping consistency.

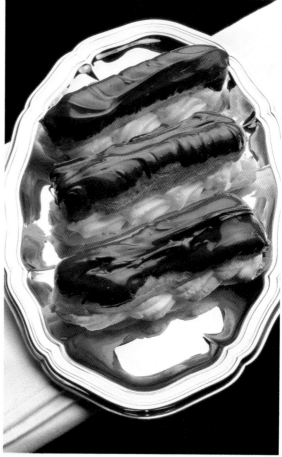

Eclairs (see page 391) made with Choux Pastry

**4.** It is important to beat the mixture vigorously at this stage to trap in as much air as possible. A hand held electric mixer is ideal for this purpose. Continue beating until the mixture develops an obvious sheen and then use as required.
**5.** Bake in an oven at 200°C (400°F) mark 6. Immediately after the choux pastry is removed from the oven it should be pierced to allow steam to escape.

**Variations**
To make a gougère, pipe or spoon the choux pastry into a ring and bake on a baking sheet or in an ovenproof dish. It can also be flavoured with finely grated cheese. Choux pastry can be baked and then filled with a savoury mixture such as fish, kidneys, chicken or ham (see Smoked Haddock Gougère, page 80).

The most elaborate use of choux pastry is the croquembouche—the table centrepiece of a French wedding or anniversary celebration. Small choux buns are stuck together with a caramel syrup to form a pyramid and then decorated with either spun sugar or sugared almonds.

## PIPING CHOUX PASTRY

**1.** To fill a piping bag, usually fitted with a plain 0.5 cm ($\frac{1}{4}$ inch) nozzle, place it in a tall jug and turn back the open end over the jug rim. Spoon the pastry mixture into the bag and squeeze it down to eliminate air bubbles.

**2.** When making éclairs, it may help to mark evenly-spaced lines on the baking sheet with the end of a wooden spoon as a guide for piping.

**3.** Hold the piping bag in one hand and, with the thumb and one finger of your other hand on the nozzle to guide it, press out the pastry. When the required length is reached, cut off the paste with a wet knife. Choux puffs and profiteroles can be piped or spooned into mounds.

*Place the piping bag in a tall jug, turning the open end over the rim.*

*Use one hand to guide the nozzle while piping choux pastry.*

# PHYLLO (FILO) OR STRUDEL PASTRY

Phyllo is a pastry of water-like thinness from the Middle East which is used for both savoury and sweet pastries, such as Baklava. It is identical to strudel pastry which originated in Europe and is used for the popular Apfel Strudel. Phyllo or strudel pastry is fairly difficult and time consuming to make. Unlike most pastries, it requires warm ingredients and, instead of light handling, it has to be kneaded and beaten. The dough is kneaded vigorously to enable the gluten in the flour to develop strength so the pastry can be stretched into a very thin, resilient sheet. For the same reason, strong plain flour is used as it yields more gluten to help produce an elastic dough. The thin sheet is either spread with a filling and rolled or folded, or it is cut into rectangles and stacked with a filling in between.

Ready-made phyllo or strudel pastry is available in sheets from continental shops and delicatessens.

| |
|---|
| 225 g (8 oz) strong plain flour |
| 2.5 ml ($\frac{1}{2}$ level tsp) salt |
| 1 egg, lightly beaten |
| 30 ml (2 tbsp) vegetable oil |
| 1.25 ml ($\frac{1}{4}$ level tsp) lemon juice |
| 75 ml (5 tbsp) lukewarm water |
| 25 g (1 oz) butter, melted |

**1.** Mix the flour and salt together in a large bowl. Make a well in the centre and pour in the egg, oil and lemon juice. Stirring with a fork, gradually add enough of the water to make a soft, sticky dough.

**2.** Work the dough in the bowl until it leaves the sides. Turn out on to a lightly floured surface and knead for 15 minutes. The dough should feel smooth.

**3.** Form it into a ball, place on a cloth and cover with a warmed bowl. Leave to 'rest' in a warm place for 30 minutes.

**4.** Warm a rolling pin and lightly flour a clean cotton cloth. Place the ball of dough on the cloth and roll out into a rectangle about 0.3 cm ($\frac{1}{8}$ inch) thick, lifting and turning to prevent it sticking to the cloth.

**5.** Brush the top of the dough with little melted butter. Gently stretch the dough by carefully lifting it on the backs of the hands and fingertips, and pulling it from the centre to the outside, trying to keep it in a rectangle.

**6.** Continue lifting and stretching the dough until it becomes paper thin and the rectangle

*Pour the egg, oil and lemon juice on the flour.*

measures no less than 75 × 50 cm (30 × 20 inches). Trim off uneven thick edges with scissors or a sharp knife.

**7.** Leave the dough on the cloth to dry and 'rest' for about 15 minutes before lifting off carefully.

**8.** Bake at 190°C (375°F) mark 5, except where otherwise specified, until lightly browned.

# CAKES

There is nothing to compare with the satisfaction of baking and serving your own homemade cake. Obviously, while it is not good to eat too many sweet things, there will always be occasions when you want to serve a cake. This chapter includes small and large cakes, rich fruit cakes and cakes for special occasions, as well as recipes for all the different types of icings and information on decorating and piping.

◆

## INGREDIENTS FOR CAKE MAKING

### FLOUR

A wide range of different types of flour is available (see page 440) and the difference between them is largely due to the varying gluten content. Gluten is an elastic, sticky substance formed when the flour is moistened. It sets when heated, trapping air in the mixture and giving it a light texture.

For cake making soft flour with a low gluten content is best. It is starchy and absorbs fat well to give a light, soft texture. Whether the soft flour is plain or self raising is largely a matter of personal taste.

**Self raising flour** is popular because it eliminates errors, the raising agents are already evenly blended throughout the flour.

**Plain flour** can be used with a raising agent and the raising agent can be varied to suit individual recipes. If you only have plain flour, use 225 g (8 oz) flour and 15 ml (1 level tbsp) baking powder to replace self raising flour in scones, 10 ml (2 level tsp) baking powder for a plain cake mixture, e.g. rock buns, and 5 ml (1 level tsp) for a rich fruit cake mixture. Sift the flour and baking powder together before use to ensure even blending.

**Wholemeal flour** can be used in some recipes (see page 440) but it gives a denser texture. Alternatively, use a mixture of plain and wholemeal flour.

It is worth sifting wholemeal flour as any air

that can be incorporated will give a better result. Sift the flour, then tip the bran from the sieve back into the bowl. Stir well.

### SUGAR AND OTHER SWEETENERS

Sugar is an important ingredient in all cakes and is essential in sponges. Brown sugars and other kinds of sweeteners can be used to add variety and extra flavour.

**Caster sugar** is the one most commonly used in cakes, especially for creamed mixtures and whisked sponge mixtures.

**Granulated sugar** produces a creamed mixture which is slightly reduced in volume, with a reasonably good texture, apart from a slight grittiness and sometimes a speckly appearance. For rubbed-in mixtures, granulated sugar is quite acceptable.

**Icing sugar** is the finest of all sugars. It is not generally used for basic cake mixtures as it produces a poor volume and hard crust. It is used for icing and decorating cakes.

**Soft brown sugar**, whether dark or light, imparts more flavour—a caramel taste—than white sugar and has a slightly finer grain. When it is used to replace caster sugar in sandwich cakes, the volume is good; these sugars cream well.

**Demerara sugar** is even coarser in the grain than granulated, which it can replace in rubbed-in mixtures. It is more suitable for making cakes by the melting method, such as gingerbreads, where heat and moisture help to dissolve it. It is unsatisfactory for creamed mixtures, because its large crystals do not break down during mixing.

**Barbados sugar** is a very dark, unrefined sugar of a similar colour to treacle. Molasses, often known as Black Barbados or demerara molasses is the least refined and is very dark and sticky. Too strong in flavour for light cake mixtures, Barbados sugar helps to give a good flavour and colour to rich fruit cakes and gingerbreads. You can modify the decided flavour by using it half-and-half with white sugar.

**Golden syrup** gives a special flavour which is particularly good with spices.

**Treacle** is a dark syrup, which is not as sweet as golden syrup. A little added to rich fruit cakes gives a good dark colour and distinctive flavour; it is also a traditional ingredient for gingerbreads and for the making of malt bread.

**Honey** is used in some recipes. It absorbs and retains moisture, keeping cakes and teabreads fresh for longer.

### FAT

Butter and margarine are the commonest fats used, but lard, blended white vegetable fat, dripping and oil may be used. Butter and block margarine are usually interchangeable, though butter gives a special flavour. The degree of hardness of block margarine varies from brand to brand; some are sold specifically for baking purposes and have been manufactured to cream easily. As a rule, butter and firm margarine should not be taken direct from the refrigerator—leave at room temperature for 30 minutes. For best results if the fat to be used in a creamed mixture is firm, beat it alone, then add the sugar and cream together.

**Soft tub margarines** are best suited to one-stage recipes (see page 384) but it is possible to experiment with using them in other recipes, though the texture will be different.

**Oil** is being more often used today, but specially proportioned recipes are needed (see page 385).

### EGGS

These may be used as a raising agent (see right) or to bind the mixture. Use size 3 or 4 eggs, unless otherwise stated.

### LIQUID

Moisture is required for the raising agents to work.

**Milk or water** are the most usual liquids used but brewed tea, cider, fruit juice and beer are included in certain specific recipes, or may be used to taste. It is often practical to use powdered skimmed milk instead of fresh. To use powdered skimmed milk, mix the measured milk with the flour and add water as required.

**Buttermilk** is used in certain kinds of bread and scones.

### RAISING AGENTS

**Baking powder** is the most commonly used. It usually consists of bicarbonate of soda and an acid-reacting chemical such as cream of tartar, and when moistened, these react together to give off carbon dioxide. Flour contains gluten, which holds this gas in the form of tiny bubbles when it is wet.

Since all gases expand when heated, these tiny bubbles formed throughout the mixture become larger during the baking, and thus the cake rises. The heat dries and sets the gluten and so the bubbles are held, giving the cake its characteristic light texture.

However, cake mixtures are capable of holding only a certain amount of gas, and if too much raising agent is used the cake rises very well at first, but then collapses, and a heavy, close texture is the final result.

**Bicarbonate of soda and cream of tartar** combined may be used in some recipes to replace baking powder. It is usually in the proportion of one part bicarbonate of soda to two parts cream of tartar.

**Eggs** By including whisked egg in a cake mixture, air is used as a raising agent, instead of carbon dioxide. When a high proportion of egg is used and the mixture is whisked, as in sponge cakes, very little, if any, other raising agent is needed to obtain the desired result.

In creamed mixtures also the eggs are beaten in and—as long as the correct proportion of egg is used and the mixture is well beaten—little additional raising agent is needed. In plain cakes, where beaten egg is added together with the liquid, the egg helps to bind the mixture, but it does not act as the main raising agent.

### SPICES AND FLAVOURINGS

**Ready-mixed spices** are handy for general flavouring, since they are carefully blended, but for some recipes it's better to have individual spices such as cinnamon, mace and nutmeg.

**Cake flavourings** are available in a variety of flavours such as coffee, rum, almond and vanilla. They are usually concentrated and should be used sparingly.

*Black Forest Gâteau (see page 404)*

**Natural flavourings** like lemon or orange, are the most pleasant to use whenever practical. Remember, when using the rind of any citrus fruit, to grate only lightly, so as to remove just the zest— the white pith imparts a bitter flavour.

### FRUIT, NUTS AND PEEL

**Fruit** Use good quality dried fruits; if necessary, leave them to plump up in hot water, drain and dry off. You can buy them ready-washed, but it is wise to give them a good looking over. Wash any excess syrup from glacé cherries before use and thoroughly dry.

**Peel** Buy 'caps' of candied orange and lemon peel and cut to the required size or use ready-mixed chopped peel. Ready-cut peel may need chopping into smaller pieces.

**Nuts** When nuts are called for in a recipe, check before you start to see whether they are to be blanched or unblanched, whole, split, flaked, chopped or ground. Nibbed, ready-chopped nuts are handy, but a blender or food processor will produce chopped or ground nuts.

### CAKE DECORATIONS
See page 418 for ingredients for cake decorations.

## CAKE MAKING METHODS

### RUBBING-IN METHOD
'Rubbing in' is a literal description of the method: the fat is lightly 'worked' into the flour between the fingers and thumbs until the mixture resembles fine breadcrumbs.

Some air is incorporated during this process, which helps to make the cake light, but the main raising agents are chemical. The proportion of fat to flour is half or less.

Add the liquid, using just enough to bring the mixture to the right consistency: too much liquid can cause a heavy, doughy texture and insufficient liquid results in a dry cake. The mixture should drop easily from the spoon when the handle is gently tapped against the side of the bowl. For small cakes and buns that are baked on a flat baking sheet, the mixture should be stiff enough to hold its shape without spreading too much during baking. A stiff consistency describes a mixture which will cling to the spoon.

Because they are low in fat, cakes made by the rubbing-in method do not keep well. They are best eaten the day they are made.

### CREAMING METHOD
Rich cakes are made by the creaming method. The fat and sugar are beaten together until as pale and fluffy as whipped cream, the eggs are beaten in and

the flour is then folded in. In some recipes the egg whites are whisked separately and folded in with the flour.

You need a mixing bowl large enough to accommodate vigorous beating without any danger of the ingredients overflowing. If beating by hand, use a wooden spoon and warm the bowl first to make the process easier.

Scrape the mixture down from the sides of the bowl from time to time to ensure no sugar crystals are left. An electric mixer or electric hand whisk is a time and labour-saving alternative to creaming by hand, but remember it cannot be used for incorporating the flour.

Use eggs at room temperature and beat thoroughly after each addition to reduce the risk of the mixture curdling. (A mixture that curdles holds less air and produces a heavy dense cake.)

As an extra precaution against the mixture curdling, add a spoonful of the sifted flour with the second and every following addition of egg and beat thoroughly. To keep the mixture light, fold in the remaining flour gradually, using a metal spoon.

### ONE-STAGE METHOD

The one-stage method is based on soft tub margarine and this type of cake is wonderfully quick and easy to prepare. There is no need for any creaming or rubbing in: all the ingredients are simply beaten together with a wooden spoon for 2–3 minutes, until well blended and slightly glossy.

This method is also ideal for making cakes in an electric mixer but be careful not to overbeat.

Self raising flour is invariably used—often with the addition of a little extra baking powder to boost the rise. You can use either caster or soft brown sugar for these quick cakes because their fine crystals dissolve easily.

These cakes are similar to those made by the creaming method, but their texture is more open and they do not keep as well. Wrap them in foil as soon as they are cold to prevent them going stale.

### MELTING METHOD

Gingerbreads and other cakes made by the melting method have a deliciously moist and sticky texture.

The inviting texture and rich dark colour of these cakes are due to the high proportion of sugary ingredients, including liquid sweeteners such as syrup or black treacle. To ensure the liquid sweetener is easily incorporated, it is warmed with the fat and sugar until blended and then added to the dry ingredients together with any eggs and the liquid.

Bicarbonate of soda is often used to raise these cakes—it reacts with natural acids present in liquid sweeteners. Spices are frequently added to enhance the flavour and also counteract the faintly bitter taste of bicarbonate of soda.

Measure the liquid sweetener carefully; too much can cause a heavy, sunken cake. Put the saucepan on the scales, set the dial to zero, then spoon in the required amount of syrup or treacle, or weigh the pan, then add the sweetener until the scales register the weight of the pan plus the required weight of syrup. Warm it very gently, just until the sugar has dissolved and the fat has melted. If allowed to boil, the mixture will become an unusable toffee-like mass.

Allow the mixture to cool slightly before pouring it on to the dry ingredients, or it will begin to cook the flour and a hard tough cake will result. The blended mixture should have the consistency of heavy batter; it can be poured into the prepared tin and will find its own level.

Most cakes made by the melting method should be stored for a day or so before cutting, to allow the crust to soften and give the flavour time to mellow.

### WHISKING METHOD

The whisking method produces the lightest of all cakes. The classic sponge is light and feathery and is made by whisking together eggs and caster sugar, then folding in the flour. There is no fat in the mixture, and the cake rises simply because of the air incorporated during whisking. For an even lighter cake, the egg yolks and sugar can be whisked together, with the whites whisked separately and folded in afterwards.

Because they have no fat they always need a filling, and do not keep well. Bake a sponge the day you wish to eat it.

A moister version of the whisked sponge is a Genoese sponge. This is also made by the whisking method, but melted butter is added with the flour. This gives a delicate sponge, lighter than a Victoria sandwich, but with a moister texture than the plain whisked sponge, and a more delicious rich and buttery taste.

When adding melted butter, make sure it is just liquid and pour into the mixture around the sides of the bowl and fold in very lightly. Don't try to substitute margarine for butter in this recipe or the flavour and texture will be lost. A Genoese sponge keeps better than a plain whisked sponge.

To make a really good sponge, the eggs and sugar must be whisked until thick enough to leave a trail when the whisk is lifted from the surface. If you use a rotary whisk or a hand-held electric mixer, place the bowl over a saucepan of hot water to speed the thickening process. When whisking in an electric table top mixer, additional heat is not required.

Do not let the bottom of the bowl touch the water or the mixture will become too hot. When the mixture is really thick and double in volume, take the bowl off the heat and continue to whisk until it is cool.

Add the flour carefully. Sift it first, then add a little at a time to the whisked mixture and fold it in until evenly blended. Do not stir or you will break the air bubbles and the cake will not rise.

### CAKES MADE USING OIL

Cakes made using oil (corn oil, for example) are very easy to mix and very successful. When using oil for making sandwich cakes, it is essential to add an extra raising agent or to whisk the egg whites until stiff and fold them into the mixture just before baking. This counteracts the heaviness of the cake that sometimes occurs when oil is used.

## CAKE TINS

Choose good-quality, strong cake tins in a variety of shapes and sizes. Non-stick surfaces clean most easily and are particularly useful in small awkwardly shaped tins. Some cake tins have a loose bottom or a loosening device to make it easier to remove the cake.

Use the size of tin specified in the recipe. Using too large a tin will tend to give a pale, flat and shrunken-looking cake; cakes baked in too small a tin will bulge over and lose their contours. If you do not have the tin specified, choose a slightly larger one. The mixture will be shallower and will take less time to cook, so test for doneness 5–10 minutes early.

**Flan rings and tins** come in many forms. Round tins with plain or fluted sides and removable bases are primarily for pastry flan cases. For sponge flans, use a special flan tin with a raised base.

**Loaf tins** are used for cakes as well as bread. The most useful sizes are 900 ml (1½ pint) 450 g (1 lb) and 1.7 litre (3 pint) 900 g (2 lb).

**Sandwich tins** are shallower round tins with straight sides for making sandwich and layer cakes, in sizes 18–25 cm (7–10 inches).

A *moule à manqué* tin is a deep sandwich tin with sloping sides.

**Small cake tins and moulds** come in sheets of six, nine or 12 or individually. There are shapes for buns, sponge fingers, madeleines, etc.

**Spring-release tins** come complete with different loose bottoms.

**Standard cake tins** For everyday use, 15 cm (6 inch), 18 cm (7 inch) and 20.5 cm (8 inch) tins are adequate; for celebration cakes you may need larger sizes that are available in a variety of shapes and sizes.

## PREPARING TINS

Follow the manufacturer's special directions regarding non-stick (silicone-finished) tins, which do not usually require greasing or lining.

### GREASING

When greasing cake tins, brush lightly with melted margarine or butter (preferably unsalted). They may also be dredged with flour as an additional safeguard against sticking; sprinkle with a little flour in the tin and shake until coated, then shake out any surplus.

For fatless sponges, use a half-and-half mixture of flour and caster sugar. You can do the same to a sponge flan tin to produce a crisper crust.

### LINING

With most cakes it is necessary to line the tins with greaseproof paper, which is usually greased before the mixture is put in, or with non-stick paper, which does not require greasing, and can be used several times.

For a Victoria sandwich cake mixture, it is sufficient to line just the base of the tin. For rich mixtures and fruit cakes, line the whole tin. The paper is usually doubled to prevent the outside of the cake from over-browning and drying out. With the extra rich fruit mixtures used for wedding and other formal cakes, which require a long cooking time, it is also advisable to pin a double strip of thick brown paper or newspaper around the outside of the tin, to help prevent the outside of the cake overcooking.

**To line a deep tin** Cut a piece (or 2 pieces, if necessary) of greaseproof paper long enough to reach around the tin and overlap slightly, and high enough to extend about 2.5 cm (1 inch) above the top edge. Fold up the bottom edge of the strip about 2.5 cm (1 inch), creasing it firmly, then open out and snip into this folded portion with scissors; this snipped edge enables the paper band to fit a square, oblong, round or oval tin neatly.

Grease the inside of the paper. Place the strip in position in the greased tin, with the cut edge flat against the base. In a rectangular tin, make sure the paper fits snugly into the corners.

Cut a double round of paper to fit inside the base of the tin. (Stand the tin on the paper, draw round it and then cut.) Put the rounds in place—they will keep the snipped edge of the band in position and make a neat lining; brush the base of the lining with melted lard.

**To line a sandwich tin** Cut a round of greaseproof paper to fit the bottom of the tin exactly. If the tin's sides are shallow and you want to raise them, fit a band of paper inside the tin, coming about 2.5 cm (1 inch) above the rim.

**To line a Swiss roll tin** Cut a piece of paper about 5 cm (2 inch) larger all around than the tin. Place the tin on it and in each corner make a cut from the angle of the paper as far as the corner of the tin. Grease the tin and put in the paper so that it fits closely, overlapping at the corners. Grease the paper and dust with a half-and-half mixture of flour and sugar sifted together. Non-stick paper is very satisfactory for lining this type of tin.

**To line a loaf tin** It is not usually necessary to line a loaf tin fully. Grease the inside, line the base only with an oblong of greaseproof paper and grease the paper.

**To line a sponge flan tin** Grease the inside well, and place a round of greased greaseproof paper over the raised part only of the tin.

## HEATING THE OVEN

Preheat the oven before starting to make cakes so that it will be at the correct temperature by the time the cake is ready to go in. Check that the shelves are in the correct position—place in the centre of the oven where possible.

### TO TEST WHETHER A CAKE IS COOKED

Small cakes should be well risen, golden brown in colour and firm to the touch—both on top and underneath—and they should begin to shrink from the sides of the tin on being taken out of the oven.

Larger cakes present more difficulty, especially for beginners, although the oven heat and time of cooking give a reasonable indication, but the following tests are a guide:

- Press the centre top of the cake very lightly with the fingertip. The cake should be spongy and should give only very slightly to the pressure, then rise again immediately, retaining no impression.
- In the case of a fruit cake, lift it gently from the oven and 'listen' to it, putting it closely to the ear. A continued sizzling sound indicates that the cake is not cooked through.
- Insert a warmed long skewer (never use a cold knife) in the centre of the cake. If any mixture is sticking to it, the cake requires longer cooking.

### COOLING

Allow the cake a few minutes to cool before turning it out of the tin; it will shrink away from the sides and is more easily removed. Turn out on to a wire rack. Allow fruit cakes to cool completely in the tin.

## CAUSES OF PROBLEMS

### TOO CLOSE A TEXTURE

- Too much liquid.
- Too little raising agent.
- Insufficient creaming of the fat and sugar.
- Creamed mixture curdled when the eggs were added (therefore holding less air).

### FRUIT SUNK TO THE BOTTOM

- Damp fruit.
- Sticky glacé cherries.
- Too soft a mixture so cannot support the weight of the fruit.
- Opening the oven door while the cake is rising.

- Using self raising flour where the recipe requires plain, or using too much baking powder—the cake over-rises and cannot carry the fruit with it.

### CAKES SUNK IN THE MIDDLE

- Mixture too soft.
- Too much raising agent.
- Oven too cool, which means that the centre of the cake does not rise.
- Oven too hot, which makes the cake appear to be done on the outside before it is cooked in the centre.
- Insufficient baking.

# SMALL CAKES

are easy to make. They may be undecorated or finished
with a variety of colourful coatings. As well as traditional small cakes like Fairy
Cakes and Maids of Honour, there are recipes for pastry cakes such as Cream Horns.

## ALMOND FINGERS

100 g (4 oz) plain flour

pinch of salt

50 g (2 oz) butter or block margarine

5 ml (1 level tsp) caster sugar

1 egg yolk

**For the filling**

45 ml (3 level tbsp) raspberry jam

1 egg white

45 ml (3 level tbsp) ground almonds

50 g (2 oz) caster sugar

few drops almond flavouring

45 ml (3 level tbsp) flaked almonds

1. Lightly grease a shallow 18 cm (7 inch) square
tin. Sift the flour and salt and rub in the butter
until the mixture resembles fine breadcrumbs. Stir
in the 5 ml (1 tsp) sugar and add the egg yolk and
enough water to mix to a firm dough.

2. Knead lightly on a floured surface and roll out
to an 18 cm (7 inch) square; use to line the base of
the tin. Spread the pastry with the jam, almost to
the edges.

3. Whisk the egg white until stiff. Fold in the
ground almonds, sugar and flavouring. Spread the
mixture over the jam.

4. Sprinkle with flaked almonds and bake in the
oven at 180°C (350°F) mark 4 for about 35 minutes
until crisp and golden. Cool in the tin, then cut
into fingers and remove with a palette knife.
*Makes 8–12*

*From the left: Maids of Honour (see page 388) and Almond Fingers.*

## MAIDS OF HONOUR

*These originated in Henry VIII's palace at Hampton Court, where they were popular with the Queen's maids of honour, hence the name.*

| |
|---|
| 568 ml (1 pint) pasteurised milk |
| 15 ml (1 tbsp) rennet |
| 212 g (7½ oz) packet frozen puff pastry, thawed |
| 1 egg, beaten |
| 15 g (½ oz) butter or margarine, melted |
| 50 g (2 oz) caster sugar |

**1.** Gently heat the milk in a saucepan until just warm to the finger. Remove from the heat and stir in the rennet. Leave for 1½–2 hours until set.

**2.** When set, put the junket into a muslin bag and leave to drain overnight. Next day, refrigerate the curd for several hours or until very firm.
**3.** Grease 12 × 6.5 cm (2½ inch) patty tins. On a lightly floured surface, roll out the pastry very thinly and using a 7.5 cm (3 inch) plain cutter, cut out 12 rounds. Line the patty tins with the pastry rounds and prick well.
**4.** Stir the egg, butter and sugar into the drained curd. Divide the mixture between the pastry cases and bake in the oven at 200°C (400°F) mark 6 for 30 minutes, until well risen and just firm to the touch. Serve warm.
*Makes 12*

## SPONGE FINGERS

| |
|---|
| 1 egg |
| 45 ml (3 level tbsp) caster sugar |
| 60 ml (4 level tbsp) strong plain flour |

**1.** Line a baking sheet with non-stick paper. Put the egg and sugar in a deep bowl and whisk until light, creamy and stiff enough to retain the impression of the whisk for a few seconds.
**2.** Sift half the flour over the mixture and fold in very lightly, using a metal spoon. Add the remaining flour in the same way. Spoon the

mixture into a piping bag fitted with a 1 cm (½ inch) plain nozzle and pipe the mixture on to the baking sheet in 7.5 cm (3 inch) lengths, leaving room for spreading.
**3.** Bake in the oven at 200°C (400°F) mark 6 for 8–10 minutes, until golden. Remove the sponge fingers carefully and cool on a wire rack.
*Note* If you wish, the ends of the fingers may be dipped into melted plain or milk chocolate, or chocolate flavoured cake covering, and allowed to harden before using.
*Makes 16*

## ROCK BUNS

| |
|---|
| 100 g (4 oz) butter or block margarine |
| 225 g (8 oz) plain flour |
| 10 ml (2 level tsp) baking powder |
| 2.5 ml (½ level tsp) mixed spice |
| grated rind of ½ a lemon |
| 100 g (4 oz) demerara sugar |
| 100 g (4 oz) mixed dried fruit |
| 1 egg, beaten |
| about 5 ml (1 tsp) milk (optional) |

**1.** Grease two baking sheets. Rub the fat into the sifted flour, baking powder and spice until the mixture resembles fine breadcrumbs.
**2.** Stir in the rind, sugar and fruit. Make a well in the centre, pour in the egg and a little milk if necessary, to give a stiff crumbly consistency. Bind together loosely using a fork.
**3.** Use two forks to shape the mixture together in rough heaps on the baking sheets. Bake in the oven at 200°C (400°F) mark 6 for 15–20 minutes.
*Makes 12*

## CHOCOLATE CRACKLES

| |
|---|
| 225 g (8 oz) chocolate chips, plain chocolate or chocolate flavoured cake covering |
| 15 ml (1 tbsp) golden syrup |
| 50 g (2 oz) butter or margarine |
| 50 g (2 oz) cornflakes |

**1.** Spread out 12 paper cases on a baking sheet. Melt the chocolate dots with the golden syrup and butter over a very low heat.
**2.** Fold in the cornflakes. When well mixed, divide between the paper cases and leave to set.
*Makes 12*

# ENGLISH MADELEINES

100 g (4 oz) butter or block margarine
100 g (4 oz) caster sugar
2 eggs, beaten
100 g (4 oz) self raising flour
30 ml (2 level tbsp) red jam, sieved and melted
50 g (2 oz) desiccated coconut
5 glacé cherries, halved
angelica leaves

1. Grease 10 dariole moulds. Cream the fat and sugar until pale and fluffy. Add the eggs, a little at a time, beating well after each addition before adding more.
2. Fold in the flour, using a metal spoon, then three-quarters fill the moulds.
3. Bake in the oven at 180°C (350°F) mark 4 for about 20 minutes, or until firm and browned. Turn them out of the moulds and leave to cool on a wire rack.
4. Trim off the bottoms, so that the cakes stand firmly and are of even height. When they are nearly cold, brush with melted jam, then holding them on a skewer, roll in coconut.

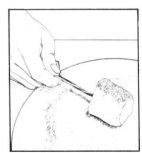

*Using a skewer, roll the jam covered Madeleines in the coconut so they are evenly coated.*

5. Top each madeleine with a glacé cherry half and two small angelica leaves.
*Makes 10*

# FAIRY CAKES

100 g (4 oz) butter or block margarine
100 g (4 oz) caster sugar
2 eggs, beaten
100 g (4 oz) self raising flour
Glacé Icing made with 350 g (12 oz) icing sugar (see page 422)

1. Spread 12 to 16 paper cases out on baking sheets, or if wished put them into patty tins.
2. Cream the fat and sugar until pale and fluffy. Add the eggs, a little at a time, beating well after each addition. Fold in the flour using a metal spoon. Two-thirds fill the cases with the mixture.
3. Bake in the oven at 190°C (375°F) mark 5 for 15–20 minutes, until golden.
4. When cold, top each cake with a little glacé icing.
*Makes 12–16*

**Variations**
Add one of the following:
● 50 g (2 oz) sultanas (known as Queen cakes)
● 50 g (2 oz) chopped dates
● 50 g (2 oz) chopped glacé cherries
● 50 g (2 oz) chocolate chips

# BOSTON BROWNIES

65 g (2½ oz) butter or block margarine
50 g (2 oz) plain chocolate
175 g (6 oz) caster sugar
65 g (2½ oz) self raising flour
1.25 ml (¼ level tsp) salt
2 eggs, beaten
2.5 ml (½ tsp) vanilla flavouring
50 g (2 oz) walnut pieces, roughly chopped

1. Grease and base line a 20.5 cm (8 inch) square tin.
2. Melt the butter and chocolate in a small bowl over a pan of hot water, then add the sugar.
3. Sift the flour with the salt and add the chocolate mixture, eggs, vanilla flavouring and walnuts.
4. Beat until smooth and pour into the tin. Bake in the oven at 180°C (350°F) mark 4 for 35–40 minutes, until the mixture is risen and beginning to leave the sides of the tin. Leave in the tin to cool, then cut into fingers or squares.
*Note* If wished cover with Chocolate Fudge Frosting (see page 424).
*Makes 12*

## ECCLES CAKES

*212 g (7½ oz) packet frozen puff pastry, thawed, or*
  *¼ quantity Puff Pastry (see page 376)*

*25 g (1 oz) butter or block margarine, softened*

*25 g (1 oz) soft dark brown sugar*

*25 g (1 oz) finely chopped mixed peel*

*50 g (2 oz) currants*

*caster sugar, to sprinkle*

**1.** Roll out the pastry on a lightly floured surface and cut into eight to ten 9 cm (3½ inch) rounds.
**2.** Mix the butter, sugar, mixed peel and currants in a bowl.
**3.** Place 5 ml (1 tsp) of the fruit and butter mixture in the centre of each pastry round. Draw up the edges of each pastry round to enclose the filling, then re-shape.

**4.** Turn each round over and roll lightly until the currants just show through. Prick the top of each with a fork. Leave to 'rest' for about 10 minutes in a cool place.
**5.** Dampen a baking sheet and transfer the rounds to it. Bake in the oven at 230°C (450°F) mark 8 for about 15 minutes until golden. Transfer to a wire rack to cool. Sprinkle with sugar while warm. *Makes 8–10*

*Gently fold the edges of the pastry so the filling is completely and securely enclosed.*

## PALMIERS

*368 g (13 oz) packet frozen puff pastry, thawed, or*
  *½ quantity Puff Pastry (see page 376)*

*caster sugar for dredging*

*150 ml (5 fl oz) double cream*

**1.** Roll out the pastry on a lightly floured surface to a rectangle measuring 30 × 25 cm (12 × 10 inches).
**2.** Dredge with caster sugar. Fold the long sides of the puff pastry halfway towards the centre.
**3.** Dredge with more caster sugar and fold again, taking the side right to the centre.
**4.** Dredge with sugar again, and fold in half lengthways to make one long strip of eight

thicknesses of pastry. Press lightly.
**5.** Cut across the pastry length into 24 equal-sized slices. Dampen a baking sheet and place the palmiers on it, cut-side down. Flatten them slightly with a palette knife or the palm of your hand.
**6.** Bake in the oven at 220°C (425°F) mark 7 for 8 minutes, until golden brown. Turn each one over and bake for a further 4 minutes. Transfer to a wire rack and leave to cool.
**7.** Whip the cream with a little caster sugar. Sandwich the palmiers together with the cream before serving. Sprinkle with caster sugar. *Makes 12*

## CREAM HORNS

*212 g (7½ oz) packet frozen puff pastry, thawed, or*
  *¼ quantity Puff Pastry (see page 376)*

*beaten egg, to glaze*

*raspberry jam*

*150 ml (5 fl oz) double cream*

*icing sugar, to dredge*

**1.** Roll out the pastry on a lightly floured surface to a strip measuring 66 × 10 cm (26 × 4 inches). Cut the pastry lengthways with a sharp knife into eight 1 cm (½ inch) ribbons.
**2.** Grease eight cream horn tins. Moisten one edge of each pastry strip and wind each around a horn tin, starting at the tip, overlapping 0.3 cm

(⅛ inch) and finishing neatly on underside. The pastry should not overlap the metal rim. Brush with beaten egg.
**3.** Dampen a baking sheet and arrange the cream horns on it, join-side down. Bake in the oven at 220°C (425°F) mark 7 for 10 minutes, until golden.
**4.** Cool for a few minutes, then carefully twist each tin, holding the pastry lightly in the other hand, to ease it out of the pastry horn. Leave the horns for about 30 minutes to cool completely.
**5.** When cold, fill the tip of each horn with a little jam. Whip the cream until stiff and fill the horns down to the jam. Sift the icing sugar over the cream horns.
*Makes 8*

## ÉCLAIRS

*Illustrated on page 379*

| quantity Choux Pastry (see page 379) |
| 300 ml (10 fl oz) double cream |
| 100 g (4 oz) plain chocolate |

**1.** Dampen a baking sheet. Put the choux pastry into a piping bag fitted with a medium plain nozzle and pipe 9 cm (3½ inches) long fingers on to the baking sheet. Trim with a wet knife.

**2.** Bake in the oven at 200°C (400°F) mark 6 for about 35 minutes, until crisp and golden.

**3.** Make a slit down the side of each bun with a sharp, pointed knife to release the steam, then transfer to a wire rack and leave for 20–30 minutes to cool completely.

**4.** Just before serving, whip the double cream until stiff and use it to fill the éclairs.

**5.** Break the chocolate into a bowl and place over simmering water. Stir until melted.

**6.** Pour into a wide shallow bowl and dip in the filled éclairs, drawing each one across the surface of the chocolate.

*Makes 12*

# SCONES AND TEABREADS are quickly and easily made and very popular, whether hot or cold. You can mix and cook them while the rest of the tea is being prepared. The raising agent may be baking powder or bicarbonate of soda and cream of tartar, with fresh milk. Similar mixtures can be used for quick teabreads made without yeast.

*Scotch Pancakes or Drop Scones (see page 393)*

Self raising flour is perfectly satisfactory for scones, although you get a slightly better rise with plain flour and a raising agent. Scones should be eaten the day they are made as they quickly go stale.

In some parts of the country, griddle scones are more frequently made than oven scones. If you do not possess a griddle, you can use a heavy-based frying pan or the solid hotplate of an electric cooker. If you use a hotplate, make sure it has a smooth surface and is clean before you start.

## CAUSES OF PROBLEMS

### HEAVY AND BADLY RISEN

- Insufficient raising agent.
- Heavy handling, especially during the kneading.
- Insufficient liquid.
- Oven too cool or the position for baking too low in the oven.

### SCONES SPREAD AND LOSE THEIR SHAPE

- Slack dough, caused by too much liquid used to make the dough.
- Too heavily greased tin. The fat melts on heating in the oven and 'pulls out' the soft dough before it has enough time to set.
- Incorrect kneading (especially of the scraps for the second rolling) or twisting the cutter round as the scones were stamped out (such scones are oval instead of round when cooked).

### VERY ROUGH SURFACE

- Insufficient kneading or badly done.
- Rough handling when transferring to the baking sheet.

## OVEN SCONES

| |
|---|
| 225 g (8 oz) self raising flour |
| 2.5 ml (½ level tsp) salt |
| 5 ml (1 level tsp) baking powder |
| 25–50 g (1–2 oz) butter or margarine |
| 150 ml (¼ pint) milk |
| beaten egg or milk, to glaze (optional) |

**1.** Preheat a baking sheet in the oven. Sift the flour, salt and baking powder together into a bowl, then rub in the fat until the mixture resembles fine breadcrumbs.
**2.** Make a well in the centre and stir in enough milk to give a fairly soft dough. Turn it on to a lightly floured surface, knead very lightly if necessary to remove any cracks, then roll out lightly to about 2 cm (¾ inch) thick, or pat it out with the hand.
**3.** Cut into 10 to 12 rounds with a 5 cm (2 inch) cutter (dipped in flour) or cut into triangles with a sharp knife. Place on the baking sheet, brush if wished with beaten egg or milk and bake towards the top of the oven at 230°C (450°F) mark 8 for 8–10 minutes, until brown and well risen.
**4.** Transfer to a wire rack to cool. Serve split and buttered.
*Makes 10–12*

**Variations**
If plain flour and baking powder are used instead of self raising flour, allow 15 ml (1 level tbsp) baking powder to 225 g (8 oz) flour and sift them together twice before using.

If you use cream of tartar and bicarbonate of soda in place of baking powder, allow 5 ml (1 level tsp) cream of tartar and 2.5 ml (½ level tsp) bicarbonate of soda to 225 g (8 oz) plain flour with ordinary milk or 2.5 ml (½ level tsp) bicarbonate of soda and 2.5 ml (½ level tsp) cream of tartar with buttermilk.

*EVERYDAY FRUIT SCONES*
Add 50 g (2 oz) currants, sultanas, seedless raisins or chopped dates (or a mixture of fruit) to the dry ingredients in the basic recipe.

*RICH AFTERNOON TEA SCONES*
Follow the basic recipe, adding 15–30 ml (1–2 level tbsp) caster sugar to the dry ingredients and using 1 beaten egg with 75 ml (5 tbsp) water or milk in place of 150 ml (¼ pint) milk; 50 g (2 oz) dried fruit may also be included.

# GRIDDLE SCONES

225 g (8 oz) self raising flour

pinch of salt

2.5 ml (½ level tsp) freshly grated nutmeg

50 g (2 oz) butter or block margarine

50 g (2 oz) caster sugar

1 egg, beaten

45–60 ml (3–4 tbsp) milk

1. Preheat and grease a griddle, or heavy-based frying pan.
2. Sift the flour, salt and nutmeg together and rub in the fat until the mixture resembles fine breadcrumbs. Stir in the sugar. Mix with the egg and milk to a firm dough.
3. On a lightly floured surface roll out to 1 cm (½ inch) thick and cut into rounds or triangles. Cook on a moderately hot griddle until brown on both sides—about 10 minutes in all.
*Makes 8–10*

## Variation
Add 50 g (2 oz) dried fruit with the sugar.

# SCOTCH PANCAKES OR DROP SCONES

100 g (4 oz) self raising flour

30 ml (2 level tbsp) caster sugar

1 egg, beaten

150 ml (¼ pint) milk

1. Lightly grease a griddle or heavy-based frying pan.
2. Mix the flour and sugar. Make a well in the centre and stir in the egg, with enough of the milk to make a batter of the consistency of thick cream. The mixing should be done as quickly and lightly as possible. Do not beat.
3. Drop the mixture in spoonfuls on to a hot surface. For round pancakes, drop it from the point of the spoon, for oval ones, drop from the side.
4. Keep the griddle at a steady heat and when bubbles rise to the surface of the pancakes and burst—after 2–3 minutes—turn the pancake over, using a palette knife. Continue cooking for a further 2–3 minutes, until golden brown on the other side.
5. Place the cooked pancakes on a clean tea towel, cover with another towel and place on a rack to cool. (This keeps in the steam and the pancakes do not become dry.) Serve with butter or with whipped cream and jam.
*Makes about 15–18 pancakes*

## Variation
For richer drop scones, add about 25 g (1 oz) fat, rubbing it into the flour. If you prefer, use 100 g (4 oz) plain flour, 2.5 ml (½ level tsp) bicarbonate of soda and 5 ml (1 level tsp) cream of tartar instead of the self raising flour.

# CHEESE SCONES

225 g (8 oz) self raising flour

pinch of salt

5 ml (1 level tsp) baking powder

40 g (1½ oz) butter or margarine

75–100 g (3–4 oz) Cheddar cheese, finely grated

5 ml (1 level tsp) mustard powder

about 150 ml (¼ pint) milk

1. Grease a baking sheet. Sift the flour, salt and baking powder together in a bowl and rub in the fat until the mixture resembles fine breadcrumbs. Stir in half the cheese, the mustard and enough milk to give a fairly soft, light dough.
2. On a lightly floured surface, roll out to about 2 cm (¾ inch) thick and cut into rounds with a 5 cm (2 inch) plain cutter. Put on the baking sheet, brush the tops with milk and sprinkle with the remaining cheese.
3. Bake in the oven at 220°C (425°F) mark 7 for about 10 minutes. Cool on a wire rack.
*Makes about 16*

## DATE BRAN MUFFINS

| |
|---|
| 100 g (4 oz) plain flour |
| pinch of salt |
| 15 ml (1 level tbsp) baking powder |
| 50 g (2 oz) bran |
| 250 ml (9 fl oz) milk |
| 25 g (1 oz) butter or margarine |
| 45 ml (3 level tbsp) caster sugar |
| 1 egg, beaten |
| 100 g (4 oz) dates, chopped |

1. Grease 16 × 6.5 cm (2½ inch) deep patty tins. Sift the flour, salt and baking powder together in a bowl. Soak the bran in the milk for 5 minutes.
2. Meanwhile, cream the fat and sugar until light, add the beaten egg gradually and mix until smooth. Add the bran mixture and stir. Add the flour mixture and dates, stirring only until just mixed.
3. Fill the tins two-thirds full and bake in the oven at 200°C (400°F) mark 6 for 20–25 minutes, until golden and well risen. Cool on a wire rack.
*Makes 16*

## MALTED FRUIT LOAF

| |
|---|
| 350 g (12 oz) plain flour |
| 2.5 ml (½ level tsp) bicarbonate of soda |
| 5 ml (1 level tsp) baking powder |
| 250 g (9 oz) sultanas |
| 30 ml (2 level tbsp) demerara sugar |
| 135 ml (9 level tbsp) malt extract |
| 2 eggs, beaten |
| 200 ml (7 fl oz) milk |

1. Grease and base-line a 1.7 litre (3 pint) loaf tin, measuring about 20 × 13 cm (8 × 5 inch) top

measurement, and grease the underside of a baking sheet.
2. Sift the flour, bicarbonate of soda and baking powder together in a bowl. Stir in the sultanas.
3. Slowly heat together the demerara sugar and malt extract. Do not boil. Pour on to the dry ingredients. Add the eggs and milk and beat well.
4. Turn the mixture into the prepared tin. Cover with the baking sheet, greased side down. Place a weight on top. Bake in the oven at 150°C (300°F) mark 2 for about 1½ hours. Turn out and cool on a wire rack. Wrap and keep for two days before eating.

## BANANA AND HONEY TEABREAD

| |
|---|
| 450 g (1 lb) bananas |
| 225 g (8 oz) self raising flour |
| 2.5 ml (½ level tsp) salt |
| 1.25 ml (¼ level tsp) freshly grated nutmeg |
| 125 g (4 oz) butter or block margarine |
| 125 g (4 oz) caster sugar |
| grated rind of 1 lemon |
| 2 eggs, size 2 |
| 120 ml (8 level tbsp) thick honey |
| 8 sugar cubes (optional) |

1. Grease and base-line a 1.7 litre (3 pint) loaf tin measuring about 20 × 13 cm (8 × 5 inch) top measurement.

2. Peel the bananas, then mash the flesh using a fork or potato masher. Mix the flour, salt and nutmeg together. Rub in the fat until the mixture resembles fine breadcrumbs.
3. Stir in the sugar, lemon rind, eggs, 90 ml (6 tbsp) honey and mashed banana. Beat well until evenly mixed. Turn the mixture into the prepared tin.
4. Bake in the oven at 180°C (350°F) mark 4 for about 1¼ hours, covering lightly if necessary. Test with a fine skewer which should come out clean when the teabread is cooked.
5. Cool slightly, then turn out on to a wire rack to cool completely. Gently warm the remaining honey, then brush over the teabread. Roughly crush the sugar lumps, and scatter over the top.

# APRICOT NUT TEABREAD

75 g (3 oz) dried apricots, cut into small pieces

75 g (3 oz) bran breakfast cereal (not flaked)

75 g (3 oz) demerara sugar

300 ml (½ pint) milk

50 g (2 oz) hazelnuts, chopped

1 egg, beaten

175 g (6 oz) self raising flour

5 ml (1 level tsp) baking powder

1. Grease and base-line a 1.7 litre (3 pint) loaf tin measuring about 20 × 13 cm (8 × 5 inch) top measurement. Set aside until required.
2. Put the apricots into a large bowl and add the bran, sugar and the milk. Cover with cling film and leave in a cool place for 3 hours.
3. Stir the hazelnuts, egg, flour and baking powder into the mixture and stir until well blended.
4. Turn the mixture into the prepared tin and bake in the oven at 190°C (375°F) mark 5 for 1–1¼ hours or until firm to the touch. Cover lightly with foil if necessary.
5. Turn out and cool on a wire rack. Store for a few days before eating.

# GINGERBREAD

450 g (1 lb) plain flour

5 ml (1 level tsp) salt

15 ml (1 level tbsp) ground ginger

15 ml (1 level tbsp) baking powder

5 ml (1 level tsp) bicarbonate of soda

225 g (8 oz) demerara sugar

175 g (6 oz) butter or block margarine

175 g (6 oz) black treacle

175 g (6 oz) golden syrup

300 ml (½ pint) milk

1 egg, beaten

1. Grease and line a 23 cm (9 inch) square cake tin. Sift together the flour, salt, ginger, baking powder and bicarbonate of soda into a large mixing bowl.
2. Put the sugar, fat, treacle and syrup in a saucepan and warm gently over a low heat until melted and well blended. Do not allow the mixture to boil. Remove from the heat and leave to cool slightly, until you can hold your hand comfortably against the side of the pan.
3. Mix in the milk and egg. Make a well in the centre of the dry ingredients, pour in the liquid and mix very thoroughly.
4. Turn into the tin and bake in the oven at 170°C (325°F) mark 3 for about 1½ hours, or until firm to the touch.
5. Turn out on to a wire rack to cool. Gingerbreads are better kept for a few days wrapped in foil or in an airtight container before eating.

**Variation**
Use half quantities of the above recipe and use a size 6 egg. Bake in an 18 cm (7 inch) deep square tin for 1–1¼ hours.

# OATMEAL PARKIN

225 g (8 oz) treacle

225 g (8 oz) golden syrup

100 g (4 oz) butter or block margarine

2.5 ml (½ level tsp) bicarbonate of soda

300 ml (½ pint) milk

1 egg, beaten

450 g (1 lb) plain flour

350 g (12 oz) medium oatmeal

5 ml (1 level tsp) salt

50 g (2 oz) sugar

5 ml (1 level tsp) ground ginger

1. Grease and base-line a 23 cm (9 inch) square cake tin. Melt the treacle, syrup and butter together. Do not boil. Blend the soda with the milk and the egg.
2. Mix all the dry ingredients together, pour in the melted butter mixture, stir well, add the egg and milk mixture, stir well.
3. Turn into the prepared tin and bake in the oven at 180°C (350°F) mark 4 for 45 minutes, until firm to the touch.
4. Turn out of the tin when cold. Store in an airtight container for at least one week before slicing and eating.

# LARGE CAKES of the 'everyday type' are very easy to bake and make really tempting teatime treats. Included in this section are deliciously light sponges and Swiss rolls, fruit and nut cakes.

## VICTORIA SANDWICH CAKE

*175 g (6 oz) butter or block margarine, softened*

*175 g (6 oz) caster sugar*

*3 eggs, beaten*

*175 g (6 oz) self raising flour*

*45–60 ml (3–4 level tbsp) jam*

*caster sugar, to dredge*

**1.** Grease and base-line two 18 cm (7 inch) sandwich tins.
**2.** Beat the butter and sugar together until pale and fluffy. Add the eggs, a little at a time, beating well after each addition. Fold in half the flour, using a metal spoon, then fold in the rest.
**3.** Divide the mixture evenly between the tins and level with a knife. Bake in the oven at 190°C (375°F) mark 5 for about 20 minutes until they are well risen, firm to the touch and beginning to shrink away from the sides of the tins. Turn out and cool on a wire rack.

**4.** When the cakes are cool, sandwich them together with jam and sprinkle the top with sugar.

**Variations**
*CHOCOLATE*
Replace 45 ml (3 level tbsp) flour with 45 ml (3 level tbsp) cocoa. Sandwich the cakes with Vanilla or Chocolate Butter Cream (see page 423).

*COFFEE*
Add 10 ml (2 level tsp) instant coffee powder dissolved in a little warm water to the creamed butter and sugar mixture with the eggs or use 10 ml (2 tsp) coffee essence. Sandwich the cakes with Vanilla or Coffee Butter Cream (see page 423).

*ORANGE OR LEMON*
Add the finely grated rind of an orange or lemon to the mixture. Sandwich the cakes together with Orange or Lemon Butter Cream (see page 423).

## VICTORIA SANDWICH CAKE MADE WITH OIL

*150 g (5 oz) self raising flour*

*5 ml (1 level tsp) baking powder*

*125 g (4 oz) caster sugar*

*105 ml (7 tbsp) vegetable oil*

*2 eggs, beaten*

*45 ml (3 tbsp) milk*

*few drops vanilla flavouring*

*45–60 ml (3–4 level tbsp) jam*

**1.** Grease and base-line two 18 cm (7 inch)

sandwich cake tins.
**2.** Sift the flour and baking powder into a bowl and stir in the sugar. Add the oil, eggs, milk and flavouring and stir with a wooden spoon until the mixture is blended and creamy.
**3.** Divide the mixture evenly between the tins and bake in the oven at 180°C (350°F) mark 4 for 35–40 minutes, until well risen, firm to the touch and beginning to shrink away from the sides of the tin.
**4.** Turn out and cool on a wire rack. When cold, sandwich together with jam.

## ONE STAGE SANDWICH CAKE

*100 g (4 oz) self raising flour*

*5 ml (1 level tsp) baking powder*

*100 g (4 oz) soft tub margarine*

*100 g (4 oz) caster sugar*

*2 eggs*

*45–60 ml (3–4 level tbsp) jam or lemon curd*

**1.** Grease and base line two 18 cm (7 inch)

sandwich cake tins.
**2.** Sift the flour and baking powder into a large bowl. Beat in margarine, sugar and eggs.
**3.** Divide the mixture evenly between the tins and bake in the oven at 170°C (325°F) mark 3 for 25–35 minutes, until they are well risen, firm to the touch and beginning to shrink away from the sides of the tin. Turn out and cool on a wire rack. When cool, sandwich with jam or lemon curd.

# WHISKED SPONGE CAKE

3 eggs, size 2
100 g (4 oz) caster sugar
75 g (3 oz) plain flour
45–60 ml (3–4 tbsp) strawberry or apricot jam, to fill
caster sugar, to dredge

1. Grease and line two 18 cm (7 inch) sandwich tins and dust with a little flour or with a mixture of flour and caster sugar.
2. Put the eggs and sugar in a large bowl and stand it over a pan of hot water. Whisk the eggs and sugar until doubled in volume and thick enough to leave a thin trail on the surface of the batter when the whisk is lifted.
3. Remove the bowl from the heat and continue whisking for a further 5 minutes, until the mixture is cooler and creamy looking.

4. Sift half the flour over the mixture and fold it in very lightly, using a large metal spoon. Sift and fold in the remaining flour in the same way.
5. Pour the mixture into the tins, tilting the tins to spread the mixture evenly. Do not use a palette knife or spatula to smooth the mixture as this will crush out the air bubbles.
6. Bake in the oven at 190°C (375°F) mark 5 for 20–25 minutes, until they are well risen, firm to the touch and beginning to shrink away from the sides. Turn out and cool on a wire rack.
7. When the cakes are cold, sandwich them together with jam and dredge with caster sugar.

**Variation**
Sandwich the cakes together with whipped cream or Butter Cream (see page 423) and cover the top with Glacé Icing (see page 422).

# SWISS ROLL

3 eggs, size 2
100 g (4 oz) caster sugar
100 g (4 oz) plain flour
caster sugar, to dredge
100 g (4 oz) jam, warmed

1. Grease a 33 × 23 cm (13 × 9 inch) Swiss roll tin. Line with greaseproof paper (see page 386) and grease the paper. Dust with caster sugar and flour.
2. Put the eggs and sugar in a bowl, place over a pan of hot water and whisk until pale and creamy and thick enough to leave a trail on the surface when the whisk is lifted.
3. Remove the bowl from the heat and whisk until cool. Sift half the flour over the mixture and fold in very lightly with a metal spoon. Sift and fold in the remaining flour, then lightly stir in 15 ml (1 tbsp) hot water.
4. Pour the mixture into the tin and tilt the tin backwards and forwards to spread the mixture in an even layer. Bake in the oven at 200°C (400°F) mark 6 for 10–12 minutes until golden brown, well risen and firm to the touch.
6. Meanwhile, place a sheet of greaseproof paper over a damp tea towel. Dredge the paper thickly with caster sugar.
7. Quickly turn out the cake on to the paper, trim off the crusty edges and spread with warmed jam.
8. Roll up the cake with the aid of the paper.

Make the first turn firmly so that the whole cake will roll evenly and have a good shape when finished, but roll more lightly after this turn.
9. Place seam-side down on a wire rack and dredge with sugar. Leave to cool for 30 minutes before serving.

**Variations**
*CHOCOLATE SWISS ROLL*
Replace 15 ml (1 level tbsp) flour with 15 ml (1 level tbsp) cocoa powder. Turn out the cooked sponge and trim as above, then cover with a sheet of greaseproof paper and roll with the paper inside. When cold, unroll and remove the paper. Spread with whipped cream or Butter Cream (see page 423) and re-roll. Dust with icing sugar.

*CHOCOLATE ICE CREAM LOG*
Make up the Chocolate Swiss Roll. When cooked, turn out, trim, sprinkle with caster sugar, cover with a tea towel and leave to cool. Halve sponge horizontally and sandwich with a 1 litre (1¾ pint) block of raspberry ripple ice cream. Serve with hot Rich Chocolate Sauce (see page 211). Serve immediately.

*GINGER SWISS ROLL*
Follow the basic recipe adding 5 ml (1 level tsp) ground ginger with the flour. Spread with 100 g (4 oz) warmed ginger marmalade instead of jam.

*Lemon Swiss Roll*

## LEMON SWISS ROLL

*3 eggs, size 2*

*100 g (4 oz) caster sugar*

*100 g (4 oz) plain flour*

*150 ml (5 fl oz) double cream*

*about 275 g (10 oz) lemon curd*

*100 g (4 oz) Glacé Icing (see page 422), to decorate*

**1.** Grease a 33 × 23 cm (13 × 9 inch) Swiss roll tin. Line with greaseproof paper (see page 386) and grease the paper. Dust with caster sugar and flour.

**2.** Put the eggs and sugar in a large bowl, place over a pan of hot water and whisk until pale and creamy and thick enough to leave a trail on the surface when the whisk is lifted.

**3.** Remove the bowl from the heat and whisk until cool. Sift half the flour over the mixture and fold in very lightly. Sift and fold in the remaining flour, then lightly stir in 15 ml (1 tbsp) hot water.

**4.** Turn the mixture into the prepared tin and level the surface. Bake in the oven at 200°C (400°F) mark 6 for 10–12 minutes until golden brown, well risen and firm to the touch.

**5.** Meanwhile, place a sheet of greaseproof paper over a damp tea towel. Dredge the paper thickly with caster sugar.

**6.** Quickly turn out the cake on to the paper, trim off the crusty edges and roll up with the paper inside. Transfer to a wire rack and leave to cool for 30 minutes.

**7.** Whip the cream until it just holds its shape. Unroll the cake and spread with three-quarters of the lemon curd. Top with cream, then roll up again and place on a serving plate.

**8.** Spoon Glacé Icing on to the Swiss Roll. Immediately, using the point of a teaspoon, draw rough lines of lemon curd across the icing and pull a skewer through to form a feather pattern (see page 422). Leave to set for 1 hour.

*Gently pull the tip of a fine skewer through the lemon curd and Glacé Icing.*

## GENOESE SPONGE

*40 g (1½ oz) butter*

*3 eggs, size 2*

*75 g (3 oz) caster sugar*

*65 g (2½ oz) plain flour*

*15 ml (1 level tbsp) cornflour*

**1.** Grease and line two 18 cm (7 inch) sandwich tins or one 18 cm (7 inch) deep round cake tin.

**2.** Put the butter into a saucepan and heat gently until melted, then remove from the heat and leave to stand for a few minutes to cool slightly.

**3.** Put the eggs and sugar in a bowl, place over a pan of hot water and whisk until pale and creamy and thick enough to leave a trail on the surface when the whisk is lifted. Remove from the heat and whisk until cool.

**4.** Sift the flours together into a bowl. Fold half the flour into the egg mixture with a metal spoon.

**5.** Pour half the cooled butter around the edge of the mixture. Gradually fold in the remaining butter and flour alternately. Fold in very lightly or the butter will sink and result in a heavy cake.

**6.** Pour the mixture into the tins. Bake sandwich cakes in the oven at 180°C (350°F) mark 4 for 25–30 minutes, or the deep cake for 35–40 minutes, until well risen, firm to the touch and beginning to shrink away from the sides of the tin. Turn out and cool on a wire rack for 30 minutes before serving.

# APPLE HAZELNUT GENOESE

*eggs*

00 g (4 oz) caster sugar

0 g (2 oz) plain flour

5 ml (1 tbsp) cornflour

5 g (1 oz) ground hazelnuts

5 g (3 oz) butter, melted and cooled

0 ml (6 tbsp) apple jelly

even-Minute Frosting (see page 424), using 30 ml
(2 tbsp) thick apple purée instead of water

. Grease two 18 cm (7 inch) straight-sided
andwich tins. Base line and grease the paper.
. Put the eggs and sugar in a bowl, place over a
an of hot water and whisk until pale and creamy
nd thick enough to leave a trail on the surface
vhen the whisk is lifted. Sift in the flour and
ornflour and add the hazelnuts, then fold in
he butter.
. Turn into the tins and bake in the oven at
80°C (350°F) mark 4 for about 25 minutes until
vell risen, firm to the touch and beginning to

*Apple Hazelnut Genoese*

shrink away from the sides of the tin.
4. Sandwich the layers with apple jelly and
prepare the Seven-Minute Frosting.
5. Cover the cake with the frosting, peaking up
the surface. Leave for 2–3 hours before serving to
allow the frosting to firm up.

# WALNUT LAYER CAKE

*eggs, separated*

00 g (4 oz) caster sugar

'5 g (3 oz) walnuts, finely chopped

'5 g (1 oz) fresh brown breadcrumbs

'5 g (1 oz) plain flour

quantity Butter Cream (see page 423), using coffee
essence instead of milk

0 ml (2 tsp) coffee essence

quantity American Frosting (see page 424)

valnut halves, to decorate

1. Grease and base-line two 18 cm (7 inch)
sandwich tins. Dust with caster sugar and flour.
2. Whisk together the egg yolks and caster sugar
until very pale. Fold in the walnuts, breadcrumbs
and flour.
3. Whisk the egg whites until stiff. Stir one large
spoonful into egg yolk mixture, then fold in the
remainder.
4. Divide the mixture equally between the tins
and level the surface. Bake at 180°C (350°F) mark 4
for about 30 minutes. Turn out and cool on a wire
rack.
5. When the cakes are cold, sandwich them

together with the Butter Cream.
6. Make the American Frosting. Coat the cake
completely, working quickly to ensure a glossy
frosting. Decorate at once with the walnut halves.

*Walnut Layer Cake*

## MARMALADE SPICE CAKE

175 g (6 oz) butter or block margarine, softened

120 ml (8 level tbsp) golden syrup

2 eggs, beaten

150 ml (10 level tbsp) medium cut orange marmalade

350 g (12 oz) self raising flour

5 ml (1 level tsp) baking powder

5 ml (1 level tsp) freshly grated nutmeg

5 ml (1 level tsp) cinnamon

1.25 ml ($\frac{1}{4}$ level tsp) ground cloves

about 150 ml ($\frac{1}{4}$ pint) milk

50 g (2 oz) cornflakes, crushed

1. Grease and base-line a 20.5 cm (8 inch) square or 23 cm (9 inch) round cake tin.
2. Beat the butter with 90 ml (6 tbsp) of the golden syrup until well mixed. Gradually beat in the eggs keeping the mixture stiff.
3. Add half the marmalade to the cake mixture. Mix in the flour sifted with the baking powder and spices, adding enough milk to give a fairly stiff consistency.
4. Turn into prepared cake tin, level the surface. Mix the cornflakes with the remaining syrup and marmalade. Carefully spread over the cake mixture.
5. Bake in the oven at 180°C (350°F) mark 4 for about 1 hour. Turn out and cool on a wire rack.

## CHOCOLATE SLAB CAKE

50 g (2 oz) plain chocolate

75 ml (5 level tbsp) cocoa powder

105 ml (7 tbsp) milk

75 g (3 oz) plain white flour

75 g (3 oz) plain wholemeal flour

10 ml (2 level tsp) ground mixed spice

10 ml (2 level tsp) baking powder

250 g (9 oz) caster sugar

3 eggs, beaten

300 g (11 oz) soft tub margarine

225 g (8 oz) icing sugar

1. Grease and base-line a roasting tin about 30.5 × 23 cm (12 × 9 inches) top measurement, 25.5 × 18 cm (10 × 7 inches) base measurement.
2. Break the chocolate into a bowl. Add 45 ml (3 level tbsp) cocoa and 60 ml (4 tbsp) of the milk and place over a pan of simmering water. Stir until smooth, then leave to cool slightly.
3. Place the flours, spice, baking powder, 175 g (6 oz) caster sugar, the eggs and 225 g (8 oz) margarine in a bowl.
4. Pour in the chocolate mixture and whisk well for about 1 minute. Turn into the prepared tin and bake in the oven at 180°C (350°F) mark 4 for about 50 minutes, until firm to the touch. Turn out and cool on a wire rack.
5. Sieve together the icing sugar and remaining cocoa. Heat the remaining margarine, caster sugar and milk until the sugar dissolves. Bring to the boil, then beat with the icing sugar until the icing begins to thicken.
6. Using a palette knife spread the icing all over the cake. Leave to set before serving.

## CHOCOLATE BISCUIT CAKE

125 g (4 oz) plain chocolate or plain chocolate
    flavoured cake covering

15 ml (1 tbsp) golden syrup

125 g (4 oz) butter or block margarine

125 g (4 oz) digestive biscuits, broken up

25 g (1 oz) seedless raisins

25 g (1 oz) glacé cherries, halved

50 g (2 oz) flaked almonds, toasted

1. Grease a loose bottomed 18 cm (7 inch) flan tin.
2. Break the chocolate into a bowl and place over a pan of simmering water. Add the syrup and butter and stir until the chocolate and butter have melted. Remove from the heat and cool slightly.
3. Mix the biscuits, fruit and almonds into the chocolate mixture. Turn the mixture into the tin, lightly level the top, then chill for at least 1 hour before serving.

## FARMHOUSE SULTANA CAKE

| |
|---|
| 225 g (8 oz) plain white flour |
| 10 ml (2 level tsp) mixed spice |
| 5 ml (1 level tsp) bicarbonate of soda |
| 225 g (8 oz) plain wholemeal flour |
| 175 g (6 oz) butter or block margarine |
| 225 g (8 oz) soft brown sugar |
| 225 g (8 oz) sultanas |
| 1 egg, beaten |
| about 300 ml (½ pint) milk |
| 10 sugar cubes (optional) |

1. Grease and base-line a 20.5 cm (8 inch) square cake tin.

2. Sift the plain flour with the spice and soda into a large mixing bowl; stir in the wholemeal flour.
3. Rub in the butter until the mixture resembles fine breadcrumbs, then stir in the sugar and sultanas.
4. Make a well in the centre of the dry ingredients and add the egg and milk. Beat gently until well mixed and of a soft dropping consistency, adding more milk if necessary. Turn into the prepared tin.
5. Roughly crush the sugar cubes with the end of a rolling pin and scatter over the cake, if liked.
6. Bake in the oven at 170°C (325°F) mark 3 for about 1 hour 40 minutes, until cooked. When tested with a fine skewer, no traces of moist cake should remain. Turn out and cool on a wire rack.

## MADEIRA CAKE

| |
|---|
| 100 g (4 oz) plain flour |
| 100 g (4 oz) self raising flour |
| 175 g (6 oz) butter or block margarine, softened |
| 175 g (6 oz) caster sugar |
| 5 ml (1 tsp) vanilla flavouring |
| 3 eggs, beaten |
| 15–30 ml (1–2 tbsp) milk (optional) |
| 2–3 thin slices citron peel |

1. Grease and line an 18 cm (7 inch) round cake tin with greaseproof paper.
2. Sift the flours together. Cream the butter and the sugar until pale and fluffy, then beat in the vanilla flavouring. Add the eggs, a little at a time, beating well after each addition.

3. Fold in the sifted flour with a metal spoon, adding a little milk if necessary to give a dropping consistency.
4. Turn the mixture into the tin and bake in the oven at 180°C (350°F) mark 4 for 20 minutes.
5. Lay the citron peel on top of the cake, return it to the oven and bake for a further 40 minutes until firm. Turn out and cool on a wire rack.

**Variations**
ORANGE MADEIRA CAKE
Add the grated rind of 2 oranges to the butter and sugar.

SEED CAKE
Add 10 ml (2 level tsp) caraway seeds with the flour. Omit the citron peel.

## RICH CHERRY CAKE

| |
|---|
| 225 g (8 oz) glacé cherries, halved |
| 150 g (5 oz) self raising flour |
| 50 g (2 oz) plain flour |
| 45 ml (3 level tbsp) cornflour |
| 45 ml (3 level tbsp) ground almonds |
| 175 g (6 oz) butter or block margarine, softened |
| 175 g (6 oz) caster sugar |
| 3 eggs, beaten |
| 6 sugar cubes |

1. Grease and base-line an 18 cm (7 inch) round cake tin. Wash the cherries and dry thoroughly.

Sift the flours and cornflour together. Stir in the ground almonds and cherries.
2. Cream the butter and sugar until pale and fluffy. Add the eggs, a little at a time, beating well after each addition. Fold in the dry ingredients.
3. Turn the mixture into the tin, making sure the cherries are not grouped together, and hollow the centre slightly.
4. Roughly crush the sugar cubes with a rolling pin and scatter these over the cake.
5. Bake in the oven at 180°C (350°F) mark 4 for 1–1½ hours, until well risen and golden brown. Turn out and cool on a wire rack.

*Dundee Cake*

## DUNDEE CAKE

| |
|---|
| *100 g (4 oz) currants* |
| *100 g (4 oz) seedless raisins* |
| *50 g (2 oz) blanched almonds, chopped* |
| *100 g (4 oz) chopped mixed peel* |
| *275 g (10 oz) plain flour* |
| *225 g (8 oz) butter or block margarine, softened* |
| *225 g (8 oz) light soft brown sugar* |
| *finely grated rind of 1 lemon* |
| *4 eggs, beaten* |
| *25 g (1 oz) split almonds, to decorate* |

**1.** Line a 20.5 cm (8 inch) round cake tin with greased greaseproof paper. Combine the fruit, chopped nuts and mixed peel in a bowl. Sift in a little flour and stir until the fruit is evenly coated.
**2.** Cream the butter and sugar until pale and fluffy, then beat in the lemon rind. Add the eggs, a little at a time, beating well after each addition.
**3.** Sift the remaining flour over the mixture and fold in lightly with a metal spoon, then fold in the fruit and nut mixture.
**4.** Turn the mixture into the tin and make a slight hollow in the centre with the back of a metal spoon. Arrange the split almonds on the top.
**5.** Bake in the oven at 170°C (325°F) mark 3 for about 2½ hours until a fine warmed skewer inserted in the centre comes out clean. Check near the end of the cooking time and cover with several layers of greaseproof paper if it is overbrowning.
**6.** Cool in the tin for 15 minutes, before turning out on to a wire rack to cool completely for 2 hours. Store in an airtight tin for at least 1 week to mature.

# HALF-POUND CAKE

225 g (8 oz) butter or block margarine, softened

225 g (8 oz) caster sugar

4 eggs, beaten

225 g (8 oz) seedless raisins

225 g (8 oz) mixed currants and sultanas

100 g (4 oz) glacé cherries, halved

225 g (8 oz) plain flour

2.5 ml (½ level tsp) salt

2.5 ml (½ level tsp) mixed spice

60 ml (4 tbsp) brandy

few walnut halves

**1.** Line a 20.5 cm (8 inch) round cake tin with greased greaseproof paper.
**2.** Cream the fat and sugar until pale and fluffy. Add the eggs, a little at a time, beating well after each addition.
**3.** Mix the fruit, flour, salt and spice and fold into the creamed mixture, using a metal spoon. Add the brandy and mix to a soft dropping consistency.
**4.** Turn the mixture into the tin, level the top and arrange the nuts on top. Bake in the oven at 150°C (300°F) mark 2 for about 2½ hours, until a fine warmed skewer inserted in the centre comes out clean. Turn out and cool on a wire rack.

Half-Pound Cake

# ONE STAGE FRUIT CAKE

225 g (8 oz) self raising flour

10 ml (2 level tsp) mixed spice

5 ml (1 level tsp) baking powder

100 g (4 oz) soft tub margarine

100 g (4 oz) soft brown sugar

225 g (8 oz) mixed dried fruit

2 eggs, beaten

30 ml (2 tbsp) milk

**1.** Grease and base line an 18 cm (7 inch) round cake tin. Sift the flour, spice and baking powder into a large bowl, add the remaining ingredients and beat until thoroughly combined.
**2.** Turn the mixture into the tin and bake in the oven at 170°C (325°F) mark 3 for about 1¾ hours, until a fine warmed skewer inserted in the centre comes out clean. Turn out and cool on a wire rack.

# FRUIT CAKE MADE WITH OIL

225 g (8 oz) plain flour

10 ml (2 level tsp) baking powder

150 g (5 oz) caster sugar

150 ml (¼ pint) vegetable oil

2 eggs

45–60 ml (3–4 tbsp) milk

450 g (1 lb) mixed dried fruit

**1.** Grease and base line an 18 cm (7 inch) cake tin. Sift together the flour, baking powder and sugar. Add the oil, eggs and 45 ml (3 tbsp) milk and beat well. Add the fruit.
**2.** Put into the tin and bake at 170°C (325°F) mark 3 for 1 hour, reduce temperature to 150°C (300°F) mark 2 and bake for a further 1¼–1½ hours.
**3.** Cool in the tin for 1 hour, then turn out. Store in an airtight container 1 day before cutting.

# SPECIAL OCCASION AND SEASONAL CAKES

A special cake can make an eye-catching centrepiece for a children's birthday tea or a dinner party. Then there are some cakes that are traditionally made at certain times of the year. Simnel Cake used to be associated with Mothering Sunday in England when girls in service were given a holiday and took a cake home with them. Nowadays, it is eaten at Easter and the marzipan balls are thought to represent the eleven faithful apostles. The White Christmas Cake is a light cake using pale fruit and Brazil nuts (for rich fruit cakes, see page 415). The Yule Log is the traditional French Christmas cake (known as *Bûche de Noël*).

## BLACK FOREST GÂTEAU

*Illustrated on page 381*

| |
|---|
| 100 g (4 oz) butter |
| 6 eggs |
| 225 g (8 oz) caster sugar |
| 75 g (3 oz) plain flour |
| 50 g (2 oz) cocoa powder |
| 2.5 ml (½ tsp) vanilla flavouring |
| two 425 g (15 oz) cans stoned black cherries, drained and syrup reserved |
| 60 ml (4 tbsp) kirsch |
| 600 ml (20 fl oz) whipping cream |
| 100 g (4 oz) Chocolate Caraque (see page 418), to decorate |
| 5 ml (1 level tsp) arrowroot |

1. Grease and base-line a 23 cm (9 inch) round cake tin. Put the butter into a bowl, place over a pan of warm water and beat it until really soft but not melted.

2. Put the eggs and sugar into a large bowl, place over a pan of hot water and whisk until pale and creamy and thick enough to leave a trail on the surface when the whisk is lifted.

3. Sift the flour and cocoa together, then lightly fold into the mixture with a metal spoon. Fold in the vanilla flavouring and softened butter.

4. Turn the mixture into the tin and tilt the tin to spread the mixture evenly. Bake in the oven at 180°C (350°F) mark 4 for about 40 minutes, until well risen, firm to the touch and beginning to shrink away from the sides of the tin.

5. Turn out of the tin on to a wire rack, covered with greaseproof paper, to cool for 30 minutes.

6. Cut the cake into three horizontally. Place a layer on a flat plate. Mix together 75 ml (5 tbsp) cherry syrup and the kirsch. Spoon 45 ml (3 tbsp) over the cake.

7. Whip the cream until it just holds its shape, then spread a little thinly over the soaked sponge. Reserve a quarter of the cherries for decoration and scatter half the remainder over the cream.

8. Repeat the layers of sponge, syrup, cream and cherries. Top with the third cake round and spoon over the remaining kirsch-flavoured syrup.

9. Spread a thin layer of cream around the sides of the cake, reserving a third to decorate. Press on the Chocolate Caraque, reserving a few to decorate the top.

10. Spoon the remaining cream into a piping bag, fitted with a large star nozzle and pipe whirls of cream around the edge of the cake. Top each whirl with a chocolate curl.

11. Fill the centre with the reserved cherries. Blend the arrowroot with 45 ml (3 tbsp) cherry syrup, place in a small saucepan, bring to the boil and boil, stirring, for a few minutes until the mixture is clear. Brush the glaze over the cherries.

**Variations**
- For a richer flavour, fill the gâteau with either Chocolate or Coffee Crème au Beurre (see page 423) instead of the cream.
- A Victoria Sandwich Cake or the Victoria Sandwich Cake Made with Oil (see page 396) can also be used instead of the cake recipe given. Make the chocolate variation of the Victoria Sandwich Cake.

## CHOCOLATE BATTENBERG CAKE

*175 g (6 oz) butter or block margarine, softened*

*175 g (6 oz) caster sugar*

*few drops vanilla flavouring*

*3 eggs, beaten*

*175 g (6 oz) self raising flour*

*30 ml (2 level tbsp) cocoa powder*

*a little milk, to mix (optional)*

*225 g (8 oz) Almond Paste (see page 420)*

*caster sugar, to dredge*

*225 g (8 oz) apricot jam, melted*

**1.** Grease and line a 30×20.5 cm (12×8 inch) Swiss roll tin and divide it lengthways with a 'wall' of pleated greaseproof paper.

**2.** Cream the butter and sugar together until pale and fluffy, then beat in vanilla flavouring. Add the eggs, a little at a time, beating well after each addition.

**3.** Gradually sift the flour over the mixture and fold it in lightly. Turn half the mixture into one side of the tin and level the surface. Sift the cocoa over the other half and fold in, adding a little milk if necessary to give a dropping consistency.

**4.** Turn the chocolate mixture into the other side of the tin and level the surface. Bake in the oven at 190°C (375°F) mark 5 for 40–45 minutes, until well risen, firm to the touch and beginning to shrink away from the sides of the tin. Turn out and set aside and leave to cool on a wire rack.

**5.** When cold, trim cakes to an equal size and cut each in half lengthways. On a working surface sprinkled with caster sugar, roll out the almond paste to a rectangle 30×40 cm (12×16 inches).

**6.** Place one strip of cake on the almond paste so that it lies up against the short edge of paste. Place an alternate coloured strip next to it.

**7.** Brush top and sides of cake with melted jam and layer up with alternate coloured strips.

**8.** Bring almond paste up and over cake to cover it. Press paste firmly on to cake, then seal and trim join. Place cake seam-side down and trim both ends with a sharp knife. Crimp top edges of paste with the thumb and forefinger and mark the top in a criss-cross pattern with a knife. Dredge lightly with caster sugar.

*Place one strip of cake against the short edge of the almond paste.*

*Arrange cake strips in alternate colours and lift over almond paste.*

## CHOCOLATE AND VANILLA ROULADE

*4 eggs*

*100 g (4 oz) vanilla-flavoured sugar*

*60 ml (4 level tbsp) cocoa powder*

*2.5 ml (½ level tsp) ground cinnamon*

*caster sugar, to dredge*

*150 ml (5 fl oz) double cream*

*icing sugar and strawberries, to decorate*

**1.** Grease a 30.5×20.5 cm (12×8 inch) Swiss roll tin. Line with greaseproof paper and grease the paper. Dust with caster sugar and flour.

**2.** Whisk the eggs and vanilla sugar in a bowl placed over a pan of hot water until pale and creamy and thick enough to leave a trail on the surface when the whisk is lifted. Sift in the cocoa powder and cinnamon and fold gently through the mixture.

**3.** Turn the mixture into the tin and bake at 200°C (400°F) mark 6 for 15 minutes, until golden.

**4.** Meanwhile, place a sheet of greaseproof paper over a damp tea towel. Dredge the paper thickly with caster sugar.

**5.** Quickly turn out the cake on to the paper, trim off the crusty edges and roll up with the paper inside. Leave to cool on a wire rack.

**6.** Whip the cream until it is just holding its shape. When the cake is cold, unroll and remove the paper. Spread with the whipped cream. Roll up and dredge with icing sugar and decorate.

*Roll up the cake with the paper inside.*

*Marbled Chocolate Cake*

## MARBLED CHOCOLATE CAKE

| |
|---|
| 50 g (2 oz) plain chocolate |
| 5 ml (1 tsp) vanilla flavouring |
| 225 g (8 oz) butter or block margarine |
| 225 g (8 oz) caster sugar |
| 4 eggs, beaten |
| 225 g (8 oz) plain flour |
| 10 ml (2 level tsp) baking powder |
| 50 g (2 oz) ground almonds |
| 30 ml (2 tbsp) milk |
| Chocolate Frosting (see page 424) |

**1.** Grease a 1.7 litre (3 pint) ring mould. Melt the chocolate with the vanilla flavouring and 15 ml (1 tbsp) water in a bowl placed over a pan of simmering water. Remove from the heat and leave to cool.

**2.** Cream together the fat and caster sugar until pale and fluffy. Add the eggs, a little at a time, beating well after each addition.

**3.** Fold the flour, baking powder and ground almonds into the creamed mixture. Stir in the milk. Spoon half the mixture evenly into the base of the prepared tin.

**4.** Stir the cooled but still soft chocolate into the remaining mixture. Spoon into the tin. Draw a knife through the cake mixture in a spiral. Level the surface.

**5.** Bake in the oven at 180°C (350°F) mark 4 for about 55 minutes, until well risen, firm to the touch and beginning to shrink away from the sides of the tin. Turn out and cool on a wire rack.

**6.** Prepare Chocolate Frosting. Pour over the cooled cake, working quickly to coat top and sides. Leave to set.

# SACHERTORTE

*200 g (7 oz) plain chocolate*

*175 g (6 oz) unsalted butter or block margarine,
softened*

*100 g (4 oz) caster sugar*

*100 g (4 oz) ground almonds*

*4 eggs, separated*

*50 g (2 oz) fresh brown breadcrumbs*

*30 ml (2 tbsp) apricot jam, melted*

*50 g (2 oz) icing sugar*

*Chocolate Caraque (see page 418), to decorate*

1. Line the base of a 23 cm (9 inch) spring release cake tin and brush with melted butter. Break half the chocolate into a bowl and place over a pan of simmering water. Stir until melted, then remove from the heat.

2. Cream 125 g (4 oz) butter and the sugar together until light and fluffy. Stir in the almonds, egg yolks, breadcrumbs and melted chocolate and beat until well combined.

3. Whisk the egg whites until stiff and fold half into the chocolate mixture, then fold in the other half. Pour into the prepared tin and level the surface.

4. Bake the cake in the oven at 180°C (350°F) mark 4 for 40–45 minutes until firm to the touch.

5. Cover with a damp tea towel, leave for 5 minutes to cool slightly, then unclip the sides and invert on to a wire rack. Remove the base. Turn the cake uppermost, cover again, and leave until cold. Brush the top with the melted apricot jam.

6. Melt the remaining chocolate with the remaining butter in a bowl over simmering water. Remove from the heat, sift in the icing sugar and mix well. Stir in 10 ml (2 tsp) hot water and leave to stand for 5 minutes.

7. Spread the icing on top of the cake, easing it gently to the edge to cover the sides. Leave to set then sprinkle with Chocolate Caraque to decorate.

*Sachertorte*

## DEVIL'S FOOD CAKE

| |
|---|
| 75 g (3 oz) plain chocolate |
| 250 g (9 oz) light soft brown sugar |
| 200 ml (7 fl oz) milk |
| 75 g (3 oz) butter or block margarine, softened |
| 2 eggs, beaten |
| 175 g (6 oz) plain flour |
| 3.75 ml (¾ level tsp) bicarbonate of soda |

**For the Fudge Icing**

| |
|---|
| 225 g (8 oz) sugar |
| 75 g (3 oz) unsalted butter |
| 196 g (6.91 oz) can condensed milk |
| 25 g (1 oz) plain chocolate |
| 50 g (2 oz) cocoa powder |

1. Grease and base-line two 19 cm (7½ inch) sandwich tins. Grease the paper and dust with caster sugar and flour.
2. Break the chocolate into a small saucepan, add 75 g (3 oz) brown sugar and the milk and heat very gently, stirring. Remove from the heat and leave to cool.
3. Cream the butter and remaining brown sugar. Gradually beat the eggs into the creamed mixture. Slowly pour in the chocolate mixture and beat until well combined.
4. Sift together the flour and bicarbonate of soda and gently fold into the mixture with a metal spoon.
5. Turn the mixture into the prepared tins and tilt to spread evenly. Bake in the oven at 180°C (350°F) mark 4 for about 35 minutes, until the cakes spring back when lightly pressed with fingertips. Turn out on to a wire rack to cool.
6. Meanwhile, make the icing. Place the ingredients in a large heavy-based saucepan with 45 ml (3 tbsp) water and heat gently until the sugar has dissolved. Bring to the boil and boil to 110°C (225°F) on a sugar thermometer, stirring frequently.
7. Remove from the heat and leave to cool for about 20 minutes to thicken.
8. Sandwich the cakes together with some of the icing. Place on a wire rack over a baking sheet and pour over the remaining icing. Allow it to trickle down the sides and, using a palette knife, spread it over the cake to give a smooth top and sides. Leave to set in a cool place, not in the refrigerator.

## RASPBERRY ROULADE

| |
|---|
| 450 g (1 lb) raspberries, hulled |
| 4 eggs, separated |
| 100 g (3 oz) caster sugar |
| 40 g (1½ oz) plain flour |
| 30 ml (2 tbsp) orange-flavoured liqueur |
| 300 ml (10 fl oz) double cream |
| 45 ml (3 level tbsp) icing sugar |

1. Grease a 33 × 23 cm (13 × 9 inch) Swiss roll tin. Line with greaseproof paper and grease the paper. Dust with caster sugar and flour.
2. Put half the raspberries into a blender and work until just smooth, then press through a nylon sieve to remove the pips.
3. Whisk the egg yolks in a deep bowl with the caster sugar until pale and creamy and thick enough to leave a trail on the surface when the whisk is lifted. Gradually whisk in the raspberry purée, keeping the mixture stiff.
4. Sift the flour over the surface and fold lightly into the egg and raspberry mixture.
5. Whisk the egg whites until stiff, and fold them gently through the raspberry mixture.
6. Turn into the prepared tin and smooth the surface. Bake in the oven at 200°C (400°F) mark 6 for about 12–15 minutes or until golden brown and firm to the touch.
7. Meanwhile, place a sheet of greaseproof paper over a damp tea towel. Dredge the paper thickly with caster sugar.
8. Quickly turn out the cake on to the paper, trim off the crusty edges and roll up with the paper inside. Carefully place on a wire rack and leave until completely cold.
9. Meanwhile, reserving six raspberries for decoration, sprinkle the rest with the liqueur and sift over the icing sugar. Whip the cream until it is just stiff enough to hold its shape.
10. When the cake is cold, unroll and remove the paper. Spread three-quarters of the cream over the top and scatter with raspberries.
11. Roll up the roulade and decorate with whirls of cream. Just before serving, dust with sieved icing sugar and decorate with the reserved raspberries.

# COFFEE PRALINE GÂTEAU

150 g (6 oz) caster sugar

75 g (3 oz) blanched almonds

75 g (3 oz) unsalted butter

3 eggs

75 g (3 oz) plain flour

15 ml (1 tbsp) coffee essence

Crème au Beurre (see page 423)

icing sugar, to dredge

**1.** Prepare the praline by heating 75 g (3 oz) sugar with the nuts over a gentle heat, without stirring, until the sugar has dissolved, then boil to a rich brown. Turn out on to an oiled baking sheet and cool. When cold, grind through a mouli grater, or crush with a rolling pin.

**2.** Melt the butter, then cool. Grease and base line a 20.5 cm (8 inch) round cake tin. Dust with a little sugar and flour. Tip out excess flour.

**3.** Whisk the eggs in a bowl over a pan of hot water with the remaining sugar until very thick. Lightly fold in the flour with 60 ml (4 level tbsp) praline followed by the cool, but still flowing, butter.

**4.** Turn into the tin and bake in the oven at 180°C (350°F) mark 4 for about 25 minutes or until light golden brown, well risen and beginning to shrink away from the sides of the tin. Turn out and cool on a wire rack.

**5.** Beat the coffee essence and half the remaining praline into the Crème au Beurre.

**6.** Cut the cake horizontally and sandwich sparingly with Crème au Beurre. Spread a little more round the edges and press praline on this. Pipe the rest of the Crème au Beurre in whirls on the top. Dust with icing sugar.

# FROSTED COCONUT CAKE

50 g (2 oz) shelled hazelnuts

225 g (8 oz) butter or block margarine, softened

225 g (8 oz) caster sugar

5 eggs

2.5 ml (½ tsp) vanilla flavouring

125 g (4 oz) plain flour

125 g (4 oz) self raising flour

40 g (1½ oz) desiccated coconut

75 g (3 oz) icing sugar

premium shred coconut

**1.** Grease and base line a 20.5 cm (8 inch) spring-release cake tin with greaseproof paper. Spread the hazelnuts in a grill pan and brown them under a hot grill. Place in a clean tea towel and rub off the skins. Leave to cool, then finely chop.

**2.** Cream the fat and sugar together until pale and fluffy. Whisk 4 whole eggs and 1 yolk together and gradually beat into the creamed mixture with the vanilla flavouring.

**3.** Sift the flours together into a large mixing

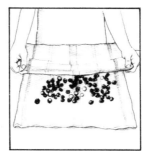

Place the browned nuts in a tea towel and rub off the skins.

bowl. Fold into the mixture with 25 g (1 oz) of the desiccated coconut, and half the nuts. Spoon into the prepared tin and bake in the oven at 180°C (350°F) mark 4 for 45 minutes.

**4.** Meanwhile, in a bowl whisk the egg white until stiff. Whisk in half the sifted icing sugar, then fold in the remaining icing sugar, desiccated coconut and hazelnuts.

**5.** Spoon the meringue topping on to the partially baked cake and scatter with premium shred coconut.

**6.** Return to the oven for 20–30 minutes, or until a fine warmed skewer inserted in the centre comes out clean. Cover lightly after 15 minutes if necessary. Cool on a wire rack.

**Variation**

Use walnuts instead of hazelnuts. There is no need to toast these.

## CARAMEL BANANA TORTE

| |
|---|
| 175 g (6 oz) self raising flour |
| 1.25 ml (¼ level tsp) baking powder |
| 1.25 ml (¼ level tsp) bicarbonate of soda |
| 50 g (2 oz) butter or margarine, cut into pieces |
| 150 g (5 oz) caster sugar |
| 350 g (12 oz) ripe bananas |
| 2.5 ml (½ level tsp) freshly ground nutmeg |
| 45 ml (3 tbsp) milk |
| 1 egg, beaten |
| 75 g (3 oz) sugar |
| 175 g (6 oz) full fat soft cheese |
| 30 ml (2 tbsp) lemon juice |
| 30 ml (2 level tbsp) icing sugar |
| 50 g (2 oz) flaked almonds, toasted |

1. Grease a 20.5 cm (8 inch) round cake tin. Base line with greaseproof paper and grease the paper.
2. Sift the flour, baking powder and bicarbonate of soda into a bowl. Rub in the butter until the mixture resembles fine breadcrumbs, then stir in the caster sugar.

3. Peel half the bananas and mash them in a bowl, then beat in the nutmeg, milk and egg and stir into the dry ingredients. Turn the mixture into the prepared tin and level the surface.
4. Bake in the oven at 180°C (350°F) mark 4 for about 40 minutes. Cool in the tin for 5 minutes before turning out on to wire rack to cool completely. Cut the cake in half horizontally.
5. Make the caramel. Put the rest of sugar into a small saucepan. Dissolve, without stirring, over gentle heat, then boil until a rich brown colour.
6. When the caramel is ready, immediately pour it over the top surface of the cake and use an oiled knife to spread the caramel over the cake. Mark into eight portions with the point of a knife.
7. Put the soft cheese, lemon juice and icing sugar into a bowl and beat together. Peel and chop the remaining bananas and add to half of the cheese mixture. Use this mixture to sandwich the cakes together.
8. Spread a little cheese mixture around the sides and cover with most of the almonds. Decorate the top with the remaining cheese mixture and the flaked almonds.

*Caramel Banana Torte*

*Passion Cake*

# PASSION CAKE

225 g (8 oz) butter or block or soft tub margarine

225 g (8 oz) light soft brown sugar

4 eggs, beaten

225 g (8 oz) self raising wheatmeal flour

5 ml (1 level tsp) baking powder

350 g (12 oz) carrots, peeled and coarsely grated

finely grated rind and juice of 1 lemon

15 ml (1 tbsp) lemon juice

125 g (5 oz) walnut pieces, chopped

75 g (3 oz) full fat soft cheese

50 g (2 oz) icing sugar

**1.** Grease and base-line a 20.5 cm (8 inch) round cake tin.

**2.** Cream the butter and sugar together until pale and fluffy. Add the eggs, a little at a time, beating well after each addition.

**3.** Fold in the flour with the baking powder. Stir in the carrots, lemon rind, 15 ml (1 tbsp) lemon juice and 100 g (4 oz) walnuts. Spoon the mixture into the tin and level the surface.

**4.** Bake in the oven at 180°C (350°F) mark 4 for about 1½ hours, until well risen and golden brown. Turn out and cool on a wire rack.

**5.** Make the icing by beating together the cheese, icing sugar and remaining lemon juice and beat until soft and creamy. Spread over the top of the cake using a palette knife. Decorate with the reserved walnuts.

**Variation**

*SPICY CARROT CAKE*

Prepare this one-stage cake using the same ingredients, substituting 225 ml (8 fl oz) vegetable oil for the fat and adding 5 ml (1 level tsp) ground mixed spice. Beat all the ingredients together until well mixed, then spoon into the prepared tin and bake in the oven for about 1½ hours, covering lightly with a piece of greased greaseproof paper, if necessary, to prevent overbrowning.

## SIMNEL CAKE

175 g (6 oz) butter or block margarine, softened

175 g (6 oz) caster sugar

3 whole eggs and 1 egg white

225 g (8 oz) plain flour

pinch of salt

2.5 ml (½ level tsp) ground cinnamon

2.5 ml (½ level tsp) grated nutmeg

100 g (4 oz) glacé cherries, washed, dried and cut into
    quarters

50 g (2 oz) cut mixed peel, chopped

250 g (9 oz) currants

100 g (4 oz) sultanas

finely grated rind of 1 lemon

milk, if necessary

450 g (1 lb) Almond Paste (see page 420)

crystallised flowers, to decorate (optional)

**1.** Grease an 18 cm (7 inch) round cake tin. Line
with greaseproof paper and grease the paper.
**2.** Cream the butter and sugar until pale and
fluffy. Lightly whisk the whole eggs and gradually
beat into the creamed ingredients.
**3.** Sift the flour, salt and spices over the surface
and fold into the mixture with a metal spoon. Add
all the fruit and the lemon rind, folding together to
give a smooth dropping consistency. If a little too
firm add 15–30 ml (1–2 tbsp) milk.
**4.** Divide the Almond Paste in half. Lightly dust
a surface with icing sugar and roll out one half to a
16 cm (6½ inch) circle.
**5.** Spoon half the cake mixture into the prepared
tin. Place the round of almond paste on top and
cover with the remaining cake mixture. Press
down gently with the back of a spoon to level the
surface.
**6.** Tie a double thickness of brown paper round
the outside of the tin. Bake in the oven at 150°C
(300°F) mark 2 for about 2½ hours. When cooked
the cake should be a rich brown colour, and firm
to the touch.
**7.** Cool in the tin for about 1 hour, then turn out.
Ease off the greaseproof paper and leave to cool
completely on a wire rack.
**8.** Divide the remaining Almond Paste in two.
Roll out one half to a 17 cm (7½ inch) circle and the
rest into eleven small balls. Lightly beat the egg
white and brush over the top of the cake. Place the
circle on top, crimp the edges, and with a little of
the egg white fix the balls around the top edge
of the cake.
**9.** Brush the Almond Paste with the remaining egg
white and place under a hot grill for 1–2 minutes
until the paste is well browned. Tie a ribbon
around the cake to serve and decorate with
crystallised flowers if wished.

## WHITE CHRISTMAS CAKE

175 g (6 oz) butter or block margarine, softened

175 g (6 oz) caster sugar

3 eggs, size 2, beaten

125 g (4 oz) dried apricots, roughly chopped

125 g (4 oz) Brazil nuts, chopped

50 g (2 oz) candied lemon peel, finely chopped

125 g (4 oz) sultanas

125 g (4 oz) plain flour

125 g (4 oz) self raising flour

Apricot Glaze (see page 419)

225 g (8 oz) Almond Paste (see page 420)

Royal Icing (see page 419), to decorate

**1.** Grease and line the bottom and sides of a
20.5 cm (8 inch) round cake tin.

**2.** Cream the fat and sugar together until pale
and fluffy. Add the beaten eggs, a little at a time,
beating after each addition.
**3.** Mix all the fruit and nuts together. Sift the
flours together and fold into the creamed mixture.
Fold in the fruit. Spoon into the prepared tin.
**4.** Bake in the oven at 180°C (350°F) mark 4 for
about 1¼ hours, covering if necessary, until a fine
warmed skewer inserted in the centre comes out
clean. Cool a little, then turn out on to a wire rack.
**5.** To finish, brush the top of the cake with
Apricot Glaze. Cover top with rolled out Almond
Paste (see page 420).
**6.** Rough ice the top of the cake (see page 421) and
leave to dry. Decorate if wished with ready made
decorations such as Christmas trees and snowmen
and tie a cake frill around the edge.

# YULE LOG

*3 eggs*

*100 g (4 oz) caster sugar*

*100 g (4 oz) plain flour*

*caster sugar, to dredge*

*chocolate Crème au Beurre (see page 423)*

*icing sugar, to decorate*

**1.** Grease a 30 × 20 cm (12 × 8 inch) Swiss roll tin. Line with greaseproof paper and grease the paper. Dust with caster sugar and flour.
**2.** Put the eggs and sugar in a large bowl, place over a pan of hot water and whisk until pale and creamy and thick enough to leave a trail on the surface of the mixture when the whisk is lifted.
**3.** Sift half the flour over the mixture and fold in very lightly with a metal spoon. Sift and fold in the remaining flour, then lightly stir in 15 ml (1 tbsp) hot water.

**4.** Pour the mixture into the prepared tin. Bake in the oven at 220°C (425°F) mark 7 for 8–12 minutes until golden brown, well risen and firm to the touch.
**5.** Meanwhile, place a sheet of greaseproof paper over a damp tea towel. Dredge the paper with a little caster sugar.
**6.** Quickly turn out the cake on to the paper and trim off the crusty edges and roll up with the paper inside. Leave to cool on a wire rack.
**7.** When cold, unroll and remove the paper. Spread one-third of the Crème au Beurre over the surface and re-roll. Refrigerate for 30 minutes until the roll is firm.
**8.** Coat with the remaining Crème au Beurre and mark lines with a fork to resemble tree bark.
**9.** Chill for 1 hour before serving. Dust lightly with icing sugar and decorate with a sprig of real or artificial holly.

## BAKING SHAPED OR LARGER CAKES

If you want to make a shaped cake, such as a number or heart, you need to know how much mixture is required to fill the special tin. This is quite simple to calculate using the guide below. This guide also applies to making a larger cake than suggested in the following novelty cake ideas.

For every 600 ml (1 pint) of water the tin will hold, you will need mixture made with the ingredients listed below, so multiply as required. Remember to fill the tin only as deep as you want the finished cake to be—not necessarily to the very top.

## VICTORIA SANDWICH CAKE MIXTURE

**makes 600 ml/1 pint cake mixture**

*50 g (2 oz) butter or block margarine*

*50 g (2 oz) caster sugar*

*1 egg*

*50 g (2 oz) self raising flour*

## FRUIT CAKE MIXTURE

**makes 600 ml/1 pint cake mixture**

*175 g (6 oz) currants*

*50 g (2 oz) sultanas*

*50 g (2 oz) seedless raisins*

*12 glacé cherries, halved*

*45 ml (3 level tbsp) chopped mixed peel*

*100 g (4 oz) plain flour*

*1.25 ml (¼ level tsp) mixed spice*

*75 g (3 oz) butter or block margarine*

*75 g (3 oz) brown soft sugar*

*1½ eggs*

Make either cake in the usual way (see pages 396 and 415). Bake the Victoria Sandwich Mixture in the oven at 180°C (350°F) mark 4 and the fruit cake mixture in the oven at 150°C (300°F) mark 1–2. The time varies according to the shape and depth of the cake.

It is difficult to give an accurate guide for cooking times for cakes baked in odd-shaped containers because the more contact the heat has with the tin sides, the faster it cooks.

It is not really feasible to cook a Victoria Sandwich Cake in a tin larger than 25 cm (10 inches) across as the edges will overcook long before the middle is done. However, fruit cake mixtures adapt well to large tins.

Bake the fruit cake in the centre of the oven and test to see if cooked by piercing with a skewer—the skewer should come out clean. Leave the cake to cool completely in the tin before turning out.

# MEDIEVAL CASTLE CAKE

You will need a 23 cm (11 inch) square cake board to stand the cake on.

*double quantity Victoria Sandwich Cake mixture (see page 396) baked in two 18 cm (7 inch) square cake tins*

*Chocolate Butter Cream using 350 g (12 oz) icing sugar (see page 423)*

*twenty-four 2.5 cm (1 inch) Chocolate Squares (see page 418)*

*green food colouring*

*50 g (2 oz) desiccated coconut*

*4 chocolate finger biscuits, halved*

*4 miniature paper flags and toy knights*

1. Cut eight 3.5 cm (1½ inch) diameter rounds from one cake with a plain pastry cutter. Place the other cake on the cake board and spread the top and sides with the Chocolate Butter Cream. Smooth the top with a palette knife.
2. Using a serrated icing comb, mark the sides of the cake. For each tower, sandwich two rounds of cake together with butter cream. Stand one tower at each corner of the cake and spread the top and sides with butter cream. Smooth over with a palette knife. Using the icing comb, mark the sides of each tower.
3. Spoon some butter cream into a piping bag fitted with a star nozzle. Pipe a shell border around the top and base edges of the castle and down each corner.
4. Pipe a star edge around the top and base edges of each tower. Place the chocolate squares, evenly spaced, along the top edge of the castle. Pipe a doorway in the centre of two opposite sides.
5. Spread the cake board with butter cream. Stir

*Medieval Castle Cake*

a little green food colouring into the desiccated coconut and sprinkle liberally over the butter cream for grass.

6. Place four chocolate biscuit halves in front of each door for the drawbridges. Place a flag in each tower. Place the toy knights in position.

**Variation**

Use orange, coffee or mocha butter cream instead of chocolate.

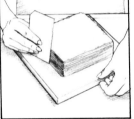

*Cover cake with butter cream and mark sides with a serrated icing comb.*

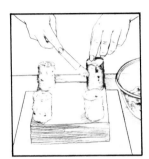

*Position towers in corners. Spread the top and sides with the butter cream.*

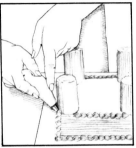

*Pipe a shell border around the top, back and down the corners.*

*Place chocolate biscuit halves in front of doors to make a drawbridge.*

# RICH FRUIT CAKES are traditional at weddings and Christenings,

anniversaries and Christmas. The centrepiece will most often be a beautiful cake decorated with Royal Icing; beneath the sugar coating will be a dark, glossy cake loaded with fruit, candied peel, nuts and spices and deliciously soaked with brandy.

Like other rich cakes, fruit cakes are made by the creaming method (see page 303), but the mixture is slightly stiffer to support the weight of the fruit. If the mixture is too wet, fruit is inclined to sink to the bottom. Remember that all dried fruit should be thoroughly cleaned and dried before use; glacé cherries should be rinsed to remove excess syrup, then dried. Toss all fruit in a little of the measured flour to make sure it is quite dry.

All fruit cakes keep well, but the richest actually improve if kept for two or three months before you cut them. Every two or three weeks, get it out, prick the surface with a fine skewer and spoon over a little brandy or other spirit.

## RICH FRUIT CAKE

1. Grease and line the cake tin for the size of cake you wish to make, using a double thickness of greaseproof paper. Tie a double band of brown paper round the outside.
2. Prepare the ingredients for the appropriate size of cake according to the chart (see page 416). Wash and dry all the fruit, if necessary, chopping any over-large pieces, and mix well together in a large bowl. Add the flaked almonds. Sift flour and spices into another bowl with a pinch of salt.
3. Put the butter, sugar and lemon rind into a bowl and cream together until pale and fluffy. Add the beaten eggs, a little at a time, beating well.
4. Gradually fold the flour lightly into the mixture with a metal spoon, then fold in the brandy. Finally fold in the fruit and nuts.

5. Turn the mixture into the prepared tin, spreading it evenly and making sure there are no air pockets. Make a hollow in the centre to ensure an even surface when cooked.
6. Stand the tin on newspaper or brown paper in the oven and bake at 150°C (300°F) mark 2 for the required time (see chart), until a fine warmed skewer inserted in the centre comes out clean. Cover with greaseproof paper after about 1½ hours.
7. When cooked, leave the cake to cool in the tin before turning out on to a wire rack. Prick the top all over with a fine skewer and slowly pour 30–45 ml (2–3 tbsp) brandy over it before storing.
8. Wrap the cake in a double thickness of greaseproof paper and place upside down in an airtight tin. Cover with foil to store.

## PLANNING A WEDDING CAKE

It is most important for the final overall result to choose the sizes of the tiers carefully, avoiding a combination that would look too heavy. Good proportions for a three-tier cake are 30.5, 23 and 15 cm (12, 9 and 6 inches); for a two-tier cake 30.5 and 20.5 cm (12 and 8 inches), 28 and 18 cm (11 and 7 inches) or 25.5 and 15 cm (10 and 6 inches).

The bottom tier should be deeper than the upper ones, therefore cakes of 25.5–30.5 cm (10–12 inches) diameter are generally made about 7.5 cm (3 inches) deep, while those 18–23 cm (7–9 inches) in diameter are 6.5 cm (2½ inches) deep, and 15 cm (6 inches) diameter cakes are 5 cm (2 inches) deep.

Don't attempt to make the larger sizes of cake unless you have an oven to cope with it, as you should allow at least 2.5 cm (1 inch) space between the oven walls and the tin. For a three-tier cake, make the two smaller cakes together and the largest one should be baked separately.

You can expect to cut 8–10 portions of cake from each 450 g (1 lb) cooked weight. (See chart on page 416.)

When the reception is large, it is well worth making and icing an extra tier for cutting behind-the-scenes.

### CAKE BOARDS AND PILLARS
Silver is the usual colour (except for a golden wedding cake). The board should be 5 cm (2 inches) larger than the cake. For a very large cake, use a board 10–12.5 cm (4–5 inches) larger than the size of the finished cake.

Pillars between the base cake and the next tier are usually 9 cm (3½ inches) high and those between the middle tier and top tier 7.5 cm (3 inches) high. They are available in white or silver polythene or white plaster.

## QUANTITIES AND SIZES FOR RICH FRUIT CAKES

To make a formal cake for a birthday, wedding or anniversary, the following chart will show you the amount of ingredients required to fill the chosen cake tin or tins, whether round or square.

*Note* When baking large cakes, 25 cm (10 inches) and upwards, it is advisable to reduce the oven heat to 130°C (250°F) mark $\frac{1}{2}$ after two-thirds of the cooking time.

| Square tin size | 15 cm (6 inches) square | 18 cm (7 inches) square | 20.5 cm (8 inches) square |
|---|---|---|---|
| **Round tin size** | 15 cm (6 inches) diameter | 18 cm (7 inches) diameter | 20.5 cm (8 inches) diameter | 23 cm (9 inches) diameter |
| Currants | 225 g (8 oz) | 350 g (12 oz) | 450 g (1 lb) | 625 g (1 lb 6 oz) |
| Sultanas | 100 g (4 oz) | 125 g (4$\frac{1}{2}$ oz) | 200 g (7 oz) | 225 g (8 oz) |
| Raisins | 100 g (4 oz) | 125 g (4$\frac{1}{2}$ oz) | 200 g (7 oz) | 225 g (8 oz) |
| Glacé cherries | 50 g (2 oz) | 75 g (3 oz) | 150 g (5 oz) | 175 g (6 oz) |
| Mixed peel | 25 g (1 oz) | 50 g (2 oz) | 75 g (3 oz) | 100 g (4 oz) |
| Flaked almonds | 25 g (1 oz) | 50 g (2 oz) | 75 g (3 oz) | 100 g (4 oz) |
| Lemon rind | a little | a little | a little | $\frac{1}{4}$ lemon |
| Plain flour | 175 g (6 oz) | 215 g (7$\frac{1}{2}$ oz) | 350 g (12 oz) | 400 g (14 oz) |
| Mixed spice | 1.25 ml ($\frac{1}{4}$ level tsp) | 2.5 ml ($\frac{1}{2}$ level tsp) | 2.5 ml ($\frac{1}{2}$ level tsp) | 5 ml (1 level tsp) |
| Cinnamon | 1.25 ml ($\frac{1}{4}$ level tsp) | 2.5 ml ($\frac{1}{2}$ level tsp) | 2.5 ml ($\frac{1}{2}$ level tsp) | 5 ml (1 level tsp) |
| Butter | 150 g (5 oz) | 175 g (6 oz) | 275 g (10 oz) | 350 g (12 oz) |
| Sugar | 150 g (5 oz) | 175 g (6 oz) | 275 g (10 oz) | 350 g (12 oz) |
| Eggs, beaten | 2$\frac{1}{2}$ | 3 | 5 | 6 |
| Brandy | 15 ml (1 tbsp) | 15 ml (1 tbsp) | 15–30 ml (1–2 tbsp) | 30 ml (2 tbsp) |
| Time (approx.) | 2$\frac{1}{2}$–3 hours | 3 hours | 3$\frac{1}{2}$ hours | 4 hours |
| Weight when cooked | 1.1 kg (2$\frac{1}{2}$ lb) | 1.6 kg (3$\frac{1}{4}$ lb) | 2.2 kg (4$\frac{3}{4}$ lb) | 2.7 kg (6 lb) |

| Square tin size | 23 cm (9 inches) square | 25.5 cm (10 inches) square | 28 cm (11 inches) square | 30.5 cm (12 inches) square |
|---|---|---|---|---|
| **Round tin size** | 25.5 cm (10 inches) diameter | 28 cm (11 inches) diameter | 30.5 cm (12 inches) diameter | |
| Currants | 775 g (1 lb 12 oz) | 1.1 kg (2 lb 8 oz) | 1.5 kg (3 lb 2 oz) | 1.7 kg (3 lb 12 oz) |
| Sultanas | 375 g (13 oz) | 400 g (14 oz) | 525 g (1 lb 3 oz) | 625 g (1 lb 6 oz) |
| Raisins | 375 g (13 oz) | 400 g (14 oz) | 525 g (1 lb 3 oz) | 625 g (1 lb 6 oz) |
| Glacé cherries | 250 g (9 oz) | 275 g (10 oz) | 350 g (12 oz) | 425 g (15 oz) |
| Mixed peel | 150 g (5 oz) | 200 g (7 oz) | 250 g (9 oz) | 275 g (10 oz) |
| Flaked almonds | 150 g (5 oz) | 200 g (7 oz) | 250 g (9 oz) | 275 g (10 oz) |
| Lemon rind | $\frac{1}{4}$ lemon | $\frac{1}{2}$ lemon | $\frac{1}{2}$ lemon | 1 lemon |
| Plain flour | 600 g (1 lb 5 oz) | 700 g (1 lb 8 oz) | 825 g (1 lb 13 oz) | 1 kg (2 lb 6 oz) |
| Mixed spice | 5 ml (1 level tsp) | 10 ml (2 level tsp) | 12.5 ml (2$\frac{1}{2}$ level tsp) | 12.5 ml (2$\frac{1}{2}$ level tsp) |
| Cinnamon | 5 ml (1 level tsp) | 10 ml (2 level tsp) | 12.5 ml (2$\frac{1}{2}$ level tsp) | 12.5 ml (2$\frac{1}{2}$ level tsp) |
| Butter | 500 g (1 lb 2 oz) | 600 g (1 lb 5 oz) | 800 g (1 lb 12 oz) | 950 g (2 lb 2 oz) |
| Sugar | 500 g (1 lb 2 oz) | 600 g (1 lb 5 oz) | 800 g (1 lb 12 oz) | 950 g (2 lb 2 oz) |
| Eggs, beaten | 9 | 11 | 14 | 17 |
| Brandy | 30–45 ml (2–3 tbsp) | 45 ml (3 tbsp) | 60 ml (4 tbsp) | 90 ml (6 tbsp) |
| Time (approx.) | 6 hours | 7 hours | 8 hours | 8$\frac{1}{2}$ hours |
| Weight when cooked | 4 kg (9 lb) | 5.2 kg (11$\frac{1}{2}$ lb) | 6.7 kg (14$\frac{3}{4}$ lb) | 7.7 kg (17 lb) |

WEDDING CAKE TIMETABLE

*WEDDING CAKE TIMETABLE*

**–3 months before** Make the cakes. When cold, rick at intervals with a fine skewer and spoon ome brandy evenly over the surface. Wrap the akes in greaseproof paper and then in double hickness foil. Store in a cool, dry place.

**4–20 days before** The baked cakes should have n even top but if not, they can be levelled with a harp knife. Cover each cake with Almond Paste see page 420) and store loosely covered with reaseproof paper in a cool dry place for 4–5 days before applying the first coat of icing.

**10–15 days before** Apply the first coat of Royal Icing (see page 420) and leave to dry for 1–2 days. Think about the design of the cake.

**8–12 days before** Apply the second coat of Royal Icing if necessary and leave to dry for 1–2 days. Make all separate or run-out decorations for the cake and leave to dry for 1–2 days.

**7 days before** Complete all further decorating a week before the cake is to be served. Do not assemble a tiered cake until the day.

# DECORATING CAKES

Icing turns a workaday cake into a loving creation. Decorations for informal cakes may be anything from a light dusting of caster ugar or a smooth coat of glacé icing to whirls of butter cream interspersed with nuts or coloured sweets. For formal cakes, you need to master piping techniques and the method of flat icing with Royal Icing.

## EQUIPMENT

imple decorations need no special equipment; all ou need are a palette knife, fork and a wire rack, lowever the right tools do help when you start to ttempt more elaborate work.

**cing comb** helps with icing the sides of a deep ake.

**cing nail** is a small metal or polythene nail with large head that is designed to hold decorations, uch as icing roses, while you make them. It nables you to hold the rose securely, and turn it vithout damaging it.

**cing ruler** is useful for flat icing a large cake. You an substitute anything with a fine straight edge, ong enough to extend both sides of the cake.

**cing turntable**, this gives you clearance from the vorking surface and enables you to turn the cake reely. If you do not have a turntable, place the ake board on an upturned plate, to give it a little ift from the working surface.

**Nozzles** can be used with paper or fabric piping bags. A fine plain nozzle for writing and piping traight lines and simple designs, plus a star or shell nozzle, are the basics—you can build up quite a variety using these. More advanced piping work demands a whole range of different shapes and sizes. For use with paper piping bags, choose nozzles without a screw band; the band is useful with a fabric bag. The following are the most useful:

- Fine plain (writing) No. 1
- Medium plain (writing) No. 2
- Thicker plain (writing) No. 3
- Six-point star
- Eight-point star (medium)
- Petal
- Shell

**Piping bags** can be made from greaseproof paper, or bought ready-made in fabric. Special icing pumps are also available.

**Silver cake board or 'drum'** sets off any iced cake. Some are made from thin card, or stronger ones are about 1 cm (½ inch) thick. Choose a board that is 5 cm (2 inches) larger than the cake, so that a border shows all round.

**Fine sandpaper** can be used to sand down any imperfections on royal icing.

## ICING CAKES

Glacé icing and frostings are most commonly used or small cakes and sponges (and also for biscuits, ee page 438). Royal icing is used with almond paste and an apricot glaze on rich fruit cakes such s Christmas and wedding cakes. Almond paste an also be used as a decoration in its own right, shaped and coloured if wished.

The cake must be completely cold before you start icing. The surface must be level; if necessary, turn the cake upside down and ice the flat bottom. If making a sandwich or layer cake, fill first. Decorate the sides, then the top.

## CAKE DECORATIONS

Add ready-made decorations before the icing hardens completely, or stick them in place with a little dab of fresh icing.

**Nuts** are a popular decoration, particularly walnuts, hazelnuts, almonds and pistachios.

**Crystallised violets and roses** can be bought in small quantities; keep them in a dark place to avoid bleaching.

**Angelica** can be cut into shapes for decoration. When buying look for a really good colour and a small amount of sugar. To remove sugar, soak briefly in hot water, then drain and dry well.

**Chocolate and coloured vermicelli** stale quickly and become speckled, so buy in small quantities as needed.

**Silver dragees (balls)** keep well in a dry place; use tweezers for handling. They come in other colours than silver.

**Hundreds and thousands** are useful for children's cakes, as are all sorts of coloured sweets, and for more sophisticated decorations, look for *sugar coffee beans*.

**Chocolate**, choose plain eating chocolate for chopping and grating. Chocolate flavoured cake covering is useful for scrolls and curls and also for melting, but the flavour is not so good. Crumbled chocolate flake makes a useful last minute decoration.

### CHOCOLATE CARAQUE

Melt 100 g (4 oz) chocolate in a bowl over a pan of hot water. Pour it in a thin layer on to a marble slab or cold baking tray and leave to set until it no longer sticks to your hand when you touch it. Holding a large knife with both hands, push the blade across the surface of the chocolate to roll pieces off in long curls. Adjust the angle of the blade to get the best curls.

### CHOCOLATE SHAPES

Make a sheet of chocolate as above and cut into neat triangles or squares with a sharp knife, or stamp out circles with a small round cutter.

Chocolate curls can also be made by paring thin layers from the edge of a block of chocolate with a potato peeler.

## PIPING

Butter cream, crème au beurre, stiff glacé icing and royal icing can all be piped. It is usual to pipe on to a base of the same kind of icing, though butter cream is sometimes piped on to glacé icing.

The icing used for piping must be completely free of lumps, or it will block the nozzle. It must also be exactly the right consistency to force easily through the nozzle, but still retain its shape.

Work with a small quantity at a time, refilling the piping bag frequently if necessary. If you are a beginner, practise on an upturned plate first. The practice icing can be scraped up while still soft and reused. Even on the real cake, if the base icing is hard mistakes can be gently scraped off and corrected by repiping.

### MAKING AND USING A PIPING BAG

Fold a 25.5 cm (10 inch) square of greaseproof paper diagonally in half, then roll into a cone. Fold the points inwards to secure them. To insert a nozzle, snip off the tip of the bag and drop the nozzle securely into position before adding the icing.

For a very fine line, just snip off the end of the bag and use without a nozzle.

Never more than half-fill the bag. When using a paper piping bag, fold the top flap down, enclosing the front edge, until the bag is sealed and quite firm; twist a fabric bag firmly closed.

To hold the bag, lay it across the palm of one hand; with a paper bag, place your thumb firmly over the top of the bag, grasp the rest with the other four fingers and apply a steady even pressure until icing starts to come out of the tip of the nozzle.

With a fabric bag grasp the bag where it is twisted with thumb and first finger and apply pressure with the remaining fingers.

### TO PIPE A STRAIGHT LINE

Place the tip of the nozzle where the line is to start. Apply slight pressure to the bag and as the icing starts to come out of the nozzle, lift the bag about 2.5 cm (1 inch) from the surface. This allows even the shakiest of hands to pipe a straight line.

Move your hand in the direction of the line, guiding it with the other hand if you want, allowing the icing to flow evenly. About 1 cm ($\frac{1}{2}$ inch) before the end of the line, stop squeezing the bag and gently lower the tip of the nozzle to the surface.

### TO PIPE DOTS

Only a slight pressure on the piping bag is required. Place the tip of the nozzle on the surface and hold he bag almost upright. Squeeze the bag gently and at the same time lift the nozzle slightly. Stop squeezing, move the nozzle slightly in a gentle shaking action to avoid a 'tail', and lift the nozzle.

Larger dots can be made by moving the nozzle in a small circle or by using a larger nozzle.

### To Pipe Stars

Fit the bag with a star nozzle. Hold the bag upright and just above the surface of the cake. Squeeze the icing out. As soon as the star is formed, stop squeezing and lift the bag away sharply.

### To Pipe Rosettes

Fit the bag with a star nozzle. Hold the icing bag upright, just above the surface of the cake. Squeeze gently and move the nozzle in a complete circle, filling in the centre. Pull the nozzle away sharply to avoid forming a point on the iced surface which would spoil the appearance of the piped rosette.

### To Pipe a Shell Border

Use either a star nozzle or a special shell nozzle; a shell nozzle will give a flatter, fuller shell with more ridges. In either case the movement is the same. Hold the bag at an angle to the surface and just above it. Squeeze until the icing begins to come from the nozzle and forms a head.

Pull the bag gently and at the same time release pressure to form the tail. Pipe the next shell just touching, and remember to release pressure each time to form the tail of the shell.

### Writing

Use a plain writing nozzle and pipe as for a straight line (see above). Practise with simple capital letters at first. Before attempting to write on the cake, draw the letters on greaseproof paper and prick them on to the base icing with a pin; use the pin pricks as a guide. For fancier writing, magazines provide a useful source of stylised lettering.

### To Pipe a Rose

Place a little icing on the top of an icing nail and stick a small square of non-stick paper on top. Fit the piping bag with a petal nozzle. Hold the bag with the thin part of the nozzle uppermost.

Pipe a cone of icing, twisting the nail between thumb and finger, to form the centre of the rose. Pipe five or six petals around the centre, overlapping each petal and piping the outer ones so that they are more open, and lie flatter.

Lift the square of paper from the nail and leave the rose uncovered for about 24 hours to dry. Attach it to the cake with a dab of icing.

### To Pipe a Daisy

Work with the thick edge of the nozzle to the centre and pipe five even-sized petals. Dry as instructed above.

## Royal Icing

4 egg whites
900 g (2 lb) icing sugar
15 ml (1 tbsp) lemon juice
10 ml (2 tsp) glycerine

1. Whisk the egg whites in a bowl until slightly frothy. Then sift and stir in about a quarter of the icing sugar with a wooden spoon. Continue adding more sugar gradually, beating well after each addition, until about three-quarters of the sugar has been added.
2. Beat in the lemon juice and continue beating for about 10 minutes, until the icing is smooth.
3. Beat in the remaining sugar until the required consistency is achieved, depending on how the icing will be used.
4. Finally, stir in the glycerine to prevent the icing hardening. Cover and keep for 24 hours to allow air bubbles to rise to the surface.
*Makes about 900 g (2 lb)*

## Apricot Glaze

100 g (4 oz) apricot jam

1. Put the jam and 30 ml (2 tbsp) water in a saucepan and heat gently, stirring, until the jam softens. Bring to the boil and simmer for 1 minute.
2. Sieve the glaze and use while still warm.
*Makes 150 ml ($\frac{1}{4}$ pint)*

## ALMOND PASTE

| |
|---|
| 225 g (8 oz) icing sugar |
| 225 g (8 oz) caster sugar |
| 450 g (1 lb) ground almonds |
| 5 ml (1 tsp) vanilla flavouring |
| 2 eggs, lightly beaten |
| 10 ml (2 tsp) lemon juice |

**1.** Sift the icing sugar into a bowl and mix in the caster sugar and ground almonds.
**2.** Add the vanilla flavouring, egg and lemon juice and mix to a stiff dough. Knead lightly, then shape into a ball. Cover until ready to use.
*Makes 900 g (2 lb)*

*COVERING A RICH FRUIT CAKE*
*WITH ALMOND PASTE*
**1.** Measure around the cake with a piece of string. Dust the working surface with icing sugar and roll out two-thirds of the paste to a rectangle, half the length of the string by twice the depth of the cake.
**2.** Trim the edges, then cut in half lengthways with a sharp knife. Place the cake upside down on a board and brush the sides with apricot glaze. Gently lift the almond paste and place it firmly in position round the cake.
**3.** Smooth the joins with a palette knife and keep the top and bottom edges square. Roll a jam jar lightly around the cake to help the paste stick more firmly.
**4.** Brush the top of the cake with apricot glaze and roll out the remaining almond paste to fit. With

*Glaze cake sides then cover with almond paste.*

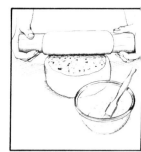

*Use rolling pin to lift almond paste on to cake.*

the help of the rolling pin, lift it on to the cake.
**5.** Lightly roll with the rolling pin, then smooth the join and leave to dry for up to 4–5 days before starting to ice.

## ICING AND ALMOND PASTE QUANTITIES

The amounts of Almond Paste quoted in this chart will give a thin covering. The quantities of Royal Icing should be enough for two coats.

| Square tin size | | 15 cm (6 inches) square | 18 cm (7 inches) square | 20.5 cm (8 inches) square | 23 cm (9 inches) square | 25.5 cm (10 inches) square | 28 cm (11 inches) square | 30.5 cm (12 inches) square |
|---|---|---|---|---|---|---|---|---|
| Round tin size | 15 cm (6 inches) round | 18 cm (7 inches) round | 20.5 cm (8 inches) round | 23 cm (9 inches) round | 25.5 cm (10 inches) round | 28 cm (11 inches) round | 30.5 cm (12 inches) round | |
| Almond Paste | 350 g (12 oz) | 450 g (1 lb) | 550 g (1¼ lb) | 800 g (1¾ lb) | 900 g (2 lb) | 1 kg (2¼ lb) | 1.1 kg (2½ lb) | 1.4 kg (3 lb) |
| Royal Icing | 450 g (1 lb) | 550 g (1¼ lb) | 700 g (1½ lb) | 900 g (2 lb) | 1 kg (2¼ lb) | 1.1 kg (2½ lb) | 1.4 kg (3 lb) | 1.6 kg (3½ lb) |

*FLAT ICING WITH ROYAL ICING*
**1.** Always apply royal icing over a layer of almond paste rather than directly on to the cake. Spoon almost half the icing on to the top of the cake and spread it evenly with a palette knife, using a padding action to remove any air bubbles that may remain.
**2.** Using an icing ruler or palette knife longer than

the width of the cake, draw it steadily, without applying any pressure, across the top of the cake at an angle of 30°. Neaten the edges with a palette knife. Leave to dry for 24 hours before icing the sides.
**3.** To ice the sides, place the board on an icing turntable or on an upturned plate. Spread the remaining icing on the side of the cake and smooth

t roughly with a small palette knife. Hold the palette knife or an icing comb upright and at an angle of 45° to the cake.

4. Draw the knife or comb towards you to smooth the surface. For a square cake, apply the icing to each side separately. Reserve the surplus icing for decorating.

5. For a really smooth finish, allow to dry for 1–2 days, then apply a second thinner coat of icing. Use fine sandpaper to sand down any imperfections in the first coat. Allow to dry thoroughly before adding piped decorations.

## ROSEBUD WEDDING CAKE

*three round cakes of the following sizes, covered in Almond Paste (see page 420); 30.5 cm (12 inch), 23 cm (9 inch), 15 cm (6 inch) on three round cake boards 40.5 cm (16 inch), 28 cm (11 inch), 20.5 cm (8 inch)*

*white Royal Icing using 2.7 kg (6 lb) icing sugar (see page 419)*

*four 9 cm (3½ inch) and four 7.5 cm (3 inch) round pillars*

*24 roses in pink icing, to decorate*

1. Flat ice the cake with two coats of Royal Icing (see page 419). Place the pillars in position on the base and middle cakes and prick around with a pin for positioning later.

2. Cut a circle of greaseproof paper to the size of the top of each cake; fold the largest two into eight segments, the smallest into six segments. Using a compass or the bottom of a glass of the right diameter, pencil a scallop on the rounded edge between the folds about 5 cm (2 inches) deep for big cakes, and about 2.5 cm (1 inch) deep for the top tier.

3. Cut out the scallops, open paper, place on cake and hold with one hand while pricking scalloped outline on to the icing.

4. Remove paper and, using an icing bag filled with white icing and fitted with a plain No. 2 icing nozzle, pipe a line along the inner edge of the scallops. Pipe a trellis inside each scallop as shown in the photograph.

5. Using an icing bag fitted with a plain nozzle (No. 1) and white icing, pipe a line 0.5 cm (¼ inch) outside the scalloped edge. Pipe two V's and three dots at the join of each scallop.

6. Place your selected pieces of ribbon and daisy edging in position around the cakes. Secure the

### ROUGH ICING WITH ROYAL ICING

1. Use two-thirds of the icing to roughly flat ice the top and sides of the cake (see left). Leave to dry for 24 hours.

2. Spoon the remaining icing on top of the flat icing and roughly smooth over it with a palette knife or spatula.

3. Using the palette knife or back of a teaspoon, pull the icing into well formed peaks. Leave to dry for 24 hours.

*Rosebud Wedding Cake*

ends in position with headed pins.

7. Using an icing bag fitted with a three-point star nozzle and white icing, pipe a shell or star border around the base of the cakes.

8. Carefully position the pillars on top of the bottom cake layer and secure them with icing. Place the second cake layer on top, then pillars, then the top cake layer.

9. Finish the decoration with a rose at the points where the scallops meet, and clusters at the base of the pillars, if wished (optional).

# GLACÉ ICING

*100 g (4 oz) icing sugar*

*few drops vanilla or almond flavouring (optional)*

*colouring (optional)*

**1.** Sift the icing sugar into a bowl. Add a few drops of vanilla or almond flavouring if wished.

**2.** Gradually add 15 ml (1 tbsp) warm water. The icing should be thick enough to coat the back of a spoon. If necessary, add more water or sugar to adjust consistency. Add colouring, if liked, and use at once.

*Makes about 100 g (4 oz)*

## Variations

### ORANGE OR LEMON
Replace the water with 15 ml (1 tbsp) strained orange or lemon juice.

### MOCHA
Dissolve 5 ml (1 level tsp) cocoa powder and 10 ml (2 level tsp) instant coffee in a little hot water and use instead of the same amount of water.

### LIQUEUR
Replace 10–15 ml (2–3 tsp) of the water with the same amount of any liqueur.

### CHOCOLATE
Dissolve 10 ml (2 level tsp) cocoa powder in a little hot water and use instead of the same amount of water.

### COFFEE
Flavour with 5 ml (1 tsp) coffee essence or dissolve 10 ml (2 level tsp) instant coffee in a little hot water and use instead of the same amount of water.

### ROSEWATER
Use 10 ml (2 tsp) rosewater instead of water.

### TO USE GLACÉ ICING
**1.** If coating both the top and sides of the cake, stand it on a wire rack with a tray underneath to catch the drips. As soon as the icing reaches a coating consistency and looks smooth and glossy, pour it from the bowl on to the centre of the cake.
**2.** Allow the icing to run down the sides, guiding it with a palette knife. Keep a little icing back to fill the gaps. Scrape up any icing which falls underneath the rack and use this also. Make sure there are no cake crumbs or it will ruin the appearance of the cake.
**3.** If the sides are decorated and only the top is to have glacé icing, pour the icing on to the centre of the cake and spread it with a palette knife, stopping just inside the edges to prevent it dripping down the sides.
**4.** If the top is to be iced and the sides left plain, protect them with a band of greaseproof paper tied around the cake and projecting a little above it.
**5.** Pour on the icing and let it find its own level. Peel off the paper when the icing is hard.
**6.** Arrange any ready-made decorations such as nuts, cherries, sweets, silver balls, etc. in position as soon as the icing has thickened and formed a

skin. Except for feather icing, leave the icing until quite dry before applying piped decorations.

### TO FEATHER ICE
**1.** Make a quantity of glacé icing and mix to a coating consistency. Make up a second batch of icing using half the quantity of sugar and enough warm water to mix it to a thick piping consistency.
**2.** Tint the second batch with food colouring and spoon into a greaseproof paper piping bag.
**3.** Coat the top of the cake with the larger quantity of icing. Working quickly, before it has time to form a skin, snip the end off the piping bag and pipe parallel lines of coloured icing about 1–2 cm ($\frac{1}{2}$–$\frac{3}{4}$ inch) apart, over the surface.
**4.** Quickly draw the point of a skewer or a sharp knife across the piped lines, first in one direction then in the other, spacing them evenly apart.

### SPIDER'S WEB
Alternatively, coat the top of the cake with the larger quantity of icing as above. Pipe concentric circles on top of the cake about 1 cm ($\frac{1}{2}$ inch) apart with the coloured icing. Quickly draw the point of a skewer or sharp knife starting from the inner circle out towards the edge, in one direction only.

# BUTTER CREAM

75 g (3 oz) butter, softened
175 g (6 oz) icing sugar
few drops vanilla flavouring
15–30 ml (1–2 tbsp) milk or warm water

**1.** Put the butter in a bowl and cream until soft. Gradually sift and beat in the icing sugar, then add the vanilla flavouring and milk or water.
*Makes 250 g (9 oz)*

## Variations

### ORANGE OR LEMON
Replace the vanilla flavouring with a little finely grated orange or lemon rind. Add a little juice from the fruit instead of the milk, beating well to avoid curdling the mixture.

### CHOCOLATE
Dissolve 15 ml (1 level tbsp) cocoa powder in a little hot water and cool before adding to the mixture.

### COFFEE
Replace the vanilla flavouring with 10 ml (2 tsp) instant coffee blended with some of the liquid, or replace 15 ml (1 tbsp) of the liquid with the same amount of coffee essence.

### MOCHA
Dissolve 5 ml (1 level tsp) cocoa powder and 10 ml (2 level tsp) instant coffee in a little warm water taken from the measured amount. Cool before adding to the mixture.

### ALMOND
Add 30 ml (2 level tbsp) finely chopped toasted almonds and mix.

### TO USE BUTTER CREAM
It can be used as a filling or icing. Spread it over the top only, or over the top and sides. Decorate by making swirl marks and mark with the prongs of a fork. For more elaborate decoration, butter cream pipes well.

# CRÈME AU BEURRE *(Rich Butter Cream)*

75 g (3 oz) caster sugar
2 egg yolks, beaten
175 g (6 oz) butter, softened

**1.** Place the sugar in a heavy-based saucepan, add 60 ml (4 tbsp) water and heat very gently to dissolve the sugar, without boiling.
**2.** When completely dissolved, bring to boiling

point and boil steadily for 2–3 minutes, to reach a temperature of 107°C (225°F).
**3.** Pour the syrup in a thin stream on to the egg yolks in a deep bowl, whisking all the time. Continue to whisk until the mixture is thick and cold.
**4.** In another bowl, cream the butter until very soft and gradually beat in the egg yolk mixture.
*Makes about 275 g (10 oz)*

## Variations

### CHOCOLATE
Melt 50 g (2 oz) plain chocolate with 15 ml (1 tbsp) water. Cool slightly and beat into the Crème au Beurre mixture.

### FRUIT
Crush 225 g (8 oz) fresh strawberries, raspberries, etc., or thaw, drain and crush frozen fruit. Beat into the Crème au Beurre mixture.

### ORANGE OR LEMON
Add freshly grated rind and juice to taste to the Crème au Beurre mixture.

### COFFEE
Beat 15–30 ml (1–2 tbsp) coffee essence into the Crème au Beurre mixture.

### TO USE CRÈME AU BEURRE
Use as butter cream on more elaborate cakes.

## COFFEE FUDGE FROSTING

| |
|---|
| 50 g (2 oz) butter or margarine |
| 125 g (4 oz) light soft brown sugar |
| 45 ml (3 tbsp) coffee essence |
| 30 ml (2 tbsp) single cream or milk |
| 200 g (7 oz) icing sugar, sifted |

1. Put the butter, sugar, coffee essence and cream in a saucepan and heat gently until the sugar dissolves. Boil briskly for 3 minutes.
2. Remove from the heat and gradually stir in the icing sugar. Beat with a wooden spoon until smooth, then continue to beat for 2 minutes until the icing is thick enough to spread. Use immediately, spreading with a wet palette knife.
*Makes about 400 g (14 oz)*

**Variation**
CHOCOLATE FUDGE FROSTING
Omit the coffee essence and add 75 g (3 oz) plain chocolate or plain chocolate flavoured cake covering with the butter in the pan.

## VANILLA FROSTING

| |
|---|
| 150 g (5 oz) icing sugar, sifted |
| 25 ml (5 tsp) vegetable oil |
| 15 ml (1 tbsp) milk |
| few drops vanilla flavouring |

1. Put the icing sugar in a bowl and beat in the oil, milk and vanilla flavouring until smooth.
*Makes about 175 g (6 oz)*

## CHOCOLATE FROSTING

| |
|---|
| 25 g (1 oz) plain chocolate or plain chocolate flavoured cake covering |
| 150 g (5 oz) icing sugar |
| 1 egg, beaten |
| 2.5 ml (½ tsp) vanilla flavouring |
| 25 g (1 oz) butter or margarine, softened |

1. Break the chocolate into pieces and place in a bowl over a pan of simmering water. Heat gently until the chocolate has melted.
2. Stir in the icing sugar, add the egg, vanilla flavouring and butter and beat until smooth.
*Makes about 200 g (7 oz)*

## AMERICAN FROSTING

| |
|---|
| 1 egg white |
| 225 g (8 oz) caster or granulated sugar |
| pinch of cream of tartar |

1. Whisk the egg white until stiff. Gently heat the sugar with 60 ml (4 tbsp) water and the cream of tartar, stirring until dissolved. Then, without stirring, bring to the boil and boil to 120°C (240°F).
2. Remove the syrup from the heat and immediately when the bubbles subside, pour it on to the egg white in a thin stream, beating the mixture. Leave to cool slightly.
3. When the mixture starts to go dull around the edges and is almost cold, pour quickly over the cake and spread evenly with a palette knife.
*Makes about 225 g (8 oz)*

## SEVEN-MINUTE FROSTING

| |
|---|
| 1 egg white |
| 175 g (6 oz) caster sugar |
| pinch of salt |
| pinch of cream of tartar |

1. Put all the ingredients into a bowl with 30 ml (2 tbsp) water and whisk lightly.
2. Place the bowl over a pan of hot water and heat, whisking continuously, until the mixture thickens sufficiently to stand in peaks. This will take about 7 minutes.
3. Pour the frosting over the top of the cake and spread with a palette knife.
*Makes about 175 g (6 oz)*

# BISCUITS AND PETITS FOURS

H omemade biscuits are quite irresistible.
There are six main types of biscuits: rolled, shaped, drop, bar, piped and refrigerator, with dozens of versions to be made from each basic recipe. The latter part of this chapter includes a selection of petits fours for serving with coffee.

◆

### FOR PERFECT BAKING

- Have all biscuits even in size and rolled to the same thickness for overall browning.
- Use a flat baking sheet with hardly any sides. High sides prevent proper browning.
- Check the biscuits just before the minimum baking time is up.
- To cool, transfer them with a wide flexible spatula to wire racks. Press down the spatula on the baking sheet and ease it under the biscuits.
- Some biscuits—especially those with syrup or honey as an ingredient—are still soft after baking, so leave them for a few minutes before lifting them off the sheet.
- Do not overlap the biscuits while cooling.

### FOR IDEAL STORING

- Line the bottom of an airtight container with greaseproof paper or non-stick paper and place a sheet between each two layers of biscuits or between each single layer of soft ones.
- Store different types of biscuit in separate containers.
- Bar biscuits can be kept in the baking tin and covered tightly with foil to save space.
- Store biscuits un-iced. Before serving dredge with sugar or cover with icing.
- Most homemade varieties will keep for up to two weeks. If plain biscuits lose their crispness, return them to a baking sheet and freshen in the oven at 170°C (325°F) mark 3 for 5 minutes without overbrowning.
- Biscuits and cookies keep well in the freezer for several months. Pack fragile ones in rigid boxes but just wrap others in foil or freezer film. Thaw in a single layer.

## ROLLED BISCUITS are the traditional basic biscuits. If you find it difficult to roll thinly, chill the dough slightly and roll out between sheets of non-stick paper. Adding extra flour to stop the sticking will make the biscuit tough and can spoil the final look. If you do use flour, be sure to brush away the surplus.

In a hot kitchen, handle these doughs a little at a time and leave the rest in the refrigerator for about 30 minutes. This prevents the biscuits from shrinking too much during baking.

## SHREWSBURY BISCUITS

*125 g (4 oz) butter or block margarine*

*150 g (5 oz) caster sugar*

*2 egg yolks*

*225 g (8 oz) plain flour*

*grated rind of 1 lemon or orange*

1. Grease two large baking sheets.
2. Cream the butter and sugar until pale and fluffy. Add the egg yolks and beat well.
3. Stir in the flour and grated lemon rind and mix

to a fairly firm dough with a round-bladed knife.
4. Turn out on to a lightly floured surface and knead lightly.
5. Roll out to about 0.5 cm ($\frac{1}{4}$ inch) thick. Cut into rounds with a 6.5 cm ($2\frac{1}{2}$ inch) fluted cutter and place on the baking sheets.
6. Bake in the oven at 180°C (350°F) mark 4 for about 15 minutes, until firm and a very light brown colour.
*Makes 20–24*

**Variations**

*SPICE BISCUITS*
Omit the lemon rind and add 5 ml (1 level tsp) mixed spice and 5 ml (1 level tsp) ground cinnamon, sifted with the flour.

*FRUIT BISCUITS*
Add 50 g (2 oz) chopped dried fruit to the mixture with the flour.

*FRUIT SQUARES*
Make up the mixture and divide in half. Roll out both portions into oblongs and sprinkle 100 g (4 oz) chopped dried fruit over one piece. Cover with the other piece and roll out the mixture 0.5 cm ($\frac{1}{4}$ inch) thick. Cut into squares.
*Makes 18–20*

*CHOCOLATE CREAM SANDWICHES*
Omit 45 ml (3 level tbsp) of the flour and sift in 45 ml (3 level tbsp) cocoa. When the cooked biscuits are cool, sandwich them together with Butter Cream (see page 423).

*RASPBERRY RINGS*
Roll out the mixture and cut into rounds, using a 6.5 cm ($2\frac{1}{2}$ inch) plain cutter. Place the rounds on a greased baking sheet, remove the centres of half the biscuits, using a 2.5 cm (1 inch) plain cutter, then bake. When the biscuits are cool, spread the solid rounds with jam and dip the rings into white Glacé Icing (see page 422). Place the iced rings on top of the rounds so that the jam shows through.
*Makes 10–12*

## PINWHEEL BISCUITS

*100 g (4 oz) butter or block margarine*

*50 g (2 oz) caster sugar*

*50 g (2 oz) cornflour*

*100 g (4 oz) plain flour*

*finely grated rind of $\frac{1}{2}$ a lemon*

*15 ml (1 tbsp) lemon juice*

*15 ml (1 tbsp) coffee essence*

*milk*

1. Grease two baking sheets.
2. Cream half of the butter and half of the sugar together in a bowl until pale and fluffy. Gradually work in half the flours with the lemon rind and juice. Knead well, then wrap in cling film and chill in the refrigerator for at least 30 minutes.

3. Meanwhile, cream the remaining butter and sugar together as before. Add the remaining flours and the coffee flavouring. Knead, wrap and chill as above.
4. Roll out both pieces of dough to oblongs 25.5 × 18 cm (10 × 7 inches). Brush a little milk over one layer and top with second piece of dough. Roll up from the narrow edge, wrap in cling film and chill for 30 minutes.
5. Cut the roll into eighteen slices and place on the baking sheets. Bake in the oven at 180°C (350°F) mark 4 for about 20 minutes. Cool on a wire rack.
*Makes 18*

# EASTER BISCUITS

*100 g (4 oz) butter or block margarine*

*75 g (3 oz) caster sugar*

*1 egg, separated*

*200 g (7 oz) plain flour*

*pinch of salt*

*2.5 ml ($\frac{1}{2}$ level tsp) ground mixed spices*

*2.5 ml ($\frac{1}{2}$ level tsp) ground cinnamon*

*50 g (2 oz) currants*

*15 ml (1 level tbsp) chopped mixed peel*

*15–30 ml (1–2 tbsp) milk or brandy*

*a little caster sugar*

**1.** Grease two baking sheets.

**2.** Cream together the butter and sugar until pale

and fluffy and beat in the egg yolk.

**3.** Sift the flour with the salt and spices and fold it into the creamed mixture, with the fruit and peel. Add enough milk to give a fairly soft dough.

**4.** Knead lightly on a floured surface and roll out to about 0.5 cm ($\frac{1}{4}$ inch) thick.

**5.** Cut into rounds using a 5 cm ($2\frac{1}{2}$ inch) fluted cutter. Place on the baking sheets and bake in the oven at 200°C (400°F) mark 6 for about 10 minutes.

**6.** Remove from the oven, brush with beaten egg white and sprinkle lightly with caster sugar.

**7.** Return to the oven for a further 10 minutes, until golden brown. Cool on a wire rack.

*Makes 16–18*

# CHOCOLATE NUT SNAPS

*1 egg, separated*

*100 g (4 oz) caster sugar*

*150 g (5 oz) plain chocolate*

*125 g (4 oz) hazelnuts, skinned and finely chopped*

*40 g (1$\frac{1}{2}$ oz) plain flour*

*200 g (7 oz) icing sugar, sifted*

**1.** Grease two baking sheets.

**2.** Whisk the egg white until stiff but not dry. Fold in the caster sugar.

**3.** Coarsely grate 75 g (3 oz) chocolate into the mixture and stir in with the hazelnuts, flour and egg yolk. Knead lightly on a well floured surface. Wrap and chill for 30 minutes.

**4.** Roll out the dough to about 5 mm ($\frac{1}{4}$ inch)

thick. Using a 5 cm (2 inch) star cutter, stamp out twenty-four shapes. Knead lightly and re-roll dough as necessary. Place on the baking sheets. Chill again for 30 minutes.

**5.** Bake in the oven at 190°C (375°F) mark 5 for about 20 minutes. Immediately ease off the baking sheet and cool on a wire rack.

**6.** Blend the icing sugar to a smooth paste with about 30 ml (2 tbsp) water. Spoon 45 ml (3 level tbsp) into a small greaseproof paper icing bag (see page 418). Melt remaining chocolate with 20 ml (4 tsp) water and stir into remaining icing.

**7.** Coat the surface of each biscuit with chocolate icing. Pipe on the white icing and pull a skewer back and forth through the icing to create a feather effect. Leave to set.

*Makes 24*

# SHORTBREAD ROUNDS

*125 g (4 oz) butter or block margarine*

*50 g (2 oz) caster sugar*

*125 g (4 oz) plain flour*

*50 g (2 oz) ground rice*

*caster sugar, to dredge*

**1.** Grease two baking sheets.

**2.** Cream the butter until soft. Add the caster sugar and beat until pale and fluffy.

**3.** Stir in the flour and ground rice, until the mixture binds together. Knead well to form a smooth dough.

**4.** On a lightly floured surface, roll out the dough thinly. Using a 7 cm ($2\frac{3}{4}$ inch) fluted cutter, stamp out about 20 rounds, rerolling the dough as necessary.

**5.** Place the rounds on the baking sheets and prick the surface with a fork. Bake in the oven at 180°C (350°F) mark 4 for about 15 minutes, or until pale golden and just firm to the touch.

**6.** Cool on a wire rack. Dredge with caster sugar. *Note* Shortbread can also be made in a floured shortbread mould which is turned out on to the baking sheet before baking.

*Makes about 20*

## Gingerbread Men

350 g (12 oz) plain flour

5 ml (1 level tsp) bicarbonate of soda

10 ml (2 level tsp) ground ginger

100 g (4 oz) butter or block margarine

175 g (6 oz) light soft brown sugar

60 ml (4 level tbsp) golden syrup

1 egg, beaten

currants, to decorate

1. Grease three baking sheets.
2. Sift the flour, bicarbonate of soda and ginger into a bowl. Rub the butter into the flour until the mixture looks like fine crumbs. Stir in the sugar. Beat the syrup into the egg and stir into the bowl.
3. Mix to form a dough and knead until smooth.
4. Divide into two and roll out on a lightly floured surface to about 0.5 cm (¼ inch) thick. Using a gingerbread man cutter, cut out figures and place them on the baking sheets. Decorate with currants. Bake in the oven at 190°C (375°F) mark 5 for 12–15 minutes, until golden. Cool slightly, then place on a wire rack.
*Makes 12*

*Gingerbread Men*

# Shaped Biscuits are made from soft doughs that need quick and deft handling. They can be moulded with the palms of the hands into small balls or barrels; dampen your palms if the dough sticks. The shaped dough may be rolled in crushed cornflakes or nuts before baking. This type of biscuit dough may also be cooked in moulds (see Madeleines, right).

## Melting Moments

100 g (4 oz) butter or block margarine

75 g (3 oz) caster sugar

1 egg yolk

few drops of vanilla flavouring

150 g (5 oz) self raising flour

crushed cornflakes

1. Grease two baking sheets.
2. Cream the butter and sugar together until pale and fluffy, then beat in the egg yolk.
3. Add the vanilla flavouring, stir in the flour to give a smooth dough and divide the mixture into approximately twenty-four portions.
4. Form each piece into a ball and roll in crushed cornflakes.
5. Place the balls on the baking sheets and bake in the oven at 190°C (375°F) mark 5 for 15–20 minutes.
6. Cool on the baking sheets for a few moments before lifting on to a wire rack.
*Makes approximately 24*

**Variation**
Instead of rolling the biscuits in cornflakes, use 50 g (2 oz) rolled oats. Press a half glacé cherry in the centre of each biscuit.

## ALMOND CRISPS

125 g (4 oz) butter or block margarine

75 g (3 oz) caster sugar

1 egg yolk

few drops almond flavouring

150 g (5 oz) self raising flour

75 g (3 oz) chopped almonds

1. Grease two or three baking sheets.
2. Cream together the butter and sugar until pale and fluffy. Beat in the egg yolk and almond flavouring and then the flour to give a smooth dough.
3. Form into a neat log shape and cut into twenty-four even slices. Shape each into a barrel, then roll in chopped almonds.
4. Place well apart on the baking sheets and bake in the oven at 190°C (375°F) mark 5 for 15–20 minutes. Cool on a wire rack.
*Makes 24*

## MADELEINES

150 g (5 oz) self raising flour

50 g (2 oz) semolina

50 g (2 oz) cornflour

225 g (8 oz) butter or block margarine

75 g (3 oz) icing sugar, plus extra, to dredge

1. Grease eighteen madeleine moulds.
2. Into a bowl, sift the flour, semolina and cornflour. Cream the butter and icing sugar together until pale and fluffy. Stir in the flour mixture, using a fork to form a soft paste.
3. Press a little of the mixture into each mould and smooth off the top. Bake in the oven at 180°C (350°F) mark 4 for 15–20 minutes. Leave to cool a little in the tins before gently easing out. When cold, dredge with icing sugar.
*Makes 18*

## CHERRY AND WALNUT BISCUITS

225 g (8 oz) plain flour

pinch of salt

75 g (3 oz) butter or block margarine

100 g (4 oz) caster sugar

grated rind of ½ a lemon

1 egg, separated

45–60 ml (3–4 tbsp) milk

100 g (4 oz) walnut pieces, finely chopped

12 glacé cherries, halved

1. Grease two baking sheets.
2. Sift the flour with the salt, rub in the butter until the mixture resembles fine breadcrumbs, then stir in the sugar, lemon rind, egg yolk and milk to give a fairly firm dough.
3. Form the dough into small balls, dip these in the slightly whisked egg white and roll them in the chopped walnuts.
4. Place the biscuits on the baking sheets and top each with a cherry half.
5. Bake in the oven at 180°C (350°F) mark 4 for 20–25 minutes, until firm and lightly browned. Cool on a wire rack.
*Makes 24*

*Madeleines, Cherry and Walnut Biscuits, Almond Crisps*

## GRANTHAM GINGERBREADS

100 g (4 oz) butter or block margarine

350 g (12 oz) caster sugar

1 egg, beaten

250 g (9 oz) self raising flour

5 ml (1 level tsp) ground ginger

1. Grease two or three baking sheets.
2. Cream the butter and sugar together in a bowl until pale and fluffy. Gradually beat in the egg.

3. Sift the flour and ginger into the mixture and work in with a fork until a fairly firm dough is obtained.
4. Roll the dough into small balls about the size of a walnut and put them on the baking sheets, spaced apart.
5. Bake in the oven at 150°C (300°F) mark 2 for 40–45 minutes, until crisp, well risen, hollow and very lightly browned.
*Makes 30*

## PEANUT BUTTER COOKIES

50 g (2 oz) crunchy peanut butter

grated rind of ½ an orange

50 g (2 oz) caster sugar

45 ml (3 level tbsp) light soft brown sugar

50 g (2 oz) butter or block margarine

1 egg

30 ml (2 tbsp) seedless raisins, chopped

100 g (4 oz) self raising flour

1. Cream together the peanut butter, orange rind, sugars and butter until pale and fluffy.
2. Beat in the egg, add the raisins and stir in the flour to give a fairly firm dough.
3. Roll the dough into small balls about the size of a walnut and place well apart on an ungreased baking sheet. Dip a fork in a little flour and press criss-cross lines on to each ball.
4. Bake in the oven at 180°C (350°F) mark 4 for 25 minutes, until risen and golden brown. Cool on a wire rack.
*Makes 25–30*

# DROP BISCUITS are made from a soft dough and are usually spooned directly on to the baking sheet. The term 'drop' is misleading, since the mixture must be stiff enough to need pushing from the spoon. The baked texture is variable; it can be soft and cake-like, crisp or even brittle. Drop biscuits are often irregular in shape as they tend to spread as they bake, but that is part of their charm.

## GINGER BISCUITS

125 g (4 oz) golden syrup

50 g (2 oz) butter or block margarine

50 g (2 oz) dark soft brown sugar

finely grated rind of 1 orange

30 ml (2 tbsp) orange juice

175 g (6 oz) self raising flour, sifted

5 ml (1 level tsp) ground ginger

1. Grease two or three baking sheets.
2. Place the syrup, butter and sugar into a medium saucepan.

3. Add the orange rind and juice to the pan. Heat very gently until the ingredients have completely melted and are evenly blended together.
4. Leave the mixture to cool slightly, then add the flour and ginger. Mix well until smooth.
5. Place small spoonfuls of the mixture on to the baking sheets, leaving room for spreading.
6. Bake in the oven at 180°C (350°F) mark 4 for about 12 minutes, until golden brown. Leave to stand for 1 minute before easing off with a fish slice. Cool completely on a wire rack.
*Makes about 24*

# CHOCOLATE CHIP COOKIES

75 g (3 oz) butter or block margarine

75 g (3 oz) caster sugar

75 g (3 oz) light soft brown sugar

few drops of vanilla flavouring

1 egg

175 g (6 oz) self raising flour

pinch of salt

50 g (2 oz) walnut pieces, chopped

50–100 g (2–4 oz) chocolate chips

**1.** Cream together the butter, sugars and vanilla flavouring until pale and fluffy, then gradually beat in the egg.
**2.** Sift the flour and salt and fold in with the nuts and chocolate chips.
**3.** Drop spoonfuls of mixture on to two greased baking sheets and bake in the oven at 180°C (350°F) mark 4 for 12–15 minutes.
**4.** Cool on the baking sheets for 1 minute, then place on a wire rack to finish cooling.
*Makes 20*

# COCONUT MACAROONS

2 egg whites

100 g (4 oz) icing sugar, sifted

100 g (4 oz) ground almonds

few drops of almond flavouring

100 g (4 oz) desiccated coconut

30 ml (2 level tbsp) shred coconut

**1.** Line two baking sheets with non-stick paper.
**2.** Whisk the egg whites until stiff but not dry. Lightly fold in the sugar.

**3.** Gently stir in the almonds, almond flavouring and desiccated coconut until the mixture forms a sticky dough.
**4.** Spoon walnut-sized pieces of mixture on to the baking sheets. Press a few strands of shredded coconut on to the top of each one.
**5.** Bake in the oven at 150°C (300°F) mark 2 for about 25 minutes. The outer crust should be golden and the inside soft. Cool on a wire rack.
*Makes 18*

# FLORENTINES

25 g (1 oz) hazelnuts, finely chopped

25 g (1 oz) blanched almonds, finely chopped

3 glacé cherries, chopped

30 ml (2 level tbsp) mixed peel, chopped

15 ml (1 level tbsp) sultanas, chopped

50 g (2 oz) butter or block margarine

50 g (2 oz) caster sugar

10 ml (2 tsp) top of the milk

100 g (4 oz) plain chocolate

**1.** Line three baking sheets with non-stick paper.
**2.** Mix together the nuts, fruit and peel.
**3.** Melt the butter in a saucepan. Stir in the sugar and bring slowly to the boil, stirring. Remove the pan from the heat immediately and then stir in the fruit and nut mixture with the milk. Allow the mixture to cool slightly, stirring occasionally, until evenly blended and no longer oily in appearance.
**4.** Spoon the mixture on to the baking sheets, allowing plenty of space to spread.
**5.** Bake in rotation in the oven at 180°C (350°F) mark 4 for about 12 minutes, until golden brown.

**6.** Using a small oiled palette knife immediately push in the edges to give a neat round shape. Allow to cool for 1–2 minutes, then using a fish slice, slide them on to a wire rack to cool.
**7.** Break up the chocolate and place in a small bowl over a pan of hot water and heat gently until the chocolate melts. Remove the bowl and stir the chocolate until cool and thick.
**8.** Spoon a little chocolate on to the smooth side of each florentine and carefully spread to coat. Leave chocolate until creamy but not set.

*Spread chocolate over the smooth side of each.*

**9.** Draw the prongs of a fork across in a wavy line. Wipe the non-stick paper clean and use a fish slice to replace the florentines on a lined baking sheet. Refrigerate until set. Store in the refrigerator, interleaved with non-stick paper.
*Makes 12*

*From the left: Cigarettes Russes, Brandy Snaps*

## BRANDY SNAPS

| |
|---|
| *50 g (2 oz) butter or block margarine* |
| *50 g (2 oz) caster sugar* |
| *30 ml (2 tbsp) golden syrup* |
| *50 g (2 oz) plain flour, sifted* |
| *2.5 ml (½ level tsp) ground ginger* |
| *5 ml (1 tsp) brandy (optional)* |
| *grated rind of ½ a lemon* |
| *150 ml (¼ pint) double cream* |

1. Grease the handles of several wooden spoons and line two or three baking sheets with non-stick paper.
2. Melt the butter with the sugar and syrup in a small saucepan over a low heat. Remove from the heat and stir in the flour and ginger, brandy if using, and lemon rind.
3. Put small spoonfuls of the mixture about 10 cm (4 inches) apart on the baking sheets, to allow.

plenty of room for spreading.
4. Bake in rotation in the oven at 180°C (350°F) mark 4 for 7–10 minutes, until bubbly and golden. Allow to cool for 1–2 minutes, then loosen with a palette knife and roll them round the spoon handles.
5. Leave until set, then twist gently to remove. (If the biscuits cool too much whilst still on the sheet and become too brittle to roll, return the sheet to the oven for a moment to soften them.) Before serving, whisk the cream until thick and fill the brandy snaps.
*Makes 10*

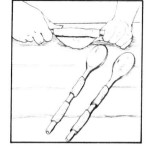

*Shape the brandy snaps whilst warm and malleable.*

## Cigarettes Russes

*25 g (1 oz) butter or block margarine*

*1 egg white*

*50 g (2 oz) caster sugar*

*25 g (1 oz) plain flour*

**1.** Grease the handles of several wooden spoons and line two baking sheets with non-stick paper.
**2.** Melt the butter and leave to cool. Whisk the egg white until stiff and fold in the sugar.
**3.** Gently stir the butter into the egg white with the flour.

**4.** Spread small spoonfuls of mixture into oblongs about 7 × 5 cm (3 × 3½ inches) on the baking sheets, not more than two per baking sheet. Bake in rotation (re-using the non-stick paper), at 190°C (375°F) mark 5 for 6–7 minutes.
**5.** Allow to stand for 1–2 seconds, then remove with a fish slice and place upside down on a flat surface.
**6.** Wind tightly round a greased wooden spoon handle. Cool slightly, ease off handles and place on a wire rack to finish cooling.
*Makes 8*

# Piped Biscuits look very impressive but do not take any more time to make than other biscuits; the mixture is simply put into a piping bag and piped in fingers or rings. They are the ideal choice when cooking for large numbers. They have a crisp yet melt-in-the-mouth texture, and can be served plain or sandwiched together with a filling.

## Chocolate Viennese Fingers

*125 g (4 oz) butter or margarine*

*25 g (1 oz) icing sugar, plus a little to dredge*

*125 g (4 oz) plain flour*

*1.25 ml (¼ level tsp) baking powder*

*few drops of vanilla flavouring*

*50 g (2 oz) plain chocolate or plain chocolate flavour cake covering*

*icing sugar, to decorate (optional)*

**1.** Beat the butter until smooth, then beat in the icing sugar until pale and fluffy.
**2.** Sift in the flour and baking powder. Beat well, adding the vanilla flavouring.
**3.** Put into a piping bag fitted with a medium star nozzle. Pipe out finger shapes, about 7.5 cm (3 inch) long, on to two greased baking sheets, spacing them well apart.
**4.** Bake in the oven at 190°C (375°F) mark 5 for 15–20 minutes. Cool on a wire rack.

*When cool, dip the ends of the fingers into the melted chocolate.*

*Chocolate Viennese Fingers*

**5.** Break up the chocolate and place in a bowl over a pan of simmering water. Heat gently until the chocolate melts. Dip the ends of each Viennese Finger in the melted chocolate. Leave to set on the wire rack. Dredge if wished.
*Makes about 20*

## LANGUES DE CHATS

50 g (2 oz) butter or block margarine

50 g (2 oz) caster sugar

1 egg

50 g (2 oz) self raising flour

Butter Cream (see page 423)

50 g (2 oz) plain chocolate or plain chocolate flavour
  cake covering

1. Grease two baking sheets.
2. Cream the butter and sugar until pale and
fluffy, then beat in the egg. Work in the flour until
the mixture is of piping consistency.

3. Put into a piping bag fitted with a 1 cm ($\frac{1}{2}$ inch)
plain piping nozzle and pipe on to the baking
sheets in fingers about 6–8 cm (2$\frac{1}{2}$–3 inches) long,
spaced widely apart.
4. Bake in the oven at 220°C (425°F) mark 7 for
about 5 minutes, until the edges of the biscuits are
colouring. Cool on a wire rack. When the fingers
are cold, melt the chocolate in a bowl over
simmering water. Allow to cool slightly. Sandwich
the fingers together in pairs with butter cream and
dip the ends of each in the melted chocolate. If left
plain, these biscuits are good with a rich sweet
such as syllabub or soufflé.
*Makes about 12*

## CHERRY GARLANDS

225 g (8 oz) soft tub margarine

50 g (2 oz) icing sugar

200 g (7 oz) plain flour

150 g (5 oz) cornflour

a few drops of vanilla flavouring

50 g (2 oz) glacé cherries, very finely chopped

glacé cherries, quartered, and angelica pieces,
  to decorate

icing sugar, to dredge

1. Grease two or three baking sheets.
2. Cream the margarine and icing sugar together

in a bowl until the mixture is pale and fluffy.
3. Beat in the flours, vanilla flavouring and
cherries. Beat until the mixture is very soft.
4. Spoon half the mixture into a piping bag fitted
with a 1 cm ($\frac{1}{2}$ inch) star nozzle. Pipe 5 cm (2 inch)
rings on to the baking sheets, allowing room for
spreading. Decorate with cherry quarters and
pieces of angelica. Repeat with remaining mixture.
5. Bake in the oven at 190°C (375°F) mark 5 for
about 20 minutes, until pale golden. Allow to firm
up slightly on the baking sheets for about 30
seconds before sliding on to a wire rack to cool.
Dredge with icing sugar.
*Makes 24*

# BAR BISCUITS are especially easy and quick to prepare. The mixture is
pressed into a large tin and cut into bars when cooked. Some bars need to cool on a
wire rack, others in the tin. Often bar biscuits cannot be stored for as long as other
types of homemade biscuits.

## FLAPJACKS

75 g (3 oz) butter or block margarine

50 g (2 oz) light soft brown sugar

30 ml (2 level tbsp) golden syrup

175 g (6 oz) rolled oats

1. Grease a shallow 18 cm (7 inch) square cake tin.
2. Melt the butter with the sugar and syrup and
pour it on to the rolled oats. Mix well, turn the
mixture into the prepared tin and press down well.

3. Bake in the oven at 180°C (350°F) mark 4
for about 20 minutes, until golden brown. Cool
slightly in the tin, mark into fingers with a sharp
knife and loosen round the edges.
4. When firm, remove from the tin, and cool on a
wire rack, then break into fingers. The flapjacks
may be stored in an airtight container for up to
a week.
*Makes 8–10*

## DATE CRUNCHIES

175 g (6 oz) self raising flour

175 g (6 oz) semolina

175 g (6 oz) butter or block margarine

75 g (3 oz) caster sugar

225 g (8 oz) stoned dates, chopped

15 ml (1 tbsp) honey

15 ml (1 tbsp) lemon juice

pinch of ground cinnamon

1. Grease a shallow 18 cm (7 inch) square tin.
2. Mix the flour with the semolina. Melt the butter with the sugar until the butter is melted and stir into the flour mixture.
3. Press half of this 'shortbread' mixture into the prepared tin. Meanwhile, heat the dates with the honey, 60 ml (4 tbsp) water, lemon juice and cinnamon, stirring well, until the mixture is soft and smooth. Spread this filling over the mixture in the tin, cover with the remaining 'shortbread' mixture and press down lightly.
4. Bake in the oven at 190°C (375°F) mark 5 for 30–35 minutes. Cut into fingers but do not remove from the tin until cold.
*Makes 12*

**Variation**
Use 75 g (3 oz) chopped dried apricots instead of the dates and cook with 200 ml ($\frac{1}{3}$ pint) water for 10 minutes until softened. Purée if wished in a blender or food processor.

# REFRIGERATOR BISCUITS These biscuits are very handy as the dough can be kept in the refrigerator and baked when required, providing oven-fresh biscuits on demand. The biscuits they make are always crisp and flavourful, their individual taste and finish depending on the extra ingredients added to the basic recipe. The dough must always be chilled until firm, so that it can be sliced as thinly and evenly as possible.

## CHOCOLATE CHEQUERBOARDS

200 g (7 oz) soft tub margarine

90 g (3½ oz) caster sugar

290 g (10½ oz) plain flour

15 ml (1 level tbsp) cocoa powder

few drops of vanilla flavouring

1 egg white, beaten

1. Lightly grease two or three baking sheets.
2. Beat together the margarine, sugar and flour to give a workable dough.
3. Remove two-thirds of the dough to another bowl. Into this, work the cocoa powder mixed to a paste with 15 ml (1 tbsp) water. Knead to an even coloured ball. Halve.
4. Work the vanilla flavouring into the remaining plain dough. With floured hands roll the vanilla dough and one piece of chocolate dough into twelve 1 × 15 cm ($\frac{1}{2}$ × 6 inch) strips (six of each dough).
5. Assemble the strips into two logs of alternating vanilla and chocolate strips to make a chequerboard pattern. Brush with a little beaten egg.
6. Halve the remaining chocolate dough. Roll out each piece into a sheet large enough to encase a log. Roll round each log and brush with beaten egg white.
7. Square up the logs and chill until very firm, about 1 hour. Cut each log into 1 cm ($\frac{1}{2}$ inch) slices. Place on the baking sheets and bake in the oven at 190°C (375°F) mark 5 for about 15 minutes. Cool on a wire rack.
*Makes 24*

## ALMOND CHOCOLATE BISCUITS

| |
|---|
| 200 g (7 oz) self raising flour |
| 150 g (5 oz) caster sugar |
| 1.25 ml (¼ level tsp) freshly grated nutmeg |
| 150 g (5 oz) butter or block margarine |
| 100 g (4 oz) ground almonds |
| 50 g (2 oz) plain chocolate or plain chocolate flavour cake covering, coarsely grated |
| 1 egg, beaten |

**1.** Grease two or three baking sheets.
**2.** Put the flour, sugar and nutmeg into a bowl. Rub the butter into the flour mixture until it resembles fine crumbs. Stir in the almonds and 25 g (1 oz) chocolate. Bind together with egg until smooth.
**3.** On a lightly floured surface, divide the mixture into two and roll each part into a 30.5 cm (12 inch) long, thin sausage shape, using greaseproof or non-stick paper.
**4.** Chill in refrigerator for about 30 minutes, until firm. Cut slices off about 1 cm (½ inch) thick and place well apart on the baking sheets. Flatten lightly with the back of the hand. Bake in rotation in the oven at 190°C (375°F) mark 5 for 15–20 minutes.
**5.** Cool until just warm, then sprinkle the remaining chocolate over. Transfer to a wire rack.
*Makes about 48*

## REFRIGERATOR BISCUITS

| |
|---|
| 150 g (5 oz) caster sugar |
| 150 g (5 oz) soft tub margarine |
| few drops of vanilla flavouring |
| grated rind of 1 lemon |
| 1 egg, beaten |
| 225 g (8 oz) plain flour |

**1.** Lightly grease two baking sheets.
**2.** Cream together the sugar and margarine until pale and fluffy. Beat in the vanilla flavouring, lemon rind and egg.
**3.** Stir in the flour and mix to a firm paste. Knead lightly, wrap and chill in the refrigerator for 30 minutes.
**4.** Roll the dough to a sausage shape—5 cm (2 inches) in diameter and 20.5 cm (8 inches) long. Wrap in greaseproof paper. Refrigerate until required (for at least 30 minutes after shaping).
**5.** When required, cut off 0.5 cm (¼ inch) slices, place on the baking sheets and bake at 190°C (375°F) mark 5 for 12–15 minutes. Cool the biscuits on a wire rack.
*Makes 32*

**Variation**
*HONEY JUMBLES*
Follow the basic recipe above as far as the end of stage 4. Slice off 0.5 cm (¼ inch) rounds. Roll into pencil-thin strips 10 cm (4 inches) long. Twist into 'S' shapes and place on lightly greased baking sheets. Chill for 30 minutes. Bake as above. While still warm, glaze well with runny honey, sprinkle with demerara sugar and grill for 1–2 minutes until caramelised. Cool.

*From the top: Refrigerator Biscuits, Honey Jumbles*

# PETITS FOURS are the delicious, rich little sweets and biscuits that are

served with coffee after dinner. Traditional petits fours always include little iced cakes made from a Genoese sponge cut into small shapes. They are coated with apricot jam and then covered with fondant, marzipan or glacé icing. They may be decorated with nuts, glacé fruits or crystallised flower petals.

Meringue mixtures are ideal and may be piped into fancy shapes, cooked, then decorated with small pieces of glacé cherry or nuts, or dipped in chocolate. Almost any small rich sweets can be included. A good selection should be colourful and varied in shape, texture and decoration. Serve with truffles, chocolates and fondants (see page 441).

## MERINGUE PETITS FOURS

*2 egg whites*

*125 g (4 oz) icing sugar*

*10–15 ml (2–3 tsp) coffee flavouring*

*glacé cherries and angelica, to decorate*

1. Line a baking sheet with non-stick paper.
2. Place the egg whites and sugar in a mixing bowl over a pan of hot water and whisk until the mixture is very thick and stands in peaks. Remove the bowl from the heat.
3. Place half the mixture in a piping bag fitted with a plain 1 cm (½ inch) nozzle and pipe small rounds of the mixture, about 2.5 cm (1 inch) in diameter, on the lined baking sheet.
4. Add the coffee flavouring to the remaining mixture and pipe an equal number of rounds. Reserve any uncooked meringue mixture.
5. Bake in the oven at 170°C (325°F) mark 3 for 10–15 minutes, until set but not coloured. Cool.
6. Use a little uncooked meringue mixture to sandwich one white and one coffee meringue together. Decorate each with a little piece of glacé cherry and angelica.
*Makes about 24*

*From the left: Meringue Petits Fours, Almond Stars (see page 438), Iced Petits Fours (see page 438)*

## ALMOND STARS

2 egg whites

150 g (5 oz) ground almonds

75 g (3 oz) caster sugar

few drops of almond flavouring

24 pieces of angelica or glacé cherries, to decorate

1. Line two baking sheets with non-stick paper. Whisk the egg whites until stiff and use a large metal spoon to fold in the almonds, sugar and almond flavouring.
2. Using a large star nozzle, pipe stars, quite close together, on to the lined baking sheets.
3. Decorate each star with a piece of angelica or a glacé cherry. Bake in the oven at 150°C (300°F) mark 2 for 15–20 minutes, until beginning to colour.

*Makes about 24*

## FROSTED FRUITS

Soft, juicy fruit such as grapes may be given a crisp, sparkling coating of sugar and served as petits fours.

Wash the fruit and dry carefully. Dip in lightly beaten egg white, toss in caster sugar and leave to dry on a wire rack. Serve the day of making.

## ICED PETITS FOURS

25 g (1 oz) butter or block margarine

40 g (1½ oz) plain flour

15 g (½ oz) cornflour

2 eggs

50 g (2 oz) caster sugar

apricot jam

50 g (2 oz) Almond Paste (see page 495)

225 g (8 oz) icing sugar, sifted

food colourings

mimosa balls, glacé cherries, angelica, grated
    chocolate, nuts or crystallised flowers, to decorate

1. For the Genoese sponge, grease and line a 20.5 cm (8 inch) square tin.
2. Heat the butter gently until it is melted and leave to cool until the sediment has settled. Sift the flour and cornflour together on to a plate.
3. Whisk the eggs and sugar together in a mixing bowl over a pan of hot water until thick and creamy. Remove from the heat and whisk until cool. Re-sift half the flour and cornflour over the surface of the egg mixture and fold in carefully with a large metal spoon.
4. Pour half the melted butter around the edge of the mixture and carefully fold in with the metal spoon. Repeat using the remaining flour and butter.
5. Pour the mixture into the prepared tin and bake in the oven at 180°C (350°F) mark 4 for 20–25 minutes, until risen and golden brown. Turn out and cool on a wire rack.
6. When the cake is cold, cut into shapes about 4 cm (1½ inches) in size, e.g. rounds, oblongs, squares, diamonds, triangles, crescents. Heat the apricot jam gently, adding a little water if the jam is very thick. Brush each petit four with the apricot glaze.
7. Divide the almond paste and add a ball or roll of almond paste to the top of each petit four.
8. For the decoration, blend the icing sugar with a little water to make glacé icing. Divide the icing and colour pale yellow, pink, green and brown and leave some white. Spoon the icing over the petits fours, making sure each one is completely covered.
9. Decorate with mimosa balls, glacé cherries, angelica, chocolate dots, nuts or crystallised flowers. Leave to set, then place in paper cases.

*Makes 25–30*

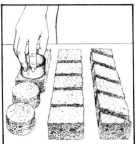

*When cold, cut the cake into a variety of even-sized shapes.*

*Ice the petits fours in different colours and then decorate. Leave until set.*

# BREAD

T he process of bread making has changed very little over the years. Most bread is made with yeast and the dough is kneaded, left to rise, and shaped before baking. A few breads are made with other raising agents and do not have to be left to rise—these are known as quick breads. Bread that has no raising agent is called unleavened bread.

◆

## INGREDIENTS FOR BREAD MAKING

### RAISING AGENTS

**Yeast** is a living plant available fresh or dried. When mixed with flour and liquid it gives off carbon dioxide, which expands, making the dough rise.

Fresh yeast is rather like putty in colour and texture, and should have a faint 'winey' smell. There should be no discoloration and it should crumble easily when broken. Although it will store for up to a month in a screw-topped jar, the best results are obtained when it is absolutely fresh, so buy it in small quantities when required.

Fresh yeast is usually blended with a liquid and then added to the flour all at once. It can also be rubbed directly into the flour or added as a batter. The batter method is known as the 'sponge dough process'; some ingredients are mixed to form a sponge, which is allowed to ferment, then mixed with remaining ingredients to form a dough.

Fresh yeast is easiest measured by weight. The amount of yeast required varies according to the richness of the dough and the type of flour used.

Dried yeast is sold in granulated form and is very convenient as it can be stored in an airtight container in a cool place for up to 6 months. Ordinary dried yeast requires sugar to activate it; the yeast granules are sprinkled over tepid liquid with the sugar and the mixture is then left to froth for about 15 minutes before using. The sugar used to activate the yeast loses its sweetness in the

frothing process so dried yeast can be used in savoury recipes. However, there are now several new varieties of dried yeast available. Some require only one rising of the dough, while others can be added directly to the flour without having to first mix with water and sugar.

Dried yeast is easiest measured in 5 ml (1 level tsp) or 15 ml (1 level tbsp) spoonfuls. As it is more concentrated than fresh yeast, generally half the amount of dried yeast is required, so that 15 ml (1 level tbsp) dried yeast has the same effect as 25 g (1 oz) fresh yeast.

**Bicarbonate of soda** is the main raising agent for quick breads. When added to liquid and heated, it gives off carbon dioxide which expands and makes the dough rise.

**Cream of tartar** is often used with bicarbonate of soda as it reacts with it to help produce carbon dioxide. It also helps to neutralise the slightly soapy taste often given by bicarbonate of soda.

**Baking powder** is a ready-made mixture of bicarbonate of soda and acid (often cream of tartar) which produces carbon dioxide when it comes in contact with moisture. Also used for quick breads.

### FLOUR

Wheat is either hard or soft depending on its gluten content. When hard wheat is milled it produces a strong flour, rich in protein, containing

*A selection of brown bread loaves and rolls*

a sticky, rubber-like substance called gluten. In bread making, the gluten stretches like elastic and as it is heated, it expands and traps in the dough the carbon dioxide released by the yeast. The gluten then sets and forms the 'frame' of the bread. It is the gluten content in a strong flour that gives the volume and open texture of bread and best results are obtained by using this flour.

When soft wheats are milled they produce a flour with different gluten properties, more suited to the making of cakes or pastries where a smaller rise and closer, finer texture are required. This ordinary soft flour, which is either plain or self raising, can be used for bread but it will give a smaller rise and closer crumbly texture with a pale, hard crust, and a disappointing result. Self raising flour, i.e. plain flour with raising agents already added can be used in recipes for quick breads.

Generally, bread made with wholemeal flour has a closer texture and a stronger, more distinctive taste than white bread.

**Wholemeal (or wholewheat) flour** contains 100 per cent of the wheat (i.e. the entire grain is milled). Bread made with this flour is coarse-textured, has a nutty taste, and is brown in colour. Strong, plain and self raising types of wholemeal flour are available.

**Brown (wheatmeal) flour** contains 80–90 per cent of the wheat (i.e. some of the bran is removed) and it is more absorbent than white flour, giving a denser-textured bread than white, but not as coarse

as wholemeal. It is available in strong, plain and self raising forms.

**White flour** contains 72–74 per cent of the wheat. The bran and wheatgerm which give wholemeal and brown flours their brown colour are removed, resulting in the white flour which is used to make fine-textured 'white' bread. Much is bleached chemically; look for the word 'unbleached' for untreated flour. It is available in strong, plain and self raising forms.

**Stoneground flour** takes its name from the specific process of grinding which heats the flour and gives it a slightly roasted, nutty flavour. Both wholemeal and brown flours can be stoneground.

**Granary flour** is strong brown flour with added malted wheat flakes giving a nutty flavour.

**Rye flour** used on its own produces rather dense, heavy bread as rye lacks sufficient protein for the formation of gluten. Finely milled rye flour gives the densest texture and bread made with coarse rye flour is rougher and more open-textured. When baking rye bread, combine the rye flour with a strong flour.

**Buckwheat flour** is slightly bitter. It lacks gluten, but gives an interesting texture to white flour doughs when mixed with them.

If you wish to eat a bread high in fibre, choose a flour with a high percentage of the wheat grain. Extra fibre can be added to bread recipes in the form of bran, bran flakes or oatmeal. Add in small quantities and use a little extra liquid for mixing.

## SALT

Salt improves the flavour of bread. It should be measured accurately, as too little causes the dough to rise too quickly and too much kills the yeast and gives the bread an uneven texture. Salt is used in the proportions of 5–10 ml (1–2 level tsp) to 450 g (1 lb) flour. Low sodium salts may also be used.

## FAT

Adding fat to the dough enriches it and gives a moist, close-textured load with a soft crust. It also helps keep the bread fresh and soft for a longer time. It is often rubbed into the flour and salt or, if a large quantity is used, it is melted and added with the liquid ingredients. If using margarine, block margarine is better than soft tub as it is easier to rub in. Oil may be used instead of fat.

## LIQUID

Water is suitable for plain bread, producing a loaf with an even texture and a crisp crust. Milk and water, or milk alone, will give a softer golden crust and the loaf will stay soft and fresher.

The amount of liquid used will vary according to the absorbency of the flour. Too much will give the bread a spongy and open texture. Wholemeal and brown flours are usually more absorbent than white.

The liquid is generally added to the yeast at a tepid temperature, i.e. 43°C (110°F). Boiling water will kill the yeast.

## GLAZES AND FINISHES

If a crusty finish is desired, bread or rolls can be brushed before baking with a glaze made by dissolving 10 ml (2 level tsp) salt in 30 ml (2 tbsp) water.

For a shiny finish, the surface should be brushed with beaten egg or beaten egg and milk.

For a soft finish, dust the bread or rolls with flour before baking. Some breads and yeast buns are glazed after baking to give them a sticky finish. To do this, brush the bread with warmed honey or a syrup made by dissolving 30 ml (2 level tbsp) sugar in 30 ml (2 tbsp) water and bringing to the boil.

There are many ways of adding interest, variety and extra fibre and vitamins to bread and rolls. After glazing and before baking, lightly sprinkle the surface with one of the following:

- Poppy, caraway, celery or fennel seeds.
- Sesame seeds. Particularly good sprinkled on to the soft baps used with hamburgers.
- Cracked wheat, barley or wheat flakes, wheat-germ, oatmeal or crushed cornflakes. Sprinkle them on top of wholemeal bread or baps.

*Liberally coat the surface with glaze, then with your desired topping.*

# MAKING BREAD

### MIXING THE DOUGH

Warmed ingredients and bowl will help to speed up the first rising process. Measure all the ingredients carefully into a large bowl. Add the yeast liquid and mix with the dry ingredients, using a wooden spoon or fork, until blended. Work the dough, using your hands, until the mixture is smooth and leaves the sides of the bowl clean.

### KNEADING THE DOUGH

Kneading is essential to strengthen the gluten in the flour, thus making the dough elastic in texture and enabling it to rise more easily.

Turn the dough on to a floured work surface, knead the dough

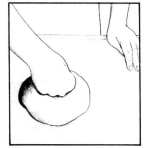

*Knead until smooth.*

by folding it towards you and quickly and firmly pushing down and away from you with the heel of the hand. Give the dough a quarter turn and continue kneading for about 10 minutes, until it is firm, elastic and no longer sticky.

**Using a dough hook** If you have a mixer with a dough hook attachment, it can take the hard work out of kneading. Follow manufacturer's instructions; working with small amounts of dough is more successful than attempting a large batch all at once. Place the yeast dissolved in the liquid in the bowl, add the dry ingredients, begin at the lowest speed and mix to form the dough. Increase the speed for the recommended time.

**Using a food processor** A food processor also takes the hard work out of yeast mixtures. Follow the manufacturer's instructions on quantities as it is important that the bowl is not overfilled. You may need to halve the recipe and prepare two batches of dough.

## RISING

The kneaded dough is now ready for rising. Unless otherwise stated, place in a bowl and cover with a clean tea towel. This will prevent a skin forming during rising. Rising times vary with temperature. Allow 1½–2 hours at room temperature for the dough to rise. It should have doubled in size and the risen dough should spring back when gently pressed with a lightly floured finger.

Good results are obtained by allowing the covered dough to rise in the refrigerator overnight or for up to 24 hours. The dough must be allowed to return to room temperature (taking several hours) before it is shaped.

The dough can be made to rise in about 45 minutes–1 hour in a warm place such as an airing cupboard or above a warm cooker.

## PREPARING TINS

While the dough is rising, grease the tins or baking sheets. Where reference is made to a 450 g (1 lb) loaf tin, capacity 900 ml (1½ pints), the approximate size to use is 16.5 × 10.5 cm (6½ × 4 inch) top measurements, and for a 900 g (2 lb) loaf tin, capacity 1.7 litres (3 pints), use one with 20 × 13 cm (8 × 5 inch) top measurements.

## KNOCKING BACK

The best texture is obtained by kneading the dough for a second time after rising. Turn the risen dough on to a lightly floured working surface and knead for 2–3 minutes to 'knock' out any large bubbles and ensure an even texture. The dough is then shaped as required (see below), placed in the prepared tins or on baking sheets, covered with a clean tea towel and left to rise again.

## PROVING OR SECOND RISE

This is the last process before baking. The shaped dough should be allowed to 'prove', that is left at room temperature until it has doubled in size and will spring back when lightly pressed with a floured finger. The dough is ready for glazing and baking.

## BAKING

Basic breads are baked in the oven at 230°C (450°F) mark 8. When cooked, the bread should be well risen and golden brown and it should sound hollow when tapped underneath with the knuckles. Larger loaves may need to be turned out of the tin and returned to the oven upside down for the last 10–15 minutes of the cooking time to ensure they are cooked through. Allow to cool on wire racks.

## TRADITIONAL BREAD AND ROLL SHAPES

**Loaf** Only fill the tin two thirds full for a perfect shape. Fold the dough in three, smooth over the top and tuck in the ends, then place into the tin.

**Tin** Roll out the dough to an oblong and roll up like a Swiss roll. Tuck the ends under and place in the prepared tin. Before baking, score the top of the loaf with a sharp knife if wished.

**Baton** Shape into a long roll with tapering ends, about 20.5 cm (8 inches) long.

**Cob** Knead the dough into a ball by drawing the sides down and tucking them underneath to make a smooth top.

**Crown** Divide the dough into 50 g (2 oz) pieces. Knead and place in a greased round sandwich tin. It is usually pulled apart into rolls when served.

**Cottage** Cut one-third off the dough. Knead both pieces well and shape into rounds, place the smaller round on top of the larger one, and place on a baking sheet. Make a hole through the middle of both pieces using the handle of a wooden spoon. Glaze with salt water before baking.

**Bloomer** Flatten the dough and roll up like a Swiss roll. Tuck the ends under and place on a baking sheet. When proved to double its size,

make diagonal slits on top with a sharp knife. Glaze the top with beaten egg or salt water before baking.

**Plait** Divide the dough into three and shape into three long rolls about 30.5 cm (12 inches) long. Pinch the ends together and plait loosely, then pinch the other ends together. Before baking, glaze with beaten egg and sprinkle with poppy seeds.

**Knots** Shape each piece of dough into a thin roll and tie into a knot.

**Rounds** Place the pieces on a very lightly floured surface and roll each into a ball. To do this, hold the hand flat almost at table level and move it round in a circular motion, gradually lifting the palm to get a good round shape.

**Rings** Make a thin roll with each piece of dough and bend it round to form a ring; dampen the ends and mould them together.

**Trefoil** Divide each piece of dough into three pieces and roll each into a ball. Place the three balls grouped together.

**Twist** Divide each piece of dough into two and shape into thin rolls. Hold one end of the two pieces of dough together and twist. Damp the ends and tuck under.

# WHITE BREAD

*15 g (½ oz) fresh yeast or 7.5 ml (1½ level tsp) dried*
  *yeast and a pinch of sugar*

*450 ml (¾ pint) tepid water*

*700 g (1½ lb) strong white flour*

*10 ml (2 level tsp) salt*

*knob of lard, butter or block margarine*

**1.** Grease a 900 g (2 lb) loaf tin, or two 450 g (1 lb) loaf tins.
**2.** Blend the fresh yeast with the water. If using dried yeast, sprinkle it into the water with the pinch of sugar and leave in a warm place for 15 minutes until frothy.
**3.** Mix the flour and salt in a large bowl and rub in the lard. Make a well in the centre of the dry ingredients and add the yeast liquid. Stir in with a fork or wooden spoon.
**4.** Work it to a firm dough using your hand, adding extra flour if the dough is too slack, until it leaves the sides of the bowl clean. Do not let the dough become too stiff as this produces heavy 'close' bread.
**5.** Turn the dough on to a floured surface and knead thoroughly for about 10 minutes, until the dough feels firm and elastic and no longer sticky. Shape it into a ball and place in a large mixing bowl. Cover the bowl with a clean tea towel to prevent a skin forming and allow to rise (see page 442) until it has doubled in size and springs back when pressed gently with a floured finger.
**6.** Turn the dough on to a lightly floured surface and knead well for 2–3 minutes, flattening it firmly with the knuckles to knock out the air bubbles. Stretch the dough into an oblong the same width as the length of the tin, fold it into three and turn it over so that the 'seam' is underneath. Smooth over the top, tuck in the ends and place in the greased loaf tin.
**7.** Cover the tin with a clean tea towel and leave to prove for about 30 minutes, until the dough comes to the top of the tin and springs back when pressed gently with a lightly floured finger. Glaze and finish as desired (see page 441).
**8.** Place the tin on a baking sheet and bake in the oven at 230°C (450°F) mark 8 for 30–40 minutes, until well risen and golden brown. When the loaf is cooked it will shrink slightly from the sides of the tin. Turn out the loaf; it will sound hollow if you tap the bottom of it. Cool on a wire rack.

**Variations**

*MILK BREAD*
Increase the lard, butter or margarine to 50 g (2 oz) and rub into the dry ingredients. Mix the dough with 450 ml (¾ pint) milk or a mixture of milk and water. This will give a close-textured loaf with a softer crust.

*ROLLS*
After knocking back the dough, divide it into about eighteen pieces and roll into any of the shapes described, left. Place on greased baking sheets about 2.5 cm (1 inch) apart. Cover the baking sheets with a clean tea towel and leave to prove until doubled in size. Remove the cover, glaze and finish as desired (see page 441). Bake in the oven at 230°C (450°F) mark 8 for 15–20 minutes, until well risen and golden brown. Cool on a wire rack.

# GRANARY BREAD

*900 g (2 lb) Granary flour*

*12.5 ml (2½ level tsp) salt*

*25 g (1 oz) lard or block margarine*

*25 g (1 oz) fresh yeast or 15 ml (1 level tbsp) dried yeast*
  *and 5 ml (1 level tsp) sugar*

*15 ml (1 level tbsp) malt extract*

*600 ml (1 pint) tepid water*

**1.** Grease two 450 g (1 lb) loaf tins.
**2.** Mix the flour and salt in a bowl and rub in the lard. Cream the fresh yeast with the malt extract and water and add to the flour. If using dried yeast, sprinkle it into the water with the sugar and leave in a warm place for 15 minutes, until frothy. Add to the flour mixture with the malt extract.
**3.** Mix to a stiff dough. Turn on to a lightly floured surface and knead for 10 minutes, until the dough feels firm and elastic and not sticky.
**4.** Cover with a clean tea towel and leave to rise in a warm place until doubled in size. Turn on to a lightly floured surface and knead for 2–3 minutes.
**5.** Divide the dough into two pieces and place in the loaf tins. Cover and leave to prove until the dough is 1 cm (½ inch) above the top of the tins.
**6.** Bake in the oven at 230°C (450°F) mark 8 for 30–35 minutes. Turn out and cool on a wire rack.

## WHOLEMEAL BREAD

*50 g (2 oz) fresh yeast or 30 ml (2 level tbsp) dried yeast*
*and 5 ml (1 level tsp) sugar*

*900 ml (1½ pints) tepid water*

*1.4 kg (3 lb) strong wholemeal flour*

*30 ml (2 level tbsp) caster sugar*

*20 ml (4 level tsp) salt*

*25 g (1 oz) lard or block margarine*

1. Grease two 900 g (2 lb) loaf tins.
2. Blend the fresh yeast with 300 ml (½ pint) of the water. If using dried yeast, sprinkle it into 300 ml (½ pint) water with the sugar and leave in a warm place for 15 minutes, until frothy.
3. Mix together the flour, caster sugar and salt in a large bowl and rub in the lard. Stir the yeast liquid into the dry ingredients, adding enough of the remaining water to make a firm dough that leaves the bowl clean.
4. Turn it on to a lightly floured surface and knead for about 10 minutes, until the dough feels firm and elastic and no longer sticky. Shape into a ball, place in a bowl, cover and leave until doubled in size.
5. Turn it on to a floured surface and knead until firm, divide into two or four pieces and flatten firmly with the knuckles to knock out any air bubbles. Knead again. Shape to fit the tins.
6. Cover with a clean tea towel and leave to prove until the dough rises almost to the tops of the tins.
7. Brush the tops of the loaves with salt glaze (see page 441) and bake in the oven at 230°C (450°F) mark 8 for 30–40 minutes. Turn out and cool on a wire rack.

## QUICK WHOLEMEAL BREAD

*15 g (½ oz) fresh yeast or 7.5 ml (1½ level tsp) dried*
*yeast and a pinch of sugar*

*about 300 ml (½ pint) tepid water*

*450 g (1 lb) strong wholemeal flour or 225 g (8 oz)*
*strong wholemeal flour and 225 g (8 oz) strong*
*white flour*

*5 ml (1 level tsp) sugar*

*5–10 ml (1–2 level tsp) salt*

*25 g (1 oz) lard or block margarine*

1. Grease two baking sheets.
2. Blend the fresh yeast with the water. If using dried yeast, sprinkle it into the water with the pinch of sugar and leave in a warm place for 15 minutes, until frothy. Mix together the flour, sugar and salt and rub in the lard. Add the yeast liquid and mix to give a fairly soft dough, adding a little more water if necessary.
3. Turn on to a floured surface and knead for about 10 minutes, until the dough feels firm and elastic and no longer sticky. Divide into two, shape into rounds and place on the baking sheets.
4. Cover and leave until doubled in size.
5. Bake in the oven at 230°C (450°F) mark 8 for about 15 minutes, then reduce the oven temperature to 200°C (400°F) mark 6 and bake for a further 20–30 minutes. Turn out and cool on a wire rack.

## FLOURY BAPS

*15 g (½ oz) fresh yeast or 7.5 ml (1½ level tsp) dried*
*yeast and a pinch of sugar*

*300 ml (½ pint) tepid milk and water mixed*

*450 g (1 lb) strong white flour*

*5 ml (1 level tsp) salt*

*50 g (2 oz) lard or block margarine*

1. Lightly flour a baking sheet.
2. Blend the fresh yeast with the liquid. If using dried yeast, sprinkle it into the milk and water with the pinch of sugar and leave in a warm place for 15 minutes, until frothy.
3. Mix together the flour and salt in a bowl and rub in the lard. Stir in the yeast liquid. Work to a firm dough, adding extra flour only if really needed, until the dough leaves the sides of the bowl.
4. Knead on a floured surface for about 5 minutes. Place in a bowl, cover with a clean tea towel and leave until doubled. Lightly knead, then cut into 8–10 pieces. Shape each into a ball, place on the baking sheet and press to flatten slightly.
5. Cover with a clean tea towel and leave to prove in a warm place until doubled in size.
6. Dredge the tops lightly with flour and bake in the oven at 200°C (400°F) mark 6 for 15–20 minutes. Cool on a wire rack.
*Makes 8–10*

# BRIDGE ROLLS

*15 g (½ oz) fresh yeast or 7.5 ml (1½ level tsp) dried*
    *yeast and a pinch of sugar*

*100 ml (4 fl oz) tepid milk*

*225 g (8 oz) white plain flour*

*5 ml (1 level tsp) salt*

*50 g (2 oz) butter or block margarine*

*1 egg, beaten*

*beaten egg, to glaze (optional)*

*From the back: Bridge Rolls and Floury Baps*

**1.** Grease a baking sheet.
**2.** Blend the fresh yeast with the milk. If using dried yeast, sprinkle it into the milk with the pinch of sugar and leave in a warm place for 15 minutes, until frothy.
**3.** Mix the flour and salt in a bowl and rub in the butter. Add the yeast liquid and egg and mix to a fairly soft dough, adding a little extra milk if necessary.
**4.** Turn on to a lightly floured surface and knead the dough for 10 minutes, until smooth. Place in a bowl and cover with a clean tea towel. Leave to rise until doubled in size.
**5.** Knead lightly on a floured surface, then cut into twelve–sixteen pieces. Make each into a tapered roll shape and place fairly close together in rows on the baking sheet.

**6.** Cover with a clean tea towel and leave to prove until doubled in size.
**7.** Brush with beaten egg if a glazed finish is required and bake in the oven at 220°C (425°F) mark 7 for about 15 minutes. Allow to cool on a wire rack before separating the rolls.
*Makes 12–16*

# DARK RYE BREAD

*275 g (10 oz) rye flour*

*275 g (10 oz) strong white flour*

*15 g (½ oz) salt*

*10 ml (2 level tsp) caraway or fennel seeds*

*150 ml (¼ pint) tepid water*

*150 ml (¼ pint) tepid milk*

*15 ml (1 tbsp) black treacle*

*25 g (1 oz) fresh yeast or 15 ml (1 level tbsp) dried yeast*
    *and 5 ml (1 level tsp) sugar*

**1.** Grease two baking sheets.
**2.** Mix together the flours and salt in a mixing bowl. Stir in the caraway or fennel seeds.
**3.** Combine the water, milk and treacle, crumble in the fresh yeast and stir until blended. If using dried yeast, sprinkle it into the water and milk with the sugar and leave in a warm place for 15 minutes, until the yeast is frothy.
**4.** Pour the liquid into the flour mixture and mix to a firm dough, adding extra flour if required. Turn the dough on to a lightly floured surface and knead for about 10 minutes, until the dough feels firm and elastic and no longer sticky.
**5.** Place in a bowl, cover with a clean tea towel and leave to rise until doubled in size. Turn the dough on to a lightly floured surface, knead well and divide into two. Shape into traditional cob or baton shapes (see page 442).
**6.** Place on the greased baking sheets and cover with a clean tea towel. Leave to prove until doubled in size and the dough springs back when lightly pressed with a floured finger.
**7.** Bake in the oven at 190°C (375°F) mark 5 for 30 minutes. Brush the tops with water, reduce the oven temperature to 180°C (350°F) mark 4 and bake for 20 minutes more. Cool on a wire rack.

# CRUMPETS

350 g (12 oz) strong white flour

15 g ($\frac{1}{2}$ oz) fresh yeast or 7.5 ml (1$\frac{1}{2}$ level tsp) dried
    yeast and a pinch of sugar

300 ml ($\frac{1}{2}$ pint) tepid water

2.5 ml ($\frac{1}{2}$ level tsp) salt

2.5 ml ($\frac{1}{2}$ level tsp) bicarbonate of soda

225 ml (8 fl oz) milk

vegetable oil

**1.** Sieve 175 g (6 oz) flour into a mixing bowl and crumble in the fresh yeast. Make a well in the centre of the flour mixture and pour in the water. Gradually mix together until smooth, beating well as the flour is worked into the liquid. Cover and leave to stand in a warm place for about 15 minutes, or until frothy.
**2.** If using dried yeast, sprinkle it into the water with the pinch of sugar and leave in a warm place for 15 minutes until frothy.
**3.** Meanwhile, sieve the remaining flour, salt and bicarbonate of soda into a large bowl, (if dried yeast is being used, all the flour will be added at this stage). Make a well in the centre, then pour in the yeast mixture and the milk. Mix to give a thick batter consistency.
**4.** Using a wooden spoon, vigorously beat the batter for about 5 minutes to incorporate air. Cover and leave in a warm place for about 1 hour, until sponge-like in texture. Beat the batter for a

further 2 minutes to incorporate more air.
**5.** Place a large, preferably non-stick frying pan on to a high heat and, using absorbent kitchen paper, rub a little oil over the surface. Grease the insides of three crumpet rings or three 8 cm (3$\frac{1}{4}$ inch) plain metal pastry cutters. Place the rings blunt edge down on to the hot surface and leave for about 2 minutes, or until very hot.
**6.** Pour the batter into a large measuring jug. Pour a little batter into each ring to a depth of 1 cm ($\frac{1}{2}$ inch). Cook the crumpets for 5–7 minutes until the surface of each appears dry and is honey-combed with holes.
**7.** When the batter has set, carefully remove each metal ring. Flip the crumpet over and cook

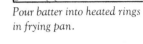

*Pour batter into heated rings in frying pan.*

the second side for 1 minute only. Cool on a wire rack.
**8.** Continue cooking the crumpets until all the batter is used. It is important that the frying pan and metal rings are well oiled each time, and heated before the batter is poured in. When required, toast the crumpets on both sides and serve hot.
*Makes about 24*

# CHEESE LOAF

450 g (1 lb) strong white flour

salt and pepper

5 ml (1 level tsp) mustard powder

100–175 g (4–6 oz) Cheddar cheese, grated

15 g ($\frac{1}{2}$ oz) fresh yeast or 7.5 ml (1$\frac{1}{2}$ level tsp) dried
    yeast and a pinch of sugar

300 ml ($\frac{1}{2}$ pint) tepid water

**1.** Grease two 450 g (1 lb) loaf tins.
**2.** Mix together the flour, salt, pepper and mustard in a large bowl. Stir in three quarters of the cheese.
**3.** Blend the fresh yeast and water together. If using dried yeast, sprinkle it into the water with the pinch of sugar and leave in a warm place for

15 minutes, until frothy. Add the yeast liquid to the dry ingredients and mix to a soft dough.
**4.** Turn on to a floured surface and knead for about 10 minutes, until the dough feels firm and elastic and no longer sticky. Cover with a clean tea towel and leave to rise in a warm place for about 45 minutes, until doubled in size. Turn on to a floured surface and knead for 5 minutes.
**5.** Divide the dough into two and shape to fit the tins. Cover with a clean tea towel and leave to prove in a warm place, until the dough reaches the top of the tins. Sprinkle the top of the loaves with the remaining cheese.
**6.** Bake in the oven at 190°C (375°F) mark 5 for 40–45 minutes, until well risen and golden brown on top. Turn out and cool the loaves on a wire rack.

# DANISH PASTRIES

25 g (1 oz) fresh yeast or 15 ml (1 level tbsp) dried yeast
    and 5 ml (1 level tsp) sugar

150 ml (¼ pint) tepid water

450 g (1 lb) plain white flour

5 ml (1 level tsp) salt

50 g (2 oz) lard

30 ml (2 level tbsp) sugar

2 eggs, beaten

300 g (10 oz) butter or margarine, softened

50 g (2 oz) sultanas

beaten egg, to glaze

Glacé Icing (see page 422) and flaked almonds, to
    decorate

**Almond paste**

15 g (½ oz) butter or margarine

75 g (3 oz) caster sugar

75 g (3 oz) ground almonds

1 egg, beaten

**Cinnamon butter**

50 g (2 oz) butter

50 g (2 oz) caster sugar

10 ml (2 level tsp) ground cinnamon

1. Blend the fresh yeast with the water. If using dried yeast, sprinkle it into the water with the 5 ml (1 tsp) sugar and leave in a warm place for 15 minutes, until frothy.
2. Mix the flour and salt, rub in the lard and stir in the 30 ml (2 level tbsp) sugar. Add the yeast liquid and beaten eggs and mix to an elastic dough, adding a little more water if necessary. Knead well for 5 minutes on a lightly floured surface, until smooth. Return the dough to the rinsed-out bowl, cover with a clean tea towel and leave the dough to 'rest' in the refrigerator for 10 minutes.
3. Shape the butter into an oblong. Roll out the dough on a floured board to an oblong about three times as wide as the butter. Put the butter in the centre of the dough and fold the sides of the dough over the butter. Press the edges to seal.
4. With the folds at the sides, roll the dough into a strip three times as long as it is wide; fold the bottom third up, and the top third down, cover and leave to 'rest' for 10 minutes. Turn, repeat, rolling, folding and resting twice more.
5. To make the almond paste, cream the butter and sugar, stir in the almonds and add enough egg

to make a soft and pliable consistency.
6. Make the cinnamon butter by creaming the butter and sugar and beating in the cinnamon.
7. Roll out the dough into the required shapes and fill with almond paste or cinnamon butter.
8. After shaping, cover the pastries with a clean tea towel and leave to prove in a warm place for 20–30 minutes. Brush with beaten egg and bake in the oven at 220°C (425°F) mark 7 for about 15 minutes. While hot, brush with thin Glacé Icing and sprinkle with flaked almonds.
Makes 16

## SHAPING DANISH PASTRIES

**Crescents** Cut out a 23 cm (9 inch) round. Divide into four segments and put a little almond paste at the base of each. Roll up from the base and curl round to form a crescent.

**Imperial stars** Cut into 7.5 cm (3 inch) squares and make diagonal cuts from each corner to within 1 cm (½ inch) of the centre. Put a piece of almond paste in the centre of the square and fold one corner of each cut section down to the centre, securing the tips with beaten egg.

**Foldovers and cushions** Cut into 7.5 cm (3 inch) squares and put a little almond paste in the centre. Fold over two opposite corners to the centre. Make a cushion by folding over all four corners, securing the tips with beaten egg.

**Pinwheels** Cut into a rectangle 25.5 × 10 cm (10 × 4 inches). Spread with cinnamon butter and sultanas, roll up like Swiss rolls and cut into 2.5 cm (1 inch) slices. Bake cut side upwards.

**Twists** Cut into rectangles as for pinwheels. Cut each rectangle lengthways to give four pieces. Spread with cinnamon butter and fold the bottom third of each up and the top third down, seal and cut each across into thin slices. Twist these slices and put on a baking sheet.

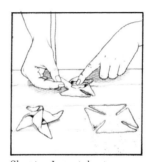
*Shaping Imperial stars.*

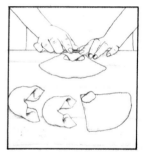
*Rolling up Crescents.*

## CROISSANTS

| | |
|---|---|
| 25 g (1 oz) fresh yeast or 15 ml (1 level tbsp) dried yeast and 5 ml (1 level tsp) sugar | |
| 225 ml (8 fl oz) tepid water | |
| 2 eggs | |
| 450 g (1 lb) strong white flour | |
| 10 ml (2 level tsp) salt | |
| 25 g (1 oz) lard or block margarine | |
| 225 g (8 oz) unsalted butter, or block margarine, at cool room temperature | |
| 2.5 ml (½ level tsp) caster sugar | |

1. Blend the fresh yeast with the water. If using dried yeast, sprinkle it into the water with the sugar and leave in a warm place for 5 minutes, until frothy.

2. Whisk one egg into the yeast liquid. Sift flour and salt into a large bowl and rub in the lard. Make a well in the centre and pour in the yeast liquid. Mix and then beat in the flour until the bowl is left clean. Turn on to a lightly floured surface, knead well for about 10 minutes until the dough is firm and elastic.

3. Roll out the dough on a clean, dry floured surface to an oblong about 51 × 20.5 cm (20 × 8 inches). Keep the edges as square as possible, gently pulling out the corners to stop them rounding off. Dust the rolling pin with flour to prevent it sticking to the dough.

4. Divide the butter into three. Dot one portion over the top two-thirds of the dough but clear of the edge. Turn up the bottom third of the dough over half the butter, then fold down the remainder. Seal the edges with a rolling pin. Turn the dough so that the fold is on the right.

5. Press the dough lightly at intervals along its length, then roll out to an oblong again. Repeat rolling and folding with the other two portions of butter. Rest dough in refrigerator for 30 minutes, loosely covered with a clean tea towel. Repeat three more times, cover and chill 1 hour.

6. Roll out the dough to an oblong about 48 × 33 cm (19 × 13 inches), lay a clean tea towel over the top and leave to rest for 10 minutes. Trim off 1 cm (½ inch) all around and divide the dough in half lengthways, then into three squares, then across into triangles.

7. Beat the remaining egg, 15 ml (1 tbsp) water and sugar together for the glaze and brush it over the triangles. Roll each triangle up from the long edge finishing with the tip underneath. Curve into crescents and place well apart on ungreased baking sheets, allowing room to spread. Cover loosely with a clean tea towel.

8. Leave at room temperature for about 30 minutes, or until well risen and 'puffy'. Brush carefully with more glaze. Bake in the oven at 220°C (425°F) mark 7 for about 15 minutes, until crisp and well browned. Cool on wire racks.
*Makes 12*

*Brioche, Individual Brioches and Croissants*

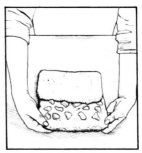

*Fold over the dough encasing the butter.*

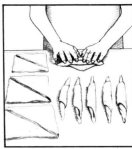

*Roll up each triangle from the long end.*

# MALT BREAD

*25 g (1 oz) fresh yeast or 15 ml (1 level tbsp) dried yeast
and 5 ml (1 level tsp) caster sugar*

*150 ml (¼ pint) tepid water*

*450 g (1 lb) strong white flour*

*5 ml (1 level tsp) salt*

*60 ml (4 tbsp) malt*

*15 ml (1 tbsp) black treacle*

*25 g (1 oz) butter or block margarine*

*15 ml (1 level tbsp) sugar for glaze (optional)*

1. Grease two 450 g (1 lb) loaf tins.
2. Blend the fresh yeast with the water. If using dried yeast, sprinkle it into the water with the 5 ml (1 level tsp) sugar and leave in a warm place for 15 minutes, until frothy.
3. Mix the flour and salt in a large bowl. Warm the malt, treacle and butter until just melted. Stir the yeast liquid and malt mixture into the dry ingredients and mix to a fairly soft, sticky dough, adding a little more water if necessary.
4. Turn on to a floured board, knead well for about 10 minutes, until the dough is firm and elastic. Divide into two pieces. Shape both into an oblong, roll up like a Swiss roll and put into the prepared loaf tins.
5. Leave to rise in a warm place until the dough fills the tins; this may take about 1½ hours, as malt bread dough usually takes quite a long time to rise.
6. Bake in the oven at 200°C (400°F) mark 6 for 30–40 minutes. When cooked the loaves can be brushed with a sugar glaze of 15 ml (1 level tbsp) sugar dissolved in 15 ml (1 tbsp) water.

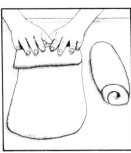

*Roll up firmly and place in loaf tins. Leave to rise.*

# BRIOCHE

*15 g (½ oz) fresh yeast or 7.5 ml (1½ level tsp) dried
yeast and a pinch of sugar*

*25 ml (5 tsp) tepid water*

*225 g (8 oz) strong white flour*

*a pinch of salt*

*15 ml (1 level tbsp) caster sugar*

*2 eggs, beaten*

*50 g (2 oz) butter or block margarine, melted*

*beaten egg, to glaze*

1. Brush a 1.1 litre (2 pint) fluted mould with oil.
2. Blend the fresh yeast with the water. If using dried yeast, sprinkle it into the water with the pinch of sugar and leave in a warm place for 15 minutes, until frothy.
3. Mix together the flour, salt and sugar. Stir the yeast liquid into the flour, with the eggs and melted butter. Work to a soft dough, turn out on to a floured board and knead for about 5 minutes, until smooth and elastic.
4. Put the dough in a large bowl, cover with a clean tea towel and leave in a warm place until it has doubled in size.
5. Knead the dough well on a lightly floured surface. Shape three quarters of it into a ball and place in the bottom of the mould. Press a hole in the centre as far as the tin base. Shape the remaining dough into a 'knob', put into the hole and press down lightly.
6. Cover the mould with a clean tea towel and leave at room temperature until the dough is light and puffy and nearly reaches the top edge of the mould.
7. Brush lightly with beaten egg and bake in the oven at 230°C (450°F) mark 8 for 15–20 minutes, until golden. Turn out and serve at once or cool on a wire rack.

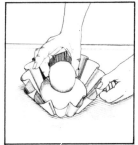

*Place three quarters of the dough in a mould, then top with remainder.*

*Note* The French traditionally serve Brioche warm for breakfast with a large cup of milky coffee and homemade fruit preserves. It is delicious with Apricot Jam (see page 457).

### Variation
*INDIVIDUAL BRIOCHES*
For small brioches divide the dough into 12 pieces, put into deep 7.5 cm (3 inch) oiled fluted patty tins, and bake as above for about 10 minutes. Serve hot or cool on wire racks.

## CHELSEA BUNS

225 g (8 oz) strong white flour

15 g (½ oz) fresh yeast or 7.5 ml (1½ level tsp) dried
  yeast and a pinch of sugar

100 ml (4 fl oz) tepid milk

2.5 ml (½ level tsp) salt

knob of butter or lard

1 egg, beaten

melted butter or block margarine for brushing

75 g (3 oz) mixed dried fruit

30 ml (2 level tbsp) chopped mixed peel

50 g (2 oz) soft brown sugar

clear honey, to glaze

**1.** Grease an 18 cm (7 inch) square cake tin.
**2.** Put 50 g (2 oz) of the flour in a large bowl
and blend together with the yeast and milk until
smooth. If using dried yeast, add a pinch of sugar.
Set aside in a warm place until frothy.

**3.** Mix the remaining flour and the salt in a large
bowl and rub in the fat. Mix in the batter with the
egg to give a fairly soft dough that will leave
the sides of the bowl clean after beating. Turn the
dough out on to a lightly floured surface and
knead for about 5 minutes until it is smooth.
**4.** Place in a bowl, cover with a clean tea towel
and leave to rise for 1–1½ hours. Knead the dough
thoroughly and roll out to an oblong 30 × 23 cm
(11¾ × 9 inches). Brush with melted butter and
cover with dried fruit, peel and brown sugar.
**5.** Roll up from the longest side like a Swiss roll,
and seal the edge with water. Cut into nine equal-
sized slices and place these, cut side down, in the
cake tin. Cover with a clean tea towel and leave to
prove in a warm place until doubled in size.
**6.** Bake the buns in the oven at 190°C (375°F)
mark 5 for about 30 minutes. While warm, brush
with a wet brush dipped in honey.
*Makes 9*

## STOLLEN

15 g (½ oz) fresh yeast or 7.5 ml (1½ level tsp) dried
  yeast

1.25 ml (¼ level tsp) caster sugar

100 ml (4 fl oz) tepid milk

225 g (8 oz) strong white flour

1.25 ml (¼ level tsp) salt

25 g (1 oz) butter or block margarine

grated rind of 1 small lemon

50 g (2 oz) chopped mixed peel

50 g (2 oz) currants

50 g (2 oz) sultanas

25 g (1 oz) blanched almonds, chopped

¼ a beaten egg

icing sugar for dusting

**1.** Grease a baking sheet.
**2.** Blend the yeast, sugar and milk with 50 g (2 oz)
of the flour. Leave in a warm place for about
20 minutes until frothy.
**3.** Mix the remaining flour and salt together in a
large bowl and rub in the fat. Stir in the fruit and
nuts.
**4.** Add the yeast batter and egg and mix
thoroughly to a soft dough. Knead on a lightly
floured surface for about 10 minutes until smooth.
**5.** Cover with a clean tea towel and leave to rise in

*Stollen*

a warm place for about 1 hour, until the dough has
doubled in size.
**6.** Knead the dough for 2–3 minutes on a
lightly floured surface. Roll into an oval shape
about 23 × 18 cm (9 × 7 inches), then mark a line
lengthways with the rolling pin and fold the dough
in half along this line. Place on the baking sheet.
**7.** Cover with a clean tea towel and leave to prove
in a warm place until doubled in size.
**8.** Bake in the oven at 200°C (400°F) mark 6 for
30 minutes, until well risen and golden brown.
Cool on a wire rack. Before serving dust thickly
with icing sugar.

# Hot Cross Buns

25 g (1 oz) fresh yeast or 15 ml (1 level tbsp) dried yeast

50 g (2 oz), plus 5 ml (1 level tsp) caster sugar

150 ml (¼ pint) tepid milk

75 ml (5 tbsp) tepid water

450 g (1 lb) strong white flour

5 ml (1 level tsp) salt

5 ml (1 level tsp) mixed spice

5 ml (1 level tsp) ground cinnamon

2.5 ml (½ level tsp) ground nutmeg

50 g (2 oz) butter, melted and cooled

1 egg, beaten

75 g (3 oz) currants

30 ml (2 level tbsp) chopped mixed peel

50 g (2 oz) Shortcrust Pastry, made with 50 g (2 oz)
    flour (see page 372)

**For the glaze**

60 ml (4 tbsp) milk and water, mixed

45 ml (3 level tbsp) caster sugar

Hot Cross Buns

1. Grease a baking sheet. Blend the yeast, 5 ml (1 level tsp) caster sugar, milk and water and 100 g (4 oz) of the flour together and leave in a warm place for about 20 minutes, until frothy.
2. Sift the remaining flour, salt, spices and 50 g (2 oz) sugar in a bowl. Stir in the butter, egg, yeast liquid, currants and peel and mix to a soft dough.
3. Turn on to a lightly floured surface and knead for about 10 minutes, until smooth and elastic and no longer sticky. Cover with a clean tea towel and leave to rise in a warm place until doubled in size. Turn the dough out on to a floured surface and knead for 2–3 minutes. Divide the dough into twelve pieces and shape into round buns.
4. Place on the baking sheet, cover and leave in a warm place until doubled in size.
5. Roll out the pastry thinly on a floured surface and cut into thin strips about 9 cm (3½ inches) long. Dampen the pastry strips and lay two on each bun to make a cross.
6. Bake in the oven at 190°C (375°F) mark 5 for 15–20 minutes, until golden brown. For the glaze, heat the milk, water and sugar together. Brush the hot buns twice with glaze, then cool.
*Makes 12*

# Devonshire Splits

15 g (½ oz) fresh yeast or 7.5 ml (1½ level tsp) dried
    yeast and a pinch of sugar

about 300 ml (½ pint) tepid milk

50 g (2 oz) butter or block margarine

30 ml (2 level tbsp) sugar

450 g (1 lb) strong white flour

5 ml (1 level tsp) salt

Devonshire or whipped cream and jam for serving

icing sugar for dusting

1. Grease two baking sheets.
2. Blend the fresh yeast with half the milk. If using dried yeast, sprinkle it into 150 ml (¼ pint) of the milk with the pinch of sugar and leave in a warm place for 15 minutes, until frothy.
3. Dissolve butter and sugar in remaining milk.
4. Mix together the flour and salt in a large bowl, make a well in the centre, add the butter mixture and yeast liquid.
5. Beat to an elastic dough, turn out on to a lightly floured surface and knead until smooth. Cover with a clean tea towel and leave in a warm place until doubled in size.
6. Turn on to a lightly floured surface and divide into fourteen–sixteen pieces. Knead lightly and shape into round buns.
7. Place on the baking sheets and flatten lightly with the hand. Cover with a clean tea towel and leave to prove in a warm place until doubled in size.
8. Bake in the oven at 220°C (425°F) mark 7 for 15–20 minutes. Cool on a wire rack. Split and spread with jam and cream. Dust with icing sugar.
*Makes 14–16*

## LARDY CAKE

15 g (½ oz) fresh yeast or 7.5 ml (1½ level tsp) dried
    yeast and a pinch of sugar

300 ml (½ pint) tepid water

450 g (1 lb) strong white flour

10 ml (2 level tsp) salt

15 ml (1 tbsp) vegetable oil, plus extra for brushing

50 g (2 oz) butter or block margarine

100 g (4 oz) caster sugar

5 ml (1 level tsp) mixed spice

75 g (3 oz) sultanas or currants

50 g (2 oz) lard

**1.** Grease a 24 × 19 cm (9½ × 7½ inch) roasting tin.
**2.** Blend the fresh yeast with the water. If using
dried yeast, sprinkle it into the warm water with
the pinch of sugar and leave in a warm place for
15 minutes, until frothy.
**3.** Sift the flour and salt into a bowl and stir
in the yeast mixture, with the oil to give a soft
manageable dough. Beat until smooth. Cover with
a clean tea towel and leave in a warm place to rise
until doubled in size.
**4.** Turn the dough out on to a lightly floured
surface and knead for 5–10 minutes. Roll out to a
rectangle about 0.5 cm
(¼ inch) thick. Cover
the top two thirds of
the dough with small
flakes of butter, 45 ml
(3 level tbsp) sugar, half
the spice and half the
dried fruit.
**5.** Fold the bottom
third up and the top
third down, sealing the
edges with a rolling pin.
Turn the dough so that

*Cover two thirds of the dough with filling.*

the folded edge is on the side. Roll out again to a
rectangle and dot the lard, 45 ml (3 level tbsp) sugar
and remaining spice and dried fruit in the same
way as before. Fold and roll as before.
**6.** Place the dough in the prepared tin, pressing it
down so that it fills the corners. Cover with a
clean tea towel and leave to rise in a warm place
until doubled in size. Brush with oil, sprinkle with
the remaining caster sugar and mark criss-cross
fashion with a knife.
**7.** Bake in the oven at 220°C (425°F) mark 7 for
about 30 minutes. Cool on a wire rack. Serve
sliced, with or without butter.

# QUICK BREADS vary from cake-like breads made with bicarbonate of
soda to the thin flat breads like chappatis which are unleavened, i.e. have no raising
agent. These breads are quick to make as they do not require the long preparation of
yeast doughs. However, they must be eaten quickly as they go stale much sooner than
yeast breads.

## CHAPPATI

225 g (8 oz) plain wholemeal flour

150–200 ml (5–7 fl oz) tepid water

30 ml (2 level tbsp) ghee (see page 571) or butter

**1.** Place the flour in a bowl and add enough
water to bind. On a lightly floured surface knead
the dough until it feels soft and pliable, the
consistency should be like that of shortcrust
pastry dough. Cover with cling film and leave to
rest for at least 15 minutes.
**2.** Heat a heavy-based frying pan or griddle.
Divide the dough into 8–10 portions and shape
into small balls. Dip the balls into a little flour,
sufficient to coat them lightly, then roll into
rounds 12.5 cm (5 inches) in diameter.

**3.** Place the rolled out chappati in the hot pan and
as soon as small bubbles start to appear on the
surface, turn it over and repeat the process. Using
a clean tea towel, carefully press down the edges of
the chappati—so the edges are cooked and the
chappati puffs up. The chappati is cooked as soon
as both sides have brown spots on the surface.
**4.** Remove from the frying pan or griddle and
smear with a little ghee or butter. Stack the
chappatis on top of each other and cover to keep
hot. Serve at once.
*Makes 8–10*
*Note* If you make the chappatis in advance, store
in an airtight container and warm up under the
grill.

# PARATHAS

Plain parathas are similar to chappati but the addition of ghee or butter and various ways of folding give parathas their distinct character.

*225 g (8 oz) plain wholemeal flour*

*200 ml (7 fl oz) water*

*45 ml (3 tbsp) ghee, melted*

1. Place the flour in a bowl and gradually add the water to form a soft pliable dough. Knead the dough for a few minutes until it leaves the sides of the bowl. Cover with cling film and leave to rest for 15 minutes.
2. Divide the dough into eight equal portions. Place each portion in the palm of the hand and roll it into a smooth ball. Dip the pieces into a little flour and coat lightly.
3. Roll the dough into 10 cm (4 inch) rounds. Smear a little ghee over the parathas. Fold one-third of the round into the centre and then the remaining one-third over the first fold, so that you have a rectangle measuring 2.5 cm (1 inch) × 10 cm (4 inches).
4. Smear a little ghee over the rectangle and repeat the folding method as described above, so you now have a small square. Dip the squares into a little flour to coat, then roll out to a larger square no larger than 12.5 cm (5 inches).
5. Heat a heavy-based frying pan or griddle. Cook the Parathas until bubbles start to appear on the surface. Cook the other side. Turn again, pressing the edges down with a clean tea towel.
*Makes 8*

# TORTILLAS

These are made from *masa harina* (fine corn meal) which can be bought at shops specialising in Mexican and Spanish food.

*250 g (9 oz) masa harina*

*2.5 ml (½ level tsp) salt*

*225 ml (8 fl oz) tepid water*

1. Mix the masa harina with the salt in a large bowl. Gradually add the tepid water, mixing lightly with a fork to make a dough that is just moist enough to hold together. If necessary, add more water, 15 ml (1 tbsp) at a time. Gather the dough lightly into a ball.
2. Knead the dough quickly and lightly in the bowl with one hand until it is smooth.
3. Divide the dough into 12 equal pieces and shape each one into a small ball. Keep covered to prevent them drying while you roll each out.
4. Flatten each ball until 0.5 cm (¼ inch) thick, then place between two sheets of waxed paper. Roll out to 15 cm (6 inch) rounds and leave between the waxed paper.
5. Heat a heavy-based frying pan or griddle. Remove the top sheet from one round and invert it into the frying pan. Peel off the second paper sheet. Cook for 30 seconds, until edges curl up.
6. Turn the tortilla over and press gently with a fish slice or spatula until bubbles form underneath it. Turn it again and cook for a further minute or until the underside is speckled with brown.
7. Remove from the frying pan. Wrap to keep it hot while you cook the remainder, stacking them in foil as they are cooked.
*Makes 12*

# BAKING POWDER BREAD

*350 g (12 oz) plain brown flour*

*20 ml (4 level tsp) baking powder*

*5 ml (1 level tsp) salt*

*100 g (4 oz) sugar*

*100 g (4 oz) sultanas*

*2 eggs, beaten*

*150 ml (¼ pint) milk*

*60 ml (4 tbsp) black treacle*

*50 g (2 oz) butter or block margarine, melted*

1. Grease a 450 g (1 lb) loaf tin.
2. Sift the flour, baking powder, salt and sugar into a bowl and stir in the sultanas. Add the eggs, milk, black treacle and butter and stir until well blended. Turn into the prepared tin.
3. Bake in the oven at 180°C (350°F) mark 4 for about 1 hour, until well risen and golden brown. Serve sliced and buttered and eat while it is very fresh.

## SODA BREAD

| |
|---|
| 450 g (1 lb) plain white flour |
| 10 ml (2 level tsp) bicarbonate of soda |
| 10 ml (2 level tsp) cream of tartar |
| 5 ml (1 level tsp) salt |
| 25–50 g (1–2 oz) lard or block margarine |
| about 300 ml (½ pint) soured milk or buttermilk |

1. Grease and flour a baking sheet.
2. Sift together the dry ingredients twice. Rub in the lard. Mix to a soft dough with the milk, adding a little at a time.
3. Shape into an 18 cm (7 inch) round and mark into triangles. Place on the baking sheet.
4. Bake in the oven at 220°C (425°F) mark 7, for about 30 minutes. Eat while very fresh.

## POTATO BREAD

| |
|---|
| 225 g (8 oz) strong white flour |
| 10 ml (2 level tsp) baking powder |
| 5 ml (1 level tsp) salt |
| 175 g (6 oz) potatoes, cooked and mashed |
| 15 ml (1 tbsp) vegetable oil |
| paprika for dusting |

1. Grease and base line a 900 ml (1½ pint) loaf tin.
2. Mix together the flour, baking powder and salt in a bowl. Rub in the mashed potato until evenly mixed with the dry ingredients.
3. Stir in the oil and 200 ml (7 fl oz) water. (This will be quite a wet dough.) Turn into the prepared loaf tin and dust the surface with paprika.
4. Bake in the oven at 230°C (450°F) mark 8 for about 25 minutes. Turn out and cool on a wire rack.

## CARAWAY RYE BREAD

| |
|---|
| 350 g (12 oz) rye flour |
| 10 ml (2 level tsp) caraway seeds |
| 2.5 ml (½ level tsp) salt |
| 5 ml (1 level tsp) baking powder |
| 50 g (2 oz) butter or block margarine |
| 142 ml (5 fl oz) soured cream |
| 150 ml (¼ pint) milk |
| 1 egg |
| milk and caraway seeds, to garnish |

1. Grease and base line two 300 ml (½ pint) Turtle pots or other ovenproof containers.

2. Combine the flour, caraway seeds, salt and baking powder in a large bowl. Rub in the butter.
3. Whisk together the soured cream, milk and egg. Stir into the dry ingredients. Bind to a smooth firm dough, adding a little water if necessary.
4. Halve the dough, and on a lightly floured surface knead each piece lightly, then place in the pots. Brush with milk and sprinkle with caraway seeds.
5. Bake in the oven at 200°C (400°F) mark 6 for 1 hour. Cover loosely with foil towards the end of cooking time if the loaf is browning too quickly. Wrap when cold; best eaten next day but will keep up to three days.

## HERBED CHEESE BREAD

| |
|---|
| 225 g (8 oz) self raising white flour |
| 7.5 ml (1½ level tsp) salt |
| 5 ml (1 level tsp) mustard powder |
| 5 ml (1 level tsp) snipped fresh chives |
| 15 ml (1 tbsp) chopped fresh parsley |
| 75 g (3 oz) double Gloucester or mature Cheddar cheese, grated |
| 1 egg, beaten |
| 25 g (1 oz) butter or block margarine, melted |

1. Grease a 450 g (1 lb) loaf tin. Mix the flour, salt and mustard in a bowl and stir in the herbs and cheese. Add the egg, 150 ml (¼ pint) water and melted butter and stir until well blended.
2. Spoon into the loaf tin and bake in the oven at 190°C (375°F) mark 5 for about 45 minutes.
3. Turn out and cool on a wire rack. Serve sliced and buttered while still warm.

# Jams, Jellies and Marmalades

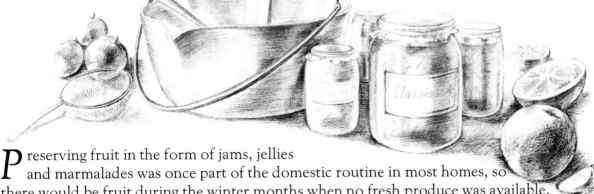

$P$ reserving fruit in the form of jams, jellies and marmalades was once part of the domestic routine in most homes, so there would be fruit during the winter months when no fresh produce was available. Although this is no longer necessary, people still enjoy making preserves free from artificial colourings and preservatives. This chapter also includes preserving fruits in alcohol, mincemeat and rumpots.

Jams and jellies are also a good way of using up gluts of fruit that you do not want to eat or freeze.

◆

## EQUIPMENT

The equipment is the same for jams, jellies and marmalades.

**A preserving pan** This makes preserve making much easier than using a large saucepan as the outward sloping sides mean you can quickly achieve the fast rolling boil necessary for jam making. In straight sided saucepans the contents tend to boil over.

Choose a preserving pan made of heavy aluminium, stainless steel or tin-lined copper. It should have a fairly thick base to prevent the jam burning and be wide enough to allow the jam to boil without splashing. A big one is best; ideally the jam should come only half way up the sides.

Preserving pans made of unlined copper or brass are safe for jam making provided they are perfectly clean and have no tarnish on them. However, these pans tend to be pricey and jams made in them will contain less vitamin C than those made in aluminium or stainless steel pans. Do not leave jam standing in a copper or brass pan for any length of time.

**Jam jars** These can be recycled endlessly provided they are free from cracks, chips or any other flaws. Commercial jam jars often have screw tops which provide a good seal—always put a wax disc on to the surface of the jam before screwing on the lid (see page 457). Jars which hold 450 or 900 g (1 or 2 lb) are the most useful as you can buy covers for them. Wash the jars well in warm soapy water and rinse thoroughly in clean, warm water. Dry off the jars in a cool oven at 140°C (275°F) mark 1 and use while still hot. In addition to jars, you will need waxed discs, cellophane covers, rubber bands and labels.

**Long-handled wooden spoon** This is for stirring jam without getting your hands too near it.

**Slotted spoon** For skimming off any scum and fruit stones from the surface of the jam.

**Sugar thermometer** This is helpful when testing for a set, see page 457.

**Wide-necked funnel** For filling jars without spilling. Failing this, use a heatproof jug.

**Nylon sieve** A metal one will discolour the fruit.

$J$AM is basically a cooked mixture of fruit and sugar. The high concentration of sugar used in jam making prevents the growth of micro-organisms and allows the jam to be kept for many months.

### CHOOSING FRUIT

Fruit for jam should be sound—poor quality fruit will not have as much flavour—and either just ripe or slightly underripe. The jam will only set if there are sufficient quantities of pectin, acid and sugar present. Some fruits are naturally rich in pectin (see chart below) and give a good set, while others do not contain as much and may need to have it boosted with added pectin. Lemon juice is most often used for this purpose, since it aids the set and often brings out the flavour of the fruit. Allow 30 ml (2 tbsp) lemon juice to 2 kg (4 lb) of a fruit with poor setting properties. Alternatively, you can buy bottled pectin—follow the manufacturer's instructions for how much to use. Sometimes an acid only is added, such as citric or tartaric acid. These contain no pectin but help to extract the natural pectin from the fruit and improve the flavour of fruits lacking in acid. Allow 2.5 ml ($\frac{1}{2}$ level tsp) to 2 kg (4 lb) of a fruit with poor setting properties.

**Homemade pectin extracts** This can be made from sour cooking apples, crab apples or apple peelings, cores and windfalls.

Wash 1 kg (2 lb) fruit and chop roughly without peeling or coring. Cover with 600–900 ml (1–$1\frac{1}{2}$ pints) water and stew gently for about 45 minutes, until well pulped. Strain through a jelly bag or muslin cloth (see page 462), then carry out a pectin test (see opposite) to ensure that there is sufficient pectin present. Allow 150–300 ml ($\frac{1}{4}$–$\frac{1}{2}$ pint) of this extract to 2 kg (4 lb) of fruit which is low in pectin. Pectin extract can also be made using the same method from fresh gooseberries and redcurrants.

### SUGAR

Sugar acts as a preservative in jam and also affects its setting quality. The exact amount of sugar needed depends on the pectin strength of the fruit, so it is essential to use the amount specified in a recipe. Too little sugar produces a poor set and the jam may go mouldy when stored. Too much sugar makes a dark sticky jam, overpowers the fruit flavour and may crystallise.

Granulated sugar is the most economical for jam making although less foamy scum is formed on the surface of the jam when lump or preserving sugar is used. However, these are more expensive and the only real benefit is that the end product is slightly clearer than when granulated sugar is used. Caster sugar can be used, but again is more expensive; brown sugar can also be used but will produce a darker jam and will affect flavour.

You can make your own reduced sugar jams similar to those on the market. Don't reduce sugar content by more than 20 per cent or the jam will be runny. As it doesn't keep well, make it in small batches and store in the refrigerator (up to 6 weeks) or a cool place (3–4 weeks).

### TESTING FOR PECTIN CONTENT

The chart shows the pectin content of fruits and vegetables used in preserving. If you are not sure of your fruit setting qualities, carry out this test.

When the fruit has been cooked until soft, but before you add sugar, take 5 ml (1 tsp) juice, put it in a glass and, when cool, add 15 ml (1 tbsp) methylated spirit. Shake the glass and leave for 1 minute. If the mixture forms a jelly-like clot the fruit has a good pectin content. If it does not form a single firm clot, the pectin content is too low and you will need extra.

## PECTIN CONTENT OF FRUITS AND VEGETABLES USED IN PRESERVING

| Good | Medium | Poor |
|------|--------|------|
| Cooking apples | Apricots | Bananas |
| Crab apples | Bilberries | Cherries |
| Cranberries | Blackberries | Elderberries |
| Currants (red and black) | Cranberries | Figs |
| Damsons | Dessert apples | Grapes |
| Gooseberries | Greengages | Japonica |
| Lemons | Loganberries | Marrows |
| Limes | Mulberries | Medlars |
| Quinces | Plums | Melons |
| Seville oranges | Raspberries | Nectarines |
| | | Peaches |
| | | Pineapples |
| | | Rhubarb |
| | | Strawberries |

## TESTING FOR A SET

Use one of these two methods:

1. The temperature test is the most accurate. Stir the jam and insert a sugar thermometer in the middle of the pan. When the reading is 105°C (221°F) a set should be obtained. Some fruits need a degree lower or higher than this, so it is sensible also to carry out the saucer test. Put a tiny amount of jam on a cold saucer or plate (leave in the refrigerator beforehand), allow it to cool, then push a finger gently through it. If the surface of the jam wrinkles, setting point has been reached. Be sure to remove the pan from the heat while doing the test so that the temperature doesn't rise and the jam become over boiled, which weakens its setting property.

2. The flake test involves lifting some jam from the pan on a wooden spoon, letting it cool a little, then dropping it back. If it has been boiled for long enough, drops of jam will run together along the edge of the spoon and form flakes which will break off sharply.

## POTTING , COVERING AND STORING

As soon as a set has been reached, remove the pan from the heat and with the slotted spoon skim off any scum. Don't pot strawberry and other whole fruit jams immediately or all the fruit will rise to the top. Leave them in the pan for about 15–20 minutes before potting. Spoon the jam into the warm jars, filling them right to the top.

Wipe the outside of the jars with a damp cloth while they are still warm and immediately put wax discs, wax side down, on the surface of the jam, making sure they lie flat. Either cover immediately with a dampened round of cellophane and secure with a rubber band or string, or leave the jam until quite cold before doing this. Label the jars and store in a cool, dry, dark place. Most jams keep well for about a year after which their flavour starts to deteriorate.

## WATCHPOINTS

Problems with jam making can be eliminated if the following simple tips are followed:

- Mould growth usually occurs because the jam has not been covered with a wax disc while still hot. Alternatively, the pots may have been stored in a place where they picked up bacteria and were not cleaned properly. Other possible causes are insufficient evaporation of water while the fruit is being cooked before sugar is added and/or too short a boiling time after the sugar was added. It is important not to eat jam that has mould growth on it as it produces toxins. Throw away the whole jar if you find any mould on the top surface.
- Bubbles in jam indicate fermentation which is usually because not enough sugar has been used or because the jam was not reduced sufficiently. Fermented jam can be boiled up again and repotted but thereafter should only be used for cooking.
- Crystallisation is usually caused by lack of enough acid or by under or over boiling the jam after the sugar has been added.
- Shrinkage of jam in pots is caused by inadequate covering or failure to store the jam in a cool, dark, dry place.

# APRICOT JAM

1.8 kg (4 lb) apricots, washed, halved and stoned

450 ml (¾ pint) water

juice of 1 lemon

1.8 kg (4 lb) sugar

knob of butter

1. Crack a few of the apricot stones with a weight, nutcracker or hammer, take out the kernels and blanch in boiling water for 1 minute.

2. Place the apricots, water, lemon juice and kernels in a preserving pan and simmer for about 15 minutes until they are soft and the contents of the pan are well reduced. Remove from the heat, add the sugar, stirring until dissolved, then add the knob of butter. Return to the heat, bring to the boil and boil rapidly for about 15 minutes, stirring frequently.

3. Test for a set and, when setting point is reached, take the pan off the heat and remove any scum that has accumulated on the surface with a slotted spoon.

4. Leave to stand for 15 minutes. Pot and cover.

*Makes about 3 kg (6½ lb)*

# Dried Apricot Jam

450 g (1 lb) dried apricots

1.7 litres (3 pints) water

juice of 1 lemon

1.4 kg (3 lb) sugar

50 g (2 oz) blanched almonds, split

knob of butter

1.  Put the apricots in a bowl, cover with the water and leave to soak overnight.
2.  Place the apricots in a preserving pan with the soaking water and lemon juice. Simmer for about 30 minutes until soft, stirring from time to time.
3.  Remove the pan from the heat and add the sugar and blanched almonds. Stir until the sugar has dissolved, then add the knob of butter. Bring to the boil and boil rapidly for 20–25 minutes, stirring frequently to prevent sticking.
4.  Test for a set and, when setting point is reached, take the pan off the heat and remove any scum with a slotted spoon.
5.  Leave to stand for 15 minutes. Pot and cover.

*Makes about 2.3 kg (5 lb)*

# Blackcurrant Jam

1.8 kg (4 lb) blackcurrants, washed and strung

1.7 litres (3 pints) water

2.7 kg (6 lb) sugar

knob of butter

1.  Place the fruit in a preserving pan with the water. Simmer gently for about 45 minutes until the fruit is soft and the contents of the pan are well reduced, stirring from time to time to prevent sticking. (As the skins of currants tend to be rather tough, it is important to cook the fruit really well before adding the sugar.)
2.  Remove the pan from the heat, add the sugar to the fruit pulp, stir until dissolved, then add the knob of butter. Bring to the boil and boil rapidly for about 10 minutes, stirring frequently.
3.  Test for a set and, when setting point is reached, take the pan off the heat and remove any scum with a slotted spoon.
4.  Pot and cover.

*Makes about 4.5 kg (10 lb)*

# Blackberry and Apple Jam

1.8 kg (4 lb) blackberries, washed

300 ml ($\frac{1}{2}$ pint) water

700 g (1$\frac{1}{2}$ lb) cooking apples (prepared weight), peeled, cored and sliced

2.7 kg (6 lb) sugar

knob of butter

1.  Place the blackberries in a large saucepan with 150 ml ($\frac{1}{4}$ pint) of the water and simmer gently until soft.
2.  Put the apples in a preserving pan with the remaining 150 ml ($\frac{1}{4}$ pint) water and simmer gently until soft, then pulp with a wooden spoon or a potato masher.
3.  Add the blackberries and sugar to the apple pulp, stirring until the sugar has dissolved, then add the knob of butter. Bring to the boil and boil rapidly, stirring frequently, for about 10 minutes.
4.  Test for a set and, when setting point is reached, take the pan off the heat and remove any scum with a slotted spoon.
5.  Pot and cover.

*Makes about 4.5 kg (10 lb)*

**Variation**

*Plum and Apple Jam*

Put 900 g (2 lb) halved and stoned plums, 900 g (2 lb) peeled, cored and sliced apples and 900 ml (1$\frac{1}{2}$ pints) water in a preserving pan and boil for about 1 hour until the fruit is tender and the contents of the pan have been reduced by half. Remove the pan from the heat and add 1.4 kg (3 lb) sugar, stirring until dissolved, then add a knob of butter and boil rapidly for 10–15 minutes. Test for a set and, when setting point is reached, take the pan off the heat, remove any scum with a slotted spoon, then pot and cover.

*Makes about 2.3 kg (5 lb)*

# WHOLE STRAWBERRY JAM

*1.1 kg (2½ lb) small strawberries, washed and hulled*
*45 ml (3 tbsp) lemon juice*
*1.4 kg (3 lb) sugar*
*knob of butter*
*227 ml (8 fl oz) bottle of commercial pectin*

**1.** Place the strawberries in an aluminium or stainless steel preserving pan with the lemon juice and sugar. Leave to stand for 1 hour, stirring occasionally.
**2.** Heat slowly, stirring, until the sugar has dissolved, then add the knob of butter.
**3.** Bring to the boil and boil rapidly for 4 minutes, stirring occasionally.
**4.** Remove the pan from the heat and stir in the pectin. Leave to stand for at least 20 minutes before potting.
**5.** Pot and cover.
*Makes about 2.3 kg (5 lb)*

*Whole Strawberry Jam*

# STRAWBERRY JAM

*1.6 kg (3½ lb) strawberries, washed and hulled*
*45 ml (3 tbsp) lemon juice*
*1.4 kg (3 lb) sugar*
*knob of butter*

**1.** Place the strawberries in a preserving pan with the lemon juice and simmer gently, stirring occasionally, for 20–30 minutes until really soft.

**2.** Take the pan off the heat, add the sugar, stirring until dissolved, then add the knob of butter. Bring to the boil and boil rapidly for about 20 minutes, stirring frequently.
**3.** Test for a set and, when setting point is reached, take the pan off the heat and remove any scum with a slotted spoon.
**4.** Leave to stand for 15 minutes. Pot and cover.
*Makes about 2.3 kg (5 lb)*

# CHERRY JAM

*1.8 kg (4 lb) cherries, e.g. Morello, stoned*
*juice of 3 lemons*
*1.4 kg (3 lb) sugar*
*knob of butter*
*75 ml (5 tbsp) kirsch (optional)*

**1.** Crack a few of the cherry stones in a nutcracker and remove the kernels.
**2.** Put the cherries, kernels and lemon juice in a pan and simmer very gently for about 45 minutes until really soft, stirring from time to time to prevent sticking.
**3.** Remove from the heat, add the sugar, stirring until dissolved, then add the knob of butter. Bring

to the boil and boil rapidly for about 30 minutes, stirring frequently.
**4.** Test for a set and, when setting point is reached, take the pan off the heat and remove any scum with a slotted spoon. Leave to stand for 15 minutes.
**5.** Stir in the kirsch, if using, then pot and cover.
*Note* Cherry stones are easy to remove with a cherry stoner or the end of a potato peeler, but if you haven't got one, use the cherries with their stones and remove them from the pan with a slotted spoon as they rise to the surface.
   As cherries are lacking in pectin, this jam will give only a light set.
*Makes about 2.3 kg (5 lb)*

## MULBERRY AND APPLE JAM

1.4 kg (3 lb) mulberries, washed

600 ml (1 pint) water

450 g (1 lb) cooking apples (prepared weight), peeled, cored and sliced

1.6 kg (3½ lb) sugar

knob of butter

1. Place the mulberries in a preserving pan with half the water and simmer gently for about 20 minutes, until they are soft and pulpy.
2. Place the apples in a saucepan with the remaining water and simmer gently for about 20 minutes until they are soft and pulpy.
3. Add the apples to the mulberries and stir in the sugar. Continue stirring until the sugar has dissolved, then add the knob of butter. Bring to the boil and boil rapidly for about 10 minutes, stirring frequently.
4. Test for a set and, when setting point is reached, take the pan off the heat and remove any scum with a slotted spoon.
5. Pot and cover.
*Makes about 2.3 kg (5 lb)*

## PEACH JAM

1.8 kg (4 lb) peaches

1 lemon

450 ml (¾ pint) water

1.4 kg (3 lb) sugar

knob of butter

227 ml (8 fl oz) bottle of commercial pectin

1. Skin, stone and chop the peaches, reserving the stones. Halve the lemon and squeeze out the juice.
2. Cut up the lemon peel and tie in a piece of muslin with the peach stones.
3. Put the peaches, lemon juice and muslin bag in a preserving pan with the water. Bring to the boil, then simmer for about 30 minutes, stirring frequently, until the peaches are tender.
4. Remove the muslin bag, squeezing well in a sieve with the back of a wooden spoon.
5. Remove the pan from the heat, add the sugar and stir until dissolved. Add a knob of butter, then bring to the boil and boil rapidly for 5–10 minutes.
6. Remove the pan from the heat, add the pectin.
7. Remove any scum with a slotted spoon and leave to stand for 15 minutes. Pot and cover.
*Note* This jam has only a light set.
*Makes about 2.7 kg (6 lb)*

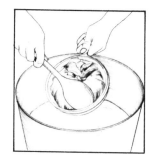

*Press firmly to extract juices from muslin bag.*

## PLUM JAM

2.7 kg (6 lb) plums, washed

900 ml (1½ pints) water

2.7 kg (6 lb) sugar

knob of butter

1. Place the plums and water in a preserving pan and simmer gently for about 30 minutes, until the fruit is really soft and the contents of the pan are well reduced.
2. Remove the pan from the heat, add the sugar, stirring until dissolved, then add the knob of butter. Bring to the boil and boil rapidly for 10–15 minutes, stirring frequently.
3. Test for a set and, when setting point is reached, take the pan off the heat.
4. Using a slotted spoon, remove the stones and any scum from the surface of the jam.
5. Leave to stand for 15 minutes. Pot and cover.
*Makes about 4.5 kg (10 lb)*

**Variations**

GREENGAGE JAM
Follow the above recipe using washed greengages, with stalks removed, instead of plums and only 600 ml (1 pint) water.

DAMSON JAM
Follow the above recipe using only 2.3 kg (5 lb) damsons and, after adding the sugar, boil for 10 minutes only.

# LIGHT SET RASPBERRY JAM

*This jam has only a light set, but has a very good colour and fresh fruit flavour.*

*1.1 kg (2½ lb) raspberries, washed*

*1.4 kg (3 lb) sugar*

**1.** Put the raspberries in a preserving pan and simmer very gently for about 10 minutes until the juice flows, then bring to the boil and boil gently for a further 10 minutes.

**2.** Warm the sugar in a heatproof bowl in the oven and add it to the fruit. Keep stirring until it has dissolved.

**3.** Bring the jam back to the boil and boil for 2 minutes.

**4.** Take the pan off the heat and remove any scum with a slotted spoon.

**5.** Leave to stand for 15 minutes. Pot and cover.

*Makes about 2.3 kg (5 lb)*

# RASPBERRY JAM

*1.8 kg (4 lb) raspberries, washed*

*1.8 kg (4 lb) sugar*

*knob of butter*

**1.** Place the fruit in a preserving pan and simmer very gently in its own juice for about 20 minutes, stirring carefully from time to time, until the fruit is really soft.

**2.** Remove the pan from the heat and add the sugar, stirring until dissolved, then add the knob of butter and boil rapidly for about 30 minutes.

**3.** Test for a set and, when setting point is reached, take the pan off the heat and remove any scum with a slotted spoon.

**4.** Leave to stand for 15 minutes. Pot and cover.

*Makes about 3 kg (6½ lb)*

**Variation**

*LOGANBERRY JAM*

Follow the above recipe, using loganberries instead of raspberries.

# RHUBARB GINGER JAM

*1.1 kg (2½ lb) rhubarb (prepared weight), chopped*

*1.1 kg (2½ lb) sugar*

*juice of 2 lemons*

*25 g (1 oz) root ginger*

*100 g (4 oz) stem or crystallised ginger, chopped*

**1.** Place the rhubarb in a large bowl in alternate layers with the sugar and lemon juice, cover and leave overnight.

**2.** Next day, peel and bruise the root ginger slightly with a weight or rolling pin, and tie it in a piece of muslin. Put the rhubarb mixture in a preserving pan with the muslin bag, bring to the boil and boil rapidly for 15 minutes, stirring frequently.

**3.** Remove the muslin bag, add the stem or crystallised ginger and boil for a further 5 minutes.

**4.** Test for a set and, when setting point is reached, take the pan off the heat and remove any scum with a slotted spoon.

**5.** Pot and cover.

*Makes about 2 kg (4½ lb)*

# GOOSEBERRY JAM

*2.7 kg (6 lb) gooseberries, topped, tailed and washed*

*1.1 litres (2 pints) water*

*2.7 kg (6 lb) sugar*

*knob of butter*

**1.** Place the gooseberries in a preserving pan with the water. Simmer gently, uncovered, for about 30 minutes, until the fruit is really soft and reduced, mashing it to a pulp with a wooden spoon and stirring from time to time.

**2.** Remove from the heat, add the sugar to the fruit pulp and stir until dissolved. Add the knob of butter, bring to the boil and boil rapidly for about 10 minutes, stirring frequently.

**3.** Test for a set and, when setting point is reached, take the pan off the heat and remove any scum with a slotted spoon.

**4.** Pot and cover.

*Makes about 4.5 kg (10 lb)*

## MARROW AND GINGER JAM

| |
|---|
| *1.8 kg (4 lb) marrow (prepared weight)* |
| *1.8 kg (4 lb) sugar* |
| *25 g (1 oz) root ginger, peeled* |
| *thinly peeled rind and juice of 3 lemons* |

**1.** Peel the marrow, remove the seeds and cut into pieces about 1 cm (½ inch) square.
**2.** Place in a basin, sprinkle with about 450 g (1 lb) of the sugar and allow to stand overnight.

**3.** Press the ginger with a weight to release the flavour from the fibres, tie it up in a piece of muslin with the lemon rind and place in a preserving pan with the marrow and lemon juice.
**4.** Simmer for 30 minutes, add the rest of the sugar and boil gently for 15–20 minutes. When setting point is reached and the marrow looks transparent take off the heat and remove scum.
**5.** Remove the muslin bag. Pot and cover.
*Makes about 3 kg (6½ lb)*

## UNCOOKED FREEZER JAM

| |
|---|
| *1.4 kg (3 lb) raspberries or strawberries, washed and hulled* |
| *1.8 kg (4 lb) caster sugar* |
| *60 ml (4 tbsp) lemon juice* |
| *227 ml (8 fl oz) bottle of commercial pectin* |

**1.** Place the fruit in a large bowl and very lightly crush with a fork.
**2.** Stir in the sugar and lemon juice and leave at room temperature, stirring occasionally, for about 1 hour until the sugar has dissolved.

**3.** Gently stir in the pectin and continue stirring for a further 2 minutes.
**4.** Pour the jam into small plastic containers, leaving a little space at the top to allow for expansion.
**5.** Cover and leave at room temperature for a further 24 hours. Label and freeze for up to 6 months.
**6.** To serve, thaw at room temperature for about 1 hour.
*Makes about 3.2 kg (7 lb)*

---

# JELLIES
The difference between jams and jellies is that with jellies only the juice is used in the end product. Jellies are slightly more difficult to make and the yield from the fruit is not as high as with jams, but they are well worth the effort. They can be served with meat, used as a glaze on flans and spread on bread and butter.

### CHOOSING FRUIT
To make a jelly you need fruit with a high pectin content to give a good set (see chart on page 456). Fruit with low pectin should be combined with high pectin ones.

### MAKING JELLIES
Prepare the fruit by washing and chopping; there is no need to peel or core. Don't use damaged fruit.

The amount of water (stated in the recipes) varies according to the water content of the fruit. Hard fruits should always be covered with water. Cooking should be slow and thorough in order to extract as much juice as possible. After 30 minutes to 1 hour, depending on the softness of the fruit, pour the contents of the pan into a scalded jelly bag suspended on a stand or upturned chair or stool. If you do not have a jelly bag, improvise with a double thickness of fine cloth such as a clean tea towel or an all-purpose kitchen cloth. Leave it to drip into a bowl until all the juice is strained off. This may take several hours or overnight if necessary. Do not touch or squeeze the bag while the juices are dripping through or the resulting jelly will be cloudy.

Measure the strained juice and add 450 g (1 lb) sugar for each 600 ml (1 pint) juice extract for pectin rich fruits and 350 g (12 oz) sugar to 600 ml (1 pint) juice for medium pectin fruits.

Stir the sugar into the juice, return to the pan and heat gently, stirring until the sugar dissolves. Boil for about 10 minutes until setting point is reached; test for this in the same way as for jam (see page 457). Remove any scum from the surface with a slotted spoon, then pot and cover as for jam (see page 457).

# MINT AND APPLE JELLY

2.3 kg (5 lb) cooking apples, washed and chopped

1.1 litres (2 pints) water

few fresh mint sprigs

1.1 litres (2 pints) distilled vinegar

sugar

90–120 ml (6–8 tbsp) chopped fresh mint

few drops of green food colouring

1. Place the apples in a large saucepan with the water and mint sprigs. Bring to the boil, then simmer gently for about 45 minutes, until soft and pulpy. Stir from time to time to prevent sticking. Add the vinegar and boil for a further 5 minutes.

2. Spoon the apple pulp into a jelly bag or cloth attached to the legs of an upturned stool, and leave to strain into a large bowl for at least 12 hours.

3. Discard the pulp remaining in the jelly bag. Measure the juice extract and put it in a preserving pan with 450 g (1 lb) sugar for each 600 ml (1 pint) extract. Heat gently, stirring, until the sugar has dissolved, then bring to the boil and boil rapidly for about 10 minutes.

*Strain the juices through a suspended jelly bag.*

4. Test for a set and, when setting point is reached, take the pan off the heat and remove any scum with a slotted spoon.

5. Stir in the mint and add a few drops of green food colouring. Allow to cool slightly, then stir well to distribute the mint.

6. Pot and cover.

**Variation**

HERB JELLIES
Other fresh herbs, such as rosemary, parsley, sage and thyme, can be used to replace the mint.

*Rosemary and Apple Jelly*

# BRAMBLE JELLY

1.8 kg (4 lb) slightly under-ripe blackberries, washed

juice of 2 lemons or 7.5 ml (1½ level tsp) citric or tartaric acid

450 ml (¾ pint) water

sugar

1. Put the blackberries, lemon juice and water into a preserving pan and simmer gently for about 1 hour, until the fruit is really soft and pulpy, stirring from time to time to prevent sticking.

2. Spoon the blackberry pulp into a jelly bag or cloth attached to the legs of an upturned stool and leave to strain into a large bowl for at least 12 hours.

3. Discard the pulp remaining in the jelly bag. Measure the juice extract and return it to the pan with 350 g (12 oz) sugar for each 600 ml (1 pint) extract. Heat gently, stirring, until the sugar has dissolved, then bring to the boil and boil rapidly for about 10 minutes.

4. Test for a set and, when setting point is reached, take the pan off the heat and remove any scum with a slotted spoon.

5. Pot and cover.

# REDCURRANT JELLY

1.4 kg (3 lb) redcurrants, washed

600 ml (1 pint) water

sugar

45 ml (3 tbsp) port (optional)

1. There is no need to remove the currants from their stalks. Place the currants in a preserving pan with the water and simmer gently for about 30 minutes, until the fruit is really soft and pulpy. Stir from time to time to prevent sticking.
2. Spoon the fruit pulp into a jelly bag or cloth attached to the legs of an upturned stool, and leave to strain into a large bowl for at least 12 hours.
3. Discard the pulp remaining in the jelly bag. Measure the juice extract and return it to the pan with 450 g (1 lb) sugar for each 600 ml (1 pint) extract.
4. Heat gently, stirring, until the sugar has dissolved, then bring to the boil and boil rapidly for about 15 minutes.
5. Test for a set and, when setting point is reached, remove the pan from the heat.
6. Stir in the port, then remove any scum with a slotted spoon.
7. Pot and cover.

# ELDERBERRY JELLY

900 g (2 lb) cooking apples, washed

900 g (2 lb) elderberries, washed

sugar

1. Remove any bruised or damaged portions from the apples and roughly chop them without peeling or coring. Place them in a saucepan with just enough water to cover and simmer gently for about 1 hour, until the fruit is very soft and pulpy.
2. Put the elderberries in another saucepan with just enough water to cover and simmer gently for about 1 hour, until the fruit is very soft and tender.
3. Combine the two lots of fruit. Spoon the fruit pulp into a jelly bag or cloth attached to the legs of an upturned stool, and leave to strain into a large bowl for at least 12 hours.
4. Discard the pulp remaining in the jelly bag. Measure the juice extract and put it in a preserving pan with 350 g (12 oz) sugar for each 600 ml (1 pint) extract. Heat gently, stirring, until the sugar has dissolved, then boil rapidly for about 10 minutes.
5. Test for a set and, when setting point is reached, take the pan off the heat and remove any scum with a slotted spoon.
6. Pot and cover.

**Variation**
*BILBERRY JELLY*
If preferred, follow the above recipe, using bilberries instead of elderberries.

# QUINCE JELLY

1.8 kg (4 lb) quinces, washed and roughly chopped

3.4 litres (6 pints) water

grated rind and juice of 3 lemons

sugar

1. Place the fruit in a preserving pan with 2.3 litres (4 pints) of the water and the lemon rind and juice.
2. Cover with foil or a baking sheet and simmer for 1 hour until the fruit is tender. Stir from time to time to prevent sticking.
3. Spoon the fruit pulp into a jelly bag or cloth attached to the legs of an upturned stool, and leave to strain into a large bowl for at least 12 hours.
4. Return the pulp in the jelly bag to the pan and add the remaining water. Bring to the boil, simmer gently for 30 minutes, then strain again through a jelly bag or cloth for at least 12 hours.
5. Discard the pump remaining in the jelly bag. Combine the two lots of juice extract and measure. Return to the pan with 450 g (1 lb) sugar for each 600 ml (1 pint) extract. Heat gently, stirring, until the sugar has dissolved, then bring to the boil and boil rapidly for about 10 minutes.
6. Test for a set and, when setting point is reached, take the pan off the heat and remove any scum with a slotted spoon.
7. Pot and cover.

# MARMALADE is made from citrus fruits. Seville or bitter oranges make the

best marmalades. Sweet oranges give marmalade a rather cloudy appearance and are best used in combination with other citrus fruits (see Three Fruit Marmalade, below).

Make your marmalade in January or February when Seville oranges are on sale or buy the fruit then and freeze it until required. It is advisable to add one-eighth extra weight of Seville or bitter oranges when freezing for subsequent marmalade making in order to offset pectin loss.

### PREPARING THE FRUIT

The peel of citrus fruits is tougher than that of other fruits and needs to be evenly shredded by hand, in the shredder attachment of a food mixer or in a food processor. You can choose the thickness of peel you prefer. To prepare in a food processor, cut the orange peels in half, fit the slicing disc and slice the peel into quarters. Transfer to a bowl. Fit the metal blade and chop batches of the sliced peel, using a pulse action, to the thickness preferred. For a good appearance, a quarter of the peels can be shredded by hand. Do not put peel through a mincer as this produces a paste-like marmalade. If you are making a large quantity and prepare some fruit a day ahead, leave the peel in water to prevent drying out.

Marmalade needs to be cooked for much longer than jams; at least one hour and often two or three.

Therefore larger quantities of water are needed to allow for evaporation.

The first cooking stage extracts the pectin, reduces the contents of the pan by about half and softens the peel. If this is not done properly the marmalade will not set. Much of the pectin in oranges is contained in the pips and membranes and it is essential to extract it all. Put all the pips and any loose membrane in a clean piece of muslin, tie it with string and dangle it in the preserving pan so you can remove it after the first cooking stage and squeeze all the juice from it into the pan.

Add the sugar at the beginning of the second cooking stage and stir until it has dissolved. Boil rapidly for 15–20 minutes until setting point is reached, then test as for jam (see page 457). Remove the pan from the heat, skim off any scum and leave the marmalade to cool for 10–15 minutes. Stir to distribute the peel and pot as for jam (see page 457).

## THREE-FRUIT MARMALADE

| 4 ripe lemons, washed and halved |
| 2 sweet oranges, washed and halved |
| 2 grapefruits, washed |
| 3.4 litres (6 pints) water |
| 2.7 kg (6 lb) sugar |

**1.** Altogether, the fruit should weigh a total of about 1.4 kg (3 lb).
**2.** Squeeze the juice and pips out of the lemons and oranges. Peel the grapefruit and remove any white pith from the flesh.
**3.** Tie the pith and pips from all the fruit in a piece of muslin. Thinly cut the peel of all the fruit and chop the grapefruit flesh roughly.
**4.** Put the peel, flesh, juice, water and muslin bag in a preserving pan. Simmer gently for 1–1½ hours, until the peel is really soft and the contents of the pan are reduced by half.
**5.** Remove the muslin bag from the pan, squeezing well and allowing the juice to run back into the pan.
**6.** Add the sugar and heat gently, stirring, until dissolved, then boil rapidly for 15–20 minutes.
**7.** Test for a set and, when setting point is reached, take the pan off the heat and remove any scum with a slotted spoon. Leave the marmalade to stand for 15 minutes, then stir to distribute the peel.
**8.** Pot and cover.
*Makes about 4.5 kg (10 lb)*

# Seville Orange Marmalade

1.4 kg (3 lb) Seville oranges, washed

juice of 2 lemons

3.4 litres (6 pints) water

2.7 kg (6 lb) sugar

## Method One

1. Halve the oranges and squeeze out the juice and pips. Tie the pips, and any membrane, in muslin.
2. Slice the orange peel and put it in a preserving pan with the fruit juices, water and muslin bag.
3. Simmer gently for about 2 hours until the peel is soft and the liquid reduced by half.
4. Remove the muslin bag.
5. Add the sugar and heat gently, stirring until it has dissolved. Bring to the boil and boil the mixture rapidly for about 15 minutes.
6. Test for a set and, when setting point is reached, take off the heat and remove any scum.
7. Leave to stand for 15 minutes, then stir gently to distribute the peel. Pot and cover.
*Makes about 4.5 kg (10 lb)*

## Method Two *(whole fruit method)*

1. Place the whole washed fruit in a saucepan with the water.
2. Cover and simmer gently for about 2 hours until tender. Remove the fruit from the pan and leave to cool, cut it up, thinly or thickly. Tie the pips in a piece of muslin.
3. Put the muslin bag in the liquid in the pan, add the lemon juice and boil for 5 minutes.
4. Put the fruit in a preserving pan, add the liquid from the saucepan, discarding the muslin bag, and boil off the excess liquid.
5. Add the sugar and heat gently, stirring until it has dissolved, then bring to the boil and boil rapidly for about 15 minutes.
6. Test for a set and, when setting point is reached, take the pan off the heat and remove any scum with a slotted spoon. Leave to stand for about 15 minutes, then stir gently to distribute the peel.
7. Pot and cover.

## Variations

### Dark Chunky Marmalade

Follow the recipe for Seville Orange Marmalade. Cut the peel into thick slices. When the sugar is added, stir until it has dissolved, bring to the boil, then simmer gently for a further 1½ hours until the colour of the marmalade has darkened. Test for a set and, when setting point is reached, take the pan off the heat and remove any scum with a slotted spoon. Stand for 15 minutes. Pot and cover.

### Whisky Marmalade

Follow the recipe for Seville Orange Marmalade. When setting point is reached, take the pan off the heat, remove any scum with a slotted spoon, then stir in 150 ml (¼ pint) whisky. Leave to stand for about 15 minutes, then stir to distribute the peel. Pot and cover.

# Diabetic Marmalade

3 large oranges, washed

3 lemons, washed

1.1 litres (2 pints) water

900 g (2 lb) Sorbitol powder

227 ml (8 fl oz) bottle of commercial pectin

1. Pare the rinds from the oranges and lemons as thinly as possible, using a sharp knife or a potato peeler, and shred the rind very finely.
2. Halve the oranges and lemons and squeeze out the juice and pips. Tie the pips and pith in a piece of muslin.
3. Put the fruit juices, shredded rind, muslin bag and water into a preserving pan. Bring to the boil, then simmer gently for 1–1½ hours, until the peel is tender and pan contents reduced by half.
4. Remove the muslin bag, squeezing out as much juice as possible.
5. Add the Sorbitol powder and stir until it has dissolved, then bring to the boil and boil rapidly for 5 minutes.
6. Remove from the heat and stir in the pectin, then remove any scum with a slotted spoon. Leave to cool for 15 minutes, then stir to distribute peel.
7. Pot and cover.
*Makes about 1.8 kg (4 lb)*
*Note* Small jars are recommended as the marmalade will not keep well once opened. Store in the refrigerator for up to 6 weeks.

*Seville Orange Marmalade*

# ORANGE SHRED MARMALADE

900 g (2 lb) Seville oranges, washed

juice of 2 lemons

2.6 litres (4½ pints) water

1.4 kg (3 lb) sugar

**1.** Peel off enough rind from the oranges, avoiding the pith, to weigh 100 g (4 oz). Cut the rind into thin strips. Cut up the rest of the fruit and simmer it in a covered preserving pan with the lemon juice and 1.4 litres (2½ pints) of the water for about 2 hours, until the fruit is really soft.
**2.** Put the shredded rind in another pan with 600 ml (1 pint) of the water, cover and simmer gently until this also is really soft.
**3.** Drain off the liquid from the shreds and reserve the shreds.
**4.** Pour the contents of the pan into a jelly bag or cloth attached to the legs of an upturned stool and leave to drip into a large bowl for 15 minutes.
**5.** Return the pulp remaining in the jelly bag to the pan with the remaining 600 ml (1 pint) water, simmer for a further 20 minutes, then pour into the jelly bag again and leave to drip for several hours.
**6.** Combine the two lots of extract and test for pectin (see page 456). If the liquid does not clot, reduce it slightly by rapid boiling, then test again. Add the sugar and stir until it has dissolved. Add the reserved orange peel shreds and boil rapidly for about 15 minutes.
**7.** Test for a set and, when setting point is reached, take the pan off the heat and remove any scum with a slotted spoon. Leave the marmalade to stand for about 15 minutes, then stir to distribute the peel.
**8.** Pot and cover.
*Makes about 2.3 kg (5 lb)*

### Variation
LEMON SHRED MARMALADE
Follow the recipe above but substitute 900 g (2 lb) lemons.

# PRESSURE COOKED MARMALADES, JAMS AND JELLIES Provided your cooker is one with a three-pressure gauge, it is a good idea to use it for preserving, as it saves quite a bit of time and the fruit retains its flavour and colour.

### MARMALADES AND JAMS
There are a few points to remember:
1. Always remove the trivet from the pressure pan.
2. Never fill the pan more than half full.
3. Cook the fruit at medium (10 lb) pressure.
4. Reduce pressure at room temperature.
5. Only the preliminary cooking and softening of the fruit must be done under pressure—never cook a preserve under pressure after adding the sugar (and lemon juice, if used), but boil it up in the open pan.
6. You can adapt any ordinary marmalade or jam recipe for use with a pressure cooker by using half the stated amount of water and doing the preliminary cooking of the fruit under pressure. With marmalade, half the required water is added when the fruit is cooked under pressure, the rest being added with the sugar.
*Notes* Soft fruits such as raspberries and strawberries need very little preliminary softening and are therefore not usually cooked in a pressure cooker.

When two or more fruits (e.g. blackberries and apples) are combined, the necessary cooking times may vary somewhat.

### JELLIES
The fruit used for making jellies can also be softened in the pressure cooker and this method is particu-larly useful for fruits which have hard skins, pips and so on.
1. Prepare the fruit according to any ordinary jelly recipe.
2. Place it in the cooker (without the trivet) and add only half the amount of water stated in the recipe.
3. Cook at medium (10 lb) pressure (see chart for the times), then reduce the pressure at room temperature.
4. Mash the fruit well and pour it into the prepared jelly bag. Finish in the ordinary way.

## PRESSURE COOKING TIMES
### MEDIUM (10 lb) PRESSURE

|  | JAM | JELLY |
|---|---|---|
| Apples | 5 | 7 |
| Blackberries and apples combined | 7 | 9 |
| Blackcurrants | 3–4 | 4 |
| Citrus fruits | 20 | 25 |
| Damsons, plums and other stone fruit | 5 | 5 |
| Gooseberries | 3 | 3 |
| Marrow | 1–2 | — |
| Pears (cooking) | 7 | 9 |
| Quinces | 5 | 7 |

Time in minutes

# FRUIT BUTTERS, CHEESES AND CURDS are all traditional country preserves which are usually only made when there is a glut of fruit, as a large quantity of fruit produces only a comparatively small amount of preserve.

### BUTTERS AND CHEESES
Fruit butters are soft and butter-like and can be used like jam. They do not keep very well so make in small quantities and use up fairly quickly.

Cheeses are very thick preserves that are often served as an accompaniment to meat, poultry and game. The preserve is so thick that it can be potted in small moulds or jars and turned out whole when required. Cheeses store much better than butters and, in fact, improve on keeping.

The fruits most commonly used for making fruit butters and cheeses are apples, apricots, blackberries, gooseberries, damsons and medlars.

**Preparation and cooking**
Fruit for butter or cheese making only needs picking over and washing, although larger fruits should be roughly chopped. Put the prepared fruit in a preserving pan or large saucepan with just enough water to cover, and simmer until really soft. Press

the fruit pulp through a nylon sieve, using a wooden spoon so that the fruit does not discolour. Measure the pulp and allow the following amounts of sugar: For butters, allow 225–350 g (8–12 oz) sugar to each 600 ml (1 pint) pulp. For cheeses, allow 350–450 g (12 oz–1 lb) sugar to each 600 ml (1 pint) pulp.

Return the pulp to the pan, add the sugar and stir until dissolved. Boil gently until the required consistency is reached. Stir continuously to prevent the preserve sticking to the bottom of the pan as it cooks and thickens. Butters should be cooked until they are like thick cream. The cooled butter should be thick so it spreads like jam.

**Potting** For butters, prepare jars or small pots and cover as for jam (see page 457).

For cheeses, brush the inside of small, prepared jars (preferably straight-sided) or moulds with oil. This enables the preserve to be turned out. Pour in the cheese, cover as for jam (see page 457) and store for 3–4 months before using.

## CURDS
Made with eggs and butter as well as sugar and fruit, curds are not a true 'preserve' and should only be made in small quantities and eaten quickly. They will keep for up to 2–3 weeks in the refrigerator.

## APPLE CHEESE

*1.4 kg (3 lb) cooking apples, windfalls or crab apples*
  *washed*

*about 1.1 litres (2 pints) water*

*2.5 ml (½ level tsp) ground cinnamon*

*1.25–2.5 ml (¼–½ level tsp) ground cloves*

*sugar*

**1.** Chop the apples without peeling or coring and put them in a large saucepan. Add just enough water to cover and simmer gently for about 1 hour, until the apples are really soft and pulpy.
**2.** Using a wooden spoon, press the apple pulp through a nylon sieve and measure the purée. Return the purée to the pan and add the spices and 450 g (1 lb) sugar for each 600 ml (1 pint) purée.

**3.** Heat gently, stirring, until the sugar has dissolved. Bring to the boil and boil gently, stirring frequently, for 30–45 minutes, until so thick that the wooden spoon leaves a clean line through the mixture when drawn across the bottom of the pan.

*Carefully test thickness with a wooden spoon.*

**4.** Pot and cover, or if preferred, prepare and fill a bowl or several small moulds from which the Apple Cheese can be turned out and served whole.
*Makes about 1.4 kg (3 lb)*

## DAMSON CHEESE

*1.4 kg (3 lb) damsons, washed*

*150–300 ml (¼–½ pint) water*

*sugar*

**1.** Place the fruit and water in a saucepan, cover and simmer gently for 15–20 minutes, until the fruit is really soft. Scoop out the stones with a slotted spoon as they come to the surface.
**2.** Using a wooden spoon, press the fruit pulp through a nylon sieve and measure the purée.
**3.** Return the purée to the pan and add 350 g (12 oz) sugar for each 600 ml (1 pint) purée.
**4.** Heat gently, stirring, until the sugar has dissolved, then bring to the boil and boil gently, stirring frequently, for 30–40 minutes, until so thick that the wooden spoon leaves a clean

line through the mixture when drawn across the bottom of the pan.
**5.** Pot and cover the cheese or, if preferred, prepare and fill a bowl or several small moulds (see above) from which the cheese can be turned out and served whole. Leave to set and cover.
*Makes about 1.4 kg (3 lb)*

**Variations**
GOOSEBERRY CHEESE
Make as above, using 1.4 kg (3 lb) gooseberries and 150 ml (¼ pint) water.

DAMSON AND BLACKBERRY CHEESE
Make as above, using 450 g (1 lb) damsons and 900 g (2 lb) blackberries.

## Lemon Curd

| | |
|---|---|
| *grated rind and juice of 4 medium lemons* | |
| *4 eggs* | |
| *100 g (4 oz) butter* | |
| *350 g (12 oz) caster sugar* | |

**1.** Place all the ingredients in the top of a double saucepan or in a bowl standing over a pan of simmering water.
**2.** Stir until the sugar has dissolved and continue heating gently for about 20 minutes, until the curd thickens.
**3.** Strain into jars and cover.
*Makes about 700 g (1½ lb)*

## Orange Curd

| | |
|---|---|
| *grated rind and juice of 2 large oranges* | |
| *juice of ½ a lemon* | |
| *225 g (8 oz) caster sugar* | |
| *100 g (4 oz) butter* | |
| *3 egg yolks, beaten* | |

**1.** Place all the ingredients in the top of a double saucepan or in a bowl standing over a pan of simmering water.
**2.** Stir until the sugar has dissolved and continue heating gently for about 20 minutes, until the curd thickens.
**3.** Strain into jars and cover.
*Makes about 450 g (1 lb)*

# Fruits in Alcohol and Mincemeats preserve

fruit with the minimum of cooking. Although they do not have the keeping qualities of jams and jellies made by the traditional boiling method, the fruits retain a flavour which is very much closer to the original taste of the fruit. Use the same equipment as for jam making, and cover and store in the same way (see page 457). All these preserves make very acceptable gifts.

## Brandied Peaches

| | |
|---|---|
| *450 g (1 lb) fresh peaches or one 822 g (1 lb 13 oz) can peach halves* | |
| *225 g (8 oz) sugar (if using fresh peaches)* | |
| *about 150 ml (¼ pint) brandy or orange-flavoured liqueur* | |

**1.** If using fresh peaches, skin the peaches by plunging them into boiling water for 30 seconds, then gently peeling off the skins. Halve the peaches and remove the stones.
**2.** Make a light syrup by dissolving 100 g (4 oz) of the sugar in 300 ml (½ pint) water. Add the peaches and poach gently for 4–5 minutes. Remove from the heat, drain and cool, then arrange the fruit in small jars.
**3.** Add the remaining sugar to the reserved syrup and dissolve it slowly. Bring to the boil and boil to 110°C (230°F), then allow to cool. Measure the syrup and add an equal quantity of brandy or liqueur. Pour over the peaches. Cover.

**4.** If using canned peaches, drain the syrup from the peaches and put it in a saucepan (this size can yields about 450 ml (¾ pint) syrup). Reduce the syrup to half the quantity by boiling gently, remove from the heat and cool.
**5.** Prick the peaches with a fine skewer or darning needle and place in small jars.
**6.** Measure the syrup and add an equal quantity of brandy or liqueur and pour over the fruit. Cover and leave for at least 3 months.

**Variations**
*Brandied Cherries*
Follow the above recipe using cherries instead of peaches.
    Use plums or greengages and armagnac instead of brandy.

*Brandied Peaches*

## MINCEMEAT

| |
|---|
| 450 g (1 lb) currants |
| 450 g (1 lb) sultanas |
| 450 g (1 lb) seedless raisins |
| 225 g (8 oz) chopped mixed peel |
| 225 g (8 oz) cooking apples, peeled, cored and grated |
| 100 g (4 oz) blanched almonds, chopped |
| 450 g (1 lb) dark soft brown sugar |
| 175 g (6 oz) shredded suet |
| 5 ml (1 level tsp) grated nutmeg |
| 5 ml (1 level tsp) ground cinnamon |
| grated rind and juice of 1 lemon |
| grated rind and juice of 1 orange |
| 300 ml (½ pint) brandy |

**1.** Place the dried fruits, peel, apples and almonds in a large bowl. Add the sugar, suet, spices, lemon and orange rind and juice and brandy, and mix all the ingredients together thoroughly.

**2.** Cover the mincemeat and leave to stand for 2 days. Stir well and put into jars. Cover. Allow at least 2 weeks to mature before using.

*Note* For mincemeat that will keep well, use a firm, hard type of apple, such as Wellington; a juicy apple, such as Bramley Seedling, may make the mixture too moist.

*Makes about 2.5 kg (5½ lb)*

---

# RUMPOT or *Rumtopf*, as it's called in Germany where it originated, is a delicious concoction of fresh fruit, sugar and rum layered up in a stone or pottery jar.

Rumpots do take a while to mature—they're normally started in early summer and the last fruits are added in the autumn, then left to mature for a month or more.

You'll need a large deep glazed stone or pottery jar with a wide neck and tightly fitting lid; a large glass jar will do.

You'll also need a small plate or saucer which will fit into the jar and can be easily removed with each addition of fruit; plus some cling film or preserving skin such as Porosan to make sure as little air as possible gets into the jar.

Use only fruit that is in perfect condition: just ripe and with no blemishes. Most fruits are suitable, except rhubarb, which tends to give a bitter taste, or apples, which may ferment. Soft fruits like raspberries, loganberries and currants are delicious but they will disintegrate with time, so don't expect them to remain whole when you come to eat the Rumpot; very watery fruits like melons should be kept to a minimum as they dilute the alcohol, which may result in a layer of mould growth or fermentation.

For every 450 g (1 lb) prepared fruit, you'll need 225 g (8 oz) caster sugar.

Thoroughly clean the jar and plate; if possible, sterilise them with a solution of sodium meta-bisulphide, which you can get from chemists and suppliers of home wine making equipment.

Carefully wash the fruit and dry on absorbent kitchen paper. Berry fruits should be hulled; currants, gooseberries and grapes should be removed from their stalks. Skin large-stoned fruits if you like, then halve them and remove the stones.

Spread the first fruit on a plate; sprinkle the sugar over and turn gently so that every part of the fruit is covered. After about an hour, transfer the fruit and sugar to the jar and spread evenly. Pour over enough alcohol to cover completely. Place the plate or saucer on top to keep the fruit submerged, then tightly cover the jar. Store in a cool, dry place until you're ready to add the next fruit. Repeat the process, replacing a clean plate or saucer each time and resealing the jar as before.

When the last batch of fruit has been added, top up with more alcohol, cover and store for at least a month. Add more liquid if necessary.

You may find mould growth in your Rumpot if the fruit is overripe or damaged, or if the container is stored in unsuitable conditions; unfortunately there's nothing you can do but throw out the contents and start again. If fermentation occurs, it's best to boil the contents in a saucepan, cool and then eat as soon as possible.

# CHUTNEYS, RELISHES AND PICKLES

Making chutneys and pickles is a traditional way of preserving fruit and vegetables with vinegar, spices and flavourings. Chutneys are gently cooked for several hours to produce a sweet and sour mixture like chunky jam. With pickles, the ingredients are either brined (soaked in a salt and water solution) and bottled, uncooked, in spiced vinegar or they are gently cooked first.

◆

## CHUTNEYS AND RELISHES differ largely in their finished texture. Chutneys are made from very finely chopped or sliced fruits and/or vegetables which are cooked very slowly to result in a smooth texture and mellow flavour. Relishes have a more chunky texture and are cooked for less time.

Ingredients for chutney are finely chopped, sliced or minced. Bruised and poorly shaped produce can be used as it will not affect the final taste or appearance.

Once mixed with vinegar, sugar, spices and salt, the chutney is simmered very slowly, uncovered, so the liquid evaporates and the mixture forms a pulp. The final consistency should be that of a thick sauce.

For relishes, the ingredients should be cut into chunks and cooked for a fairly short time to retain their shape. It is possible to make some relishes without any cooking.

### EQUIPMENT

**Preserving pan**, enamel-lined, aluminium or stainless steel pans are best. Brass, copper and iron ones tend to impart a metallic flavour. For the same reason, use nylon rather than metal sieves.

**Jars** can have screw tops (the plastic-lined ones used for things like instant coffee are best—it is important that the chutney, relish or pickle does not touch a metal lid, as the acid in the vinegar will cause oxidisation) or be covered with greaseproof paper and a circle of muslin dipped in melted paraffin wax or preserving skin (brand name Porosan).

Chutneys and relishes must be covered carefully to prevent the vinegar evaporating and the finished preserve shrinking.

Before using the jars, wash them well in warm soapy water, then rinse thoroughly in clean warm water. Dry off in a cool oven at 140°C (275°F) mark 1. Use while still hot when potting hot mixtures or the jars might crack.

### STORING

Chutneys should be stored in a cool, dark, dry place and allowed to mature for 2–3 months before eating.

# APPLE CHUTNEY

| 1.4 kg (3 lb) cooking apples, peeled, cored and diced |
| --- |
| 1.4 kg (3 lb) onions, skinned and chopped |
| 450 g (1 lb) sultanas or seedless raisins |
| grated rind and juice of 2 lemons |
| 700 g (1½ lb) demerara sugar |
| 600 ml (1 pint) malt vinegar |

**1.** Put the apples, onions, sultanas, lemon rind and juice, sugar and vinegar in a preserving pan.
**2.** Bring to the boil, then reduce the heat and simmer, uncovered, stirring occasionally, for about 3 hours, until the mixture is of a thick consistency, with no excess liquid remaining.
**3.** Spoon the chutney into prepared jars and cover immediately with airtight and vinegar-proof tops.
*Makes about 2.7 kg (6 lb)*

**Variations**
*SMOOTH APPLE CHUTNEY*
A blender or food processor can be used to produce a smoother texture, if preferred. In this case, bring all the ingredients, except the sultanas or raisins, to the boil and simmer until really soft. Allow to cool slightly, then pour into the blender goblet or processor bowl, a little at a time, and blend until smooth. Return to the saucepan with the sultanas or raisins and cook for a further 15 minutes or until thick. Pot and cover in the usual way.

*GOOSEBERRY CHUTNEY*
Follow the recipe above, replacing the apples with 1.4 kg (3 lb) gooseberries, topped, tailed and washed.

# HOT INDIAN CHUTNEY

| 700 g (1½ lb) cooking apples, peeled, cored and sliced |
| --- |
| 450 g (1 lb) onions, skinned and finely chopped |
| 700 g (1½ lb) soft brown sugar |
| 1.3 litres (2½ pints) malt vinegar |
| 450 g (1 lb) seedless raisins, chopped |
| 4 garlic cloves, skinned and crushed |
| 20 ml (4 level tsp) salt |
| 30 ml (2 level tbsp) ground ginger |
| 45 ml (3 level tbsp) mustard powder |
| 30 ml (2 level tbsp) paprika |
| 15 ml (1 level tbsp) ground coriander |

**1.** Place all the ingredients in a preserving pan.
**2.** Bring to the boil, then reduce the heat and simmer gently for about 3 hours, uncovered, stirring occasionally, until no excess liquid remains and the chutney is thick and pulpy.
**3.** Spoon into prepared jars and cover immediately with airtight and vinegar-proof tops.
*Makes about 2 kg (4½ lb)*

# MARROW AND APPLE CHUTNEY

| 1.8 kg (4 lb) marrow, peeled and chopped |
| --- |
| 75 g (3 oz) salt |
| 900 g (2 lb) cooking apples, peeled, cored and finely chopped |
| 450 g (1 lb) shallots or onions, skinned and chopped |
| 450 g (1 lb) soft brown sugar |
| 1.1 litres (2 pints) distilled vinegar |
| 5 ml (1 level tsp) ground ginger |
| 15 g (½ oz) Pickling Spice (see page 198) |

**1.** Put the marrow pieces into a large bowl in layers with the salt and leave for 12 hours or overnight.
**2.** Next day, rinse the marrow pieces, drain off the water and put them into a preserving pan.
**3.** Add the apples, shallots, sugar, vinegar, ginger and spice. Bring to the boil, then reduce the heat and simmer gently, uncovered, for about 2 hours, stirring from time to time, until the chutney becomes thick with no excess liquid.
**4.** Pour into prepared jars while still warm and cover immediately with airtight and vinegar-proof tops.
*Makes about 2.7 kg (6 lb)*

## PEAR CHUTNEY

| |
|---|
| 1.4 kg (3 lb) pears, peeled, cored and sliced |
| 450 g (1 lb) cooking apples, peeled, cored and chopped |
| 225 g (8 oz) seedless raisins, chopped |
| 225 g (8 oz) sultanas |
| 450 g (1 lb) onions, skinned and chopped |
| 1.1 litres (2 pints) malt vinegar |
| 450 g (1 lb) demerara sugar |
| 1.25 ml (¼ level tsp) cayenne pepper |
| 2.5 ml (½ level tsp) grated nutmeg |
| 10 ml (2 level tsp) salt |

1. Place all the fruit and vegetables in a preserving pan with the vinegar, sugar, spices and salt.
2. Bring to the boil, then reduce the heat and simmer gently, uncovered, stirring occasionally, for about 2½ hours until the mixture is thick and no excess liquid remains.
3. Spoon the chutney into prepared jars and cover immediately with airtight and vinegar-proof tops.
*Makes about 2.3 kg (5 lb)*

## PEACH CHUTNEY

| |
|---|
| 1 small piece root ginger, peeled and bruised |
| 6 ripe peaches, stoned, skinned and sliced |
| 100 g (4 oz) sultanas |
| 2 large onions, skinned and finely chopped |
| 15 ml (1 level tbsp) salt |
| 375 g (12 oz) demerara sugar |
| 300 ml (½ pint) malt vinegar |
| 15 ml (1 level tbsp) mustard seeds |
| grated rind and juice of 1 lemon |

1. Tie the root ginger in a piece of muslin and place in a preserving pan with all the remaining ingredients.
2. Bring to the boil, reduce the heat and simmer, uncovered, for about 1¾ hours, stirring occasionally, until no excess liquid remains and the mixture is thick.
3. Remove the muslin bag. Spoon the chutney into prepared jars and cover immediately with airtight and vinegar-proof tops.
*Makes about 1.1 kg (2½ lb)*

## SWEET MANGO CHUTNEY

| |
|---|
| 1.8 kg (4 lb) yellow mangoes, peeled, stoned and sliced |
| 2 small cooking apples, peeled, cored and chopped |
| 2 medium onions, skinned and chopped |
| 100 g (4 oz) seedless raisins |
| 600 ml (1 pint) distilled vinegar |
| 350 g (12 oz) demerara sugar |
| 15 ml (1 level tbsp) ground ginger |
| 3 garlic cloves, skinned and crushed |
| 5 ml (1 level tsp) grated nutmeg |
| 2.5 ml (½ level tsp) salt |

1. Place all the ingredients in a preserving pan.
2. Bring to the boil, then reduce the heat and simmer gently, uncovered, stirring occasionally, for about 1½ hours, until no excess liquid remains and the mixture is thick and pulpy.
3. Spoon the chutney into prepared jars and cover immediately with airtight and vinegar-proof tops.
*Makes about 2 kg (4½ lb)*

*From the left: Sweet Mango Chutney, Hot Indian Chutney*

## RED TOMATO CHUTNEY

| |
|---|
| 30 ml (2 level tbsp) mustard seeds |
| 15 ml (1 level tbsp) whole allspice |
| 1.8 kg (4 lb) red tomatoes, skinned |
| 5 ml (1 level tsp) cayenne pepper |
| 225 g (8 oz) demerara or granulated sugar |
| 20 ml (4 level tsp) salt |
| 450 ml (¾ pint) distilled vinegar |

1. Tie the mustard seeds and allspice in a piece of muslin and place in a preserving pan with the skinned tomatoes and the cayenne pepper.
2. Simmer gently for about 45 minutes, breaking down the tomatoes with a wooden spoon, until reduced to a pulp.
3. Add the sugar, salt and vinegar. Continue simmering for about 2½ hours, until no excess liquid remains and the mixture is thick.
4. Remove the muslin bag. Spoon into prepared jars and cover immediately with airtight and vinegar-proof tops.
*Makes about 900 g (2 lb)*

## GREEN TOMATO CHUTNEY

| |
|---|
| 4 small pieces of root ginger, bruised |
| 450 g (1 lb) cooking apples, peeled, cored and minced |
| 2 medium onions, skinned and minced |
| 1.4 kg (3 lb) green tomatoes, thinly sliced |
| 225 g (8 oz) sultanas |
| 225 g (8 oz) demerara sugar |
| 10 ml (2 level tsp) salt |
| 450 ml (¾ pint) malt vinegar |
| 2.5 ml (½ level tsp) cayenne pepper |
| 5 ml (1 level tsp) mustard powder |

1. Tie the root ginger in a piece of muslin and place in a preserving pan with all the remaining ingredients.
2. Bring to the boil, then reduce the heat and simmer gently, uncovered, for about 2 hours, stirring occasionally, until the ingredients are tender, reduced to a thick consistency and no excess liquid remains.
3. Remove the muslin bag, spoon the chutney into prepared jars and cover immediately with airtight and vinegar-proof tops.
*Makes about 1.4 kg (3 lb)*

## MUSTARD RELISH

| |
|---|
| 175 g (6 oz) cucumber, finely chopped |
| 1 medium onion, skinned and finely chopped |
| 225 g (8 oz) cauliflower, broken into florets |
| 100 g (4 oz) tomatoes, skinned and roughly chopped |
| 1 medium green pepper, seeded and finely chopped |
| 1 medium red pepper, seeded and finely chopped |
| 225 g (8 oz) fresh gherkins, thickly sliced |
| 25 g (1 oz) salt |
| 15 ml (1 level tbsp) mustard seeds |
| 250 g (9 oz) sugar |
| 30 ml (2 tbsp) flour |
| 2.5 ml (½ level tsp) mustard powder |
| 2.5 ml (½ level tsp) ground turmeric |
| 450 ml (¾ pint) malt vinegar |

1. Place all the vegetables in a large bowl. Dissolve the salt in 1.1 litres (2 pints) water and pour over the vegetables. Cover and leave to stand overnight.
2. Next day, drain and rinse the vegetables well. Mix the mustard seeds, sugar, flour, mustard powder and turmeric together in a large saucepan, then gradually stir in the vinegar. Bring to the boil, stirring. Add the drained vegetables and simmer, uncovered, for 30 minutes. Stir gently from time to time to prevent sticking.
3. Spoon the relish into prepared jars and cover immediately with airtight and vinegar-proof tops.
*Makes about 1.4 kg (3 lb)*

# CUCUMBER AND CELERY RELISH

3 cucumbers

2 large onions, skinned and chopped

4 large celery sticks, trimmed and diced

1 medium green pepper, seeded and diced

30 ml (2 level tbsp) salt

100 g (4 oz) sugar

45 ml (3 level tbsp) mustard powder

75 ml (5 level tbsp) flour

5 ml (1 level tsp) ground turmeric

300 ml (½ pint) cider vinegar

1. Cut the cucumbers into 0.5 cm (¼ inch) cubes and place in a bowl.
2. Add the onions, celery, green pepper and salt to the cucumber and stir. Leave to stand for 30 minutes, then drain.
3. Mix the sugar, mustard, flour and turmeric together in a saucepan, then gradually stir in the cider vinegar.
4. Add the chopped vegetables and cook over a medium heat for about 30 minutes, stirring to prevent burning.
5. Spoon the relish into prepared jars and cover immediately with airtight and vinegar-proof tops.
*Makes about 1.6 kg (3½ lb)*

# TOMATO RELISH

1.4 kg (3 lb) tomatoes, skinned and sliced

450 g (1 lb) cucumber or marrow, peeled, seeded and roughly chopped

50 g (2 oz) salt

2 garlic cloves, skinned and finely chopped

1 large red pepper, seeded and roughly chopped

450 ml (¾ pint) malt vinegar

15 ml (1 level tbsp) mustard powder

2.5 ml (½ level tsp) ground allspice

2.5 ml (½ level tsp) mustard seeds

1. Layer the tomatoes and cucumber in a bowl, sprinkling each layer with salt. Cover and leave overnight.
2. Next day, drain and rinse well and place in a large saucepan. Add the garlic and pepper.
3. Blend the vinegar with the dry ingredients and stir into the pan. Bring slowly to the boil, then reduce the heat and simmer gently, uncovered, for about 1 hour, stirring occasionally, until the mixture is soft.
4. Spoon the relish into prepared jars and cover immediately with airtight and vinegar-proof tops.
*Makes about 1.4 kg (3 lb)*

PICKLES are made by preserving raw or lightly cooked vegetables or fruit in clear spiced vinegar. They can be sweet or sharp or a blend of both and are usually served as accompaniments to cold meats. Only crisp fresh fruits and vegetables should be pickled. The equipment is the same as for chutneys and relishes (see page 473). In addition you will need a large bowl for brining.

### THE RIGHT VINEGAR

Vinegar is used to preserve pickles. You can buy ready-spiced vinegar for pickling or make your own (see page 478). In general, distilled vinegar makes light coloured pickles like onions and cauliflower look more attractive but malt vinegar tends to have a better flavour. Wine vinegar can also be used.

### BRINING

For a sharp-flavoured pickle, the vegetables are usually brined first to remove surplus water as this diluted the vinegar and prevents it acting as a preservative. Table salt is suitable for brining.

Sweet pickles tend to be made of fruit which does not need brining and is usually cooked lightly before pickling so that the surplus moisture evaporates.

**Dry brining** (for cucumber, marrow, tomatoes and red cabbage). Prepare the vegetables according to the recipe and layer them in a bowl with salt, allowing 15 ml (1 level tbsp) to each 450 g (1 lb) vegetables. Cover and leave overnight.

**Wet brining** (for cauliflower, walnuts and onions). Prepare the vegetables according to the recipe and place in a large bowl. Cover with a brine solution made by dissolving 50 g (2 oz) salt in 600 ml (1 pint) water to each 450 g (1 lb) vegetables. Put a plate over the surface to keep the vegetables submerged in the liquid, cover and leave overnight.

### PACKING AND STORING

After dry or wet brining, the vegetables should be rinsed well in cold water, drained, then packed into jars to within 2.5 cm (1 inch) of the top.

Pour over the spiced vinegar, making sure it covers all the vegetables, and add at least 1 cm (½ inch) to allow for evaporation. Leave a little space at the top of the jar to prevent the vinegar coming into contact with the jar lid.

Cover as for chutneys and relishes (see page 473) and store in a cool dry dark place. Allow to mature for 2–3 months before eating. The exception is pickled red cabbage which begins to lose its crispness after 2–3 weeks.

## SPICED VINEGAR

| |
|---|
| 1.1 litres (2 pints) vinegar |
| 30 ml (2 tbsp) blade mace |
| 15 ml (1 tbsp) whole allspice |
| 15 ml (1 tbsp) cloves |
| 2 cinnamon sticks |
| 6 black peppercorns |
| 1 small bay leaf |

1. Place the vinegar, spices and bay leaf in a saucepan, bring to the boil, then allow to cool.
2. Cover to preserve the flavour and leave the vinegar to marinate for about 2 hours.
3. Strain the vinegar through a piece of muslin into a jug, then pour into bottles and seal with airtight and vinegar-proof tops.
*Note* A better result is obtained if the spices stand in unheated vinegar for 1–2 months.

If the individual spices are not available, use 25–50 g (1–2 oz) pickling spice. Different brands of pickling spice will vary considerably; for example, some contain whole chillies, giving a hotter flavour. See page 198 for homemade Pickling Spice.

## SWEET SPICED VINEGAR

| |
|---|
| 1.7 litres (3 pints) vinegar |
| 450 g (1 lb) sugar |
| 7.5 ml (1½ level tsp) salt |
| 5 ml (1 tsp) Mixed Spice (see page 198) |
| 5 ml (1 tsp) black peppercorns |
| 8–10 cloves |

1. Place the vinegar, sugar, salt and spices in a saucepan, bring to the boil, then pour into a bowl.
2. Cover to preserve the flavour and leave to marinate for 2 hours. Strain the vinegar through a piece of muslin into a jug, then pour into bottles and seal with airtight and vinegar-proof tops.

## PICKLED GHERKINS

| |
|---|
| 450 g (1 lb) gherkins |
| 50 g (2 oz) salt |
| 600 ml (1 pint) light malt vinegar |
| 5 ml (1 level tsp) whole allspice |
| 5 ml (1 level tsp) black peppercorns |
| 2 cloves |
| 1 blade of mace |

1. Put the gherkins in a large bowl. Dissolve the salt in 600 ml (1 pint) water and pour the brine solution over the gherkins. Leave to soak for 3 days.

2. Rinse, drain and dry the gherkins well, then pack them carefully in large jars. Pour the vinegar into a saucepan, add the spices and boil for 10 minutes. Pour over the gherkins, cover tightly and leave in a warm place for 24 hours.
3. Strain the vinegar out of the jars into a saucepan, boil it up and pour it over the gherkins again. Cover tightly and leave for another 24 hours.
4. Repeat this process until the gherkins are a good green colour.
5. Finally, pack the gherkins in prepared jars, cover with vinegar, adding more if required, and cover with airtight and vinegar-proof tops.

*From the left: Pickled Gherkins and Pickled Onions*

## PICKLED ONIONS

1.8 kg (4 lb) pickling onions
450 g (1 lb) salt
1.1 litres (2 pints) Spiced Vinegar (see left)

1. Place the onions, without skinning, in a large bowl. Dissolve half the salt in 2.3 litres (4 pints) water, pour the brine over the onions and leave to marinate for 12 hours.
2. Skin the onions, then cover with fresh brine, made with the remaining salt and the same amount of water, and leave for a further 24–36 hours.
3. Drain and rinse the onions well and pack them into jars. Pour the Spiced Vinegar over the onions and cover the jars immediately with airtight and vinegar-proof tops.

## PICKLED RED CABBAGE

about 1.4 kg (3 lb) firm, red cabbage, finely shredded
2 large onions, skinned and sliced
60 ml (4 level tbsp) salt
2.3 litres (4 pints) Spiced Vinegar (see left)
15 ml (1 level tbsp) soft brown sugar

1. Layer the cabbage and onions in a large bowl, sprinkling each layer with salt, then cover and leave overnight.
2. Next day, drain the cabbage and onion thoroughly, rinse off the surplus salt and drain again. Pack into prepared jars.
3. Pour the vinegar into a saucepan and heat gently. Add the sugar and stir until dissolved. Leave to cool, then pour over the cabbage and onion and cover immediately with airtight and vinegar-proof tops.
*Note* Use within 2–3 weeks as the cabbage tends to lose its crispness.

## PICKLED BEETROOT

*beetroot*

*Spiced Vinegar (see page 478)*

1. Weigh the beetroot and wash them carefully, taking care not to damage the skins. Wrap them in foil and bake in the oven at 180°C (350°F) mark 4 for 2–3 hours, depending on size, until tender.
2. Leave the beetroot to cool, then skin and thinly slice them. Pack the slices into jars and cover with cold Spiced Vinegar.
3. Cover the jars immediately with airtight, vinegar-proof tops.

For longer keeping, dice the beetroot, pack loosely, cover with boiling vinegar and seal.

**Variation**
Alternatively, make a brine solution, allowing 50 g (2 oz) salt dissolved in 600 ml (1 pint) water to each 450 g (1 lb) beetroot.
Put the beetroot in a large saucepan, cover with the brine solution and simmer gently for 1½–2 hours, depending on the size, until tender. Cool, skin and slice. Pack into jars and cover as above.

## PICKLED MUSHROOMS

*900 ml (1½ pints) malt vinegar*

*2 shallots, skinned and chopped*

*4 blades of mace*

*few fresh marjoram sprigs*

*5 ml (1 level tsp) ground pepper*

*10 ml (2 level tsp) salt*

*900 g (2 lb) small button mushrooms, wiped*

1. Pour the vinegar into a large saucepan and add the shallots, mace, marjoram and seasoning.
2. Bring to the boil and add the mushrooms. Simmer gently, uncovered, for about 10 minutes, until tender and slightly shrunk.
3. Remove the mushrooms with a slotted spoon and pack into prepared jars. Pour over the hot vinegar and cover immediately with airtight and vinegar-proof tops.

## PICKLED EGGS

*600 ml (1 pint) white wine or cider vinegar*

*6 garlic cloves, skinned*

*25 g (1 oz) Pickling Spice (see page 198)*

*small piece of orange rind*

*1 blade of mace*

*6 fresh eggs, hard-boiled and shelled*

1. Put all the ingredients, except the eggs, in a heavy-based saucepan.
2. Bring to the boil, then reduce the heat, cover and simmer gently for 10 minutes. Leave to cool, then strain some of the spiced vinegar into a large wide-mouthed jar.
3. Put in the eggs and top up the jar with more spiced vinegar.
4. Cover with airtight and vinegar-proof tops and leave for at least 6 weeks before using.

## 'BREAD AND BUTTER' PICKLE

*3 large ridge or smooth-skinned cucumbers, sliced*

*4 large onions, skinned and sliced*

*45 ml (3 level tbsp) salt*

*450 ml (¾ pint) distilled vinegar*

*150 g (5 oz) sugar*

*5 ml (1 level tsp) celery seeds*

*5 ml (1 level tsp) mustard seeds*

1. Layer the cucumber and onion slices in a large bowl, sprinkling each layer with salt. Leave for

1 hour, then drain and rinse well.
2. Put the vinegar, sugar, celery and mustard seed into a saucepan and heat gently, stirring, until the sugar has dissolved, then bring to the boil and cook for 3 minutes.
3. Pack the vegetable slices into prepared jars and add enough hot vinegar mixture to cover.
4. Cover immediately with airtight, vinegar-proof tops.
*Note* This pickle must be stored in a dark place or the cucumber will lose its colour.

# PICCALILLI

2.7 kg (6 lb) mixed marrow, cucumber, beans, small
    onions and cauliflower (prepared weight)

350 g (12 oz) salt

250 g (9 oz) sugar

15 ml (1 level tbsp) mustard powder

7.5 ml (1½ level tsp) ground ginger

2 garlic cloves, skinned and crushed

1.4 litres (2½ pints) distilled vinegar

50 g (2 oz) flour

30 ml (2 level tbsp) ground turmeric

**1.** Seed the marrow and finely dice the marrow
and cucumber. Top, tail and slice the French
beans, skin and halve the onions and break the

cauliflower into individual florets.
**2.** Layer the vegetables in a large bowl, sprinkling
each layer with salt. Add 3.4 litres (6 pints) water,
cover and leave for 24 hours.
**3.** Next day, remove the vegetables, rinse and
drain well.
**4.** Blend the sugar, mustard, ginger and garlic with
1.1 litres (2 pints) of the vinegar in a preserving
pan. Add the vegetables, bring to the boil, reduce
the heat and simmer, uncovered, for 20 minutes,
until the vegetables are cooked but still crisp.
**5.** Blend the flour and turmeric with the
remaining vinegar and stir into the vegetables.
**6.** Bring to the boil and cook for 2 minutes.
Spoon into prepared jars and cover immediately
with airtight and vinegar-proof tops.

# MIXED PICKLE

1.1 kg (2½ lb) mixed cauliflower, cucumber, small
    onions, green or red peppers and French beans
    (prepared weight)

150 g (5 oz) salt

1.4 litres (2½ pints) Spiced Vinegar (see page 478)

**1.** Break the cauliflower into florets, peel and dice
the cucumber, skin the onions, seed and slice the

peppers and top, tail and slice the beans.
**2.** Layer the vegetables in a large bowl, sprinkling
each layer with salt. Add 1.4 litres (2½ pints) water
and leave overnight.
**3.** Next day, rinse the vegetables, drain well and
dry on absorbent kitchen paper.
**4.** Pack the vegetables into jars and cover with
spiced vinegar. Cover the jars immediately with
airtight and vinegar-proof tops.

# PICKLED PLUMS

450 g (1 lb) granulated sugar

thinly pared rind of ½ a lemon

2 cloves

1 small piece root ginger, peeled and bruised

300 ml (½ pint) malt vinegar

900 g (2 lb) plums

**1.** Place all the ingredients, except the plums, in a
saucepan. Heat gently, stirring, until the sugar has
dissolved, then bring to the boil.
**2.** Remove from the heat, leave until cold, then

strain, return to the pan and bring to the boil
again.
**3.** Prick the plums, place them in a deep bowl,
pour over the spiced vinegar, cover and leave for
5 days.
**4.** Strain the vinegar into a saucepan, bring to the
boil and pour over the fruit again. Cover and leave
for another 5 days.
**5.** Strain the vinegar into a pan and bring to the
boil again. Pack the plums into prepared jars,
pour the boiling vinegar over and cover the jars
immediately with airtight and vinegar-proof tops.

# PICKLED DATES

1.3 litres (2½ pints) distilled vinegar

40 g (1½ oz) pickling spices

350 g (12 oz) soft brown sugar

1.4 kg (3 lb) dates, halved and stoned

**1.** Place the vinegar, spices and sugar in a saucepan. Heat gently, stirring, until dissolved, then
boil for 45 minutes until reduced by half.
**2.** Place the dates into prepared jars, pour the hot
syrup over them and leave to cool. Cover the jars
with airtight and vinegar-proof tops.

*Pickled Orange Rings*

## PICKLED ORANGE RINGS

6 firm oranges, washed and sliced into 0.5 cm (¼ inch)
   rounds

900 ml (1½ pints) distilled vinegar

700 g (1½ lb) sugar

20 ml (4 level tsp) ground cloves

7.5 cm (3 inch) cinnamon stick

5 ml (1 level tsp) cloves

**1.** Put the fruit into a large saucepan with just
enough water to cover and simmer gently for
45 minutes, until the rind is really soft.
**2.** Remove the oranges with a slotted spoon

and add the vinegar, sugar, ground cloves and
cinnamon to the juice in the pan. Bring to the boil,
reduce the heat and simmer gently for 10 minutes.
**3.** Return the orange rings to the pan, a few at
a time, and cook gently until the rind becomes
transparent. Using a slotted spoon, lift the orange
rings from the syrup and pack them into prepared
jars.
**4.** Continue to boil the syrup for about
15 minutes until it begins to thicken, then leave to
cool and pour it over the orange rings.
**5.** Add a few cloves to each jar and cover
immediately with airtight and vinegar-proof tops.

## SPICED PEARS

900 g (2 lb) firm eating pears, peeled, cored and
   quartered

450 ml (¾ pint) cider vinegar

450 g (1 lb) sugar

1 cinnamon stick

10 cloves

1 small piece of root ginger

**1.** Place the pears in a saucepan, cover with
boiling water and cook gently for about 5 minutes
until almost tender, then drain.

**2.** Pour the vinegar into a pan and add 300 ml
(½ pint) water, sugar, cinnamon, cloves and root
ginger. Heat gently, stirring, until the sugar has
dissolved, then boil for 5 minutes.
**3.** Add the pears and continue cooking until the
pears are tender.
**4.** Remove the pears with a slotted spoon and
pack into prepared jars. Strain the vinegar syrup
to remove the spices and pour over the pears to
cover.
**5.** Cover the jars immediately with airtight and
vinegar-proof tops.

# BOTTLING AND PRESERVING

Bottling is a process of preserving by sterilisation and an economical way of using windfall fruit or produce which is in season and plentiful. It kills yeasts and moulds already present in the food by heating the jars of fruit in the oven, in a water bath on top of the stove or in a pressure cooker and then sealing the jars when hot.

It is not possible to use bottling as a method of preserving meat, fish, poultry or vegetables in the home. In order to kill the bacteria which can lead to food poisoning, the food must be preserved in acid conditions—which is why most fruits can be bottled successfully—or heated to extremely high temperatures. Heat processing carried out at home, even when using a pressure cooker, is inadequate and cannot ensure that bottled vegetables are free from bacteria. Extra acid needs to be added when bottling tomatoes but almost any type of fruit can be bottled, providing the general rules for preparing and processing are followed. As with any other preserving process, the fruit must be fresh, sound, clean and properly ripe—neither too soft, nor too hard. Choose fruits of a similar shape, size and ripeness for any one bottle.

### BOTTLING JARS

These are wide-necked jars with glass caps or metal discs, secured by screw-bands or clips or a polypropylene screw-band. These all fit the jars. These bands can be used in a pressure cooker but are not really suitable for prolonged heating in the oven. If the cap or disc has no integral rubber gasket, a thin rubber ring is inserted between it and the top of the bottle. Neither the rubber rings nor the metal discs with fitted seals should be used more than once. Jars can be obtained in different sizes ranging from 450 g (1 lb) upwards.

Before use, check all jars and fittings for any flaw and test to make sure they will be airtight. To do this, fill the jars with water, put the fittings in place, then turn them upside-down. Any leak will show in 10 minutes.

Jars must be absolutely clean, so wash them well and rinse in clean hot water. There is no need to dry them—the fruit slips into place more easily if the jar is wet.

### SYRUP FOR BOTTLING

Fruit may be preserved in either syrup or water, but syrup imparts a much better flavour and colour (see recipe on page 486).

### PACKING THE FRUIT

Pack the fruit into the jars in layers so it is firmly wedged in place.

Prepare the fruit according to the chart on page 485. Put the fruit in the jars layer by layer, using a packing spoon or the handle of a wooden spoon to push down the fruit. When a jar is full, the fruit should be firmly and securely wedged in place, without bruising or squashing. The more closely the fruit is packed, the less likely it is to rise after the shrinkage which may occur during processing.

**Normal pack** Most fruit should be packed as above and the jars then filled up with syrup or water before or after processing.

**Tight pack** Fruit such as gooseberries and chopped rhubarb may be packed much more tightly, leaving space for only a very little syrup or water to be added. Fruit packed in this way is best used as a dessert without further cooking. If packed in the normal way, use gooseberries and rhubarb in pies or other made-up dishes which require further cooking.

**Solid pack** Apple slices and tomato halves may be packed so tightly into jars that they need no syrup or water added either before or after processing.

### PROCESSING

Bottles can be sterilised in the oven, in a water bath or in the pressure cooker.

**Oven method** The advantages of the oven method are that jars can be processed at one time and no special equipment is needed. It is, however, not quite so exact as the water bath method, as it is not easy to maintain a constant temperature throughout the oven and it is easier to over-cook the fruit. If you use this method, use only one shelf of the oven, placed just below the centre. Don't crowd too many jars in the oven at one time or the heat will fail to penetrate the fruit evenly.

**Wet pack oven method** Heat the oven to 150°C (300°F) mark 2. Fill the packed jars with boiling syrup or water to within 2.5 cm (1 inch) of the top. Put on the rubber rings and glass caps or metal discs but not screw-bands or clips. Place the jars 5 cm (2 inches) apart in a roasting tin lined with newspaper to catch any liquid which may boil over. Put in the centre of the oven and process for the time stated in the table (see page 488). Remove jars one by one, placing them on a wooden surface, and put on clips or screw-bands, screwing the bands as tightly as possible. Place hot jars on a wooden surface after processing so they do not crack. Leave until cold before testing for a good seal (see page 486).

**Dry pack oven method** Heat the oven to 130°C (250°F) mark ½. Pack the bottling jars with fruit but do not add any liquid. Put on the caps but not rubber rings, discs with rings, screw-bands or clips. Place the jars 5 cm (2 inches) apart on a solid baking sheet lined with newspaper. Put in the centre of the oven and process for the time stated in the table (see page 488). Remove jars one at a time to a wooden surface. Fill up at once with boiling syrup.

When the jars have been filled with syrup, give each one a quick, vigorous twist to remove as many air bubbles as possible. Fill the jars to the brim before putting on the fittings. Place the rubber bands (dipped first in boiling water), caps or metal discs in position and secure with clips or screw the bands on tightly. Leave to cool.

The dry pack oven method is not recommended for fruits which discolour in the air, for light stone fruit and citrus fruit.

**Water bath method** The water bath method is a more exact method of sterilisation, but needs special equipment—a large vessel about 5 cm (2 inches) deeper than the height of the bottling jars, a sugar thermometer and bottling tongs. The vessel can be a very large saucepan, a zinc bath or a zinc bucket; it must have a false bottom such as a metal grid, or even a folded coarse cloth.

**Slow water bath** Pack the jars with fruit, then fill up with cold syrup. Put the rubber bands and glass caps or metal discs and screw-bands or clips in place, then turn the screw-bands back a quarter-turn. Place the jars in the large vessel and cover with cold water, immersing them completely if possible, but at least up to the necks. Heat gently on top of the cooker, checking the temperature of the water regularly. Raise the temperature gradually from cold to 54°C (130°F) in 1 hour, then to the processing temperature given in the chart (see page 487) within a further 30 minutes. Maintain the temperature for the length of time in the chart.

Remove the jars and place on a wooden surface. Tighten the screw-bands immediately. When cool, test for a seal.

**Quick water bath** Fill the packed jars with hot (not boiling) syrup, cover and place in the vessel of warm water. Bring the water to simmering point in 25–30 minutes, and keep simmering for the time stated in the table (see page 487).

### PULPED FRUIT

Soft and stone fruits can be bottled as pulp. Prepare as for stewing, then add only the minimum of water and stew until just cooked. Soak the rubber bands, glass caps or metal clips in boiling water. If desired, the fruit can be sieved at this point and then reheated to boiling point. While still boiling, pour into hot jars and place the rubber bands and glass caps or metal discs and screw-bands in position.

Immerse the jars in a deep pan and add hot water up to the necks. Raise the temperature to boiling point and maintain for 5 minutes. Remove the jars and allow to cool.

## Preparing Fruit for Bottling

| FRUIT | PREPARATION |
| --- | --- |
| Apples | *Normal pack*   Peel, core and cut into thick slices or rings; during preparation put into a brine solution made with 15 g ($\frac{1}{2}$ oz) salt to 1.1 litres (2 pints) water. Rinse quickly in cold water before packing into jars.<br>*Solid pack*   Prepare slices as above, remove from brine and dip in small quantities in boiling water for $1\frac{1}{2}$–3 minutes, until the fruit is just tender and pliable. Pack as tightly as possible into the jars. |
| Apricots | *Whole*   Remove stalks and wash fruit.<br>*Halves*   Make a cut round each fruit up to the stone, twist the two halves apart and remove the stone. Crack some stones to obtain the kernels and include with the fruit. Pack quickly, to prevent browning. |
| Blackberries | Pick over, removing damaged fruits, and wash carefully. |
| Blackberries with apples | Prepare apples as for solid pack (see Apples) before mixing with the blackberries. |
| Blackcurrants | String, pick over and wash. |
| Cherries | *Whole*   Remove stalks and wash fruit.<br>*Stoned*   Use a cherry stoner or small knife to remove stones. Collect any juice and include with the fruit. If liked, add 7 g ($\frac{1}{4}$ oz) citric acid to each 4.5 litres (1 gallon) syrup (with either black or white cherries), to improve the colour and flavour. |
| Damsons | Remove stems and wash fruit. |
| Gooseberries | Small green fruit are used for pies and made-up dishes; larger softer ones are served as stewed fruit. Top, tail and wash. To prevent shrivelling if fruit is preserved in syrup, the skins can be pricked. |
| Mulberries | Pick over, handling fruit carefully. Try to avoid washing it. |
| Peaches | Immerse the fruit in a saucepan of boiling water for 30 seconds, then rinse in cold water and peel off the skin. Peaches can be bottled whole but are more usually cut in half (see Apricots). Bottle quickly before fruit discolours. |
| Pears (dessert) | Peel, halve, remove cores with a teaspoon. During preparation, keep in a solution of 15 g ($\frac{1}{2}$ oz) salt and 7 g ($\frac{1}{4}$ oz) citric acid per 1.1 litres (2 pints) water. Rinse quickly in cold water before packing. Add 1.25 ml ($\frac{1}{4}$ level tsp) citric acid or 15 ml (1 tbsp) lemon juice to each 450 g (1 lb) jar. |
| Pears (cooking) | As these are very hard, prepare as for dessert pears but, before packing, stew gently in a sugar syrup—100–175 g (4–6 oz) sugar to 600 ml (1 pint) water—until just soft. Add 1.25 ml ($\frac{1}{4}$ level tsp) citric acid or 15 ml (1 tbsp) lemon juice to each 450 g (1 lb) jar. |
| Pineapple | Peel, trim off leaves, remove central core and as many 'eyes' as possible. Cut into rings or chunks. |
| Plums and Greengages | *Whole*   Remove stalks and wash fruit.<br>*Halves*   Make a cut round the middle of each fruit to the stone, twist the halves and remove the stone. Crack some stones to obtain the kernels and include with the fruit. |
| Quinces | Prepare as for pears. Always pack into small jars, as they are usually used in small quantities only, e.g. as flavouring in apple dishes. |
| Raspberries/Loganberries | Remove the hulls and pick over the fruit. Avoid washing if possible. |
| Redcurrants | String, pick over and wash. |
| Rhubarb | The thicker sticks are generally used for made-up dishes; the more delicate, forced rhubarb is used as stewed fruit. Cut rhubarb into 5 cm (2 inch) lengths. To make it pack more economically and taste sweeter when bottled, it may be soaked first; pour hot syrup over and leave overnight. Pack rhubarb in jars and use the syrup to top up the jars. |
| Strawberries | These do not bottle well. |

*Freshly bottled gooseberries, apricots and cherries*

### PRESSURE COOKER METHOD

This method shortens the time and also ensures that the temperature is controlled exactly. The cooker must have a low (5 lb) pressure control. Any pressure cooker will take the 450 g (1 lb) bottling jars, but you will need a cooker with a domed lid when using larger bottling jars.

Prepare the fruit as for ordinary bottling, but look at the additional notes in the chart opposite. Pack the fruit into clean, warm jars, filling them right to the top. Cover with boiling syrup or water to within 2.5 cm (1 inch) of the top of the jars. Put on the rubber bands, glass caps or metal discs, clips or orange screw-bands, screwing these tight, then turning them back a quarter-turn. Next, as an extra

precaution, heat the jars by standing them in a bowl of boiling water.

Put the inverted trivet into the pressure cooker and add 900 ml (1½ pints) water, plus 15 ml (1 tbsp) vinegar to prevent the pan from becoming stained. Bring the water to the boil. Pack the bottles into the cooker, making sure they do not touch by packing newspaper between. Fix the lid in place, put on the heat without the weight and heat until steam comes steadily from the vent. Put on the low (5 lb) pressure control and bring to pressure on a medium heat. Reduce the heat and maintain the pressure for the time given in the chart (see right). Any change in the pressure will cause liquid to be lost and under-processing may be the unfortunate result.

Remove the pan carefully and reduce the pressure at room temperature for about 10 minutes. Place the jars one by one on a wooden surface and tighten the screw-bands. When cool, test for a seal.

### TESTING FOR A GOOD SEAL

Test for correct seal by removing the screw-band or clip and trying to lift the jar by the cap or disc. If this holds firm, it shows that a vacuum has been formed as the jar cooled and it is hermetically sealed. If the cap or disc comes off, there is probably a flaw in the rim of the jar or on the cap. If, however, several bottles are unsealed, the processing procedure may have been faulty. Use the fruit from the jars at once; it can be re-processed but the result is loss of quality.

### STORING

Store bottled fruits without clips or screw-bands as this can stretch them. If you do leave screw-bands on, smear each one with a little oil and screw on loosely. This prevents rust and makes for ease of opening later. Store the bottled fruit in a cool, dark place.

## SUGAR SYRUP

*225 g (8 oz) sugar*

*600 ml (1 pint) water*

Dissolve the sugar in half the water. Bring to the boil for 1 minute, then add the remaining water. (This method cuts the time required for the syrup to cool.) If the syrup is to be used while still boiling, keep a lid on the pan to prevent evaporation, which would alter the strength.

Finely pared lemon and orange rind, fruit liqueurs or whole spices can be added to the syrup if liked.

Honey or brown sugar may be substituted for granulated sugar, though brown sugar will turn the syrup brown. Golden syrup may also be used. In this case, put the syrup and water into a pan, bring to the boil and simmer for 5 minutes before using the syrup. The flavour will, of course, be different.

## Processing Times for Pressure Cooker Method

Prepare the fruit as for ordinary fruit bottling, unless otherwise stated. Bring to pressure and process for the time given in the chart.

| Fruit | Processing time in minutes at low (5 lb) pressure | Fruit | Processing time in minutes at low (5 lb) pressure |
|---|---|---|---|
| Apples (quartered) | 1 | Plums or apricots (stoned and halved) | 1 |
| Apricots or plums (whole) | 1 | | |
| Blackberries | 1 | Rhubarb (in 5 cm (2 inch) lengths) | 1 |
| Loganberries | 1 | Strawberries | Not recommended |
| Raspberries | 1 | Soft fruit, solid pack: put the fruit in a large bowl, cover with boiling syrup—175 g (6 oz) sugar to 600 ml (1 pint) water—and leave overnight. Drain, pack jars and cover with same boiling syrup. Process as usual. | 1 |
| Cherries | 1 | | |
| Currants (red and black) | 1 | | |
| Damsons | 1 | | |
| Gooseberries | 1 | | |
| Pears, eating | 5 | | |
| Pears, cooking (very hard ones can be pressure-cooked for 3–5 minutes before packing in jars). Add 1.25 ml ($\frac{1}{4}$ level tsp) citric acid or 15 ml (1 tbsp) lemon juice to each 450 g (1 lb) fruit. | 5 | Pulped fruit, e.g. apples: prepare as for stewing. Pressure cook with 150 ml ($\frac{1}{4}$ pint) water at high (15 lb) pressure for 2–3 minutes, then sieve. While still hot, fill jars and process. | 1 |

## Temperatures and Processing Times for Water Bath Method

These are the temperatures and processing methods recommended by Long Ashton Research Station.

| TYPE OF FRUIT | SLOW METHOD | QUICK METHOD |
|---|---|---|
| | Raise from cold in 90 minutes; maintain as below | Raise from warm to simmering in 25–30 minutes; maintain for: |
| **Soft fruit, normal pack:** Blackberries, currants, loganberries, mulberries, raspberries; Gooseberries and rhubarb (for made-up dishes); Apples, sliced | 74°C (165°F) for 10 minutes | 2 minutes |
| **Soft fruit, tight pack:** As above, including gooseberries and rhubarb (for stewed fruit) **Stone fruit, whole:** Apricots, cherries, damsons, greengages, plums and quinces | 82°C (180°F) for 15 minutes | 10 minutes |
| Apples, solid pack; Apricots, halved; Nectarines; Peaches; Pineapples; Plums, halved | 82°C (180°F) for 15 minutes | 20 minutes |
| Figs Pears: Add 1.25 ml ($\frac{1}{4}$ level tsp) citric acid or 15 ml (1 tbsp) lemon juice to each 450 g (1 lb) fruit | 88°C (190°F) for 30 minutes | 40 minutes |

## Temperatures and Processing Times for Oven Method

These are the temperatures and processing times recommended by the Long Ashton Research Station.

| TYPE OF FRUIT | WET PACK | | DRY PACK | |
|---|---|---|---|---|
| | Preheat oven to 150°C (300°F) mark 1. Process time varies with quantity in oven, as below. | | Preheat oven to 130°C (250°F) mark $\frac{1}{2}$. Process time varies with quantity in oven, as below. | |
| | Quantity | Time | Quantity | Time |
| **Soft fruit, normal pack:** | | | | |
| Blackberries, currants, loganberries, mulberries, raspberries; | 450 g–1.8 kg (1–4 lb) | 30–40 minutes | 450 g–1.8 kg (1–4 lb) | 45–55 minutes |
| | 2.3–4.5 kg (5–10 lb) | 45–60 minutes | 2.3–4.5 kg (5–10 lb) | 60–75 minutes |
| Gooseberries and rhubarb (for made-up dishes); | As above | As above | As above | As above |
| Apples, sliced | 450 g–1.8 kg (1–4 lb) | 30–40 minutes | Not recommended | |
| | 2.3–4.5 kg (5–10 lb) | 45–60 minutes | | |
| **Soft fruit, tight pack:** | | | | |
| As above, including Gooseberries and rhubarb (for stewed fruit) | 450 g–1.8 kg (1–4 lb) | 40–50 minutes | 450 g–1.8 kg (1–4 lb) | 55–70 minutes |
| | 2.3–4.5 kg (5–10 lb) | 55–70 minutes | 2.3–4.5 kg (5–10 lb) | 75–90 minutes |
| **Stone fruit, dark, whole**: Cherries, damsons, plums | As soft fruit (tight pack) | | As soft fruit (tight pack) | |
| **Stone fruit, light, whole:** Apricots, cherries, greengages, plums, quinces | As above | | Not recommended | |
| Apples, solid pack; Apricots, halved; Nectarines; Peaches; Pineapples; Plums, halved | 450 g–1.8 kg (1–4 lb) | 50–60 minutes | Not recommended | |
| | 2.3–4.5 kg (5–10 lb) | 65–80 minutes | | |
| Figs | 450 g–1.8 kg (1–4 lb) | 60–70 minutes | 450 g–1.8 kg (1–4 lb) | 80–100 minutes |
| | 2.3–4.5 kg (5–10 lb) | 75–90 minutes | 2.3–4.5 kg (5–10 lb) | 105–125 minutes |
| Pears: Add 1.25 ml ($\frac{1}{4}$ level tsp) citric acid or 15 ml (1 tbsp) lemon juice to each 450 g (1 lb) fruit | As Figs | | Not recommended | |

**When the seal fails** Check the neck of the jar for chips, cracks or other faults. Inspect the sealing disc to make sure that there are no faults or irregularities in the metal or the rubber rim. The instructions for each method of sterilising must be followed exactly—it is very important to tighten tops at once. If the seal fails, use at once.

**When fruit rises in the jar** This does not affect the keeping qualities, but it does spoil the appearance. It is due to over-processing, too high temperature, loose packing, over-ripe fruit or too heavy syrup.

**When mould appears or fermentation takes place** These are caused by poor-quality fruit, insufficien sterilising or a badly sealed bottle. Do not eat.

**When fruit darkens** If only the top pieces are attacked, it can be due to their not being fully covered by liquid or to under-processing. If dark ened throughout, this is probably due to using poor produce, to over-processing or failure to store in a cool, dark place. Do not eat the fruit.

# OTHER PRESERVING METHODS Curing, smoking, salting,
drying and storing are the original preservation methods. Except storing, they are all types of dry preserving—for without moisture, micro-organisms cannot grow and eventually spoil foods. Storing vegetables and fruits under certain conditions enables them to be kept fresh for longer. Salting, storing and drying processes are economical and simple.

## CURING

Curing is the method of salting and smoking fish or meat to preserve it. This method of preserving is not often carried out at home as few people now have the time or opportunity. The raw materials can be expensive and commercially cured foods are more convenient and safer to eat. Curing is therefore not recommended as a method of home preserving.

### SMOKING

Smoking is the method of preserving meat and fish by drying them in the smoke of a wood fire. The flavour of the food depends on the type of wood used—oak, beech and juniper, for example, all give their own special flavour. Some old houses had chimneys specially constructed for smoking and in others a special outhouse was used.

A type of home smoker is now on the market and is particularly suitable for fish, poultry, cheese, sausage and meat. Food smoked in this way is for immediate consumption and not for preservation.

### SALTING

This method of preserving fish and meat dates back to Roman times. It was widely used until the advent of refrigeration. For best results at home, salting is limited to certain fish, vegetables and nuts. Choose rock, kitchen or block, or sea salt; kitchen or block salt is cheaper and perfectly adequate. Do not use free-running table salt.

## SALTING BEANS

*450 g (1 lb) kitchen salt for each 1.4 kg (3 lb) French or runner beans*

Choose small, young, fresh and tender French or runner beans; it isn't worth preserving old, stringy ones. Cut off the stalks, wash and string if necessary. French beans can be left whole, but runner beans should be sliced.

Place a layer of salt in a glass or stoneware jar, then a layer of beans. Fill the jar with alternate layers, pressing the beans down well and finishing with a layer of salt. Cover with a moisture-proof covering—cork or plastic material—and tie tightly. Leave for a few days to allow a strong brine solution to form. The beans will shrink considerably as the salt draws out the moisture from them, and so the jars can be filled up with more layers of beans and salt—always finishing with salt. Store in a cool, dry, dark place. Use within 6 months.

To cook, remove some beans from the jar. (Put a layer of salt on top of the remaining beans and re-cover the jar.) Wash thoroughly several times in cold water, then soak for 2 hours in warm water. Cook as for fresh beans, but in boiling *unsalted* water, until tender. Drain and serve in the usual way.

## DRYING

Some foods, such as apples, pears, plums, mushrooms, herbs and onions, are more suitable than others for drying and can be dried at home using basic kitchen equipment.

Select good quality fruit that is just ripe. Avoid any with blemishes or bruises.

In the home, any source of heat can be utilised for drying, providing it is applied with ventilation. Unfortunately the average oven does not have a low enough temperature setting to dry foods slowly and instead tends to bake and shrivel the food. However, the heat left in the oven after cooking can be used to dry food. A warm airing cupboard or the area over a central heating boiler is ideal because there is a continuous supply of gentle heat and the air can circulate freely. The prepared food should be placed on a wire rack or cooling tray during the drying process.

## DRYING FRUIT

**Apples and pears** Prepare by peeling and coring. Slice apples into rings about 0.5 cm (¼ inch) thick, and cut pears in half or into quarters using a stainless steel knife. Put the prepared fruit in a solution of 50 g (2 oz) salt to 4.5 litres (1 gallon) water, to prevent discoloration. Leave them in the solution for 5 minutes, then dry on a clean tea-cloth.

Spread the fruit on baking sheets or trays, or thread rings of fruit on thin sticks and place across a roasting tin. Dry in a cooling oven (oven with heat turned off), in an airing cupboard or over a central heating boiler until leathery in texture. This will take 6–8 hours. When dried, remove the fruit from the heat and allow to cool. Pack into jars, tins, or paper-lined boxes—they should not be airtight containers—and store in a cool, dry, well-ventilated place.

**Plums and apricots** For best results, cut the fruit in half and remove the stones, although smaller fruit can be dried whole. Wash the fruit, dry carefully and arrange, cut sides up, on trays or baking sheets. Dry as for apples and pears.

**To cook dried fruit** Soak in cold water overnight or for several hours before use. Drain the fruit well before using for stewed fruit or in puddings and pies.

## DRYING VEGETABLES

**Mushrooms** Wipe with a damp cloth; do not wash. Leave whole or cut into slices or quarters. Dry as for apples. Add dried mushrooms to soups, stews and casseroles. Soak dried mushrooms in just enough water to cover for 30 minutes before frying or grilling.

**Onions** Remove the skins and cut into 0.5 cm (¼ inch) slices. Separate into rings and dip each ring into boiling water for 30 seconds. Drain, dry and spread on trays or thread on to thin sticks. Dry as for apples. Soak dried onions in hot water for 30 minutes, then drain and dry on absorbent kitchen paper before frying or grilling.

## DRYING HERBS

Herbs should be picked on a dry day, when the dew has lifted, before the sun dispels the volatile oils. The best time is shortly before they flower—usually June or July—when they contain the maximum amount of oil. Pick off any damaged leaves and rinse quickly in cold water.

Herbs can be dried in the sun over a period of 4–5 days. However, this method tends to result in loss of the colour and aromatic properties of some herbs. It is much quicker and better to dry them in an airing cupboard or the oven on the lowest possible setting, both with the door left slightly ajar to allow air to circulate. Place the herbs on wire racks covered with muslin or cheesecloth which lets the air through. Herbs will dry in an airing cupboard in 3–5 days or in the oven in 2–3 hours. Turn the herbs gently from time to time to ensure quicker, more even drying.

Herbs can also be dried very successfully in a microwave oven. Place the herbs on absorbent kitchen paper, in a single layer, and cook on high for 2–3 minutes, depending on the quantity. When cool, crumble between your fingers and store.

Herbs are dry when the stem and leaves become brittle but remain green and will crumble easily when rubbed between the fingers. If you are not quite sure about this, check by putting the dried herbs into a glass jar, cover it and watch for a few days to see if moisture appears. If it does, turn them out and continue the drying process. If the leaves turn brown you know that they have been over-dried and are of no further use.

It is also possible to dry herbs by hanging bunches in a dry place for about 2 weeks. Pick the stems as long as possible, tie them loosely in small bunches and suspend them out of direct sunlight. If this is difficult, place them in brown paper bags and hang them up. After three days check the herbs at regular intervals until they are dry.

Once dried, you can strip the leaves from the stems and crumble them for storage. Don't rub so hard that they turn to dust as some of the flavouring properties will be lost. The exception are bay leaves which should be left whole as they contain large amounts of oil and, if crushed, they will release it before it is required. Store dried herbs in small screw-topped jars. Dried herbs can be dipped in boiling water for 1 minute to bring back their colour.

## STORING

There are various methods and techniques of storing some root vegetables, hard fruits and nuts to keep them in good condition. (Green vegetables and soft fruits do not store well.) The ideal storage area should be cool, moist and dark. A cellar, shed or outbuilding with an earth, brick or concrete floor is ideal. It must be well ventilated and protected from frost and mice. It may be necessary to dampen the floor to keep the atmosphere moist. If kept in a warm, dry atmosphere—such as an upstairs room—the fruit and vegetables will quickly shrivel and dry up.

# SWEETS

Sweet making at home is fun and the sweets make very attractive presents. The sweets in this chapter range from simple uncooked peppermint creams, which can be made by children with a little supervision, to more complicated fudges and toffees, requiring undivided attention and patience, as well as a certain amount of special equipment.

◆

## EQUIPMENT

**Sugar boiling thermometer** This is the only really accurate way of measuring the temperature of the liquid when making cooked sweets and can mean the difference between success and failure. Accurate measurement is imperative with some sweets to get the right consistency so be sure to have one you can clearly read.

Buy one which is easy to read and graduates from 16°C (60°F) to 182°C (360°F) or 232°C (450°F). These thermometers are usually mounted on brass with a brass or wooden handle. Some have a sliding clip so that they can be fixed to the edge of the pan.

A new thermometer should be seasoned by placing in cold water, bringing the pan to the boil and leaving it in the water to cool. Check what it reads when the water is boiling to see if it is accurate. It should read 100°C (212°F).

When using a thermometer, shake it well first and be sure that the bulb is completely immersed in the mixture. Always read a thermometer at eye level.

It is important to warm a sugar thermometer before dipping it in the hot liquid (if you put it straight in the tube could burst). While you are not using it, stand the thermometer in a mug of hot water. Once you have finished measuring, clean the thermometer very thoroughly as any sugar crystals left on it could spoil the next batch of sweets.

**Saucepan** Should be strong and thick based to prevent burning and sticking. Non-stick pans are not suitable as the high temperatures reached may damage the lining. Good materials are cast aluminium, stainless steel, copper and brass.

**Spatula** Should be made of wood. It is for working fondant mixtures and beating fudges.

*From the left: sugar thermometer, cherry stoner, slotted and long-handled spoons, funnel, nylon sieve, cellophane covers and rubber bands.*

**Flexible blade palette knife** Should have a stainless steel blade. It is used for lifting and shaping sweets.

**Scissors** Strong kitchen scissors are useful for cutting toffee and jellies.

**Cutters** Little shaped cutters make it easy to cut fondants, marzipans and other soft mixtures.

**Working surface** A marble slab gives the best results for turning toffees and other boiled mixtures, but is expensive to buy new. If you make a lot of sweets (and pastry for which a marble slab is also good) look for stonemasons' offcuts or a piece from an old washstand or table.

Alternatively, an enamelled surface will produce a good result, or you can use a heavy wooden chopping board as long as it is dampened or well greased before use. Some laminated surfaces can be used but check with the maker that they can withstand temperatures of up to 138°C (290°F).

### SPECIALIST EQUIPMENT

**Rubber fondant mat** This consists of a sheet of rubber about 2.5 cm (1 inch) thick with shaped impressions into which you run liquid fondant, jelly or chocolate. When it is set, you can 'pop' the shapes out like ice cubes by bending the rubber.
**Cream rings** Useful for moulding peppermint creams and other round sweets.
**Dipping forks** Small forks with two or three wire prongs or a loop at the end. Use them for lifting sweets out of coating fondant or chocolate. The prongs or loop can also be used for making raised designs on the top of sweets.

**Caramel bars** Used for toffee and caramel making. They are small bar-shaped moulds that can be adjusted to give the exact size and thickness required.
**Caramel markers** Different sizes of squares that are used to mark toffees and fudges before they set. The marked divisions make it easy to break the mixture into individual sweets.
**Fondant funnels** Specially designed funnels with a plunger which controls the flow of liquid and make it easy to fill small moulds. An ordinary metal funnel with a small spout may be used instead.
**Modelling tools** In wood or strong plastic with shaped heads. Used for shaping and marking marzipan and fondant sweets.
**Moulds** Come in a wide range of shapes and sizes for making all kinds of sweets from Easter eggs to liqueur chocolates. Available metal, flexible or rigid plastic or rubber and give very professional looking results.
**Tins** Square or rectangular tins between 2 and 4 cm ($\frac{3}{4}$ and 1 inch) deep are useful for setting fudges, caramel and toffees. Those with non-stick linings are easiest to work with.

## SUGAR BOILING

Sugar boiling is the basis of nearly all sweet making. The sugar is first dissolved in the liquid, then brought to the boil, 100°C (212°F). The temperature continues to rise as the water evaporates and the syrup thickens and becomes darker. The following are the most important stages; they are best checked with a sugar thermometer but simple tests are described for those who do not own one.
**Smooth** 102°C–104°C (215°F–220°F) Used for crystallising purposes. The mixture looks syrupy. To test, dip your fingers in water and then very quickly in the syrup. The thumb will slide smoothly over the fingers but sugar will cling to them.
**Soft ball** 116°C–118°C (240°F–245°F) Used for fondants and fudges. Test by dropping a little of the syrup into very cold water. It should form a soft ball. At 116°C (240°F) the soft ball will flatten when you take it out of the water; the higher the temperature the firmer the ball.
**Firm or hard ball** 120°C–130°C (250°F–265°F) Used for caramels. When dropped into cold water the syrup forms a ball which is hard enough to hold its shape, although still pliable.
**Soft crack** 132°C–143°C (270°F–290°F) Used for toffees. When dropped into cold water the syrup separates into hard but not brittle threads.
**Hard crack** 149°C–154°C (300°F–310°F) Used for

hard toffees. When dropped into cold water the syrup separates into hard and brittle threads.
**Caramel** 174°C (345°F) Used for pralines and caramels. The syrup turns golden brown when it reaches this temperature.

### AVOIDING CRYSTALLISATION

Sugar must be dissolved and boiled with great care, as syrup has a tendency to re-crystallise if incorrectly handled. The main causes of crystallisation are agitation of the mixture by stirring or beating whilst the sugar is dissolving and the presence of solid particles during boiling.

### WATCHPOINTS

- Make sure the pan is clean.
- Make sure the sugar has dissolved completely before boiling.
- If crystals do form, brush the sides of the pan with a brush dipped in cold water.
- Do not stir the mixture unless the recipe specifically instructs you to. If necessary, use a wooden spatula to tap the grains of sugar on to the bottom of the pan to hasten dissolving.
- Once the sugar has dissolved, boil rapidly to the required temperature. When it is reached, remove the pan from the heat immediately.

## STORING SWEETS

Homemade sweets should be stored in a cool place in tightly covered containers. Uncooked sweets and unboiled marzipan do not keep well—use within a week. Toffees and caramels should be wrapped in cling film to prevent them going soft. Different types of sweets should be stored separately until served, to prevent flavours mixing.

Chocolates should be covered with cling film and stored in an airtight tin. Don't keep them long or they will lose their gloss. Truffles and chocolates with a high percentage of cream in them should be stored in the fridge.

Once fudge has been cut, store it between sheets of waxed paper in an airtight tin. Cooked fudges will keep for 2–3 weeks.

# FONDANTS form the basis of many sweets and chocolate centres. The mixture is also used for icing cakes. Fondants may be dipped in melted chocolate (see page 501) or decorated with crystallised flower petals, nuts or glacé fruits. Any fondant that is not required for immediate use may be stored in a covered jar or tin.

## BOILED FONDANT

150 ml ($\frac{1}{4}$ pint) water

450 g (1 lb) granulated sugar

45 ml (3 level tbsp) powdered glucose

**1.** Put the water and sugar in a heavy-based saucepan and heat gently until the sugar has dissolved. Bring the syrup to the boil, add the glucose and boil to a temperature of 116°C (240°F) (soft ball stage).
**2.** Sprinkle a little water on a marble slab, pour on the syrup and leave for a few minutes to cool.
**3.** When a skin forms round the edges, use a wooden spatula to collect the mixture, then turn and work, using a figure-of-eight movement.
**4.** Continue to work the syrup, collecting it into as small a mass as possible, until it changes its consistency, becoming opaque and firm. The fondant can be melted down after 'working', poured into a rubber mat and left to set.
**5.** Scrape it off the slab and knead it in the hands until it is even-textured throughout.
*Note* If no slab is available the fondant can be turned and very gently kneaded in a bowl; leave it in the bowl for 15 minutes to cool, turn and very gently knead it in the bowl until thick, then knead it on greaseproof paper.
*Makes about 550 g (1$\frac{1}{4}$ lb)*

## UNCOOKED FONDANT

450 g (1 lb) icing sugar, sifted, plus extra for dusting

45 ml (3 tbsp) liquid glucose or good pinch of cream of tartar

1 egg white, lightly whisked

few drops of flavouring, such as lemon, orange or coffee

few drops of food colouring, such as yellow, orange or brown

**1.** Place the icing sugar and glucose in a bowl and stir in sufficient egg white to make a pliable mixture.
**2.** Transfer to a surface dusted with icing sugar and knead well, then add a few drops of flavouring and colouring and gently knead.
**3.** Roll out and use as required.
*Makes about 450 g (1 lb)*

## PEPPERMINT CREAMS

few drops of peppermint flavouring

225 g (8 oz) fondant (see above)

**1.** Knead together the peppermint flavouring and the fondant until smooth and evenly coloured.
**2.** Roll it out to 0.5 cm ($\frac{1}{4}$ inch) thick on a surface lightly dusted with icing sugar and cut into rounds.
**3.** Put into paper cases and leave for 24 hours until thoroughly dry.

# UNCOOKED PEPPERMINT CREAMS

450 g (1 lb) icing sugar, sifted

5 ml (1 tsp) lemon juice

1 egg white, lightly whisked

few drops peppermint flavouring or oil of peppermint

green food colouring (optional)

**1.** In a bowl, mix the sugar with the lemon juice and enough egg white to make a pliable mixture.

Flavour with peppermint and tint a pale green if liked.

**2.** Knead on a surface dusted with icing sugar and roll out to 0.5 cm ($\frac{1}{4}$ inch) thick. Cut into rounds with 2.5 cm (1 inch) cutter, or form into balls and flatten slightly with a rolling pin.

**3.** Leave for 24 hours until thoroughly dry.

*Makes about 450 g (1 lb)*

**Variation**

*WALNUT CREAMS*

**1.** Knead a few drops of coffee essence or strong black coffee into some Uncooked Fondant (see page 493).

**2.** Shape into balls about 2.5 cm (1 inch) in

diameter, press a half walnut into each and put the sweets into paper cases.

**3.** Leave for 24 hours to set and dry. The creams may be half dipped in chocolate.

*From the back: Neapolitan Slices, Marzipan Fruits and Flowers and Walnut Creams*

# MARZIPAN

MARZIPAN is not difficult to prepare and by using edible colourings, moulding the marzipan into different shapes or combining it with other ingredients such as dried or glacé fruits and nuts, you can make a wide variety of sweets. There are two types of marzipan: boiled, which is best for flowers and sweets that need a good deal of handling (see recipe, below) and unboiled which is quicker to make, but needs careful handling to prevent cracking (for recipe see Simple Marzipan or Almond Paste, below). You can, if wished, use ready-made bought marzipan.

## BOILED MARZIPAN

*450 g (1 lb) preserving or granulated sugar*

*150 ml (¼ pint) water*

*pinch of cream of tartar*

*350 g (12 oz) ground almonds*

*2 egg whites*

*75 g (3 oz) icing sugar, sifted*

**1.** Put the sugar and the water in a heavy-based saucepan and dissolve over a low heat. When the syrup reaches boiling point, add the cream of tartar and boil to 116°C (240°F) (soft ball stage).

**2.** Remove the pan from the heat and stir rapidly until the syrup begins to 'grain'.
**3.** Stir in the ground almonds and egg whites and cook for a few minutes over a low heat, stirring.
**4.** Pour on to an oiled marble or enamel slab or wooden chopping board, add the icing sugar and work well with a palette knife, lifting the edges of the mixture and turning them into the centre.
**5.** As soon as the mixture is sufficiently cool, knead it until smooth. Additional icing sugar may be kneaded in if the mixture is too wet.
*Makes about 900 g (2 lb)*

## SIMPLE MARZIPAN OR ALMOND PASTE (unboiled)

*225 g (8 oz) icing sugar, sifted*

*225 g (8 oz) caster sugar*

*450 g (1 lb) ground almonds*

*5 ml (1 tsp) vanilla flavouring*

*2 eggs, lightly beaten*

*lemon juice*

**1.** Mix the icing sugar with the caster sugar and ground almonds.
**2.** Add the vanilla flavouring, with sufficient beaten egg and lemon juice to mix to a stiff dough.
**3.** Form into a ball and knead lightly.
*Makes 900 g (2 lb)*

## Variations

### MARZIPAN FRUITS AND FLOWERS

To make fruits and flowers, take small balls of marzipan and mould them into the desired shapes with the fingers. Using a small paint brush and food colourings, tint them all over or add shading. (If making one fruit only, add the colouring to the marzipan before shaping.) Finish off as follows:
**Oranges and other citrus fruit**: to obtain a pitted surface, roll the fruit lightly on the finest part of a grater. Press a clove in one end.
**Strawberries and raspberries**: roll them in caster sugar to give them a bumpy surface. Colour a little marzipan green for the hull and assemble or use small pieces of angelica.
**Apples and pears**: press a clove into the top and bottom.

### NEAPOLITAN SLICES

**1.** Divide some marzipan into three equal pieces and knead a few drops of contrasting food colourings into two of them.
**2.** Roll out each coloured ball into 2 strips 1 cm (½ inch) thick and about 2.5 cm (1 inch) wide.
**3.** Cut each strip in half lengthways and trim with a sharp knife so that they are exactly the same size.
**4.** Roll out the uncoloured piece of marzipan very thinly to the same length as the strips and about 11.5 cm (4½ inch) wide.
**5.** Lay the coloured bars along it, two underneath and two on top to make a chequered pattern, and wrap the uncoloured marzipan around the bars so that the whole thing resembles a small Battenberg cake. Cut into 0.5 cm (¼ inch) slices.

# Toffee

*T*OFFEE can be made successfully in your own kitchen, but don't expect it to be exactly like the commercially-made variety. It does, however, need care and accuracy. The temperature to which toffee needs to be boiled varies according to type, and care must be taken to prevent the hot sugar syrup from burning. A large heavy-based saucepan is essential, and to prevent the mixture from boiling over, the inside of the pan should be brushed with water just above the level of the sugar syrup. Do not stir the mixture unless the recipe states that you should, otherwise the toffee will crystallise and spoil the final result.

The toffee should be allowed to boil very slowly indeed. Remove the pan from the heat just before the required temperature is reached to avoid overheating, leaving the thermometer in the syrup just to make certain. The mixture should be poured into the tins immediately and marked into squares or fingers with an oiled knife before the toffee sets. When set, toffees and caramels should be wiped carefully with absorbent kitchen paper to remove any oil, then wrapped individually in waxed papers.

This section also includes other sweets which need careful boiling such as Turkish Delight and Coconut Ice Bars.

## Treacle Toffee

| |
|---|
| *450 g (1 lb) demerara sugar* |
| *150 ml (¼ pint) water* |
| *1.25 ml (¼ level tsp) cream of tartar* |
| *75 g (3 oz) butter* |
| *100 g (4 oz) black treacle* |
| *100 g (4 oz) golden syrup* |

**1.** Lightly oil an 18 cm (7 inch) shallow square tin.
**2.** Put the sugar and water in a large heavy-based saucepan and heat gently until the sugar has dissolved.
**3.** Add the remaining ingredients and bring to the boil. Brush the inside of the pan with water just above the level of the sugar syrup. Boil to 132°C (270°F) (soft crack stage).
**4.** Pour into the prepared tin, cool for 5 minutes, then mark into squares with an oiled knife and leave to set.
*Makes about 800 g (1¾ lb)*

## Peanut Brittle

| |
|---|
| *350 g (12 oz) unsalted peanuts, chopped* |
| *400 g (14 oz) granulated sugar* |
| *175 g (6 oz) light soft brown sugar* |
| *175 g (6 oz) corn or golden syrup* |
| *150 ml (¼ pint) water* |
| *50 g (2 oz) butter or margarine* |
| *1.25 ml (¼ level tsp) bicarbonate of soda* |

**1.** Lightly oil an 18 cm (7 inch) shallow square tin.
**2.** Spread the peanuts out on a baking tray and warm in the oven at 130°C (265°F) mark ½ for 20 minutes.
**3.** Put the sugars, syrup and water in a large heavy-based saucepan and heat gently until the sugar has dissolved. Add the butter, bring to the boil. Brush the inside of the pan with water just above the level of the sugar syrup. Boil very gently to 149°C (300°F) (hard crack stage).
**4.** Carefully stir in the bicarbonate of soda and warmed nuts.
**5.** Pour the toffee slowly into the prepared tin and mark into bars with an oiled knife when almost set.
*Note* To store, place the pieces of Peanut Brittle in single layers, between sheets of greaseproof paper, in an airtight tin.
*Makes about 1.1 kg (2½ lb)*

**Variation**
The peanuts can be replaced with toasted almonds.

## BUTTERSCOTCH

450 g (1 lb) demerara sugar

150 ml (¼ pint) water

50–75 g (2–3 oz) unsalted butter

1. Lightly oil a 15 cm (6 inch) shallow square tin.
2. Put the sugar and water in a heavy-based saucepan and heat gently until the sugar has dissolved. Bring to the boil and boil to 138°C

(280°F) (soft crack stage), brushing down the sides of the pan occasionally with a brush dipped in cold water.
3. Add the butter a little at a time, stir until dissolved before adding more, then pour the mixture into the prepared tin.
4. Cut into pieces when almost set.
*Makes about 450 g (1 lb)*

## TOFFEE APPLES

450 g (1 lb) demerara sugar

50 g (2 oz) butter or margarine

10 ml (2 tsp) vinegar

150 ml (¼ pint) water

15 ml (1 tbsp) golden syrup

6–8 medium apples and the same number of wooden
    sticks

1. Place the sugar, butter, vinegar, water and syrup gently in a heavy-based saucepan and heat until the sugar has dissolved. Bring to the boil,

then brush the inside of the pan with water just above the level of the sugar syrup. Boil rapidly for 5 minutes until the temperature reaches 143°C (290°F) (soft crack stage).
2. Wipe the apples and push the sticks into the cores, making sure they are secure.
3. Dip the apples into the toffee, twirl around for few seconds to allow excess toffee to drip off, then leave to cool and set on a buttered baking sheet or waxed paper.
*Makes 6–8*

## PEPPERMINT HUMBUGS

450 g (1 lb) granulated sugar

150 ml (¼ pint) water

1.25 ml (¼ level tsp) cream of tartar

15 ml (1 tbsp) golden syrup

few drops of peppermint flavouring

few drops of brown food colouring

1. Lightly oil a marble or wooden chopping board.
2. Put the sugar and the water in a large heavy-based saucepan and heat gently until the sugar has dissolved. Mix the cream of tartar with 15 ml (1 tbsp) water and add to the pan with the golden syrup. Brush the inside of the pan with water just above the sugar level. Bring the mixture gently to 154°C (310°F) (hard crack stage).
3. Pour the syrup on to the slab and allow to cool a little.
4. Using oiled palette knives, fold the sides of the toffee into the centre and add a few drops of peppermint flavouring. When the mixture is cool

enough to handle, cut off one-third and, with oiled hands, twist into a rope about 51 cm (20 inches) long. Fold in half and twist and pull out again. Continue to do this until it is pale in colour and elastic and shiny.
5. Add a few drops of food colouring to the

*Brush pan with cold water.*

remaining toffee and gently form into a thick roll.
6. Divide the pulled toffee into four ropes and press these against the sides of the thick darker rope. Pull out gently to the required thickness and twist. The larger the size of humbug you want, the thicker you will need to make the roll.
7. Using oiled scissors, cut into humbugs or cushions. Leave to set on a buttered baking sheet or waxed paper.
*Makes about 450 g (1 lb)*

*Turkish Delight*

## TURKISH DELIGHT

| 300 ml (½ pint) water |
| 25 g (1 oz) gelatine |
| 450 g (1 lb) granulated sugar |
| 1.25 ml (¼ level tsp) citric acid |
| few drops of red food colouring |
| few drops of rose water |
| **For the sherbet mix** |
| 50 g (2 oz) icing sugar |
| 2.5 ml (½ level tsp) bicarbonate of soda |
| 1.25 ml (¼ level tsp) citric acid |

**1.** Pour the water into a heavy-based saucepan. Sprinkle over the gelatine. Stir gently to ensure that all the grains are covered. Leave to soak for about 10 minutes or until the gelatine is sponge-like.

**2.** Over a very gentle heat, slowly dissolve the gelatine. When clear and liquid, add the sugar and citric acid. Stir gently until the sugar dissolves. (Take care not to splash the sugar up the sides of the pan, as this may cause the mixture to crystallise).

**3.** Bring the contents of the pan to the boil and boil over a moderate heat for about 20 minutes or until the mixture is syrupy and a pale straw colour (do not stir the mixture, or the scum which appears on the surface will then be distributed through it and give a cloudy jelly).

**4.** Remove the pan from the heat, let the bubbles subside, then skim any scum from the surface of the mixture. Leave the mixture to stand for about 25 minutes, until cool, thick and almost set. Stir in sufficient red food colouring to give a pale pink colour and add rose water to taste.

**5.** Base line a 185 mm × 185 mm (7¼ × 7¼ inch) square tin. Oil the base and sides well. Carefully pour in the Turkish Delight mixture. Leave until completely cold, then place in the refrigerator and leave overnight to set.

**6.** Meanwhile, sieve together the icing sugar, bicarbonate of soda and citric acid for the sherbet coating. Store in a polythene bag.

**7.** The next day sprinkle half the quantity of sherbet mix on to a sheet of greaseproof paper. Peel off the lining paper, then turn the Turkish Delight over to coat the other side.

**8.** Rinse a large sharp knife in cold running water, then use to cut the Turkish Delight into 2.5 cm (1 inch) squares. Place in a bowl, shake over the remaining sherbet mix until completely coated.

**9.** To store, line an airtight container with greaseproof paper, put in the Turkish Delight, sprinkling over any remaining sherbet.
*Makes 49 squares*

## COCONUT ICE BARS

| 450 g (1 lb) granulated sugar |
| 150 ml (¼ pint) milk |
| 150 g (5 oz) desiccated coconut |
| few drops of red food colouring |

**1.** Lightly oil an 18 cm (7 inch) shallow square tin.
**2.** Put the sugar and the milk in a heavy-based saucepan and heat gently until the sugar has dissolved. Bring to the boil and boil gently for about 10 minutes, or until 116°C (240°F) (soft ball stage) is reached.

**3.** Remove from the heat and stir in the coconut.
**4.** Pour half the mixture quickly into the prepared tin. Add a few drops of food colouring to the second half and pour quickly over the first layer.
**5.** Leave until half set, mark into bars and cut or break when cold.
*Makes about 550 g (1¼ lb)*

# FUDGE

$F{\small UDGE}$ is very popular and is also quite simple to make. It can be flavoured with such things as chocolate, coffee, nuts or glacé fruits. Cooked fudge is made from sugar, butter and milk or cream that is gently heated and then boiled to the required temperature. Either caster or granulated sugar may be used. When making fudge, stir the mixture to dissolve the sugar, then bring to the boil without stirring. Continue boiling until the correct temperature is reached, stirring occasionally to prevent sticking. When the required temperature is reached, the mixture is beaten with a wooden spoon to give the characteristic creamy texture. Immediately as the fudge begins to thicken, it should be poured into the prepared tins. Mark it into squares just before it begins to set. A knife dipped in hot water makes cutting easier.

## VANILLA FUDGE

450 g (1 lb) granulated sugar

75 g (3 oz) butter or margarine

150 ml (¼ pint) milk

175 g (6 oz) can evaporated milk

2.5 ml (½ tsp) vanilla flavouring

1. Lightly oil an 18 cm (7 inch) shallow square tin.
2. Put the sugar, butter and milks in a heavy-based pan and heat gently, stirring, until dissolved.
3. Bring to the boil without stirring, then continue boiling until a temperature of 116°C (240°F) is reached stirring occasionally to prevent sticking.
4. Remove the pan from the heat, add the vanilla flavouring and beat the mixture with a wooden spoon until thick and grainy. Pour the mixture into the prepared tin and leave until almost set, about 5–10 minutes.
5. Using a sharp knife, mark the soft fudge into squares, then leave to cool completely before cutting and removing from the tin. Store for up to 2–3 weeks in an airtight container.
*Makes 800 g (1¾ lb)*

**Variation**
CHERRY FUDGE
Follow the above recipe as far as the end of stage 3. Stir in 100 g (4 oz) chopped glacé cherries in place of vanilla flavouring. Complete as above.

## CHOCOLATE FUDGE

450 g (1 lb) granulated sugar

150 ml (¼ pint) milk

150 g (5 oz) butter or margarine

150 g (5 oz) plain chocolate

50 g (2 oz) honey

1. Lightly oil an 18 cm (7 inch) shallow square tin.
2. Heat all the ingredients gently in a large heavy-based saucepan, stirring until the sugar has dissolved.
3. Bring to the boil without stirring, then continue boiling until a temperature of 116°C (240°F) is reached, stirring occasionally to prevent sticking.
4. Remove from the heat, stand the pan on a cool surface for 5 minutes, then beat the mixture until thick, creamy and beginning to 'grain'.
5. Pour into the prepared tin, mark into squares when almost set and cut when cold.
*Makes about 800 g (1¾ lb)*

*Vanilla Fudge and Chocolate Fudge*

$T$RUFFLES are mouthwatering sweets believed to have originated in France, where larger truffles were served as part of a selection of cakes and biscuits at teatime. Although traditionally associated with Christmas, smaller truffles make ideal after-dinner sweets. They are usually chocolate based with added flavourings such as rum, brandy, coffee, fruit and nuts. When completely set, they are tossed in chocolate or cocoa powder, coconut or chopped nuts, or dipped in chocolate.

## RICH CHOCOLATE RUM TRUFFLES

225 g (8 oz) plain chocolate

2 egg yolks

25 g (1 oz) butter

10 ml (2 tsp) rum

15 ml (1 tsp) single cream

drinking chocolate powder

1. Melt the chocolate in a bowl over hot water, making sure the bottom of the bowl does not touch the water, then add the egg yolks, butter, rum and cream.
2. Stir until the mixture is thick enough to handle.
3. Cool slightly, then form into balls and roll in chocolate powder.
4. Leave until firm, then put in paper cases.
*Makes about 225 g (8 oz)*

**Variation**
RICH CHOCOLATE BRANDY TRUFFLES
Replace the rum with brandy.

## MOCHA TRUFFLES

225 g (8 oz) plain chocolate

60 ml (4 tbsp) condensed milk

few drops of coffee flavouring or strong black coffee

cocoa powder

1. Break the chocolate into small pieces and melt it in a bowl over hot water, making sure the bottom of the bowl does not touch the water.
2. Stir in the condensed milk and a few drops of coffee flavouring.
3. Allow the mixture to cool slightly, then form the mixture into small balls.
4. Roll in cocoa powder and leave until set.
*Makes about 225 g (8 oz)*

## ALMOND TRUFFLES

100 g (4 oz) fresh or stale cake crumbs

100 g (4 oz) caster sugar

100 g (4 oz) ground almonds

120 ml (8 tbsp) apricot jam, heated and sieved

10–15 ml (2–3 tsp) rum or sherry

75–100 g (3–4 oz) chocolate vermicelli

1. Crumble the cake crumbs finely and add the sugar, ground almonds and 75 ml (5 tbsp) apricot jam to bind it and give a fairly sticky mixture.
2. Add rum or sherry to taste.
3. Shape into small balls, dip them into the remaining jam and roll them in the chocolate vermicelli. Harden, then put into paper cases.
*Makes about 350 g (12 oz)*

## CHOCOLATE NUT TRUFFLES

100 g (4 oz) plain chocolate, finely grated

25 g (1 oz) chopped mixed nuts

50 g (2 oz) icing sugar

1–2 drops of vanilla flavouring

about 15 ml (1 tbsp) single cream

chocolate vermicelli

1. Put the chocolate, nuts and sugar into a bowl and add 1–2 drops of vanilla flavouring and enough cream to bind all the ingredients together.
2. Form into small balls, roll them in chocolate vermicelli and put into paper cases when firm.
*Makes about 225 g (8 oz)*

# DIPPED CHOCOLATES

These are perhaps the most 'professional' looking chocolates you will make at home. Ordinary block or plain or milk chocolate flavoured cake covering will do, but dipping is a time-consuming operation and it is as well to help ensure good results by using couverture chocolate available from delicatessens and specialist suppliers. It can also be found at larger supermarkets.

When melting the chocolate, it should be broken into small pieces and placed in a bowl over a saucepan of cold water. Make sure that the base of the bowl does not touch the water and that it is wedged into the pan so that no steam escapes round the sides of the bowl. (Humidity spoils the texture and gloss of finished chocolates and dipping is best done on a warm, dry day when there is no other steamy cooking taking place in the kitchen.)

Heat the water gently but don't allow it to boil. Remove the pan from the heat and stir the chocolate until it is completely melted. If it starts to harden again before you have finished dipping, simply reheat it gently in the same way. If the chocolate is too warm, it will dry cloudy and white; if too cool, it will coat the centres too quickly.

Many fondants, fudges and caramels make ideal centres for dipped chocolates. The table below gives some suggested combinations of centre, coating and decoration so you can select the type of chocolates you want to make. Place the centres on a baking sheet and warm them slightly before you begin.

When the chocolate is ready, lower the centres into it one at a time using a dipping fork. Lift each centre out, shake off any surplus chocolate by knocking the fork gently against the edge of the basin and place the sweet on a baking sheet lined with waxed paper.

While the chocolate is still soft, make a pattern by pressing the dipping fork lightly on the top and lifting it off again gently, or press on a decoration, or pipe the top of the sweet with a little contrasting chocolate. When the chocolates have dried thoroughly, put them into individual paper cases.

## FINISHING SUGGESTIONS

| Centre | Coating | Decoration |
| --- | --- | --- |
| Peppermint Creams | Plain chocolate, completely or half dipped | Press the top with a dipping fork |
| Coffee Fondants | Plain chocolate | Piped milk chocolate or an almond half |
| Orange Fondants | Plain chocolate | Candied orange peel |
| Walnut Creams | Plain chocolate, half dipped | Piece of walnut |
| Marzipan Balls | Plain chocolate | Blanched almond |
| Chocolate Nut Truffles | Plain chocolate | Chocolate vermicelli |

# CHOCOLATE EASTER EGGS

Tin or plastic moulds are essential for making eggs; they are available in various sizes. Use good quality couverture chocolate or plain or milk chocolate flavoured cake covering and prepare it as for chocolate dipping (see above for detailed instructions).

Wipe the inside of the moulds with absorbent kitchen paper, then half fill each mould with chocolate and tilt to allow the chocolate to run to the edge of the mould and coat it evenly. Repeat this two or three times, then pour the surplus back into the chocolate pan. Run a finger round the edge of the mould to remove surplus chocolate, then put the mould, domed side up, on a cool flat surface. As the shells cool, they will contract slightly and may be removed by pressing gently at one end. The outer glazed surface caused by contact with the mould must not be handled more than can be helped. The shells can be joined by lightly touching the two halves on to a warm, flat tin, so that just sufficient chocolate melts to enable them to set firmly together. Press gently to seal before setting aside to allow the chocolate to harden.

Wrap the eggs in foil, or decorate them with brightly coloured ribbon, sifted icing sugar or fine lines of chocolate piping.

## RICH CHOCOLATE CUPS

| |
|---|
| 150 g (5 oz) couverture chocolate |
| 100 g (4 oz) plain chocolate, grated |
| 100 g (4 oz) icing sugar, sifted |
| about 10 ml (2 tsp) rum |
| few pistachio nuts or lightly toasted almonds, finely chopped |

1. Melt the couverture chocolate in a bowl over hot water and brush it over the inside of about 16 small foil cases. Leave them to dry.
2. Mix the grated chocolate and icing sugar in a bowl, with sufficient rum to form a stiff paste.
3. Fill the cases with this mixture, then cover them with a little more melted couverture chocolate.
4. When nearly set, sprinkle with a little of the finely chopped pistachio nuts.
Makes about 16

Chocolate Nut Truffles (see page 500) and Rich Chocolate Cups

# CANDIED FRUITS
Candying is a method of preserving fruits by the use of sugar syrup. They can then be served as a dessert or eaten as sweets. The peel of citrus fruits such as oranges and lemons can also be candied and is widely used in making cakes, cookies and puddings and in mincemeat. Candying essentially consists of soaking the fruit in a syrup, the sugar content of which is increased daily over a stated period of time until the fruits are completely impregnated with sugar. They can then be left plain or be given a crystallised or glacé finish.

Candied fruits are expensive to buy because of the labour involved and the amount of sugar used. The process should not, however, be beyond the skill of the home cook, provided certain basic rules are followed. Crystallised ginger cannot be done satisfactorily at home though. The most suitable fruits to candy are those with a really distinctive flavour—pineapples, peaches, plums, apricots, oranges, cherries, crab-apples, pears. Both fresh and canned fruits may be used, but different types should not be candied in the same syrup.

### PREPARATION OF THE FRUIT AND SYRUP

**Fresh fruit** The fruits must be ripe, but firm and free from blemishes. Prepare them according to kind. Small whole crab-apples, apricots and plums should be pricked all over with a stainless steel fork; cherries must be stoned; peaches and pears peeled and halved or cut into quarters. The fruits which are peeled and cut up need not be pricked with a fork.

Place the prepared fruits in sufficient boiling water to cover them and cook gently until just tender. Overcooking spoils the shape and texture,

while undercooking results in slow penetration of the syrup and causes dark colour and toughness. Tough fruits such as apricots may take 10–15 minutes, whereas soft ones will probably need only 2–4 minutes.

**Canned fruits** Use good quality fruit. Pineapple chunks or small rings, plums, sliced and halved peaches and halved apricots are all suitable for preserving with this method.

**The syrup** Granulated sugar is generally recommended for the preparation of the syrup. Part of the sugar may be replaced by glucose. The chart which follows (see page 504) gives full details of the proportion of sugar to liquid at the different stages.

*FINISHING THE CANDIED FRUIT*

When the fruits are thoroughly dried, pack them in cardboard or wooden boxes, between layers of waxed or non-stick paper, or give them one of the following finishes before packing.

**Crystallised finish** Take the pieces of candied fruit and dip each quickly into boiling water; drain off excess moisture, then roll each piece in caster sugar.

**Glacé finish** Prepare a fresh syrup, using 450 g (1 lb) sugar and 150 ml (¼ pint) water, bring to the boil and boil for 1 minute. Pour a little of the syrup into a cup. Dip the candied fruit into boiling water for 20 seconds, then dip one piece at a time into the syrup in the cup, using a dipping fork or skewer. Place the fruit on a wire rack to dry. Cover the rest of the syrup in the pan with a damp cloth and keep it warm (a double pan is useful for this purpose). As the syrup in the cup becomes cloudy, replace it with fresh syrup from the pan.

## CHESTNUTS IN SYRUP

225 g (8 oz) granulated sugar

225 g (8 oz) glucose or dextrose

180 ml (¼ pint plus 2 tbsp) water

350 g (12 oz) whole chestnuts, peeled and skinned
(weight after preparation) or 350 g (12 oz) canned
chestnuts, drained

vanilla flavouring

1. Put the granulated sugar, glucose or dextrose and water into a saucepan large enough to hold the chestnuts and heat gently until the sugars have dissolved, then bring to the boil.
2. Remove from the heat, add the chestnuts and bring to the boil again. Remove from the heat, cover and leave overnight, preferably in a warm place.
3. Next day, re-boil the chestnuts and syrup in the pan, without the lid. Remove from the heat, cover and again leave standing overnight.
4. On the third day, add 6–8 drops of vanilla flavouring and repeat the boiling process.
5. Warm two 450 g (1 lb) bottling jars in the oven, fill with the chestnuts and cover with syrup. Cover with airtight tops.
6. Test that the bottling jars are airtight by removing the screw-band or clip and trying to lift the jar by the cap or disc. If this holds firm it shows that a vacuum has been formed as the jars have cooled and they are hermetically sealed.
*Note* This recipe gives a delicious result, but the chestnuts are not exactly like commercially prepared Marrons Glacés, which cannot be reproduced under home conditions.

## CANDIED PEEL

Orange, lemon and grapefruit peel are all suitable. This recipe is suitable for 6 oranges or lemons or 4 grapefruit, or a mixture.
1. Wash or scrub the fruit thoroughly, halve it and remove the pulp. Larger pieces of peel retain their moisture better, so do not cut it up.
2. Simmer the peel in a little water for 1–2 hours until tender. (Change the water two or three times when cooking grapefruit peel.) Drain well.
3. Make the liquid up to 300 ml (½ pint) with water. Add 225 g (8 oz) sugar, dissolve over a low heat, then bring to the boil. Add the peel and leave for 2 days.
4. Drain off the syrup, dissolve another 100 g (4 oz) sugar in it and simmer the peel in this syrup until semi-transparent. The peel can be left in this thick syrup for 2–3 weeks.
5. Drain off the syrup, place the peel on a wire rack, cover and leave to dry. Store in screw-topped jars.
*Note* This recipe is ideal for using in Mincemeat (see page 472) or Christmas Pudding (see page 327). To use in these or other baking recipes, coarsely chop into small dice when required. Use in cakes, biscuits or other puddings.

# PROCESSING CHART FOR CANDIED FRUIT

Using 450 g (1 lb) prepared fruit (see notes on page 503)

| FRESH FRUIT | | CANNED FRUIT | | |
|---|---|---|---|---|
| Day | Syrup | Soak for | Day | Syrup | Soak for |

| Day | Syrup | Soak for | Day | Syrup | Soak for |
|---|---|---|---|---|---|
| 1 | Drain 300 ml ($\frac{1}{2}$ pint) liquid from fruit, add 175 g (6 oz) sugar for 50 g (2 oz) sugar and 100 g (4 oz) glucose, dissolve, bring to the boil and pour over fruit. | 24 hrs | 1 | Drain off canning syrup and make up to 300 ml ($\frac{1}{2}$ pint); add 225 g (8 oz) sugar for 100 g (4 oz) sugar and 100 g (4 oz) glucose, dissolve, bring to the boil and pour over fruit. | 24 hrs |
| 2 | Drain off syrup, add 50 g (2 oz) sugar, dissolve, bring to the boil and pour over fruit. | 24 hrs | 2 | Drain off syrup, add 50 g (2 oz) sugar, dissolve, bring to the boil and pour over fruit. | 24 hrs |
| 3 | Repeat Day 2 | 24 hrs | 3 | Repeat Day 2 | 24 hrs |
| 4 | Repeat Day 2 | 24 hrs | 4 | Repeat Day 2 | 24 hrs |
| 5 | Repeat Day 2 | 24 hrs | 5 | Repeat Day 2, using 75 g (3 oz) sugar | 48 hrs |
| 6 | Repeat Day 2 | 24 hrs | 6 | — | — |
| 7 | Repeat Day 2 | 24 hrs | 7 | Repeat Day 2, using 75 g (3 oz) sugar | 4 days |
| 8 | Repeat Day 2, using a further 75 g (3 oz) sugar | 48 hrs | | | |
| 9 | — | — | | | |
| 10 | Repeat Day 8 | 4 days | | | |
| 11 | — | — | 11 | Dry in oven at lowest setting or cover lightly and leave in a warm place (this may take from a few hours to 2–3 days) until quite dry; turn them 2–3 times | — |
| 12 | — | — | | | |
| 13 | — | — | | | |
| 14 | Dry as for canned fruit | — | | | |

## Notes

**Amount of syrup** If the syrup is not sufficient to cover the fruit, make up more in the same strength, but remember that the amount of sugar to be added later must be increased accordingly. For example, if you increase the amount used for fresh fruit to 450 ml ($\frac{3}{4}$ pint) juice and 250 g (9 oz) sugar, then on Day 2 you will have to add 75 g (3 oz) sugar and on Day 8 add 125 g (4$\frac{1}{2}$ oz) sugar.

**Soaking time** It is important that the fruit should soak for a full 24 hours (or as specified) before the next lot of sugar is added.

**Adding sugar** On the days when the added sugar is increased to 75 g (3 oz), first dissolve the sugar, then add the fruit and boil it in the syrup for 3–4 minutes.

**Day 14 (fresh) Day 11 (canned)** Once the syrup has reached the consistency of honey, the fruit may be left to soak for as little as 3 days or up to 2–3 weeks, according to how sweet you like the candied fruit to be.

# HOME FREEZING

Owning a freezer means you can buy food (such as meat) in bulk, shop less often, have a store of pre-cooked dishes or produce readily available and preserve produce straight from the garden or when it is cheap at the height of the season. Meals for unexpected guests are no longer a problem and you can spread the work of catering for a large party over a period of weeks. This chapter will help you choose the freezer best suited to your needs and use it to maximum efficiency.

◆

Freezing is the easiest method of preserving food and, as long as the simple basic rules are followed, the food retains its colour, texture, taste and nutrients.

Most foods are largely made up of water, even something like lean meat contains about 70 per cent water. Freezing converts this water to ice crystals. Freezing the food quickly results in tiny ice crystals, retained within the cell structure, so that when thawed, the structure is undamaged and the food value remains unchanged.

However, slow freezing results in the formation of large ice crystals, which damage the cell structure and cause loss of nutrients. As this damage is irreversible, slow-frozen food shows loss of texture, colour and flavour when thawed.

Foods like cucumber and strawberries, which have a high water content and delicate structure, never freeze successfully because the tiniest crystal formation breaks down their structure.

The success of freezing as a method of food preservation depends on the fact that low temperatures destroy some micro-organisms and prevent the growth of others. They in fact become dormant. However enzymes (chemicals naturally present in food which cause the destruction of vitamins, texture and colour) are not destroyed by freezing but slowed down.

### BUYING A FREEZER

There are various types of freezers to choose from and it is largely a matter of personal choice.

**Upright freezers** These range in size from small, table-top models to large upright ones. They have front opening doors—large freezers sometimes have two doors—take up less floor space than chest freezers and are less obtrusive.

Upright freezers, fitted with shelves and/or pull-out baskets, are easy to load and unload. In some models, each shelf or basket is fronted by its own flap which shuts out warm air when the door is opened. Upright freezers need defrosting more often than the chest type—although frost-free models are available, they are more expensive both to buy and to run.

**Chest freezers** Size for size, chest freezers are cheaper than upright models, and running costs are lower. They have an additional advantage too: more food will fit into the same amount of space, since large items can be accommodated with small ones tucked round them, unrestricted by shelves and baskets. However, they take up considerably more floor space; are more difficult to keep organised, and small people and those with bad backs find it difficult to reach down to the bottom of the cabinet.

**Refrigerator/freezers** A unit which incorporates a refrigerator and a freezer, one built above the other, is popular in small kitchens with little space. The refrigeration and freezing capacities are roughly equal in many models, although it is also possible to buy units which have bigger freezers than refrigerators, and vice versa.

**Second-hand freezers** Second-hand freezers are sometimes available through dealers or advertisements. Check that what you are offered is a genuine home freezer, not an old commercial food conservator. Check that the lid or door fits well and that reliable servicing facilities are available.

**What size freezer?** What size freezer you need depends on a number of factors: for instance, how often you shop; whether you plan to freeze precooked dishes or merely to store basic ingredients; how many people there are in the household, and whether you will be freezing your own produce.

Freezer capacity is quoted in either cubic litres or feet. To make a rough comparison divide the number of litres by 30 to give the number of cubic feet (1 cubic foot is equal to 28.3 litres and will hold 9–11 kg (20–25 lb) of food.

As a general rule, allow 56 litres (2 cubic feet) per person plus an extra 56 litres (2 cubic feet), but do think carefully about your particular needs before deciding. Talk to friends who own freezers to see whether they are satisfied with the size they have. If in doubt, buy a model that is 28–56 litres (1–2 cubic feet) larger than you think you need — it's better to have more space than you need than not enough.

**Star symbols** All freezers must carry this star symbol ★★★ which indicates that they are capable of freezing fresh food. An appliance with three stars or less is suitable only for storing ready-frozen food as follows:

★ for 1 week
★★ for 1 month
★★★ for 3 months

### DEFROSTING

Upright freezers need defrosting two or three times a year; chest freezers once, or at the most twice, a year. As a general guide, defrost your freezer when the frost on the shelves reaches a thickness of 0.5 cm ($\frac{1}{4}$ inch). Follow the manufacturer's instructions for your particular freezer as the procedure varies with different models.

Try to defrost when stocks are low or when it is a cold day. Put the contents of the freezer into the refrigerator or wrap in newspapers or blankets.

You will need a plastic spatula to tap the frost loose as it melts, some old towels to mop up with and bowls of hot water to speed up the process. When the freezer is free of frost, wash it out with a solution of 15 ml (1 level tbsp) bicarbonate of soda to 1 litre ($1\frac{3}{4}$ pints) warm water, then dry it thoroughly before switching on again.

### POWER CUTS

Most power cuts do not last for long and the food in your freezer should be safe.

If there is advance warning of a power cut, turn on the fast-freeze switch, but before you do make sure the freezer is as full as possible. Fill any gaps with rolled up newspaper, old towels or plastic boxes filled with cold water.

Cover the freezer with a blanket or rug to increase its insulation, but make sure you leave the condenser and pipes on the back uncovered. Do not open the door during a power cut as this lets warm air into the freezer.

After the power has been restored, leave the fast-freeze on for at least 2 hours. Food in a chest freezer will be undamaged for about 48 hours if you have had advance warning and 30–35 hours if there has been no warning. An upright freezer will keep its contents safe for about 36 hours with advance warning, 30 hours without.

### MOVING HOUSE

It is best to move a freezer when it is empty, although some removal firms have the facility to plug a loaded unit into an electrical supply in their van. Bear in mind that a freezer full of food is very heavy and might be damaged during transportation. It is better to use its contents and transport it empty.

When moving a freezer, it should be kept as upright as possible and never tipped to an angle of more than 30°, as this could cause an airlock in the cooling system. When it is unloaded and installed in your new home, switch on the freezer to check that all the lights are working.

### TWENTY RULES FOR FREEZING

**1.** Freeze only good quality foods—what comes out is only as good as what went in.
**2.** Handle food as little as possible.

**3.** Pack food for freezing in small quantities. It will thaw more quickly and you only need to defrost what you need.

**4.** Pack and seal food carefully. Food that is exposed to air or moisture will deteriorate and there is a risk of cross flavouring.

**5.** Never put anything hot or even warm into a freezer. It will raise the temperature of other items in the freezer and may cause deterioration. Once food has been cooked or blanched, cool it rapidly in a bowl of iced water.

**6.** Freeze food as quickly as possible so that it retains its texture.

**7.** Follow the manufacturer's instructions on use of the fast-freeze switch and where in the cabinet to freeze down food.

**8.** Do not pack food too closely together, spread it out until it is frozen.

**9.** Move newly-frozen items from the fast-freeze area, if your freezer has one, once they are frozen.

**10.** Remember to switch the fast-freeze control back to normal setting once food has been frozen.

**11.** Do not keep opening the door of your freezer; it raises the temperature inside the cabinet. Decide what you want to get out and remove it quickly.

**12.** Use a freezer thermometer to help you maintain a steady storage temperature of $-18°C$ (0°F). Move it around within the freezer to check that the temperature is maintained throughout the cabinet.

**13.** Label and date food so that you can rotate stock efficiently. Consider keeping a freezer log book to stop you going through the contents to see what you have stored.

**14.** Defrost the freezer when stocks are low and preferably on a cold day. Do the job as fast as you can so that the contents can be put back quickly.

**15.** Tape the address of the service organisation to an inconspicuous spot on the freezer casing or inside the adjacent kitchen cupboard door.

**16.** Know what to do in emergencies such as a power cut or freezer breakdown (see opposite).

**17.** If you are storing a large quantity of food, particularly expensive ingredients, consider taking out special freezer insurance to cover you against loss.

**18.** If your freezer is in a garage or outhouse, fit a freezer alarm to it so that you have immediate warning if anything goes wrong, and fit a lock.

**19.** Plug in a built-in alarm on the freezer to warn you if the fuse blows.

**20.** Keep your freezer full to reduce the running costs. Fill gaps with basics like bread, or if you are running down your stock to defrost, fill the gaps with old towels or crumpled newspaper.

## HOW TO FREEZE

Never freeze more than one tenth of your freezer's capacity in any 24 hours, otherwise heat will be absorbed by the freezer's refrigeration system and also by the food already frozen. If, for instance, you have a 50 kg (110 lb) freezer (approximately 170 litres or 6 cubic feet), you should only freeze about 5 kg (11 lb) of food at a time.

**Using the fast-freeze switch** The fast-freeze switch works by over-riding the thermostat. It allows the temperature in the freezer to fall well below $-18°C$ (0°C)—the normal storage temperature (which is controlled by the thermostat). The food freezes faster in the colder temperature, forming smaller ice crystals, so that the texture of the food will be better when thawed. Reducing the temperature means, too, that the food already in the freezer gets colder and will be less affected by the higher temperature of the fresh food. Turn on the fast-freeze switch about 6 hours before you plan to put in food to be frozen, then leave it on for 12–24 hours to freeze the food.

It is possible to freeze food without using the fast-freeze switch, but the faster the food is frozen the better the texture when thawed.

### FREEZING SOLIDS

Package solids tightly, so that you expel as much air as possible, wrapping them in foil or freezer wrap, which fits where it touches. If filling a rigid container and the food only comes halfway up, fill up the vacant space with crumpled foil or non-stick paper. However, if possible, avoid half-empty containers as they waste freezer space.

### FREEZING LIQUIDS

Liquid expands one tenth when frozen, so it's essential to leave at least 1 cm ($\frac{1}{2}$ inch) of 'headspace' in a container holding about 300 ml ($\frac{1}{2}$ pint) and about 2.5 cm (1 inch) for a container holding 600 ml (1 pint). Unless you leave room for expansion, items such as soups, sauces and fruits packed in syrup will push off their lids.

If you use a glass container, make sure it has straight sides, as it is easier to get the contents out again.

**Freezing solids plus liquids** Combinations of solids and liquids, such as stews and casseroles, or fruit in syrup, should if possible have a layer of liquid on the top with no pieces of food sticking out. Leave

1 cm ($\frac{1}{2}$ inch) headspace. Solids which rise about the surface of the liquid, such as fruit salad, need an inner covering of crumpled non-stick paper before wrapping.

**Pre-forming** This is ideal for storing liquid foods such as fruit purées, casseroles and stocks in a polythene bag, rather than a rigid container. The food is placed in a polythene bag-lined container, frozen until solid, then removed from the container and replaced in a regular shape.

### STORAGE TIMES

Bacteria cannot multiply in or on frozen food, so there is no danger of the food becoming a health hazard, no matter how long it is stored. However, freezing does not kill bacteria and food contaminated before freezing will still be contaminated after it has been thawed. As with all perishable foods, if frozen food is thawed and then kept at room temperature, bacteria will develop and it will become a health hazard.

Different foods have different recommended storage times. These are determined by the length of time they can be stored frozen without any detectable change in food value, taste, colour and texture. They can be stored longer than the recommended times without becoming harmful to health, but the flavour and texture will not be as good.

## PACKAGING

Good packaging is vital if frozen food is to remain in good condition. Freezing converts the water content of the food to ice crystals which must be retained, as they are converted back to moisture when the food is thawed. Badly-packed food will dry out, causing white patches known as 'freezer burn'. There is also the risk that strong-smelling foods will transfer their odours to other foods. Although it is important to store all frozen food correctly, any food which is to be stored for a long time must be extremely well wrapped, since it will tend to get pushed around when other items are put into and removed from the freezer.

**Polythene bags and sheeting** These should be of fairly heavy gauge polythene unless they are to be used for overwrapping, when a thinner gauge will do. Exclude as much air as possible before sealing. They must be sealed by twist ties or by heat-sealing with an iron. When using the latter method, shield the polythene with a piece of paper before applying the iron. Have an assortment of sizes on hand. A self sealing bag is obtainable.

**Cling film/freezer wrap** Plastic film is very useful when wrapping food for the freezer. Use it as a lining if you want to pack acidic fruits in foil and also for wrapping individual portions of foods which can then be stored together in a polythene bag and removed one at a time.

**Foil** This is ideal for wrapping awkward shaped items and can be moulded closely around the food to ensure air does not get in. Use a single layer of the standard thickness or a double layer if you are using thin kitchen foil.

Foil should not be used for wrapping acidic fruits which may react with it. If you think the foil is likely to become punctured in the freezer, over-wrap large items with a polythene bag.

Foil is also useful for lining casserole dishes when preparing food. Once the dish has been cooked and frozen, the foil lining containing the food can be removed from the casserole. Overwrap the parcel and store in the freezer until needed, then unwrap, reheat and serve.

**Foil dishes** Foil dishes come in a range of sizes and shapes and you can cook, freeze and reheat food in them.

**Plastic containers** Plastic containers are more expensive than other types of freezer packaging, but will last for years. Some varieties may lose their airtight seal after a while and need sealing with freezer tape to prevent air affecting the contents. While you may want special plastic shapes for some food, ice cream bombes for instance, square and rectangular containers make better use of freezer space than round ones.

**Other packaging** Packaging containers from some bought foods are useful in the freezer. Good examples are soft margarine and cottage cheese tubs, ice cream cartons, yogurt and cream pots and foil dishes. Make sure they are scrupulously clean and do not expect to use them more than two or three times. Use freezer tape for an airtight seal.

Specially toughened glass dishes are handy for mousses and desserts which are to be served in the dish, but they must be freezer-proof.

In addition to wraps, bags and boxes, you will also need sheets of waxed or non-stick paper; plastic or paper-covered wire twist ties, which can be bought ready-cut or on a roll; freezer tape; labels; a chinagraph pencil or waterproof felt-tipped pen.

### LABELLING

It is essential to label everything that goes into your freezer, stating what it is and the date it went into the freezer, unless it is a commercial packet which clearly states what the contents are, in which case just put the date. Use a chinagraph pencil or waterproof felt-tipped pen for labelling.

You can buy freezer labels in different colours so that you can code things for easier finding—for example red for meat, green for vegetables, and so on.

## FREEZING VEGETABLES

Vegetables should be frozen really fresh, not more than 12 hours after harvesting. Refer to vegetable chapter for basic preparation of vegetables (see page 213). All vegetables will keep better if they are blanched before freezing. Blanching means immersing food in boiling water for a short time to inactivate enzymes that would otherwise cause deterioration of flavour, texture, colour and nutritional value.

Blanching also kills many micro-organisms that spoil food and forces out air from inside the vegetables. Air trapped inside the cell walls expands on cooking and ruptures them, so that they leak and give off scum. Although some vitamin C is destroyed during blanching, more is lost with un-blanched vegetables, as destructive enzymes remain active while the vegetables are frozen. The vitamin loss can be minimised by blanching in fast boiling water for exact times (see the individual entries in the chart, see page 510).

Have ready a large bowl of ice-cold water. Using a saucepan large enough to hold a wire basket or colander, add about 4 litres (7 pints) water and 10 ml (2 level tsp) salt for every 450 g (1 lb) vegetables and bring to the boil. Place the vegetables in the wire basket and immerse in the boiling water. Bring back to the boil quickly and blanch for the recommended length of time, see page 213 (starting the time from when the water re-boils).

Remove the basket and plunge into the ice-cold water. Drain well and pack immediately in poly-thene bags or rigid containers; seal and label. The blanching water can be used six or seven times, then replaced with fresh water.

**Storage time**
The maximum recommended storage time for vege-tables is 10–12 months; 6–8 months for vegetable purées.

### COOKING VEGETABLES
Blanching partially cooks the vegetables, so they need shorter cooking time when taken from the freezer. Cook all vegetables from frozen.

**Unblanched vegetables** Some people prefer not to blanch vegetables and the following can be frozen without blanching and kept for the times stated:

| | | | |
|---|---|---|---|
| Brussels sprouts | 3 days | Peppers | 3 months |
| Broad beans | 3 weeks | Peas | 6–9 months |
| Runner beans | 1 month | Carrots | 12 months |
| Sweetcorn | 1 month | Spinach | 12 months |

## FREEZING VEGETABLES

| Vegetable | Preparation | Blanching time |
|---|---|---|
| Artichokes, globe | Wash in cold water, add a little lemon juice to the blanching water, blanch, cool, and drain upside-down on absorbent kitchen paper. Pack in rigid containers. | Blanch a few at a time for 8–10 minutes |
| Asparagus | Grade into thick and thin stems but don't tie into bunches. Wash in cold water, blanch, cool and drain. Tie into small bundles. | Thin stems—2 minutes Thick stems—4 minutes |
| Aubergines | Peel and cut roughly into 2.5 cm (1 inch) slices. Blanch, cool and dry on absorbent kitchen paper. Pack in layers in rigid containers, separated by non-stick paper. | 3–4 minutes |
| Avocados | Prepare in pulp form: peel and mash, adding 15 ml (1 tbsp) lemon juice to each avocado. Pack in small containers. | |
| Beans, French, runner, broad | French: trim ends and blanch Runner: slice thickly and blanch Broad: shell and blanch In each case, cool, drain and pack. | 2–3 minutes 2 minutes 3 minutes |

## FREEZING VEGETABLES—contd.

| Vegetable | Preparation | Blanching time |
|---|---|---|
| Beetroot | Choose small beetroot up to 5 cm (2 inches) in diameter. Wash well and rub skin off after blanching. Beetroot under 2.5 cm (1 inch) in diameter may be frozen whole; others should be sliced or diced. Pack in rigid containers. *Note* Short blanching and long storage can make beetroot rubbery. | Small whole— 5–10 minutes Large—cook until tender— 45–50 minutes |
| Broccoli | Wash in salted water, and cut into small sprigs. Blanch, cool and drain. Pack in boxes in 1–2 layers, tips to stalks. | Thin stems—3 minutes Medium stems—4 minutes Thick stems—5 minutes |
| Brussels sprouts | Make small cuts in stem. Blanch, cool and drain. | Small—3 minutes Medium—4 minutes |
| Cabbage, green, red | Wash thoroughly, shred. Blanch, cool and drain. Pack in polythene bags or rigid containers. | 1–2 minutes |
| Carrots | If left whole scrape after blanching. Slice or cut into small dice. Blanch, cool, drain and pack. | 3–5 minutes |
| Cauliflower | Break into small florets about 5 cm (2 inches) in diameter. Add the juice of a lemon to the blanching water to keep them white; blanch, cool, drain and pack. | 3 minutes |
| Celeriac | Cook until almost tender, peel and slice. Cool, then pack. | |
| Celery | Cut into 2.5 cm (1 inch) lengths. Use for cooked dishes. | 2 minutes |
| Chestnuts | Wash, cover with water, bring to the boil, drain and peel. Pack in rigid containers. Can be used to supplement raw chestnuts in recipe. Can also be cooked and frozen as purée for soups and sweets. | 1–2 minutes |
| Chillies | Remove stalks and scoop out the seeds and pithy part. Blanch, cool, drain and pack. | 2 minutes |
| Corn on the cob | Select young yellow kernels, not starchy, over-ripe or shrunken. Remove husks and 'silks'. Blanch, cool and dry. Pack individually in freezer polythene or foil. *Note* There may be loss of flavour and tenderness after freezing. | Small—4 minutes Medium—6 minutes Large—8 minutes |
| Courgettes | Wash and cut into 1 cm ($\frac{1}{2}$ inch) slices. Blanch, cool, drain and pack. | 1 minute |
| Fennel | Trim and slice thinly. Blanch, cool, drain and pack. | 2 minutes |
| Kohlrabi | Choose small roots, 5–7 cm (2–3 inches) in diameter. Cut off tops, peel and dice. Blanch, cool, drain and pack. | $1\frac{1}{2}$ minutes |
| Leeks | Cut into 1 cm ($\frac{1}{2}$ inch) slices and wash well. Sauté for 4 minutes in butter or oil, drain, leave to cool, pack and freeze. Only suitable for casseroles or as a base to Vichysoisse. | |
| Mange-tout (sugar peas) | Trim the ends. Blanch, cool, drain and pack. | 1 minute |
| Marrow | Choose young marrows. Peel, cut into 1–2.5 cm ($\frac{1}{2}$–1 inch) slices, blanch, cool, drain and pack. | 3 minutes |
| Mushrooms | Choose small button mushrooms. Leave whole, wipe clean but don't peel or blanch. Fry in butter or margarine for 1 minute. Mushrooms larger than 2.5 cm (1 inch) in diameter are suitable only for slicing and using in cooked dishes. | |

## FREEZING VEGETABLES—contd.

| Vegetable | Preparation | Blanching time |
|---|---|---|
| Onions | Peel, finely chop, blanch and pack in small rigid containers for cooking later; packages should be overwrapped to prevent the smell filtering out. Button onions may be blanched whole and used in casseroles. | 2 minutes<br>Button onions—4 minutes |
| Parsnips | Choose young parsnips, trim, peel and cut into narrow strips. Blanch, cool, drain and pack. | 2 minutes |
| Peas, green | Shell and blanch. Shake the blanching basket from time to time to distribute the heat evenly. Cool, drain and pack in polythene bags or rigid containers. | 1–2 minutes |
| Peppers, sweet, green, red, yellow | Wash well, remove stems and all traces of seeds and membranes. Can be blanched as halves for stuffed peppers, or in thin slices for stews and casseroles. For better colour, when storage is less than 6 months, do not blanch. | 3 minutes |
| Potatoes | Best frozen cooked as Croquettes or Duchesse Potatoes (see page 240) or as partially-cooked chips (fully-cooked ones are not satisfactory).<br>New: Choose small even-sized potatoes. Wash, cook fully and cool.<br>Chipped: Soak in cold water for about 30 minutes, drain and dry. Part-fry in deep fat for 2 minutes, cool and freeze for final frying later. | |
| Spinach | Blanch in small quantities, cool quickly and press out excess moisture, or purée. Pack in rigid containers or polythene bags. | 2 minutes |
| Tomatoes | Tomatoes are most useful if frozen as purée. Small whole tomatoes packed in bags and frozen can be used in cooked dishes.<br>Purée: Skin the tomatoes, simmer in their own juice for 5 minutes, until soft. Rub through a nylon sieve or purée in a blender or food processor, cool and pack in small containers. | |
| Turnips | Trim and peel. Cut into small dice, about 1 cm ($\frac{1}{2}$ inch). Blanch, cool, drain and pack in rigid containers.<br>*Note* Turnips may be fully cooked and mashed before freezing. Pack in rigid containers, leaving 1 cm ($\frac{1}{2}$ inch) headspace. | $2\frac{1}{2}$ minutes |

**Unsuitable for freezing** (except as soups and purées): Chicory, cucumber, endive, kale, lettuce, radishes, Jerusalem artichokes.

## FREEZING FRUIT

Fruit for freezing should be just ripe and free from blemishes. It should be frozen as soon as possible after picking. Refer to fruit chapter for basic preparation of fruit (see pages 309–318). The various ways of preparing fruit for freezing are as follows:

**Dry pack** Fruits like blackcurrants, gooseberries, blackberries and raspberries can be frozen just as they are. Spread the fruit on baking trays or sheets lined with non-stick or greaseproof paper and put into the freezer until frozen—this is known as open freezing—then pack the fruit in polythene bags. The fruit will stay separate in the bags, so that small amounts can be removed as needed without having to thaw all of it.

**Dry sugar pack** If preferred, fruits like the above can be sprinkled with sugar before freezing, then as they thaw the fruit and sugar make a syrup. Spread the fruit in a shallow dish, sprinkle over caster sugar, allowing 100 g (4 oz) sugar to each 450 g (1 lb) fruit (unless individual chart entry states otherwise). Mix together gently until evenly coated, then pack in rigid containers, leaving 1–2 cm ($\frac{1}{2}$–$\frac{3}{4}$ inch) headspace.

**Cold syrup** Firm-textured fruits like peaches and apricots are best frozen in a sugar syrup. Fruits that discolour, such as apples and pears, should also be soaked in a solution of lemon juice first. Use the juice of one lemon to each 1 litre (1$\frac{3}{4}$ pints) water used. When preparing large quantities of fruit, make the syrup the day before and leave to chill overnight, as it has to be used cold.

As a rough guide, for every 450 g (1 lb) fruit, allow 300 ml ($\frac{1}{2}$ pint) syrup (made up to the strength indicated in the individual entries in the chart). Dissolve the sugar in the water, bring to the boil, remove from the heat, add lemon juice where indicated, cover and leave to cool. Pour the syrup over the fruit or place the fruit in a container with the syrup. Light-weight fruits which tend to rise in liquids can be held below the surface by using a dampened and crumpled piece of non-absorbent paper on top of the mixture. Leave 1–2 cm ($\frac{1}{2}$–$\frac{3}{4}$ inch) headspace for expansion.

**Purée** Over-ripe fruit can be puréed and frozen to make good stand-by sauces and desserts.

**Storage time**
The maximum recommended storage time for most fruits is 9–12 months; 6–8 months for dry pack fruits and purées; 4–6 months for fruit juices.

*THAWING AND COOKING FRUIT*
If the fruit is to be served raw, thaw it slowly in the unopened container and eat while still slightly chilled; turn it into a dish only just before serving. Fruits which tend to discolour, e.g. peaches, should be thawed more rapidly and kept submerged in the syrup while thawing. Allow 6–8 hours per 450 g (1 lb) fruit in the refrigerator or 2–4 hours at room temperature. Dry sugar packs thaw rather more quickly than fruit in syrup. For quick thawing, place the container in slightly warm water for 30 minutes–1 hour.

If the fruit is to be cooked, thaw it until the pieces are just loosened. Cook as for fresh fruit, but don't forget that it will already be sweet if it has been packed in dry sugar or syrup.

## FREEZING FRUIT

| Fruit | Preparation |
|---|---|
| Apples, sliced | Peel, core and cut into 0.5 cm ($\frac{1}{4}$ inch) slices. Drop into water and lemon juice. Blanch for 2–3 minutes and cool in ice-cold water before packing; useful for pies and flans. |
| puréed | Peel, core and stew in the minimum amount of water—sweetened or unsweetened. Purée or mash. Leave to cool before packing. |
| Apricots | Plunge them into boiling water for 30 seconds to loosen the skins, then peel. Then prepare in one of the following ways: (a) Cut in half or slice into syrup made with 450 g (1 lb) sugar to 1 litre (1$\frac{3}{4}$ pints) water with the juice of a lemon added to prevent browning. Immerse the apricots by placing a piece of clean, crumpled, non-absorbent paper on the fruit, under the lid. (b) Leave whole and freeze in syrup. After long storage, an almond flavour may develop around the stone. (c) Purée cooked apricots. |
| Blackberries | Wash and dry fruit. Dry pack or dry sugar pack. Pack in rigid containers. |
| Blackcurrants | Use one of the following methods: (a) Dry pack method for whole fruit. (b) Purée—cook to a purée with very little water and brown sugar, according to taste. |
| Blueberries or Bilberries | Use one of the following methods: (a) Dry pack. (b) Dry sugar pack—lightly crush berries, mix with sugar until dissolved and then pack in rigid containers. (c) Cold syrup—900 g (2 lb) sugar dissolved in 1 litre (1$\frac{3}{4}$ pints) water. |
| Cherries | Use one of the following methods: (a) Dry pack. (b) Dry sugar pack—stoned cherries; pack in containers cooked or uncooked; best used stewed for pie fillings. (c) Cover with cold syrup—450 g (1 lb) sugar to 1 litre (1$\frac{3}{4}$ pints) water; leave headspace. Take care not to open until required, as fruit loses colour rapidly on exposure to the air. |
| Damsons | The skins are inclined to toughen during freezing. Best packing methods are: (a) Purée. (b) Halve, remove the stones and pack in cold syrup—450 g (1 lb) sugar to 1 litre (1$\frac{3}{4}$ pints) water; they will need cooking after freezing and can be used as stewed fruit. (c) Poached and sweetened. |
| Figs | Wash gently to avoid bruising. Remove stems. Use one of the following methods: (a) Dry pack, either whole or peeled, then pack in polythene bags. (b) Peel and pack in cold syrup—450 g (1 lb) sugar to 1 litre (1$\frac{3}{4}$ pints) water. (c) Leave whole and wrap in foil; suitable for dessert figs. |

## FREEZING FRUIT—contd.

| Fruit | Preparation |
|---|---|
| Gooseberries | Use one of the following methods: (a) Dry pack; use for pie fillings. (b) Cold syrup—900 g (2 lb) sugar to 1 litre (1¾ pints) water. (c) Purée—stew fruit in a very little water, rub through a nylon sieve and sweeten. |
| Grapefruit | Segment and pack. Use one of the following methods: (a) Cold syrup (equal quantities of sugar and water—add any juice from the fruit to the syrup). (b) Dry sugar pack—225 g (8 oz) sugar to 450 g (1 lb) fruit, sprinkled over fruit; when juices start to run, pack in rigid containers. |
| Grapes | The seedless variety can be packed whole; others should be skinned, pipped and halved. Pack in cold syrup—450 g (1 lb) sugar to 1 litre (1¾ pints) water. |
| Greengages | Halve, remove stones and pack in syrup—450 g (1 lb) sugar to 1 litre (1¾ pints) water, with the juice of 1 lemon added. Place in rigid containers. Do not open pack until required. Skins tend to toughen. |
| Lemons and Limes | Use one of the following methods: (a) Squeeze out juice and freeze it in ice-cube trays; remove frozen cubes to polythene bags for storage. (b) Dry pack—whole lemons, slices or segments. (c) Remove all pith from the peel, cut into julienne strips, blanch for 1 minute, cool and pack; use for garnishing dishes. |
| Loganberries | Remove stalks and dry pack in rigid containers. Dry sugar pack. |
| Mangoes, Papaya | Peel and slice ripe fruit into cold syrup—450 g (1 lb) sugar to 1 litre (1¾ pints) water; add 30 ml (2 tbsp) lemon juice to each 1 litre (1¾ pints) syrup. Serve with additional lemon juice. |
| Melons | Only cantaloup and honeydew melons freeze quite well (though they lose their crispness when thawed). (a) Cut in half and seed, then cut flesh into balls, cubes or slices and put into cold syrup—450 g (1 lb) sugar to 1 litre (1¾ pints) water. (b) Dry pack method, with a little sugar sprinkled over. Pack in bags. |
| Oranges | Pack as for grapefruit, or use one of the following methods: (a) Squeeze out and freeze tne juice; add sugar if desired and freeze in small quantities in containers or in ice-cube trays. (b) Grate peel for orange sugar as for lemon sugar. (c) Seville oranges may be scrubbed, packed in suitable quantities and frozen whole until required for making marmalade. (Do not thaw whole frozen fruit in order to cut it up before cooking as some discoloration often occurs—use whole fruit method for marmalade (see page 465). It is advisable to add one-eighth weight of Seville or bitter oranges or tangerines when freezing for subsequent marmalade making, in order to offset pectin loss.) |
| Peaches | Really ripe peaches are best skinned and stoned under running water, as scalding will soften and slightly discolour the flesh. Plunge firm peaches in boiling water for 30 seconds, then skin. Brush with lemon juice. (a) Pack halves or slices in cold syrup—450 g (1 lb) sugar to 1 litre (1¾ pints) water, with the juice of 1 lemon added. Pack in rigid containers, leaving headspace. (b) Purée peeled and stoned peaches; mix in 15 ml (1 tbsp) lemon juice and 100 g (4 oz) sugar to each 450 g (1 lb) fruit—suitable for sorbets. |
| Pears | It is really only worthwhile freezing pears if you have a big crop from your garden, as they discolour rapidly, and the texture of thawed pears can be unattractively soft. Peel, quarter, remove core and dip in lemon juice immediately. Poach in syrup—450 g (1 lb) sugar to 1 litre (1¾ pints) water—for 1½ minutes. Drain, cool and pack in the cold syrup. |
| Pineapple | Peel and core, then slice, dice, crush or cut into wedges. (a) Pack unsweetened in layers, separated by non-stick paper, in rigid containers. (b) In cold syrup—450 g (1 lb) sugar to 1 litre (1¾ pints) water, including any pineapple juice from the preparation—in rigid containers. (c) Dry sugar pack crushed pineapple in rigid containers. |
| Plums | Halve and discard stones. Freeze in cold syrup—450 g (1 lb) sugar to 1 litre (1¾ pints) water with the juice of 1 lemon. Pack in rigid containers. Do not open pack until required, as the fruit loses colour. |
| Redcurrants | Dry pack. |
| Rhubarb | Trim into 1–2.5 cm (½–1 inch) lengths. Blanch in boiling water for 1 minute and cool quickly. (a) Pack in cold syrup, using equal quantities sugar and water. (b) Dry pack; use for pies and crumbles. |
| Strawberries and Raspberries | Remove stalks. Raspberries freeze well. Whole strawberries can be a disappointment; they are best frozen as a purée. Use one of the following methods: (a) Dry pack. (b) Dry sugar pack. (c) Purée; sweeten to taste—about 50 g (2 oz) sugar per 225 g (8 oz) purée; add a little lemon juice to strawberry purée. |

Fruits not suitable for freezing: bananas, pomegranates, kiwi fruit.

## FREEZING MEAT AND POULTRY

Many butchers will supply bulk meat at a good discount on normal retail prices, and will cut it into usable-sized joints. Sometimes butchers will also blast-freeze the meat, so that you get it ready frozen. Alternatively, ready-frozen meat is sold as whole carcasses, halves or quarters, or in bulk packs. Fresh meat needs very little preparation; trim off excess fat and, whenever possible, remove any bones as well. These only take up freezer space and are better used for making stocks for soups (see page 19), which are much more economical to store.

It is essential to package meat well, excluding as much air as possible to prevent the fat going rancid and the meat drying out. Use heavy duty polythene bags. Separate chops and steaks with layers of greaseproof or non-stick paper.

*FREEZING POULTRY*

Commercial quick-frozen raw poultry is so readily available, it's only an advantage to freeze it at home if the price is favourable.

A chicken takes up less freezer space if it is jointed first. Use the carcass for making stock (see page 19), then freeze the stock.

Wrap chicken quarters or joints individually in foil or polythene bags, label, then combine into a larger package to save time hunting for individual packs.

Cold roast or poached chicken should be cooled as quickly as possible after cooking. Wrap small amounts in foil, with any stuffing packed separately, and freeze at once. To avoid excessive drying, freeze it with gravy or stock.

A turkey takes up valuable freezer space, so it's not good planning to store one for too long.

Turkeys can be jointed and stored like chicken. Cooked turkey can also be frozen like chicken; cut the meat off the bone and discard any fat.

Choose young duckling and geese for freezing. Look for ones without too much fat, though very lean birds may be dry. Freeze as for chicken, packing the giblets separately.

**Storage time**

The recommended storage time for chicken, duckling and geese is 12 months; turkey 6 months; giblets 2–3 months and cold cuts of meat 2–3 months.

*FREEZING GAME*

Venison must be hung before freezing, then frozen in usable joints as for meat. Hares and rabbits should also be prepared as for cooking fresh. As most recipes call for portions, it's sensible to pack them this way, discarding the more boney parts. Pack and freeze the game as for meat.

Game birds actually improve with freezing. Hang, undrawn, until sufficiently high, then pluck, draw, wash well and dry thoroughly. Pack in foil or freezer bags and freeze.

**Storage time**

The maximum recommended storage time for venison is 12 months; hares and rabbits 6 months; game birds 9 months.

*FREEZING BACON*

Only very fresh bacon should be frozen, the longer bacon has been cut or kept in the shop, the shorter its storage life in the freezer.

Commercial vacuum-packed bacon is good for freezing as the maximum amount of air has already been extracted from the inside wrapping. Alternatively, freeze top-quality bacon, closely wrapped in freezer cling film or foil and overwrapped in polythene bags. If wished, rashers can be interleaved with waxed or non-stick paper. Wrap bacon chops individually in foil, then pack together in a polythene bag. Joints up to 1.5–2 kg (3–4 lb) should be wrapped in foil, then overwrapped in a polythene bag.

**Storage time**

The recommended storage time for bacon is: vacuum-packed bacon 3 months; smoked rashers, chops, gammon steaks and joints 2 months; unsmoked rashers, chops, gammon steaks and joints 1 month.

## MEAT AND MEAT PRODUCTS STORAGE TIME

| Food | Recommended storage time | Food | Recommended storage time |
|---|---|---|---|
| Beef | 8 months | Curry | 4 months |
| Lamb | 6 months | Ham | 2 months |
| Mince | 3 months | Meat pies | 3 months |
| Offal | 3 months | Pâté | 1 month |
| Pork | 6 months | Sliced meat— | |
| Sausages | 3 months | with gravy | 3 months |
| Veal | 6 months | without gravy | 2 months |
| Casseroles— | | Cottage pie | 3 months |
| with bacon | 2 months | Soup | 3 months |
| without bacon | 3 months | Stock | 6 months |

# GUIDE TO FREEZING MISCELLANEOUS FOODS

| Food and Storage Time | Preparation | Freezing | Thawing and Serving |
|---|---|---|---|
| **Fish, uncooked** Whole salmon, fresh water fish: 2 months Oily fish: 2 months White fish and steaks: 2–3 months Caviar: do not freeze | Must be really fresh. Wash and remove scales by scraping tail-to-head with back of knife. Gut. Wash thoroughly under running water. Drain and dry on absorbent kitchen paper. | For best results, place whole fish unwrapped in freezer until solid. Remove and dip in cold water. This will form thin ice over the fish. Return to freezer; repeat process until the ice glaze is 0.5 cm ($\frac{1}{4}$ inch) thick. Wrap in freezer wrap; support with a thin board. Separate steaks with double layer of cling film; overwrap in foil or freezer wrap. | Allow to thaw for 24 hours in a cool place before cooking. Once thawed, use promptly. Fish steaks should be cooked from frozen. |
| **Sauces, Soups Stocks** Sauces, soups: 3 months Stock: 6 months | All are very useful as standbys in the freezer. | When cold, pour into rigid containers, leaving headspace, seal well. | Either thaw for 1–2 hours at room temperature, or heat gently from frozen until boiling point. |
| **Cream** fresh: 3 months commercially-frozen: up to 1 year | Use only whipping or double cream. Whipped cream may be piped into rosettes on non-stick paper. | Transfer cream to suitable container, leaving space for expansion. | Thaw at room temperature for 45–60 minutes. Put rosettes in position as decoration before thawing. Thaw for 30 minutes. |
| **Cakes, baked** including sponge flans, Swiss rolls, layer cakes and large gateaux: 3 months. Fruit cakes: | Bake in usual way. Leave until cold on a wire rack. Swiss rolls are best rolled up in cornflour, not sugar, if to be frozen without filling. Do not spread or layer with jam. | Wrap plain cake layers separately, or together with cling film or waxed paper between layers. Pack decorated cream cakes in rigid boxes to protect them. | Thaw smaller cakes for 1–2 hours at room temperature; larger gateaux 3–4 hours—cream cakes may be sliced while frozen for a better shape and quicker thawing; fruit cakes 4–5 hours. |
| **Bread** 1–2 months | Freshly-baked bread, both bought and homemade, can be frozen. Crisp, crusty bread stores well up to 1 week, then the crust begins to 'shell off'. | In original wrapper for up to 1 week; for longer periods, seal in foil or polythene. Homemade bread: freeze in foil or polythene bags. | Leave to thaw in the sealed polythene bag or wrapper at room temperature 3–6 hours. Sliced bread can be toasted from frozen. |
| **Herbs** Up to 6 months | Wash and trim if necessary. Dry thoroughly. | Freeze in small bunches in a rigid foil container or bag. | Can be used immediately. Crumble while still frozen. |
| **Cheese** 3–6 months | Full fat soft cheeses and cream cheeses are suitable for freezing. Hard cheeses become crumbly if stored too long, but are fine grated for cooking. Cottage cheese and low fat soft cheeses are not suitable for freezing. | Wrap in freezer film or polythene bag. | Thaw for 24 hours in refrigerator and allow to come to room temperature before serving. Use grated cheese straight from frozen. |

## THAWING AND COOKING FROM FROZEN

Some foods can be cooked from frozen, others need to be thawed. Foods can be thawed slowly or quickly; those thawed slowly have a slightly better texture.

**Meat** Small cuts of meat like chops, steaks, mince, sausages and liver can be cooked gently from frozen, if there is no time for thawing. When cooking, you will need to cook for almost twice as long as usual. Start cooking at a low temperature and increase the temperature half way through the cooking time. Some whole joints of meat can also be cooked from frozen, provided you use a meat thermometer to check that they are cooked right through. Cooking times for frozen joints over 2.8 kg (6 lb) are very difficult to calculate. To prevent the outside being overcooked before the inside is thawed, it is better to thaw large joints before cooking.

Rolled joints such as breast of lamb, whether stuffed or not, must be thawed before cooking. This is because all the surfaces of the meat have been handled and rolled up, so it is important to ensure thorough cooking to destroy any bacteria which might be present in the meat.

**Bacon** Must be thawed before cooking.

**Stews, pre-cooked pies and casseroles** There is a danger that these will not heat through properly if they are cooked from frozen. Thaw at cool room temperature.

**Fish** Whole large fish should be thawed out as slowly as possible to retain moisture and texture. Small fish and cuts are best cooked from frozen.

**Vegetables** These should be cooked from frozen. Try slow-cooking them in a heavy saucepan with a knob of butter or margarine instead of water, to preserve the vitamins.

**Fruit** If it is going to be eaten without further preparation, fruit needs very gentle thawing to prevent it from going too soft and mushy. If wished, it can be eaten while there is still a little ice.

**Bread and rolls** Thawing in a warm oven makes them crisp and smell like newly baked bread.

### SLOW THAWING

The slowest way of thawing is in the refrigerator or at cool room temperature. Always leave food in its original wrapping, otherwise meat will bleed and lose some of its quality and colour; fruit will lose its juice and suffer in texture; fish will dry out. Allow plenty of time; as little as 450 g (1 lb) of food can take anything up to 6 hours to thaw.

### QUICK THAWING

Food thawed at normal room temperature takes about half the time. In an emergency, submerge the package in a bowl of cold water or hold it under running cold water. Once thawed, treat as fresh.

### COOKING AND REHEATING FROM FROZEN

In general, foods that can be cooked or reheated from frozen should be heated as rapidly as possible, as this preserves the flavour and texture. As the food thaws, gently separate the pieces.

### THAWING MEAT

Meat can be thawed at room temperature, but there is less risk of contamination if it is thawed in the refrigerator. If the juices which have come from the meat during thawing are used in cooking, they should be cooked as soon as possible. Thawed meat can be cooked and then refrozen, if wished.

### THAWING POULTRY

All frozen poultry must be completely thawed before cooking, so leave plenty of time. Thaw poultry weighing up to 2.7 kg (6 lb) in the refrigerator and poultry weighing over that at room temperature. If the giblets are inside the body cavity, remove them as soon as possible.

The bird is completely thawed when no ice crystals remain in the body cavity and the limbs are flexible. Once thawed, poultry should be cooked as soon as possible.

### APPROXIMATE THAWING TIMES: FOR MEAT

| Type of cut | Time per 450 g (1 lb) | |
| --- | --- | --- |
| | In a refrigerator | At room temperature |
| Joints | | |
| 1.4 kg (3 lb) or more | 6–7 hours | 2–3 hours |
| less than 1.4 kg (3 lb) | 3–4 hours | 1–2 hours |
| Steaks, chops, stewing steak | 5–6 hours | 2–4 hours |

### FOR POULTRY

| Weight | Oven-ready | |
| --- | --- | --- |
| up to 1.8 kg (4 lb) | 12 hours | in the refrigerator |
| 2.7 kg (6 lb) | 15 hours | |
| 4.5 kg (10 lb) | 18 hours | |
| 6.8 kg (15 lb) | 24 hours | at room temperature |
| 9 kg (20 lb) | 30 hours | |

# COOKING IN A MICROWAVE OVEN

Cooking in a microwave oven is quick, clean and easy. The oven runs off an ordinary household socket outlet and is very economical to operate. It can cook foods such as fish and vegetables in minutes so the nutrients and flavour are retained. It can thaw, cook from frozen or reheat food on a plate. However, there are certain foods it cannot cook, such as Yorkshire puddings, deep-fat fried foods and meringues, and some things where the texture or appearance is not very good; meat, pastry, cakes and breads do not brown, so it is best used in conjunction with a conventional oven.

♦

Microwaves are a form of electrical energy similar to those used for transmitting radio and television. The waves are of a high frequency and short length—hence the name. Microwaves cannot pass through metal—they are reflected off it—so they are safely contained within the oven cavity. They are in no way harmful.

Inside a microwave oven is a magnetron, which converts electricity into microwaves. The microwaves pass through substances such as china and glass, but they are absorbed by the moisture molecules in food. They make the molecules vibrate at such a rapid rate that they produce intense heat, which cooks the food. Microwaves penetrate all the surfaces of the food simultaneously, to a depth of about 5 cm (2 inches) and the heat then spreads to the rest of the food.

### CHOOSING A MICROWAVE OVEN

There are three different types of microwave oven to choose from: the countertop portable type, a built-in microwave in a conventional cooker or a combination type of oven that can be switched either to microwave or to convection (circulation of hot air by a fan) cooking.

The main points to consider when choosing an oven are the power settings, controls, timer settings and internal fittings.

The most useful type of oven is one with variable power, ranging from full (usually 600–700 watts) down through various levels to defrost and warm (usually 200–300 watts). A wide choice of settings enables you to cook items very accurately.

Controls should be clear and easy to use; there is a choice of touch pads, buttons or dials. Some microwave ovens have memory programmes which can be set automatically to cook foods you eat often.

Timer settings should allow you to set the oven for small accurate timings, such as 3 seconds (for bringing eggs from the refrigerator to room temperature) as well as longer times for cooking joints of meat.

All microwave ovens incorporate a turntable or

stirrers which distribute the microwaves, so the food cooks evenly. If you buy a model without either of these, you can buy a rechargeable turntable. All models have an internal light which goes on when the oven is switched on, so you can see the food while it is cooking. This is essential as the food cooks so quickly.

All ovens have vents either at the back, side or top, which allow moisture to escape during cooking. It is important that these are not obstructed by putting the oven under a low shelf or in too small a space.

### SAFETY
Provided you buy an oven which meets the British Standard specifications, it is one of the safest kitchen appliances. It has no moving parts or sharp edges and the dishes in which the food is cooked remain relatively cool.

Have your oven checked once a year, or as often as the manufacturer recommends, for leakage as this could affect the cooking results. Call in the manufacturer's service agent, who will have a special precision meter for doing this. Do-it-yourself meters are available, but they tend to be inaccurate.

If the oven is dropped or has something dropped on it, have it checked before using it. Although microwave ovens are portable appliances, it is best not to move them around too much.

Microwave ovens can affect older types of cardiac pacemaker. If necessary, consult your doctor about this and warn any visitors who have one to stay out of the kitchen while the oven is switched on.

### CARING FOR A MICROWAVE OVEN
The most important thing to remember is never to switch on the microwave oven when it is empty. If there is nothing to absorb the microwaves, they bounce back to the magnetron and will shorten its life. Leave a cup of water in the oven when not in use, then no damage will occur if the oven is accidentally turned on.

Wipe the oven with a damp cloth after each use and mop up spillages immediately or they will continue to absorb microwaves. Foods do not burn on to the interior of the oven but if any spilled food does stick, do not scrape it off with a sharp instrument as this could damage the interior and distort the pattern of microwaves.

To clean the oven, place a large bowl of water inside it and turn the oven on to full power until the water gives off steam. Remove the bowl and wipe the oven with a damp cloth wrung out in washing up liquid, then rinse with clear water and dry with a clean cloth.

### SUITABLE CONTAINERS
A wide variety of containers can be used in a microwave oven. Round containers are best, followed by square ones; rectangular ones are the least efficient. Choose containers with straight sides which allow you to spread the food in an even layer.

The containers must not contain metal; microwaves reflect off metal dishes, causing arcing (small sparks) which will damage the magnetron. Metal also acts as a barrier to the microwaves, preventing the food getting hot.

**China, glass and some pottery dishes** are suitable as long as they do not have metal trims and the pottery is not porous. To test if a dish is suitable, fill a heatproof cup with water and stand it in the dish to be tested. Put the dish in the oven and switch on to full power for 1–2 minutes. If the dish is cool and the water hot, the dish is safe to use. If the dish is hot and the water cool, it means the dish has been absorbing the waves and it is not suitable. If both dish and water are warm, the dish is safe to use but food will take longer to cook and it is preferable to use a more suitable container.

**Plastics** can be used in a microwave, though some plastics become distorted. Test for 15 seconds on full power with a little water in the dish to see if it is suitable. Also, avoid cooking food with a high proportion of fat and sugar in plastic as these ingredients become extremely hot in the oven and may distort the plastic.

**Other materials** which are suitable include wicker and wood, which can be used for short periods, as for warming up bread rolls. Absorbent kitchen paper is useful for covering fatty foods, such as bacon rashers, as it absorbs the fat and makes it crisper. Cling film is ideal for covering food.

It is a good idea to have a plentiful supply of containers which can go into the freezer as well as the microwave oven. Special microwave ware is available, in both permanent and disposable forms, and most of the containers can be used in the freezer as well. These containers are made of special materials which allow microwaves to pass through quickly so the food cooks faster than in ordinary glass or china.

The range includes useful shapes like ring moulds, muffin pans, loaf dishes and pudding basins. Disposable plastic dishes, ovenproof boards, roasting bags and boil-in bags are also available.

## OTHER MICROWAVE ACCESSORIES

**A browning dish** may be supplied with your oven or may be bought separately. It is made from ceramic or glass with a special coating which absorbs microwaves when placed in the oven with full power on. It becomes very hot and can be used to pre-brown the surface of foods like steak, burgers, sausages and chops, which do not brown otherwise when cooked in a microwave oven.

**Microwave roasting racks** are also available. They are made of ceramic or microwave-proof plastic with ridges which keep the meat, poultry or other foods above their juices while cooking.

**A temperature probe** is useful for cooking large joints. Some ovens have them built-in, with others you may need to buy one separately. A conventional meat thermometer must not be used as the mercury is affected by the microwaves.

## COOKING IN A MICROWAVE

Cooking in a microwave oven is very different from cooking by other methods and does require practice and special techniques. Your oven will probably come with its own recipe book, whose timings will be gauged exactly for that model.

In general, foods cook in a microwave oven in between a quarter and a third of their conventional cooking time, but this varies according to the density, quantity and temperature of the food when it goes into the oven.

Microwaves are attracted to water bearing molecules. Fats and sugars will reach a higher temperature as in conventional cooking, so should be watched carefully. Bones in meat conduct heat and are best removed if possible. If meat is cooked with the bone in, the part nearest the bone should be covered with a small smooth piece of foil half-way through the cooking time to prevent it overcooking. Foods covered by a skin or membrane, such as sausages, egg yolks, potatoes and liver should be pricked with a wooden cocktail stick to prevent a build-up of steam bursting them.

Make sure the container is the right size for the amount of food to be cooked. If it is too small, the food will bubble over the edges on to the base of the oven; if too large, the food will spread out too thinly and overcook in seconds.

The way food is arranged on a dish also affects the way it cooks. Place items like chicken pieces and chops in a circle with the thinner ends towards the centre, so that the thicker ends receive the most microwave energy. Other foods are best arranged in a circle around the edge of the dish. Some food will need turning, stirring or rearranging while cooking—a recipe will specify when necessary.

Most foods are best covered, either with a tight fitting lid or cling film or with absorbent kitchen paper if you want a crisp finish, as with bacon rashers. Take care when removing a lid or cling film after cooking, as the steam will be hot.

## STANDING TIME

Standing time is an important factor in both cooking and thawing (see below) in a microwave. Once the heat action has started inside the food, it continues even after the power has been turned off. Most recipes specify the length of standing time and it is important to follow this, even if the food still looks uncooked when the power is turned off.

## WHAT DOES AND DOES NOT COOK WELL

Fish and vegetables cook particularly well in a microwave oven and there is no loss of flavour or texture. Meat and poultry also cook well—care must be taken with unevenly-shaped joints to ensure even cooking.

Casseroles and soups can be made in a microwave oven, but those requiring long, slow cooking to tenderise cheap cuts of meat and give depth of flavour are best cooked in a conventional oven or in a slow cooker and reheated in a microwave when required.

Many puddings can be made in a microwave oven; it is particularly good for steamed puddings and fruit ones, using either fresh or dried fruit. Cakes can be cooked in a microwave oven, but will look very pale because of the fast cooking and lack of applied surface heat. Ingredients (or flavourings) such as chocolate or ginger can be added or the finished cake can be iced. Bread and pastry are best cooked in a conventional oven, but can be warmed through in a microwave oven.

Egg and cheese dishes need to be cooked on a low setting and watched carefully, as they will become rubbery if overcooked. Sauces are excellent cooked in a microwave oven. It can also be used for small batches of preserves; sweets, such as fudges; and for blanching vegetables for the freezer.

Dishes like soufflés and Yorkshire puddings, which need to rise, are not satisfactory. Rice and pasta take just as long as on the top of the stove.

## THAWING IN A MICROWAVE OVEN

Frozen food can be thawed in a microwave oven in minutes. Some ovens have a special control for automatic thawing. If your oven does not have this control, food can be thawed by turning on full power briefly, then leaving the food to stand.

# COOK'S TIPS FOR THE MICROWAVE

- To warm rolls, place four in a wicker serving basket and microwave on HIGH for 20–30 seconds.

- To make quick Melba toast, toast the bread on both sides, then using a sharp knife, slice the bread in half horizontally. Place the untoasted side up on a microwave baking sheet or large plate and microwave on HIGH for 30–40 seconds until dry and crisp.

- To soften butter to a spreading consistency, microwave on MEDIUM for 30 seconds.

- To prevent egg yolks from bursting during cooking, prick the yolk carefully with a wooden cocktail stick, skewer or fork.

- To reheat pancakes, wrap them in a clean tea towel and microwave on HIGH for 2 minutes or until warmed through.

- To soften brown sugar which has become hard and lumpy, microwave it on HIGH for 40–50 seconds in the original packaging.

- If golden syrup or honey has crystallised the texture can be restored by microwaving on HIGH for 1–2 minutes. Always remove metal lids and if necessary transfer the syrup or honey to a glass jar.

- To plump sultanas or raisins, cover with water and microwave on HIGH for 5 minutes. Stir, leave to stand, then drain and dry with absorbent kitchen paper before using.

- To toast flaked almonds, place them on a large plate and microwave on HIGH for 8–10 minutes, stirring frequently until golden brown.

- Lemons and other citrus fruit will yield more juice if microwaved on HIGH for 30 seconds before squeezing.

- To soften ice cream for serving, microwave in its container on MEDIUM for 30–90 seconds, then leave to stand for 1 minute.

- Quickly reheat pre-cooked pies by placing them on absorbent kitchen paper to absorb moisture.

- Thin slices of meat will reheat more evenly than thickly cut slices. Add gravy or a sauce to provide moisture and prevent the meat from drying out.

- Take care when making milk drinks in the microwave as milk can boil over as in conventional cookery. Leave a reasonable space at the top of the mug to prevent this.

# CATERING FOR LARGE NUMBERS

*T*oday entertaining is as formal or casual as you want it to be. This is just as well since most hosts also combine the functions of cook, butler and bottle washer. A little planning and advance preparation is necessary for successful entertaining, whether it is a small barbecue or a formal dinner party. The more work you can do before a dinner party, the more relaxed you will be on the day.

◆

## INVITATIONS

Written invitations are the best way of asking a number of people to a party, whether it's a crowd of children or teenagers, or an adult drinks or buffet supper. It forces people to reply, so that you have an idea how many people are likely to turn up, and it also acts as a reminder to them of the type of party and the time and place.

Send out invitations 2–3 weeks before the event. It is perfectly in order to ask people to reply by telephone. Keep a list by your telephone of those invited and tick them off as they answer.

For dinner parties, invite people by telephone about 10–14 days in advance and indicate if it is to be a dressed-up or casual occasion. Ask your guests if there are any foods which they don't eat for dietary or religious reasons, or simply because they don't like them, to save any embarrassing moments at dinner and wasting food.

## PLANNING THE MENU

Deciding what food you will serve when guests come is one of the most pleasurable parts of entertaining. Try and plan a menu so that dishes are a balance of light and heavy, rich and simple. Choose foods that are in season and plan your menu around the best produce available.

Think about how the food will look when it is prepared; colour and presentation should vary so each dish is a surprise to eye and palate alike. Try to choose colours and textures that complement each other; it is only too easy to find that you have produced a meal that is all pale dishes (cream soup, blanquette de veau and lemon soufflé) which is bland and uninteresting.

Balance the food in terms of richness, so that you don't serve three hefty courses and cheese. If you have two hot courses, it's a good idea to serve a cold dessert or if you serve a cold soup, follow with a hot main course. Avoid serving similar ingredients in several courses—if you serve tomato soup, do not follow with pasta and tomato sauce. If you have cheese in the first or main course, don't serve it after the dessert as well.

Consider how rushed you're going to be on the day. If you're giving a dinner party after work, plan food that can be made in advance, such as a casserole or curry, or put together very quickly. Don't cook dishes which require a lot of last minute attention, such as stir-frying and flambéing. Nothing kills a party faster than frequent disappearances of the cook, unless you entertain in the kitchen while cooking.

### CROCKERY AND CUTLERY

When deciding on the menu, think about the mechanics of eating the food. If you are using paper plates for a buffet supper, don't serve a hot wet dish that will make them curl and droop. If it's fork and finger food, make sure that everything is served in bite-sized pieces which won't need cutting.

For dinner parties, bear in mind the limitations of your crockery and cutlery. While it's possible for someone to dash out during the main course to wash up the starter plates so they can be used for cheese, it's not ideal. Plan your food so that course can succeed course without the need for this.

### ADVANCE PLANNING

Save time on the day by doing as much preparation in advance as possible. Make a list of what you need to buy and work out when you will do the shopping. Don't forget things like savoury nibbles to go with pre-food drinks, coffee, chocolates, flowers and liqueurs if you plan to serve them.

If you are freezing any dishes, cook and freeze them in advance and work out when they will need to be taken out of the freezer. Remember that many dishes such as pâtés, casseroles and some cold puddings can be made in advance and stored in the refrigerator with no ill effects.

It's not always easy to get ahead with table laying or plate and cutlery sorting for a party if you need to use the things right up to the meal before. But you can make sure that glasses are polished, cutlery is clean, tablecloth and napkins pressed, salt and pepper mills and ice trays filled and so on.

On the day, before the guests arrive, have the coffee organised, set out the first course if possible, preheat plates, have the wine open and the ice cubes out. If you are having a dinner party of more than six people, decide in advance where you want people to sit and direct them to their places or write place cards for everyone.

### BUYING THE DRINK AND HIRING GLASSES

When you have decided on your food, select the wine. For a buffet party where you are not sure how much people will drink, ask your local off licence to supply you with drink on a sale or return basis. If you are getting your wine from them, off licences will usually lend glasses free of charge provided you agree to pay for breakages. Otherwise, hire glasses or—if you entertain a lot—consider

*A delicious buffet for 20; see page 524 for the full menu.*

investing in a few dozen cheap glasses of your own.

For teenage or outdoor parties, disposable plastic glasses are a sensible buy, but remember that these are much less stable than real glass.

## QUANTITY GUIDE
## DRINKS TO THE BOTTLE
(using a standard size 100 ml ($3\frac{1}{2}$ fl oz) wine glass)

| | |
|---|---|
| Sherry, port, vermouth | 12 glasses |
| Single measure of spirits | 30 |
| 'Split'—200 ml (8 fl oz) soda, tonic, ginger ale | 2–3 |
| Table wine (75 cl) | 6 |
| Table wine (1 litre) | 8 |
| Fruit juices—600 ml (1 pint) | 4–6 |
| Fruit cordial—1 litre ($1\frac{3}{4}$ pints) bottle diluted with 4 litres (7 pints) water | 20–26 |
| Punch—1.7 litres (3 pints) | 6–8 |

## HOSTING A PARTY

It is difficult to be a good host at a large party—even if there are two of you—if you are also involved in serving food and pouring drink. If it is not a buffet party, consider either hiring professional waitresses or seeing if local neighbours' children or students would be prepared to help. There is little point in giving a party if you spend all your time pushing dishes in and out of the oven or wrestling with a corkscrew.

With buffet parties, introduce as many people as possible to each other early on and leave groups to form and reform as they please after that. Obviously you should rescue anyone who looks as if they would like a change of companion and ensure that nobody is left out on their own.

A buffet party is the ideal way to entertain a large number of people. Plan the menu well in advance to allow time to decide on the quantity of food you will need (use the following charts as a guide).

As a general rule, the more people you are catering for the less food per head you need to provide—however, its better to have too much than too little. The maximum number you should try and cater for is fifty (unless you are experienced).

It is easier to serve mostly cold dishes when entertaining a large number of people, but try and include one or two hot dishes. When planning the menu, choose dishes that can be cooked and/or frozen ahead of time, such as flans, pâtés, tarts, pastries, sandwich fillings, cakes and gateaux, leaving time for preparing perishable ingredients like salads on the day of the party.

Take into consideration the amount of refrigerator space you have, otherwise you may find yourself with too many perishable items and no storage. Use space in a friend's refrigerator or store covered dishes in a cool place, such as a garage.

# Buffet Menu for 20

Garlic Bread × 2
Eastern Casserole of Lamb × 2
Brown Rice Pilaff
White Cabbage with Orange and Peanut Dressing
Three Bean Salad
Apricot Meringue Tranche × 2
Strawberries with Raspberry Sauce

◆

## Count-Down Timetable

**Two days before the party**
Three Bean Salad: Soak the kidney beans
overnight.

**One day before the party**
Garlic Bread: Make 2. Wrap in foil and store in a
cool place.
Eastern Casserole of Lamb: Make double
quantities. Cover with cling film and refrigerate.
White Cabbage with Orange and Peanut Dressing:
Prepare salad and pour over dressing. Cover with
cling film and refrigerate.
Three Bean Salad: Prepare salad and pour over
dressing. Cover with cling film and refrigerate.
Apricot Meringue Tranche: Make double
quantities. The meringue layers can be made even
earlier, if wished. When cold, store in an airtight
container or wrap in foil. Prepare the apricots.
Strawberries with Raspberry Sauce: Hull the
strawberries, keep cool. Purée and sweeten the
raspberries, keep covered with cling film in a
separate bowl.

**On the day of the party**
Garlic Bread: Warm in the oven 15 minutes before
serving.
Eastern Casserole of Lamb: Remove from the
refrigerator 2 hours before the party and allow to
come to room temperature. In one large saucepan
(or two smaller ones with half the casserole in
each), reheat slowly on the top of the stove for
45–60 minutes, stirring occasionally.
Brown Rice Pilaff: Prepare and bake $1\frac{1}{2}$–2 hours
before the party. If the pilaff needs to be
kept warm, reduce oven heat to lowest setting
15–30 minutes before the end of the cooking time.
Salads: Remove from the refrigerator 2 hours
before serving, keep covered. Stir and garnish
1 hour ahead.
Apricot Meringue Tranche: Whip the cream and
assemble the tranches not more than 2 hours
beforehand.
Strawberries with Raspberry Sauce: Pour the
raspberry sauce over the strawberries and chill
covered in the refrigerator for 1–2 hours before
serving.

## Hot Garlic Bread

*1 large French loaf*

*100–175 g (4–6 oz) butter or margarine*

*2 garlic cloves, skinned and crushed*

*salt and pepper*

**1.** Cut the loaf into 2.5 cm (1 inch) thick slices.
**2.** Cream the butter in a bowl until soft. Add the
garlic and salt and pepper and beat together.

**3.** Spread liberally between the slices. Wrap loaf
loosely in foil and bake at 180°C (350°F) mark 4
for about 15 minutes until soft.
*Serves 8–10*

**Variation**
Hot Herb Bread
Follow the recipe above, omitting the garlic and
adding 30 ml (2 tbsp) fresh chopped herbs, e.g.
parsley, chives, thyme.

# EASTERN CASSEROLE OF LAMB

450 g (1 lb) tomatoes, skinned and quartered

45 ml (3 tbsp) vegetable oil

1.4 kg (3 lb) lean boned lamb or mutton, cut into large chunks

3 medium onions, skinned and sliced

30 ml (2 level tbsp) ground coriander

10 ml (2 level tsp) ground cumin

5 ml (1 level tsp) ground ginger

1.25 ml (¼ level tsp) ground turmeric

1.25 ml (¼ level tsp) cayenne pepper

30 ml (2 level tbsp) flour

15 ml (1 level tbsp) tomato purée

450 ml (¾ pint) Chicken Stock (see page 19)

75 g (3 oz) sultanas

salt and pepper

**1.** Rub the tomato seeds through a sieve and reserve the juice.
**2.** Heat the oil in a large flameproof casserole. Add the meat, a few pieces at a time and fry until well browned, then remove from the casserole. Brown the onions in the fat remaining in the casserole.
**3.** Add the coriander, cumin, ginger, turmeric and cayenne pepper and cook for 2 minutes, then stir in the flour and cook gently for 2 minutes. Add the remaining ingredients and the reserved tomato juice and season well. Replace the meat, cover the casserole and cook in the oven at 170°C (325°F) mark 3 for about 1¾ hours for lamb, 2½ hours for mutton.
*Note* The flavour of this casserole is improved if it is made a day ahead, to allow the spices to blend with the lamb, and reheated.
*Serves 10*

# BROWN RICE PILAFF

30 ml (2 tbsp) vegetable oil

4 medium onions, skinned and finely chopped

1 large red pepper, seeded and finely chopped

1 garlic clove, skinned and crushed

5 ml (1 level tsp) ground turmeric

900 g (2 lb) long grain brown rice

1.8 litres (3¼ pints) Chicken Stock (see page 19)

30 ml (2 tbsp) white wine vinegar

salt and pepper

**1.** Heat the oil in a large saucepan, add the onion and red pepper and fry gently for 5 minutes.
**2.** Stir in the garlic, turmeric, rice, stock and vinegar. Bring to the boil and season.
**3.** Transfer the pilaff to an ovenproof dish and cover tightly with foil. Bake in the oven at 180°C (350°F) mark 4 for about 1¼ hours. Fork through before serving.
*Serves 20*

# WHITE CABBAGE WITH ORANGE AND PEANUT DRESSING

1.4 kg (3 lb) crisp white cabbage, finely shredded

10 oranges, peeled and pith removed

100 g (4 oz) salted peanuts, finely chopped

5 ml (1 level tsp) mustard powder

15 ml (3 level tsp) celery seeds

15 ml (3 level tsp) sugar

10 ml (2 level tsp) grated onion

120 ml (8 tbsp) vegetable oil

60 ml (4 tbsp) white wine vinegar

salt and pepper

chopped fresh parsley, to garnish

**1.** Put the cabbage into a large bowl.
**2.** Segment the oranges over the bowl to catch the juice, then add to the cabbage with the peanuts.
**3.** Make the dressing by combining the salt, pepper, mustard powder, celery seeds, sugar, onion, oil, vinegar and seasoning in a bowl or screw-topped jar and whisk or shake together until well blended.
**4.** Pour the dressing over the salad and toss well. Leave overnight for the flavours to blend.
**5.** Toss the salad and sprinkle with parsley before serving.
*Serves 20*

## Three Bean Salad

225 g (8 oz) red kidney beans, soaked overnight

900 g (2 lb) broad beans, shelled

900 g (2 lb) French beans, trimmed

150 ml (¼ pint) French Dressing (see page 260)

chopped fresh parsley, to garnish

1. Drain the kidney beans and rinse well. Put in a large saucepan, cover with water and bring to the boil. Boil vigorously for 10 minutes, then reduce the heat and simmer for about 1 hour, until tender. Drain well.
2. Meanwhile, cook the broad beans in boiling salted water for 15–20 minutes, until just tender. Cook the French beans in boiling salted water for 5–10 minutes. Drain the beans and while still hot combine with the kidney beans and French Dressing. Leave to cool.
3. Sprinkle with parsley just before serving.
*Serves 20*

## Apricot Meringue Tranche

4 egg whites

225 g (8 oz) caster sugar

75 g (3 oz) ground almonds

25 g (1 oz) flaked almonds

50 g (2 oz) granulated sugar

700 g (1½ lb) fresh ripe apricots, halved and stoned

30 ml (2 tbsp) almond-flavoured liqueur

150 ml (5 fl oz) double cream

1. Draw two rectangles 30.5 × 10 cm (12 × 4 inches) on sheets of non-stick paper. Place upside down on baking sheets.
2. Whisk the egg whites until stiff, but not dry. Whisk in 60 ml (4 level tbsp) caster sugar, whisking until the meringue stands in stiff peaks. Fold in the remaining caster sugar and the ground almonds.
3. Spoon the meringue into a piping bag fitted with a 1 cm (½ inch) plain nozzle. Pipe in lines across the width of each rectangle marked on the non-stick paper. Sprinkle flaked almonds over one layer.
4. Bake in the oven at 100°C (200°F) mark low for about 2 hours. Peel the paper off and leave the meringue to cool on a wire rack.
5. Meanwhile, put the granulated sugar in a saucepan with 200 ml (7 fl oz) water and heat until the sugar has dissolved. Add the apricots and poach in the syrup until just tender.
6. Reserve ten apricot halves. Drain the remainder and purée in a blender or food processor with the liqueur, until just smooth. Leave until cold.
7. Lightly whip the cream until it stands in soft peaks, then spread over the plain meringue layer. Spoon over the apricot purée and top with the second meringue layer. Refrigerate for 2 hours.
8. Decorate with the reserved apricot halves just before serving.
*Serves 8*

## Strawberries with Raspberry Sauce

1.8 kg (4 lb) small strawberries, hulled

900 g (2 lb) raspberries

100 g (4 oz) icing sugar, sifted

1. Place the strawberries in a large serving bowl.
2. Purée the raspberries in a blender or food processor until just smooth, then rub through a nylon sieve to remove the pips.
3. Whisk in the icing sugar and pour over the strawberries. Chill well before serving.
*Serves 20*

# BUFFET MENU FOR 50

PÂTÉ EN CROÛTE × 3
CHICKEN GALATINE × 4 *(see page 152)*
POACHED SEA TROUT IN ASPIC WITH MAYONNAISE × 4 *(see page 78)*
ORIENTAL SALAD × 2
PARTY COLESLAW
FENNEL AND RADICCHIO SALAD
GREEN SALAD WITH CROÛTONS
BREADS AND CRACKERS WITH BUTTER
STRAWBERRY AND ORANGE MOUSSE × 4 *(see page 357)*
EXOTIC FRUIT SALAD × 4
PROFITEROLES × 4 *(see page 337)*
WHOLE RIPE BRIE

◆

## COUNT-DOWN TIMETABLE

**Two days before the party**
Pâté en Croûte: Make three; prepare and cook the filling.
Chicken Galantine: Make four. When cold, wrap each one individually and refrigerate.
Profiteroles: Make four quantities of choux puffs, bake and when cold store, without filling, in an airtight tin.

**One day before the party**
Pâté en Croûte: Make the pastry, encase the pâté and bake. Leave to cool, then refrigerate.
Poached Sea Trout in Aspic with Mayonnaise: Cook, cool and refrigerate without skinning. Prepare the Mayonnaise, cover and store in the refrigerator.
Oriental Salad: Make double quantity. Prepare the vegetables and store in polythene bags in the refrigerator. Make the dressing and refrigerate in a screw-topped jar.
Party Coleslaw: Prepare the vegetables and store in polythene bags in the refrigerator.
Fennel and Radicchio Salad: Prepare the vegetables and store in polythene bags in the refrigerator. Make the dressing and refrigerate in a screw-topped jar.
Green Salad with Croûtons: Prepare the vegetables and store in polythene bags in the refrigerator. Make the dressing and refrigerate in a screw-topped jar. Make the croûtons and store in an airtight tin.
Strawberry and Orange Mousse: Make four and refrigerate, undecorated.
Profiteroles: Make four quantities of chocolate

sauce. Cover and keep in a cool place.
Brie: Remove from the refrigerator.

**Early on the day of the party**
Poached Sea Trout: Finish with aspic and keep in a cool place.

**Four hours before the party**
Party Coleslaw: Add the dressing and keep covered in a cool place, not necessarily the refrigerator.
Exotic Fruit Salad: Make four quantities, cover with cling film and keep in a cool place.

**Two hours before the party**
Pâté en Croûte: Slice, arrange on plates and cover with cling film.
Chicken Galatine: Slice, arrange on plates and garnish. Cover with cling film.
Poached Sea Trout in Aspic with Mayonnaise: Garnish.
Oriental Salad: Add the peanuts and dressing to the salad, toss well and cover with cling film.
Profiteroles: Reheat the chocolate sauce. Fill the profiteroles with cream and chill for 1 hour.

**One hour before the party**
Fennel and Radicchio Salad: Toss all the ingredients together and cover with cling film.
Green Salad with Croûtons: Finish salad and cover with cling film. Toss again just before serving and sprinkle with croûtons.
Strawberry and Orange Mousse: Decorate and keep in the refrigerator until ready to serve.

## PÂTÉ EN CROÛTE

450 g (1 lb) chicken livers, trimmed

75 g (3 oz) streaky bacon rashers, rinded and chopped

1 medium onion, skinned and chopped

1 garlic clove, skinned and crushed

100 g (4 oz) butter or margarine, softened

salt and pepper

3 eggs

150 ml (5 fl oz) double cream

30 ml (2 tbsp) medium sherry

350 g (12 oz) shortcrust pastry made with 350 g (12 oz)
    flour

beaten egg, to glaze

1. Put the livers, bacon and onion in a blender or food processor with the garlic, butter and seasoning. Blend until smooth. Add the eggs, cream and sherry and blend for 2–3 seconds.

2. Pour into a greased and base-lined 1.1 litre (2 pint) loaf tin, preferably non-stick. Cover, then stand the tin in a roasting tin and add enough water to come half-way up the sides of the loaf tin. Cook in the oven at 150°C (300°F) mark 2 for about 1½ hours.
3. Remove the loaf tin from the roasting tin, place a weight on the top and leave overnight.
4. On a lightly floured surface, roll out the pastry to a rectangle large enough to enclose the pâté completely. Roll out the trimmings and use to make decorations.
5. Turn the pâté out and encase in the pastry, decorate and glaze. Place on a baking sheet and bake in the oven at 200°C (400°F) mark 6 for about 30 minutes.
6. Cool on a wire rack, then chill for 1–2 hours. Serve sliced.
*Serves 12–15*

## ORIENTAL SALAD

2 heads Chinese leaves, total weight about 2 kg (4½ lb),
    roughly chopped

450 g (1 lb) beansprouts

4 medium red peppers, seeded and finely shredded

300 ml (½ pint) vegetable oil

90 ml (6 tbsp) soy sauce

10 ml (2 tsp) runny honey or soft brown sugar

30 ml (2 tbsp) white wine vinegar

salt and pepper

100 g (4 oz) unsalted peanuts

1. Mix together the Chinese leaves, beansprouts and peppers in a large bowl.
2. Place all the remaining ingredients, except the peanuts, in a bowl or screw-topped jar and whisk or shake together until well blended.
3. To serve, add the peanuts and dressing to the salad and toss well.
*Serves 25*

## PARTY COLESLAW

1.5 kg (3 lb) white cabbage, finely shredded

6 celery sticks, trimmed and sliced

450 g (1 lb) carrots, peeled and grated

1 medium onion, skinned and chopped

75 g (3 oz) seedless raisins

142 ml (4 fl oz) soured cream

15 ml (1 tbsp) lemon juice

150 ml (¼ pint) Mayonnaise (see page 161)

salt and pepper

1. Mix together the cabbage, celery, carrots, onion and raisins in a large bowl.
2. Blend the soured cream with the lemon juice, Mayonnaise and seasoning. Pour over the salad and mix well.
*Serves 25*

# FENNEL AND RADICCHIO SALAD

2 large iceberg lettuces, shredded

2 medium heads of radicchio or 450 g (1 lb) red
  cabbage, shredded

2 medium onions, skinned and sliced

1 fennel bulb, trimmed and finely chopped

150 ml (¼ pint) sunflower oil

50 ml (2 fl oz) red wine vinegar

15 ml (1 level tbsp) whole grain mustard

salt and pepper

**1.** Mix together the lettuces, radicchio, onions
and fennel in a large bowl.
**2.** Place the oil, vinegar, mustard and seasoning in
a bowl or screw-topped jar and whisk or shake
together until well blended.
**3.** Stir the dressing into the salad and toss well.
*Serves 25*

# GREEN SALAD WITH CROÛTONS

8 cos or large Webb's lettuces, torn into bite-sized
  pieces

4 bunches watercress, washed and trimmed

4 cucumbers, chopped

4 medium peppers, seeded and chopped

3 celery heads, trimmed and chopped

45–60 ml (3–4 tbsp) vegetable oil

4 slices of bread, crusts removed and cut into 1 cm
  (½ inch) cubes

100 g (4 oz) blue cheese, crumbled

900 ml (1½ pints) French Dressing (see page 160)

chopped fresh parsley, to garnish

**1.** Mix together the lettuces, watercress,
cucumbers, peppers and celery in a large bowl.
**2.** Heat the oil in a frying pan, add the bread
and fry until crisp and golden brown. Drain the
croûtons on absorbent kitchen paper.
**3.** Add the blue cheese to the dressing, pour over
the salad and toss well.
**4.** Sprinkle over the croûtons and garnish with
parsley just before serving.
*Serves 50*

# EXOTIC FRUIT SALAD

1 medium pineapple, skin removed and cut into 1 cm
  (½ inch) cubes

1 mango, peeled and sliced

1 papaya, peeled and sliced

3 nectarines, sliced

100 g (4 oz) black or green grapes, halved and seeded

1 Ogen melon, halved and seeded

juice of 3 large oranges

juice of 1 lemon

45 ml (3 tbsp) orange-flavoured liqueur

fresh mint sprigs, to decorate

**1.** Mix together the pineapple, mango, papaya,
nectarines and grapes in a large bowl.
**2.** Scoop out the melon flesh with a melon baller
and add to the bowl, then scrape out the remaining
flesh, chop and add to the fruit.
**3.** Mix together the orange juice, lemon juice
and liqueur. Pour over the fruit, cover with cling
film and chill in the refrigerator for 2–3 hours.
Decorate with mint before serving.
*Note* The salad can be kept in a cool place, not
necessarily the refrigerator, for 3–4 hours after
chilling.
*Serves 10*

## APPROXIMATE QUANTITIES FOR BUFFET PARTIES

| STARTERS | Ingredients | Portions | Notes |
|---|---|---|---|
| Fish cocktail | 50 g (2 oz) peeled shrimps, prawns, crab or lobster meat, 2 lettuce leaves, about 40 ml (1½ fl oz) sauce | 1 | Serve in stemmed glasses, garnished with a shrimp or prawn. Serve with lemon wedges. |
| | 700 g (1½ lb) fish (as above), 1 large lettuce, 450 ml (¾ pint) sauce | 12 | |
| Pâtés—allow 3 half slices hot toast per person to serve with the pâté | 75–100 g (3–4 oz) | 1 | |
| | 1.1 kg (2½ lb) | 12 | |
| Smoked salmon (serve with toast as above or brown bread and butter) | 40–50 g (1½–1 oz) | 1 | |
| | 550 g (1¼ lb) | 12 | |
| | 1.1 kg (2½ lb) | 25 | |
| Other smoked fish, such as smoked trout, mackerel | 100 g (4 oz) | 1 | |
| | 1.1 kg (2½ lb) | 12 | |
| | 2–2.5 kg (4½–5 lb) | 25 | |
| Soups—cream, clear or iced | 150–200 ml (5–7 fl oz) | 1 | |
| | 2.3 litres (4 pints) | 12 | |
| | 4.5 litres (8 pints) | 25 | |

| MAIN DISHES | | | |
|---|---|---|---|
| Delicatessan meats—ham, tongue, salami | 75–100 g (3–4 oz) | 1 | |
| | 1 kg (2¼ lb) | 12 | |
| | 2.3 kg (5 lb) | 25 | |
| Salmon | 100–175 g (4–6 oz) | 1 | |
| | 1.4–1.8 kg (3–4 lb) | 12 | |
| Roast turkey | 3.6–5 kg (8–11 lb) | 10–15 | |
| | 6.8–9 kg (15–20 lb) | 20–30 | |
| Chicken—whole | three 2.7 kg (6 lb) birds | 24  26 | Serve hot or cold. |
| —joint | 150–225 g (5–8 oz) | 1 | |

| SALAD VEGETABLES | | | |
|---|---|---|---|
| Carrots | 900 g (2 lb), grated | 12 | |
| | 1.8 kg (4 lb), grated | 25 | |
| Celery | 2–3 heads | 12 | |
| | 5 heads | 25 | |
| Cucumbers | 1–1½ cucumbers | 12 | |
| | 2–3 cucumbers | 25 | |
| Lettuce | 2–3 lettuces | 12 | Dress at last minute. |
| | 5–6 lettuces | 25 | |
| Boiled potatoes | 700 g (1½ lb) | 12 | For potato salads. |
| | 1.4 kg (3 lb) | 25 | |
| Tomatoes | 700 g (1½ lb) | 12 | |
| | 1.4 kg (3 lb) | 25 | |

## APPROXIMATE QUANTITIES FOR BUFFET PARTIES—contd.

| DRESSINGS | Ingredients | Portions | Notes |
|---|---|---|---|
| French Dressing (see page 260) | 300 ml ($\frac{1}{2}$ pint) | 12 | |
| | 450–600 ml ($\frac{3}{4}$–1 pint) | 25 | |
| Mayonnaise (see page 261) | 600 ml (1 pint) | 12 | |
| | 900 ml–1 litre ($1\frac{1}{2}$–$1\frac{3}{4}$ pints) | 25 | |

| DESSERTS | | | |
|---|---|---|---|
| Meringues | 6 egg whites, 350 g (12 oz) caster sugar, 600 ml (20 fl oz) whipped cream | 40 (small) meringue halves | Sandwich meringue halves together with the whipped cream not more than 2 hours before serving. |
| Trifle | Old English Trifle (see page 349) | 6 | |
| | Old English Trifle × 2 | 15 | |
| Profiteroles | 1 quantity of Choux Pastry (see page 379), 150 ml (5 fl oz) whipped cream, 1 quantity of Rich Chocolate Sauce (see page 211) | 6 | Fill the profiteroles with the whipped cream not more than 2 hours before serving. |
| | 2 quantities of Choux Pastry, 300 ml ($\frac{1}{2}$ pint) whipped cream, 2 quantities of Chocolate Sauce | 12–15 | |
| Fruit Salad | Fruit Salad × 4 (see page 341), 900 ml ($1\frac{1}{2}$ pints) cream | 25 | Can be prepared a day ahead, but bananas should be added just before serving. |
| Ice Cream (bought or homemade) | 1 litre ($1\frac{3}{4}$ pints) (see pages 359–362) | 12 | Transfer from the freezer to the refrigerator 30 minutes before serving to soften. |
| | 2.3 litres (4 pints) | 25–30 | |

| SAVOURIES | | | |
|---|---|---|---|
| Cheese Straws | Cheese Straws × 2 (see page 49) | 48 | |
| Sausage Rolls | Sausage Rolls × 4 (see page 145) | 64 | |
| Bouchées | Bouchées × 2 (see page 51) 2 quantities of filling | 50 | |
| Smoked Salmon Pinwheels | Smoked Salmon Pinwheels × 1 (see page 50) | 96 | |
| Asparagus Rolls | Asparagus Rolls × 2 (see page 50) | 50 | |
| Cocktail sausages | 450 g (1 lb) | 32 | |
| Quiche | one 20.5 cm (8 inch) quiche | 6–8 | |

| BREAD, CRACKERS AND SANDWICHES | | | |
|---|---|---|---|
| Bread loaves | 1 large loaf, about 800 g (28 oz) | 20–24 slices | |
| | 1 small loaf, about 400 g (14 oz) | 10–12 slices | |
| | 1 long sandwich loaf, 1.4 kg (3 lb) | 50 slices | |

## APPROXIMATE QUANTITIES FOR BUFFET PARTIES—contd.

### BREAD, CRACKERS AND SANDWICHES—contd.

|  | Ingredients | Portions | Notes |
|---|---|---|---|
| Slices of bread | 1–1½ slices | 1 | Cut into triangles when serving with a meal. |
| French bread | 1 large loaf | 12–15 | |
|  | 1 small loaf | 6–8 | |
| Cheese biscuits or crackers | 3 biscuits | 1 | |
|  | 60 biscuits | 30 | |
| **BUTTER OR MARGARINE** | 15–25 g (½–1 oz) butter or margarine | 1 | If bread is served with the meal. |
|  | 25–40 g (1–1½ oz) butter or margarine | 1 | If serving cheese as a course. |
|  | about 100 g (4 oz) butter or margarine | spreads 10–12 sandwiches | |
|  | about 100 g (4 oz) butter or margarine | spreads 10–12 bread rolls | |

### CHEESE

|  | Ingredients | Portions | Notes |
|---|---|---|---|
| Cheese (for biscuits) | 25–40 g (1–1½ oz) | 1 | When serving cheese at the end of the meal, choose one blue-veined, one hard and one cream cheese. |
|  | 700–900 g (1½–2 lb) | 25 | |
| Cheese (for wine and cheese parties) | 75 g (3 oz) | 1 | Serve a selection of at least four types. |
|  | 2–2.3 kg (4½–5 lb) | 25 | |

## APPROXIMATE COFFEE AND TEA QUANTITIES

|  | 1 Serving | 24–26 Servings | Notes |
|---|---|---|---|
| **COFFEE** ground | 200 ml (⅓ pint) | 250–275 g (9–10 oz) coffee 3.4 litres (6 pints) water 1.7 litres (3 pints) milk 450 g (1 lb) sugar | If you make the coffee in advance, strain it after infusion. Reheat without boiling. |
| **TEA** Indian | 200 ml (⅓ pint) | 50 g (2 oz) tea 4.5 litres (8 pints) water 900 ml (1½ pints) milk 450 g (1 lb) sugar | It is better to make tea in several pots rather than one outsized one. |
| China | 200 ml (⅓ pint) | 50 g (2 oz) tea 5.1 litres (9 pints) water 2–3 lemons 450 g (1 lb) sugar | Infuse China tea for 2–3 minutes only. Put a thin lemon slice in each cup before pouring. Serve sugar separately. |

# Wines and Liqueurs

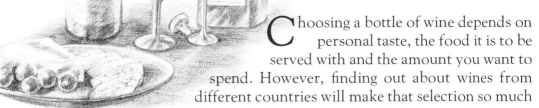

Choosing a bottle of wine depends on personal taste, the food it is to be served with and the amount you want to spend. However, finding out about wines from different countries will make that selection so much easier. Rich and warming liqueurs, each with their own distinctive flavour, provides a satisfying conclusion to any meal.

◆

WINES vary according to the varieties of grape used; where and how they are grown; how the wines are made and treated; and according to the weather in each year. Not only can wines from the same grape varieties grown in different countries be completely different from each other, the same wine from the same vineyards will vary from vintage to vintage, too.

Wine is fermented grape juice. The fermentation turns grape sugar into alcohol. The amount of alcohol in wine may vary from as little as 5 or 6 per cent by volume (the amount is usually shown on labels) to 16 per cent. In wines such as port and sherry, additional alcohol is added to arrest fermentation and preserve more of the wine's natural sweetness. These are *fortified* wines, with alcoholic strengths from 17 to 22 per cent.

### WHAT'S ON THE LABEL

Most wine-producing countries have increasingly complex wine-labelling laws intended in part to give consumers more accurate information, but often more importantly to protect growers from over-production or unfair competition from inferior products. Each country's system is different.
**France** All France's best wine-producing regions are subject to regulations of *Appellations Contrôlées*. An *Appellation Contrôlée* (A.C.) is a guarantee of origin, of production method, of grape varieties

used and quantities produced, but not of quality itself. The A.C. may apply to one small vineyard or to an extensive district. The system varies from region to region. Burgundy has very detailed and precise *appellations* for its best vineyards; in Bordeaux, it is the property or château of origin that matters. In both cases, and many others, there are grades of *appellation* going from simple A.C. Bordeaux or Bourgogne, via more closely designated districts and individual communes, right up to the most highly prized individual vineyards. Wine regions without the quality and traditions required for an A.C. will be ranked as *Vins Délimités de Qualité Supérieure* (V.D.Q.S.). Minor wines of some quality have the lower title *Vins de pays*. Anything else can only be described as *Vin de table*.
**Germany** German wine law is completely different. It is based on the ripeness of the grapes at harvest time and a fairly comprehensive system of quality-testing by expert analysis and tasting. Wine from grapes ripe enough to need no additional sugar is

*Qualitätswein mit Prädikat (Q.m.P.)*: in ascending order of richness *Kabinett*, *Spätlese*, *Auslese*, *Beeren-auslese*, or *Trockenbeerenauslese*. Wine from good vineyards that has needed extra sugar is *Qualitäts-wein bestimmter Anbaugebiete (Q.b.A.)*. All *Qualitäts-wein* is officially checked, tested and tasted. The label will show the wine-producing region and either a *Bereich* (district) or a town or parish name (suffixed -er) followed by a vineyard name. Unfortunately, consumers without a reference book or detailed knowledge have no way of telling whether the vineyard name is that of an *Einzellage* (individual vineyard) or of a *Grosslage* (name covering a group of vineyards). *Einzellage* wines are the best. The name of the grape varieties may also appear. The pre-eminent grape is Riesling. The lowliest wine is simply described as *Deutscher Tafelwein*.

**Italy** The would-be equivalent of the French A.C. is the *Denominazione di Origine Controllata (D.O.C.)*, but *D.O.C.*s have been awarded to many areas whose wines are of only local interest, and some of the best wines do not qualify for *D.O.C.* A higher category, *Denominazione di Origine Controllata e Garantita (D.O.C.G.)* is restricted to a few top-quality zones in Italy. Italian wine names, usually simple, may be geographical, historical, folklorical, or by grape variety. The same name may apply to a wine which is red, white or pink; sweet or dry; sparkling or still. *Classico* means the wine comes from the central, and usually best, part of the region. *Riserva* means the wine has been aged for a statutory period in wood.

**Spain** The Spanish system (*denominación de origen*) delimits many areas of no more than local interest. *Crianza* shows that wine has been aged; *Reserva* that it is good quality wine matured long in cask; *Gran Reserva* better and longer.

**Portugal** The outdated system of controlled appellation is still being overhauled. *Garrafeira* indicates a reserve wine with long bottle age.

**California** The wines are named with producers' or brand names, often linked with that of the grape variety.

## THE AGE OF THE WINE

Most wine is sold when it is ready to drink. Blended wines from chain stores are intended, and best used for prompt consumption. But fine wines need bottle age, which may vary from 5 to as many as 20 or more years for great Bordeaux, Hermitage, or vintage port. Your wine merchant, or his list, should advise about the quality and maturity of vintage wines. All but the finest white wines, and all cheap reds, should be drunk as young as possible.

## HOW TO SERVE WINE

All white wines should be served chilled, dry whites at 8–9°C (46–48°F), sweeter and sparkling ones at 5–6°C (41–43°F).

The lighter and younger red wine is, the cooler it should be served. Beaujolais, Loire reds and *vins de pays* 10–12°C (50–54°F), ordinary reds 13–14°C (55–57°F), meaty reds 14–16°C (57–61°F), finest reds 16–18°C (61–64°F). Wine temperature should be regulated by placing it in a fridge or warm room sufficiently in advance of use.

## HOW TO STORE WINE

All bottled wine needs is to be kept lying on its side in a cool, dark, draught-free place with the minimum of vibration and no exposure to sudden changes in temperature. A cellar with a steady temperature of 11°C (52°F) is ideal, but cardboard boxes anywhere with a constant temperature between 8°C (46°F) and 20°C (68°F) will serve.

## THE WINE FOR THE FOOD

The classically accepted partnerships are:
- with oysters: Chablis or dry Champagne
- with soup: dry sherry or dry Madeira
- with fish: dry white wines or dry Champagne
- with roasts or game: red Burgundy, full claret, Rioja, Barolo
- with sweets: Sauternes or fine sweet hock
- with cheese: Port, brown sherry or Madeira, claret

However, there are no rules about wines to be served with food; it is a very personal matter. Helpful guidelines are light wines before fuller ones; dry before sweet; red before sweet white; lesser wines before fine ones. When one wine only is served throughout a meal it should be the wine most appropriate to the main course.

**Dry white wines** which stimulate the palate are good as an aperitif or with hors d'oeuvres or shellfish (Chablis, Muscadet, Portuguese Vinho Verde, Champagne or other sparkling wine if dry).

**Dry or medium dry white wines** suit plainly cooked veal, chicken and fish dishes and drink well throughout the meal (white Burgundy, Sancerre, Alsace Riesling, Moselle, Soave, Verdicchio).

**Rosé wines, of a medium dryness** are pleasant summer wines for cold plates and picnic dishes (Tavel, Rosé de Cabernet).

**Lighter bodied red wine** is pleasant with lamb chops, veal escalopes and milder casserole dishes (light clarets, Beaujolais, Valpolicello, Bardolino).

**Fuller red wine** suits red meats, rich stews, casseroles, game dishes (St. Emilion and Pomerol

*A Selection of International Wines*

among the clarets; red Burgundy, Côtes du Rhône, Chianti, Rioja).

**Sweet white wines** are drunk chilled, on their own or to go with certain sweet puddings and dessert fruits (Sauternes, sweeter hocks, Muscat de Beaumes de Venise.

## FRANCE

**Bordeaux** produces the complete range of quality from light, quick-maturing reds to the greatest clarets, and from modest dry whites to the world's greatest sweet ones.

The great red wines are the classified growths (*crus classés*) of Haut-Médoc: St. Estèphe, Pauillac, Margaux and St. Julien; of Graves, St. Emilion

and Pomerol. Fine reds come from Médoc and the *crus grands bourgeois*, *bourgeois* and *exceptionnels* of Haut-Médoc, lesser Graves, outlying districts of St. Emilion, Lalande-de-Pomerol and Fronsac. Good are the reds of Bourg, Blaye and Bordeaux Supérieur, drunk at 3 to 5 years old. Below that, stick to reliable shippers' blends.

The great dessert whites are the classified growths of Sauternes and Barsac. Unclassified wines of those *appellations* are fine, as are those of Sainte Croix-du-Mont, Loupiac and Cérons. Première Côtes de Bordeaux are sound. The fine dry whites are classified growths of Graves.

**Burgundy** The greatest reds come from the Côte de Nuits. *Grands crus* need 10 years' maturity;

*premiers crus* up to 12; village wines (such as Gevrey-Chambertin or Vosne-Romanée) about 6. The big wines from the Côte de Beaune are the *premiers crus* prefixed Corton, and the reds of Pommard, slightly weightier than Volnay. Great whites are the *premiers crus* of the Montrachet family and of Meursault.

**Chablis** Distinctive white with a greenish glint, often big in character though very dry.

**Beaujolais** Light, short-lived, fruity reds. Drink *nouveau* or *primeur* by Easter of the year after the vintage. The principal *crus*, in descending order of speed with which they should be drunk: Chiroubles, Brouilly, Côte de Brouilly, St. Amour, Fleurie, Julienas, Chenas, Morgon, Moulin à Vent (keeps up to about 7 years).

**Champagne** Comes only from a carefully defined area around Reims, and is the world's greatest sparkling wine. Vintages are only declared in the best years.

**Loire** Crisp dry whites from Sancerre and Pouilly Fumé. Similar but less well known are Quincy, Reuilly and Menetou-Salon. Vouvray may be dry, medium or sweet. Most are medium, the greatest sweet and capable of long ageing. Other good sweet whites come from Coteaux du Layon, Bonnezeaux, Quarts de Chaume, and Moulin Touchais. The best dry white of Anjou is Savennières. Good light, dry, quaffing wines are Muscadet and Gros Plant, both better if described as '*sur lie*'. Best reds are Bourgeuil and Chinon, best drunk quite young and cool; the lighter Saumur Champigny; and, in propitious years only, red Sancerre. Rosé d'Anjou is pretty but commonplace, a summer refresher.

**Rhône** Good value robust reds, some elegant whites and serious rosés. The great reds come from Côte Rôtie, St. Joseph, Cornas, Hermitage and some estates of Châteauneuf-du-Pape. Also fine are Gigondas, Vacqueyras and Crozes-Hermitage. Compared with these long-lived wines, Côtes du Rhône-Villages, Lirac and the lesser Côtes du Rhône, or inexpensive Côtes du Ventoux and Côtes du Lubéron, are now increasingly made for early drinking.

**Alsace** Fruity and fragrant white wines, named simply according to grape variety. Pinot blanc, soft and nutty; Sylvaner, light, crisp and uncomplicated; Muscat, fragrant aperitif wine; Tokay, buttery, rich and capable of accompanying meat; Gewürztraminer, powerful spicy flavour; Riesling, classically elegant. Late-harvested sweet wines are made in good years. Edelzwicker (also sold as Flambeau or Crystal d'Alsace) is a blend.

**South-west France** Another area of improvement. Seek out Fronton, Buzet, Duras, Marmandais and Bergerac for light, Bordeaux-like wines; Madiran and Cahors for reds of more body; Monbazillac for sweet whites.

**Midi-Provence, Languedoc, Roussillon** Three-quarters of French wine comes from here, and considerable efforts are being made to improve the better *Vins de pays*. The best reds are soft, fruity and fresh for early drinking; better whites, clean and flavoursome. Best bets are Coteaux d'Aix-en-Provence, Bandol, Vin du Sable du Golfe de Lyon, Minervois and Corbières.

## GERMANY

**Rheingau** This region produces the finest Rhine wines, or Hocks, largely from Riesling grapes.

**Rheinhessen and Rheinpfalz** Large producing regions, planted principally with Sylvaner and Müller-Thurgau, which produce many Liebfraumilch blends, pleasant wine of neutral character. Bereich Nierstein is very popular, but of very mixed quality.

**Baden** Straightforward, rather heavy or soft wines. Most successful German *trockens* come from here.

**Mosel–Saar–Ruwer** Mittel-Mosel, the central area, produces the best wines—more acid and zesty than Rhine wines. Bernkastel has the best wines. Piesport is also justifiably famous. Saar wines, including those of Wiltingen, Ayl and Ockfen, are brilliant and austere. Ruwer wines (Eitelsbach, Mertesdorf and Kasel) are fine and delicate.

## ITALY

**Alto Adige** Wines with this D.O.C. can be of any of seventeen varieties. The best reds, Lago di Caldaro and Santa Maddalena, are soft and slightly almondy.

**Piedmont** Big, full-bodied reds pre-eminently from the Nebbiolo grape. The classic wines are Barolo and the more amenable Barbaresco, also Gattinara and Nebbiolo Piedmontese. The other important, but less distinguished, red grape is Barbera, grown best round Alba, Asti and Monferrato. Asti Spumante is a sweet and fruity sparkler, low in alcohol. The best white is Gavi dei Gavi, but it is unjustifiably expensive.

**Lombardy** Some red wines (Valtellina, Sassella, Grumello, Inferno) that are comparable with the great Piedmontese reds.

**Veneto** Light reds—notably Valpolicella and Bardolino—of grace and charm, with slightly bitter tastes, best drunk young. Raboso is more powerful and needs age. Soave is famous, but variable, often bland, sometimes firm, well balanced and flowery.

**Friuli—Venezia Giulia** The most successful varieties are Pinot Grigio and Merlot, the most successful production area is Collio.

**Tuscany** Most elegant of Italian reds—Chianti, the stronger and more fragrant Brunello di Montalcino, and related Vino Nobile di Montepulciano.

**Umbria** The classic white is Orvieto, traditionally semi-sweet, but now commonly dry. The red worth remembering is Rubesco di Torgiano, which is comparable with Chianti Classico.

**Marches** The only widely known wine is the Verdicchio dei Castelli di Jesi, a fresh, pale white.

**Lazio** Frascati, soft-ripe and honey coloured, is more often pasteurised and neutral now. Marino is often a better buy. Est! Est!! Est!!! is more remarkable as a name than a wine.

**Sicily** Corvo is the island's most popular wine; Regaleali and Rapitalá are the best and most enjoyable whites to drink.

**Sardinia** Cannonau, a full-flavoured red, and Torbato di Alghero and Vermentino, flavoursome, fresh whites are the best known.

### SPAIN

Rioja and Penedès are the most important regions producing quality wines. Other full-bodied reds include those of Navarra (Castillo de Tiebas), Valladolid (Vega Sicilia, Protos) and Jumilla. Rueda now produces fresh young whites. All mature Spanish table wines of high quality tend to have a characteristic vanilla flavour derived from keeping in oak, though some fresh and fruity whites are now also being made for quicker consumption. Cava sparkling wines are made by the champagne method, but not as distinguished.

### PORTUGAL

An under-rated producer. Solid red wines and fruity dry whites come from the Dão region. Bucellas is an elegant, classic white. The reds of the newly demarcated Bairrada region and of Colares require long ageing to be at their best, and dependable quality blends include Periquita, Pasmados and Serradeyres. Mateus rosé is a popular carbonated semi-sweet rosé. Vinho verde is made from under-ripe grapes.

### CALIFORNIA

The wine industry has been much modernised in the past decade, and has taken the world by storm with good quality wines. Improvements continue to be made. The most successful varieties to date are Cabernet Sauvignon, the variable native Zinfandel, Chardonnay (outstanding) and Sauvignon (or Fumé) Blanc.

### AUSTRALIA

Wines to rival California's but less for export. Labels tend to be very informative and helpful. Prizes in shows for once mean a great deal. Reds tend to be powerful, broad and fat flavoured, particularly those made from Shiraz grapes. Cabernet Sauvignons are rich and blackcurrant. Among whites, Chardonnays and Rhine Riesling wines show great character. There are also gorgeous deep brown, sweet Muscat wines from Victoria.

### NEW ZEALAND

The most rapidly advancing wine industry in the world, using classic varieties in modern and experimental methods to produce distinctive, characterful wines. Stronger in white wines than red, with the Gewürztraminer particularly successful.

### CENTRAL EUROPE AND BALKANS

Wines from these countries offer great value for money, with quality tending generally to improve. Save in Greece, labelling follows the common German pattern of matching place name with grape variety. Austrian wines are similar to German, but lighter and cheaper. The *Weingutesiegel* (W.G.S.) means the wine has been officially tested and approved. Hungary provides lively whites and some sturdy, warming reds, and also the famous Tokay sweet wine, which resembles an oxidized Sauternes. Romanian wines are sound, good value, but undistinguished. Yugoslavia sells reliable Riesling, Cabernet, Pinot blanc and Traminer, while Bulgaria offers bargain Cabernet, Merlot and Chardonnay. Greece has been in a backwater, but has some reliable, cheap brands. Retsina tastes of turpentine because of added resin, and needs to be drunk very cold with Greek food. Cyprus has improving standards and reliable brands of robust cheap red. Commandaria is a bargain dessert wine.

### SOUTH AFRICA

The only exports are tested quality wines, and good vintages are the rule. Inexpensive blended wines are excellent value, and there are fine estate wines. The successful varieties to seek are Chenin Blanc (Steen), Colombard, Rhine Riesling, Fumé Blanc, Chardonnay—whites; and Cabernet Sauvignon, Shiraz, Tinta Barocca and the native Pinotage—reds.

### OTHER WINE-PRODUCING COUNTRIES

English wines are produced on a small scale, but are highly priced for their quality. Swiss wines are sound, but expensive and little seen. North African reds are full-bodied and robust. Argentina and Chile both produce excellent Cabernet Sauvignon wines, and Argentina some successful Chardonnay.

Wines may also be found from Mexico, Israel, Turkey, Egypt, Lebanon (Château Musar is excellent), the Soviet Union and China.

## SPARKLING WINES

Many sparkling wines—Champagne is of its own unique quality and price—are made by the champagne method, and state this on the label. The other main method is the *cuve close* (or sealed vat).

Asti Spumante is made by a process that combines the two methods. Most German *Sekt* (sparkling wine) is made by the *cuve close* method.

## FORTIFIED WINES

The most famous are sherry, port, Madeira and Marsala. Strict legislation protects these names in Europe so that sherry can only come from the Jerez region of Spain and port from Portugal.

### PORT

Port is made from grapes grown in the upper valley of the Douro river and is shipped from Oporto.
**Vintage port** is the great wine, unique in style. It spends most of its life in a bottle and that can be for 10–20 or even more years for a fine vintage. Must be decanted, or filtered free of sediment.

*When decanting port, it is important to keep the bottle level. This prevents the sediment passing into the decanter.*

**Wood ports** are blends of wines of different years and ages which are matured in cask; they may be ruby, tawny, 'crusted' or vintage-character. *Ruby* is generally a blend of young wines; *tawny* can be either a fine old matured port which started as a ruby or a blend of ruby port and older or white wine. *White port*, made entirely from white grapes, is pale gold and slightly dry.

### SHERRY

Sherry comes from the vineyards around the towns

of Jerez de la Frontera, Puerto de Santa Maria and Sanlucar de Barrameda, which is on the sea and where, specifically, Manzanilla is produced.

Sherry is a blend of wines, matured by what is called the *solera* system, to ensure a continuing supply of wines of the same style and quality. There are five main types of sherry.
**Fino**, driest to the taste, pale gold in colour, this is a wine best drunk chilled.
**Manzanilla** is a special type of fino, bone-dry and with a slight salt tang flavour to it.
**Amontillado** at its finest is a matured fino, with deep fragrance and a slightly 'nutty' flavour.
**Oloroso** is tawny-gold sherry with a rich bouquet and not by nature sweet at all, although many are sweetened for export as cream sherries.
**Brown sherries** are dark and sweet.

### MADEIRA

Madeira, named for the Portuguese island where it is made, is wine fortified by the addition of cane spirit and matured by cooking in heated lofts known as *estufagem*. Traditionally the varieties of Madeira are:
**Sercial**, the driest and lightest wine, a suitable aperitif, slightly chilled.
**Verdelho**, medium dry, darker in colour.
**Bual**, velvety, medium-sweet, deep golden-brown, suitable with dessert fruit and nuts.
**Malmsey**, the sweetest Madeira, rich and honeyed.

### MARSALA

Marsala, the famous wine of Sicily is made from a blend of local wines, brandy and unfermented grape juice. There are dry as well as sweet Marsalas.

## APERITIFS

Patent aperitifs are either wine or spirit based. French and Italian vermouths are among the most widely used wine-based aperitifs. Other aperitifs,

generically called bitters, are made from distilled spirits distinctively flavoured with roots, herbs and barks.

## VERMOUTHS

Dry, medium or sweet, they may be served chilled and straight or with ice cubes and/or soda water and a slice of lemon; or to make mixed drinks (dry white with gin for a dry Martini; sweet red with whisky for a Manhattan, for instance). Chambéry is the most subtle, delightful vermouth of France and has its own *appellation d'origine*. Made from light, dry wine of the southern Alps, its pink version, Chamberyzette, is flavoured with wild strawberries. Noilly Prat is the other bone-dry, pale, best-known French vermouth. Cinzano, Martini and Gancia are famous Italian vermouth names. They can be red (sweet), white (dry) or *bianco* (meaning white, but on the sweet side of medium).

## BITTERS

Campari, the best-known Italian bitters, is usually mixed with soda, as is the French Amer Picon. Campari mixed with red Italian vermouth, a splash of soda and a slice of lemon makes the popular drink called Americano. Suze is a very bitter, yellow, gentian-based aperitif, good as a restorative. Fernet-Branca and Underberg are ferocious looking-and-tasting medicinal bitters.

**Anis** drinks—Pernod, Pastis, Ricard, Ouzo—are aniseed/liquorice-flavoured greenish liquors that turn milky when water is added.

# LIQUEURS are *digestifs*, and so ideal as after-dinner drinks, though increasingly used in cooking sweet dishes, too. Alcohol, an essential ingredient in all liqueurs, may be in the form of grape spirit, grain spirit or fruit spirit. Sweetening is added and the variety of flavourings come from herbs, spices or fruit. Brandy is a spirit distilled from wine and is included here because of its popularity as an after-dinner drink.

The list shows the more familiar liqueurs in this country, although many fascinating local ones can be discovered during travel to regions of their origin.

**Advocaat** A Dutch liqueur, thick and creamy, made from fresh egg yolks and brandy.

**Amaretto di Saronno** Italian fruit liqueur, flavoured with apricot kernels.

**Anisette** A colourless aniseed-flavoured liqueur that comes from France, Spain and Italy. Marie Brizard, from Bordeaux, is the most famous.

**Aquavit** Scandinavian national drink, made from

*A Colourful Selection of Liqueurs*

grain, rye or potato and variously flavoured with caraway, aniseed or dill.. Always served iced, but really best with open sandwiches or piquant snacks.

**B and B** Drier version of Bénédictine, in which the liqueur is ready-mixed half and half with brandy.

**Bailey's Irish Cream** A low-strength liqueur of chocolate-flavoured whiskey and double cream.

**Bénédictine** The most renowned and popular of herb-based liqueurs.

**Bourbon whiskey** More full flavoured, robust and fruity than Scotch, but with less finesse.

**Brandy** There are many grape brandies, and the noble ones come from Cognac. From southern Bordeaux comes Armagnac, where it is proudly called D'Artagnan's Brandy. It has a distinctive herby, sometimes smoky flavour and aroma.

Fruit brandies are sometimes misnamed. The terms 'Cherry Brandy', 'Apricot Brandy', 'Peach Brandy' are established names for sweet *liqueurs* made respectively from the fruits mentioned.

**Calvados** (applejack) is an apple brandy that takes its name from Calvados, the centre of the Normandy apple orchards.

**Cassis** A blackcurrant flavoured liqueur from Dijon, often added to dry white wine for a pretty, cooling summer drink called Kir.

**Chartreuse** One of the most famous herb-flavour liqueurs originally compounded by the Carthusian monks at Chartreuse, near Grenoble. The yellow type is sweeter, the green higher in alcohol.

**Cointreau** is a popular orange curaçao.

**Crème de Cacao** A very sweet chocolate-coloured and cocoa-flavoured liqueur from the West Indies, sometimes drunk through a layer of cream.

**Crème de Menthe** Green in colour with a pronounced peppermint flavour.

**Curaçao** The original orange curaçao was made from citrus fruit from the island of Curaçao but the term is now generic and is used for various orange-flavoured liqueurs.

**Drambuie** a Scottish liqueur, golden coloured, with the flavour of whisky and heather honey.

**Eaux-de-vie** (Waters of Life) are fruit brandies. The best known are *kirsch* (cherry); *framboise* (raspberry); *fraise* (strawberry); *myrtille* (bilberry); *mirabelle* (golden plum); *quetsch* (Switzen plum); *prunelle* (sloe); *poire Williams* (pear); *houx* (holly berry); *coing* (quince); *alisier* (rowanberry); and in Germany and Switzerland *Enzian* (gentian).

**Galliano** A golden spicy herbal Italian liqueur, made famous in Harvey Wallbanger cocktails.

**Glayva** Scottish, whisky-based liqueur flavoured with honey and herbs.

**Goldwasser** Aniseed-flavoured liqueur from Germany; colourless, with little gold particles in it.

**Grand Marnier** The best known French brand of orange-flavoured liqueur in the curaçao family.

**Irish Mist** Irish whiskey and heather honey.

**Izarra** Green and yellow herbal liqueurs based on armagnac and with a bouquet of mimosa honey, from the Basque country.

**Kahlúa** A Mexican coffee liqueur, quite different from Tia Maria.

**Kirsch** is an *eau de vie*, or stone fruit brandy, in which the crushed kernels are included with the fruit juice—in this instance cherry.

**Kümmel** A caraway-flavoured, colourless liqueur of Dutch origin.

**Lovage** Herbal alcoholic cordial of low strength, drunk as a digestif in the West Country.

**Malibu** A mixture of coconut and rum.

**Malt Whisky** A more soporific after-dinner digestif than Cognac.

**Mandarin Napoleon** Belgian proprietary liqueur, of tangerines macerated in aged Cognac.

**Maraschino** A bitter-sweet, water white liqueur made with maraschino cherries and their crushed kernels. It originated in Yugoslavia.

**Parfait Amour** An exotic, sweet citrus-oil based liqueur made in several colours, mainly violet. It is scented and slightly spiced.

**Pisco** A South American brandy made from muscat wine, aged in clay jars and traditionally said to have the taste and aroma of beeswax.

**Royal Mint Chocolate** A popular modern liqueur with a subtle flavour blend.

**Sambuca** Italian liqueur tasting of elderberry and liquorice. It is traditional to float coffee beans on each glass and set fire to the liqueur for a few minutes to roast them, and release their flavour.

**Slivovitz** is a colourless, dry plum brandy, notably from the Balkans.

**Sloe Gin** Rich, ruby red liqueur made by steeping sloe berries in gin. The traditional 'stirrup cup' of Old England.

**Southern Comfort** The most popular of America's indigenous liqueurs—a whiskey flavoured with peaches, oranges and herbs.

**Strega** An aromatic herb liqueur made from a centuries old Italian recipe combining the flavours of some 70 herbs and barks.

**Tia Maria** A Jamaican rum liqueur, based on coffee extracts and local spices.

**Triple Sec** A strong white curaçao.

**Van Der Hum** South African liqueur, tasting of the *naartje*, or tangerine.

**(La) Vieille Cure** A very potent liqueur made from some 50 aromatic plants and roots.

# COCKTAILS, CUPS AND PUNCHES

This chapter contains a selection of the many drinks—cocktails, cups, punches both hot and cold, and mulls—which are based on spirits, sherry, port, wine, cider and ale. (The spirits used include whisky, gin, brandy, rum and vodka.) For non-alcoholic squashes and punches see the latter part of the next chapter. Where 'splits' are used, these are 240 ml (8½ fl oz) bottles.

◆

COCKTAILS are alcoholic drinks based on mixtures of different wines, spirits and liqueurs, sometimes with the addition of fruit juice, coffee or cream. They are drunk on their own, never with meals. Although mixing cocktails is relatively simple in itself, there are a number of basic rules.

All cocktails are served cold and lots of ice is needed to chill them. Crushed ice is more efficient at cooling than large blocks, so make your ice in a tray with fairly small sections and crush it, either with a special ice crusher or wrapped in a tea towel and crushed with a kitchen mallet or rolling pin. The ice should not melt in the drink, but remain in the base to cool it, so do not get it out of the freezer until it is needed. Measuring is critical when making cocktails to get the right balance of ingredients. The classic cocktail measure—which you can buy—is 40 ml (1½ fl oz) but as long as you use a *consistent* measure for each ingredient you can use something like a medicine beaker, small glass or even an egg cup. Ideally, cocktails are mixed in a special shaker which incorporates a strainer, so that when it is poured out the ice which has chilled the drink remains behind.

They can also be mixed in a jug, in which case you will need a strainer, preferably the special bar type known as a hawthorne. In addition, you will need a long-handled spoon for stirring and measuring small quantities of flavourings, a corkscrew, bottle opener, sharp fruit knife, citrus squeezer and chopping board.

Cocktails are made either by shaking, which produces a really cold but cloudy drink or by stirring which keeps it clear. Stir gently when fizzy liquids are involved or they will quickly go flat. Some cocktails which include fresh fruit need to be made in a blender or food processor in order to purée it.

Classic cocktail glasses are stemmed with a straight-sided bowl that is considerably wider at the top than the base. Their capacity is about 75–100 ml (3–4 fl oz) and they are used for short drinks.

Long cocktails are served in tall, straight-sided glasses called highballs or Collins glasses. Their capacity is about 200–300 ml (7–10 fl oz). Other glasses used for cocktails include whisky tumblers, wine glasses and champagne saucers and flutes. Glasses should be chilled in the refrigerator for at least an hour before cocktails are poured into them. If you want to frost the rims for a decorative effect, dip them first into egg white and then into caster sugar before chilling.

*'Frost' in caster sugar.*

Part of the charm of cocktails is their range of colours and the garnishes used in them.

Depending on the type of drink, you can garnish it with maraschino cherries, little cocktail onions, olives, fresh fruit—especially citrus fruit—mint or cucumber. Spices such as nutmeg are sometimes sprinkled on to cream cocktails.

Cocktails are often drunk through a straw and some cocktail glasses incorporate built-in glass straws. You can use wooden or coloured plastic cocktail sticks to spear some of the garnishes and give a decorative finishing touch with a small, coloured paper parasol.

Each of the following cocktail recipes will serve one person. Multiply the amounts according to the number of people you are serving.

## BRANDY ALEXANDER

*1 part brandy*

*1 part crème de caçao*

*1 part double cream*

*a pinch of grated nutmeg*

**1.** Mix together the brandy, crème de caçao and cream and shake well.
**2.** Dust with a little nutmeg and serve.

**Variation**
For a Gin Alexander, replace the brandy with gin.

## BLACK RUSSIAN

*2–3 ice cubes*

*2 parts vodka*

*1 part coffee-flavoured liqueur*

**1.** Put the ice cubes in a tumbler and pour over the vodka and coffee-flavoured liqueur.

**Variation**
For a White Russian float a measure of cream on top.

*From the left: Black Russians and Brandy Alexander*

# RUSTY NAIL

*2–3 ice cubes*

*2 parts whisky*

*1 part Drambuie*

**1.** Put the ice cubes in a tumbler and pour over the whisky and Drambuie.

**2.** Stir and serve on the rocks.

# WHISKY SOUR

*juice of ½ a lemon*

*5 ml (1 level tsp) sugar*

*1 measure rye whisky*

*crushed ice*

**1.** Mix together the lemon juice, sugar and whisky and shake well with the ice.

**2.** Serve in a whisky tumbler.

# TOM COLLINS

*2–3 ice cubes*

*juice of 1 lemon*

*15 ml (1 level tbsp) sugar*

*1 measure whisky*

*1 orange slice*

*soda water*

**1.** In a shaker, mix the ice cubes, lemon juice, sugar and whisky until a frost forms.

**2.** Pour into a glass and add a slice of orange.

**3.** Top with soda water and stir before serving.

# PINK GIN

*2–3 drops Angostura bitters*

*1 measure gin*

*2–3 measures iced water*

**1.** Put the bitters into a glass and turn it until the sides are well coated.

**2.** Add the gin and top up with iced water to taste.

*From the left: Dry Martini and Sweet Martini Cocktail*

# DRY MARTINI

*2 parts French vermouth*

*1 part dry gin*

*crushed ice*

*1 stuffed olive or lemon rind curl*

**1.** Shake the vermouth and gin together with some crushed ice in a shaker.

**2.** Pour into a glass and float a stuffed olive or a curl of lemon rind on top. The proportions of a martini are a matter of personal taste; some people prefer 2 parts of gin to 1 of vermouth, others equal parts of gin and vermouth.

**Variation**

SWEET MARTINI COCKTAIL

Follow the recipe above, but use sweet vermouth and decorate with a cocktail cherry.

# BLOODY MARY

*1 measure vodka*

*2 measures tomato juice*

*dash of Worcestershire sauce*

*squeeze of lemon juice*

*crushed ice*

**1.** Shake all the ingredients with the crushed ice in a shaker, then strain into a cocktail glass.

## SCREWDRIVER

*2–3 ice cubes*

*1 measure vodka*

*juice of 1 orange*

*1 orange slice, to decorate*

1.  Put the ice cubes into a tall glass and pour in the vodka and orange juice. Stir lightly and decorate with a slice of orange.

## HARVEY WALLBANGER

*2 parts vodka*

*6 parts orange juice*

*crushed ice*

*1 part Galliano*

1.  Pour the vodka and orange juice over the ice in a tall glass and float the Galliano on top.

## DAIQUIRI

*juice of ½ a lime or ¼ of a lemon*

*5 ml (1 level tsp) sugar*

*1 measure white rum*

*crushed ice*

*extra fruit juice and caster sugar for frosting*

1.  Mix the fruit juice, sugar and rum and shake well with the crushed ice in a shaker.
2.  Dip the edges of the glass in a little more fruit juice and then into caster sugar to frost the rim before filling.

## PINA COLADA

*3 parts white rum*

*4 parts pineapple juice*

*2 parts coconut cream*

*crushed ice*

*1 pineapple slice and 1 cherry, to decorate*

1.  Blend together the rum, pineapple juice, coconut cream and crushed ice.
2.  Pour into a large goblet or a hollowed-out pineapple half.
3.  Decorate with a slice of pineapple and a cherry. Serve with straws.

## MARGARITA

*lemon juice*

*salt*

*4 parts tequila*

*1 part curaçao*

*1 part lemon or lime juice*

1.  Dip the edges of a chilled glass into lemon juice and then salt.
2.  In a shaker, mix the tequila, curaçao and lemon juice.
3.  Strain into the chilled glass and serve.

## TEQUILA SUNRISE

*5 ml (1 tsp) grenadine*

*1 part tequila*

*2 parts orange juice*

*ice cubes*

1.  Carefully pour the grenadine into the bottom of a chilled glass.
2.  Stir the tequila and orange juice with ice in a mixing glass and strain into the glass so that it splashes on to the grenadine.
3.  Add ice cubes and serve.

## BUCKS FIZZ

*1 part fresh orange juice*

*2 parts champagne*

1.  Chill the ingredients.
2.  Fill a champagne glass about one-third full with orange juice and top up with champagne.

## BLACK VELVET

*1 part Guinness*

*1 part champagne*

1.  Chill the ingredients.
2.  Pour equal quantities of Guinness and champagne into beer tankards and serve.

# CUPS AND PUNCHES are subtle mixtures of wines and/or spirits
flavoured with fruit or spices. They may be served hot or cold and are usually made in
large quantities for parties.

When serving cups and punches, allow 200 ml (7 fl oz) per glass.

## MIDSUMMER NIGHT'S DREAM

*1 bottle Reisling*

*1 bottle Beaujolais*

*750 ml (25 fl oz) lemonade*

*50 ml (2 fl oz) orange-flavoured liqueur*

*1 dessert apple, cored and sliced*

*melon pieces*

*orange slices, quartered*

*a few strawberries*

*crushed ice*

*about 30 ml (2 tbsp) sugar*

**1.** Pour the wines, lemonade and the orange-flavoured liqueur over the fruit and ice in a bowl. Chill and add sugar to taste.
**2.** Serve ice-cold.
*Makes about 2.3 litres (4 pints)*

*From the left: Bucks Fizz and Midsummer Night's Dream*

## WHITE WINE CUP

*crushed ice*

*3 bottles white wine*

*¾ bottle dry sherry*

*60 ml (4 tbsp) orange-flavoured liqueur*

*4 'splits' tonic water*

*3 cucumber slices, an apple slice and a borage sprig
    per jug, to garnish*

**1.** Mix all the ingredients together and chill before serving. Decorate with garnish.
*Makes about 3.7 litres (6½ pints)*

## GLUHWEIN

*600 ml (1 pint) red wine*

*75 g (3 oz) brown sugar*

*2 cinnamon sticks, each 5 cm (2 inches) long*

*1 lemon stuck with cloves*

*150 ml (¼ pint) brandy*

**1.** Put all the ingredients except the brandy in a saucepan, bring to simmering point, cover and simmer gently for 2–4 minutes.
**2.** Remove from the heat, add the brandy, strain and serve at once.
*Makes about 750 ml (1¼ pints)*

## BRANDY CIDER CUP

*600 ml (1 pint) tea*

*50 g (2 oz) sugar*

*juice of 2 oranges*

*90–120 ml (6–8 tbsp) brandy*

*1 litre (1¾ pints) cider*

*1 lemon, thinly sliced*

**1.** Infuse the tea for a few minutes and strain it on to the sugar in a bowl.
**2.** Cool and add the orange juice and brandy.
**3.** Just before serving, add the cider and decorate with the lemon slices.
*Makes about 2 litres (3½ pints)*

## SLOE GIN

450 g (1 lb) sloes

75–100 g (3–4 oz) sugar

almond flavouring

1 75 cl bottle gin

**1.** Remove the stalks and wash the sloes. Prick them all over with a darning needle and put into a screw-topped bottle.
**2.** Add the sugar and a few drops of almond flavouring. Fill up the bottle with gin, screw down tightly and leave in a dark place for 3 months, shaking occasionally.
**3.** At the end of this time, open the bottle and strain the liquor through muslin until clear.
**4.** Re-bottle and leave until required.

## CLARET CUP

25 g (1 oz) sugar

thinly pared rind and juice of 1 lemon and 2 oranges

2 bottles claret

4 'splits' tonic water

few thin cucumber slices

borage sprigs (optional)

**1.** Put the sugar and the lemon and orange rinds in a saucepan and simmer for about 10 minutes.
**2.** Cool and add the strained juice of the lemon and oranges, together with the claret. Chill well.
**3.** Just before serving, add the tonic water, cucumber and borage, if using.
*Makes about 2.3 litres (4 pints)*

## DR JOHNSON'S CHOICE

1 bottle red wine

12 sugar cubes

6 cloves

150 ml (¼ pint) orange-flavoured liqueur

150 ml (¼ pint) brandy (optional)

freshly grated nutmeg

**1.** Heat the wine, sugar and cloves to near boiling point, then pour in 600 ml (1 pint) boiling water.
**2.** Pour in the orange-flavoured liqueur and the brandy, if using.
**3.** Pour into glasses and sprinkle with nutmeg.
*Makes about 1.7 litres (3 pints)*

## VIN BLANC CASSIS (KIR)

4 parts dry white wine (Chablis or similar)

1 part crème de cassis

**1.** Thoroughly chill the wine before combining it with the cassis. Serve in a claret glass.

## MULLED WINE

300 ml (½ pint) water

100 g (4 oz) sugar

4 cloves

1 cinnamon stick, 5 cm (2 inches) long

2 lemons, thinly sliced

1 bottle burgundy or claret

1 orange or lemon, thinly sliced, to decorate

**1.** Boil the water, sugar and spices together. Add the lemon slices, stir and leave to stand for 10 minutes.
**2.** Add the red wine, return to the heat and heat gently but do not boil.
**3.** Strain the wine into a bowl and serve hot, decorated with orange or lemon slices.
*Makes about 1.1 litres (2 pints)*

## JULGLOGG (CHRISTMAS WINE)

1 bottle aquavit or gin

2 bottles burgundy

75 g (3 oz) seedless raisins

100 g (4 oz) sugar

15 ml (1 level tbsp) cardamom seeds (optional)

6 cloves

1 cinnamon stick, 5 cm (2 inches) long

small piece of lemon rind

**1.** Pour half the aquavit into a saucepan with the burgundy and add the raisins and sugar.
**2.** Tie the spices and lemon rind in muslin and add to the pan. Cover, bring very slowly to the boil and simmer for 30 minutes.
**3.** Add the remaining aquavit and remove from the heat. Take out the bag of spices just before serving and ignite the mixture with a match.
**4.** Serve in tumblers or punch glasses.
*Makes about 2.4 litres (4½ pints)*

# TEA, COFFEE
## AND OTHER DRINKS

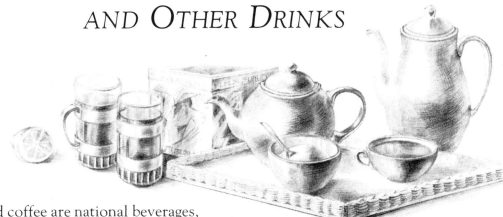

T ea and coffee are national beverages,
but knowing which type to choose can be confusing.
This chapter gives a guide to the different varieties and explains how to
prepare them for the best flavour. The latter part of the chapter includes popular
milk and egg drinks and soft drinks.

◆

TEA Although tea has been drunk in China for many centuries, it was only brought
to the UK in the 17th century and quickly gained popularity to become the popular
drink it is today. Tea is made from the dried, top leaf shoots of a type of camellia
sinensis. Originally all tea for the UK came from China and Java but now most comes
from India, Sri Lanka and Africa.

**Green tea** is the original tea. The leaves are picked, withered on racks and steamed to stop oxidisation/fermentation. They produce a weak brew which is best drunk on its own or with lemon.

**Oolong tea** is semi-fermented; after withering, the leaves are slightly crushed and half-fermented before being dried. This process produces a brown tea with delicate flavour.

**Black tea** is the most popular type sold in the UK. The leaves are fermented until they are a dark brown and then dried.

**Smoked tea** is produced in much smaller quantities. A few teas are given a distinctive, slightly tarry flavour by being dried over smoke.

Indian, Ceylon and African teas are sold black and usually blended in the UK and sold under brand names whose flavour and quality are consistent. Most popular brand teas are a blend of different types. The best teas are those sold under their own names. The following is a list of some of those most readily available.

**Assam** Strong tea with a rich malty flavour. It is often blended with other teas.

**Ceylon** Although Ceylon is now called Sri Lanka, the tea has not been renamed. A light flavoursome tea with a slightly lemony or astringent taste.

**Ching Wo** Black China tea which can be drunk with milk.

**Darjeeling** Indian high-grown tea with a brisk flavour. Often known as the Champagne of tea.

**Earl Grey** A tea flavoured with oil of bergamot. It is best drunk without milk.

**English Breakfast** Two different types: originally a fragrant blend of China teas, now usually a stronger blend of Ceylon and Assam tea.

**Formosa Oolong** A delicate semi-fermented tea with a peachy flavour. The only oolong tea to be found in the west.

**Gunpowder** Top quality green tea which gets its name from its metallic grey sheen.

**Jasmine** Green or black tea, or a mixture, with jasmine flowers. Goes well with Chinese food and is best without milk or sugar.
**Keemun** Considered the best China tea available in the UK. Has an aromatic flavour strong enough to be drunk with milk.
**Lapsang Souchong** A pungent China tea with a smoked flavour.
**Lemon tea** Usually a black tea mixed with lemon peel and scented with lemon oils. Can be served hot or cold without milk.
**Nilgiris** A bright black tea from India.

### USING TEA
Tea is usually drunk hot, with either milk or lemon or on its own, but it can also be used cold as an ingredient in punches, ice creams and some other dishes. Tea should be bought in small quantities and stored in an airtight, light proof container to preserve the aroma and strength. When making a pot of tea, allow 5 ml (1 tsp) per person and once there are more than three people, add a further spoonful for the pot.

Warm the pot and put in the measured quantity of tea. Boil freshly drawn water (not hot tap water, as it will have been stored in the tank and will have lost flavour) and pour on to the leaves. Leave to infuse for 4–5 minutes for Indian teas; 2–3 minutes for China teas, then strain into cups.

### HERB AND FLOWER TEAS
Many herbs and flowers produce flavoursome, aromatic teas (known as tisanes) and some are deemed to have medicinal or cosmetic properties. Health food shops usually stock good supplies. They are made in the same way as standard teas and usually served hot without milk after being infused in the pot.

## RUSSIAN TEA

1. Make a strong infusion of black tea, according to packet instructions, adding an extra 5 ml (1 tsp) tea to the given proportions.
2. Over the back of a spoon, half-fill some glasses with tea and fill to the top with hot water. Add lemon slices and sugar to taste.

This is the traditional way of making Russian tea, but some people just make a weak brew of tea and add the lemon and sugar.

Rum can replace lemon as a flavouring.

In Russia and the Balkan countries, jam is often served as a sweetener in tea.

## SPICED INDIAN TEA

*600 ml (1 pint) water*

*3 green cardamoms*

*2.5 ml (½ level tsp) fennel seeds (optional)*

*2 cloves*

*1 small cinnamon stick*

*10–15 ml (2–3 level tsp) tea or 2 tea bags*

*45–60 ml (3–4 tbsp) milk*

*sugar (optional)*

1. Pour the water into a saucepan, add the spices, cover the pan and bring to the boil. Reduce the heat, add the tea and let the tea simmer gently for about 5–7 minutes.
2. Add the milk and required amount of sugar if using.
3. Increase the heat and bring the tea back to the boil. Remove from heat, strain into cups and serve at once.
*Serves 4*

## ICED TEA

1. Make tea in the usual way. Chill, then pour over the back of a spoon into a glass which has been half-filled with crushed ice.
2. Add sugar to taste and a slice of lemon to the glass.
3. Re-chill before serving.
*Note* Iced herbal teas, known as *tisanes*, are a refreshing summer drink. These can be made in the same way as Iced Tea using fresh or dried herbs. Chamomile, hibiscus, lime, flowers, lemon verbena, peppermint and rosehip are all suitable for serving iced.
*Serves 1*

**Variation**
Add a sprig of mint before serving.

*From the left: Russian Tea, Iced Tea and Spiced Indian Tea*

## FRESH FRUIT AND MINT TEA PUNCH

| |
|---|
| 600 ml (1 pint) boiling water |
| 25 ml (5 level tsp) tea |
| 50 g (2 oz) sugar |
| 450 ml (¾ pint) orange juice |
| ice cubes |
| ½ a lemon, sliced |
| ½ an orange, sliced |
| 50 g (2 oz) strawberries, sliced |
| mint leaves |

1. Pour the water on to the tea, stir and allow to infuse for 3–5 minutes. Stir again, strain into a bowl containing the sugar and stir until this is dissolved.
2. Add the orange juice and leave until cold.
3. To serve, pour over the ice cubes in a punch bowl and add the sliced fruit and the mint leaves.
*Makes about 1.1 litre (2 pints)*

COFFEE has been imported into the UK for the past three hundred years. It is grown in a number of tropical countries and comes from the berries of the coffee tree. As they ripen, they turn first green and then red to reddish-black. Coffee beans are extracted from bright red berries, each containing two small oval green seeds encased in a fine silvery skin which is protected by a tough outer husk. Once the seeds are ripe, they are picked and the red pulp is removed. They then undergo a wet or dry process to remove all traces of the pulp, are dried in the sun and finally have the skins removed by machine. After this the beans are graded according to size and quality.

Because the coffee beans are affected by climate, soil, picking, processing, storing and transport, the flavour of the coffee will vary from shop to shop. The buyers of the beans and, where appropriate, the blenders, are the people who aim for consistency of taste, particularly if the beans are destined to become instant coffee. The best, most finely flavoured varieties are known as *arabicas* and grow at altitudes of 2000 to 6500 feet above sea level. *Robusta* varieties are coarser, with a poorer flavour, and grow between sea level and 2000 feet.

### BUYING COFFEE

You can buy green beans and roast them yourself either in the oven or in a special electric roaster, but it is more reliable to get them in small quantities from a specialist coffee merchant, good grocer or supermarket. For best flavour, the beans should be freshly roasted and used within a few days, at most a week. If you do not have regular access to a good supplier, buy larger quantities periodically and store them in a freezer. The beans will keep for 6 months frozen with virtually no loss of flavour.

Coffee is also sold ready ground in vacuum sealed containers which often specify the method which should be used for making the coffee (e.g. filter). Instant coffees come in powder or freeze-dried granule form, the latter being better flavoured and more expensive. There is also coffee essence (usually mixed with chicory) which has a sweet distinctive flavour. The essence is best used in cooking or for making quick iced coffee.

All coffee beans naturally contain caffeine but for those who want to avoid this for medical reasons or because it makes them feel hyped-up, decaffeinated coffee is available in beans, ground and instant forms with only marginal loss of the original flavour. The subtle variations of flavour of individual coffees are endless. It is worth trying them separately and in a blend until you find the one you like best. Among the types of coffee available are:

**Brazilian** The flavour is very smooth and mild and has no bitterness or acidity.

**Chagga** Chagga coffee is produced by the Wa-Chagga tribe living on the slopes of Mount Kilimanjaro in Tanzania. The beans are picked and washed in the mountain streams from the Kibo Glacier and then dried in the mountain air. This is a full bodied and usually medium to dark roast.

**Colombian** Colombian coffee is from South America and has a strong flavour with little acidity.

**Continental blend** A blend of dark roasted coffees with a strong flavour. Usually drunk at breakfast.

**Java** A mature coffee from the East Indies with

a subtle, mellow flavour. It is most suitable for drinking 'black' as an after-dinner coffee.

**Kenya** A very aromatic coffee with a pleasant sharpness. At its best when served 'black' as an after-dinner coffee.

**Mocha** Mocha is the traditional Turkish coffee. The flavour, traditionally described as 'gamey', is strong and subtle.

**Mysore** This coffee is a rich, full flavoured coffee from Southern India.

**Vienna** This coffee is often sold already blended to give a smooth, subtly strong flavour.

The best way to find out the kinds you like is to talk to a specialist coffee merchant and to buy small quantities of different types and experiment.

### MAKING COFFEE

If you buy coffee beans you need a coffee grinder, either electric or manual. You may also need special equipment for making the coffee unless you use the time-honoured method of pouring boiling water on to grounds in a jug, then straining.

Electric filter coffee machines work by heating the water and then pouring it through ground coffee in a filter into a container on a heated plate. You can also buy plastic filter cones for use with filter papers on jugs but this method does not keep the coffee hot.

Espresso machines work by forcing water through coffee grounds under pressure. They may be electric or for use on a hob.

Other methods include plunger pots, glass vacuum machines (Cona), drip pots and electric percolators, while for Turkish or Greek coffee you need a special small, long handled pan which is wider at the bottom than the top.

The most suitable grinds for some common methods of brewing coffee are as follows:

## COFFEE GRINDING GRADES

| Method | Grinding Grade |
| --- | --- |
| Filter/drip | Fine to medium |
| Jug | Coarse |
| Turkish | Fine |
| Plunger method | Medium |
| Glass balloon/vacuum (Cona) | Medium fine or fine |
| Espresso | Very fine |
| Percolator | Medium or coarse |

Allow 50 g (2 oz) coffee per 600 ml (1 pint) water. Coffee may be drunk black (without milk) or white with the addition of milk—allow 1 part hot milk to 2 parts coffee—or cream. Some people like to sweeten it with sugar or honey and some add alcohol (see below). Coffee should be served hot but not boiling and should not be kept hot for too long after making or the flavour will deteriorate.

## IRISH OR GAELIC COFFEE

*1 part Irish whiskey*

*5 ml (1 level tsp) brown sugar*

*3–4 parts double strength coffee*

*15–30 ml (1–2 tbsp) double cream, chilled*

**1.** Gently warm a glass, pour in the whiskey and add the sugar.
**2.** Pour in black coffee to within 2.5 cm (1 inch) of the brim and stir to dissolve the sugar.
**3.** Fill to the brim with cream, poured over the back of a spoon, and allow to stand for a few minutes.
*Serves 1*

*Pour the cream over the back of a spoon so it stays on the surface.*

**Variations**
*LIQUEUR COFFEE ROUND THE WORLD*
All the following are made as for Irish Coffee. Allow 1 measure of the liqueur or spirit to about 4 measures of double-strength black coffee, with sugar to taste—usually about 5 ml (1 level tsp)— and some thick double cream to pour on top; these quantities will make 1 glassful.
Cointreau Coffee (made with Cointreau)
Caribbean Coffee (made with rum)
German Coffee (made with kirsch)
Normandy Coffee (made with Calvados)
Russian Coffee (made with vodka)
Calypso Coffee (made with Tia Maria)
Witch's Coffee (made with strega; sprinkle a little grated lemon rind on top)
Curaçao Coffee (made with curaçao; stir with a stick of cinnamon)

## Coffee à la Brûlot

1 orange

2 cinnamon sticks, each 5 cm (2 inches) long

4 cloves

3 sugar cubes

150 ml ($\frac{1}{4}$ pint) brandy

600 ml (1 pint) double-strength coffee

1. Pare off the coloured rind of the orange skin in one long, thin ribbon.

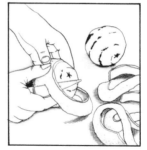

*Pare the orange rind.*

2. Place the rind, cinnamon, cloves and sugar in a pan, pour in the brandy, warm and ignite it. While the brandy is still flaming, add the coffee; as the flame subsides, ladle the coffee into coffee cups.

*Serves 6*

## Iced Coffee

50 g (2 oz) ground coffee

900 ml (1$\frac{1}{2}$ pints) water

sugar to taste

ice cubes

double cream, whipped

1. Make some strong black coffee with the coffee and water.
2. While it is still hot, sweeten to taste with sugar. Cool and chill.
3. Pour into glasses, add an ice cube and top with whipped cream to serve.
*Serves 4*

## Turkish Coffee

*The correct utensil to use is a copper coffee pot with a long handle and no lid, but you can use a small saucepan.*

15–20 ml (3–4 level tsp) finely ground Turkish coffee

5 ml (1 level tsp) sugar

150 ml ($\frac{1}{4}$ pint) water

few drops of rose water

1. Put all ingredients except the rose water in the coffee pot or saucepan and heat, stirring, until the mixture boils and looks frothy.
2. Remove from the heat and when the froth subsides, replace on a brisk heat. Bring to the boil three times in all.
3. Remove from the heat, add a few drops of rose water to perfume the coffee and strain it into a warm jug or small cups. Turkish coffee is drunk black.
*Serves 1*

*Turkish Coffee served with Turkish Delight (see page 498)*

# MILK AND EGG DRINKS This section gives recipes for some

favourite cold and hot milk drinks and typical flips and nogs. There are also various proprietary preparations, including cocoa, different kinds of drinking chocolate and malt drinks; directions for making these are given on the containers.

## MILK SHAKES

Mix the milk with strong coffee, chocolate powder, fruit juice, fruit purée or syrup, or use a special milk shake flavouring. Blend until frothy either with a rotary whisk or a blender or food processor. For an ice-cold milk shake, add 15–30 ml (1–2 tbsp) ice cream to each glass before serving.

## ICED STRAWBERRY SHAKE

*300 ml (½ pint) milk*

*50 g (2 oz) strawberries, hulled and mashed*

*30 ml (2 tbsp) ice cream*

**1.** Whisk all the ingredients together with a rotary whisk until frothy, or blend at maximum speed for 1 minute in a blender or food processor.
**2.** Pour into a large glass.
*Serves 1*

**Variations**
Replace the strawberries with raspberries, mashed to a purée, or 1 banana, peeled and mashed.

## COFFEE MILK SHAKE

*150 ml (¼ pint) milk*

*150 ml (¼ pint) black coffee*

*30 ml (2 tbsp) ice cream*

**1.** Whisk all the ingredients together with a rotary whisk until frothy, or blend at maximum speed for 1 minute in a blender or food processor.
**2.** Pour into a large glass.
*Serves 1*

## PORT WINE FLIP

*1 egg*

*5 ml (1 level tsp) icing sugar*

*150 ml (¼ pint) port*

*1 ice cube*

*freshly grated nutmeg*

**1.** Put the egg, sugar, port and ice cube into a cocktail shaker, blender or food processor and shake or blend well.
**2.** Strain into a glass and sprinkle with a little nutmeg before serving.
*Serves 1*

## EGG NOG

*1 egg*

*15 ml (1 level tbsp) sugar*

*50 ml (2 fl oz) sherry or brandy*

*300 ml (½ pint) milk*

**1.** Whisk the egg and sugar together and add the sherry or brandy.
**2.** Heat the milk without boiling and pour it over the egg mixture. Stir well and serve hot in a glass.
*Serves 1*

# Soft Drinks

Homemade soft drinks are full of flavour and make refreshing thirst-quenchers on hot summer days. This section includes children's favourites such as lemonade, ginger beer, ice cream soda and fruit squashes and punches.

Where 'splits' are referred to in some of the drinks, these are 240 ml (8¼ fl oz) bottles. Sterilise bottles, where necessary, as for jam jars (see page 455).

## Quick Lemon Squash

juice of ½ a lemon

sugar to taste

soda water

1. Put the lemon juice and sugar into a glass and fill to the top with soda water.
Serves 1

## 'Still' Lemonade

3 lemons

175 g (6 oz) sugar

900 ml (1½ pints) boiling water

1. Remove the lemon rind thinly with a potato peeler.

2. Put the rind and sugar into a bowl or large jug and pour on the boiling water. Cover and leave to cool, stirring occasionally.
3. Add the juice of the lemons and strain the lemonade. Serve chilled.
Makes about 1.1 litres (2 pints)

## Bitter Lemon

2 lemons

600 ml (1 pint) water

100 g (4 oz) sugar

1. Cut the lemons into pieces, put in a saucepan with the water and bring to the boil.

2. Reduce the heat and simmer gently for 10–15 minutes, until the fruit is soft.
3. Add the sugar and stir until dissolved.
4. Remove from the heat, cover and cool. Strain before using.
   This drink is delicious with soda water and/or gin.
Makes about 900 ml (1½ pints)

## Ice Cream Soda

1 glass soda water

15 ml (1 tbsp) ice cream

1. Whisk the soda water and ice cream together with a rotary whisk until frothy or blend at maximum speed for 1 minute in a blender or food processor.
2. Pour into a large glass and serve at once.
Serves 1

**Variations**
GRAPEFRUIT OR LIME SODA
Follow the method above and whisk together ½ glass soda water, 30 ml (2 tbsp) grapefruit juice or 15 ml (1 tbsp) lime juice and 15 ml (1 tbsp) ice cream.

GINGER SODA
Follow the method above and whisk together ¾ glass ginger beer, ¼ glass lemonade and 15 ml (1 tbsp) ice cream.

## ORANGE and GRAPEFRUIT SQUASH

900 g (2 lb) sugar

1.1 litres (2 pints) water

20 ml (4 level tsp) tartaric acid

finely grated rind and juice of 2 large oranges

finely grated rind and juice of 1 grapefruit

1. Put the sugar and water into a saucepan and stir over a gentle heat until the sugar has dissolved.

Bring to the boil and simmer for 10 minutes.
2. Put the tartaric acid and the orange and grapefruit rinds into a large bowl or jug, pour over the syrup and leave to stand overnight.
3. Add the fruit juice, strain and pour into a sterilised bottle. Serve diluted with water or soda water.
*Makes about 1.7 litres (3 pints)*

## PINEAPPLE CRUSH

600 ml (1 pint) pineapple juice

juice of 1 orange

juice of 1 lemon

sugar

1.1 litres (2 pints) ginger ale (chilled in the bottle)

1. Combine the fruit juices, sweeten to taste with sugar and chill.
2. Just before serving, add the ginger ale.
*Makes about 1.7 litres (3 pints)*

## ORANGEADE

2 oranges

1 lemon

50 g (2 oz) sugar

600 ml (1 pint) boiling water

1. Thinly pare off the coloured orange rind, free of any pith.
2. Put the rinds and sugar into a bowl and pour over the boiling water.
3. Leave to cool, stirring occasionally, then add the strained juice of the oranges and lemon.
*Makes about 900 ml (1½ pints)*

## QUICK GINGER BEER

rind and juice of 1 large lemon

25 ml (5 level tsp) cream of tartar

450 g (1 lb) sugar

25 g (1 oz) root ginger, peeled

2.3 litres (4 pints) boiling water

2.3 litres (4 pints) cold water

15 g (½ oz) fresh yeast

1 slice toast

*Use a rolling pin to bruise the root ginger.*

*Syphon from the bowl into sterilised bottles.*

1. Place the lemon rind, cream of tartar and sugar in a large bowl or plastic bucket. Bruise the ginger and add to the bowl.
2. Pour over the boiling water and stir until sugar is dissolved. Add the cold water and lemon juice and cool until just warm to the hand.
3. Spread the yeast on the toast and float it on the mixture. Cover with a clean cloth and leave in a warm place for 24 hours until frothy.
4. Remove any scum from the top of the mixture,

discard the toast and syphon the beer into sterilised bottles, avoiding any sediment.
5. Seal the bottles with screw tops or corks secured with wire. Leave for three days in a cool place before drinking. Drink within three days or the ginger beer tends to taste very yeasty and becomes too fizzy.
*Makes about 5.1 litres (9 pints)*

## CITRUS PUNCH

*juice of 2 grapefruit*

*juice of 2 lemons*

*juice of 5 oranges*

*150 ml (¼ pint) pineapple juice*

*sugar*

*4 'splits' tonic water (chilled in the bottle)*

*1 lemon, thinly sliced, to decorate*

**1.** Strain the fruit juices into a bowl, mix well and chill.
**2.** Just before serving, add the sugar and tonic water and decorate with lemon slices.
*Makes about 1.6 litres (2¾ pints)*

*Strain through a sieve.*

## SPICY FRUIT PUNCH

*600 ml (1 pint) orange juice*

*300 ml (½ pint) pineapple juice*

*grated rind and juice of 1 lemon*

*2.5 ml (½ level tsp) freshly grated nutmeg*

*2.5 ml (½ level tsp) ground mixed spice*

*6 cloves*

*600 ml (1 pint) water*

*175 g (6 oz) sugar*

*1.1 litres (2 pints) ginger ale (chilled in the bottle)*

*crushed ice*

**1.** Mix the fruit juices, lemon rind and spices in a large jug.
**2.** Put the water and sugar into a saucepan and heat gently to dissolve the sugar. Cool slightly and add to the other ingredients in the jug. Chill.
**3.** Strain the liquid and add the ginger ale and some crushed ice before serving.
*Makes about 2.8 litres (5 pints)*

## PINE-LIME SPARKLE

*600 ml (1 pint) pineapple juice*

*45 ml (3 tbsp) fresh lemon juice*

*150 ml (¼ pint) lime juice cordial*

*50 g (2 oz) icing sugar*

*2 'splits' bitter lemon (chilled in the bottle)*

*lime slices (optional)*

**1.** Put the pineapple and lemon juices and the lime cordial in a bowl and stir in the icing sugar. Chill.
**2.** Just before serving add the bitter lemon and some lime slices, if wished.
*Makes about 1 litre (1¾ pints)*

*Pine–Lime Sparkle*

# EQUIPPING YOUR KITCHEN

K itchen equipment is big business today. There is a tool for every task, and electrical machines for all manner of speedy processes. Choosing what you really need from the array in the shops is difficult. Use the following guidelines to help you judge what to buy.

- Will you really use it enough to justify the purchase price?
- Does it do anything you couldn't do just as quickly and easily with a sharp knife?
- Do you have space to store it where it will be accessible when needed?

♦

## COOKING APPLIANCES

It is generally assumed that every kitchen needs a cooker complete with hob, oven and grill. This is, in fact, not so since the wide range of small cooking appliances available can be combined to produce the same results as a cooker. So if you are a cook who rarely uses an oven, or are setting up home on a limited budget, it is worth considering some of the alternatives to a cooker discussed in this chapter.

Conventional cookers will still be most people's choice, and the first decision to make when choosing is about fuel. Electricity is available in all areas but gas may not be. If your heart is set on gas it is worth finding out about the possibility of bottled gas. There is also the choice of a solid fuel range or wood-burning stove, but the economics of this will depend on what you use to heat water and/or a heating system.

Your second choice will be between a split-level oven and hob, sited separately or one above the other, or a free-standing, all-in-one cooker. The space you have may well dictate this since a split-level model requires about three times the space of a free-standing cooker if hob and oven are not sited one over the other. The main advantage of a split-level cooker is that you can have, for example, a gas hob and an electric oven (useful in power cuts) or vice versa. You do not have to bend to the oven (useful for back pain sufferers) and you can site each piece of equipment at the point where it most suits you to use it. Think carefully about what cooker you want and spend time in gas and electricity showrooms and department stores looking at the models available. Don't be swayed by fancy features which you may, in fact, never use. Consider fitting a cooker hood over your hob whether it is separate or integral. It may be the type that ducts air outside the home or have an activated charcoal filter which recirculates

the air when cleaned. The former type is better if you can fit it to an outside wall, but both types do a good job of removing steam and smells which makes the kitchen a pleasanter place to work in and also keeps it cleaner.

Electric hobs, both split-level and on free-standing cookers, may have radiant, sealed or ceramic rings. Radiant rings are the most common type and consist of a coil of sheathed element. They heat up and cool down quickly and spillage is caught in a bowl or tray underneath which can be cleaned easily. Spillage directly on to the rings will burn itself off. Some radiant rings have a dual circuit, which means that just the centre section can be used for small pans. Otherwise the cooker may have large and small rings.

Sealed-disc rings are made of smooth metal with a central indentation and there are generally large and small ones on a cooker. They heat up more slowly than radiant rings but retain heat longer. Any spillage will run on to the hob, where it can be wiped up.

Ceramic hobs consist of a flat ceramic top with heating elements underneath. The cooking areas are marked on top. Ceramic hobs make a neat, smooth run of units in a kitchen. The cooking areas heat up more slowly than radiant rings but retain heat longer.

Gas hobs usually have four burners, some-times of different sizes. They may be sealed so that spillage can be wiped up or have individual spillage bowls, which are removable. Gas burners provide instant heat and are easily and quickly regulated to provide the required heat. Some have a set position for simmering. Gas hobs may have automatic ignition, whereby the flame comes on when the control is operated; or semi-automatic ignition, where the gas supply is activated by a control knob and you then turn the appropriate knob for the burner required.

Some gas hobs incorporate automatic re-ignition, which means the burner will re-ignite automatically if accidentally extinguished. Some have a thermostatically controlled burner, which can be set to keep the contents of a pan at the required temperature.

More sophisticated versions of the split-level hob are modular units. These consist of such items as twin rings, rectangular cooking plates, ceramic hob with cooking areas, deep-fat fryers, pan rests, barbecue grills and with some systems a hob ventilator/extractor. The idea is that you can select the modular units you want and site them together or separately at convenient places in your kitchen.

## OVENS

**Electric ovens** may be conventional, conventional-with-microwave or oven-with-grill or side-by-side. Some models have two ovens, others just one. British conventional-type ovens have two elements, one at each side of the oven, covered by removable panels. Continental and American conventional ovens have the elements at top and bottom, which means that the heat distribution is different so food may need to be positioned differently and cooking temperatures and times altered.

**Fan ovens** may be fan assisted, which circulates air directly around the oven, or fan ducted, which blows air through ducts on to the individual shelves. The cooking capacity is greater than with conventional ovens, the heat can be set lower and the cooking time is shorter. If you are used to a conventional oven it may take you some time to become accustomed to one with a fan and you may initially have some failures when baking. Once you have mastered your particular model you will find it maintains an even temperature throughout the oven, so that you can utilise every part of it at once—good for batch baking.

**Gas ovens** may also be of the conventional type, fan assisted or with a built-in microwave.

Some cookers have self-clean/stay-clean linings, which means that deposited soil is burned off during cooking. These only work at medium and high temperatures, so if all your oven cooking is done at low temperatures, you will need to burn off soil at a higher temperature from time to time.

Pyrolytic cleaning is done at very high temperature and is found on only a few cookers. The oven door is shut and a safety lock activated while the cleaning is in progress. Soiling carbonises and

any heat, smoke and odour is dispersed. When cleaning is completed there may be a little ash remaining in the oven, but this is easily brushed out. To economise on electricity it is a good idea to start the cleaning process immediately after high temperature cooking.

**Grills** On most British-made floor-standing electric cookers the grill is either under the hob or at eye level. On split-level models it is either above or below the main oven. Most under-hob grills extend across the full width of the cooker and the drop-down door fitted to the grill compartment serves as a resting place for dishes when turning or serving food. Some grills are divided so that just half the grill area can be used if necessary. Usually the half grill for small loads is to one side, but on some models it is in the centre, which provides a slightly larger heated area as the heat tends to travel a little to either side.

On most floor-standing gas cookers the grill is at eye level, but there is usually at least one model available with it at waist level. Special wall-mounted grill units are available for split-level arrangements and include pull-out shelves for easy inspection of food, and sometimes rotisseries. Grill pans for both types of cooker may have one or two handles, a pull-out, stay-out runner system that enables both hands to be free to cope with the food, and the ability to vary the distance from the heat source, either by different side runners or a reversible trivet. Most gas grills provide a plate-warming facility.

On built under cookers the grill is usually inside the oven at the top. Having the grill in the oven means that the two cannot be used simultaneously and that the oven door may need to be left ajar during grilling—not always convenient in a small kitchen.

**Rôtisseries** These are either supplied with the cooker or come as optional extras, to be fitted in the oven or grill compartment. Some also have facilities for kebab skewers.

**Meat probe** A few cookers have a metal probe attached to the oven interior which when inserted into the joint will signal when the meat has reached the desired stage of cooking by means of a buzzer. The required state of 'doneness' is set beforehand on the special meat probe dial, usually located on the control panel.

**Thermostat controls** The oven temperature is controlled by the thermostat, which maintains the temperature set on the dial. On cookers with electronic touch controls a touch pad is used to select the temperature. In a gas oven there are definite heat zones; the top is the hottest, the centre corresponds with the thermostat setting and the lower part is coolest.

**Warming drawer** Most electric cookers have some space for plate-warming in the grill compartment, as do gas cookers, but a separate warming drawer with a low wattage element is fitted below the oven in some free-standing cookers.

**Storage space** This is supplied on some free-standing cookers and is useful for baking trays, cake tins, etc. It is either a cavity at the base of the cooker enclosed behind a removable or drop-down door, or a pull-out drawer.

**Automatic oven timer** Most electric and gas cookers, both built-in and free-standing, are now fitted with an auto-timer. Controls are set to 'start' and 'stop' and 'cooking time'. The oven will then switch on, heat up to temperature and switch off as required.

**Minute minder** This is often included with the auto-timer but may be separately positioned. Usually settings are from 1 to 60 minutes and a pinger or buzzer sounds when the time is up.

**Clocks** These are included on most models, either incorporated with the auto-timer or separate.

**Oven lights** These are particularly useful when a glass door is fitted.

**Hob light** This is controlled by a separate switch and is an advantage if the cooker is positioned in a dark area.

**Wheels and removable oven and inner glass doors** The above features are worth looking for when choosing a gas or electric cooker since they make cleaning the cooker and behind it easier.

### MICROWAVE COOKERS

Microwave cookers can be used as supplements to conventional cookers or instead of them. They run off a 13 amp socket outlet, can be placed on any flat surface, cook in a quarter to a third of the time conventional cooking takes and save energy. Until fairly recently they were regarded as a sci-fi miracle and not something most people would want in their home. But provided you are prepared to adapt your cooking techniques there are very few dishes that can't be cooked in a microwave cooker and many which positively benefit from the speed it offers in terms of retaining texture and flavour. Good examples are vegetables and fish. For more on microwave cookery see page 517.

The main problem with microwave cookers is that the terms used on the different brands have not been standardised. Thus the setting 're-heat' on one model may be the equivalent of 'roast' on another. It is therefore important to familiarise yourself thoroughly with the instruction book supplied with your model and to experiment with the recipes contained in it. As you become more accustomed to this type of cooking it will become simple to use recipes from general microwave cookery books and also to adapt recipes you have formerly prepared with a conventional cooker.

Note that you cannot use metal containers in a microwave oven since these reflect the microwaves and prevent them penetrating the food. China, pottery and glass containers are all suitable, although some eathenware products contain metal particles which can rule them out. Microwaves also pass through wood and cane which makes it possible to heat things like bread rolls in their serving containers. As a general guideline, rigid plastics are safe in a microwave oven but flexible ones are not, although this will to some extent depend on the level at which you are cooking and what you are cooking. Foods with a high fat or sugar content get much hotter than other foods and can cause distortion in plastics which would be perfectly safe with other items.

Depending on the degree of sophistication of the model you buy you may need accessories such as a turntable, browning dish or cooking probe. Study the manufacturers' brochures and before purchasing think carefully; do you wish to use your microwave cooker merely for defrosting and re-heating or do you plan to do a lot of cooking from scratch? If the former, a basic model will be fine but for more sophisticated cooking, a more advanced model will probably be more use. Be prepared for some failures when you start since the techniques and timing are radically different from those used with a conventional cooker.

**Mini-ovens** Free-standing table-top ovens come complete with shelves, roasting tin or grill pan and sometimes automatic timers. They run off a 13 amp socket outlet and take surprisingly large quantities of food. Grilling works by blowing hot air over the food rather than exposing it to radiant heat, so although things like bacon, sausages and toast brown adequately, chops and steaks tend to have a steamed appearance.

### MULTI-COOKERS (ELECTRIC FRYPANS)

Multi-cookers look like large frying pans and are extremely versatile pieces of cooking equipment. They work off a 13 amp socket outlet and can be used to fry, roast, bake, casserole, steam and griddle. The lid has a vent which can be closed for moist cooking and opened when steam needs to be let out. A big plus with these pans is that when the thermostatically controlled heating element is removed, the pans themselves can be washed in the normal way with no need to worry about water penetrating the electrical connections.

Multi-cookers may be square or round and come with plain or non-stick finishes. Square ones are easier to fit baking racks into (if not supplied, choose one that fits snugly and raises the food about 1 cm (½ inch) off the base) while non-stick linings, although useful when frying, can become scratched if the pan is used frequently with racks and cake tins inside it.

### ELECTRIC CASSEROLES

Electric casseroles, sometimes called slow cookers or crockpots, run off a 13 amp socket outlet and thus provide controlled gentle cooking at about a third of the cost of heating a large conventional oven. They are particularly useful for people who are out all day since there is no risk of burning or boiling dry—most dishes will keep in perfect condition for a few hours longer than is needed to cook them. Slow cookers are in fact useful for anyone who wants to get food preparation out of the way but have a meal ready later on.

Electric casseroles come in various sizes, so choose one that suits your household. A model with a removable pot, which can be taken out of the casing and used to serve at table, is more useful than one with a fixed pot and also easier to clean. An automatic model that will turn itself from the high to the low setting without you needing to remember it or be there is also helpful, especially if you want to put the cooker on and go out. Some models need to be pre-heated on the high setting before the prepared food is put into the casserole.

All slow cooking is done with the lid on except when you are making yogurt or serving mulled wine. It is important not to raise the lid during cooking to see how things are getting on as this will introduce cold air into the casserole and mean you need to add about half an hour's extra cooking time. Note too that draughts and a cold kitchen will affect the electric casserole's efficiency, and if these conditions are present you should allow more cooking time.

Familiarise yourself with the manufacturer's instructions and practise with some of the recipes supplied. You will quickly be able to work out the cooking times required for preparing your usual dishes in the electric casserole. Do not use the electric casserole to re-heat either frozen or re-frigerated food. If you are adding red kidney beans to a dish, always boil them for at least 10 minutes on the hob before adding them to the slow cooker to destroy a particular toxic enzyme which will not be destroyed by the heat of the appliance. (This does not apply to canned red kidney beans, which have undergone heat treatment during processing.)

Put less liquid in an electric casserole than you would in a casserole to be cooked in the oven as there is virtually no evaporation. Season carefully as the long, slow method of cooking intensifies the individual flavours of ingredients. Under-season initially and check before serving.

If you are not going to eat the contents of the electric casserole when ready, turn the food out of the casserole and cool it quickly before storing in the refrigerator. Do not leave food in the electric casserole to be re-heated later.

Although it is possible to cook a casserole from scratch in an electric casserole, you will achieve a better flavour and colour by browning the meat and vegetables first in a pan on the hob.

### INFRA-RED GRILLS (CONTACT GRILLS)

These come with a hinged pair of non-stick heated plates between which you can cook any flat food (chops, burgers, steak), doing both sides simultaneously. They can also cook foil-wrapped vegetables and fish.

Some come supplied with a baking tin, which increase their versatility by producing what is, in effect, a mini-oven between the heated plates. You can buy a separate baking tin if your model is not supplied with one.

Infra-red grills run off a 13 amp socket outlet, so are cheap to run and are a useful buy for anyone who doesn't need to cook food in large quantities. They are also good buys for people with built under continental ovens who find the grilling position inconvenient.

### SANDWICH TOASTERS

Until the advent of the electric sandwich toaster, making toasted sandwiches was a chore involving several different tasks. Now all that is necessary is to spread your two pieces of bread with butter or margarine, place one buttered side down in the toaster, add the chosen filling, top it with the other slice of bread, buttered side up, close the toaster and cook for a couple of minutes. These machines are cheap to buy and run and come in a variety of sizes, from small models that make two sandwiches at a time—suitable for most homes—up to ones that make eight sandwiches at a time.

Some models come with removable plates, which makes cleaning easy, and one or two have interchangeable plates, so that by slotting in another pair you can make waffles or grill steaks and burgers in your sandwich toaster and increase its versatility.

Most models have non-stick plates and claim to seal the sandwich all the way around so that even really runny fillings don't trickle out. Look for models that divide sandwiches into two or four pieces and seal each of these. This makes the sandwiches much easier to eat. Models that just seal around the outside of the bread can cause problems when the sandwich is cut. Before choosing, look at the depth of the indentations that hold the sandwiches. In general the deeper the better as this means you can get more filling in. If the depth is too great in relation to the overall size of the indentation, this can cause the bread to break as you push it down to get the filling in.

### DEEP-FAT FRYERS

Electric deep-fat fryers offer much the safest method of frying since they are thermostatically controlled, so the risk of fat over-heating and catching fire is eliminated. (Deep frying on hobs is one of the biggest single causes of accident in the home.) Capacities range from 1 to 4 litres (2–7 pints) of oil, so think carefully when purchasing; the larger models can take up a lot of space on a worktop or in a cupboard, however, you will find that frying is so quick that doing two or three basketfuls is not a problem.

Look for a model with a filter in the lid as this will cut down on cooking odours, especially important if you work in a kitchen-cum-eating area. Filters need changing after 20 to 40 uses depending on the various types of food that have been fried.

Bear in mind that the oil used in a deep-fat fryer can be re-used a number of times. Wait until it is cool and then strain it before storing it either in a container (make sure it is really cool before pouring it back into a plastic bottle) or in the fryer itself, in which case remember it is there before you move it around for storage.

### ELECTRIC WOKS

These offer the same facilities as woks designed for use on a conventional cooker, but have the advantage of allowing you to cook in them at the table. They can also be used for many of the functions of a multi-cooker, e.g. stewing, steaming, poaching and simmering. If you are buying an electric wok, check that it heats to a high temperature, otherwise stir-frying may be slow and you would be better off with an ordinary wok used on the top of your conventional cooker.

## OTHER EQUIPMENT

### KETTLES

The choice lies between electric and non-electric kettles. Obviously the former are more expensive, but provided you buy a model with an automatic cut-out they are safer in that they will not boil dry.

Whichever type you choose, look for a well-balanced, stable shape, a comfortable handle raised sufficiently high above the lid so that your knuckles don't get burned and ease of filling (whether through spout or lid). If you only require small quantities of boiled water at a time look at jug kettles, which can boil as little as one cup.

### COFFEE MAKERS

Although there is a lot talked about the right way to make real coffee it is perfectly simple once you have selected your method and the equipment it requires.

Good coffee can be prepared using just a jug, but this requires the coffee to be strained and does not keep it hot, so it must be drunk at once.

Making coffee through a filter can be done over a jug, which again does not keep it hot, or in an electric machine, which will both boil the water and keep the made coffee hot. These electric machines come with a variety of refinements such as an insulated jug, a built-in coffee grinder, a clock/alarm and a coffee strength regulator.

Another type of electric coffee maker is the percolator, but this tends to boil the coffee, which purists claim spoils the flavour.

For Italian-style espresso you can buy electric machines, small metal models that force boiling water through the coffee grounds. These work on the hob and because they are made of metal will keep the coffee hot for a short time after it has been made.

### BLENDERS, FOOD PROCESSORS AND MIXERS

Chopping, grating, slicing and so on, can take up a lot of time when you are preparing food. Obviously all of these tasks can be done with manual tools such as graters, knives and mandolines, but while manual work is fine for small quantities an electric appliance does make life easier when more than the odd carrot or lump of cheese is involved.

Blenders, food processors and mixers have functions that to some extent overlap. Whether you need all three or just one or two will depend on the kind of food preparation you do and the quantities you do it in.

Blenders are marvellous for making batter, mayonnaise, pâté, purées and soup as well as preparing baby foods. Some models can cope with dry ingredients, others require liquid before they can operate. Check before buying how the blades are set. Some are too high to cope with one-yolk mayonnaise or small quantities of baby food.

Although food processors can perform all of the functions of blenders plus some others, they do not always obtain the same smooth texture when puréeing.

When choosing a blender look for compact design, simple control and a robust goblet with a handle. It is also useful if the goblet is calibrated so you can measure liquids directly into it. Do not be led into buying a blender because it has a vast range of speeds, as results are not altered by blending at different speeds and it doesn't mean you can prepare greater quantities or different foods. In general, it is not worth buying a blender with a working capacity of less than 1 litre (2 pints) as it is always possible to blend small quantities provided the blades are covered by the food. If you frequently blend small quantities look for a model with low-set blades. If you own a dishwasher, buy one with a dishwasher-proof goblet.

Food processors are a more recent development than blenders and mixers and claim to be able to perform all the functions of both—e.g. slice, grate, chop, cream, knead and beat. They consist of a bowl that is fitted on to a motor housing. You select the appropriate blade or cutting disc for the task in hand, put the ingredients in the bowl, fit the lid and the ingredients are processed in seconds. In fact, you will need to practise for a while before experience can tell you how long it takes to process different types of food. Just a few seconds too long can mean the difference between chopping meat and turning it into a paste. Some food processors don't whip cream or egg whites, however, but they do, on the whole, make perfectly acceptable cakes, although sponges don't turn out as fluffy and well risen as when mixed by hand or with electric beaters. If you use your food processor a great deal it is a good idea—storage permitting—to buy one or two extra bowls to save washing-up frequently.

Free-standing and hand-held mixers once had a place in almost every kitchen and many people still find that for their style of cooking these are a better buy than a food processor. Certainly if you can afford the attachments (and have somewhere to store them) a free-standing mixer becomes a remarkably versatile machine. They are still the best buy when it comes to stirring, beating and whisking, and they can cope with family-sized quantities of things like cake mixture which the standard-sized food processors can't manage. They work more slowly than food processors, but this can be an advantage in that it reduces the risk of over-processing ingredients. Many mixers come with a liquidiser attachment. It performs the same functions as a blender but does not have its own motor.

Hand-held mixers are very compact—even those with stands take up less space than free-standing models. They are a good buy if you have a limited budget, a tiny kitchen or don't do enough cooking to justify the purchase of more expensive mechanical help.

Their advantages are that they can be used with any size bowl—you just move the beaters around to ensure that all the ingredients are combined—and you can even use them over a pan on the hob, when making sauces for example. Take care to keep the flex off the heat source when doing this. With small quantities use one beater.

Mini choppers are small but powerful machines based on the design of a blender. They usually comprise a blender and a small container for chopping in—in effect a mini food processor. They are very efficient at chopping, shredding and blending a wide variety of ingredients, but do not mix. They make a useful supplement to a hand-held mixer.

### KITCHEN TOOLS

The preceding pages have dealt with the various types of electric and gas kitchen equipment. Obviously there is a whole range of manual tools designed for specific jobs. Knives are perhaps the most important kitchen tools and it is essential to choose those which are the right size for the task in hand, which are sharp with a strong blade, and comfortable to hold.

Right is a list of equipment that The Good Housekeeping Institute considers essential, plus a list of items which may or may not be necessary for your kind of cooking. Before making any purchases, think carefully about if you will actually use the item.

# KITCHEN TOOLS

## Basic cookware

Milk saucepan
Frying pan with lid
2 × 1.7 litre (3 pint)
 saucepans with lids
3.4 litre (6 pint)
 saucepan with lid
4.5 litre (8 pint)
 saucepan with lid
Colander
Roasting tin and trivet
2 × baking sheets
2 × sandwich tins
Deep cake tin
900 g (2 lb) loaf tin
Bun/muffin tin
Wire cooling rack
Flan ring or tin
Yorkshire pudding tin
Casseroles
Soufflé dish
Deep pie dish
Shallow pie dish
Basins
Mixing bowl
Carving dish

## Additional cookware

Chip pan and basket
Double boiler
Steamer or steaming
 basket
Omelette pan
Egg poacher
Fish kettle
Pressure cooker
Griddle
Wok and stand
Blanching basket
Stockpot
Swiss roll tin
Dariole moulds
Spring-form tin
Spring-form tube tin
Madeleine sheet
Tartlet moulds
Charlotte mould
Terrine mould
Raised pie mould
Jelly mould
Cream horn tins

Savarin mould
Bombe mould
Ramekins
Gratin dish
Flan dish
Chicken brick
Marble pastry slab
Mandoline grater
Oven thermometer
Meat thermometer

## Basic utensils

Balloon whisk
Rotary whisk
Apple corer
Potato peeler
Egg slicer
Bottle opener
Corkscrew
Pan trivets
Bread board and knife
2 chopping boards
Box grater
Mincer
Kitchen scissors
Cooking tongs
Palette knife
Ladle
Fish slice
Slotted spoon
Potato masher
Flexible spatula
Wooden spoons
Wooden spatulas
Strainer
Sieve
Salad shaker
Flour dredger
Pastry brush
Pastry wheel
Rolling pin
Assorted biscuit and
 pastry cutters
Pie funnel
Salt and pepper mills
Garlic press
Lemon squeezer
Kitchen knives (including:
 general kitchen knife,
 cook's knife, paring
 knife, boning knife,

grapefruit knife, small
 fruit/vegetable knife)
Carving knife, fork and
 steel
Knife sharpener
Knife rack or block
Kitchen scales
Measuring jug
Measuring spoons
Skewers
Cook's timer
Vegetable brush
Ice cube trays

## Additional utensils

Pastry blender
Pastry brush
Kebab skewers
Cannelle knife
Splash guard
Bean slicer
Cheese slicer
Skimmer
Jar opener
Milk saver
Ceramic baking beans
Poultry scissors
Nutmeg grater
Manual pasta maker
Potato/melon baller
Butter curler
Shortcake mould
Pestle and mortar
Herb chopper
Cherry stoner
Citrus zester
Birch whisk
Spaghetti rake
Rotary grinder
Meat mallet
Gravy ladle
Ice cream scoop
Chocolate dipping fork
Potato baker
Crinkle cut chipper
Cheese wire
Vegetable shredder
Freezer thermometer
Deep-frying thermometer
Nutcrackers
Larding needle

Trussing needle
Bulb baster
Biscuit cutters

## Storage

Plastic storage boxes
Salt crock
Airtight storage containers
Herb and spice containers,
 possibly on rack
Bread bin
Flour bin/crock
Egg rack

## Basic electrical
## equipment

Food mixer
Blender/liquidiser
 or Food processor
Coffee maker
Kettle
Toaster

## Additional electrical
## equipment

Sandwich toaster
Contact grill
Coffee grinder
Ice cream maker
Juice extractor
Multi-cooker
Electric casserole
Deep-fat fryer
Yogurt maker
Electric carving knife

## Specialised equipment

*For cake icing and decoration*
Piping bag and nozzles
Icing turntable
Icing ruler
Serrated scraper
Icing nails

*For jam and jelly making
 and preserving*
Jelly bag and stand
Preserving pan
Sugar thermometer
Bottling jars and rings
Jam funnel

# PAN AND CASSEROLE CHOICE Although saucepans are
now designed as fashion items for the kitchen, the really important thing is how they cook, not how they look. Paying more usually means better quality, better finish and longer life, but a cheap, relatively lightweight set of pans may be a good first-time buy and can be replaced with something superior when it wears out.

It is important to choose the right type of pan for your cooker. Most pans will work on gas and radiant electric cookers, but ceramic hobs, sealed electric hotplates and ranges require heavy pans with flat bases in order that good contact is made between the pan base and the heat source.

Although pans are sold in ranges from small to large sizes it is not necessary to buy all your pans from one range unless you particularly want them to match—for example if they will be stored where they can be seen.

The materials from which pans are made affect their cooking properties. Aluminium conducts heat evenly and does not hot-spot. Pans of medium and heavy gauge will last well and keep their shape, lightweight aluminium pans are only suitable for use on gas and have a short life. One disadvantage of aluminium is its tendency to discolour and pit, but this can be avoided with proper care or by choosing aluminium pans that have a non-stick lining. Some aluminium pans have an external coating of coloured vitreous enamel—Vitramel®—which makes their appearance less dull. Avoid pans whose finish is merely sprayed-on polyamide as this tends to scratch.

**Cast iron** and **cast aluminium** pans are marvellous for long, slow cooking because of their weight and thickness. Both materials are good conductors of heat and many are coated with vitreous enamel, which looks more attractive and makes them easier to clean.

All cast metal is heavy and these pans are not a suitable choice for anyone who has difficulty in lifting things, particularly as these pans may break if dropped on to a hard floor.

**Copper** is the chef's choice of pan material because it conducts heat so well. It is also expensive. It comes in both heavy and light grades and needs to be coated with tin, nickel or aluminium to prevent the copper reacting with certain foods and producing an unpleasant taste. You need a fair amount of elbow grease if you wish to maintain the appearance of the copper.

**Ceramic and porcelain** casseroles can usually also be used as pans on top of the hob. Check that they are marked flameproof. They tend to hot-spot on

the hob so are really more suitable as casseroles.

**Glass** saucepans enable you to see what's cooking but also tend to hot-spot in the same way as ceramic. They are easier to clean than ceramic saucepans.

**Stainless steel** is an expensive material but very durable and easier to care for. Stainless steel is not itself a good conductor of heat and so pans made from it usually have another metal such as aluminium or copper bonded on to the base or sandwiched into it. Avoid stainless steel pans with a sprayed-on copper coating as this has virtually no effect on cutting down hot-spotting.

**Vitreous enamel** (Vitramel®) steel pans are not as efficient on the hob as other metals. They tend to heat up quickly but to hot-spot and food sticks to them. More expensive Vitramel® pans have a special metallic coating on the base which helps spread heat more evenly and cut down on hot-spotting. Choose Vitramel® pans with a metal rim around the top and lid. These are vulnerable areas which if knocked could chip.

Vitramel® is the trademark of the Vitreous Enamel Development Council and denotes good-quality enamel and its application.

## SIZE AND QUANTITY
How large and how many pans you require will depend on the size of your household and the amount of cooking you do. It is best to start off with the minimum of pans you think you'll require and add to them when other needs become apparent.

As a rough guide, most homes will need a milk saucepan, a frying pan with lid, two 1.7 litre (3 pint) saucepans with lids and one or two larger saucepans with lids—one 3.4 litre (6 pint) and one 4.5 litre (8 pint) for example.

Other more specialist pans, such as an omelette pan, egg poacher, double boiler, steamer, preserving pan and wok, can be bought when needed.

## NON-STICK LININGS
These prevent foods from sticking to the pan surface and make cleaning much easier. Today's non-stick coatings are much harder wearing than

their predecessors and should last years if treated with care. Use wooden or plastic utensils.

### POINTS TO CONSIDER

Once you have chosen your materials look at the pans themselves to check the kind of detail that makes the difference between good and bad.

**Stability** Flat bases are essential for even heat penetration. Check for this by standing the pan on a flat surface (the shop's counter) and press on either side in turn to see if it wobbles.

**Lids** should fit well but move just enough to allow steam to escape. Test by angling the pan slightly. The lid should only move fractionally and not at all if there are special steam vents. Check that the rim of the lid is easy to clean with no hidden traps.

**Knobs** are best made of heat-resistant material so you can raise a lid without using a glove. Ideally they should have a heat-resisting collar to prevent you burning your knuckles when raising the lid. If it is a screw-on knob check that the screw can be tightened—it is bound to work loose with use. Knobs on pans intended to go in the oven need to be made of suitable materials and the same applies to those intended to be put in the dishwasher.

**Handles** should be a good length and comfortable to hold. Check for ease of holding and balance in the shop (try a pretend pour). Common faults are a too narrow handle or one that's too long. If there are thumb and finger grips make sure they are in the right place. Large pans holding 3 litres (6 pints) or more should have a short handle opposite the usual long one, so you can use both hands to lift them when full.

Handles need to be heat resistant. Look for flame guards at the join, especially on wooden handles. Riveted handles cannot be tightened so, in the long term, screwed ones are a better buy.

**Shape** Look to see if there is a slight curve inside where the sides meet the base—this makes the pan easier to clean. Bulge-shaped pans are good for sauces and beating things as spoons fit snugly into the bulge but are more difficult to clean than straight-sided pans.

**Pouring** You need to pour from practically every pan at some time or other. Some pans have two pouring lips, some only one (not practical for left-handers) but best of all is a continuous pouring rim, so you can pour from every point.

**Storage** Think about your storage space before buying; some pans need a lot of cupboard and shelf space. Some stack on top of each other.

## CASSEROLES

Casseroles are made of the same materials as saucepans plus earthenware, stoneware and pottery, which are never suitable for use on the hob.

The ideal casserole is one which you can use on top of the stove or in the oven and which also looks good enough to bring to the table. You need

casseroles which won't chip or break easily and which are simple to clean.

When choosing casseroles look for the same points as when choosing pans. Check that the handles and knobs are a suitable shape to be grasped with a thick oven glove when hot.

## PRESSURE COOKERS

A pressure cooker can be used to cook under pressure and also as an ordinary large pan and is thus a useful addition to most kitchens. Pressure cooking saves time, retains nutrients and can be used to cook more than one food at a time. Because of its speed it is an economical method of cooking and useful for cooking root vegetables and pulses quickly and for tenderising meat.

Pressure cooking works on a very simple principle. The atmospheric pressure inside the sealed saucepan is increased when steam from the boiling liquid is allowed to escape only at a controlled rate. Water normally boils at 100°C (212°F) but at this high pressure the boiling point is increased to between 110°C–120°C (230°F–248°F) so food cooks more quickly.

Pressure cookers are made of stainless steel or aluminium and come supplied with a trivet and small baskets for cooking different foods. Some models have non-stick linings, but this is not necessary as all pressure cooking involves a minimum of 250 ml ($\frac{1}{2}$ pint) liquid, not fat or oil alone.

The different pressures are produced by weights representing pounds per square inch (no metrication here as yet). Low and medium pressures are used for soups, jams, bottling and steamed mixtures with raising agents. High pressure is used for everything else. Most pressure cookers use 4, 10 and 15 lb weights, although some use 8 and 12 lb. However, these in between weights can make it hard to follow general pressure-cookery books and restrict you to the manufacturers' own recipes.

# STORING FOOD

*H*owever large or small your kitchen you will need to organise space to store food, including that which you use every day and items which spend longer in the cupboard as they are used only in small quantities or for emergency meals. Storage for perishable foods, eg meat, fish, dairy products, fruit and vegetables, is of vital importance since these, if kept too long, will develop bacteria, mould and enzymes (called micro-organisms) whose activity will cause these foods to go off. The best place to keep them is in a refrigerator, failing this a ventilated food cupboard or cool larder. If you have neither, these products should be bought daily when needed, to ensure safe eating. In general, it is advisable to buy perishable foods as you need them and in small quantities to ensure that surplus doesn't sit around too long before being eaten. Perishable foods intended for long-term storage can be kept in a freezer.

◆

## THE REFRIGERATOR

The average domestic refrigerator maintains a temperature of 2°C–7°C (35°F–45°F) which is sufficiently low to stop micro-organisms developing. It won't destroy any micro-organisms already present in the food, so you should take care to buy perishables when they are as fresh as possible and get them into cool storage quickly.

We list here some tips for getting the best out of your refrigerator.
**1.** Open the door as infrequently as possible as every time you do this, warm air enters the fridge and raises the temperature which affects both the food and the amount of electricity used.
**2.** Cover all food before you put it in the refrigerator and if it's just been cooked allow it to cool first. Hot or uncovered foods cause the frozen food compartment to become frosted up and this frost forms an insulating layer which prevents the refrigerator from working efficiently.
**3.** Learn which foods keep best in different parts of the refrigerator:
(a) Raw foods like meat, bacon, poultry and fish should go into the coldest part, directly under the frozen food compartment. If your containers don't have lids, use kitchen foil or plastic film to cover food. When not covered, the smell and flavour of strong foods like fish and onions will transfer to things like cheese and butter.
(b) Cooked meats and made-up dishes should go on the middle shelves.
(c) Vegetables and salad ingredients should go at the bottom in the special crisper, if there is one.

(d) The butter compartment is generally inside the door where the temperature is higher so the butter won't get too hard.
**4.** Remove cooked foods which are to be served cold and cheese from the refrigerator half an hour before serving to allow them to come up to room temperature and regain their flavour.
**5.** Wipe up all spills immediately, so they don't have time to solidify. Keep a weather eye open for oddments tucked away in corners and see that they're either eaten quickly or thrown out.
**6.** Defrost the refrigerator regularly unless it does this automatically. Clean it with a weak solution of bicarbonate of soda in warm water. Ordinary soap and detergent tend to leave a penetrating smell which may be absorbed by the stored foods.
**The star rating** given by refrigerator and frozen food manufacturers is a useful guide to how long you can keep frozen food in the frozen food compartment of a refrigerator. It works like this:

### FROZEN FOOD STORAGE TIMES

| Maximum temperature of frozen food compartment | Maximum storage time for: | |
|---|---|---|
| | frozen foods | ice cream |
| * −6°C (21°F) | up to 1 week | 1 day |
| ** −12°C (10°F) | up to 1 month | up to 2 weeks |
| *** −18°C (0°F) | up to 3 months | up to 3 months |

A refrigerator may have a one, two or three star rating. See the chart above for temperatures and food storage times.

## REFRIGERATOR STORAGE TIMES

| Food | How to store | Days |
|---|---|---|
| **Meat, raw** | | |
| Joints | Rinse blood away; wipe dry, cover loosely with polythene or foil | 3–5 |
| Chops, cut meat | Cover as above | 2–4 |
| Minced meat, offal | Cover as above | 1–2 |
| Sausages | Cover as above | 3 |
| Bacon | Wrap in foil or polythene, or put in plastic container | 7 |
| **Meat, cooked** | | |
| Joints | Wrap tightly in foil or polythene, or put in lidded container | 3–5 |
| Sliced ham | As above | 2–3 |
| Continental sausages | As above | 3–5 |
| Casseroles | In lidded container | 2–3 |
| Pâté | Covered | 7 |
| **Poultry, raw** | | |
| Whole or joints | Draw, wash, wipe dry. Wrap loosely in polythene or foil | 2–3 |
| **Poultry, cooked** | | |
| Whole or joints | Remove stuffing; when cool, wrap or cover as for cooked meats | 2–3 |
| **Made-up dishes** | Cover when cool | 1 |
| **Fish, raw** (white, oily, smoked) | Cover loosely with foil or polythene | 1–2 |
| **Fish, cooked** | As above, or in covered container | 2 |
| **Shellfish** | Eat the day it is bought—don't store | |
| **Vegetables, salads** | | |
| Prepared green and root vegetables, green beans, celery, courgettes, aubergines, peppers | In 'crisper' drawer, or in plastic container, or wrapped in polythene | 5–8 |
| Sweetcorn, mushrooms, tomatoes, radishes, spring onions | Clean or wipe as necessary; store in covered container | 5–7 |
| Lettuce, cucumber, cut onions, cut peppers, parsley | As above | 4–6 |
| Cress, watercress | As above | 2 |
| **Fresh fruit** | | |
| Cut oranges, grapefruit, lemons | In covered container | 3–4 |
| Strawberries, redcurrants, raspberries, peaches | As above | 1–3 |
| Grapes, cherries, gooseberries, cut melon | As above | 5–7 |
| Rhubarb, cleaned | As above | 6–10 |
| **Eggs** | | |
| Fresh, in shell | In rack, pointed end down | 14 |
| Yolks | In lidded plastic container | 2–3 |
| Whites | As above | up to 7 |
| Hard-boiled, in shell | Uncovered | up to 7 |
| **Fats** | | |
| Butter, margarine | In original wrapper, in special compartment of refrigerator | 14–21 |
| Cooking fats | As above | 28 |
| **Milk, etc** | | |
| Milk | In original container, closed | 3–4 |
| Cream | As above | 2–4 |
| Soured cream, buttermilk, yogurt | As above | 2–4 |
| Milk sweets, custards | Lightly covered with foil or film | 2 |

## REFRIGERATOR STORAGE TIMES—*continued*

| Food | How to store | Days |
|---|---|---|
| **Cheese** | | |
| Parmesan, in piece | In cling film, foil, or airtight container | 21–28 |
| Hard cheeses | As above | 7–14 |
| Semi-hard cheeses | As above | 7–10 |
| Soft (cream or curd) cheeses | As above | 5–7 |
| **Bread, rolls, etc** | | |
| Any type of bread | In original waxed paper or polythene wrapper, or in foil | 7 |
| Sandwiches | Wrap in foil or use tightly-lidded plastic box; do not store if filling contains mayonnaise | 1–2 |
| **Leftovers** | | |
| Casseroles, pies, vegetables, cooked fruit | In original dish, tightly covered, or in plastic container | 2–4 |
| Canned foods, opened | Leave in can but cover; fruits and fruit juices, which tend to alter slightly in flavour, are best put in another container | As for freshly cooked foods |
| Cooked vegetables | In cling film, foil or airtight container | 1–2 |
| **Standbys** | | |
| Batter, uncooked | In covered jug or plastic container | 1–2 |
| Pancakes, cooked | Interleaved with greaseproof paper and foil-wrapped | 7 |
| Dry pastry mix | In screwtop jar or plastic container | up to 14 |
| Pastry, raw | Wrapped in foil | 2–3 |
| Grated cheese | In lidded jar or plastic container | up to 14 |
| Stock, soup | In covered jug | 1–2 |
| Tomato purée | Cover with thin layer of vegetable oil | up to 14 |

## THE LARDER OR FOOD CUPBOARD

Ideally the temperature here should not exceed 10°C (50°F) and there should be some ventilation. Any outlet or window should be covered with gauze or perforated zinc to keep out insects and it is also wise to draughtproof the door to prevent heat from the kitchen getting into the larder and to reduce condensation. If you're fitting it out from scratch vary the heights between shelves. The shelves should be covered with easily cleaned materials such as self-adhesive plastic, laminated plastic, ceramic tiles or spongeable shelf paper and all spills wiped up immediately. Perishable foods should be checked daily and store cupboard cans and packets should be used in rotation. A good way to keep a check on them is to date each one as you buy it.

Packaged dry ingredients can be kept quite safely in the original packets until opened, after which the contents should be transferred to a storage jar with a well fitting lid. Really airtight lids are essential only for strong-smelling foods like coffee, herbs and spices, which lose their aroma when exposed to the air, and for things like salt and baking powder which absorb moisture and easily become caked.

Cereal products such as flour and semolina keep well but should be watched for insect infestation. Affected foods should be thrown out at once and stocks checked to ensure that damage has not spread. The high fat content of wholemeal flour and oatmeal may cause rancidity so buy in fairly small quantities and use up quickly.

Canned fruit is best used within a year as the contents may deteriorate in colour after this time even though the food value is not altered. Condensed milk will begin to discolour after 6–9 months. Dried full-cream milk will keep for a few weeks after opening, but then tends to go rancid.

Always discard any cans that have 'blown', recognisable by bulging ends and leaking or rusty seams. Bacteria can penetrate them so the contents are no longer sterile.

## LARDER AND FOOD CUPBOARD STORAGE TIMES

| Food | Storage life | Storage comments |
|---|---|---|
| Flour, white<br>wheatmeal<br>wholemeal | Up to 6 months<br>Up to 3 months<br>Up to 1 month | Once opened, transfer to container<br>with close-fitting lid |
| Baking powder, bicarbonate of soda,<br>cream of tartar | 2–3 months | Dry storage essential; if opened, put in<br>container with close-fitting lid |
| Dried yeast | Up to 6 months | As above |
| Cornflour, custard powder | Good keeping qualities | As above |
| Pasta | As above | As above |
| Rice, all types | As above | As above |
| Sugar, loaf, caster, granulated | As above | Cool, dry storage; if opened, transfer<br>as above |
| Sugar, icing, brown | Limited life—tends to absorb moisture | Buy in small quantities, as required |
| Tea | Limited life—loses flavour if stored<br>long | Buy in small quantities; store in airtight<br>container in dry, cool place |
| Instant and ground coffee in sealed can<br>or jar | Up to 1 year | Cool, dry storage; once opened, re-<br>seal securely; use quickly |
| Coffee beans, loose ground coffee | Very limited life; use immediately | Buy as required; use airtight container |
| Instant low-fat skimmed milk | 3 months | Cool, dry storage is vital; once opened,<br>re-seal securely; use fairly quickly |
| Breakfast cereals | Limited life | Buy in small quantities. Cool, dry<br>storage |
| Dehydrated foods | Up to 1 year | Cool, dry storage. If opened, fold packet<br>down tightly and use within a week |
| Herbs, spices, seasonings | 6–8 months | Cool, dry storage, in airtight container.<br>Keep from light. Buy in small quantities |
| Nuts, ground almonds, desiccated<br>coconut | Limited life—depends on freshness<br>when bought. Fat content goes rancid<br>if kept too long | Lidded container |
| Dried fruits | 2–3 months | Cool, dry storage |
| Jams, etc | Good keeping qualities | Dry, cool, dark storage |
| Honey, clear or thick | As above | Dry, cool storage. After about 1 year,<br>appearance may alter, but still eatable |
| Golden syrup, treacle | As above | As above |
| Evaporated milk | 6–8 months | Safe even after some years, but<br>darkens, thickens and loses flavour.<br>Once opened, treat as fresh milk |
| Canned fruit | 12 months | As above |
| Canned vegetables | 2 years | As above |
| Canned fish in oil | Up to 5 years | As above |
| Canned fish in tomato sauce | Up to 1 year | As above |
| Canned meat | Up to 5 years | As above |
| Canned ham | 6 months | As above. Cans holding 900 g (2 lb) or<br>more should be kept in the refrigerator |
| Pickles, sauces | Reasonably good keeping qualities | Cool, dry, dark storage |
| Chutneys | Limited life | As above |
| Oils, olive, corn | Up to 18 months | Cool, dry storage |

# GLOSSARY

This glossary is a brief guide to the most commonly employed cooking methods, terms and ingredients whose functions are not immediately obvious. Where appropriate, a cross reference is made to a fuller explanation in another part of the book.

◆

**Agar agar** Powder, sticks or shreds made from seaweed and used as a jelling agent.

**Altitude** Affects cooking times and temperatures. The higher the altitude the lower the temperature at which water boils.

**Antipasto** Italian phrase for a selection of hot or cold hors d'oeuvre. Literally means before the meal.

**Arrowroot** Can be used as an alternative to cornflour as a thickening agent in liquids, such as sauces.

**Aspic jelly** Savoury jelly used for setting and garnishing savoury dishes.

**Au gratin** Describes a dish which has been coated with sauce, sprinkled with breadcrumbs or cheese and finished by browning under the grill or in the oven. The low-sided dishes in which this is done are called *gratin dishes*.

**Bain-marie** A low-sided container which is half-filled with water kept just below boiling point. Containers of food are placed in it to keep warm or cook without overheating. A bain-marie is used for cooking custards and other egg dishes and keeping sauces warm. No special container is needed; a roasting tin will do.

**Baking** Cooking in the oven by dry heat.

**Baking blind** The method used for cooking flans and tarts without their fillings (see page 371).

**Baking powder** A raising agent consisting of an acid and an alkali which react to produce carbon dioxide. This expands during baking and makes cakes and breads rise.

**Barding** Covering the breast of poultry or game birds with pieces of bacon or fat to prevent the flesh drying out during roasting.

**Basting** Spooning the juices and melted fat over meat, poultry or game which is being roasted to keep it moist. Use a large spoon or a special bulb baster.

**Bean curd** Also known as *tofu* and widely used in vegetarian and oriental cooking. It is made from a pressed purée of soya beans and sold fresh, dried and in cans.

**Beating** A method of incorporating air into an ingredient or mixture by agitating it vigorously with a spoon, fork, whisk or electric mixer. Also done to soften ingredients.

**Béchamel** Flavoured white sauce; one of the four basic types (see page 202).

**Beurre manié** Equal parts of flour and butter kneaded together to form a paste. Used for thickening soups, stews and casseroles at the end of cooking.

**Bicarbonate of soda** Sometimes used in baking to act as a raising agent.

**Blanching** Immersing food briefly in boiling water to whiten it, as in sweetbreads, or to remove skin e.g. peaches and tomatoes. Vegetables which are to be frozen and kept for a certain length of time are blanched to destroy enzymes and preserve the colour, flavour and texture.

**Blanquette** Stew made from white meat such as veal or from poultry in a white sauce enriched with cream and egg yolk.

**Blender** An electric machine consisting of a goblet with rotating blades in the base. Used for puréeing wet mixtures and grinding dry ingredients. Ideal for making fresh breadcrumbs.

**Boiling** Cooking in liquid at 100°C (212°F). The main foods that are boiled are vegetables, rice, pasta and suet puddings. Syrups and glazes that need reducing and thickening are also boiled as are some sauces.

**Boning** Removing the bones from meat or poultry, cutting the flesh as little as possible, so that it can be rolled or stuffed.

**Bottling** The term used for preserving food or preserves in glass jars under sterile conditions (see page 483). This is the final stage of home wine making.

**Bouchée** Small round piece of cooked puff pastry served with a filling on top or inside. Should be no more than 4 cm (1½ inch) diameter so that it can be eaten in one mouthful (its literal meaning).

**Bouquet garni** Small bunch of herbs—usually a mixture of parsley stems, thyme and a bay leaf—

tied in muslin and used to flavour soups and stews.

**Bourguignonne** Term applied to dishes in which burgundy and small braised button onions are used e.g. boeuf bourguignonne.

**Braising** Cooking method used for cuts of meat, poultry and game which are too tough to roast. It is also good for some vegetables. Use a pan or casserole with a tightly fitting lid so that little liquid is lost through evaporation. Place the meat on a bed of chopped vegetables (called a *mirepoix*), add just enough liquid to cover the vegetables and cook on the hob or in the oven.

**Brining** Immersing food in a salt and water solution.

**Brioche** An enriched yeast dough mixture baked in the shape of a cottage loaf. French in origin and usually eaten warm for breakfast.

**Brochette** Skewer, spit.

**Broiling** American term for grilling.

**Broth** Another word for stock.

**Brûlée** Applying heat to a sugar crust on top of a sweet dish to caramelise it.

**Brut** Means unsweetened and is a term used to describe dry wine and champagne.

**Canapé** Small appetisers, usually served with drinks and often consisting of a topping on a bread or pastry base.

**Candying** Method of impregnating fruit, pieces of fruit or peel with sugar to preserve them.

**Caramel** Substance obtained by heating sugar syrup very slowly until a rich brown colour.

**Carbonade** Rich stew or braise of meat which includes beer.

**Casserole** Strictly speaking, a dish with a tightly fitting lid used for cooking meat and vegetables. Now applied to the food cooked in this way.

**Celsius** Also known as Centigrade. A scale for measuring temperature in which the freezing point of water is 0° and the boiling point 100°. Used for the oven settings on modern electric cookers.

**Chantilly** Whipped cream which has been slightly sweetened and may be flavoured with vanilla.

**Charcuterie** Cooked pork products such as sausages and terrines.

**Charlotte** A hot or cold moulded dessert. For a hot charlotte the mould is lined with bread and for a cold charlotte it is lined with sponge fingers.

**Chasseur** Literally hunter-style. Describes dishes cooked with mushrooms, shallots and white wine.

**Chaudfroid** Jellied sauce with a béchamel sauce base, used for coating cold fish, poultry and game.

**Chilling** Cooling food without freezing.

**Chining** Severing the rib bones from the backbone by sawing through the ribs close to the spine. Joints such as loin or neck of lamb, veal or pork are best chined as this makes them easier to carve into chops or cutlets after cooking.

**Chopping** Cutting food into small neat pieces without damaging the tissues.

**Chorizo** Spanish sausage made of smoked pork and pimiento. Sold ready cooked.

**Chowder** An American dish somewhere between a soup and a stew, usually based on fish e.g. clam chowder.

**Citric acid** A mild acid, used mainly for preserving soft fruit drinks and in home wine making.

**Clarifying** Process of removing sediment or impurities from a food. Butter and dripping may be clarified so that they can be used for frying at higher temperatures.

*To clarify butter*, heat until melted and all bubbling stops. Remove from the heat and stand until the salt and sediment have sunk to the bottom, then gently pour off the fat, straining it through muslin. Chill and use as required. Clarified butter is also known as ghee.

*To clarify dripping*, melt the fat, then strain it to remove any particles. Pour over two to three times its volume of boiling water and allow to cool. The fat will rise to the top and become firm. Lift it off and wipe the underside with absorbent kitchen paper to remove any sediment.

Clarifying also means to clear a liquid such as consommé by adding egg white. The coagulation of the egg white throughout the liquid gathers up all the bits into a scum which can be discarded.

**Clotting** A gentle heat applied to cream which produces the thick clotted cream of the south-west of England.

**Cocotte** Small earthenware, ovenproof container of single portion size. Also called a *ramekin*.

**Coddling** Method of soft boiling eggs.

**Colander** Perforated metal or plastic draining basket.

**Compote** Mixture of fruit stewed in sugar syrup. Served hot or cold.

**Concasser** Chopped roughly.

**Conserve** Whole fruit jam.

**Consistency** Term used to describe the texture of a mixture, e.g. firm, dropping, runny.

**Consommé** Concentrated stock which has been clarified.

**Corned beef** Pieces of beef cured in salt and sugar, pressed together into blocks and canned.

**Cornstarch** American name for cornflour.

**Court bouillon** Seasoned liquid in which meat, poultry, fish or vegetables are boiled or poached.

**Couscous** Processed semolina in tiny pellets. Also the name of North Africa's national dish.

**Crackling** The crisp skin on roasted pork.

**Cream of tartar (tartaric acid)** A raising agent which is an ingredient of baking powder and self raising flour.

**Creaming** Beating together fat and sugar until the mixture resembles whipped cream in texture and colour (pale and fluffy). Used in cakes and puddings which require the incorporation of a lot of air.

**Crêpe** French term for a pancake.

**Crimping** Trimming cucumber, radishes, etc with a canelle knife (a knife with a V-shaped blade which removes neat strips) or fork to produce a deckled finish when cut; decorating the edges of a pie, tart or shortbread by pinching it at regular intervals to give a fluted effect.

**Croquette** Mixture of meat, fish, poultry, cooked potatoes or vegetables bound together and formed into roll or cork shapes, coated with egg and breadcrumbs and shallow or deep-fried.

**Croûte** A circle or rectangle of fried or toasted bread on which game and some main dishes and savouries are served. A pastry crust, usually crescent shaped, served with savoury dishes.

**Croûtons** Small pieces of fried or toasted bread which are served with salads and soup.

**Curd** The parts of milk which coagulate when a vegetable or mineral acid is added to them. Also refers to a creamy preserve made from fruit (usually lemon or orange) and sugar, eggs and butter.

**Curdle** To separate fresh milk or a sauce either by adding acid (such as lemon juice) or by heating excessively. Also used to refer to creamed mixtures which have separated when the egg has been beaten in too quickly.

**Cure** To preserve fish, meat or poultry by salting, drying or smoking.

**Dal** The Indian term for pulses.

**Daube** Meat or vegetables which have been braised in stock.

**Deep fat** Hot oil or fat in which the food is totally immersed for frying.

**Dégorger** To draw out moisture, e.g. salting aubergines to remove bitter juices.

**Dice** To cut into small cubes.

**Dough** A thick mixture of uncooked flour and liquid, usually combined with other ingredients. The term is used to refer to mixtures such as pastry, scones and biscuits as well as those made with yeast.

**Drawing** Removing the entrails from poultry and game.

**Dredging** Sprinkling food lightly with flour, sugar or other powdered coating. Fish and meat are often dredged with flour before frying, while cakes, biscuits and pancakes may be sprinkled with caster or icing sugar after cooking.

**Dressing** Plucking, drawing and trussing poultry and game. Garnishing a dish. Coating a salad.

**Dripping** Fat obtained from roasting meat or pieces of fat which are rendered down deliberately (see also Rendering).

**Dropping consistency** Term used to describe the correct texture of a cake or pudding mixture just before cooking. Test for it by taking a spoonful of the mixture and holding the spoon on its side above the bowl. The mixture should fall off of its own accord within 5 seconds.

**Drying** Preserving food by dehydration. It is usually done commercially (e.g. dried milk granules, dried peas) but it is possible to dry herbs and fruit at home.

**Egg and crumbing** Method of coating fish, cutlets, rissoles, croquettes, etc before frying or baking.

**Emulsion** Mixture of two liquids which do not automatically dissolve into each other, e.g. oil and water. They can be made to emulsify by vigorous beating or shaking together. See French Dressing (page 260) and Mayonnaise (page 261).

**En croûte** Term describing food which is wrapped in pastry before cooking.

**En papillote** Food which is precooked, then wrapped and heated in foil or greaseproof paper for a brief period and served in the parcel.

**Enzyme** Substances present in all foods which have not been subjected to processing and which work within them continuously. Most enzymes are killed by cooking (see also Blanching).

**Escalope** Slice of meat such as veal, turkey or pork cut from the top of the leg and often egged and crumbed, then fried or grilled.

**Espagnole** Classic rich brown sauce, one of the four basic types (see page 204).

**Extract** Concentrated flavouring which is used in small quantities, e.g. meat extract, yeast extract.

**Faggot** A mixture of pork offal, onion and breadcrumbs which is baked and eaten with gravy. Small bunch of herbs tied like a miniature faggot of wood, such as a bouquet garni.

**Fahrenheit** System of measuring temperature which is gradually being replaced with Celsius. Its freezing point is 32° and boiling point 212°.

**Farce** Alternative French term for stuffing.

**Farina** Fine flour made from wheat, nuts or potatoes.

**Fermenting** Term used when enzyme activity alters a food consistency, e.g. when making bread, yogurt or wine.

**Fillet** A term used for the undercut of a loin of

beef, veal, pork or game, for boned breasts of poultry and for boned slices of fish.

**Fines herbes** Mixture of chopped herbs, usually parsley, tarragon, chives and chervil.

**Flame (flambé)** Flavouring a dish with alcohol which is then ignited so that the actual alcohol content is burned off. Traditionally done to Rich Christmas Pudding (see page 327) and Crêpes Suzette (see page 328).

**Folding in (cutting and folding)** Method of combining a whisked or creamed mixture with other ingredients so that it retains its lightness. Used mainly for meringues, soufflés and certain cake mixtures. Folding is done with a metal spoon.

**Fondue** Dish cooked at table over a fondue burner into which the diners dip food speared on long pronged fondue forks.

**Fool** Cold dessert consisting of puréed fruit with whipped cream or custard blended into it.

**Forcemeat** Stuffing for meat, fish or vegetables (see page 183).

**Fricassée** White stew of chicken, rabbit, veal or vegetables, finished with cream and egg yolks (see also Blanquette).

**Frosting** American term for icing cakes. Method of decorating the rim of a drinks glass.

**Frothing** Dredging the surface of roast meat, usually game, with flour and heating to a brown colour in a hot oven.

**Frying** Method of cooking food in hot fat or oil. There are two methods. Shallow frying in a little fat in a shallow pan and deep frying where the food is totally immersed in oil.

**Galantine** Dish of white meat which has been boned, sometimes stuffed, rolled, cooked, pressed and glazed to be served cold.

**Garnish** Edible decoration such as parsley, watercress, hard-boiled egg or lemon added to a savoury dish to enhance its appearance.

**Gelatine** Animal-derived jellying product.

**Génoise (Genoese)** Sponge cake made with a whisked egg mixture enriched with melted butter.

**Ghee** Clarified butter widely used in Indian cookery (see also Clarifying).

**Gill** Liquid measurement equivalent to 150 ml ($\frac{1}{4}$ pint).

**Glacé** French word meaning iced or glossy, e.g. Glacé Cherries and Glacé Icing (see page 422).

**Glaze** Foods used to give a glossy coating to sweet and savoury dishes to improve their appearance and sometimes flavour. Ingredients for glazes include beaten egg, egg white, milk and syrup.

**Gluten** A constituent of wheat and other cereals. The amount present in varying flours create the different textures of cakes and breads.

**Granita** A half-frozen water ice.

**Grating** Shredding cheese, carrots and other hard substances with a manual or electric grater.

**Grecque, à la** Strictly, should be of Greek origin but seldom the case. Now more often the name given to dishes of French origin. Usually refers to vegetables cooked in stock with olive oil and spices.

**Griddle** Flat, heavy, metal plate used on top of the cooker for cooking scones.

**Grinding** Reducing foods to small particles in a food mill or electric grinder. Done mainly to coffee beans, nuts and spices.

**Grissini** Long, slim and brittle Italian bread sticks.

**Hanging** Leaving meat or game suspended in a cool dry place to allow air to circulate around it to tenderise the flesh and develop the flavour.

**Hard sauce** Creamed butter and sugar flavoured with brandy, rum or whisky and chilled until firm—also called brandy or rum butter. Served with hot puddings.

**Hors d'oeuvre** Often used as a term for a starter but, strictly speaking, means a selection of cold foods served together as an appetiser.

**Hulling** Removing the *calyx* from soft fruits, e.g. strawberries.

**Infusing** Method of imparting flavour to a liquid. Flavourings, herbs, spices or coffee beans are soaked in milk or water.

**Jardinière** Refers to dishes garnished with mixed fresh spring vegetables or green peas and sprigs of cauliflower.

**Jugged** Method of cooking hare, in a tall covered pot until very tender and rich dark brown in colour. The blood is added at the end of the cooking time.

**Julienne** Vegetables or fruit rind cut into very fine strips to use as a garnish or ingredient.

**Kebab** Cubes of meat, fish, shellfish, fruit and vegetables which are cooked on a skewer under a grill or on a barbecue.

**Kosher** Food prepared according to orthodox Jewish laws.

**Kugelhopf** Sweetened yeast cake which contains dried fruit and is baked in a special fluted tin.

**Langues de chats** Literally means cats' tongues. Small thin flat crisp biscuits served with ice cream and mousse.

**Larding** Inserting small strips of fat bacon into the flesh of game birds, poultry and dry meat before cooking. It is done with a special larding needle.

**Leaven** The raising agent in dough, usually yeast or baking powder.

**Liaison** Something which is used for thickening or binding. Usually flour, cornflour, arrowroot, rice or potato flour or egg yolk.

**Lukewarm** About blood temperature, approximately 37°C (98.4°F).

**Macédoine** Mixture of fruit or vegetables cut into even-sized dice. Usually used as a garnish.

**Macerating** Softening foods by soaking in liquid.

**Marinating** Soaking meat, poultry or game in a mixture of oil, wine, vinegar and flavourings to tenderise it and add flavour. The mixture is known as a *marinade*.

**Marmite** A French metal or earthenware pot used for long slow cooking of casseroles on top of the stove or in the oven.

**Medallions** French term for small rounds of meat, usually beef or veal.

**Meringue** Egg white whisked until stiff, mixed with caster sugar and dried slowly in a low oven until crisp.

**Meunière** Refers to food cooked in butter, seasoned with salt, pepper and lemon juice and finished with parsley. Usually applied to fish dishes.

**Milling** Reducing to a powder or paste (see also Grinding).

**Mincing** Chopping or cutting into small pieces. May be done with a knife, a manual mincing machine or in a food processor.

**Mirepoix** Mixture of cut vegetables, usually carrot, celery and onion with a little added ham or bacon used as a bed on which to braise meat.

**Mocca** A term which has come to mean a blend of chocolate and coffee.

**Monosodium glutamate** A powder which enhances the flavour of ingredients it is added to. A principal ingredient in processed foods and Chinese cookery.

**Navarin** Lamb stew with onions and potatoes.

**Noisettes** Neatly trimmed and tied pieces of lamb or beef, not less than 1 cm (½ inch) thick.

**Panada** Thick sauce used for binding croquettes and similar mixtures.

**Par-boiling** Boiling food for part of its cooking time before finishing it by another method.

**Paring** Peeling or trimming vegetables or fruit.

**Pasteurising** Sterilising milk by heating to 60–92°C (140–180°F) to destroy bacteria.

**Pasty** Individual savoury pastry pie made without a dish on a baking sheet.

**Pâte** Pastry, particularly Pâte Sucrée (see page 373), a sweet flan pastry.

**Pâté** A savoury mixture made from minced meat and/or vegetables cooked to form a solid mass. Fish pâtés are cooked or uncooked.

**Patty** Small pie or vol au vent, often of puff pastry.

**Paunching** Removing the stomach and intestines of a rabbit or hare.

**Paupiettes** Slices of meat or fish rolled around a stuffing.

**Pectin** Substance found in most fruit and some vegetables which is necessary for setting jams and jellies.

**Pickling** Preserving food in vinegar (see page 477).

**Piping** Forcing cream, icing, mashed potato, cake mixtures and meringues through a nozzle on the end of a bag to create fancy patterns.

**Pith** White lining under the rind of citrus fruit.

**Plucking** Removing feathers from poultry and game.

**Poaching** Cooking food in an open pan covered with seasoned, just simmering, liquid.

**Pope's eye** The small circle of fat in the centre of a leg of lamb or pork. The name for prime rump steak in Scotland.

**Pot roasting** Method of cooking meat in a pan with fat and a little liquid.

**Potage** A thick soup.

**Praline** Almonds caramelised in sugar, then crushed and used to flavour sweet dishes.

**Preserving** Keeping food in edible condition by refrigerating, freezing, cooking, pickling, crystallising, bottling, drying or smoking.

**Pressure cooking** Cooking food quickly in steam under pressure.

**Prosciutto** Italian raw smoked ham.

**Proving** The term used for leaving bread dough to rise after shaping.

**Pulping** Crushing or cooking food to a soft consistency. Pulp is also the fleshy area of fruit and vegetables.

**Pulses** Generic name given to the dried seeds of pod bearing plants. These peas, beans and lentils are used for their high protein content.

**Quenelles** Fish, meat or poultry which has been blended to a fine forcemeat, shaped into rounds or ovals, then cooked in liquid and served either as a garnish for soup or as a main course.

**Ramekin** Individual round ovenproof dish.

**Réchauffé** French term for reheated leftovers.

**Reducing** Boiling a liquid to evaporate water from it and produce a more concentrated flavour.

**Rendering** Extracting fat from meat trimmings by cutting them into small pieces and heating in a cool oven at 150°C (300°F) mark 2 until the fat runs out and can be strained.

**Rennet** Extract from calf's stomach which will curdle or coagulate milk for junket and cheese-making. Vegetarian rennet is also available.

**Rice paper** Edible paper made from the pith of a

Chinese tree. Used as an edible base for sticky baked goods such as macaroons.

**Roasting** Cooking meat in an oven or over an open flame (see page 92).

**Roulade** Meat, cake or soufflé mixture served in a roll.

**Roux** Mixture of equal amounts of fat and flour cooked together to form the base of sauces.

**Rubbing in** Method of incorporating fat into flour when a short texture is wanted with pastry, cakes or biscuits.

**Salmi** A stew made from game birds; the bird is partly roasted and then cooked with wine or port (see page 175).

**Salting** Method of preserving food in layers of salt.

**Sautéing** Cooking food in a small quantity of fat in a sauté pan (a frying pan with straight sides and a wide base), which browns the food quickly.

**Scalding** Pouring boiling water over food to clean it, loosen hairs or remove the skin. Food should not be left in boiling water or it will begin to cook. It is also the term used for heating milk to just below boiling point, to retard souring or infuse it with another flavour.

**Scalloping** Decorating the double edge of a pastry pie with small horizontal cuts which are pulled up with the back of a knife to produce a scalloped effect (see page 370).

**Scoring** To cut narrow parallel lines in the surface of food to improve its appearance or help it cook more quickly (see also Crackling).

**Searing** Browning meat quickly in a little hot fat before grilling or roasting.

**Seasoned flour** Flour mixed with a little salt and pepper and used for dusting meat and fish before frying.

**Seasoning** Adding salt, pepper, herbs and spices for added flavour.

**Shredding** Grating cheese or raw vegetables into fine pieces.

**Sieving** Pushing food through a perforated sieve to get a soft, even texture.

**Sifting** Sieving dry ingredients to remove lumps.

**Simmering** Keeping liquid just below boiling point.

**Singeing** Using a flame to burn off any residual traces of feather on plucked game or poultry.

**Skimming** Removing froth, scum or fat from the surface of stock, gravy, stews and jam. Use either a skimmer, a spoon or absorbent kitchen paper.

**Skinning** Removing the skin from meat, fish, poultry, fruit or vegetables.

**Smoking** Curing food by exposure to wood smoke.

**Souring** Adding acid to cream to give it a sour taste.

**Sousing** Pickling in brine or vinegar.

**Spit** Rotating rod on which meat, poultry or game is cooked either in the oven or over a fire.

**Steaming** Cooking food in the steam of rapidly boiling water.

**Steeping** Covering food with hot or cold water and leaving it to stand, either to soften it or extract its flavour and/or colour.

**Sterilising** Destroying bacteria by heating.

**Stewing** Long, slow cooking method where food is placed in liquid which is kept at simmering point. Good for tenderising coarse meat and vegetables.

**Stir-frying** Quick method of frying in shallow fat. The food must be cut into small, even-sized pieces and moved around constantly until coated. Stir-fried food is usually cooked in a *wok*.

**Stock** The liquid produced when meat, bones, poultry, fish or vegetables are simmered in water with herbs and flavourings for several hours to extract their flavour (see page 19).

**Suet** Hard fat found around the kidneys in beef or mutton. Usually bought in packets rather than fresh. Use in pastry and steamed puddings.

**Sweating** Gently cooking food (usually vegetables), covered, in melted fat until the juices run.

**Syrup** Concentrated solution of sugar in water, used in making water ices, drinks and fruit dishes.

**Tenderising** Beating raw meat with a spiked mallet or rolling pin to break down the fibres and make it more tender for grilling or frying.

**Tepid** Approximately at blood heat.

**Terrine** China or earthenware dish used for pâtés. Also used to refer to the food cooked in it.

**Texturised vegetable protein (TVP)** Meat substitute made from vegetables, usually soya beans. Takes on the flavour of anything it is cooked with.

**Truffle** Rare black or white fungus of the same family as the mushroom. Due to the cost, truffles are used mainly for garnishing.

**Trussing** Tying or skewering into shape before cooking. Applies mainly to poultry and game.

**Unleavened** Bread without a raising agent.

**Vanilla sugar** Sugar in which a vanilla pod has been stored to release its flavour.

**Vol au vent** Round or oval puff pastry case which is filled with diced meat, poultry, fish or vegetables in sauce.

**Whipping or whisking** Beating air rapidly into a mixture either with a manual or electric whisk.

**Wok** Chinese pan used for stir-frying. The food cooks on the sloping sides of the pan as well as in the rounded base.

**Zest** The coloured outer layer of citrus fruit which contains essential oil.

# INDEX